Property and Conveyancing Library

Renewal of Business Tenancies

Fourth Edition

Property and Conveyancing Library

Renewal of Business Tenancies

Fourth Edition

Kirk Reynolds Q.C., M.A. (Cantab.)
A bencher of the Middle Temple

Wayne Clark, LL.B. (Lond.), B.C.L. (Oxon.)
Barrister

SWEET & MAXWELL

THOMSON REUTERS

First Edition	1997
Second Edition	2002
Third Edition	2007
Fourth Edition	2012

Published in 2012 by Sweet & Maxwell, 100 Avenue Road, London NW3 3PF part of Thomson Reuters (Professional) UK Limited (Registered in England & Wales, Company No 1679046.
Registered Office and address for service: Aldgate House, 33 Aldgate High Street, London EC3N 1DL)

For further information on our products and services, visit *www.sweetandmaxwell.co.uk*

Typeset by Letterpart Ltd, Reigate, Surrey

Appendices typeset by Servis Filmsetting Ltd, Stockport, Cheshire.

Printed and bound in Great Britain by CPI Group (UK) Ltd, Croydon, CR0 4YY.

No natural forests were destroyed to make this product; only farmed timber was used and re-planted.

A CIP catalogue record of this book is available for the British Library.

ISBN: 978-0414-024243

Preface

The major change to this Book brought about in this Edition will not be immediately apparent to most of our readers. It is the move from the traditional printed book (which has been the only format in which it was available in previous Editions and Supplements) to the online digital version which will be available to subscribers, in parallel to the print edition.

Our publishers believe that the print version will remain popular with the majority of our readers for some time, since it has many merits, but that others will be attracted by the new features available to online subscribers, particularly the highly convenient and comprehensive search facilities linking the text to a data base of reported cases and statutory material.

Turning now to matters of substance, there are a number of cases, noted and digested for the first time in this Edition, which deserve special mention.

The decision of Sales J. in the *Humber Oil Terminal* case clarifies many points about the working of the new Interim Rent provisions, as well as more wide-ranging issues of principle about how the Court is to disregard any part of the rental value which is attributable to a tenant's improvement, while giving the landlord a fair figure for the value of what he has contributed. This interesting decision is currently under appeal.

In an earlier round in the same dispute, Vos J. and the Court of Appeal had to consider the interrelationship between the Competition Act 1998 and ground (g) of s.30(1) (which entitles a landlord, in certain circumstances, effectively to "take over" the tenant's business). The complicated provisions of ground (g), which are already the subject of much case law, have been further clarified in the case of *Frozen Value Limited v Heron Foods Limited.*

In *Edwards & Walkden (Norfolk) Limited v City of London*, where leases of various properties in Smithfield Market were renewed under the Act, the Court took the unusual course of converting fixed service charges in the current tenancies into variable service charges in the new tenancies.

In *Crossco No.4 Unlimited v Jolan* it was held that the absence of a board resolution did not prevent a landlord from succeeding under ground (g).

In *Newham LBC v Van Staden*, the Court of Appeal reached a controversial decision as to the impact of a definition of the term as including "any period of holding over" on the parties' attempt to exclude, by agreement under s.38A, the security of tenure provisions of the Act.

The text is up to date to October 1, 2012.

KIRK REYNOLDS QC

WAYNE CLARK
Falcon Chambers
Falcon Court
London EC4Y 1AA

Foreword to the third edition

Part II of the Landlord and Tenant Act 1954 has now been with us for more than half a century. Over that half century, the courts have handed down many, many judgments which have either expounded the relevant legal principles or given insight into the practical operation of the Act. In recent years the explosion in law reporting, accompanied by the general availability of unreported cases, has meant that there is a vast amount of judicial utterance which is available to be consulted and deployed.

The 1954 Act was significantly amended by the Regulatory Reform (Business Tenancies) (England and Wales) Order 2003. Even if the original provisions of the 1954 Act had been thoroughly explored by the courts so that there were not many issues of principle left unresolved, the 2003 amendments have opened up several new important areas of controversy which remain to be argued and, one expects, in time settled by the courts.

The 1954 Act, as amended, is considered and applied by lawyers and other property professionals up and down the country every day of the working week. The County Court has a regular stream of cases under the Act. Appeals to the High Court and to the Court of Appeal are likely to continue unabated.

Against this background, the practitioner and the courts need, and deserve, a legal textbook on Pt II of the 1954 Act, as amended, which is comprehensive, up to date, and written with clarity and authority. To be comprehensive, the textbook must deal not only with the statutory provisions, but also the vast number of judicial decisions. It is also immensely helpful when a legal textbook not only states the established law with complete accuracy, but also identifies areas of controversy with a full discussion of the competing arguments and the authors' considered views on the points in issue.

This text book is a high quality work which succeeds in meeting all of the above requirements. Previous editions of this work rapidly established themselves as an essential tool for all practitioners in this area of law and practice. This new edition builds on all the successes of the past and integrates into the text all of the new developments, growing in bulk as it does so. This new edition is every bit as essential, and as welcome, as previous editions have been.

The Honourable Mr Justice Morgan
September 2007
Royal Courts of Justice
London

TABLE OF CONTENTS

5. RESPONSE TO THE NOTICE OR REQUEST

6. APPLICATIONS FOR NEW TENANCIES AND TERMINATION APPLICATIONS

12. COMPENSATION FOR DISTURBANCE

13. IMPROVEMENTS

APPENDICES

Appendix 1
Statutes

Appendix 2
Statutory Regulations

TABLE OF CASES

TABLE OF STATUTES

TABLE OF STATUTORY INSTRUMENTS

CHAPTER 1

DOES THE ACT APPLY?[1]

1. CHECKLIST OF CONDITIONS TO BE FULFILLED

The following checklist is provided for easy reference, in order to determine whether the Act applies. Each point in the checklist is considered in greater detail in the following paragraphs of this chapter. It should be noted that the provisions of the 1954 Act cannot be prevented from applying to a transaction either by reason of the agreement of the parties (unless the agreement is one which complies with the provisions of s.38[2]), or by estoppel: *London & Associated Investment Trust Plc v Calow*[3] (digested in para.1–16). **1–01**

In order for the Act to apply it is necessary to answer all of the following questions in the affirmative:

- Is there an existing tenancy (other than a tenancy at will)?[4]
- Does the tenancy include "premises" which are capable of being occupied?[5]
- Are the premises occupied?[6]
- Is the occupation that of the tenant (or of a company in which the tenant has a controlling interest within s.23(1A)(a),[7] or where the tenant is a company, of a person with a controlling interest in the company within s.23(1A)(b),[8] or of a beneficiary under a trust within s.41(1),[9] or of an associated company of the tenant within s.42(2))?[10]
- Is the occupation for the purposes (or partly for the purposes) of a "business"?[11]
- Is that business carried on by the tenant[12] or by a beneficiary under a trust within s.41(1)[13] or by a company in which the tenant has a controlling

[1] All sections referred to in the text are to the 1954 Act, (as amended) unless otherwise stated.
[2] As to which see para.2–03 et seq.
[3] [1986] 2 E.G.L.R. 80 Ch. D.
[4] This condition is considered in detail in para.1–17 et seq.
[5] This condition is considered in detail in para.1–26 et seq.
[6] This condition is considered in detail in para.1–42 et seq.
[7] This condition is considered in detail in para.1–86 et seq.
[8] This condition is considered in detail in para.1–86 et seq.
[9] This condition is considered in detail in para.1–92 et seq.
[10] This condition is considered in detail in para.1–107 et seq.
[11] This condition is considered in detail in para.1–111 et seq.
[12] This condition is considered in detail in para.1–122 et seq.
[13] This condition is considered in detail in para.1–123 et seq.

interest within s.23(1A)(a),[14] or, where the tenant is a company, by a person with a controlling interest in the company within s.23(1A)(b),[15] or by an associated company of the tenant within s.42(2))?[16]

- Is the business use permitted (either expressly or as a result of consent or acquiescence) under the subsisting terms of the tenancy?[17]
- Does the tenancy fall outside the following specific exceptions under s.43[18]:
  - (i) a tenancy of an agricultural holding;
  - (ii) a tenancy created by a mining lease;
  - (iii) a tenancy for specified public uses;
  - (iv) a tenancy granted in consequence of employment;
  - (v) a tenancy for a term of years certain not exceeding six months?
- Does the tenancy fall outside the special circumstances relevant to s.28[19] (agreement for grant of a future tenancy) and s.57 (ministerial certificate on grounds of public interest)[20] or s.36(2) (where the court has ordered a new tenancy but the tenant has applied for the order to be revoked)?[21]

2. THE 2003 ORDER

1–02 The provisions of Pt II of the Landlord and Tenant Act 1954 have been substantially amended with effect from June 1, 2004 by The Regulatory Reform (Business Tenancies) (England and Wales) Order (SI 2003/3096).[22] The significance of these changes justifies one in referring to the new procedures as a new regime, in contrast to the provisions which will continue to apply to notices served prior to that date.

3. IS THERE A "TENANCY"?

Definition of tenancy

Includes agreements for lease and tenancies by estoppel

1–03 By virtue of s.23(1), the Act applies only to tenancies. "Tenancy" is defined in s.69(1). As well as including tenancies and sub-tenancies properly so called,[23] it

[14] This condition is considered in detail in para.1–125.

[15] This condition is considered in detail in para.1–125.

[16] This condition is considered in detail in para.1–126.

[17] This condition is considered in detail in para.1–129 et seq.

[18] These exceptions are considered in detail in para.1–141 et seq. The fact that the premises are licensed for the sale of intoxicating liquor on the premises previously prevented the Act applying—this is no longer the case: see the Landlord and Tenant (Licensed Premises) Act 1990 and para.1–151.

[19] This condition is considered in detail in para.15–14 et seq.

[20] See para.1–153.

[21] This condition is considered in detail in para.1–154.

[22] This Order is referred to in the text as "the 2003 Order."

[23] In order to take effect at law a lease has to be in writing and signed by the parties as a deed: ss.52 and 53 of the Law of Property Act 1925. The lease need not be by deed or in writing if the term does

also includes tenancies created pursuant to the Act and agreements for a tenancy or sub-tenancy, which will, if capable of specific performance, take effect in equity[24]—*Tottenham Hotspur Football & Athletic Co Ltd v Princegrove Publishers Ltd*[25] (digested in para.1–05). The Act applies to a tenancy by estoppel[26]: *Bell v General Accident Fire and Life Assurance Corp Ltd*[27](digested in para.1–138); *London & Associated Investment Trust Plc v Calow*[28] (digested in para.1–16). Thus even if the landlord who grants the lease does not himself have title to do so, the estoppel which arises between the parties is such that both they and their successors in title would be estopped from denying that the grant was effective to create the tenancy that it purported to create.[29] In *Bell v General Accident Fire & Life Assurance Corp Ltd*, (digested in para.1–138), the tenancy was granted by an intergroup company of the freehold owner and thus the grantor had no freehold or other title to the property to grant the lease. However, it was held that the doctrine of estoppel operated to prevent the tenant under the lease from denying the grantor's title and there was no reason why the 1954 Act should not apply to tenancies by estoppel. The tenant's argument that the 1954 Act did not apply to tenancies by estoppel was based upon the language of the statutory definition of "landlord" in s.44(1) and of "tenancy" in s.69(1). Section 44(1) requires the "landlord" to be, in effect, the owner of the fee simple in the premises, or of any other interest which satisfies the conditions of s.44(1). Section 69(1) defines "tenancy" as being "a tenancy created immediately or derivatively out of the freehold . . .". The tenant argued that, although the doctrine of estoppel prevented the tenant from disputing the grantor's title to the grant of

---

not exceed three years and takes effect in possession (i.e. starts immediately) at a rent which is the best reasonably obtainable (i.e. without a fine): s.54 of the LPA 1925. See also fn.24 with respect to the registration requirements in connection with registered land and first registration.

[24] Under the doctrine in *Walsh v Lonsdale* (1882) L.R. 21 Ch. D. 9. Note, a tenancy granted out of a registered estate will be required to be registered at HM Land Registry if in excess of seven years in order for the legal estate to pass: s.27(2)(b)(ii), Land Registration Act 2002. Until registration the lease will take effect in equity only: s.27(1) of the LRA 2002. Where the lease is granted out of an unregistered estate the grant of the lease will trigger the requirement for first registration of the estate out of which the lease has been granted: s.4(1)(c)(i) of the LRA 2002. If the grantor does not apply to register his estate, the grant of the lease takes effect as a contract made for valuable consideration to grant or create the legal estate concerned: s.7(2)(b) of the LRA 2002.

[25] [1974] 1 W.L.R. 113; [1974] 1 All E.R. 17.

[26] As to tenancies by estoppel, see *Bruton v London and Quadrant Housing* [2000] 1 A.C. 406 HL. It is not the estoppel which creates the tenancy but the tenancy which creates the estoppel. The estoppel arises when one or other of the parties wants to deny one of the ordinary incidents or obligations of the tenancy on the ground that the landlord had no legal estate. The basis of the estoppel is that having entered into an agreement which constitutes a lease or tenancy, he cannot repudiate that incident or obligation: Lord Hoffmann in *Bruton v London & Quadrant Housing Trust* [2000] 1 A.C. 406 HL at 415, 416. Until the acquisition of the legal estate the tenancy exists by estoppel. Upon the acquisition of the legal estate the tenancy is fed and as between the parties there exists an estate. There is no need for there to be a re-execution of the tenancy upon acquisition of the legal estate: *First National Bank Limited v Thompson* [1996] Ch. 231 CA (where the court held that there was no need for re-execution of the legal charge in order for the charge to be a legal charge from the date of acquisition of the legal estate by the mortgagor). The tenancy by estoppel is not binding on third parties. Once the interest of the licensee comes to an end the occupier's lease will not be binding on them: *Kay v Lambeth LBC and London and Quadrant Housing Trust* [2004] H.L.R. 56 CA.

[27] [1998] 1 E.G.L.R. 69 CA.

[28] [1986] 2 E.G.L.R. 80.

[29] *Bell v General Accident Fire and Life Assurance Corporation Limited* [1998] 1 E.G.L.R. 69 CA.

the lease, it did not prevent it from contending that the grantor was not the "landlord" within the statutory definition or that the tenancy by estoppel was not a "tenancy" within the statutory definition at the date of grant. On the tenant's argument there was, at the date of grant, no "landlord" and no "tenancy" of the business premises within the meaning of the 1954 Act. This argument was rejected by the court.[30]

1–04 The statutory definition expressly provides that it does not include a mortgage term or any interest arising in favour of a mortgagor by his attorning tenant to his mortgagee.[31]

1–05 ***Tottenham Hotspur Football & Athletic Co Ltd v Princegrove Publishers Ltd***[32]
As a compromise of the tenant's application for a new tenancy, it was agreed that the landlord would grant to the tenant a tenancy for one year certain from which the security of tenure provisions of the Act would be excluded and an order by consent was made to that effect. The court further ordered that the agreement be authorised pursuant to s.38(4) and that the agreement should be contained in the new lease. No formal lease was ever executed, but the tenant remained in possession under the terms of the agreement and the order, paying the rent accordingly. On the expiry of the year certain the tenant refused to give up possession and the landlord brought proceedings for possession. It was held that the effect of the tenant going into possession under the agreement was, pursuant to the doctrine in *Walsh v Lonsdale*, to put the tenant in the same position as if an instrument giving effect to the agreement had been executed and thus the provisions of ss.24–28 had been excluded and the landlord was entitled to possession.

Does the agreement need to be in writing?

1–06 To come within the Act, an "agreement" for a tenancy need not be in writing unless so required by common law or statute. Although s.69(2) of the 1954 Act defines "agreement" between the landlord and the tenant as meaning an agreement "in writing between them", it is thought that this refers only to agreements made for the purpose of the Act. This was conceded by counsel in *Wheeler v Mercer*[33] (digested in para.1–18) to be the effect of the words. So interpreted, s.69(2) is dealing with agreements between landlord and tenant such as one contemplated, e.g. by ss.32 to 35 inclusive. This interpretation is supported by the fact that the "landlord" referred to in s.69(2) is a reference to the

---

30 Mummery L.J. in his judgment said:

"The effect of the common law doctrine of estoppel is to bid you to treat an imaginary state of affairs as real, i.e. that Fire [the grantor] was entitled to the fee simple or such other interest in the premises as would have enabled it to grant the term of years by the 1978 lease. The consequences of treating the imaginary state of affairs as real must also be imagined as real, unless there is a prohibition against doing so. One of those 'real' consequences is that the tenants were not legally entitled, as against Fire, to assert that the title to the premises was vested in anyone other than Fire; or that someone other than Fire was the landlord; or that no tenancy existed between them and Fire."

31 See the definition of "tenancy" in s.69(1) of the Act.

32 [1974] 1 W.L.R. 113; [1974] 1 All E.R. 17.

33 [1957] A.C. 416.

"landlord" as defined in s.44. Thus, the "landlord" as there defined is not necessarily the immediate landlord, whereas a tenancy is normally created by the immediate landlord. Furthermore, the words "between the landlord and the tenant" do not appear in the definition of "tenancy" in s.69(1). It follows that a "tenancy" within the Act may be made orally or arise by implication (e.g. arising by the payment and acceptance of rent in the case of a holding over). By statute, an agreement for a lease made on or after September 27, 1989 must be made in writing and all the terms which the parties have expressly agreed must be incorporated in one document or, where contracts are to be exchanged, in each: ss.2(1), 5(3), (4)(a) of the Law of Property (Miscellaneous Provisions) Act 1989. These requirements do not, however, apply in relation to an agreement to grant a short lease, that is to say, one taking effect in possession for a term not exceeding three years (whether or not the lessee is given power to extend the term) at the best rent which can be reasonably obtained without taking a fine: s.2(5)(a) of the 1989 Act.[34]

Distinguished from licence

Grant of exclusive possession hallmark of tenancy

The Act does not apply to licences. Whether a particular agreement for the occupation of land creates a tenancy or a licence depends not upon the label attached to it by the parties,[35] but upon whether it creates in substance the rights and obligations of landlord and tenant or those of licensor and licensee.[36] In *National Car Parks Ltd v Trinity Development Co (Banbury) Ltd*,[37] the agreement, which was one to administer a car park, provided that "This licence is not intended by either party hereto to confer upon the licensee any right or interest in the nature of a tenancy and gives no proprietary interest to the licensee in the licensed premises". Judge Rich QC, sitting as a deputy judge of the High Court, said: "*... this clause indicates the intention of the parties, and it is not to be assumed that they failed in such intention ...*" In the Court of Appeal it was said that: **1–07**

[34] On the provisions of the 1989 Act see generally *Hill & Redman's Law of Landlord and Tenant* (London: LexisNexis), paras 1002–1089.

[35] For an early case illustrating this principle, see *Addiscombe Garden Estates v Crabbe* [1958] 1 Q.B. 513 (digested at para.1–11) where Jenkins L.J. said at 522:

"The whole document must be looked at; and if, after it has been examined, the right conclusion appears to be that, whatever label may have been attached to it, it in fact conferred and imposed on the grantee in substance the rights and obligations of a tenant, and on the grantor in substance the rights and obligations of a landlord, then it must be given the appropriate effect, that is to say, it must be treated as a tenancy agreement as distinct from a mere licence."

[36] The Court of Appeal has, however, on several occasions indicated that, where the contract is negotiated between two substantial parties of equal bargaining power and with the benefit of legal advice, and the contract negotiated contains not merely a label but a clause that sets out in unequivocal terms the parties' intention as to its legal effect, the court would require some persuading that its true effect was directly contrary to that expressed intention: *Clear Channel UK Ltd v Manchester City Council* [2006] 1 E.G.L.R. 27 CA per Parker L.J. at [29] followed in *Scottish Widows Plc v Stewart* [2006] EWCA Civ 999.

[37] [2001] 1 E.G.L.R. 43.

> "*The court must, of course, look at the substance but as I see it it does not follow from that that what the parties have said is totally irrelevant and to be disregarded. For my part, I would agree with the judge that some attention must be given to the terms which the parties have agreed. On the other hand it must be approached with healthy scepticism, particularly, for instance, if the parties' bargaining positions are asymmetrical.*[38]"

Since the landmark decision of the House of Lords in *Street v Mountford*,[39] the test for distinguishing a licence from a tenancy is whether the arrangement under consideration was intended[40] to create legal relations between the parties and granted exclusive possession for a period and at a rent.[41] Although that case concerned residential premises, and the terminology used in the speech of Lord Templeman is more apt to distinguish a lodger from a residential tenant than a commercial licensee from a commercial tenant, the same test is equally applicable to business property.

In *Bruton v London and Quadrant Housing*[42] Lord Hoffmann said:

> "The decision of this House in *Street v Mountford* is authority for the proposition that a 'lease' or 'tenancy' is a contractually binding agreement, not referable to any other relationship between the parties, by which one person gives another the right to exclusive occupation of land for a fixed or renewable period or periods of time, usually in return for a periodic payment in money. An agreement having these characteristics creates a relationship of landlord and tenant to which the common law or statute may then attach various incidents. The fact that the parties use language more appropriate to a different kind of agreement, such as a licence, is irrelevant if upon its true construction it has the identifying characteristics of a lease. The meaning of the agreement, for example, as to the extent of the possession which it grants, depend upon the intention of the parties, objectively ascertained by reference to the language and relevant background... But the classification of the agreement as a lease does not depend upon any intention additional to that expressed in the choice of terms. It is simply a question of characterising the terms which the parties have agreed. This is a question of law. In this case, it seems to me that the agreement, construed against the relevant background, plainly gave Mr Bruton a right to exclusive possession. There is nothing to suggest that he was to share possession with the trust, the council or anyone else. The trust did not retain such control over the premises as was inconsistent with Mr Bruton having exclusive possession, as was the case in *Westminster City Council v Clarke*.[43] The only rights which it reserved were for itself and the council to enter at certain times and for limited purposes. As Lord Templeman said in *Street v Mountford* such an express reservation 'only serves to emphasise

---

[38] Arden L.J. [2002] P. & C.R. 18 at [26].

[39] [1985] A.C. 809 HL.

[40] The intention is ascertained objectively. Thus, the fact that the parties state that the agreement is not intended to create a tenancy is not conclusive and does not preclude a finding that the agreement is in fact the grant of a tenancy: *Facchini v Bryson* [1952] 1 T.L.R. 1386 CA; *Street v Mountford* [1985] A.C. 809 at 819. However, in *Clear Channel UK Ltd v Manchester City Council* [2006] 1 E.G.L.R. 27 CA, Parker L.J. observed in connection with a contract negotiated between two substantial parties of equal bargaining power and with the benefit of full legal advice that:

"... I do [not] intend to cast any doubt whatever upon the principles established in *Street v Mountford*. On the other hand, the fact remains that this was a contract negotiated between two substantial parties of equal bargaining power and with the benefit of full legal advice. Where the contract so negotiated contains not merely a label but a clause that sets out in unequivocal terms the parties' intention as to its legal effect, I would in any event have taken some persuading that its true effect was directly contrary to that expressed intention." (at [29])

[41] In fact the right to receive rent is not an essential feature of a lease: *Ashburn Anstalt v Arnold* [1988] 2 W.L.R. 706; [1988] 2 All E.R. 147 CA. Its absence does not mean that a licence and not a tenancy has necessarily been created: *Ashburn Anstalt v Arnold*.

[42] [2000] 1 A.C. 406 HL.

[43] [1992] 2 A.C. 288 HL. In this case a local authority provided a room in a hostel to a single homeless man pursuant to their statutory duty to do so. They reserved the right to change the room

the fact that the grantee is entitled to exclusive possession and is a tenant'. Nor was there any other relationship between the parties to which Mr Bruton's exclusive possession could be referable."

Negating exclusive possession

In considering whether exclusive possession has been conferred, the most important consideration is likely to be the degree of control over the premises and the use retained by the owner.[44] This will ordinarily require a detailed consideration of the terms of the contract between the parties.[45] For example, the reservation of a unilateral right on the part of the landowner to move the occupier to other premises, subject to the reservation being a sham,[46] negates the grant of exclusive possession: *Westminster City Council v Clarke*,[47] *Dresden Estates Ltd v Collinson*[48] (digested in para.1–14). Similarly, a clause in an agreement which provided that the occupier should not interfere with the owners' right to **1–08**

---

which he occupied at any time or require him to share a room with someone else. They also controlled the extent of the use by forbidding visitors without consent and by requiring that the occupier was in the premises by a stated time each evening.

[44] Where the landowner provides services which require unrestricted access to and use of the premises occupied, the occupier may well be a licensee only. The mere fact that the occupier does not utilise the services does not elevate his position to that of a tenant: *Uratemp Ventures Ltd v Collins* [2000] 1 E.G.L.R. 156 CA (unaffected by the subsequent overruling of this decision by the House of Lords on a different point: [2002] 1 A.C. 301 HL).

[45] As to whether management agreements truly reflect the parties' intentions or constitute the grant of a tenancy, see the cases in para.1–82 et seq. below. See also *Wang v Wei* [1976] 1 E.G.L.R. 66.

[46] The most often cited definition of sham is that by Diplock L.J. in *Snook v London and West Riding Investments Ltd* [1967] 2 Q.B. 786 at 802C–802E:

"It is I think necessary to consider what (if any) legal concept is involved in the use of this popular and pejorative word. I apprehend that if it has any meaning in law, it means acts done or documents executed by the parties to the sham which are intended by them to give to third parties or to the court the appearance of creating between the parties legal rights and obligations different from the actual legal rights and obligations (if any) which the parties intended to create. But one thing, I think is clear, in legal principle, morality and the authorities . . . for acts or documents to be a 'sham', with whatever legal consequences follow from this, all the parties thereto must have a common intention that the acts or documents are not to create the legal rights and obligations which they give the appearance of creating."

In *National Westminster Bank Plc v Jones* [2001] 1 B.C.L.C. 98 Ch D, Neuberger J. said:

"It is equally clear, to my mind, that the mere fact that a tenancy, or any other contractual transaction, is entered into for such an artificial purpose, namely to avoid the contractual or statutory rights which a third party would otherwise enjoy, does not by any means of itself render the transaction a sham."

In considering whether an agreement is a sham it is permissible to examine external evidence including the parties' explanations and circumstantial evidence such as evidence of the subsequent conduct of the parties: *Hitch v Stone (Inspector of Taxes)* [2001] EWCA Civ 63 CA; *Brumwell v Powys CC* [2011] EWCA Civ 1613 CA at [28].

[47] [1992] 2 A.C. 288 HL (residential premises).

[48] (1987) 55 P. & C.R. 47; [1987] 1 E.G.L.R. 45 (commercial premises). See also *McCarthy v Bence* [1990] 1 E.G.L.R. 1 CA. In that case there was a share milking agreement, under which the land owners would make available land for the stocking of cows together with the necessary buildings. The agreement provided that the owners could alter the fields upon which the cows could be kept. Clause 1 of the agreement in that case stated:

"This [the provision of the land for the cows] will not involve exclusive occupation and I may alter the area of land and the fields available from time to time but will not do anything thereby to prejudice the arrangement."

possession and control of the premises was held to be inconsistent with the grant of exclusive possession: *Shell-Mex and BP Ltd v Manchester Garages*[49] (digested in para.1–12). Alternatively, the occupation may be explicable on a basis other than on that of the existence of a landlord and tenant relationship. As Lord Hoffmann mentioned in the *Bruton* decision (para.1–07 above), if the occupation is ancillary to a relationship of vendor and purchaser, the grant of a tenancy may be negatived: *Essex Plan Ltd v Broadminster*.[50] A limitation on hours of use may indicate that exclusive possession has not been granted: *Manchester City Council v National Car Parks*[51] (digested in para.1–13).

1–09 Caution should, of course, be observed in relation to the detailed facts and judicial statements of principle in those cases which preceded *Street v Mountford*,[52] although it is considered that most if not all of them would have been decided in the same way: see also *Wang v Wei*,[53] *University of Reading v Johnson-Houghton*,[54] and *Vandersteen v Agius*.[55]

It is to be noted in that case that there was no suggestion of this clause being a sham. However, the argument was put that as a matter of fact the occupier had been granted exclusive possession. The Court of Appeal held on analysis that this was not the case. It was conceded on behalf of the owner that the power to move the occupier to alternative accommodation could be exercised only reasonably and not arbitrarily. It is also worth noting *Fatac Ltd (In Liquidation) v Commr of Inland Revenue*[2002] NZCA 269 CA, where the New Zealand Court of Appeal referred to *Dresden v Collinson* [1987] 1 E.G.L.R. 45, without disapproval, as an illustration of the fact that the right to require the occupier to move from one part of the premises to another at the owner's direction tended to negate exclusive possession.

[49] [1971] 1 W.L.R. 612; [1971] 1 All E.R. 841. See also *Esso Petroleum Co Ltd v Fumegrange Ltd* [1994] 2 E.G.L.R. 90; *National Car Parks Ltd v Trinity Development Co (Banbury) Ltd* [2001] EWCA Civ 1686; [2002] 2 P. & C.R. 18 CA.

[50] (1988) 56 P. & C.R. 353; *Cameron Ltd v Rolls-Royce Plc* [2008] L. & T.R. 22 (agreement for lease providing for licence pending grant held to be licence). Similarly payment of mesne profits pending the execution of an order for possession will not give rise the grant of a new tenancy as the occupation is referrable to the order rather than an intention to grant a new tenancy. However, an increase in the mesne profits to be paid by the occupier other than at a rate permitted by the order may give rise to the grant of a new tenancy: *Leadenhall Residential 2 Ltd v Stirling* [2002] 1 W.L.R. 499; [2001] 3 All E.R. 645 CA.

[51] [1982] 1 E.G.L.R. 94 CA. However, a mere limitation on hours does not of itself negate the grant of exclusive possession. Thus, in *Westminster CC v Southern Railway Co Ltd* [1936] A.C. 511 HL access to a station bookstall restricted to the hours of operation of the station did not prevent the operator from being a tenant. See also *Graysim Holdings Ltd v P&O Property Holdings Ltd* [1993] 1 E.G.L.R. 93, first instance, where stallholders were held to be tenants notwithstanding that access to and trade from their respective stalls was limited to specified hours of the day. A limitation on hours may be ignored as a sham: *Aslan v Murphy (No.1)* [1990] 1 W.L.R. 766; [1989] 3 All E.R. 130 CA (clause preventing occupation for 90 minutes a day).

[52] [1985] A.C. 809 HL.

[53] [1976] 1 E.G.L.R. 66 (so-called management agreement held to be a tenancy).

[54] [1985] 2 E.G.L.R. 113.

[55] (1993) 65 P. & C.R. 266 CA (where the court was satisfied that the arrangement to provide services was separate from that relating to the accommodation and thus entry by the landowner was done pursuant to an agreement to clean and provide ancillary services and not in the capacity of a landlady with a business lodger).

Advertising hoardings, front of house rights and stalls

The nature of the right granted may negate the grant of exclusive possession.[56] Thus agreements giving permission to erect or affix advertisements or advertising hoardings have been held to create licences on the basis that exclusive possession has not been granted of the land.[57] The position is a fortiori where the land upon which the advertising hoarding is to be placed has not been identified by the parties.[58] Similarly, the grant of "front of house rights" for the provision of refreshments in a theatre has been held to be a licence.[59] Rights granted in respect of stalls, such as a market stall, or franchise agreements have also been considered to exclude, by their nature, the grant of exclusive possession.[60] However, each case depends upon its own facts and it is possible for such rights **1–10**

---

[56] The grant of a right to "gallops" for training horses has been held to grant a tenancy: *University of Reading v Johnson-Houghton* [1985] 2 E.G.L.R. 113. See para.1–26 et seq. on the question of whether such a demise constitutes "premises" for the purposes of the Act.

[57] *Wilson v Tavener* [1901] 1 Ch. 578 (grant of right to erect a hoarding upon the forecourt of a house and use of gable end of cottage held to be a licence); *Provincial Bill Posting Co v Low Moor Iron Co* [1909] 2 K.B. 344 (agreement to take "the exclusive right of posting bills and exhibiting advertisements upon" certain land for a period of seven years. The hoardings were substantial with supporting posts being driven into the ground to a depth of four to five feet, tied together with cross-pieces and secured to back posts some 12 feet behind. Agreement held to be licence as there was "no exclusive right to the occupation of any definite portion of land"); *King v David Allen & Sons Billposting Ltd* [1916] 2 A.C. 54 (right to put advertisements on flank wall of cinema held to be a licence); *United Kingdom Advertising Co Ltd v Glasgow Bag-Wash Laundry* 1926 S.C. 303; *Kewal Investments v Arthur Maiden* [1990] 1 E.G.L.R. 193. Contrast *Taylor v Pendleton Overseers* (1887) L.R. 19 Q.B.D. 288 (advertising agreement held to be tenancy), which case was said in *Kewal Investments v Arthur Maiden* to be one on its own special facts. (In *Kewal* there was a grant of permission for an advertising station consisting of five 16-sheet panels at the site in question, and to exhibit advertising posters on it, and have access to the advertising stations at all reasonable times for the purpose of inspecting, maintaining and repairing it, held to be a licence.)

[58] *Clear Channel UK Ltd v Manchester City Council* [2006] 1 E.G.L.R. 27 CA. The local authority entered into an agreement with Clear Channel under which the latter would construct and operate M-shaped advertising stations placed on concrete bases at various sites owned by the local authority. No formal agreement had been concluded, but it was common ground that the parties' rights and obligations were set out in a draft agreement. That agreement referred to some 13 sites the locations of which were not precisely defined, being identified only by the relevant street. The agreement stated that it "shall constitute a licence in respect of each Site and confers no tenancy". The Court of Appeal held that Clear Channel had a licence only; the sites referred to in the agreement were not the areas of the bases but larger, undefined areas of land owned by the local authority, and that there was no intention to grant exclusive possession.

[59] *Clore v Theatrical Properties Ltd* [1936] 3 All E.R. 483 CA (licence notwithstanding words of demise); *Daly v Edwards* (1900); affirmed *Edwardes v Barrington* (1901) 85 L.T. 650 ("Free and exclusive licence and right to the refreshment rooms" held to be licence); *Frank Warr & Co v London CC*[1904] 1 K.B. 713 (agreement related to the Globe Theatre, Strand, London, whereby lessees of theatre "let... the free and exclusive right to all refreshments... with the necessary use of the refreshment rooms and bars and cloakrooms and wine cellars... together with... the free right... of free access to and from all parts of the house, including the front of the theatre ..." agreement held to be a licence); *Payne-Jennings & Killick v Bright Enterprises* (1959) 173 E.G. 917. Contrast *Radaich v Smith*, where the grantee of the sole right for five years to supply refreshments to the public using the premises was held, by the High Court of Australia, to be a tenant. As to whether such persons can in any event be said to be in occupation of the land in question, see *Commissioners of Customs & Excise v Sinclair Collis Ltd* [2001] UKHL 30; [2001] S.T.C. 989, discussed in para.1–50.

[60] *R. v Morrish* (1863) 32 L.J.M.C. 245; *Rendell v Roman* (1893) 9 T.L.R. 192 (exhibitions); *Wigan Borough Council v Green & Son (Wigan) Ltd* [1985] 2 E.G.L.R. 242 (market stalls); *Ross Auto Wash*

to amount to a tenancy, notwithstanding that a trader's access to the stall is restricted to certain hours of the day.[61] In *Graysim Holdings Ltd v P&O Property Holdings Ltd*[62] a market hall contained 35 individual stalls. The stalls were fixed and of wooden construction. They consisted of studs to which partitioning had been attached. The stalls were fitted with roller blinds which were so designed that at the end of a day's trading they could be secured by the trader padlocking the blind to the counter or some other part of the stall. Some of the security-minded stallholders had more elaborate systems, but each trader secured his own stall with his own padlock and key. The tenant of the market hall provided a number of facilities and services to the stallholders, including the provision and maintenance of lavatories, bin rooms and the employment of a market superintendent, who collected the rent, and service charge, and effected minor repairs and maintenance services to the demised premises. Trading hours were limited and it was only during such hours that stallholders had access to the demised premises. The tenant prescribed the goods that could be sold by the stallholders. It was also part of the superintendent's duties to maintain discipline amongst traders and to ensure that the aisles were clear for shoppers. It was held that the stallholders were tenants of their respective stalls.

1–11 ***Addiscombe Garden Estates Ltd v Crabbe***[63] By an agreement in writing, landowners agreed to allow the trustees of the Shirley Park Lawn Tennis Club to use and occupy a club-house, changing-room and tennis courts for a fixed period of two years in consideration of a monthly payment. The document described itself as a "licence" and was drafted in such a way that the words "landlord" and "tenant" and cognate terms were successfully avoided. It was nonetheless held by the Court of Appeal that the agreement created a tenancy, not a licence, and that the tenancy was a business tenancy within the Act because the members of the club were a body of persons which was carrying on an activity in the shape of a lawn tennis club within the meaning of s.23(2).

1–12 ***Shell-Mex and BP Ltd v Manchester Garages***[64] Shell-Mex were the freeholders of a filling station which was occupied by Manchester Garages under a lease as to part of the land which was used for the storage of motor vehicles and general servicing work, and under an agreement described as a licence as to the part of the land on which there were three petrol pumps, a kiosk, a car display canopy and offices. Both pieces of land were occupied by Manchester Garages for the purposes of their business. The agreement was expressed to be a licence, and Manchester Garages agreed, inter alia, to use every endeavour and due

---

v Herbert [1979] 1 E.G.L.R. 95 (market stalls, digested in para.1–84); *Smith v Northside Developments* [1987] 2 E.G.L.R. 151 at 283 (part of shop premises at Camden Lock).

[61] *Joel v International Circus and Christmas Fair* (1920) 124 L.T. 459 (erecting and operating a stall at a trade exhibition); *Westminster City Council v Southern Railway Co* [1936] 2 A.C. 511 HL (railway station bookstall).

[62] [1993] 1 E.G.L.R. 93, first instance. The important finding was that the individual stall holders had exclusive possession, as this meant that the lessee of the market hall was not in occupation for business purposes: see para.1–65, et seq.

[63] [1958] 1 Q.B. 513 CA.

[64] [1971] 1 W.L.R. 612; [1971]; 1 All E.R. 841 CA.

diligence to sell and foster the sale of Shell-Mex's products and not to impede in any way the officers, servants or agents of Shell-Mex in the exercise by them of Shell-Mex's rights of possession and control of the premises. The Court of Appeal held that the agreement created a licence, and not a tenancy, because of the personal tie, because Shell-Mex retained possession and control of the premises, because there was no proviso for re-entry and because it was doubtful whether the agreement was assignable. The dominant purpose of the transaction as a whole was the promotion of the sale of Shell-Mex's products. A licence rather than a tenancy was best fitted to the character of that transaction.

Manchester City Council v National Car Parks[65] The owners of certain premises agreed to grant to National Car Parks the right to use them as a car park for a term of six months between limited hours of the day. The agreement was expressed to be a licence. The Court of Appeal held that there were commercial reasons why the agreement was unlikely to be a tenancy, and that the restrictions on opening showed that National Car Parks were not granted and were not intended to be granted exclusive possession. The agreement was to be construed as a licence. **1–13**

Dresden Estates v Collinson[66] By an agreement in writing described as a "licence" and referring throughout to the parties as "licensor" and "licensee", the licensee agreed, by cl.2 of the agreement, "to permit the licensors with necessary workmen and contractors and equipment to enter on the premises to carry out work deemed necessary by the licensors to the premises or to the adjoining premises or services". Clause 4 of the agreement conferred upon the licensors the right "... from time to time on giving the required notice to require the licensee to transfer his occupation to other premises within the licensor's adjoining property" and upon "... giving the required notice to the licensee increase the licence fee to such amount as may be specified in such notice". It was held that although cl.2 was consistent with a grant of a tenancy, the terms of cl.4 militated very strongly against the grant of exclusive possession and the occupier was accordingly a licensee. **1–14**

Dellneed v Chin[67] Mr Chin, the leasehold owner of restaurant premises in Soho, London, entered into a management agreement with a company. The management agreement was a "mai toi" agreement, a form of agreement well known in the Chinese community and referring literally to a table use or table rent agreement. The company spent £22,000 on furniture and £11,000 on equipment and prior to signing the agreement entered the premises for the purposes of redecorating them. The management agreement provided for the company to take over the management of the business in consideration of a weekly sum and payment of all outgoings. The company was entitled to retain all profits. The company was solely responsible for the employment and dismissal of staff. Mr Chin reserved to himself a right to enter the premises at any time to **1–15**

65 [1987] 1 E.G.L.R. 75.
66 [1982] 1 E.G.L.R. 94 CA. See also fn.48 above.
67 [1987] 1 E.G.L.R. 75.

ensure that the business was operated efficiently and the company was complying with its obligations under the agreement. He was not, however, required to provide any services to the premises and reserved no right to do so in the agreement. The agreement was for a fixed term and shortly prior to its expiry Mr Chin informed the company that he required vacant possession on its termination. It was held that the company was a subtenant of Mr Chin, for on the true construction of the terms of the agreement and, on the evidence, the relationship between the parties was not that of an owner and manager; the company was starting up its own restaurant business, albeit with equipment provided by Mr Chin and with the benefit of the name, reputation and goodwill attaching to those premises. To the extent the agreement on its face purported to represent the company as manager it did not reflect the parties' true intention which was to grant the company exclusive possession of the premises at a rent, for a term.

1–16 ***London & Associated Investment Trust Plc v Calow***[68] Calow, a solicitor, was a director of the plaintiff company. He was looking for offices to set up business. F, who was the leasehold owner of the first and second floors of an office building, was prepared to let the two top floors provided security of tenure the provisions of the 1954 Act were excluded by order of the court. It was agreed by Calow and the plaintiff that the plaintiff was to take underleases of the two floors and Calow would then be granted a sub-underlease of the second floor only. In April 1980, F granted the plaintiff an underlease of the second floor for a term of five years from December 1, 1979, expiring on November 30, 1984.[69] The underlease was excluded from the provisions of ss.24 to 28 of the 1954 Act by order of the court. It was a term of the underlease that any sub-underlease be granted outside the security of tenure provisions of the 1954 Act.

A draft sub-underlease was prepared but was never executed. The draft sub-underlease was for a term expiring on November 29, 1984. It was a term of the draft sub-underlease that if Calow ceased to be a director of the plaintiff company, the sub-underlease would determine automatically. No order was obtained from the court in respect of the proposed sub-underlease excluding the security of tenure provisions of the 1954 Act. Calow had entered into occupation of the second floor in January 1980 for the purposes of decorating it. No money was paid to the plaintiff until execution of the underlease when he paid in full his share of the rent, service charges and other outgoings applicable to the second floor. Calow was in sole occupation of the second floor with the exception of a reception area which was used by the plaintiff for receiving visitors to their first floor premises. The plaintiff also used some office machinery in another of the second floor offices. Further, by arrangement with Calow, the plaintiff would use Calow's office as a conference or boardroom. The use of the reception area continued for a period of two years.

Calow continued in occupation of the premises paying the plaintiff the rent, service charges and other outgoings applicable to the premises until October 24, 1983, when Calow resigned his directorship of the plaintiffs. Calow vacated the premises on December 31, 1983. No notice either at common law or under the

68 [1986] 2 E.G.L.R. 80.

69 A lease of the first floor was also granted but the lease is not material to the decision.

1954 Act was given. Calow paid all sums due to the plaintiff up to the date of his vacating the premises. The plaintiff claimed that Calow was liable for rent, service charges and other outgoings from January 1, 1984, to November 29, 1984 (being the term date of the draft sub-underlease). Calow argued that he had a licence and could therefore terminate his occupation at any time, or, alternatively, if he were a tenant, that the plaintiffs were estopped from contending that the provisions of the 1954 Act applied to it.

The issues before the High Court were whether Calow was a licensee or tenant; and, if a tenant, the terms of that tenancy and whether Calow remained liable up to November 29, 1984.

It was held:

(1) The principles laid down in *Street v Mountford*[70] applied equally to business premises.[71]
(2) Calow had exclusive possession of the premises. The use by the plaintiff of the premises did not amount to sharing possession; it was an arrangement for specific and well-defined limited purposes.
(3) Calow had taken the premises for a defined term at a rent.
(4) Calow was accordingly a tenant.
(5) Calow's tenancy was either on the terms of the draft sub-underlease or was an annual periodic tenancy on such terms of the draft sub-underlease as were consistent with an annual periodic tenancy.
(6) Therefore, whatever the terms of the tenancy after Calow's resignation it continued pursuant to s.24 and Calow was accordingly liable up to November 29, 1984 (the judge was not asked to consider Calow's liability after November 29, 1984).
(7) The plaintiffs were not estopped from contending that the tenancy continued after December 31, 1983, pursuant to the 1954 Act as:
    (i) there was no agreement between the plaintiff and Calow to exclude the 1954 Act—this was something which was required by F;
    (ii) no representation was made by the plaintiff that an order of the court was not required;
    (iii) the provisions of the 1954 Act cannot be prevented from applying to a tenancy either by agreement between the parties or by estoppel.[72]

---

[70] [1985] A.C. 809 HL.

[71] In *Mann Aviation Group (Engineering) Ltd (In Administration) v Longmint Aviation Ltd* [2011] EWHC 2238 (Ch), Sales J. said:

"[34] In circumstances where the owner of land and the person who occupies that land intend their relationship to be one of landlord and tenant (rather than a relationship of landowner and licensee, whether contractual or otherwise), and substantial periodic rental payments are made, the law is clear. A periodic tenancy will be found to arise by implication from those circumstances: *Street v Mountford* [1985] AC 809, 818E-F. In my view, the position is the same whether one is looking at occupation of a residential property or at occupation of a commercial property: *London & Associated Investment Trust plc v Calow* (1986) 53 P & CR 340, [1986] 2 EGLR 80; *Woodfall's Law of Landlord and Tenant,* para 1.022, fn 4, para 1.023."

[72] On this issue the judge said:

"This is not one of those exceptional cases where you can contract out of or be estopped from setting up some provision for your protection which is conferred by an Act of Parliament, for the simple reason, as Mr. Reynolds put it to me, that here there is a positive prohibition against

Does not include tenancy at will

1–17 It is now clearly established that tenancies at will do not come within the Act. This is so whether the tenancy at will arises by implication of law (*Wheeler v Mercer*[73] (digested in para.1–18)) or by express agreement (*Manfield v Botchin*[74] (digested in para.1–19) and *Hagee (London) Ltd v AB Erikson and Larson*[75] (digested in para.1–20)). Entry into occupation of land pending negotiation for the grant of a lease "is one of the classic circumstances in which a tenancy at will exists"—per Nicholls L.J. in *Javad v Aqil*[76] citing *Hagee (London) Ltd v AB Erikson and Larson.*[77] So too entry pursuant to an agreement for a lease gives rise to a tenancy at will, unless there are circumstances from which the court may infer that the parties intended to grant a periodic tenancy.[78] The payment in advance of a periodic rent is not inconsistent with the grant of a tenancy at will; the payment of such a rent is but one, albeit an important one, of the circumstances to consider in determining the fair inference to be drawn as to the parties' intentions: *Javad v Aqil*; *Cardiothoracic Institute v Shrewdcrest*[79] (digested in para.1–19). A tenant holding over after the expiry of a lease with the consent of his landlord is likewise a tenant at will until some other interest is created, either by express grant or by implication by the payment and acceptance of rent: *Cardiothoracic Institute v Shrewdcrest, Javad v Aqil, Longrigg, Burrough & Trounson v Smith,*[80] *London Baggage Co (Charing Cross) Ltd v Railtrack Plc.*[81]

1–18 ***Wheeler v Mercer***[82] The quarterly periodic tenancy of the tenant was determined by notice to quit with effect from September 29, 1953. The tenant made a claim for a new lease under the provisions of the Landlord and Tenant Act 1927 (since repealed). Protracted negotiations for a new lease ensued. On April 6, 1955 the landlord asked the tenant to vacate immediately. In possession proceedings the defendant pleaded that she held the premises under a tenancy at will arising by implication of law and as such was entitled to the protection of the

---

contracting out, which is only relaxed in certain ways indicated in the section. Given that there is a positive prohibition against contracting out in the section, there is no need to enquire for whose benefit that has been provided. Given that express statutory prohibition against contracting out, there is no room for estoppel in this field" (at [83], [84]).

[73] [1957] A.C. 416 HL.

[74] [1970] 2 Q.B. 612.

[75] [1976] Q.B. 209 CA. As Denning M.R. said (at [215]) "If the tenant takes such a tenancy [i.e. an express tenancy at will], he runs the risk of being turned out, but so long as he does it on proper advice with his eyes open, he is bound by it. I would only add that a tenancy at will of this kind is rare. The court will look into it very closely to see whether or not it really is a tenancy at will, or whether it is a cloak for a periodic tenancy."

[76] [1991] 1 W.L.R. 1007; [1991] 1 All E.R. 243 CA.

[77] [1976] Q.B. 209 CA.

[78] *Hamerton v Stead* (1824) 3 B. & C. 478; *Braythwaite v Hitchcock* (1842) 10 M. & W. 494.

[79] [1986] 1 W.L.R. 368; [1986] 3 All E.R. 633.

[80] [1979] 2 E.G.L.R. 42 CA.

[81] [2004] 1 W.L.R. 320. Where a period of holding over as tenant at will after the expiration of the term was disregarded in determining whether the tenant was in occupation for business purposes for the purposes of s.38(2): see para.12–68.

[82] [1957] A.C. 416 HL.

Act. The House of Lords held that a tenancy at will by implication of law was not protected by the Act since (inter alia) s.25 showed that the definition of "tenancy" in s.69 as a tenancy created "by a tenancy agreement" was not intended to include such a tenancy.

Manfield & Sons v Botchin[83] The owners of three shops had been anxious to redevelop them for some time, but had encountered difficulties in obtaining planning permission. One of the shops was empty and, in order to derive income from it until such time as they were able to go ahead with their development, they entered into a written agreement which included the following terms: 1–19

> "The [landlords] shall let and [the tenant] shall take the said premises on a tenancy at will commencing on December 5, 1964 at a rental to be calculated at a rate of £1,560 per annum and paid on demand at such time or times as [the landlords] may think fit provided always that if [the landlords] should demand the aforesaid rent at fixed periods such demand or acceptance of rent shall not be deemed to create any periodic tenancy."

The agreement imposed a limited decorating obligation on the tenants and restricted user to the sale of gifts and antiques. There was no proviso for re-entry and it was expressly declared that the tenant's occupation "shall not be such as is protected by part two of the Landlord and Tenant Act 1954". On this basis the tenant remained in occupation for four-and-a-half years, paying rent on a monthly basis. When the landlords obtained planning permission they served notice to quit, but the tenant did not vacate. The court held that the agreement was to be construed as a tenancy at will and that an express tenancy at will was not a "tenancy" as defined by s.69, because s.25 contains no provision whereby such a tenancy can be ended by notice given by the landlord.

Hagee (London) Ltd v AB Erikson and Larson[84] The leasehold owner of premises granted a tenancy at will at an annual rent, payable quarterly in advance, by an agreement which stated that the tenants had an exclusive right of occupation. The Court of Appeal held that this was an express tenancy at will and was not protected by the Act. 1–20

Cardiothoracic Institute v Shrewdcrest[85] The claimant, which was a medical organisation, was the owner of a former convent, which it intended at all material times to redevelop for its own purposes at some uncertain time in the future. The defendant conducted a business of providing students with hostel accommodation and it entered into a series of tenancy agreements in respect of the convent for short fixed terms, from which the security of tenure provisions of the Act were excluded by agreement and with the leave of the court. At the end of the last of these (in October 1983), the plaintiff and the defendant entered into protracted negotiations for a further unprotected tenancy and the defendant remained in occupation carrying on its business and paying rent on a regular basis. The judge found that the defendant was throughout this period at pains to emphasise its lack 1–21

---

[83] [1970] 2 Q.B. 612.

[84] [1976] Q.B. 209 CA.

[85] [1986] 1 W.L.R. 368; [1986] 3 All E.R. 633.

of security of tenure (in order to avoid having to comply with certain statutory requirements); that both parties anticipated that the necessary formalities to obtain an exclusion order from the court would be completed; and that the plaintiff made it plain that any tenancy to be granted would only be on that basis. When the plaintiff sought possession, the defendant claimed to be a tenant protected by the 1954 Act. However the court decided that holding over pending negotiation was the classic circumstance in which a tenancy at will would be implied by law, and the facts of the case established that that was the parties' intention. The effect of the payment and acceptance of rent was not to create a periodic tenancy, because the evidence showed that that was not the parties' intention.

Tenancy ceasing to exist

1–22 The Act will cease to apply in circumstances where the tenancy has ceased to exist, such as where the tenant has terminated it by notice to quit or has surrendered the tenancy, or where the tenancy or a superior interest from which it is derived has been forfeited. The position where the tenancy has been forfeited but the tenant has a right to seek relief from forfeiture is discussed in para.6–49.

Sub-tenancies

1–23 One unexpected effect of the definition of "tenancy", which includes sub-tenancies, is that even a tenant whose tenancy is not, for any reason, one to which the Act applies, may create a sub-tenancy within the Act. For example, a tenant who does not occupy any part of the premises for business purposes can create a protected sub-tenancy of the whole or part. A tenant within one of the exceptions contained in s.43(1) and discussed in paras 1–141 to 1–151 can, it appears, create a sub-tenancy which will not itself fall within any of the exceptions and which will, accordingly, be protected. It also appears that a tenant whose security of tenure under ss.24 to 28 of the Act has been excluded by agreement in accordance with s.38A can himself create a protected sub-tenancy. No protection is conferred on the so called sub-tenant where the transaction in question is correctly to be analysed as an assignment, as where the term of the purported sub-tenancy is equal in duration to the term of the tenancy. In such a case the interest which has been assigned will have the same unprotected status as it had before the purported grant of the sub-tenancy: *Parc (Battersea) Ltd (In Receivership) v Hutchinson*[86] (digested in para.2–33).

[86] [1999] 2 E.G.L.R. 33 Ch D.

"Unlawful" sub-tenancies

It should be noted that the Act applies equally to lawful and to unlawful sub-tenancies, that is to say sub-tenancies which have been granted in breach of a covenant against sub-letting: *D'Silva v Lister House Developments Ltd.*[87] The effect of this is that if an unlawful sub-tenancy has been granted, the landlord will be without remedy unless he forfeits the head lease (and with it the sub-tenancy). A problem arises where the superior landlord has lost the right to forfeit or where the sub-tenancy is granted at a date so close to expiry of the tenancy that the superior landlord has, in practice, no opportunity to forfeit (e.g. if the sub-tenancy is granted one day before expiry of the tenancy). In such a case the superior landlord may be able to oppose the grant of a new tenancy to the sub-tenancy in reliance upon s.30(1)(c) ("any other reason connected with the tenant's use and management of the holding").[88] This is an additional reason why the prudent landlord will serve a notice pursuant to s.40 enquiring whether any sub-tenancies have been granted (see para.4–01 et seq). **1–24**

Statutory tenancies

The question arises whether a statutory tenancy deriving from the security of tenure provisions of the Rent Act 1977 or the Rent (Agriculture) Act 1976 is a "tenancy" within the meaning of s.69(1) and could thus attract the protection of the Act if the statutory tenant were to start to use the demised premises for business purposes. It is submitted that a statutory tenancy of this kind, being a mere personal status of irremovability and not being an estate or interest in land, is not a tenancy for these purposes. In *Durman v Bell*[89] the Court of Appeal held that a former agricultural worker who had a statutory tenancy under the 1976 Act of premises, which he not only occupied as his residence but also for business purposes, did not automatically lose his statutory tenancy as a result of the business. Some commentators[90] have treated *Durman v Bell* as being direct authority for the submission made above, but it is suggested that a close examination of the two judgments in that case, while wholly consistent with this submission, directly support only the narrower proposition that the business use does not automatically put an end to a statutory tenancy. The wider question of whether mixed business and residential use prevents the application of various relevant statutory provisions is discussed in para.1–36 et seq. **1–25**

---

[87] [1971] Ch. 17; [1970] 2 W.L.R. 563; [1970] 1 All E.R. 858 disapproving the county court decision in *Earl of Radnor v Lovibond & Co* (1958) 108 L.J. 204. *D'Silva v Lister House* is unaffected on this point by *Longman v Viscount Chelsea* [1989] 2 E.G.L.R. 242 CA. *D'Silva v Lister House* has been followed by Morgan J. in *Brimex Ltd v Begum* [2007] EWHC 3498 (Ch); [2009] L. & T.R. 21.

[88] Ground (c) is discussed further in para.7–42 et seq.

[89] [1988] 2 E.G.L.R. 117 CA.

[90] *Woodfall: Landlord and Tenant* (London: Sweet & Maxwell), Vol.2, para.22.033; Haley, *The Statutory Regulation of Business Tenancies*, 1st edn (Oxford: OUP), para.3–35, fn.158; and the first edition of this book, para.1.1.7.

4. DOES THE TENANCY INCLUDE "PREMISES" CAPABLE OF BEING OCCUPIED?

Meaning of "premises"

1–26 The Act applies only where the property comprised in the tenancy "is or includes premises": s.23(1). "Premises" is not defined, but the cases make it clear that it is not to be given a narrow meaning so as to comprise only land which is built upon, but rather its wider conveyancing sense, so as to include bare land as well as buildings. Thus the Act has been held to apply to open land used for the training of horses (*Bracey v Read*[91] (digested para.1–28) and *University of Reading v Johnson-Houghton*[92]), to former brick pits used for the purposes of a gun club (*Botterill v Bedfordshire CC*[93] (where the point was not, however, disputed)) and a car park used for the parking of vehicles belonging to partners in a firm of solicitors (*Harley Queen v Forsyte Kerman (A Firm)*[94] (digested in para.1–29)).

1–27 Where furniture or other chattels are held on a separate lease from the business premises the lease of the chattels is not protected by the 1954 Act: *Mirabeau v Sheckman.*[95]

1–28 ***Bracey v Read***[96] The landlord let two pieces of downland, to be used as "gallops" for exercising horses, to the tenant, a trainer of race horses. There were no buildings on the downland. The landlord served a common law notice to quit which the tenant contended was invalid, claiming the protection of the 1954 Act. It was conceded that he occupied the gallops for business purposes. It was held that the word "premises" in s.23 was to be construed as including bare land and, accordingly, the tenancy was protected by the Act.

1–29 ***Harley Queen v Forsyte Kerman (A Firm)***[97] The landlord served a notice to quit to terminate a quarterly tenancy of a numbered parking bay in a basement garage of a block of flats. The tenant, a firm of solicitors in nearby offices, claimed that the tenancy was protected by the Act. The tenancy agreement contained a covenant by the tenant to use the premises as a private garage for one motorcar. The county court judge held, dismissing the landlord's claim for possession, that the tenancy was protected, since the premises were occupied by a partner's car for the purposes of the firm's business and the covenant was not a prohibition on business use. In any event, the landlord had acquiesced in any breach.

---

[91] [1962] 3 W.L.R. 1194; [1962] 3 All E.R. 472 (reported also at [1963] Ch. 88 but not on this point).

[92] [1985] 2 E.G.L.R. 113.

[93] [1985] 1 E.G.L.R. 82 CA.

[94] [1983] C.L.Y. 2077.

[95] [1959] E.G.D. 133.

[96] [1963] 3 W.L.R. 1194; [1962] 3 All E.R. 472 (reported also at [1963] Ch. 88 but not on this point). See also *Commissioners of Customs and Excise v Sinclair Collis Ltd* [2001] UKHL 30 considered at para.1–50.

[97] [1983] C.L.Y. 2077.

Incorporeal hereditament

The Act may apply to a grant which consists solely of an easement for a term of years certain (often referred to, loosely, as "a lease of an easement"): *Pointon York Group Plc v Poulton*.[98] It was formerly considered that an easement such as a right of way did not comprise "premises" which are capable of being occupied within the meaning of s.23: *Land Reclamation Co Ltd v Basildon DC*[99] (digested in para.1–32), However, the Court of Appeal has held in *Pointon York Group Plc v Poulton*,[100] that Parliament did not intend in s.23 of the Act to provide for a meaning of "premises" different to that under the Landlord and Tenant Act 1927 as decided in *Whitley v Stumbles*,[101] where the House of Lords held that an incorporeal hereditament constituted "premises" for the purpose of s.17 of the 1927 Act. Thus, in *Pointon* the Act was held to apply where the tenant used parking spaces, limited to normal office hours only, in connection with its business. **1–30**

The right or easement must, however, be one which is capable of "occupation" by the tenant. In *Pointon*[102] the court held that on the true construction of the rights granted by the tenant's lease, the tenant was during normal business hours entitled to use the parking spaces to the exclusion of all others, and thus the right amounted to a right to occupy the spaces for discontinuous periods of parts of a **1–31**

---

[98] [2006] 3 E.G.L.R. 37; [2007] 1 P. & C.R. 115 CA.

[99] [1979] 1 W.L.R. 767; [1979] 2 All E.R. 993; [1979] 1 E.G.L.R. 85 CA. On a proper consideration of this case the Court of Appeal in *Pointon York Group Plc v Poulton* above said that the court did not decide that an incorporeal hereditament could never be "occupied". What the court held, it was said, was that the right of way granted in that case was not occupied. Buckley L.J. at 775 specifically recognised that "It may be that, if the right of way were an exclusive right, the circumstances might result in the exercise of the easement amounting to occupation of the land over which it passes: see *Holywell Union v Halkyn District Mines Drainage Co* [1895] A.C. 117, but that is not this case." In *Nevill Long & Co (Boards) Ltd v Firmenich & Co* [1983] 2 E.G.L.R. 76 CA (digested in paras 1–35 and 3–197); Fox L.J. said at 77 "It is quite true that, as decided in *Land Reclamation Co Ltd v Basildon Council*, a right of way is not property which can be described as 'occupied' by the tenant and if it is the only property comprised in the tenancy is outside the Act." It would not seem that this dictum was referred to in *Pointon York Group Plc v Poulton* [2006] 3 E.G.L.R. 37; [2007] 1 P. & C.R. 115 CA.

[100] [2006] 3 E.G.L.R. 37; [2007] 1 P. & C.R. 115 CA.

[101] [1930] A.C. 544 HL. The case concerned an incorporeal right of fishing. That right was demised with a lease of a hotel. Section 17 of the Landlord and Tenant Act 1927 defined the holdings to which the relevant part of the 1927 Act applied as "any premises held under a lease . . . and used wholly or partly for carrying on thereat any trade or business . . .". The House of Lords held that there was no reason for supposing that the expression "any premises held under a lease" in s.17 of the 1927 Act did not include "not merely the actual buildings in which trade is carried on, but also the land surrounding them, the easements granted as appurtenant to them, and any other incorporeal hereditaments which may form part of the premises in the strict legal sense of the term which are the subject matter of the habendum." It was said that any other construction would defeat the plain purpose of the Act, which was to provide, in the circumstances defined in the Act, the tenant with the right to continue to carry on his trade or business in the premises in the legal sense in which he was carrying them on under the lease for which he sought that renewal.

[102] [2006] 3 E.G.L.R. 37; [2007] 1 P. & C.R. 115 CA.

day. The position would be different in the case of a right to use a way leading from one place to another which members of the public or persons other than the tenant may also use.[103]

1–32 If the incorporeal hereditament is not one which on its true construction is capable of being occupied, it will nevertheless be protected where it is included together with other premises in a tenancy to which the Act applies: *Jones v Christy*[104] (digested in para.1–33); *Nevill Long & Co (Boards) Ltd v Firmenich & Co*[105] (digested in paras 1–35 and 3–197). However, a mere licence, for instance, to maintain advertising signs on the outside of a building forming part of the demised premises, will not be part of "the premises" protected by the Act but such a right may be included as one of the terms of the new tenancy on renewal under the Act: see *Re No. 1 Albemarle Street*[106] (digested in para.8–16).

1–33 ***Jones v Christy***[107] The user covenant of the tenant's lease provided that he was not to use the demised premises other than as a private residence for the profession of a veterinary surgeon. The lease also granted fishing rights in a stretch of river water. The tenant did not practise as a veterinary surgeon but carried on the activity of letting the fishing rights to others, for a profit, using a room in the demised premises as a drying room. The landlord opposed the grant of a new tenancy under ground (c) (other reasons or breaches) of s.30(1). The county court judge held that the letting of fishing rights was not a business. The tenant appealed. It was held:

(1) The letting of the fishing rights had been done on such a scale that the tenant was carrying on a business.
(2) The fishing rights, being an incorporeal hereditament, could not have been occupied for the purposes of a business.[108]
(3) However, the tenant, by occupying and using the room in the demised premises in connection with the business, was thereby occupying the premises for the purposes of a business and accordingly the tenancy was protected by the Act.
(4) The tenant was in breach of the covenant in the lease not to use the demised premises or any part thereof other than as a private residence of a veterinary surgeon and in light of s.30(1)(c) he ought not to be granted a new tenancy.

---

[103] See above, Arden L.J. at [29].
[104] (1963) 107 S.J. 374 CA.
[105] (1984) 47 P. & C.R. 59 CA.
[106] [1959] 2 W.L.R. 171; [1959] 1 All E.R. 250.
[107] Arden L.J. in *Pointon York Group Plc v Poulton* [2006] 3 E.G.L.R. 37; [2007] 1 P. & C.R. 115 CA said of this decision that "... [it] contains the expression of doubt by Lord Denning M.R. as to whether the mere letting of fishing rights could be 'occupation' for the purpose of the 1954 Act. His observation referred to the letting of fishing rights on their own since he goes on to say that, since the fishing rights had been used for the purposes of a business in connection with a room that was also let by the same lease, the letting of the fishing rights could in fact be the subject of a new tenancy within the 1954 Act. This case therefore deals with occupation of a particular type of incorporeal hereditament let on its own. It does not establish that no incorporeal hereditament can be occupied, still less that it cannot form part of 'the premises' for the purposes of s.23(1) if enjoyed in connection with land" at [26].
[108] See now *Pointon York Group Plc v Poulton*[2006] 3 E.G.L.R. 37; [2007] 1 P. & C.R. 115 CA.

Waiver or acquiescence by the lessors in the breach could not be inferred, for a waiver in the past of such a breach, being a continuing breach of covenant, could not affect the future.

Land Reclamation Co Ltd v Basildon DC[109] The claimant company carried on a waste disposal business on land, the sole access to which was by way of private road on the defendant council's land. The council had entered into a document called a lease whereby "in consideration of the rent and covenants hereinafter reserved... (the council) hereby demises unto the company full rights... to pass... along the private road... for all purposes in connection with the use of the company's land". The company claimed to have a tenancy protected by the Act. The Court of Appeal held that the word "occupy" in s.23(1) was not apt to describe the enjoyment of some incorporeal right such as an easement of way; here, the right of way was not exclusive to the company and was not even continuous in time and was accordingly not property comprised in the lease and not "premises" within s.23. **1–34**

Nevill Long & Co (Boards) Ltd v Firmenich & Co[110] The tenant of premises which were protected by the Act enjoyed rights of way over other land which gave access to the rear of the premises. During the tenancy, the freehold owner of the premises sold the reversion of the leased premises to one company and sold the freehold of the land over which the rights of way were enjoyed to another. The tenant sought a declaration that the right of way included in the lease would continue after expiry of the term pursuant to the Act. The Court of Appeal held that although the right of way by its incorporeal nature was incapable of occupation, the Act could apply to a right of way where it was additional to other property comprised in the tenancy which included premises occupied by the tenant for the purposes of his business. **1–35**

Mixed tenancies

Section 23(1) does not require that the entirety of the property comprised in the tenancy should be occupied for business purposes. It suffices if the property comprised in the tenancy "includes" premises which are so occupied. Thus the Act will apply to premises which are used for mixed residential and business purposes, at least if the business activity is a significant purpose of the occupation and not merely incidental to the residential use. Thus, a lease of a shop with residential accommodation above used by the tenant as his home will be a business tenancy.[111] In *Cheryl Investments Ltd v Saldanha*[112] (digested in **1–36**

[109] [1979] 1 W.L.R. 767; [1979] 2 All E.R. 993; [1979] 1 E.G.L.R. 85 CA.

[110] [1983] 2 E.G.L.R. 76; (1984) 47 P. & C.R. 59 CA. See para.3–197 on the issue of severed reversions on which *Nevill Long* is also relevant.

[111] *Broadway Investments Hackney Ltd v Grant* [2006] EWCA Civ 1709; [2007] 1 P. & C.R. 18 CA, where the permitted use was for business purposes and the premises were in fact used for the permitted use pursuant to a positive user covenant. Lloyd L.J. said that he could see "no possible argument... for saying that Part II of the 1954 Act did not apply" at [33]. Lloyd L.J. said:

> "This is a tenancy under which not only was Mr Grant allowed to use the ground floor and basement for business purposes, and for no other purpose, but he was positively required to do so....

para.1–39) the view was expressed that a professional man who takes a tenancy of a residential property for the very purpose of carrying on his profession in one room and residing in the rest of the house with his family, like the doctor who has a consulting room in his house, has a tenancy protected under the 1954 Act, for the occupation for the purposes of a business is as significant as the purpose of occupying the property as a residence. Neither is merely incidental to the other. However, if a business man takes work home in the evening which he does in a study set aside for that purpose, he could scarcely be said to be occupying the premises for the purposes of a business, any more than the person who watches the television regularly every evening can be said to be occupying his house for the purposes of watching television. It is only if the business activity is part of the tenant's aim and object in occupying the premises that the 1954 Act will apply. As is so often the case in matters of this kind it will in the end come down to a question of degree.[113]

1–37 A tenancy cannot be a regulated tenancy within the meaning of the Rent Act 1977[114] nor an assured tenancy within the meaning of the Housing Act 1988[115] if it is a tenancy to which the 1954 Act applies. Whether a tenancy is one within the Rent Act 1977 depends upon whether the premises were let as a dwelling. Thus one's attention is directed to the object of the letting at its commencement.[116] The mere unilateral cessation of business use and the commencement of use for residential purposes will not suffice to render the tenancy one let as a dwelling: *Phaik Seang Tan v Sitkowski*.[117] There must be either a surrender and re-grant or a contractual variation of the terms of the tenancy so as to enable the conclusion to be drawn that the premises have been let as a separate dwelling; it may be possible for the court to infer such a contract from the conduct of the parties:

He has in fact done so, according to his own evidence, from the time when the premises were fit for such use. No doubt part of his purpose in taking the Lease was to provide himself with a home, but the terms of the Lease are not compatible with a proposition that, once the shop was open for business, his use of that part of the premises was only incidental to his use of the other part of the premises as his home, or that running the shop was not part of the reason for, or part of his arm and object in occupying the premises" at [32].

[112] [1978] 1 W.L.R. 1329; [1979] 1 All E.R. 5; [1978] 2 E.G.L.R. 54 CA.

[113] In *Wright v Mortimer* (1996) 28 H.L.R. 719 CA, the landlord contended that the tenant of a maisonette was a business tenant because he was enjoying the premises for the purposes of his profession as an art historian. Some 30% of his work as a writer took place in the demised premises but he had no secretary, office or office equipment and it was not essential to his writing for him to occupy the maisonette. The demised premises were not used as his business address nor did he carry out any fine art dealing, consulting or advisory works there. The county court held that the business activities were merely incidental to the residential occupation. The Court of Appeal refused leave to appeal.

[114] s.24(3) of the Rent Act 1977. See s.18(1) of the Rent Act 1977 as to the meaning of "regulated tenancy".

[115] Housing Act 1988, Sch.1, para.4.

[116] *Wolfe v Hogan* [1949] 2 K.B. 194 CA.

[117] [2007] 1 W.L.R. 1628. It was said that the position may be different where the premises were originally let for purely residential purposes and the tenant subsequently uses them wholly or partly for business purposes and then ceases the business user, as in those circumstances: "it would not be particularly odd if a tenant, who initially had protection of the 1977 Act, could, by his unilateral action, switch to the 1954 Act, and could then unilaterally switch back to the 1977 Act whose protection he enjoyed initially; whereas it could fairly be said to be odd if a tenant, who initially had 1954 Act protection, could unilaterally switch to 1977 Act protection": Neuberger L.J. at [72].

Tomkins v Basildon DC[118] (digested in para.1–39). The cessation of business use for a period of 14 years with the continued acceptance of rent by the landlord throughout that period was, without more, sufficient to give rise to inference that the landlord had positively assented to the change of user: *Phaik Seang Tan v Sitowski*.[119] Under the 1954 Act one's attention is drawn to the purpose for which the premises are being occupied at the relevant time. It follows that where premises which were let as a dwelling under a protected tenancy within the Rent Act 1977 are subsequently used for the purposes of a business to a degree which brings them within the 1954 Act, the tenancy will cease to be a protected tenancy.

Three practical points can be suggested in relation to the question of whether premises, which were originally let as a dwelling under a protected tenancy within the Rent Act 1977, have subsequently, by their use for the purposes of a business, been brought within the 1954 Act. First, *Cheryl Investments Ltd v Saldanha* and *Royal Life Saving Society v Page*[120] (digested in para.1–39) were cases where the terms of the letting did not prohibit business user. If the business user is prohibited by the terms of the tenancy the Act may be excluded by virtue of the provisions of s.23(4) (see paras 1–129 et seq.). Secondly, the residential occupier probably cannot acquire 1954 Act protection if he is a statutory tenant, as opposed to a protected tenant, for the 1954 Act applies only to contractual interests. Thus, a statutory tenant who commenced occupation of the premises for the purposes of a business to a degree which would otherwise bring them within the 1954 Act, does not automatically cease to be a statutory tenant: *Durman v Bell*[121] (a case concerning the Rent (Agriculture) Act 1976). Thirdly, a distinction must be drawn between (1) cases in which the tenant is himself a residential occupier, and (2) cases in which others (the tenant's employees) are residing in the property but the tenant nevertheless claims to be in occupation for the purposes of a business. The judgments in *Cheryl Investments Ltd v Saldanha* illustrate that in the first case the business activity must be "a significant purpose" of the tenant's occupation for the 1954 Act to apply. In the second case, however, the test is rather stricter. The test is whether the occupation is necessary for the furtherance of the tenant's business, rather than merely for the convenience of the tenant's business: *Trustees of the Methodist Secondary Schools Trust Deed v O'Leary*[122] (digested in para.1–139). The second category of cases is discussed in para.1–107 et seq., below. 1–38

Cheryl Investments Ltd v Saldanha; Royal Life Saving Society v Page[123] In two appeals heard together by the Court of Appeal the tenants claimed that they were protected by the Rents Acts, not by the 1954 Act. In the first action, S, whose premises were a flat consisting of a double bedroom with bathroom and 1–39

[118] [2002] 3 E.G.L.R. 33 CA.
[119] As Neuberger L.J. said: "... it is well established that, simply by accepting rent with knowledge of the breach, a landlord does not waive the right to forfeit the lease for a continuing breach of a user covenant. By the same token, there has to be something more than mere knowledge of the change of use coupled with acceptance of rent to operate as a positive consent to the change." at [79].
[120] [1978] 1 W.L.R. 1329; [1979] 1 All E.R. 5; [1978] 2 E.G.L.R. 54 CA.
[121] [1988] 2 E.G.L.R. 117 CA.
[122] [1993] 1 E.G.L.R. 105.
[123] [1978] 1 W.L.R. 1329; [1979] 1 All E.R. 5; (1978) 2 E.G.L.R. 54 CA.

toilet, was an accountant and partner in a firm engaged in commerce. The firm had no trade premises and the partners carried on its business from their homes. In particular, Shad installed a telephone in his flat and had placed a table in the hall with "all the usual office equipment" including a typewriter, files and headed notepaper and he was seen to receive frequent visitors with briefcases. In the second action, P was the assignee of a tenant to whom the premises, a maisonette, had originally been "let as a separate dwelling". P, a doctor, had consulting rooms in Harley Street where he held daily clinics, but, having contemplated seeing patients occasionally at the maisonette, he had at the time of the assignment sought and gained the landlords' consent to "carrying on his profession" in the maisonette. He had, however, only seen one person per year there, the last being 18 months ago. The Court of Appeal held that the vital factor was the purpose for which the premises were occupied and not the use to which they were put, although the purposes may be evidenced by actual use. In the first appeal, it was plain that S was occupying the premises for the dual purposes of his dwelling and his business and, since the business use was a significant purpose of his occupation, his was a business tenancy within s.23, and not therefore entitled to Rent Act protection. In the second appeal, the only significant purpose of the doctor's occupation was as his home and such use as he made for his profession was merely incidental to that use; accordingly, he was entitled to stay on as a statutory tenant under the Rent Acts. A mere intention to carry on some business at the premises unaccompanied by any action putting into effect that intention is not enough.

1–40 ***Gurton v Parrott***[124] The tenant of residential premises groomed, bred and kennelled dogs in outbuildings and the land on which they stood. The county court judge held that this constituted a business. The tenant had started kennelling the dogs for friends and subsequently obtained a local authority licence permitting up to 46 dogs to be kennelled. The activity was seasonal, mainly during the summer holidays. She made, as found by the county court judge, a not insignificant turnover from the business. However, the county court judge found that the aim and object of the tenant in occupying the property was for the purpose of a residence only and that the running of the business on the property was merely incidental, something akin to a hobby, taking advantage of the facilities offered by the existing outhouses and other small amount of land, which might otherwise have been used as a yard or garden. Accordingly, he held that she was protected by the Rent Act, not the 1954 Act. The Court of Appeal refused to interfere with his finding.

1–41 ***Tomkins v Basildon DC***[125] In 1978, T had along with B been granted a tenancy of a house with dog kennels. The user covenant provided that the premises were to be used for the carrying on of the trade or business of keeping and training greyhounds and for residential accommodation incidental thereto. It was not disputed that as originally granted the tenancy was one to which the 1954 Act applied. By 1986 the business user had ceased. B died in 1995. When L, a local

124 [1991] 1 E.G.L.R. 98.
125 [2002] 3 E.G.L.R. 33 CA.

authority, sought possession in 1998, T claimed that she had a secure tenancy protected by the Housing Act 1985 as the tenancy was one under which a dwelling-house was let as a separate dwelling. The county court judge held that such a letting arose as a result of the dealings between the parties and in particular:

(1) the cessation of the commercial activity in 1986;
(2) the knowledge of L of the cessation of that activity;
(3) the election by L to treat the letting as one for residential purposes and in particular:
    (a) an internal file note to the effect that the review of the rent under the lease was to be on the basis of a non-commercial approach;
    (b) an internal file note from the finance officer who stated that he had no objection to the lease being converted to a housing tenancy;
    (c) a description by the finance officer of the premises as "residential accommodation together with dog kennels at the rear";
(4) the fact that the rating authority no longer classified the premises as "non-domestic";
(5) the non-charging of VAT on the rent, given that VAT cannot be charged on rent paid for residential property.

On appeal both parties and the Court of Appeal were content to treat the passage[126] in Slade L.J.'s judgment in *Russell v Booker*[127] as accurately stating the law as to the circumstances in which a tenancy may subsequently become one "let as a separate dwelling".[128] The Court of Appeal held that the findings of the judge did not warrant his conclusion that there had been a contractual variation of

---

[126] See fn.128 where the learned Lord Justices' dicta are set out.

[127] [1982] 2 E.G.L.R. 86 at 89, 90.

[128] Slade L.J. said:"We take the decision of this court in *Whitty v Scott-Russell*, read in conjunction with its decision in *Wolfe v Hogan*, as authority for the following propositions, which fall to be applied in the present case:

(1) Where the terms of a tenancy agreement provide for or contemplate the use of the premises for some particular purpose, then, subject to the qualification mentioned in (2) below, that purpose is the essential factor in deciding the question whether or not the house can be said to have been let 'as a separate dwelling-house' so as to fall within the Rent Acts.

(2) Nevertheless, where the original tenancy agreement provided for or contemplated the use of the premises for some particular purpose, but, by the time when the possession proceedings are begun, that agreement has been superseded by a subsequent contract providing for a different user, the subsequent contract may be looked at in deciding the latter question.

(3) If a tenant changes the user of the premises and the fact of the change is fully known to, and accepted by, the landlord, it may be possible for the court to infer a subsequent contract to let them 'as a separate dwelling-house', although this would be a contract different in essentials from the original tenancy agreement.

(4) However, unless a contract of the last-mentioned nature can be spelt out, a mere unilateral change of user will not enable a tenant to claim the protection of the Rent Acts in a case where the terms of the tenancy agreement itself provide for and contemplate the use of the premises for some particular purpose which does not attract the protection of those Acts—for example as a shop or agricultural holding.

(5) Where the tenancy agreement itself does not provide for or contemplate the use of the premises for any particular purpose, actual subsequent user has to be looked at in determining whether a house is 'let as a separate dwelling-house', so as to attract the protection of the Rent Acts."

the lease. All of the matters other than head (4) were internal to L, and head (4) was a communication of the position of the rating authority not that of L. Even if the communication had been by L the position as to the classification of the premises for rating purposes was irrelevant to the terms of the tenancy. As to head (5), the non-charging of VAT was neutral. The highest it could be put was that the landlord for the time being was content not to enforce the positive covenant so far as it related to the commercial user, and was content to review the rent under the lease on the basis of the actual as opposed to the permitted user. The commercial user did not cease to be the relevant user: T could at any time recommence the commercial user. Accordingly, the premises had not become "let as a separate dwelling".

5. ARE THE PREMISES "OCCUPIED"?

Meaning of "occupied"

Physical presence and control

1–42 The Act applies only to premises which are "occupied" by the tenant for business purposes. "Occupied" is not defined, but has been considered and applied in many cases and has been authoritatively construed by the House of Lords in *Graysim Holdings Ltd v P&O Property Holdings Ltd*[129] (digested in para.1–63). In that case Lord Nicholls, with whom all the Law Lords agreed, said:

> "As has been said on many occasions, the concept of occupation is not a legal term of art, with one single and precise legal meaning applicable in all circumstances. Its meaning varies according to the subject matter. Like most ordinary English words 'occupied', and corresponding expressions such as occupier and occupation, have different shades of meaning according to the context in which they are being used. Their meaning in the context of the Rent Acts, for instance, is not in all respects the same as in the context of the Occupiers' Liability Act 1957."

He went on to state that:

> "In Part II of the 1954 Act 'occupied' and 'occupied for the purposes of a business carried on by him' are expressions employed as the means of identifying whether a tenancy is a business tenancy and whether the property is part of the holding and qualifies for inclusion in the grant of a new tenancy. In this context 'occupied' points to some business activity by the tenant on the property in question. The Act seeks to protect the tenant in his continuing use of the

---

In *Phaik Seang Tan v Sitkowski* [2007] 1 W.L.R. 1628 CA, it was said that the decision in *Russell v Booker*, although bearing a superficial similarity with a mixed business and residential use case, was of no assistance, as it was one involving agricultural holdings, and in *Maunsell v Olins* [1975] A.C. 373 HL, the majority of the House of Lords held that, in the statutory context of the then s.18(5) of the Rent Act 1968 (now s.137(3) of the Rent Act 1977, albeit amended following the *Maunsell* decision) "premises" could not be treated as "a dwelling house" where the letting concerned is of an agricultural holding even if it includes a dwelling. Although the *Maunsell* case has been reversed by legislation (in relation to sub-tenancies of dwelling houses) the reversal does not apply or bear on the grant of tenancies of agricultural holdings: Neuberger L.J. at [48]. Although a whole host of authorities was considered by Neuberger L.J., *Tompkins v Basildon DC* does not appear to have been referred to.

[129] [1995] 3 W.L.R. 854; [1995] 4 All E.R. 831 HL.

> property for the purposes of that activity. Thus the word carries a connotation of some physical use of the property by the tenant for the purposes of his business."

Occupation is a matter of fact; it is to be distinguished from the concept of possession, which connotes the legal right to be in occupation of land rather than the fact of actual occupation. The question arises, both in the context of s.23(1) in considering whether the tenant occupies with the consequence that the Act applies, and in the context of s.30(1)(g) where a landlord asserts an intention to "occupy" for the purposes of his own business. The word "occupied" in the context of the 1954 Act connotes "an element of control and user involved in the notion of physical occupation. That does not mean physical occupation every minute of the day, provided the right to occupy continues".[130] Physical presence is unnecessary if the premises are being used in the ordinary course or conduct of the tenant's business, provided that the premises are occupied by no other business occupier and are not used for any non-business purpose: *Bacchiocchi v Academic Agency Ltd*,[131] *Pointon York Group Plc v Poulton*.[132] However, it would seem from the authorities that physical presence may be readily satisfied. Thus, the following have been held to be sufficient: **1–43**

(1) the presence of a carpet layer fitting carpets for the occupation by the tenant albeit engaged by the outgoing sub-tenant in fulfilment of his obligations under the sub-lease, and the visits of the tenant's personnel on two occasions to plan and approve the carpeting: *Pointon York Group Plc v Poulton*[133];
(2) the retention of rubber shoes in a basement of a shop albeit that the tenant had ceased to trade from the premises: *I&H Caplan v Caplan (No.2)*[134] (digested in para.1–46).

As has been pointed out on more than one occasion by the courts, it is not possible to determine whether the tenant is in occupation of the premises by itemising the circumstances found to be present in individual cases where the tenant is held in fact to be in occupation for that purpose and by determining how **1–44**

---

[130] Eveleigh L.J. in *Hancock and Willis v GMS Syndicate Limited* [1983] 1 E.G.L.R. 70 (digested in para.1–45). The presence of, e.g. an advertising hoarding or a vending machine, on land is unlikely to constitute occupation of the land: see para.1–50. An agreement for the use of land for advertising is likely to constitute a licence in any event: see para.1–10.

[131] It has been held that the observations contained within this case as to the meaning of "occupied", albeit in the context of s.38, apply to a consideration of the meaning of "occupied" under s.23. It was said that "On well established principles of statutory interpretation, unless the context otherwise requires, the word 'occupy' must bear the same meaning in s.23 as it does in s.38. No reason has been shown why it should not do so" per Arden L.J. in *Pointer York Group Plc v Poulton* [2006] 3 E.G.L.R. 37 CA at [35]. The *Bacchiocchi* decision is considered in detail in paras 1–60 to 1–61.

[132] [2006] 3 E.G.L.R. 37; [2007] 1 P. & C.R. 115 CA per Arden L.J. at [31].

[133] [2006] E.G.L.R. 37; [2007] 1 P. & C.R. 115 CA. This was the finding of the judge at first instance: [6]. The Court of Appeal held, upholding the judge, that the activities of the tenant and the carpet layer were incidental to the tenant's business: the tenant was checking that the premises were properly equipped and suitable for the business he wished to carry on there and the carpet layer was performing an activity for the purpose of the tenant's business even though he was employed by the sub-tenant for the purpose of their fulfilling their covenants under the sub-tenancy.

[134] [1963] 1 W.L.R. 1247; [1963] 2 All E.R. 930.

many or how few of those circumstances are present in the instant case. As Lord Nicholls put it in *Graysim*[135]: "The circumstances of two cases are never identical and seldom close enough to make comparisons of much value." Nevertheless, the cases show that certain elements have been treated as being relevant to the question of whether "occupation" has been proved, namely:

(1) physical presence or absence of the alleged occupier[136];
(2) the exercise of control over those using the premises;
(3) the provision of services by the alleged occupier which require him to be physically on the premises;
(4) the time devoted to the activity carried on.

The matter was summarised by Ralph Gibson L.J. in *Wandsworth LBC v Singh*[137] (digested in para.1–49 below) thus:

> "If it is shown that the tenant, having possession of the premises and having given to no person the right to exclude the tenant from any part of the premises or to limit the tenant's access thereto, is by himself, his servants, or agents physically present on the premises to such extent and exercising control of them to such extent as would reasonably be expected having regard to the nature of the premises and the terms of the tenancy, and is so present and exercising control for the purposes of the business or activity carried on by the tenant, then for my part it would seem likely at least that an observer knowing the facts and applying the ordinary and popular meaning of the phrase 'occupation for the purposes of a business or activity', would hold that tenant to be in occupation."

The Courts have shown a remarkable degree of flexibility in the concept of "occupation". It has been held that the tenant was in occupation albeit:

(a) the premises were occupied by persons who were not directly employed by the tenant: *Linden v DHSS*[138] (digested at para.1–45);
(b) the tenant held a closing down sale and, but for a small quantity, had sold and removed most of his stock: *I&H Caplan Ltd v Caplan (No.2)*[139] (digested at para.1–46);
(c) the tenant had ceased business activity from the premises for a period of 12 days prior to the expiry of the term: *Bacchiocchi v Academic Agency Ltd*[140];
(d) the tenant had sub-let the property and only had a three day reversion during which it was fitting out the premises for occupation: *Pointon York Group Plc v Poulton.*[141]

1–45 ***Linden v DHSS***[142] The Secretary of State for the Department of Health and Social Security was the tenant of a house, converted into eight flats, which was used to accommodate persons employed in NHS hospitals in the area. The

[135] [1996] A.C. 329 HL.
[136] See paras 1–42 and 1–43.
[137] [1991] 2 E.G.L.R. 75 CA.
[138] [1986] 1 W.L.R. 164; [1986] 1 All E.R. 691.
[139] [1963] 1 W.L.R. 1247.
[140] [1998] 1 W.L.R. 1313. See also paras 1–59 and 1–61.
[141] [2007] 1 P. & C.R. 6 CA.
[142] [1986] 1 W.L.R. 164; [1986] 1 All E.R. 691.

persons were not directly employed by the Secretary of State but by the local health authority who managed the accommodation on a day-to-day basis. It was held that the local health authority (as opposed to the individual occupiers) occupied the premises and so occupied them as agent for the Secretary of State. Scott J. said:

> "I think the present case is on the borderline but on balance in my opinion, the authority is in occupation of [the property] for the purposes of s.56(3). The features of the case which lead me to that conclusion are, particularly, that one or more of the flats were usually to be found to be vacant and under the control only of the authority; that the authority retains keys to all the flats and visits them regularly; that under the agreements exclusive possession is not given to the occupants; that the authority provides not simply furniture but crockery and blankets at the premises; and that the authority's maintenance of the flats includes decorating and the carrying out of quite trivial repairs. The evidence shows, in my view, [that the property] needs not just a landlord but a manager. On the evidence that is the function discharged by the authority. The conclusion is . . . that the authority is in occupation of [the premises] . . ."

I&H Caplan Ltd v Caplan (No.2)[143] The tenants carried on the business of selling clothing, hosiery and shoes. Their application for a new tenancy under the Act was successfully opposed by the landlords under ground (g) of s.30(1) (own occupation). The tenants appealed to the Court of Appeal. At the same time they decided to cease trading at the premises and advertised a closing down sale. The greater part of the stock, left after the sale, was removed the following week, having been sold to another company. From this date until the appeal was heard later in the year, the premises were empty apart from a quantity of rubber footwear left in the basement. The tenants' intention was that, if successful in their appeal, they would discontinue their own line of business but use the premises as a ladies' gown shop. The tenants won in the Court of Appeal and took immediate steps to start trading. The House of Lords subsequently held in favour of the tenants on another point. In separate proceedings, the High Court had to determine whether the tenants had, in any event, lost their right to a new tenancy because they had not been in "occupation" after the original dismissal of their application by the High Court. The court held that while it was a continuing condition of the tenant's entitlement to a new tenancy that he should, throughout the proceedings, be a tenant protected by the Act, such protection was not lost simply by ceasing physically to occupy the premises, provided the continuity of business user was not broken. Although the facts of the case were borderline, the "thread of continuity of business user" remained unbroken, so the tenants were entitled to succeed. **1–46**

Hancock & Willis v GMS Syndicate[144] The tenants, a firm of solicitors, held a lease of premises consisting of a ground floor, basement and two vaults, and a rear area between those vaults in the basement. The ground floor and basement were used for the purposes of the tenant's business, while the rear addition and one of the vaults were furnished with tables and chairs and were used for twice-monthly staff lunches: the other vault was used as a wine cellar. The **1–47**

143 [1963] 1 W.L.R. 1247; [1963] 2 All E.R. 930. This case is also digested on the issue of what constitutes the "holding" for the purposes of the Act at para.8–09.

144 [1983] 2 E.G.L.R. 75 CA.

tenants' staff moved to other accommodation. Thereafter the premises were used only for the lunches and the storage of files. The tenants' furniture and carpeting remained at the premises. The tenants then granted a licence for a fixed term of six months to a company to occupy "at all times of day and night". The licence permitted the company to occupy the ground floor and basement although it was agreed that the wine cellar was not included in the licence and that the tenants should have the right to use the rear addition and the second of the vaults twice monthly for staff lunches. Throughout the period of the licence the tenant's use of the premises was so limited, except for occasional access. The company moved their own furniture into the premises in addition to that left by the tenants, but at all times the tenants retained the key to the premises. The question arose whether the tenants still "occupied" the premises. The court held that the "thread of continuity" of business user had existed prior to the grant of the licence to the company but that, by granting the licence, the tenants had effectively prevented themselves from making any real use of the premises during its currency. The company had exclusive occupation and the tenants could only enter with the company's consent. The tenants could not be said to be in constructive occupation of the premises by virtue of the presence on the premises of the tenants' furniture and files, for the tenants reserved no right to enter to inspect the files and it was wrong to regard the premises as being used for the storage of the tenants' office furniture, for the company had use of the furniture by the terms of the licence and thus during the currency of the licence the furniture was to be treated as the furniture of the company and not that of the tenants.

Nature of activity

1–48 The tenant's presence or exercise of control may be discontinuous and occur only as required by the nature of the activity for the purposes for which the tenant goes on to the land. Thus in *Bracey v Read*[145] (digested in para.1–28) the user of the land by the tenant for gallops for racehorses was treated (by way of a concession) to be occupation by the tenant for the purposes of s.23 of the 1954 Act, and in *Wandsworth LBC v Singh*[146] (digested in para.1–49) the local authority were held to be in occupation of a small public open space, having regard to the nature of the premises and the terms of the tenancy, albeit the sub-contractors employed by the local authority for the horticultural work visited the site about once a fortnight for about 32 weeks in the summer and the local authority's parks maintenance manager or one of his assistants inspected it irregularly only when passing.

1–49 ***Wandsworth LBC v Singh***[147] The local authority was lessee of an area of open space. They laid out the land as a small park and this was used by the local inhabitants. The horticultural work was sub-contracted out by the local authority. The contractors visited the site 16 times in the summer or, in practice, once a fortnight for some 32 weeks. The local authority parks maintenance manager or one of his assistants inspected the site when passing, although this was not on a

145 [1962] 3 W.L.R. 1194; [1962] 3 All E.R. 472.
146 [1991] 2 E.G.L.R. 75 CA.
147 [1991] 2 E.G.L.R. 75 CA.

regular basis. The local authority incurred the expense of the provision and maintenance of seating and planting, pruning and replacement where necessary of trees, shrubs and plants. Regular redecoration of the site was carried out on a five-year cycle. The gates to the park were from time to time locked and when so locked prevented the public from enjoying the open space. The question arose whether the local authority's lease was a business tenancy within s.23. It was held that the physical presence and control necessary for occupation under s.23 did not have to be continuous, provided that the right to occupy continued. The local authority was physically present upon and exercised control over the land by their servants or agents as would be reasonably expected having regard to the nature of the premises. The local authority did all that was required of them to maintain the place in decent order for use by the public. Accordingly it was held that the local authority had a business tenancy.

Must be control of "premises"

The mere use of an object situated on the land resting thereon principally by its own weight, e.g. a vending machine, is unlikely to constitute occupation of the land itself. In *Sinclair Collis Ltd v Customs and Excise Commissioners*[148] the court was concerned with whether an agreement to install a cigarette-vending machine in a public house constituted a licence to occupy land, and therefore was exempt from VAT. The Court of Appeal held that the machine was occupying the land it stood on. The House of Lords disagreed. Lord Millet said: **1–50**

> "As I have pointed out, each machine remains the property of the company but once installed it is in the custody and possession of the site owner. The floor under the machine is, of course, occupied by the machine, but it is impossible to describe the company as in occupation of this area. It cannot enter the area itself or admit others to do so without moving the machine, and since the subject matter of the alleged letting is the space occupied by the machine from time to time, this means that the company cannot itself enter the subject matter of the letting or admit others to do so at all. The site owner, by contrast, is in possession not only of the machine but of the floor underneath it. If he wishes to clean or renew the carpet he is free to do so and to move the machine temporarily for this purpose.
> The company cannot sensibly be described as occupying any part of the premises by its machine. Such a concept can hardly apply where the part of the premises in question has no independent existence of its own, being defined by the dimensions of the machine and its location from time to time. There is in my view no close analogy with a kiosk or shop counter which is capable of separate occupation by a lessee and his licensees. The agreement between

---

[148] [2001] UKHL 30. This case concerned the operation and effect of art.13B(b) of the EC Sixth Directive and the provisions of the UK Value Added Tax Act 1994, intended to give effect to community law concerning exemption from VAT. The issue related to whether an agreement for the siting of cigarette machines by a tobacco company on a third party's land could constitute "the leasing or letting of immovable property" within art.13B(b). The decision of the House of Lords on the actual facts of the case was, by a three-to-two majority, to refer the question to the European Court of Justice (the decision of the Court of Justice is at [2003] S.T.C. 898; [2003] ECR 1-5965. The court's judgments echo the opinions expressed by the House of Lords). There was a three-to-two split in the opinion of the members of the judicial committee as to the application of the exception from VAT on the particular facts of the case. In *Clear Channel UK Ltd v Manchester City Council* [2004] 1 E.G.L.R. 128, first instance, it was said by Etherton J. that as the case turned upon the proper interpretation of the European Directive, and, in particular, the correct approach to the interpretation of an exemption from VAT, it was dangerous to attempt to extract any general principle from the case. The point did not arise for consideration on appeal: [2006] 1 E.G.L.R. 27 CA.

> the company and the site owner is not, in my view, an agreement for the letting of defined areas of land with a right to place machines on them, but a right to bring machines onto the site owner's premises and place them in suitable positions there. The site owner remains in sole occupation of the whole of his premises including the areas from time to time occupied by machines. The company for its part retains the property in the machines and has rights of access to them, but is given no right to occupy any part of the premises."

Lord Scott said:

> "...two elements, possession and control, seem to me to be the important ingredients of a relationship between an individual and land apt to be described as 'occupation'. A 'licence to occupy' is, in my opinion, to be read as meaning a licence to go into possession, not necessarily exclusive possession, or to go on to the land and take some degree of control of it. If neither of these features is present, the licence cannot, in my opinion, properly be described as a licence to occupy.
> Accordingly, a person entitled to place an advertisement on a wall cannot, in any meaningful sense, be described as being in occupation of the space occupied by the advertisement. The commissioners' practice in regard to advertisements is, in my opinion, correct. It is not concessionary. It is a recognition that the right granted is not a 'letting' of land and that the exercise of it does not involve the occupation of land. For the same reasons the grant of a right for a salesperson with a tray suspended from his or her neck to wander around a public house or the foyer of a theatre offering for sale the contents of the tray would not constitute the grant of a licence to occupy. There would be no part of the premises of which the salesperson could be said to be in possession or control or, therefore, in occupation. Nor, in my opinion, would the result be any different if the salesperson were obliged under the agreement to be stationed in a specific corner of the premises. There would still be nothing that could reasonably be thought to constitute 'occupation' or a 'letting' of land."

Problem areas

1–51 Difficult problems may occur where physical occupation has ceased for reasons beyond the tenant's control, or where the continuity of occupation is interrupted. These matters are dealt with in para.1–52 et seq. The question of "shared occupation" or "dual occupation" is considered separately in para.1–64 et seq.

Where the tenant has physically ceased to occupy the premises

Seasonal business

1–52 Where the tenant's business is of a seasonal nature, the tenant will, depending upon the gap between the activities and the history of the occupation, be likely to be held to be in occupation during the out-of-season period. As was stated by Salmon L.J. in *Artemiou v Procopiou*[149] (digested in para.7–276):

> "Anyone who goes into occupation of premises in which a seasonal business is carried on is occupying them all year round for the purposes of the business; if not it is difficult to see for what other purposes he would be occupying them during the out-of-season months."

If the thread of continuity of business user has been broken, the mere fact that the tenant intends to restart the business is not enough to bring the business within

[149] [1966] 1 Q.B. 878 CA.

the protection of the Act. Thus in *Teasdale v Walker*[150] (digested in para.1–83) the tenant of seafront premises at Skegness, having broken the continuity of business user by granting a sub-tenancy under the guise of a management agreement, was held not to be in occupation of the premises for the purposes of the 1954 Act, notwithstanding the tenant's intention to restart the business in the following season.

Cessation of occupation through matters outside the tenant's control

If the tenant is required to vacate the premises because of matters outside his control, e.g. because the premises are destroyed by fire, the tenant will retain the protection of the 1954 Act so long as he continues to assert and claim his right of occupation: *Morrisons Holdings Ltd v Manders Property (Wolverhampton) Ltd*[151] (digested in para.1–54); *Flairline Properties Ltd v Hassan*[152] (digested in para.1–55). Similarly, if the tenant vacates because of the need for repairs which are the landlord's liability, but not otherwise: *Demetriou v Poolaction.*[153] **1–53**

Morrison Holdings Ltd v Manders Property (Wolverhampton) Ltd[154] The tenants of shop premises were unable to carry on business when their premises were affected by an adjacent catastrophic fire. They wrote to the landlords expressing their desire "to get back into trade as soon as possible" and inviting the landlords to reinstate the premises as they were bound to do under the terms of the lease. Although the tenants were physically unable to occupy the building, they retained possession of the keys, and left some fixtures and fittings there. Instead of reinstating the premises, the landlords, who were redeveloping their other extensive property holdings, gave notice terminating the tenancy pursuant to a break clause operable in the event of substantial damage rendering reinstatement uneconomic, and demolished the premises. The tenants subsequently applied for a new tenancy under the Act which the landlords resisted on ground (f) of s.30(1) (demolition and reconstruction). On the hearing of a preliminary point, the county court judge decided that since the tenants had vacated the whole of the premises before their application, they had no locus standi to apply for a new tenancy. This decision was reversed by the Court of Appeal, which held that it was sufficient that a tenant showed that he had continued to assert and claim his right to occupancy where events over which he had no control had led him to absent himself from the premises. The landlords were not, by their actions in demolishing the premises, to be allowed to destroy the tenants' locus standi. **1–54**

Flairline Properties Ltd v Hassan[155] The tenant's restaurant premises were seriously damaged by fire in April 1995 and were as a consequence rendered unusable. The tenancy expired by effluxion of time in March 1997. The premises **1–55**

[150] [1958] 1 W.L.R. 1076; [1958] 3 All E.R. 307 CA.
[151] [1976] 1 W.L.R. 533; [1976] 2 All E.R. 205 CA.
[152] [1999] 1 E.G.L.R. 138 QBD.
[153] [1991] 1 E.G.L.R. 100 CA.
[154] [1976] 1 W.L.R. 533; [1976] 2 All E.R. 205 CA.
[155] [1999] 1 E.G.L.R. 138 QBD.

were not physically occupied after the fire. The tenant retained the key to the premises and stored there kitchen equipment, furniture and other items. In October 1995 the local planning authority refused consent to the landlord's application for conservation area consent and planning permission to demolish and rebuild the fire-damaged roof and part of the external wall at the premises. The refusal was solely on the ground that the degree of demolition proposed to the external wall was excessive. The planning authority did, however, indicate that if the landlord's plans were revised to involve less demolition the application would be acceptable. In August 1996 the tenant entered into an agreement to take a lease of premises nearby for a term of 25 years. He spent some £750,000 in refurbishing the new premises and commenced trading in September 1997. The landlord claimed possession on the basis that the tenant's tenancy had expired by effluxion of time as the tenant was not in occupation for business purposes at the term date. It was, however, held that, as the tenant had continued to assert an intention to occupy the premises for the purposes of a restaurant upon their being reinstated, the tenant had not lost the protection of the Act. In particular:

(1) it was sufficient to establish his intention to occupy, where events over which the tenant has no control have led him to absent himself from the premises, that he has intended to return to reoccupy the premises once they have been reinstated;
(2) the tenant was not required to establish that the intention which he possessed had the quality required for a landlord's intention to redevelop for the purposes of ground (f) of s.30(1) (demolition and re-construction), in particular that there was a reasonable prospect that the planning authority would allow the premises to be reinstated (although in fact on the evidence before the court it was possible to conclude that there was a reasonable likelihood that once the landlord had submitted a modified scheme approval would be forthcoming and thus there was a reasonable likelihood of the tenant reopening the premises in the foreseeable future).

Voluntary vacation

1–56 If the tenant vacates voluntarily, the question of whether the thread of business continuity has been broken is a question of fact: see *I&H Caplan Ltd v Caplan (No.2)*[156] (digested in para.1–46) and *Hancock & Willis v GMS Syndicate*[157] (digested in para.1–47). As Sir Gordon Willmer said in *Morrison Holdings Ltd v Manders Property (Wolverhampton) Ltd*[158] (digested in para.1–54):

> "So far as the law is concerned, I think it can be taken as axiomatic that in order to be in occupation one does not have to be physically present every second of every minute of every hour of every day. All of us remain in occupation, for instance, of our houses even while we are away doing our day's work. It follows, therefore, that occupation necessarily must include an element of intention as well as a physical element. If I leave my premises and emigrate to the United States of America with no intention of returning, it can well be said that I no longer remain in occupation. But if as a shop keeper I close my shop for a fortnight in the summer to

156 [1963] 1 W.L.R. 1247; [1963] 2 All E.R. 930.
157 [1983] 1 E.G.L.R. 70 CA.
158 [1976] 1 W.L.R. 533; [1976] 2 All E.R. 205 CA.

> enable my staff to have a holiday, I apprehend that no one would contend that during that fortnight I ceased to be in occupation of my shop."

If the thread of business continuity has been broken, the mere fact that the tenant intends to recommence business user will not be sufficient to confer protection of the Act. The position is a fortiori if the intention is a conditional one: *Teasdale v Walker*[159] (digested in para.1–83) and *Aspinall Finance v Viscount Chelsea*[160] (digested in para.1–57). It appears that the court is more generous to the tenant in this respect where the cessation of occupation has been involuntary. In *Flairline Properties Ltd v Hassan*[161] (digested in para.1–55), where the cessation of business occupation was involuntary, the court rejected the landlord's submission that the tenant in such circumstances must show not merely that he intended to reoccupy, but also that he had a reasonable prospect of bringing this about.

Aspinall Finance Ltd v Viscount Chelsea[162] The tenant of premises used as a gaming club voluntarily ceased occupation of the premises in order to move the business to a more desirable location and in the process gave up the gaming licence from the licensing authority in respect of the demised premises. It was the intention of the tenant to reopen the demised premises as a gaming club and that intention had never changed. In order to obtain a licence from the licensing authority a certificate of consent from the Gaming Board was required and the Gaming Board had indicated that it was not prepared formally to consider its position as to the grant of a certificate in respect of the demised premises until the tenant had a new lease of them. The tenant applied to the court for a new lease under the Act. It was held that the tenant was not in occupation for business purposes and, although it had an intention or desire to reoccupy, that was not one which it was in a position to implement. **1–57**

Where the tenant in renewal proceedings is faced with the landlord's opposition to the renewal, he may have taken precautionary measures in anticipation of having to give up possession, such as the removal of stock or redeployment of staff. However, in such circumstances the court may be more ready to find that there has been no cessation of the continuity of business user because, as was said by Cross J. in *I&H Caplan Ltd v Caplan (No.2)*[163] (digested in para.1–46), it would be unreasonable to argue that such measures amount to a cesser of physical occupation depriving the tenant of the protection of the Act. **1–58**

Winding down business occupation

The question whether the tenant is in occupation for business purposes has also had to be considered by the courts in the rather different context of establishing the amount of compensation for disturbance to which the tenant is entitled under s.37.[164] If the tenant has been in occupation of the holding for more than 14 years **1–59**

159 [1958] 1 W.L.R. 1076; [1958] 3 All E.R. 307 CA.
160 [1989] 1 E.G.L.R. 103.
161 [1999] 1 E.G.L.R. 138 QBD.
162 [1989] 1 E.G.L.R. 103.
163 [1963] 1 W.L.R. 1247; [1963] 2 All E.R. 930.
164 See paras 12–31 et seq., 12–58/59 and 12–65 et seq.

prior to the termination of his current tenancy he will be entitled to double the amount of compensation to which he would otherwise be entitled. In this context the question arises whether a tenant who has ceased physical occupation shortly prior to the termination of the tenant's tenancy (whether that be the contractual term date or the date of termination specified in the landlord's s.25 notice) the tenant may, nevertheless, be treated as having remained in occupation for the purposes of a business if the closure can be viewed as part and parcel of the normal business activity of winding down the business in order to provide for an orderly quitting of the premises. It is a question of fact and degree whether the period of non-activity reasonably incidental to the winding down for the purpose of ending all business activity on the day the tenant is required to quit breaks the thread of business continuity. It is clearly a commercial absurdity to suggest that the tenant should remain in occupation until the clock strikes midnight on the last day. Thus common sense dictates that there should be an allowance for cessation of business activity for the purpose of quitting pursuant to the statutory scheme but without prejudicing the tenant's rights, e.g. to compensation. Thus cessation of business use 12 days prior to the end of the lease did not prevent the tenant, who had occupied premises for 20 years for business purposes, from claiming double compensation under s.37 of the Act: *Bacchiocchi v Academic Agency Ltd.*[165] In that case Ward L.J. said that the proper approach in considering whether there had been cessation of business activity, where the period of inactivity was pursuant to the commercial decision to cease trading from those premises, required one to consider the following questions:

(1) What was the purpose of leaving the premises unattended? Was it linked to or part and parcel of the business activity which was then necessarily geared to winding down preparatory to vacating for good?
(2) What was the intention lying behind the decision to leave the premises unattended? Was it total abandonment not only of the premises but also of the accruing right to compensation, or was the intention to quit in orderly fashion in order to comply with the statutory obligation to do so?
(3) As a matter of fact and degree, was the period of non-activity reasonably incidental to the winding down for the purpose of ending all business activity on the day the tenant was required to quit?
(4) Bearing in mind the elasticity of the thread of continuity,[166] did the thread stretch from the commencement of the business for the quitting of the premises looking at it as a coherent whole?

Non-occupation for a period of five months was held to be a period of non-activity which broke the thread of continuity of business user: *Sight & Sound Education Ltd v Books Etc Ltd*[167] (digested in para.12–33).

1–60 In none of the cases has the court had to deal with winding down business occupation in respect of large office premises. In *I&H Caplan Ltd v Caplan*

[165] [1998] 1 W.L.R. 1313; [1998] 2 All E.R. 241.
[166] See *I&H Caplan Ltd v Caplan (No.2)* [1963] 1 W.L.R. 1247; [1963] 2 All E.R. 930 (digested in para.1–46).
[167] [1999] 3 E.G.L.R. 45.

(No.2)[168] the court was concerned with shop premises on the first, ground and basement floors. In *Bacchiocchi v Academic Agency Ltd*[169] the court was concerned with a basement restaurant and *Sight & Sound Education Ltd v Books Etc Ltd*[170] was dealing with a book store. Premises which are tens of thousands of square feet cannot be vacated within a week, two weeks or probably even a month. Meticulous planning has to be undertaken to remove staff and fixtures and fittings. It is unclear what approach the court would take if presented with a set of facts where the tenant had vacated several weeks before the term date where that was the only practical means of providing for an orderly removal.[171]

The *Bacchiocchi v Academic Agency Ltd*[172] decision above needs to be considered very carefully. It would appear, on one reading, to uphold the view that a tenant is still protected by the 1954 Act notwithstanding that he has ceased all business activity and has vacated the premises with no intention to return. This could give rise to difficulties in relation to the continuation of the tenancy under s.24 of the 1954 Act. The Court of Appeal has held in *Esselte AB v Pearl Assurance Plc*[173] (digested in para.2–53) that in order for a continuation tenancy in accordance with the Act to arise the tenant must be in occupation for the purposes of a business at the term date otherwise the tenancy will end. The court rejected the view that the tenancy would continue so long as it was at some time during its life one to which the Act applied. Protection requires business occupation. The result of the *Esselte* decision is that if a tenant has failed to serve a notice pursuant to s.27(1) of the Act, by which he notifies the landlord that he does not wish his tenancy to continue pursuant to s.24 of the Act after the term date, the tenancy would, nevertheless, still end if, at the term date, the tenant was not in occupation for the purposes of a business.[174] *Bacchiocchi v Academic Agency Ltd* may now make it difficult to determine, in the absence of a notice served under s.27(1), whether the cessation of business occupation has been sufficient to prevent a statutory continuation. The decision would appear to make it prudent to serve a notice pursuant to s.27(1) to prevent inadvertent statutory continuation.[175] **1–61**

---

[168] [1963] 1 W.L.R. 1247; [1963] 2 All E.R. 930.
[169] [1998] 1 W.L.R. 1313; [1998] 2 All E.R. 241.
[170] [1999] 3 E.G.L.R. 45.
[171] The issue becomes an important one where the tenant's lease contains a clause, as was the case before the Court of Appeal in *Bacchiocchi*, which excludes the tenant's the right to compensation. Such a clause is only struck down if it can be shown that the tenant has been in business occupation for the period of five years immediately preceding the termination of the tenant's tenancy, i.e. up to the termination date provided for by the 1954 Act.
[172] [1998] 1 W.L.R. 1313; [1998] 2 All E.R. 241.
[173] [1997] 1 W.L.R. 891; [1997] 2 All E.R. 41; [1997] 1 E.G.L.R. 73 CA.
[174] This remains the position after the 2003 Order amendments. Section 27(1A) makes express provision to reflect the *Esselte* decision.
[175] This remains the case notwithstanding the terms of s.27(1A) which provides "Section 24 of this Act shall not have effect in relation to a tenancy for a term of years certain where the tenant is not in occupation of the property comprised in the tenancy at the time when, apart from this Act, the tenancy would come to an end by effluxion of time."

Sub-letting

1–62 One set of circumstances in which the tenant may have ceased to occupy the whole or the major part of the premises is where his business consists of sub-letting to business or residential sub-tenants. This is dealt with in detail in para.1–67.

1–63 A further problem arises where the tenant wishes to re-occupy the premises upon the expiration of a sub-tenancy and there is a nominal reversion only, often a matter of days. The tenant's main concern here is to ensure that he does enough in relation to re-occupying the premises upon the termination of the sub-tenancy to satisfy the court that he is in occupation for business purposes as at the term date of the tenancy. It would seem that with respect to office premises, if the tenant intends to occupy the premises for business purposes and undertakes steps which can be said to be incidental to the tenant's business activities, such as fitting out the premises for business purposes by the provision of carpets, computer cables, telephones and the like, this would seem to be sufficient: *Pointon York Group Plc v Poulton*.[176]

Third party rights

1–64 Ordinarily the tenant will be the occupier, being the person who under the terms of the lease is entitled to exclusive possession of the demised premises. This will be so even though the lease reserves to his landlord the usual rights to enter and inspect and repair, and even though the lease contains a user covenant, strictly limiting the use which the tenant may make of the demised property. In such cases the property is occupied by the tenant because he has a degree of sole use of the property sufficient to enable him to carry on his business there to the exclusion of everyone else. However, there may be occasions when there may be more than one person exercising or entitled to exercise rights over the same property. In such cases there is competition for the role of occupier. A particular problem which has had to be considered by the courts (including the House of Lords) has been the position which arises when the business of one person consists of permitting others to use his property for their own purposes (which may be business, residential or other purposes), so that in the result both exercise rights over the same property for their respective purposes.

Arrangements for third party use where tenant remains in occupation

1–65 A tenant may effect an arrangement with a third party (not amounting to a sub-letting) pursuant to which there is conferred upon the third party rights which entitle it to undertake an activity from within the demised premises albeit those rights do not amount to the grant of exclusive possession. In these circumstances it would seem that so long as the tenant can be said to be in occupation it matters not that there may be another person using the premises for business purposes. The provision by a tenant of a retail store of a small space for a counter to enable

[176] [2006] 3 E.G.L.R. 37; [2007] 1 P. & C.R. 115 CA.

product promotion (e.g. of a fragrance) for a limited period by a third party readily springs to mind. Alternatively, a tenant of a hotel may provide rooms and facilities once a month for an antiques fair or a farmer may permit his fields to be used for car boot sales.[177] In two cases very far removed on their facts from those sorts of commercial arrangements the Court of Appeal had, it would seem, little difficult with the concept of dual occupation. Thus, in *Hills (Patents) Ltd v University College Hospital Board of Governors*[178] the activities of a board of hospital governors were so substantial that they were to be treated as in occupation of the hospital for the purposes of s.30(1)(g) notwithstanding the fact that the governors were by statute entrusted with the task of managing the hospital on behalf of the Minister of Health and the Minster would, through the agency of the board, also be occupying the same. Denning L.J. said that the fact that the Minister may have also occupied the premises did not affect the board's ability to occupy, for whereas possession in law is single and exclusive, occupation may be shared with others or had on behalf of others.[179] Similarly in *Willis v British Commonwealth Universities Association (No.1)*[180] the landlord intended to provide accommodation, equipment and staff for a central organisation for university admissions (being an "activity" for the purposes of s.23) and was treated as intending to occupy the premises for business purposes for the purposes of s.30(1)(g) notwithstanding the fact that the actual administration of the university admissions was to be undertaken by another body from within the same premises.

In *Graysim Holdings Ltd v P&O Property Holdings Ltd*[181] (digested in para.1–70) it was said that when a landowner permits another to use his property for business purposes, the question of whether the landowner is sufficiently excluded, and the other is sufficiently present, for the latter to be regarded as the occupier in place of the former is a question of degree. It has been said that the question is not "is there a high degree of management" but "does that high degree of management involve or require some degree of occupation or control of the [relevant property] whether affecting exclusivity of possession or otherwise?": *Smith v Titanate Ltd*.[182] It is not, however, possible for the same property to form the holding of two business *tenancies*, each with statutory protection. This principle does not of course preclude a tenant remaining in occupation where third parties are entitled to and exercise rights over the property, and this is particularly so where the arrangement does not amount to the grant of a sub-tenancy. In *Lee-Verhulst (Investments) Ltd v Harwood Trust*[183] (digested in **1–66**

[177] Two examples provided by Lord Nicholls in *Graysim Holdings v P&O Property Holdings Ltd* [1996] A.C. 329 at 335G.

[178] [1956] 1 Q.B. 90 CA.

[179] Words to similar effect were uttered by Salmon L.J. in *Willis v British Commonwealth Universities Association*. Neither was commented upon in the House of Lords in *Graysim Holdings Ltd v P&O Property Holdings Ltd* (as to which see further below). The *Hills v University College Hospital Board* decision, along with *Willis v British Commonwealth Universities Association*, were cited in argument only.

[180] [1965] 1 Q.B. 140 CA.

[181] Lord Nicholls gave the only speech.

[182] [2005] 2 E.G.L.R. 63 at [21] per H.H. Judge Cooke (digested in para.1–75).

[183] [1973] Q.B. 204 CA.

para.1–72) the court held that in the case of a tenant carrying on the business of letting 20 furnished bed sits for which the tenant provided services, the tenant remained in occupation of the whole building. This decision is on its facts unexceptional on the basis that the residents were licensees only.[184] In *Smith v Titanate*[185] H.H. Judge Cooke held that *Lee-Verhulst (Investments) Ltd v Harwood* had not been overruled by the House of Lords and we respectfully agree.[186] *Lee-Verhulst (Investments) Ltd v Harwood* is the only reported example of the tenant licensor being held to have remained in occupation.

Where tenant's business is sub-letting

1–67 Where the business carried on by the tenant is that of sub-letting the whole or parts of the premises whether for business or residential purposes, the tenant cannot, save in very exceptional circumstances,[187] be in occupation of the whole or the parts in question for the purposes of the Act. The House of Lords established the relevant principles in *Graysim Holdings Ltd v P&O Property Holdings Ltd*[188] (digested in para.1–70) and the earlier cases must be considered in the light of that decision.

1–68 An alternative line of reasoning, considered by Lord Nicholls in *Graysim*, based on the decision in *Bagettes Ltd v GP Estates Co Ltd*[189] (digested in para.1–71), supports the same conclusion but with somewhat different practical results. This alternative reasoning would start by accepting that where part at least of the premises were retained as common parts the tenancy was protected as to the common parts, but would go on to hold that no grant of a new tenancy of those common parts should be made because no business would be carried on from them once the sub-let parts had been excluded from the holding. There would have ceased to be any "holding" for the purposes either of seeking the grant of a

---

[184] Per Lord Nicholls [1996] A.C. 329 at 337. However, in the course of his judgment in *Lee-Verhulst (Investments) Ltd v Harwood* Sachs L.J. said, at 215D–215E, that if, contrary to his view, the occupants of the rooms were sub-tenants, there would be a "shared" occupation: the sub-tenants of the rooms would have exclusive residential occupation, and the tenant company would have such occupation as was required for the purposes of the business. Lord Nicholls felt "unable to agree with this proposition" (at 338).

[185] [2005] 2 E.G.L.R. 63 CC (Central London).

[186] Although *William Boyer and Sons Ltd v Adams* (1976) 32 P. & C.R. 89 is probably to be viewed as having been overruled. In that case, Mr Adams was a tenant of a former farmhouse and outbuildings. He lived in the farmhouse and sub-let the outbuildings for use as light industrial units. Templeman J. held that Mr Adams was entitled to the protection of Pt II of the Act of 1954 in respect of the whole of the premises, *including the sub-let units*. The judge, at 91, treated the *Lee-Verhulst* decision as authority for the proposition that occupation of part of a property by a tenant is not necessarily inconsistent with occupation of the whole, including the part, by his landlord for the purposes of the landlord's business.

[187] This qualification of "exceptional circumstances" is made in the text because Lord Nicholls said that "Although there will usually be little difficulty in landlord and tenant cases, this may not always be so. I would not rule out the possibility that, exceptionally, the rights reserved by a landlord might be so extensive that he would remain in occupation of the demised property." (at 336). He did not elaborate on what the exceptional circumstances may be.

[188] [1996] A.C. 329 HL.

[189] [1956] 2 Ch. 290 CA.

new tenancy or for the purposes of seeking compensation in respect of the retained parts. The position was stated succinctly by Jenkins L.J., in *Bagettes Ltd v GP Estates Co Ltd:*

> "Once the flats which it is his business to sublet are excluded from his tenancy the remaining parts of the premises, though still in his occupation, are no longer occupied by him for the purposes of any business. Once the flats are gone the business for the purposes of which he formerly occupied the remainder of the premises, that is to say, the provision of services for the tenants of the flats sublet, as part of the entire business of letting and managing those flats, is gone also, and is incapable of continuance or revival."

Summary of Position

The following general propositions can, it is suggested, be derived from the cases: **1–69**

(1) A tenant will not be "occupying" premises if they are sub-let (rather than licensed) to a sub-tenant who is himself a business tenant protected by the Act, save in very exceptional circumstances.[190] This was expressly decided by the House of Lords in *Graysim Holdings Ltd v P&O Property Holdings Ltd*[191] (digested in para.1–70). For examples, see *Trans-Britannia Properties v Darby Properties*[192] (digested in para.1–73) (which is a pre-*Graysim* decision and which must now be read as an example of the impossibility of the tenant and sub-tenant both being in occupation of the relevant business premises) and *Bassari Ltd v Camden LBC*[193] (digested in para.1–74).

(2) Nor will the tenant be occupying premises if he has sub-let rather than licensed them for residential purposes. This was decided by the Court of Appeal in *Bassari Limited v London Borough of Camden*[194] (digested in para.1–74).

(3) It seems to follow that wherever a tenant has sub-let premises he cannot ordinarily be said as a matter of law to be "occupying" the sub-let premises.

(4) Even where the tenant has not sub-let all of the premises and remains in occupation of some part, that occupation must not be of a nature which will necessarily cease to be for business purposes when the new tenancy of "the holding" is granted. Thus if the holding consists solely of the common parts and the remainder is being sub-let such that the tenant is not in occupation, the holding is of such a character that it is necessarily brought to an end by the separation of the holding from the remainder of the premises comprised in the lease (see *Bagettes Ltd v GP Estates Co Ltd*,[195] digested in para.1–71).

(5) Occupation by a third party of premises under a licence otherwise than for the purpose of carrying on a business belonging to the tenant itself is not per se sufficient to make the tenant the occupier of the premises under a

---

190 As to which, see fn.187 above.

191 [1996] A.C. 329 HL.

192 [1986] 1 E.G.L.R. 151 CA.

193 [1999] L. & T.R. 45 CA.

194 [1999] L. & T.R. 45 CA.

195 [1956] 2 Ch. 290 CA.

tenancy within the meaning of the Act: *Hancock & Willis v GMS Syndicate*[196] (digested in para.1–47). In that case the Court of Appeal held that a tenant who had granted a licence of the premises to a third party who occupied them for the purposes of his own business did not exercise sufficient rights of control and user of the premises to be said to "occupy" them.

(6) Suggestions in some of the authorities that one can have a sharing of occupation in the sense that the same premises are occupied within the meaning of the 1954 Act by two or more persons for the carrying on of their respective businesses are inconsistent with *Graysim*.

(7) Subject to the foregoing, it is a matter of fact and degree in each case whether the tenant "occupies" the premises. The question is not "is there a high degree of management" but "does that high degree of management involve or require some degree of occupation or control of the [relevant property] whether affecting exclusivity of possession or otherwise?": *Smith v Titanate Ltd.*[197]

1–70 ***Graysim Holdings Ltd v P&O Property Holdings Ltd***[198] The tenant was in business as a market operator and manager. The tenant took a 21-year lease of a shell building, which it covenanted to use and occupy as a general market. The building was fitted out as a market hall with 35 individual stalls. Each stall consisted of studs, to which partitions had been attached, and was fitted with a roller blind which could be secured by the stallholder by pad-locking the blind to the counter or some other part of the stall. The judge at first instance found that each stallholder had exclusive possession of his stall. It was assumed in the Court of Appeal that each stallholder was, therefore, a sub-tenant of the tenant. The tenant provided a number of facilities and services to the stallholders, including the provision and maintenance of lavatories, bin rooms and the employment of a market superintendent, who collected the rent and service charge, and effected minor repairs and maintenance services to the demised premises. Trading hours were limited and it was only during such hours that stallholders had access to the demised premises. The tenant prescribed the goods that could be sold by the stallholders. It was also part of the superintendent's duties to maintain discipline amongst traders and to ensure that the aisles were clear for shoppers. The judge held that the tenant was not in occupation for the purposes of a business carried on by it. The Court of Appeal reversed his decision. Although the stallholders had exclusive possession of the stalls, this did not prevent the tenant from occupying the premises as a whole for the purposes of s.23(1). There was a sufficient degree of presence and manifestation of control in respect of the whole; it exercised to the full in respect of the whole premises extensive management and control necessitated by the business. On appeal to the House of Lords it was held:

(1) Where the tenant of a business tenancy sub-let parts of the premises on sub-tenancies which were themselves business tenancies protected by the

196 [1983] 1 E.G.L.R. 70 CA.

197 [2005] 2 E.G.L.R. 63 at [21].

198 [1996] A.C. 329 HL.

1954 Act, the sub-let premises ceased to be part of the tenant's "holding". In such circumstances there could be no "shared occupation" or "dual occupation" of the same premises (by tenant and sub-tenant) as had been suggested in some of the earlier cases.

(2) Accordingly, where the tenant's business consists of sub-letting, and he has sub-let the whole of the premises (or all except the common parts) his tenancy will cease to be protected by the Act.

Bagettes Ltd v GP Estates Co Ltd[199] The tenant was in the business of sub-letting residential flats. The only parts of the premises which were in its actual occupation were the common parts, such as the caretaker's rooms, boiler rooms and certain of the flats which were empty. The Court of Appeal held that, although the tenant company might be said to occupy those common parts, it did not do so for the purposes of its business since the purpose of such occupation would cease once the sub-let flats were excluded from the premises comprised in the tenancy. (For an alternative explanation of, and further support for, the result reached in this case, see the discussion of the *Graysim* case in para.1–67 above.) **1–71**

Lee-Verhulst (Investments) Ltd v Harwood Trust[200] Twenty separate fully furnished apartments were sub-let or licensed by the tenant to individual occupiers. In that case the Court of Appeal considered whether the tenant company could be said to be in occupation of the parts which were sub-let or licensed. Because of the range of services afforded by the tenant company to the actual occupiers and the degree of management control exercised over the sub-let or licensed parts it was held that the tenant company was sharing occupation of the premises with the residential occupiers. **1–72**

Trans-Britannia Properties v Darby Properties[201] The landlord demised to the tenants certain premises upon which the tenants constructed 46 lock-up garages, which they sub-let to individuals who used them to park private motor vehicles. There was no living accommodation on the site, and no office, and the services rendered by the tenants to the occupiers consisted of repairing the garages and in particular the doors and locks, and keeping the site free from rubbish. There was no water or electricity on the site. The tenants retained keys to each garage, but there was no evidence that they ever obtained access except with the permission of the individual occupier. At the expiry date of the lease some of the garages were vacant, but the majority were sub-let. The county court judge held that the tenants were in occupation of the demised premises for the purposes of a business carried on by them because: (1) the tenants were in rateable occupation of the site; (2) they occupied one garage as a store; (3) they let out the garage space and cleaned and maintained and serviced the site; (4) they had access keys to the garages; and (5) they appeared to keep "a fairly close watch" on the garages. The Court of Appeal reversed the county court judge's decision, holding that on the facts there was insufficient occupation by the tenant for the purposes of s.23. The **1–73**

199 [1956] 2 Ch. 290 CA.
200 [1973] Q.B. 204 CA.
201 [1986] 1 E.G.L.R. 151 CA.

fact of rateable occupation was not significant; there was no evidence of any obligation to render significant services and the tenant never claimed or exercised any right to enter the garages save with the consent of the occupiers, and their own employees only visited the site once a fortnight.

1–74 ***Bassairi Ltd v Camden LBC***[202] The demised premises consisted of a basement, a ground floor shop and four floors of residential accommodation above the shop. The tenant sub-let the basement and ground floor to sub-tenants for the purposes of a hairdressers' business. The upper floor was converted into nine bedsits or studio flats with some shared facilities. Eight of these flats were occupied by individual residents and one was retained by the tenant and used as a store room. In relation to the residential element services were provided by the tenant including the supply of toiletries such as shampoo, soap, cleaning materials, toilet paper and toothpaste together with a cleaning service and an answering service for the telephone, dry cleaning, a laundry service, television, tea and coffee, continental breakfast and the use of a bible together with a microwave for a couple of the occupiers. The tenant admitted that it was not in occupation of the basement and shop part of the premises but claimed to be in business occupation of the nine flats. It was held that:

(1) The occupiers of the residential premises were tenants as opposed to licensees.
(2) In light of *Graysim Holdings Ltd v P&O Property Holdings Ltd*[203] (digested in para.1–70) the tenant was unable as a matter of law to occupy the eight sub-let flats and those flats could not form part of the holding within the meaning of s.23 of the Act because there could not be dual occupation by the tenant and the sub-tenant of the flats let to the sub-tenants.
(3) Even if the occupiers were licensees as opposed to tenants the evidence was not such as to justify a finding that the tenant's degree of control was such as to justify a finding that the tenant was in occupation. There was no evidence that the services referred to were in fact supplied nor that the tenant retained the right to enter the flats.
(4) In relation to the one retained flat it was said that on the basis of *Graysim*, above, there could not be a part of the premises retained for the purposes of sub-letting the remainder of the premises, which would be the subject of any business tenancy, because a new tenancy of the retained part could not be used for the business of sub-letting, the sub-tenants having ceased, *ex hypothesi*, to be the sub-tenants of the tenant. The Court of Appeal dismissed the appeal.

1–75 ***Smith v Titanate Ltd***[204] L sought to oppose T's claim to enfranchise under the Leasehold Reform Act 1967 by arguing that T held a tenancy which fell within Pt II of the Landlord and Tenant Act 1954. If it did T would have to satisfy a

---

[202] [1999] L. & T.R. 45 CA.
[203] [1995] 3 W.L.R. 854; [1995] 4 All E.R. 831 HL.
[204] [2005] 2 E.G.L.R. 63 County Court (Central London).

residency condition which, being a company, it could not fulfil. T held a lease of 52 years of a building from which it conducted its business of operating serviced accommodation. The building was sub-let into six flats which were either Assured Shorthold Tenancies or a simple one-page agreement (for very short lettings of several weeks or a few months). The flats were let furnished, with telephones, TVs, heating and lighting and hot water. The services provided included tea and coffee, together with a change of linen twice week and a daily change of towels. T had an office in the building which was attended during working hours by a manager who supervised the services and cleaning. It was held that T was not in occupation for the purposes of a business within the meaning of s.23 of the 1954 Act.

Where the third party is a manager or other agent

The tenant though not physically in occupation may be occupying through a manager or other agent. The only difficulty in such cases is whether the arrangement with the third party manager or agent is truly such or whether the relationship is one which on a true consideration of its terms ousts the tenant from occupation, e.g. if the management agreement is in fact the grant of a sub-tenancy: see *Parkes v Westminster Roman Catholic Diocese Trustee*[205] (digested in para.1–77); *Teesside Indoor Bowls v Stockton-on-Tees BC*[206] (digested in para.1–78); and *Dellneed v Chin*[207] (digested in para.1–15) by way of example.[208] **1–76**

Parkes v Westminster Roman Catholic Diocese Trustee[209] The tenant applied to renew its tenancy of a country club with a club house, bowling green and tennis courts. The landlord, the Westminster Roman Catholic Diocese Trustee, opposed the application under s.30(1)(g) (own occupation). The intention proved at trial was to use the premises as a community centre; the clubhouse would be turned into a church room for meetings after services in the nearby church; and the tennis courts would be used for elderly or young people. The actual activities of running the community centre would be carried on by the parish priest and his committee. The landlord was a company limited by guarantee in which was vested, on trust, all the property and assets of the Roman Catholic Church in the diocese of Westminster. It was held the business or activities to be carried on would be "carried on by the landlord" as required by s.30(1)(g), for the parish priest and his committee would be acting as the landlord's agents and would on its part carry out its activities pursuant to the trust deed. **1–77**

(It should be noted that the landlord was unable to rely on the trust provisions of s.41(2) of the 1954 Act because that section operates only where there are "beneficiaries". There are no specific beneficiaries of a charitable trust (see

205 (1978) 36 P. & C.R. 22 CA.

206 [1990] 2 E.G.L.R. 87 CA.

207 (1987) 53 P. & C.R. 172.

208 For other cases on management agreements, see *Teasdale v Walker* [1958] 1 W.L.R. 1076 CA (digested in para.1–83) and *Ross Auto Wash Ltd v Herbert* [1979] 1 E.G.L.R. 95 (digested in para.1–84).

209 [1978] 2 E.G.L.R. 50 CA. As to other cases on agency, see para.1–82 et seq.

para.1–81). Accordingly, the landlord had to show that they themselves intended to occupy the premises for the purposes of a "business" to be carried on by them.)

1–78 ***Teesside Indoor Bowls v Stockton-on-Tees BC***[210] The landlord local authority intended to occupy the tenant's holding, a bowling club, for its own purposes. The local authority decided to enter into a management agreement with an experienced bowling company, as they considered that they did not have the necessary experience or flair to run the bowling club themselves. The local authority retained policy decisions like pricing of membership fees, green fees, locker fees and bar, but the rules of the club were to be drawn up by the company. There was no allegation that the agreement was a sham. The Court of Appeal rejected the argument that the premises were intended to be occupied by the members of the club for the purposes of the club's business or for the purposes of the management company's business. The premises were intended to be occupied by the local authority for the purposes of the local authority's business or for the purpose of the business of the local authority carried on through the management company as the local authority's agent.

Relevant time

1–79 The question whether the tenant is in occupation, and thus whether the tenancy is within the Act, is to be judged from time to time. During the contractual term, it is usually irrelevant whether the Act applies and the tenant may cease occupation (so that the Act ceases to apply) and then resume it during the contractual term so that it once again applies. However, in order to take advantage of the provisions for the continuation of tenancies, the tenant must be in occupation for business purposes on the contractual expiry date of the term. In order to be entitled to the grant of a new tenancy he must also be in occupation at all times thereafter. The cessation of business occupation occurring both before and after the contractual term date (where the tenancy has continued pursuant to s.24 of the Act) is considered in Ch.2.

6. IS THE OCCUPATION THAT OF THE TENANT?

Occupation "by the tenant"

1–80 The Act applies only where premises are occupied "by the tenant": s.23(1). In the case of a joint tenancy "the tenant" for the purposes of the Act means all the joint tenants in whom the legal estate is vested (*Jacobs v Chaudhuri*,[211] digested in para.6–28), and thus, prima facie, all would have to occupy in order to secure protection of the Act. However, as the tenancy in those circumstances would be held on an implied trust, occupation by all or any of the joint tenants will suffice to attract the protection of the Act: s.41(1).[212]

210 [1990] 2 E.G.L.R. 87 CA.
211 [1968] 2 Q.B. 470 CA.
212 See para.1–92 et seq.

Special considerations arise where the tenant is not personally in occupation. The various circumstances in which this situation can occur are considered in the following paragraphs. **1–81**

Occupation by a manager or other agent[213]

In *Pegler v Craven*,[214] Jenkins L.J. said: **1–82**

> "The conception of 'occupation' is not necessarily and in all the circumstances confined to the actual personal occupation of the person termed the occupier himself. In certain contexts and for certain purposes it obviously extends to vicarious occupation by a caretaker or other servant or by an agent."

Where the tenant relies upon the vicarious occupation of a manager, the management agreement must be examined. The labels used by the parties are not conclusive—the respective obligations and functions of the tenant and the "manager" must be assessed and if, in reality, the manager is occupying for the purposes of his own business, the tenant will not be protected by the Act. In the case where a management agreement has been entered into, the question is whether it is, in reality, the grant of a sub-tenancy. If it is, it is not the tenant in occupation but the "manager" under the sub-tenancy. A business which is carried on by an individual at his own financial risk is normally indicative of his acting as principal and not as agent.[215] All of the agreements entered into between the parties need to be considered. Thus, where the occupier agreed with a local authority to manage a caravan park paying £32,890 per annum to the local authority, under an Operator's Agreement which contained detailed obligations as to what he was to do in running the park, and at the same time entered into an employment contract to work on the park as a part time security guard, and entered into an agreement to occupy a bungalow on the site "for the better performance of his duties," it was held that the true effect of the arrangements was that the occupier was managing the caravan park business as agent of the local authority rather than on his own account: *Brumwell v Powys CC*.[216]

Teasdale v Walker[217] The tenant had used the premises near the seafront at Skegness to hold mock auctions. Initially the tenant conducted the auctions herself, and then employed somebody to run them; in both cases, she kept the profits. However, the tenant then had to move to Derby, due to the illness of her mother. She therefore entered into a written agreement with G by which he became entitled to occupy the premises and to conduct the mock auctions on his own account on payment to the tenant of the sum of £750 for the year. The **1–83**

[213] In addition to the cases digested here, see also *Parkes v Westminster Roman Catholic Diocese Trustee* [1978] 2 E.G.L.R. 50 CA (digested in para.1–77) and *Teesside Indoor Bowls Ltd v Stockton-on-Tees BC* [1990] 2 E.G.L.R. 87 CA. (digested in para.1–78); *Dellneed v Chin* [1987] 1 E.G.L.R. 75 CA (digested in para.1–15).

[214] [1952] 1 All E.R. 685 CA.

[215] *Brumwell v Powys CC* [2011] EWCA Civ 1613; [2012] L. & T.R. 14 CA at [43].

[216] [2011] EWCA Civ 1613; [2012] L. & T.R. 14 CA. It was said that the Operator's Agreement formed one part of a single transaction given effect by three agreements.

[217] [1958] 1 W.L.R. 1076; [1958] 3 All E.R. 307 CA.

agreement referred to the tenant as "employer" and to G as "manager". G's salary was expressed to consist of the whole of the profits of the business except the £750 and he was to have full liberty to conduct the business of the tenant in whatever manner he considered fit without any hindrance or interference on the part of the employer. G was to pay for all goods supplied for the purposes of the business and was liable for all the outgoings in respect of the premises including the rent, rates and water rates for the year. The landlord served a notice under s.25 and the issue arose whether the tenant occupied the premises for the purposes of her business. The Court of Appeal held that "occupation" is not confined to the actual occupation of the person termed the occupier, but extends to vicarious occupation by a caretaker or other servant or by an agent. However, the tenant could not be said to be occupying the premises through G as her manager. Insofar as the agreement referred to the tenant as "employer" and G as "manager", it was a complete fiction and the "management" agreement was a sham.

1–84 ***Ross Auto Wash v Herbert***[218] The tenant had a tenancy of a shopping precinct, from which various licensees conducted their individual businesses. The tenant entered into an agreement with X whereby X agreed to "carry out on . . . behalf [of the tenant] the management and servicing of the business, and in particular . . . to collect the concession licensees' fees and arrange for payment of outgoings". It was expressly stated that X was "appointed manager only and full possession and control of the premises remains with [the tenant]". The tenant retained control over the granting of individual licences, and personally provided a number of services including the effecting of insurance, the arrangement of advertising and credit facilities and the payment of heating, lighting, rates, taxes and other outgoings. X received some of the licence fees, although no specific arrangement had been made about how much of those fees X could keep. X also paid for some of the outgoings, in particular, the cost of decoration. The tenant had originally intended to assign his lease to X, but that proposal had fallen through because the landlord had refused consent. Upon the tenant's application for a new tenancy under the Act, the issue arose as to whether the tenant (as opposed to X) was occupying the premises for the purpose of his business. The High Court held that the reality of the position was that stated in the management agreement and that X was manager only of the tenant's business of granting licences. Accordingly, the tenant was in occupation for the purposes of the Act and was protected.

1–85 ***Cafeteria (Keighley) Ltd v Harrison***[219] The trustees of the deceased landlord sought to resist an application for a new tenancy on the basis of ground (g) of s.30(1). They, being children of the deceased, together with another brother, all being beneficiaries of the deceased's estate under his will, intended to carry on the deceased's business. One of the trustees lived in Yorkshire, the other in Nottingham, while the brother lived in South Africa. The county court judge granted the tenant a new tenancy on the ground that the trustees and the brother could not occupy the premises for the purposes of the business due to their geographical situation. On appeal it was held that:

---

[218] [1979] 1 E.G.L.R. 95.

[219] (1956) 168 E.G. 668 CA.

(1) Although the trustees and brother were unavailable, due to their geographical situation, to go to the premises at any time for the purposes of the business, this did not prevent them from establishing the requisite ability to occupy for the purposes of s.30(1)(g), for a landlord who intended to occupy premises for the purposes of a business did not have to occupy in person; the premises could be occupied through an agent or manager.

(2) However, as no arrangements were made for a manager to be appointed the intention to occupy had not been proved. The appeal was dismissed.[220]

Occupation by tenant's company

Pre-2003 Order

It was formerly the position[221] that where the tenant operated a business through a company, it was the company rather than the tenant who was to be regarded as the occupier of the premises at which the business was carried on. The mere fact that the tenant was a controlling shareholder of the company did not enable the court to treat the company as the tenant's alter ego, managing the business for and on behalf of the tenant.[222] **1–86**

This was so no matter how much energy and money the tenant may have put into the business and notwithstanding the hardship that the tenant would suffer by being deprived of the benefit of the expenditure he had incurred by what may have seemed to be a legal technicality. The attitude of the court was that if persons choose to carry on their operations through the medium of a limited company obtaining the advantages in respect of responsibility for the debts thereby conferred, they could not really complain if they had to face some disadvantages also.

Position with effect from June 1, 2004

Article 13 of the 2003 Order amended s.23(1) of the 1954 Act by inserting new subss.(1A) and (1B). These provide: **1–87**

> "(1A) Occupation or the carrying on of a business –
> (a) by a company in which the tenant has a controlling interest; or
> (b) where the tenant is a company, by a person with a controlling interest in the company, shall be treated for the purposes of this as equivalent to occupation or, as the case may be, the carrying on of a business by the tenant.
>
> (1B) Accordingly references (however expressed) in this Part of this Act to the business of, and to use, occupation or enjoyment by, the tenant shall be construed as including

[220] The trustees being the legal owners of the deceased's freehold interest and thus competent landlords might have invoked s.30(1)(g) as trustee landlords rather than relying on their position as beneficiaries under the trust pursuant to s.41(2) of the Act. The fact that the brother, who was not a trustee, was mentioned as a potential occupier, indicates that the application for the new tenancy was being resisted on the basis of an intended occupation qua beneficiaries. The distinction is not made clear in the report. Where the landlord's interest is the creation of a trust under a will it does not fall foul of the five-year rule contained in s.30(2): see s.41(2).

[221] That is prior to the coming into force of the 2003 Order with effect from June 1, 2004.

[222] The cases are considered and digested in the second edition of this work at paras 14–31 to 14–34.

references to the business of, or to use, occupation or enjoyment by, a company falling within sub-s.(1A)(a) above or a person falling within sub-s.(1A)(b) above."

1–88 These provisions are intended to overcome the difficulties arising in two situations:

(1) The tenant is the sole shareholder of a company. The tenant, rather than carrying on business in his own name, carries on business through the company. The tenant will now be protected.[223] The decisions in *Pegler v Craven*[224]; *Cristina v Seear*[225]; and *Nozari-Zadeh v Pearl Assurance*[226] have been reversed.

(2) The tenant is a company. The business is in fact carried on by the principal shareholder. The company is non-trading; it is simply the property-holding vehicle of the tenant. Without having to consider whether or not the company holds the lease on trust for the purposes of enabling the controlling shareholder to be protected pursuant to the provisions of s.41 of the 1954 Act (together with the difficulties which that may entail), the company tenant will have protection pursuant to s.23(1A).

"Controlling interest"

1–89 A person has a controlling interest in a company if, had that person been a company, the other company would have been a subsidiary within the meaning of s.1159 of the Companies Act 2006[227]: s.46(2) as inserted by art.17 of the 2003 Order.

"Person"

1–90 Section 23(1)(A)(b) treats occupation and the carrying on of a business by a "person" having a controlling interest in the tenant company as the occupation and carrying on of the business of the tenant. "Person" does not include a company but is confined to individuals. Although not expressly stated to be so, it is apparent from the provisions of s.46(2) that this is the case. Section 46(2) provides that "... a person has a controlling interest in a company if, *had he been a company*, the other company would have been its subsidiary..." (emphasis added). Thus, where the tenant is a company and the premises are occupied by an associated company, the tenant obtains protection only if it can rely on s.41 (property held on trust) or s.42 (occupation by group company).

---

223 Although s.23(1A)(a) protects occupation "by a company in which the tenant has a controlling interest", nevertheless, the application for the new tenancy must still be made in the name of the tenant. There is no amendment to s.29 to enable a tenant who qualifies for 1954 Act protection pursuant to s.23(1A)(a) to make the application in the name of the company rather than the name of the tenant. See para.6–34.

224 [1952] 1 All E.R. 685 CA.

225 [1985] 2 E.G.L.R 128 CA.

226 [1987] 2 E.G.L.R. 91 CA.

227 Previously s.736 of the Companies Act 2005.

The amendments relating to companies and their controlling shareholders are also reflected in two other provisions, s.30, dealing with grounds of opposition and s.34, relating to improvements.[228] 1–91

Occupation by beneficiaries

By virtue of s.41(1), where a tenancy is held on trust, occupation by all or any of the beneficiaries under trust is to be treated for the purposes of s.23 as equivalent to occupation by the tenant. The wide wording s.41(1), which would appear on first sight to embrace anybody who has any sort of beneficial interest under the trust, has been considerably cut down by the decisions of the court. (The relevant cases were decided under s.41(2)[229] but the wording in s.41(1) is identical.) The effect of these decisions is that the "beneficiary under the trust" must be one who is entitled by the terms of the trust, either absolutely or at the trustees' discretion, to occupy the premises: *Frish Ltd v Barclays Bank Ltd*[230] (digested in para.1–100); *Carshalton Beeches Bowling Club v Cameron*[231] (digested in para.1–101); *Meyer v Riddick*[232] (digested in para.1–103). 1–92

The trust need not be an express trust. Where a tenancy has been acquired as a partnership asset, the inference may be drawn that it has been acquired on the basis of an implied or constructive trust of which the partners are the beneficiaries: *Hodson v Cashmore*[233] (digested in para.1–102). A declaration of trust requires to be manifested or proved by writing, signed by some person able to declare it: s.53(1)(a) of the Law of Property Act 1925. Section 53(2) of the Law of Property Act 1925 excludes implied, resulting or constructive trusts from the operation of s.53(1) of the Law of Property Act 1925. However, there must be evidence from which one can draw the inference of an implied, resulting or constructive trust. Thus where the tenant permitted land to be occupied by a collective carrying on the project of a community free farm, which was a project of a loose association which gave the opportunity to groups of unemployed individuals to work on the restoration of derelict buildings upon the land and to enable it to be used to house animals, it was held that no trust could be established in favour of the collective. This was so even assuming that a loose grouping of like minded individuals who share common objectives could be viewed as a body of persons for whom the land could be held on trust. No rent was paid by the collective nor did any of the members of the collective contribute their work in order to obtain a proprietary interest in the property carrying with it a liability to indemnify the trustees against liability for the rent: *Secretary of State for Transport v Jenkins*.[234] 1–93

---

228 As to which, see paras 7–254 et seq. and para.8–143.

229 Which treats, for the purposes of s.30(1)(g), the intended occupation of beneficiaries under a trust, as the intended occupation of the trustee landlord: see para.7–258.

230 [1955] 3 W.L.R. 439; [1955] All E.R. 185 CA.

231 [1978] 1 E.G.L.R. 107 CA.

232 [1990] 1 E.G.L.R. 107 CA.

233 (1972) 226 E.G. 1203; [1973] E.G.D. 485.

234 (2000) 79 P. & C.R. 118 CA.

1–94 The fact that the beneficiary must be occupying pursuant to his equitable interest means that one must look under the terms of the trust to see whether there is anyone intended to take a personal benefit. If there is not, then the mere fact that the trustees may permit another to control and manage the demised premises does not enable the trustees to rely upon s.41(1) of the 1954 Act. Thus, where trustees of a charitable trust dedicated the matters concerning the school to a board of management, the fact that the board of management via an employee occupied a dwelling house for the purposes of his duties as caretaker to the school did not mean that the trustees could rely upon s.41, for it was the board of management, through the caretaker, who were in occupation of the property and the board of management was not intended to take any personal benefit under the trust: *Trustees of the Methodist Secondary Schools Trust Deed v O'Leary*,[235] (see para.1–139). Sir Christopher Slade commented in that case on the "knotty problems" which may arise where tenanted properties are held by trustees on trust not for individuals but for public charitable purposes. A public charitable trust does not have "beneficiaries" in whose favour the provisions can operate. Lord Denning M.R. in *Parkes v Westminster Roman Catholic Diocese Trustee*[236] (digested in para.1–77) was of the view that the provisions of s.41(2) (which enable a landlord to rely upon the proposed occupation of beneficiaries in opposing under para.(g) of s.30(1) of the Act) did not apply to charitable trusts. There appears to be no reason why this is not equally applicable to the provisions of s.41(1).

1–95 It would seem that there is nothing to prevent s.41(1) from applying to a situation where the trustees, who are also beneficiaries, occupy the demised premises for the purposes of their own businesses, e.g. three dentists all of whom occupy the premises carrying on their individual practices though not in partnership (see *Harris v Black*[237] (digested in para.6–30). However see para.1–122 as to whether "a" business is being carried on.

1–96 A lease cannot be granted to an unincorporated association.[238] Thus a lease which is expressed to be granted to an unincorporated association cannot create any estate in land. It will not, however, be construed as a grant to the persons who sign the counterpart.[239] The lease must, therefore, be held by an individual or individuals on behalf of the association. In relation to a club the lease will usually be taken by officers of the club, who will be trustees of the lease for the members of the club, e.g. see *Teba Fabrics v Conn*.[240]

1–97 The position most often encountered in practice is that of joint tenants where only one or some of them are in occupation. It is clear at common law that beneficial joint tenants or tenants in common have the right to possession of the entire

---

[235] (1992) 66 P. & C.R. 364; [1993] 1 E.G.L.R. 105 CA.

[236] [1978] 2 E.G.L.R. 50.

[237] (1983) 46 P. & C.R. 366 CA.

[238] *Camden LBC v Shortlife Community Housing* (1993) 25 H.L.R. 330; *Onyx (UK) Ltd v Beard* [1996] E.G. 55 (C.S.) Ch. D.

[239] *Camden LBC v Shortlife Community Housing*(1993) 25 H.L.R. 330.

[240] (1958) 121 E.G. 495; *Addiscombe Garden Estates Ltd v Crabbe* [1958] 1 Q.B. 513 CA (digested at para.1–11).

property and to the use and enjoyment of it in a proper manner.[241] If the trustees/beneficiaries attempt to formalise the occupation, e.g. by the grant of a commercial lease, the occupation of the beneficiary under that lease will not enable the trustees to rely on the provisions of s.41(1), for the occupation is qua sub-tenant protected by the 1954 Act, rather than qua beneficiary.

Another common situation where a trust was sought to be raised was where the tenant carried on the business via a limited company of which the tenant was the controlling shareholder. As has been seen (paras 1–83 et seq.), the tenant was not prior to June 1, 2004 regarded as being in occupation, for the company had an independent legal personality and the occupation and the carrying on of the business was that of the company and not the tenant. The requirement to search for a trust relationship[242] between the company and the controlling shareholder in order to confer protection on the tenant will now no longer arise in light of the provisions contained in s.23(1A).[243] **1–98**

It is to be noted that s.41(1) does not, for all purposes, substitute the beneficiaries for the tenant. Thus any notice served in accordance with the Act must be served by or upon "the tenant" which will be the trustees, not the beneficiaries. Similarly, the making of any application for a new tenancy must be by the trustees rather than any of the beneficiaries, save in the case of partners where the special provisions of s.41A of the 1954 Act may apply. **1–99**

Frish Ltd v Barclays Bank Ltd[244] The question arose whether the landlords were able to make out the ground of opposition to the tenant's application for a new tenancy set out in ground (g) of s.30(1) (own occupation). The landlords held their interests upon discretionary trusts for sale in favour of the settlor during his lifetime and, thereafter, his children and remoter issue. The trustees' proposal for the purposes of ground (g) was that the premises should be occupied by the settlor for the purposes of his business, he taking a seven-year lease at a full rent from the trustees. The Court of Appeal had to decide whether, on a true construction of s.41(2), the settlor was, in these circumstances a "beneficiary under the trust", upon whose proposed occupation the landlord could rely for the purposes of ground (g). The court held that the word "beneficiary" must, in **1–100**

241 *Bull v Bull* [1955] 1 Q.B. 234; [1955] 2 W.L.R. 78; [1955] 1 All E.R. 253 CA, per Denning L.J at 237. This right exists irrespective of the quantum of the tenant in common's undivided share. It is clear that no tenant in common may go so far as to turn out another co-tenant of the property: *Bull v Bull* at 237. Where land is held on a trust of land post 1996, the Trust of Land and Appointment of Trustees Act 1996 confers on a beneficiary who is beneficially entitled to an interest in possession in the land to occupy it: Trust of Land and Appointment of Trustees Act 1996 s.12. This right is subject to the trustees' powers to exclude or restrict the right in certain circumstances: Trust of Land and Appointment of Trustees Act 1996 s.13.

242 There is no decided case in the context of the 1954 Act as to the circumstances in which a trust could be held to have arisen for the benefit of a company of which the tenant is the controlling shareholder. If there was a declaration of trust then, of course, there is no problem. In the absence of a formal instrument of trust, the question is then one of whether such a trust could be implied from the circumstances. See the very short report of *Beech v Bloomfield* [1953] C.L.Y. 1988; C.P.L. 672 CC, where one of two directors of a company carrying on a retail grocery business was held to be a bare trustee for the company. The facts and reasoning which led to this conclusion are not, however, stated.

243 See para.1–87 et seq.

244 [1955] 2 Q.B. 541 CA.

context, be given a limited meaning, for its literal meaning would allow trustee landlords to rely upon the intended occupation of anyone who happens to have a beneficial interest under the trusts, however remote and contingent, and who could make a commercial bargain with the landlords which was attractive to them. Accordingly the landlords' ground of opposition failed because the proposed occupation would be subject to the lease and not by virtue of any interest arising under the trust.

1–101 ***Carshalton Beeches Bowling Club v Cameron***[245] The premises, occupied by the tenant for its business as a bowling club, comprised a bowling green and the first floor of a house. The rest of the house, together with another house nearby, had been used for many years as a school. The landlord died and by her will left her property, as part of her residuary estate, to her nephew Peter Henry and her niece, Lady Cameron, in equal shares. Peter Henry and Lady Cameron agreed that the estate would be wound up by transferring the two school properties to Peter Henry for a consideration. The tenant's application for a new tenancy was opposed by the deceased landlord's executors on ground (g) of s.30(1) (own occupation). At trial it was proved that Peter Henry, who was going to carry on the school, would take over the first floor for use as a proprietary club for parents of children at the school and would use the bowling green as part of the school amenities. The Court of Appeal held that Peter Henry was not, in the circumstances, a "beneficiary under a trust" for the purposes of s.41(2) so that his intended occupation was insufficient for the purposes of ground (g). In order to come within the subsection, it was necessary that the executors were entitled under the will to let Peter Henry into occupation qua beneficiary. This they could not do because there was insufficient property in the residuary estate to appropriate the school properties to Peter Henry and still satisfy Lady Cameron's half-share. Even when the intended transfer (for a consideration) to Peter Henry had taken place he would still be unable to rely upon ground (g) because he would then be a "landlord by purchase" (as to which, see paras 7–264 and 7–278).

1–102 ***Hodson v Cashmore***[246] The deceased tenant, a partner in a firm of architects, held a yearly tenancy granted in the 1960s of chambers in the Temple, from which the firm practised. On the tenant's death the trustees of the Inner Temple, as landlord, served a common law notice to quit on the personal representatives of the tenant. The tenant's surviving partner, who continued the practice, claimed the protection of the Act on the ground that the tenancy was a partnership asset and was thus held by the personal representatives on trust for him. The common law notice was accordingly invalid. The court held that, although the partnership deed threw no light on the matter and the payment of rent and stamp duty out of partnership funds was itself insufficient to make the tenancy a partnership asset, the evidence nonetheless indicated that the deceased tenant and his partner had regarded the acquisition of the tenancy as being on behalf of and for the benefit of

245 [1978] 1 E.G.L.R. 80 CA.
246 (1972) 226 E.G. 1203.

the firm and it was accordingly held on trust for the surviving partner within s.41(1) and the tenancy was protected by the Act.

Meyer v Riddick[247] The landlords of business premises were Mr and Mrs N and Mr R. They were joint tenants at law holding the freehold on trust for themselves as tenants in common in equity, each being entitled to a one-third share of the proceeds of sale. The landlords opposed the tenant's application for renewal of the business tenancy under para.(g) of s.30(1) of the Act (own occupation). At the hearing of the tenant's application the evidence given was that Mr N and Mr R, who were solicitors, intended to occupy the premises for the purposes of a solicitor's business to be carried on by them in conjunction with several other partners in a firm. The landlords would grant a lease of the premises to the four partners of the firm, two of whom were to be Mr R and Mr N. The lease was to be a commercial lease. Although the three owners of the land were not all intending to occupy, it was argued that, as two of the beneficial owners were intending to occupy, their occupation was to be treated by virtue of s.41(2) as that of the landlord. The Court of Appeal held that although Mr R and Mr N, as beneficiaries under the statutory trust for sale, were entitled to occupy the premises (although not to the exclusion of Mrs N), their intended occupation was not by virtue of their beneficial interest. The only means by which they intended to confer upon themselves and their co-partners exclusive occupation, to the exclusion of Mrs N, was by the grant of a commercial lease and thus the occupation was qua lessee, not qua beneficiary. **1–103**

Occupation by associated company

Section 42 provides for the situation where the tenancy is held by a member of a group of companies as defined in s.42(1). For the purposes of s.42 two bodies corporate shall be taken to be members of a group if and only if one is a subsidiary of the other or both are subsidiaries of a third body corporate [or the same person has a controlling interest in both]. The expression "subsidiary" has the same meaning as in s.1159 of the Companies Act 2006[248]: s.46 of the 1954 Act. Where a tenancy is held by a member of the group, occupation by another member of the group is to be treated for the purpose of s.23 as equivalent to the occupation of the tenant. Section 42(2)(c) provides that an assignment of the tenancy from one member of the group to another shall not be treated as a change in the person of the tenant. For discussion of the implications of this provision see para.1–124, below. **1–104**

In *Frish Ltd v Barclays Bank Ltd*[249] (digested in para.1–100) it was suggested that "the essential thing by virtue of which the occupation is to be had under section 42 is the qualification as an associated company," and the exact machinery whereby that occupation is achieved is irrelevant. This was a comment made in connection with the corresponding provisions applying to the position where the **1–105**

[247] [1990] 1 E.G.L.R. 107 CA.
[248] See Appendix, para.A1.082.
[249] [1955] 2 Q.B. 541 CA.

reversionary interest is held by a member of a group of companies (s.42(3)), but there is no reason to think that the suggestion is not equally applicable to s.42(2). However, it is questionable how far this can be taken. It is clear, e.g. that an associated company would not qualify under s.42(2) if its only right to occupy derived from the fact that it had been granted a sub-tenancy. The sub-tenant's position is fully protected by virtue of the sub-tenancy and, as with s.41(1), where the essential thing is that the occupation is pursuant to the terms of the trust, it is clear that the occupation by the associated company is not *qua* associated company but qua sub-tenant. As Evershed M.R. said in *Frish Ltd v Barclays Bank Ltd*, the conception under s.41 and s.42 is to be uniform and if that is so the intended occupation of the associated company must be by virtue of its quality or right as an associated company. He went on:

> "what is intended is that the protection for the tenancy is not to be lost by the circumstance that the tenant is company A, but actual occupant is company B, not by virtue of a sub-tenancy (because, as I have said in the case of a trust, if there was a sub-tenancy, then the sub-tenancy would qualify as the tenancy for s.23), but by virtue of the commercial association between companies A and B."

1–106 Section 42(1) was amended by the 2003 Order. As noted above "subsidiary" has the same meaning as in s.1159 of the Companies Act 2006. Such subsidiary companies remain group companies. However, the terms of s.42 of the 1954 Act as amended by the 2003 Order extends the concept of group companies to include companies where the same person has a controlling interest in both of the companies (i.e. the tenant and the company occupying): art.16 of the 2003 Order amending s.42(1).

7. IS THE OCCUPATION FOR THE PURPOSES (OR PARTLY FOR THE PURPOSES) OF A BUSINESS?

Test of "purposes" of occupation

1–107 By virtue of s.23(1), the Act only applies where premises are occupied by the tenant "and are so occupied for the purposes of a business carried on by him or for those and other purposes". It is to be noted that, although the tenant must occupy the premises in question (or part thereof), the business need not be carried on there: see *Bracey v Read*[250] (digested in para.1–28) and *Hunt v Decca Navigator Co*[251] (digested in para.7–243). In *Groveside Properties Ltd v Westminster Medical School*[252] (digested in para.1–110), below, Kerr L.J. emphasised that the question of whether the tenant was occupying the premises interacted with the question of whether that occupation was for business purposes or not, so that the two questions must be looked at "together and in the round". (On occupation see paras 1–42 et seq. generally.)

250 [1962] 3 W.L.R. 1194; [1962] 3 All E.R. 472.
251 (1972) 222 E.G. 625.
252 [1983] 2 E.G.L.R. 68.

Where the tenant is not personally in occupation of the demised premises but uses them for his staff the question arises whether the occupation is for the tenant's business. In *Chapman v Freeman*[253](digested in para.1–109) Lord Denning suggested a strict test, stating that nothing short of necessity would suffice. However, the broader test of whether the occupation is in "furtherance of the tenant's business activities" was the preferred approach in *Groveside Properties Ltd v Westminster Medical School*[254]; *Linden v DHSS*[255] (digested in para.1–45) and *Methodist Secondary Schools Trust Deed Trustees v O'Leary*[256] (digested in para.1–139). Thus, a school caretaker living in the residential property leased by the tenant school was occupying the same on behalf of the school board of management, in that the requirement to be available as near as possible to the school to react to any emergency, including emergencies outside normal hours, was in furtherance of the school's activities: see *Trustees of the Methodist Secondary Schools Trust Deed v O'Leary*.[257] **1–108**

Chapman v Freeman[258] The tenant was the owner of a small residential hotel. The landlord granted him a tenancy of a nearby cottage, which the tenant used to house some of his hotel staff, who were not charged any rent for their occupation. The tenant claimed that his tenancy was protected by the Act. At trial it was conceded that the tenant himself occupied the cottage, but the Court of Appeal held that his occupation was not "for the purposes of a business carried on by" him because it was merely a matter of convenience that the staff should be housed in the cottage. To be protected the tenant would have to go further and show that the occupation was in furtherance of his business activities, e.g. where it is necessary for the staff to be near at hand in order to perform their duties. **1–109**

Groveside Properties Ltd v Westminster Medical School[259] Where a medical school was the tenant of a flat which it used to accommodate some of its students, it was held by the Court of Appeal to have retained sufficient presence and control of the flat to be in occupation of it. Its occupation in order to fulfil its objective of providing accommodation in a small collegiate atmosphere for students of medical science was occupation for the purposes of a business carried on by it. Fox L.J. said: **1–110**

> "It seems to me that the running of a major medical school must be an activity within s.23(2). Was then the flat occupied for the purposes of that activity? On the evidence I can only conclude that it was. The activity is medical education. If, as the evidence establishes, the fostering of a corporate spirit among the students is an important part of their educational process, and the achievement of such a spirit is materially assisted by the provision of accommodation in the flat, I think it follows that the occupation of the flat is for the purposes of the activity carried on by the school. The occupation of the flat was designed to promote the orderly and contented residence of the students."

253 [1978] 1 W.L.R. 1298; [1978] 3 All E.R. 878 CA.
254 [1983] 2 E.G.L.R. 118 CA.
255 [1983] 2 E.G.L.R. 68 CA.
256 [1993] 1 E.G.L.R. 105 CA.
257 [1993] 1 E.G.L.R. 105 CA.
258 [1978] 1 W.L.R. 1298; [1978] 3 All E.R. 878 CA.
259 [1983] 2 E.G.L.R. 68.

Meaning of "business"

1–111 "Business" is defined by s.23(2) to include "a trade, profession or employment" and "any activity carried on by a body of persons, whether corporate or unincorporate". As the Court of Appeal stated in *Abernethie v Kleiman Ltd*[260] (digested in para.1–114), it follows from this definition that "business" has a different meaning in relation to a body of persons than it has in relation to an individual. For this reason, the question of what constitutes "business" carried on by an individual is discussed in paras 1–113 to 1–115 followed by a detailed consideration in paras 1–116 to 1–117 of the wider range of activities carried on by a body of persons also coming within the definition. Although the word "include" suggests that the definition is not exhaustive, the effect of the definition is that an individual must show that he carries on a "trade profession or employment"; a body of persons, whether corporate or incorporate, can, in addition, establish that it carries on business if it carries on an "activity". The range of activities carried on by a body of persons which can come within the definition of "business" is illustrated by the cases and has been held to include a teaching hospital[261] and provision of accommodation, equipment and staff for another corporate body. The effect of s.56(3) is that the activities of a government department are deemed to be a "business" within s.23.

1–112 Although the actual making of a profit is not essential, the term "business" connotes some commercial activity with the ambition of making a gain or a profit: *Rolls v Miller*.[262] Thus an enterprise which is not carried on with a view to profit and not carried on as a trading activity, but rather in a spirit of public benevolence, is not the carrying on of a "business": *Secretary of State for Transport v Jenkins*.[263] In that case the tenant maintained the land as a community free farm, which gave an opportunity to groups of unemployed individuals to work on the restoration of derelict buildings enabling it to be used to house animals, and it was held that the tenant was not carrying on a business. However, an activity which is carried on as a trading activity and with a view to making a profit or surplus is nonetheless a business albeit the profit or surplus is not distributed. Thus a company limited by guarantee which managed sports grounds was held to be carrying on a business within the Act although it was a non-profit-making organisation, in the sense that no dividends were paid and there are no issued shares, and the profit made was reinvested in the business by continually upgrading and refurbishing the sports grounds and their facilities: *Hawkesbrook Leisure Ltd v The Reece-Jones Partnership*.[264]

Tenant an individual

1–113 In relation to an activity carried on by an individual, that activity must constitute a "trade, profession or employment". Those three categories are exhaustive of the

260 [1970] 1 Q.B. 10; [1969] 2 W.L.R. 1364; [1969] 2 All E.R. 790 CA.
261 *Willis v British Commonwealth Universities Association (No.1)* [1965] 1 Q.B. 140 CA.
262 (1884) L.R. 25 Ch. D. 206. See also paras 13–12 to 13–16.
263 (2000) 79 P. & C.R. 118 CA.
264 [2003] EWHC 3333 (Ch); [2004] 2 E.G.L.R. 461.

meaning of "business" in relation to an activity' carried on by an individual: *Lewis v Weldcrest*[265] (digested in para.1–115). The pursuit by a person gratuitously of a spare-time activity in his own home is not a "trade, profession or employment": *Abernethie v Kleiman Ltd*[266] (digested in para.1–114). As Widgery L.J. said in that case, the Act:

> "was intended to pick up a very wide range of tenancies which previously had no sort of protection at all. Shops, factories, professional offices, cinemas, tennis clubs and the like were all without protection before 1954, except for the very limited coverage provided by the Landlord and Tenant Act 1927, and, it being the intention of Parliament to give protection to this wide range of commercial activity, the definition [of business] had to be a wide one. But it certainly does not follow from that that Parliament intended to push the tentacles of this Act into domestic lettings and the activities that a man carries on in his private rooms as part of his hobby or recreation . . . By and large . . . what a man does with his spare time in his home is most unlikely to qualify for the description 'business' unless it has some direct commercial involvement in it, whether it be a hobby or a recreation or the performance of a social duty."

In many cases the question whether the tenant is carrying on a trade, profession or employment is a question of degree. Thus, for instance, whether the taking in of lodgers can be a trade depends to a large extent on the number of lodgers, the size of the premises and the sort of sums and services which are involved.

Abernethie v Kleiman Ltd[267] The tenant ran a greengrocer's business and had **1–114** for some years held a Sunday school, usually in the loft but occasionally in the shop part of the premises. The tenant ceased the greengrocer's business and used the shop part for residential purposes, but carried on the Sunday school. No charge was made for the Sunday school, though subscriptions to a scripture mission were welcome. The Court of Appeal held that the Sunday school was not a "business" within the definition in s.23(2). It was not a "trade or profession", for it was carried on amateurishly and for no money reward. Nor was it an "employment" because it was only for one hour a week and voluntary. It was not necessary to consider whether it was an "activity" because that part of the definition applied only where it was carried on by a "body of persons".

Lewis v Weldcrest[268] The tenant of a four-bedroomed residential house herself **1–115** occupied one bed-sitting room and shared the kitchen, bathroom and one other room with her five lodgers. She cooked some meals for them. The county court judge found that the tenant, who was making little or nothing out of the lodgers, took them in as an expedient in order to enable her to live in her house as her dwelling. The Court of Appeal held that the question was whether the tenant could be said to be carrying on a "trade, profession or employment". The question was one of degree and, bearing in mind the number of lodgers, the size of the premises and the sorts of sums and services which were involved, the tenant was not carrying on a trade, let alone a profession or employment, so she was not carrying on a "business" within the meaning of s.23(2).

---

[265] [1978] 1 W.L.R. 1107; [1978] 3 All E.R. 1226 CA.
[266] [1970] 1 Q.B. 10 CA.
[267] [1970] 1 Q.B. 10 CA.
[268] [1978] 1 W.L.R. 1107; [1978] 3 All E.R. 1226 CA.

Tenant a body of persons

1–116 The expression "body of persons" connotes some involvement or participation in a common activity other than the mere joint ownership of property; accordingly joint tenants are not ipso facto a body of persons: *Secretary of State for Transport v Jenkins*.[269] Although there need not be a precise identity between the persons who are in occupation as tenants and the persons who carry on the activity, nevertheless, the activity must be carried on by the tenants. Thus where joint tenants permitted a community free farm project to be undertaken from their land, in which the tenants themselves participated being a loose association of individuals who were working on the restoration of derelict buildings to be used to house animals, it was held that the activity was not that of the tenants having invited others to assist them in carrying on that activity, but of the loose association or collective, which collective was not acting as their agent.[270]

1–117 Where the tenant is a body of persons (whether corporate or unincorporate) the tenant is carrying on a business if it carries on an "activity". In *Hillil Property & Investment Co Ltd v Naraine Pharmacy Ltd*[271] (digested in para.1–119) the Court of Appeal held that an "activity" connotes some general use by the persons occupying and not some particular, casual operation. The activity must be something which is relative to the conceptions involved in the words "trade, profession or employment". Thus the dumping of rubbish and building materials at an empty shop in fitting out another shop of the tenant was held not to be an "activity". It is, however, clear from the decided cases that the word "activity" is of wide import and ranges from the use of premises as a club (being an obvious example) to the use of premises for a community centre including religious instruction and social events (*Parkes v Westminster Roman Catholic Diocese Trustee*[272] (digested in para.1–77)) and has been held to include a teaching hospital (*Willis v British Commonwealth Universities Association*)[273] and provision of accommodation, equipment and staff for another corporate body (*Hills v University College Hospital Board of Governors*).[274]

Members' clubs carry on an "activity"

1–118 A club is also carrying on a "business" though conducted solely for the benefit of their members. In *Addiscombe Garden Estates Ltd v Crabbe*,[275] (digested in para.1–11) the court rejected the argument that "activity" should be construed as meaning "such activity". Thus, a club is still within the protection of the Act albeit there is no trade with non-members, e.g. as when a golf club charges non-members a fee for playing on its course. Accordingly, where the trustees of a tennis club had a tenancy of the club-house, changing-room and tennis courts, the

---

[269] (2000) 79 P. & C.R. 118 CA.

[270] *Secretary of State for Transport v Jenkins* (2000) 79 P. & C.R. 118 CA.

[271] [1979] 2 E.G.L.R. 65 CA.

[272] [1978] 2 E.G.L.R. 50 CA.

[273] [1965] 1 Q.B. 140 CA. See also *Groveside Properties Ltd v Westminster Medical School* [1983] E.G.L.R. 68 CA (digested in para.1–110).

[274] [1956] 1 Q.B. 90 CA.

[275] [1958] 1 Q.B. 513 CA.

Court of Appeal held that their tenancy was a business tenancy within the Act because the members of the club were a body of persons which was carrying on an activity in the shape of a lawn tennis club: *Addiscombe Garden Estates Ltd v Crabbe*.[276]

Hillil Property & Investment Co Ltd v Naraine Pharmacy Ltd[277] The tenant had a tenancy of two adjoining shops in the same street. It carried on the business of a pharmacy in one of the shops and when the other shop (which had been sub-let) fell vacant the tenant decided to join the two shops structurally together, in order to provide bigger and better premises for the carrying on of its pharmacy. The tenant took a tenancy of another shop in the same street, which was not immediately contiguous to the other two shops, for the purpose of storing materials while the building operations were carried out. At the date when the term of the tenancy of the third shop was due to expire it was being used as a dumping ground for waste materials from the other two shops. The Court of Appeal held that even on the basis that the builders, in dumping the material at the shop, were doing so as the agents of the tenants, nonetheless the dumping was not an "activity". That expression connotes some general use by the persons occupying and not some particular, casual operation. However, the question of whether the storing of waste materials was an "activity" missed the point. The tenants' business was that of a pharmacy (which is, of course, "trade" within the definition of the section) and the question for the court was whether the storing of spoil was done for the purposes of that trade. Quite different considerations would have arisen if the tenant's business had consisted of collecting, storing and disposing of waste. 1–119

Provision of accommodation

It is clear that the provision of accommodation (which might consist of residential or commercial premises) may be a "business" within the meaning of the Act: *Bagettes Ltd v GP Estates Co Ltd*[278] (digested in para.1–71) and *Graysim v P&O Property Holdings Ltd*,[279] (digested in para.1–70). A statement which seems, at first sight, to contradict this, appears in *Horford Investments v Lambert*,[280] where Russell L.J. said: 1–120

> "A letting of a dwelling-house from which the tenant intends to make a profit from subletting is not a letting of the premises for business purposes. No business is there carried on."

However, it must be remembered that in *Horford Investments v Lambert* the court was considering the question of whether a lease of two flats was "let as a separate dwelling" within the terms of s.1(1) of the Rent Act 1968 (now s.1 of the Rent Act 1977) and in accordance with the well-known Court of Appeal authority of

276 [1958] 1 Q.B. 513 CA.
277 [1979] 2 E.G.L.R. 65 CA.
278 [1956] 2 Ch. 290 CA.
279 [1996] A.C. 329 HL.
280 [1976] Ch. 39 CA.

Wolfe v Hogan[281] the court first looks to the user covenant in the lease to ascertain the purpose of the letting. It would therefore appear that all that Russell L.J. is saying is that a covenant in a residential lease permitting the lessee to sub-let cannot be construed as meaning that the letting is thereby one for business purposes. In other words, the existence of a covenant to sub-let cannot of itself justify the finding that the tenant is carrying on a "business"; sub-letting in fact can, however, constitute a business.

The practical importance of this is much diminished by the decision of the House of Lords in *Graysim*, above, and of the Court of Appeal in *Bassari Ltd v Camden LBC*[282] (digested in para.1–74) which lay down the principle that a tenant whose business is sub-letting is not "occupying" the premises which are sub-let.[283] The discussion is still relevant however where the business involves the provision of accommodation through licences or other informal arrangements not amounting to sub-lettings.

Mixed purposes

1–121 It is not necessary that the occupation should be exclusively for business purposes; the definition in s.23(1) makes it clear that it is sufficient if occupation is for business purposes "and other purposes".

8. IS THE BUSINESS CARRIED ON BY THE TENANT?

The business carried on must be that of the tenant

1–122 There is a close connection between the question of who is carrying on the business and the question of who is the occupier. In *Pegler v Craven*,[284] decided under the Leasehold Property (Temporary Provisions) Act 1951, it was held that that Act had no application where the tenant was an individual but the business was that of a limited company of which he was a shareholder.[285] In *Teasdale v Walker*[286] (digested in para.1–83), above, the Act was held not to apply where the business was carried on not by the tenant, but by a so-called "manager", who was in reality carrying on his own business independently of the tenant. In *Ross Auto Wash v Herbert*[287] (digested in para.1–84) on the other hand, it was held that, where the tenant bona fide employed a manager to manage certain premises, the tenant was occupying them for the purpose of a business carried on by him. It is to be noted, however, that the tenant need not be the sole participant in the

[281] [1949] 1 All E.R. 570 CA.

[282] [1999] L. & T.R. 45 CA.

[283] Although Lord Nicholls expressly stated that there may be exceptional circumstances in which a landlord still remained in occupation notwithstanding the existence of a sub-letting, the authors are unaware of any case since *Graysim* where such exceptional circumstances have been held to have existed. See para.1–67 fn.187.

[284] [1952] 1 All E.R. 685 CA.

[285] The occupation and the carrying on of a business by a company in which the tenant has a controlling interest now gives rise to protection of the Act: see para.1–87 et seq.

[286] [1958] 1 W.L.R. 1076; [1958] 3 All E.R. 307 CA.

[287] [1979] 1 E.G.L.R. 95.

business, for the Act clearly contemplates that a business carried on by the tenant in partnership is within the Act: s.41A: *Re Crowhurst Park*.[288] This is readily applied where only one business is being carried on by the tenant and the partners, but what is not clear is what happens if the "tenant" consists of two or more persons each of whom occupies the premises carrying on his own individual businesses not in partnership with one another. It is doubtful whether, in such a case, what is carried on is "a" business.[289]

Business of beneficiary

By virtue of s.41(1), where the tenancy is held on trust, the business of one of the beneficiaries is deemed to be the business of the tenant for the purposes of s.23(1) (see para.1–92 et seq.). Occupation of a beneficiary is, similarly, deemed to be that of the tenant. Examples of situations where the tenancy would be held on trust include: an express trust; the case where there are joint tenants; the case where the tenancy is held as a partnership asset; and possibly the case where the tenancy is held by an individual, but the business is carried on by a company which is responsible for the rent and other outgoings.[290] **1–123**

A curious point arises from the wording of s.41(1)(c), which provides that, where the tenancy is held on trust, a change in the persons of the trustees shall not be treated as a change in the person of the tenants. This subsection has not been the subject of judicial interpretation but, if construed literally, it would appear to suggest that if A and B hold the tenancy as trustees they remain "the tenant" for all purposes during the term, even if subsequently the tenancy is assigned to new trustees, C and D. If that is correct, it appears that (e.g.) a s.25 notice would be properly addressed to A and B rather than to C and D. Clearly this could lead to most anomalous results, for instance, if A and B have both died. However, for the reasons given in the discussion in para.1–126 below, of the closely analogous provisions of s.42(2)(c), it appears that the purpose of this subsection was quite limited and that it was concerned only with transitional provisions which are now of no continuing significance. It is therefore considered unlikely that the literal interpretation mentioned above would receive judicial approval. **1–124**

Business of tenant's company or business of person having controlling interest in the tenant (where a company)

The carrying on of a business (1) by a company in which the tenant has a controlling interest or (2) where the tenant is a company, by a person with a controlling interest in the company, is treated for the purposes of s.23 as equivalent to the carrying on of a business by the tenant: s.23(1A). The provisions of s.23(1A) are discussed in paras 1–87 et seq. **1–125**

---

[288] [1974] 1 W.L.R. 583 at 589 per Goulding J.; [1974] 1 All E.R. 991.

[289] This point was not taken although it appears to have been available in *Harris v Black* (1983) 46 P. & C.R. 366 CA (digested in para.6–30).

[290] On the question as to when a trust will arise by implication, see para.1–92 et seq.

Business of associated company

1–126 Section 42 provides that the conduct of a business, by one member of a group of companies of which the tenant is a member, is deemed to be the conduct of the business of the tenant.[291]

Section 42(2)(c) provides that an assignment of the tenancy from one member of the group to another shall not be treated as a change in the person of the tenant. The effect of this provision is not clear. On a literal reading it would appear to indicate that if a tenancy is granted to Company A, but subsequently assigned to Company B (a member of the same group of companies), Company A is nonetheless to be treated for all purposes under the Act as the tenant. Thus, e.g. a notice under s.25 should be addressed to Company A rather than to Company B. Indeed, the provision is not expressly limited to the purposes of the Act. Thus, it might be argued that in the case of an assignment from Company A to Company B in breach of covenant, the landlord would be unable to forfeit because the assignment should be treated as not having taken place. However, this literal interpretation would not seem to be tenable in the light of the report of the debate in *Hansard*, cols 409–410, July 27, 1954, which shows that s.42(2)(c) was intended to deal with a problem arising under the transitional provisions. Paragraph 4 of Sch.9 conferred the right to a new lease upon a tenant whose tenancy had determined prior to the coming into force of the Act but who was holding over on a periodic basis. One of the requirements of para.4 of Sch.9 was that the tenant had to be the same as, or a successor in business to, the tenant under the fixed-term tenancy. It was considered that this could cause a problem if there was a change in the identity of the tenant under the previous fixed-term tenancy and the tenant under the holding over periodic tenancy. The matter was expressed by the Solicitor General in moving this part of the Bill in the following terms:

> "[section] 26 confers the right on the tenant of business premises to take the initiative in having the tenancy replaced by a new tenancy. The right is confined to the tenant under a tenancy which was granted for a term exceeding one year. Where such a tenancy comes to an end after the Bill has become law, it will be automatically continued under Part I . . .
> Where, however, a tenancy was granted for a term of years and the term expires before the coming into operation of the Bill, the law implies that if the tenant retains possession and the landlord accepts rent a new tenancy from year to year is thereby created. Such a new tenancy would not be within the terms of [section] 26(1), and therefore would not give rise to a right to request a new tenancy under Part I, but for para.4 of the Ninth Schedule. In other words, para.4 secures that the tenant who holds over after a fixed term tenancy comes to an end will have the right conferred by [section] 26, irrespective of whether the fixed term tenancy came to an end before or after the coming into operation of the Bill.
> The notion of the tenant holding over is expressed in para.(c) of para.4 as a requirement that the tenant under the current tenancy must be the same as, or a successor in business to, the tenant under the fixed term tenancy. It is at this point that a group of companies requires special treatment. If, for instance, after the expiry of the fixed term and before the passing of the Bill a new subsidiary was formed for the purpose of holding all the land belonging to the group and the tenancy was then assigned to that new subsidiary, the requirement that the tenant must be the same would not be fulfilled unless the change of tenant were ignored. The same would apply if the fixed term tenancy was vested in the subsidiary and the subsidiary

[291] Compare para.1–86 et seq. on the question of occupation.

> was for some reason dissolved after the expiry of the term. By ignoring the change of tenant in such cases, [s.42(2)(c)] secures the benefit of para.4 of the Ninth Schedule to a group of companies."

Should the rival interpretations ever come before the court, it is considered that this material would be admissible to resolve the question under the rule in *Pepper v Hart*.[292]

Need not be carried on at the premises

It was noted in para.1–107 that the business need not be carried on at the premises. Contrast the provisions of s.30(1)(g) and s.17(1) of the Landlord and Tenant Act 1927 (see paras 7–246 and 13–12, respectively). **1–127**

Relevant date

The question of whether or not the business is being carried on by the tenant may arise at various dates, with different consequences. For a full discussion of the legal effect of the tenancy ceasing to be one to which the Act applies, see para.2–45 et seq. **1–128**

9. Is business use permitted (either expressly or as a result of consent or acquiescence) under the subsisting terms of the tenancy?

User in breach of prohibition

By virtue of s.23(4) the Act does not apply where the business is being carried on "in breach of a prohibition (however expressed) of use for business purposes". However, that expression is given a somewhat limited meaning. It does not include a prohibition of "use for the purposes of a specified business" nor of "use for the purposes of any but a specified business". However, it does include a prohibition of "use for the purposes of some one or more of the classes of business specified in s.23(2)". Such a prohibition may be implied: e.g. in *Trustees of the Methodist Secondary Schools Trust Deed v O'Leary*[293] (digested in para.1–139), a clause requiring the tenant "to use the demised premises for the purpose of a private residence in single occupation only" was held to prohibit business use. The effect of this can be illustrated by the following table. **1–129**

Covenant	Effect
(1) General prohibition of use for business purposes: "Not to use for business purposes".	Act excluded.

292 [1993] A.C. 593 HL.
293 [1993] 1 E.G.L.R. 105 CA.

(2) General prohibition (implied) Act excluded of use for business purposes: "To use the premises for the purposes of a private residence only".	Act excluded.
(3) Requirement to use for specified business: "To use as a launderette".	Act applies even if not used as launderette but used for some other business.
(4) Prohibition of use for particular business: (a) "Not to use as a launderette". (b) "Not to use as barrister's chambers".	(a) Act applies even if used as a launderette. (b) Act applies even if used as barrister's chambers.
(5) Not to use for one of the classes of: "business" in s.23(2): "Not to use for any profession".	Act applies if used for trade or business or an activity by a body or persons but Act excluded if used for a profession.
(6) Prohibition of use for business purpose save for one specified type of use within one of the classes of "business" in s.23(2): "Not to use for any trade, profession or employment or business activity save for the profession of a barrister." Or: "Not to use save for the profession of a barrister".	Act applies if used for the profession of a barrister. Act probably applies if used for any other profession. Act probably excluded if used for any trade employment or business activity (not being a profession).

Prohibition must "subsist"

1–130 It is further to be noted that s.23(4) only applies to a prohibition "which subsists under the terms of a tenancy". Clearly, the subsection would not apply if the landlord and tenant had agreed to vary the terms of the tenancy so as to permit a business use which was previously prohibited. It probably also does not apply if the prohibition is one which is limited to certain circumstances which have not yet arisen or have ceased to exist. Possible examples are a prohibition which is subject to a precondition which has not yet been fulfilled, or a prohibition which is expressed to cease upon the happening of a certain event, such as an assignment of the tenancy, or if the prohibition is expressed to arise only if, e.g. the tenancy is vested in a company as opposed to an individual.

Prohibition must be under terms of current tenancy

Section 23(4) only applies to a prohibition which subsists "under the terms of the tenancy". In *D'Silva v Lister House Developments Ltd*,[294] there was a covenant in a head lease which prohibited use for business purposes. No such covenant was included in the sub-tenancy. It was held that s.23(4) had no application, because it does not apply to a prohibition which is not immediately binding upon the tenant. (This decision remains unaffected on this point by the Court of Appeal decision in *Longman v Viscount Chelsea*,[295] which disapproved *D'Silva* on other points.) The position may be different if the sub-tenant has actual or constructive notice of such a covenant existing in the head lease and is thus bound in equity by that restrictive covenant under the rule in *Tulk v Moxhay*.[296] It would appear that in any event this decision has no application to tenancies to which the Landlord and Tenant (Covenants) Act 1995 applies, by virtue of s.3(5) of that Act.[297] **1–131**

Prohibition must extend to whole of property

Section 23(4) only applies to a prohibition which extends to the whole of the property comprised in the tenancy. Thus, e.g. a covenant which requires ground floor premises to be used as a shop, and the upper floors to be used for residential purposes only, is not a prohibition within the subsection. Such a prohibition may, however, affect the question of what is "the holding" for the purposes of s.23(3): see *Narcissi v Wolfe*[298] (digested in para.8–10) and para.8–06 generally. **1–132**

Effect of consent or acquiescence

Consent

Business user in breach of a relevant prohibition will not affect the application of the Act if it has been consented to by the immediate landlord *or* his predecessor in title. It was stated in *Bell v Alfred Franks & Bartlett Co Ltd*[299] (digested in para.1–138) that "consent" involves more than standing by without objecting; it requires: **1–133**

---

294 [[1970] 2 W.L.R. 563; [1970] 1 All E.R. 858 Ch D.

295 [1989] 2 E.G.L.R. 189 CA.

296 (1848) 18 L.J. 83 Ch D.

297 This section provides that:

"Any landlord or tenant covenant of a tenancy which is restrictive of the user of the land shall, as well as being capable of enforcement against an assignee, be capable of being enforced against any other person who is the owner or occupier of any demised premises to which the covenant relates, even though there is no express provision in the tenancy to that effect."

It has been held that the expression "any demised premises" means the premises demised by the lease in question. It does not refer to *any* premises demised by the landlord and thus a covenant by the landlord not to permit a competitive use in adjoining premises is unenforceable by the tenant of the demised premises against the tenant of the adjoining premises: *Oceanic Village Ltd v United Attractions Ltd* [2000] Ch. 234.

298 [1959] 3 W.L.R. 431; [1959] 3 All E.R. 71 Ch D.

299 [1980] 1 W.L.R. 340; [1980] 1 All E.R. 356 CA.

> "a positive, demonstrative act, something of an affirmative kind. It is not to be implied, because the resort of implication betokens an absence of express affirmation. The only sense in which there can be implied consent is where a consent is demonstrated, not by language but by some positive act other than words which amounts to an affirmation of what is being done and goes beyond mere acquiescence in it."[300]

Acquiescence

1–134 The subsection further provides, however, that use in breach of a relevant prohibition will not prevent the application of the Act if there has been "acquiescence" by the immediate landlord. In *Bell v Alfred Franks*[301] (digested in para.1–138), "acquiescence" was stated to involve a passive failure to do anything about the user with knowledge thereof. Thus acceptance of rent, or serving a s.25 notice and not opposing renewal, would amount to an acquiescence if there was prior knowledge of the facts which gave rise to the breach: *Trustees of the Methodist Secondary Schools Trust Deed v O'Leary*[302] (digested in para.1–139). Compare *Real and Leasehold Estates Investment Society v Medina Shipping*,[303] where Denning M.R. said that "acquiescence involves more than knowledge of the breach. There must be knowledge of and acquiescence in the breach such that one could infer therefrom a consent...". Knowledge of the breach by the porter or a member of the landlord's staff was said to be insufficient, as neither would have authority to acquiesce in such a breach. The erection of a business plate of which the landlord is unaware will not give rise to acquiescence in the prohibited user: *Brown v Myerson*[304] (digested in para.1–140).

User in breach of planning

1–135 It has been held in the county court that a user in breach of covenant, albeit acquiesced in by the landlord, will not give rise to 1954 Act protection if the user is in breach of planning permission: *Daimar Investments v Jones*[305] (digested in para.1–137). This appears to have been distinguished in *Jackson v Stagg*.[306] The soundness of the decision in *Daimar* is to be doubted, since the relevance of the planning permission to the question of acquiescence is not obvious. (But note that the absence of planning permission may, however, give rise to a ground for refusing a new tenancy, see *Turner & Bell v Searles (Stanford-le Hope)*[307] (digested in para.7–48).)

---

300 Per Shaw L.J. in *Bell v Alfred Franks* [1980] 1 W.L.R. 340; [1980] 1 All E.R. 356 CA.

301 [1980] 1 W.L.R. 340 CA.

302 [1993] 1 E.G.L.R. 364 CA.

303 [1969] E.G.D. 601 CA.

304 Unreported July 21, 1998.

305 (1962) 112 L.J. 424.

306 Unreported January 14, 1974, but referred to in an article in 125 New L.J. 1277. (Consent to user giving rise to protection, notwithstanding absence of planning permission for use.)

307 [1977] 1 E.G.L.R. 58 CA.

Predecessors in title

It is to be noted that although the Act will apply where there has been consent by the immediate landlord or a predecessor in title, it will not apply where there has been merely acquiescence by a predecessor in title and not acquiescence by the immediate landlord (the policy behind this distinction is explained in *Bell v Alfred Franks*[308] (digested in para.1–138)). One effect of this is that a tenancy, to which the Act applies because the landlord has acquiesced in an unlawful business user, will cease to be a tenancy to which the Act applies if the landlord sells the reversion and the new landlord does not himself acquiesce in that use. The position of such a tenant is accordingly precarious. It may even be that a landlord who has acquiesced in unlawful business user (but not consented thereto) can remove the tenant from the protection of the Act by transferring the reversion to a connected company or individual. It remains to be seen how the courts would react to such a ruse. **1–136**

Daimar Investments v Jones[309] A tenant of shop premises obtained a separate weekly tenancy of the floors above, and covenanted with the landlords to use them only as a private dwelling house. Subsequently, however, the tenant used those floors to store furniture for his business. The landlord's managing agent noticed the change of use, but continued to accept rent. The landlords later assigned to the plaintiff who took proceedings for possession against the tenants. By s.12 of the Town and Country Planning Act 1947, which was then in force, the conversion of the dwelling into business premises constituted a "development" which required planning permission. The county court judge held that although ordinarily the agent's acquiescence in the business user would be taken as waiving the breach of covenant on the landlord's behalf, no such waiver could be relied upon where the obtaining of permission to the relevant change of use was mandatory. Possession was granted. **1–137**

Bell v Alfred Franks & Bartlett Co Ltd[310] A flat and garage were demised by a lease which provided that the tenants were to "use the said garage for standing a private car only . . . and the flat only as a private dwelling house". The lease was subsequently varied to allow the standing of two private cars. The landlord took an assignment of the reversion in 1975; for some long time before that assignment, a director of the tenant company had used the garage from time to time to take in and store samples collected from the tenant's business. Two cars were put there in order to assist the objects of the tenants by carrying prospective customers to and fro and also for the purpose of conveying samples. The landlord's predecessor in title had been able to observe what was happening there; he saw parcels containing samples left at the garage, he had conversations **1–138**

---

308 Shaw L.J. said at 57:

"It is quite clear that what s.23(4) intended was to ensure that the immediate landlord should not be bound by mere—and I use that word deliberately—'mere' acquiescence on the part of the immediate predecessor in title, because that goes far to giving to the tenant a protection and exposing the immediate landlord to an undue risk to which he ought not to be exposed."

309 (1962) 112 L.J. 424.

310 [1980] 1 W.L.R. 340; [1980] 1 All E.R. 356 CA.

with the tenant's director which had reference to the contents of the parcels and he also saw the two cars used by the tenant. Various points arose as to whether or not the Act applied. The Court of Appeal held that the bringing of samples in cartons and so forth constituted a business use, even though it was intermittent and not continuous, and that "private" in the context of the lease meant use for some personal domestic purpose. Accordingly, the use was in breach of covenant as was the use of the garage to keep the two cars in question, since they were used to a substantial degree for the business of the tenants. While the knowledge of the landlord's predecessor in title gave rise to an inference that there had been "acquiescence", no positive "consent" had been proved. Accordingly, the tenancy was not protected by the Act.

1–139 ***Trustees of the Methodist Secondary Schools Trust Deed v O'Leary***[311] A school via its management board employed a caretaker in the house demised by the landlord. The tenancy of the house provided that the premises would be used "for the purposes of a private residence in single occupation only". The caretaker was required to live in the house so as to be as near as possible to the school to react to an emergency, including emergencies outside normal school hours. This was held to constitute occupation for the purposes of a business in accordance with the test laid down by the majority in *Chapman v Freeman*[312] (digested in para.1–109). Such use was held to be a breach not only of the covenant but also of an implied prohibition, having regard to the nature of the covenant, not to use the premises for business purposes within the meaning of s.23(4) of the Act. Although the caretaker had been in occupation for a period of 18 years prior to the hearing of the trustees' application for renewal, the landlord was unaware that the caretaker was so employed or that the property was being used for the purposes of the caretaker to be on call at all times to deal with emergencies. The landlord thought that the caretaker was one of the school's maintenance staff. It was held that, notwithstanding the fact that the landlord had accepted rent throughout the entire period of the caretaker's occupation, and had served a s.25 notice not opposing renewal, the landlord did not know the facts which gave rise to the breach of covenant and, in those circumstances, there could be no acquiescence.

1–140 ***Brown v Myerson***[313] The tenant carried on the business of a licensed conveyancer. Such a use was prohibited by the terms of her tenancy. The tenant contended that she was a business tenant, albeit the business user was in breach of covenant. She alleged that there was acquiescence claiming that she had put up a small plate on the front door and had a larger announcement that she was a licensed conveyancer on the premises. The landlord gave evidence that he did not go through the front door, that he had made two or three visits to the property and had never seen the announcement that she was a licensed conveyancer, which might have alerted him to the fact that she was carrying on her business there. The judge believed the landlord. Accordingly he found that there was no

311 [1993] 1 E.G.L.R. 105 CA.
312 [1978] 1 W.L.R. 1298 CA.
313 Unreported July 21, 1998.

acquiescence. The Court of Appeal declined to grant leave to appeal holding that there was no arguable ground on which it could be said there was acquiescence by the landlord in the breach of the user covenant.

10. DOES THE TENANCY FALL OUTSIDE THE SPECIFIED EXCEPTIONS SET OUT IN SECTION 43?

Agricultural holdings excepted

The Act does not apply to agricultural holdings: s.43(1)(a). "Agricultural holding" is defined by s.69(1) of the Act to have the same meaning as in the Agricultural Holdings Act 1986. The Act does not apply to tenancies which would be agricultural holdings had it not been that the relevant Minister had given his approval to their exclusion: s.2(1) of the Agricultural Holdings Act 1986. Nor does it apply to tenancies which would have been tenancies of an agricultural holding but for the exclusions contained in s.2(3) of the 1986 Act. **1–141**

For the purposes of the 1986 Act an "agricultural holding" is the aggregate of land (whether agricultural land or not) comprised in a tenancy which is a contract for an agricultural tenancy, not being a contract under which the land is let to the tenant during his continuance in the office, appointment or employment under the landlord (s.1(1) of the 1986 Act). The words "whether agricultural land or not" contemplate mixed user. A contract of tenancy relating to land is a contract for an agricultural tenancy if, having regard to all relevant circumstances, the whole of the land comprised in the contract, subject to such exceptions only as do not substantially affect the character of the tenancy, is let for use as agricultural land (s.1(2) of the 1986 Act). Where there is mixed use, whether the land constitutes an agricultural holding depends upon whether, in substance, the land comprised in the tenancy taken as a whole, is agricultural land. Whether or not the premises are let for and used as an agricultural holding may be derived from: (1) the express terms of the tenancy; (2) the actual contemplated use of the land at the date of the contract and subsequently; and (3) any other relevant circumstances (s.1(2) of the 1986 Act). Thus the nature of the tenancy and its entitlement to protection under the 1986 Act may change. An agricultural holding may, of course, be used for the purposes of a business, e.g. use of land as a garden centre may be an agricultural holding or may be merely a retail shop. The protection of the 1986 Act may be lost through abandonment of agricultural use,[314] and this is the case irrespective of whether the landlord has consented to it or not. However, the court is unlikely to treat the tenancy as having ceased to be within the protection of the Agricultural Holdings Act: *Short v Greeves*[315] (digested in para.1–143). **1–142**

Short v Greeves[316] The tenant occupied a garden centre consisting of some 6.2 acres pursuant to a tenancy which, at the time of the grant, was a tenancy of an **1–143**

---

[314] *Wetherall v Smith* [1980] 1 W.L.R. 1290; [1980] 2 All E.R. 530 CA.

[315] [1988] 1 E.G.L.R. 1 CA.

[316] [1988] 1 E.G.L.R. 1 CA.

agricultural holding. He grew roses, wall flowers, and primulas and some conifers. There was a greenhouse on the land the front part of which was used for retail sales. The plants were grown in the open but near the greenhouse plants were in containers for sale. Subsequently the tenant commenced selling garden sundries, which were brought onto the land for sale from elsewhere, such as garden seeds, gnomes, bags of peat, paving, earthenware pots, timber garden sheds, etc. At the date of the hearing approximately 1.2 acres of the land was used as a thriving shop selling predominantly goods which had not been grown on the land. The landlord failed in his argument that a substantial part of the land was used for non-agricultural purposes. Although the sale of imported plants and other goods had increased, the business was still based on the sale of grown produce and a substantial part of the land was used for the purposes of horticulture.

1–144 The effect of the 1986 Act is to convert tenancies to which the Act applies to yearly periodic tenancies either at the expiration of the term (where the tenancy is in excess of two years: s.3 of the 1986 Act) or immediately (where the tenancy is less than a tenancy from year to year: s.2(1) of the 1986 Act). A tenancy exceeding one year but not exceeding two years in duration is an "agricultural holding" within the meaning of the Agricultural Holdings Act 1986 but falls outside the security of tenure provisions applicable to tenancies of agricultural holdings. However, it will not be protected by the 1954 Act: *EWP v Moore*.[317]

1–145 The Agricultural Tenancies Act 1995, which came into force on September 1, 1995, makes fundamental changes to the law relating to lettings of agricultural land. In general the 1986 Act does not apply to a new letting to a new tenant after September 1, 1995. The 1995 Act creates a new concept of "farm business tenancy". By s.43(1)(aa) of the 1954 Act it is provided that the Act does not apply to a farm business tenancy. By s.69(1) of the Act it is provided that a "farm business tenancy" has the same meaning as in the Agricultural Tenancies Act 1995. "Farm business tenancy" is defined in s.1 of the 1995 Act.

Mining leases excepted

1–146 The Act does not apply to a tenancy created by a mining lease: s.43(1)(b). By virtue of s.46 of the 1954 Act "mining lease" has the same meaning as in s.25(1) of the Landlord and Tenant Act 1927.The scope of this definition is discussed in paras 13–07 et seq. The meaning of "mining lease" has been considered by the Court of Appeal in *O'Callaghan v Elliott*[318] It was held that it did not matter that at the date of grant the premises were not being mined; it was sufficient that the grant was for those purposes. Mining did not therefore have to take place upon the premises. In that case the reason for the exclusion was expressed to be that such a lease diminishes the value of the subject matter of the demise by the extraction of minerals from the land and the longer the lease continues the more it diminishes the value.

[317] [1992] 2 W.L.R. 184; [1992] 1 All E.R. 880 CA.
[318] [1966] 1 Q.B. 601 CA.

Tenancies in consequence of employment excepted

The Act does not apply to tenancies granted in consequence of the tenant's office, appointment or employment from the grantor, being a tenancy which is terminable by reference to the ending of that office, appointment or employment: s.43(2). There is no authority on the meaning of "office", "appointment" or "employment". It is at least arguable that a tenancy granted as part of any arrangement giving the tenant the exclusive right to distribute the landlord's products in a particular locality would be such an "appointment". Where such a tenancy was granted after the commencement of the Act, the exception applies only when the tenancy was granted by an instrument in writing which expresses that purpose. **1–147**

Tenancies for six months or less excepted

Subject to exceptions, the Act does not apply to tenancies granted for a term certain not exceeding six months: s.43(3).[319] "Term certain" is not defined but it seems clear from the context that a periodic tenancy is not a "term certain". A term expressed to be for 12 months and thereafter from year to year has been held not to be a "term of years certain" within the meaning of s.38(4), which allowed the exclusion with the consent of the court of the security of tenure provisions of the Act in relation to "a term of years certain": *Nicholls v Kinsey*[320] (see para.2–05). It is probable that a tenancy for six months subject to prior determination by the landlord or the tenant would be a "term certain" for these purposes. There was a conflict of judicial dicta whether a term of years subject to a break clause is "a term of years certain" for the purposes of s.38(4) but for the reasons given in para.2–09 it is now clear that such a tenancy does come within the expression: see *Metropolitan Police District Receiver v Palacegate Properties Ltd*.[321] **1–148**

There are two exceptions from this exception

(1) First, where there is a provision in the tenancy "for renewing the term" or extending it "beyond six months from its beginning". The reference to the "beginning" of the term is presumably to the date of grant of the tenancy in question and not to the date from which the term is expressed to commence; otherwise, whether the tenancy came within the Act or not would depend upon a mere matter of drafting. Thus, it is thought that a tenancy granted on October 30, 2007 and expressed to be for a term of four-and-a-half months from September 29, 2007 with provision for an **1–149**

[319] As to whether time-sharing arrangements are within the Act, see *Landlord and Tenant Review* (1999) 3 pp.48–50.

[320] [1994] E.G.L.R. 131 CA. The provisions of s.38(4) have been repealed by the 2003 Order. The exclusion of the security provisions is now by agreement rather than by order of the court: s.38A. However, an agreement for s.38A may be made only in respect of "a term of years certain": s.38A(1). See para.2–05 et seq.

[321] [2001] Ch. 131; [2000] 3 W.L.R. 519; [2000] 3 All E.R. 663 CA.

extension for a further month, would not fall within the Act, because although it could be extended for more than six months from September 29, 2007 there would, even with the extension, be a period of less than six months between October 30, 2007 and the latest date on which the tenancy would determine. An interesting anomaly would appear to arise if the renewal is for a period of less than six months, albeit the renewal will have the effect of extending the original tenancy beyond six months from its beginning, e.g. a tenancy for a fixed term of five months with a right to renew for a period of four months. The Act would apply to the original tenancy, because it is a tenancy which "contains a provision for a renewal of term or for extending it beyond six months from its beginning". In these circumstances it is advisable for the tenant to seek renewal under the 1954 Act rather than rely on the contractual right to renewal, for the renewed tenancy, being less than six months and with no right of renewal or extension, may be caught by the exclusion.

(2) Secondly, where the tenant, or a predecessor in his business, has been in occupation for a period which exceeds 12 months. There appears to be no requirement that a predecessor in the business was a tenant during the time of his occupation. It has been held that "the tenant" in s.43(3)(b) refers however only to the person who was the tenant for the purposes of the Act, namely a tenant under a fixed-term tenancy or a periodic tenancy, and does not include a licensee, a trespasser or a tenant at will. Thus occupation by the tenant, otherwise than as a tenant under a tenancy to which the Act applies, would not be occupation which is relevant for these purposes: *Cricket Ltd v Shaftesbury Plc*[322] (digested in para.1–150). Presumably the question whether this exception applies is to be answered at the date of the relevant grant. This would, apparently, allow the grant of three successive protected terms each being less than six months in duration. At the date of grant of the third term the tenant would have been in occupation for slightly less than 12 months.

1–150 ***Cricket Ltd v Shaftesbury Plc***[323] The tenant was granted two successive tenancies. The first was from November 26, 1997 to July 30, 1998. The second was from May 1, 1998 to September 30, 1998. Accordingly the tenant had by this stage been the tenant under two tenancies each of which did not exceed six months. Thereafter the tenant remained in occupation as a tenant at will. The landlord claimed to have determined the tenancy at will and sought possession. The tenant contended that as he had been in occupation for a period which exceeded 12 months by the time the landlord claimed possession, the landlord could not rely upon s.43(3)(b) for that ceased to apply once the tenant had been in occupation for more than 12 months. This argument was rejected by the court. It was held that, in order for tenant's contention to succeed, it had to be shown that "the tenant" had been in occupation for the requisite period. "The tenant" meant the person who was the tenant for the purposes of the Act, namely, a tenant under a fixed-term tenancy or a periodic tenancy, but not a licensee, trespasser or a

322 [1999] 3 All E.R. 283; [1999] 2 E.G.L.R. 57 Ch D.

323 [1999] 3 All E.R. 283; [1999] 2 E.G.L.R. 57 Ch D.

tenant at will. The tenant had not on any day after September 30, 1998 been in occupation as "the tenant" but merely as a tenant at will. Furthermore, where the tenant holds over after the expiry of a tenancy for a term certain exceeding six months and the holding over has the effect of the tenant's occupation, when combined with the period of a fixed-term tenancy, exceeding 12 months, the fulfilment of the 12 months' occupation does not retrospectively revive the expired term so as to bring it within the protection of the 1954 Act.

Licensed premises now within the Act

Prior to the Landlord and Tenant (Licensed Premises) Act 1990, which came into force on January 1, 1991, the 1954 Act did not apply to "a tenancy of premises licensed for the sale of intoxicating liquor for consumption on the premises", subject to numerous exceptions: s.43(1)(d). Since the 1990 Act, and subject to transitional provisions the effect of which is for practical purposes largely spent, it is no longer material to the application of the Act that the premises have an on-licence. **1–151**

11. WHERE THERE HAS BEEN AN AGREEMENT FOR A FUTURE TENANCY WITHIN SECTION 28

It is provided by s.28 that the Act shall not apply to a tenancy once an agreement for a future tenancy complying with the terms of that section has been entered into. The terms of s.28 are considered in detail in para.15-14 et seq. **1–152**

12. WHERE A CERTIFICATE HAS BEEN GIVEN ON GROUNDS OF PUBLIC INTEREST

Sections 57 and 58 contain detailed provisions modifying the application of the Act on grounds of national security or other public interest where the interest of the landlord belongs to or is held for the purposes of a government department, local authority statutory undertaker or development corporation.[324] Other special provisions extend to premises where the landlord is the Minister of Technology or the Urban Regeneration Agency (s.60) the Welsh Development Agency (s.60A) and the Development Board for Rural Wales (s.60B). **1–153**

[324] Neither of the authors have encountered in their many years of practice reliance upon these sections.

13. WHERE THE COURT HAS ORDERED A NEW TENANCY BUT THE ORDER HAS BEEN REVOKED ON THE TENANT'S APPLICATION UNDER SECTION 36(2)

1–154 For the procedure whereby the tenant who has obtained an order for the grant of a new tenancy may apply for that order to be revoked, see paras 10–10, et seq. and 14–119, et seq. If an order for revocation has been made, the current tenancy will not be one to which the Act applies, but will continue by virtue of s.36(2) for such period as the court may specify.

14. MISCELLANEOUS

1–155 There are various miscellaneous exclusions from protection consisting of:

(1) a tenancy granted to a dockyard contractor in respect of any land in a designated dockyard[325];
(2) a tenancy granted to a contractor in respect of any land and premises designated under the Atomic Weapons Establishment Act 1991[326];
(3) a concession lease granted by the Secretary of State under the Channel Tunnel Act 1987[327];
(4) new leases of flats granted pursuant to s.56 of the Leasehold Reform, Housing and Urban Development Act 1993[328];
(5) tenancies to which the Railways Act 1993,[329] s.31 applies;
(6) a lease granted by the secretary of state of the Greenwich Hospital[330];
(7) a lease of land granted by the secretary of state for the purposes of providing or providing and running a prison[331];
(8) to a tenancy granted by the secretary of state in any case where the property comprised in the tenancy is or includes premises which, in accordance with any agreement relating to the tenancy (whether contained in the instrument creating the tenancy or not) are to be occupied for the purposes of a vehicle testing business.[332]

---

325 s.3(2) of the Dockyard Services Act 1986.
326 s.3(1) and Sch. para.3 to the 1991 Act.
327 See s.16(2) of the Channel Tunnel Act 1987.
328 By virtue of s.59(2) of the 1993 Act.
329 s.31 of the 1993 Act.
330 Armed Forces Act 1996 s.30(7). The Greenwich Hospital consists of (a) the site known as the Royal Naval College, including the premises known as the Trident Hall and the Trafalgar Quarters; (b) the premises known as the Dreadnought Seamen's Hospital and (c) the premises known as the Devonport Nurses' Home: Armed Forces Act 1996 s.30(1).
331 Criminal Justice Act 1991 s.84(3).
332 Transport Act 1982 s.14(1).

Chapter 2

THE CONTINUATION OF TENANCIES

1. Tenancies which are continued

Tenancies within the Act

2–01 Subject to the exception noted in the next paragraph, the effect of s.24(1) is that a tenancy, to which the Act applies, continues unless and until it is terminated in accordance with the provisions of the Act. Section 24 expressly preserves certain common law modes of termination which are explained in para.3–01 et seq. The Act also sets out various statutory modes of determination which are dealt with in para.3–38 et seq.

Exclusion of continuation provisions

Pre-June 2004

2–02 Prior to January 1, 1970, it was not possible for the parties to a proposed tenancy to exclude by agreement the continuation provisions of the Act, since such an agreement would have been avoided by s.38(1). However, s.5 of the Law of Property Act 1969 amended s.38 adding a new subs.(4), so as to permit the prospective landlord and tenant to obtain the court's authorisation to the exclusion of the security of tenure which the tenancy to be granted would otherwise attract. The jurisdiction of the court to grant an exclusion order has been repealed with effect from June 1, 2004 subject to transitional provisions. The former provisions are considered in detail in paras 2.1.2.1 et seq. of the 2nd edition of this work to which the reader is referred.

Post June 1, 2004

2–03 By the amendments made by the 2003 Order (arts 21 and 22) the jurisdiction for granting an exclusion order has been taken away from the court.[1] The exclusion of security of tenure is now a matter of agreement between the parties, subject to compliance with the relevant procedural requirements. Article 21 of the 2003

[1] s.38(4) has been repealed and the new regime is now contained in s.38A(1) and (3). For a detailed consideration of possible problems with the new regime concerning exclusion agreements, see the series of articles in the *Estates Gazette* by Fenn, Colby and Highmore, [2004] 22 E.G. 132; [2004] 23 E.G. 116; [2004] 25 E.G. 166.

Order repeals s.38(4), save in respect of transitional cases.[2] Thus under the new regime there is no question of the court sanctioning an exclusion agreement; it is simply a matter of the parties agreeing that the provisions of ss.24 to 28 are to be excluded, and complying with the relevant procedural requirements described below.

Section 38A(1)

2–04 It is provided by s.38A(1) that:

> "The persons who will be the landlord and the tenant in relation to a tenancy to be granted for a term of years certain which will be a tenancy to which this Part of this Act applies may agree that the provisions of sections 24 to 28 of this Act shall be excluded in relation to that tenancy."

There are procedural requirements to be followed: s.38A(3). It is to be noted that save for the fact that the exclusion is now by agreement (subject to a notice procedure), the tenancies which may be the subject of an exclusion agreement are no different to the tenancies which could be the subject of the court's authorisation under s.38(4). Thus:

(1) the tenancy must be one which is to be "a term of years certain";
(2) the exclusion agreement must be one made between "the persons who will be the landlord and tenant" in relation to such a tenancy.

"Term of years certain"

2–05 The tenancy which may be the subject of an exclusion agreement must be one which is "to be granted for a term of years certain".[3] In *Re Land and Premises at Liss, Hants*,[4] it was held that this expression includes not merely a term of more than one year but also a fixed term of less than one year. A term expressed to be for 12 months and thereafter from year to year was not a "term of years certain" within the meaning of s.38(4) and thus an order of the court purporting to exclude the provisions of ss.24 to 28 of the Act in respect of such a tenancy was void and of no effect: *Nicholls v Kinsey*.[5] It will of course be a question of construction in any particular case whether or not the grant was of "a term of years certain". In *Metropolitan Police District Receiver v Palacegate Properties Ltd*,[6] where that question of construction was considered, it was sought to be argued that the *habendum* created a fixed term followed by a tenancy from year to year. The *habendum* provided that the tenant was:

---

[2] By art.21(2) to the 2003 Order it is provided that if a person has, before the coming into force of the 2003 Order, entered into an agreement to take a tenancy, any provision in that agreement which requires an order under s.38(4) of the Act to be obtained in respect of the tenancy continues to be effective notwithstanding the repeal of s.38(4) and the court retains jurisdiction to make such an order.
[3] The expression "term of years certain" is also to be found in ss.24(3), 26(1), 27(1), 27(2) and 33 and a similar expression "term certain" is used in s.43(3)
[4] [1971] 3 W.L.R. 77; [1971] 3 All E.R. 380.
[5] [1994] 1 E.G.L.R. 131 CA.
[6] [2001] Ch. 131; [2000] 1 E.G.L.R. 63 CA.

> "To hold the same unto the tenant for the term of 5 years commencing on 23rd day of April One thousand and ninety three ("the Term") and thereafter determinable by 6 months prior written notice on the part of the landlord taking effect at any time after 1st June 1995 as hereinafter provided."

There was in addition a further clause in the lease providing for either party to determine the term by giving not less than six months notice in writing expiring at any time after December 25, 1994. It was argued that the *habendum* was to be construed as applying after the expiry of the term of five years, with the tenancy continuing as a yearly tenancy unless and until terminated by notice to quit. The word "thereafter", it was argued, meant after the expiry of "the term of five years". This was rejected by the court. The *habendum* contemplated written notice being given after June 1, 1995 which was well within the five-year term. The word "thereafter" referred not to a time after the term of five years but a date after April 23, 1993. The presence of a separate right to terminate conferred on both parties did not defeat that construction.

If the tenant's lease defines the "term" granted so as to include an indefinite period after the expiry of the contractual term, the term will not be a "term of years certain" and thus any contracting out of such a tenancy will be of no effect: *Newham LBC v Thomas van Staden*[7] (digested in para.2–08). There the term was defined to include "any period of holding over or extension of it whether by statute or at common law or by agreement" and the Court of Appeal held that this term was not a "term of years certain." **2–06**

In order to consider the impact of *Newham LBC v Thomas van Staden* one must keep very much in mind a distinction between the definition of "term" identifying the contractual term for the purposes of grant and the definition of "the term" for the purposes of obligation. The issue is one of construction: any provision which extends the term to include a period of holding over for the purposes of grant will be problematic. Such words will not, however, be problematic if all they do is extend the term *for the purposes of obligation*. Thus if, as a matter of construction, one can construe the words of the grant contained within the relevant lease so as to exclude from the process of calculating the period of the grant any period of holding over or extension, the problem presented by *Newham LBC v Thomas van Staden* will be avoided. **2–07**

Newham LBC v Thomas van Staden[8] Newham granted a tenancy to van Staden for a 21-month term. The tenancy was granted prior to the 2003 Order and a Court Order excluding protection was obtained. The lease provided for the grant to be "from and including 1 January 2003 to 28 September 2004 (hereinafter called 'the term' which expression shall including any period of holding over or extension of it whether by statute or at common law or by agreement)". Van Staden remained in occupation after the expiry of the contractual term. Newham served a notice on van Staden pursuant to the terms of the lease. They contended that any tenancy arising after the contractual expiry was also contracted out. The Court of Appeal held that the term was not a term of **2–08**

---

[7] [2008] EWCA Civ 1414; [2009] 1 E.G.L.R. 21.

[8] [2008] EWCA Civ 1414; [2009] 1 E.G.L.R. 21.

years certain within the then provisions of the 1954 Act (equivalent to s.38A(1)) and thus had not been contracted out of the protection of the 1954 Act. The Court of Appeal held:

(i) the words "which expression shall include" were not mere surplusage as contended for by the landlord but had to be given effect;
(ii) the words had the effect of providing for a term to include an indefinite period of holding over; and
(iii) the effect was that there was no term of years certain. Although arguably such a grant could be void for uncertainty, the Court did not consider that argument as it had not been put before them.

2–09 Until the decision in *Metropolitan Police District Receiver v Palacegate Properties Ltd*,[9] there was some uncertainty about whether a lease subject to a break clause was a term certain. In *Scholl Manufacturing Co v Clifton (Slim-Line)*[10] (digested in para.3–188), Diplock L.J. expressed the opinion that a term of years subject to a landlord's option to break was nonetheless a term of years certain. Harman L.J. expressed the contrary view. The third member of the court did not express any opinion on this point. Certain passages in the judgment of Russell L.J. in *Lewis v MTC Cars Ltd*[11] (digested in para.10–49) lend some support to Harman L.J.'s view, which can also be justified on the grounds of the apparent policy behind the then s.38(4).[12] This policy may have been that, provided landlord and tenant entered into the transaction with their eyes open, there was no objection to a tenant who had the certainty of the agreed contractual term also knowing that at its end he should not be entitled to apply for a new tenancy. It may, on the other hand, have been thought undesirable that a tenant with so precarious an estate as a weekly or monthly tenancy could be perpetually in doubt as to when that tenancy would come to an end and his business cease. If that is the policy, it may be said that a term of years subject to a break clause operable by the landlord is more closely analogous to a periodic tenancy than it is to a term of years without break. Strong support for the view of Diplock L.J. is to be derived from the definition of "notice to quit" in s.69(1) which indicates that the expression "term of years certain" was intended to include a fixed term containing a break clause. Moreover, the same expression "term of years certain" occurs in ss.24(3), 26(1), 27(1), 27(2) and 33 and a similar expression "term certain" is used in s.43(3). If those words do not include any fixed term which has a landlord's break clause, the implications would be far-reaching. Furthermore, a construction based on Harman L.J.'s view would give rise to great practical difficulties. It is quite usual for a tenancy to contain a break clause operable by a landlord and it would be inconvenient if the continuation provisions of the Act could not be excluded from such a tenancy. The authors in previous editions of the work had consistently stated their view that the opinion expressed by Diplock L.J. was to be preferred and the Court of Appeal so held in *Metropolitan Police*

[9] [2001] Ch. 131; [2000] 1 E.G.L.R. 63 CA.
[10] [1967] Ch. 41 CA.
[11] [1975] 1 W.L.R. 457; [1975] 1 All E.R. 874 CA.
[12] *Scholl Manufacturing Co v Clifton (Slim-Line)*was concerned with the provisions of s.38(4) (now repealed) although, as noted previously, the relevant wording in s.38A is identical to that in s.38(4).

District Receiver v Palacegate Properties Ltd.[13] In that case the Court of Appeal held that a term of five years subject to termination by prior notice of six months was, nevertheless, a "term of years certain" within the then provisions of s.38(4).[14] The Court of Appeal expressed the view that insofar as Harman L.J. in *Scholl Manufacturing Co v Clifton (Slim-Line)* was using the expression "term certain" as a term of art, the opinion of Diplock L.J. was to be preferred, and accordingly the presence of a break clause did not prevent the term being a term of years certain for the purposes of s.38(4) of the Act. This decision therefore concludes the argument in favour of the view that a tenancy for a term of years subject either to a landlord's or a tenant's right to break is a "term of years certain" within the meaning of s.38(4). It is considered that this decision is equally authoritative as to the meaning of the very same phrase in s.38A(1).

A claim to a quarterly tenancy pursuant to the doctrine of proprietary estoppel is not a claim to a term certain: *Manton Securities Ltd v Nazam.*[15] **2–10**

Can security of tenure be excluded if the proposed tenancy is not one to which the Act would otherwise apply at the date of its grant?

In every case where the parties seek to enter into an agreement excluding the security of tenure provisions of the Act they must anticipate that, at least potentially, the tenancy into which they are about to enter will attract the security of tenure of the 1954 Act. At the date of the making of the order no tenancy, of course, exists. Sometimes, however, the parties will seek to enter into an exclusion agreement excluding security of tenure from the tenancy even though, for some reason existing at the date of the grant, it would not or might not be one to which the Act applied. However s.38A(1) enables the parties to exclude the security of tenure provisions "in relation to a tenancy to be granted for a term of years certain which will be a tenancy to which this part of this Act applies". This wording would seem to cause difficulties if the proposed tenancy is not of that description at the date of the agreement. In *Son of Pub Master v Measures*,[16] it was held that an exclusion order made pursuant to s.38(4) in relation to a tenancy which at the date of execution was not a tenancy to which the Act applied, but which subsequently did come within the Act, was nevertheless a valid exclusion order. In that case the tenant operated the premises as a pub and, at the date of execution of the lease, such a tenancy fell outside the security of tenure provisions of the 1954 Act by reason of s.43(1)(d) of the Act.[17] However, the premises subsequently fell within the protection of the Act having regard to the exceptions to that subsection. The landlord was successful in its argument that the tenancy was, nevertheless, excluded from protection of the 1954 Act by reason of the order of the court. What appears to have persuaded the judge as to the validity of the order was the possibility in the circumstances of the case in question of the tenant undertaking works so as to fall within the exceptions to s.43(1)(d). **2–11**

---

13 [2001] Ch. 131; [2000] 1 E.G.L.R. 63 CA.
14 Repealed by the 2003 Order but the relevant wording is now to be found in s.38A(1).
15 [2008] EWCA Civ 805; [2008] P. & C.R. D46.
16 An unreported county court decision by Judge Hague QC, dated May 11, 1994.
17 Repealed by Landlord and Tenant (Licensed Premises) Act 1990 ss.1 and 2.

Exclusion of security where parties are already landlord and tenant

2–12 A question which is sometimes raised is whether the landlord and tenant can enter into an exclusion agreement under s.38A(1) where there already exists between the parties a relationship of landlord and tenant. The fear that the parties may be unable to do so in such a case is based upon the words in s.38A(1) that the exclusion is in respect of a tenancy to be granted between the persons "who will be the landlord and the tenant" and because the exclusion is in relation to "a tenancy to be granted". However, it is considered that this argument is ill founded. The fact that the parties are already landlord and tenant in relation to an existing tenancy is irrelevant, for it is still accurate to say that they will be the landlord and tenant in relation to the tenancy in respect of which the exclusion agreement is made. This view is, at least indirectly, supported by *Cardiothoracic Institute v Shrewdcrest*[18] (digested in para.1–21), where three consecutive applications in respect of short-term tenancies were granted. No point was taken that the exclusion orders under s.38(4) were of no effect by reason of the fact that the parties were already in a relationship of landlord and tenant.

Procedural requirements for agreement

2–13 Any agreement excluding ss.24 to 28 will be void unless:

(1) the landlord has served on the tenant a notice in the form,[19] or substantially in the form,[20] set out in Sch.1 to the 2003 Order (s.38A(3)(a)); and
(2) the requirements specified in Sch.2 to the 2003 Order are met (s.38A(3)(b)).[21]

Time for service

2–14 The starting position under the 2003 Order is that the Sch.1 notice should be served 14 days prior to entry by the tenant into the tenancy or (if earlier) the date on which the tenant becomes contractually bound[22] to do so. The provisions of Sch.2 to the 2003 Order draw a distinction between the requirements to be followed where the Sch.1 notice is served 14 days before that date (set out in paras 2–16 and 2–17) and where the notice is served less than 14 days prior to that date (set out in paras 2–18 and 2–19). As there are different procedural requirements depending on when the Sch.1 notice is received it would be foolhardy to serve notice by post. Receipt of a declaration from the tenant is not of course conclusive evidence that he did in fact receive the notice 14 days prior to the relevant date.

[18] [1986] 1 W.L.R. 368; [1996] 3 All E.R. 633.

[19] As to the form, see Appendix, para.A2.050.

[20] s.38A(3)(a) expressly provides that the form may be substantially in the form set out in Sch.1.

[21] As to which, see para.2–16.

[22] As to the meaning of this expression, see para.2–21 et seq.

Form of Schedule 1 notice

The notice is required to be in the form or substantially in the form set out in Sch.1 to the 2003 Order: s.38A(3)(b). Schedule 1 requires no information as to the terms of the tenancy into which the tenant is about to enter. Nothing is required to be said about the demised premises, the rent or the terms of the tenancy.[23] The notice contains three elements: **2–15**

(1) the name and address of the tenant to whom the notice is to be given;
(2) the name and address of the landlord who is serving the notice;
(3) the information (or "health warning") to the tenant informing him as to the fact that he is about to enter into a tenancy which has no security of tenure, the time limits within which the notice he has received was required to be served upon him, and the possible declarations that he will be required to enter into.

Problems ought not to arise so long as the prescribed information is replicated in the notice. Legal stationers have produced appropriate forms of notice and these should be used as a matter of practice.

Requirements where at least 14 days' notice is given

The requirements of Sch.2 to the 2003 Order are as follows: **2–16**

(1) the Sch.1 notice (or one substantially to like effect) that is required to be served by the landlord pursuant to s.38A(3)(a) must be served not less than 14 days[24] before the tenant enters into the tenancy or (if earlier) becomes contractually bound[25] to do so[26];
(2) the tenant or a duly authorised agent of the tenant must, before he enters into the tenancy, or (if earlier) becomes contractually bound to do so, make a declaration in the form[27] or substantially in the form, set out in para.7 to Sch.2.[28] If a statutory declaration is made when an ordinary declaration will do this matters not; a statutory declaration is substantially in the same form as that of an ordinary declaration: *Chiltern Railway Co Ltd v Patel*[29];

---

[23] See the notice in Appendix, para.A2.050.

[24] This would not seem to need to be a clear period of 14 days. Thus a notice served on the 1st of the month with respect to a tenancy to be entered into on the 14th of the month is nevertheless a notice of 14 days: see *Hogg Bullimore v Cooperative Insurance Society* (1985) 50 P. & C.R. 105 where a s.25 notice given on April 2, 1984 specifying October 2, 1984 was nevertheless held to be one giving not less than six months' notice of termination for the purposes of the Act. It will be important for the landlord to ensure that the tenant received the notice not later than 14 days prior to entry into the tenancy (or agreement as the case may be) for the 14-day period determines the nature of the declaration to be provided by the tenant. The wrong form of declaration will render the exclusion agreement void.

[25] As to the meaning of "contractually bound" see para.2–21 et seq.

[26] para.2 to Sch.2 to the 2003 Order.

[27] As to the form of declaration, see Appendix, para.A2.052.

[28] para.3 to Sch.2 to the 2003 Order. As to the Form of Declaration, see para.2–17.

[29] [2008] EWCA Civ 178; [2008] 2 E.G.L.R. 33 CA. As Lord Neuberger said:

(3) a reference to the landlord's notice and the tenant's declaration must be contained in or endorsed on the instrument creating the tenancy[30];
(4) the agreement, or a reference to the agreement, under s.38A(1) must be contained in or endorsed upon the instrument creating the tenancy.[31]

The form of declaration required by Schedule 2 where at least 14 days notice is given

2–17 The declaration is set out in para.7 to Sch.2 to the 2003 Order. It provides for the tenant to declare a number of things, namely:

(1) that he has been served with the requisite notice in the form or substantially in the form contained in Sch.1 not less than 14 days before the relevant date;
(2) that he has read the notice served upon him by the landlord and accepts the consequences of entering into the agreement to exclude ss.24–28;
(3) the name of the tenant and the address of the property which is to form the subject matter of the letting and that he proposes to enter into a tenancy of those premises;
(4) the duration of the term and its commencement date;
(5) that he proposes to enter into an agreement with the named landlord for the provisions of ss.24–28 to be excluded in relation to the tenancy.

The declaration is required to reproduce the Sch.1 form of notice.[32] Where the tenant was served with a notice 14 days before the tenancy was entered into but signed a statutory declaration in the presence of a solicitor, which is required only where less than 14 days notice is given (see para.2–14 et seq.), it was held that ss.24–28 were nevertheless validly excluded. The more stringent measure of a statutory declaration performed the statutory task of alerting the tenant to what she was doing; it mattered not that the declaration went further than was necessary: *Patel v Chiltern Railway Co Ltd*.[33]

Requirements where less than 14 days' notice is given

2–18 If the landlord has not served on the tenant a Sch.1 notice prior to the period starting 14 days before the tenant enters into the tenancy or (if earlier) becomes

"The fact that a document is a statutory declaration obviously does not prevent it from being a declaration. The fact that, under para 8 [of Sch.1 to the 2003 Order] the declarant 'solemnly and sincerely declares' rather than merely 'declares' the fact that the declaration is said to be made pursuant to the 1835 Act, and the fact that the form is witnessed by a solicitor or a commissioner for oaths, cannot in any way prevent a para 8 declaration from being substantially in the form of a declaration under para 7. The para 8 form carries the same message of the para 7 form, but in a more emphatic and solemn form. What the judge referred to . . . as a general principle of our law that the greater includes the less does seem to me to be in point." (at [16])

[30] para.5 to Sch.2 to the 2003 Order.

[31] para.6 to Sch.2 to the 2003 Order.

[32] It does not require a copy of the form of notice which was actually served upon the tenant to be annexed to the declaration.

[33] [2008] 2 E.G.L.R. 33 CA.

contractually bound to do so, the agreement to exclude the security of tenure provisions will, nevertheless, be valid provided[34]:

(1) the Sch.1 notice required to be served is in fact served on the tenant before the tenant enters into the tenancy or (if earlier) becomes contractually bound to do so; and
(2) the tenant, or his duly authorised agent, before that time, makes a statutory declaration under the Statutory Declarations Act 1835 in the form,[35] or substantially in the form, set out in para.8 to Sch.2 to the 2003 Order.

The statutory declaration requires the tenant to declare[36]:

(a) that he is proposing to enter into the tenancy of premises and for the term specified;
(b) that he proposes to enter into an agreement excluding the provisions of ss.24–28;
(c) that the landlord has served a notice in the form,[37] or substantially in the form, set out in Sch.1 to the 2003 Order; and
(d) that the tenant has read the notice and that he accepts the consequences of entering into it.

The declaration is required to reproduce the Sch.1 form of notice.[38]

Where para.4 of Sch.2 applies, i.e. where the Sch.1 notice is served less than 14 days before the tenancy or the contract to take the tenancy is entered into, it is still necessary to comply with the remaining requirements of Sch.2, namely: **2–19**

(1) a reference to the landlord's notice and the tenant's statutory declaration must be contained in or endorsed on the instrument creating the tenancy[39];
(2) the agreement, or a reference to the agreement, under s.38A(1) must be contained in or endorsed upon the instrument creating the tenancy.[40]

Difference between the 14 days' notice and less than 14 days' notice requirements

The difference between the procedures applicable to the case where at least 14 days' notice has been given and the case where it has not is the requirement (in **2–20**

34 s.38A(3)(a) and para.4 to Sch.2 to the 2003 Order.
35 As to which see Appendix, para.A2.053.
36 para.8 to Sch.2 to the 2003 order.
37 See Appendix, para.A2.050.
38 It should be noted that the declaration sets out verbatim the form of the Sch.1 notice but does not require the actual form of notice which was served upon the tenant to be annexed. If the actual notice does not correspond to the form of the Sch.1 notice it does not matter so long as the actual notice was in a form substantially to like effect as the Sch.1 notice.
39 para.5 to Sch.2 to the 2003 Order.
40 para.6 to Sch.2 to the 2003 Order.

the latter case) for a *statutory* declaration to be given.[41] The content of the statutory declaration required by para.8 is exactly the same as the declaration required by para.7. The only difference therefore between the two cases is that where the 14 days requirement has not been complied with the declaration has to be a statutory declaration, that is to say, it has to be sworn in front of someone who is empowered to administer oaths and such a person will usually be a solicitor.[42]

"Contractually bound"

2–21 As mentioned above,[43] in order to satisfy the 14-days' notice requirement, the notice must be served not less than 14 days before the tenant enters into the tenancy or (if earlier) becomes contractually bound to do so[44] and the tenant or a duly authorised agent of the tenant must, before he enters into the tenancy, or (if earlier) becomes contractually bound to do so, make a declaration in the form[45] or substantially in the form, set out in para.7 to Sch.2.[46] What does "contractually bound" mean? If the meaning of that phrase is sufficiently wide to encompass a conditional agreement for lease, it will be impossible to enter into an agreement for lease conditional on compliance with the statutory requirements.[47] On balance the authors take the view that the policy of the Act, and its new provisions for excluding security of tenure, favour the view that such conditional agreements should not mean that the parties are already "contractually bound", but a decision of the Court is needed before the point can be stated with any certainty.

2–22 Even if "contractually bound" refers only to the position where the parties are unconditionally bound to enter into a lease, a landlord must ensure that he does not inadvertently fail to comply with the requirements of the legislation before the condition is satisfied. For instance, if an agreement for lease were conditional only on the grant of planning permission, the landlord would have to ensure, in order for the lease to be one outside the Act, that the notice and declaration/statutory declaration was served/received in good time before satisfaction of the condition. This problem would usually be dealt with by making the agreement subject to a further condition such as discussed in para.2–24 below.

---

[41] It is to be noted that in both cases the declaration or statutory declaration may be made by a duly authorised agent of the tenant.

[42] No advice is required to be given by the person administering the oath and thus as has been said by one commentator "One can only wonder, therefore, what benefit would be achieved by this additional procedural step, and how in fact the tenant is given greater protection": Hunter, J., *Business Tenancies: A Guide to The New Law*, 1st edn (London: Law Society Publishing), p.33.

[43] See para.2–16.

[44] para.2 to Sch.2 to the 2003 Order.

[45] As to the form of declaration see para.2–17 and see Appendix, para.A2.055.

[46] para.3 to Sch.2 to the 2003 Order.

[47] Some commentators do consider that the phrase "contractually bound" includes conditional agreements. Hunter, J., *Business Tenancies: A Guide to The New Law*, 1st edn (London: Law Society Publishing), p.30 says that: "The effect of the words 'becomes contractually bound to do so' may be such that conditional agreements for lease will be a thing of the past. The requirement is that before an agreement for lease is entered into, the Schedule 2 requirements as to the notice and declaration must be met. It may be that a conveyancing solution will be contrived, but that remains to be seen."

Prior to the 2003 Order, an agreement for lease, where the lease was intended to be one outside the security of tenure provisions of the Act, usually provided for it to be conditional on the grant by the court of an exclusion order. After the 2003 Order careful drafting will be required to ensure that the statutory requirements can be fulfilled before the condition is satisfied. Thus one would expect the condition to be worded so as to be satisfied only upon the expiry of 15 days from the date of receipt of a declaration[48] or immediately upon the receipt of a statutory declaration from the tenant.[49] The tenant will become contractually bound (unconditionally) on satisfaction of the condition and the statutory requirements will, therefore, have been fulfilled before the tenant became "contractually bound" to take the lease. **2–23**

The view that "contractually bound" excludes conditional agreements for lease may assist in the debate as to what to do with options,[50] guarantees[51] and disclaimer provisions, where the tenant or guarantor is to take a new lease either upon service of a notice by the tenant (in the case of an option) or the landlord (in the case of tenant default/disclaimer). When an option is exercised it gives rise to a binding agreement for lease. When the landlord serves upon the guarantor notice requiring the guarantor to take a lease upon disclaimer of the lease by the liquidator, the service of the notice gives rise to a binding agreement for lease: *Re Company (No.00792 of 1992) Ex p. Tredegar Enterprises*.[52] Is it necessary in either case to serve upon the tenant or guarantor a Sch.1 notice with respect to the new tenancy prior to entering into the lease, under which the option (whether "call" or "put") is exercised? If conditional contracts are caught by the words "contractually bound," the answer is probably yes. However, if conditional contracts are not within that phrase, the potential problems with options and guarantors can be overcome by drafting, so as to make any agreement which is to arise upon exercise conditional on the s.38A procedure being fulfilled.[53] **2–24**

Variations after Schedule 1 notice has been served

Case law under the old regime suggests that a landlord should be cautious where variations are agreed either to the contract which has been entered into or to the terms of the lease intended to be granted once the Sch.1 notice has been served. **2–25**

(i) Variation of the agreement for lease Let us assume a variation of the completion date under the contract but no variation of the terms of the tenancy which is to be taken. This will give rise to a new contract. Must a new Sch.1 **2–26**

[48] In accordance with para.3 of Sch.2 to the 2003 Order (i.e. where a 14 day notice was given).

[49] In accordance with para.4 to Sch.2 to the 2003 Order (i.e. where less than 14 days notice is given).

[50] Hunter, J., *Business Tenancies: A Guide to The New Law*, 1st edn (London: Law Society Publishing), p.38.

[51] See [2004] 25 E.G. 166.

[52] [1992] 2 E.G.L.R. 39 Ch. D.

[53] The difficulty here of course is that the tenant is the person responsible for providing the declaration. It may be possible to provide for a covenant on his part in the lease (under the terms of which the new lease is to arise) to provide the declaration if called upon to do so by the landlord. An alternative would be for the terms of the lease to provide that the declaration may be provided by X, being a representative of the landlord, who is duly authorised by the tenant/guarantor.

notice be served prior to the variation?[54] The argument that there is no need to do so relies upon the fact that one was served (albeit in relation to the earlier contract) prior to the varied contract coming into being. Paragraph 2 of Sch.2 requires the Sch.1 notice to be served before the tenant becomes contractually bound to enter into the tenancy to which the notice applies; it can, therefore, be argued that such a notice was served prior to the varied contract coming into being (the effect of which varied contract is that the tenant becomes contractually bound to enter into the tenancy) albeit originally with respect to the earlier contract. Furthermore, the proposed tenancy to be entered into by the tenant remains unaltered. On the other hand, it can be said that the Sch.1 notice relates only to a tenancy to be granted under the original contract not to a tenancy to be granted pursuant to the varied contract, albeit the tenancy is to be on the same terms. It should not be difficult to comply with the requirements of s.38A of the Act where the variation which gives rise to the alleged new contract is in correspondence, for a mere agreement in correspondence is insufficient to comply with s.2 of the Law of Property (Miscellaneous Provisions) Act 1989.[55]

2–27 **(ii) Variation of terms of tenancy to be entered into** The Court of Appeal in *Metropolitan Police District Receiver v Palacegate Properties Ltd*[56] considered whether an exclusion order approved by the court in relation to a tenancy which was subsequently granted in varied terms, was effective. The question centred upon the words in s.38(4)(since repealed), "in relation to that tenancy". The court held that, for the exclusion order to be valid, the terms of the tenancy as actually entered into had to bear a similarity to those before the court. Section 38A(1) retains the same expression: the notice which is served is a notice "in relation to" the tenancy to be taken. It would seem to follow that the tenancy the subject of the exclusion agreement in accordance with s.38A(1) and (3) must bear a similarity to the tenancy actually taken. Thus, under the old regime, if the tenancy to be granted was to be varied, say, by providing that the lease to be taken was to contain a landlord's break clause, then it would seem, on the *Palacegate Properties* authority, that a new order of the court would have to be obtained in order to ensure that the tenancy entered into was excluded from protection. Accordingly, it would seem to follow that under the new regime a new Sch.1 notice and declaration should equally be served/provided in relation to an agreement to take a lease subsequently varied to provide for the incorporation in the proposed lease of a landlord's break notice. However, how is this achieved in practice? The landlord must avoid agreeing to grant the tenancy in the varied terms until the procedural requirements are completed in relation to this new contract which is about to be entered into. If the parties have entered into an agreed variation of the contract satisfying s.2 of the Law of Property (Miscellaneous Provisions) Act 1989 before a new Sch.1 notice is served, then the tenant will be able to enforce it and the new tenancy in varied terms will be

[54] *McCausland v Duncan Lawrie Ltd* [1997] 1 W.L.R. 38. The terms of the agreed variation will need to comply with the provisions of s.2 of the Law of Property (Miscellaneous Provision) Act 1989.

[55] *Commission for the New Towns v Cooper (Great Britain) Ltd* [1995] Ch. 259 CA; [1995] 2 W.L.R. 677; [1995] 2 All E.R. 929.

[56] [2001] Ch. 131 CA, discussed at para.2.1.2.8 of the 2nd edition of this Work.

protected by the 1954 Act. Having to wait 14 days in order to serve a fresh Sch.1 notice may enable the tenant to change his mind and revert back to the original contract.

It may be said that the policy objective of the new changes was simplification and that with respect to the examples given above no further Sch.1 notice is required to be given, as there is nothing linking the Sch.1 notice to the terms of the tenancy. A Sch.1 notice does not in fact require any reference to be made to the terms of the tenancy.[57] Thus security of tenure will be excluded, it could be argued, from any tenancy entered into after the giving of the Sch.1 notice if the provisions of Sch.2 are satisfied, no matter that the terms were not agreed when the notice was given or that they subsequently change at some point. Support for this view may be derived from the Department of the Environment's comments in their document "Outcome of Consultation Exercise on Procedural Reforms".[58] The department's conclusion on the *Palacegate Properties* case was that: **2–28**

> "The Department does not see a need to revise its proposals on account of the *Palacegate Properties* case, which concerned a subsequent change in lease terms. The policy objective is simply to ensure that the tenant is aware of the implications of any proposal to exclude security of tenure. While it considers that tenants would be well advised to reappraise the proposed exclusion of security of tenure in relation to any subsequent changes in the overall package, this is outside the scope of the main policy objective."

The court's reluctance to adopt an over technical approach, described below, may be said to support this argument.

Furthermore, the Court of Appeal have said in relation to the old wording of s.38(4) concerning contracting out, that an over technical approach should not be taken with respect to the Act. Thus, it was held that an application to the court remained valid as being made by those persons who may be the landlord and who may be the tenant, although in the lease as it was ultimately granted one or more of them did not appear as a party. Accordingly, where the tenancy was initially to be granted to G with C acting as surety and an exclusion order was obtained with respect to such a tenancy, the subsequent grant of the lease to C alone did not invalidate the exclusion order: *Brighton & Hove City Council v Collinson*.[59] **2–29**

(iii) Variation of tenancy after execution of lease. Where the tenancy has been entered into and the landlord and the tenant subsequently agree to vary the tenancy it is thought that the security of tenure provisions remain excluded from the tenancy, as varied, except in a case where the variation is so radical as to amount to a surrender of the original tenancy and a re-grant of another in the varied terms: *Friends Provident Life Office v British Railways Board*.[60] In that case it was said that a surrender and re-grant by operation of law arose only **2–30**

[57] This is not so in the case of the *declaration* whether statutory or otherwise, although even here only the property and the length of the term need to be referred to. The other terms and conditions of the tenancy and the rent payable do not need to be referred to in the declaration.

[58] Dated February 2002, para.15.

[59] [2004] EWCA Civ 678; [2004] L. & T.R. 24.

[60] [1996] 1 All E.R. 336; [1995] 2 E.G.L.R. 55 CA.

where the variation affected the legal estate and either increased the extent of the premises demised or the term for which they were held.

The effect of the exclusion agreement

2–31 Where the parties have entered into an agreement excluding ss.24 to 28, the tenancy is still, strictly speaking, one to which the Act applies, but the effect of exclusion is, inter alia, to prevent the tenancy being continued by s.24(1). The practical effect of this is that the tenant is not entitled to security of tenure nor to compensation for disturbance. However, the fact that the tenancy is still one to which the Act applies may be of relevance in determining whether some other statutory code of protection falls to be applicable in relation to the demised premises. Thus if a tenancy is one to which the Act applies it cannot be a regulated tenancy protected by the Rent Act 1977,[61] a secure tenancy protected by the Housing Act 1985[62] or an assured tenancy protected by the Housing Act 1988.[63]

Assigning a contracted-out tenancy

2–32 An assignee of a tenancy which is contracted out of the provisions of ss.24 to 28 has no greater security of tenure than the original tenant. This is equally the case where the assignment occurs by operation of law: *Parc Battersea Ltd v Hutchinson*[64]; *St Giles Hotel Ltd v Microworld Technology Ltd.*[65]

2–33 ***Parc Battersea Ltd v Hutchinson***[66] On December 4, 1997 the landlord granted a lease of premises to M Ltd for a term expiring on March 31, 1998. The tenancy was excluded from the operation of ss.24 to 28 of the 1954 Act. On December 8, 1997, M Ltd orally agreed to sub-let part of the land leased for a rent of £300 a month. It was expressly agreed that M Ltd would not serve notice to quit expiring before March 31, 1999. The agreement was never reduced into writing but H went into occupation of the premises on December 18, 1997 and paid rent in accordance with the terms agreed.

Upon the expiry of M Ltd's lease the landlord sought possession against H. H contended that he was protected by the 1954 Act. It was held:

(1) the true nature of the tenancy granted to H was a tenancy for a term certain expiring on March 31, 1998; such an agreement, albeit created by parol, granted a legal interest in favour of H: s.54(2) of the Law of Property Act 1925;

---

61 s.24(3) of the 1977 Act.
62 Sch.1 para.11 to the Housing Act 1985.
63 Sch.1 para.4 to the Housing Act 1988.
64 [1999] L. & T.R. 554; [1999] 2 E.G.L.R. 33 Ch. D.
65 [1997] 2 E.G.L.R. 105 CA.
66 [1999] L. & T.R. 554; [1999] 2 E.G.L.R. 33 Ch. D.

(2) the grant of the sub-lease being for a period equal to or exceeding the remainder of the term of M Ltd's lease in relation to the part demised to H, took effect not as a sub-lease but as an assignment of the remainder of the grantor's term: *Milmo v Carreras*[67];

(3) although the sub-lease, viewed as an assignment, was made orally, an oral tenancy for a period exceeding the remainder of the grantor's term fell within s.53(1)(a) being a disposal of an interest by operation of law within the terms of that sub-section;

(4) accordingly, as H effectively took an assignment of part of the premises demised to M Ltd, H had no statutory protection as the assignment was of part of premises demised by a lease which was excluded from the security of tenure provisions of the 1954 Act.

Nature of continuation tenancy

The effect of s.24(1) has been said to be to continue the tenant's common law tenancy, but with a statutory variation as to the mode of determination: per Denning L.J. in *HL Bolton Engineering Ltd v TJ Graham & Sons Ltd.*[68] This description of the operation of the provision has been followed by Harman J. in *Weinbergs Weatherproofs v Radcliffe Paper Mill Co*[69] and approved by the Court of Appeal in *Cornish v Brook Green Laundry*[70] and by the House of Lords in *Bowes Lyon v Green*[71] (digested in para.3–90). The continuation of the tenancy is thus different in nature from a statutory tenancy under the Rent Acts, which is a personal right of irremovability and not a tenancy at all. The tenancy continued by s.24 of the Act is a continuation of the estate in land and is capable therefore of being assigned or forfeited for breach of covenant. Thus, as the tenant after the contractual expiry date is entitled to hold under the tenancy, the court will not normally infer from the payment and acceptance of rent the creation of a new tenancy at common law: *Lewis v MTC Cars*[72] (digested in para.10–49). **2–34**

As statute prolongs the tenancy (until determined in accordance with one of the prescribed modes) all the terms and conditions of the contractual tenancy, save those relating to termination, will continue to govern the continuation tenancy. For example a tenant is entitled to retain the use of the landlord's fixtures which cannot, therefore, be removed by the landlord at the expiration of the contractual term: *Poster v Slough Estates Ltd.*[73] In that case a superior landlord had granted a tenancy under which the tenant had affixed tenants fixtures which, on ordinary principles, he would have been entitled to remove at the end of his tenancy, which was not protected by the Act. However, because the sub-tenancy which he had granted included the fixtures and was itself protected by the Act, the sub-tenant **2–35**

[67] [1946] 1 K.B. 306 CA.

[68] [1957] 1 Q.B. 159 CA (this case is digested at para.7–169 on the issue of "intention", and at para.7–279 on the issue of the meaning of "purchase" within s.30(2)).

[69] [1958] Ch. 437.

[70] [1959] 1 Q.B. 394 CA.

[71] [1963] A.C. 420 HL.

[72] [1975] 1 W.L.R. 457; [1975] 1 All E.R. 874 CA.

[73] [1968] 1 W.L.R. 1515; [1968] 3 All E.R. 257 Ch. D.

was entitled to continue to use the fixtures during his continuation tenancy. See also *New Zealand Government Property Corp v HM&S Ltd*[74] (digested in para.8–127), the effect of which is that tenant's right to remove tenant's fixtures will not end at the contractual expiry date but will continue during the period of continuation under s.24.

2–36 Similarly, the rent continues to be that payable under the terms of the tenancy. This has, however, since the amendment of the Act in 1969 been subject to the landlord's right to seek the payment of an interim rent pursuant to s.24A.[75] As an alternative to relying upon the right to seek an interim rent some landlords incorporate a clause into the tenancy providing for an upwards-only rent review on the last day of the contractual term. The advantages of this "last day review" are that it avoids the need for applying for an interim rent to cover any period of holding over after the expiry of the contractual term and may be on the basis of assumptions different to those required to be made by the court under s.24A of the Act. A last day review provision is certainly worth considering when negotiating the terms of a tenancy. However, now that a tenant has a right to seek an interim rent, the advantages of it are limited.[76] It has been held that a landlord cannot implement the rent review provisions in a lease during the period of continuation where the rent review date is by reference to a specified period of "the term", for this refers only to the contractual term: *Willison v Cheverell Estates Ltd*.[77]

2–37 The continuation under s.24 is a continuation of the tenancy of the entirety of the premises demised albeit the tenant may only be occupying part of the demised premises. For example, the tenant of a shop with an upper residential part may be occupying only the shop and the residential part may be sub-let. The tenancy is one to which the Act applies because part of the property (namely the shop) is occupied by the tenant for the purposes of a business carried on by him.[78] The effect is that the tenancy of the whole will be continued. Thus, the tenant will continue to be the immediate landlord of the sub-tenant and continue to be entitled to receive the rent due from the sub-tenant.

It is most important to recognise that, as the continuation from the contractual expiry date is of the estate not the contract, it is the person in whom the estate is vested at that time who is liable for the rent during the continuation period. An original tenant, therefore, who has assigned his tenancy before the contractual expiry date will not be liable after that date for rent due: *City of London Corp v Fell*.[79] As was stated by Nourse L.J. in the Court of Appeal:

> "... where an original tenant has assigned the tenancy before the end of the contractual term the tenancy which section 24(1) provides shall not come to an end is, and can only be, the tenancy of the assignee. Since the contractual obligations of the original tenant form no part of the legal relationship between the landlord and the assignee, and since they are not independently

---

[74] [1982] 2 W.L.R. 837; [1982] 1 E.G.L.R. 52 CA.

[75] The provisions of which have been radically altered by the 2003 Order. See Ch.9.

[76] For the advantage of the review rent will last only for so long as the tenant does not seek an interim rent. As to the tenant's right to seek an interim rent, see para.9–02 et seq.

[77] [1996] 1 E.G.L.R. 116 CA.

[78] See para.1–36 fn.111.

[79] [1994] 1 A.C. 458 HL.

> continued by the subsection, they are in no way affected. If, as here, the original tenant has covenanted to pay rent only during the contractual term, the landlord cannot recover from him any rent payable in respect of a period after that date.[80]"

Prior to the Landlord and Tenant (Covenants) Act 1995, there was no reason why the parties could not, by express words, agree contractually that the original tenant would remain liable for rent during the period of continuation under s.24. Thus, for instance, one could have expressed the term as including "not only the term hereby granted but also the period of any holding over or of any extension thereof whether by statute or common law", which was the wording used in *Herbert Duncan v Cluttons*.[81] Where the Landlord and Tenant (Covenants) Act 1995 applies to the tenancy the obligation to pay rent, however worded, will cease to bind the original tenant after an assignment.[82] Even where wording is used as in *Herbert Duncan v Cluttons* it is a matter of construction whether the original tenant or any intermediate assignee is liable to pay an interim rent during the continuation of a tenancy entered into before the 1995 Act came into operation. This is illustrated by the decision in *Herbert Duncan v Cluttons*, where it was held that although the original tenant had agreed to pay the rent during the term as defined he did not covenant to pay any other rent and in particular did not covenant to pay an interim rent determined pursuant to the provisions of s.24A. The fact that the then provisions of s.24A(2) of the Act deemed the interim rent to be "the rent payable under the tenancy" did not enable the landlord to translate the contract into one for payment of an interim rent. Although this case concerned the provisions of s.24A in their form prior to the coming into force of the amendments made by the 2003 Order, the principle illustrated by it applies equally to seeking to provide for a contractual requirement to pay an interim rent under the new provisions contained within ss.24A to 24D. **2–38**

In the case of a tenancy to which the 1995 Act applies, any obligation of the original tenant to pay an interim rent however expressed will cease to be binding after an assignment subject to the tenant entering into an authorised guarantee agreement.[83] Where the parties agreed that the tenant was liable to pay commission during the term of any "substituted" lease, it was held that the tenant's liability to pay commission continued during both the period of continuation under s.24 and the term of a new lease: *Berthon Boat Co Ltd v Hood Sailmakers Ltd*[84] (digested in para.2–43). **2–39**

Subject to the Landlord and Tenant (Covenants) Act 1995, the position of a surety, whether of the original tenant or of the tenant during the period of the continuation of the tenancy under s.24, is dependent upon the terms of the contract entered into by the surety with the landlord. Thus in *Junction Estates v* **2–40**

---

[80] [1993] Q.B. 589 at 604D.

[81] [1993] Q.B. 589 CA (this was heard with *City of London v Fell*, although only the latter was appealed to the House of Lords).

[82] See s.5 of the Landlord and Tenant (Covenants) Act 1995. These provisions apply to "new tenancies", being tenancies granted after January 1, 1996, unless it is granted in pursuance of an agreement entered into before that date or an order of a court made before that date: Landlord and Tenant (Covenants) Act 1995 s.1(3).

[83] Pursuant to s.16 of the Landlord and Tenant (Covenants) Act 1995.

[84] [2000] 1 E.G.L.R. 39.

Cope[85] the guarantor's liability was in respect of the period of the contractual term only, as was the case in *A Plesser & Co v Davis*.[86]

2–41 ***Junction Estates v Cope***[87] The landlords granted a lease of business premises for a term of seven years expiring on December 25, 1970. There were two guarantors of the original tenant covenanting:

> "in consideration of the demise . . . jointly and severally . . . with the landlord that the tenant will pay the rent hereby reserved on the days and in the manner aforesaid and will perform and observe all the tenant's covenants hereinbefore contained and that in default in such payment of rent or in the performance or observance of such covenants as aforesaid the guarantors will pay and make good to the landlord on demand all losses damage costs and expenses thereby arising or incurred by the landlord."

The original tenant assigned the lease during the contractual term. Upon the expiry of the term the tenancy continued pursuant to s.24. The tenant failed to pay the rent and the landlord sued the guarantors for the outstanding monies. It was held that the language of the guarantee made it clear that the guarantors were liable for the payment of the rent reserved by the lease during the seven-year term only and not for the payment of rent during the period that the tenancy was continued by s.24.

2–42 A tenant who sub-lets for a term longer than that which he possesses effects an assignment by operation of law.[88] However, as a tenancy protected by the Act may continue beyond its term date a sub-tenancy created out of it to continue beyond the term date does not operate as an assignment: *William Skelton & Son Ltd v Harrison & Pinder Ltd*[89] (digested in para.3–201). There is no reason why this principle is not equally applicable to the grant of a sub-tenancy during a period of continuation under s.24. The continuation tenancy under s.24 of the Act is of uncertain duration, lasting until terminated in accordance with the Act. Of course, if the sub-tenancy is a tenancy of the whole, then the tenant will cease to be in occupation of the property for the purposes of a business. This cesser of business occupation will not put an end to the tenancy automatically (s.24(3)(a)), but it is terminable by the landlord by notice of not less than three and not more than six months notice in writing: s.24(3)(a) of the Act.

2–43 ***Berthon Boat Co Ltd v Hood Sailmakers Ltd***[90] The tenant entered into a lease and by a collateral agreement entered into on the same date and in consideration of the grant agreed to pay "throughout the term of the lease or any lease which may be substituted therefore" commission based on certain specified sales. Subsequently a new lease was granted which took effect as a surrender and re-grant by implication of law. Upon expiry of the contractual term of the new lease it was continued by s.24. A dispute arose between the landlord and the

---

85 (1974) 27 P. & C.R. 482.

86 [1983] 2 E.G.L.R. 70.

87 (1974) 27 P. & C.R. 482.

88 *Milmo v Carreras* [1946] 1 K.B. 306; *Parc Battersea Ltd v Hutchinson* [1999] 2 E.G.L.R. 33 (digested in para.2–33).

89 [1975] Q.B. 361.

90 [2000] 1 E.G.L.R. 39 QBD.

tenant as to whether the collateral agreement had come to an end upon the contractual expiry date of the new lease. The court held that, upon a true construction of the collateral agreement, the tenant was liable to pay the commission during the continuation period and would be liable to continue to pay the commission through the term of any tenancy granted by order of the county court, in any proceedings that followed, because both the continuation tenancy and any such new tenancy came within the meaning of the word "substituted".[91]

Break clauses

If a landlord exercises a right to break the term of a lease to which the Act applies, the effect is to bring the contractual term to a premature end but not to determine the tenancy. Section 24 continues the tenancy unless it is terminated in accordance with the provisions of the Act, but does not prevent the bringing to an end of the contractual relationship. The landlord will still have to terminate the tenancy in accordance with the Act but his s.25 notice will need only comply with the requirements of the Act. **2–44**

2. EFFECT OF THE ACT CEASING TO APPLY

Condition of continuation

The Act may cease to apply to a tenancy for a number of reasons, e.g. where the tenant ceases to carry on business or where the tenant goes out of occupation. The general rule is that it is a continuing condition of the tenant's right to protection under the Act that the tenant remains in occupation of the premises for the purposes or partly for the purposes of a business: *I&H Caplan Ltd v Caplan (No.2)*[92] (digested in para.1–44). It is necessary to consider separately the effect of this continuing condition ceasing to be satisfied during the contractual period of the tenancy and during any continuation period under s.24 of the Act, and to consider the different effects of cesser on fixed terms and periodic tenancies and of any steps which may have been taken under the Act prior to cesser. **2–45**

Cessation of business user prior to the contractual term date

Effect of Act ceasing to apply during contractual term of fixed term tenancy where no section 25 notice or section 26 request has been served

During the term of a tenancy granted for a term of years certain, the question whether the Act applies or not is rarely of significance, although it will, e.g. affect **2–46**

[91] This case would appear to be wrongly decided as the "term" ended with the contractual tenancy—*City of London Corp v Fell* [1994] 1 A.C. 458 HL—and neither a continuation tenancy nor a new tenancy is a substitution for the original term. Although it appears that the argument was put that the reference to the "term" was to the contractual term only no reference appears to have been made to *City of London Corp v Fell*. See para.2–37.

[92] [1963] 1 W.L.R. 1247; [1963] 2 All E.R. 930.

the question whether an agreement to surrender the tenancy is enforceable.[93] It is, however, of critical importance as the term draws towards an end. If the tenancy is one to which the Act applies at the expiry date of the contractual term, then the continuation provisions of s.24(1) will come into play.

2–47 Before the decision of the Court of Appeal in *Long Acre Securities Ltd v Electro Acoustic Industries Ltd*,[94] (digested in para.2–52) it was considered that if the tenant was not in occupation for the purposes or partly for the purposes of a business at the expiration of the contractual term, the tenancy would come to an end on the term date. However, Dillon L.J., in giving the judgment of the court in the *Long Acre Securities* case, stated that the tenant could not stop a continuation tenancy arising under s.24 and, therefore, put an end to his liability to pay rent, just by quitting the premises before the contractual term date. The reason given for this was a tenancy to which the Act applied was a continuing tenancy from the outset and, thus, could not be brought to an end otherwise than in accordance with the Act, and cessation of occupation for business purposes was not one of the modes of termination provided for by the Act.[95]

2–48 The decision was criticised[96] as one which appeared to have overlooked the fact that s.24 applies only to "a tenancy to which this Part of this Act applies", and the Act applies only if the tenancy includes premises which are occupied by the tenant for the purposes or partly for the purposes of a business carried on by him. An unsuccessful attempt was made at first instance in *Esselte AB v Pearl Assurance Plc*[97] to confine the *Long Acre Securities* decision to its particular facts.[98] However, when *Esselte AB v Pearl Assurance Plc* (digested in para.2–53) came before the Court of Appeal[99] it overruled the *Long Acre Securities* decision, holding that it was inconsistent with and made in ignorance of an earlier binding decision of the Court of Appeal, namely *Morrison Holdings Ltd v Manders Property Ltd*[100] (digested in para.1–54).

2–49 In *Morrison Holdings Ltd v Manders Properties Ltd*[101] the tenant's lease was due to expire on December 24, 1977 subject to a break clause exercisable by the landlord should the demise and other neighbouring premises be substantially destroyed or damaged by fire. A fire occurred on May 20, 1974 so as to render the demised premises unfit for occupation of the tenants for the purposes of their

---

[93] See para.3–07 et seq.

[94] [1990] 1 E.G.L.R. 91; (1991) 61 P. & C.R. 177 CA.

[95] In the early decision *Nu Flats & Properties Ltd v Sheckman* [1954] E.G.D. 133, Finnemore J. appears to give some support for the view of Dillon L.J.

[96] *Woodfall: Law of Landlord and Tenant* (London: Sweet & Maxwell) (the relevant text is no longer to be found in the current looseleaf, presumably in light of the subsequent decisions of the Court of Appeal).

[97] [1995] 2 E.G.L.R. 61 Ch.

[98] It was argued that it was to be viewed as merely deciding that if, at the time the landlord served a s.25 notice, the tenant was in occupation for the purposes of a business carried on by him but subsequently vacated prior to the contractual term date, the tenancy did not end on the contractual term date but on the date of termination specified in the s.25 notice, unless the tenant effectively brought forward that date by service of a notice under s.27 of the Act.

[99] [1997] 1 W.L.R. 891; [1997] 2 All E.R. 41 CA.

[100] [1976] 1 W.L.R. 533; [1976] 2 All E.R. 205 CA.

[101] [1976] 1 W.L.R. 533; [1976] 2 All E.R. 205 CA.

business. On May 22, 1974, the landlord served notice to operate the break clause and on June 17, 1974, demolished the premises to which the tenants had not returned. On July 1, 1974, the landlord served a notice under s.25 to determine the tenancy. On October 17, 1974, the tenants applied to the court for the grant of a new tenancy. The court came to the conclusion that the tenants' cesser of occupation did not amount to its abandonment so as to preclude any locus standi to apply for the new tenancy. Scarman L.J. in the course of his judgment said:

> "Of course, if the tenants were out of occupation or had abandoned their right of occupation at the time the notice was served, it would determine the contract of tenancy, since the tenancy would no longer be one to which Part I of the Act applied. But if the tenants still occupied or claimed their right of occupation at the time the notice was served, then the notice would not avail because it was not a notice as required by the Act."[102]

Morritt L.J. in *Esselte AB v Pearl Assurance Plc* (digested in para.2–53) said that although the *Morrison Holdings v Manders* decision related to the locus standi of a tenant not in occupation to bring proceedings under s.24(1) seeking the grant of a new tenancy, rather than the effect on the termination of the contractual tenancy of the tenant ceasing to occupy the demised premises, this feature did not alter the fact that it was an essential part of the reasoning of the Court of Appeal in arriving at that conclusion that if a tenant had ceased to occupy the premises for the purposes of its business then the protection which the Act would otherwise afford would be lost. Thus as the Lord Justice said:

> "It must follow from this proposition that a tenancy for a term which would determine by effluxion of time if it were not one to which the Act applies will so determine if at the expiration of the term the tenant has ceased to occupy it for the purposes of any business."[103]

In *Surrey CC v Single Horse Properties Ltd*[104] (digested in para.2–54). The Court of Appeal applying *Esselte AB v Pearl Assurance Plc*[105] held that a tenancy ceases at the contractual term date if the tenant is not in occupation for the purposes of a business, and this is so even where the tenant has served a counter-notice to the landlord's s.25 notice and made an application to the court for renewal. Arden L.J. said: **2–50**

> "In my judgment, since, as I have explained, section 25 refers back to section 24, the conclusion in the Esselte case must apply for the purposes also of section 25(1). A notice under section 25(1) is thus of no effect if the tenancy is not continued by section 24(1). The tenancy is not so continued if it expires on the term date by effluxion of time: see the Esselte case. Whenever the notice is served, there would be nothing for the landlord's termination to 'bite on'." (at [37])

A new s.27(1A) has been added by the 2003 Order. It provides: **2–51**

---

[102] [1976] 1 W.L.R. 533, at 540.
[103] [1997] 1 W.L.R. 891 at 903.
[104] [2002] EWCA Civ 367; [2002] 1 W.L.R. 2106. This case was concerned with whether the principle established in *Esselte AB v Pearl Assurance Plc* applied to a case where the tenant had actually applied for the grant of a new tenancy prior to the contractual term date and ceased to occupy the premises for business purposes prior to the contractual term date. This involved the further consideration of the application of s.64. See further para.2–58 et seq.
[105] [1995] 2 E.G.L.R. 61.

> "Section 24 of this Act shall not have effect in relation to a tenancy for a term of years certain where the tenant is not in occupation of the property comprised in the tenancy at the time when, apart from this Act, the tenancy would come to an end by effluxion of time."

Section 27(1A) reflects the decisions of the Court of Appeal in *Esselte AB v Pearl Assurance Plc*[106] (digested in para.2–53) and *Surrey CC v Single Horse Properties Ltd*[107] (digested in para.2–54). There is no continuation of the tenancy under s.24 unless the tenant is in occupation for the purposes or partly for the purposes of a business carried on by the tenant, as at the date on which the tenancy would otherwise expire by effluxion of time, irrespective of:

(1) any later date of termination specified in the landlord's s.25 notice; or
(2) any later date of commencement of the new tenancy specified in the tenant's s.26 request; or
(3) the fact that the tenant has made an application to the court for renewal.[108]

2–52 ***Long Acre Securities Ltd v Electro Acoustic Industries Ltd***[109] The term of a tenancy of business premises was due to expire on March 25, 1988. The premises were at some stage used by the tenant for business purposes. The landlord served a s.25 notice on March 3, 1988, specifying March 1, 1989 as the date of termination. The landlord was, therefore, in effect trying to obtain rent for a further year. The tenant on March 4, 1988 served a notice pursuant to s.27(2) of the 1954 Act determining the tenancy with effect from June 24, 1988. The county court judge found that there was no business occupation on March 25, 1988, and accordingly held that the tenancy (and the obligation to pay rent) had therefore ended on that date. The Court of Appeal, however, held that the tenant's liability for rent continued beyond the contractual term date up to June 24, 1988 (the date specified in the tenant's s.27(2) notice) but not (as the landlord had claimed) up to March 25, 1989 (the date specified in the s.25 notice). As noted above this decision has since been overruled.

2–53 ***Esselte AB v Pearl Assurance Plc***[110] The tenant of business premises, the contractual term of which expired on February 15, 1993, vacated the premises, as found by the judge at first instance, on December 6, 1992. The tenant served notices pursuant to s.27(2) on the landlord on January 16, 1993 to determine both the tenancies on June 24, 1993. The tenant paid rent up to February 14, 1993 and the landlord claimed that the tenant should also pay rent up to June 24, 1993. The tenant argued that the tenancy did not continue pursuant to the provisions of s.24(1) of the Act as that applied only in relation to "tenancies to which this Part of this act applies" under s.23 and, therefore, the tenant had to be in occupation for the purposes of a business at the contractual term date in order for the tenancy to continue. The Court of Appeal held that the tenancy determined with effect from February 15, 1993.

---

106 [1997] 1 W.L.R. 891; [1997] 2 All E.R. 41 CA.
107 [2002] EWCA Civ 367; [2002] 1 W.L.R. 2016.
108 See further, para.2–56.
109 [1990] 1 E.G.L.R. 91 CA.
110 [1997] 1 W.L.R. 891; [1997] 2 All E.R. 41 CA.

Surrey CC v Single Horse Properties Ltd[111] The tenant held office premises under a lease granted on July 24, 1975 for 25 years ending on June 24, 2000. It occupied the building as offices in connection with its functions as a local education authority. The tenancy was one to which the 1954 Act applied while such occupation continued. On December 3, 1999, the landlord served a notice dated November 30, 1999 under s.25 on the tenant. This notice terminated the tenancy on June 24, 2000. On January 26, 2000, the tenant served a counter-notice to the effect that it was not willing to give up possession on the termination date. On March 21, 2000, it applied to the county court for a new tenancy under the Act. On April 10, 2000, the landlord served an answer. On May 15, 2000, the district judge gave directions by consent with a view to trial of the application in September or October 2000. However, on June 13, 2000, the tenant vacated the building. On June 16, 2000 its agents notified the landlord that it had done so and returned the keys. Accordingly, the tenant did not occupy the premises on the term date (June 24, 2000). On August 3, 2000 the landlord applied for an order in the following terms: **2–54**

> "The [tenant's] application for a new tenancy be struck out. The said tenancy the subject of the application do continue with rent payable thereunder for a period of three months from the making of this order."

The ground on which the application was made was that the tenant had vacated the premises. On August 22, 2000, the district judge made an order in the terms sought by the landlord. Since the order provided that the tenancy was to continue with rent payable thereunder for a period of three months from the date of the order, the tenant was liable to pay rent from June 24, 2000 to November 22, 2000, even though it had not been in occupation of the premises for any part of that period. On September 7, 2000 the tenant applied for an order varying the district judge's order so as to delete that part of it which provided for payment of rent after June 24, 2000. The application was dismissed on October 25, 2000. The tenant appealed to the judge. He made an order dismissing the appeal. The Court of Appeal reversed the judge and held that the tenancy had ended on the contractual term date, June 24, 2000, notwithstanding the fact that the tenant had made an application for renewal which was extant at the date of the term date.

Questions arising out of Esselte AB v Pearl Assurance Plc and Surrey CC v Single Horse Properties Ltd

It is clear from s.27(1A) that if the tenant is not in occupation for the purposes of a business at the term date, his tenancy will end. There are, however, a number of interesting questions which are left unresolved by the two decisions of the Court of Appeal. **2–55**

Uncertainty as to whether tenant is in occupation The first is, what is a landlord to do if he is unsure within the period of 12 months preceding the contractual term date whether or not the tenant is in occupation for the purposes of a business and, therefore, whether the tenancy is one to which the Act applies? **2–56**

[111] [2002] 1 W.L.R. 2016; [2002] 2 E.G.L.R. 43 CA.

Until the contractual term date the tenancy is continuing by virtue of the contract of tenancy and there is nothing to stop the tenant, after the service of a s.25 notice served at a time when the tenant was not in occupation, resuming occupation and regaining the protection of the Act. This was a matter touched on by Morritt L.J. in *Esselte AB v Pearl Assurance Plc*. He said:

> "If the tenant is in occupation for the statutory purposes the landlord may serve a notice under section 25(1) to determine the tenancy at the term date. If the landlord is doubtful whether or not the tenant is in occupation for the statutory purposes then I see no reason why, as Counsel for Pearl submitted, he should not serve a notice under section 25(1) without prejudice to his principal contention that as the tenant is not in occupation no such notice is required."[112]

This leaves open the question of the precise legal status of a s.25 notice served in such circumstances. As it is clear that the Act only applies if the tenant is in occupation for business purposes, it is difficult to see how a notice served at a time when the tenant is not in occupation can be a valid s.25 notice. In *Cheryl Investments Ltd v Saldanha*,[113] (digested in para.1–39) Geoffrey Lane L.J. observed that:

> "If at the time the [section 25] notice is served the business occupation has ceased, there is no 'tenancy to which this Part of this Act applies' and nothing on which a section 25 notice by the landlord can bite. It seems therefore that the business occupation must exist both at the time the contractual tenancy comes to an end and at the date of service of the notice of determination."[114]

However, Geoffrey Lane L.J.'s dictum ought to be contrasted with what is said in the judgment of Pearce L.J. in *Teasdale v Walker*[115] (digested in para.1–83). In the course of giving the judgment of the court, Pearce L.J. expressed the view that where a s.25 notice has been served at a time when the tenant is not in occupation for the purposes of a business, but he subsequently resumes occupation, the s.25 notice bites at that time and the tenant is then entitled to apply for a new tenancy. Support for the view of Geoffrey Lane L.J. is provided by the judgment of Arden L.J[116] in *Surrey CC v Single Horse Properties Ltd.*[117]

2–57 **Termination by cessation of occupation** The second interesting question which arises out of *Esselte AB v Pearl Assurance Plc* (digested in para.2–53), is whether in all circumstances a tenant to whose tenancy the Act applies can prevent it being continued by s.24 by the simple expedient of ceasing business occupation on or before the contractual term date. It is necessary to distinguish a number of situations:

(1) The simplest case is where cesser occurs prior to the contractual term date before either party has served any notice or request under ss.25, 26 or 27.

---

[112] [1997] 1 W.L.R. 891 at 898.
[113] [1978] 1 W.L.R. 1329; [1979] 1 All E.R. 5 CA.
[114] [1978] 1 W.L.R. 1329 at 1338.
[115] [1958] 1 W.L.R. 1076; [1958] 3 All E.R. 307 CA.
[116] Quoted in para.2–46 above.
[117] [2002] EWCA Civ 367; [2002] 1 W.L.R. 2016.

This is now catered for by s.27(1A). The tenancy will not be continued beyond the contractual expiry date in such circumstances.

(2) The second situation differs in that the landlord has prior to the contractual term date, served a s.25 notice to expire at some later (post-contractual term) date. This was the precise situation which existed in the decision of *Long Acre Securities v Electro Acoustic* (digested in para.2–52). In *Sight & Sound Education Ltd v Books Etc Ltd*[118] (digested in para.12–33) it appears to have been accepted by all parties[119] that where the landlord served a s.25 notice specifying a date of termination later than the contractual term date, the tenancy would nevertheless cease on the contractual term date if the tenant had ceased to occupy the premises for business purposes prior to that date.[120] This was also the view of the deputy judge in *Arundel Corp v Financial Trading Co Ltd*.[121] The subject of discussion here has now been settled by the Court of Appeal in *Surrey CC v Single Horse Properties Ltd*[122] (digested in para.2–54). The court held, applying *Esselte AB v Pearl Assurance Plc*[123] (digested in para.2–53), that a tenancy ceases at the contractual term date if the tenant is not in occupation for the purposes of a business, and this is so even where the tenant has served a counter-notice to the landlord's s.25 notice and made an application to the court for renewal.

(3) The third situation differs in that the tenant has prior to the contractual term date made a s.26 request specifying some later date. Here it would seem possible to argue that, by invoking his rights under s.26, the tenant has precluded himself from determining the tenancy at any date by ceasing business occupation, especially in view of the wording of s.26(5) which

---

118 [1999] 3 E.G.L.R. 45 Ch. D.

119 Counsel on behalf of the tenant seems to have accepted that the tenancy did end on the contractual term date by reason of the tenant's non-occupation and did not argue the contrary. It was not in the interest of the landlord on the facts of that case to argue otherwise. The case is equally explicable on the basis that the tenancy did not end on the contractual term date and that the tenant was not entitled to double compensation as the tenant was not in occupation for business purposes for the period of 14 years immediately preceding the date of termination of the current tenancy within s.37(3). See para.12–31 et seq.

120 Judge Robert Pryor QC, without it would appear hearing full argument on the point said:

"As I have said, the tenant vacated shortly before September 28, 1997, the original contractual term date, and the consequence of that was that, having vacated with no intention to resume occupation, the tenant ceased to enjoy the protection of the 1954 Act. The Act ceased to apply and so the contractual arrangements reasserted themselves, if one can put it in that way, with the result that the tenancy, or tenancies, expired by effluxion of time on September 28, 1997. That is the consequence of a decision of the Court of Appeal in *Esselte AB v Pearl Assurance plc*. The result, summarising it, therefore was that the tenant vacated, the tenancy came to an end, the tenant's obligation to pay rent came to an end and the tenant's right of occupation came to an end. The tenant could not have remained in occupation or resumed occupation after September 28, 1997, having discontinued its proceedings and vacated, without being a trespasser."

121 Unreported March 27, 2000, Technology and Construction Court, Mr Blunt QC sitting as a deputy judge. In this case the judge accepted the argument that notwithstanding service of a s.25 notice specifying a date of termination later than the contractual term date, where a tenant ceased to occupy premises for business purposes before the expiry of the contractual term the Act had no application to the tenancy and it terminated by effluxion of time on the contractual expiry date. The judge in fact found that the tenant had not ceased to occupy the premises at the term date and thus the tenancy continued pursuant to s.24.

122 [2002] EWCA Civ 367; [2002] 1 W.L.R. 2016.

123 [1997] 1 W.L.R. 891; [1997] 2 All E.R. 41 CA.

provides that "where a tenant makes a request for a new tenancy . . . the current tenancy shall terminate immediately before the date specified . . .". It is considered that in light of *Surrey CC v Single Horse Properties Ltd*, the position is the same as that under (2), namely that service by the tenant of a s.26 request does not prevent the tenant from bringing about an earlier termination of the term simply by vacating prior to the contractual expiry date. The tenancy will by reason of the non-occupation cease on the contractual term date, notwithstanding the fact that the s.26 request may specify a date for commencement of the new lease which is later than the contractual term date.

(4) Finally, it is necessary to consider the position where the tenant has, pursuant to s.27(2), served a notice prior to the contractual term date terminating the tenancy at some later date. This is precisely what happened in *Esselte AB v Pearl Assurance Plc* where it was held that cessation of business use prevented the tenancy being continued notwithstanding service of the s.27(2) notice. In that case, however, the notice pursuant to s.27(2) was served at a time when the tenancy was not one to which the Act applied. As cessation of business occupation prevents a tenancy from continuing pursuant to s.24 after the term date, then it would seem to follow that, equally, the service of a s.27(2) notice should not continue the tenancy if the tenant is not in occupation at the term date.[124] It is considered that after *Surrey CC v Single Horse Properties Ltd* this represents the correct position, and remains the position notwithstanding the amendments to the Act by the 2003 Order.

Effect of Act ceasing to apply during contractual term of fixed term tenancy where a section 25 notice or section 26 request has been served but no application for a new tenancy/termination application has been made

2–58 A tenancy protected by the Act comes to an end on the date specified in the relevant s.25 notice or, in the case of a s.26 request, immediately before the date specified for the commencement of the new lease (s.26(5)), unless the tenant or landlord makes an application for the grant of a new tenancy or the landlord makes a termination application. The position which arises where the tenancy ceases to be one which the Act applies if after service of such a notice or request but before any application is made is considered in para.2–57 sub-para.(2). The Court of Appeal decision in *Surrey CC v Single Horse Properties Ltd*[125] (digested in para.2–54) makes it clear that in these circumstances the tenancy will end on the contractual term date notwithstanding service of a s.25 notice and notwithstanding the fact that that notice may specify a date of termination later than the contractual term date.[126] Whether the tenant may seek to shorten the date of termination specified in a s.25 notice by serving a s.27 notice is considered in

[124] See the discussion at sub-para.(2), above. As to the effect of a s.25 notice specifying a term of termination later than the term date.

[125] [2002] EWCA Civ 367; [2002] 1 W.L.R. 2016.

[126] As noted above, in para.2–57 sub-para.(2), there were two first instance decisions which had reached this conclusion prior to *Surrey CC v Single Horse*.

paras 3–101 and 3–108. The tenant cannot seek to shorten the date of termination by serving a s.27 notice where the tenant has himself served a s.26 request: s.26(4).

Effect of Act ceasing to apply during contractual term of fixed term tenancy where a section 25 notice or section 26 request has been served and an application for renewal/termination has been made

Where a s.25 notice or s.26 request has been served and an application has been made and thereafter, but prior to the expiry of the contractual term date, the tenancy ceases to be one to which the Act applies by reason of a cesser of business occupation by the tenant, the application becomes liable to be struck out: *Domer v Gulf Oil (Great Britain)*[127]; *I&H Caplan Ltd v Caplan (No.2)*[128] (digested in para.1–46). **2–59**

Section 64 provides that if: **2–60**

> "apart from this section the effect of the notice or request would be to terminate the tenancy before the expiration of the period of three months beginning with the date on which the application is finally disposed of, the effect of the notice or request shall be to terminate the tenancy at the expiration of the said period of three months and not at any other time."

If the application is struck out, the tenancy will prima facie continue for a further period of three months specified by s.64 together with a period of 21 days[129] (or such other period as the court may specify) for appeal thereafter unless at the date of the striking out there is more than three months remaining before the termination date specified in the relevant notice or request, in which case the tenancy will determine on the date specified in the notice or request. However, until the decision in *Surrey CC v Single Horse Properties Ltd*[130] (digested in para.2–54) the question arose as to whether, where the three-month period provided for by s.64 expired after the contractual term date, the tenancy expired on the date specified by the section or, by reason of the tenant's non-occupation, at the contractual term date. It was held that, unless the tenant is in occupation for business purposes at the contractual term date, the tenancy will end on that date and will not be continued, irrespective of the fact that the tenant has made an application for renewal.[131] Arden L.J. said:

---

[127] (1975) 119 S.J. 392; 125 N.L.J. 309.

[128] [1963] 1 W.L.R. 1247; [1963] 2 All E.R. 930.

[129] The time for appealing specified in CPR r. 52.4(2): Civil Procedure (Amendment No.4) Rules 2005 (SI 2005/3515), r.11(c)(ii); and see para.14–137 et seq.

[130] [2002] EWCA Civ 367; [2002] 1 W.L.R. 2016.

[131] The matter had been the subject of an unreported first instance decision in *Arundel Corp v Financial Trading Co Ltd* (Unreported March 27, 2000, Technology and Construction Court, Mr Blunt QC). The deputy judge accepted, albeit with some reservation, the argument, in reliance upon *Esselte AB v Pearl Assurance Plc*, that notwithstanding the fact that the tenant had made an application for a new lease before the contractual expiry date, if the tenant ceased to occupy premises for business purposes before the expiry of the contractual term the Act had no application to the tenancy and it terminated by effluxion of time on the contractual expiry date. He said:

"Nor is it clear to me precisely why, where a section 25 notice has been served, the tenancy is not continued under Section 64(1). The argument advanced by FTC is that where a tenant for a fixed term ceases to occupy premises for the purposes of his business before the expiration of the term the

> "In my judgment, since as I have explained, section 25 refers back to section 24, the conclusion in the *Esselte* case must apply for the purposes also of section 25(1). A notice under section 25(1) is thus of no effect if the tenancy is not continued by section 24(1). The tenancy is not so continued if it expires on the term date by effluxion of time: see the *Esselte* case. Whenever the notice is served, there would be nothing for the landlord's termination to 'bite on'. [The] argument [of Counsel for the Landlord] amounts to reading into Part II of the 1954 Act a concept whereby a tenancy is continued beyond its term date if by then the tenant has invoked the jurisdiction of the court by making an application to it. In my judgment, there is no room in section 25 for such a concept.
>
> It follows from this conclusion that in the present case the section 25(1) notice was of no effect for the purpose of terminating the tenancy and that accordingly it did not have the effect of terminating the tenancy within three months of the final disposal of the tenant's application to the court as required by section 64(1)(c). Accordingly, section 64(1)(c) was not satisfied, and there was not, and could not be, any interim continuation of the tenancy under the operative part of section 64(1)"[132] (at [37] and [38]).

2–61 A resumption of occupation by the tenant for business purposes will not revive the application, for once the continuity of occupation has been lost the tenant loses his right to pursue his application. Section 24(3)(a) of the Act, which provides that "where a tenancy to which this Part of this Act applies ceases to be such a tenancy, it shall not come to an end by reason only of a cesser" does not assist, because, first, the provisions of s.24(3)(a) apply only to a period of cessation of occupation after the expiry of the contractual term (*Esselte AB v Pearl Assurance Plc*)[133] (digested in para.2–53) and because secondly it was held in *I&H Caplan v Caplan (No.2)*[134] (digested in para.1–46) to apply only to the position prior to an application made by the tenant for a new tenancy. It is considered that the resumption of business occupation before the contractual term date in these circumstances cannot give the tenant what is in effect a second bite of the cherry. The thread of business continuity having been broken and the tenant's claim for renewal being struck out, the tenancy will, having regard to the provisions of s.64, have been terminated in accordance with the Act.

Effect of Act ceasing to apply during contractual term of periodic tenancy where no section 25 notice or section 26 request has been served

2–62 It is an essential characteristic of a periodic tenancy that it will continue until determined by an appropriate notice to quit whether or not the Act applies to that

---

tenancy ceases to be one to which Part I of the Act applies so that it terminates by effluxion of time: there is thus no tenancy upon which the Landlord's section 25 notice to determine can operate and the section 25 notice is immaterial and has no effect: the mechanism of section 64 (which would otherwise continue the tenancy where the tenant has applied to the court for a new tenancy) operates by deferring the effect of the section 25 notice: thus as the section 25 notice has no operation after cesser of occupation, section 64 does not continue the tenancy. This argument can be criticized on the basis that it assumes what it sets out to prove, namely that the continuation provisions in section 64 are sub-ordinate to the provisions contained in section 24. Nevertheless, the decision of the Court of Appeal in *Esselte* is clear . . . and . . . it must be applied."

The judge in fact found as a fact that the tenant had not ceased to occupy the premises at the term date and thus the tenancy continued pursuant to s.64.

[132] This reasoning would also apply to a landlord's termination application made after service of a s.25 notice followed by a cessation of business occupation by the tenant.

[133] [1997] 1 W.L.R. 891; [1997] 2 All E.R. 41 CA. See para.2–67 et seq. It is considered that this is equally true of the provisions of s.27(2). See para.3–116.

[134] [1963] 1 W.L.R. 1247; [1963] 2 All E.R. 930.

tenancy. However, a periodic tenancy to which the Act applies cannot be determined by an ordinary common law notice to quit given by the landlord. If the landlord desires to determine it he must instead serve a s.25 notice: *Commercial Properties v Wood*[135] (digested in para.3–178). As to the length of notice to be given for the purposes of s.25, see para.3–176 et seq. If the tenancy is not one to which the Act applies there is, of course, no reason why an ordinary common law notice to quit cannot be given. As with the position in relation to a fixed-term tenancy, where the landlord serves such a common law notice to quit at a time when the tenancy is not protected by the Act, the tenancy will come to an end on the date specified in the notice and resumption of business occupation by the tenant after the giving of the notice will not affect its validity: s.24(3)(b) (see para.2–66).

A periodic tenant who wishes to determine his tenancy can only do so by serving a common law notice to quit even if his periodic tenancy is one to which the Act applies. An exception to this rule is where the periodic tenancy is one to which the Act applies and is a tenancy from year to year arising after the expiration of a term certain, in which case he may determine the tenancy by serving a s.26 request and may thereafter, if he wishes, apply for a new tenancy under the Act: s.26(1). **2–63**

Effect of Act ceasing to apply during contractual term of periodic tenancy where a section 25 notice or section 26 request has been served but no application for a new tenancy/termination has been made

In order to terminate a periodic tenancy in accordance with the Act the landlord must serve a s.25 notice. The tenant can terminate a periodic tenancy by serving a common law notice to quit, but this will not be a mode of termination which entitles him to apply for a new tenancy. A s.26 request cannot be served by a periodic tenant unless the periodic tenancy is one from year to year and has arisen after the expiry of a fixed-term tenancy pursuant to the terms of that tenancy: s.26(1) of the Act and see para.3–210. If after the giving of the s.25 notice, but before the date of termination specified in it has been reached, the tenancy ceases to be one to which the Act applies by reason of the cesser of business occupation by the tenant, it is unclear whether the tenancy will expire on the date specified in the s.25 notice. If that date is the same date which could validly have been in a common law notice to quit, there seems no reason in principle why the s.25 notice should not take effect as a common law notice to quit: s.69(1). If, however, the date specified would not have been a date at which the tenancy could have been validly terminated by a common law notice to quit, a difficult question arises as to whether the cessation of business occupation renders the s.25 notice ineffective. The fact that this uncertainty exists may indicate that a prudent landlord should serve both a s.25 notice and a common law notice to quit making it clear that the latter will be relied upon only if the Act ceases to apply. **2–64**

135 [1968] 1 Q.B. 15 CA.

Alternatively, it should be possible to ensure that the date of termination specified in the s.25 notice would coincide with the appropriate common law date of termination.

Effect of cesser of business occupation in respect of a periodic tenancy where a section 25 notice or section 26 request has been served and an application for a new tenancy/termination has been made

2–65 Assume a tenancy from year to year. A s.25 notice may be given either to hit the common law date of termination or a later date: *Commercial Properties v Wood*[136] (digested in para.3–178). As a yearly tenancy at common law requires six months notice to quit[137] it is possible for the tenant to make an application for renewal before the expiry of the notice. If after making that application the tenant ceases to occupy the premises for business purposes the question which arises is whether the tenancy ends on the date at which the tenancy would otherwise come to an end at common law (assuming that the s.25 notice may operate as such or if the landlord has, in addition, served a notice to quit at common law at the same time as the s.25 notice: see para.2–62) or will continue in accordance with s.64 until three months after final disposal. The position is very similar to that considered in respect of fixed-term tenancies (para.2–58 et seq.). In the light of *Surrey CC v Single Horse Properties Ltd*[138] (digested in para.2–54) it would seem that, if the s.25 notice is equated to a notice to quit (or a common law notice has also been served as suggested in para.2–64) then, unless the tenant is in occupation for business purposes at the date of the expiry of the notice, the tenancy will end and will not be continued, irrespective of the fact that the tenant has made an application for renewal or the landlord has made a termination application.

Cessation of business user post contractual term date

Section 24(3)

2–66 Section 24(3) provides as follows:

- "Notwithstanding anything in subsection (1) of this section–
  - (a) where a tenancy to which this Part of this Act applies ceases to be such a tenancy, it shall not come to an end by reason only of the cesser, but if it was granted for a term of years certain and has been continued by subsection (1) of this section then (without prejudice to the termination thereof in accordance with any terms of the tenancy) it may be terminated by not less than three nor more than six months' notice in writing given by the landlord to the tenant;

---

[136] [1968] 1 Q.B. 15 CA.

[137] See *Woodfall: Law of Landlord and Tenant* (London: Sweet & Maxwell) Vol.1, para.17, paras 17–206 to 17–207.

[138] [2002] EWCA Civ 367; [2002] 1 W.L.R. 2016.

(b) where, at a time when a tenancy is not one to which this Part of this Act applies, the landlord gives notice to quit, the operation of the notice shall not be affected by reason that the tenancy becomes one to which this Part of this Act applies after the giving of the notice."

Applies only where cessation of business occupation occurs after expiry of contractual term

It would appear from the Court of Appeal decision in *Esselte AB v Pearl Assurance Plc* (digested in para.2–53) that s.24(3)(a) of the Act applies only where the cessation of business occupation has occurred after the tenancy has continued beyond the contractual term date pursuant to the provisions of s.24(1). In *Esselte AB v Pearl Assurance Plc*, Morritt L.J. said: **2–67**

> "In my view s.24(3) (a) is of particular significance for it assumes that a fixed term tenancy, to which the Act has ceased to apply, will come to an end unless continued by sub-s.(1). This could not have been the case if the formula 'a tenancy to which this Part of this Act applies' should be read as including a tenancy to which this Act has applied. Thus the cases in which the tenancy has been continued by sub-section (1) must be confined to those in which the Act ceased to apply after they had been so continued. In those cases the paragraph prescribes how the continuing tenancy may subsequently be determined."[139]

Further, s.24(3) applies only where no claim for a new tenancy has been made by the tenant: *I&H Caplan v Caplan (No.2)*[140] (digested in para.1–46). **2–68**

Where a lease has been disclaimed by reason of the tenant's insolvency, an opportunity may arise to terminate the continuation tenancy by service of a notice under s.24(3)(a). An interesting example of the application of s.24(3)(a) arose in *Re Blenheim Leisure (Restaurants) Ltd.*[141] Neuberger J. had to consider an application to restore Blenheim Leisure (Restaurants) Ltd ("BLR") to the Registrar of Companies.[142] Notices had been served on the Crown pursuant to s.24(3)(a)[143] of the 1954 Act terminating BLR's tenancies of nightclubs which were continuing under s.24 of the 1954 Act and which had previously been vested in BLR but which had become vested in the Crown by reason of the dissolution of BLR.[144] The Crown did not disclaim the lease. The Crown was not of course in occupation of the premises for business purposes. The landlord, unusually, joined **2–69**

---

[139] [1997] 1 W.L.R. 891 at [897].

[140] [1963] 1 W.L.R. 1247; [1963] 2 All E.R. 930.

[141] [2007] B.C.C. 821 Neuberger J. Where a company is dissolved the leasehold interest of the company vests in the Crown as *bona vacantia*: Companies Act 2006 s.1012.

[142] Pursuant to s.653(3) of the Companies Act 1985 (see now ss.1028 and 1032 of the Companies Act 2006). By s.653(3) it was provided that:

"On an office copy of [an order for restoration] being delivered to the registrar of companies for registration the company [to which the order relates] is deemed to have continued in existence as if its name had not been struck off; and the court may by the order give such directions and made such provisions as seem just for placing the company and all other persons in the same position (as nearly as may be) as if the company's name had not been struck off."

[143] Which enables a notice to be served by the landlord terminating the s.24 tenancy where the tenancy ceases to be one to which the Act applies by reason of non-occupation for business purposes. The section is set out in para.2–66.

[144] Where a company is dissolved the leasehold interest of the company vests in the Crown as *bona vacantia*: Companies Act 2006 s.1012.

in the application to resist the restoration. One of the arguments presented to Neuberger J. in opposing restoration was that if allowed the tenancies would be restored to BLR and the notices served on the Crown rendered nugatory. Neuberger J. put it in this way, citing argument of counsel on behalf of the landlords:

> "In this case, [it is said on behalf of the landlord] . . . that, because of the effect of the 1954 Act and the notices which were served on the Crown by the Respondents, there will be no tenancies of any of the clubs if BLR is not restored to the register, whereas there will be if they are . . ."

Neuberger J. did not dissent from this conclusion.[145] If, as appears to be the case, the restoration revests the tenancy in the tenant with effect from the date of striking off what is the position? If at the contractual term date the tenant was in occupation for business purposes there is no reason why the tenancy should not have continued pursuant to s.24 notwithstanding the subsequent non-occupation by the tenant by reason of the tenant's insolvency. It would seem, however, that the court pursuant to the provisions of the Companies Act may direct that any notices served under the 1954 Act are to treated as effective notwithstanding the restoration.[146]

Service of contractual break notice to terminate when tenancy is not one to which the Act applies

2–70 Often fixed-term tenancies of business premises contain contractual provisions enabling the landlord to break the term before its expiry. If a contractual break notice is served in accordance with the terms of the lease and at the date of service the tenant is not in occupation for the purposes of a business but subsequently resumes occupation before the break date, it is considered that the break notice will, nevertheless, take effect because s.24(3)(b) expressly provides that where a "notice to quit" is given by the landlord at a time when the Act does not apply to the tenancy it will take effect notwithstanding that the tenancy subsequently becomes one to which the Act applies. A "notice to quit" is defined in s.69 as meaning "a notice to terminate a tenancy (whether a periodical tenancy or a tenancy for a term of years certain) given in accordance with the provisions (whether express or implied) of that tenancy". Thus the contractual break notice is a "notice to quit" within s.24(3)(b). The object of s.24(3)(b) has been expressed in the following terms[147]:

> "I think the object of that sub-section is clear enough. It is not intended merely as a transitional provision to cover notices to quit that are served before the coming into force of the Act; it is intended as a permanent provision of the Act and its object is to deal with the situation in

---

[145] The effect of the restoration can be quite dramatic. Thus in *Allied Dunbar Assurance Plc v Fowle* [1994] B.C.C. 422 QBD, it was held that restoration of a company where the company's lease had been disclaimed by the Crown reinstated the liability of the sureties under the lease notwithstanding the fact that but for the restoration the disclaimer would have discharged their liability under the lease.

[146] See s.653(3) of the Companies Act 2005 (now ss.1028(3) and 1032(3) of the Companies Act 2006).

[147] Devlin J. in *Orman Brothers Ltd v Greenbaum* [1954] 3 All E.R. 731, approved by the Court of Appeal [1955] 1 All E.R. 610 CA.

> which there is a change of user between the serving of the notice and its taking effect, a change of user which might bring the tenancy within the Act. Thus, if instead of reading 'tenancy is not one to which this part of this Act applies' I call it, not precisely but no doubt for general purposes sufficiently accurately, a 'business tenancy', then the sub-section would read in this way: 'where, at a time when a tenancy is not a business tenancy, the landlord gives notice to quit, the operation of the notice shall not be affected by reason that the tenancy becomes a business tenancy after the giving of the notice'. That is a plain, simple and, no doubt, necessary provision."

Where the tenancy has ceased to be one to which the Act applies the tenant has a right to terminate the tenancy equivalent to that conferred on the landlord by s.24(3)(a). By s.27(2) it is provided that a tenancy, granted for a term of years certain, which is continuing by virtue of s.24[148] shall not come to an end by reason only of the tenant ceasing to occupy the property but may be brought to an end on any day by not less than three months' notice in writing given by the tenant to the immediate landlord.[149] **2–71**

Effect of cesser of business occupation after the contractual term date of a fixed term tenancy where no section 25 notice or section 26 request has been served

Where the tenant ceases to occupy the premises for the purposes or partly for the purposes of a business the tenancy will continue notwithstanding the cesser of business user: s.24(3) (a) of the Act.[150] The landlord can in those circumstances terminate the tenancy either if the terms of the lease enable him to serve a notice to quit (most unusual) or, alternatively, by serving a notice in writing pursuant to the provisions of s.24(3)(a) of the Act, which must be one of not less than three months nor more than six months. A resumption of occupation after the date of service of such a notice will not affect its validity. In *Teasdale v Walker*[151] (digested in para.1–83), Pearce L.J. said: **2–72**

> "It is, we think, clear that during the [tenant's] occupation a three or six months' notice [under s.24(3)(a)] could have been given, and the fact that the tenancy became one to which the Act applies (e.g., by subsequent resumption by the tenant of occupation for the purposes of a business carried on by her) would not have affected the operation of that notice (section 24(3) (b))."

It would be tempting simply to rely upon this statement as concluding the question, but it is necessary to examine Pearce L.J.'s dictum more critically because it appears to have been based upon the view that a notice given under s.24(3)(a) is a "notice to quit" within s.24(3)(b). However, "notice to quit" is defined in s.69 as meaning "a notice to terminate a tenancy (whether a periodical tenancy or a tenancy for a term of years certain) given in accordance with the provisions (whether express or implied) of that tenancy". A notice under s.24(3)(a) is not a notice to quit within that definition. Notwithstanding this criticism, it is considered that the landlord may serve a notice under s.24(3)(a)

---

148 It is to be noted that the right to terminate the tenancy arises only after the term date has expired, the tenancy having previously been continued under s.24, i.e. there was business occupancy at the term date.

149 s.27(2) is discussed in greater detail in para.3–109 et seq.

150 See para.2–66. See also s.27(2).

151 [1958] 1 W.L.R. 1076; [1958] 3 All E.R. 307 CA.

upon cesser of business occupation and that Pearce L.J.'s view that resumption of business occupation after service of a s.24(3)(a) notice will not prevent such a notice from taking effect can be supported otherwise than by treating the notice as a "notice to quit". Although s.24(3)(a) does not deal expressly with the question of resumption of occupation, it was unnecessary to do so in the context of a notice under subs.(3)(a) while it was necessary to do so in the context of a notice under subs.(3)(b). The latter is dealing with a notice which is one served pursuant to the terms of the relevant tenancy (e.g. a break clause or a notice to quit in respect of a periodic tenancy), and specific statutory provision was required to prevent other provisions of the Act from affecting the validity of a unilateral act of one of the parties under the terms of the contract. A notice under s.24(3)(a) is a mode of termination provided for by the Act and, therefore, no express reference to resumption of occupation was needed.

2–73 If there is a cesser of business occupation by the tenant but the landlord does not serve a notice under either s.24(3)(a) or (b), it appears from the decision in *Teasdale v Walker*[152] (digested in para.1–83) that the resumption of occupation for the purposes of a business will ensure that the tenancy once again becomes one to which the Act applies. Although the facts of *Teasdale v Walker* were held not to establish a resumption of occupation for business purposes, the Court of Appeal stated, albeit obiter, that if the facts had been different the tenancy would have again come within the Act. Pearce L.J. in giving the judgment of the court was of the view that if a s.25 notice has been given, a resumption of occupation by the tenant subsequently would have entitled the tenant to apply for a new tenancy in accordance with the terms of the Act, because s.25 contains no provision equivalent to s.24(3)(b).

2–74 A tenant may also terminate the tenancy which is continuing under the Act notwithstanding the cessation of business occupation by serving on his immediate landlord a notice of not less than three months: s.27(2). If a notice is served under s.27(2), and the rent is payable in advance, the tenant is entitled to an apportionment of the rent and any rent paid by the tenant in excess of the amount apportioned to the period before termination is recoverable by him: s.27(3).[153] This apportionment provision does not apply to a notice served by a landlord under s.24(3)(a).

Effect of cesser of business occupation after the contractual term date of a fixed term tenancy where a section 25 notice or section 26 request has been given but no application for a new tenancy has been made

2–75 The position we are considering here is one where the tenancy has been continued under s.24, a s.25 notice or s.26 request has been served but the date of termination specified in the relevant notice or request has not yet expired and there is a cesser of business occupation by the tenant. In these circumstances the tenancy will be continued pursuant to s.24(3)(a)[154] and it is considered that the

---

152 [1958] 1 W.L.R. 1076; [1958] 3 All E.R. 307 CA.

153 See further, para.3–117.

154 As to which, see para.2–66.

tenancy will come to an end on the date specified in the relevant notice or request which was valid at the time it was served. The landlord may, it is considered, bring forward the date of termination by service of a notice under s.24(3)(a) of the Act. It is considered that resumption of business occupation by the tenant will not affect the validity of the notice served pursuant to that subsection.[155] Equally a tenant may, if the facts warrant it, serve a notice pursuant to s.27(2) to bring the tenancy to an end earlier than that specified in the landlord's s.25 notice.[156] No s.27(2) notice can, however, be served where the tenant has served a s.26 request: s.26(4).

Effect of cesser of business occupation after the term date of a fixed term tenancy where a section 25 notice or section 26 request has been given and an application for a new tenancy has been made

The position is not identical to that where the tenant's application for renewal has been made before the term date.[157] The reason for this is that as the cesser of business user occurs after the continuation under s.24 no question arises as to whether the tenancy may end on a date other than that provided for by the s.25 notice as extended by s.64. In these circumstances the tenancy will continue pursuant to the provisions of s.64[158] and the tenancy will end in accordance with s.64 upon the application being finally disposed of. **2–76**

Effect of cesser of business occupation in respect of periodic tenancy after the expiry of a common law notice to quit where no section 25 notice or section 26 request has been served

The position considered here is most unusual and unlikely to arise in practice.[159] The landlord, rather than serving a straightforward s.25 notice, serves a common law notice to quit thus determining the contract but giving rise to continuation of the tenancy under s.24. In practice most landlords would simply serve a s.25 notice. If during the continuation of the tenancy under s.24 there is a cesser of business occupation, the question arises as to whether s.24(3)(a) assists the tenant. This, as has been previously noted, provides that "where a tenancy to which this Act applies ceases to be such a tenancy, it shall not come to an end by reason only of the cesser . . . " It has been suggested that in these circumstances cesser of business occupation will result in the tenancy coming to an end immediately. The authors respectfully disagree with this view. As has already been noted, it is clearly stated in s.24(3) that all tenancies to which the Act applies **2–77**

---

155 See para.2–72.

156 See further, para.3–113. But not, it is considered, for a date later than that specified in the landlord's s.25 notice.

157 Considered in para.2–59 et seq.

158 The tenancy will not end by reason only of the cesser: s.24(3)(a) and s.27(2). Note, however, the provision for service of the notice referred to in s.24(3)(a) will not apply: see para.2–68.

159 The authors have encountered this position once in practice. An analogous position arises where the landlord serves a break notice upon the tenant under a fixed-term tenancy without at the same time serving a statutory notice of termination. The break notice is effective to terminate the term but the tenancy continues thereafter pursuant to s.24: *Weinbergs Weatherproofs v Radcliffe Paper Mill Co* [1958] Ch. 437.

shall not come to an end only by reason of the cesser of business occupation. This is reiterated in s.27(2) as amended by the 2003 Order. However, this potentially raises a conundrum: if the tenancy does not cease, how is it to be brought to an end? It is only in respect of fixed-term tenancies that a s.24(3)(a) notice (served by the landlord) or s.27(2) notice (served by the tenant) can be served. However, as it is of the essence of a periodic tenancy that either the landlord or the tenant can determine the same by notice to quit,[160] there is no reason why the landlord or tenant cannot simply bring the tenancy to an end by service of a notice to quit in the ordinary way.[161] Section 24(2) expressly preserves the common law mode of termination by notice to quit, and it is suggested that, in the circumstances envisaged, such a right should apply to the tenancy once it has ceased to be a tenancy to which the Act applies.[162]

Effect of cesser of business occupation in respect of a periodic tenancy after the expiry of a common law notice to quit where a section 25 notice or section 26 request has been served but no application for a new tenancy has been made

2–78 As with the position considered in para.2–72, the circumstances in which this problem will arise will be rather unusual. If the tenant has remained in occupation after the expiry of a common law notice to quit served by the landlord, the tenancy will be continuing pursuant to s.24. If thereafter the landlord were to serve a notice pursuant to s.25 and the tenant were to vacate prior to the date of termination specified within it, the tenancy will not end until the specified date. The reason for this is that whilst the tenancy is continuing under s.24 the cessation of business occupation has no impact upon the continuation of the tenancy: s.24(3).[163]

Effect of cesser of business occupation in respect of a periodic tenancy after the expiry of a section 25 notice or section 26 request where an application for a new tenancy has been made

2–79 Assume a tenancy from year to year. The landlord serves a s.25 notice on the tenant. The tenant makes an application for a new tenancy. After the expiry of the termination date specified in the s.25 notice the tenant vacates. It is considered that in these circumstances the tenancy will expire in accordance with s.64. There

---

160 *Prudential Assurance Co Ltd v London Residuary Body* [1992] 2 A.C. 386 HL.

161 However, the problem with this argument is that the landlord has already served a notice to quit to terminate the contractual term and the continuation tenancy is not a continuation of a tenancy from, e.g. year to year but of a tenancy which was previously one from year to year. The tenancy is continuing under s.24 but not as a periodic tenancy.

162 Unless one were to recognise the entitlement for the landlord to serve what in effect amounts to a further notice to quit there may be no basis upon which the landlord can bring the tenancy to an end. He cannot serve a s.25 notice for the tenancy is not one to which the Act applies. Thus, unless a ground for forfeiture exists (assuming the tenancy is one which contains such a right of re-entry) the landlord may be in some difficulty.

163 The provision for service of a notice of three months provided for by s.24(3)(a) applies only where the tenancy was one which was granted for a term of years certain.

is no alternative argument available to the tenant that the tenancy should be treated as having ended on the s.25 notice date as the cessation of business occupation occurred after that date.

CHAPTER 3

THE TERMINATION OF TENANCIES

1. COMMON LAW MODES OF TERMINATION PRESERVED BY SECTION 24(2)

General

Even where the tenancy is one to which the Act applies, so that the ordinary common law rules on expiry by effluxion of time and termination by notice to quit given by the landlord are not to take effect, s.24(2) preserves certain of the common law modes of termination. **3–01**

Notice to quit given by tenant

The tenancy can be brought to an end by a notice to quit given by the tenant. "Notice to quit" is defined in s.69(1) to mean a notice to terminate a tenancy (whether a periodic tenancy or a tenancy for a term of years certain) given in accordance with the provisions (whether express or implied) of that tenancy. Clearly this includes both a notice to quit properly so called and a notice given pursuant to a tenant's option to break.[1] If the tenancy contains no express or implied provisions for its determination by notice, the tenancy will not come to an end by the tenant informing the landlord that he intends to vacate the premises, even if the landlord agrees to this. This would be an agreement to surrender and thus rendered void by s.38(1).[2] **3–02**

To prevent the evasion of the protection of the Act by landlords requiring tenants to give notice to quit before the term is entered into, it is expressly provided by s.24(2)(a) that a notice to quit given by a tenant within one month of his entering into occupation in right of the tenancy will not bring it to an end.[3] **3–03**

Where the landlord has served a s.25 notice or the tenant has served a s.26 request, it is probably the case that the tenant can seek, where the tenancy makes **3–04**

---

[1] The question whether the tenant who has the benefit of a contractual break clause can, in addition, take advantage of the protection of the Act by making a s.26 request for a new tenancy as from the break date (or later) is considered in para.3–217.

[2] See para.3–07 et seq.

[3] The period of the tenant's "occupation in right of the tenancy" is calculated from the date of grant as opposed to its expressed commencement date. A term is only vested from the date of grant notwithstanding that the date of commencement pre-dates the grant: *Bradshaw v Pawley* [1980] 1 W.L.R. 10; [1979] 3 All E.R. 273.

express provision for earlier determination by notice, to bring the tenancy to an end at the earlier date provided for by the terms of the contract by serving a notice to quit.[4]

Surrender

3–05 The tenancy can be brought to an end by surrender. This means an actual surrender, which can be by deed[5] or by operation of law, e.g. where the tenant vacates the premises and the landlord accepts the keys. The case of *HL Bolton Engineering Co Ltd v TJ Graham & Sons Ltd*,[6] provides an example of a surrender by operation of law. It is to be distinguished from an agreement to surrender, which is rendered void by s.38(1) unless it has, prior to the coming into force of the amendments brought about by the 2003 Order,[7] been authorised by the court pursuant to s.38(4),[8] or post the coming into force of the amendments, by agreement of the parties.[9] All agreements to surrender, whether expressed to take effect forthwith[10] or upon a future date, are rendered void.

3–06 Prior to June 1, 2004[11] even an actual surrender by deed would not take effect where the instrument of surrender "was executed before, or was executed in pursuance of, an agreement made before the tenant had been in occupation in right of the tenancy for one month": s.24(2)(b).[12] The object of this provision was to prevent the tenant contracting out of his rights before the beginning of his tenancy, either by executing an instrument of surrender or by agreeing to execute such an instrument. However, as with effect from June 1, 2004 all agreements to surrender a tenancy to which the Act applies are valid provided the parties have complied with certain procedural requirements before the agreement is entered into. The provisions of s.24(2)(b) have been repealed.

---

[4] See the decision in *Long Acre Securities v Electro Acoustic Industries Ltd* [1990] 1 E.G.L.R. 91 (digested in para.2–52). Although this decision was overruled (on the question of whether or not business occupation was required at the contractual term date in order for a continuation tenancy to arise) in the later decision of the Court of Appeal in *Esselte AB v Pearl Assurance Plc* [1997] 1 W.L.R. 891; [1992] 2 All E.R. 41 CA (digested at para.2–53), it highlights the fact that where there are several modes of termination (albeit in that case *statutory* modes of termination) there is no reason why, where one has been implemented, another may be used to bring about an earlier determination of the tenancy.

[5] Law of Property Act 1925 s.52.

[6] [1957] 1 Q.B. 159 CA (this case is digested in para.7–169 on the meaning of "intention" in s.30(1) and in para.7–279 on the meaning of "purchase" within s.30(2)).

[7] Being June 1, 2004.

[8] See para.3–20.

[9] See para.3–21 et seq.

[10] See para.3–07 and *Tarjomani v Panther Securities Ltd* (1983) 46 P. & C.R. 32 (digested in para.3–10). It appears from that decision that such an agreement was, with respect to such agreements entered into prior to June 1, 2004, void whenever entered into, but any surrender executed pursuant thereto would be effective unless the agreement was entered into before expiry of the one-month period having regard to the provisions of s.24(2)(b) (repealed with effect from June 1, 2004 by the 2003 Order). The period of the tenant's "occupation in right of the tenancy" was calculated from the date of the grant of the tenancy as opposed to its expressed commencement date: see fn.3 above.

[11] The coming into force of the provisions of the 2003 Order.

[12] Now repealed.

Agreement to surrender

Agreement to surrender void

The effect of s.38(1) is to render void[13] any agreement which relates to a tenancy[14] within the Act which "purports to preclude the tenant from making an application or request under" the Act. The words "purports to" have been construed as being equivalent to "has the effect of": *Joseph v Joseph*[15] (digested in para.3–08); *Allnatt London Properties Ltd v Newton*[16] (digested in para.3–09). Accordingly, any agreement which would have the effect of putting an end to the tenancy (and thus preventing the tenant from making an application or a request) is rendered void by s.38(1), as well as agreements which by their terms expressly forbid the making of a request or an application. However, there must be an agreement. Thus, a provision in a lease requiring the tenant to first offer to surrender[17] his tenancy in order to be able to assign or underlet is not struck down, as the agreement to surrender arises only if the offer made by the tenant is accepted.[18] The section renders void not only an agreement for a surrender in the future but also an agreement for an immediate surrender: *Tarjomani v Panther* **3–07**

[13] See the suggestion in *Woodfall: Law of Landlord and Tenant* (London: Sweet & Maxwell), Vol.2, para.22–038, fn.1, that "void" may mean "voidable" at the option of the tenant, citing *R. v Hipswell* (1828) 8 B. & C. 466 and *Davis v Bryan* (1827) 6 B. & C. 651.

[14] It is to be noted that the agreement to surrender is still struck down even if it relates to those parts not occupied by the tenant. The section strikes down any agreement which "relates to a tenancy to which the Act applies". The Act applies where only part of the premises are occupied for business purposes: s.23(1).

[15] [1967] Ch. 78 CA.

[16] [1981] 2 All E.R. 290; [1983] 1 E.G.L.R. 73.

[17] The first attack on offer back clauses was to argue that they sought to pre-determine the grounds upon which it could be said that the landlord could reasonably refuse consent and that this was contrary to the then provisions of s.19 of the Landlord and Tenant Act 1927. However, the validity of offer back clauses as imposing a condition precedent to the right to assign arising, and thus free of any restriction as to reasonableness, was established in the early authority of *Adler v Upper Grosvenor Street Investments Ltd* [1957] 1 All E.R. 229 and subsequently by the Court of Appeal in *Bocardo SA v S&M Hotels Ltd* [1980] 1 W.L.R. 17 CA. Notwithstanding the amendments to the 1927 Act by the Landlord and Tenant Act 1988, it is still the case that the imposition of a condition precedent to the right to assign arising does not trigger the statutory duty imposed by the Landlord and Tenant Act 1988: *Crestfort Ltd v Tesco Stores Ltd* [2005] EWHC 805 (Ch); [2005] 3 E.G.L.R. 25.

[18] *Allnatt London Properties Ltd v Newton* [1981] 2 All E.R. 290 (first instance); [1983] 1 E.G.L.R. 73. In that case both courts held (and the Court of Appeal so held without going into the consequences) that the agreement reached by the landlord in accepting the tenant's offer to surrender was rendered void by s.38 of the 1954 Act. Megarry V.C. opined that in those circumstances the landlord could not insist on taking the property back, because there was no binding agreement to surrender. On the other hand, there was nothing that the tenant could do, because his right to assign, albeit with the landlord's consent, only arose if the landlord did not accept the offer to surrender, but he had, however, accepted it. The decision in *Allnatt London Properties Ltd v Newton* was considered by the Court of Appeal in *Tiffany Investments Ltd v Bircham & Co Nominees (No.2) Ltd* [2003] EWCA Civ 1759; [2004] 2 E.G.L.R. 31. In that case, which was concerned with residential premises under Pt I of the 1954 Act, the lease conferred a right of pre-emption on the lessor if the lessee should wish to dispose of the lease. By the provisions of s.17 of the 1954 Act it is provided that the provisions "of this Part of this Act shall have effect notwithstanding any agreement to the contrary". The Court of Appeal held that the clause was not rendered void by s.17 and, following *Allnatt v Newton*, held that although an agreement might be avoided by s.17, the obligation to make the offer was not.

Securities Ltd[19] (digested in para.3–10). It is considered that as an agreement which falls within s.38(1) is void, the agreement is not revived by the tenancy ceasing to be one to which the Act applies. Thus, an agreement providing for a surrender if the tenant shall cease business occupation cannot be enforced if at some time prior to the satisfaction of the condition triggering the requirement to surrender the tenancy was once one to which the Act applied.[20] It has been held that an agreement to surrender is struck down with respect to a tenancy to which the Act applies even if the agreement affects only those parts of the demised premises which are not occupied by the tenant for business purposes: *Ultimate Leisure Ltd v Tindle*.[21]

3–08 ***Joseph v Joseph***[22] As part of an agreement relating to the dissolution of a partnership, it was agreed that the tenants of business premises would surrender the residue of their lease to the landlord on a future date. When they failed to do so, the landlord sought an order for possession and damages. The Court of Appeal held that such an agreement was one which "purports to preclude" the tenant from making an application for a new tenancy at some future date within the meaning of s.38(1) and was accordingly rendered void by that subsection.

3–09 ***Allnatt London Properties Ltd v Newton***[23] The tenant had a lease of business premises for a term of 21 years. The alienation clause in the lease provided as follows:

> "Not (subject to the proviso to this clause) to assign underlet part with the possession or occupation of the demised premises as a whole provided always that if at any time and so often as the tenant shall desire to assign or underlet the demised premises as a whole the tenant shall make to the landlords an offer in writing . . . to surrender the lease with vacant possession and otherwise free from encumbrances on a date three months from the date of the said written offer in consideration of the payment by the landlords to the tenant of a sum representing the net premium value (if any) of this lease for the unexpired residue of the term . . . such value to be agreed or determined as provided in this clause."

It was provided further that if the landlords should refuse such offer or should not accept the same within 21 days the tenants should be at liberty to apply for consent in writing to assign or underlet the demised premises as a whole and that such consent should not be unreasonably withheld. The tenant desired to assign and asked the landlord to consent. The landlord refused, and required the tenant to offer a surrender. This he duly did and the landlord accepted the offer. The tenant wanted £45,000 for the surrender, but the landlord was willing to pay only £10,000. The tenant withdrew the offer. The landlord claimed a declaration that

[19] (1983) 46 P. & C.R. 32.

[20] Although it may be said in respect of the example given in the text, that the agreement is conditional and thus only specifically enforceable upon satisfaction of the condition and that, as the condition once satisfied brings the tenancy outside the Act, the agreement to surrender is not struck down by s.38. However, s.38 does not refer to "specifically enforceable" agreements; it applies to agreements to surrender and this would appear to include agreements which are conditional.

[21] Unreported November 29, 2006 Patten J. This was not an issue raised on appeal: [2007] EWCA Civ 1241; [2007] All E.R. (D) 399.

[22] [1966] 3 W.L.R. 631; [1966] 3 All E.R. 486 CA.

[23] [1981] 2 All E.R. 290; [1983] 1 E.G.L.R. 73.

the agreement was enforceable, specific performance of the agreement, and damages. The tenant counterclaimed a declaration that, so long as his tenancy was protected by the 1954 Act, he was at liberty to assign or sub-let the whole of the premises with the landlord's consent (such consent not to be unreasonably withheld) without first offering any surrender.

It was held (by Sir Robert Megarry V.C. and the Court of Appeal) that the court was bound by the decision in *Joseph v Joseph* that the words in s.38(1) "which purports to" mean "which has the effect of". The agreement to surrender would have the effect of precluding the tenant from making an application or request for a new tenancy and was thus rendered void. However, it was held (by Sir Robert Megarry V.C., the point not being pursued on appeal) that s.38(1) did not invalidate any part of the clause in the lease, which stood at one remove from any subsequent agreement to surrender which was itself struck down by s.38(1); thus the tenant remained bound by the absolute prohibition on assignment.

Tarjomani v Panther Securities Ltd[24] The tenant of business premises, being in arrears with his rent, agreed with the landlord by letter to surrender his lease in consideration for being released from all outstanding rent and other arrears. The tenant signed the agreement and was permitted 28 days to leave. The tenant remained in possession and continued trading. When the landlord sought possession the tenant contended that the agreement to surrender was unenforceable. It was accepted that the letter did not constitute an effective express surrender, because it was not by deed as required by s.52(1) of the Law of Property 1925. It was contended, however, that it operated in equity as an immediate surrender and accordingly that s.38(1) had no application. It was held that an ineffective surrender of the legal estate cannot take effect in equity as an immediate effective surrender under the principle of *Walsh v Lonsdale*.[25] In any event, that principle depended upon the existence of a specifically enforceable contract but there was no specifically enforceable contract as s.38(1) applied to agreements for an immediate surrender as well as an agreement to surrender in the future. Accordingly the agreement fell foul of s.38(1). **3–10**

Grant or agreement to grant new lease

Is the grant of or an agreement to grant a new lease to the tenant caught by s.38(1)? The answer one would have thought would have been obvious. However, in *Gibbs Mew Plc v Gemmell*[26] it was sought to be argued that the grant to a protected business tenant of a tenancy at will, the effect of which gave rise to a surrender by operation of law of the tenant's existing lease thereby putting an end to the tenant's protection, was void. It was argued that the tenancy at will was an agreement relating to the prior tenancy (in that its effect was to bring about a surrender of that tenancy) and thus the grant had the effect of precluding the tenant from making an application under the 1954 Act in respect of that business tenancy. The Court of Appeal held that in fact the tenant was estopped from **3–11**

---

[24] (1983) 46 P. & C.R. 32.
[25] (1882) L.R. 21 Ch. D. 9.
[26] [1999] 1 E.G.L.R. 43 CA.

denying that there had been a surrender of the earlier tenancy. Therefore, s.38 had no application. However, it was said that even if s.38 could apply in these circumstances, s.38(1) did not prevent an actual surrender by operation of law.

3–12 Even where an agreement to grant a new lease is not one pursuant to which the landlord is to acquire the tenant's lease, because the landlord is proposing to grant a new interest to the tenant, the agreement will have the effect upon its completion, by operation of law, of terminating the tenant's existing interest. The view that an agreement to grant a lease has the effect of an agreement to surrender the tenant's existing lease appears to be supported by the provisions of s.28 of the Act.[27] This section provides that an agreement for the grant to the tenant of a future tenancy of the holding, or of the holding with other land, on terms and from a date specified in the agreement, has the effect that the current tenancy continues until that date but no longer and shall not be a tenancy to which the Act applies. This overcomes any potential difficulty with s.38(1) in relation to the enforcement of the agreement to grant the new lease.

Any agreement

3–13 The section refers to "any agreement relating to a tenancy to which the Part of this Act applies . . ." In the context of the virtually identical provisions of s.23(1) of the Leasehold Reform Act 1967 it has been held that an agreement relates to the tenancy even though the tenant is not a party to it and the agreement is made between the landlord and a third party: *Rennie v Proma Ltd.*[28] Similarly, in *Ralwood v Adams*[29] a tripartite agreement between landlord, tenant and the local authority pursuant to which the tenant was required to cease business user was held to be caught by s.38(1). In *Ultimate Leisure v Tindle*[30] the court was quite prepared to conclude that an agreement by L's tenant (T) with a prospective purchaser (P) to surrender part of the premises demised was caught, albeit on one reading of the obligations under the purchase agreement the obligation by T to surrender was made only with P.

3–14 A lease which is to be excluded from the security of tenure provisions of ss.24 to 28 of the 1954 Act pursuant to s.38A(1) is nevertheless a tenancy "which will be a tenancy to which this Part of this Act applies"[31] for a tenancy is one to which the Act applies if it satisfies the terms of s.23(1) of the Act. Thus, is it necessary in respect of a tenancy which is to be granted containing an agreement to surrender but which will exclude the security of tenure provisions of ss.24–28 for the parties also to comply with the notice requirements of s.38A(2) and (4)? The notice requirements cannot, in respect of an agreement to surrender, be completed prior to the grant of a tenancy, and thus an agreement to surrender contained within a lease which has already been executed may be said to be void, for the agreement, which will be contractually binding as soon as the lease has been

---

[27] Section 28 is considered at para.15–14 et seq.

[28] [1990] 1 E.G.L.R. 119 CA (conveyance of freehold to tenant subject to third party's consent, held that third party's consent was caught by s.23(1) of the 1967 Act).

[29] Unreported August 1998, HC, H.H. Judge Green QC, sitting as a deputy judge of the High Court.

[30] [2007] EWCA Civ 1241; [2007] All E.R. (D) 399.

[31] See para.2–31.

executed, is one which does not comply with ss.38A(2) and (4). However, it is considered that an excluded lease may contain an agreement to surrender without the parties having to concern themselves with s.38(2) and (4). A lease takes effect from its grant and not e.g. from the date of commencement specified for the term (*Roberts v Church Commissioners for England*[32]). Logically, at the very moment of execution, the agreement to surrender as between the persons who are landlord and tenant (and which would otherwise have to have complied with s.38(4)) is not one which "purports to preclude the tenant from making an application" etc. within s.38(1), for the parties have already by the agreement excluded the security of tenure provisions of the Act from the tenancy. The tenancy, when granted, is not one in respect of which any application for renewal or request for renewal could be made.

Section 38(1) may have unforeseen consequences in relation to the grant of *temporary* permissions to undertake business use. In *Frankel & Nelson v Biniski Mizgalski*[33] it was held that a contractual provision which entitled the landlord to require the tenant to cease business use of the premises was void under s.38(1). The tenant of residential premises sought and obtained permission from the landlord to use part of the premises as medical consulting rooms. The licence granted by the landlord was terminable upon 25 weeks' notice. The landlord's attempt to require the tenant to cease carrying on business use failed. The effect of this decision would appear to be that a landlord can never grant the tenant a terminable consent to use property for business purposes. **3–15**

Of particular interest arising out of *Frankel & Nelson v Biniski Mizgalski*is the fact that s.38(1) was held equally to apply to covenants contained within the headlease to use the premises only for residential purposes. The mesne landlord was himself a tenant under the terms of a headlease which required premises to be used for residential purposes only. The head landlord had granted licence to the mesne landlord to permit the tenant to use part of the premises as medical consulting rooms. The licence granted by the head landlord was similarly terminable by notice. The head landlord determinated the licence as between the parties to the headlease. Section 38(1) was inapplicable as between the head and mesne landlords, for the mesne landlord was not in occupation for the purposes of a business under the terms of the headlease. The argument was put that, accordingly, the tenant was caught by the restrictive covenants contained in the headlease which prohibited use as medical consulting rooms. This argument was rejected on the basis that the restrictive covenants under the headlease were themselves agreements "relating to the tenancy" and were void under s.38(1). **3–16**

Other arrangements

The policy behind s.38(1) might also lead the courts to hold void other arrangements which have the practical effect of removing the tenant's security of **3–17**

---

32 [1972] 1 Q.B. 278 CA.

33 Unreported December 1998, HC.

tenure, such as an agreement between the landlord and the tenant for the landlord to take an assignment of the business tenancy one month before the expiry of the term.

3–18 A common situation which arises in practice concerns the entry into an agreement between the landlord and the tenant for the grant of premises in a new development to be undertaken by the landlord, with the delivery up of the tenant's current premises upon completion of the newly developed premises. How does the landlord ensure that the tenant vacates the old premises and how does the tenant ensure that the landlord accepts delivery up of the old premises? An agreement for the tenant to surrender the old premises upon notice being given by the landlord of the new premises being available will not be good enough, for such an agreement will be an agreement to surrender and caught by s.38(1). If the parties are, for whatever reason, unable to comply with the procedure provided for by s.38A(4) (e.g. because of the need to enter into the agreement immediately), one possible way of overcoming the difficulties encountered by s.38(1) would be to provide that the agreement for lease to be conditional upon the tenant having surrendered the lease of the old premises. The conditional agreement for lease then only becomes enforceable upon the condition being fulfilled which, *ex hypothesi*, arises only upon the surrender of the lease of the old premises.[34]

3–19 Another common problem encountered in practice arises where a potential purchaser of the landlord's reversionary interest wishes to enter into an agreement with the tenant, e.g. to grant the tenant a new tenancy upon acquisition of the reversionary interest. It would seem clear that no binding agreement can be entered into by the prospective purchaser with the tenant, for any such agreement does not fall within the provisions of s.38A(2), for that section sanctions agreements to surrender only as between "the persons who are the landlord and the tenant in relation to a tenancy to which this Part of this Act applies".[35]

Agreement to surrender: parties' agreement

3–20 **Pre-June 1, 2004** By virtue of s.38(4)(b), which was introduced by the Law of Property Act 1969, the landlord and the tenant in relation to a tenancy to which the Act applies were able to make joint application to the court to authorise them to enter into an agreement which would otherwise be struck down by s.38(1). If the court granted that application and an agreement was subsequently entered into in the form of such instrument as specified by the court, the agreement to surrender was enforceable according to its terms. These provisions have been repealed with effect from June 1, 2004.

---

[34] Although see fn.20 above.

[35] This was equally the position under s.38(4) (now repealed). The sanction of the court to an agreement to surrender was possible only in relation to parties who were the landlord and tenant as at the date of the application and court order: s.38(4)(b).

Post June 1, 2004 By the 2003 Order (art.22) a new s.38A is inserted into the 1954 Act. The court's jurisdiction to make an order has been repealed.[36] By s.38A(2) the persons who are[37] the landlord and the tenant in relation to a tenancy to which Pt II applies may now agree that the tenancy[38] will be surrendered on such date or in such circumstances as may be specified and on such terms (if any) as may be so specified. Such an agreement is valid provided the conditions set out below are satisfied without the parties having to first obtain the court's sanction. 3–21

Surrender as to part

It might be argued that the reference in s.38(1) to the agreement being one for "the surrender of the tenancy" leads to the conclusion that an agreement relating to a surrender of part only of the demised premises is excluded from the prohibition. This could be said to be consistent with s.38A(4), which renders void only those agreements falling within s.38A(2), which enables the parties to agree to "the tenancy" being surrendered. The alternative and better argument is that the general prohibition in s.38(1) also prohibits an agreement to surrender part, because an agreement to surrender part certainly has the effect of precluding the tenant from making an application or serving a request with respect to the tenancy as a whole: see para.3–07. If this is correct, then it would seem logical to construe s.38A(2) to permit an agreement to surrender part, where the provisions of s.38(4) have been complied with. 3–22

Procedural requirements to validate agreements to surrender

Any agreement between the landlord and the tenant shall be void unless: 3–23

(1) the landlord has served on the tenant a notice in the form,[39] or substantially in the form, set out in Sch.3 to the 2003 Order (s.38A(4)(a)); and
(2) the requirements specified in Sch.4 to the 2003 Order are met (s.38A(4)(b)).

[36] By art.21(2) of the 2003 Order. The transitional provisions in art.29(4) of the 2003 Order do not apply here. Those provisions provide that if a person has, before the coming into force of the 2003 Order, entered into an agreement to take a tenancy, any provision in that agreement which requires an order under s.38(4) of the Act to be obtained in respect of the tenancy continues to be effective notwithstanding the repeal of s.38(4) and the court retains jurisdiction to make such an order. This wording does not cover an agreement to surrender.

[37] The amendments retain the old wording. Thus, the agreement to surrender can only be entered into between parties who are landlord and tenant. No agreement providing for a surrender can be entered into between parties who will be landlord and tenant with respect to a tenancy agreement they are about to enter into.

[38] See para.3–22 as to whether an agreement to surrender part only of the premises demised is caught by s.38.

[39] See Appendix, para.A2.054. The form of notice provides only for the name and address of the tenant and the name and address of the landlord. The notice is headed "Form of Notice that an Agreement to Surrender a Business Tenancy is to be made". However, there is no space for describing the property which is to be the subject of the agreement nor the terms of the agreement. The notice provides in the notes a warning to the tenant as to the consequences of entering into the surrender agreement and encourages the tenant to seek professional advice.

3–24 The requirements for a valid agreement without sanction of the court mirror those contained within Sch.2 to the 2003 Order for agreements excluding ss.24 to 28. Accordingly:

(1) the landlord must serve on the tenant a notice in the form[40] or substantially in the form, contained within Sch.3 not less than 14 days before the tenant enters into the agreement under s.38A(2) of the Act, or (if earlier) becomes contractually bound[41] to do so[42];
(2) the tenant[43] must make a declaration before entering into the agreement or (if earlier) before he becomes contractually bound to do so in the form,[44] or substantially in the form, set out in para.6 to Sch.4 to the 2003 Order.[45]

If the landlord has not served a 14-day notice, nevertheless, the agreement will still be valid if:

(a) the notice is actually served upon the tenant before he enters into the agreement to surrender or (if earlier) becomes contractually bound to do so;
(b) the tenant makes a statutory declaration in the form, or substantially in the form,[46] set out in para.7 to Sch.4 to the 2003 Order.

---

[40] See Appendix, para.A2.054. The form of notice provides only for the name and address of the tenant and the name and address of the landlord. The notice is headed "Form of Notice that an Agreement to Surrender a Business Tenancy is to be made". However, there is no space for describing the property which is to be the subject of the agreement nor the terms of the agreement. The notice provides in the notes a warning to the tenant as to the consequences of entering into the surrender agreement and encourages the tenant to seek professional advice.

[41] See paras 2 and 3 of Sch.4 to the 2003 Order: Appendix, para.A2.055.

[42] So long as a notice is served in accordance with Sch.3 (or a form substantially to like effect) it would seem to matter not that the terms of the surrender agreement are subsequently varied after notice is served: see the corresponding provisions relating to exclusion agreements at para.2–25 et seq. The form of notice is such that the terms of the agreement do not need to be recited in the notice. In fact no space is provided in the form of notice for the terms of the agreement to be recited: see fn.39 above. As the form of notice is simply to provide the tenant with a warning as to the consequences of entering into a surrender agreement and to advise the tenant to seek professional advice, the agreement can, it is suggested, go through a myriad of changes without requiring the landlord to serve a fresh Sch.3 notice.

[43] The form of declaration contained within para.6 of Sch.4 makes provision for the declaration to be signed by a duly authorised agent. The form of authority does not have to be appended to the declaration nor is provision made for the authority to be disclosed to the landlord. Of course as the landlord is the person most concerned to ensure that the agreement to surrender is valid it is appropriate for a landlord, where the declaration has been signed by someone other than the tenant, to insist that a copy of the letter of authority be disclosed when the declaration is given to him.

[44] See Appendix, para.A2.056. It has been held with respect to the corresponding provisions dealing with the entry into agreements excluding ss.24–28, that the signing of a statutory declaration rather than a simple form of declaration, which was all that was necessary in the circumstances of the case, did not invalidate the exclusion agreement: *Patel v Chiltern Railway Co Ltd* [2008] E.G.L.R. 33 CA. See paras 2–16 and 2–17.

[45] The form of declaration provides space for the names and addresses of the parties and the address of the premises. The form contains a reproduction in blank of the Sch.3 prescribed form. Thus, the declaration does not require the actual notice to be appended to the declaration nor for the Sch.3 notice which is reproduce to be filled in.

[46] See para.A2.057.

Upon entering into the agreement after compliance with the notice/declaration requirement, it should be noted that it is provided that a reference to the notice and declaration or statutory declaration (as the case may be), must be contained in or endorsed on the instrument creating the agreement under s.38A(2).[47] **3–25**

Meaning of "contractually bound to do so"

The words "or (if earlier) becomes contractually bound to do so" are a little odd in the context of an agreement to surrender. This wording mirrors that used in the context of agreements excluding security of tenure under ss.24 to 28.[48] In that context one can well understand the requirement for those words, for often parties enter into agreements for lease rather than proceeding directly to grant. However, in the context of agreements to surrender it is very unlikely that the parties will actually enter into an agreement which provides for the parties to enter into *an agreement* to surrender. A scenario which is possibly contemplated by these words involves the giving of a notice first offering to surrender the premises as a condition of the right to assign/underlet. The agreement will arise on acceptance of the offer.[49] Accordingly, although the requirements of Schs 3 and 4 to the 2003 Order need not be complied with prior to the grant of the lease simply because it incorporates a surrender back clause, it would seem that in order for any contract arising out of the surrender back clause to be effective the statutory procedure must be complied with. This may of course give rise to difficulties in practice as the landlord is often under a short time limit within which to accept the offer. **3–26**

It is considered that the new provisions do not affect the validity of an actual surrender which is effected whether by deed or by operation of law,[50] save where the surrender occurs by reason of an agreement to grant the tenant a new tenancy.[51] **3–27**

Forfeiture

The landlord may bring to an end the tenancy otherwise than in the manner provided by the Act if he has grounds enabling him to forfeit the lease.[52] The tenant will be entitled to apply for relief, although it is a matter for the discretion of the court whether to grant or refuse relief in any particular case. In the case of a term of years certain of which a substantial part remains unexpired, the landlord will decide on ordinary commercial principles whether or not to rely upon any grounds of forfeiture which may be available, and the question whether the tenancy is or is not one to which the Act applies will be largely irrelevant. In the case of a periodic tenancy, or of a fixed term where the expiry date is approaching, the tactical considerations are different. **3–28**

---

[47] para.5 of Sch.4 to the 2003 Order: see para.A2.056.
[48] See para.2–21 et seq.
[49] See para.3–07, fn.18.
[50] See para.3–05 et seq.
[51] See para.3–11.
[52] On the effect of a forfeiture taking place after the tenant has applied to the court for a new tenancy, see para.6–49 et seq.

3–29 Usually the matters which give rise to the right of forfeiture will overlap, at least to some extent, with one or more of the grounds of opposition set out in s.30(1). For example, if the premises are in disrepair towards the end of the term, the landlord will normally be entitled to forfeit after he has served a notice under s.146 of the Law of Property Act 1925. The same disrepairs could be relied upon to oppose the tenant's application for a new tenancy pursuant to ground (a) of s.30(1).[53] Breaches of covenant which are not serious enough to justify forfeiture, and aspects of the tenant's use and management of the demised premises which do not amount to a breach of covenant, may be taken into consideration in determining whether the tenant ought to be granted a new tenancy.

3–30 Opposition under the Act has certain advantages over forfeiture. First, under the Act the court is not obliged to grant a renewal albeit the tenant may have remedied the breaches of covenant. For instance, if the landlord claims possession by reason of the non-payment of rent the tenant in action for forfeiture is entitled to relief virtually as of right, for the right of re-entry is viewed simply as security for the payment of the rent and if the tenant pays the rent and the landlord's costs the tenant will, save in exceptional circumstances, obtain relief. Other breaches of covenant are usually treated as irrelevant to the tenant's claim for relief.[54] If the landlord opposes renewal in reliance upon ground (b) (persistent failure to pay rent) the fact that the tenant may have paid the rent by the date of the hearing is simply one of the factors to which the court will have regard in considering whether the tenant is to be entitled to a renewal. Secondly, the opposition to a renewal may be maintained in circumstances where a claim for forfeiture would fail. The right to forfeit may be waived. Waiver prevents the landlord from forfeiting at all. The fact that the right to forfeit for a breach of covenant may have been waived does not, however, stop the landlord from opposing renewal in reliance on the breach of covenant. The existence of the waiver and the circumstances in which it occurred (for a waiver may occur by simple inadvertence) will be material to the exercise of the court's discretion as to whether or not to order a renewal.

3–31 ***Norton v Charles Deane Productions***[55] The landlord demised business premises under four separate leases consisting of four houses which had no physical internal communication. By cl.4(2) of the leases the tenant covenanted not to do or permit to be done on the demised premises or any part thereof anything which might be a nuisance, damage, inconvenience or annoyance to the lessors, or the owners or occupiers of any adjoining premises. The premises were to be used as a high-class residential hotel. The leases were assigned to a company and a director of the company. The landlord served a s.146 notice complaining of various breaches of cl.4(2). It was held:

---

[53] For further consideration of the tactical problems, see para.7–24 et seq.

[54] *Gill v Lewis* [1956] 2 Q.B. 1 CA. In the county court the tenant is given an automatic right to relief in respect of a claim for possession on the ground of non-payment of rent: County Court Act 1984 s.138.

[55] (1969) 214 E.G. 559.

(1) The leases would not be forfeited as the allegations of breach (as specified in the notice) had not been proved, or had not been properly pleaded.
(2) A new tenancy would not, however, be granted because in all the circumstances the defendants' use and mismanagement of the demised premises was such that they ought not to be granted a new tenancy.

Forfeiture and sub-tenancies

The rule at common law is that, once a superior tenancy has been forfeited, all sub-tenancies derived from it fall with it.[56] Sub-tenants have the right to apply for relief from forfeiture by virtue of s.146(4) of the Law of Property Act 1925. Unlike the position under s.146(2), where it is the tenant (as opposed to a sub-tenant) who is applying for relief, the effect of relief is not automatically to reinstate the sub-tenancy as it existed before the forfeiture. **3–32**

On the contrary, relief takes effect as a fresh grant and the court is given a discretion as to the terms of the lease between the landlord and the person who was previously his sub-tenant, subject to a stipulation that no sub-tenant shall be entitled to require a lease longer than he had under his original sub-tenancy. It will sometimes be the case that the terms of the sub-tenancy are quite different from those of the forfeited head tenancy; the head tenancy may have been granted many years before the sub-tenancy so that the terms of the latter would be more modern; the head tenancy or the sub-tenancy may impose obligations on the head tenant and sub-tenant which are more or less burdensome. Thus it may be that the head landlord would derive a benefit or suffer a detriment if the court were to order relief in favour of the sub-tenant upon the same terms as the sub-tenancy, or the same terms as the head tenancy.[57] Although there is authority giving some guidance on the way in which the court will exercise its discretion over the terms upon which it will grant relief to a sub-tenant following forfeiture of the head tenancy,[58] there is no case under the 1954 Act where the same problem is specifically considered, although the Court of Appeal has in *Cadogan v Dimovic*[59] (digested in para.3–33) considered the position where the landlord forfeited the superior tenancy at a time when the sub-tenancy was being continued by virtue of the provisions of the Act.

Cadogan v Dimovic[60] The landlord forfeited a head lease. A sub-tenant (whose sub-tenancy was protected by the Act) applied for relief from forfeiture under s.146(4) of the Law of Property Act 1925. By the time the sub-tenant's application was heard, the contractual term of his sub-tenancy had expired. The county court judge dismissed the application holding that, since s.146(4) **3–33**

[56] *Pennell v Payne* [1995] Q.B. 192 CA; *Barrett v Morgan* [2000] 2 A.C. 264 HL. It is not possible for the parties to validly contract otherwise: *PW & Co v Milton Gate Investments Ltd* [2003] EWHC 1994 (Ch); [2004] Ch. 142.

[57] A similar position can arise under the 1954 Act where the head landlord and the sub-tenant come into direct relationship, not because of forfeiture of the head tenancy, but because it expires by effluxion of time while the sub-tenancy is continued pursuant to the Act: see para.10–30 et seq.

[58] *Ewart v Fryer* [1901] 1 Ch. 499.

[59] [1984] 1 W.L.R. 609; [1984] 2 All E.R. 168 CA.

[60] [1984] 1 W.L.R. 609; [1984] 2 All E.R. 168 CA.

prevented the grant by way of relief of a lease "for any longer term than [the applicant] had under his original sub-lease", the court had no jurisdiction. This decision was reversed by the Court of Appeal, which held that the words in s.146(4) referred to the position immediately before forfeiture of the head lease, at which time the sub-tenancy would have continued until brought to an end under the provision of the 1954 Act. Accordingly, the court had jurisdiction to make a vesting order for a new term of appropriate duration, but within the limits of the extension imposed by the 1954 Act. It is not reported what term was granted to the tenant to give effect to the order for relief, as the matter was remitted to the judge in chambers to determine the terms of relief.

Notice to quit served by mesne landlord on superior landlord

3–34 It has now been established by *Pennell v Payne*[61] that when a landlord who is himself a tenant terminates his tenancy by notice to quit served on his landlord, any tenancy which he has created also determines. Since this is not a common law mode of determination expressly preserved by s.24(2), it is thought that if the sub-tenancy in such a case is one to which the Act applies, its contractual term is thereby determined but it continues under s.24(1) until determined in accordance with the Act.

Death of tenant

3–35 The death of the tenant will not terminate the lease. The tenancy will vest in the tenant's personal representatives (either the executors pursuant to the will or the administrator pursuant to the grant of letters of administration on an intestacy). The death of the tenant is obviously of importance if the tenancy is continuing pursuant to s.24, for it may be that the death will result in a cessation of occupation for business purposes. Where the tenant dies intestate and letters of administration have not been taken out any notices should be served direct on the Public Trustee at the Public Trust Office, PO Box 3010, London WC2A 1AX[62]: *Practice Direction* [1995] 3 All E.R. 192.

Bankruptcy and liquidation

3–36 Upon the bankruptcy of the tenant the tenant's lease does not determine but will vest in the trustee in bankruptcy once appointed.[63] Any disposition by the bankrupt after the presentation of the petition for bankruptcy and prior to the vesting in the trustee, without the leave of the court, is void.[64] Property held by

---

[61] [1995] 2 Q.B. 192 CA.

[62] [1995] 3 All E.R. 192. See s.18, Law of Property (Miscellaneous Provisions) Act 1994. The notice should be addressed to "The Personal Representative of [full name of deceased] of [deceased's last known place of residence]". The notice should *not* be addressed to the Public Trustee or c/o the Public Trustee.

[63] s.306 of the Insolvency Act 1996.

[64] s.284(3) of the 1986 Act.

the bankrupt on trust for others is excluded from the transfer to the trustee.[65] This includes property in which the bankrupt is beneficially entitled.[66] This exclusion will accordingly cover the case of a person who constitutes one of two or more joint tenants who hold the lease on a trust of land.[67]

On the making of a winding-up order the property of a company does not vest in the liquidator. The liquidator may, however, apply to the court for an order vesting property of the company in the liquidator.[68] **3–37**

2. STATUTORY MODES OF TERMINATION

General

Unless the tenancy has come to an end by virtue of one of the common law modes of determination preserved by s.24(2) which have been discussed in paras 3–01 et seq., "a tenancy to which this Part of this Act applies shall not come to an end unless terminated in accordance with the provisions of this Part of this Act": s.24(1) The various ways in which, in accordance with the provisions of the Act, such a tenancy may be terminated are hereinafter described as the "statutory modes of termination". They are summarised in paras 3–39 to 3–48 and discussed in greater detail in the remainder of this Part. **3–38**

Summary of modes of termination

Tenant serves notice pursuant to section 27(1)

Where the tenant has served a valid notice pursuant to s.27(1) to the effect that he does not desire his tenancy to be continued by the Act, it will come to an end on the contractual term date (see para.3–104 et seq.). **3–39**

Tenant serves notice pursuant to section 27(2)

Where the tenant serves a valid notice pursuant to s.27(2) the tenancy will come to an end on the date therein specified (see para.3–109 et seq.). **3–40**

Landlord serves section 25 notice

Where the landlord has served a valid notice pursuant to s.25, but neither the tenant nor the landlord has made an application for a new tenancy pursuant to s.24(1), and the landlord has not made a termination application, the tenancy will come to an end on the date specified in the s.25 notice subject possibly to prior termination if the tenant gives notice under s.27(2) (see paras 3–113 and 3 206). **3–41**

---

[65] s.283(3)(a) of the 1986 Act.

[66] *Re A Solicitor* [1952] 1 All E.R. 549.

[67] ss.34 and 36 of the Law of Property Act 1925, as amended by the Trustees of Land and Appointments Act 1996.

[68] s.145(1) of the Insolvency Act 1986.

Tenant serves section 26 request

3–42 Where the tenant has made a valid request for a new tenancy pursuant to s.26, but neither the landlord nor the tenant has made an application to the court pursuant to s.24(1), and the landlord has not made a termination application, the tenancy will come to an end immediately before the date specified in the s.26 request for the commencement of the new tenancy (see para.3–223).

Parties reach agreement for future tenancy

3–43 Where the landlord and the tenant have reached an agreement for a future tenancy pursuant to s.28 the current tenancy determines on the date agreed for the commencement of the future tenancy (see para.15–14 et seq.).

Disposal of application for new tenancy

3–44 Where an application has been made to the court under s.24(1) whether by the landlord or the tenant and that application has been "finally disposed of" within the meaning of s.64(2), the current tenancy will determine three months after final disposal,[69] unless that date is earlier than the date of termination specified in the relevant s.25 notice or s.26 request, in which case it will determine on the later date (see para.3–227 et seq.).

Landlord succeeds on termination application

3–45 Where the landlord has, after service of a s.25 notice by him or in response to the tenant's s.26 request (after service of a counter-notice by the landlord pursuant to s.26(6)), made an application for termination under s.29(2) and he succeeds in that application, the court shall make an order for the termination of the current tenancy in accordance with s.64 without the grant of a new tenancy (see para.10–01).

Court of the view that landlord would have succeeded on grounds of opposition

3–46 In the special circumstances envisaged in s.31(2) the court may order that the date of termination specified in the landlord's s.25 notice or, as the case may be, the tenant's s.26 request, be such later date as the court may determine, being a date not later than one year than the date so specified, and the tenancy shall come to an end on that date without the grant of a new tenancy (see para.7–290 et seq.).

Tenant applies for revocation of order granting new tenancy

3–47 If the tenant, within 14 days after the making of an order by the court for the grant of a new tenancy applies for it to be revoked the court shall revoke the order and the tenant's current tenancy will come to an end on a date specified by the court: s.36(2) (see para.10–10).

[69] Together with the time for appealing, see paras 3–229 and 14–137 et seq.

Government/public bodies

Special provisions enable government departments and other public authorities to terminate tenancies in particular circumstances (see para.1–153). **3–48**

3. SERVICE OF NOTICES

Service pursuant to section 23 of the 1927 Act

By virtue of s.66(4), the provisions as to the giving of notices contained in s.23 of the Landlord and Tenant Act 1927 apply for the purposes of the 1954 Act. **3–49**

The methods of service set out in s.23 are permissive not mandatory: *Galinski v McHugh*[70] (digested in para.3–81). If some other method of service is chosen, difficulties may arise in proving proper service, see, e.g. *Chiswell v Griffon Land & Estates Ltd*[71] (digested in para.3–80). **3–50**

Section 23(1) permits the following methods of service: **3–51**

(1) Personal service.
(2) Leaving the document at the "last known place of abode in England and Wales" of the person on whom it is to be served.
(3) By sending the notice through the post in a registered letter or by recorded delivery[72] addressed to the person on whom it is to be served at the "last known place of abode". Or, in the case of a local or public authority or statutory or public utility company, it may be addressed to the secretary or other proper officer at the principal office of such authority or company.
(4) In the case of a notice to a landlord it may be served on any duly authorised agent.[73]

The advantage of utilising one of the statutory modes of service is that the risk of non-receipt is on the recipient, so that service is effected albeit it may be shown that the notice was never received by the tenant.[74]

Personal service

Personal service means what it says. A notice served on an agent is not personal service but this does not matter, because service on the duly authorised agent is sufficient: *Galinski v McHugh* (digested in para.3–81).[75] A company cannot be served personally: *Stylo Shoes Ltd v Prices Tailors Ltd* (digested in para.3–60).[76] **3–52**

---

70 [1989] 1 E.G.L.R. 109 CA.
71 [1975] 1 W.L.R. 1181; [1975] 2 All E.R. 665 CA.
72 See Recorded Delivery Service Act 1962 s.1.
73 The fact that the section expressly permits service on the agent of the landlord does not by necessary implication exclude service on the tenant's agent: *Galinski v McHugh* [1989] 1 E.G.L.R. 109 CA.
74 This is discussed at length in para.3–69.
75 See fn.70.
76 [1960] Ch. 396.

Leaving notice at last known place of abode

3–53 In *Price v West London Investment Building Society Ltd*[77] (digested in para.3–69), it was held that "place of abode" included a tenant's business address as well as his personal residence. Thus, a notice addressed to the tenant at a hotel which were demised to the tenant was effective service albeit the tenant in fact lived in Malta: *Italica Holdings SA v Bayadea*[78] (digested in para.3–56). The registered office of a company may be its place of abode: *National Westminster Bank v Betchworth Investments*.[79] It has been held that where joint tenants were husband and wife and the s.25 notice was addressed to them both but served under cover of a letter addressed only to the husband at the matrimonial home, the notice was not left at the wife's last known place of abode within the meaning of s.23 of the 1927 Act: *Rostran v Michael Nairn and Co Ltd*.[80] If the notice is in fact delivered to the tenant's last known place of abode it does not matter that it was incorrectly addressed: *Stylo Shoes Ltd v Prices Tailors Ltd* (digested in para.3–60).[81]

3–54 The "last known" place of abode does not mean the last place which the tenant had notified to his landlord as being the appropriate address to which notices should be sent. The reference to the "last known place of abode" was put in to deal with the case where the landlord was unaware of a change of abode on the part of the tenant and in such a case a notice will be properly served if it is sent to the last place of which the landlord knew as a place of abode of the tenant: *Price v West London Investment Building Society Ltd* (digested in para.3–69).[82]

3–55 A requirement that a notice be "left at" premises does not prescribe any particular method of leaving.[83] Thus it may be hand delivered, or delivered by post, recorded delivery or some other method.[84] The method adopted must, however, be a proper one in the sense that it is one which a reasonable person, minded to bring the document to the attention of the person to whom the notice is addressed, would adopt: *Lord Newborough v Jones*.[85] In that case, a notice to quit an agricultural holding was held to have been properly served, albeit in slipping the letter under the door, the notice (accidentally and unknowingly to the sender) was pushed under the linoleum placed on the floor and did not come to the attention of the tenant until it was too late. Similarly, it has been held in the case of a communal block of flats, that service through the letter box on the ground floor, where it would fall either onto the hall floor or into a basket inside the letter box, was sufficient to qualify as being left at the tenant's last known place of abode, where the tenant occupied only part of the building. It was sufficient that could go to communicate to the tenant residing there: *Trustees of Henry Smith's Charity v*

[77] [1964] 1 W.L.R. 616; [1964] 2 All E.R. 318 CA.
[78] [1985] 1 E.G.L.R. 70.
[79] [1975] 1 E.G.L.R. 57 CA.
[80] [1962] E.G.D. 284.
[81] [1960] Ch. 396.
[82] [1964] 1 W.L.R. 616; [1964] 2 All E.R. 318 CA per Diplock, L.J. with whom Willmer L.J. agreed.
[83] *Warnborough Investments Ltd v Central Midlands Ltd* [2007] 1 L. & T.R. 10 Ch at [78].
[84] *Kinch v Bullard* [1999] 1 W.L.R. 423 per Neuberger J. at 427. See also *Stylo Shoes Ltd v Price Tailors Ltd* [1960] Ch. 396 (digested at para.3–60).
[85] [1975] Ch. 90 CA.

Kyriakou.[86] Subject to that qualification it probably matters not where the notice is left. In *Katana v Catalyst Communities Housing Ltd*,[87] there were two separate tenancies of different parts of a former petrol filling station. Mr Katana's premises, used as a car wash, were at the front of the site. There was an office on the forecourt forming part of the demise which contained a letter box. The landlord served the s.25 notice on Mr Katana by attaching one copy to the exterior of a kiosk and also by putting one copy through a letter box within the kiosk rather than through the letter box in the office. The kiosk formed part of the demised premises. Patten L.J. said, on an application for permission to appeal, that the 1954 Act did not make a distinction for the purposes of deemed service between one part of the premises and another. As the s.25 notice had been attached to the windows of the kiosk and a copy was put through the letter box of the kiosk there was effective service for the purposes of s.23 of the 1927 Act. This was to be contrasted with the second tenant, Mr Abrahams. He occupied premises to the rear of the site. Access to his premises was through a gate which was only open during business hours. His s.25 notice was also left at the kiosk. As the kiosk did not form part of his demise but that of Mr Katana the notice had not been served on him unless it could be shown that it had actually been received by him.

Leaving a notice includes leaving it with a person who is actually on the premises. Where a notice is handed to someone at the premises it will be treated as being "left at the last known place of abode" if delivered to a person "in regard to whom there is reasonable ground for supposing that he or she will hand it to the lessee, if the lessee should be available for that purpose."[88] Thus, a letter taken in by an employee of the tenant will have been left for the tenant.[89] Leaving a notice with the person at the customer relations desk at the premises has also been held to be good enough.[90] It is probably otherwise if it is left in the hands of a person who, to the knowledge of the parties, is a mere visitor and happens at that moment to be leaving the premises.[91] **3–56**

If the notice is served by leaving it at the addressee's last known place of abode it is given on the date it is so left: *Price v West London Investment Building Society Ltd*[92] (digested in para.3–59). The notice will be given with effect from the date **3–57**

[86] [1989] 2 E.G.L.R. 110 CA.

[87] [2010] EWCA Civ 370. The decision in *Catalyst Communities Housing Ltd v Katana* although of some interest is actually not an authority for any proposition of law. Under the Practice Direction (CA: Citation of Authorities) [2001] 1 W.L.R. 1001 a judgment on an application for permission to appeal cannot be cited unless it contains an express statement to the effect that it is intended to establish a new principle or to extend the present law. No such express statement is contained in judgment.

[88] Humphreys J. in *Cannon Brewery Co v Signal Press Ltd* (1929) 139 L.T. 384 at 385, in respect of the provisions of s.196(3) of the Law of Property Act 1925.

[89] *Price v West London Investment Building Society Ltd* [1964] 1 W.L.R. 616; [1964] 2 All E.R. 318 CA (digested in para 3–59).

[90] *Warnborough Investments Ltd v Central Midlands Ltd* [2007] 1 L. & T.R. 10 Ch. D (Rent review notice held to be served by being left at the demised premises albeit the premises had to the knowledge of the landlord been sub-let).

[91] Humphreys J. in *Cannon Brewery Co v Signal Press Ltd* (1929) 139 L.T. 384 at 385.

[92] [1964] 1 W.L.R. 616; [1964] 2 All E.R. 318 CA.

of being so left notwithstanding the fact that the recipient never receives it after it is delivered because, e.g. it is destroyed[93] or mislaid.[94]

3–58 ***Italica Holdings SA v Bayadea***[95] The landlord sent to the tenant of hotel premises in London a notice pursuant to s.25. The notice was served by recorded delivery addressed to the tenant at the hotel. The tenant failed to serve a counter-notice. The tenant did not reside in England but in Malta. When the landlord sought possession the tenant contended that he had never received the notice and that it had not been sent to his "last known place of abode" within the meaning of s.23 of the 1927 Act. It was held that the notice was so served and, therefore, properly served notwithstanding that the notice may never have reached the premises. The hotel premises qualified as the "last known place of abode" of the tenant notwithstanding that the tenant had ceased to reside in the United Kingdom as:

(1) the hotel premises were the only connection, apart from family links, which the tenant retained with this country; accordingly, so far as the landlord was concerned, the hotel premises were the only possible candidate as being the place at which the tenant carried on business;
(2) the premises were the place at which the relevant business was carried on, namely the business which attracted the protection of the Act;
(3) the premises were the only territorial link which the tenant retained with England and Wales.

3–59 ***Price v West London Investment Building Society***[96] A landlord of business premises served on the tenant a notice under s.25. The notice was sent by registered post addressed to the tenant at the business premises. The notice was duly delivered at the premises on March 23, 1963 (being taken in by an employee of the tenant), but by some misfortune it did not reach the tenant personally until March 29, 1963. On May 28, 1963, the tenant served a counter-notice on the landlord. It was held that the phrase "place of abode" in s.23(1) of the Landlord and Tenant Act 1927 was to be construed with reference to the subject matter with which in the particular case the phrase is concerned, and accordingly for the purposes of the Act the phrase refers not only to the personal residence of the tenant concerned (of which the landlord may be entirely ignorant), but also to the business address, which the landlord is much more likely to know and where, for the purposes of the provisions of the Act, the tenant is much more likely to be found.

---

93 *Kinch v Bullard* [1998] 4 All E.R. 650; [1998] 3 E.G.L.R. 112 Ch D (a decision on the similar wording of the Law of Property Act 1925 s.196(3). Severance of joint tenancy held to have been effected upon the notice of severance being put through the letter box by the postman at the intended recipient's last known place of abode, notwithstanding that the notice was in fact received by the sender who had changed her mind as to the severance and duly destroyed the notice).

94 *Price v West London Investment Building Society* [1964] 1 W.L.R. 616, where the notice was mislaid. It did not reach the tenant personally until he happened to find it mixed up with a lot of circulars and the like which were connected with his business. It is implicit in the finding that the notice was given when left and that the actual receipt by the intended recipient was irrelevant.

95 [1985] 1 E.G.L.R. 70.

96 [1964] 1 W.L.R. 616; [1964] 2 All E.R. 318 CA.

The giving of the notice was complete when the registered letter was taken in and signed on March 23, 1963, and consequently the tenant's counter-notice was out of time.

Stylo Shoes Ltd v Prices Tailors Ltd[97] A landlord in November 1958 purported to serve a s.25 notice determining the plaintiff's tenancy by sending it by registered post to the secretary of the plaintiff's company at its supposed registered office in Huddersfield. The company had, in fact, in February 1957, transferred its registered office and principal place of business to an address in Leeds. The postmaster in Huddersfield forwarded the letter to the new address in Leeds where the tenant company did in fact receive it. The tenants gave a counter-notice, but stated in a covering letter that they contested the validity of the s.25 notice. Although the judge had no doubt that a company could be a "person" for the purposes of the section, it could not be served personally. Although the notice had been sent by registered post it had not been addressed to the company's registered office. However, the sequence of the registered posting to Huddersfield followed by the postmaster's forwarding to Leeds qualified as "leaving at the last known place of abode". The court was unable to accept the argument that the failure to specify the correct address was fatal to the defendants. The vital thing was that the letter was in fact delivered to the tenant's last known place of abode. **3–60**

Statutory or public utility companies

A "statutory company" means a company constituted by or under an Act of Parliament to construct, work or carry on any gas, water, electricity, tramway, hydraulic power, dock, canal or railway undertaking.[98] The expression "public utility company" means any company within the meaning of the Companies (Consolidation) Act 1908, or a society registered under the Industrial and Provident Societies Acts 1893 to 1913, carrying on any such undertaking.[99] It is to be noted that the application of the provisions of s.23 are not limited to such companies, as a company is "a person" within the meaning of the section: *Stylo Shoes v Prices Tailors*[100] (digested in para.3–60). **3–61**

Service on agent

Service on the tenant's agent will be sufficient: *Railtrack Plc v Gojra*.[101] The fact that s.23 of the 1927 Act expressly permits service on an agent of the landlord does not by necessary implication render impermissible service on an agent of the tenant: *Galinski v McHugh*[102] (digested in para.3–81) and *Italica Holdings SA v Bayadea*[103] (digested in para.3–58). **3–62**

[97] [1960] Ch. 396.
[98] Landlord and Tenant Act 1927 s.25(1).
[99] Landlord and Tenant Act 1927 s.25(1).
[100] [1960] 2 W.L.R. 8; [1959] 3 All E.R. 901.
[101] [1998] 1 E.G.L.R. 63 CA.
[102] [1989] 1 E.G.L.R. 109 CA.
[103] [1985] 1 E.G.L.R. 70.

Service by registered post or recorded delivery

3–63 Section 12 of the 1927 Act specifies service by registered post. Service by recorded delivery service is, however, equally effective.[104] As to the question of the date at which service of a notice by recorded delivery or registered post is effected and the risk of non-receipt, see para.3–69 et seq.

Other modes of service

3–64 If service is not effected by one of the statutory means, it will be necessary to prove that it was actually received by the addressee: *Stylo Shoes v Prices Tailors*[105] (digested in para.3–60) and *Deerfield Travel Services v Leathersellers Co*[106] (digested in para.13–26).

Service by fax

3–65 It is considered that service of the statutory forms of notice by fax would be held to be valid. In *Hastie & Jenkerson v McMahon*[107] it was held that service by fax of a list of documents was good service in accordance with the then rule of the Supreme Court since it was received in a legible state. Woolf L.J. said:

> "The purpose of serving a document is to ensure that its contents are available to the recipient and whether the document is served in the conventional way or by fax the result is exactly the same. Counsel on behalf of the Defendant submits that what is transmitted by fax is not the document but an electronic message. However, this submission fails to distinguish between the method of transmission and the result of the transmission by fax. What is produced by the transmission of the message by fax admittedly using the recipient's machine and paper is the document which the other party intended should be served.... What is required is that a legible copy of the document should be in the possession of the party to be served. This fax achieves [this] ..."

---

[104] Recorded Delivery Service Act 1962 s.1.

[105] [1960] Ch. 396.

[106] (1983) 46 P. & C.R. 132 CA.

[107] [1990] 1 W.L.R. 1575; [1991] 1 All E.R. 255 CA. See also *EAE (RT) Ltd v EAE Property Ltd* 1994 S.L.T. 627 (fax notification was sufficient to comply with the requirement of the rent review clause for a notice in writing) and *PNC Telecom Plc v Thomas* [2002] EWHC 2848 (Ch) (a faxed letter was notice for the purposes of s.368 of the Companies Act 1985 requesting the company to convene an extraordinary general meeting to propose to shareholders ordinary resolutions and in particular in that case for the removal and appointment of directors. The argument of P&C, the company, was that the requisition required by s.368 of the Companies Act 1985 must be deposited either in person or by post at the registered office and that transmission by fax was not permissible. The original was not received at P&C's registered office until November 26, 2002. The faxed requisition was in fact received on November 8, 2002). In the Australian decision of *Jalun Pool Supplies Pty Ltd v Onga Pty Ltd* [1999] S.A.S.C. 20 the Supreme Court of South Australia decided that it was sufficient that the document was received electronically albeit a physical copy was not available until later. In that case the document had to be received before the "close of business". Close of business was held by the court to be 5.30pm. The explanation for the delay was that there was a build up of facsimile messages at about 5.00pm when a number of messages were being sent at once. The messages were stored in a memory function and were reproduced in documentary form some time after the electronic receipt. The document was received electronically at 5.02pm but the copy was not available until 5.30pm. Debelle J. held that it was unnecessary for the service of the document by facsimile transmission to require the document to be in a complete and legible state.

The court did, however, reserve the position in relation to documents which initiate court proceedings. This reservation has not, however, found its way into the CPR: see r.6.2 and PD to Pt 6, paras 3.1 to 3.4.

Service by email

The argument against an electronic document as forming written notice is that an electronic document in its digital form does not qualify as writing.[108] This view was rejected by the Law Commission for England and Wales.[109] The Commission was of the view that while an electronic document may not be in writing, the screen display will satisfy the definition of writing.[110] In that respect, an electronic message is no different from a message contained in a document which could easily be delivered but not read. The fact that it remains unread does not affect its validity.[111] In the courts in the US analogies have been drawn between sending a facsimile and sending an email.[112] In Canada it has been held[113] that an enforceable contract can be created by email. The court concluded that the electronic contract "must be afforded the sanctity that must be given to any agreement in writing". **3–66**

Change in identity of landlord

Section 23(2) of the 1927 Act provides that, until a tenant has received notice that his landlord has ceased to be entitled to the rents and profits (e.g. by virtue of a transfer of the reversion), he is entitled, for the purposes of service of notices, etc. to treat that person as still being the landlord. A notice of change in the person entitled to the rents and profits pursuant to s.23(2) will not be effective unless it also informs the tenant of the name and address of the person who has become entitled: *Meah v Sector Properties Ltd*[114] (digested in para.3–68).The notice must state that the new landlord has become the person entitled to receive the rents.[115] This does not fully safeguard the position of a tenant under the Act, because his **3–67**

[108] In reality an electronic document is a series of numbers stored in the computer's memory. The binary code which represents the electronic information is not stored on the computer as one document but in a series of numbers which is only understandable to a person once the appropriate software has read and translated the numbers into words: Reed C., *Digital Information Law: Electronic Documents and Requirements of Form* (London: Centre for Commercial Law Studies, 1996).

[109] In their paper, "Electronic Commerce: Formal Requirements in Commercial Transactions—Advice from the Law Commission" (2001).

[110] For the purposes of the meaning of "writing" in the Interpretation Act 1978.

[111] See the Commission Advice at paras 3.5–3.10.

[112] *Shattuck v Klotzbach*, 2001 Mass. Super. LEXIS 642, 14 Mass. L. Rep. 360 (Mass. Super. Ct. 2001) where the parties created an agreement of sale by email. The court had no difficulty in concluding, and in fact the court accepted without argument, that the emails were "writing" for the purposes of the Statute of Frauds. The more difficult question for the court was whether the emails were signed in compliance with the Statute of Frauds.

[113] *Rudder v Microsoft Corp* (1999), 47 C.C.L.T. (2d) 168; 2. C.P.R. (4th) 474 (Ont. SC); 40 C.P.C. (4th) 394 (Ont. SCJ).

[114] [1974] 1 W.L.R. 547; [1974] 1 All E.R. 1074 CA.

[115] *Railtrack Plc v Gojra* [1998] 1 E.G.L.R. 63 CA per Evans L.J. The court left open the question whether a notice under the subsection can only be given after the change of landlord had occurred.

immediate landlord may cease to be "the landlord" within the definition in s.44 without ceasing to be entitled to the rent and profits.[116]

3–68 ***Meah v Sector Properties Ltd***[117] The tenant was the underlessee under an underlease of 14 years expiring on June 24, 1971. The reversion had been assigned on more than one occasion. It was vested in D Ltd until April 3, 1970, when it was assigned to O Ltd. On that same day, O Ltd contracted to assign it to L, but completion did not take place until January 28, 1971. BM were the managing agents of the property until the assignment to L when the managing agents became KTA. R was the solicitor to the tenant throughout. In June 1969, BM notified R that D Ltd had acquired the freehold reversion and that future rents should be paid to them as the reversioners' agents. But they gave no similar notice at any time that on April 3 the reversion was assigned to O Ltd and the tenant and R remained in ignorance of that fact. Therefore, the rent continued to be paid to BM, but this did not matter as they had in fact been retained as managing agents of the property by O Ltd. Indeed, there was no evidence that the tenant ever learnt of the existence of O Ltd.

However, on December 15, 1970, BM wrote to R pointing out that L had contracted to buy the freehold. That letter gave the name and address of L's managing agents. R on receiving notification of what was afoot wrote immediately to KTA to say that the tenant proposed to request a new tenancy. R also telephoned KTA on December 21, 1970, and on the same day telephoned BM. The Court of Appeal thought that it was permissible to infer from R's telephoning BM that KTA had told him that, completion of the assignment to L not having yet taken place, BM were still the managing agents of the property. On the same day R wrote to BM enclosing a tenant's request under s.26, requesting a new tenancy commencing on June 24, 1971. The request was addressed to "BM as agents for D Ltd". At no material time were the reversioners opposed to the granting of a new tenancy to the tenant and negotiations over the terms continued throughout the relevant period. On January 28, 1971, the tenant was informed that the reversion had been assigned to L and that future rents were to be paid to KTA as his agents. The tenant did not apply to the court for a new tenancy within the period specified by s.29(3).

L assigned his interest to the landlord on January 14, 1972. The landlord claimed possession arguing that, in the circumstances, by reason of the combined effect of ss.24(1), 26(5) and 29(3) the tenant's tenancy had expired on June 23, 1971. The judge made a possession order. On appeal by the tenant it was held:

(1) It was for the tenant to prove that O Ltd had not duly authorised BM to receive a request under s.26 on their behalf. The whole course of events, including the action of BM and the reversioners' solicitors, indicated that BM were either initially or at least retrospectively so authorised. Nor did the fact that the request was addressed to "BM as agents for D Ltd" prevent the request from being validly served on BM as agent of O Ltd, who was in fact the owner, for the tenant intended the notice to be served on O Ltd.

[116] See para.3–87 et seq. as to the meaning of "the landlord".

[117] (1974) 229 E.G. 1097 CA.

(2) Section 23(2) was excluded only if the notice of change supplied, inter alia, "notice of the name and address of the person who has become entitled to the rents and profits". The letter of December 15, 1970, did not supply any of the information required by s.23(2) and accordingly was not excluded and thus if service of the request to "BM as agents for D Ltd" was service on D Ltd, that was deemed to be effective service on O Ltd.

Date of service and risk of non-receipt

Risk of non-receipt: using registered or recorded mail as permitted by section 23 of the Landlord and Tenant Act 1927

Early authority It was stated in *Sun Alliance v Hayman*[118] that when a notice is served in accordance with s.23 it is both "given" and "received". This analysis does not assist in cases where it is essential to establish the exact date upon which a notice has been "given", because it will often have been sent on one particular day but not received until a later day.[119] The question of when a notice is being given becomes particularly important if the document in question is not received by the intended recipient. The question arises as to who runs the risk of non-receipt. Obiter dicta of Megaw L.J. in *Chiswell v Griffon Land and Estates Ltd*[120] (digested in para.3–80) and of Slade L.J. *Galinski v McHugh*[121] (digested **3–69**

[118] [1975] 1 W.L.R. 177; [1975] 1 All E.R. 248 CA.

[119] It does not enable one to say whether the notice is given when received or received when given.

[120] [1975] 1 W.L.R. 1181; [1975] 2 All E.R. 665 CA. Megaw L.J. said:

"... the provisions of section 23 of the Landlord and Tenant Act 1927 are incorporated in the 1954 Act by section 66(4) of the latter Act. The provisions of section 23 of the 1927 Act lay down the manner in which service can be effected. It is provided, as what I may call at any rate the primary means of effecting service, that it is to be done either by 'personal' service or by leaving the notice at the last-known place of abode, or by sending it through the post in a registered letter, or (as now applies) in a recorded delivery letter. If any of those methods is adopted, they being the primary methods laid down, and, in the event of dispute, it is proved that one of those methods has been adopted, then sufficient service is proved. Thus, if it is proved, in the event of dispute, that a notice was sent by recorded delivery, it does not matter that the recorded delivery letter may not have been received by the intended recipients. It does not matter, even it were to be clearly established if it had gone astray in the post. There is the obvious, simple way of dealing with a notice of this sort. But, as I think may be assumed for the purposes of this appeal, if the person who gives the notice see fit not to use one of those primary methods, but to send the notice through the post, not registered and not by recorded delivery, that will nevertheless be good notice, if in fact the letter is received by the person to whom the notice has to be given. But a person who chooses to use that method instead of one of the primary methods is taking the risk that, if the letter is indeed lost in the post, notice will not have been given. I am prepared to assume, for the purpose of this appeal, that in those circumstances section 26 of the Interpretation Act 1889 [now s.7 of the Interpretation Act 1978] applies. On these hypotheses, it is permissible to give the notice by means of a letter posted in the ordinary post. So the result of s.26 may be that once it is proved that such a notice, in proper form, has been duly posted, there is a presumption that the notice has been effected at the time when that letter, so posted, would be delivered in the ordinary course of post. But, of course, the result of adopting that method must be that, if the letter is not in fact delivered, or its receipt is denied and cannot be proved, then notice has not been given."

[121] [1989] 1 E.G.L.R. 109 CA, Slade L.J. said that:

"... section 23(1) [of the 1927 Act] is intended to assist the person who is obliged to serve the notice, by offering him choices of mode of service which will be deemed to be valid service, *even if in the event the intended recipient does not in fact receive it*" (original emphasis).

in para.3–81) suggested that the risk of non-receipt, where one of the statutory methods of service has been used, is upon the recipient not the sender. The obiter dicta of Megaw L.J. in *Chiswell v Griffon*[122] was followed at first instance in *Italica Holdings SA v Bayadea*[123] and by Wilson J. in *Railtrack Plc v Gojra*.[124] Megaw L.J.'s comments were, however, obiter, as in the case before him none of the methods prescribed by s.23(1) of the 1927 Act was adopted. Again, in *Galinski v McHugh* the comments of Slade L.J. were obiter, for the landlord in that case (concerned with the service of a notice under s.4 of Pt I of the 1954 Act) did not use one of the methods of service prescribed by s.23(1) of the 1927 Act.

3–70 **Section 7 of the Interpretation Act 1978** The presumptions as to service and the time of delivery contained in what is now s.7 of the Interpretation Act 1978 need to be noted.[125] It provides:

> "Where an Act authorises or requires any document to be served by post (whether the expression 'served' or the expression 'give' or 'send' or any other expression is used) then, unless the contrary intention appears, the service is deemed to be effected by properly addressing, pre-paying and posting a letter containing the document and, unless the contrary is proved, to have been effected at the time at which the letter would be delivered in the ordinary course of post."

3–71 The section makes a distinction between and provides for presumptions as to the fact of service and as to the time at which service has been effected. In the absence of proof to the contrary, service will be deemed to be effected on the day when in the ordinary course of post the document would be delivered. If the contrary can be proved, although the document will be deemed to have been served by reason of the statutory provision, it would have been proved that it was not served in time. This distinction is one which has been adopted in several Divisional Court decisions.[126]

---

[122] See para.3–20.

[123] [1985] 1 E.G.L.R. 70.

[124] [1998] 1 E.G.L.R. 63 CA at 65.

[125] Megaw L.J. in the *Chiswell v Griffon* decision, when dealing with the situation that arises if a person using the *ordinary post* serves a notice that is lost in the post, said that notice will not then have been given, and, as he indicated, he was prepared to assume that, in those circumstances, s.26 of the Interpretation Act 1889 applied. (That section has been re-enacted as s.7 of the Interpretation Act 1978.) By implication it would not therefore apply where one of the statutory methods of service was adopted.

[126] Thus in *R. v County of London Quarter Session Appeals Committee Ex p. Rossi* [1956] 2 W.L.R. 800; [1956] 1 All E.R. 670 CA, Parker L.J. said:

"The section [i.e. s.26 of the Interpretation Act 1889, which in all material respects is identical to s.7 of the Interpretation Act 1978], it will be seen, is in two parts. The first part provides that the dispatch of a notice or other document in the manner laid down, shall be deemed to be service thereof. The second part provides that unless the contrary is proved that service is effected on the day when in the ordinary course of post the document would be delivered. The second part, therefore, concerning delivery as it does, comes into play and only comes into play in a case where under the legislation to which the section is applied the document has to be received by a certain time. If in such a case the 'contrary is proved', that is, that the document was not received by that time or at all, then the position appears to be that through under the first part of the section the document is deemed to have been served, it has been proved that it was not served in time."

The reference to "contrary" in "contrary being proved" in s.7 of the Interpretation Act 1978 has been said to be a reference to the contrary of the deeming provision that the letter in question was

The application of s.7 of the Interpretation Act 1978 in the context of s.23 of the 1954 Act was considered by the Court of Appeal in *Lex Service v Johns*.[127] Glidewell L.J. considered that s.23 of the 1927 Act had to be interpreted in the light of s.7 of the Interpretation Act. Having reviewed the authorities, including *R. v London County Quarter Sessions Appeals Committee Ex p. Rossi*[128] and *Chiswell v Griffon*[129] (digested in para.3–80) he concluded that the real issue in the case before him was whether for the purposes of s.7 of the Interpretation Act 1978 the evidence of the defendant that he did not receive the letter and the associated evidence proved the contrary, that is to say was contrary evidence which contradicted the statutory provision that *service* is deemed to be effected.[130] He was of the view that if there were evidence of a document having been received by some person but it were proved that that person was not the person upon whom the document was required to be served and that the person who received the document had not brought it to the attention of the person upon whom it was required to be served, then the document had not been properly served. But in the absence of such evidence then the contrary was not proved.[131] 3–72

Recent authority *Lex Service Plc v Johns*[132] has, however, been held to be *per incuriam*, since the Court of Appeal did not have cited to it the earlier decision of 3–73

delivered in the ordinary course of post. The reference to the contrary being "proved" requires no more than evidence which supports a finding on the balance of probabilities that the letter was not delivered. There is no burden upon the addressee of the letter in question to lead positive evidence as to what happened to the letter and/or a burden upon the addressee to show that the sender of the letter was aware that it had not been delivered: *Calladine-Smith v Saveorder Ltd* [2011] EWHC 2501 (Ch); [2011] 3 E.G.L.R. 55.

127 [1990] 1 E.G.L.R. 92 CA. The landlord terminated the tenant's periodic tenancy by service of a common law notice to quit and a s.25 notice. Both notices had been posted by the recorded delivery service addressed to the demised premises. The tenant did not receive either of the notices but the postman's recorded delivery receipt book showed that a document, numbered the same as the receipt for the recorded delivery of the letter, was received by somebody whose signature was illegible. There was evidence that other businesses were carried on in buildings behind the demised premises which at the relevant time apparently had no proper address, save "behind" or "at the rear of" the demised premises. The tenant sought to invite the court to draw the inference that the notices were delivered at the other premises and that somebody there may have received them. There was no specific evidence, however, to that effect. It was held that the tenant had not, pursuant to the terms of s.7 of the Interpretation Act 1978 "proved the contrary" as to the time of service being other than that at which the letter would be delivered in the ordinary course of post.

128 [1956] 2 W.L.R. 800; [1956] 1 All E.R. 670 CA.

129 [1975] 1 W.L.R. 1181; [1975] 2 All E.R. 665 CA.

130 Although the learned Lord Justice appears by reference to confine himself to the circumstances in which the presumption as to "service" may be rebutted rather than the question of the time of delivery he had held earlier, that there was evidence of a sheet from the postman's recorded delivery receipt book showing the receipt for the recorded delivery of the letter and the two notices and was received by somebody whose signature was illegible. "In other words, all the requirements for recorded delivery of a document or letter are proved to have been carried out." Thus the document appears to have been served and his comments as to the contrary being proved must refer to *time of service*.

131 So far as Balcombe L.J. was concerned, the contrary could not be proved simply by the intended recipient denying having received the relevant document. However, he was implicitly accepting that in circumstances other than those before him, the contrary could be proved where the issue was one as to *the time of service*.

132 [1990] 1 E.G.L.R. 92 CA.

the Court of Appeal in *Galinski v McHugh*[133] (digested in 3–81). The Court of Appeal has now authoritatively determined that, where one of the primary methods of service provided for by s.23 is adopted, the risk of non-receipt is on the addressee: *CA Webber (Transport) Ltd v Railtrack*[134] (digested in para.3.75). It was held that s.7 of the Interpretation Act has no application to the provisions of s.23 of the Landlord and Tenant Act 1927. Peter Gibson L.J. in *Webber (Transport) Ltd v Railtrack*[135] said:

> "I conclude on this review of the authorities that, save only for *Lex Service*, the consistent view taken by the courts has been that where a notice is served by a primary method authorised by s.23, such as by recorded delivery post, it matters not whether the notice was received and that there is no scope for the application of s.7 [*of the Interpretation Act 1978*], the risk of non-receipt being cast on the intended recipient. The date of service is the date when the server entrusts the notice to the post for recorded delivery, and that provides certainty for those who are required to serve documents . . . *Lex Service* has been criticized, and I have expressed my opinion that it was decided *per incuriam*. Accordingly, it seems to me that, having regard to the cogent and consistent (save for *Lex Service*) reasoning in the authorities, it is not open to this court now to return to the line apparently taken in *Lex Service* that s.23 is subject to s.7" (at [41]).

3–74 **Date of Service** The date at which service is effected where recorded delivery or post is adopted is the date at which the notice is entrusted to the post office; it matters not that the notice is returned undelivered: *CA Webber (Transport) Ltd v Railtrack.*[136]

---

133 See also the earlier decision of the Court of Appeal in *Blunden v Frogmore Investments Ltd* [2002] EWCA Civ 573; [2002] E.G.L.R. 29, where service of a s.25 notice was held to be valid notwithstanding non-delivery and the return of the notice to the post office. However, it is to be noted that in that case no argument was run that s.7 of the Interpretation Act 1978 applied.

134 [2004] 1 W.L.R. 320; [2004] 1 E.G.L.R. 49 CA. The authorities relating to the interrelation of Interpretation Act 1978, s.7 and s.23 had been fully considered at first instance before the decision in *CA Webber (Transport) Ltd v Railtrack* by Smedley J. in *Commercial Union Life Assurance Ltd v Moustafa* [1999] 2 E.G.L.R. 37 QBD. The court considered that *Galinski v McHugh* and *Lex Services v Johns* were irreconcilable with one another although Interpretation Act 1978, s.7 was not in issue and does not appear to have been referred to in the *Galinski v McHugh* decision. It was significant, it was said, that there was no reference anywhere in *Lex Services v Johns* to the court having been referred to *Galinski v McHugh*, which had been decided some nine months or so previously and it had to be borne in mind that the decision in *Galinski v McHugh* was given by a court composed of three Lord Justices and that it was subsequently followed in *Railtrack Plc v Gojra*. Accordingly, it seemed to Smedley J., that he had to follow the decision of the Court of Appeal in *Galinski v McHugh*. He accordingly held that a notice under s.17 of the Landlord and Tenant (Covenants) Act 1995, to which the modes of service provided for by s.23(1) of the 1927 Act apply (Landlord and Tenant (Covenants) Act 1995 s.27(5)), which requires notice to be given prior to the expiry of six months from the date that the debt fell due in order for the landlord to sue for the debt, was validly served if it was sent by recorded delivery to its recipient at his last known place of abode, whether it was received by that recipient or not. Thus notwithstanding the fact that the s.17 notice was returned after the expiry of the six-month period to the sender undelivered, having been sent by recorded delivery addressed to the tenant's last known place of abode before the expiry of the six-month period, with an endorsement on the envelope indicating that there had been no answer and the envelope was endorsed "Not called for", the notice was nevertheless deemed to have been served prior to the expiry of the period of six months.

135 [2004] 1 W.L.R. 320; [2004] 1 E.G.L.R. 49 CA. See also the earlier first instance decision of *Beanby Estates Ltd v Egg Stores (Stamford Hill) Ltd* [2003] 1 W.L.R. 2064; [2003] 3 E.G.L.R. 85 (Neuberger J.) (digested at para.3–76).

136 See fn.135.

CA Webber (Transport) Ltd v Railtrack[137] R, the landlord of business premises, served s.25 notices relating to two adjoining units let to W specifying January 22, 2002 as the date of termination. The notices were sent by recorded delivery on Friday July 20, 2001. W by an arrangement with the Post Office did not receive mail on Saturday. W in fact received the notices on either Monday July 23, or Tuesday July 24, 2001. W contended that the s.25 notices were invalid as they specified a date of termination less than six months from the date that they were given and so failed to conform with the requirements of s.25(4) of the 1954 Act. **3–75**

It was held by the Court of Appeal that the s.25 notices were valid:

(1) section 7 of the Interpretation Act 1978 did not apply to s.23 of the Landlord and Tenant Act 1927. Insofar as *Lex Services v Johns*[138] decided otherwise it was inconsistent with the decision of the Court of Appeal in *Galinski v McHugh*[139] and was *per incuriam*;

(2) that the words "sending through" the post in s.23 did not imply some sort of onward transmission. The word "through" in the phrase "sending... through" connoted a method of sending; it said nothing about onward transmission. All that the sender by recorded post can do is to entrust the notice to the post office: that is the act described in s.23;

(3) the interpretation adopted by the court to s.23, so as to exclude the application of s.7 of the Interpretation Act 1978, was not an infringement of the tenant's human rights under arts 1 and 6 of the First Protocol to the Human Rights Act 1998. The aim of s.23 was to assist the server of the notice and to establish a fair allocation of the risk of failure of communication and avoid disputes of fact, where the true facts are likely to be unknown to the server of the notice and difficult for the court to ascertain. In those circumstances it is neither unreasonable nor disproportionate to achieve certainty for landlords and tenants alike by interpreting s.23 as excluding the applicability of s.7 of the Interpretation Act 1978.

Beanby Estates Ltd v Egg Stores (Stamford Hill) Ltd[140] L sent a s.25 notice on January 7, 2002 by recorded delivery. It was actually received by the tenant on January 9, 2002. The tenant served a counter-notice and applied for a new tenancy on May 8, 2002. L argued that the proceedings were issued too late as the notice was served on January 7, 2002. Neuberger J. held that the proceedings were made too late, as the s.25 notice was served on January 7, 2002, not on January 9. **3–76**

Is receipt necessary in order for delivery to be effective? In *Stephenson v Orca Properties*[141] it was held that where service is effected by recorded delivery, delivery cannot, in the ordinary course of post, be effected unless someone signs **3–77**

[137] [2004] 1 W.L.R. 320; [2004] 1 E.G.L.R. 44 CA.

[138] [1990] 1 E.G.L.R. 92 CA.

[139] [1989] E.G.L.R. 109 CA (digested in para.3–81).

[140] [2003] 1 W.L.R. 2064; [2003] 3 E.G.L.R. 85.

[141] [1989] 2 E.G.L.R. 129. This decision does not appear to have been cited to the court in *Commercial Union Assurance Ltd v Moustafa*.

a receipt. If no one is available to sign or is willing to sign a receipt, delivery will not be effected.[142] However, that decision was concerned not with s.23 of the 1927 Act but with the interpretation of s.196(4) of the Law of Property Act 1925. Section 196(4) of the Law of Property Act 1925 provides:

> "(4) Any notice required or authorised by this Act to be served shall also be sufficiently served, if it is sent by post in a registered letter addressed to the lessee, lessor, mortgagee, mortgagor, or other person to be served, by name, at the aforesaid place of abode or business, office, or counting-house, and if that letter is not returned by the postal operator (within the meaning of the Postal Services Act 2000) concerned undelivered; and that service shall be deemed to be made at the time at which the registered letter would in the ordinary course be delivered."

Section 23 of the Landlord and Tenant Act 1927, unlike s.196(4), makes no express provision as to the time at which the letter is deemed to be served if not returned undelivered. As interpreted by the Court of Appeal, in *CA Webber (Transport) Ltd v Railtrack* (digested in para.3–75), s.23 is not subject to s.7 of the Interpretation Act 1978[143] which contains words similar to those of s.196(4). Thus, a notice served by recorded delivery or post in accordance with s.23 is served on the date it is entrusted with the post office: it matters not if the notice is undelivered, e.g. by going astray in the course of post or returned undelivered. *Beanby Estates Ltd v Egg Stores (Stamford Hill) Ltd*[144] (digested in para.3–76) is a good example of this. In *Stephenson v Orca Properties* the issue was whether a notice initiating a rent review, which had to be served on the tenant before midnight on Sunday June 30, 1985, was deemed to have been validly served by that date having been sent by recorded delivery on Friday June 28. The evidence was that the post office had attempted to deliver the notice on June 29 but had found that the offices to which the letter was sent were not open. The letter was therefore returned to the delivery office and a successful delivery was effected on July 1. Scott J. held that the trigger notice had not been served in time. He said that in the case of delivery by recorded delivery:

> "Delivery cannot, in the ordinary course of post, be effected unless someone signs a receipt. If no one is available to sign or is unwilling to sign a receipt, delivery will not be effected . . .. Delivery in the ordinary course of post requires, where recorded delivery letters are concerned, an available recipient; it cannot take place at a time when there is no available recipient."

3–78 *Stephenson v Orca Properties* was not followed by Patten J. in *WX Investments Ltd v Begg*[145] (digested in para.3–79). In that case Patten J. held that, in determining for the purposes of s.196(4) of the Law of Property Act 1925 when delivery is treated as having taken place, it is necessary to decide when delivery in the ordinary course of post would have taken place. This does not require the presence of an available recipient. The fiction created by the deeming provision extends to what would in the ordinary course of post be the likely date of delivery. To make the presumption of delivery an effective one, s.196(4) requires an assumption to be made that an available recipient was present on that

[142] In *Lex Services v Johns* [1990] 1 E.G.L.R. 92 CA, Glidewell L.J. suggests that one of the requirements for delivery was a signature (albeit illegible) for receipt.
[143] As to which see para.3–70.
[144] As to which see para.3–70.
[145] [2002] EWHC 925 (Ch); [2002] 3 E.G.L.R. 47.

occasion. Once the statutory presumption comes into play with the operation of the deeming provision, the date on which the recorded receipt was in fact signed is irrelevant.

WX Investments Ltd v Begg[146] On September 22, 1997, L served a trigger notice on T initiating a review of the rent. T had 14 days within which to serve a counter-notice. T sent a counter-notice by first class recorded delivery on September 24, 1997. Attempts were made by the Post Office to effect delivery on September 25 and September 30, 1997 but without success. The counter-notice was finally delivered on October 10, 1997, a date nominated by L with the post office which had offered to deliver the notice on a date specified by L. The lease incorporated the provisions of s.196(4) of the Law of Property Act 1925.[147] Patten J. held that delivery of the counter-notice was deemed to have taken place on September 25, 1997. **3–79**

Chiswell v Griffon Land and Estates Ltd[148] The tenant, in response to the landlord's s.25 notice, posted a counter-notice. The tenant did not adopt any one of the modes of service permitted by s.23 of the Landlord and Tenant Act 1927. Instead he placed the counter-notice in a pre-paid envelope properly addressed to the landlord's solicitors. The counter-notice was never received by the landlord's solicitors and thus it was concluded that, as a matter of reasonable probability, the letter had gone astray in the post. It was held by the Court of Appeal that the tenant's application for a new tenancy had properly been dismissed, the judge having found on a balance of probability that, within the terms of s.26 of the Interpretation Act 1889 (now s.7 of the Interpretation Act 1978) the contrary had been proved. **3–80**

Galinski v McHugh[149] The landlord served on the tenant's solicitors a notice pursuant to s.4 of Pt I of the Landlord and Tenant Act 1954 proposing a statutory tenancy in place of the original tenancy, which, under the provisions of Pt I of the 1954 Act, had continued after the expiry of the contractual term. The tenant had two months in which to give formal notice to claim to enfranchise the freehold. No such notice was served. Section 4 of the 1954 Act required notice to be "given to the tenant". The provisions of s.23(1) of the 1927 Act applied for the purposes of Pt I of the 1954 Act by s.66(4) of the 1954 Act. It was held by the Court of Appeal that although s.23(1) of the 1927 Act expressly permitted service on any agent of the landlord this did not by necessary implication render impermissible service on an agent of the tenant. As the judge at first instance had found as a fact that the tenant's solicitors had ostensible authority to accept service, the s.4 notice was properly served. **3–81**

---

146 [2002] EWHC 925 (Ch); [2002] 3 E.G.L.R. 47 (Patten J.).

147 As to which see para.3–77.

148 [1975] 1 W.L.R. 1181 CA.

149 [1989] 1 E.G.L.R. 109 CA.

Risk of receipt out of time: other modes of service

3–82 The above discussion[150] is concerned with service of documents by the primary methods prescribed by s.23 of the 1927 Act. Where none of those methods is adopted the time of service will be a question of fact and, if service has been effected by ordinary post, there is no reason why the provisions of s.7 of the Interpretation Act 1978 ought not to apply. Of course, in the context of using a method of service other than that prescribed by s.23, the risk of receipt out of time is on the sender rather than the intended recipient. In *Price v West London Investment Building Society Ltd*[151] (digested in para.3–59) it was held that a s.25 notice had been served on the date when it was delivered to the tenant's premises and received by the tenant's employee there.

3–83 **Contractual provisions as to service** A contractual provision as to service may have the same effect as s.23 of the Landlord and Tenant Act 1927. In *Blunden v Frogmore Investments Ltd*[152] (digested in para.3–84) cl.6.9 of the lease provided that:

> "In addition to any other prescribed mode of service any notices requiring to be served hereunder shall be validly served if served in accordance with section 196 of the Law of Property Act 1925 as amended by the Recorded Delivery Act 1962 or in the case of the Tenant if left addressed to it or if there shall be more than one to any of them, on the Demised Premises or sent to it him or any of them by post or left at the last known address or addresses of it him or them in Great Britain."

It was held that service in accordance with that provision was effective notwithstanding non-receipt by the intended recipient. It was said that a condition of non-return could not be read in to cl.6.9, as existed in s.196(4) of the Law of Property Act 1925, nor could "sent... by post" be read as meaning "sent and delivered".

3–84 ***Blunden v Frogmore Investments Ltd***[153] B was a tenant of a unit in a building which had been damaged by a terrorist bomb. The lease provided in cl.6.4 that the lease could be determined by the landlord, F, if there occurred destruction or damage such as to render the demised premises or the building wholly or substantially unfit for occupation, by giving to the tenant not later than six months after the date of the destruction or damage notice in writing to this effect. The explosion occurred on June 15, 1996. On December 4, 1996, 11 days before the expiry of the six-month period F, by its solicitors, served three letters on B. The letters were sent by recorded delivery and certificates of proof of posting were obtained. The letters contained two notices: one being a notice (embodied in

[150] At paras 3–67 to 3–79.

[151] [1964] 1 W.L.R. 616; [1964] 2 All E.R. 318 CA.

[152] [2002] EWCA Civ 573; [2002] 2 E.G.L.R. 29; [2003] 2 P. & C.R. 6. See also *Ener-G Holdings Plc v Philip Hormell* [2012] EWCA Civ 1059 (a non-landlord and tenant case concerning a contractual provision providing for deemed service).

[153] [2002] EWCA Civ 573; [2002] 2 E.G.L.R. 29; [2003] 2 P. & C.R. 6.

a letter) under cl.6.4 and the other being under s.25 of the 1954 Act terminating the lease and opposing renewal under s.30(1)(f) of the Act. The three addresses to which the letters were sent consisted of:

(1) the postal address of the demised premises;
(2) the private address given in the lease as B's residence;
(3) a private address given by B to F's general manager of the building.

In addition, copies of the notices were affixed to the outside of the demised premises.

B's evidence was that at the time the notices were sent he was living with his brother at a private address different to those to which the notices were addressed. Further, it was impossible for him to receive mail at the demised premises as, because of the damage caused by the bomb, it was out of bounds to the tenants of the building and the general public.

All three letters were returned to F's solicitors by the post office. F argued that the notices were validly served, relying on the provisions of cl.6.9 of the lease and s.23 of the Landlord and Tenant Act 1927. Clause 6.9 of the lease is set out in para.3–81.

The Court of Appeal held that the notices were validly served because:

(a) it was unnecessary for the statutory notice to comply with cl.6.9, as the statutory notice could do double duty, both as a contractual break notice and a statutory notice, following *Scholl Manufacturing Co v Clifton (Slim-Line)*[154] (digested in para.3–188);
(b) the contractual provisions of cl.6.9 applied notwithstanding the fact that as, a matter of literal interpretation, neither notice was "required" to be served;
(c) F achieved good service by post under the express terms of cl.6.9 despite the non-delivery of the letter to B's private address; no condition of non-return could be read into cl.6.9, as existed in s.196(4) of the Law of Property Act 1925, nor could "sent . . . by post" be read as meaning "sent and delivered";
(d) F achieved good service under s.23 of the Landlord and Tenant Act 1927 despite the non-delivery and return of the letters. In particular no argument was run that s.7 of the Interpretation Act 1978 applied albeit cl.6.4 was time specific;
(e) F did achieve good service by affixing the notice to the demised premises, per Robert Walker L.J.; Carnworth and Schiemann L.JJ. reserved their position on whether or not effective notice had been served by this means.

---

[154] [1967] Ch. 41 CA.

The computation of time

3–85 For the purposes of the Act "month" means a calendar month: Interpretation Act 1978 ss.5 and 22(1) and Sch.2 para.4(1). In *Dodds v Walker*,[155] the House of Lords explained the "corresponding date rule" applicable to the computation of times in such cases. That rule is as follows:

(1) Where there is a date in the month during which the notice is to expire which "corresponds" to the date in the month in which the notice is served, then the notice should specify that "corresponding date". Accordingly, if one had to give one month's notice from July 31, the appropriate date to specify would be August 31, because both July and August are months which have 31 days.
(2) If there is no "corresponding date" in the month in which the notice is to expire, because that month contains fewer days than the month in which the notice is served, then the notice should be expressed to expire on the last day of the month in which the notice expires. Thus, if one were giving one month's notice from August 31, it should be expressed to expire on September 30.

4. PERSON BY AND TO WHOM NOTICE IS TO BE GIVEN

3–86 A valid s.25 notice must be given by "the landlord" to "the tenant" and likewise a valid s.26 request must be made by "the tenant" to "the landlord". It is therefore necessary to consider the meaning of "the landlord" and "the tenant" as defined by the Act. It should be noted, however, that notices under s.27(1) and (2) are to be given to the immediate landlord.

Meaning of "landlord"

3–87 "The landlord" is not necessarily the tenant's immediate landlord but is the person who, at the time the matter is being considered, fulfils the conditions[156] set out in s.44(1). Such a person is also referred to for the purposes of Sch.6 as "the competent landlord". It is suggested that the following is a convenient method of ascertaining who is "the landlord" in relation to a particular tenancy, where there is a tier of reversionary interests:

(1) Start at the bottom of the tier of interests, that is to say with the immediate landlord. Consider the nature of his interest. Is it:
    (a) The fee simple?
    (b) The residue of a term of years with more than 14 months unexpired?
    (c) The residue of a term of years with less than 14 months expired, but which is a tenancy to which the Act applies and in respect of which no s.25 notice has been served and no s.26 request made?

[155] [1981] 1 W.L.R. 1027; [1981] 2 All E.R. 609 HL.

[156] As to a person being estopped from denying that he is the landlord, see para.3–93.

(d) A periodic tenancy (whether protected by the Act or not) in respect of which no notice (whether a common law notice to quit or a s.25 notice or a s.26 request) has been served?

(e) A tenancy which is being continued under s.24 of the Act in respect of which no s.25 notice has been served or s.26 request made?

If the interest in question is in one of the above categories, the owner of the interest is "the landlord" for the purposes of s.44. If the interest is not in one of the categories, the owner is not "the landlord".

(2) Assuming the immediate landlord not to have an interest bringing him within the definition, one goes to the next landlord up in the chain and asks the same questions of his interest. If that interest comes within one of the categories then he is "the landlord". If not, one carries on up the chain until a person fulfilling the definition is found.

It the previous editions of this work[157] it was said that "It is a matter of some doubt whether there is yet another category, namely a tenancy for a term of years certain to which the Act does not apply and which has less than 14 months unexpired. Although authority suggests that the owner of such an interest is not within the definition of "landlord" (see *Skelton v Harrison & Pinder*[158] (digested in para.3–201)), the contrary can be argued since it is impossible to say that such an interest will definitely come to an end within 14 months because circumstances may subsequently alter so as to bring the tenancy back within the Act." **3–88**

On reflection it is considered that the inquiry denoted by s.44 is an enquiry as to who is "the landlord" at a particular date. It involves considering an interest which "for the time being" fulfils certain conditions. Accordingly, the court will determine whether the tenant has a tenancy of less or more than 14 months at the relevant date that the issue (i.e. who is the landlord for the purposes of s.44) is to be determined without having regard to future possibilities. The matter was considered in *Bowes-Lyon v Green*[159] (digested in para.15–17). Although *Bowes-Lyon v Green* was concerned with s.44 prior to its amendment by the Law of Property Act 1969, which amended s.44(1)(b), the reasoning of the House of Lords applies equally, it is considered, to the current provisions of s.44.[160] **3–89**

In *Bowes-Lyon v Green*[161] the superior landlord ("SL") had granted the tenant ("T") a tenancy of the ground and basement floors of premises for a term expiring on April 1, 1959. T had sub-let to the appellant ("A"). The sub-tenancy was of the ground floor only. The sub-tenancy expired contractually on March 31, 1959. On March 19, 1958 SL granted a reversionary lease of the ground floor to A effective from April 5, 1959 for a term of seven years, which was less than 14 months before the contractual expiry date of T's lease. Both T's tenancy and A's sub tenancy were protected by the 1954 Act. A resisted T's claim for one quarter's rent due on June 24, 1959 arguing that the agreement between him and SL to **3–90**

157 See, e.g. 3rd edn, para.3.84.

158 [1975] Q.B. 361.

159 [1963] A.C. 420 HL.

160 The relevant wording under consideration by the House of Lords is not materially different.

161 [1963] A.C. 420 HL.

grant the reversionary lease was an agreement falling within s.28 of the 1954 Act such that A's sub-tenancy did not continue beyond the contractual term date of the sub-lease. The agreement would only come within s.28 if at the time it was entered into SL was the competent landlord[162] within s.44. A contended that he was not T's sub-tenant as at the time of the grant of the reversionary lease, as although T's tenancy was within the 1954 Act it was possible that it would not continue, e.g. by T vacating. It was held that T remained competent landlord of A *at the time that the reversionary lease was entered into* and thus SL was not the "competent landlord" for the purposes of s.28 at the date that the reversionary lease was entered into. Lord Reid said:

> "... what you are directed by the earlier part of the section to look for is an interest which *for the time being* fulfils the conditions. That must, I think, mean an interest which fulfils the conditions on the day with regard to which it must be determined who is 'the landlord.' On that day in this case the respondent [i.e. T] held a protected tenancy because she was carrying on business in a part of the premises let to her and it was only a future possible act on her part which could convert it into an unprotected tenancy. Unless that occurred it could be said with certainty that her tenancy would not come to an end by effluxion of time within 14 months because it would be continued for an indefinite time by the Act. On this view you look at the position on the relevant day and you can say definitely that, unless that position changes, any particular tenancy will or will not come to an end within 14 months by effluxion of time. On the other view there is no such clear-cut answer; all you can say is either that the tenancy cannot come to an end by effluxion of time within 14 months or that it may or may not do so depending on events which may be likely or extremely unlikely to happen." (at 435)[163]

Equitable interests

3–91 The "landlord" in s.44(1) is referring to the legal not the equitable owner. As Nourse L.J. put it in *Pearson v Alyo*[164]: "The subsection is concerned only with legal owners. The Act would be unworkable if it were otherwise." Although the "landlord" is unconcerned with the beneficial interests behind the legal estate it is considered that a mesne landlord holding under an agreement for lease which is capable of being specifically enforced would, nevertheless, qualify (assuming the length of term intended to be granted exceeded the statutory minimum) as the "landlord" in s.44(1). Thus if F, the freehold owner, agreed to grant to T a lease of business premises for a period of 10 years and, notwithstanding the fact that the completion date had passed, the lease had not been completed but was capable of being specifically enforced, and T had sub-let the premises, it would be T not F who would be the sub-tenant's landlord within s.44(1). Support for this view is derived from *Shelley v United Artists Corp Ltd*[165] (digested in para.14–45) where

---

[162] Any agreement between the landlord and the tenant for the purposes of s.28 must be one between the "competent landlord" within s.44 and the tenant: see para.15–15.

[163] See also Lord Morris at 443.

[164] [1990] 1 E.G.L.R. 114 CA. It was held that a s.25 notice served by one of two joint landlords holding on trust for one of them, who happened to be the sole beneficial owner, was invalid. The fact that the sole beneficial owner served the notice mattered not. The "landlord" was the trustees and both need to be named in the notice. See also *Biles v Caesar* [1957] 1 W.L.R. 156 CA at 158 per Denning L.J. referring to the "landlord" being the person in whom the legal title is vested.

[165] [1990] 1 E.G.L.R. 103 CA.

the Court of Appeal held that a specifically enforceable option to take a new lease could be added to the landlord's existing leasehold interest for the purposes of s.44.

Trustees

Where the legal estate is held on trust then the trustees are the landlord and not the beneficiaries under the trust: *Dun & Bradstreet Software Services (England) Ltd v Provident Mutual Life Assurance Association*,[166] where a break notice served in the name of the beneficiary of the leasehold interest rather than the trustee, would, but for an estoppel, have been invalid by reason thereof. **3–92**

Representation as to being "landlord"

The court in *Shelley v United Artists Corp Ltd*[167] (digested in para.14–45) also held that a landlord which serves a s.25 notice thereby asserts that it is "the landlord" within the meaning of s.44 and that this is a continuing representation which becomes a misrepresentation (unless corrected) if the landlord subsequently ceased to fulfil the s.44 definition.[168] This, in turn, can give rise to an estoppel preventing the person who is the "landlord" from denying that proceedings against the previous "landlord" are valid and binding, as it did on the particular facts of *Shelley*. **3–93**

Receivers and mortgagees

Section 67 makes special provision for the case where the interest of the landlord is subject to a mortgage and the mortgagee is in possession, or a receiver has been appointed. In such circumstances, it is the mortgagee or receiver who is "the landlord" for the purposes of the Act: *Meah v Mouskos*,[169] where it was held by the Court of Appeal that proceedings under the Act (which had validly been commenced at a time before the receiver was appointed) should be amended to join the receiver. **3–94**

---

[166] [1998] 2 E.G.L.R. 175 CA. See also para.3–102.

[167] [1990] 1 E.G.L.R. 103 CA.

[168] In *Lay v Ackerman* [2004] EWCA Civ 184; [2004] L. & T.R. 29; [2005] 1 E.G.L.R. 139, the landlord, a body of trustees, had served on the tenant a counter-notice pursuant to s.45 of the Leasehold Reform, Housing and Urban Development Act 1993 (in connection with the tenant's claim for an extended lease under that legislation), incorrectly naming another body of trustees as landlord. There was no issue over the fact that the actual landlord had in fact served the counter notice. Neuberger L.J. said of the *Shelley v United Artists* decision:

"In my judgment, the appellants' case here is stronger than that of the successful tenant in *Shelley*. If a landlord serves a notice on a tenant wrongly identifying a third party as 'the landlord', there is a plain and unambiguous representation to the tenant, who *ex hypothesi*, knows the representation is made by the landlord (because he is confident that the notice was served on behalf of the actual landlord) to the effect that the third party is the landlord. The tenant is plainly entitled to rely upon that statement, as against the actual landlord, at least until the landlord has unambiguously put the tenant right." at [52].

[169] [1964] 2 Q.B. 23 CA.

Statutory tenant

3–95 A statutory tenant under the Rent Act does not fulfil the definition of "landlord" in s.44 because he is not "the owner of" any "interest in the property" comprised in the current tenancy: *Piper v Muggleton*.[170]

Registered land: general

3–96 If one is dealing with unregistered land, there is no difficulty in ascertaining when the landlord becomes the competent landlord for the conveyance will transfer the legal estate. In the context of registered land there may be a delay in the passing of the legal estate having regard to the requirement of registration. The legal estate in registered land passes only upon registration,[171] that is, when the purchaser's name is entered on the Proprietorship Register.[172] As there is an interval of time between the date of application for the registration and the actual date of registration, s.74 of the Land Registration Act 2002 provides that the legal estate is deemed to have passed retrospectively on the day on which the application for registration was deemed delivered.[173] There is no problem over service of a s.25 notice once registration has been completed. However, difficulties may arise in circumstances where a notice is served prior to registration having been completed. It is clear that at the date of the notice, the transferee is not, in fact, the competent landlord, for the legal estate has not yet been vested in him. Thus, for instance, it has been held that until registration the transferee cannot serve a valid notice to quit: *Smith v Express Dairy Company Ltd*[174]; nor forfeit the lease: *Crumpton v Unifox Properties Ltd*.[175] It can be

---

170 [1956] 2 Q.B. 569 CA.

171 See by way of example, *Brown & Root Technology Ltd v Sun Alliance* [2001] Ch. 733 CA (exercise of option by assignor of lease valid, for until registration the assignor remained the "lessee" albeit the assignor had done everything that was necessary to give rise to an effective assignment).

172 ss.27(1), (4) and Sch.2 paras 2 and 3 of the Land Registration Act 2002, effective from October 10, 2003 (Land Registration Act 2002 (Commencement No.4) Order 2003 (SI 2003/1725)); *Frederick Lawrence Ltd v Freeman Hardy & Willis Ltd* [1959] Ch. 731 at 748, per Romer L.J. (digested in para.7–258); *Brown Root Technology Ltd v Sun Alliance* [2001] Ch. 733 CA.

173 As to the time at which applications are deemed to be delivered, see Land Registration Rules r.15.

174 [1954] J.P.L. 45.

175 [1992] 2 E.G.L.R. 82 CA. See, however, *Scribes West Ltd v Relsa Anstalt (No.3)* [2004] EWCA Civ 1744; [2005] 1 E.G.L.R. 22 where the Court of Appeal held that an equitable owner was entitled to forfeit by reason of the provisions of s.141 of the Law of Property Act 1925. In that case company A was the registered proprietor of premises subject to a lease. On February 28, 2001 it assigned its reversionary interest to company B by way of a standard Land Registry TR1. The form recorded the receipt of the purchase price of £131 million and included a statement that "the transferor assigns to the transferee the benefit of any rights claims title or covenants to which it is entitled in respect of the property". On the same day company B gave notice of the assignment to the tenant and required the tenant to pay the rent to it. On July 16, 2001 it peaceably re-entered the premises for non-payment of rent. On July 25, 2001 it granted a new lease of the premises to a third party. On January 2, 2002 the transfer was registered at the Land Registry. The Court of Appeal held that the forfeiture was valid notwithstanding the fact that company A remained the registered proprietor (and therefore the legal owner) at the relevant date. Company B was the equitable owner of the premises and was entitled (by virtue of the assignment of rights coupled with notice) to receive the rent from the tenant. It was held that the operation of s.141(2) of the Law of Property Act 1925 (under which a right of re-entry is capable of being enforced "by the person from time to time entitled, subject to the term, to the income

argued, however, that the effect of registration being retrospective to the date of the making of the application validates the service of the s.25 notice. The position is unclear, but the authors' view is that the validity of the notice must be considered at the date when it was served and since at that date as registration had not been completed, the notice has been served by a person who was not the "competent landlord".

L can give a notice in respect of premises of which he is the registered proprietor **3–97** albeit, as a matter of unregistered conveyancing, L may have no title to the land in question. L is competent landlord by virtue of the provisions of the Land Registration Act 2002. L, unless and until the registered title is rectified, is deemed to have vested in it the premises referred to or, alternatively, T will be estopped from denying L's title: *Prudential Assurance Co Ltd v Eden Restaurants (Holborn) Ltd*[176] (digested in para.3–98).

Prudential Assurance Co Ltd v Eden Restaurants (Holborn) Ltd[177] T's lease **3–98** demised premises including an area of a basement shaded green on the lease plan, referred to as "the green land". Upon the landlord serving a notice pursuant to s.25 of the 1954 Act, T contended that the notice was invalid as L did not have title to the green land, contending that as it was below the surface of the public highway, it was vested in the local highway authority. L in fact held the premises under a lease. The freehold title was registered but none of the entries in respect of the titles included the green land. L's lease was also registered. L's lease also purported to demise to L the green land.

It was held by the Court of Appeal:

(1) that by virtue of L's registered title and the relevant provisions of the Land Registration Act, L was deemed to be registered proprietor of the whole of the demised premises demised, including the green land, and that this was so, even if it could be demonstrated by T as a fact that the freehold title to the green land was not owned by L or the freeholder but was owned by the local highway authority. There had never been any application to rectify the relevant entries in the register and unless and until rectified, by force of statute, L was deemed to have vested in it by virtue of the Land Registration Act the green land;

(2) although T's lease was granted by the freehold owner, and thus T would be estopped from impeaching the freeholder's title thereto, as L was effectively a successor in title, albeit by the grant of a lease of the reversion standing in the shoes of the freehold owner during the term of L's lease, T was equally estopped from impeaching, as against L, title to the green land: *Rennie v Robinson*[178];

---

of the whole or any part, as the case may require, of the land leased") was not confined to the legal owner. The word "entitled" it was said drew no distinction between legal and equitable interests: it connoted no more than an enforceable right to the relevant income.

176 [2000] L. & T.R. 480 CA.

177 [2000] L. & T.R. 480 CA.

178 (1823) 1 Bing. 147

(3) accordingly, L was competent landlord for the purposes of the 1954 Act in respect of all the premises demised, including the green land.

Registered land: disposition of legal estate requiring first registration

3–99 The new Act came into force on October 13, 2003[179] subject to transitional provisions.[180] Registration of title at the Land Registry is compulsory in all areas.[181] The registration of individual titles is, however, provided for only after certain specified transactions: Land Registration Act 2002 s.4. This section provides for the circumstances in which an unregistered estate must be registered.[182] Section 4 may be expanded by order: LRA 2002 s.5. Section 7(1) of the Land Registration Act 2002 provides that upon a disposition of the legal estate requiring first registration, the legal estate passes on the transfer, subject to the legal estate being divested from the purchaser if there is a failure to apply for registration within two months[183] of the date of transfer, subject to that period being extended. The consequence of non-registration is that, in the case of a transfer of the freehold, the legal estate, having passed to the purchaser, will automatically pass back and the vendor will remain trustee of the legal estate for the purchaser.[184] The failure to effect a registration of the grant of a lease requiring registration,[185] is that it will take effect as a contract made for valuable consideration to grant the legal estate concerned.[186]

---

[179] The Land Registration Act 2002 received Royal Assent on February 26, 2002 and came into force with effect from October 13, 2003: Land Registration Act 2002 (Commencement No.4) Order 2003 (SI 2003/1725) (with the exception of s.98(1) and Sch.6, para.5(4) and (5) of the Act).

[180] LRA 2002 Sch.12.

[181] The Land Registration Order 1989 (SI 1989/1347), which came into force on January 1, 1990, extended compulsory registration to all remaining districts in England and Wales by December 1, 1990.

[182] It reflects and expands the provisions of the Land Registration Act 1925 s.123 (as substituted by the LRA 1997 s.1 effective from April 1, 1998 (SI 1997/3036)).

[183] See LRA 2002 s.6.

[184] LRA 2002 s.7(2)(a) This reflects what was understood to be the position under LRA 1925 s.123: *Pinekerry v Kenneth Needs (Contractors)* (1992) 64 P. & C.R. 245 CA at 247.

[185] Those leases which are required to be registered are set out in s.4(1)(c)–(f), LRA 2002. Of particular note are:

(1) The grant out of a qualifying estate of a term of years absolute not being less than seven years from the delivery date of the grant. The grant must be for valuable or other consideration or by way of gift or in pursuance to a court order: s.4(1)(c).

(2) The grant out of a qualifying estate of an estate in land for a term of years absolute to take effect in possession after the end of the period of three months beginning with the date of the grant: s.4(1)(d). (This provision is intended to catch reversionary leases. The reversionary lease will not be an overriding interest under Sch.1, para.1 (a leasehold estate in land granted for a term not exceeding seven years from the date of the grant, except for a lease the grant of which falls within s.4(1)(d), (e) or (f)) or Sch.3, para.1 (a leasehold estate in land granted for a term not exceeding seven years from the date of the grant, except for (a) a lease the grant of which falls within s.4(1)(d), (e) or (f), or (2) a lease the grant of which constitutes a registrable disposition).

A "qualifying estate" is an unregistered legal estate which is (i) a freehold estate in land or (ii) a leasehold estate in land for a term which, at the time of the transfer, grant or creation, has more than seven years to run: LRA 2002 s.4(2).

[186] LRA 2002 s.7(2)(b).

If the purchaser, having served a s.25 notice within the two-month period, fails to apply for registration, so that at the end of the two-month period the legal estate is then divested from him and revested in the vendor as trustee, it would appear that such a s.25 notice is valid, for at the date when the notice was served the purchaser was the competent landlord for the purposes of s.44. The tenant would, in those circumstances, have to be careful to ensure that any proceedings were issued against and served on the appropriate person. No such problem arises if the application for registration is made in due time. **3–100**

Meaning of "tenant"

The term "tenant" is not expressly defined.[187] It presumably bears its ordinary meaning of the persons or person in whom the tenancy is vested.[188] Outside the special provisions of s.41A, it is essential for all joint tenants to join together in the giving of notices: *Harris v Black*[189] (digested in para.6–30). Notices should be addressed to them all: *Booth v Reynolds*[190] (digested in para.3–103). Where the tenant dies, his personal representatives become the tenant for the purposes of the Act: *Re Crowhurst Park*.[191] **3–101**

It often arises that one is required to serve a notice on behalf of or upon trustees. It would appear to be sufficient to refer to the identity of the "tenant" as the "trustees of [name of trust/settlement]" without the need to identify the trustees individually: *Hackney African Organisation v London Borough of Hackney*.[192] A notice signed by one of several trustees for and on behalf of the others is valid. Although joint tenants are well advised to make the position clear in the body of the document itself it is unnecessary for a notice served by one of several trustees to state in the body of the notice that he has been so authorised by the others and that it was served on behalf of them all. Provided only and always that the notice, properly construed, is recognisable as a notice on the part of all the trustees jointly that should be sufficient for the purposes of the statute.[193] **3–102**

---

[187] See also paras 3–138 and 6–24 for further discussion on the meaning of "tenant".

[188] The special provisions of s.41A dealing with the position where the business has been carried on by joint tenants in partnership are discussed in paras 6–31 et seq.

[189] (1983) 46 P. & C.R 366 CA; *Hackney African Organisation v London Borough of Hackney* [1999] L. & T.R. 117; [1999] 77 P. & C.R. D. 18 CA, where it was said that the words in s.41(1)(c), which provides that "a change in the persons of the trustees shall not be treated as a change in the persons of the tenant", did not dispense with the need for trustees holding a lease jointly to act together in seeking a renewal of that lease: per Simon Brown L.J. Joint tenants in partnership are discussed in paras 6–31 et seq. (1974) N.L.J. 119.

[190] (1974) N.L.J. 119.

[191] [1974] 1 W.L.R. 583.

[192] [1999] 77 P. & C.R. D. 18 CA.

[193] *Hackney African Organisation v London Borough of Hackney* [1999] L. & T.R. 117; [1999] 77 P. & C.R. D. 18 CA. In this case the court was concerned with a counter-notice served by one of four trustees. It was signed by the chairman of the Trust, named him alone as the tenant and gave as the tenant's address his own personal address. It was, however, sent with a covering letter on the trust's notepaper and signed by the chairman as "chair" of the relevant organisation and described it as "our counter-notice". The remaining trustees subsequently confirmed that they empowered the chairman to act on their behalf in connection with the service of the notice. It was held that the subsequent statement established that the chairman was acting with the authority of his fellow trustees and it was

3–103 ***Booth Investments Ltd v Reynolds***[194] A husband and wife were joint tenants of a tenancy of business premises. The husband carried on business alone as he and his wife had separated. The landlord's s.25 notice was addressed to and served on the husband only. It was held that the s.25 notice was invalid as it had to be addressed to all persons who constituted the tenant. The s.25 notice could not be validated by s.41A of the 1954 Act as the husband and wife had never carried on business in partnership.

5. SECTION 27 NOTICES

Notice under section 27(1)

3–104 The tenancy will not continue by virtue of s.24(1) if the tenant gives notice pursuant to s.27(1). Such a notice may be given by any tenant under a tenancy to which the Act applies provided it is a term certain.[195] The notice must be given to the immediate landlord and must be given not later than three months before the date on which, apart from the Act, the tenancy would come to an end by effluxion of time. The notice should state that the tenant does not desire the tenancy to be continued. Such a notice cannot be given until the tenant has been in occupation in right of the tenancy for one month. Notwithstanding the decision in *Esselte AB v Pearl Assurance Plc*[196] (digested in para.2–53) it may still be prudent for a tenant to serve a s.27(1) notice albeit the tenant intends to cease occupying the premises for business purposes at the contractual term date. It will ensure that the tenancy will not continue under s.24(1) after the term date whether or not the tenant, for whatever reason, remains in occupation thereafter for business purposes (e.g. if the tenant has miscalculated how long it will take him to vacate the premises). It is the authors' view that a tenant who serves a s.27(1) notice is liable to double rent under Distress for Rent Act 1737, s.18 as it is considered that the statutory notice is not a notice to quit within the meaning of the section.

3–105 A tenant may not serve a notice within s.27(1) after he has made a request for a new tenancy—see s.26(4).

3–106 One matter that now remains left open in light of the Court of Appeal decision in *Esselte AB v Pearl Assurance Plc*[197] (digested in para.2–53) is whether a tenant can serve a s.27(1) notice after the tenant has received a s.25 notice from his landlord and thereby shorten the date of termination. The authors' view is that the tenant ought to be able to serve such a notice, for this is a mode of termination

unnecessary for the counter-notice to expressly state that the named trustee and signatory did indeed have authority of his fellow trustees. Furthermore, the context in which the counter-notice came to be signed (there being existing proceedings between the parties where it was clear that the signatory was a trustee) and the fact that the covering letter made it plain that the notice was in fact served by the trustee organisation for their benefit, and not the chairman's own, the counter-notice was to be construed as one given by the chairman on behalf of the relevant organisation and thus on behalf of his fellow trustees as well as himself.

194 (1974) N.L.J. 119.

195 For a discussion of the meaning of "term certain", see para.2–05 et seq.

196 [1997] 1 W.L.R. 891; [1997] 2 All E.R. 41 CA.

197 [1997] 1 W.L.R. 891; [1997] 2 All E.R. 41 CA.

provided for by the Act. Where there are two modes of determination, one of which provides for an earlier date of termination than the other, there is no reason why the tenant should not be able to utilise the method providing for the earlier date notwithstanding his earlier exercise of the other method providing for a later date of termination. It is considered doubtful, however, whether a tenant can serve a s.27(1) after he has made an application for a new tenancy (this assumes, of course, that all the appropriate steps, including the making of the application, have occurred three months prior to the contractual term date). It is considered, by parity of reasoning with *I&H Caplan Ltd v Caplan (No.2)*[198] (digested in para.1–46) that in these circumstances the termination of the tenancy is dealt with by s.64.

Section 27(1A)

A new s.27(1A) has been added by art.25 of the 2003 Order. It provides: **3–107**

> "Section 24 of this Act shall not have effect in relation to a tenancy for a term of years certain where the tenant is not in occupation of the property comprised in the tenancy at the time when, apart from this Act, the tenancy would come to an end by effluxion of time."

Section 27(1A) reflects the decisions of the Court of Appeal in *Esselte AB v Pearl Assurance Plc*[199] (digested in para.2–53) and *Surrey CC v Single Horse Properties Ltd*[200] (digested in para.2–54). There is no continuation of the tenancy under s.24 unless the tenant is in occupation for the purposes or partly for the purposes of a business carried on by the tenant, as at the date on which the tenancy would otherwise expire by effluxion of time, irrespective of: **3–108**

(1) any later date of termination specified in the landlord's s.25 notice; or
(2) any later date of commencement of the new tenancy specified in the tenant's s.26 request; or
(3) the fact that the tenant has made an application to the court for renewal.

Notice under section 27(2)

Date of termination to be specified

Where a tenancy granted for a term of years certain is being continued by virtue of s.24, the tenant may terminate it by not less than three months notice given to the immediate landlord to expire at any time. It was formerly the position that the notice had to specify a date of termination which was a quarter day but this requirement was amended by the 2003 Order—see s.27(2). Such a notice may not be given unless the tenant has been in occupation in right of the tenancy for one month. The subsection expressly contemplates that the notice may be given before or after the term date of the tenancy. This enables the tenant, in effect, to **3–109**

198 [1963] 1 W.L.R. 1247, [1963] 2 All E.R. 930.
199 [1997] 1 W.L.R. 891; [1997] 2 All E.R. 41 CA.
200 [2002] EWCA Civ 367; [2002] 1 W.L.R. 2106.

choose how long he wishes his tenancy to be continued by s.24. If he wishes no continuation, he will give a notice pursuant to s.27(1). If he wants, e.g. a short period of continuation, he will give a notice to that effect before the contractual expiry date. If he does not wish to commit himself at an early stage, he can wait until the tenancy is being continued by virtue of s.24(1) and then choose which day he wishes the continuation to cease.

3–110 In the absence of authority the full implications of a s.27(2) notice are unclear. Although the authors have not encountered such a notice in practice, there is nothing within s.27(2) preventing the tenant from serving a notice of say two years in an attempt to continue to his advantage the terms of the tenant's current tenancy. The subsection simply provides for a minimum period of notice. No maximum is expressed. A tenant might well wish to serve a notice of say two year's duration, for various reasons. First, it gives the tenant certainty. He may want only a short term by way of renewal. Rather than fight the landlord in court he can obtain such a term by the simple expedient of serving a notice. Secondly, no interim rent is payable, as an application for an interim rent can be made only where a s.25 notice or s.26 request has been served: s.24A(1).

3–111 If such a two-year notice is served how can a landlord respond? Can the landlord serve a six month s.25 notice, effectively requiring the tenant to go to court? One argument against the landlord being able to serve a s.25 notice is that the tenant's s.27(2) notice has crystallised the date of termination of the tenancy. Accordingly, as a s.25 notice cannot be given more than 12 months and not less than six months before the termination date, the landlord is effectively prevented from serving a notice for the first year during which the tenant's s.27(2) notice is running. In the absence of direct authority, the authors can only express their view that it would be contrary to the policy of the Act to allow the tenant to prevent the landlord from invoking the procedures of the Act at such date as he would ordinarily have been able to. This approach, the authors believe, is consistent with the approach taken by the courts in cases raising similar problems under the old regime, such as *Long Acre Securities Ltd v Electro Acoustic Industries Ltd*[201] (digested in para.2–52).

Notice can be served albeit the tenancy is not one to which Act applies

3–112 In the second edition of this work[202] the authors were of the view that a notice could be given pursuant to s.27(2) even if the tenancy was not one to which the Act applied, so it could be given, e.g. where the tenancy was being continued by s.24(3) even though the tenancy had ceased to be one to which the Act applied. Section 27(2) as amended by the 2003 Order makes it clear that the tenancy shall not come to an end automatically upon cessation of business occupation. It reiterates, effectively, the provisions of s.24(3)(a) concerning the continuation of the tenancy upon the cessation of business occupation. Section 24(3)(a) provides *the landlord* with an opportunity of serving a notice to terminate the tenancy

[201] [1990] 1 E.G.L.R. 91.

[202] See para.2–62 et seq.

where the tenancy ceases to be one to which the Act applies.[203] There was, prior to the amendments, no corresponding express provision for *the tenant* to do so, although having regard to the wording in s.27 it was arguable that the tenancy, albeit no longer one to which the Act applied, could be brought to an end by service of a notice pursuant to s.27(2) in its unamended form.[204]

After service of section 25 notice?

It is considered that, notwithstanding the fact that the Court of Appeal have in *Esselte AB v Pearl Assurance Plc*[205] (digested in para.2–53) effectively overruled *Long Acre Securities v Electro Acoustic Industries*[206] (digested in para.2–52) a tenant may serve a s.27(2) notice when the landlord has served a s.25 notice as was in fact decided by the *Long Acre Securities* case. As has previously been stated (see para.3–106) the authors see no reason why, where there are two modes of termination provided for by the statute, the date providing for the earlier termination should not prevail. The opportunity to serve such a notice may be of some assistance to a tenant. **3–113**

Example T holds shop premises under a lease with a term date of September 1, 2012. On June 1, 2012, L serves a s.25 notice of 12 months length, specifying as the date of termination June 1, 2013. T is unable to serve, at the date of receipt of L's s.25 notice, a s.27(1) notice, as such a notice must be served not later than three months before the term date. T may not wish to vacate by September 1, 2012, as to do so would be inconvenient. If T does not wish to stay in occupation until June 1, 2013 but he does wish to take advantage of the Christmas period, there would appear nothing stopping T serving a notice to terminate his tenancy on say, January 15, 2013, pursuant to s.27(2) which would terminate the tenancy earlier than L's s.25 notice. **3–114**

After service of section 26 request?

The tenant has no right to serve a notice under s.27(2) if he himself has made a request for a new tenancy pursuant to s.26: s.26(4). **3–115**

After making of application for a new tenancy?

It is a matter of some doubt whether a tenant can give a notice pursuant to s.27(2) after he has made an application for a new tenancy. The argument in favour of the view that he can do so is based upon a literal interpretation of the words of the subsection. It says that a tenant may serve such a notice at any time when "the **3–116**

[203] This notice must be not less than three months nor more than six months: see para.2–66 et seq.

[204] A notice under s.27(2) may be given where the tenancy is one granted for a term of years certain and is one "continuing by virtue of s.24 of the Act". A tenancy which ceases to be one to which the Act applies after having continued under s.24 (e.g. by the tenant having been in occupation at the term date subsequently ceasing to occupy the premises for business purposes) is, nevertheless, still one which is continuing by virtue of s.24 for it is continuing by virtue of s.24(3).

[205] [1997] 1 W.L.R. 891.

[206] [1990] 1 E.G.L.R. 91 CA. See the discussion at paras 2–46 to 2–51.

tenancy is continuing by virtue of section 24". Once the tenant has made an application for a new tenancy, the current tenancy is continued by virtue of s.24 (in conjunction with s.64 which alters the date on which the relevant s.25 notice or s.26 request should take effect). There are five matters which suggest that a s.27(2) notice cannot be served where an application has been made for the grant of a new lease:

(1) There would be two conflicting dates of termination.
(2) The corresponding provisions of s.24(3)(a) (enabling service of a notice by the landlord) have been held[207] not to apply where the tenant has made an application for the grant of a new tenancy. Section 27(2) in its form as amended by the 2003 Order now expressly refers to the fact that the tenancy shall not come to an end by reason of the cesser and to that extent it replicates s.24(3) and provides *the tenant*[208] with a right to terminate the tenancy by serving three-months notice. The position of the tenant is thus now no different to that of the landlord under s.24(3)(a). Thus, it may be said that the draftsman must have had in mind the application of that section and just as the landlord is not given a statutory right to serve notice under s.24(3)(a) where the tenancy ceases to be one to which the Act applies during the pendency of proceedings neither is the tenant; the opportunity to confer such a right was not taken and s.27(2) was and is not intended to confer on the tenant a right additional to that provided for by s.64 for the termination of the tenancy during the pendency of proceedings.
(3) One would have to make a distinction between applications which were preceded by a s.25 notice, where s.27(2) could apply and applications preceded by a s.26 request, where s.27(2) cannot apply.[209] There is no good reason why such a distinction should be drawn.
(4) The tenant could in all cases, where the application for renewal has been dismissed or the application for termination has succeeded, foreshorten the period of the continuation of the tenancy so as to exclude from the period of continuation the time for appealing.[210]
(5) It has been said that: "The manifest object of section 64 as a whole was to ensure that during the periods, sometimes prolonged, whilst litigation between landlord and tenant was pending and neither party knew whether a

---

[207] In *I&H Caplan v I&H Caplan (No.2)* [1963] 1 W.L.R. 1247, see para.2–68.

[208] s.24(3)(a) confers on *the landlord* only the right to serve a notice terminating the continuation tenancy.

[209] The reason for this is that s.26(4) provides:

"(4) A tenant's request for a new tenancy shall not be made if the landlord has already given notice under the last foregoing section to terminate the current tenancy, or if the tenant has already given notice to quit or notice under the next following section; and no such notice shall be given by the landlord or the tenant after the making by the tenant of a request for a new tenancy."

The "next following section" is of course s.27. Thus, no notice may be served by a tenant under s.27(2) where he has served a s.26 request nor may a s.26 request be served where he has previously served a notice pursuant to s.27.

[210] For the period under s.64 is three months together with the time for appeal, which is 21 days (see para.3–227 et seq.). The period of the notice under s.27(2) is three months only to terminate at any time. This reason applies only where the application was preceded by a s.25 notice rather than a s.26 request for a s.27(2) notice cannot be served where the tenant has served a s.26 request: see para.3–115.

new tenancy would be granted, there should yet be certainty as between them relating to their interim obligations."[211] However, upholding the tenant's right to serve a s.27(2) notice during the pendency of proceedings generates complete uncertainty with respect to any application[212] (whether made by landlord or tenant).[213]

It is provided that, where a tenancy is terminated under s.27(2), any rent payable in respect of a period which begins before, and ends after, the tenancy is terminated shall be apportioned and any rent paid by the tenant in excess of the amount apportioned to the period before termination shall be recoverable: s.27(3). Thus, if a rent under a tenancy continuing under s.24 is payable on the usual quarter days and the tenant were to serve a s.27(2) notice, say, on June 6, 2013 to expire on September 1, 2013, the tenant is required only to pay rent for the period from June 24, 2013 to September 1, 2013. If he pays the entire quarter's rent due on June 6, 2013 before the tenancy terminates on September 1, 2013, he is entitled to repayment of the rent attributable to the period September 1, 2013 to September 28, 2013 (being the end of the period of the June quarter's rent). The apportionment provision does not apply to a landlord's notice served pursuant to s.24(3)(a).[214] **3–117**

6. SECTION 25 NOTICES

Requirements for valid section 25 notice

It must be given by or on behalf of the "landlord", within the meaning of section 44

The meaning of "landlord" has been discussed above.[215] It goes without saying that a notice served by someone other than the "landlord" within the meaning of s.44 will not be valid: *Yamaha-Kemble Music (UK) Ltd v ARC Properties Ltd*,[216] **3–118**

[211] *Zenith Investments (Torquay) Ltd v Kammins Ballroom Co Ltd (No 2)* [1971] 1 W.L.R. 1751 at 1757, per Sachs L.J.

[212] That is an application made in response to a s.25 notice for a s.27(2) notice cannot be served if the tenant has served a s.26 request: see para.3–115.

[213] A landlord would never know when the tenancy may end notwithstanding the existence of proceedings, for the tenant may at any time terminate the tenancy under s.27(2). Moreover, the uncertainty is exacerbated by the fact that the notice under s.27(2) is to be served on the "immediate landlord" not the competent landlord. It is the competent landlord who is the appropriate party to the proceedings. Although the "immediate landlord" and the "competent landlord" may be one and the same they need not be. Furthermore, the notice under s.27(2) is one which is to be "not less than three months' notice". Thus, the tenant could, absurdly, extend the continuation of his tenancy by serving say a one-year's notice under s.27(2) albeit he is entitled only to three months plus the time for appealing under s.64. S.64 only extends the date of the s.25 notice if the date of termination specified ends earlier than three months plus time for appealing. The tenant can serve a longer notice and obtain the benefit of the protection of s.27(2). In these circumstances, s.27(2) is not simply a means of terminating the tenancy but of obtaining a further period of protection under the Act.

[214] As to notices served under s.24(3)(a), see para.2–66 et seq.

[215] See para.3–87.

[216] [1990] 1 E.G.L.R. 261.

where a notice served by the assignor of the reversionary interest after the assignment to a wholly owned subsidiary was held to be invalid.

Notice given in the name of someone other than the landlord

3–119 It is not uncommon for a notice, often in error, to name the wrong person as landlord. This gives rise to two issues. First, does the naming of a third party as landlord invalidate the notice? Absent estoppel, the arguments deployed to uphold the validity of a notice in these circumstances have been two-fold: (1) that the giver of the notice is acting as a general agent for the true landlord; (2) that, albeit no general agency can be established, the naming within the notice of a third party as landlord would not in fact mislead a reasonable recipient. This is commonly known as the *Mannai* test, named after the decision of the House of Lords in *Mannai Investment Co Ltd v Eagle Star Life Assurance Co Ltd*.[217] The question of general agency is conceded in paras 3–121 to 3–128. The application of the *Mannai* test is considered in paras 3–129 to 3–133, 3–190 and 3–191.

3–120 The second issue is whether, assuming the error in the notice does not invalidate it, the notice was served by the correct landlord. It is clear that it must be "the landlord" who serves the notice. That does not mean that, in order for a notice to be valid, the landlord must serve it personally, or that the landlord need even sign it (for it may be signed by his duly authorised agent). What is required is that the notice is served with the authority of the landlord, and not somebody else. It will usually be clear from the evidence. Indeed where the landlord has, in relation to relatively routine (albeit very important) matters such as service of statutory and contractual notices in relation to properties, left the day-to-day decisions and actions in relation to notices in the hands of their solicitors, the fact that the notice has been served with the authority of the landlord is wholly in accordance with common sense.[218]

General agency

3–121 The Court of Appeal in *Lemmerbell Ltd v Britannia LAS Direct Ltd*[219] (digested in para.3–128) considered, albeit in the context of a break clause, the circumstances in which a notice served by someone other than the correct party may be valid. The following propositions may be derived from that decision:

(1) generally the notice must be given by the landlord. A notice given by someone who is not the landlord will be invalid;
(2) a notice may be validly given by an agent acting on behalf of the landlord so long as it states that it is being given by X on behalf of the landlord and X is duly authorised. This is the common case with solicitors naming the landlord in the s.25 notice and signing the notice for and on behalf of the landlord as duly authorised agent;

---

217 [1997] A.C. 749 HL. It has been held that the *Mannai* approach to the consideration of the validity of break notices applies equally to statutory notices: *York v Casey* [1998] 2 E.G.L.R. 25 CA.
218 Neuberger L.J. in *Lay v Ackerman* [2004] L. & T.R. 29; [2005] 1 E.G.L.R. 139 CA at [27].
219 [1999] 3 E.G.L.R. 67 CA.

(3) a notice which is given in the name of someone other than the landlord without stating that that person is acting as an agent will be valid (on the basis of a general agency) if:
   (a) the giver was in fact duly authorised to give it; and
   (b) the circumstances are such that the recipient can act upon the notice safely in the knowledge that it will be binding on the principal of the giver;

(4) those circumstances include cases where:
   (a) the recipient knows that the giver was authorised to give the notice;
   (b) the principal has held out of the giver of the notice as authorised to give the notice;
   (c) the recipient has been led to believe that the giver of the notice is the principal.

A general agency is an unusual commercial relationship, particularly where a tenant is the principal, the agent having authority to do anything in relation to the subject matter of the agency, even to the extent of destroying that subject matter, without reference to the principal. The inference of such an agency, in the absence of express authority creating the agency, requires clear evidence to support it. The mere payment of rent coupled with occupation does not necessarily indicate that the payer has the tenant's authority to terminate the estate: *Dun & Bradstreet Software Services (England) Ltd v Provident Mutual Life Assurance Association*.[220] **3–122**

The circumstances in which notices served in the name of someone other than the landlord have or have not been upheld are illustrated by *Lemmerbell Ltd v Britannia LAS Direct Ltd*[221] (digested in para.3–128) and the cases in para.3–124 et seq. **3–123**

Jones v Phipps[222] The landlords, who were trustees of the marriage settlement of Sir Maxwell Graves, left to him, the life tenant under the settlement, the entire management of a farm. The court inferred that it was with the sanction of the landlords that Sir Maxwell had dealt with the farm on his own and negotiated with the tenant as to the terms and continuance of the holding. It was held that it was incidental to his authority as agent for the landlord that he should determine the tenancy by notice to quit at such time as he should think proper. The tenant had always considered Sir Maxwell to be the legal owner of the farm. The court also held that Sir Maxwell, being a general agent and not one holding a special or limited authority, was able to serve a valid notice to quit in his own name without referring to his agency. It was emphasised by the court that the notice was to be such that the tenant could act upon it safely, that is one which the tenant had reason to believe was binding on the landlord. **3–124**

---

220 [1998] 2 E.G.L.R. 175 CA.
221 [1998] 3 E.G.L.R. 67 CA.
222 (1868) L.R. 3 Q.B. 567.

3–125 ***Harmond Properties v Gajdzis***[223] A notice to quit was served on a tenant by solicitors stating that they were acting "on behalf of your landlord Mr R.P. Harvey". Mr Harvey was in fact not the landlord but the general agent of the landlord company of which he was a director. He had carried out the letting and acted as if he were the landlord in every way. It was held that the notice was valid, the solicitors being the solicitors acting for the landlord company, which knew through its director, Mr. Harvey, that they were employed by him to give notices to quit.

3–126 ***Townsend Carriers Ltd v Pfizer Ltd***[224] A break notice had been served not by the tenant company but by an associated company, not on the landlord company but on an associated company. The tenant and the landlord had consigned the whole conduct and management of the tenancy and of the tenancy itself to agents on their behalf, allowing their respective associated companies to deal with the property as if they were landlord and tenant respectively in respect of matters such as an increase in rent and variations of the lease. It was held that the break notice had been validly served.

3–127 ***Peel Developments (South) Ltd v Siemens Plc***[225] A break notice was served by the tenants on a subsidiary of the landlord company. That subsidiary was found to have acted as managing agent of the property. It was held that, on the evidence the management of the property was carried out by the subsidiary, and that the subsidiary was the general agent of the landlord. Accordingly, the notice was validly served on the subsidiary.

3–128 ***Lemmerbell Ltd v Britannia LAS Direct Ltd***[226] LAS Direct Ltd ("Direct") was tenant under two leases which contained a break clause enabling them to determine the term on September 28, 1995 upon giving six-months written notice. The tenant's solicitors wrote to the landlord's solicitors expressing themselves as acting on behalf of Direct and Life Association of Scotland Ltd ("Life"), informing the landlord that the demised premises were to be used by employees of Life. It was explained to the landlord's solicitors that Life and Direct were wholly owned subsidiaries of LAS Holdings Ltd and confirmation was sought that the landlord had no objection to that use. No response was received. Both leases remained vested in Direct and there was no request for consent to an assignment and no assignment was effected. Life served break notices upon the landlord in accordance with the terms of the lease purporting to terminate the leases with effect from September 28, 1995. The notice was said to be on "behalf of [Life], successors in title to . . . [Direct]". There were six matters which were relied upon to infer general agency and thus validate the notices:

---

[223] [1968] 1 W.L.R. 1858; [1968] 3 All E.R. 263 CA.
[224] [1977] 1 E.G.L.R. 37 Ch D.
[225] [1992] 2 E.G.L.R. 85.
[226] [1998] 3 E.G.L.R. 67 CA. See also *Dun & Bradstreet Software Services (England) Ltd v Provident Mutual Life Assurance Association* [1998] 2 E.G.L.R. 175 CA.

(1) the director of the landlord's parent company was authorised to collect rent, at the request of Life, from Life and to address correspondence relating to the payment of rent to Life, rather than to Direct;
(2) thereafter demands for rent and insurance premiums in respect of the demised premises were addressed not to Direct, but to Life;
(3) correspondence in relation to insurance of the demised premises was with Life not Direct;
(4) Chestertons, who were instructed on behalf of both Life and Direct, wrote to the landlord, asking it to address invoices in respect of work to be done on the demised premises for the purposes of making them secure to Life, not Direct;
(5) there was no evidence of dealing by the landlord with Direct itself in relation to the leases at any time after the letter written by the solicitors to Life and Direct;
(6) the landlord evinced no surprise when it received the notices given in the name of Life as lessee.

There was no evidence of the administrative arrangements between Direct and Life and Life had not been appointed by Direct as its agent. Any agency was, therefore, to be implied from the course of conduct by the principal and the agent. The Court of Appeal held that Life was not the general agent of Direct. In fact Direct had in 1993 ceased to trade and was a dormant company. It had not been shown that Direct consciously allowed Life to manage the demised premises nor was it sent copies of any communications by Life relating to the demised premises.

The Court of Appeal held that in the circumstances no general agency could be inferred. The description of Life as a successor in title to Direct and the evident belief of Life that it was tenant was inconsistent with the notion that Life was acting as the agent of Direct in serving the break notices. Furthermore, it could not be said that the landlord could act safely upon the notice being one which they had reason to believe was binding on Direct. The landlord was aware that no consent had been given to any assignment by Direct, but that was not inconsistent with there having been an effective assignment. Without the production to them of an assignment, the landlord could not know if Life was the right person to be giving the notices.

Reliance on the *Mannai* principle If no general agency can be established, a notice in the name of someone other than the landlord may be upheld as a matter of construction. An error in a notice would not invalidate it if it would not mislead the reasonable recipient: *Mannai Investment Co Ltd v Eagle Star Life Assurance Co Ltd*.[227] In that case a tenant had been granted two leases for 10 years from January 13, 1992, each with a provision entitling the tenant to **3–129**

[227] [1997] A.C. 749 HL. It has been held that the *Mannai* approach to the consideration of the validity of break notices applies equally to statutory notices: *York v Casey* [1998] 2 E.G.L.R. 25 CA. There have been numerous cases since applying *Mannai* to statutory notices. See also fn.346. The suggestion in *York v Casey* by Peter Gibson L.J. at 27 that *Mannai* would apply only if the error in the notice is obvious or evident has not been followed: *Ravenseft Properties v Hall* [2002] H.L.R. 624 CA at [27]; *Fernandez v McDonald* [2003] 4 All E.R. 1033 CA at [20].

determine by giving notice to take effect at the expiry of the third year of the term, i.e. January 13, 1995. The tenant served notices referring to the clause pursuant to which the tenant was entitled to break the lease. The notices were gave notice to determine the leases "on 12 January 1995". The majority of the House of Lords held that the notices were valid, notwithstanding the mistake. It was said that a reasonable recipient of the two notices in the position of the landlord would have been in no doubt as to what was intended, namely to determine the leases on January 13. Lord Steyn said at 767D:

> "The question is not how the [recipient] landlord understood the notices. The construction of the notices must be approached objectively. The issue is how a reasonable recipient would have understood the notices. And in considering this question the notices must be construed taking into account the relevant objective contextual scene."

A little later at 768D–G he said:

> "It is important not to lose sight of the purpose of a notice under the break clause. It serves one purpose only: to inform the landlord that the tenant has decided to determine the lease in accordance with the right reserved. That purpose must be relevant to the construction and validity of the notice. Prima facie one would expect that if a notice unambiguously conveys a decision to determine a court may nowadays ignore immaterial errors which would not have misled a reasonable recipient . . .
> Even if such notices under contractual rights reserved contain errors they may be valid if they are 'sufficiently clear and unambiguous to leave a reasonable recipient in no reasonable doubt as to how and when they are intended to operate' . . ." per Slade L.J. (CA).

At 772G–H, Lord Steyn observed:

> "The question is not whether 12 January can *mean* 13 January: it self-evidently cannot. The real question is a different one: does the notice construed against its contextual setting unambiguously inform a reasonable recipient how and when the notice is to operate *under the right reserved*?"

3–130 In *Lay v Ackerman*,[228] Neuberger L.J. said:

> "The correct approach on the basis of the decision and reasoning in *Mannai* is as follows. One must first consider whether there was a mistake in the information contained in the notice (as there was as to the date in *Mannai*, and there was as to the landlord, in the present case).[229] If there was such a mistake, one must then consider how, in the light of the mistake, a reasonable person in the position of the recipient would have understood the notice in the circumstances

---

[228] [2004] L. & T.R. 29; [2005] 1 E.G.L.R. 139 CA. In this case the landlord, The Trustees of the Portman Family Settled Estates served a counter-notice pursuant to s.45 of the Leasehold Reform, Housing and Urban Development Act 1993, by their duly authorised solicitors. However, the solicitors in error named the landlord as the Trustees of the Portman Family Collateral Settlement. The counter-notice was upheld.

[229] There may still be a mistake albeit the name of the incorrect landlord is inserted deliberately. As Neuberger L.J. said:

"it appears to me that the answer to the question whether the mis-identification of the landlord was 'deliberate' or not depends on how one puts the question. If one were to ask whether the solicitors who prepared the Counter-Notice intended to identify the landlord in the Counter-Notice as the PFCS Trustees [being the incorrect name], the answer would be in the affirmative. To that extent the mis-identification was deliberate. On the other hand, if one was to ask whether the solicitors had intended to identify someone other than the actual landlord as the landlord, the answer would be in the negative. To that extent the mis-identification was a mistake." (at [38])

> of the particular case. Finally one must consider whether, as a result, the notice would have been understood as conveying the information required by the contractual, statutory or common law provision pursuant to which it was served." (at [40])

In *Lemmerbell Ltd v Britannia LAS Direct Ltd*[230] (digested in para.3–128) the Court of Appeal rejected the argument that a reasonable recipient would have construed the break notice as having been given on behalf of the true tenant, as the notice on its face said that the notice had been given by Life as successor in title to Direct and that, if true, could only have come about as a result of an assignment albeit no consent had been given to an assignment. The reasonable recipient could not know, in the absence of proof of the assignment, whether Life was the lessee. If there had been no assignment the reasonable recipient could not know whether the solicitors who had given the notice for and on behalf of Life were authorised by Direct to act for it and to serve the notice, contrary to the express terms of the notice. Thus it was not obvious, from the notice, that there was an error in the name of the lessee nor was it obvious who the actual current lessee was nor whether Life's solicitors were duly authorised by anyone other than Life.[231] Thus it was impossible as a matter of construction to cure the defect by substituting Direct for Life as the person on whose behalf the solicitors were giving notice. **3–131**

The *Mannai* test for determining validity of a notice is an objective one.[232] Thus the reaction of the actual recipient to the notice which has been served is irrelevant.[233] Accordingly, a letter of response from the recipient's solicitor is probably inadmissible on the issue of validity.[234] **3–132**

Where the name of the landlord is someone other than the true landlord the recipient may be estopped from denying the validity of the notice. Whether any estoppel may be made out depends on the facts of any particular case.[235] **3–133**

Misdescription of landlord's name

A misdescription in the landlord's name does not necessarily invalidate the notice. Thus, where the notice described the landlord as "Norfolk Square No.2 Ltd" but the name of the landlord was in fact "Norfolk Square Hotels No.2 Ltd" the notice was not invalid for that reason: *M&P Enterprises (London) v Norfolk Square Hotels*[236] (digested in para.3–203). Whether a misdescription invalidates **3–134**

---

[230] [1998] 3 E.G.L.R. 67 CA.

[231] Thus it is considered that it should, as a matter of principle, be easier for a notice misdescribing the recipient to be more easily upheld that a notice misdescribing the sender. The recipient knows who he is and what if anything has happened to the tenancy vested in him. See, however, *R. (on the application of Morris) v London Rent Assessment Committee* [2002] EWCA Civ 276; [2002] 2 E.G.L.R. 13.

[232] See the quotation from Lord Steyn's speech at para.3–129 above. See also para.3–190.

[233] *Lancecrest Ltd v Asiwaju* [2005] EWCA Civ 117; [2005] L. & T.R. 22 at [38] to [42] per Neuberger L.J. (a case concerned with the validity of a counter-notice under a rent review clause).

[234] *Lay v Ackerman* [2004] L. & T.R. 29; [2005] 1 E.G.L.R. 139 at [80] per Neuberger L.J. For the facts of this case see fn.228 above.

[235] As to estoppel see para.3–232 et seq.

[236] [1994] 1 E.G.L.R. 129.

the notice is to be tested by asking whether it would mislead the reasonable recipient: *Mannai Investment Co Ltd v Eagle Star Life Assurance Co Ltd*.[237]

3–135 It is to be noted that the 2004 Regulations[238] require "the landlord" to be identified in the notice. In *Morrow v Nadeem*,[239] (digested in para.3–249) which is a pre-*Mannai* decision, a notice served pursuant to s.25 of the 1954 Act was held to be invalid in circumstances where the landlord was described as the individual who was effectively the sole shareholder and director of the landlord company, rather than the landlord company itself. The notice in that case was in a form prescribed by the Landlord and Tenant (Notices) Regulations 1957 (SI 1957/1157). Furthermore, it would seem that the recipient tenant of the notice could not have been clear that the notice was authorised by the person who was in fact the landlord. In other words, at the time of the service of the s.25 notice, the tenant could not have been sure that the person who was in fact the landlord had authorised its service. All she knew was that an individual had served the notice holding himself out as her landlord, but what she could not have been sure of, at the time she received the notice, was that, if the landlord was another person, such as the company, the notice was actually served with that other person's authority. No argument to that effect appears to have been raised.

Joint landlords

3–136 If the landlord consists of two or more persons they must all join in the giving of the notice: *Pearson v Alyo*.[240] This is so notwithstanding the fact that only one of the "joint tenants" of the legal estate may be solely and absolutely beneficially entitled: *Pearson v Alyo*. However, in *Leckhampton Dairies Ltd v Artus Whitfield Ltd*[241] a s.25 notice given by one of two joint landlords without the consent of the other was held to be valid. It is not clear from the facts of the report whether the notice named only one of the landlords in the notice or, alternatively, named both joint owners, but was served by one only without the consent of the other. In either event, it is considered that the decision cannot stand with *Pearson v Alyo*. If the reversionary interest is held under separate titles, so that there is a severed reversion, difficulties may be encountered in serving a valid s.25 notice: see para.3–193 et seq.

Notice should be signed by the landlord or his duly authorised agent

3–137 The notice should be signed by the landlord(s) or his duly authorised agent: *Tennant v London CC*[242] (digested in para.3–251). The signing of the notice is not, however, essential, at least where it is apparent from a covering letter from whom the notice emanates: *Stidolph v American School in London Educational*

---

[237] [1997] A.C. 749 HL.
[238] That is Landlord and Tenant Act 1954 Pt II (Notices) (Regulations) 2004 (SI 2004/1005). See para.3–145 et seq.
[239] [1986] 1 W.L.R. 1381.
[240] [1990] 1 E.G.L.R. 114 CA.
[241] (1986) 83 L.S.G. 875; (1986) 130 S.J. 225.
[242] (1957) 121 J.P. 428 CA.

Trust.[243] It was unnecessary in the circumstances of the case in *Stidolph* to decide whether the notice by itself would have been valid, although Cross L.J. remarked that the other enclosure was "quite sufficient to fill in the gap in the notice", from which it might be inferred that the unsigned notice by itself would have been insufficient. A counter-notice signed only by one of four tenant trustees was held to be valid albeit the counter-notice[244] did not expressly state it was served by one on behalf of the four as it was recognisable from the terms of the notice and the factual matrix in which it was served that it was a counter-notice on behalf of all four trustees: *Hackney African Organisation v London Borough of Hackney*.[245] If there is no authority to sign the notice it will, however, be invalid: *London CC v Farren*.[246] The tenancy agreement cannot regulate the form of a s.25 notice or the means of signature of such a notice, for its terms are superseded by the provisions of the Act: *London CC v Farren*.[247]

It must be "given" to the "tenant"[248]

In considering whether the notice has been "given" to the "tenant" there are, in fact, two separate questions which need to be considered. First, has the notice been addressed to the "tenant"? Secondly, if it has, has it been served upon the "tenant"? A notice which is not addressed to the actual tenant may, nevertheless, still be valid on the basis of general agency[249] or in reliance on the *Mannai* test.[250] In those circumstances the question of whether the tenant has been served becomes central and is highlighted by *Railtrack Plc v Gojra*.[251] In that case the tenant addressed a s.26 request to British Railways Board, the undertaking of which had been transferred to Railtrack Plc, which was the landlord within s.44. By statute that request was to be treated as if it had been addressed to Railtrack Plc. The request was sent in an envelope and it and the covering letter were addressed to "the solicitors department, British Railways Board." The British Railways Property Board, which was a division of the British Railways Board, continued to be responsible for the management of the premises. It was held on the facts that the Board was agent for service and it mattered not that was not addressed to the "solicitors department". It was said that "service of a document intended to have legal effect was rightly effected on the British Railways Board and sensibly marked for the attention of its solicitors' department". **3–138**

[243] (1969) 20 P. & C.R. 802; (1969) 113 S.J. 689 CA.

[244] A counter-notice is no longer required to be served by a tenant in response to a s.25 notice: see para.5–02.

[245] (1999) 77 P. & C.R. D. 18 CA. See also para.3–102, fn.193.

[246] [1956] 1 W.L.R. 1297; [1956] 3 All E.R. 401 CA.

[247] [1956] 3 All E.R. 401 CA.

[248] As to the meaning of "tenant", see para.3–101.

[249] As to which, see para.3–121 et seq.

[250] As to which, see para.3–129 et seq.

[251] [1998] 1 E.G.L.R 63 CA.

Joint tenants[252]

3–139 Where the tenant consists of two or more joint tenants, then, save where the tenants are in partnership[253] it is essential that the s.25 notice be addressed to all of them: *Booth v Reynolds*[254] (digested in para.3–103). However, where the lease is held by several trustees it would appear sufficient for the notice to describe the tenant as "the trustees for the time being of the [relevant organisation]": *Hackney African Organisation v London Borough of Hackney*.[255] Not only must the notice be addressed to all of the joint tenants but, furthermore, it would appear that the notice must be served upon all of them: *Booth v Reynolds* (digested in para.3–103).

3–140 In *Rostron v Michael Nairn & Co Ltd*,[256] Cross J. considered the position which would have arisen if (contrary to his finding) the tenancy of the demised premises had been vested in a husband and his wife jointly. In such a case, a notice addressed to both joint tenants but served under cover of a letter addressed only to the husband at the matrimonial home would not have been "left" at the wife's last known place of abode within the meaning of s.23 of the Landlord and Tenant Act 1927 and would not, therefore, have been "given". He remarked that it would have had to have been established that the husband either had shown the notice to his wife, or that she had constituted him as her agent to receive such notices. The judge expressed the further view, however, that if the notice had actually been given to the wife it did not matter that it was not addressed to her.

Addressee other than the tenant

3–141 Where someone other than the tenant has been named in the notice the misnomer will not invalidate the notice if:

(1) it is not such as to mislead the reasonable recipient: *Mannai Investment Co Ltd v Eagle Star Life Assurance Co Ltd*[257]; or
(2) the recipient is the general agent of the actual tenant. Such general agency will arise where there has been a long course of dealing during which the agent has been treated or regarded as the tenant: *Jones v Phipps*[258] (digested in para.3–124); *Harmond Properties v Gajdzis*[259] (digested in para.3–125); *Re Knight & Hubbard's Underlease*[260]; *Townsend Carriers Ltd v Pfizer Ltd*[261] (digested in para.3–126); *Peel Developments (South) Ltd*

[252] See also paras 6–26 et seq.
[253] See para.6–31.
[254] (1974) New. L.J. 119.
[255] [1999] L. & T.R. 117 CA.
[256] [1962] E.G.D. 284.
[257] [1997] A.C. 749 HL. It has been held that the *Mannai* test applies to statutory notices: *York v Casey* [1998] 2 E.G.L.R. 25 CA. See para.3–129 et seq.
[258] (1868) L.R. 2 Q.B. 567.
[259] [1968] 1 W.L.R. 1858; [1968] 3 All E.R. 263.
[260] [1923] 1 Ch. 130.
[261] [1977] 1 E.G.L.R. 37.

v Siemens Plc[262] (digested in para.3–127); *Dun & Bradstreet Software Services (England) Ltd v Provident Mutual Life Assurance*[263]; *Lemmerbell Ltd v Britannia LAS Direct Ltd* (digested in para.3–128).[264]

An example of the *Mannai* approach upholding the validity of a s.25 notice (albeit a decision made prior to *Mannai*), where the name of the tenant specified was other than the tenant, is *Bridgers v Stanford*.[265] In that case a s.25 notice addressed not to the tenant but to the company carrying on the tenant's business (both companies being subsidiaries of a third company and the names of both companies having been used interchangeably in correspondence with the landlord) was held valid, as the misstatement of the tenant's name it was said, in the circumstances, would not mislead a reasonable recipient. **3–142**

Bankruptcy

Where the tenant is declared bankrupt and the lease vests in the trustee in bankruptcy, the notice should be addressed to and served on the trustee in bankruptcy: *Gatwick Investments v Radivojevic*.[266] **3–143**

Liquidation

The property of the company upon liquidation does not vest in the liquidator upon appointment[267] and therefore any notice should be addressed to and served upon the company. **3–144**

It must be given "in the prescribed form", that is to say in the form prescribed by regulations made from time to time by the Secretary of State for the Environment

Current regulations The 2003 Order does not alter the provisions as to the date of termination to be specified by the landlord in his s.25 notice. Thus the date to be specified of not less than six and not more than 12 months provided for in subs.(2) to s.25 remains. The notice is, as under the regime operating pre-June 1, 2004, required to be in a prescribed form: s.66(1) of the 1954 Act. The form of notice with regard to notices served post June 1, 2004 is now prescribed by the Landlord and Tenant Act 1954 Pt II (Notices) (Regulations) 2004 (SI 2004/1005). There are two forms of notice. One where the landlord opposes renewal (Form 2) and another where he does not (Form 1).[268] A form "substantially to the like effect" is sufficient: see reg.2(2) of the 2004 Regulations. **3–145**

---

262 [1992] 2 E.G.L.R. 85.
263 [1998] 2 E.G.L.R. 175 CA.
264 [1998] 3 E.G.L.R. 67 CA.
265 [1991] 2 E.G.L.R. 265 CA.
266 [1978] C.L.Y. 1768.
267 See para.3–36.
268 These forms are to be found in Appendix, paras A2.034 and A2.032, respectively.

3–146 The 2004 Regulations, like their predecessor, the Landlord and Tenant Act 1954 Pt II (Notices) Regulation1983 (SI 1983/133),[269] prescribed form contains a warning notice, referred to in *Sabella Ltd v Montgomery*,[270] as an "act quick" notice, which provides in lettering in upper case in a prominent box an explanation of the rights and obligations of the tenant, and, in particular, that the notice is intended to bring the tenancy to an end and an exhortation to the tenant to read the notes and to act quickly.

3–147 **Use of old form** It might have been thought that the form prescribed by the 1983 Regulations was so different in format from all previous versions that a notice served on an old form of notice would be invalid. Such a view was, for some time, thought to be regarded as being wrong in view of the interlocutory decision of Glidewell L.J. in refusing leave to appeal in *Morris v Patel*.[271] However, it was held in *Sabella Ltd v Montgomery*[272] that a notice served in a form preceding the form introduced by the 1983 Regulations, was invalid, as the old form did not provide the recipient with the substance of the information required by the new form and in particular omitted the "act quick" warning notice contained in the form of notice prescribed by the 1983 Regulations. It is considered that a notice served in the form prescribed by the 1983 Regulations rather than the current 2004 Regulations[273] will be invalid not least because it will fail to deal with the requirements of the new s.25(6)–(8).[274]

3–148 **Omissions in particulars** Omissions of various particulars required to be contained in a notice will invalidate the notice if it fails to give "the proper information to the tenant which will enable the tenant to deal in a proper way with the situation, whatever it may be, referred to in the statement of notice" (*Barclays Bank Ltd v Ascott*[275] (digested in para.3–149); approved in *Tegerdine v Brooks*[276]; *Morrow v Nadeem*[277] (digested in para.3–249; *Bridgers v Stanford*[278]). Thus notices have been held to be valid notwithstanding the fact that:

(1) The notice incorrectly specified the county court jurisdiction limit: *Bond v Graham*[279] and *British Railways Board v AJA Smith Transport*[280] (digested in para.3–252) (these cases would not now arise having regard to the fact that the county court no longer has any relevant rateable value jurisdiction limit).

---

[269] As modified by the Landlord and Tenant Act 1954 Pt II (Notices) (Amendment) Regulations 1989 (SI 1989/1548).
[270] [1998] 1 E.G.L.R. 65 CA.
[271] [1987] 1 E.G.L.R. 75 CA.
[272] [1998] 1 E.G.L.R. 65 CA.
[273] See para.3–145.
[274] As to which, see para.3–155 et seq.
[275] [1961] 1 W.L.R. 717; [1961] 1 All E.R. 782.
[276] (1978) 36 P. & C.R. 261; (1977) 245 E.G. 51 CA.
[277] 1986] 1 W.L.R. 1381; [1987] 1 All E.R. 237 CA.
[278] [1991] 2 E.G.L.R. 265 CA.
[279] [1975] 2 E.G.L.R. 63.
[280] [1987] 1 E.G.L.R. 75.

(2) The notice omitted certain information or notes for the benefit of the recipient on the back of the form where those notes were irrelevant to the circumstances of the case: *Barclays Bank Ltd v Ascott*[281] ((digested in para.3–149) the omission of notes relating to the situation where the landlord was opposing the grant of a new tenancy but the landlord was not in fact opposing renewal).

Barclays Bank Ltd v Ascott[282] Two notes to the s.25 notice had been omitted. They were, however, irrelevant to the recipient's rights or obligations and their omission, therefore, did not invalidate the notice. One was irrelevant as it related to a notice where the landlord opposed the grant of a new tenancy, which the landlord in that case was not doing. The second note dealt with the position where there was an uncertainty as to who was the competent landlord. This too did not arise in the case. It was held that the tenant had been given the substance of the information to enable the tenant to deal with the notice in the appropriate way. **3–149**

The notice must since June 1, 2004 provide the particulars required by ss.25(6), (7) and (8). Those subsections provide that the notice "shall not have effect" unless the requirements of those subsections are complied with.[283] It is considered that a failure to provide those particulars will thus invalidate the notice. **3–150**

Form substantially to like effect The 2004 Regulations make it clear that the prescribed form must be used or a form substantially to like effect.[284] Thus, the comparison to be made is between the notice served and the prescribed form, and it is immaterial that any addition or omission has had no material effect upon the actual recipient.[285] If the notice is not the same as or substantially to the same effect, it is invalid and it cannot be saved by establishing that the recipient did not suffer any prejudice: *Sabella Ltd v Montgomery*[286] above. Thus the fact that the absence of an "act quick" warning notice has not in fact prejudiced the tenant because the tenant consulted solicitors and took appropriate action within the timetable required by the 1954 Act, is an irrelevant consideration in determining the validity of the notice: *Sabella Ltd v Montgomery* disapproving *Morris v Patel*.[287] A difference between the prescribed form and the form actually used can **3–151**

[281] [1961] 1 W.L.R. 717; [1961] 1 All E.R. 782.
[282] [1961] 1 W.L.R. 717; [1961] 1 All E.R. 782.
[283] These are considered in para.3–149 et seq.
[284] reg.2(2) of the Landlord and Tenant Act 1954 Pt II (Notices) (Regulations) 2004 (SI 2004/1005).
[285] In *Sun Alliance & London Assurance Co Ltd v Hayman* [1975] 1 W.L.R. 177; [1975] 1 All E.R. 248 CA the majority of the Court of Appeal suggested that a notice would still be valid, even though misleading, if it would mislead in the same way if in the proper form. The extent to which the reasonable tenant would be misled by the notice not being in the prescribed form is relevant in determining whether the form can be said to be substantially to the like effect as the prescribed form. The effect of the dicta in *Sun Alliance and London Assurance Company Ltd v Hayman* is that if the notice is not more misleading than it would have been if in the prescribed form, albeit the prescribed form itself may be misleading, the notice will be valid. The court was not saying, as the Court of Appeal in *Tegerdine v Brooks* [1978] 1 E.G.L.R. 33 CA, suggests, that the mere fact that the tenant would be misled by the notice is irrelevant in determining the validity of the notice.
[286] [1998] 1 E.G.L.R. 65 CA.
[287] [1998] 1 E.G.L.R. 65 CA.

only be disregarded when the information given as to the particular recipient's rights and obligations under the 1954 Act is in substance as effective as that set out in the form. Material which is irrelevant to the recipient's rights or obligations may be omitted. Once differences have been ascertained, then the decision as to whether the two are substantially to like effect will depend upon the importance of the differences rather than their number or amount: *Sabella Ltd v Montgomery*.

It generally must be given in relation to a tenancy to which the Act applies

3–152 If the notice is served at a time when the Act has ceased to apply to the tenancy there would appear nothing on which the notice can "bite". See para.2–52 et seq. for a discussion of whether a s.25 notice may "bite" if the tenancy subsequently becomes or ceases to be one to which the Act applies.

It must specify a date of termination which must be one of the dates permitted by section 25

3–153 This question is discussed in detail in para.3–170 et seq.

With respect to any notice served prior to June 1, 2004, the notice must have been one which required the tenant, within two months after the giving of the notice, to serve a counter notice notifying the landlord in writing whether or not, at the date of termination, he is willing to give up possession of the property comprised in the tenancy: section 25(5)

3–154 This requirement is no longer applicable with regards to notices served after June 1, 2004. The tenant is not now required to serve a counter-notice in response to a landlord's s.25 notice. Section 25(5) is repealed: art.4 of the 2003 Order.[288]

It must comply with the requirements of sections 25(6),(7) and (8)

3–155 New provisions are introduced as to the contents of s.25 notices: ss.25(6), (7) and (8).[289] The landlord is required in his s.25 notice to state:

(1) whether or not he is opposing the grant of a new tenancy (s.25(6));
(2) if he is opposing the grant of a new tenancy, the ground or grounds of opposition under s.30(1) upon which he relies (s.25(7));
(3) if he does not oppose the grant, his proposals for renewal the landlord's proposals as to:
    (a) the property to be comprised in the new tenancy (being either the whole or part of the property comprised in the current tenancy);
    (b) the rent to be payable under the new tenancy; and
    (c) the other terms of the new tenancy (s.25(8)).

[288] The position prior to June 1, 2004 is dealt with in the 2nd edn of this work at para.3–147.
[289] art.4(2) to the 2003 Order.

Section 25(6),(7) and (8) all provide that the s.25 notice "shall not have effect" unless the requirements of the sub-section are met.

Compliance with section 25(8)

One can envisage interesting questions arising as to whether or not there is compliance with s.(8). **3–156**

Rent

Undoubtedly there will be issues as to whether or not the rent to be specified has to be a realistic assessment of the open market rent. Contrast the provision under the 1993 Leasehold Reform Housing and Urban Development Act: *Cadogan v Morris*.[290] In this decision the Court of Appeal held that a tenant's notice under s.42(3)(c) of the Leasehold Reform Housing and Urban Development Act 1993 seeking a 90-year extended lease, required the premium which the tenant stated he was prepared to pay for the new extended lease to be a realistic one. Thus, specifying a premium of £100 when the realistic figure lay between £100,000 and £300,000 rendered the tenant's notice invalid. The position under the 1993 Act is, however, distinguishable, as under that Act if a landlord fails to serve a counter-notice in response to the tenant's notice of claim the court has no discretion as to the terms on which the freehold is claimed: *Willingale v Globalgrange Ltd*.[291] This is not the position under the 1954 Act.[292] Where the tenant has served a s.26 request, the landlord is not in fact required to serve a counter-notice. The landlord is only required to do so where he opposes renewal: s.26(6). **3–157**

In order to avoid the landlord being limited to the rent specified in the s.25 notice it may be considered appropriate to qualify the rental figure stated so as to accommodate the fact that the valuation date for s.34 is the commencement of the new lease, which may be many months away. Thus, it may be thought appropriate to state the following: **3–158**

> "£X. The landlord, however, reserves the right to alter the proposed rental at any trial of any claim for renewal arising out of the service of this section 25 notice to reflect the open market rent at the valuation date in accordance with section 34 of the Act."

---

[290] [1999] 1 E.G.L.R. 59 CA.

[291] [2000] 2 E.G.L.R. 55 CA.

[292] And thus the position is analogous to *9 Cornwall Crescent London Ltd v Kensington and Chelsea RLBC* [2005] EWCA Civ 324; [2006] 1 W.L.R. 1186, where the Court of Appeal distinguished *Cadogan v Morris* in the context of the service of a landlord's counter-notice under s.21 of the Leasehold Reform, Housing and Urban Development Act 1993, as the figure specified in the counter-notice could not by default by the tenant become the figure for the price for the freehold. Thus, it was held that the figure need not be realistic, simply one specified in good faith.

Terms

3–159 How extensive must the description of the terms of the new tenancy be? Is it necessary, for instance, for a draft lease to be submitted or is it sufficient, as is often the case in relation to the information provided by the landlord in the landlord's acknowledgement of service, to refer to the terms being "on the landlord's standard form of commercial lease"? It is certainly arguable that it is insufficient to refer in a very general way to a pro forma lease without providing the tenant with any detail as to what the landlord's modern form of lease actually contains.

3–160 Yet another question is whether the "other terms" must be terms which, if the matter were to go to court, the court could order. For example, if the landlord stated that he would be seeking an order excluding the security of tenure under the Act that would obviously be a term which the parties could agree but it would not be one which, in default of agreement, the court could order. Similarly if the landlord stated that he sought to grant a 20-year term, which is a term longer than the maximum term which, in default of agreement, the court could order. Since the statement of the landlord's terms arises in the context of a notice where the order of a new tenancy by the court will not be opposed, it is clearly arguable that the inclusion of either of these proposed terms by the landlord in his s.25 notice would invalidate it.

Inconsistent expressions of intention

3–161 The form prescribed by the 1989 Regulations[293] provided alternative sets of wording (one of which should be deleted) enabling the landlord by striking through one of them to express an intention to oppose or not oppose renewal. In *Lewis v MTC Cars Ltd*[294] (digested in para.10–49) the landlord failed to delete the sentence saying that he would not oppose the grant of a new tenancy, but did state a ground of opposition within s.30(1). It was held that the notice was valid because the statement of the ground of opposition made it clear that the landlord did, indeed, intend to oppose the grant of a new tenancy. A notice which states an intention to oppose the grant of a new tenancy but fails to state any ground of opposition is invalid: *Barclays Bank Plc v Bee*[295] (digested in para.3–162). A fortiori if a notice which fails both to delete either of the relevant alternatives and to state any ground of opposition. Where the landlord served upon the tenant under cover of one letter two notices, one opposing renewal, which was invalid by reason of the fact that it failed to specify any ground of opposition and the other, a valid notice, not opposing renewal, both notices were invalid. The two documents were entirely inconsistent with one another as a reasonable recipient

[293] para.5 of Form 1 to the Landlord and Tenant Act 1954, Pt II (Notices) (Amendment) Regs (now repealed). See now Form 2 to the 2004 Regs which avoids this potential problem: para.A2.034.
[294] [1975] 1 W.L.R. 457.
[295] [2002] 1 W.L.R. 332 CA.

could not conclude, having regard to the relevant objective contextual scene in which the notices were served, that the that invalid notice should be ignored: *Barclays Banks Plc v Bee*.[296]

3–162 ***Barclays Bank Plc v Bee***[297] The landlord under cover of a single letter served upon the tenant two notices pursuant to s.25. The first notice opposed renewal but did not specify any ground of opposition. The second notice did not oppose renewal. It was obvious that a mistake had been made as the letter referred only to one notice being enclosed and requested acknowledgement by returning one copy. Neither was a copy of the other. One of them should not have been sent. Upon the error being brought to the landlord's attention by the tenant the landlord served a third notice opposing renewal on grounds (f) and (g) of s.30(1). The landlord prior to the service of the various notices expressed the view to the tenant that it was his intention to carry out development work on the property but had indicated that this would commence in two to three years time. It was not in dispute between the parties that the first notice was invalid. The tenant argued that the second notice was valid and that accordingly the landlord was unable to rely on the third notice to oppose renewal. It was agreed that, subject to the landlord's argument as to validity, the second notice was a valid notice. The Court of Appeal held that the two notices when read together were inconsistent. Albeit the tenant knew that the landlord intended to redevelop, the reasonable recipient of the notices would have been left in doubt as to the landlord's intention in respect of the renewal. It was the case as a matter of law that a s.25 notice once served could not be amended.[298] The landlord could not, therefore, have in fact amended the first notice to add grounds of opposition. However, a reasonable recipient of the notice need not be taken to know that the first notice was incapable of amendment. Thus objectively the notices were entirely inconsistent and the central message to the tenant was hopelessly and instantaneously confused. Accordingly, as the first two notices served were invalid the landlord was able to oppose renewal by relying on the third notice served.

Infelicitous wording

3–163 In *Housleys v Bloomer-Holt*[299] (digested in para.7–109) the landlords stated their intention to oppose on the grounds that they intended to carry out "substantial work of reconstruction" and in *Philipson-Stow v Trevor Square*[300] the landlord stated an intention to oppose on the grounds of "substantial works of redecoration". Although both phrases differed from the form of words used in s.30(1)(f), both notices were held to be valid. This particular problem should not arise under the prescribed form, which requires simply that the relevant paragraph of s.30(1) be specified, rather than that the full wording should be set out.

---

296 [2002] 1 W.L.R. 332 CA.
297 [2002] 1 W.L.R. 332 CA.
298 See para.3–162.
299 [1966] 1 W.L.R. 1244; [1966] 2 All E.R. 966 CA.
300 [1981] 1 E.G.L.R. 56.

Honest belief in grounds specified

3–164 It is considered that the landlord must have an honest belief in the ground stated: *Stradbroke v Mitchell*[301] (digested in para.3–167) which applied to a case under the Agricultural Holdings Act a dictum of Lord Denning in a 1954 Act case, *Betty's Cafes Ltd v Phillips Furnishing Stores Ltd*.[302] In *Betty's Cafes* a landlord opposed the tenant's application for a new lease of a cafe in Bradford on ground (f), namely that on termination of the current tenancy the landlord intended to reconstruct the premises, and could not reasonably do so without obtaining possession. That ground was, as required by s.26(6) of the Act, stated in the landlord's counter-notice opposing the grant of the new tenancy. The question at issue was whether the landlord was required to have formed that intention at the date of giving the notice of opposition or whether, as the House of Lords held, the landlord could succeed in his opposition if he proved that he held the intention at the date of the hearing. However, though agreeing with this conclusion, Lord Denning expressed the view that the landlord's statement of his grounds of opposition in his notice must be honest and truthful.[303]

3–165 In *Marks v British Waterways Board*[304] (digested in para.7–138) Mr Marks, the tenant, held a sub-lease of business premises, of which the British Waterways

---

[301] [1991] 1 E.G.L.R. 1 CA.

[302] [1959] A.C. 20 at 51 and 52. Contrast the position in respect of the service of s.26 requests and whether the tenant's proposals for the grant of a new tenancy need to be genuine, considered in *Sun Life Assurance Plc v Thales Tracs Ltd* [2001] EWCA Civ 704; [2007] 1 W.L.R. 1562 (digested in para.3–220). See para.3–219 sub-para.(7).

[303] He said:

"Such being the true interpretation of these notices, I am of opinion that they must be given honestly and truthfully. They are not to be regarded merely as pleadings preparatory to a trial—in which parties, I regret to say, sometimes deny the truth, or refuse to admit it, if it suits their plan of campaign. These notices are intended to be acted on before there is a trial at all. On the receipt of such a notice, the tenant has to decide his course of action—for instance, whether to accept the alternative accommodation that is offered, or whether to accept the landlord's word that he intends to occupy the premises himself, or as the case may be. In every case he has to decide whether to apply for a new lease or not. It would be deplorable if a landlord could be allowed to get an advantage by misrepresenting his state of mind or any other fact. Suppose he said in his notice: 'I intend to reconstruct the premises' or 'I intend to occupy for the purposes of my own business', when he, in fact, had no such intention at all. On the faith of such a statement, the tenant might be induced to abstain from applying to the court for a new tenancy, because he would think it no use to do so. He would know that he would have to pay the costs if he lost. Just imagine the tenant's consternation if, at the end of the tenancy, after he had left, the landlord did not reconstruct the premises or occupy them himself, but straightway let in someone else. Would the tenant have no redress? I should have thought it clear that the notice would be bad—voidable—liable to be set aside for fraudulent misrepresentation: see *Lazarus Estates, Ltd v Beasley* ([1956] 1 All E.R. 341; [1956] 1 Q.B. 702). If it was avoided, the original tenancy would continue. The landlord would get no advantage from his misrepresentation—which is as it ought to be. If it was too late to avoid the notice, the landlord would be liable at common law in damages for fraud; just as he would be under section 55 if the misrepresentation was made to the court. Provided, however, that the notice is a good and honest notice when it is given, then it is clear, to my mind, that the ground stated therein must be established to exist at the time of the hearing... What is the result of this? If the notice had been a dishonest notice in which the landlord company had fraudulently misrepresented their intention—or, I would add, if there had been a material misrepresentation in it—I should have thought it would be a bad notice."

[304] [1963] 3 All E.R. 28; [1963] 1 W.L.R. 1008 CA.

Board was a freeholder. Mr Marks served notice on his lessor requesting a new tenancy under the 1954 Act. At that time, the sub-lessor had agreed to surrender his lease to the British Waterways Board. The board wished to obtain possession of the premises in order to demolish and reconstruct. The sub-lessor served a counter-notice stating that this was the intention of "the landlords". By the time of the hearing, the surrender had been effected, and British Waterways Board was Mr Marks's landlord. The Court of Appeal held that the counter-notice was valid and effective. In his judgment Lord Denning M.R. said[305]:

> "... the notice opposing the new tenancy, a landlord's notice, is to be regarded as in the nature of a pleading ... It is sufficient as long as it gives notice to the tenant of the case which he has to meet. So long as it is not deceptive or misleading, it avails the subsequent owner of the property who is the landlord at the date of the hearing."

Harman L.J. said[306]:

> "... one must not mislead the tenant; one must not say anything which is fraudulent, but, if the notice is given in good faith and the facts about reconstruction can be substantiated by the person who is the landlord when the hearing comes on, then the counter-notice really has served the purpose which the legislature can be said to have required it to serve."

Pearson L.J. made the same point[307]:

> "What one has to inquire into in regard to the notice given under section 26 is whether it was given bonafide; whether it was an honest notice. It may be that there are some further requirements with regard to it. It may be that it would be void if it were deceptive or misleading, or if it contained some material misrepresentation."

In *Stradbroke v Mitchell*[308] (digested in para.3–167) Glidewell L.J. said:

> "In my view [the] authorities establish the proposition that a landlord's counter-notice under section 26(6) of the 1954 Act is invalid and of no effect if the statement contained in it of the landlord's intention is fraudulent, not honestly made. The notice with which we are here concerned is a notice of the same sort as a notice under section 26(6). It is not a mere notice to quit. In my view, a notice to quit which states that it is given for one of the reasons set out in the various cases in Schedule 3 to the 1986 Act is invalid and of no effect if it contains a statement which is false and made fraudulently by the giver of the notice, i. e. knowing the statement to be untrue, or reckless whether it is true or false."

As a consequence of the decisions mentioned in paras 3–164 to 3–165 above the practice of specifying grounds of opposition for tactical purposes, being grounds other than those upon which the landlord could genuinely rely, has all but fallen into disuse. It is to be noted that the apparent introduction by these cases of a requirement for the validity of a notice, that the landlord genuinely intends to rely on the ground specified, does not invalidate a notice where there has been a subsequent change of mind. When the landlord serves his notice he is expressing a statement as to his then state of mind. Such a statement is a statement of fact: **3–166**

[305] [1963] 3 All E.R.28 at 31; [1963] 1 W.L.R. 1008 at 1015.
[306] [1963] 3 All E.R. 28 at 33; [1963] 1 W.L.R. 1008 at 1018.
[307] [1963] 3 All E.R. 28 at 35; [1963] 1 W.L.R. 1008 at 1020.
[308] [1991] 1 W.L.R. 469; [1991] 1 All E.R. 676.

> "The state of a man's mind is as much a fact as the state of his digestion. It is true that it is very difficult to prove what the state of a man's mind at a particular time is, but if it can be ascertained it is as much a fact as anything else."[309]

Thus, if the landlord genuinely specifies ground (b) (persistent non-payment of rent) in addition to say ground (f) (demolition or redevelopment) but subsequently abandons reliance upon ground (b), because, for instance, he considers that on reflection the persistence of the non-payment, although present, is unlikely to persuade the court that they should refuse the renewal, the landlord has nevertheless served a valid notice. At the time of the service of the notice he had grounds to rely upon ground (b) and his reliance upon it reflected his then state of mind; there was no misrepresentation as to his state of mind at the date of the service of the notice.

3–167 ***Stradbroke v Mitchell***[310] The tenancy of two farms included a number of cottages, which were subject to a covenant in the tenancy agreement preventing their assignment or under-letting except to workmen on the farms. The landlord served a notice to quit on the defendant under s.26(2) of and Case E in Sch.3 to the Agricultural Holdings Act 1986 alleging breaches of the covenant against sub-letting in respect of five cottages on the farms. Under s.26(2) and Case E of the 1986 Act a landlord of an agricultural holding was entitled to possession if at the date of the giving of the notice the landlord's interest in the holding had been materially prejudiced by a breach of covenant by the tenant which was not capable of being remedied. As regards the breaches alleged in the notice, the landlord had given his consent to sub-letting of three of the cottages, the sub-letting of a further cottage was not in breach of the covenant and the only apparent breach, the sub-letting of the fifth cottage, had been remedied by the date of the notice. The tenant contended that the notice to quit was not valid because, inter alia, the landlord had acted fraudulently in serving it because it contained false misrepresentations. The landlord contended that the truth or falsity of the statement of reasons attached to a notice to quit were merely an indication of the grounds the landlord would seek to prove and did not affect the validity of the notice. The Court of Appeal held that the notice to quit was invalid as:

(1) the statements in it were calculated to deceive in that they were assertions that the landlord honestly believed that he had good grounds to terminate the tenancy and the fact that the tenant was not deceived was irrelevant;
(2) it contained a statement which was false and made fraudulently by the landlord by reason of knowing the statement to be untrue or being reckless whether it was true or false. The landlord had been so fixed on his objective of getting the cottages back from the defendant that he had been reckless whether the statements made in his notice to quit were true or not and in those circumstances the false statements made in the notice to quit that there had been a breach of covenant were fraudulent.

[309] Bowen L.J. in *Edgington v Fitzmaurice* (1885) L.R. 29 Ch D. 459 CA.
[310] [1991] 1 W.L.R 469; [1991] 1 All E.R. 676.

No amendment of notice

It is important for the landlord to ensure that he specifies the correct grounds upon which he intends to rely, for a valid s.25 notice cannot be unilaterally withdrawn[311] nor amended: *Hutchinson v Lambeth*[312] (digested in para.3–169). **3–168**

Hutchinson v Lambeth[313] A county court judge on an application for a new tenancy, resisted by the landlord on grounds (a) and (b) of s.30(1), permitted the landlord to amend his answer so as to incorporate ground (c) (allegations of nuisance) even though these grounds had not been specified in the s.25 notice. The Court of Appeal held that the judge had no jurisdiction to permit the amendment but the amendment, although irregular, was not sufficient to justify a retrial, as the evidence of nuisance was relevant to the exercise of the judge's discretion under grounds (a) and (b) of s.30(1) (those grounds being discretionary). **3–169**

The notice must accurately specify the premises comprised in the tenancy

There are two senses in which a notice may fail to do so. First, it may misdescribe the premises comprised in the tenancy; and secondly, it may purport, or appear to purport, to terminate the tenancy in respect of part only of the premises comprised in the tenancy. **3–170**

Misdescription

The s.25 notice need not describe the property in minute detail nor follow exactly the parcels clause of the lease. It is considered that the test, as in all matters concerning defects alleged to invalidate the notice, is whether the notice was clear and plain to a reasonable tenant reading it so that the tenant could not be misled by it; that is to say, would a reasonable tenant considering the notice know that it was intending to terminate the whole of the tenancy of the premises demised by the relevant lease?[314] A typographical error is in most cases unlikely to mislead a reasonable tenant receiving it. Thus where a s.25 notice referred to the demised premises as "12 Sussex Gardens" instead of "92 Sussex Gardens" it was agreed by counsel for the landlord and tenant, which concession was approved by the judge, that the error did not invalidate the notice: *M&P Enterprises (London) v Norfolk Square Hotels*[315] (digested in para.3–203). However, an omission of part of the demised premises is more serious. Thus where the premises were situated on both the fourth and ninth floors of a building, a reference in the notice to only the fourth floor invalidated the notice: *Kaiser Engineers and Contractors Inc v ER Squibb & Sons Ltd*.[316] In that case it **3–171**

[311] See the cases in relation to s.26 requests under para.3–219 sub-para.(7), below.
[312] [1984] 1 E.G.L.R. 75 CA.
[313] [1984] 1 E.G.L.R. 75 CA.
[314] See *Mannai Investment Co Ltd v Eagle Star Life Assurance Co Ltd* [1997] A.C. 749 HL and para.3–129 et seq.
[315] [1994] 1 E.G.L.R. 129 at 130E and 131C.
[316] (1971) 218 E.G. 1731.

was not clear to a reasonable tenant that it was being asked to give up the entirety of the premises demised by the tenancy. However, an omission of part of the premises demised is not fatal if it is obvious that the landlord was intending to terminate the whole. Thus where the s.25 notice followed the wording of the parcels clause with the omission of a small area of land at the rear formerly consisting of a garage, all of which premises were occupied by the tenant as a supermarket, it was held that no reasonable tenant would have had the slightest hesitation in knowing that the s.25 notice was intended to terminate the whole of the tenancy: *Safeway Food Stores v Morris*.[317] On the other hand, where the premises consisted of offices on the ninth and storage accommodation on two other floors, together with a car parking space, the reference in the s.25 notice to the ninth-floor accommodation only was held to invalidate the notice: *Herongrove v Wates City of London Properties*.[318] It may be that the notice, rather than omitting the full description, refers to more property than that which was demised to the tenant. But where it was the landlord who occupied the balance of the accommodation not demised to the tenant but nevertheless referred to in the s.25 notice, the notice was held to be valid, for the tenant must have known that the landlord himself was occupying the balance of the accommodation not demised and so must have known that the notice could apply only to that part of the property demised to the tenant: *Bridgers v Stanford*.[319]

Notice referring to part only of the tenancy

3–172 The notice must terminate the whole of the tenancy. Thus, as has been seen above, if, as a matter of construction, the description of the premises in the notice refers to part only of the premises demised, the notice will be ineffective, albeit the terms of the contract expressly confer upon the landlord a right to break part only of the premises demised by the lease: *Southport Old Links v Naylor*.[320] However, if the lease, as a matter of construction, grants two tenancies, there is no difficulty in the landlord terminating only one of the tenancies created by the lease: *Moss v Mobil Oil Co Ltd*.[321] Whether the lease gives rise to two tenancies rather than one is a question of construction. The existence of a contractual break clause will not be sufficient: *Southport Old Links v Naylor*. In *Moss v Mobil Oil Co Ltd*, the demise consisted of two separate petrol filling stations which were physically separate and the lease provided that:

> "In this lease . . . all other covenant agreements and conditions contained herein and in the Schedules hereto shall be read and construed as if separate and independent leases had been entered into in respect of each of the demised premises and not as one demise."

It was held that the lease albeit one document created two demises.

---

[317] [1980] 1 E.G.L.R. 59.
[318] [1988] 1 E.G.L.R. 82.
[319] [1991] 2 E.G.L.R. 265.
[320] [1985] 1 E.G.L.R. 66 CA.
[321] [1981] 1 E.G.L.R. 71 CA.

Notice referring to more than one demise

It has also been held that in the unusual circumstances where the same tenant holds more than one tenancy of several properties from the same landlord, that one notice in respect of more than one of the tenancies is valid: see *Tropis Shipping Ltd v Ibex Properties Ltd*.[322] **3–173**

Several notices in respect of one demise

If the landlord purports to terminate the tenancy by the service of two or more notices, with each notice referring to a part of the single demise (e.g. different floors within a building), the notices are invalid unless they are to be treated as a single notice in respect of the demise. In *M&P Enterprises (London) Ltd v Norfolk Square Hotels Ltd*[323] (digested in para.3–203) an unsuccessful attempt was made to treat four separate s.25 notices relating to different parts of the demised premises, each being served by one of the four owners of the reversion, as a single s.25 notice terminating the tenant's tenancy. In *St Ermins Property Co Ltd v Patel*[324] two notices under s.4 of Pt 1 to the 1954 Act, each referring to one of the two maisonettes comprising the building and which were in fact held under a single demise, were held to be invalid. An attempt by the landlord to uphold the two notices by reference to the *Mannai Co Ltd v Eagle Star Life Assurance Co Ltd*[325] decision was rejected. Sir Martin Nourse said: **3–174**

> "If that principle [Mannai] is to be applied to this case, the Landlord must establish that a reasonable recipient in the position of the Tenants and with knowledge of the true nature of the continuation tenancy and the essential pro-visions of the 1954 Act would, on reading the two notices . . . , have been left in no doubt that the Landlord wished to determine the tenancy by a single notice in respect of the premises as a whole but had wrongly done so by two notices in respect of the lower and upper maisonettes respectively. That statement of what the Landlord must establish is a sufficient demonstration of its inability to bring this case within a principle which was invented in order to cure a wrong date inserted in a notice determining a lease in circumstances where it was obvious both that the date had been inserted by mistake and what the date intended to be inserted was. I am unable to see how a recipient of the notices, reasonable or unreasonable, could have been left in any doubt that what the Landlord wished to do was to do what he did and serve two notices and not one".

A section 25 notice may not be served if the tenant has already made a request for a new tenancy

See s.26(4). **3–175**

[322] [1967] E.G.D. 433.
[323] [1994] 1 E.G.L.R. 129.
[324] [2001] EWCA Civ 804.
[325] [1997] A.C. 749 HL. As to the *Mannai* test, see para.3–129.

The notice must be given not more than 12 nor less than 6 months before the date of termination specified therein.

3–176 Subject to one special provision under s.25(3)(b), which is discussed in para.3–181 below, it is not necessary that a clear period of 6 or 12 months be given. A s.25 notice which specifies a date of termination which is six months from the date when the notice is given, excluding the date of service, is valid: *Hogg Bullimore & Co v Cooperative Insurance Society*.[326] In that case the notice was given on April 2, 1984 and specified October 2, 1984 as the date of termination and was held to be a good notice.

Date to be specified: periodic tenancies and tenancies with break clauses

3–177 Section 25(3) provides for the date of termination to be specified in the case of a tenancy which, apart from the Act, could have been brought to an end by notice to quit given by the landlord, that is to say a periodic tenancy or a tenancy for a fixed term containing a landlord's option to break. In such a case the date of termination to be specified must not be earlier than the earliest date on which, apart from the Act, the tenancy could have been brought to an end by notice to quit given by the landlord, supposing him to have given that notice on the date that he serves the s.25 notice. Such a notice is, of course, also required, by virtue of s.25(2), to be not more than 12 nor less than 6 months in duration. It is not necessary for the date of termination to be exactly the date which would have had to be specified in a common law notice to quit; it is sufficient if it is not earlier than that date.

3–178 ***Commercial Properties v Wood***[327] Business premises were held on a tenancy from month to month. The tenancy commenced on the 18th of each month and could thus be determined (at common law) by not less than one month's notice expressed to expire on the first day of any month. On October 4, 1965, the landlord served notice under s.25 determining the tenancy on April 11, 1966. The notice was good because it complied with the wording of the Act. The date specified (April 11, 1966) was "not earlier" than the earliest date on which the landlord could, by giving notice on October 4, have ended the periodic tenancy (i.e. December 1, 1965).

Examples

3–179 The provisions can be illustrated by the following examples.

3–180 **Quarterly tenancy** In the case of a quarterly tenancy, the common law rule is that not less than one-quarter's notice must be given, to expire on one of the usual quarter days. If one considers the position at common law on, say, January 1, the earliest date upon which a quarterly tenancy could be terminated by giving a notice on that date would be June 24. Under s.25 a notice given on January 1

[326] (1984) 50 P. & C.R. 105.

[327] [1968] 1 Q.B. 15 CA.

would have to specify a date which was (1) not earlier than June 24 and (2) not earlier than six months from January 1 and (3) not later than 12 months from January 1. Accordingly, the landlord could specify any date between July 1 and January 1 of the next year.

Fixed term subject to landlord's break In the case of a tenancy for a term of years certain with a right to break at September 29 in a particular year, a landlord considering his position at common law on January 1 in that year would be able to serve a notice to expire on September 29. Under s.25 he could specify any date which was (1) not earlier than September 29 and (2) not earlier than six months from January 1 and (3) not later than 12 months from January 1. Accordingly, he could serve a notice specifying any date between September 29 and January 1 of the next year. **3–181**

In the case of a tenancy where more than six months notice to quit is required, s.25(3)(b) provides that, instead of 12 months being the longest period permitted for the notice, it must not be longer than the length of notice to quit required, plus six months. For example, in the case of a term of years certain which permitted the landlord to serve a break notice of 13 months' duration, he would be entitled, if he so desired, to serve a notice not more than 19 months before the date of termination specified therein. The minimum length of notice which could be given in these circumstances would be 13 months, in order to comply with the terms of the tenancy. The date of termination would, of course, have to be a date which was not earlier than the date upon which the common law break notice could have taken effect.

Statutory notice perform double duty

The landlord is able to exercise the break clause by serving a s.25 notice only; the s.25 notice can do double duty: see para.3–180 et seq. If the landlord takes the unusual step of serving first a contractual break notice and then, on a later date, a s.25 notice, he may encounter the argument that the s.25 notice is invalid. Such an argument centres upon the wording of s.25(3)(a), namely, that the date of termination to be specified must not be "earlier than the earliest date on which apart from this Part of this Act the tenancy could have been brought to an end by a notice to quit given by the landlord on the date of the giving of the notice under this section". If, at the date when the s.25 notice is given, the latest date has passed at which a notice could have been given at common law determining the tenancy on the date specified, it could be argued that the s.25 notice does not comply with this wording. That argument was, however, rejected by the county court in *Jones v Daniels & Davidson (Holdings)*,[328] the facts of which are adapted for the purposes of the following example. **3–182**

Example The tenancy is a tenancy from year to year, with its anniversary date on September 29. Accordingly, at common law, a notice to quit could be given not later than March 25 in any year specifying as the date of termination September 29 in that year. If the landlord gave such a notice, it would not **3–183**

[328] [1981] C.L.Y. 1513.

determine the tenancy for the purposes of the Act (assuming it to be one to which the Act applied). However, a s.25 notice given subsequent to such a common law notice at any time on or before March 29 could validly specify September 29 as a date of termination, notwithstanding that a common law notice specifying that date could not then have been given.

Date to be specified: "any other tenancy"

3–184 Section 25(4) provides for the date of termination to be specified in relation to "any other tenancy". In effect this applies to all tenancies for fixed terms which do not allow the landlord to serve a break notice. In such a case the date of termination must not be earlier than the date on which, apart from the Act, the tenancy would come to an end by effluxion of time. The notice must also comply with the requirements of s.25(2) as to its minimum and maximum duration. A s.25 notice which specifies the last day of the term is good: *Re Crowhurst Park*.[329] There may, in some cases, be an element of doubt as to what is the last day of the term, as where the term is expressed as being a number of years "from" a particular date and it is unclear whether that date is intended to be included in the term or not: *Ladyman v Wirral Estates*,[330] followed and approved by the Court of Appeal in *Whelton Sinclair v Hyland*.[331] It is good practice, if there is any doubt at all as to what is the last day of the term, to add on a couple of extra days to the earliest date which could have been specified in the notice. This also gives some leeway in case of delays in actual service of the notice.

Date to be specified: where contractual term has expired

3–185 It follows that in every case where the contractual date of termination has passed and the tenancy is being continued by s.24, the s.25 notice can specify any date which complies with the minimum and maximum requirements of s.25(2).

Landlord's option to break: effect of notice

3–186 Where the lease contains a landlord's option to break, service of a break notice which complies with the terms of the lease takes effect as a determination of the

---

[329] [1974] 1 W.L.R. 583; [1974] 1 All E.R. 991.

[330] [1968] 2 All E.R. 197. Ordinarily the word "from" would require the day on which the term commenced to be excluded. Thus, if a tenancy were expressed to be for a term of five years to commence on, e.g. August 1, 2009, the tenancy would, prima facie, commence on the very next day such that the tenancy would expire on August 1, 2014, i.e. the whole of August 1, 2014 is part of the term. In *Humber Oil Terminals Trustee Ltd v Associated British Ports* [2012] EWHC 1336 (Ch), the lease was expressed to be for a term "on and from" the January 1, 1970 "for the term of forty years". It was held that a s.25 notice specifying December 31, 2009 was invalid as the tenancy did not end until January 1, 2010. The judge held that "the use of the phrase 'on and from' January 1, 1970 . . . most naturally falls to be construed to mean that the period of the demise is the period 'on' January 1, 1970 and for 40 years 'from' January 1, 1970. That period expired on January 1, 1970." (at [213] per Sales J.)

[331] [1992] 2 E.G.L.R. 158 CA, where it was held that the general rule of construction relating to "from" is normally displaced in leases where the commencement date corresponds with one of the quarter days. In such a case the term includes the date of commencement.

contractual term on the date specified in the notice. If the tenancy is one to which the Act applies, it will thereafter continue by virtue of s.24(1). If the landlord then wishes to determine the continuation tenancy, he must serve a s.25 notice in the usual way: see *Castle Laundry (London) v Read*.[332] Often, the landlord can serve a s.25 notice in the prescribed form so as to take effect both as a contractual break notice and a notice under s.25: see *Scholl Manufacturing Co v Clifton (Slim-Line)*[333] (digested in para.3–188) and *Weinbergs Weatherproofs v Radcliffe Paper Mill Co*[334]; *Keith Bayley Rogers & Co v Cubes Ltd*[335] (digested in para.3–189); *Aberdeen Steak Houses Group Plc v Crown Estate Commissioners*[336]; and *Blunden v Frogmore Investments Ltd*.[337] Such a notice must comply both with the contractual requirements of the lease and the statutory requirements of s.25.[338] It may be, however, that the contractual provisions of the lease entitle the landlord to break only in particular specified circumstances, such as where he desires to increase the rent. Since it would be inappropriate to state in a s.25 notice that it is being given because the landlord wishes to increase the rent, it will be best in such circumstances for the landlord to serve two notices, one complying with the terms of the break clause and another in the form prescribed by s.25. In any event, it is always wise, when the landlord is both exercising a contractual right to break and terminating the tenancy pursuant to s.25, that he should make it clear in a covering letter that his s.25 notice is intended to achieve both purposes. (As to the date to be specified in a s.25 notice which does "double duty" as a contractual break notice, see para.3–175).

Where there is a chain of interests such as a head tenant and an occupying undertenant, with a break clause contained in the head tenancy, the superior landlord, in order to be "competent landlord" in respect of the occupying undertenant will first have to operate the break in the head tenancies, for by s.44 (see para.3–85) the landlord entitled to give a s.25 notice is the owner of the fee simple or of a tenancy which will not come to an end within 14 months of effluxion of time or by virtue of a notice to quit already given by the landlord. In *Keith Bayley Rogers & Co v Cubes Ltd*[339] (digested in para.3–189) Templeman J. stated that where a landlord has power to serve, in sequence, a notice exercising the break clause followed by a notice under s.25, and he launches both notices on the same day, it is to be assumed that the notices were delivered in the correct sequence; it is not necessary to pester the postman to see which notice was delivered first.[340] **3–187**

---

[332] [1955] 1 Q.B. 586.

[333] [1967] Ch. 41 CA.

[334] [1958] Ch. 437.

[335] (1976) 31 P. & C.R. 412.

[336] [1997] 2 E.G.L.R. 107 CA.

[337] [2002] EWCA Civ 573; [2002] 2 E.G.L.R. 29.

[338] See para.7–189 as to the considerations to which regard should be had when serving a break notice on redevelopment grounds.

[339] (1975) 31 P. & C.R. 412.

[340] In *Eaglehill Ltd v J Needham Builders Ltd* [1973] A.C. 992 at 1011 HL the principle was formulated by Lord Cross as follows:

> "If two acts have been done one of which ought to have been done after the other if it was to be valid and the evidence which could reasonably be expected to be available does not show which was done first, they will be presumed to have been done in the proper order."

3–188 ***Scholl Manufacturing Co v Clifton (Slim-Line)***[341] The lease contained a break clause which provided that either party could determine the lease on March 25, 1966 by giving to the other six months previous notice in writing. On May 11, 1965 the landlord served upon the tenant a notice under s.25 terminating the tenancy on March 25, 1966. Accompanying the notice was a letter which stated that:

> "... we enclose here-with a landlord's notice to terminate the business tenancy in respect of [the demised premises] ... This formal notice is given at an early date in order that we may, as far as possible, arrange for the termination of the lease to the best advantage of our mutual interest".

No counter-notice under the Act was given by the tenants but they denied that the contractual term had been effectively broken. The Court of Appeal held that "notice to quit" within s.69 of the 1954 Act included the notice given pursuant to a break clause and as the date specified in the s.25 complied with the terms of the contract and the requirements of the Act the notice was a good notice effective to bring the contractual term to an end and to terminate the tenancy in accordance with the Act. In any event the notice coupled with the letter was sufficient to bring to the mind of the tenants the landlord's desire to put an end to the lease at the date which the break clause allowed.

3–189 ***Keith Bayley Rogers & Co (A Firm) v Cubes Ltd***[342] The lease permitted the landlord to break it on six-months' notice to expire on June 24, 1974. The tenant had underlet the premises to Keith Bayley Carroll and Co which was likewise subject to a break with effect from June 24, 1974. On August 16, 1973, the freehold owners, Cubes Ltd, sent to the tenant a notice under s.25 addressed (1) to the tenant, (2) to a company which had formerly had an interest in the lease or underlease, and (3) to the occupying undertenants, "whoever is the tenant". The s.25 notice specified June 24, 1974 as the date of termination. In the covering letter sent to the tenant Cubes Ltd stated, "you will see that we have joined you in the notice, together with [the company] and also that the occupiers Keith Bayley Carroll and Co although we must point out to you the only persons who will be entitled to any tenancy are those in occupation". Cubes Ltd sent an identical notice on the same date to the occupying undertenants. It was held it was clear that anyone receiving the notice, alternatively the notice together with the covering letter, could be in no doubt that the landlords were desirous of terminating the lease pursuant to the break clause. The s.25 notice was, therefore, sufficient to do double duty.

---

[341] [1967] Ch. 41 CA.

[342] (1976) 31 P. & C.R. 412.

Attacks on the validity of section 25 notices

Test for validity

In a number of cases, the validity of s.25 notices has been attacked. The test which has been evolved is whether the notice would be clear to a reasonable tenant and whether it is plain enough not to mislead him: *Carradine Properties Ltd v Aslam*[343] followed and approved in *Germax Securities Ltd v Spiegal*,[344] *Bridgers v Stanford*.[345] The House of Lords have approved this test in relation to break notices: *Mannai Investment Co Ltd v Eagle Star Life Assurance*.[346] In *Lewis v MTC Cars*[347] (digested in para.10–49) Templeman J. said that the test was whether the notice was sufficiently clear so that the tenant knew "what the landlord was up to". Another judicial formulation of the same test is whether the notice "has given the proper information to the tenant which will enable the tenant to deal in a proper way with the situation, whatever it may be, referred to in the . . . notice", per Barry J. in *Barclays Bank Ltd v Ascott*[348] approved in *Tegerdine v Brooks*[349] and *Morrow v Nadeem*[350] (digested in para.3–249). There is a strong line of authority suggesting that, whichever test is adopted, it must be applied objectively. The question is not whether the tenant was actually misled, but whether a reasonable recipient to the notice could have been misled (see *Sun Alliance & London Assurance Co Ltd v Hayman*[351]; *Tegerdine v Brooks*[352] and *Pearson v Alyo*[353]). In *Pearson v Alyo*, Nourse L.J. said: 3–190

> ". . . it must be emphasised that the validity of a s.25 notice is to be judged and judged objectively, at the date at which it was given. The question is not whether the inaccuracy actually prejudices the particular person to whom the notice is given but whether it is capable of prejudicing a reasonable tenant in the position of that person".

In *Mannai Investment Co Ltd v Eagle Star Life Assurance Co Ltd*[354] Lord Steyn said:

> "The question is how the landlord understood the notices. The construction of the notices must be approached objectively. The issue is how a reasonable recipient would have understood the notices."

---

343 [1976] 1 W.L.R. 442; [1976] 1 All E.R. 573.

344 [1979] 1 E.G.L.R. 84.

345 [1991] 2 E.G.L.R. 265 CA.

346 [1997] A.C. 749. This test has been held to apply to statutory notices: *York v Casey* [1998] 2 E.G.L.R. 25 CA. See also *John Lyon's Free Grammar School v Secchi* (2000) 32 H.L.R. 820 CA; *Burman v Mount Cook Ltd* [2002] Ch. 256 CA; *Ravenseft Properties Ltd v Hall* [2002] H.L.R. 33 CA; *McDonald v Fernandez* [2003] 4 All E.R. 1033 CA; *Lay v Ackerman* [2004] L. & T.R. 29; [2005] 1 E.G.L.R. 139 CA. These are cases concerning statutes other than Part II of the 1954 Act. The *Mannai* test is considered at length at para.3–129 et seq.

347 [1974] 1 W.L.R. 1499; First instance, affirmed [1975] 1 W.L.R. 457 CA.

348 [1961] 1 W.L.R. 717; [196] 1 All E.R. 782.

349 (1977) 36 P. & C.R. 261 CA.

350 [1986] 1 W.L.R. 1381 CA.

351 [1975] 1 W.L.R. 177 at 185 e–f.

352 (1977) 36 P. & C.R. 261 at 266, per Cairns L.J.

353 [1990] 1 E.G.L.R. 114 CA.

354 [1997] A.C. 749 HL.

This objective approach to the question of the validity of a notice was questioned, in a decision which pre-dates *Mannai*, by Scott L.J. in the Court of Appeal in *Land v Sykes*.[355] Considering the decision of *Carradine Properties Ltd v Aslam*,[356] which clearly refers to an objective test in considering the validity of the notice, he said:

> "... if a notice to quit in fact communicates the correct information to the recipient tenant, I do not think that it is any business of the courts, or that there is any requirement of the law of landlord and tenant that operates, to deprive the notice of validity by reference to what some hypothetical reasonable tenant might have thought the notice meant. I agree that if objectively construed in light of the facts known to both landlord and tenant the meaning of the notice is clear, that is an end of the matter. But if, in fact, the tenant was not con-fused, I for my part think that that would suffice."

Land v Sykes[357] was concerned with the validity of a statutory notice under the Agricultural Holdings Act 1986, but there is no reason why Scott L.J.'s comments are not equally applicable to all forms of notices to quit, including notices under the 1954 Act. However, any suggestion of a subjective approach to the validity of notices under the Act has clearly been rejected.

Material to be taken into account

3–191 In applying the objective test as to how the reasonable recipient would have understood the notice served, regard is to be had to "the relevant objective contextual scene."[358] "... The question is what reasonable persons, circumstanced as the actual parties were, would have had in mind. It follows that one cannot ignore that a reasonable recipient of the notices would have had in the forefront of his mind the terms of the leases."[359] However, in considering the validity of a s.25 notice albeit the reasonable recipient of the notice need not be taken to know that a notice which fails to specify a ground of opposition could not be amended, the existence of an invalid notice may be taken into account, in considering the validity of an otherwise valid notice served at the same time as an invalid notice, as "it makes a statement as much as a covering letter would do": *Barclays Bank Plc v Bee*[360] (digested in para.3–162).

Cases illustrating attacks on validity of notices

3–192 The variety of defects or alleged defects raised before the court is considerable, as the following summary of the principal reported cases on the topic indicates.

***Barclays Bank Ltd v Ascott*[361] (digested in para.3–149)** The s.25 notice stated that the landlord would not oppose the grant of a new tenancy if the tenant could

[355] [1992] 1 E.G.L.R. 1 CA.
[356] [1976] 1 W.L.R. 442.
[357] [1992] 1 E.G.L.R. 1 CA.
[358] Lord Steyn at 767, *Mannai Investment Co Ltd v Eagle Star Life Assurance Co Ltd* [1997] A.C. 749 HL.
[359] [1997] A.C. 749 at 768.
[360] [2002] 1 W.L.R. 332 CA, per Arden L.J.
[361] [1961] 1 W.L.R. 717.

find a guarantor, but did not state expressly whether the tenant was opposing the grant of the new tenancy and did not indicate, as required, if opposing, on what ground under s.30 of the 1954 Act the landlord was opposing; the notice was held to be invalid.

Bolton v Oppenheim[362] The notice stated that the landlord intended to oppose and set out the ground (f) of s.30(1), but omitted to state that the landlord "could not reasonably do (the work) without obtaining possession"; the notice was held valid. A similar result was reached in *Biles v Caesar*.[363]

Barclays Bank Plc v Bee[364] **(digested in para.3–162)** The tenant received under cover of one letter two notices, one opposing renewal, which was invalid by reason of the fact that it failed to specify any ground of opposition and the other, a valid notice, not opposing renewal. Both notices were held to be invalid as the two documents were entirely inconsistent with one another.

Bond v Graham[365] **and *AJA Smith Transport v British Railways Board***[366] **(digested in para.3–252)** A notice on an out-of-date form was held to be valid.

Bridgers v Stanford[367] A notice addressed not to the tenant but to a company carrying on the tenant's business, where both companies were subsidiaries of a third and the names of both companies were used inter-changeably in correspondence with the landlord, was held to be valid.

Falcon Pipes v Stanhope[368] The landlord failed to date the notice; the notice was held to be valid.

Germax v Spiegal[369] Here date on which the notice was given was incorrectly stated in the body of the notice, but a covering letter made it clear what the correct date was; the notice was held to be valid.

Harvey Textiles Ltd v Hillel[370] A notice under s.25 was valid where the ground of opposition was framed in terms of ground (g) of s.30(1) even though it did not make it clear that it was the landlord's intention to carry out the business of a company controlled by him within s.30(3) rather than personally.

---

362 [1959] 1 W.L.R. 913; [1959] 3 All E.R. 90 CA.
363 [1957] 1 W.L.R. 156; [1957] 1 All E.R. 151 CA.
364 [2002] 1 W.L.R. 332 CA.
365 [1975] 2 E.G.L.R. 63.
366 [1981] 2 E.G.L.R. 69 CA.
367 [1991] 2 E.G.L.R. 265 CA.
368 [1967] E.G.D. 804; 204 E.G. 1243; (1967) 117 N.L.J.1345.
369 [1979] 1 E.G.L.R. 84 CA.
370 [1979] 1 E.G.L.R. 74.

Lewis v MTC (Cars)[371] **(digested in para.10–49)** The landlord had not deleted the part of the prescribed form, stating that he would not oppose an application for a new tenancy but had stated a ground of opposition. The notice was held to be valid.

Morrow v Nadeem[372] **(digested in para.3–249)** The name of the landlord was given as someone who was not, in fact, the landlord and it was held that the notice was invalid.

M&P Enterprises (London) v Norfolk Square Hotels[373] **(digested in para.3–203)** A s.25 notice describing the landlord as Norfolk Square No.2 Ltd when its true name was Norfolk Square Hotel No.2 Ltd was not invalid for that reason.

Nasim v Wilson[374] The view was expressed that a notice which was not signed by the landlord was probably valid.

Pearson v Alyo[375] **and *Smith v Draper***[376] **(digested in para.3–248)** A s.25 notice naming only some of the joint landlords was held to be invalid.

Philipson-Stow v Trevor Square[377] **and *Housleys v Bloomer-Holt***[378] **(digested in para.7–109)** The ground of opposition specified in the notice did not follow the proper wording under s.30(1)(f), but the notices were held to be valid.

Sabella Ltd v Montgomery[379] A s.25 notice which did not contain the "Act Quick" warning notice and failed to refer to the notes dealing with the ground of opposition relied upon by the landlord (albeit subsequently abandoned) was invalid.

Safeway v Morris[380] The premises were inaccurately described, but the notice was held to be valid.

Stidolph v American School[381] The notice was unsigned, but a covering letter made it clear that it was served on behalf of the landlord; the notice was held to be valid.

---

371 [1975] 1 W.L.R. 457; [1975] 1 All E.R. 874 CA.
372 [1986] 1 W.L.R. 1381; [1987] 1 All E.R. 237 CA.
373 [1994] 1 E.G.L.R. 129.
374 (1975) 119 S J. 611.
375 [1990] 1 E.G.L.R. 114 CA.
376 [1990] 1 E.G.L.R. 69 CA.
377 [1981] 1 E.G.L.R. 56.
378 [1966] 1 W.L.R. 1244; [1966] 2 All E.R. 966 CA.
379 [1998] 1 E.G.L.R. 65 CA.
380 [1980] 1 E.G.L.R. 59.
381 (1969) 20 P. & C.R. 802 CA.

Sun Alliance v Hayman[382] The complaint was that the notice was in the form prescribed in 1957, whereas it should have been in the (different) form prescribed in 1967; the notice was held to be valid.

Sunrose v Gould[383] The date of termination specified was simply "15th July", without stating a year; the notice was held to be valid.

Tegerdine v Brooks[384] One of the notes was omitted from the prescribed form; the notice was nonetheless held to be valid.

Yamaha-Kemble Music (UK) Ltd v ARC Properties Ltd[385] A notice served by the assignor of the reversionary interest after the assignment to a wholly-owned subsidiary was held to be invalid, as it was not served by the "landlord".

Severed reversion

General position

Particular problems arise where, at the date for service of a s.25 notice, the reversion expectant upon the termination of the tenancy is vested in two different landlords. In essence the question is who may serve a valid s.25 notice. The cases illustrate the various ways in which the problem has arisen in practice, and the solutions proposed by the courts. The landlords of the severed parts may, it seems, combine and give a single notice in respect of the whole of the premises comprised in the tenancy. In *Nevill Long & Co (Boards) Ltd v Firmenich & Co*[386] (digested in para.3–197), Fox L.J. said (at 66): **3–193**

> "We should add that it seems to us that the Defendants and Meek [the owners of the reversion] together could constitute 'the landlord' for the purposes of section 25 (either by serving a single notice or separate notices operating at the same time) since together they are entitled to the entirety of the land comprised in the relevant reversion."

The service of a s.25 notice by one only of the persons constituting the landlord will be invalid: *EDF Energy Networks (EPN) Plc v BOH Ltd*[387] (digested in para.3–198). The requirement for the different persons in whom the reversion is vested to join together in serving a notice is made clear in respect of a notice served post June 1, 2004: s.44(1A). In one case, *M&P Enterprises (London) v Norfolk Square Hotels*[388] (digested in para.3–203), an unsuccessful attempt was made to treat four separate s.25 notices relating to different parts of the demised premises, each being served by one of the four owners of the reversion, as a single s.25 notice terminating the tenant's tenancy. The provisions of s.140 of the

382 [1975] 1 W.L.R. 177; [1975] 1 All E.R. 248 CA.
383 [1962] 1 W.L.R. 20; [1961] 3 All E.R. 1142 CA.
384 [1978] 1 E.G.L.R. 33 CA.
385 [1990] 1 E.G.L.R. 261.
386 [1983] 2 E.G.L.R. 76.
387 [2009] EWHC 3193 (Ch); [2010] L. & T.R. 14. There was no appeal on this point: [2011] EWCA Civ 19 at [20].
388 [1994] 1 E.G.L.R. 129.

Law of Property Act 1925, which permit a reversioner of part to serve a "notice to quit" in respect of the severed part, do not apply to enable one only of the reversioners to serve a s.25 notice in respect of that part of the premises affecting him: *Dodson Bull Carpet Co Ltd v City of London Corp*[389] (digested in para.3–196). The section is not a general deeming provision that, where there has been a severance of the reversion, the severed part is the only property originally comprised in the lease. The section cannot be interpreted so as to remove protected statutory rights of tenants: *Nevill Long & Co (Boards) Ltd v Firmenich & Co*[390] (digested in para.3–197).

3–194 A severed reversion can arise in a number of ways, e.g.:

Where the tenant sublets premises with adjoining premises of which he is also tenant from a different landlord, and the tenant's interest in adjoining premises comes to end earlier than the other. The landlord and the tenant will, when there is less than 14 months unexpired in the tenancy of the adjoining premises, be "the landlord" within s.44 of the sub-tenant: *Dodson Bull Carpet Co v City of London Corp*[391] (digested in para.3–196).

Where the landlord has a leasehold interest and effects a surrender of part of his headlease such that upon surrender the "landlord" within s.44 is the headlessee of part and the freehold owner of that part surrendered by the headlessee.

Where the tenant's demise includes rights of way and the land over which the way runs is transferred to a third party: *Nevill Long & Co (Boards) Ltd v Firmenich & Co*[392] (digested in para.3–197); *EDF Energy Networks (EPN) Plc v BOH Ltd*[393] (digested in para.3–198).

3–195 Where the reversion is severed and the tenant acquires part of the reversion it does not necessarily follow that the tenant's tenancy in respect of the part so acquired is deemed to have been merged with the freehold. Where there is no evidence of a person's intention as to merger there is a presumption against any merger if it would be against that person's interests: *EDF Energy Networks (EPN) Plc v BOH Ltd*[394] (digested in para.3–198).

3–196 ***Dodson Bull Carpet Co Ltd v City of London Corp***[395] Two separate premises had been demised by a single lease. As the result of the falling in of various superior interests, the position at the date of expiry of that lease was that two different entities fulfilled the definition of "landlord" within the meaning of the Act in respect of the two properties. One of those "landlords" purported to serve a s.25 notice in respect of the property of which he was the reversioner, but the court held that the notice was invalid because the landlord of one of the severed

389 [1975] 1 W.L.R. 781; [1975] 2 All E.R. 497.
390 [1983] 2 E.G.L.R. 76.
391 [1975] 1 W.L.R. 781; [1975] 2 All E.R. 497.
392 [1983] 2 E.G.L.R. 76.
393 [2009] EWHC 3193 (Ch); [2010] L. & T.R. 14. The issue on appeal was whether or not the tenant's acquisition of the freehold of the land demised gave rise to a surrender of his leasehold interest, which the Court of Appeal held it did not: [2011] EWCA Civ 19; [2011] L. & T.R. 15.
394 [2011] EWCA Civ 19; [2011] L. & T.R. 15, following well established authority: *Ingle v Vaughan Jenkins* [1900] 2 Ch. 368 and *Capital & Counties Bank Ltd v Rhodes* [1903] 1 Ch. 631.
395 [1975] 1 W.L.R. 781; [1975] 2 All E.R. 497.

parts of the tenancy could not serve a valid s.25 notice to terminate the tenancy as to that part. An attempt was made to rely on the provisions of s.140 of the Law of Property Act 1925, which provides that a reversioner may exercise his rights of re-entry or serve a notice to quit in respect of his severed part "as if the land comprised in each severed part... had alone originally been comprised in the lease". The judge held that this had no application to a s.25 notice because it was not a right of re-entry or notice to quit within the meaning of s.140. He left open the question whether, in such a case, the two landlords of the severed parts could combine and together give a notice in respect of the whole of the premises comprised in the tenancy. The judge said that the true position might be that no notice at all could be given until there was once again a single landlord entitled to an interest expectant in reversion to the entirety of the premises comprised in the tenancy.

Nevill Long & Co (Boards) Ltd v Firmenich & Co[396] The tenancy had consisted of (1) the demise of certain premises which the tenant occupied for business purposes and (2) a right of way over adjoining land owned by the landlord for the benefit of those premises. By the date of expiry of the contractual term, the landlord had sold his interest in the land over which the right of way existed. The new owner of that land argued that the tenant's rights in respect of the right of way over that land had ceased because it was to be treated as a separate tenancy of the right of way only, which was not capable of being protected by the Act: see *Land Reclamation v Basildon*[397] (digested in para.1–34). The Court of Appeal accepted that the premises comprised in the tenancy included not merely the premises demised, but also the rights of access included therein. Accordingly, they held that, as between the landlord and his purchaser there had, indeed, been a severance of the reversion as between the land demised and the land over which the right of way was enjoyed. However, they went on to hold that this did not adversely affect the position of the tenant. So far as he was concerned he still had one tenancy and the severance of the reversion was relevant only so far as concerned the rights as between the two landlords. It followed, in the view of the court, that neither the owner of the land demised nor the owner of the land burdened by the easement was alone "the landlord" within the meaning of s.44. **3–197**

EDF Energy Networks (EPN) Plc v BOH Ltd[398] The tenant, an electricity supplier, was granted a tenancy over three contiguous plots of land (1, 2 and 3) with a right of way and right to lay cables granted over another neighbouring plot, plot 4. The tenant built and operated an electricity sub-station on plot 2. The freehold to all 4 plots was sold and the tenant acquired the freehold of plot 2. Plots 1, 3 and 4 became vested in B. The effect of the sale of the freehold to B and to the tenant was that if the tenant's tenancy continued in respect of plot 2, there was a severed reversion. The trial judge had held that a s.25 notice must be **3–198**

[396] [1983] 2 E.G.L.R. 76.
[397] [1979] 1 W.L.R 767 CA. See now *Pointon York Group Plc v Poulton* [2006] EWCA Civ 1001; [2007] 1 P. & C.R. 115, discussed, at para.1–30 et seq.
[398] [2011] EWCA Civ 19; [2011] L. & T.R. 15.

given by all reversioners upon the lease and this would have thus required a notice to be served by the tenant (qua landlord of plot 2) and B[399] (as landlord of plot 4, being land over which the tenant had rights). B sought to argue that the tenant's lease of plot 2 had come to an end by merger upon the acquisition of the freehold of plot 2 by the tenant. The trial judge held that there was no merger. It was only this issue that came before the Court of Appeal. The court upheld the judge's determination. As there was no merger of the tenant's tenancy in respect of plot 2, the tenant's rights continued such that the tenant's consent (qua landlord of plot 2) to serving any notice to terminate the tenant's tenancy was required. Accordingly, B's attempt to serve a s.25 notice terminating the tenant's tenancy was ineffective.

3–199 The problem of severed reversions can arise quite inadvertently where the tenant occupies adjoining premises and lets both the tenanted premises and his own premises to a third party (see para.3–194). Modern commercial leases should contain a covenant against sub-letting the tenanted premises together with the tenant's adjoining premises but it certainly appears something worthy of consideration, in order to protect the landlord from inheriting a severed reversion.[400]

Where tenancy of part is not within the Act

3–200 A landlord of a severed part of the reversion which is subject to a tenancy which is not within the Act can, however, serve a valid notice to terminate under s.24(3)(a): *Skelton v Harrison & Pinder*[401] (digested in para.3–201).

3–201 ***Skelton v Harrison & Pinder***[402] The superior landlord granted a 21-year lease of factory premises to his company, WAS, expiring on April 24, 1970. In 1962, WAS wanted to grant a 21-year lease of the ground floor only of the factory to HP, WAS remaining in occupation of the remainder of the factory premises for the purposes of a business carried on by them. The parties sought to achieve the desired duration of term by providing for an "underlease" of the ground floor, to be granted by WAS to HP for the remainder of WAS's term less three days, and for a "reversionary lease" to be granted from then on by the superior landlord to HP until 1983. The head tenancy of WAS continued beyond April 24, 1970 by reason of the fact WAS were in occupation for the purposes of a business. HP were, however, by reason of the reversionary lease granted by the superior landlord, entitled to the reversion immediately expectant upon WAS's head tenancy insofar as it related to the ground floor. WAS were not in occupation of the ground floor and, accordingly, HP sought to terminate WAS's tenancy in so far as it related to the ground floor by serving a notice under s.24(3)(a) on March 28, 1972, terminating the tenancy of the ground floor of the factory premises with

[399] *EDF Energy Networks (EPN) Plc v BOH Ltd*[2009] EWHC 3193 (Ch); [2010] L. & T.R. 14.

[400] In previous editions of this work it was noted that such covenants were "rarely (if ever)" incorporated. However, the authors have noticed a marked increase in the number of commercial leases where the alienation covenant prohibits a letting with adjoining premises.

[401] [1975] Q.B. 361.

[402] [1975] Q.B. 361.

effect from July 1, 1972. The reversion of WAS's lease was severed in that insofar as it related to the ground floor, WAS's landlord was HP It was held that by the operation of s.140 of the Law of Property Act 1925, the right inter alia to determine WAS's lease in respect of the ground floor by notice to quit remained annexed to the severed part of the reversionary estate and HP were consequently entitled to give WAS whatever notice to quit the head lease specified. Since WAS were not in occupation of the ground floor and since there was now a separate reversion to it, their tenancy thereof had ceased to enjoy the protection of the Act and thus s.24(3)(a) applied to allow a notice to quit to determine the tenancy, provided the duration of the notice was correct. As that had been done, WAS's interest in the ground floor had ceased.

Two tenancies as a matter of construction

The problem relating to severed reversions may be overcome if, as a matter of construction, the severed interest can be viewed as giving rise to two tenancies, albeit embodied in one lease (see *Moss v Mobil Oil Co Ltd*[403]). The existence of a contractual break clause is unlikely to be sufficient to enable the court to construe the lease as giving rise to two tenancies rather than one: *Southport Old Links v Naylor*.[404] **3–202**

M&P Enterprises (London) v Norfolk Square Hotels[405] The tenant was demised five buildings under one lease. Four of the buildings were contiguous and formed one hotel. Another building separate from the others was also run as a hotel. The reversion was owned by four companies. The landlords served four separate s.25 notices upon the tenant. Each notice referred to each building owned by each of the landlords (one company owned two buildings). Each s.25 notice specified the same date of termination, and the same address of its agents (the landlords' solicitors). Each s.25 notice opposed the grant of a new lease under s.30(1)(g). The notices were served under cover of a letter which, referring to the demised premises by title, said "We refer to the above matter and enclose herewith notices under section 25 of the Landlord and Tenant Act 1954". It was held that the four notices could not be construed together so as to operate as a single notice. They were referred to in the covering letter as "notices" and it would not be clear to a reasonable recipient whether the premises were being treated as subject to a single tenancy. **3–203**

One matter that remains for judicial determination are the practical implications of a severed reversion when it comes to the court having to grant a new tenancy. Does the court grant one tenancy directing the two respondents to join together or does it grant separate tenancies from each landlord? It is considered that the former is most likely having regard to the fact that the two landlords constitute the "competent landlord". Section 36(1) provides that "the landlord shall be bound to execute on making favour of the tenant" the lease determined by the **3–204**

[403] [1991] 1 E.G.L.R. 71 CA. See para.3–172 et seq.
[404] [1985] 1 E.G.L.R. 66 CA.
[405] [1994] 1 E.G.L.R. 129.

court. "The landlord" is, of course, the landlord under s.44 and it is the two landlords together who fulfil this definition.

The 2003 Order

3–205 The problem relating to severed reversions has not been removed by the 2003 Order. On the contrary, art.27(2) of the 2003 Order makes it clear that where different persons own interests in different parts of the tenant's property, the reference to "landlord" is a reference to all those persons collectively: s.44(1A) (inserted by art.27(2) of the 2003 Order).

One of the amendments that has been made to deal with a severed reversion is to provide for an apportionment of rent as between the respective owners of the property interests. Section 35(1) (which gives the court power, in default of agreement, to determine the other terms of new tenancy) is amended, so that the terms of the tenancy to be ordered by the court, may "where different persons own interests which fulfil the conditions specified in s.44(1) of this Act in different parts of" the property which is the subject matter of the tenancy, include "terms as to the apportionment of the rent": s.35(1) as amended by art.27(3) of the 2003 Order.

Where a tenant makes a claim for compensation pursuant to s.37 of the Act, s.37(3B) makes it clear that the compensation for each part separately held is to be determined separately and recoverable only from the person who is the "landlord" for the purposes of s.44 with respect to that part.[406]

Effect of service of section 25 notice

3–206 Prior to the repeal of the requirement for the tenant to serve a counter-notice in response to a landlord's s.25 notice,[407] if the tenant failed to serve a counter-notice in response to the s.25 notice or, having served a counter-notice, failed to make an originating application within the statutory period (s.29(3)), the tenancy ended on the termination date specified in the s.25 notice. This problem does not now arise in light of the fact that the tenant is no longer required to serve a counter-notice. The s.25 notice once served cannot be unilaterally withdrawn.[408] Nor can the landlord seek to amend the grounds of opposition contained in the s.25 notice: see *Hutchinson v Lambeth*[409] (digested in para.3–169 above). There are, however, limited circumstances in which a s.25 notice may be withdrawn.[410] It is to be noted that specifying a ground of opposition which the landlord knows not to exist will be a ground stated in bad faith and, by analogy to the decision of the Court of Appeal on notice to quit under the Agricultural Holdings Act 1986, it is considered that the notice will be invalid: see *Rous v*

---

406 See para.3–87 as to the meaning of "landlord".

407 See para.5–01.

408 See the cases discussed in para.3–214/215 in relation to s.26 requests.

409 [1984] 1 E.G.L.R. 75 CA.

410 See para.7–08.

Mitchell.[411] A successor in title to the landlord may take advantage of the grounds of opposition stated in the s.25 notice: see para.7–132.

Service of fresh notice without prejudice

It often happens that the tenant raises the argument that the s.25 notice served by the landlord is invalid, without necessarily disclosing the alleged defect, or that the landlord does not accept that the notice is defective. There is no objection to the landlord serving a second notice without prejudice to the validity of the first and if it so happens that the first is invalid there is no reason why the second will not be considered a valid notice in those circumstances: see *Keith Bayley Rogers & Co (A Firm) v Cubes Ltd*[412] (digested in para.3–189) and *Smith v Draper*[413] (digested in para.3–248). **3–207**

7. SECTION 26 REQUESTS

Section 26 provides a method whereby certain classes of tenant of business premises may take steps to determine, by notice, a tenancy to which the Act applies. It is, to that extent, the tenant's equivalent to the landlord's right to terminate a tenancy by notice under s.25. **3–208**

Tenants entitled to make section 26 requests

Where there is a tenancy to which the Act applies which was granted for a term certain exceeding one year or granted for a term of years certain and thereafter from year to year, the tenant may make a request for a new tenancy unless barred from doing so by the circumstances mentioned in para.3–213 below. **3–209**

Tenants not entitled to make section 26 requests

It follows from the limited definition of those tenants who are entitled to make requests pursuant to s.26(1) that no such request may be made by a periodic tenant or a tenant who has a fixed term for a year or less. **3–210**

Termination by tenants not entitled to make section 26 requests

Since the making of a s.26 request is the only way in which a tenant can initiate the machinery whereby he can obtain a new tenancy from the court, it follows that a tenant who has a tenancy to which the Act applies, but who is not entitled to make such a request, will never be in a position to make an application, unless the **3–211**

---

[411] [1991] 1 E.G.L.R. 1 CA. See the discussion at para.3–164 et seq. and *Sun Life Assurance Plc v Thales Tracs Ltd* [2001] EWCA Civ 704; [2001] W.L.R. 1562 (digested in para.3–220) in the context of s.26 requests where a different result was reached having regard to the wording of the section.

[412] (1975) 31 P. & C.R. 412.

[413] [1990] 2 E.G.L.R. 69 CA.

landlord serves a s.25 notice upon him. The policy is apparently that a tenant who has only a short-term or a periodic tenancy should not be entitled to improve his position by seeking a fixed term for up to 15 years pursuant to the Act, if the landlord is content to leave matters as they are. Such tenants do, of course, retain security of tenure–the periodic tenant by the nature of his tenancy which continues from period to period at common law; and the tenant who has a term less than one year by virtue of the continuation provisions of s.24(1). The periodic tenant can give a contractual "notice to quit" to the landlord under s.24(2) (see para.3–02); and the tenant with a term of less than one year can, if he so desires, prevent a continuation or put an end to the continuation tenancy by the appropriate notice pursuant to s.27(1) or (2). However, if they do so their tenancies will come to an end and they will have no right to apply to the court for a new one (see paras 3–104 and 3–109).

Circumstances in which no request may be made

3–212 Even one of the class of tenants who are entitled, in principle, to make a s.26 request, may not do so in the following circumstances.

If the tenant has already made a section 26 request

3–213 The tenant is not entitled to make successive requests albeit that at the date of the each request he is a tenant of premises to which the Act applies: *Stile Hall Properties Ltd v Gooch*[414] (digested in para.3–214).

3–214 ***Stile Hall Properties Ltd v Gooch***[415] The tenant made a request for a new tenancy, but did not make application to the court within the relevant time limit. Before the date specified in the request, but after the expiry of the four-month period within which an originating application for the grant of a new lease ought to have been made as a result of the first request, the tenant purported to make a second request specifying a later date. Although the tenant was (unlike the tenant in *Meah v Sector*[416] (digested in para.6–25)) still a tenant at the time that the second request was made, the Court of Appeal held that it was contrary to the scheme of the Act for a tenant to be able to make successive requests and thus to extend the tenancy beyond the date stated in the first request upon which it would otherwise have come to an end.

3–215 In *Polyviou v Seeley*,[417] it was sought to distinguish *Stile Hall v Gooch*, on the grounds that both the first request and the second request in that case specified the same date for the termination of the current tenancy. The Court of Appeal held that there was no material distinction between the two cases. It is thought that the

---

[414] [1980] 1 W.L.R. 62.
[415] [1980] 1 W.L.R. 62.
[416] [1974] 1 W.L.R. 547; [1974] 1 All E.R. 1074 CA.
[417] [1980] 1 W.L.R. 55; [1979] 3 All E.R. 853 CA.

scheme of the Act requires that, once a valid s.26 request has been made, it cannot be unilaterally withdrawn or the same effect achieved by any procedural device.[418]

The tenant is not entitled to make a request under section 26 if the landlord has already given notice under section 25: section 26(4)

Service of a s.25 notice by the tenant's landlord precludes the tenant from serving a s.26 request: s.26(4). The tenant is not entitled to make a s.26 request if he has already given notice to quit: s.26(4) **3–215A**

Given the limited class of tenants entitled to make a request for a new tenancy, the circumstances in which a tenant can give a notice to quit are limited to those where there is a tenancy granted for a term of years certain and thereafter from year to year and a fixed term exceeding one year, which contains a tenant's break clause. **3–216**

Prior to the decision of Rattee J. in *Garston v Scottish Widows Fund & Life Assurance Society*[419] it was thought that a tenant might be able to make a s.26 request to take effect as at the date when he could exercise a contractual right to break his fixed term, thereby ending his liability to pay rent at the contractual rate while preserving his rights under the Act to seek a tenancy at a rent which (subject to the prevalent economic conditions such as those of the mid-1990s) might well be considerably lower. The *Garston* decision precluded the tenant from "having the best of both worlds" in this way; no s.26 request can be made specifying a date earlier than the term date of the lease. A request purporting to specify the date at which that term can be broken does not comply with the proviso to s.26(2). The decision of Rattee J. was upheld by the Court of Appeal[420] for the reasons given by the learned Judge.[421] **3–217**

The tenant is not entitled to make a s.26 request if he has served notice to terminate his tenancy pursuant to s.27(1): see s.26(4). **3–218**

Requirements of a valid section 26 request

In order to be valid, a s.26 request must comply with the following requirements: **3–219**

(1) It must be made by or on behalf of the "tenant".[422]
(2) It must be given to the "landlord" as defined by s.44.[423]

---

[418] See also *Meah v Sector Properties Ltd* [1974] 1 W.L.R. 547; [1974] 1 All E.R. 1074 CA (digested in para.6–25).
[419] [1996] 1 W.L.R. 834; [1996] 4 All E.R. 282 Ch D.
[420] [1998] 1 W.L.R. 1583; [1998] 3 All E.R. 596 CA.
[421] See also the discussion in para.3–221.
[422] As to the meaning of "tenant", see para.3–101.
[423] As to the meaning of "landlord", see para.3–87.

A misdescription of the landlord's name will not invalidate the request if the misnomer would not mislead the reasonable recipient: *Sun Life Assurance Plc v Thales Tracs Ltd*[424]

(3) It must be made in the prescribed form.

As under the old regime the request is required to be in a prescribed form: s.66(1) of the 1954 Act. The form of request is prescribed by the Landlord and Tenant Act 1954 Pt II (Notices)(Regulations) 2004, (SI 2004/1005), Form 3 to Sch.2.[425]

A form "substantially to the like effect" is sufficient: see reg.2(2). On the question of what is substantially to the like effect as the prescribed form, see the cases on s.25.[426]

(4) The request must set out the tenant's proposals as to the property to be comprised in the new tenancy, which must be either the whole or part of the property comprised in the current tenancy: s.26(3).

(5) It must set out the tenant's proposals as to the rent to be payable under the new tenancy: s.26(3).

(6) It must set out the tenant's proposals as to the "other terms" of the new tenancy: s.26(3).

The "other terms"[427]for this purpose include the duration of the new tenancy proposed by the tenant. Thus a request for a new tenancy "upon the terms of the current tenancy" is valid, since it is to be construed as requesting the same duration as the current tenancy: *Sidney Bolsom Investment Trust Ltd v E Karmios & Co Ltd.*[428]

(7) Must the tenant's proposals be genuine?

In *Sun Life Assurance Plc v Thales Tracs Ltd*[429](digested in para.3–220) it was held at first instance that where, prior to the service of the s.26 request, the tenant has no intention of seeking a renewal, the proposals for a new tenancy specified pursuant to s.26(3) of the 1954 Act are not genuinely held, for by making those proposals for a new tenancy, it is implicit that the tenant is representing that he wants a new tenancy and if he does not hold such an intention at the date of the s.26 notice there is a material misrepresentation. This decision has been reversed by the Court of Appeal. It was said in the Court of Appeal that a proposal, as with a request, simply described the doing of an act. They were "performance words" which described an act and which therefore did not require consideration as to its truth. As Dyson L.J. said:

> "Both 'request' and 'proposal' are what [counsel for the tenant] called 'performance words'. They describe an act. They do something. It is not meaningful to ask whether a request or a proposal says anything about the state of mind of the person who makes the request or puts forward the proposal. The meaning of a request and a proposal is judged objectively by examining them. The state of mind of the person who makes the request and the

[424] [2000] 1 E.G.L.R. 138, first instance. This point was not the subject of appeal [2001] EWCA Civ 704; [2001] E.G.L.R. 57 (digested in para.3–220).

[425] See Appendix para.A2.035.

[426] para.3–151.

[427] As to the requirement to specify "other terms" in a s.25 notice see para.3–159 et seq.

[428] [1956] 1 Q.B. 529 CA.

[429] [2001] 1 W.L.R. 1562; [2001] 2 E.G.L.R. 57 CA.

> proposal is irrelevant to their meaning. Nor is it meaningful to consider whether they are true. On the other hand, there are different kinds of words that do say some-thing about the state of mind of the person using them. Thus, for example, if a person says that he believes or intends something, he is undoubtedly saying something about his state of mind. It is meaningful, and may be relevant, to consider the truth of a statement of belief or intention."

(8) The s.26 request must specify the date upon which the tenant desires the new tenancy to begin: see s.26(2).
The requirements for what date may be specified are discussed in para.3–221.

Sun Life Assurance Plc v Thales Tracs Ltd[430] T occupied business premises pursuant to two leases which expired on December 24, 1998. T was aware that L wanted to redevelop T's premises and was likely to oppose renewal. T accordingly entered upon negotiations with the owner of adjoining premises and on November 13, 1997 exchanged contracts with the adjoining owner to acquire the freehold interest of property which would be suitable for T's purposes. T went into occupation of the adjoining premises on December 22, 1997. On January 9, 1998 T served s.26 requests in relation to two demised premises addressed to "Sun Life Long Term Business Fund". T's landlord was in fact Sun Life Assurance Plc. L objected to the s.25 notices as being addressed to the wrong person. Further s.26 requests were served addressed to Sun Life Assurance Society Plc. L served a counter-notice opposing renewal under para.(f) of s.30(1) of the 1954 Act. It was held: **3–220**

(1) (at first instance, this not being the subject matter of appeal) that albeit the first s.26 request was addressed to "Sun Life Long-Term Business Fund", rather than "Sun Life Assurance Plc", the misdescription of the landlord did not mislead and was a case of a mere misnomer which could be disregarded by the court, following *Nittan (UK) v Solent Steel Fabrications*[431];
(2) there is no express statutory requirement specifying any particular state of intention on the part of the tenant at the time when he serves his request pursuant to s.26; the tenant's proposals referred to in s.26(3)need not be "genuine proposals". The fact that the tenant had in fact taken steps to find alternative premises and had an intention not to renew the leases at the time of service of the s.26 notices was irrelevant to the tenant's entitlement to compensation. The s.26 notices were accordingly valid.

Date to be specified

The date to be specified in the s.26 request is governed by the provisions of s.26(2). Like s.25(3),[432] it provides that such date must not be less than six, nor more than 12, months from the date of making the request and it is further provided that the date specified must not be earlier than the date on which, apart **3–221**

[430] [2001] 1 W.L.R. 1562; [2001] 2 E.G.L.R. 57 CA.
[431] [1981] 1 Lloyd's Rep. 633 at 639 CA.
[432] See para.3–176 et seq.

from the Act, the current tenancy would come to an end by effluxion of time[433] or could be brought to an end by notice to quit given by the tenant. This proviso has been construed by Rattee J. in *Garston v Scottish Widows Fund & Life Assurance Society*[434] so as to prevent a tenant who has a fixed term subject to a tenant's break from making a request which specified a date earlier than the contractual term date. In that decision the learned judge construed the proviso to s.26(2) as follows:

> "The actual words of the proviso on their natural construction contemplate one relevant date only in respect of a given tenancy, and the two alternative definitions of that date are to take account of the fact that the relevant tenancy may be (a) one granted simply for a term of years, in which case the relevant date under the proviso will be the date on which it would come to an end by effluxion of time, or (b) one granted, for a term of years certain and thereafter from year to year in, which case . . . the tenancy will never come to an end by effluxion of time; and the only possible relevant date specified in the proviso to section 26(2) is the date on which, as at the date of the request under section 26(1), the existing tenancy could be brought to an end by notice to quit given by the tenant. Thus, in the case of a tenancy granted, for a term of years exceeding one year, the date for the commencement of a new tenancy could not be earlier than the date on which the current tenancy would, apart from the Act of 1954, come to an end by effluxion of time".

There is no provision such as is found in s.25(3)(b) to provide for the case where the notice to quit which can be given to the tenant is required to be of long duration.

3–222 **Example** If a lease of 14 years entitles the tenant to continue thereafter from year to year but to determine that yearly tenancy by giving more than 12 months' notice, the tenant would be unable to make a s.26 request because such a request may not specify a date more than 12 months after the making thereof. He could, of course, give a notice to quit breaking the lease contractually, but this would have the effect of debarring him from subsequently making a s.26 request: see s.26(4) (and para.3.7.4(iii)). Similarly, it appears that there would be no continuation under s.24(1), because that subs. takes effect subject to s.24(2), which preserves the common law termination of the tenancy by notice to quit given by the tenant.

Effect of making request

Termination of tenant's tenancy

3–223 The effect of making a request for the grant of a new tenancy is that the tenant's current tenancy will terminate immediately before the date specified for the

[433] See para.3–177. In *Tekegac v Emmott* [2008] P.L.S.C.S. 186 CC, T had a tenancy of 12 years running "from the 9th day of December" 1994. T served a s.26 request specifying December 9, 2006 as the date for the commencement of the new tenancy. A tenancy of 12 years commencing from December 9, 2006 would actually expire on midnight December 9/10, 2006 so that the tenant had the whole of the 9th. The notice was held to be valid on the statutory wording, as a s.26 request must not specify a "date earlier than" that upon which the contractual term expired; to specify the last day, i.e. the 9th, was permissible.

[434] [1996] 1 W.L.R. 834; [1996] 4 All E.R. 282 Ch D.

commencement of the new tenancy if no application to the court for a new tenancy is made within the appropriate statutory period (being the statutory period provided for by s.29A(1)[435]): s.26(5). If a claim for a new tenancy, either by the landlord or the tenant, is duly made within this time, the current tenancy will be continued by s.64.

Service of counter-notice by landlord

The landlord is entitled within two months after the making of the request to notify the tenant of the landlord's opposition to renewal, stating the grounds on which the landlord opposes: s.26(6).[436] **3–224**

Termination by other means notwithstanding section 26 request

As has already been noted,[437] a tenant cannot make a request under s.26 if his landlord has already given a s.25 notice: s.26(4). Conversely, a tenant who has served a s.26 request thereby prevents his landlord from serving a valid s.25 notice (see s.26(4)). As the tenant may serve a s.26 request specifying a date of commencement not more than 12 months after the date on which the request is given, there are many tactical considerations as to whether the landlord or the tenant should get in first. These tactical considerations are discussed in para.4–19 et seq. It is considered that a tenant cannot unilaterally withdraw a valid s.26 request. **3–225**

The service of a request does not, it is considered, prevent the tenant from subsequently determining the tenancy by service of a notice to quit. The circumstances in which a tenant would wish to take advantage of the preservation of the right to terminate by service of a common law notice to quit after having served a s.26 request could arise only in very exceptional circumstances. One could, for instance, envisage a situation where one had a fixed term of years expressed to continue thereafter from year to year with a contractual right to break upon serving three months notice at any time. The tenant could, it is considered, after having served a s.26 request of 12 months duration accelerate the date of termination by serving a notice to quit of three months.[438] **3–226**

8. TERMINATION BY "FINAL DISPOSAL" OF APPLICATION

"Final disposal"

Section 64

By s.64 it is provided that: **3–227**

---

[435] As to which, see para.6–17 et seq.

[436] See para.5–03 et seq.

[437] See para.3–215A.

[438] As to the question of there being several methods of termination giving rise to different dates of termination, see the discussion at paras 3–106 and 3–113 in connection with the service of notice pursuant to s.27(1) and (2).

"(1) In a case where–

(a) a notice to terminate a tenancy has been given under Part I or Part I of this Act or a request for a new tenancy has been made under Part I thereof, and

(b) an application to the court has been made under the said Part I or under section 24(1) or 29(2) of this Act as the case may be, and

(c) apart from this section the effect of the notice or request would be to terminate the tenancy before the expiration of the period of three months beginning with the date on which the application is finally disposed of, the effect of the notice or request shall be to terminate the tenancy at the expiration of the said period of three months and not at any other time.

(2) The reference in paragraph (c) of subsection (1) of this section to the date on which an application is finally disposed of shall be construed as a reference to the earliest date by which the proceedings on the application (including any proceedings on or in consequence of an appeal) have been determined and any time for appealing or further appealing has expired, except that if the application is withdrawn or any appeal is abandoned the reference shall be construed as a reference to the date of the withdrawal or abandonment."

3–228 The "final disposal" of an application for a new tenancy is the commonest way in which a tenancy will come to an end. This is the combined effect of ss.24 and 64. Final disposal may be the result of:

(1) the striking out of the tenant's application for renewal;
(2) the dismissal of the tenant's application for renewal;
(3) the discontinuance of the tenant's application for renewal or, with the consent of the tenant,[439] the landlord's application for renewal;
(4) the grant of the application, whether pursuant to an application for renewal by either the landlord or tenant;
(5) the determination in favour of the landlord of the landlord's termination application[440];
(6) the determination of any appeal arising out of the application.

Time of "final disposal"

3–229 As can be seen above it is expressly provided by s.64(2) that the reference to "final disposal" shall be construed as a reference to the earliest date on which the proceedings have been determined and any time for appealing has expired, except that where the proceedings have been withdrawn or an appeal abandoned, the reference shall be construed as a reference to the date of such withdrawal or abandonment. In the ordinary case, therefore, 21 days (i.e. the time during which an appeal from the High Court or the county court to the Court of Appeal might be lodged[441]) is to be added to the three months mentioned in s.64. Where the tenant makes an application for permission to appeal out of time and permission is refused, the "final disposal" is calculated from the date upon which the time for appealing expired, and not the date when the application to extend time was dismissed: *Shotley Point Marina (1986) Ltd v Spalding*.[442] The reason is that the

[439] A landlord cannot withdraw an application made by him pursuant to s.24 for renewal without the tenant's consent: s.24(2C). See further on this, para.6–10 et seq.

[440] Made pursuant to s.29(2).

[441] Civil Procedure Rules r.52.4. See para.14–137 et seq. as to the time for appealing.

[442] [1997] E.G.L.R. 233.

wording in s.64(1), namely "any proceedings on or in consequence of an appeal", refer to an appeal and not an attempt to bring an appeal. The court is never seized of an appeal where permission is required until leave has been granted. It was held upon consideration of RSC Order 59 r.4 that the court (whether of first instance or the Court of Appeal) had no power to abridge the time for appealing (which would accelerate the termination of the current tenancy under s.64(1)): *Re 20 Exchange Street, Manchester*.[443]

Where permission to appeal is obtained the tenancy will continue automatically until three months after the date on which the appeal is finally determined. However where the landlord has established to the court's satisfaction one or more substantive grounds for opposing the grant of a new tenancy, which are not the subject of an appeal, nevertheless, where the tenant appeals in relation to one of those substantive grounds, the tenant's current tenancy continues automatically. Thus, for instance, where the landlord succeeds under paras (d) and (f) the tenant may wish to appeal the issue in relation to para.(d) in order to ensure that he obtains compensation under s.37.[444] Thus, an appeal which only goes to an issue of compensation and not to the question of whether a new tenancy should be granted nevertheless continues the tenancy in accordance with s.64. This difficulty was noted by Brooke L.J. in *Mark Stone Car Sales Ltd v Howard de Walden Estates Ltd*.[445] He considered that "imaginative judicial interpretation of the present wording of the might lead to a solution that the 'application' within the meaning of that was finally disposed of when a Court's unappealed decision put paid to any question of the grant of a new tenancy". However, he thought it much better if there was an amendment to the present wording of the statute. **3–230**

Effect of "final disposal"

The effect of final disposal of the application is that the current tenancy comes to an end three months after the date of final disposal, except in the rare case where the date specified in the relevant s.25 notice or s.26 request is a later date, in which case it will come to an end on that later date: See *Re 88 High Road, Kilburn*[446] (digested in para.8–149). **3–231**

9. ESTOPPEL, WAIVER AND ELECTION

It is not appropriate in a book of this nature to deal with the complicated subject of the law of estoppel, and the associated topics of election, waiver and acquiescence, in the same detail as can be found in specialist books on the **3–232**

[443] [1956] 1 W.L.R. 765; [1956] 2 All E.R. 509n.
[444] As to which, see Ch.12 generally.
[445] (1997) 73 P. & C.R. D43.
[446] [1959] 1 W.L.R. 279; [1959] 1 All E.R. 527. (Note, the case digest is on a different point, relating to the length of term to be granted and the incorporation of a rent review clause.) As to the position where the application is finally disposed of prior to the contractual term date and the tenant vacates before the contractual term date, see para.2–59 et seq.

topic.[447] Nonetheless, it has often been argued in cases under the Act that one party or the other has waived the right to take a particular point, or is estopped from taking it, or has elected not to take it, or has acquiesced in the other party's conduct in such a way as to prevent him from taking it. For this reason, we intend to set out, in broad and general terms, the principal elements of law to be derived from the cases; to illustrate circumstances in which such arguments have arisen in the context of the Act; and to point to some practical consequences and problems which may confront practitioners.

Election

3–233 In *Stevens & Cutting Ltd v Andersen*[448] (digested in para.3–246), Stuart-Smith L.J. stated the principles relevant to the doctrine of election in the following terms:

> "A party may be deprived of the right to pursue a certain course of conduct if, when faced with two alternative and inconsistent courses of action, he chooses one rather than the other and his election is communicated to the other party. It is, however, now established that before he can be said to have elected, the party electing must know not only of the facts giving rise to the right but that he has the right."

3–234 Stuart-Smith L.J. referred to election between "courses of action". This is an expression used in many expositions of the principle.[449] There is, however, a volume of binding authority showing that for many purposes (including determining the time at which an election must be made), it is necessary to distinguish election between remedies from election between rights.[450] The distinction between rights and remedies can of course be obscured by terminology: every remedy is in one sense a right (even if its grant is discretionary), but not every right is a remedy. It has been said that the distinction is clear if "right" is used to indicate a substantive right such as entitlement to a leasehold interest or to the benefit of a contract.[451] If a would-be purchaser is induced by a misrepresentation to enter into a contract, he has a choice whether to treat himself as no longer bound by the contract, or to affirm it (in either case he will usually also be entitled to claim damages for any loss caused by the misrepresentation). That is an election between rights. If he chooses to affirm the contract and the other party defaults, the purchaser may sue for specific

---

[447] Spencer Bower, G. et al., *Spencer Bower on the Law Relating to Estoppel by Representation*, 4th edn (London: Bloomsbury Professional, 2004); Wilkin, S. and Ghaly, K., *Law of Estoppel, Variation and Waiver*, 3rd edn (London: John Wiley & Sons, 2012); *Halsbury's Laws of England* (4th edn, Vol.16, reissue).

[448] [1990] 1 E.G.L.R. 95 CA.

[449] See, Lord Scarman in *China National Foreign Trade Transportation Corp v Evlogia Shipping Co SA of Panama (The Mihalios Xilas)* [1979] 1 W.L.R. 1018 at 1034, and Lord Goff in *Motor Oil Hellas (Corinth) Refineries SA v Shipping Corp of India (The Kanchenjunga)* [1990] 1 Lloyd's Rep. 391 at 398.

[450] See especially Lord Atkin in *United Australia Ltd v Barclays Bank Ltd* [1941] A.C. 1 at 29–30; Lord Wilberforce in *Johnson v Agnew* [1980] A.C. 367 at 396; and Lord Nicholls in *Tang Man Sit v Capacious Investments Ltd* [1996] A.C. 514 at 521–522.

[451] Robert Walker L.J. in *Ballard (Kent) Ltd v Oliver Ashworth (Holdings) Ltd* [1999] 2 E.G.L.R. 23 CA.

performance or for damages. That is an election between remedies. Normally, election between remedies need not be made until judgment.[452] Election proceeds upon the premise that the party said to be fixed by the waiver must have possessed two (or more) substantive but inconsistent rights. In such a case, his choice by overt act, communicated to the other party to rely on one such right, precludes him from later claiming the benefit of another. Thus where the notice which has been served is valid and effective to bring the tenancy to an end, the landlord possess no right to treat the tenancy as continuing, and accordingly there is no choice of substantive rights whatever: *Ballard (Kent) Ltd v Oliver Ashworth (Holdings) Ltd*[453] (digested in para.3–235). The position, it is considered, is different if the landlord's s.25 notice or the tenant's s.26 request is defective, for the recipient has the choice between either accepting its validity, and thus bringing an end to the tenancy (subject to the provisions of the 1954 Act) or rejecting the notice/request as invalid and keeping the tenancy alive[454]: *Bristol Cars Ltd v RKH (Hotels) Ltd.*[455]

Ballard (Kent) Ltd v Oliver Ashworth (Holdings) Ltd[456] The tenant served a break notice in accordance with the terms of the lease. The landlord's solicitors wrote stating that they were treating the notice as defective and invalid, and warned the tenant that if it continued to maintain the validity of the notice, but failed to vacate the premises, the landlord would collect double rent under s.18 of the Distress for Rent Act 1737. The tenant remained in possession of the premises for just over a year after the break date. The landlord brought proceedings to recover the contractual rent for that period plus interest. The tenant contended that the tenancy was at an end. The landlord amended its statement of claim to claim in the alternative double rent under the Distress for Rent Act 1737; in response, the tenant amended its defence and counterclaim to plead waiver by election of any claim under the 1737 Act, in that the landlord, by its claim for contractual rent, had elected to treat the tenant as tenant under the lease. The Court of Appeal held that the tenant was not entitled to succeed on the principle of election as, the break notice being valid, the landlord had no choice of substantive rights whatever; the tenant's break notice was good and the landlord had no right to treat the tenancy as continuing. **3–235**

The party electing must know not only of the facts giving rise to the right but that he has the right: *Peyman v Lanjani*.[457] In that case, Stephenson L.J. pointed out that there are some cases where the landlord is presumed to know his legal rights, e.g. his right to forfeit the lease in the event of breach. He pointed out that: **3–236**

---

[452] Sometimes, however, election between substantive rights and between procedural remedies will necessarily coincide. The most obvious example is in the law of landlord and tenant when a landlord decides not to claim that a lease has been determined by forfeiture; by that decision he necessarily also elects not to seek an order for possession of the demised premises.
[453] [2000] Ch. 12; [1999] 2 E.G.L.R. 23 CA.
[454] One cannot choose to treat a valid notice as invalid but one may accept as valid an otherwise invalid notice.
[455] [1979] 2 E.G.L.R. 56 CA.
[456] [2000] Ch. 12; [1999] 2 E.G.L.R. 23 CA.
[457] [1985] Ch. 457 CA.

> "when a party has legal advice, he will be more easily presumed to know the law and evidence or special circumstances may be required to rebut the presumption [that he was aware of his right arising from the facts of which he had knowledge]".

As Farquharson L.J. said in *Stevens & Cutting v Anderson*[458] (digested in para.3–246):

> "If [the relevant party] was ignorant of the relevant facts constituting the breach which give him his right of election or of the rights he is entitled to following the breach, then he will not be so bound and can take a different decision when these matters become known to him."

He added that "where a party has made such an election it is not necessary to show that the other party has suffered detriment or damage as a result of it". In this important respect the doctrine of election differs from most forms of estoppel.[459]

Estoppel

3–237 There are various forms and descriptions of estoppel, and the modern tendency is, perhaps, to treat the question of whether or not an estoppel has been successfully raised in broader and more general terms than was previously the case. Nonetheless, the relevant authorities contain convenient statements of the elements which give rise to an estoppel. In *Stevens & Cutting Ltd v Anderson*[460] (digested in para.3–246), Stuart-Smith L.J. said:

> "In order to found an estoppel three things must be established: a representation offact; reliance upon the representation by the person to whom it is made; and detriment resulting from such reliance."

This is a statement of the principles relevant to the common law doctrine of estoppel *in pais*. Referring to the equitable doctrine, Stuart-Smith L.J. said:

> "In the case of promissory estoppel, there must be a promise intended by the promisor to affect his legal relationship with the promisee upon the faith of which the promisee has acted to his detriment."

3–238 In relation to both kinds of estoppel, the representation (or promise) must be clear and unequivocal. The recipient of a notice has no duty to the sender to inform him of the defects within it and accordingly mere silence in response to a statement by the sender that the notice will be assumed to be valid will not found an estoppel: *Lemmerbell Ltd v Britannia LAS Direct Ltd*[461] (digested in para.3–128). In that case the solicitors for the tenant (who had served a defective break notice) stated that "... we must press you to let us know if you find

---

458 [1990] 1 E.G.L.R. 95 CA.

459 See para.3–239 et seq.

460 [1990] 1 E.G.L.R. 95 CA.

461 [1998] 3 E.G.L.R. 67 CA. See also the earlier decision at first instance, *Patel v Peel Investments (South)* [1992] 2 E.G.L.R. 116 Ch D, where Morritt J. said (in respect of an alleged estoppel over defects in a rent review notice) that "it is entirely proper for a landlord not to point out to a tenant what he needs to do to protect his position."

anything wrong with the contracted [sic] notice to determine referred to . . . If we do not hear from you on this we shall assume the notice to determine is valid." It was held that the failure to respond (other than merely to acknowledge receipt) to the request was not a representation as to the validity of the notice. However, if upon a request being made a positive response is received as to the validity of the notice the representation is sufficient to found an estoppel; a statement that there is no objection to the notice is not to be treated as a representation of law but is a representation of fact: *Dun & Bradstreet Software Services (England) Ltd v Provident Mutual Life Assurance Association*.[462]

In relation to both kinds of estoppel, detriment must be shown and will not readily be inferred (compare the conclusion of the Court of Appeal in *Stevens & Cutting v Anderson*[463] (digested in para.3–246) with that of the court in *Bristol Cars Ltd v RKH Hotels Ltd*[464] (digested in para.3–250)). Serving a counter-notice and making a claim for a new tenancy may not be sufficient acts of detriment: *Wroe (t/a Telepower) v Exmos Cover Ltd*[465] (digested in para.3–255). However, it has been held that incurring lawyers' fees and surveyors' fees in reliance upon the validity of a s.25 notice may constitute detriment for the purposes of founding an estoppel: *John Lyon's Free Grammar School v James*[466] (digested in para.3–254). **3–239**

Yet another form of estoppel is estoppel by convention, which was described by Lord Denning M.R. in *Amalgamated Investment & Property Co Ltd v Texas Commerce International Bank Ltd*[467] as follows: **3–240**

> "When the parties to a transaction proceed on the basis of an underlying assumption . . . on which they have conducted the dealings between them—neither of them will be allowed to go back on that assumption when it would be unfair or unjust to allow him to do so."

Where reliance is placed upon estoppel by convention the necessity for proof of some clear and unequivocal statement becomes of less importance. The court must determine what the state of affairs in which the parties have accepted and decide whether there is sufficient certainty and clarity in the terms of the convention to give rise to any enforceable equity.[468] In a case under the Act, *Benedictus v Jalaram*[469]), Bingham L.J. described a similar rule as follows:

> "If in the course of litigation a party (A) accepts the truth of an assertion of fact expressly or impliedly made by his opposing party (B) and founds on that fact formally to claim relief to which he would not be entitled if that fact were not true (A knowing if the fact is true or not, whether or not B knows), and if the litigation is thereafter conducted on the basis of the truth of that fact, A may not thereafter assert the falsity of that fact and retract his acceptance and its truth where the effect would be both to deny B a remedy which would have been available to B had A asserted the falsity of that fact from the beginning and to deny B a remedy to which A's acceptance of that fact entitled him."

---

[462] [1998] 2 E.G.L.R. 175 CA.
[463] [1990] 1 E.G.L.R. 95 CA.
[464] [1979] 2 E.G.L.R. 56.
[465] [2000] 1 E.G.L.R. 66 CA.
[466] [1995] 3 W.L.R. 908; [1995] 4 All E.R. 740 CA.
[467] [1981] 3 W.L.R. 565; [1981] 3 All E.R. 577 CA.
[468] *Troop v Gibson* [1986] 1 E.G.L.R. 1 CA per Ralph Gibson L.J.
[469] [1989] 1 E.G.L.R. 251 CA.

3–241 The doctrine of res judicata may prevent the tenant from asserting rights inconsistent with those under the 1954 Act. Thus where the landlord obtained an order for an interim rent under s.24A the tenant was estopped per *rem judicatam* from claiming Rent Act protection on the landlord's claim for possession: *De Vere Hotels & Restaurants v Culshaw*.[470]

Waiver and acquiescence

3–242 The doctrines of "waiver" and "acquiescence" overlap to a considerable degree, with the doctrines of election and the various forms of estoppel described above. Waiver is not at all a precise term of art.[471] It can be used to describe the effect of an election (especially in the old expression "waiver of forfeiture", which in the law of landlord and tenant is apt to describe a landlord's decision not to terminate a lease by re-entry for breach of covenant and not to seek the remedy of an order for possession; he may still be able to seek some other remedy, usually damages for breach of covenant). However the expression "waiver" is often used in a wider sense of any deliberate decision by a party not to stand on his strict rights (for instance, as in *Kammins Ballrooms Co Ltd v Zenith Investments (Torquay) Ltd*[472] (digested in para.3–245), not to take a technical point as to the validity of a notice). In that case Lord Diplock regarded this second type of waiver as being a form of estoppel, and said that ordinary principles of estoppel apply to it.[473]

Cases decided under the Act

3–243 The cases under the Act were arguments based upon election, estoppel, waiver, or the like and are many and various, but can be loosely grouped according to their principal subject matter.

Prematurity of claim

3–244 We start with two cases where the landlord sought to contend that a tenant's application for a new tenancy should be struck out on the grounds of prematurity, having been made earlier than two months after service of the relevant s.25 notice, and where the tenant contended that the landlord was not entitled to take that point.

---

[470] (1972) 116 S.J. 681 CA.

[471] See for instance Lord Diplock in *Kammins Ballrooms Co Ltd v Zenith Investments (Torquay) Ltd* [1971] A.C. 850 at 882; [1970] 2 All E.R. 871 at 894 and Lord Goff in *Motor Oil Hellas v (Corinth) Refineries SA* [1990] 1 Lloyd's Rep. 391 at 397–398; also Spencer Bower, G. et al., *Spencer Bower on the Law Relating to Estoppel by Representation*, 3rd edn (London: Bloomsbury Professional, 2004); pp.291–92 (see now, 3rd edn, (1977) pp.316–17), quoted by Viscount Dilhorne in *Kammins Ballrooms Co Ltd v Zenith Investments (Torquay) Ltd* [1970] 2 All E.R. 871 at 886; [1971] A.C. 850 at 872–873.

[472] [1971] A.C. 850 HL.

[473] See [1970] 2 All E.R. 871 at 894–895; [1971] A.C. 850 at 883.

Kammins Ballrooms Co Ltd v Zenith Investments (Torquay) Ltd[474] The tenant made a premature originating application. The landlords filed an answer to the originating application in which they stated the ground of opposition which they had specified in the s.25 notice to the renewal. The answer contained no reference to the application having been made too soon. The landlord's solicitors then wrote offering compensation as provided in the Act if the tenants agreed to vacate. The parties' solicitor then concurred in asking the county court registrar to fix a date for the hearing of the originating application. No reference to the applicant's application having been made too soon was made. It was not until after it was too late to make a further application that the point was taken that the originating application was pre-mature and, therefore, invalid. The majority of the House of Lords held that there had been no "waiver" nor was the landlord estopped. **3–245**

So far as estoppel was concerned, there was no representation to the tenants to the effect that the landlords were not going to take a point of prematurity nor any representation to the effect that the applicant's tackle was all in order. The letter written offering compensation was not a representation that the only ground of opposition to the application would be that specified in the answer nor was the service of the answer implicitly admitting the validity of the application. As Lord Morris said,

> "in stating the grounds upon which [the landlord] would oppose . . . they did not preclude themselves from taking the prior point that the application was not made within the statutory time limit. There is no evidence that the landlords ever made a decision to abandon any point which was open to them or adopt it at some course which was inconsistent with or which negatived their reliance upon a point under s.29(3) if and when they became alive to it".

As far as Lord Morris was concerned the filing of the answer was not a "waiver", for the form was in the prescribed form and the form did not specifically require that a point such as that which the landlord was now taking was to be set out in the answer.

Stevens & Cutting v Anderson[475] The tenant made a premature application for a new tenancy. No objection was taken to the originating application as being premature in the landlord's answer. The answer simply opposed renewal under s.30(1)(a) and (c). The answer also contained an application for interim rent under s.24A of the 1954 Act. **3–246**

Negotiations had been conducted by the parties for renewal from 1985 until October 1987. The county court judge found that the tenant was led to believe that new leases might well be obtained through negotiation. On December 14, 1987 the landlord's solicitor had his attention drawn by counsel to the fact that the originating application was premature. The landlord's solicitor gave evidence to the effect that although he knew in general terms the time-scale laid down, he had not until then observed that the date set out on the face of the originating application showed that the application was premature. This was accepted by the judge. The landlord's solicitor notified the tenant's solicitors the very next day

[474] [1971] A.C. 850 HL.
[475] [1990] 1 E.G.L.R. 95 CA.

that the landlord was taking the point as to the prematurity of the originating application. The Court of Appeal held that there had been no election by the landlord. Although, ordinarily, it would be presumed that a solicitor would know the law, this presumption was rebutted by the evidence which the judge had accepted. The landlord's solicitor had acted promptly upon becoming aware of the point. So far as estoppel was concerned, there had been no representation or promise that the landlord would not rely on any ground of opposition other than those referred to under s.30(1) of the 1954 Act.

The fact that the parties entered into negotiations and in particular the finding of the judge that the tenant had been led to believe that new leases might well be obtained by negotiations or, alternatively, if not that there was some prospect of success before the court if negotiations failed, was not a representation either expressly or by conduct that if negotiations failed the landlord would not oppose the grant of a new lease. In those circumstances it was difficult to spell out the landlord's behaviour in conducting without prejudice negotiations a promise that the only grounds of opposition to a new tenancy would be those already raised under s.30(1) of the 1954 Act.

Defects in notices

3–247 The second category of cases concerns defects in notices upon which (it was argued) one party or the other was prevented from relying.[476]

3–248 ***Smith v Draper***[477] The landlord consisted of three individuals who held their interests jointly. The solicitors who acted on behalf of the landlord served a s.25 notice which, however, named only two out of the three as the landlord. The tenant's solicitors contended that the notice was invalid but, without prejudice to that contention, gave a counter-notice and commenced proceedings for a new tenancy. The landlord's solicitors served a second (valid) notice, without prejudice to their contention that the first notice was valid. This notice contained a ground of opposition in addition to those specified in the first notice. A counter-notice was duly served to the second notice.

The landlord's solicitors wrote formally abandoning the first notice but the tenant's solicitors failed to make an application for a new tenancy based upon the second notice. The landlords contended that, as the first notice was invalid and the second notice was valid, the landlords were entitled to possession in view of the failure to apply for a new tenancy in response to the second notice. The Court of Appeal held that the landlords were entitled to possession as the tenant had not agreed to treat the first notice as valid nor were the landlords estopped from relying upon the invalidity of the first notice.

3–249 ***Morrow v Nadeem***[478] The landlord as named in the s.25 notice was the controlling shareholder of a company, the company being the true landlord. The

[476] For a case on whether the landlord was estopped from denying that a counter-notice had been served by the tenant, see *Mehmet v Dawson* [1984] 1 E.G.L.R. 74 CA. A tenant is no longer required to serve a counter-notice in response to a s.25 notice: para.5–01.

[477] [1990] 2 E.G.L.R. 69 CA.

[478] [1986] 1 W.L.R. 1381; [1987] 1 All E.R. 237; [1986] 2 E.G.L.R. 73 CA.

tenant, in response to the s.25 notice, gave counter-notice stating that she was unwilling to give up possession and the notice was addressed to the solicitors as agents for the person named in the s.25 notice. The tenant duly made an originating application for the grant of new tenancies and named as the respondent the controlling shareholder. The purchaser of the reversionary interest then applied to be substituted as the respondent to the proceedings on the ground that it became successor to the reversionary interest. An order was made substituting him as respondent. The tenant shortly thereafter raised the issue that the s.25 notice was invalid. The invalidity had come to the tenant's solicitors' attention by reason of the fact, that when the purchaser of the reversionary interest acquired that interest, his solicitors wrote informing the tenant's solicitors that he became successor in title to the company but had no knowledge of the individual respondent and invited the tenant to accept that, as no point had been taken as to the validity of the s.25 notice, he was to be viewed as competent landlord at the time the counter-notices and application were issued. It was in response to that letter that the point was then taken and thus there was no agreement to the invitation made by the landlord's solicitors.

The Court of Appeal held that the notices did not name the competent landlord but went on to consider whether there was a "waiver" of the defect. There was no suggestion in the correspondence at any time until the amendment to the originating application that the validity of the notice was being or would be challenged. However, Nicholls L.J. stated that neither the tenant nor her solicitors were at any time aware of the true identity of the landlord and the steps taken in the proceedings were taken in ignorance of the fact that the person named in the s.25 notice was not the competent landlord. There was, moreover, no reason why the notice should not be taken at face value and acted upon on that footing and this was done without dissent from the landlord's solicitors. Accordingly there had been no waiver.

Bristol Cars Ltd v RKH Hotels Ltd[479] The tenant served a defective s.26 request, specifying a date of termination less than six months from the date of the giving of the notice. No counter-notice was served specifying a ground of opposition. The tenant applied for a new tenancy and there were further negotiations about the rent. Directions were given by the court and the application was adjourned sine die. The landlord applied for an interim rent under s.24A and obtained an extension of time within which to file an answer. When the landlord sought to contend that the s.26 request was invalid it was held that the landlord had waived the defect. Templeman L.J. with whom Megaw L.J. agreed, analysed the case in terms of estoppel rather than waiver by election. The landlords had in effect led the tenants to believe that they would not and could not oppose the grant of a new tenancy and, by the time the landlords had sought to assert the contrary, "the position of the tenants had so altered that it would be unfair to allow the landlords now to contest the validity of the request and then to oppose the grant of a new tenancy". The landlords were estopped certainly not later than the date when they applied for an interim rent, as such an application could be made only on the basis of a valid s.26 request. **3–250**

[479] [1979] 2 E.G.L.R. 56 CA.

(An alternative ground, as far as Templeman L.J. was concerned, was that there had been a waiver in the sense of an election when the landlord made an application for an interim rent. However, some doubt must be cast upon this having regard to the fact that it was dealt with on the basis that the landlords did not know that they had the legal right to object to the validity.[480]) Bridge L.J. viewed the case simply as one of election.

3–251 ***Tennant v London County Council***[481] The landlord authority served a s.25 notice on the tenant. The notice was not signed by the person duly authorised by the authority's standing orders. He had delegated this task to one of his assistants, who therefore signed the notice "pp [the authorised person]". On May 4, 1956 the tenant issued his application for the grant of a new tenancy and on September 20, 1956 the landlord, in an affidavit in response, revealed the facts relating to the signing of the s.25 notice on November 9, 1956. The tenant contended in an affidavit that the assistant did not have sufficient authority to sign the s.25 notice, with the consequence that it was invalid. On December 20, 1956 the tenant issued a writ claiming a declaration to this effect. The Court of Appeal held that the s.25 notice was valid but added that the tenant had ample material on the face of the document itself to indicate to any person interested in the matter that there might be a case for investigation as to the circumstances in which the document came to be signed as it was so that, by not objecting but instead taking steps to obtain a renewal, the tenant had waived any defect in the notice.

3–252 ***British Railways Board v AJA Smith Transport***[482] The landlord's notice under s.25 served on the tenant was in Form 7 prescribed by Appendix 1 to the Landlord and Tenant (Notices) Regulations 1957 (SI 1957/1157), as amended, save that note 3 in the form referred to the county court rateable value jurisdiction limit as £2,000 instead of £5,000, being the figure substituted in the 1957 Regulations by the Landlord and Tenant (Notices) Regulations 1973 (SI 1973/792). Regulation 4 of the 1957 Regulations provided that a notice served under s.25 was either to be in Form 7 or in a form substantially to the like effect. The tenant had made an application to the court for the grant of a new tenancy. This was refused and the tenant appealed. (See para.7–150). It was only at this stage, that is on appeal to the Court of Appeal, that the tenant became aware of the possibility of the invalidity of the s.25 notice. The Court of Appeal invited the tenant to amend its notice of appeal so that it could consider the validity of the s.25 notice. Counsel for the tenant submitted that the Court of Appeal did not have jurisdiction to order such an amendment. The Court of Appeal, without making any finding on the amendment issue, permitted the tenant to contest the appeal in the form of the unamended notice of appeal. The tenant thereafter continued to pursue its application for a new tenancy although counsel for the tenant reserved the right to pursue the question of the validity of the s.25 notice in future proceedings if a new tenancy was not granted. The tenant's appeal was

---

[480] It is essential in order for there to be an election that the party knows of his strict legal rights: see para.3–233 et seq.

[481] (1957) 121 J.P. 428; 55 L.G.R. 421 CA.

[482] [1981] 2 E.G.L.R. 66.

dismissed and thus it failed in its application for a new tenancy. The landlord then sought declarations from the High Court that the notice was effective to terminate the tenancy.

The court held that the s.25 notice was substantially to the like effect as the prescribed form. However, assuming it were invalid the tenant had by the stage of the proceedings in the Court of Appeal (on the appeal against the refusal to grant the tenant a new tenancy), at the latest, when the tenant knew all the material facts and knew that a new tenancy could only be claimed if a valid s.25 notice had been served, elected to pursue the claim for a new tenancy. That conduct was inconsistent with any right to dispute the validity of the s.25 notice and the tenant was according estopped from doing so now, notwithstanding the express reservation of the right to contest its validity.

Watkins v Emslie[483] An owner of land claimed possession against the occupier, Mrs Emslie. She contended that she was a tenant protected by the Act. Prior to the court's decision in the case, Mrs Emslie served a s.26 request upon the landowner. She failed, however, to make any application to the court for a new tenancy under the Act. The court determined that Mrs Emslie was a tenant and dismissed the landowner's claim for possession. The landowner's advisers then wrote to Mrs Emslie, saying that they would be instructed to serve a "notice to quit" upon her. After the date specified in the s.26 request, the landowner commenced a second possession action, claiming that Mrs Emslie's tenancy had been determined pursuant to s.26 and that he was now entitled to possession. Mrs Emslie defended the proceedings, contending that her s.26 request had been invalid because she was not a tenant for a term of years certain exceeding one year but was either a monthly or weekly periodic tenant, and had thus not been able to make a valid request under s.26. The landowner contended that she was estopped from putting forward this contention, because he had refrained from himself serving a s.25 notice upon her in reliance upon the fact that she had already made her s.26 request. The Court of Appeal held that there was no evidence that this was the reason why the landowner had not served his own notice. He had not done so because he had been contending that Mrs Emslie was not a tenant at all. Moreover, the suggestion that he would be serving a "notice to quit" (by which must have been meant a s.25 notice) was inconsistent with treating the s.26 request as valid because s.26(4) provides that no s.25 notice can be given after making by the tenant of a request for a new tenancy under s.26. No estoppel had been established. **3–253**

John Lyon's Free Grammar School v James[484] The tenant, who lived and practised as a solicitor at the tenanted premises, had served a notice of leasehold's claim under the Leasehold Reform Act 1967 in 1991 claiming to enfranchise. This notice was held in court proceedings to have been ineffective because the rateable value of the premises was too high. By the then provisions of para.2 of Sch.3 to the 1967 Act a claim to acquire the freehold was of no effect if made more than two months after a landlord's notice to terminate the tenancy under **3–254**

---

[483] [1982] 1 E.G.L.R. 81 CA.

[484] [1996] Q.B. 163 CA.

s.25 of the 1954 Act; and, on the other hand, a landlord's notice terminating a tenancy under that section was of no effect if served during the currency of the claim to acquire the freehold. After the determination by the court as to the validity of the tenant's notice of leaseholder's claim, the landlord on September 2, 1991 served a notice under s.25. The tenant did not challenge that counter-notice but served a counter-notice and starting proceedings for a new tenancy. The s.25 notice was served in Form 1 in Sch.2 to the Landlord and Tenant 1954 Pt II (Notices) Regulations 1983 (as amended). The notice was in the wrong form. It ought to have been in Form 13, as the premises were premises to which the Leasehold Reform Act 1967 could apply.

On November 1, 1993 the Leasehold Reform, Housing and Urban Development Act 1993 took effect removing the limit on rateable value for the purposes of enfranchisement under the 1967 Act. Four days later the tenant gave to the landlords a second enfranchisement notice. Since the 1993 notice was given more than two months after service of the s.25 notice, the 1993 notice will have been of no effect if the s.25 notice was valid. However, a tenant's claim is of no effect if made more than two months after a s.25 notice has been given.

It was said that the service of the counter-notice by the tenant that he was not willing to give up possession would have been purposeless unless the s.25 notice was valid. That it was given was explicable only as a response to the requirement of notification under s.25(5) and thus its service has seen the validity of the s.25 notice. The defect to the s.25 notice was plain on its face as it was one not to be used where the tenancy was one to which the 1967 Act may apply.

It was indisputable that the landlord had relied on the s.25 notice. By incurring lawyers' and surveyors' fees the landlord suffered obvious detriment albeit that by an award of costs they might be reimbursed at least in part. They had refrained from serving another s.25 notice in the correct form and had done so in faith of the tenant's representation that he was treating the s.25 notice as valid. Since the tenant knew that the wrong form had been served, while it was evident that the landlord did not, it was not unconscionable for the tenant to raise its invalidity and there was no unfairness in the tenant being bound by the consequence of treating it as valid.

Denial of tenant's status

3–255 ***Wroe v Exmos Cover Ltd***[485] W was granted an agreement dated September 23, 1994 described on its face as a "licence for the use of Business Premises". The agreement was made between E as licensor and W and his wife as licensee. The use of the rooms was restricted to business use. The licence period was 12 months. It was renewed such that the licence was to end with effect from March 31, 1997. Upon requesting delivery up of possession, W contended that the occupation was that of tenant not licensee. The licensor, E Ltd, was concerned about the grant of any tenancy to W as E Ltd had only a leasehold interest in the premises, which lease contained an absolute prohibition against granting sub-tenancies of part of the premises demised. After September 29, 1997 W remained in occupation. He sought to tender a cheque described as "rent" but this

[485] [2000] 1 E.G.L.R. 66 CA.

was returned. E Ltd wrote stating that they had no power to offer a tenancy as they were not allowed to do so under the terms of their lease. Monies continued to be tendered and rejected. On November 24, 1997 a director of E Ltd wrote to W's solicitors stating:

> "I want to be fair but it is now nearly eight months since I told [W] I wanted my old office back in six months. [W's] motives are perfectly understandable of course, but without any response at all I am left with no alternative but to get on. To do this apparently we have to accept he is holding over under the Landlord and Tenant Act from 1st October 1997 as a tenant and now do so. We enclose a copy of the notice . . . served on him today under section 25 of the Landlord and Tenant Act 1954 and this gives him a further six months to make the permanent office arrangements I should have thought are in his interests."

A s.25 notice dated November 24, 1997 was served on W. The notice purported to terminate W's "tenancy" on May 31, 1998. It indicated that if W made an application under the 1954 Act for the grant of a new tenancy, the application would be opposed under the ground mentioned in para.(g) of s.30(1) of the 1954 Act. Thereafter, until August 1998, the matter proceeded on the basis that the room occupied by W was held on a tenancy to which the 1954 Act applied. A counter-notice was served and W alone made an application for the grant of a new tenancy. E Ltd could have taken the point that the application ought to have been made by W and his wife, they being the persons with whom the agreement of September 23, 1994 had been made. However, that point was not taken by E Ltd. The answer served by E Ltd did not deny the existence of a current tenancy or that the grant of a tenancy would put E Ltd in breach of the covenant against sub-letting in its own lease. The opposition to a new tenancy was confined to the ground stated in the notice given under s.25 of the 1954 Act.

On June 11, 1998, the court ordered a preliminary issue as to whether or not E Ltd could make good its opposition to a new tenancy on ground (g) of s.30(1) of the 1954 Act. This was not opposed by E Ltd. The hearing of the preliminary issue occurred on August 10, 1998. During the course of the hearing the judge took the point that W did not have a tenancy but was merely a licensee. W contended that, whatever the effect of the agreement made, the letter of November 24, 1997 created an estoppel, which prevented E Ltd from denying the existence of a tenancy. The county court judge held that the agreement of September 23, 1994 created a licence not a tenancy. There was no appeal in relation to that conclusion. However, the judge held that the letter of November 24, 1997 did not create an estoppel.

The Court of Appeal rejected W's appeal. They held:

(1) the letter of November 24, 1997 was an unequivocal representation that at least in relation to the termination of W's right to occupy the room he would be treated by E Ltd as if he were holding over under a tenancy to which the 1954 Act applied;

(2) the letter did not, however, contain any representation that the application for a new tenancy would not be opposed. The most that could be said was that the letter together with a s.25 notice, read together, suggested that

opposition to a new tenancy would be found only on ground (g) of s.30(1) of the 1954 Act; and would not be found on an argument that the 1954 Act had no application at all;

(3) however, W did not take any steps in reliance upon the representation which would make it unfair or inequitable, to allow E Ltd to contend that there had never been a tenancy. It was impossible for W to say that he remained in occupation of the room after November 24, 1997 in reliance on the letter of that date. W's solicitors had made it clear in earlier correspondence and in subsequent correspondence that he was asserting the right to remain in occupation until the expiry of the period specified in a valid notice given in accordance with the 1954 Act. He did not remain in occupation in reliance on the letter of November 24, 1997, nor in reliance on the s.25 notice that was served at the time of that notice. He remained in occupation because, independently of the letter or the notice, he was advised by his solicitors that he was entitled to do so;

(4) the service of a counter-notice by W and the making of an originating application for a new tenancy were not acts of detriment in reliance on the representation made to him. W applied for a new tenancy because he wanted a new tenancy. The landlord's s.25 notice provided the opportunity to make the application; but it did not, in any sense, encourage W to take that course. It was made clear to him in the notice itself that an application for a new tenancy would be opposed. There was no evidence to suggest that W would not have made the application if he had not been led by W to think that it would oppose only on ground (g), and not on the ground that there was no current tenancy within the Act;

(5) nor could it be said that it was a case in which E Ltd had elected between two inconsistent remedies; nor that it sought to approbate and reprobate. The most that could be said was that it had made a procedural mistake. It should have raised the issue licence or tenancy answer to W's application for a new tenancy; and it should not have invited the court to determine the s.30(1)(g) point as a preliminary issue in advance of the question of whether or not there was a current tenancy to which the 1954 Act could apply. However, that mistake did not preclude E Ltd from raising the issue licence or tenancy and the judge was entitled to invite consideration of that question in the circumstances that went to the route of the court's jurisdiction.

Opposing Renewal

3–256 The tenant may argue that the landlord cannot by reason of what he has said or done seek to oppose renewal.[486]

3–257 ***Spence v Shell UK***[487] The tenant's lease of a motor service station and garage contained an option to renew. The option was, however, poorly drafted and was

[486] See also *Wroe (t/a Telepower) v Exmos Cover Ltd* [2000] 1 E.G.L.R. 66 CA (digested in para.3–255).

[487] [1980] 2 E.G.L.R. 68 CA.

probably void for uncertainty. The landlord and the tenant, being concerned about this possibility, entered into negotiations for the grant of a new option to give effect to the parties' original intention to enter into a valid option. After negotiations lasting two years, the landlord informed the tenant that it was no longer proceeding with a new option. It served a s.25 notice stating that it would oppose any application for a new tenancy under ground (f) of s.30(1) (demolition and reconstruction). The Court of Appeal held that the landlords were not estopped from opposing the grant of a new lease under ground (f) since there had been no clear and unambiguous promise or assurance that in the event of negotiations for the grant of a new option breaking down they would not oppose an application for a new tenancy under the Act.

Crossco No.4 Unlimited v Jolan Ltd[488] The landlord and tenant were companies which were controlled originally by the same persons. The tenant's lease contained a break clause operable by the landlord on three months' notice. Upon a complicated demerger, on a commercial basis, of the a number of companies and entities of which the freehold owner but the tenant formed part, the lease remained vested in the original tenant and the freehold became vested in a company wholly owned by Jolan Ltd. The new landlord operated the break clause and opposed renewal under para.(f) s.30(1) of the 1954 Act. The tenant traded from the ground floor of the premises demised by the lease. The tenant argued that the landlord was estopped from terminating the tenancy with respect to the ground floor.[489] The claim was put on the basis of proprietary estoppel, promissory estoppel, and estoppel by convention. The tenant also argued that there was a constructive trust pursuant to which it was unconscionable for the landlord to assert ownership to the freehold without providing the tenant with a lease of the ground floor without a break clause. The judge held: **3–258**

That there was no representation or assurance during the demerger negotiations by the landlord that the tenant could remain on the ground floor for the remainder of the length of the term of the lease and without the break clause.

The tenant had mistakenly believed that the lease did not contain a break clause but that was not the result of anything which the landlord had said prior to the demerger. There was no implied representation or assurance by the landlord that the mistaken belief (which the judge held the landlord was unaware of) was a justified belief.

(i) No constructive trust arose.[490] The tenant had made a unilateral mistake about the terms of the lease and that mistake was not induced by any

[488] [2011] EWHC 803 (Ch); [2011] EWCA Civ 1619; [2012] 1 P. & C.R. 16.

[489] Other arguments which the judge also rejected were that the parties to the demerger had entered into a binding contract that the ground floor was not to be the subject of any right to determine. Alternatively, that the transfer to Jolan Ltd should be rectified so as to remove the right to determine the lease in respect of the ground floor.

[490] The case law draws a distinction between the case of an arrangement under which the property was later acquired and a case where one party already owned property and then made a non-binding arrangement with another under which arrangement, if it had been performed, the other would have acquired rights in the future: see *Cobbe v Yeoman's Row Management Ltd* [2008] UKHL 55; [2008] 1 W.L.R. 1752 per Lord Scott at [30]–[37].

representation or assurance form the landlord nor caused or contributed by the landlord. Nor did the landlord know that the tenant had made a mistake about the terms of the lease. The tenant knew it did not have a binding agreement for a deed of variation or lease relating to the ground floor premises and there was no reliance on there being a binding agreement for a variation or new lease. The tenant's reliance was upon the terms of the existing lease but in the mistaken belief that that was not subject to a break clause. It was accordingly, not unconscionable for the landlord, following the demerger, to assert the existence of the freehold title and to rely on the terms of the existing lease.

(ii) On the evidence before the court the landlord had a firm and settled intention to carry out work falling within s.30(1)(f) of the 1954 Act.[491]

The tenant appealed to the Court of Appeal on the issues of proprietary estoppel and constructive trust. The court held that the tenant's mistake (of which the landlord was unaware) could not make landlord's conduct unconscionable. The intention of the parties had been to reduce their agreement to a formal written contract, and it was clear that the mutual intention of the parties had been that they not to be bound until then.

On the issue of estoppel, the judge had been entitled to conclude that none of the element of proprietary estoppel were made out.

Denial of new lease

3–259 In some cases the parties may have reached what is believed by the tenant to be an agreement for the grant of a new lease only for the landlord to then seek to withdraw from the arrangement on the basis that there is no binding agreement between them. If the negotiations between the parties are "subject to contract," or subject to some equivalent qualification, the tenant is unlikely to be able to hold the landlord to the deal.[492] In *Att Gen of Hong Kong v Humphreys Estate*[493] Lord Templeman expressed the view that it is unlikely that a party to negotiations set out in a document expressed to be "subject to contract" would be able to satisfy the court that the parties had subsequently agreed to convert the documents into a contract or that some form of estoppel had arisen to prevent both parties from refusing to proceed with the transactions envisaged by the document. The House of Lords has made it clear that where parties have been dealing on the basis that their negotiations are "subject to contract", proprietary estoppel will not ordinarily be available: see *Cobbe v Yeoman's Row Management Ltd.*[494] The result is not unconscionable because the disappointed party will always have known that that was the position.

---

[491] On this aspect of the case see para.7–167.

[492] An agreement "subject to contract" or "subject to lease" negates an intention to create legal relations: *D'Silva v Lister House Developments Ltd* [1971] Ch. 17; *Longman v Viscount Chelsea* (1989) 58 P. & C.R. 189 CA; *Akiens v Salomon* [1993] 1 E.G.L.R. 101 CA. See also para 15–03 et seq.

[493] [1987] A.C. 114 PC at 127H.

[494] [2008] UKHL 55; [2008] 1 W.L.R. 1752.

A party is not necessarily precluded from raising a proprietary estoppel by the use of the expression "subject to contract" if the claimant is able to establish that the defendant had made a representation and had encouraged, on the part of the claimant, a belief or expectation that he would not withdraw from the 'subject to contract' agreement or rely on the "subject to contract" qualification.[495]

JT Developments v Quinn[496] The tenant failed to serve a counter-notice in response to a s.25 notice. The s.25 notice did not oppose renewal but, in light of the fact that no counter-notice had been served, the tenant had lost its right to a renewal. However, after the time for serving a counter-notice had expired, the tenant telephoned the landlord and during the course of the conversation between the parties, the landlord represented that the tenant would obtain a new lease on the same terms as an adjoining tenant with an adjustment as to rent. No precise figures as to rent were mentioned, although sufficient information was given to enable the precise figure, which depended upon measurement of the premises, to be calculated. Nothing was said in the course of this telephone conversation as to the doing of any work to the premises by the tenant. No letter in confirmation of what was agreed or said in the conversation was written by either party. The tenant subsequently carried out work of improvement to the demised premises. The landlord inspected the demised premises to measure the same for the purposes of determining the amount of the rent under the new tenancy. No steps were taken thereafter by either side to settle the terms of the new lease or to continue negotiations for a lease. However, the tenant again approached the landlord on the telephone, who stated that he gave his word that the tenant was getting a new tenancy "as already discussed, the same as the adjoining tenant". The landlord sought possession after the expiry of the s.25 notice. The court held that there was no oral agreement concluded between the parties for the grant of a new lease. However, the court held that the tenant had acquired an equity which needed to be satisfied by reason of the doctrine of proprietary estoppel. The landlord had given the tenant an assurance during the course of the initial telephone conversation which had been acted upon. The landlord had encouraged an expectation that the tenant would have a new lease on the demised premises and the tenant on the faith of that promise or expectation, with the knowledge of the landlord, and without objection by him, laid out money upon the demised premises. **3–260**

[495] *Yeoman's Row Management Ltd v Cobbe* [2006] EWCA Civ 1139, [2006] 1 W.L.R. 2964, per Mummery L.J. at [57]. This comment would appear to remain good notwithstanding the fact that the actual decision in the case (that a proprietary estoppel did arise) was reversed by the House of Lords: [2008] UKHL 55; [2008] 1 W.L.R. 1752.

[496] [1991] 2 E.G.L.R. 257 CA. Contrast this decision with *Akiens v Solomon* (considered at para.15–07) where an agreement between the parties "subject to lease" did not prevent the landlord from relying upon the tenant's failure to make his application in time.

In a non-1954 Act context (but in respect of which a claim for a binding agreement for lease failed by reason of the qualified nature of the negotiations) see *Brent LBC v O'Bryan* (1993) 65 P. & C.R. 258 CA; *James v Evans* [2001] 3 E.G.L.R. 1; *Edwin Shirley Productions Ltd v Workspace Management Ltd* [2001] 2 E.G.L.R. 16; *Adegbulu v Southwark LBC* [2003] EWHC 1930 (Ch).

3–261 ***Haq v Island Homes Housing Association***[497] The tenant of shop premises, after the expiry of his contractual term and after notices and counter notices had been served under the 1954 Act, agreed subject to contract with his local authority landlord to extend his shop premises onto adjoining land owned by the Council and for him to be granted a 60-year term at an agreed rent. Works were required for the extension. It was agreed that, before the works commenced, a licence for works and an agreement for lease should be executed and that the new lease would be granted following completion of the works and the tenant's existing tenancy would be surrendered. The tenant, to the knowledge of the Council, entered the adjoining land and executed the relevant work before execution of any documents. The tenant started to trade from the enlarged premises. The Council sold the reversion to a Housing Association which was prepared to grant a 15-year term to the tenant of the extended premises in accordance with the 1954 Act. The tenant claimed that he was entitled to a 60-year term of the extended premises on that basis that he had undertaken the relevant work in reliance on the representation made by the Council to grant the new lease and that the Council were to be taken to have waived the requirement for execution of the relevant documentation.

The Court of Appeal held (reversing the judge at first instance) that the tenant had not made out the requirements for proprietary estoppel. The negotiations were at all times subject to contract. Albeit the Council must have been taken to have granted the tenant an implied licence to enter to carry out the work and waive the requirement for execution of the necessary licence before commencing work, the Council could not be taken to have waived the subject to contract status of the arrangements and thus the requirement that an agreement for lease should be agreed and executed as a precondition to the grant of the lease.

Practical points on estoppel under the Act

3–262 A number of points of practical importance for practitioners can be derived from the decided cases under the Act.

(1) A party seeking to raise an estoppel should consider carefully what evidence is necessary in order to satisfy the court as to each of the required elements of an estoppel. In *Stevens & Cutting v Anderson*[498] (digested in para.3–246), the landlord called evidence from its solicitor as to what he had understood and believed the position to be. This enabled the landlord to rebut the presumption that the landlord, knowing the facts which gave rise to its right, also knew that it had the right. The tenant, on the other hand, called no evidence to show detriment and, in the absence of specific evidence, the court was not prepared to presume detriment.

(2) A party will often be able to prevent an estoppel arising against it by clearly indicating to the other party that the action which it is taking is expressly without prejudice to its position if its understanding of the facts or the law should subsequently be held to have been erroneous. The most common

[497] [2011] EWCA Civ 805; [2011] 2 P. & C.R. 17.

[498] [1990] 1 E.G.L.R. 95 CA.

examples in practice are where a notice, or counter-notice, or application is of doubtful validity, but it is necessary to take some steps in response to it without waiving the possible invalidity. It is not always possible to prevent an estoppel arising by this method: see *British Railways Board v Smith*[499] (digested in para.3–243), above. In that case it was insufficient that the tenant had, at a late stage in the proceedings, sought to keep open its options. The appropriate form of action will depend upon all the circumstances, but in all cases any point as to invalidity should be taken promptly, before any step is taken which is inconsistent with that contention, and it may be necessary that the point be expressly taken in the relevant court proceedings in the form of a claim for alternative relief.

(3) In many cases the parties may wish to avoid the complications of arguments as to the invalidity or possible invalidity of notices or applications. There is nothing to prevent both parties expressly agreeing that an otherwise doubtful notice or step will be treated as being valid; thereafter neither party can depart from that agreement and arguments as to estoppel should not arise: see, e.g. *Elsden v Pick*.[500]

(4) Quite apart from the technicalities of the law of estoppel, a more general principle may be derived from the decision of the Court of Appeal in *Benedictus v Jalaram*.[501] A party who wishes to contest the validity of a notice but also wishes to protect his position in case it turns out that the notice is valid should make it abundantly clear in any proceedings issued under the Act that those proceedings are without prejudice to his alternative contention. Even if the point as to invalidity has been raised, e.g. in an affidavit, or in correspondence, the issue of proceedings relying upon the notice in question may be taken to be an election to treat it as valid, as seems to have happened in *Tennant v London CC*[502] (digested in para.3–251) and *Stylo Shoes Ltd v Prices Tailors Ltd*[503] (digested in para.3–60).

(5) A landlord who serves a s.25 notice is thereby asserting that he is the "competent landlord" entitled to give it and that is a continuing representation upon which the tenant is entitled to rely. If the landlord ceases to be the "competent landlord" he should inform the tenant of this fact, otherwise he may be estopped from afterwards contending that the tenant's proceedings have not been commenced against the correct landlord: *Shelley v United Artists Corp Ltd*[504] (digested in para.14–45).[505]

---

499 [1981] 2 E.G.L.R. 69.

500 [1980] 1 W.L.R. 898 CA (a case under the Agricultural Holdings Act 1948).

501 [1989] 1 E.G.L.R. 251 CA.

502 55 L.G.R. 421; (1957) 121 J.P. 428 CA.

503 [1960] 2 W.L.R. 8; [1959] 3 All E.R. 901.

504 [1990] 1 E.G.L.R. 103.

505 See also para.3–87 et seq, above, on the meaning of "landlord".

CHAPTER 4

SERVING NOTICES—TIMING AND TACTICS

1. OBTAINING INFORMATION

Scope of section 40(1): information required by landlord

The pre-2003 Order position

Section 40(1) in its form prior to the amendments made by the 2003 Order provided a means whereby landlords of business premises could obtain information on two matters. **4–01**

(1) The first matter in respect of which the tenant could be made to provide information was whether he occupied the premises or any part thereof wholly or partly for the purposes of a business carried on by him. This followed the wording of s.23(1) and the answer to this question was intended to inform the landlord whether or not the tenant in question had a tenancy to which the Act applied. This information is something which the landlord can continue to seek under the new regime. As has been noted in Ch.1, tenancies can go in and out of the Act (at least for the purposes of the tenant's ability to apply for a new tenancy), so the provision of this information pursuant to s.40(1) informs the landlord what is the true position at the date when the information is furnished. If necessary, the landlord can serve a further notice if he has reason to believe that the position has changed.

(2) The second matter upon which a landlord could require information was whether any sub-tenancy was in existence, and, if so, what premises were comprised in the sub-tenancy, what was the term thereof, by what notice (if any) it was terminable, what was the rent payable, who was the sub-tenant, and (to the best of the knowledge and belief of the tenant) whether the sub-tenant was in occupation of the premises and, if not, what was the sub-tenant's address. The importance of this to the landlord was that, if he served a s.25 notice upon his tenant, he became the "landlord" for the purposes of the Act in respect of the sub-tenant as well.[1] Somewhat curiously, there was no provision requiring the tenant:

   (a) to state whether (to the best of his knowledge and belief) the sub-tenant was carrying on a business;

[1] See para.3–87 et seq.

(b) to divulge any of the other terms of the sub-tenancy, e.g. whether there was a clause therein permitting or prohibiting business use.
(c) to provide information about inferior interests. The landlord could require information from any tenant or sub-tenant of the premises or any part thereof, but the duty of each tenant or sub-tenant was confined to the furnishing of information about any immediate sub-tenant of his. The landlord would accordingly have to make successive enquiries where there was a long chain of inferior interests.

It will be seen below that the new provisions brought into force rectify (a), partially improve (b), by requiring information to be provided about the terms of the sub-tenancy, but make no modification affecting (c).

The 2003 Order

4–02 The 2003 Order replaced the then existing s.40 with a new provision which is intended to enable landlords and tenants to obtain more information than was previously the position under the old regime. A person who is an owner of an interest in reversion expectant (whether immediately or not) on a tenancy of any business premises may serve on the tenant a notice in the prescribed form[2] requiring him to provide in writing the following information, namely[3]:

(1) whether the tenant occupies the premises or any part of them wholly or partly for the purposes of a business carried on by him;
(2) whether his tenancy has effect subject to any sub-tenancy on which his tenancy is immediately expectant[4] and, if so:
    (a) what premises are comprised in the sub-tenancy;
    (b) for what term it has effect (or, if it is terminable by notice, by what notice it can be terminated);
    (c) what is the rent payable under it;
    (d) who is the sub-tenant;
    (e) (to the best of his knowledge and belief) whether the sub-tenant is in occupation of the premises or any part of the premises comprised in the sub-tenancy and, if not, what is the sub-tenant's address;
    (f) whether an agreement is in force excluding in relation to the sub-tenancy the provisions of ss.24 to 28 of the 1954 Act; and
    (g) whether a notice has been given under ss.25 or 26(6) (i.e. a landlord's counter-notice), or a request has been made under s.26 of this Act, in relation to the sub-tenancy and, if so, details of the notice or request; and
(3) (to the best of his knowledge and belief) the name and address of any other person who owns an interest in reversion in any part of the premises.

---

[2] As to which see para.4–11.
[3] s.40(1) and (2).
[4] The words "immediately expectant" has the effect of limiting the information to be provided to that of the tenant's immediate sub-tenant only and not of any interests inferior to that sub-tenancy.

The ability to require the provision of the information referred to in paras (2)(f), (g) and (3) is new. This was not information which, under the old regime, the tenant could be required to provide to the landlord.

Time for tenant to respond to section 40 notice

Section 40(1), as substituted, provides that the tenant is under a duty to provide the information upon receipt of the notice.[5] The information is required to be given within the period of one month beginning with the date of service of the notice: s.40(5). If, having given the information, the tenant becomes aware, within the period of six months beginning with the date of service of the notice, that any information which has been given in pursuance of the notice is not, or is no longer, correct, he is under a duty to correct the information within the period of one month beginning with the date on which the tenant becomes aware of the error: s.40(5)(b). This duty to correct and update information once provided did not exist under the old regime. **4–03**

Time for service of section 40 notice by landlord

A notice cannot be served by a reversioner more than two years prior to the date on which, apart from the Act, the tenancy would come to an end by effluxion of time or could be brought to an end by notice to quit given by the landlord: s.40(6). This reflects the position as under the old regime. For the service of notices generally, see s.23 of the Landlord and Tenant Act 1927.[6] **4–04**

Scope of section 40(2): information required by tenant

Position pre-2003 Order

Section 40(2) allowed certain classes of tenant to enquire about the nature of the interest held by their immediate or superior landlords. The right to require such information was limited to those tenants who are within the provisions of s.26(1). This remains unaltered. Those from whom such information could be required were, by virtue of s.40(3), all those having reversionary interests expectant on the tenancy (whether immediately or not) and any mortgagee in possession in respect of such an interest. The information which could be obtained was: **4–05**

(1) whether such a person was the owner of the fee simple or a mortgagee in possession of such an owner; and, if not,
(2) (to the best of the knowledge and belief of the landlord) who was the person who was the landlord's immediate landlord, what was the term of

[5] s.40(5).
[6] See paras 3–49 et seq. above.

the landlord's tenancy and what was the earliest date (if any) at which the landlord's tenancy was terminable by notice to quit "given by the landlord".[7]

Section 40(2), however, omitted to provide for the tenant to be informed what notices (if any) had been served by or upon his landlord or superior landlord, which is material to the question of who fulfils the definition in s.44. This gap was to some extent filled by the decision of the Court of Appeal in *Shelley v United Artists Corp*[8] (digested in para.14–45). This omission has now been rectified under the new provisions.

Position post-2003 Order

4–06 A tenant for a term of years exceeding one year or granted for a term of years certain and thereafter from year to year (i.e. a tenant under such a tenancy as is mentioned in s.26(1))[9] may serve on a reversioner or a reversioner's mortgagee in possession a notice in the prescribed form[10] requiring him to provide in writing the following information[11]:

(1) whether he is the owner of the fee simple in respect of the premises or a part of them or the mortgagee in possession of such an owner;
(2) if he is not, then (to the best of his knowledge and belief):
  (a) the name and address of the person who is his or, as the case may be, his mortgagor's immediate landlord in respect of those premises or of the part in respect of which he or his mortgagor is not the owner in fee simple;
  (b) for what term his or his mortgagor's tenancy has effect and what is the earliest date (if any) at which the tenancy is terminable by notice to quit given by the landlord; and
  (c) whether a notice has been given under s.25 or s.26(6) of the Act, or a request has been made under s.26 of the Act, in relation to the tenancy and, if so, details of the notice or request;
(3) (to the best of his knowledge and belief) the name and address of any other person who owns an interest in reversion in any part of the premises; and
(4) if he is a reversioner, whether there is a mortgagee in possession of his interest in the premises and, if so (to the best of his knowledge and belief) what is the name and address of the mortgagee: s.40(3) and (4).

4–07 The "mortgagee in possession" includes a receiver appointed by the mortgagee or by the court who is in receipt of the rents and profits and a "reversioner's mortgagee in possession" means any person being a mortgagee in possession in

[7] It is thought that this last phrase is a reference to a notice to quit given by the landlord's immediate landlord, rather than a reference to a notice to quit which can be given by the immediate landlord to his landlord.
[8] [1990] 1 E.G.L.R. 103 CA.
[9] See para.3–209.
[10] See para.4–11.
[11] s.40(3) and (4).

respect of such an interest: s.40(8). A "sub-tenant" includes a person retaining possession of any premises by virtue of the Rent (Agriculture) Act 1976 or the Rent Act 1977 after the coming to an end of a sub-tenancy: s.40(8).

The ability to require the information to be given under paras (2)(c), (3) and (4), set at para.4–06, above, is new. This information could not be required to be given under the old regime. The tenant needs all this information in order to carry out the process of ascertaining who is 'the landlord' within the definition in s.44.[12] It is essential for the tenant to know this in order to discover who is the person to whom he should make any request for a new tenancy pursuant to s.26 and who should be named as respondent to any application for a new tenancy which he may subsequently make. **4–08**

Time for landlord to respond to section 40 notice

Section 40(1), as substituted, provides that the landlord is under a duty to provide the information upon receipt of the notice.[13] The information is required to be given within the period of one month beginning with the date of service of the notice: s.40(5). If, having given the information, the landlord becomes aware, within the period of six months beginning with the date of service of the notice, that any information which has been given in pursuance of the notice is not, or is no longer, correct, he is under a duty to correct the information within the period of one month beginning with the date on which the landlord becomes aware of the error: s.40(5)(b). This duty to correct and update information once provided did not exist under the old regime. **4–09**

Time for service of section 40 notice by tenant

A notice cannot be served by a tenant more than two years prior to the date on which, apart from the Act, the tenancy would come to an end by effluxion of time or could be brought to an end by notice to quit given by the landlord: s.40(6). This reflects the position as under the old regime. For the service of notices generally, see s.23 of the Landlord and Tenant Act 1927.[14] **4–10**

Section 40 notices: formal requirements

Section 40 lays down certain formal requirements for the service of notices requiring information. The forms which are to be used to request information are prescribed: s.66(1) of the 1954 Act. The forms of notice with regard to notices served post June 1, 2004 pursuant to s.40(1) (request by landlord/superior landlord) or s.40(3)(request by tenant) are now prescribed by the Landlord and Tenant Act 1954 Pt II (Notices)(Regulations) 2004 (SI 2004/1005).[15] **4–11**

---

12 As to the meaning of "landlord", see para.3–87 et seq.
13 s.40(5).
14 See paras 3–49 et seq. above.
15 See Forms 4 and 5 to the 2004 Regs, Appendix, paras A2.037 and A2.038, respectively.

Tactical considerations

4–12 The provisions of s.40 are not relied upon as often as one might perhaps expect, for there may be tactical reasons why a landlord or tenant may prefer to rely upon information already in his possession or on information which can be obtained by inspection, rather than serve a formal notice. The service of a s.40 notice is a clear indication that the landlord or tenant has it in mind subsequently to serve a s.25 notice or make a s.26 request based upon the information. This warning signal may remind the recipient of the notice of his own rights under the Act and thus enable him to get in first with his own notice or request. The tactical advantages which can be obtained by stealing a march on the other party in this way are explained below.[16] On the other hand, the advantages to be derived from the service of a formal s.40 notice are considerable. There may be no other practical way of obtaining the information. If incomplete or erroneous information is supplied, the landlord or tenant will have his remedies.[17] The effect of the service of a s.40 notice may be to force the landlord or the tenant to make admissions about his position by which he will be bound and which can be relied upon if proceedings ensue.

Failure to provide information

4–13 It may, of course, happen that a landlord or tenant will deliberately or by neglect fail to respond to a s.40 notice or will supply incomplete or erroneous information. There was, prior to the amendments brought into force by the 2003 Order, probably no practical means of enforcing compliance with a s.40 notice in such circumstances, other than to threaten the defaulter with a claim for damages. Although s.40 provided no express sanction for a failure to respond to a notice, it did provide that the effect of service thereof was that it became "the duty" of the recipient to provide the information. In principle, there would appear to have been no reason why an action for damages for breach of this statutory duty could not lie, if erroneous or incomplete information was supplied which resulted in loss.

4–14 The Act as amended by the 2003 Order continues to make express provision for the recipient to be under a "duty" to provide the information requested. However, unlike the provisions of s.40 in their pre-June 1, 2004 form, the amendments made by the 2003 Order make express provision as to what is to happen if there is a failure to provide the information requested within the period provided for by the statute, s.40B which provides:

> "A claim that a person has broken any duty imposed by section 40 of this Act may be made the subject of civil proceedings for breach of statutory duty; and in any such proceedings a court may order that person to comply with the duty and may make an award of damages."

4–15 There would appear to be nothing stopping a landlord from providing for the lease to contain an appropriately the worded covenant by the relevant party to

---

[16] See para.4–19 et seq.

[17] As explained in para.4–13 et seq.

comply with the requirements of statute, breach of which would give rise to a claim for damages. Compare the position considered by the Court of Appeal in *Shelley v United Artists*[18] (digested in para.14–45) where there was held to be a continuing representation by a landlord who had served a s.25 notice that he at all material times remained the "landlord" for the purposes of s.44. Presumably (although it did not arise on the particular facts of this case) a claim for damages for misrepresentation would lie in an appropriate case.

Recipient no longer the landlord or tenant

Where a recipient of a notice whether under s.40(1) or (3) has transferred his interest[19] he can avoid having to provide the relevant information by informing the sender of the notice in writing of the fact of the transfer and of the name and address of the person to whom the transfer was effected: s.40A(1). Once such a notice is given[20] to the recipient, the recipient ceases to be under any duty imposed by s.40 of the Act. **4–16**

Transfer of sender's interest

If the person who sends a notice, whether under s.40(1) or (3), subsequently transfers his interest and the sender is informed either by the sender or the transferee of the fact of the transfer and of the transferee's name and address, the appropriate person for the purposes of s.40 and subs.(1) of s.40A is the transferee: s.40A(2). If the recipient of the notice is unaware of the transfer at the time he provides the relevant information, the supply of that information to the transferor will discharge the statutory duty: s.40A(3). **4–17**

2. POSITION WHERE NO NOTICE OR REQUEST SERVED

Tenancy continues

As already stated,[21] if the tenancy is one to which the Act applies and no s.25 notice is served or s.26 request made, the current tenancy continues indefinitely upon the same terms and at the same rent,[22] but subject to termination in accordance with the Act. This is unlikely to be attractive to the landlord if rental values have risen since the current tenancy was negotiated, or to the tenant if rental values have fallen. Another reason why the tenant may wish to obtain a new tenancy pursuant to the Act would be if, e.g. he is considering an assignment. **4–18**

---

[18] [1990] 1 E.G.L.R. 103 CA.

[19] This presumably requires an effective transfer at law, so that until registration at HM Land Registry, the transferor of registered land remains under a duty to provide the relevant information.

[20] The notice does not in fact have to have been received in order to be given if one of the methods of service in s.23 of the Landlord and Tenant Act 1927 is adopted: see para.3–69.

[21] See paras 2–34 et seq.

[22] An interim rent is payable only once a s.25 notice or s.26 request is served: s.24A(1).

3. WHETHER AND WHEN TO SERVE A SECTION 25 NOTICE OR SECTION 26 REQUEST: TACTICS FOR LANDLORD AND TENANT

Getting in first?

4–19 The key decision, which has to be taken by a landlord or tenant as the termination of the current tenancy approaches, is whether he should attempt to get in first with his notice or request, before one is served on him by the other party. As already noted, it is provided by s.26(4) that the tenant has no right to make a request after he has been given a s.25 notice by his landlord and that the landlord likewise has no right to serve a notice pursuant to s.25 once he has received a s.26 request. It does not, of course, inevitably follow that it is always in the best interests of landlord and tenant to "get in first". For example, if the landlord has not yet fully informed himself whether the Act applies to the tenancy, he may find that, by serving a s.25 notice on the tenant, he lays himself open to the argument that he is estopped from contending that the tenancy is outside the Act.[23] Further, if a notice is given precipitously, it may be that either landlord or tenant has had insufficient time to consider fully the other tactical advantages and disadvantages mentioned in the following paragraphs.

First notice or request decides date of termination

4–20 The main tactical advantage which flows from being the first person to serve a notice or make a request is the control which it gives over the date to be specified for termination of the current tenancy. As already noted (in paras 3–177 and 3–221), such date must, generally, be not less than 6, nor more than 12, months after the date of giving the notice or making the request. Accordingly, there is an element of flexibility given to whoever serves the first notice, which is illustrated below.

Obtaining rental advantage

4–21 Prior to the amendments brought about by the 2003 Order it was the case that either the landlord or tenant could obtain a rental advantage depending on the date specified in the relevant notice or request, especially where a substantial part of the premises was sub-let. This flowed from the fact that, while the tenancy continued pursuant to s.24(1) and s.64, rent was payable at the rate reserved by the current tenancy, subject only to the right of the landlord to apply for an interim rent pursuant to s.24A. As explained later (para.9–12), the interim rent could not, prior to June 1, 2004, become payable from a date earlier than the date specified in the relevant notice or request. Thus, it was to the tenant's benefit (where rental values had risen since the rent payable was last fixed) for that date to be as late as possible and to the landlord's for it to be as early as possible. The converse was, of course, true where rental values had fallen. Further, since any

---

[23] See para.3–232 et seq., and *Wroe (t/a Telepower) v Exmos Cover Ltd* [2000] 1 E.G.L.R. 66 CA, (digested in para.3–255).

sub-tenant would be liable to pay an interim rent to the tenant while the tenancy and the sub-tenancy continued pursuant to s.24, the benefit to the tenant could be magnified during such period as the sub-tenant was obliged to pay an interim rent to the tenant but the tenant was not obliged to pay an interim rent to the landlord.

The position post the coming into force of the new provisions for the payment of interim rent has eliminated the possible rental advantage to be gained by the date of termination/commencement specified in the s.25 notice or s.26 request. The reason for this is that either the landlord or the tenant can apply for payment of an interim rent and the date from which the interim rent is payable is not the date specified in the notice but the earliest date which could have been specified in the notice or request when served.[24] This can be illustrated by an example.

Example

Pre-June 1, 2004 If there was a tenancy which was due to expire on September 29, 2003, and there was a sub-tenancy of the bulk of the premises which was due to expire on September 28, 2003, the position at March 27, 2003, was as follows (assuming the Act to apply both to the tenancy and the sub-tenancy and that no notices or requests have been given or made): the tenant was still the sub-tenant's "landlord", and was accordingly entitled to serve him with a s.25 notice specifying as the date of termination September 28, 2003. The tenant was also entitled to make a s.26 request, specifying as the date of the commencement of the new tenancy March 27, 2004. If the tenant served a s.25 notice on his sub-tenant[25] and assuming the sub-tenant made an application for a new tenancy and the tenant applied for an interim rent from the earliest possible date, the tenant would be in the happy position (if rents had risen) between September 28, 2003 and March 27, 2004, of receiving an interim rent from the sub-tenant while paying only the old rent to the landlord. **4–22**

Post-June 1, 2004 If there is a tenancy which is due to expire on September 29, 2012, and there is a sub-tenancy of the bulk of the premises which is due to expire on September 28, 2012, the position as at March 27, 2012 is as follows (assuming the Act to apply both to the tenancy and the sub-tenancy and that no notices or requests have been given or made): the tenant is still the sub-tenant's "landlord" and is accordingly entitled to serve him with a s.25 notice specifying as the date of termination September 28, 2012. The tenant is also entitled to make a s.26 request on his landlord up the chain, specifying as the date of commencement of the new tenancy March 27, 2013. If the tenant does so, then assuming both tenant and sub-tenant made applications for renewal and both the landlord and the tenant applied for interim rents from the earliest possible date, the tenant would be in the position (if rents have risen) of receiving an interim rent from the sub-tenant but would also have to pay the landlord an interim rent **4–23**

[24] This date will of course be the same where the notice or request is one of six months but not otherwise e.g. in the case of a notice or request of 12 months the interim rent will run from a date six months earlier than that specified: see para.9–12 et seq.

[25] If the tenant serves a s.26 request up the chain he will cease to be the competent landlord for the purposes of seeking an interim rent as against the sub-tenant: see paras 3–87 and 9–04.

from September 29, 2012 because that was the earliest date which could have been specified when the tenant served the s.26 request upon his landlord.

Obtaining double compensation

4–24 In a case where the landlord intends to oppose the grant of a new tenancy on the grounds specified in paragraphs (e) (current tenancy created by sub-letting of part), (f) (demolition and reconstruction) and (g) (own occupation) of s.30(1) or one of them, the compensation payable to the tenant under s.37 can, in certain circumstances, be doubled by a few days' difference in the date of termination specified. The reason for this is that double compensation is payable if the tenant or a predecessor in title in his business has been in occupation for a period of 14 years or more (see para.12–31 et seq.). It is expressly provided by s.37 that this period of 14 years is to be counted back from the date specified in the relevant s.25 notice or s.26 request. The practical effects of this can be illustrated by an example.

Example

4–25 If one assumes that a term of 14 years from September 29, 1999, was granted on that date, but that the tenant did not, for some reason, start trading until December 20, 1999,[26] the tenant would, on December 25, 2012, be entitled to make a request under s.26 to expire on December 25, 2013, in which case he would be entitled to double compensation, if the landlord specified one of the relevant grounds of opposition in his counter-notice. However, if the landlord got in first and served a s.25 notice to expire on December 18, 2013, specifying a relevant ground of opposition, the tenant would be entitled only to single compensation.

4–26 It should also be noted that, as is explained below,[27] the questions of what constitutes "the holding", in respect of which compensation is payable, and of its rateable value, are judged at the date of service of the landlord's s.25 notice, or (probably) the making of the tenant's s.26 request, as the case may be. Where the tenant is out of occupation of a substantial part of the holding, but would be able to resume possession without difficulty, he may be able to increase the compensation payable to him greatly by reoccupying the whole of the premises and thus increasing "the holding", provided that he does so before any s.25 notice is served or s.26 request is made.

---

[26] It may be that in light of the decision in *Bacchiocchi v Academic Agency Ltd* [1998] 1 W.L.R. 1313; [1998] 2 All E.R. 241 CA and *Pointon York Group Plc v Poulton* [2006] EWCA Civ 1001; [2007] 1 P. & C.R. 115, it is arguable that if the tenant was in occupation of premises for the purposes of fitting out in order to be able to trade, the tenant is to be treated as in occupation for business purposes. The Court of Appeal in *Bacchiocchi v Academic Agency Ltd*, overruled the decision in *Department of the Environment v Royal Insurance Plc* [1987] 1 E.G.L.R. 83. In that case the tenant had been in occupation for 14 years, less one day at the commencement of the tenancy which the tenant had utilised for fitting out. It was held that only single compensation was payable, since there was no room for the application of the de minimis principle and the tenant had not been in occupation for the required 14-year period.

[27] See para.12–46. As to the meaning of "holding" see para.8–06.

Qualifying to oppose under section 30(1)(g)

The question whether the landlord is entitled to oppose a new tenancy on the ground specified in para.(g) of s.30(1) (own occupation) may be affected by the date of termination specified in the relevant notice or request. The reason is that, in order to rely upon this ground of opposition, the landlord must show that he has not become the landlord by purchase at any time after the date commencing five years prior to the date of termination specified in the notice or request.[28] This can be illustrated by an example. **4–27**

Example

If one supposes that the landlord purchased the reversion expectant upon a tenancy to which the Act applies on January 15, 2009, and that the term is due to expire on September 29, 2013, the position of the parties on, say, January 20, 2013, is as follows: The landlord can serve a s.25 notice expressed to expire on January 16, 2014. Since this is more than five years after the date on which he purchased the reversion, he is entitled to rely on ground (g). However, the tenant could himself make a request, stating as the date of commencement of the new tenancy January 14, 2014. If he does so, the landlord will be debarred from relying on ground (g). Of course, if the tenant were to do this the court might mitigate the hardship to the landlord in appropriate circumstances, by granting the tenant only a very short term[29] or inserting a break clause.[30] **4–28**

Deciding which ground to specify

One of the most important considerations for a landlord in deciding whether to serve a notice under s.25 is whether its timing will embarrass him in seeking to rely upon a ground of opposition. A landlord can only rely upon a ground of opposition which has been specified in his s.25 notice (see paras 3–162 and 7–02). It follows that a landlord, before serving a s.25 notice, must consider carefully whether he will wish to oppose an application for a new tenancy and, if so, upon what ground. Since the relevant date for testing the question whether the landlord has a sufficient intention for the purposes of grounds (f) (demolition and reconstruction) and (g) (own occupation) is the date of the hearing, this will involve a certain amount of consideration; after all, circumstances may change in the future. It is not unknown for landlords to serve s.25 notices at the earliest possible point, stating that they will not oppose the grant of a new tenancy, and subsequently to sell the reversion to a person who wishes to redevelop. In such circumstances, the new landlord is bound by the notice which has been given.[31] The court will not always assist a landlord who has for some reason failed to specify the ground upon which he would like to rely by granting a short tenancy **4–29**

---

[28] See para.7–264 et seq.

[29] See *Upsons v Robins* [1956] 1 Q.B. 131; [1955] 3 W.L.R. 584; [1955] 3 All E.R. 348 CA.

[30] See para.8–42 et seq.

[31] The provisions for withdrawal of a s.25 notice contained in the Sch.6 apply only in circumstances where a superior landlord has become the competent landlord: see paras 7–08 and 7–09.

or including a break clause: compare *Amika Motors v Colebrook Holdings*[32] (digested in para.8–84), with *JH Edwards v Central Commercial*[33] (digested in para.8–83), below.[34] Conversely, the tenant may wish to embarrass a landlord who has not made up his mind as to which ground of opposition (if any) he will rely upon, by making a s.26 request. If the landlord is to rely upon a ground of opposition in these circumstances, he must specify it in a counter-notice served within two months of the making of the tenant's request.[35]

Rushing the landlord

4–30 Where the landlord has decided to specify a ground of opposition, the timing of the s.25 notice and the date specified therein can be of some importance. The following example, which it is hoped bears some relation to the realities of life, illustrates the ways in which a tenant can rush his landlord and thus embarrass him in proving an intention to redevelop.

Example

4–31 Suppose a tenancy for a term is due to expire on September 29, 2013, and the premises are ripe for redevelopment. On April 12, 2013, the landlord publishes in the local newspaper (as he is required to do by s.66 of the Town and Country Planning Act 1990) notice of his intention to apply for planning permission to demolish and reconstruct the premises. The tenant can serve on April 12, 2013 a s.26 request to expire on October 13, 2013; he can apply to the court for a new tenancy on June 13, 2013[36]; he can ask (assuming that the landlord has specified ground (f) in his counter-notice) for the trial of a preliminary issue as to whether that ground has been made out; and he can reasonably expect that issue to be tried by, say, September 30, 2013. On that time scale, the landlord might have great difficulty in satisfying the court that it had a sufficient intention to demolish the premises. A tenant could prior to the amendments to the Act made by the 2003 Order also spin out proceedings so as to prolong his own rights of occupation, delay the landlord's development and thereby (possibly) obtain some financial inducement to vacate the premises.[37]

---

[32] [1981] 2 E.G.L.R. 62 CA.
[33] [1984] 2 E.G.L.R. 103 CA.
[34] Also, see paras 8–39 and 8–77 et seq.
[35] See para.5–03 et seq.
[36] Being the expiry of the two month period for service of a counter-notice. Of course if the landlord had served a counter-notice relying on ground (f) the tenant will be able to make an application immediately after service of the counter-notice. Thus if the landlord had served a counter-notice two weeks after receipt of the s.26 request, i.e. on April 26, 2013 the tenant could make his application for renewal on April 27, 2013. See para.6–05.
[37] For example of potential time-scales, see para.11–02 et seq.

Where landlord may need to rely on section 31(2)

Although the date specified in the s.25 notice or s.26 request is not usually relevant for the purposes of s.30(1) and the grounds of opposition specified therein, because the date for testing intention is the date of the hearing, it can be of importance where the landlord seeks to rely upon s.31(2). This subsection is discussed in detail below.[38] In broad terms it enables a landlord, who is unable to establish fully grounds (d) (suitable alternative accommodation), (e) (current tenancy created by sub-letting of part), or (f) (demolition and reconstruction) at the date of the hearing, to seek a declaration from the court that, if the matter had been viewed at a later date, he would have succeeded in establishing that intention. The court is not permitted to look into the indefinite future, but is limited to a period not exceeding one year from the date specified for termination of the tenancy in the relevant s.25 notice or s.26 request. The practical considerations which arise where a landlord feels that he may have to rely upon s.31(2) are illustrated by the following example. **4–32**

Example

Suppose a tenancy of premises which are ripe for redevelopment for a term due to expire on September 29, 2013, but where the landlord's plans for demolition and reconstruction are at a very rudimentary stage. If the landlord can be confident at the date when he is considering the matter, say April 1, 2013, that there is little likelihood of the tenant making a request under s.26, he would be best advised to do nothing, because time can only improve his case. However, if he decides now to serve a s.25 notice (perhaps because he has reason to believe that the tenant is contemplating making a s.26 request) it will be to his advantage to give notice of 12-months' duration, i.e. specifying April 1, 2014. If the tenant duly applies for a new tenancy, the question of whether the landlord has established his intention will be considered at the trial in, say, December 2007. By that date the landlord may still have insufficiently formed an intention to demolish and reconstruct so as to satisfy ground (f). However, under s.31(2) the court can be invited to consider whether he would have established that ground if he were to get possession not on termination of the current tenancy but on April 1, 2015 (that is to say one year after the date specified in the s.25 notice). If, instead, the landlord had served the shortest possible notice, namely one expressed to expire on October 1, 2007, the court would have been limited to considering the question whether he would have satisfied the ground on a future date, being a date not later than October 1, 2014. By serving the long notice the landlord has, in effect, gained an extra six months for the purposes of s.31(2), Conversely, it would be in the tenant's interests in such circumstances to make a request specifying the earliest possible date. **4–33**

[38] See para.7–290 et seq.

Sub-tenants

4–34 Special considerations arise where the tenancy is one to which the Act applies but the tenant has sub-let parts of the premises on sub-tenancies which are also within the Act. Since, in accordance with normal conveyancing practice, each of those sub-tenancies will have been granted for a term shorter than that of the tenancy (even if only by one day) it necessarily follows that the earliest date upon which the tenant can serve a s.25 notice on the sub-tenants is earlier (even if only by one day) than the earliest date upon which his landlord can serve a s.25 notice on him. Until the tenant receives a s.25 notice he remains "the landlord" of the sub-tenants within the meaning of s.44.[39] Once he has himself been served with a s.25 notice, he ceases to be "the landlord" and is accordingly powerless to serve any s.25 notice on his sub-tenants: his superior landlord may do so if he chooses. The tenant will have to consider carefully the amounts of the present and anticipated rents payable both under his own tenancy and the sub-tenancies before deciding whether or not to serve s.25 notices on his sub-tenants as soon as he is able to do so. If he does so and his landlord subsequently serves him with a s.25 notice, the notices served on the sub-tenants will nonetheless remain valid and the tenant and the sub-tenants will be entitled to apply for new tenancies of their respective holdings. The landlord will be entitled to apply for an interim rent pursuant to s.24A from the earliest date which could have been specified in his s.25 notice.[40] The tenant will certainly be entitled to apply for interim rents from his sub-tenants, if he is still "the landlord" at the date that he makes such application, and could possibly persuade his landlord to apply for interim rents from the sub-tenants if the tenant has ceased to be "the landlord". Whoever makes the application, the sub-rents are payable to the tenant so long as the tenancy continues.[41] In any event, by serving the notices the tenant will at least avoid the position, which would be disastrous, if rents have risen steeply and if the landlord insisted that the tenant take a new tenancy of the whole of the premises (as he is entitled to do under s.32(2)) without serving notices on the sub-tenants. If that happened, the tenant would not be in a position to serve s.25 notices on the sub-tenants until the new tenancy had been granted to him. This might involve a substantial deficit between the rent which he had to pay and that received from sub-tenants for at least six months. It is uncertain whether a tenant in such circumstances could argue successfully that the rent which he should pay to the landlord for that six-month period should be less that it would otherwise be because of the burden of the sub-tenants. Whether vacant possession is to be assumed in fixing the rent under s.34 and the circumstances in which a variable interim rent may be fixed by the court are discussed below.[42]

4–35 For reasons of timing, a landlord may wish to serve s.25 notices on sub-tenants immediately after he serves notice on the tenant, rather than to run the risk of a sub-tenant making a request under s.26 specifying a date inconvenient to the

[39] See para.3–87.

[40] See para.9–12 et seq.

[41] For further discussion of this position, see para.9–04 et seq.

[42] See para.8–120 et seq. (on the issue of vacant possession) and para.9–40 et seq. (on the issue of a variable interim rent).

landlord. Although a landlord can now make an application for renewal or termination the landlord cannot obtain possession earlier than the date of commencement for the new lease specified in the sub-tenants s.26 request.

Example

Suppose a tenancy of 10 years from March 25, 2004 in respect of premises which are now ripe for redevelopment. The landlord as at September 29, 2013 serves a s.25 notice relying on ground (f) specifying March 29, 2014 as the date of termination and makes a termination application on September 30, 2013. The landlord would expect to have that application heard well before March 25, 2014. However, if the premises are sub-let as to part and the landlord fails to serve a s.25 notice on the sub-tenant, the sub-tenant could, by getting in first with his s.26 request, specify September 29, 2014. The landlord will, notwithstanding the fact that he can make a termination application against the sub-tenant immediately after service of a counter-notice, be unable to implement his plans (assuming he succeeds in his termination applications) until, at the earliest, the expiry of the sub-tenancy on September 29, 2014. **4–36**

CHAPTER 5

RESPONSE TO THE NOTICE OR REQUEST

1. TENANT'S COUNTER-NOTICE NO LONGER REQUIRED

Responding to landlord's section 25 notice

It was essential, prior to June 1, 2004, that a tenant who had received a s.25 notice and who wished to apply for a new tenancy should, within two months of the giving of the notice, serve a written response stating that he was not prepared to give up possession—what was sometimes referred to as a "negative counter-notice". This was because s.29(2), in its form prior to June 1, 2004, provided that an application for a new tenancy which was made in consequence of a s.25 notice "shall not be entertained unless the tenant has duly notified the landlord that he will not be willing at the date of termination to give up possession of the property comprised in the tenancy".[1] **5–01**

Requirement for counter-notice repealed

A tenant is not now required to serve a counter-notice in response to a landlord's s.25 notice. Section 25(5), which provided that every s.25 notice should inform the tenant of the need to serve a counter-notice, has been repealed.[2] **5–02**

2. LANDLORD'S COUNTER-NOTICE

Where a tenant has made a request for a new tenancy pursuant to s.26, the landlord may give notice within two months that he will oppose any application to the court for the grant of a new tenancy: s.26(6). The 2003 Order has not removed the requirement for the landlord to serve a counter-notice in response to a tenant's s.26 request if he wishes to oppose renewal. There is one slightly odd omission in the 2003 Order as to the provision of information required to be provided by the landlord in response to the s.26 request. Under the new s.25(8) a **5–03**

---

[1] The subsection was unhappily worded. Although it referred to the landlord being "duly" notified, neither that subsection, nor any other, specifically laid down a time limit within which the counter-notice was to be given. However, it was provided by s.25(5) (since repealed) that every s.25 notice must contain a statement that the tenant was obliged to notify the landlord within two months of the giving of the notice whether or not he was willing to give up possession of the property comprised in the tenancy. Putting the two subsections together, the Court of Appeal in *Chiswell v Griffon* [1975] 1 W.L.R. 1181; [1975] 2 All E.R. 665 CA held that the reference to the landlord being "duly" notified meant that he must be notified within two months of the giving of the s.25 notice.

[2] art.4 of the 2003 Order.

landlord is obliged in his s.25 notice, where he is not opposing renewal, to state his proposals as to the property to be comprised in, the rent for, and other terms of the new tenancy. Interestingly, if the renewal procedure is initiated by the tenant serving a s.26 request and the landlord does not oppose renewal in response to a tenant's s.26 request and so states in his counter-notice under s.26(6), the 2003 Order does not require the counter-notice to contain information similar to that contained in s.25(8). It is difficult to see any good reason for this failure to mirror exactly in the procedure under s.26 the procedure as it would be if commenced under s.25.

To be given by "landlord"

5–04 Any counter-notice must be served by "the landlord", as defined by s.44 (see para.3–87 et seq.). A landlord who subsequently acquires the reversion will be bound by any counter-notice which has been given.

To be given to "tenant"

5–05 The counter-notice must be given to "the tenant" (for the meaning of which, see para.3–101 et seq.).

Form of counter-notice

5–06 Section 26(6) provides that any counter-notice served by the landlord shall state on which of the grounds mentioned in s.30(1) of the Act the landlord will oppose the application. No form of counter-notice is prescribed.

Failure to serve counter-notice

5–07 If the landlord does not serve a counter-notice stating that he will oppose the grant of a new tenancy and on what grounds, he will not be able to oppose the tenant's application.

Positive counter-notice

5–08 There is no provision enabling or requiring a landlord to serve a "positive counter-notice", that is to say one stating that he will not oppose the grant of a new tenancy. It is doubtful whether a landlord would be bound (in the absence of estoppel) if he chose to make such a statement, but changed his mind within the two-month period.[3] The wording of s.26(6) is of some interest in determining the ability of a landlord to make an application for renewal/termination. Section

[3] Compare *Re 14 Grafton Street* [1971] 2 W.L.R. 159; [1971] 2 All E.R. 1 and *Pennycook v Shaws (EAL) Ltd* [2004] Ch. 296 CA, where the rather differently worded provisions of s.25(5) (repealed with effect from June 1, 2004) were under consideration. In those cases it was held that service of a positive counter-notice by a tenant was irrevocable once served.

29A(3) provides that where the tenant has made a request for a new tenancy under s.26, the court shall not entertain an application under s.24(1) which is made before the end of the period of two months beginning with the date of the making of the request, unless the application is made after the landlord has given notice under s.26(6). If the landlord cannot serve a positive counter-notice it would seem that the landlord would have to wait for the two month period to expire before being able to initiate a renewal claim. Thus, tactically, there would appear to be an inherent delay in a landlord being able to "get on" with the tenant's renewal where he does not oppose the same, depending on whether the 1954 Act procedure is triggered by a s.25 notice or a s.26 request. If a s.25 notice not opposing renewal is served, in light of the repeal of the requirement for a tenant to serve a counter-notice, the landlord can now commence his renewal claim immediately after service of the s.25 notice.[4] If a landlord wished to avoid the two-month period, it is conceivable that he could serve a counter-notice under s.26(6) and then immediately serve a renewal claim, informing the tenant that the landlord abandons his opposition.

No provision for withdrawal of counter-notice

There is no provision for the superior landlord to withdraw any counter-notice given to the sub-tenant in response to the s.26 request, though he may be able to make himself competent landlord before any counter-notice is served, in which case he will have the right to serve it himself. Compare the position with regard to withdrawal of s.25 notices (para.7–08 et seq.). **5–09**

[4] See para.6–53 et seq.

CHAPTER 6

APPLICATIONS FOR NEW TENANCIES AND TERMINATION APPLICATIONS

1. ENTITLEMENT TO MAKE APPLICATION

In this Chapter matters which relate to the entitlement to make a claim for a new tenancy or a termination application, such as by whom it is to be made and when it is to be made, are considered. The procedure for making the claim or the termination application, including such matters as the form of the claim, where it is to be made and the evidence to be submitted with it, are dealt with in detail in Ch.14. Under the old regime, only the tenant could make an application to the court for the grant of a new tenancy. Articles 3 and 5 of the 2003 Order[1] amended the provisions of the Act and introduced quite new provisions enabling a landlord also to make an application for renewal or to terminate the tenant's tenancy. This represents one of the most substantial differences between the old regime and the new regime. In essence the amended sections of the Act provide that: **6–01**

(1) the tenant may apply to the court for the grant of a new tenancy[2];
(2) a landlord may apply to the court to have the tenancy renewed[3];
(3) a landlord may apply to the court to terminate the tenancy without renewal.[4]

To avoid the problems which would arise from proceedings initiated by both landlord and tenant, it is provided that neither may make any of these applications if the other has already done so.[5]

Claims for renewal

Tenancy must be one to which Act applies

By virtue of s.24(1), a tenant under a tenancy to which the Act applies may apply to the court for a new tenancy.[6] In order for a valid application to be made it is essential that, at the date the application itself is made, the tenancy is one to **6–02**

[1] art.4 of the 2003 Order amended the provisions as to the requirements for a s.25 notice.
[2] See para.6–03 et seq.
[3] See para.6–07 et seq.
[4] See para.6–13 et seq.
[5] As to priority see fn.21 and para.6–14.
[6] See Ch.1 generally as to the conditions to be fulfilled if the Act is to apply.

which the Act applies. It is to be noted that tenants, whose tenancies are being continued by s.24(3)(a) in circumstances where the tenancy has ceased to be one to which the Act applies, are not entitled to apply for a new tenancy.[7] Nor are tenants who have entered into an agreement with the landlord pursuant to s.38A for the provisions of ss.24 to 28 to be excluded.

The tenant will only be able to pursue an application which he has made if the tenancy continues to be one to which the Act applies up to the date of the hearing.[8] Now that a landlord may make an application for renewal, it is unclear how the landlord's application for renewal is to be disposed of if the tenancy ceases to be one to which the Act applies pending trial and the tenant does not agree to its withdrawal.[9]

By tenants

Generally

6–03 With regard to an application by the tenant:

(1) it may be made at any time by the tenant where the landlord has given notice under s.25;
(2) where the tenant has served a s.26 request, it cannot be made before the end of the period of two months beginning with the date of the making of the request unless the landlord has served a counter-notice to the request, in which case the application can be made at any time after service of the counter-notice: ss.24(1) and 29A(3);
(3) it cannot be made later than the end of "the statutory period", being the date which is no later than the date of termination specified in the landlord's s.25, where served or the date of commencement specified in the tenant's s.26 request, where served: s.29B[10];
(4) it cannot be made by the tenant if the landlord has already made an application for renewal and the application has been served: s.24(2A)[11];
(5) it cannot be made if the landlord has already made an application for termination pursuant to s.29 and the application has been served: s.24(2B)[12];

---

[7] It is a continuing condition of the tenant's rights to protection under the Act that he remains in occupation of the premises for the purposes or partly for the purposes of a business. See *I&H Caplan Ltd v Caplan (No.2)* [1963] 1 W.L.R. 1247; [1963] 2 All E.R. 930 (digested in para.1–46).

[8] See para.2–55.

[9] The tenancy does not determine simply because the tenancy has ceased to be one to which the Act applies: see para.2–66 relating to cessation post the contractual term. The tenant may not be prepared to consent as he may be wishing to take advantage of the operation of s.64, e.g. the tenant may have sub-let at a profit rental. See further para.6–11.

[10] As inserted by art.5 of the 2003 Order. The statutory period may be extended by agreement: s.29B. See further para.6–17 et seq.

[11] As inserted by art.3(2) of the 2003 Order.

[12] As inserted by art.3(2) of the 2003 Order.

(6) the tenant can withdraw the application without the landlord's consent.[13]

No requirement for negative counter-notice to be given by tenant

Prior to June 1, 2004, by the combined effect of s.29(2) and s.25(5), it was provided that where an application was made in consequence of a notice given under s.25 it would not be entertained unless the tenant had served a negative counter-notice within two months of the giving of the s.25 notice.[14] The requirement for service of a counter-notice was repealed with respect to s.25 notices served post June 1, 2004. **6–04**

Where tenant serves a section 26 request

Although there is no provision for service by a tenant of a counter-notice to a landlord's s.25 notice, any application by the tenant for renewal cannot be made until after the expiry of the two-month period for service of a counter-notice by the landlord or the actual service of a counter-notice by the landlord, whichever be the earlier: s.29A(3). An application made exactly two months beginning with the date of the making of the s.26 request will be valid: *EJ Riley Investments Ltd v Eurostile Holdings Ltd*[15] (digested in para.6–06). **6–05**

EJ Riley Investments Ltd v Eurostile Holdings Ltd[16] The landlord served a s.25 notice dated March 22, 1983, on the tenant on March 23, 1983. The tenant made an application for the grant of a new tenancy on May 23, 1983. The county court judge held that the tenant's application was premature. The issue on appeal was whether the tenant's application was "made not less than two months... after the giving of the landlord's notice under section 25 ..." within the meaning of s.29(3) of the Act in its form prior to amendments made by the 2003 Order. It was held that the words "not less than two months" within s.29(3) could not be construed as meaning "more than two months". Applying the corresponding date rule[17] the tenant's application was made on a date which was two months, no more no less, after March 23, 1983, and accordingly the application was not premature. **6–06**

By landlord

Generally

A landlord may apply to the court for a renewal of the tenant's tenancy: s.24(1). As to such an application: **6–07**

---

[13] This follows from the fact that there is no provision to the contrary and as a matter of procedure there is nothing preventing a claimant to a Pt 8 claim from withdrawing the same: see para.14–95 et seq.

[14] See para.5–01 et seq.

[15] [1985] 1 W.L.R. 1139; [1985] 3 All E.R. 181; [1985] 2 E.G.L.R. 124 CA.

[16] [1985] 1 W.L.R. 1139; [1985] 3 All E.R. 181; [1985] 2 E.G.L.R. 124 CA.

[17] See para.3–85.

(1) it may be made at any time by the landlord if the landlord has given notice under s.25 or the tenant has served a request under s.26: s.24(1).[18] The court shall not however entertain an application under s.24(1) which is made before the end of the period of two months beginning with the date of the making of a tenant's s.26 request, unless the application is made after the landlord has given a counter-notice under s.26(6)[19];
(2) it cannot be made later than the end of "the statutory period", being the date which is no later than the date of termination specified in the landlord's s.25 or the date of commencement specified in the tenant's s.26 request: s.29B[20];
(3) it cannot be made by the landlord if the tenant has already made such an application: s.24(2A);
(4) it cannot be made if the landlord has already made an application for termination pursuant to s.29 and the application has been served: s.24(2B)[21];
(5) the landlord cannot withdraw the application without the tenant's consent: s.24(2C);
(6) the tenant may ask the court to dismiss any such application by the landlord if he informs the court that he does not want a new tenancy: s.29(5).

Service of counter notice not required

6–08 Notwithstanding the repeal of the requirement for a tenant to serve a counter-notice to a landlord's s.25 notice,[22] the requirement for the landlord to serve a counter-notice to the tenant's s.26 request if he wishes to oppose renewal remains.[23] The landlord has two months within which to serve the notice but may, of course, serve it at any time within that two-month period. As no application can be made until service of the counter-notice or the period for its service has expired, whichever be the earlier, the landlord can to an extent dictate when proceedings may be issued and ensure that any application he wishes to make gets in first.

6–09 The wording of s.26(6) is of some interest in determining the ability of a landlord to make an application for renewal. Section 29A(3) provides that where the

[18] As amended by art.3(1) of the 2003 Order.

[19] s.29A(3).

[20] s.29A(3). As to the "statutory period" see further para.6–17 et seq.

[21] The order of priority of the applications is determined by reference to the order of service rather than issue. The rules of the CPR provide for service to be effected within four months of issue: see paras 14–56 and 14–65. The period for service is retained by the amendments made to CPR 56 and the Practice Direction to take account of the 2003 order. As noted in para.6–53 et seq. below, the landlord can it seems always get in first having regard to how the provisions of the new legislation operate. Presumably the reference to service here is a reference to service on all of the defendants. Thus, one may have a situation where the claim form for renewal needs to be made against both the immediate landlord and the superior landlord as the interest which the tenant seeks by way of renewal will be for a term longer than the immediate landlord's interest: see para.10–42 et seq. If the claimant has served only one of the two defendants has the application been served for the purposes of s.24(2B)? It has been served but served on only one of the relevant defendants.

[22] See para.5–02 above.

[23] See para.5–03 above.

tenant has made a request for a new tenancy under s.26, the court shall not entertain an application under s.24(1) which is made before the end of the period of two months beginning with the date of the making of the request, unless the application is made after the landlord has given notice under s.26(6). If the landlord cannot serve a positive counter-notice[24] under s.26(6) it would seem that the landlord would have to wait for the two-month period provided for its service to expire before being able to initiate a renewal claim. Thus, tactically, there would appear to be an inherent delay in a landlord being able to "get on" with a renewal where he does not oppose it, depending on whether the 1954 Act procedure is initiated by a s.25 notice or a s.26 request. If a s.25 notice not opposing renewal is served, in light of the repeal of the requirement for a tenant to serve a counter-notice, the landlord can commence his renewal claim immediately after service of the s.25 notice.[25] If a landlord wished to avoid the two-month period before he can issue unopposed renewal proceedings in response to a s.26 request, it is conceivable that he could serve a counter-notice under s.26(6) and then immediately serve a renewal claim, informing the tenant that the landlord abandons his opposition.

Withdrawal of landlord's application for renewal

As noted above the landlord cannot withdraw the application without the consent of the tenant: s.24(2C). The purpose behind this provision is to prevent the landlord withdrawing the claim for renewal at a point in time when the tenant would be otherwise unable to protect himself, e.g. if the landlord were to withdraw the claim after the expiry of the statutory period.[26] **6–10**

It is unclear how the landlord's application for renewal is to be disposed of if the tenancy ceases to be one to which the Act applies pending trial and the tenant does not agree to its withdrawal.[27] There seem to be several possible courses of action: **6–11**

(1) the landlord seeks an order for the application to be dismissed;
(2) the landlord amends the claim to seek a declaration that the tenant is not entitled to a renewal by reason of the cessation of business occupation and issues a CPR Pt 24 claim in respect of it. This appears a rather convoluted way of dealing with the matter.

If the tenant does consent to the withdrawal of the application it is considered that the tenant cannot thereafter, assuming the statutory period has not expired, make a second application himself for renewal, because an ability to make a second application after withdrawal of the landlord's application for renewal does not sit **6–12**

[24] See para.5–08.
[25] See para.6–53.
[26] As to the meaning of "statutory period", see para.6–17 et seq.
[27] The tenancy does not cease simply because the tenancy has ceased to be one to which the Act applies: see para.2–66 et seq., relating to cessation post the contractual term. The tenant may not be prepared to consent as of course he may be wishing to take advantage of the operation of s.64, e.g. the tenant may have sub-let at a huge profit rental. See further para.3–229 et seq.

well with s.64. If the landlord's application for renewal has been withdrawn it has been "finally disposed of" for the purposes of s.64 and the tenant's current tenancy will end in three months and 21 days (the current period for appeal) in accordance with that section. Thus, even if the tenant were to make an application there will come a time, it would seem, when that second renewal application could be struck out as the tenant will, within three months and 21 days of the withdrawal of the landlord's application, cease to have a tenancy which can form the subject matter of a valid application.

Landlord's termination application

6–13 This is dealt with by s.29(2) of the Act. A landlord may apply to the court for an order for the termination of the tenant's current tenancy without the grant of a new tenancy. As to such an application for termination:

(1) It may be made only if the landlord has given notice under s.25 of the 1954 Act that he is opposed to the grant of a new tenancy to the tenant or, if the tenant has made a request for a new tenancy in accordance with s.26 and the landlord has given a counter-notice under s.26(6) opposing renewal: s.29(2).[28]
(2) It cannot be made if either the landlord or the tenant has already made an application for renewal under s.24(1): s.29(3).[29]
(3) The landlord cannot withdraw the application for termination unless the tenant consents[30]: s.29(6).[31]
(4) The application for termination must not be made later than the statutory period: s.29A(1). "The statutory period" is the date of termination specified by a landlord in his s.25 notice or the date of the commencement of the new lease specified by the tenant in his s.26 request: s.29A(2).[32]

Priority of termination application

6–14 As mentioned above a landlord's termination application cannot be made if either the landlord or the tenant has already made an application for renewal under s.24(1): s.29(3). An important difference is to be noted between the wording in

---

[28] The landlord's ability to commence termination proceedings arises only where the landlord is relying on one of the grounds of opposition contained in s.30(1) of the Act: see further para.14–31 et seq. Thus, if the landlord were to allege that the tenant was not entitled to protection at all, e.g. by reason of the cessation of business occupation, this is not covered by the provisions of s.29(2). There is, however, nothing stopping a landlord in these circumstances from issuing proceedings for a declaration that the Act does not apply to the tenancy or opposing an application made by the tenant on the ground that the tenant is not protected by the Act.

[29] The existence of the right to make a termination application does not prevent the landlord from opposing a tenant's application for renewal, for the landlord can, in the tenant's proceedings, oppose the application as he could previously under the regime which operated before June 1, 2004.

[30] The landlord's termination application may be withdrawn only with the consent of the tenant. There is no indication as to what constitutes "consent". There is no requirement for the consent to be in writing although an oral consent is very unlikely in practice.

[31] As to withdrawal see further, para.6–15.

[32] As to the meaning of "statutory period" see para.6–17 et seq.

s.29(3) and s.24(2A)[33] and 24(2B).[34] Nothing is said in s.29(3) about *service* of the earlier application by the tenant for renewal in order for the latter to have priority over the landlord's termination application. Thus, priority as between the tenant's renewal application and the landlord's termination application appears to be determined by the date of the *making* of the application for renewal rather than its service.[35] This leaves open the possibility of the landlord making a termination application at a time when the renewal application had already been made but not served. In these circumstances the tenant's renewal application takes priority and the court would presumably strike out the landlord's termination application.

Withdrawal of termination application: tenant's status

If the landlord withdraws his termination application with the consent of the tenant what is the tenant's status? Section 29(4) provides that where the landlord makes an application for termination and "establishes, to the satisfaction of the court, any of the grounds . . . within s.30 of this Act, the court shall make an order for termination . . .".[36] It then provides that "if not [i.e. the landlord does not so establish] it shall make an order for the grant of a new tenancy and accordingly for termination of the current tenancy immediately before commencement of the new tenancy."[37] It would seem reasonably arguable that where the landlord has withdrawn the termination application he has not satisfied the court of one of the relevant grounds of opposition. However, the difficulty is that there is no mechanism in the withdrawal process for the court to order a new tenancy. It would seem that the most sensible way to proceed would be for the tenant to agree to withdrawal of the landlord's termination application but only on condition that the landlord informs the court that the parties agree that the tenant is to be granted a new tenancy and invites the court to order (1) a withdrawal of the landlord's termination application and (2) directions with respect to the determination by the court of the tenant's new tenancy. **6–15**

Withdrawal of termination application: tenant refuses to agree

If the tenancy ceases to be one to which the Act applies pending the termination application and the tenant refuses to give his consent to the withdrawal of the **6–16**

---

[33] Which provides that: "Neither the tenant nor the landlord may make an application under subsection (1) above if the other has made such an application and the application has been served."

[34] Which provides that: "Neither the tenant nor the landlord may make such an application if the landlord has made an application under section 29(2) of this Act and the application has been served."

[35] The other provisions dealing with priority refer to service. Thus:

(1) a tenant's application for renewal cannot be made if the landlord has already made an application for renewal *and the landlord's application has been served*: s.24(2A);

(2) a tenant's application for renewal cannot be made if the landlord has already made an application for termination pursuant to s.29 *and the application has been served*: s.24(2B);

(3) a landlord's application for renewal cannot be made if the tenant has already made such an application *and the application has been served*: s.24(2A);

(4) a landlord's application for renewal cannot be made if the landlord has made an application for termination pursuant to s.29 *and the application has been served*: s.24(2B).

[36] s.29(4)(a).

[37] s.29(4)(b).

application, it is unclear how the landlord can bring an end to the termination application and ensure that s.29(4)(b) does not apply.[38]

Time for making application for renewal or termination

The statutory period

6–17 An application by the tenant or landlord for renewal under s.24(1) or by the landlord for termination is to be made no later than the end of the "statutory period": s.29A(1). The "statutory period" is the date of termination specified in the landlord's s.25 notice or the date for commencement of the new lease specified in the tenant's s.26 request: s.29A(2). The parties are able to extend the statutory period by which an application may be made for renewal/termination, but any such agreement must be made before the end of the statutory period and any subsequent agreement for extension must be made before the end of the period specified in the current agreement: s.29B(1) and (2).[39] The date of termination/commencement specified in any agreement between the parties pursuant to s.29B is treated as the date of termination/commencement for the purpose of ss.25 and 26 respectively: s.29B(4).

6–18 Nothing is said in s.29B as to the form in which an agreement for an extension is to be made. However, by s.69(2) of the Act it is provided that "References in this Act to an agreement between the landlord and the tenant (except in... subsections (1) and (2) of section 38 thereof) shall be construed as references to an agreement in writing between them." There is some debate as to whether an agreement confirmed only in emails would be sufficient and that the prudent course is to ensure that any agreement is recorded in a letter.[40] There is much to be said for this course of action. Thus, if dictating a letter over the telephone to

---

[38] See also the discussion relating to the tenant's refusal to consent to a withdrawal of the landlord's renewal application: para.6–10 et seq.

[39] Occasionally agreements were, in accordance with a suggestion first made in (1981) 78 L.S.G. 853, entered into between landlord and tenant under the old regime in place before June 1, 2004 to extend the four-month time limit contained within the then provisions of s.29(3) for making an application for a new tenancy, although it was not clear how widespread that practice was. There was no doubt that such an agreement was effective for that purpose—on the basis of the decision of the House of Lords in *Kammins Ballrooms v Zenith Investments* [1971] A.C. 850 HL (digested in para.3–245). However, where such an agreement had been entered into there was a danger that negotiations may have been so prolonged that no application had been made by the date specified in the relevant s.25 notice or s.26 request, as the case may be. Once that date had passed without an application having been made, the tenancy determined. Once the tenancy had determined, the tenant ceased to be entitled to make an application for a new tenancy pursuant to s.24(1), because such an application could only be made by the tenant under such a tenancy: see *Meah v Sector Properties Limited* [1974] 1 W.L.R. 547; [1974] 1 All E.R. 1074 CA (digested in para.6–25). It is considered that a similar problem arises in connection with applications made after the expiry of the statutory period. See para.6–21.

[40] Hunter, *Business Tenancies, The Guide to the New Law*, 1st edn (London: The Law Society, 2004), p.15.

the secretary of the intended recipient is not "written notification"[41] an email may equally well not constitute writing for the purposes of the Act.[42]

The effect of an extension, as noted above, is to make the extended date the date on which the tenancy is to be treated as terminating in accordance with the landlord's s.25 notice or the tenant's s.26 request as the case may be: s.29B(4). By s.31(2) of the Act,[43] if the court is of the view that the landlord would establish any of the grounds under para.(d), (e) and (f) of s.30(1) of the Act if the date of termination specified in the landlord's s.25 notice or tenant's s.26 request, as the case may be, had been such later date as the court may declare, being a date which is not more than a year from the date of termination/commencement so specified, the tenant's current tenancy shall continue until the date so determined by the court but shall not be one to which the Act applies. It would seem that in calculating the date which is 12 months from the date of termination/commencement specified, one starts from the extended date under s.29B. **6–19**

Premature applications

The only occasion under the new regime on which an application for renewal may be made prematurely is if it is made before service of a landlord's counter-notice in response to a tenant's s.26 request contrary to the provisions of s.29A(3).[44] Under the law as it stood prior to June 1, 2004, it was decided by the House of Lords in *Kammins Ballrooms v Zenith Investments*[45] (digested in para.3–245) that a failure to observe the time limit contained within s.29(3) (in its then form[46]) was an irregularity which could be waived by the landlord. It was subsequently decided by the Court of Appeal in *Zenith Investments v Kammins Ballrooms*[47] (digested in para.6–22) that, even though the application in that case was irregular because it had been made prematurely and even though the **6–20**

---

[41] See *Tennaro v Majorarch* [2003] EWHC 2061 (Ch), Neuberger J. holding that the dictation by the vendor's solicitor to the secretary of the purchaser's solicitors of the fact that a transfer of the freehold had been completed was not "written notification" of the transfer having been completed as required by the terms of the parties' contract. See also *Holwell Securities Ltd v Hughes* [1974] 1 W.L.R. 155, where Russell L.J. said at 159E–159F: "A person does not give notice in writing to another person by sitting down and writing it out and then telephoning to that other and saying 'Listen to what I have just written'."

[42] See, however, para.3–66.

[43] As to these provisions, see para.7–290 et seq.

[44] s.29A(3) provides that "Where the tenant has made a request for a new tenancy under section 26 of this Act, the court shall not entertain an application under s.24(1) of this Act which is made before the end of the period of two months beginning with the date of the making of the request, unless the application is made after the landlord has given a notice under s.26(6) of this Act." With regards to termination applications the Act provides that a landlord simply cannot make such an application unless he has, where the tenant has served a s.26 request, given a counter-notice under s.26(6): s.29(2)(b). If the landlord has served a s.25 notice he may make a termination application at any time so long as it is not made after the expiry of the statutory period: s.29A(1)(b).

[45] [1971] A.C. 850 HL.

[46] Which provided that "No application under subsection (1) of section 24 of this Act shall be entertained unless it is made not less than two nor more than four months after the giving of the landlord's notice under section s.25 of this Act or, as the case may be, after the making of the tenant's request for a new tenancy."

[47] [1971] 1 W.L.R. 1751; [1971] 3 All E.R. 1281 CA.

landlords had not in fact waived that irregularity, it was nonetheless an "application" within the meaning of s.24(1), with the result that the current tenancy was continued until three months after the dismissal by the House of Lords of the irregular application.[48] It is considered that the *Kammins* decision applies to the provisions of s.29A(3). There is no material difference between s.29(3) in its pre-June 1, 2004 form, where the words used were that "No application [for renewal] shall be entertained, unless [made within the specified time limits]" and s.29A(3) of the current Act which provides that "the court shall not entertain an application [for renewal] which is made before [the specified time limit]."

Late applications[49]

6–21 Under the provisions of s.29(3), in their form before June 1, 2004, the tenant's application for renewal had to be made no later than the period of four months after the service of the landlord's s.25 notice or the tenant's s.26 request. It was provided that "No application . . . shall be entertained . . ." unless made before the expiry of the four-month period the tenant had made the appropriate application. The court, it was said, had no jurisdiction to extend the time limit without the consent of the landlord: *Hodgson v Armstrong*[50] (digested in para.6–45). The Act now makes express provision for an agreement to extend the "statutory period": s.29B. However, as noted above, the House of Lords in *Kammins Ballrooms v Zenith Investments*[51] (digested in para.3–245) held that a failure to observe the time limit contained within s.29(3) (in its then form[52]) was an irregularity which could be waived by the landlord. Although the wording of s.29A(3) is not dissimilar to that of s.29(3),[53] the difficulty which a tenant faces in relying on a waiver argument to validate an application made after the statutory period or any extension thereof agreed in accordance with s.29B, is that if no application has been made prior to the expiry of that period the tenant's tenancy will simply have come to an end, for the statutory period is the date of termination of the tenant's tenancy. Once the statutory period or any extended period has passed without an application having been made, the tenancy determines.[54] Once the tenancy has determined, the tenant ceases to be entitled to make an application for a new

[48] If a party does not object to the prematurity of the application he may be estopped from seeking to strike it out on that basis. However, the service of an answer which included a claim for interim rent did not amount to a waiver of the premature application in *Stevens & Cutting v Anderson* [1990] 1 E.G.L.R. 95 CA (digested in para.3–246). Contrast *Bristol Cars Ltd v RKH Hotels Ltd* (digested in para.3–250), where the making of an application for interim rent was held to constitute a waiver of a defect in the tenant's s.26 request.

[49] This particular problem is likely to arise only in connection with a tenant's application. It is difficult to see why a landlord would make an application after the expiry of the statutory period as he has no interest in doing so, for the statutory period equates to the date of termin-ation of the tenant's current tenancy specified in the s.25 notice or the s.26 request. Thus, a tenant who has not made an application by that date has no tenancy in respect of which the tenant can make an application.

[50] [1967] 2 Q.B. 299 CA.

[51] [1970] A.C. 850 HL.

[52] See fn.46 above.

[53] See para.6–20 above.

[54] See paras 3–41 and 3–42.

tenancy pursuant to s.24(1), because such an application may only be made by the tenant under such a tenancy—see *Meah v Sector Properties Ltd*[55] (digested in para.6–25).

Zenith Investments (Torquay) Ltd v Kammins Ballrooms Co Ltd (No.2)[56] The tenant, having made a request for a new tenancy pursuant to s.26, applied for a new tenancy less than two months after the date of request. By virtue of s.29(3), an application made prematurely (or late) "shall not be entertained by the Court". The House of Lords held in *Kammins v Zenith*[57] (digested in para.3–245) that the requirements of s.29(3) were procedural only and were thus capable of being waived but that, on the facts, the landlord had not waived them. The landlord claimed mesne profits in respect of the period from April 12, 1969 (the date specified in the tenant's request), to September 20, 1970, when the tenant yielded up possession. The tenant contended that it was liable only to pay rent at the rate reserved under the tenancy. It was held that the "application" referred to in s.64 included an application such as the present which was vulnerable to a particular defence (i.e. that it was premature), but which the other party could, by waiver, render invulnerable to that defence. It was incorrect in this context to refer to a "valid application" as opposed to an "invalid application". It is not possible to say that a bona fide application which fails because the opposing party raises a successful defence is not an application under the Act. **6–22**

Only one application for renewal may be made

It must inevitably be the case that a tenant may only make one application for a new tenancy. If it were otherwise there would be the possibility of two applications being "finally disposed of" on different dates with the result that s.64 would produce two conflicting dates for the termination of the current tenancy. Since the Court of Appeal has ruled (in *Zenith Investments v Kammins Ballrooms*[58] (digested in para.6–22)) that a premature application constitutes an "application" for the purposes of ss.24 and 64, the same sort of conflict would arise if a second application at a later date were entitled to be made. The machinery is only workable upon the basis that only one valid application may be made. It may therefore be that, even if the tenants in *Kammins Ballrooms v Zenith Investments*[59] (digested in para.3–245) had discovered their mistake in making a premature application before the final date upon which an application could have been made, they would have been unable to remedy that position by making a **6–23**

---

[55] [1974] 1 W.L.R. 547; [1974] 1 All E.R. 1074 CA. There, an application for a new tenancy was made almost three years out of time and long after the applicant had ceased to be a tenant. The Court of Appeal struck out the application and Megaw L.J. further stated that it was not an application which had the effect, within the principle of *Zenith Investments v Kammins Ballrooms* [1971] 1 W.L.R. 1751; [1971] 3 All E.R. 1281 (digested in para.6–22), of continuing the tenancy pursuant to s.64. The distinction between the *Zenith Investments v Kammins Ballrooms* case and that of *Meah v Sector Properties Ltd* is that in the latter case the person who purported to make the application was not even a tenant when it was made.

[56] [1971] 1 W.L.R. 1751; [1971] 3 All E.R. 1281.

[57] [1971] A.C. 850 HL

[58] [1971] 1 W.L.R. 1751; [1971] 3 All E.R. 1281.

[59] [1971] A.C. 850 HL.

second valid application. However, it is to be noted that Lord Reid in *Kammins Ballrooms v Zenith Investments*[60] appears to have been of the view that if the mistake as to the prematurity of the application had come to the tenant's attention the tenant could have made a fresh application within the time permitted by s.29.[61]

2. REQUIREMENTS OF A VALID APPLICATION

Tenant's application for renewal

Must have the status of tenant

6–24 In order to be valid an application must be made by a tenant who is entitled to make it; that is to say by the person or persons in whom is vested a tenancy to which the Act applies: s.24(1).[62] No application can, therefore, be made after the date specified in the s.26 request for the tenant has ceased to have any proprietorial interest in the premises which form the subject of the application: *Meah v Sector Properties Ltd*.[63]

6–25 ***Meah v Sector Properties Ltd***[64] The tenant had served a s.26 request determining its tenancy on June 24, 1971 but failed to make any application for a new tenancy. Long after that date the landlord obtained an order for possession and after that order had been made, but before it was enforced, the tenant purported to make an application for a new tenancy based on its s.26 request. The landlord applied to strike out the tenant's application but this was refused by the judge who held that it would be open to the tenant to argue that the landlord had waived the time limits in s.29(3). The Court of Appeal held that the application should be struck out because the tenant's tenancy had determined on the date specified in his s.26 request, so that at the date of his application to the court he had ceased to be the tenant of the property and therefore had no standing under s.24(1) to apply for a new tenancy. His purported application therefore properly fell to be struck out.

Trustees/joint tenants

6–26 Where a tenancy is held upon trust the proper persons to make the application are the trustees, not the beneficiaries, even if it is intended to rely upon the provisions

[60] [1971] A.C. 850. Lord Reid said that the landlord's solicitors "had been advised by counsel to take a preliminary abjuration that the appellants' application was invalid as having been made less than two months after the making of their request for a new tenancy. By that time it was too late to remedy this by making a new application." See also Lord Morris at 861: "It was then too late for the tenants to make a new application within the four months' period. They could so easily have done so within that period if they had been made aware that it was going to be said that their speed in going to court had precluded the court from hearing them."

[61] [1971] A.C. 850 at 858.

[62] For the meaning of "tenant" see also paras 3–101 and 3–138 et seq.

[63] [1974] 1 W.L.R. 547.

[64] [1974] 1 W.L.R. 547.

of s.41(1), which deem occupation and/or carrying on of a business by the beneficiaries to be the occupation and/or carrying on of a business by the tenant: *Jacobs v Chaudhuri*[65] (digested in para.6–28). The possible anomaly arising out of s.41(1)(c) has already been discussed. The literal construction of that subsection would appear to lead to the result that if A and B were the original trustees, but the tenancy was subsequently assigned to new trustees C and D, any application for a new tenancy would have to be made by A and B, not by C and D. As the authors have already stated in that discussion, they doubt whether such a construction would be accepted by the court.[66] In *Hackney African Organisation v London Borough of Hackney*,[67] the lease was held by four trustees. The application was made in the name of "the Hackney African Organisation (Dr. A.A. Seray-Wurie, Chairman and Trustee)" and para.1 of the document, denoting the person applying, was named as "Adu Aezick Seray-Wurie, Chairman and Trustee of the Hackney African Organisation". The particulars to the claim described the tenant, naming the four original trustees, to whom the grant had been made, and the current trustees. The claim was signed only by the chairman. It was held that the claim was valid and it was unnecessary to join the other three current trustees to the proceedings.

Where the tenancy is vested in joint tenants,[68] any application for a new tenancy must normally be made by both of them: *Jacobs v Chaudhuri*[69] (digested in para.6–28). **6–27**

Jacobs v Chaudhuri[70] The landlord demised a theatre to the applicant and his partner as joint tenants. They carried on business in partnership. Upon dissolution of the partnership one of the tenants (the applicant) bought out the other so that he had the sole beneficial interest in the business carried on in the premises. The applicant made an originating application in his own name. It was held that there was no jurisdiction to grant a new tenancy to the applicant as one of two or more joint tenants was not "the tenant" within the meaning of s.24(1). (Note, however, the statutory amendment discussed below in para.6–31, which renders this decision no longer good law on its facts.) **6–28**

Trustee unwilling to join in in making application

A potential problem occurs if one of the trustees is unwilling to join in the making of the application. Trustees must act together. The remedy against a recalcitrant co-trustee is to seek an interim injunction requiring him to co-operate in **6–29**

65 [1968] 2 W.L.R. 1098; [1968] 2 All E.R. 124 CA.

66 In *Hackney African Organisation v London Borough of Hackney* [1999] L. & T.R. 117 CA, Simon Brown L.J. said that the words in s.41(1)(c) which provide that "A change in the persons of the trustees shall not be treated as a change in the person of the tenant" did not dispense with the need for trustees holding a lease jointly to act together in seeking a renewal of that lease.

67 [1999] L. & T.R. 117 CA.

68 A trust of land will arise whether the joint tenants held the beneficial interest jointly or in common (as is presumed in the case of partners): see Megarry and Wade, *The Law of Real Property*, 8th edn (London: Sweet & Maxwell), paras 13–051—13–054.

69 [1968] 2 Q.B. 470.

70 [1968] 2 Q.B. 470.

protecting the right of renewal. The Court of Appeal has held that, although the court had jurisdiction to make an order at the suit of a trustee compelling his co-trustee to join him in signing a counter-notice to a landlord's s.25 notice[71] and in applying to the court for a new tenancy, whether to grant such an order was a matter for the discretion of the court depending on a consideration of all the circumstances: *Harris v Black*[72] (digested in para.6–30).

6–30 ***Harris v Black***[73] The plaintiff and defendant were joint tenants of business premises, which they held as trustees for themselves on the statutory trusts imposed by s.35 of the Law of Property Act 1925. They had previously been partners in a firm of solicitors but, due to disputes between them, the partnership had been dissolved and they had continued to carry on independent practices in separate parts of the premises. The landlord served a s.25 notice addressed to the plaintiff and defendant. The plaintiff wished to serve a counter-notice and to make an application for a new tenancy. The defendant refused to sign the counter-notice or to join with the plaintiff in making the application. The plaintiff sought an interlocutory mandatory order directing him to do so. The trustee did not hold the business tenancy on trust for other beneficiaries. It appeared that the defendant had a larger beneficial interest in the property than the plaintiff; the parties had been at loggerheads; the defendant was unwilling to incur the financial and other commitments which were involved in a new lease; and no special circumstances existed, e.g. relating to the particular terms on which the partnership had been dissolved. In those circumstances the order would not be granted.

Partnerships and section 41A

6–31 An exception to the rule that the application must be made by the "tenant" is created by s.41A, which was introduced by the Law of Property Act 1969, to reverse the decision in *Jacobs v Chaudhuri*[74] (digested in para.6–28). In order for s.41A to apply, the following conditions must be fulfilled:

(1) there must be a tenancy which is held jointly by two or more persons;
(2) the property comprised in the tenancy must be or include premises occupied for the purposes of a business;
(3) that business (or some other business) must at some time during the existence of the tenancy have been carried on in partnership by all the persons who were then the joint tenants (alone or with others) and the tenancy must at that time have been a partnership asset;

[71] At a time when service by a tenant of a counter-notice to the landlord's s.25 notice was required.
[72] (1983) 46 P. & C.R. 366 CA. See also *Cork v Cork* [1997] 1 E.G.L.R. 5, where an interim injunction was granted against an agricultural joint tenant requiring him to join with his co-tenant to sign a counter-notice under s.26(1) of the Agricultural Holdings Act 1986 in response to the landlord's notice to quit.
[73] (1983) 46 P. & C.R. 366 CA.
[74] [1968] 2 Q.B. 470 CA.

(4) the business (that is to say the business for the purposes of which the property is now occupied) must now be carried on by one or some of the original joint tenants (not necessarily in partnership). These are defined as "the business tenant";
(5) none of the other original joint tenants must now be in occupation in right of the tenancy, carrying on his own business.

It is to be noted that whereas conditions (1), (2), (4) and (5) relate to the position at the end of the current tenancy, condition (3) is one which is to be fulfilled at some time during the current tenancy. These complex provisions are best illustrated by an example.

Example Let us suppose that a tenancy of office premises was granted in 2000 to A, B and C, who were in partnership together with D as chartered accountants. Provided that the tenancy was held as partnership property the condition under (3) above is fulfilled. In 2005, A leaves the partnership and sets up business elsewhere, but the tenancy remains vested in A, B and C. In 2006, C and D dissolve the partnership with B and join A in his new business. B alone remains in occupation of the offices, but ceases to be a chartered accountant and becomes a management consultant. B will be able to rely upon s.41A because the tenancy is still held by joint tenants, namely A, B and C, and B is one of those joint tenants although he is no longer in partnership with anybody and is carrying on a different business from that carried on by the former partnership. In this example, therefore, it is B who is "the business tenant" within the meaning of s.41A(2). Accordingly, B can, without the concurrence of the other joint tenants make a s.26 request and give a notice under s.27(1) or (2)—see s.41A(3) which requires that such request or notice must state that it is given by virtue of s.41A and set out all the relevant facts. Further, the landlord is entitled (but not bound) to address his s.25 notice to B alone rather than to A, B and C: s.41A(4). Any application for a new tenancy may be made by B alone, instead of being made by A, B and C. Where an application is made by B alone, all references in the Act to "the tenant" include references to him alone. It is only B who is liable for the payment of rent and discharge of other obligations under the current tenancy for any rental period beginning after the date specified in the s.25 notice or s.26 request. **6–32**

It is provided by s.41A(6) that the court may impose conditions as to guarantors, sureties or otherwise as appears equitable, having regard to the fact that not all the joint tenants will be tenants under the new tenancy. The court's general power to include a term that a guarantor be provided is covered later in this work.[75] **6–33**

Controlling interests in companies

It has been seen[76] that the occupation or the carrying on of a business by a company in which the tenant has a controlling interest, or where the tenant is a company, by a person with a controlling interest in the company, is treated as the equivalent to the occupation or, as the case may be, the carrying on of a business **6–34**

[75] See para.8–69 et seq.
[76] See para.1–86 et seq.

by the tenant.[77] These provisions do not, however, substitute the company or the person with the controlling interest, as the case may be, as the appropriate claimant for the renewal. The application must in circumstances where these provisions apply still be made by the company that constitutes the tenant at law.

"Landlord" to be defendant to tenant's application

6–35 In order to be valid, an application must name as defendant the person who is, at the date the application is made, the "landlord" as defined by the Act.[78] For the procedure where the landlord has died and his interest is vested in his personal representative, see CPR Pt 19 r.8.

Landlord's application for renewal or termination

"Landlord" is claimant

6–36 The person who is the competent landlord at the making of the application is to be named as the claimant. This will usually be the person in whom the reversion immediately expectant upon determination of the tenant's lease is vested. It may not be.[79]

"Tenant" to be defendant

6–37 The person who would otherwise constitute the claimant if an application were made by the tenant would ordinarily be the defendant to any application for renewal or termination made by the landlord.[80]

Partnerships and section 41A

6–38 Although some amendment has been made to s.41A by the terms of the 2003 Order[81] a landlord who issues an application for renewal or termination cannot name as defendant only those persons that constitute for the purpose of s.41A the "business tenants".[82] Thus, a landlord must name all those persons who constitute the tenant whether or not the partnership has been dissolved and whether or not there may only be one person carrying on business in his own right who would constitute the "business tenant" for the purposes of s.41A.

---

[77] s.23(1A).

[78] See para.3–87.

[79] As to the meaning of "competent landlord" see para.3–87.

[80] The reader is thus referred to the discussion concerning who is the "tenant" in paras 3–101 and 3–138 et seq. and para.6–24 et seq.

[81] So as to provide that the new tenancy be granted only to the business tenants within the meaning of s.41A or to them jointly with others: s.41A(6).

[82] s.41A(5) refers to "an application under section 24(1) of this Act for a new tenancy may, instead of being made by all of the joint tenants, *be made by the business tenants* alone . . ."

3. Form of application

Renewal

The form of the claim form to be used to make the application for a new tenancy is prescribed. It is provided that the claimant must use the Pt 8 procedure.[83] The claim form must contain the particulars provided by the rules.[84] In *Williams v Hillcroft Garage*,[85] it was held that a failure to comply with the requirement to give certain particulars in the application did not render it a nullity, so as to justify it being struck out. Presumably, an intended application may be issued in a form which is so defective as to make it difficult to recognise it as being an application made under s.24 and in such a case the court might be justified in striking it out. A more detailed discussion of the claim form and its contents is contained in Ch.14.[86] **6–39**

However, where the tenant makes an application for a new tenancy where the grant of the tenancy is opposed, the claimant must use the Pt 7 procedure as modified by CPR 56 and the Practice Direction thereto. This is slightly odd as the tenant doesn't know at the date of issue that the landlord will definitely oppose. The landlord may well in his defence to the Pt 7 claim abandon the opposition. **6–40**

Termination application

The form of the claim form to be used to make the termination application is prescribed. It is provided that the claimant must use the Pt 7 procedure.[87] The claim form must contain the particulars provided by the rules.[88] **6–41**

4. Making of application

When made

In order to be valid, an application must be "made" within the prescribed time.[89] There is little guidance as to what constitutes the making of an application. Clearly, if an appropriate document is received by the court, together with the appropriate fee, and is then stamped and issued by that court, an application will **6–42**

[83] CPR r.56.3(3) and PD 56, para.2.1.

[84] PD 56 paras 3.4 (all cases), 3.5 (where the tenant is making the claim) and 3.7 (where the landlord is making the claim). Detailed consideration of the terms of the claim form is given in para.14–20 et seq.

[85] (1971) 115 S.J. 127; (1971) 22 P. & C.R. 402 CA. Although this decision was prior to the coming into force of CPR Pt 56 and the Practice Direction thereto (being October 15, 2001) and previously there was, strictly speaking, no prescribed form of application, it was provided by Ord.97 r.6 of the Rules of the Supreme Court (in relation to applications made in the High Court) and by Ord.43 r.6 of the County Court Rules 1981 (in relation to an application made to the county court) that any application under s.24 should contain certain particulars. See also paras 14–24 and 14–25.

[86] See para.14–20 et seq.

[87] CPR r.56.3(4) and PD 56 para.2.1A.

[88] PD 56, paras 3.4 and.3.9. See further para.14–31 et seq.

[89] As to the time within which an application must be made, see para.6–17 et seq.

have been "made".[90] If the applicant fails to tender the correct fee it has, nevertheless, been held that the application was "made" when received by the court: *Phillips & Sons Ltd v Milne*[91] (digested in para.6–44). Where the time fixed for making the application expires on a day on which the court office is closed,[92] and for that reason the application cannot be issued on that day, the application is in time if the application is filed on the next day on which it is open: *Hodgson v Armstrong*[93] (digested in para.6–45). The court so concluded by reference to general principle namely, that where a statute prescribed a period within which an act was to be done and the act was one which could only be done on the day on which the court offices were closed for the whole of the last day of the prescribed period, the period will be extended until the next day on which the court offices were open. The decision was not dependent upon the CCRs which were then applicable, albeit they formed a second reason for the decision. The decision in *Hodgson v Armstrong* and the general principle referred to has been approved and followed in *Pritam Kaur v S Russell & Sons Ltd*[94] and *Bannister v SGB Plc*.[95] There is nothing in the CPR that suggests that the general principle set out in *Hodgson v Armstrong* is inapplicable under CPR (see CPR r.2.8(5)). In *R. v Gravesend County Court Ex p. Patchett*[96] it was held that the application[97] (which was a landlord's claim for an interim rent) is made only when some positive act or process is performed by the court. Thus, where the application sat at the court office without being issued, albeit as a result of an error of the court, the application for an interim rent had not been made and the court had no jurisdiction to backdate the application. It is considered that this decision is

[90] By CPR r.7.2 it is provided: "(1) Proceedings are started when the court issues a Claim Form at the request of the Claimant.

(2) A Claim Form is issued on the date entered on the form by the court."

CPR Pt 8 PD8A provides (para.4.1) that "Part 7 and Practice Direction 7A contain a number of rules and directions applicable to all claims, including those to which Part 8 applies. Those rules and directions should be applied where appropriate". CPR r.2.6 requires the court seal on issue of the claim form. In the *White Book* notes to CPR r.2.6.1 it is stated "a seal on a document indicates that it has been issued by the Court". The Pt 8 claim form to the CPR does make provision for a seal. In the Glossary to the CPR the definition of "seal" provides: "a seal is a mark which the Court puts on a document to indicate that the document has been issued by the Court".

It is to be noted that the 1954 Act does not require the claim to have been "issued", simply that it is made.

[91] (1962) 106 S.J. 731 CC.

[92] If the office is closed because the applicant has arrived after closing hours (i.e. the day is not a bank holiday or other dies non) it has been held in the context of a claim under s.113 of the Planning and Compulsory Purchase Act 2004 that merely putting the application through the letter box of the court did not constitute the making of an application: *Barker v Hambleton DC* [2011] EWHC 1707 (Admin).

[93] [1967] 2 Q.B. 299 CA.

[94] [1973] 2 W.L.R. 147; [1973] 1 All E.R. 617 CA.

[95] [1997] 4 All E.R. 129; See also *Aadan v Brent LBC* (2000) 32 H.L.R. 848 CA (21-day period for appealing decision under the Housing Act 1996 expired on a Saturday. Appeal filed on the following Monday held to be within time). The general principle was expressly approved by Lord Neuberger in *Mucelli v Albania* [2009] UKHL 2; [2009] 1 W.L.R. 276 at [83–84] (a case dealing with time limits for an appeal to the High Court against an extradition order).

[96] [1993] 2 E.G.L.R. 125 QBD.

[97] Which was made by the landlord's solicitors by post.

questionable in light of the Court of Appeal decision in *Aly v Aly*,[98] which decided that where the applicant has done everything that is required of him, the application is made when received by the court office and not when the process is subsequently issued by the court.[99]

R. v Gravesend County Court Ex p. Patchett[100] The landlord, having served a s.25 notice terminating the tenant's tenancy with effect from December 9, 1989, wrote to the county court (on February 6, 1990) in which the tenant had issued an originating application for a new tenancy, enclosing an application (being an application in the course of proceedings) for an interim rent. The application was not dealt with by the court. It was not issued and no notice was given to the tenant. It was not until some time in August 1990 that the application was dated and issued by the court. The court, at the request of the landlord's solicitors, backdated the application to February 6, 1990. It was held that the court had no jurisdiction to backdate the application and that it could not be said to have been made until the court took steps to issue it in August 1990. **6–43**

Phillips & Sons Ltd v Milne[101] On February 7, 1962, the tenant's solicitors sent to the registrar of the county court an originating application accompanied by a fee of £2. The court received it on the next day, but did not issue it because the fee was insufficient. The tenant's solicitors were informed of this and sent the balance of the fee, but failed to identify the matter to which it related. When this was rectified, the application was issued, outside the four-month period provided by s.29(3). The county court judge held the application had been "made" when it was received by the court, notwithstanding the insufficiency of the fee, and was thus valid. **6–44**

Hodgson v Armstrong[102] The four-month period for applying for a new tenancy under s.29(3) would ordinarily have expired on April 19, 1965. In fact, the county court was closed for Easter from April 15 until it reopened on April 20. Accordingly, the tenant's solicitor found the county court office closed when **6–45**

---

98 (1983) 128 S.J. 65; (1984) 81 L.S.G. 283 CA. This decision would not appear to have been referred to the court in *R. v Gravesend County Court Ex p. Patchett*. In *Aly v Aly* an application by post was made pursuant to a Queen's Bench practice direction, which included a statement that the application would be treated as having been made "at the date and time of the actual receipt of the requisite documents in the Central Office" (see *Practice Direction* [1976] 2 All E.R. 312 at 314; [1976] 1 W.L.R. 489 at 490). The documents arrived on September 28, which would have been in time, but the summons was not stamped for issue until October 4, which was too late. The Court of Appeal decided that the application must be taken to have been made when it arrived in the office and not when the summons was issued. In getting the documents to the court by September 28, the applicant had done all that was required of him. It was said that he should not be penalised because the court did not stamp his summons until some days later.

99 Although it may be the case that a distinction should be made between postal applications and personal applications, in the case of personal applications it has been said that they must actually be issued in order to be considered to have been made within time, if the staff are able to issue the application of everyone who has got into the office or into the queue waiting to get in before the designated closing time: *Kurz v Stella Musical Veranstaltungs* [1992] 1 All E.R. 630, per Hoffmann J.

100 [1993] 2 E.G.L.R. 125 QBD.

101 (1962) 106 S.J. 731 CC.

102 [1967] 2 Q.B. 299 CA.

he chose to issue the application on April 15. On that day he posted it to the county court. The post office had been instructed by the county court to hold all mail over the period of closure, so that letter was not delivered until April 20. The Court of Appeal held that since the county court had, by its instructions, constituted the post office its agents to keep mail on its behalf, the application was duly "made" on April 17. By virtue of the CCR then in force (see now CPR r.2.8(5)) where the last day for making an application falls on the day when the court office is closed, the application is made in time if made on the next day the office is open.

Claim made in wrong court

6–46 A claim (whether for renewal or a termination application) should normally be brought in the county court.[103] It is only exceptional circumstances which justify issuing in the High Court.[104] Although a county court is held for a particular district, the jurisdiction is a general one. Thus, if a claim for a new tenancy is made to a county court in the wrong district in time but forwarded (by that court) to the county court in the correct district so as to arrive out of time it is, nevertheless, valid as having been made in time: *Sharma v Knight*.[105]

Whether application is in the nature of an offer

6–47 An interesting point was raised (but not decided) in *Lovely and Orchard Services v Daejan Investments Ltd*[106] where the tenant in his application proposed a rent which he subsequently decided was too high. Without amending his application, he put in evidence supporting a lower figure. The landlord promptly purported to "accept" the "offer" to pay rent at the higher figure. The court declined to say one way or the other whether the proposal in the application was an offer capable of acceptance in this way, but the existence of the argument should be noted and a cautious approach should therefore be adopted in framing the terms of the application. That said, any "acceptance" of the terms as expressed in the tenant's application is unlikely to give rise to a binding contract for a new lease in light of

---

[103] PD 56 para.2.2. See further para.14–06.

[104] PD 56 para.2.2. See also para.14–03.

[105] [1986] 1 W.L.R. 757 (pre-CPR) CA. See also *St Giles Hotel Ltd v Microworld Technology Ltd* [1997] 2 E.G.L.R. 105 where an application for an order excluding the tenancy from the provisions of ss.24–28 was made in the wrong court, it was said that the jurisdiction conferred by the County Courts Act 1984 is conferred on the county court and following *Faulkner v Love* [1977] 2 W.L.R. 3477; [1977] 1 All E.R. 791 CA, an order made by the wrong county court was not a nullity but merely an irregularity. Millet L.J. said "... where no objection to the jurisdiction of the court is made at the time and the court not noticing the defect proceeds to make an order, that order is not only valid as made within the jurisdiction, but also should not be taken as irregular since the court ought to be treated as having impli-citly ordered the proceedings to continue in the court in which they were commenced."

[106] [1978] 1 E.G.L.R. 44.

the provisions of s.2 of the Law of Property (Miscellaneous Provisions) Act 1989.[107] But such an acceptance may be an "agreement" for the purpose of ss.32 to 35 of the Act.[108]

Lovely and Orchard Services v Daejan Investments Ltd[109] The tenant issued proceedings for a new tenancy by an originating summons dated August 7, 1975, which contained the following paragraph: **6–48**

> "The Plaintiff's proposals for a new tenancy are 1. Period: 15 years from the date of termination of the current tenancy; 2. Rent: £27.500 p.a. with rent reviews every five years. 3. Other terms as in the [current tenancy]."

In May 1976 the tenant filed another affidavit decreasing its proposal to £15,300 per annum. On February 23, 1977, the landlord's solicitors wrote to the tenant's solicitors, stating that they accepted the "offer" contained in the originating summons dated August 7, 1975, "namely to take a lease of [the premises] for a period of 15 years from 14th October, 1975, at a rent of £27,000 per annum with rent reviews and otherwise on the terms as in the [current tenancy]". It was held that, assuming, without deciding, that the originating summons contained an offer which was capable of acceptance, it was to be construed as an offer to take a lease of 15 years from the end of the current tenancy as determined by s.64, not an offer to take a lease of 15 years from October 14, 1975 (the date specified in the s.25 notice). Accordingly, the landlord's solicitors' letter of February 23, 1977, was not an acceptance of any offer contained in the originating summons, but was itself a counter-offer.

Striking out applications

Tenant's application for renewal

An application may be struck out on a variety of grounds. It may be that it was made out of time, or is vitiated by some other serious procedural error. It may be that the tenant fails to comply with some order or direction of the court. Or it may be that the tenancy ceases to be one to which the Act applies: *I&H Caplan Ltd v Caplan (No.2)*[110] (digested in para.1–46). Where the current tenancy is forfeited after an application has been made, the court will not strike out the application unless it is clear that relief from forfeiture is not being sought, or would not be granted: *Meadows v Clerical Medical & General Life Assurance Society*[111] (digested in para.6–50). Normally the application would be adjourned pending the outcome of any application seeking relief. **6–49**

107 See para.15-21 fn.63.
108 See para.15-21.
109 [1978] 1 E.G.L.R. 44.
110 [1963] 1 W.L.R. 1247; [1963] 2 All E.R. 930.
111 [1980] 2 W.L.R. 639; [1980] 1 All E.R. 454.

6–50 ***Meadows v Clerical Medical & General Life Assurance Society***[112] The landlord, as competent landlord under s.44, served a s.25 notice on the sub-tenant. The tenant (i.e. the sub-tenant's immediate landlord) served a writ on the sub-tenant claiming forfeiture. Judgment was entered by consent for forfeiture of the sub-lease, but the sub-tenant claimed relief from forfeiture, which application stood adjourned generally. Subsequently the sub-tenant applied by originating summons for a new tenancy to the High Court. The landlord sought to strike out the originating summons under the inherent jurisdiction of the court. It was held that where the current tenancy has been forfeited, but the tenant has without undue delay made an application for relief from forfeiture which is still subsisting, the tenancy has not "come to an end by forfeiture" within the meaning of s.24(2) and the tenant is entitled to apply for a new tenancy pursuant to s.24(1). The process of forfeiture is not complete until the application for relief and up to that stage "the tenancy has a trance-like existence pendente lite; none can assert with assurance whether it is alive or dead . . . at least it cannot be said to be dead beyond hope of resurrection". Accordingly, the originating summons would not be dismissed, without prejudice to any fresh application by the landlord to dismiss if the forfeiture became fully effective.

6–51 The decision in *Meadows v Clerical Medical & General Life Assurance Society*,[113] accords with the case of *Zenith Investments Ltd v Kammins Ballrooms*[114] (digested in para.6–22), where it was held that an application for a new tenancy which had been made prematurely was nonetheless an "application" for the purposes of ss.24 and 64. In the *Meadows* case, of course, the application was made by a party who, at the date it was made, was not even "a tenant". However, Sir Robert Megarry V.C. held that it was sufficient that, because of the possibility of relief, the tenant was at least potentially a tenant. It would be different if the application was made by someone who was not, and could never become, a "tenant" within the meaning of the Act, as where the current tenancy had already been brought to an end by a request served pursuant to s.26: *Meah v Sector Properties Ltd*[115] (digested in para.6–25).

Landlord's application for renewal/termination

6–52 If the tenancy ceases to be one to which the Act applies because the tenant has ceased to occupy the premises for business purposes, the landlord can only withdraw the application for renewal/termination with the consent of the tenant.[116] There does not appear to be a clear cut mechanism enabling a landlord to dispose of the application in these circumstances.[117]

---

112 [1980] 2 W.L.R. 639; [1980] 1 All E.R. 454.
113 [1980] 2 W.L.R. 639; [1980] 1 All E.R. 454.
114 [1971] 1 W.L.R. 1751 CA.
115 [1974] 1 W.L.R. 547; [1974] 1 All E.R. 1074 CA.
116 s.24(2C) in the case of the landlord's application for renewal and s.29(6) in the case of the landlord's termination application.
117 See para.6–10 et seq. and para.6–16.

5. TACTICAL USE OF NEW PROVISIONS BY TENANT OR LANDLORD

Landlord can always "get in" first

An application by the tenant or landlord for renewal under s.24(1) or by the landlord for termination is to be made no later than the end of "the statutory period", i.e. the date of termination specified in the landlord's s.25 notice or the date for commencement of the new lease specified in the tenant's s.26 request: s.29A(2).[118] The tenant's application for renewal cannot, however, be made earlier than two months after the date of the making of the s.26 request where he has implemented the 1954 Act procedure by serving a s.26 request, unless the application is made after the landlord has given notice under s.26(6). In other words, if the landlord serves his counter-notice early, e.g. within say one week of receipt of the tenant's s.26 request, the tenant can make his application for renewal immediately. **6–53**

What is interesting about these provisions is that: **6–54**

(1) Subject to service of an appropriate s.25 notice, there is no limitation upon the date before which the landlord can make an application either for termination or for renewal. If the landlord has served a s.25 notice he does not have to wait for the tenant to serve a counter-notice, for the obligation to serve a counter-notice has now been abolished: s.25(5) of the 1954 Act being repealed by art.4(1) of the 2003 Order.
(2) The landlord does not need to serve a counter-notice to the tenant's s.26 request in order to make an application for renewal, although the application cannot in these circumstances be made earlier than two months after service of the tenant's s.26 request: s.29A(3).

Accordingly, a landlord may make an application for renewal: **6–55**

(1) immediately after he has served a s.25 notice;
(2) immediately after the expiration of two months from service of the tenant's s.26 request, where the landlord has not served a counter-notice, to the tenant's s.26 request;
(3) immediately after he has served a counter-notice to the tenant's s.26 request.

Further, a landlord may make an application for termination:

(a) immediately after he has served a s.25 notice;
(b) immediately after he has served a counter-notice to the tenant's s.26 request.

Thus, there is always an opportunity for the landlord to get in first, whether the application is one for termination or renewal. As there is no need for a tenant to **6–56**

[118] As to "the statutory period" see para.6–17 et seq.

serve a counter-notice to a landlord's s.25 notice, the landlord can prepare his application for renewal or termination and serve it immediately upon service of the s.25 notice, so as to initiate an application for termination/renewal of the current tenancy. Similarly, as a tenant cannot, where he has served a s.26 request, make an application for renewal until the landlord has given a counter-notice under s.26(6) or two months has expired from service of the s.26 request, the landlord can, again, take advantage of the fact that the service of a counter-notice on his part limits the time before which the tenant can make any application for renewal. Thus, again, the landlord can, immediately upon service of a counter-notice under s.26(6), initiate an application for termination or renewal as the case may be.

Tactical use to minimise compensation

To prevent the tenant obtaining compensation: by the landlord making an application for renewal

6–57 Article 19 of the 2003 Order introduced new provisions for the circumstances in which compensation is to be paid. There are now three "compensation cases" set out in s.37(1A) to (1C).[119] The third compensation case is as follows:

> "(1C) The third compensation case is where–
> (a) the landlord's notice under section 25 of this Act or, as the case may be, under section 26(6) of this Act, states his opposition to the grant of a new tenancy on any of the compensation grounds[120] and not on any other grounds specified in section 30(1) of this Act; and
> (b) either–
> (i) no application is made by the tenant under section 24(1) of this Act or by the landlord under section 29(2) of this Act; or
> (ii) such an application is made but is subsequently withdrawn."

6–58 It is unclear what is to happen if a landlord, who has opposed on one of the compensation grounds in his s.25 notice, rather than instituting an application to terminate the current tenancy, issues proceedings for renewal.[121] If the tenant proceeds with the renewal, obviously no compensation would be payable as the tenant has not quit the holding.[122] But what if the tenant wants to vacate, and had intended to claim compensation on the basis that he would simply let the landlord's s.25 notice take effect or agree to the landlord's claim for termination?[123] It would appear arguable in these circumstances that, notwithstanding the nature of the landlord's application, upon the dismissal of the landlord's application for renewal[124] the tenant should be entitled to compensation. A dismissal of a landlord's application for renewal, where the landlord has

[119] For a detailed consideration of these provisions, see para.12–02 et seq.

[120] Being grounds (e), (f) and (g) of s.30(1) of the Act.

[121] As has been noted in the text at para.6–53 et seq., the landlord always has the first opportunity to issue an application whether it be for renewal or termination.

[122] This being a requirement for the payment of compensation within s.37(1).

[123] Which is the "second compensation case" provided for by s.37(1B).

[124] The tenant can inform the court that he does not want a new tenancy in which case the court will dismiss the landlord's application: s.29(5).

opposed renewal in his s.25 notice or counter-notice under s.26(6), is not dealt with by s.37(1A)–(1C). However, arguably, the conditions for payment of compensation within s.37(1c) have arisen, in that the landlord has specified the appropriate compensation grounds in his s.25 notice and no application has been made by the tenant for renewal or by the landlord for termination under s.29(2).

However, a further example may illustrate that the position is not so clear. Let us assume that the landlord has genuinely changed his mind. He does not wish to oppose albeit he has stated in his s.25 notice that he will do so on compensation grounds. There is an application for renewal by the landlord. The application proceeds and the court makes an order for a new lease after a disputed hearing. The tenant does not like the terms imposed and seeks an order for revocation under s.36(2) of the Act. Can the tenant claim compensation under s.37(1C)? The authors consider that the tenant should not obtain compensation in these circumstances. Albeit, on a literal interpretation of s.37(1C), the tenant could be said to fall within the terms of the subsection, the difficulty for the tenant is that s.36(2) says that, upon the order for revocation being made, the tenancy ceases to be one to which the Act applies. If this is right, can it be said that the tenant has "quit the holding" within s.37(1) when the concept of a "holding" is one which is understandable only in the context of a tenancy to which the Act applies? **6–59**

To prevent the tenant obtaining compensation: by the landlord making an application for termination

A possible tactical use of the new provisions is for the landlord to issue a termination application in order to avoid the tenant simply walking away at the end of the lease and receiving his compensation. Under the Old Regime, if a tenant had received a s.25 notice opposing renewal on grounds giving rise to an entitlement to compensation he could, if he wished, simply accept the situation and make no application for a new tenancy, safe in the knowledge that he would be entitled to compensation on quitting. Section 37, as substituted by art.19 of the 2003 Order provides, insofar as is material: **6–60**

> "1(B) The second compensation case is where on the making of an application under section 29(2) of this Act the court is precluded . . . from making an order for the grant of a new tenancy by reason of any of the compensation grounds and not of any other grounds specified in section 30(1) of this Act."

The terms of s.37(1c) providing for the third compensation case are set out in para.6–57 above.

On a consideration of those two provisions it will be appreciated that the landlord can by instituting proceedings for termination, force the tenant to go to court to obtain his compensation. This is troublesome for a tenant, particularly in light of the fact that an application for termination can be made at any time up to the date of termination specified in the landlord's s.25 notice.[125] A tenant, who thinks he can simply walk away and obtain compensation in reliance on the landlord's s.25 notice, may be shocked to be met with an application by the

[125] This being "the statutory period": see s.29(A)(2) and para.6–17 et seq.

landlord for termination shortly before the termination date (assuming this corresponds, as it will in most cases, with the date on which the tenancy is to expire by effluxion of time).

6–61 **Example** The problem may be illustrated by the following example. L serves a s.25 notice specifying compensation grounds and specifying September 29, 2007 as the date of termination, that also being the date upon which the tenancy would otherwise expire by effluxion of time. T does not respond, as he knows L will succeed, since L's intention is to demolish the whole of the premises comprised in the tenancy. T vacates and moves to new premises one month before the term date. On September 22, 2007, being seven days before the expiry of the statutory period, L issues an application for termination under s.29(2). The 2003 Order does not reverse the effect of *Esselte AB v Pearl Assurance Plc*[126] (digested in para.3–53) or *Single Horse Properties Ltd v Surrey CC*,[127] (digested in para.2–54) so that, by reason of these authorities, unless T resumes possession before the term date, which is hardly practical, his tenancy will come to an end on the contractual term date. He would not appear to be entitled to any compensation. The circumstances do not fit either the second or third compensation cases.[128] As there is no continuation tenancy after the expiry of the contractual term date, T can obtain a dismissal of L's application. However, this would not appear to fit into the third compensation case, as the application has not been "withdrawn". Dismissal is not a withdrawal.[129] Nor can it be said that any dismissal of L's termination claim falls with the second compensation case. If, notwithstanding the fact that T's tenancy has come to an end, he continues to fight L's claim in the hope of getting compensation, L will simply contend that the tenant is not entitled to a new tenancy as the tenant's current tenancy has come to an end. Thus it cannot be said that such a dismissal comes within the second compensation case, as the court is not "precluded" from granting a new tenancy by reason of the grounds of opposition; the court is precluded by reason of the fact that the tenant no longer has a tenancy capable of renewal.[130] The only way around this tactical use of a termination application by a landlord is for the tenant to issue a protective application for renewal. He then withdraws it having vacated prior to the term date. He will then fall within the third compensation case.

Tactical use to affect assessment of, or liability for, rent

6–62 **(1) Deferring the date for assessment of the rent for the new tenancy** In a buoyant rental market a landlord may wish to defer the date for assessment of the rent under s.34. If he makes an application for termination, even though he knows that his grounds of opposition will not succeed and the tenant is desperate for

---

[126] [1997] 1 W.L.R. 891.

[127] [2002] EWCA Civ 367.

[128] Set out in paras 6–57 and 6–60 above. Nor does it in fact fit the first compensation case. The first compensation case is where the tenant has made an application for renewal, which is successfully opposed by the landlord, which is not the position under consideration: s.37(1A).

[129] See para.14–95 et seq.

[130] See para.6–49.

renewal, the court cannot deal with any application for renewal[131] until that application has been disposed of. Section 29(4)(b) of the 1954 Act provides that if the landlord shall not establish to the satisfaction of the court the grounds of opposition relied upon "it shall make an order for the grant of a new tenancy and accordingly for the termination of the current tenancy immediately before the commencement of the new tenancy". Undoubtedly the court will order appropriate directions for determination of the application for renewal after disposing of the application for termination. This will take time and by the date the rent is assessed the market will have risen further.

(2) Extending the tenant's liability for rent The position can best be illustrated by this example. T is tenant under a fixed-term tenancy but wishes to vacate although L would like him to stay. Assume that L serves a s.25 notice specifying December 25, 2012 as the date of termination and assume that the contractual term date is September 29, 2007. If T remains in occupation past the term date, intending to vacate in the week preceding December 25, 2012, it is open to L, after T has vacated but before December 25, 2012 to issue an application for renewal. T's tenancy will not end on December 25, 2012 as "a tenancy granted for a term of years which is continuing by virtue of s.24 of this Act shall not come to an end by reason only of the tenant ceasing to occupy the property comprised in the tenancy": s.27(2). T's tenancy was continuing under s.24 by reason of T's occupation after the term date. It is questionable whether T can serve a notice under s.27(2) of three months since, after the issue of L's application, the tenancy is continuing by ss.24 and 64.[132] T may not even know that L has made the application, for L has two months within which to serve it. Once T knows of it he can make an application to the court for it to be dismissed: s.29(5). However, s.64 will continue the tenancy for three months after dismissal. Thus T could end up having to pay rent for possibly an additional six months (taking into account L's time for service, T organising himself to obtain a dismissal and the three months and three weeks[133] provided for by s.64(1)). **6–63**

6. PROTECTION OF APPLICATION FOR RENEWAL/TERMINATION UNDER THE LAND REGISTRATION ACT 2002

Pending land action

The interest belonging to a person in actual occupation, so far as it relates to land of which he is in actual occupation, is an overriding interest for the purposes of the Land Registration Act 2002.[134] An "interest" for the purposes of the 2002 Act includes "a pending land action within the meaning of the Land Charges Act **6–64**

[131] The tenant cannot make an application for renewal where there is an application for termin-ation made by the landlord which has been served upon the tenant: s.24(2B).

[132] As to this issue see para.3–116.

[133] Being the period for appeal. See para.14–137 et seq.

[134] Land Registration Act 2002 Sch.1 para.2 (First Registration) and Sch.3 para.2 (Disposition of Registered Estates).

1972."[135] A "pending land action" is defined by the Land Charges Act as meaning "any action or proceeding pending in court relating to land or any interest in or charge on land".[136] However, pending land actions are excluded as overriding interests for the purposes of the Land Registration Act 2002.[137] Thus, the only way in which the tenant can seek to protect his "interest" is for to make some entry in the register to protect it.

6–65 In relation to a pending land action with respect to unregistered land, the tenant should enter a caution against first registration. A person may lodge a caution against first registration if he claims, inter alia, to be entitled to "an interest affecting a qualifying estate".[138] The effect of entering such a caution is that the registrar must give notice of the application for first registration and of the cautioner's right to object.[139]

6–66 Where the landlord has a registered estate, a notice[140] may be entered on the register to protect the tenant's interest. The form of notice may be either an agreed notice or a unilateral notice.[141] The notice will confer priority on the tenant's interest, if valid.[142]

Failure to protect interest

6–67 If the tenant has failed to protect his interest by an appropriate form of notice, and the landlord disposes of the reversion, it would seem that the tenant's application for renewal is not binding on the new landlord, who can then seek an order for its dismissal.[143]

---

[135] LRA 2002 s.87(1)(a).

[136] Land Charges Act 1972 s.17(1).

[137] Land Registration Act 2002 s.87(3).

[138] Land Registration Act 2002 s.15(1).

[139] LRA 2002 s.16(1). The caution procedure is merely a device to enable the cautioner to object to the registration for the purposes of protecting the applicant's interest on first registration in the register of the legal estate which is to be registered by reason of the first registration requirements of the Act.

[140] Interests in registered land may also be protected by a restriction but (1) a restriction may be entered only where the landlord's estate is registered (LRA 2002 s.40(1)) and (2) although a restriction may be entered by the registrar to protect a right or claim in relation to a registered estate (LRA 2002 s.42(1)(c)) he may not exercise that power for the purpose of protecting the priority of an interest which is, or could be, the subject of a notice: LRA 2002 s.42(2).

[141] Land Registration Act 2002 s.34(2). An agreed notice may be sought albeit the registered proprietor does not consent to the application. The party seeking the agreed notice needs provide to the registrar the sealed claim form and notice of issue: Land Registry. Practice Guide 19 para.3.6.2. The registrar will need to be satisfied that the applicant's claim is valid: LRA 2002 s.34(3)(c) and Land Registration Rules 2003 r.81. A unilateral notice may be entered without the consent of the registered proprietor and the registrar does not have to be satisfied as to its validity: Land Registration Act 2002 s.35; Land Registration Rules r.83 providing for it to be in form UN1.

[142] LRA 2002 ss.32 and 29.

[143] Neither of the authors has encountered a situation in practice where (1) the tenant's application for renewal has been protected by an appropriate entry at the Land Registry, or (2) of an assignee of the reversion arguing that the tenant's application is not binding on him for want of protection.

It is unclear what a tenant should do in response to a landlord's application for renewal. This too constitutes a pending land action and ought to be protected. The tenant is, albeit by reason of the actions of the landlord, seeking a renewal of his tenancy. **6–68**

CHAPTER 7

GROUNDS OF OPPOSITION

1. ENTITLEMENT TO OPPOSE APPLICATION

Section 30(1) provides that a landlord "may oppose" an application under s.24 or make a termination application under s.29(2). It follows that a landlord is free to choose whether he will or will not oppose a renewal of the tenant's tenancy. **7–01**

2. LANDLORD CONFINED TO GROUNDS SPECIFIED

The landlord may oppose only on such of the grounds set out in s.30(1) "as may be stated in" the s.25 notice or counter-notice given under s.26(6), as the case may be. It follows that the landlord must consider at the date when he serves his notice or counter-notice whether he will wish to oppose and, if so, upon which ground. If no ground or the wrong ground is specified, the landlord will not subsequently be able to amend his s.25 notice or counter-notice: *Hutchinson v Lambeth*[1] (digested in para.3–169). **7–02**

The special provisions entitling a superior landlord to withdraw a notice in certain circumstances are considered below (see para.7–08 and 7–09). **7–03**

The practical consequences of failure to specify the correct ground are illustrated by the case of *Nursey v P Currie (Dartford) Ltd*[2] (digested in para.7–234), below, where a landlord had proved an intention to demolish premises so as to bring him within ground (f) (demolition and reconstruction), but was unable to rely upon that ground because he had, in his notice, only specified ground (g) (own occupation), which he failed to establish. It is of particular importance for a landlord to consider what, if any, ground of opposition to specify, because of the rule that a successor in title is entitled to rely upon, and is bound by, any ground of opposition specified in a s.25 notice given by his predecessor: see *Marks v British Waterways Board*[3] (digested in para.7–138); *XL Fisheries v Leeds Corp*[4] (digested in para.7–137); and *Wimbush & Son v Franmills Properties*.[5] The **7–04**

---

1 [1984] 1 E.G.L.R. 75 CA.
2 [1959] 1 W.L.R. 273; [1959] 1 All E.R. 497 CA.
3 [1963] 1 W.L.R. 1008; [1963] 3 All E.R. 28 CA.
4 [1955] 3 W.L.R. 393; [1955] 2 All E.R. 875 CA.
5 [1961] 2 W.L.R. 498; [1961] 2 All E.R. 197.

question whether the landlord must have a bona fide intention to rely upon any ground of opposition which he specifies at the date he gives the s.25 notice is discussed below.[6]

Only statutory grounds to be relied upon

7–05 The landlord may only specify in his s.25 notice and/or counter-notice one or more of the seven specific grounds set out in s.30(1). Each of these grounds is discussed in detail below. The landlord is obliged, in the case of a claim by the tenant for renewal (under CPR Part 7),[7] and whether the matter is proceeding in either the High court or county court, to file an acknowledgement of service within 14 days of the claim form stating whether he intends to contest the claim and if he does oppose it, on which grounds.[8] It follows that, although a landlord may not rely upon any ground which he has not stated in his s.25 notice or counter-notice, he is not bound to rely upon such grounds as he has stated and may, therefore, abandon grounds as the case proceeds. Where the landlord has abandoned a ground of opposition in his acknowledgement of service it is unclear whether he can seek to revive it later.[9]

Particularising the ground

7–06 It has been noted[10] that tenants have attempted on a number of occasions to attack the validity of a s.25 notice on the ground that it did not specify with sufficient particularity the ground of opposition upon which the landlord intended to rely. Thus, in *Biles v Caesar*,[11] the tenant argued that the landlord was confined to that part of ground (f) which he had pleaded, namely that he intended to carry out "substantial work of reconstruction", and was not entitled to show that, e.g. he also intended to carry out works of demolition. The Court of Appeal held that the landlord was not confined to the particular subsidiary part of para.(f) which he had put in his s.25 notice; it was sufficient that he indicated his intention to rely upon ground (f). Such a point is unlikely to arise under the form of notice prescribed by the Landlord and Tenant Act 1954 Pt 2 (Notices) Regulations 2004, because that form[12] simply provides for the landlord to specify the appropriate letter denoting which paragraph under s.30(1) he intends to rely upon.

---

6 See para.7–07.

7 As to the procedure with respect to termination applications, see para.14–31 et seq.

8 See para.14–77.

9 CPR PD 56 para.3.6. This paragraph sets out various matters which need to be included in the acknowledgement of service and which are similar to those required by the previous rules. See paras 14–74 and 14–77.

10 See para.3–190 et seq.

11 [1957] 1 W.L.R. 156; [1957] 1 All E.R. 151 CA.

12 Form 2 to Sch.2 to the Regs, Appendix A2.034.

Bona fides

As has been noted,[13] a landlord is entitled to include in his s.25 notice or counter-notice a ground of opposition which he personally does not intend to rely upon, but which he anticipates may be required by a successor in title. A landlord may also be tempted to insert a ground upon which he does not really intend to rely, for tactical reasons. For example, if a landlord wishes to rely upon ground (f) and puts only that in his notice, he will become liable to pay compensation to the tenant even if the tenant makes no application for a new tenancy because he wishes to move to new premises. If, however, that landlord had also stated in his s.25 notice that he intended to rely upon ground (a) (breach of repairing obligations), compensation would not be payable to the tenant unless he applied for a new tenancy[14] and the landlord proved the ground of opposition under ground (f), but not under ground (a). The tenant might well be unwilling to go to the trouble of making an application simply in order to obtain his compensation. If, as in this example, the landlord had no real intention of relying upon ground (a), there is a serious danger that the inclusion of this ground for tactical reasons would invalidate the s.25 notice. An extensive discussion of this subject is to be found at para.3–164 et seq. **7–07**

Withdrawal of section 25 notice

Paragraph 7 of Sch.6 imposes a duty on a landlord whose interest may come to an end within 16 months (or any further time by which it may be continued under s.36(2) or s.64 of the Act) forthwith to send to his immediate landlord a copy of any s.25 notice which he serves upon his sub-tenant or of any s.26 request which he has received from him. The immediate landlord is then under an obligation forthwith to pass the copy notice to his superior landlord, irrespective of the length of his own tenancy, and so on up the chain. If within two months after the giving of the s.25 notice the superior landlord becomes "the landlord" as defined by s.44 and gives notice in the prescribed form to the tenant that he withdraws the s.25 notice previously served, it will cease to have effect: para.6 of the Schedule.[15] The reason for this is that the superior landlord would otherwise be bound by the notice served upon the sub-tenant which might not contain the ground or grounds of opposition upon which he wished to rely.[16] **7–08**

There is no provision for the superior landlord to withdraw any counter- notice given to the sub-tenant in response to the s.26 request, though he may be able to make himself competent landlord before any counter-notice is served and before time for service has expired, in which case he will have the right to serve it himself. **7–09**

---

[13] See para.7–04.

[14] Or the landlord made a termination application under s.29(2).

[15] For a further discussion see para.10–52.

[16] See paras 7–02 to 7–04.

3. GROUND (A)—FAILURE TO REPAIR

The statutory wording

7–10 Under para.(a) of s.30(1), a landlord is entitled to oppose an application for a new tenancy upon the following ground[17]:

> "Where under the current tenancy the tenant has any obligations as respects the repair and maintenance of the holding, that the tenant ought not to be granted a new tenancy in view of the state of repair of the holding, being a state resulting from the tenant's failure to comply with the said obligations."

Existence of obligation

7–11 The first requirement of ground (a) is that the tenant should have an obligation in respect of the repair and maintenance of the holding. "Repair" is defined in s.69(1) to include any work of maintenance, decoration or restoration and references to repairing, to keeping or yielding up in repair and to state of repair shall be construed accordingly. Normally, the tenant's obligation will arise under an express repairing covenant contained as a term of the tenancy, but the words of para.(a) are wide enough to include an implied obligation to repair and an obligation to comply with any statutory duty which involves the repair or restoration of the building.

7–12 One problem on which there is no authority is whether an obligation to repair on a periodic basis continues during the continuation tenancy. For example, a lease may contain an obligation on the part of the tenant to redecorate the interior of the premises in every third year of the term created by the lease. Ground (a) refers to an obligation "under the current tenancy" and it is clear that s.24(1) continues the current tenancy during the period of statutory continuation so far as the tenant in possession is concerned.[18] In the authors' opinion the answer to the problem would depend on the interpretation of the particular covenant of the current tenancy under consideration. The wording of the covenant may indicate that the obligation will continue so long as the current tenancy continues. Thus, a covenant to redecorate during every third year of the term created by the lease may not continue during the continuation tenancy, whereas a covenant to repair in, say, 2008 and every third year thereafter might well be held to. Support for this view is to be found in *Willison v Cheverell Estates Ltd*,[19] where it was held that a landlord could not implement the rent review provisions in the lease during

---

[17] For a consideration of the evidence to be relied upon by the parties in support of, or in opposition to this ground, see para.11–36 et seq.

[18] The position of an original tenant who has assigned, and of a guarantor, may well be different (especially where the Landlord and Tenant (Covenants) Act 1995 applies) but their respective positions are not relevant to the present discussion. The 1995 Act applies to tenancies granted after January 1, 1996 (the date of the coming into force of the 1995 Act) unless it was granted in pursuance of an agreement entered into before that date or an order of the court made before that date: Landlord and Tenant (Covenants) Act 1995 s.1.

[19] [1996] 1 E.G.L.R. 116 CA.

the period of continuation where the rent review date was calculated by reference to a specified period of "the term", for this was a reference only to a period during the contractual term.

Extent of obligation

Paragraph (a) is concerned only with obligations in respect of "the holding" (for the meaning of "the holding" see para.8–06 et seq.). The effect of this can be illustrated by an example. **7–13**

Example Suppose a tenancy of a shop and residential upper part contains a tenant's full repairing obligation in respect of the whole of the demised premises. If the tenant occupies the shop part for business purposes, but sub-lets the upper part to a residential tenant, his holding will consist of the shop only. If, therefore, the shop premises are kept in good repair, the landlord will not be able to rely on para.(a), even if the residential upper part is in a state of substantial disrepair. This, of course, does not prejudice the immediate landlord so far as he has a common law right of re-entry for disrepair, nor, it is thought, will it prevent the landlord from relying on the ground set out in para.(c) (other reasons or breaches) in respect of those breaches of obligations which do not fall within para.(a).[20] **7–14**

It should be noted that the obligation is one which relates to "the repair and maintenance" of the holding. "Maintenance" presumably extends the obligation to premises which are not, in ordinary language, capable of repair, such as an open site or garden as well as to operations (such as having a lift checked periodically) which might not come within the word "repair". **7–15**

State of disrepair

The next requirement under para.(a) is that, as a result of the tenant's failure to comply with the said obligation, the holding is in an unsatisfactory "state of repair". It is not thought that there is any significance in the omission by the draftsman of the words "and maintenance" from the expression "state of repair", so that this limb of para.(a) will apply to the case of an open site or garden or piece of plant or machinery which is inadequately maintained. **7–16**

Court may look at all circumstances

The court is entitled to refuse to grant a new tenancy "in view of the state of repair of the holding". In *Eichner v Midland Bank Executor and Trustee Co*[21] (digested in para.7–22) it was held that these words do not confine the court, in deciding whether or not to refuse a tenancy on the ground specified in para.(a), to a consideration of the breach of repairing obligation complained of. The court is entitled to look at all the circumstances in connection with the breaches and to **7–17**

---

[20] See para.7–42 et seq.

[21] [1970] 1 W.L.R. 1120; [1970] 2 All E.R. 597 CA.

consider the conduct of the tenant as a whole in regard to his obligations under the tenancy. In *Hutchinson v Lambeth*[22] (digested in para.3–169) the judge wrongly allowed the landlord to amend his answer to rely upon ground (c) (which he had not specified in his s.25 notice) in addition to grounds (a) and (b), which he had specified. The Court of Appeal, while agreeing that the amendment should not have been allowed, refused to overturn the judge's refusal of a new tenancy since the matters relied upon in relation to ground (c) were also relevant to the grounds which had been properly pleaded.

Exercise of court's discretion

7–18 The words "ought not" have been held to confer a discretion on the court as to whether or not it should refuse a new tenancy, once the basic facts under para.(a) have been established: *Lyons v Central Commercial Properties Ltd*[23] (digested in para.7–21). That case also gave guidance on the way in which the discretion should be exercised. Morris and Ormerod L.JJ. took the view that the discretion was a wide one insofar as the court could take into account all relevant circumstances, including what was likely to happen if a new tenancy was granted. Their statements of the principles on which the court should act are important, and merit quotation in full:

Morris L.J. said:

> "I do not think that it is desirable to say more than that once a court has found the facts as regards the tenant's past performance and behaviour and any special circumstances which exist, then, while remembering that it is the future that is being considered, in that the issue is whether the tenant should be refused a new tenancy for the future, the court has to ask itself whether it would be unfair to the landlord, having regard to the tenant's past performance and behaviour, if the tenant were to enjoy the advantage which the Act gives to him."

Ormerod L.J. said:

> "Without attempting to define the precise limits of that discretion, the judge, as I see it, may have regard to the conduct of the tenant in relation to his obligations, and the reasons for any breach of covenant which has arisen."

Harman J., however, considered the discretion to be "narrow", to be "limited to the question . . . whether, having regard to the tenant's past conduct as a tenant it would be equitable to exclude the landlord from his property for a further term or foist the tenant on him contrary to the contract". The discretion was, in Harman J.'s opinion, to be contrasted with the wider discretion conferred under ss.33 and 35. In *Eichner v Midland Bank Executor and Trustee Co*[24] (digested in para.7–22) the Court of Appeal stated that Ormerod L.J.'s statement of how the discretion was to be exercised was to be preferred to that of Harman J. It is the authors' view that Harman J.'s approach would no longer be followed by the courts.

---

[22] [1984] 1 E.G.L.R. 75 CA.
[23] [1958] 1 W.L.R. 869; [1958] 2 All E.R. 767 CA.
[24] [1970] 1 W.L.R. 1120.

As Morris L.J. pointed out in the passage from *Lyons v Central Commercial Properties Ltd*[25] (digested in para.7–21) quoted above, it is the future that is being considered and it follows that the court may very well be impressed if the tenant, while admitting that he has been in breach of his repairing obligations in the past, has complied with a schedule of dilapidations by the date of the hearing. Alternatively, the court may accept an undertaking[26] or impose a condition that a schedule be complied with as a term of the grant of the new tenancy: see, e.g. the county court decision in *Nihad v Chain*[27] (digested in para.7–23). Nonetheless, it appears from what all three judges had to say in *Lyons v Central Commercial Properties Ltd*[28] (digested in para.7–21) that the tenant has no guarantee that this past misconduct will be forgiven and a new tenancy granted to him upon terms that he complies with his covenants in the future. **7–19**

As part of the exercise of the judge's discretion, the judge should ask himself whether the landlord's interest is likely to be prejudiced by the occurrence of the matters relied upon as constituting reasons within s.30(1): see *Beard v Williams*[29] (digested in para.7–49). **7–20**

Lyons v Central Commercial Properties Ltd[30] A lease of shop premises was granted to the tenant's mother for a term of 21 years and the mother granted an underlease to the tenant for a term expiring in March 1956. In 1954 discussions began between the landlord, the tenant, and Littlewoods Mail Order Store Ltd, involving the assignment by the tenant of his underlease to Littlewoods, the surrender thereof by Littlewoods to the landlord and the grant of a new lease by the landlord to Littlewoods. The negotiations came to nothing and the landlord served a schedule of dilapidations on the tenant. The tenant made a request for a new tenancy pursuant to s.26 and the landlord served a counter-notice specifying the ground of opposition set out in s.30(l)(a) (disrepair). The tenant's application was adjourned pending further tripartite negotiations, which by this time involved the grant to Littlewoods of a 99-year building lease of the shop and other premises. **7–21**

For some reason Littlewoods broke off negotiations and the tenant's application was duly heard in the county court. The tenant gave evidence that he had built up a profitable business with considerable goodwill and stated that he was willing to give an undertaking to carry out all the works for which he was liable under the underlease. The county court judge refused to grant a new tenancy. He said in his judgment:

> "... if this were the case of a small man likely to lose his livelihood I would, despite the breaches, grant a new lease ... I have come to the conclusion that this action is brought not to secure the sitting tenant but to secure the premises for Littlewoods ... There were severe

[25] [1958] 1 W.L.R. 869; [1958] 2 All E.R. 767 CA.

[26] See *John Kay Ltd v Kay* [1952] 2 Q.B. 258 at 271, 272 CA, where the court was concerned with the wording of s.12(3)(a) of the Leasehold Property (Temporary Provisions) Act 1951, considered in fn.66 to para.7–54.

[27] [1956] E.G.D. 234 CC.

[28] [1958] 1 W.L.R. 869; [1958] 2 All E.R. 767 CA.

[29] [1986] 1 E.G.L.R. 148 CA.

[30] [1958] 1 W.L.R. 869; [1958] 2 All E.R. 767 CA.

> breaches of covenant. Although the tenant had nearly a year to remedy the breaches he did not do so. The applicant is not the sort of person who is likely to be a tenant to whom I should give relief."

The Court of Appeal held that the judge had erred in thinking that the negotiations with Littlewoods had any bearing on the matter. However (Morris L.J. dissenting), in view of the material facts found by the judge, in particular that there were severe breaches, that the tenant had done nothing in nearly a year to remedy them and that he was not the sort of person who should be given relief, the judge's refusal of a new tenancy would be confirmed.

7–22 ***Eichner v Midland Bank Executor and Trustee Co***[31] The user covenant in a lease required the tenant to use and occupy the premises "as a private dwelling house only and not for any business", but permitted the tenant "to have a private workshop and/or laboratory together with a study for his own personal use for his own profession as a Chemist" in a particular part of the premises. The tenant used part of the premises for his profession as a chemist, but he also manufactured plastic foam and carried on a translation business, with 15 to 20 translators working in the surrounding area. The landlord served a schedule of dilapidations and a s.25 notice which stated that the landlord would oppose any application for a new tenancy on ground (a) in s.30(1), namely breach of repairing obligation, and on ground (c), specifying as the relevant breach of covenant manufacturing the foam and carrying on the translation business and assigning underletting or parting with possession to a particular company or alternatively to a named individual. The tenant duly applied for a new tenancy. The judge found that the dilapidations had been remedied, that the parting with possession was not serious and that the manufacture of plastic foam was not serious enough for the court to refuse a new lease. However, he found that the carrying on of the translation business was a serious breach. In refusing to grant a new tenancy, the judge stated that he had also taken into consideration the tenant's history of paying rent and his ability to pay rent in the future, as well as the very unhappy landlord and tenant relationship over the years. He said: "It must be considered very carefully whether it is fair to saddle the landlord with a tenant with whom he is in constant litigation."

On appeal, the Court of Appeal upheld the judge's decision. In exercising its discretion about whether the tenant ought not to be granted a new tenancy on the ground specified in s.30(l)(a), (b) and (c), the court is entitled to consider all the circumstances in connection with the breaches of covenant and the conduct of the tenant as a whole in regard to his obligations under the tenancy. The view of Ormerod L.J. in *Lyons v Central Commercial*, that "the judge may have regard to the conduct of the tenant in regard to his obligations", was to be preferred to Harman J.'s dictum in the same case that "the discretion vested in the court under s.30(l)(a), (b) and (c) is narrow. It is limited to the question whether having regard only to the grounds set out a new tenancy ought not to be granted".

[31] [1970] 1 W.L.R. 1120; [1970] 2 All E.R. 597 CA.

Nihad v Chain[32] Where the tenant was admittedly in breach of covenant to repair, the court decided nonetheless to grant him a new tenancy having regard to his willingness that the new lease should contain a repairing covenant and proviso for re-entry, plus a covenant obliging him forthwith to put the premises in repair in accordance with the terms of the repairing covenants in the previous lease. **7–23**

Contrast with relief from forfeiture

The tenant's position is weaker in resisting opposition under ground (a) than it is when he is applying for relief from forfeiture based on breach of repairing obligations. In the latter case, relief is virtually automatic upon terms that the repairs are done; under ground (a) the court's discretion will not be automatically exercised in favour of the tenant even where an undertaking is given to remedy the disrepair. In the authors' opinion, the reason for this is that in the case of forfeiture the court is restoring a term of years freely granted by the landlord, but under the Act it is being asked to impose upon a landlord a new obligation to grant a tenancy in favour of a tenant who has been in breach of his obligations under the existing contract. Thus, although a landlord would be well advised to compile a schedule of dilapidations for the purposes of substantiating ground (a), he will often refrain from serving that schedule under cover of a s.146 notice with a view to forfeiture. The effect of forfeiting will be to delay the 1954 Act proceedings, to enable the tenant to claim relief from forfeiture as soon as the s.146 notice is served, to obtain relief once he has carried out the repairs, and to put the landlord in the position of arguing before the court that, although the tenant has purged past breaches and the premises are now in a state of perfect repair, nonetheless a new tenancy should not be granted. This is a weak tactical position, as can be seen from the dicta of Viscount Simonds in *Betty's Cafes*.[33] **7–24**

If the court is minded to grant a new tenancy it is considered advisable from the landlord's point of view that the landlord obtains within the new lease a covenant to carry out the repairs within a fixed period from the date of grant, in order to take advantage of s.3(1) of the Leasehold Property (Repairs) Act 1938. This section provides that the 1938 Act does not apply to a breach of a covenant or agreement insofar as it imposes on the lessee an obligation to put premises in repair that is to be performed upon the lessee taking possession of the premises or within a reasonable time thereafter. Although there has been no decision on this point, it is considered that the reference to "taking possession" must be a reference to the tenant taking possession under the new lease and that it does not matter that he has already been in possession under the old lease. **7–25**

---

32 [1956] E.G.D. 234 CC.

33 *Betty's Cafes Ltd v Phillips Furnishing Stores Ltd* [1959] A.C. 20 HL at 36:

"At the hearing the Judge . . . will necessarily take into consideration the state of disrepair, not only at the date of the notice [under s.25], but also at the date of hearing."

Relevant date

7–26 In *Betty's Cafes Ltd v Phillips Furnishing Stores Ltd*,[34] the House of Lords had to consider what was the relevant date at which to judge the question of whether a landlord had the relevant intention under ground (f) (demolition and reconstruction). In considering this question, some of their Lordships also made observations about the relevant date upon which it should be judged whether the other grounds of opposition had been made out. In relation to ground (a) Viscount Simonds made the point that it was unreal to suppose that a landlord would specify ground (a) if the state of repair at the date of the s.25 notice gave him nothing to complain of, at least upon the assumption that the landlord was acting in good faith (see para.7–07). However, the judge would not be confined, in exercising his discretion whether or not to grant a new tenancy, to a consideration of the state of repair of the holding at the date of service of the s.25 notice; he would necessarily take into consideration the state of repair or disrepair as it was at the date the matter came before him. Lord Morton agreed, stating that the court would have regard both to the state of repair at the date of the notice and to the state of repair at the date of the hearing. Lord Keith was also of the view that the court might take account of the fact that the tenant had purged past breaches of his contract of tenancy under ground (a) by the time the case came into court. The judgments of Lords Somervell and Denning do not expressly deal with ground (a), but the general tenor of their speeches is in accordance with those of the majority of the House.

4. GROUND (B)—PERSISTENT ARREARS

The statutory wording

7–27 Under para.(b) of s.30(1), the landlord may oppose an application for a new tenancy on the following ground[35]:

> "That the tenant ought not to be granted a new tenancy in view of his persistent delay in paying rent which has become due."

"Persistent"

7–28 This ground can only be relied upon where there has been "persistent" delay in paying rent. In order to show this, it may be necessary for a landlord to establish a long history of arrears. Alternatively, it may be sufficient to produce evidence that one or two instalments of rent have been in arrear for a very long period. The word "persistent" may have the undertone of a deliberate or reckless attitude on the part of the tenant, so that a long history of arrears which could be explained by inefficiency or forgetfulness might not entitle the landlord to rely upon ground (b).

---

[34] [1959] A.C. 20 HL.

[35] For a consideration of the evidence to be relied upon by the parties in support of or in opposition to this ground, see para.11–39 et seq.

Rent must have "become due"

The word used in the paragraph is "rent". The authors' tentative view is that this would include all sums reserved as rent, including (e.g.) insurance rent and service charge.[36] Whether it would include such sums if not expressly reserved as rent is more doubtful. **7–29**

The relevant duty is in relation to rent which "has become due". It should be noted that it is not a requirement of this ground that the rent should have been so far in arrears as to give the landlord a right to forfeit, let alone that he should actually have taken forfeiture proceedings. These two factors would, however, be relevant in relation to the exercise of the court's discretion in the manner noted in the next paragraphs. Similarly, the fact that the landlord did not object to the tenant's delay and indicated to the tenant, by serving a draft lease upon the tenant shortly prior to the s.25 notice, that the landlord would not oppose under ground (b) did not estop the landlord from relying on this ground of opposition but was a matter to which the court could have regard in the exercise of its discretion: *Freeman v Barclays Bank*[37] (digested in para.7–36). Contrast *Hazel v Akhtar*[38] (digested in para.7–39) where it was held that the acquiescence of the landlord in the tenant's persistent failure to pay on time estopped both the landlord and his successor in title from relying on para.(b) unless reasonable notice was given to the tenant to revert to strict compliance with the lease. The service of a notice under s.25 opposing compliance with the lease was required. *Freeman v Barclay's Bank* was not, it would appear, cited to the court. **7–30**

Court entitled to look at all relevant circumstances

The words "in view of" are used in ground (b) as in ground (a). It would appear that the court is entitled to take a general view under ground (b) on whether the tenant should in all the circumstances be granted a new tenancy, as is unquestionably the case under ground (a) (see para.7–17 et seq.). **7–31**

Court's discretion

The words "ought not" (noted above in para.7–18) confer a discretion on the court whether or not to grant a new tenancy. In *Hurstfell v Leicester Square Property Co*[39] (digested in para.7–38) it was accepted before the county court judge that, although the onus lay on the landlord to persuade the court not to grant a new tenancy, the tenant was obliged (1) to explain the reasons for the past **7–32**

---

[36] *Escalus Properties Ltd v Robinson* [1995] 2 E.G.L.R. 23 CA.

[37] [1958] E.G.D. 93 CA.

[38] [2001] EWCA Civ 1883; [2002] 1 E.G.L.R. 45. See also para.7–34. This is consistent with the early county court decision of *Davis & Cooper v Geker & Co* Unreported, digested at para.7–34, where the landlord's indulgence over the tenant's rent arrears militated against his opposition to the tenant's renewal.

[39] [1988] 37 E.G. 109 CA.

failures and (2) to satisfy the court that if a new lease were granted, there would be no recurrence of the late payments of rent. The Court of Appeal did not disagree with this concession.

7–33 The earlier reported cases under ground (b) show the court taking a hard line in relation to tenants who have been in persistent arrears with their rent, but the more lenient attitude taken in the most recent cases underlines the fact that a discretion is being exercised and each case must be judged on its own facts. The Court of Appeal will only interfere with the judge's exercise of his discretion "if it is apparent that the judge made an error of principle; if he exercised his discretion in a way which was patently perverse or if he took into account an irrelevant factor or failed to take into account a relevant factor": *Rawashdeh v Lane*.[40]

7–34 ***Davis & Cooper v Geker & Co***[41] Where the landlord had over a period of about five years treated the tenant with such leniency and courtesy in the matter of arrears of rent that it could also be said that the landlord had invited irregularity and laxity in payment, it was held that it would be wrong to refuse the tenant's application for a new lease, for the landlord could be safeguarded against future lack of promptness in paying rent by granting to the tenant a new tenancy for one year only, including a term in the new lease for a provision that rent be payable in advance, for payment of a rent deposit and providing for the proviso for re-entry to be effective upon rent being in arrears for seven days.

7–35 ***Horowitz v Ferrand***[42] A business tenant with several years' history of rent arrears applied to the court for a new tenancy which the landlord opposed under s.30(1)(b). The evidence was that the rent had always been forthcoming, but was usually late, forcing the landlord to call or send for it. The judge dismissed the application for a new tenancy, holding that the rent need not be substantially in arrears nor need the arrears last for a long time for the case to be invoked. The landlord was not expected to be subject to the work and irritation of "dunning a tenant for his rent".

7–36 ***Freeman v Barclays Bank Ltd***[43] The landlord opposed the grant of a new tenancy under, inter alia, ground (b) (persistent delay in paying rent) of s.30(1). The tenant had for a period of five years before the hearing been in persistent and substantial arrears. The landlord did not serve its s.25 notice until two years after the contractual expiry date. The landlord had corresponded with the tenant over that period and did not raise the tenant's delay in paying rent as a disqualification for renewal. On the contrary, shortly prior to the service of the s.25 notice, the landlord forwarded to the tenant a draft lease, some of the terms of which were objected to by the tenant. It was held that the landlord's attitude and approach did not prevent the landlord from relying upon ground (b).

---

[40] [1988] 2 E.G.L.R. 109 CA.

[41] Unreported, but referred to in Blundell & Wellings, *The Landlord and Tenant Acts, including Business Tenancies*, 1st edn (London: Sweet & Maxwell, 1958), p.327.

[42] [1956] C.L.Y. 4843; [1952] 33 T.C. 221.

[43] [1958] E.G.D. 93 CA.

Hopcutt v Carver[44] The county court judge dismissed a tenant's application for a new tenancy because of his persistent delay in paying rent. The Court of Appeal dismissed the tenant's appeal, because the judge had had evidence on which to arrive at his conclusions and no ground had been shown for interfering with the exercise of his discretion. **7–37**

Hurstfell v Leicester Square Property Co[45] The landlord opposed renewal of the tenant's business tenancy on the ground of persistent delay in paying rent (s.30(1)(b) of the Act). The tenant had taken an assignment of the lease in question in 1982 but the delay in payment of rent did not start until 1984. The rent was payable on the usual quarter days and from 1984 to the date of the service of the landlord's s.25 notice, February 16, 1987, the tenant was late with every quarter's rent. The rent was on one occasion 19 weeks late; on another 17 weeks; on three other occasions it was 9 or 10 weeks late; and on the other occasions the delay was four, five and six weeks. The tenant had made losses in 1984, 1985 and 1987 but broke even in 1986. The most recent accounts available showed that there was a modest profit for the early part of the financial year 1987–88. The Court of Appeal refused to interfere with the learned county court judge's decision in granting a new tenancy in the exercise of his discretion, for it held that it was not possible to say that there was no evidence on which the judge was entitled to conclude as he did. **7–38**

Hazel v Akhtar[46] The tenant held premises under a lease dated April 8, 1984 for a term of 16 years from August 18, 1984. The tenant had been late in paying the quarterly rent on every payment. The landlord did not object to this until there was a transfer of the reversion one year prior to the expiry of the term. A schedule of arrears was prepared for the period March 1997 to December 2000 which showed that the rent was in arrears for a period between 1 to 21 days for each quarter. Rent was paid by cheque and a period was allowed for the cheque to clear. There had been no complaints from the landlord nor request or demand that the rent be paid more timeously. **7–39**

The tenant did not pay the rent for the March quarter of 1999 until July as it was not until that time that he became aware of the change of the reversion and the name of the landlord's new agents. In July 1999 he received a letter demanding not only the June quarter but also the previous two quarters which he had already paid. The June quarter was paid by cheque on July 15, 1999. The new landlord's agents, some seven days later, again demanded rent for the March and December quarters on 1999 which had already been paid. The letter threatened resort to bailiffs or litigation if payment was not effected.

The county court judge held that there had been a persistent failure to pay rent and refused a new tenancy under, inter alia, ground (b) in the exercise of his direction.

On appeal, the Court of Appeal, in reversing the judge's decision and granting a new tenancy held:

---

[44] (1969) 209 E.G. 1069 CA.

[45] [1988] 2 E.G.L.R. 189 CA.

[46] [2001] EWCA Civ 1883; [2002] 1 E.G.L.R. 45.

(1) it was inappropriate to add as part of the time during which the rent was in arrears the period for the cheque to clear. The practice of accepting payment of rent by cheque "was equivalent to saying that the [landlords] were prepared to accept conditional payment by means of the tenant's cheque received on the due date"[47];

(2) the previous landlord's conduct was such that, notwithstanding the fact that the tenant's failure to pay on the due date involved repeated minor breaches in the tenant's obligation under the lease, they had assented to the practice of "slightly late" payments, by cheque, and thus the landlords were, in legal and equitable terms, estopped from insisting that the tenant should revert to strict compliance with the lease unless they gave reasonable notice to him to that effect;

(3) the new landlords as assignees of the reversion were subject to the same restraint as the previous landlord;

(4) the letter in July, wrongfully demanding the two previous quarters, was not notice that strict compliance with the terms of the lease was required for the future. This was equally the case notwithstanding the fact that the tenant had continued to pay late after the landlord had served notice pursuant to the Act terminating the tenant's lease and opposing the grant of a new tenancy under para.(b);

(5) the judge had misdirected himself in holding that the whole history of rent payments was evidence of "persistent" failure and had made a serious error of fact in relation to the July 1999 correspondence, which clearly influenced his decision;

(6) the tenant's offers to secure prompt payment or to provide security for future payments did not influence the court and were not, in the present case, required to be imposed as conditions for the grant of a new lease.

7–40 These cases suggest the practical point that a tenant who has had a bad past record is well advised to ensure, once he has received a s.25 notice specifying ground (b), that he pays rent regularly and that he makes sufficient proposals by way of undertaking, or submission to terms imposed by the court, to guarantee that he is unlikely to be in arrears in the future. Payment of rent in advance for a

---

[47] There is a considerable body of authority, which the court does not appear to have been referred to, on the question of payment of rent by cheque. Where, by reason of a previous course of conduct, a landlord has accepted payment of rent by cheque sent by post, that method of payment may be held to be agreed between the parties as acceptable. If payment of rent by cheque sent in the post is an accepted method of payment the rent is paid when the rent is posted, subject only to it being honoured: *Norman v Ricketts* (1886) 3 T.L.R. 182; *Beevers v Mason* (1979) 37 P. & C.R. 452 CA; *Luttenberger v North Thoresby Farms Ltd* [1992] 1 E.G.L.R. 261 CA. The rationale behind the principle of payment being effective from the date of posting is one of agency. The landlord has expressly or impliedly authorised the method of payment, i.e. payment by post and the post office transmits the letter as the landlord's agent in such circumstances: *Re Deveze Ex p. Cote* (1873) 9 Ch. App. 27. It would also appear that the same principle applies to a post-dated cheque, so that if payment is made by cheque through the post, albeit the cheque is post-dated, if it is honoured upon presentation, the date of payment is to be treated as being effective from the date of the cheque upon its being honoured on presentation: *D'Jan v Bond Street Estates* [1993] E.G.C.S. 43 CA; *Commercial Union Life Assurance Co Ltd v Label Ink Ltd* [2001] L. & T.R. 29. See also, more recently, *Day v Coltrane* [2003] 1 W.L.R. 1379 CA and *Avocet Industrial Estates LLP v Merol Ltd* [2012] L. & T.R. 13.

substantial period ahead, or the giving of security, will often persuade a court to give even a bad payer a second chance. In *Rawashdeh v Lane*,[48] however, the Court of Appeal refused leave to appeal against the county court judge's dismissal of an application on ground (b) where the tenant had offered security for the future payment of rent.

Relevant date As noted above (in para.7–26), the members of the House of Lords made observations in *Betty's Cafes*[49] on the relevant dates upon which the grounds of opposition should be established. Viscount Simonds and Lords Morton and Keith treated ground (b) as being exactly analogous to ground (a). Lord Somervell dealt expressly with ground (b), stating that although a notice based on that ground: **7–41**

> "would not be given unless there had been past delay in paying rent, events between the notice and the hearing would be relevant to the decision whether the court ought to grant the tenancy. The tenant may, after the notice has been given, have improved or aggravated his position as a payer".

The court would have to consider as at the time of the hearing whether he had "persistently delayed in paying his rent".

5. GROUND (C)—OTHER REASONS OR BREACHES

The statutory wording

Under para.(c) of s.30(1), the landlord is entitled to oppose the grant of a new tenancy on the following ground[50]: **7–42**

> "That the tenant ought not to be granted a new tenancy in view of other substantial breaches by him of his obligations under the current tenancy, or for any other reason connected with the tenant's use or management of the holding."

The first limb of this ground relates to "other substantial breaches" and the second to "other reasons".

"Other" than ground (a) or ground (b)

The word "other" in the first limb is clearly a reference back to grounds (a) and (b), that is to say ground (c) is dealing with breaches other than of a repairing obligation in relation to the holding or persistent arrears of rent. Thus, e.g. in relation to a breach of a user covenant, if the tenant was required to use premises as an annex to a "nature cure centre" and instead used those premises as a laundry and massage parlour, this may entitle the landlord to oppose under ground (c) as **7–43**

---

[48] [1988] 2 E.G.L.R. 109 CA.

[49] *Betty's Cafes Ltd v Phillips Furnishing Stores Ltd* [1959] A.C. 20 HL.

[50] For a consideration of the evidence to be relied upon by the parties in support of, or in opposition to this ground, see para.11–42 et seq.

long as the landlord can prove the breaches: *Jones v Jenkins*.[51] It would seem to follow from the wording of the first limb that a notice specifying only ground (c) would not entitle a landlord to complain of any breaches in respect of which he could have specified ground (a) or ground (b). However, the converse is not the case: a landlord who has specified grounds (a) and (b) can put in evidence in support of those grounds matters which would have come within ground (c) even when he has not specified ground (c): *Hutchinson v Lambeth*[52] (digested in para.3–163).

"Substantial"

7–44 Only "substantial" breaches can be complained of under the first limb. It is thought that this word will be given the same meaning as it was in a different context in *Palser v Grinling*[53]; that is to say, it does not merely mean not de minimis, but means "great, weighty, big or solid".

Relevant breaches

7–45 Despite the reference to "breaches" in the plural, it is not thought that the landlord would necessarily be precluded from relying upon ground (c) in relation to one single substantial breach of covenant. The ground is not, in terms, confined to subsisting breaches; that is to say breaches in respect of which the landlord has an enforceable right of re-entry. The situation could, therefore, arise where a landlord had by inadvertence waived his right of forfeiture in respect of a serious breach committed by the tenant, but could nonetheless rely upon it under ground (c) in order to oppose the grant of a new tenancy. This distinction between the common law doctrine of forfeiture and the powers of the court under the Act can be justified upon the ground that forfeiture involves the premature termination of the term agreed by the parties as a penalty upon the tenant, whereas the court is deciding under ground (c) whether it should force a landlord to grant a new tenancy to a person who has been in breach of covenant in the past.[54]

Not confined to "holding" under first limb

7–46 It is to be noted that, unlike ground (a), the "other breaches" referred to in the first limb of ground (c) are not confined to those which relate to "the holding". It would seem to follow that in the example given in para.7–14 the landlord would be entitled to complain of the disrepair of the residential upper part under ground (c), although not under ground (a). This reinforces the importance from the

---

[51] [1986] 1 E.G.L.R. 113 CA. See also *Jones v Christy* (1963) 107 S.J. 374 CA (digested in para.1–33).
[52] [1984] 1 E.G.L.R. 75 CA.
[53] [1948] 1 All E.R. 1 HL.
[54] See para.7–24.

landlord's point of view of considering most carefully at the time that he serves his s.25 notice the precise ground or grounds upon which he wishes to rely at the hearing.

Other reasons

The second limb of para.(c) relates to "other" reasons; that is to say reasons which have not already been covered by grounds (a), (b) and the first limb of ground (c). Since these three heads exhaustively cover all the tenant's obligations under his tenancy, it follows that the second limb necessarily comprehends only matters which do not arise as a matter of obligation between landlord and tenant. It includes all matters concerning the tenant's use of the holding: *Fowles v Heathrow Airport Ltd.*[55] Thus, where the satisfactory continuation of the tenant's business depended upon the tenant's living arrangements, those living arrangements are "another reason" connected with the tenant's use or management of the building within the meaning of s.30(1)(c): *Beard v Williams*[56] (digested in para.7–49). The court will not grant a new tenancy for a use which is in breach of planning control: *Turner & Bell v Searles (Stanford-le-Hope)*[57] (digested in para.7–48); followed in *Fowles v Heathrow Airport Ltd.*[58] It is not necessary for it to be shown that the renewal of the tenancy will necessarily involve an illegal user of the land for a new tenancy to be refused: *Fowles v Heathrow Airport Ltd.*[59] The width of this second limb of ground (c) can be illustrated by reference to two decisions of the Court of Appeal referred to in the paragraphs following. 7–47

Turner & Bell v Searles (Stanford-le-Hope)[60] Premises were let on an oral monthly tenancy to the tenant, which occupied them as a depot in connection with its coach transport business. The local planning authority subsequently served an enforcement notice requiring that use to be discontinued, and an appeal to the Secretary of State was dismissed. Accordingly, after the date on which the enforcement notice became effective, the continued use of the premises by the tenant became a criminal offence under s.89(5) of the Town and Country Planning Act 1971.[61] The local planning authority did not, in fact, bring any prosecution, apparently because it was reluctant to force the tenant out of business. The landlord served a notice under s.25 specifying ground (c). At the hearing of the tenant's application for a new tenancy the tenant's witness made it clear that the tenant intended to carry on the illegal use, if granted a new tenancy. The Court of Appeal held that the wide words at the end of paragraph (c) entitled the court to look at everything which it thought relevant in connection with the tenant's use or management of the holding past, present and future which might enable the court fairly to exercise its discretion. In any event, it was the duty of the court, whether or not the point was taken by the parties, to raise any question 7–48

---

55 [2008] EWCA Civ 1270; (2009) 1 P. & C.R. D. 20.
56 [1986] 1 E.G.L.R. 148 CA.
57 [1971] 2 E.G.L.R. 58 CA.
58 [2008] EWCA Civ 1270; (2009) 1 P. & C.R. D. 20.
59 [2008] EWCA Civ 1270 at [20].
60 [1977] 2 E.G.L.R. 58 CA.
61 See now s.179 of the Town and Country Planning Act 1990.

of illegality or immorality and it would be absurd for the court to order the parties to enter into an illegal and unenforceable contract.

7–49 ***Beard (formerly Coleman) v Williams***[62] The tenant carried on the business of breeding greyhounds from certain fields and stables. The tenant had, in breach of the terms of the tenancy, resided in a van on the field. In April 1984 the tenant was required by court order to remove the van. This he did and placed it outside the holding, about 100 yards away from the dog kennels. As the tenant was no longer residing on the field he lost his training licence. The van was, however, sufficiently close to the kennels so as to enable the tenant to carry on his breeding activities satisfactorily. If the tenant was required to move his van any further away, it would have had an adverse effect on his business. The precise location of the van was not clear from the evidence, but it appeared that, wherever it was, it was stationed unlawfully, although no steps had been taken by the police or local authority or private persons to have it removed.

The landlord served upon the tenant a notice pursuant to s.25 specifying ground (c) (other reasons or breaches) of s.30(1). The county court judge refused the grant of a new tenancy on the ground that to do so would sanction the tenant's illegal residence and this illegality was a reason, in the words of s.30(1)(c), "connected with the tenant's use or management of the holding".

On appeal it was held:

(1) It could not be said that the tenant's use of the land demised was illegal. The unlawful character of the living arrangements which enabled him to carry on his business did not prevent the court from granting a new tenancy, for the grant of a new tenancy did not sanction those unlawful arrangements (*Turner & Bell v Searles* distinguished).

(2) However, the precarious nature of the tenant's living arrangements constituted a "reason" connected with the tenant's use or management of the holding within s.30(1)(c), for, if the tenant was required to move from his existing place of abode, his business would, on the evidence, deteriorate rapidly, with the obvious prejudice to the landlord.

(3) On the question of the exercise of the court's discretion as to whether or not the tenant ought to be granted a new tenancy, it was unclear from the county court judge's notes which matters, other than illegality, he took into account. Although the Court of Appeal could itself exercise the discretion, the facts on which the court could exercise that discretion were not, on the evidence, known and accordingly the matter was to be remitted to the county court judge to reconsider his decision in the light of the observations of the Court of Appeal.

---

62 [1986] 1 E.G.L.R. 148 CA.

Must relate to "holding" under second limb

The "other reasons" must be connected with the use and management of the holding.[63] However, it is not necessary that the acts complained of should themselves take place on the "holding". It is sufficient if a connection between them and the use and management of the holding is established: *Beard v Williams*[64] (digested in para.7–49), above. **7–50**

It is also to be noted that the use and management which can be complained of is "the tenant's" use and management. Thus it would appear that, if part of the premises have been sub-let and the sub-tenant is using his premises in an objectionable way, the landlord would not be able to rely on the second limb of ground (c) against the tenant, because the use and management of the sub-let part is not that of the tenant and the matter objected to does not relate to the use and management of "the holding". If, of course, the tenant's user clause was framed in such a way as to make him responsible for the default of the sub-tenant, the landlord could rely upon the first limb of ground (c). **7–51**

Fault necessary under second limb?

On a literal reading of ground (c) it is not necessary for the landlord to show that the tenant is in any way at fault in relation to the "other reason" connected with the use and management of the holding. It could, accordingly, be argued that the landlord might rely upon ground (c) where the use to which the tenant was putting the holding was one permitted by the terms of the tenancy, but which for some other reason was socially undesirable, perhaps because of a change in the nature of the locality. Lord Denning in *Cheryl Investments v Saldanha*[65] (digested in para.1–39) even went so far as to suggest that a tenant, who had (lawfully) changed his user of the premises so that it ceased to be Rent Act protected and came within the 1954 Act might thereby be subject to ground (c). Although this accords with a literal construction of ground (c), the authors believe that a court is likely to hold that some degree of fault must be established, since if a tenancy is refused upon this ground the tenant will not be entitled to compensation. The other grounds in respect of which no compensation is payable all involve fault on the part of the tenant. **7–52**

Court entitled to look at all relevant circumstances

The words "in view of" are used in ground (c) as in grounds (a) and (b). It would appear that the court is entitled to take a general view under ground (c) whether the tenant should in all the circumstances be granted a new tenancy, which is unquestionably the case under ground (a) (see para.7–17 et seq.). **7–53**

---

[63] For the meaning of "the holding", see para.8–06 et seq.
[64] [1986] 1 E.G.L.R. 148 CA.
[65] [1978] 1 W.L.R. 1329; [1979] 1 All E.R. 5 CA.

Court's discretion

7–54 As noted above (paras 7–18 to 7–20), the words "ought not" confer a discretion on the court to grant or refuse a new tenancy once the basic facts under ground (c) have been established. Reference should be made to those paragraphs for the way in which the discretion should be exercised and in particular the relevance which an undertaking from the tenant for the future, or the imposition of terms, may have to the court's decision.[66] If the "literal construction" (see para.7–52) is the correct one, the fact that a tenant is not at fault would no doubt be most material to the court's discretion.

Relevant date

7–55 In *Betty's Cafes*,[67] Viscount Simonds and Lords Morton and Keith treated the question of the relevant date upon which the matters under ground (c) had to be established as being exactly analogous to the position under grounds (a) and (b) (see paras 7–26 and 7–41). Lords Somervell and Denning had nothing to say on the subject.

---

[66] See also *John Kay Ltd v Kay* [1952] 2 Q.B. 258 at 271, 272 CA, where the court was concerned with the wording of s.12(3)(a) of the Leasehold Property (Temporary Provisions) Act 1951, which provided that "The court shall not order the grant of a new tenancy if it is satisfied—(a) that the tenant has broken any of the terms or conditions of the expiring tenancy, and that in view of the nature and circumstances of the breach a new tenancy ought not to be granted . . .". Evershed M.R. said:

"The Judge found that there has been breaches of the repairing covenant. A reference to para.(a) in subsection (3) shows that that of itself does not suffice, because a court must also be satisfied, in view of the nature and circumstances of the breach, that a new tenancy ought not to be granted. Again I refrain from attempting any exhaustive exposition of the significance of that phrase, but plainly the second half of the paragraph involves the Judge in the duty of considering whether, it the tenancy is extended as suggested, the breach is such as will really prejudice the proper interests of the landlord. In regard to that the judge goes on to say: 'But I have decided that I cannot hold that in view of the nature and circumstances of the breach a new tenancy ought not to be granted'; and then he proceeds to give his reasons, and I think they are satisfactory reasons. 'The tenants' (he proceeds) 'are a company with substantial assets but I see no reason to think that the landlords would be in any way prejudiced by the granting of a temporary new tenancy in so far as concerns their prospects of having the necessary repairs done, or payment on account of dilapidations made in due course; and I bear in mind the tenants' undertaking at the hearing to get the most urgent repairs dealt with forthwith.' It is not suggested that the premises had got into a disreputable condition; indeed, the attractive offers which other persons apparently made for a lease of them negatived, I should have thought, such a view. I think the judge rightly concluded that, having regard to the extent of the business of the tenants, and taking into account that they had undertaken forthwith to do some urgent repairs, the existence of these breaches ought not to prevent him from making an order, and he did not think, as a ground for that conclusion, that the landlords would suffer prejudice or damage as a consequence".

[67] *Betty's Cafes Ltd v Phillips Furnishing Stores Ltd* [1959] A.C. 20 HL.

6. GROUND (D)—SUITABLE ALTERNATIVE ACCOMMODATION

The statutory wording

Under para.(d) of s.30(1), a landlord may oppose an application on the following ground[68]: **7–56**

> "That the landlord has offered and is willing to provide or secure the provision of alternative accommodation for the tenant, that the terms on which the alter-native accommodation is available are reasonable having regard to the terms of the current tenancy and to all other relevant circumstances, and that the accommodation and the time at which it will be available are suitable for the tenant's requirements (including the requirement to preserve goodwill) having regard to the nature and class of his business and to the situation and extent of, and facilities afforded by the holding."

Whether prior offer necessary

The landlord[69] must "have offered" to provide, or secure the provision of, alternative accommodation for the tenant. What is the latest date by which the landlord must have made an offer? In *Chaplin (M) Ltd v Regent Capital Holdings Ltd*[70] (decided in 1983), H.H. Judge Aron Owen sitting at Clerkenwell County Court held that it was unnecessary for the landlord to have made the offer of alternative accommodation before service of the landlord's s.25 notice. The requirement to "have offered" alternative accommodation was satisfied if the offer was made before the issues between the parties were joined in the pleadings. Accordingly, the judge held that an offer of alternative accommodation contained in a letter under cover of which the s.25 notice was served complied with the requirements of s.30(1)(d). This decision conflicts with the dictum of Lord Denning in *Betty's Cafes*[71] at 50, where he said: **7–57**

> "If a landlord opposes on the ground that 'I have offered you alternative accommodation and am willing to provide it', he clearly means that *in the past*, at some time before the notice, he *has offered* alternative accommodation, and that *in the present*, at the time of giving the notice, he is willing to provide it." [Emphasis Lord Denning's.]

However, the county court judge drew attention to Viscount Simonds' statement in *Betty's Cafes* that it would not "be reasonable to reduce the time within which the landlord should have the opportunity of finding and offering alternative accommodation" and pointed out that where the renewal procedure had been initiated by the tenant under s.26 the landlord may encounter practical difficulties if he had to show that he "has offered" alternative accommodation before the expiry of the two-month period within which he had to serve his counter-notice. **7–58**

---

[68] For a consideration of the evidence to be relied upon by the parties in support of, or in opposition to this ground, see para.11–45 et seq.

[69] This is the person falling within s.44: see para.3–87.

[70] [1994] 1 E.G.L.R. 249 CC.

[71] *Betty's Cafes Ltd v Phillips Furnishing Stores Ltd* [1959] A.C. 20 HL at 50.

It is, therefore, not authoritatively established whether or not the offer of alternative accommodation must be made before the date of giving of the s.25 notice or relevant counter-notice.[72]

May the landlord revise the offer?

7–59 It is unclear whether the offer, when made, must satisfy all or any of the conditions of suitability and reasonableness which must be established at the date of the hearing. In the *Chaplin*[73] decision above, the judge held that the conditions of suitability and reasonableness need to be satisfied only at the date of the hearing and not prior to that date. If this is correct a landlord may first offer (at whatever is the relevant date) alternative accommodation which is unsuitable and on unreasonable terms at the date of the offer, albeit available (so as to comply with the requirement to "have offered" alternative accommodation). It is unclear whether, as the judge held in the *Chaplin* case, "the offer must be kept open from the time made and throughout and must not be withdrawn" or whether the landlord may then substitute at a later date another offer of alternative accommodation in respect of which the landlord has better prospects of satisfying the requirements of suitability and reasonableness at the hearing. It seems to the authors that the latter interpretation accords better with the policy of the Act and its inherent flexibility, which the judge himself recognised as being an important justification for his non-literal interpretation. As was argued by counsel for the landlord in the *Chaplin* case, not to permit an alteration of the landlord's offer would prevent him from accommodating a change in circumstances. The statutory timetable is such that a considerable period of time, usually many months, inevitably elapses between the giving of a notice by the landlord under s.25 or s.26(6) of the Act and the hearing of the application in court. During that time, circumstances can change enormously. It would be an impossible, or almost impossible, feat for a landlord to make an offer which is "spot on" from inception and will remain so throughout the lengthy period that is going to elapse. Furthermore, an extension of that period is postulated by s.31(2) of the Act. That subsection, contains a provision which, in the circumstances and time-limit set out, has the effect of prolonging the date at which the court is to be satisfied that the ground has been established, to a future date when that ground will be satisfied. It would seem absurd that the landlord can establish the ground of opposition within the months post-dating the trial by a revision of the alternative accommodation so as to satisfy the court at the later date referred to in s.31(2) but not by making the same revision before trial.

7–60 The ability to revise the offer once made also accords with the dicta of Viscount Simonds in *Betty's Cafes*,[74] which suggest that the landlord is entitled

[72] In the more recent decision of *Knollys House Ltd v Sayer* [2006] P.L.S.C.S. 55 CC the judge stated that it was sufficient in order to satisfy the requirement of "has offered" that such an offer was made before judgment. The authors respectfully doubt the correctness of this decision in the light of the discussion in paras 7.57 and 7.58 and of the *Chaplin (M) Limited v Regent Capital Holdings Ltd* [1994] 1 E.G.L.R. 249 decision.

[73] [1994] 1 E.G.L.R. 249 CC.

[74] [1959] A.C. 20 HL.

subsequently to substitute different alternative accommodation to that offered (see para.7–64). Viscount Simonds in considering the relevant date at which the landlord's intention for para.(f) should be established considered a number of other grounds of opposition. In doing so he considered that para.(d) was of assistance. He said:

> "Perhaps a brighter light is thrown by para.(d), which opens with the words 'that the landlord has offered and is willing', etc. Here the perfect and the present tense are used. Leave out the perfect and look only at the present tense: 'the landlord is willing'. It would be a hardship and worse on the tenant, if the relevant date were any other than that of the hearing; it is to his advantage that the opportunity of accepting an offer of alternative accommodation should be open to the last moment . . . nor would it be reasonable to reduce the time within which the landlord should have the opportunity of finding and offering alternative accommodation. If the tenant complains that he has had too little time to consider its suitability, his grievance can be met by an appropriate adjournment. In para.(d), therefore I find support, if it be needed, for the view that the word 'intends' in para.(f) means intends at the date of the hearing.[75]"

This passage suggests that the landlord should not be shut out in relation to a revised offer albeit made at the hearing. **7–61**

In *Mark Stone Car Sales Ltd v Howard de Walden Estates Ltd*[76] the tenant sought to argue that the court was confined to considering only the terms of the landlord's original offer and any revision thereof by the landlord during the course of the hearing was to be ignored. The court declined to consider this issue, the matter being sought to be raised only for the first time on appeal (not having been raised at trial). In the course of giving judgment in favour of the landlord in revoking the leave that had been granted to the tenant to appeal on this issue, Brooke L.J. pointed out that:

> ". . . The Act, as at present worded, does not make it clear whether the trial judge is limited to considering the terms of the original offer of alternative accommodation which is made to the tenant before the service of a landlord's counter-notice or whether he is allowed to consider the terms of an offer made for the first time before issue is joined in the pleadings, as Judge Aron Owen held in 1983 in *M. Chaplin Ltd v Regent Capital Holdings Ltd* . . ., or whether he can consider the terms of an improved offer made by the land-lords before the end of the trial (subject of course to a special order as to costs), as both Counsel and the trial Judge assumed in the present proceedings."

In the county court decision of *Knollys House Ltd v Sayer*[77] multiple offers were made and there was no argument by the tenant that the court was not entitled to consider all offers made.

Nature of offer

It is considered that, whether or not the judge in *Chaplin (M) Ltd v Regent Capital Holdings Ltd*[78] was right as to the relevant date at which the "offer" must be made, the offer must be one which is capable of acceptance by the tenant. Thus, it would seem that an offer made "subject to contract" is not one capable of **7–62**

---

[75] [1959] A.C. 20 at 36.
[76] (1997) 73 P. & C.R. D43.
[77] [2006] P.L.S.C.S. 55 CC.
[78] [1994] 1 E.G.L.R. 249 CC.

acceptance and would thus not satisfy the statutory provisions. Whether the offer must specify in every detail matters such as the precise rent to be paid is unclear. It is presumably sufficient to offer a tenancy of defined premises at a specific rental figure "or such other rental as the court may determine", as was in fact done in the *Chaplin* case, where the judge determined, upon the evidence before him, what was a reasonable rent for the alternative premises. Whatever the form the offer takes it must be an offer by him to provide the alternative accommodation. One often sees landlords trawling through particulars of appropriate alternative accommodation and sending these to the tenant for the tenant's consideration. However, unless the landlord proposes to purchase or lease the same, simply pointing out to the tenant that such accommodation exists is not going to assist the landlord. The landlord must be able to establish that *he* is willing to provide or secure the provision of the alternative accommodation.

Landlord must be "willing" at date of hearing

7–63 The landlord must also show that he is "willing to provide or secure the provision of alternative accommodation for the tenant". As appears from the decision of the House of Lords in *Betty's Cafes*,[79] the question of whether the landlord "is willing" is to be tested as at the date of the hearing. In the *Chaplin*[80] case, the judge commented that "the present tense . . . connotes a confirmed willingness".

Date at which condition of availability must be satisfied

7–64 Although it is clear that the willingness must be present at the date of the hearing and that the accommodation must be "available" at all material times. Viscount Simonds says in *Betty's Cafes* that it would not "be reasonable to reduce the time within which the landlord should have the opportunity of finding and offering alternative accommodation". This suggests that it is possible for the landlord, having made an offer of alternative accommodation, which has presumably then become unavailable for some reason, to use the time up to the date of the hearing to find other suitable alternative accommodation. Although Lord Keith stresses that there must be a "continuing willingness", he says that the question "What is to happen if the alternative accommodation offered disappears after the date of the section 25 notice?" is a problem that may some day have to be considered. It is to be noted that these observations seem to be based on the premise that the offer has been made prior to service of the s.25 notice, contrary to the view of the judge in *Chaplin.* None of the other speeches in *Betty's Cafes* appears to deal expressly with the point. The authors reach the conclusion, based upon what Viscount Simonds said, that it is sufficient if the landlord proves at the date of the hearing that he is, at that date, willing to provide accommodation and that the accommodation will be available at a defined date in the future. This, however, raises certain practical problems in relation to the other parts of ground (d). The ground talks of the terms "on which the alternative accommodation is available"

79 [1959] A.C. 20 HL.
80 [1994] 1 E.G.L.R. 249 CC.

being reasonable. The word "is" is unfortunate if the accommodation does not have to be available at the date of the hearing. How is the reasonableness of the terms to be judged if the premises are not available and thus the terms upon which they will be available are not known at the date of the hearing? The answer is probably that the landlord, in showing that he is "willing", has to be specific about particular accommodation which is on offer and about the terms on which it is on offer. He need not show that it is "available" in the sense that the tenant could occupy it on the date of the hearing. He merely has to show that it will be available at the termination of the current tenancy and that when it is available it will be available on reasonable terms. This view is reinforced by the later reference in ground (d) to "the time at which it will be available".

Terms on which accommodation available

Generally

The terms on which the alternative accommodation is available must be "reasonable having regard to the terms of the current tenancy and to all relevant circumstances". This follows the wording of s.35, which governs the terms of a new tenancy to be granted by the court, and it is accordingly thought that the court will be guided by the same considerations as are explained in *O'May v City of London Real Property Co Ltd*[81] (digested in para.8–47). This necessarily involves a comparison between the terms of the current tenancy and those which are offered, so that the question whether the terms are reasonable is not considered in isolation, but as a matter of comparison. Probably the word "terms" includes the amount of rent. **7–65**

A landlord is not, however, required to offer to provide as part of the alternative accommodation items equivalent to those which constitute tenant's fixtures and fittings in the existing holding: *Knollys House Ltd v Sayer*,[82] a decision of the Central London County Court, where it was said that the "holding" demised did not include tenant's fixtures and fitting, and thus the accommodation to be provided, and which was to suitable for the tenant's requirements, did not require anything more than the "facilities afforded by the holding". As the fixtures and fittings did not form part of the holding (as that expression is defined in the 1954 Act) such did not need to offered to be provided by the landlord with respect to the alternative accommodation.[83] **7–66**

Fitting out

It is unclear whether a landlord is required, in order to succeed under ground (d), to offer to pay for the cost of the fitting out of the alternative accommodation, **7–67**

[81] [1982] 2 W.L.R. 407; [1982] 1 All E.R. 660 HL. See para.8–46 et seq. for a full discussion of this important case.

[82] [2006] PLSCS 55.

[83] See also the decision of Sales J. in *Humber Oil Terminals Trustee Ltd v Associated British Ports* [2012] EWHC 1336 (Ch) as to what is to be considered part of "the holding" for the purposes of determining an interim rent. This is discussed at para.9–34 et seq.

whether that payment is direct, e.g. by way of a capital sum or indirect, e.g. by way of the provision of a rent free period as a term of the lease of the alternative accommodation. The authors do not suggest that there is a clear and easy answer to this question. In the view of the authors a number of factors come into play[84]:

(1) The tenant is not entitled to a rent free period or cost of fit out on any renewal of the holding and thus it may be said that there is no justification for requiring the landlord to offer such on the alternative accommodation.
(2) On the other hand a rent free period for fitting out may be offered in the open market to any incoming tenant. The reference to "all other relevant circumstances" would indicate that the Court could have regard to the open market and the existence of fit out periods provided in the open market. If this is so, it may be said that the tenant should have the same advantage as any other prospective tenant of the proposed alternative accommodation, particularly given that he has to uproot himself against his wishes.
(3) Equally, it may be argued that the court is not required to slavishly follow the practice in the open market given that it is concerned not with what would be offered in the open market, but what is reasonable for the tenant to be offered having regard to the terms of the current tenancy and other relevant circumstances.
(4) The provision of a fit out period could be said to be the payment, essentially, of a premium to the tenant to vacate. The statute reflects the "premium" that is required, if any, to be paid. In the case of ground (d) there is no "premium", i.e. it is a non-compensatable ground and thus a requirement to provide for the costs of fitting out or to provide a fit out period would essentially provide compensation via a back door.

Suitability

7–68 The question of suitability arises under two heads: both the nature of the accommodation itself and the time at which it will become available must be "suitable for the tenant's requirements (including the requirement to preserve goodwill)".

Time at which accommodation will become available

7–69 Paragraph (d) does not specify a time at which the accommodation should be available upon the termination of the tenant's current tenancy, save that the time at which it is to be available must be suitable for the tenant's requirements, including the requirement to preserve goodwill. Paragraph (d) is to be contrasted

[84] In Haley, *The Statutory Regulation of Business Tenancies*, 1st edn (Oxford: OUP), para 8.06 it is said that "The expense to be incurred in moving premises is not, however, a factor which will affect reasonableness nor, it is submitted, suitability. It is, instead, an inevitable risk which all tenants face at the expiry of their contractual terms". However, this seems to me to miss the point that but for the landlord's ground of possession the tenant would not be obliged to vacate. If he were to do so of course he does so voluntarily and thus voluntarily takes on the risk. However, under para.(d) the landlord is imposing that risk on him.

with other mandatory grounds within s.30(1). The other mandatory grounds, such as (f) and (g) refer to the intention being one "at the termination of the current tenancy." It has been held in the context of paragraph (f) that one does not have to intend to start immediately on the termination of the current tenancy but it is sufficient if one intends to do so within a reasonable time of termination: *Livestock Underwriting Agency Ltd v Corbett and Newson Ltd*[85] (where a start within three months of the termination of the current tenancy was held to be within the statutory wording).

In an ordinary case, for example, where the tenant is a multiple retailer, it may be that a short interval between the termination of the old tenancy and the commencement of the new tenancy at the alternative accommodation would not actually adversely affect the tenant. By contrast, there may be cases where there cannot be any form of interruption in the service the tenant provides, e.g. if it were performing a statutory function. If this is the case, the tenant may quite properly contend that anything other than a smooth transfer from one set of premises to the next would be unsuitable.

Goodwill

It is difficult to define the exact meaning of "goodwill" for the purposes of ground (d). It cannot mean adherent goodwill, in the sense of goodwill which is particular to the holding, because that kind of goodwill must, by definition, be destroyed by a move from the holding. It may, however, extend to goodwill which is not particular to the holding itself, but is related to the general locality, so that a loyal clientele might be prepared to patronise a restaurant if it moved across the street, but not if it moved to a different part of town; the other part of town might be equally suitable for restaurant use in general, but the particular goodwill of that restaurant would be destroyed by the move. Where the business itself is such as to generate its own goodwill irrespective of the particular locality, it is suggested that the court will only be concerned to see whether the location of the offered premises is generally suitable to the tenant's business. Often, therefore, a major company with no local reputation will have no goodwill to take. On the other hand there may be a business which has established a certain local reputation which may be badly affected by even a relatively slight change of location. **7–70**

Other matters to which the court will have regard

In judging the question of suitability under both heads, the court is specifically required to have regard to the following matters: **7–71**

(1) The nature and class of the tenant's business. This involves no comparison with existing accommodation, but rather a consideration of whether the available accommodation is suited to the tenant's particular business.
(2) The situation and extent of the holding. This presumably requires some comparison with what the tenant has already, since the reference to the

[85] (1955) 165 E.G. 469 CC.

"holding" must be a reference to that part of the premises comprised in the current tenancy which the tenant occupies for business purposes (see para.8–06 et seq.). The "situation" clearly includes the geographical location of the holding and may also include its situation in a particular multi-storey building. In *Chaplin (M) Ltd v Regent Capital Holdings Ltd*[86] accommodation on the second floor was held to be suitable as an alternative to the existing ground-floor accommodation. The reference to "extent" may indicate that the tenant should not normally be expected to move into accommodation which is less commodious than his holding. It may also suggest that if he is cramped for space in his existing holding he cannot expect to be offered more spacious alternative accommodation, even if more spacious accommodation would be more suitable to the nature and class of his business. It should, however, be noted that in *Chaplin*[87] the judge accepted a submission that "the alternative accommodation does not have to mirror exactly the existing accommodation".

(3) The facilities afforded by the holding. Once again, this requires a process of comparison, which can cut both ways. The facilities available in the holding may be inadequate for a business of the nature and class of the tenant's business, but that does not necessarily mean that the tenant can insist on having better facilities in the alternative accommodation. A landlord is not, however, required to offer to provide those matters which constitute tenant's fixtures and fittings: *Knollys House Ltd v Sayer*[88] It is unclear whether, as under the Rent Acts, part of the "holding" can constitute "alternative" accommodation; the county court has so held: see *Lawrence v Carter*.[89]

7–72 The tenant's own belief as to the unsuitability of the alternative accommodation, if unsubstantiated by tangible evidence, is to be ignored. In *Tak Pin Yeung v Waller Investment Trust*[90] the tenant contended that the alternative accommodation was unsuitable because its Feng Shui was decidedly inferior to that of the existing accommodation.[91] The tenant believed that the positive chi energy in the demised premises had a direct impact on his financial prosperity and general well being. Negative chi could bring about financial ruin, disharmony, illness, accident and even death. The tenant called evidence to show that the alternative accommodation had negative chi. The judge rejected as a reason for its unsuitability the tenant's belief as to the absence of positive chi. There was no evidence of unsuitability in a tangible sense. The unsuitability was a product of the tenant's state of mind engendered by a belief that the new premises

86 [1984] 1 E.G.L.R. 249 CC.

87 [1984] 1 E.G.L.R. 249 CC.

88 [2006] P.L.S.C.S. 55. See para.7–66.

89 [1956] E.G.D. 229; (1956) 106 L.J. 269 CC.

90 Unreported 2002, County Court decision of H.H. Judge Hallgarten QC.

91 Underlying the principle of Feng Shui is the idea of "chi", which is the all pervasive life force which exists, it is said, everywhere and permeates both ourselves and our homes and physical surroundings. The art of Feng Shui in its application to business premises is to organise the premises in such a way as to encourage positive chi energy.

contradicted the principles of Feng Shui. This was not a ground for rejecting the alternative accommodation. The learned judge said:

> "There is nothing objectively offensive in [the alternative accommodation]. The Claimant simply believes that, having regard to a number of factors taken into account by the Feng Shui master, including his own date and time of birth, he and his family will not prosper there ... Respect for the claimant's belief, or indeed the underlying belief system, does not, in my view, mean that a court is obliged to impose on a landlord cultural norms which would stifle economic development ... I do not consider that where the subsection refers to the "situation" of the holding it refers to other than the purely physical situation of the proposed new premises. In my view, the words cannot be read so as to extend to the situation as it affects the claimant spiritually or psychologically".

Court has no discretion

Ground (d) is not discretionary: if it is established, the court must refuse to grant a new tenancy: per Birkett L.J. in the Court of Appeal in *Betty's Cafes*.[92] Compensation is not payable.[93] **7–73**

Relevant date

The various dates relevant to the establishment of the ground under para.(d) have already been considered (see paras 7–58, 7–60, 7–63 and 7–64). **7–74**

Tenant's position where landlord succeeds

Paragraph (d) does not expressly provide for what is to happen when the landlord has proved his willingness at the hearing, with the result that the tenant's application for a new tenancy is dismissed. The tenant is, of course, free to accept the position and to vacate the holding at the termination of his current tenancy rather than taking up the alternative accommodation offered. What is, however, not clear is to what extent the landlord is bound to provide or secure the provision of the alternative accommodation which he has offered, and which he has proved, to the satisfaction of the court, that he is willing to provide. Is this to be taken as an offer which is open up to the date of judgment? Or for a reasonable time thereafter? Or until such time as the court may determine? Or until the reasonable date upon which the court has been satisfied that it will be available? If the landlord's prior offer is different from the offer which he makes at the hearing, then do both offers remain open and, if so, for how long? Do the formal requirements of the Law of Property (Miscellaneous Provisions) Act 1989 apply to the offer and its acceptance? Is a successor in title to the landlord bound by any offer made? These difficulties remain to be resolved. **7–75**

---

92 [1956] 1 W.L.R. 678; [1957] 1 All E.R. 1 CA.

93 See Ch.12.

7. GROUND (E)—CURRENT TENANCY CREATED BY SUB-LETTING OF PART

The statutory wording

7–76 Under para.(e) of s.30(1), a landlord may oppose an application for a new tenancy on the following ground[94]:

> "Where the current tenancy was created by the sub-letting of part only of the property comprised in a superior tenancy and the landlord is the owner of an interest in reversion expectant on the determination of that superior tenancy, that the aggregate of the rents reasonably obtainable on separate lettings of the holding and the remainder of that property would be substantially less than the rent reasonably obtainable on a letting of that property as a whole, that on the termination of the current tenancy the landlord requires possession of the holding for the purpose of letting or otherwise disposing of the said property as a whole, and that in view thereof the tenant ought not to be granted a new tenancy."

Current tenancy must be a sub-letting of part

7–77 The first condition for the application of ground (e) concerns the nature of the current tenancy. It must have been created by a sub-letting of part only of premises comprised in a superior tenancy. By way of illustration, if A demised a ground-floor shop and first-floor office to B, who then sub-let the office to C, the first condition in ground (e) would be fulfilled in respect of C's sub-tenancy.

"Landlord" must be superior landlord

7–78 The second condition for the application of ground (e) concerns the nature of the interest of the "landlord", as defined in s.44 (see para.3–85). The landlord must be the owner of an interest expectant on the termination of the superior tenancy out of which the sub-tenancy was created. To return to the illustration above, A (not B) would fulfil this condition in respect of C's current tenancy, assuming that A is the "landlord" as defined. In *Greaves v Stanhope*[95] it was held that the surrender of the superior tenancy prior to service of the s.25 notice prevented the landlord from relying upon ground (e). He was not able to show that he "is" the owner of the relevant interest.

Effect on rental value

7–79 The third condition for the application of ground (e) requires the carrying out of an exercise in comparative valuation.

(1) First, one must suppose that there are separate lettings of:
   (a) the "holding", that is to say that part of the property comprised in the current tenancy which is occupied by the tenant for business purposes (see para.8–06); and

---

94 For a consideration of the evidence to be relied upon by the parties in support of, or in opposition to this ground, see para.11–50 et seq.
95 (1973) 228 E.G. 725.

(b) of the rest of the property comprised in the superior tenancy.

It is the valuer's task to say what rents would be achieved on those separate lettings. They are added together.

(2) It is then necessary to carry out a second valuation exercise upon the supposition that the property comprised in the superior tenancy is being let as a whole. The valuer's task is to say what rent would be achieved upon that supposed letting.

(3) The figure ascertain in (2) is then compared with the aggregated figure assessed under the first valuation and, if the aggregated figure is "substantially less", the third condition under ground (e) is made out. In *Greaves v Stanhope*,[96] the landlord failed to establish that the aggregate of the rents would be "substantially" less.

To return to our illustration, if the rent obtainable on a separate letting of the office was £1,500 per annum and that obtainable on a separate letting of the shop were £2,000 per annum, A would have to show that, by letting the shop and offices as a whole to one tenant, he would obtain a rent which was substantially greater than £3,500 per annum.[97] **7–80**

Landlord's requirement

The fourth condition to be fulfilled under ground (e) concerns the landlord's requirement. He must show that "on the termination of the current tenancy" he "requires possession of the holding for the purpose of letting or otherwise disposing of the said property as a whole". It is thought that in order to satisfy this condition the landlord will have to show both that he genuinely intends to let or otherwise dispose of the property as a whole and that he will be in a position to do so once he has determined the current tenancy. This necessarily involves him showing that he will be able to obtain vacant possession of those parts of the property which are not comprised in the "holding". Presumably, therefore, ground (e) will not be applicable unless the superior tenancy is one to which the Act does not apply, or the landlord can show that he will be able to determine it. **7–81**

Does the court have a discretion?

Finally, once the above conditions have been satisfied, the question for the court is whether "in view thereof the tenant ought not to be granted a new tenancy". The words "ought not" have been held, in relation to grounds (a), (b) and (c), to confer a discretion on the court (see para.7–18). Assuming that these words also confer a discretion under ground (e), it is difficult to foresee, in the absence of any judicial guidance, upon what principles that discretion would be exercised. Unlike grounds (a), (b) and (c), no element of fault on the part of the tenant is **7–82**

---

[96] (1973) 228 E.G. 725.

[97] For some guidance on the meaning of "substantial", see para.7–44.

involved under ground (e), so that it may be that the court simply considers all the circumstances, including the circumstances in which the sub-tenancy was created, and balances the hardship to the landlord of having to let on two separate lettings against the hardship to the sub-tenant of being deprived of a new tenancy. Compensation is payable.[98]

Relevant date

7–83 The question arises of the date or dates at which a landlord, who seeks to rely on ground (e), must show that he comes within the various parts of the ground. Clearly the first condition[99]—the nature of the current tenancy—is a matter of past history.

7–84 The second condition[100]—the nature of the landlord's interest—must clearly be fulfilled at the date when he gives his notice. It might also be thought that the words "the landlord is the owner of an interest in reversion expectant on the termination of that superior tenancy . . ." suggest that the landlord must fulfil that condition not only at the date that he gives his notice, but also at all material times up to and including the date of the hearing. That interpretation, however, would lead to the anomalous result that if the "superior tenancy" expired by effluxion of time before the date of the hearing, the landlord could not rely upon ground (e), but if it had not so expired he could. Whether this would happen in any particular case would be entirely fortuitous, depending on how quickly it was possible to obtain a date for hearing.

7–85 As for the relevant date for assessing the valuation consequences of separate lettings as opposed to a letting of the whole,[101] it would appear logical that this should be judged at the date of the hearing. If some other date were the relevant date, it might be that, because of a change in market conditions, the landlord would not in fact obtain a substantially greater rent on a letting of the whole, judged at the date of the hearing, although he could have expected to do so judged at an earlier date, e.g. of the s.25 notice. In those circumstances, there would seem to be no reason to deprive the tenant of a new tenancy since the landlord would, as things had turned out, obtain no real benefit.

7–86 Similarly, it is thought that the question of the genuineness and practicability of the landlord's requirement to let as a whole[102] would be judged at the date of the hearing, by analogy with the similar question of the genuineness and practicability of the landlord's "intention" under grounds (f) and (g).[103]

---

[98] See Ch.12.

[99] See para.7–74.

[100] See para.7–75.

[101] See para.7–76.

[102] See para.7–78.

[103] See para.7–134 et seq.

8. GROUND (F)—DEMOLITION AND RECONSTRUCTION

The statutory wording

Under para.(f) of s.30(1), a landlord may oppose an application for a new tenancy on the following ground[104]: **7–87**

> "That on the termination of the current tenancy the landlord intends to demolish or reconstruct the premises comprised in the holding or a substantial part of those premises or to carry out substantial work of construction on the holding or part thereof and that he could not reasonably do so without obtaining possession of the holding."

Statement of ground (f) in section 25 notice

A landlord, who has stated in his s.25 notice that he intends to rely upon ground (f), must prove an intention to carry out works which fall within the various categories set out in that ground. Prior to the Landlord and Tenant Act 1954 Pt II (Notices) Regulations 1983 the prescribed form provided for the relevant ground to be set out verbatim. However, even in relation to this form it was decided that the landlord is not confined to the kinds of work that he has referred to in his notice: see *Biles v Caesar*,[105] where the landlords had stated that they intended to "demolish and reconstruct the whole of the premises", but at trial proved only an intention to reconstruct a substantial part of the premises. This problem ought not to arise under the current Regulations (the Landlord and Tenant 1954 Pt 2 (Notices) Regulations 2004) , for as with the earlier 1983 Regulations, the form[106] provides only for the appropriate paragraph letter of the ground to be specified. **7–88**

Works within ground (f): a suggested approach

It is suggested that the following approach to the question of whether a particular set of works intended to be carried out by the landlord establishes ground (f) is indicated by the various authorities which are discussed in detail in succeeding paragraphs: **7–89**

(1) The starting point is to identify the totality of the works intended to be carried out.
(2) Next, it is necessary to decide whether any of those works are to be excluded from the ambit of ground (f) because they are works which the landlord is entitled to carry out under the terms of the current tenancy, or are works of repair which either landlord or tenant is obliged to carry out under the terms of the current tenancy, or are works which are not to be carried out on "the holding".

---

[104] For a consideration of the evidence to be relied upon by the parties in support of, or in opposition to, this ground, see para.11–53 et seq.
[105] [1957] 1 W.L.R. 156; [1957] 1 All E.R. 151 CA.
[106] Form 2 to Sch.2 to the Regs, Appendix A2.038.

(3) The remaining works must then be considered under the various individual categories of work mentioned in ground (f), in order to decide which works qualify for inclusion. At this stage works which are "part-and-parcel" of qualifying works, such as essential preliminaries or finishing works, will themselves qualify for inclusion.
(4) Finally, the works identified by operation of the above stages are to be considered and the question for the court is whether they satisfy ground (f).

Stage (1) of the above is largely self-explanatory, but stages (2), (3) and (4) require detailed examination.

The works intended

7–90 Little difficulty should arise in practice at the first stage of identifying the totality of the works which the landlord intends to carry out, although the special meaning of the word "intends" (discussed in paras 7–134 et seq.) should be borne in mind. It is also important to remember that it is not open to the tenant, in challenging ground (f), to contend that the landlord ought to be doing different or other work: *Decca Navigator Co v Greater London Council*[107] (digested in para.7–196).

Works which are to be excluded

7–91 It is convenient to start the next part of the analysis by considering the question whether any of the works which the landlord intends to carry out must be eliminated for any reason from further consideration.

Work must be to the holding

7–92 A category of work which must be ignored for the purposes of ground (f) is work which does not consist of work on or to "the holding". As Lord Evershed M.R. pointed out in *Joel v Swaddle*[108] (digested in para.7–132), "we are bound to confine our attention for this purpose to the holding itself". (For the meaning of "holding", see para.8–06 et seq.) However, the work does not have to be effected upon the whole or a substantial part of the holding. The issue of substantiality relates to the work or the premises comprised in the holding affected by the work, not the extent of the holding upon which that work is to be effected.[109] Thus, in

[107] [1974] 1 W.L.R. 748; [1974] 1 All E.R. 1178 CA.

[108] [1957] 1 W.L.R. 1094; [1957] 3 All E.R. 325 CA.

[109] However, if the landlord does not undertake work to a substantial part of the holding he is likely to be faced with a defence being mounted in reliance upon s.31A, see para.7–192 below. A good example of this is *Fernandez v Walding* [1968] 2 W.L.R. 583; [1968] 1 All E.R. 994 CA, which is a decision prior to the enactment of s.31A. In that case the tenant occupied two-fifths of the front section and the whole of the middle section of a factory. The landlord intended to construct an additional storey over the front section and a wall separating the front and middle sections. The judge granted the tenant a new tenancy of the middle section alone, having found that he was satisfied that the landlord could reasonably carry out all the work he wanted to by obtaining possession of the front section of the factory. The Court of Appeal reversed his decision holding that the court had no

Housleys v Bloomer-Holt[110] (digested in para.7–109) the work affected only one-third of the holding, but as the premises occupying that one-third were going to be demolished, it was held that the landlord succeed under ground (f) as he intended thereby to demolish "the whole of the premises comprised in the holding".

The "holding" will not include the tenant's chattels or fixtures which are capable of removal by the tenant: see para.7–111. **7–93**

Must affect structure

Albeit several of the decisions refer to the demolition and reconstruction of the "structure": e.g. *Percy E Cadle & Co v Jacmarch Properties*[111] (digested in para.7–116); *Joel v Swaddle*[112] (digested in para.7–132); *Romulus Trading Co Ltd v Trustees of Henry Smith's Charity*[113] (digested in para.7–125); *Barth v Prichard*[114] (digested in para.7–124), there is nothing in the wording of s.30(1)(f) which requires the demolition or construction of structural or load-bearing features as a condition of its applicability: *Pumperninks of Piccadilly Ltd v Land Securities Plc*[115] (digested on this point at para.7–98); *Ivorygrove Ltd v Global Grange Ltd*[116] (digested in para.7–120). In the *Pumperninks*decision Chadwick L.J. said: **7–94**

> "What is plain, from [the passages in the various cases] is that cases on the meaning of 'demolish' or 'reconstruct' for the purposes of s.30(1)(f) turn on their particular facts. In each case the relevant questions are: (i) what are the physical features of the property comprised in the tenancy; (ii) what, amongst those features, is capable of being demolished and reconstructed; (iii) is what is being done to those features which are capable of being demolished and reconstructed, taken as a whole, properly to be described as demolition or reconstruction of those features or a substantial part of them? It is, I think, wrong to start from the premise that physical features which are not load-bearing are incapable of being demolished and reconstructed; although it may well be that, in the particular case where there are load-bearing features, work which does not involve the demolition or reconstruction of any of those load-bearing features will not meet the test under (iii). But there is no reason why, in a case where there are physical features which are capable of being demolished and reconstructed, but none which are load-bearing, the test under (iii) should not apply, or should not be met in appropriate circumstances."

---

jurisdiction to grant a new tenancy of part only of the holding. However, after s.31A the tenant in this case may have succeeded in opposing the landlord's ground (f) either by providing means of access to enable the work to the front section or by seeking a tenancy of an economically separable part, i.e. the middle section alone.

[110] [1966] 1 W.L.R. 1244; [1966] 2 All E.R. 966 CA.

[111] [1957] 1 Q.B. 323 at 328, 329–330.

[112] [1957] 1 W.L.R. 1094 at 1100.

[113] [1990] 2 E.G.L.R. 75 at 77. It was said that for works to qualify as "reconstruction" they must be "works involving a substantial interference with the structure of the building, but structure is not necessarily confined to outside or other loadbearing walls" per Farquaharson L.J. But this must not be applied too narrowly. Farquaharson L.J. stated in the same case that works of preparation ancillary to such works are properly included, as is work "closely associated with" the qualifying works, such as the plastering of a new load-bearing wall, as well as the wall itself.

[114] [1990] 1 E.G.L.R. 109 at 111, per Stocker L.J. who said that some form of building upon the premises which involved the structure was required.

[115] [2002] Ch. 332 CA.

[116] [2003] EWHC 1409 (Ch); [2003] 1 W.L.R. 2090.

7–95 In *Ivorygrove Ltd v Global Grange Ltd*[117] (digested in para.7–120) the landlord proposed to undertake a substantial scheme of work to upgrade a hotel, increasing the size but reducing the number of bedrooms and providing all with en-suite facilities. Lawrence Collins J. said that the concepts of demolition and reconstruction did not inevitably involve load-bearing structures. Section 30(1)(f) does not refer to the "structure". Whether the relevant parts of the premises were load-bearing was simply one of the factors to be taken into account in determining the jury question of whether there is demolition or reconstruction, or demolition or reconstruction of a substantial part, or substantial work of construction on the holding or part of it, and not a pre-condition of the applicability of s.30(1)(f). In *Ivorygrove*, there were works which did in fact affect the structure. In *Pumperninks of Piccadilly Ltd v Land Securities Ltd*[118] (digested on this point at para.7–98) the demise consisted of an eggshell only, i.e. the inner skin of the premises, and contained no structural elements. The landlord intended to undertake works the effect of which was essentially to remove that skin so as to make the premises demised part of a larger open space. The court held that the works fell within para.(f). In *Graysim Holdings Ltd v P&O Property Holdings Ltd*[119] it was held that demolition and/or construction need not be confined to load-bearing walls. It was appropriate to describe the removal of the existing interior of a market hall as an exercise in demolition followed by a reconstruction of a substantial part of the premises. It was equally appropriate to describe all of the proposed works as the carrying out of a substantial work of construction on the holding. They were very extensive works which would result in a brand new market hall. There was no appeal from his decision on this aspect.[120]

Conclusion

7–96 The effect of these various decisions is therefore considered to be as follows:

(1) the concepts of demolition and reconstruction do not inevitably involve load-bearing structures. Section 30(1)(f) does not refer to the "structure". There is no requirement for the relevant parts of the holding affected by the work being load-bearing as a pre-condition of the applicability of s.30(1)(f). Physical features which are not load-bearing are capable of being demolished and reconstructed;
(2) whether the relevant parts of the holding are load-bearing is simply one of the factors to be taken into account in determining the question of whether there is demolition or reconstruction, or demolition or reconstruction of a substantial part, or substantial work of construction on the holding or part of it;
(3) where the holding includes structural parts it is arguable that reconstruction (or demolition) requires some demolition or alteration to a load-bearing

[117] [2003] EWHC 1409 (Ch) ; [2003] 1 W.L.R. 2090.
[118] [2002] Ch. 332; [2002] 3 All E.R. 609. The case is also digested at para.7–197 on the issue of the tenant's reliance on s.31A.
[119] [1993] 1 E.G.L.R. 96, Mr Anthony Grabiner QC, first instance.
[120] [1994] 1 W.L.R. 992 CA and [1996] A.C. 329 HL.

part of the structure (or enclosing walls, floor and ceiling even if not load-bearing or structural) included in the demised property;

(4) work associated with demolition and reconstruction, such as works of preparation ancillary to such works, or re-plastering and rewiring, or the laying of cables and drains, may be considered when looking at the totality of the work to determine whether the work is construction or is substantial or is on a substantial part of the premises;

(5) the removal and replacement of partitions other than demountable partitions may constitute demolition of the premises or a substantial part thereof.

Internal demise only

What if the premises as demised exclude any structural or load-bearing elements? How can one be said to undertake work to the structure when no part of the structure is demised? It has been held that a landlord may still succeed under ground (f) notwithstanding a demise of an internal skin only. In *Pumperninks of Piccadilly Ltd v Land Securities Plc*[121] (digested on this point at para.7–98) it was said that the landlord had established his ground of opposition under ground (f) albeit the tenant's demise consisted of an internal skin only. The court followed the approach of the earlier decision of the Court of Appeal in *City Offices (Regent Street) v Europa Acceptance Group*[122] in connection with the operation of a redevelopment break clause. In that case the landlord was entitled to break the lease if it proposed to undertake works of "redevelopment or reconstruction of the demised premises". The demised premises were described as an "air space within an enclosing skin", described by the court as an "eggshell". The premises consisted of a self-contained office on the second floor of a building to which the landlord was proposing to undertake works costing some £20 million. This involved retaining the listed facades to the building, removing internal partitions, suspended ceilings and central heating installations which were to be replaced and to cut through the floor and ceiling slabs to provide access for service pipes and the like. A wall which "formed one of the walls immediately behind the inner plaster skin of part of the demised premises was to be removed". The Court of Appeal held that the works proposed by the landlord constituted works of "reconstruction" notwithstanding the fact that the lease did not include any part of the structure of the building.[123] 7–97

[121] [2002] Ch. 332 CA.

[122] [1990] 1 E.G.L.R. 63 CA.

[123] Nicholls L.J. said:

"The word 'reconstruction' in [the relevant clause] falls to be construed in its context. The context here is a lease of property which does not include any part of the structural framework of the building. The demise essentially is of an air space with fixtures and fittings in a skin comprising . . . plaster coverings of the party walls and of the structural walls and the coverings of the ceilings and the coverings of the floors, including the screed thereon. [The relevant clause] contemplates the possibility of the reconstruction or, I should add, the redevelopment of that particular unit—that 'eggshell' as it has been described. The works proposed to be done will involve the physical removal of most of the eggshell and its replacement, insofar as there will be a replacement, with something different. The floor coverings will be removed and the replacement coverings will result in a slightly higher floor-level. New and lower suspended ceilings will be installed. The walls surrounding the

7–98 ***Pumperninks of Piccadilly Ltd v Land Securities Plc***[124] T's lease of a shop demised:

> "ALL THAT shop and premises situate on the ground floor of the Building . . . including the shop front and fascia thereof and pavement lights (if any) or such interest as the Lessors may have therein TOGETHER with the Lessors fixtures or fittings therein or thereon and the appurtenances thereunto appertaining . . . but there shall be excluded from the demise hereby made the excluded parts of the said premises (hereinafter called 'the excluded parts') defined in the First Schedule hereto AND which said premises (less the excluded parts) are hereinafter referred to as the 'demised premises.'"

The first schedule provided that:

> "'the excluded parts' shall mean the main structure of the Building of which the demised premises form part (but not the internal or external surfaces claddings finishes thereto or thereon within or contiguous to the demised premises) which main structure comprises without prejudice to the generality of the foregoing [*and the general description was then particularised*]."

The upshot of these provisions of the lease was that T's demise was what was known as an "egg-shell" demise, i.e. one which demised only the internal skin of the part of the building occupied. L proposed to do work to T's shop. The overall effect of the work involved the removal of every physical built thing in the demise; effectively the egg-shell and thus the material enclosing the demised premises would be removed and what was T's shop would become part of an open space, which would include adjacent units, to be fitted out by any new occupier or occupiers, providing a floor, a ceiling, plastering or other wall covering and such internal partitions as may be appropriate.

T argued, inter alia,[125] that the work did not fall within ground (f). The judge at first instance held that the work fell within para.(f) as it involved demolition of the demise. He said:

> "I do not think that in the case of an eggshell demise, which includes no load bearing element, there are for that reason no premises capable of demolition. The structure is the fabric which encloses the demise in so far as it is itself demised. In my judgment the physical boundaries of the demise, be they constituted by walls, ceiling or floor, or only their surfaces, are premises within the meaning of the paragraph [(f)] at least if they are of such physical quality as to be sensibly capable in ordinary language of being constructed or part of the construction, or of being demolished. I think in the present case that the tile work which lines the wall, the wooden floorboards covered by a metallic surface which constitute the demised floor and the roller shutter which provides the enclosure of the fourth side of the shop are all capable of being described as constructed or at least meaningfully of being demolished, and they

lease property at the foot of the stem of the letter 'T' will be removed and not replaced, thus creating a single, open floor space embracing in part the lease property and in part other property. The external walls which are not being replaced—will be dry lined, thus reducing the usable lettable space of the lease property in those areas. Further, and importantly, the external brickwork walls fronting onto the two light wells will be demolished and taken away, leaving the lease property open and exposed to the elements for many months while the works proceed. New curtain walls will then be constructed and these will give the lease property an enlarged usable lettable area . . . in short, as the works proceed, the demolition work will involve the physical demolition of most of the eggshell as part of the larger scheme and the rebuilding something significantly different."

[124] [2002] Ch. 332 CA. This is also an important decision on the application of s.31A(1) of the Act. It is digested with respect to this aspect at para.7–189.

[125] T also relied on s.31A(1)(a). On this aspect of the decision, see para.7–197.

> constitute the premises which I hold the landlord has proved he is intending to demolish; and, in the case of the roller shutter, to reconstruct by inserting a new shop front. I take this view of the roller shutter notwithstanding that it appears to be removable from within the runners on each side, which are no doubt affixed to the building at least in part because it is a replacement of the shop front which itself constituted the envelope of the demise. It is in that sense, therefore, part of the fabric or structure of the demise. On the other hand I would not regard its replacement, as proposed, by a shop front consisting of glass within an aluminium frame which would be a day's work costing some £4,200, as 'substantial work of construction' within the second limb of s.30(1)(f). The work of demolition and reconstruction, however, is to the whole of what constitutes the premises so that for the reasons set out in *Housleys Ltd v Bloomer-Holt Ltd*[126] the works intended are within the first limb of the paragraph."

On appeal, T argued that the work did not come within ground (f). It was held:

(1) that the ordinary meaning of the words "demolish" and "reconstruct" were wide enough to apply to an eggshell; an eggshell is capable of being demolished and reconstructed; *City Offices (Regent Street) v Europa Acceptance Group*[127] applied. None of the reported decisions dealt with an eggshell tenancy, where a part of a building was demised but the demise excluded the load-bearing structure of the building and included nothing which performed a structural function in relation to the building. Accordingly, none of the passages in those cases were authority for the proposition advanced on behalf of T that in s.30(1)(f) premises refers only to parts of a built structure which perform some structural function. Chadwick L.J. agreed with the learned judge's description of demolition above;

(2) that the works intended by the landlord (leaving aside the work relating to the roller-blind which involved demolition or re-construction) were works which involved demolition of the premises comprising the holding, or a substantial part of those premises, because, either: (a) as found by the judge they involved the demolition of the eggshell that was demised, or (b) they involved the demolition of that eggshell together with the rights of support which render the eggshell demised capable of occupation and use by a tenant. For the purposes of deciding the appeal it mattered not which was the correct approach;

(3) where the demised property includes structural parts of the building it is arguable that there can never be reconstruction (or demolition) unless there is some demolition or alteration to a load-bearing part of the structure (or enclosing walls, floor and ceiling even if not load-bearing or structural) included in the demised property.

Landlord entitled to carry out works

As Farquaharson L.J. pointed out in *Romulus Trading Co Ltd v Trustees of Henry Smith's Charity*[128] (digested in para.7–125): **7–99**

[126] [1966] 2 All E.R. 966; [1966] 1 W.L.R. 1244.

[127] [1990] 1 E.G.L.R. 63.

[128] [1990] 2 E.G.L.R. 75.

> "It is clear on any basis that certain works must be excluded when a judge is considering the application of (ground (f)). Thus where the landlord has a right of entry under the lease they do not come within ground (f) because he does not need to obtain possession of the holding to carry them out..."

The explanation for this lies in the wording of ground (f), and the case law in which it has been construed. The question of whether the landlord needs to obtain possession is discussed in detail in para.7–102.

Work of repair

7–100 It is thought that work which falls within the tenant's repairing covenant under the current tenancy would not qualify for the purposes of ground (f). This would be the case wherever the landlord had reserved an express right of entry to do such work (although it should be noted that no such right is implied) but would anyway seem to follow from the fact that such work is not work which the landlord needs to do himself as opposed to compelling the tenant to perform his obligation. In *Barth v Pritchard*[129] (digested in para.7–124), Stocker L.J. seems to have accepted a submission to the effect that works which the tenant was required to carry out under an obligation to reinstate contained in a licence "is not work which the appellant landlords need to do if their scheme is carried out".

7–101 If the work falls within the landlord's repairing covenant under the current lease, there appear to be two reasons why such work should be disregarded from consideration. First, it is thought that a tenant would be able successfully to argue that the landlord did not require possession (see para.7–102). Even if the current tenancy contains no express right of entry, a right of entry is implied wherever a landlord has undertaken an obligation to repair the demised premises: *Saner v Bilton*.[130] Secondly, it would also seem that a landlord would not be allowed to rely upon his own wrong insofar as he was seeking to include for the purposes of ground (f) work which only needed to be done because of his own breach of covenant.

Requirement for possession

7–102 In order to rely upon ground (f), the landlord must show "that he could not reasonably [carry out the proposed works] without obtaining possession of the holding". It is to be noted that it is "the holding" which is relevant, not any other premises, even though they might be comprised in the current tenancy. The word "possession" means not physical possession, but the legal right to enter upon the premises: *Heath v Drown*[131] (digested in para.7–103). Clearly, a landlord cannot carry out works "without obtaining possession" under ground (f) if the terms of the tenancy are such that he is not legally entitled to enter upon the holding in order to carry out the works. Where, however, the terms of the current tenancy

---

129 [1990] 1 E.G.L.R. 109 CA.

130 (1878) 7 Ch. D. 815 and see Dowding and Reynolds, *Dilapidations: The Modern Law and Practice*, 5th edn (London: Sweet & Maxwell, 2012), para.22–31.

131 [1973] A.C. 498; [1972] 2 W.L.R. 1306; [1972] 2 All E.R. 561 HL.

contain a reservation of the right to enter to do the relevant work then it is to be assumed that a similar reservation would be carried into the new tenancy and that the landlord would accordingly not need to obtain possession in order to carry out the works, because he is entitled to do so pursuant to the reservation.[132] In the absence of such a reservation, a landlord who has established an intention to do works falling within ground (f) must inevitably succeed in showing that he cannot carry them out without obtaining possession of the holding, subject to the special provisions of s.31A. However, the presence of a reservation in the tenant's current lease will not mean that the landlord fails to establish that he reasonably requires possession of the holding. If the end result of the works is such that the tenant would no longer be able to carry on his business in the reconstructed premises the landlord has been held to require "possession" notwithstanding a reservation apparently wide enough to authorise the entry: *Leathwoods Ltd v Total Oil Great Britain Ltd*[133] (digested in para.7–106). The reservation may be such as to authorise entry to carry out the relevant work, but conditional upon the landlord "making good all damage to the demised premises occasioned by any such entry". In such a case the landlord will succeed in establishing that he reasonably requires possession if he shows that he does not intend and cannot realistically be called upon to make good the damage caused, as the damage is an inherent part of the demolition and reconstruction proposed. Thus, where the landlord's proposed development consisted of the partial demolition of two walls of a shop, the permanent removal of the shop front and lavatory, the removal of two pillars and three old steel joists and the replacement thereof with a new single span joist and the re-siting of the gas and electrical services, it was held that the landlord could not be said to be entitled to exercise his legal rights under the reservation: *Shade v Eric Wright Commercial Ltd.*[134]

Heath v Drown[135] The landlord intended to carry out extensive structural **7–103**
works to the front wall of the building of which the demised premises formed part. The works would have made it impossible for the tenant to remain in occupation for business purposes for a period of between four and nine months. However, the terms of the current tenancy reserved to the landlord "the right at all reasonable hours upon notice to enter upon the demised premises with workmen and appliances for the purposes of carrying out any necessary repairs making good all damage occasioned to the demised premises by any such entry" to the building. It was conceded at trial that the intended work was work which could be lawfully carried out under the terms of this reservation. Accordingly, the House of

---

[132] As to work of repair, see paras 7–100 et seq.

[133] [1985] E.G.L.R. 237.

[134] [2001] EWCA Civ 950. In *Heath v Drown* (digested in para.7–103) the landlord's work consisted of work of repair. It was conceded that the clause was sufficient to enable the landlord to carry out the proposed work. At the end of the operation the premises would exist exactly as they existed before. Thus, although the matter was not argued, there could be no suggestion that the landlord's work was outside the ambit of the clause on the basis that the landlord was not going to be in a position to repair damage caused, as the work proposed consisted of the making good of defects without any alteration to the premises.

[135] [1970] A.C. 498; [1972] 2 W.L.R. 1306; [1972] 2 All E.R. 561, HL.

Lords held that it was not necessary for the landlord to have legal possession of the holding, with the result that it failed to establish the necessary intention under ground (f).

7–104 ***Price v Esso Petroleum Co Ltd***[136] Under the terms of a tenancy of a petrol service station the landlord reserved "the right to enter the service station at any time with workmen and others for the purpose of carrying out such improvements, additions and alterations to the service station as [the landlord] may consider reasonable, after consultation with [the tenant]". The Court of Appeal held that the landlord's proposed works, which involved the total demolition of the existing premises and their replacement with a petrol filling station of a new design, were "improvements" within the reservation, and that the landlord accordingly failed to establish that it needed legal possession in order to implement its proposals.

7–105 ***Little Park Service Station v Regent Oil Co Ltd***[137] The tenant occupied a petrol filling station pursuant to a 21-year lease subject to breaks at the end of the fifth, tenth and fifteenth years. The lease contained a covenant by the tenant "To permit [the landlord] at any time and times during the term and at their own expense to make such structural and other alterations to the premises as they may consider to be necessary or desirable . . .".

The landlord served a notice under s.25 specifying the ground of opposition in ground (f). The county court judge found that the landlord intended the total demolition of the existing building and the construction of a new filling station. He also found that it would be possible to carry out the work without closing down the station but, if it were closed for about a week (which the tenant was willing to do), there would be a saving in cost of £1,000. He concluded that "from a factual point of view only, the landlord had not shown that it could not reasonably carry out the works without obtaining possession". However, since he held that the landlord could not do the work as a matter of right, but only by the tenant's permission, he found that the landlord could not do the work without obtaining possession and dismissed the tenant's application.

The Court of Appeal held that the judge had been wrong to conclude that the landlord could not carry out the works as a matter of right under the current tenancy and under any new tenancy granted by the court. By virtue of the clause allowing the landlord the right to enter and do works, the existing tenancy did not give the tenant the right of exclusive possession.[138]

---

[136] [1980] 2 E.G.L.R. 58 CA.

[137] [1967] 2 Q.B. 655; [1967] 2 W.L.R. 1036; [1967] 2 All E.R. 257 CA.

[138] Although not overruled or even doubted in *Heath v Drown* (where it was discussed in several of the speeches), this judgment reveals a somewhat different approach to that of the House of Lords. In particular the House of Lords has reinstated the requirement that there must be a legal right for the landlord to do the work under the terms of the current tenant in order for it to be found that he does not require "possession". The subsequent insertion of s.31A by the Law of Property Act 1969 should be noted, as should the cases discussed in paras 7–192 et seq. below.

Leathwoods Ltd v Total Oil Great Britain Ltd[139] The tenant carried on the business of a garage for the sale and repair of motor vehicles, together with a petrol-filling service station. The landlord served a s.25 notice opposing the grant of a new tenancy on grounds (f) (demolition and reconstruction) and ground (g) (own occupation) of s.30(1). The landlord gave evidence that he intended to develop a modern service station. To effect this proposal he intended to demolish all the existing buildings on the premises and to construct new pipe islands with a canopy over for sales and new tankage, together with new buildings to contain the control area, shop, office, store, staff-room and toilets, and a car-wash building adjacent. The number of pumps was to be increased and their layout altered. The existing facility for sale and repair of motor vehicles was to go. Planning permission for the proposals had been granted. The cost of the re-development was estimated at £200,000. After completion of the re-development the landlord intended to occupy the premises through its trading division. The board of the landlord had resolved to implement the proposals. **7–106**

By cl.2(16)(a) of the tenant's lease the tenant covenanted:

> "To permit the landlords and its agents to enter the premises for or in connection with the carrying out of any improvement or addition to or alteration of the premises which the landlord may consider desirable."

By cl.2(10) of the tenant's lease it was provided:

> "That the premises shall not without [the landlord's consent . . .] be used for any purpose other than that of a filling and service station together with the sale and repair of motor vehicles."

By the first schedule to the lease the premises were defined as:

> "ALL THAT piece or parcel of land . . . TOGETHER WITH the petrol-filling and service station erected thereon on part thereof and known as . . ."

On the hearing of a preliminary issue as to whether the landlord had made out one or both of its grounds of opposition it was held that:

(1) Although the landlord could, on a construction of the terms of cl.2(16)(a) of the lease, have been entitled to enter upon the premises to carry out the intended works, for all the works proposed were either improvements, additions or alterations, the effect of carrying out the works would be to deprive the tenant of the facilities needed to carry on its business, such that any grant of a new lease would render the landlord in breach of its covenant not to derogate from its grant. In those circumstances, notwithstanding the decisions in *Heath v Drown*[140] (digested in para.7–103) and *Price v Esso*[141] (digested in para.7–104) it was clear the landlord required not only physical occupation of the premises but also legal possession and, therefore, succeeded in establishing its case under ground (f).

139 [1985] 2 E.G.L.R. 237 CA.

140 [1973] A.C. 498; [1972] 2 W.L.R. 1306; [1972] 2 All E.R. 561 HL.

141 [1980] 2 E.G.L.R. 58.

(2) The landlord intended to occupy the holding albeit it intended to demolish all the existing buildings thereon for, following *Cam Gears v Cunningham*[142] (digested in para.7–235), the object of ground (g) is not to hand the holding back to the landlord in a sterilised form, so that he is prevented from making any alteration thereon for the purposes of carrying on his intended business. *Nursey v Currie*[143] (digested in para.7–234) was confined to cases where the "holding" comprises buildings only.

Categories of work within ground (f)

A landlord may show all or some of the following work:

(1) That he intends to demolish the whole of the premises comprised in the holding

7–107 It has been said that demolition involves the physical act of destruction.[144] A landlord does not, however, have to rely on para.(f) if the thing intended to be "demolished" has ceased to exist. In *Aireps Ltd v Bradford City Council*[145] the letting consisted of an airline check-in desk. The tenant at the request of the landlord had vacated and the desk had been removed. It was held that there was no need for the landlord to rely on ground (f) as the tenant could have no protection in relation to the premises (the airline desk) which did not exist.[146]

"Premises" means that part of the property comprised in the holding which is, by virtue of its physical nature, capable of being demolished. This may consist of a building or a wall: *Housleys Ltd v Bloomer-Holt Ltd*[147] (digested in para.7–109). In *Turner v Wandsworth LBC*[148] (digested in para.7–163) the

---

[142] [1981] 1 W.L.R. 1011; [1981] 2 All E.R. 560 CA.

[143] [1959] 1 W.L.R. 273; [1959] 1 All E.R. 273; [1959] 1 All E.R. 497 CA.

[144] *Ivorygrove Ltd v Global Grange Ltd* [2003] EWHC 1409 (Ch); [2003] 1 W.L.R. 2090 (digested at para.7–120) at [55], per Collins J.

[145] [1985] 2 E.G.L.R. 143 CA.

[146] There was no argument that the letting was only of a chattel not of realty.

[147] [1966] 1 W.L.R. 1244; [1966] 2 All E.R. 966 CA. Sellers L.J. said at 1250:

"The fact is that what was to have been demolished was all that there was to demolish on the site, the garage and the wall, and that seems to be demolishing the whole of the premises as far as any structure was to be demolished. It seems to me that that fulfils the requirements sufficiently. I am not concerned at the moment to consider what would be the position if the structure to be demolished had been some very small dog-kennels or very small part on a very large area. It was in fact, quite apart from the wall, a garage occupying one-third of the site which was to be demolished, and that, construing this as I would construe it, is demolishing the premises comprised in the holding."

In similar vein Diplock L.J. at 1252 said:

"It is to be observed that the garage and the wall were the only parts of the holding which were capable of being demolished: the rest of it was ordinary earth, perhaps with cinders upon it. It was contended by [Counsel for the landlord], and in my view rightly, that that intention constitute an intention to demolish 'the premises comprised in the holding'. It is, I think plain, on the true construction of paragraph (f), that 'the premises' there referred to must be limited to that part of the holding which is capable of being demolished and capable of being reconstructed. Here, as I have already said, the garage and the wall were the only parts of the holding which were capable of being demolished and therefore were 'the premises comprised in the holding'."

[148] [1994] 1 E.G.L.R. 134 CA.

tenant's premises occupied a strip of land near to some railway lines. It was a long and narrow strip. It had some buildings; there was some old hardstanding, which had been there for some time; the buildings were either prefabricated or of concrete blocks, no more than one storey high. The rest of the strip was rough vegetation, which was used for grazing. The landlord entered into an agreement with a company which ran a neighbouring private school. The terms of the agreement were to dig up the old hardstanding on the site, demolish the buildings, put down some tarmacadam or concrete for a car park on part of the site, and arrange for the rest to be planted with grass and trees so that there would be an attractive, levelled site. On doing that, the company would be entitled to a lease for four years.[149] It was held that the proposed work was work of "demolition" of the premises comprised in the holding. When the landlord is relying upon total demolition, no question of "substantiality"[150] arises.

Planning permission for demolition of "any buildings other than a dwelling house or building adjoining a dwelling house" or "the whole or any part of any gate, fence, wall or other means of enclosure" is not required: see s.55(2) of the Town and Country Planning Act 1990 (as amended by the Planning and Compensation Act 1991) and the Town and Country Planning (Demolition— Descriptions of Development) Direction 1995 which came into force on June 3, 1995. One must keep carefully in mind the different concept of demolition for the purposes of ground (f) and the question of whether or not planning permission will be required for such work. Thus where the landlord proposed to demolish all structures on the site, consisting of a lawn tennis club, club house and storage space, as well as breaking up six grass and four hard courts including the ground to a depth of between 4in and 9in (100mm to 225mm) it was held that it was wrong to conclude that planning permission would not be required, for (1) the breaking up and digging out of the tennis courts could not, in the context of s.55(2) of the Town and Country Planning Act 1990,[151] be said to constitute "demolition" and (2) could not be said to be demolition of a "building" within the meaning of that statute. Accordingly, the landlord needed to establish that it had a reasonable prospect of obtaining planning permission which it was agreed it would not be able to do in the absence of establishing that the entirety of the works it wished to undertake fell within the exception to "development" in s.55(2) of the 1990 Act: *Coppen v Bruce-Smith*.[152] **7–108**

Housleys Ltd v Bloomer-Holt Ltd[153] The premises consisted of a yard, on which stood a brick boundary wall and the only building was a wooden garage covering about one-third of the site. The rest of the yard was bare earth, partly **7–109**

[149] As to building leases, see para.7–140 et seq.

[150] As to demolition of a substantial part, see para.7–113 et seq.

[151] Which provides certain specified works and uses do not constitute "development", including by para.(g) demolition of any description of buildings specified in the 1995 Direction.

[152] [1999] 77 P. & C.R. 239 CA. It is to be noted that in *Coppen v Bruce-Smith* the landlord could, if it had considered the matter earlier, have confined its claim under ground (f) to the demolition of the buildings situated on the holding in reliance on *Housleys Ltd v Bloomer-Holt Ltd* [1966] 1 W.L.R. 1244 CA. However, to so confine the claim gave rise to the question of the application of s.31A of the Act which had not been investigated in the court below.

[153] [1966] 1 W.L.R. 1244; [1966] 2 All E.R. 966 CA.

surfaced with cinders bounded by a brick wall. The landlord, who owned adjoining premises, wished to enlarge their premises for the purposes of their business of saw-millers and timber merchants. They intended, upon obtaining possession, to demolish the existing buildings on the tenant's site and the wall and then to concrete the whole of the site to enable lorries to manoeuvre and turn. The county court judge held that the landlord did not come within s.30(1)(f) on the basis that the landlord proposed "no reconstruction at all. Laying concrete is not in the contemplation of the Act. There is no demolition of a substantial part of the premises. The landlords do not intend to build on the site." The Court of Appeal allowed the appeal holding that the judge had looked at the wrong thing.

7–110 Where the tenant is entitled under the terms of the current tenancy to carry out works of alteration to the premises, it may be open to him to pre-empt the landlord's ground of opposition under ground (f) by carrying out the landlord's proposed works or something like them before the date of the hearing. The facts of *Housleys v Bloomer-Holt*,[154] above, may be adapted to illustrate this point. Suppose that the premises comprised in the holding are an open car park with one prefabricated building used for garaging cars. If the landlord's proposal was to demolish that building and to use the whole of the area of the car park for parking in the open air he would succeed under ground (f): see the facts of *Housleys v Bloomer-Holt*. However, the tenant might very well have been prepared to sacrifice the garage building in order to defeat the landlord's ground of opposition. This he could do by himself demolishing the building before the hearing (assuming that the terms of his tenancy permitted him to do so). The landlord would be unable to prove a sufficient intention because there would be nothing for him to demolish.[155]

7–111 Where the buildings on the premises constitute tenant's chattels or tenant's fixtures (the right at law to remove which at the expiry of the lease not having been excluded by its terms), a landlord cannot make out an intention (tested on the hypothesis that there will be no renewal) to demolish the premises comprised in the holding for at the termination of the tenancy there will be no buildings on the holding. The buildings will not be available for demolition because they will not be there: *Wessex Reserve Forces and Cadets Association v White*[156] (digested in para.7–112).

7–112 ***Wessex Reserve Forces and Cadets Association v White***[157] There were several buildings on the holding comprising tenant's chattels or fixtures capable of removal by T.[158] By the terms of the tenant's lease it was provided that "on the

[154] [1966] 1 W.L.R. 1244; [1966] 2 All E.R. 966 CA.

[155] If the tenant proposes terms enabling the landlord to carry out the work (but with a view to the tenant then undoing them) the tenant is most unlikely to succeed in establishing that the landlord does not require possession in order reasonably to carry out the work: see *Pumperninks of Piccadilly Ltd v Land Securities Plc* [2002] Ch. 332; [2002] 3 All E.R. 609 (digested on this point at para.7–188). See para.7–192 et seq. generally.

[156] [2005] EWHC 983 (QB); [2005] 3 E.G.L.R. 127, upheld on appeal: [2006] 2 P. & C.R. 45 CA.

[157] [2005] EWHC 983 (QB); [2005] 3 E.G.L.R. 127, upheld on appeal: [2006] 2 P. & C.R. 45 CA.

[158] In fact there were six buildings one of which was a stone shed or stall with a corrugated asbestos roof on it. This structure formed part of the demise. The court said that either (1) this was caught by the obligation on the tenant to clear the site at the end of the lease, or (2) the tenants were prepared to

termination of the tenancy [the tenant would] remove all buildings and other erections and works . . . on the said land . . .". L in order to come within para.(f) of s.30(1) of the 1954 Act had to show an intention with respect to "the premises comprised in the holding". This referred to the physical premises comprised in the tenancy at the date of the hearing (although restricted to those premises which are capable of demolition, reconstruction, etc). In respect of property constituting tenant's chattels or fixtures a landlord would generally be unable to establish a reasonable prospect of carrying out ground (f) works to them since the tenant would usually remove its chattels and fixtures upon termination of the tenancy. As T had given evidence that this was his intention L failed.[159]

(2) That he intends to demolish a substantial part of the premises comprised in the holding

While a landlord who proves an intention under (1) above (see para.7–107) to demolish the whole of the premises will, in practice, be almost bound to succeed under this limb of ground (f), a landlord whose intention is only to demolish a part of the premises will have to satisfy the court that that part is "substantial". Whether the part that is intended to be demolished is a substantial part of the premises comprised in the holding is a question of fact and degree upon which the Court of Appeal will not readily upset the trial judge's decision: *Atkinson v Bettison*[160] (digested in para.7–114). **7–113**

---

do that if that was what the landlords wanted or (3) possession was not required in order to effect demolition as demolition could be effected from the highway without the need to go on to the rest of the holding or (4) the tenant was content to agree to the inclusion of terms within the new lease to provide access and facilities for the purposes of effecting the demolition so as to bring into operation s.31A.

[159] An interesting question in this case was what T was entitled to by way of the grant of a new tenancy (if L failed in its ground of opposition). Chadwick L.J. said:

"[30] ... The effect of that provision [s.35 of the 1954 Act], read with s.29, is that, if the landlord has failed to make out a ground of opposition under s.30(1), the court must order the grant of a new tenancy; but, when deciding what the terms of the new tenancy are to be, the court must have regard to the terms of the current tenancy and to all relevant circumstances. In particular the court must have regard to the requirement, in s.32(3), that the rights enjoyed by the tenant in connection with the holding are to be included in any new tenancy.

[31] It follows that it will be a matter for the court, on further consideration of the application for a new tenancy made in the present proceedings to decide whether any new tenancy will or will not permit the maintenance and use of buildings on the property demised for the purposes of carrying on Air Training Corps activities. That is a matter on which, for my part, I express no view at all.

[32] But even if, on the grant of a new tenancy, the court were to take the view that the tenant should be required to demolish the buildings which were on the land at the end of the old tenancy and not to erect any new buildings, the tenant would still be entitled (if it wished) to have a grant of the holding on those terms. A tenancy on those terms might or might not be of value to the association. The tenant is not obliged to take the new tenancy on the terms which the court dictates. It has a choice, exercisable within a short period of some 14 days, not to take a tenancy on those terms. So that it is impossible to say -even if the grant of a new tenancy required the removal of the buildings - that the right to have a new tenancy on those terms would not be a valuable right. It is a right conferred by parliament on this tenant and of which it should not be deprived without cause."

[160] [1955] 1 W.L.R. 1127; [1953] 3 All E.R. 340 CA.

7–114 ***Atkinson v Bettison***[161] The tenant's premises consisted of three floors. The landlord's proposed works were confined to the ground floor, involving the removal of the existing shop front and its replacement with an arcade entrance suitable for a jeweller's shop, together with the removal of a wall at the back. The county court judge held that these works did not constitute a reconstruction of a substantial part of the premises, a decision with which the Court of Appeal declined to interfere.

(3) That he intends to reconstruct the whole of the premises comprised in the holding

7–115 "Reconstruct" as distinguished from "demolish" involves a substantial interference with the structure of the premises, usually involving the demolition of part of the premises and then the rebuilding of those parts interfered with probably in a different form: *Percy E Cadle & Co v Jacmarch Properties*[162] (digested in para.7–116); *Ivorygrove Ltd v Global Grange Ltd*[163] (digested in para.7–120). As Ormerod L.J. observed in *Cook v Mott*[164] (digested in para.7–126), "it would be difficult to reconstruct something unless first of all there was a construction which was wholly or partially demolished".

Thus work to be undertaken to bare land by way of infilling would not be work of "reconstruction": *Botterill v Bedfordshire CC.*[165] It is insufficient that the works effect a mere change in identity of the relevant premises: *Percy E Cadle & Co v Jacmarch Properties.*[166]

7–116 ***Percy E Cadle & Co v Jacmarch Properties***[167] The tenant's premises consisted of the ground and basement floors of a building. The ground floor was split into two parts. The front part was used as a tobacconist's shop while the back was used as a men's hairdressers. Access to the basement was by means of steps outside the ground floor. The basement was used for storage. The landlord's proposal was to convert the two floors into one self-contained unit (incorporating the first floor of the building, which was occupied by another tenant[168]). New inner staircases were to be installed and a new floor was to be laid in the basement. It was intended to put new lavatories into the first floor. The Court of Appeal upheld the judge's decision that the landlord had failed to prove an intention under ground (f).

161 [1955] 1 W.L.R. 1127; [1953] 3 All E.R. 340 CA.
162 [1957] 1 Q.B. 323 at 328.
163 [2003] EWHC 1409 (Ch); [2003] 1 W.L.R. 2090.
164 (1961) 178 E.G. 637 CA.
165 [1985] 1 E.G.L.R. 82 CA. Compare, however, *Cook v Mott* (digested in para.7–126), below and *Housleys v Bloomer-Holt* (digested in para.7–109).
166 [1957] 2 W.L.R. 80; [1957] 1 All E.R. 148 CA.
167 [1957] 2 W.L.R. 80; [1957] 1 All E.R. 148 CA.
168 Work to the first floor would not of course be work to the "holding".

(4) That he intends to reconstruct a substantial part of the premises comprised in the holding

Similar considerations apply as under heads (2) and (3) above: see *Joel v Swaddle*[169] (digested in para.7–132). In *Fernandez v Walding*[170] factory premises were constructed in three sections. The tenant occupied the last two-fifths of the front section, and the entirety of the middle section. The carrying out of work to the whole of the front section by adding a second storey and, in addition, installing between the front and middle sections a wall to separate the same which involved digging suitable foundations was held to be work to a substantial part of the holding. The carrying out of work to convert a 60-bedroom hotel, without en suite facilities, arranged over four adjoining houses, into a 38-bedroom hotel with en suite facilities, was held not to be work of demolition or reconstruction to a substantial part of the premises comprised in the holding; the removal and replacement of the partitions reinforced with plywood to stiffen them was not work of reconstruction or work of substantial construction: *Marazzi v Global Grange Ltd*[171] (digested in para.7–119). A different conclusion was reached in *Ivorygrove Ltd v Global Grange Ltd*[172] (digested in para.7–120) which was a case involving the same landlord and a very similar scheme of work with respect to an adjoining hotel. 7–117

Betty's Cafes Ltd v Phillips Furnishing Stores Ltd[173] Two adjoining premises consisted of five floors. They had a doorway between them giving access at ground floor level. The basement contained a boiler and was used for storage. The ground floor was used as a shop for the sale of bread, chocolates and sweets and there was a cafe for light meals for which the first floor was also used. A ballroom was on the second floor and the top floor was a kitchen. The landlord intended to remove all existing staircases and lift, to be replaced with a larger staircase of reinforced concrete together with a larger lift which necessitated the bricking-up of existing windows in the back wall of the premises. The party walls between the premises were to be removed at ground floor level so as to convert it into a large open space and the ground floors of the premises were to be levelled. The kitchen on the top floor was to disappear and lavatories were to be installed. All the floors in the premises were to be cut about to a considerable extent and this may have required the strengthening of the upper floors. 7–118

At first instance, Danckwerts J. held that the works amounted to a reconstruction of a substantial part of the premises and involved substantial work of construction. He held however that the landlord had not shown that it intended to carry out these works at the material time which (he held) was the date of service of the s.25 notice.

---

169 [1957] 1 W.L.R. 1094 CA.

170 [1968] 2 W.L.R. 583; [1968] 1 All E.R. 994 CA. This decision is discussed at para.7–92, fn.109.

171 [2002] EWHC 3010 (Ch); [2003] 34 G. 59.

172 [2003] EWHC 1409 (Ch); [2003] 1 W.L.R. 2090.

173 [1956] 1 W.L.R. 678; [1956] 2 All E.R. 497 (first instance); [1959] A.C. 20; [1958] 2 W.L.R. 513; [1958] 1 All E.R. 607 HL.

The House of Lords reversed Danckwerts J.'s decision on the question of the date at which the intention had to be proved but there was no appeal against his finding on the sufficiency of the works. (See para.7–136 for a discussion of the main point.)

7–119 ***Marazzi v Global Grange Ltd***[174] T was tenant of hotel premises. The hotel consisted of four adjoining houses. The three upper floors of the houses were accessed by staircases. There were 60 bedrooms, most of which had hand basins only but not en suite facilities. The rooms had been created by stud partition walls. These partitions did not originally have any load-bearing purpose or function, although it was agreed between the parties' experts that some of them may have come to perform such a function due to the deflection of the building over time. There were some public rooms on the ground floor, with kitchen and laundry facilities in the basement.

L opposed renewal under ground (f) of s.30(1) of the Act. L intended to upgrade the hotel, enlarging but reducing the number of bedrooms, so that there would be only 38 bedrooms all with en suite facilities. This involved:

(1) the removal of the stud partitions and their replacement so as to enlarge the bedrooms. Plywood was to be inserted to stiffen the partitions;
(2) the levelling of floors on two storeys with the incorporation of plywood. This involved lifting the floorboards from the joists, installing a sheet of plywood and then nailing the floorboards back down again;
(3) the renewal, modernisation, rearrangement and extension of the utility services (principally involving the installation of the bathrooms and a larger drain to service the hotel and enlarged public sewer connection because of the increase in the number of bathrooms);
(4) the removal of a basement wall in one of the houses and its replacement with a steel beam;
(5) the installation of a lift;
(6) the removal of part of the roof associated with the lift;
(7) the removal and restoration of part of a staircase in one of the houses;
(8) the opening and restoration of one external door and window.

The evidence was that the works would cost some £2 million and would take one year to effect.

The county court judge held that:

(a) items (1) to (3) above did not constitute work of demolition or reconstruction;
(b) item (1) was not substantial work of construction;
(c) items (4) to (8) were works of demolition or reconstruction but were not works to a substantial part of the holding;
(d) although the cost and the time suggested that the work would be substantial, the ultimate issue was the true character of the physical work.

---

174 [2002] EWHC 3010 (Ch); [2003] 2 E.G.L.R. 42.

On appeal Park J. held that, as it could not be said that the judge's decision was wrong, the appeal was to be dismissed. Albeit a different judge may have come to a different conclusion, the judge's findings were not outside the range within which there was a legitimate room for differences of opinion.

Ivorygrove Ltd v Global Grange Ltd[175] L was the leasehold owner of a hotel made of four interconnecting houses situated on basement, ground and three upper floors. It had obtained planning permission and listed building consent for the approved scheme, which involved creating 43 en suite bedrooms from 73 bedrooms. Consent was also obtained for a "revised scheme" of works which included the construction of a larger lift shaft. L obtained financing for the proposed works and the freeholders confirmed their consent to the proposed works. **7–120**

The external walls and party walls between the four houses were of load-bearing brick masonry. The internal walls were mainly of timber stud, supporting the floors and roofs. Each house retained its staircase with brick surrounds; one had a lift. Internally the houses had been substantially altered upon conversion to hotel use. The original rooms had been subdivided and partitioned. The hotel bedrooms mainly had either a washbasin only or no facilities. A few had en suite bathroom or shower. In order to create the reduced number of bedrooms, doorways were to be blocked up and internal walls demolished. Some of the internal walls were originally load-bearing. These were the minority of internal walls and occurred mainly in the basement. By deflection of the floors, which had occurred on the third floor and to a lesser extent on the second and first floor, some of the internal partitions had become load-bearing. Floors would be strengthened with plywood. This required the taking up and relaying of all of the floorboards. New partitions would be created with plywood stiffening. In the basement, the kitchen would be opened up with structural steel support. A second structural steel support would be inserted to the enlarged opening for the disabled lavatories. Excavations would be done to lay new drains and a connection to the public sewer. A dumb waiter would be installed. Two conservatories would be built. Windows of the upper floors of one of the houses were to be replaced to match the remainder. On the first to third floors, large areas of partitioning would be removed.

The existing partitions were mainly of plasterboard though some were brick, particularly in the basement. They were substantial, and not like demountable office partitions and had to be knocked down with a sledgehammer, so disturbing skirting, walls and ceiling finishes. The new partitions would not be like demountable office partitions, but substantial structures stiffened by plywood, insulated and plastered. They were to be rebuilt in a different position, requiring substantial making good. The internal walls, excluding the party wall, amounted to 2,587 square metres. Of these 1,275 square metres (49 per cent) would be demolished and 860 square metres (33 per cent) of new walls were to be built.

175 [2003] EWCA 1409 (Ch); [2003] 1 W.L.R. 2090.

Completely new services would have to be put in for the new bathrooms and generally. In order to run those services there would be numerous holes in both load bearing and non-load bearing walls and in the floors. The services would run both horizontally and vertically.

The revised scheme had the following main additional elements: the lift shaft would be demolished and reconstructed, and a larger lift would be installed; the new lift would travel one floor further, to the basement; the lift motor room and roof overrun would be demolished and a new flat roof would be built below parapet level; a disabled hoist in one of the houses; lavatories in the basement and second floor bedrooms; an increase in the size of the first floor corridor and bedrooms on the first and second floors by demolishing and rebuilding 11 existing partition walls and alteration of stairs to rear extension rooms.

The report of the jointly instructed engineer was to the following effect: (A) There were no structural problems in the houses, but the structure would be affected by the proposed works both because partition walls had come to be load bearing due to deflection on the upper floors and because building services needed to be routed through the structure, (B) the proposed works would affect all parts of the interior of the premises; (C) the proposed bathroom finishes, which consisted of high quality but brittle tiling, required stiffening of the floors, but a client would be advised against these finishes because of the danger of cracking in spite of stiffening; (D) extensive opening up was not necessary before the work began on site, but extensive opening up would be necessary after work began; (E) the differences between the engineers as to the amount of stiffening and reinforcement needed was because they were adopting different approaches, neither of which was wrong in engineering terms but each of which was appropriate to the commercial objects of the party instructing him: for a client with the landlord's commercial objective the proposed stiffening of the floor with plywood and plywood in the new stud partitions and additional reinforcements to beams would be reasonable and necessary; and (F) from an engineering point of view the works could be phased either in one or two houses at a time.

The costs experts on both sides agreed as follows: with vacant possession of all four houses, the total estimated cost of refurbishment and upgrading the premises was £4.2 million. The length of time which that work would take was 44 weeks. The engineers agreed the cost of works which the court might consider to be structural at £454,867 (forming 10 per cent or 11 per cent of the entire scheme), consisting of:

(1) alterations to masonry walls; renewal of basement floor; reconstruction of lift shaft; new structural steelwork; and structural wall reinforcement (£207,332);
(2) joist strengthening and levelling (£72,801);
(3) removal of non-load bearing walls (£24,205);
(4) plywood flooring (£75,809);
(5) construction of new conservatories (£25,007);
(6) crack stitching to external walls (£13,765); and
(7) construction of new partitions (£35,948).

A substantial proportion of the £4.2 million figure would qualify if works ancillary to the foregoing were included, and on the judge's estimate this was something of the order of £3 million.

H.H. Judge Green QC held that the works intended to be carried out satisfied s.30(1)(f), namely that they were works of demolition and reconstruction of a substantial part of the premises and were also a substantial work of construction on the holding. The judge had described the work to stiffen the floorboards as "structural work on any definition." As to the partitions he said:

> "A jury would consider that the demolition of the partitions and their rebuilding in a different position were works which came within both limbs of the section, and the works were substantial in the light of the physical quantity of the work, its cost and the time it took, of which the first was by far the most important."

Mr and Mrs Marazzi, tenants of another hotel subject to a similar scheme of works, had brought separate proceedings against L (see the summary of *Marazzi v Global Grange*,[176] para.7–119). However, the judge in the *Marazzi* case had held that the proposed works did not fall within s.30(1)(f) of the Act, and neither the works to the flooring nor to the partitions was held to be qualifying work. The judge was referred to the *Marazzi* case but found that the *Marazzi* case was different.

The issue on appeal was whether the judge correctly directed himself on the legal principles and whether the decision he came to was open to him on the evidence.

T argued that:

(a) the judge misdirected himself and/or erred in law in finding that L's proposed removal and/or erection of partition walls would constitute works for the purpose of the ground in s.30(1)(f) and he ought to have directed himself that, for the purposes of this ground, some form of building upon the premises which involved the structure was required and that partition walls did not fall within the definition of construction, or alternatively, the judge gave undue weight to this element of the proposed scheme;

(b) the judge misdirected himself and/or erred in law in finding that general refurbishment works fell within s.30(1)(f), since for the purposes of this ground, it is not sufficient for a landlord to include in his scheme of intended works a core of construction work so as to enable virtually every other item comprised in the scheme to be taken into account, or, alternatively, the judge gave undue weight to the refurbishment element of the proposed scheme; and

(c) no reasonable judge would have concluded that the scheme of works was substantial in either context in s.30(1)(f).

Dismissing the appeal, Lawrence Collins J. held:

(i) The test for review of a judge's decision had been variously stated as being whether the judge came to a conclusion which was clearly wrong or to

[176] [2002] EWHC 3010 (Ch).

which no reasonable man could have come, or whether there was evidence upon which he could have arrived at such a conclusion, or whether there was any wrong approach or wrong appreciation of the evidence or assessment of it, or omission to consider any evidence.[177]

(ii) For there to be reconstruction, there must be substantial work of construction, and "reconstruction" means "rebuild".[178] Demolition involves the physical act of destruction, and reconstruction is equivalent to rebuilding, and contemplates a state of affairs where there has been a measure of demolition falling short of total demolition.[179] "Reconstruction" connotes a physical reconstruction of the premises, and means a substantial interference with the structure of the premises and then a rebuilding of such part of the premises as has been demolished by reason of the interference with the structure.[180]

(iii) It is necessary to look at the whole of the work, and then decide as a matter of fact and common sense whether it amounts to demolition or reconstruction of a substantial part of the premises, or the carrying out of substantial work of construction on them.[181]

(iv) Work associated with demolition and reconstruction, such as works of preparation ancillary to such works, or re-plastering and rewiring, or the laying of cables and drains, may be considered when looking at the totality of the work to determine whether the work is construction or is substantial or is on a substantial part of the premises.[182] But that does not mean that the landlord has only to include in his scheme of intended work a substantial core of constructional work for every item comprised in the scheme to be taken into account.[183]

(v) The concepts of demolition and reconstruction do not inevitably involve load bearing structures. Section 30(1)(f) does not refer to the "structure", albeit several of the decisions refer to the "demolition and reconstruction of the structure"[184]: e.g. there is nothing in the wording of s.30(1)(f) which requires the demolition or construction of structural or load-bearing

---

[177] Following *Percy E Cadle & Co v Jacmarch Properties* [1957] 2 W.L.R. 80; *Romulus Trading Co Ltd v Trustees of Henry Smith's Charity* [1990] 2 E.G.L.R. 75; *Marazzi v Global Grange Ltd* [2002] EWHC 3010 (Ch). The decision will not be reviewed except in the case of a misdirection, or a total lack of evidence to support the conclusion: *Bewlay (Tobacconists) Ltd v British Bata Shoe Co Ltd* [1959] 1 W.L.R. 45 at 48. "Ultimately, it is a jury question": *Romulus Trading Co Ltd v Trustees of Henry Smith's Charity* [1990] 2 E.G.L.R. 75 at 78, per Mustill L.J.

[178] Following *Percy E Cadle & Co v Jacmarch Properties* [1957] 1 Q.B. 323 at 328.

[179] Following *Percy E Cadle & Co v Jacmarch Properties* [1957] 1 Q.B. 323 at 329.

[180] At 329 and at 330, per Ormerod L.J., approved in *Joel v Swaddle* [1957] 1 W.L.R. 1094 at 1100.

[181] Following *Joel v Swaddle* [1957] 1 W.L.R. 1094 at 1099; *Bewlay (Tobacconists) Ltd v British Bata Shoe Co Ltd* [1959] 1 W.L.R. 45 at 49; *Cerex Jewels v Peachey Property Corp*[1986] 2 E.G.L.R. 65 at 69.

[182] Following *Cerex Jewels v Peachey Property Corp* [1986] 2 E.G.L.R. 65; *Romulus Trading Co Ltd v Trustees of Henry Smith's Charity*[1990] 2 E.G.L.R. 75; *Cook v Mott* [1961] E.G.D. 637.

[183] Following *Romulus Trading Co Ltd v Trustees of Henry Smith's Charity* [1990] 2 E.G.L.R. 75 at 78. It is a matter of degree depending on the circumstances of each case: *Cook v Mott* [1961] E.G.D. 637.

[184] Referring to *Percy E Cadle & Co v Jacmarch Properties* [1957] 1 Q.B. 323 at 328, 329 at 330; *Joel v Swaddle* [1957] 1 W.L.R. 1094 at 1100; *Romulus Trading Co Ltd v Trustees of Henry Smith's Charity* [1990] 2 E.G.L.R. 75 at 77; *Barth v Pritchard* [1990] 1 E.G.L.R. 109 at 111, Stocker L.J.

features as a condition of its applicability. To do so would treat the references in the authorities to "structure" the cases[185] in as if they were statutes. It would be quite wrong to import into s.30(1)(f) not only the word "structure", which does not appear there, nor, still less, the case law on the meaning of structure in other statutory contexts. Whether the relevant parts of the premises are load-bearing is simply one of the factors to be taken into account in determining the jury question of whether there is demolition or reconstruction, or demolition or reconstruction of a substantial part, or substantial work of construction on the holding or part of it, and not a pre-condition of the applicability of s.30(1)(f).

(vi) Where partitions are concerned, it will be a matter of fact and degree whether their replacement and re-configuration will be within either limb of s.30(1)(f). As the judge recognised, s.30(1)(f) will not apply to demountable office partitioning. But it was open to him to find that the nature of the work, and the role of the partitions, fell within s.30(1)(f). It was also open to him to find that view confirmed when there was taken into account the construction of the larger lift, the excavations and underpinning required, the construction of two steel beams, the openings made in some load-bearing internal walls, and the amount of strengthening to the floors and laying of the new drains.

(vii) It was plainly open to the Judge on the agreed evidence to find that there was a bedrock of work to the structure totalling over £450,000, which on any view was a "substantial work of construction". That work included the installation of the larger lift shaft and lift, and associated works; the stiffening of the upper three floors to cope with the deflection; the insertion of two steel beams in the basement; and demolition at basement level of masonry and possibly load-bearing. The holding of the judge on the bedrock works was sufficient to dispose of the case, but it was also open to him on the evidence to find that the bulk of the work was so connected with the structural work that it could be taken into account in determining substantiality in both its aspects, namely that the relevant work of construction was substantial or that a "substantial part" of the property was affected.

(viii) The difference in result between this case and the *Marazzi* (digested in para.7–119) case[186] was not satisfactory given the substantially similar facts. Nevertheless, as noted in the appeal of the *Marazzi*case, the task was not to decide on the fulfilment of the conditions in s.30(1)(f) but to decide whether the judge had directed himself correctly and whether the decision was properly open to him. The cases were not heard together, and in *Ivorygrove*,[187] L had the benefit of additional expert evidence and was able to bring forward material to show H.H. Judge Green that Judge Dean's misgivings in *Marazzi* about the expert evidence in the *Marazzi* case were not justified. Moreover, it is clear from several passages in Park J.'s

[185] Such as *Percy E Cadle & Co v Jacmarch Properties* [1957] 1 Q.B. 323 at 329 (as approved by Lord Evershed M.R. in *Joel v Swaddle* [1957] 1 W.L.R. 1094 at 1100).

[186] [2002] EWHC 3010 (Ch).

[187] [2003] EWHC 1409 (Ch).

judgment in the *Marazzi* case on appeal that he was very mindful that his task was not to decide on the fulfilment of the conditions in s.30(1)(f), but to decide whether the judge had directed himself correctly and whether the decision was properly open to him. Park J. also made it clear in several passages that, if he had been the judge of fact, he might well have been persuaded to come to a different conclusion himself, both as regards the work as a whole, and on the issue of the partition walls.

(5) That he intends to carry out substantial work of construction on the holding

7–121 **"Meaning of construction"** In *Barth v Pritchard*[188] Stocker L.J. gave guidance as to the sort of works which came within, or fell outside, the meaning of the word "construction". He said:

> "One of the difficulties . . . is that there is no statutory definition of the word 'construction' and dictionary definitions such as 'to build up', 'compile', 'put together the parts of' (Chambers) or 'to make or form by fitting the parts together', 'to frame, build, erect' (Shorter Oxford) beg rather than resolve the problem. A bookcase, purpose built in situ, would fall within these definitions, but it is not contended that to erect such a bookcase would constitute construction for the purpose of section 30(1) (f) . . . I consider that whether or not works fall within the definition of 'construction' must depend upon the facts in each case in which the problem falls to be considered . . . If it is necessary to decide whether or not in any given case it is necessary for works to involve directly the structure of the building in some way, my own view would be that this is implicit in the generality of section 30(1) (f). In other words, that some form of building upon the premises which involves the structure is required. I would not consider wooden partitions, however extensive, as falling within the definition of 'construction', but the situation would have to be reviewed in accordance with the facts of any given case."

It is clear that the work may still qualify albeit elements of the holding affected are neither load bearing nor do they perform some structural function: *Ivorygrove Ltd v Global Grange Ltd*[189] (digested in para.7–120). Whether the relevant parts of the premises are load-bearing is simply one of the factors to be taken into account in determining the question of whether the works fall within para.(f); it is not a precondition to the applicability of s.30(1)(f).[190]

7–122 Work of construction does not require the building of a structure above the holding. In *Housleys v Bloomer-Holt*[191] (digested in para.7–109) it was suggested that the laying of concrete on an open yard previously covered in cinders which would provide a turning circle for lorries, the yard constituting approximately two-thirds of the holding, might amount to a "substantial work of construction", although it was not strictly necessary to decide the point for the purposes of the decision. Sellers L.J. said:

> "The whole of the area was to be concreted in a sufficiently substantial way to carry this traffic which would come in. While it is not necessary in this case, I should have thought that there was only one view to be taken on that-that there was a substantial work of construction which was intended to be carried out . . . the judge said, I think erroneously, 'laying concrete is not in the contemplation of the Act', and 'landlords do not intend to build on the site'. That seems to

[188] [1990] 1 E.G.L.R. 109 CA.
[189] [2003] EWHC 1409 (Ch); [2003] 1 W.L.R. 2090.
[190] *Ivorygrove Ltd v Global Grange Ltd* [2003] EWHC 1409 (Ch) per Lawrence Collins J. at [67].
[191] [1966] 1 W.L.R. 1244; [1966] 2 All E.R. 966 CA.

> me unnecessary. One can view 'construction' without the building of a structure above the site in that way as a building: and the laying of concrete-the laying of a substantial roadway, the laying of a runway, or other substantial work of concreting-may well be within the contemplation of the Act . . . and may well be 'substantial work of construction'".

As to the laying of electricity cables, soil pipes and drains and the making of roads, see *Cook v Mott*[192] (digested in para.7–126).

Works which qualify as work of "construction" As was pointed out in *Romulus Trading Co Ltd v Trustees of Henry Smith's Charity*[193] (digested in para.7–125), the Court of Appeal has to be careful not to review the findings of the trial judge as to what constitutes work of construction or reconstruction unless he is plainly wrong. Thus it was said that works consisting of the removal and replacement of a considerable number of internal partition walls "might be properly so described in the setting of one building but not in another". Courts might very well come to different conclusions on this basis. **7–123**

Bearing in mind that each case will turn upon its own facts, it is nonetheless considered possible to make the following general observations, based upon the detailed discussion set out in *Barth v Pritchard*[194] (digested in para.7–124); *Romulus Trading Company Ltd v Trustees of Henry Smith's Charity*; *Marazzi v Global Grange Ltd* (digested in para.7–119) and *Ivorygrove Ltd v Global Grange Ltd* (digested in para.7–120):

(1) Work for which either the landlord or the tenant is responsible under the terms of the lease, e.g. works of repair to remedy dilapidations, will not be qualifying works.[195]
(2) Work which the landlord is entitled to carry out under the terms of the lease pursuant to a right of entry is not qualifying work.[196]
(3) The installation of fittings and equipment within an existing building is not qualifying work: *Barth v Pritchard*.[197]
(4) Wooden partitions, however extensive, are unlikely to constitute work of "construction".[198]

---

[192] (1961) 178 E.G. 637.
[193] (1990) 60 P. & C.R. 62 CA.
[194] [1990] 1 E.G.L.R. 109 CA.
[195] As to which, see paras 7–100 and 7–101 above.
[196] As to which, see para.7–99 above.
[197] [1990] 1 E.G.L.R. 109 CA.
[198] In *Marazzi v Global Grange Ltd* [2002] EWHC 3010 (Ch) bedrooms in a hotel had been created by stud partition walls. These partitions did not originally have any load-bearing purpose or function, although it was agreed between the parties' experts that some of them may have come to perform such a function due to the deflection of the building over time. The landlord intended to remove some of these partitions and stiffen others with plywood. The county court judge held that this was not qualifying work of any description within para.(f). Park J. on appeal said that it could not be said that the judge was obviously wrong on this issue. He said:

"The statute refers to demolition or reconstruction of 'a substantial part' of the premises. In my view, [the submissions of counsel on behalf of the landlord, that the removal of some existing partitions and the installation of some new partitions was demolition or reconstruction] may be in difficulty if one considers carefully what is, or are, the part or parts, of the premises contended to have been demolished or reconstructed by the removal of some old partition walls and the installation of some new ones. [Counsel on behalf of the landlord] says that the parts of the premises are the

(5) The removal of partitions or the sealing up of openings in structural walls is qualifying work.[199]

(6) The provision of new toilets is work of installation not work of construction (*Barth v Pritchard*) although it has been said that the installation of a new drainage and hot and cold water systems and bathrooms where they did not exist before is work of construction (*Romulus Trading Company Ltd v Trustees of Henry Smith's Charity*[200]).

(7) Installing pipework and cables underneath and through floors, or in casing along the wall and in cut and chase gullies in plasterwork is not work of "construction", save that such works will need to be considered as part of the whole works if ancillary to works which are properly regarded as works of construction.

(8) Interference with the floor slab or floorboards will be qualifying work.

(9) Installation of new staircases or the removal of such will be qualifying work.

---

partitions themselves. This is upon the basis that everything that is in a building and that is a fixture is a part of it. In a formal sense, that is correct, but I incline to the view that that is not what the draftsman had in mind by referring to 'part' of the premises. I think that he had in mind a specific area of the premises, such, for example, as a particular floor. Let me take as an example the third floor of the hotel. [The Landlord] intends to remove some partition walls in the third floor, but it does not intend to demolish the third floor. It intends to install some new partition walls in the third floor, but I would not describe that as 'reconstructing' the third floor (that floor being a 'part' of the hotel). It seems to me to be more in the nature of altering the internal layout within the third floor, something that, to my mind, is not the same thing as reconstructing the third floor. The same applies to other areas of the building in relation to which similar question may be considered: changes to the partitioning alter the layout of the area, but do not reconstruct it.

I do accept that there can be a question of degree here. If the plans were to gut the whole interior of the hotel and rebuild the interior, that obviously would be reconstruction. But in the actual case the essence of the internal structure remains."

[199] In *Ivorygrove Ltd v Global Grange Ltd* [2003] EWHC 1409 (Ch); [2003] 1 W.L.R. 2090; [2004] 1 All E.R. 144 the landlord intended to carry out work not dissimilar to that in the *Marazzi* case (see fn.198 on the matter of partitions). In *Ivorygrove* the evidence was that the existing partitions were mainly of plasterboard though some were brick, particularly in the basement. They were substantial, and not like demountable office partitions and had to be knocked down with a sledgehammer, so disturbing skirting, walls and ceiling finishes. The new partitions would not be like demountable office partitions, but substantial structures stiffened by plywood, insulated and plastered. They were to be rebuilt in a different position, requiring substantial making good. The county court judge held that said:

"A jury would consider that the demolition of the partitions and their rebuilding in a different position were works which came within both limbs of the section, and the works were substantial in the light of the physical quantity of the work, its cost and the time it took, of which the first was by far the most important."

Lawrence Collins J, in considering the appeal from the county court judge, having decided that whether the relevant parts of the premises to which work is being effected are load-bearing parts is simply one of the factors to take into account in determining whether the work was work falling within ground (f) said:

"**[68]** It also follows that, where partitioning is concerned, it will be a matter of fact and degree whether their replacement and reconfiguration will be within either limb of section 30(1)(f). Plainly, as the judge recognised, section 30(1)(f) will not apply to demountable office partitioning. But I am satisfied that it was open to him to find that the nature of the work, and the role of the partitions, engaged section 30(1)(f)."

[200] At first instance.

(10) The provision of new accommodation within an existing structure, e.g. by the creation of new brick partitions, will be qualifying work.
(11) The fitting of fire lobbies or doors is not qualifying work.

Barth v Pritchard[201] The tenant's premises consisted of six floors of a building, only two of which, at first and fourth floor level, constituted the "holding" for the purposes of ss.23(3) and 32(2).[202] The tenant was occupier of an adjoining building and had made openings between the two at first and fourth floor levels. The landlord served a s.25 notice opposing renewal under para.(f) (demolition and reconstruction). The landlord's works were not confined to the "holding". In respect of the "holding", however, the works consisted of the provision and fixing of new sanitary fittings for two toilets which were to be installed on the fourth floor which involved the construction of timber-framed, plasterboard-faced partitions to form new cubicles; to provide and fix a new gas-fired boiler and to construct a new boiler room in timber-framed plasterboard; and to brick up the openings that were made between the two buildings. The county court judge held that works of construction required some structural work, and that mere decoration or the installation of fittings within an existing structure did not come within the statutory wording. The installation of the lavatories and the central heating boiler did not amount to structural work. Although the blocking up of the means of access between the buildings was structural it was not substantial. On appeal the landlord contended that the judge ought to have held that the works amounted to works of construction when viewed as a whole. **7–124**

The Court of Appeal dismissed the appeal and held that (1) building works could not constitute works of construction if none of the works in isolation themselves constituted works of construction; it was only in the context of works which were or might be properly regarded as construction works that other works which were not themselves construction fell to be considered when the works were regarded as a whole; (2) the tenor and purpose of s.30(1)(f) was related to "building works" affecting in some way the structure of the building itself, either internally or externally; (3) that the works of rein-stating the openings were in fact work required to be undertaken by the tenant pursuant to an obligation to reinstate under the terms of its lease and accordingly those works could not fall within the scheme of the works to be considered by the court and (4) none of the works constituted works of construction, as none involved directly the structure of the building but were more properly classified as works of "refurbishment" or "improvements".

Romulus Trading Co Ltd v Trustees of Henry Smith's Charity[203] The holding consisted of premises known as 13 Sumner Place and 47 Old Brompton Road, South Kensington. The works which the landlords intended to carry out involved the conversion of 13 Sumner Place into two maisonettes, and a self-contained flat. One of the maisonettes was to be on the ground floor and basement, the **7–125**

201 [1990] 1 E.G.L.R. 109 CA.
202 As to s.32(2) see para.8–19.
203 [1990] 2 E.G.L.R. 75.

second on the first and second floor, while the flat was to occupy the third floor. Specifically the proposed work was as follows:

Basement.
Excavation of entire floor to allow installation of new drainage and damp-proof membrane. Provision of new floor slab. Injection of all walls to provide damp-proof course. Demolition of partitions and construction of new partitions to convert to bed-sitting-rooms and one communal bathroom into three bedrooms and two bathrooms.
Ground floor.
Alterations to partitioning to create independent access to the upper floors and direct access from Old Brompton Road into the ground floor and basement maisonette. Installation of new windows on the Old Brompton Road elevation; creation of new cloakroom/WC and closing of doorway linking 13 Sumner Place with 47 Old Brompton Road.
First floor.
Alteration to partitioning to render the floor area self-contained from the staircase; demolition of partitions and structural walls to create new dining-room together with installation of a new floor at a higher level; installation of partitioning to create an internal stairwell and new kitchen; creation of new double door openings into the reception room; and construction of a new staircase internal to the flat to link the first and second floors.
Second floor.
Construction of a new rear extension and demolition of the existing rear wall to create space for a new bathroom to be en-suite with the rear room; erection of partitioning to self contain the accommodation from the communal staircase and new partitioning to create a new internal staircase and new arrangement of accommodation. (As existing, the second floor was two bed-sitting rooms and a kitchen, each with access to the common parts and as proposed there would be three bedrooms, two bathrooms and an internal staircase.)
Third floor.
Demolition of almost all partitions and new partitioning throughout. (As existing there were two bed-sitting-rooms, a bathroom and kitchen, each with direct access to the staircase. As proposed there would be a self-contained flat comprising one reception room, one kitchen, one bedroom and one bathroom.)
Generally.
The existing staircase was to be removed in its entirety and a new staircase installed in a slightly different position to maximise the space available. The majority of wall plaster would be removed throughout the property and renewed; all floorboards would be lifted throughout the property to enable full timber treatment; independent central heating would be installed to each flat. All existing plumbing and drainage would be removed and new plumbing and drainage installed; all existing wiring would be stripped out

> and replaced with new wiring; the roof would be stripped and reslated including new batons and insulation and the property would be regenerated throughout internally and externally.

The county court judge held that ground (f) was not established. The landlord appealed. The Court of Appeal remitted the case for rehearing. Whilst the judge had identified those works which were within ground (f) and those which were not, he had not made any specific finding as to whether the former amounted to "works of reconstruction of a substantial part of the premises comprised in the holding". There was evidence before the judge upon which he could have properly come to the conclusion that the landlord had not established a case under ground (f), but in the absence of the necessary explicit findings the case had to be remitted.

Cook v Mott[204] The premises consisted of part of a house and land, on which the tenant had constructed wooden dog kennels on concrete foundations. The landlord's intention was to convert part of the house into two flats, and to develop the land for use as a caravan site by removing the kennels, raising the level of the land, constructing a road and laying soil and water pipes and electricity cables. The Court of Appeal upheld the county court judge's decision that the landlord had proved an intention within ground (f). The making of the road and the laying of cables, pipes and drains were "work of construction"; the removal of the wooden kennels was work of "demolition". **7–126**

(6) That he intends to carry out substantial work of construction on part of the holding

It is to be noted that it is the "work of construction" which must be substantial, not the part of the holding upon which it is to be carried out. For example, the "holding" might consist of a large open car park. If the landlord proved an intention to build a substantial building upon only a small part of the car park, he will have proved an intention to carry out substantial work of construction, even though it is only a small part of the holding. **7–127**

"Work must be to the holding" It must not be forgotten that whichever category of work one is looking at the relevant work must be carried out on "the holding"[205]; what the landlord intends to construct elsewhere is irrelevant for this purpose. **7–128**

Change of identity insufficient It was emphasised in the Court of Appeal in *Percy E Cadle & Co v Jacmarch Properties*[206] (digested in para.7–116), above, that the court is concerned to examine the physical works intended to be carried out by the landlord and to decide whether those physical works taken as a whole satisfy the requirements of ground (f). The fact that the works will involve a **7–129**

---

204 (1961) 178 E.G. 637; [1961] E.G.D. 294 CA.

205 See para.7–92. See para.8–06 as to the meaning of "the holding".

206 [1957] 2 W.L.R. 80; [1957] 1 All E.R. 148 CA.

change in the identity of the holding, because they involve it becoming part of a large unit, will not itself entitle the landlord to succeed under ground (f) if the actual physical work does not come within ground (f).

Substantiality

7–130 Whether the works amount to "substantial" works is a matter of fact and degree.

7–131 ***Bewlay (Tobacconists) Ltd v British Bata Shoe Co Ltd***[207] The premises comprised a retail shop adjoining the landlord's shop. The landlord intended to amalgamate the two shops. This involved putting in a new shop front; changing the means of access from the street; removing three-quarters of the (non-load-bearing) wall dividing the premises from the next door premises and replacing it with screens, and doing a small amount of demolition and reconstruction to the lavatory accommodation. The Court of Appeal upheld the county court judge's decision that the intention had been made out.

7–132 ***Joel v Swaddle***[208] The holding consisted of a ground-floor shop with two rooms at the rear used for storage purposes, all of which were separated from one another and the remainder of the building by brick walls. There was a side passage to a yard at the rear. The landlord proposed to turn the ground floor and yard into a single enclosed space to be used as an amusement arcade. This work involved the removal of all the brick walls in the holding to be substituted by rolled steel joists across the roof of the premises, supported on substantial pillars, capable of bearing the girders and enabling structural support to be given to the first floor. The floor was to be lowered by eight inches. A new shop front was to be installed. The Court of Appeal reversed the decision of the county court judge that this work did not amount to reconstruction of a substantial part of the premises comprised in the holding.

7–133 One point which remains undecided on the authorities is whether each category of work mentioned in ground (f) must be considered separately. In *Bewlay (Tobacconists) Ltd v British Bata Shoe Co Ltd*[209] (digested in para.7–127), Lord Evershed M.R. made it clear that it was not correct to look at each item of work in isolation, but he left open the question as to.

> "what the answer would be in a case where the work proposed involved demolition of some part of the premises, with nothing whatever in the way of reconstruction of that part, and where the part so demolished could not be regarded as substantial–whether it would be legitimate then to add that part to some other part of the premises which was the subject of constructional work, and which in turn was not itself substantial."

In *Joel v Swaddle*[210] (digested in para.7–128), Romer L.J. said that:

---

207 [1959] 1 W.L.R. 45; [1958] 3 All E.R. 652 CA.
208 [1957] 1 W.L.R. 1094; [1957] 3 All E.R. 325 CA.
209 [1959] 1 W.L.R. 45; [1958] 3 All E.R. 652 CA.
210 [1957] 1 W.L.R. 1094; [1957] 3 All E.R. 325 CA.

> "the proper way of ascertaining whether what is proposed to be done will be work of 'reconstruction' of premises is to look at the position as a whole and compare the results on the premises of carrying out the proposed work with the condition and state of the premises before the work was done; in other words, you want to regard the whole position as one total or entire picture."

However, the apparent width of this approach was substantially restricted by the Court of Appeal in *Barth v Pritchard*[211] (digested in para.7–124). There, Stocker L.J. said that he did not read these authorities "as indicating that proposed works, considered as a whole, could amount to construction if none of the items considered separately could be so regarded". He stated that it was only in the context of works which were, or might be, properly regarded as construction works that other works which were not themselves construction fell to be considered when the works were regarded as a whole. In *Romulus Trading Co Ltd v Trustees of Henry Smith's Charity*[212] (digested in para.7–125), the Court of Appeal was reluctant to lay down any general rule in view of the fact that they were remitting the case for rehearing by the county court judge on what Mustill L.J. described as being "ultimately . . . a jury question". Nonetheless, the court did reject as being "far too wide" the following submission:

> "That . . . the correct approach when deciding whether a particular scheme of works is within either part of section 30(1) (f) (i.e. whether it is work of demolition or reconstruction on the one hand or work of construction on the other) is to look at the scheme as a whole. Some of the work may be works of reconstruction (or construction) which are indisputably within the section, some of the work may be ancillary thereto, while some may be work of refurbishment which were clearly outside the subsection. Counsel argues that as long as some of the work amounts to work of construction or reconstruction the fact that the scheme also contains work which does not qualify should not prevent the trial judge taking an overall view of the scheme and asking himself whether in substance the works so regarded amount to works of reconstruction or construction with paragraph (f). He supports this submission by pointing out that it is not generally possible to evaluate the scheme by going through its components, deciding which works are covered by paragraph (f) and which are not, and then having regard only to the former when deciding whether the works are works of construction or reconstruction."

The perhaps startling effect of this approach can be best understood by considering the detailed description of the work, as set out in the digest at para.7–125, which the Court of Appeal felt might properly be held to be insufficient for the purposes of grounds (f) by the trial judge, to whom the case was remitted.

Meaning of "intends": the first aspect

Firm and settled intention required

Under ground (f), the landlord must show that he "intends" to carry out the relevant work. The same word is used in ground (g) (own occupation) and the test of intention evolved by the courts under the two grounds is similar, if not identical. There are two interrelated aspects of intention which have been **7–134**

[211] [1990] 1 E.G.L.R. 109 CA.
[212] [1990] 2 E.G.L.R. 75.

considered by the courts. The first aspect, relates to whether the landlord can show that he has reached a firm and bona fide decision to carry out the proposed works. In *Fleet Electrics v Jacey Investments*[213] Lord Evershed M.R. said:

> "It is not now in doubt that the import of the word 'intend' in section 30(1) (f) of the Act is that at the appropriate date or dates . . . there must be a firm and settled intention not likely to be changed, or in other words that the proposal for doing the work has moved 'out of the zone of contemplation . . . into the valley of decision'".

Those last words were taken from the well-known judgment of Asquith L.J. in *Cunliffe v Goodman*.[214]

First aspect of "intention" determined subjectively

7–135 The first aspect of "intention" is a subjective assessment of the state of mind of the landlord: *Zarvos v Pradhan*[215] (digested in para.7–160). If a judge makes a finding that the landlord does not genuinely intend that which he says he intends, then the judge is finding that he does not believe what the landlord says. If that is his finding he should make it plain in his judgment that he does not believe him and wherever possible explain why he does not believe him: *Zarvos v Pradhan*.[216]

When and by whom intention to be formed

7–136 The House of Lords, in the *Betty's Cafes* case[217] decided that the question whether the landlord had formed such an intention was to be judged as at the date of the hearing; it is not necessary for the landlord to have made a definite decision by the date of the giving of the s.25 notice. Accordingly, in *Betty's Cafes*it was sufficient that the landlord passed a resolution to implement the proposed works during the course of the hearing. See also *Brainhills Ltd v Town Tailors Ltd*[218] where a resolution of company was passed during the course of an adjournment. However, some limit must be placed on the principle that it is open to the landlord to prove his intention at any stage of the hearing. Thus, in *A&B Gallant*

[213] [1956] 1 W.L.R. 1027 at 1032; [1956] 3 All E.R. 99 CA.

[214] [1950] 2 K.B. 237 at 254.

[215] Albeit a case under ground (g) the approach to intention is identical to that under ground (f): [2003] EWCA Civ 208; [2003] 2 E.G.L.R. 37. Ward L.J. said:

"The judicial gloss put on those ordinary words [of ground (g)] arises out of Asquith's LJ's explanation [in *Cunliffe v Goodman*] of the connotation of the word 'intends'. Hence the first element of the subjective intention, the genuine settled commitment to the project, and the second, a check on the reality which is demonstrated by showing, objectively, that there is the real possibility of carrying it into fruition. Pie in the sky will not be enough."

If a judge makes a finding that the landlord does not genuinely intend that which he says he intends, then the judge is finding that he does not believe what the landlord says. If that is his finding he should make it plain in his judgment that he does not believe him and wherever possible explain why he does not believe him: *Zarvos v Pradhan* [2003] EWCA Civ 208 per Ward L.J. at [45].

[216] [2003] EWCA Civ 208 per Ward L.J. at [45].

[217] *Betty's Cafes Ltd v Phillips Furnishing Stores Ltd* [1959] A.C. 20 HL.

[218] [1956] E.G.D. 195 CA.

v British Home Stores[219] the county court judge refused to admit during the course of the landlord's submissions in reply a company resolution that had been passed by the landlord shortly before. However, it is for the parties to assist the court in furthering the overriding objective contained in CPR r.1.1, to deal with cases justly, by raising the issues they wish to take at an early stage. Thus, where the landlord opposed under para.(g), relying on the provisions of s.30(3),[220] it was a proper exercise of the court's discretion to adjourn to enable the landlord to produce evidence to meet the objection that he did not have a controlling interest in the company which was to occupy, where that objection was taken for the first time in the tenant's closing submissions: *Ambrose v Kaye*.[221]

It follows from the fact that the intention is to be judged at the date of the hearing that the relevant intention is not necessarily that of the landlord who gave the s.25 notice, but of the person who is the "landlord" within the meaning of s.44 at the date of the hearing: *XL Fisheries v Leeds Corp*[222] (digested in para.7–137); *Morris Marks v British Waterways Board*[223] (digested in para.7–138). Where after the service of the s.25 notice one of two joint landlords died the relevant intention was that of the survivor, the person in whom the legal title was vested, notwithstanding the fact that the survivor held that legal estate on trust on behalf of himself and the estate of the deceased: *Biles v Caesar*.[224] As is apparent from *Biles v Caesar*[225] the relevant intention is that of the legal owner at the date of the hearing.[226] It is considered that there is no reason why the landlord cannot intend to carry out the work in partnership or as part of a joint venture.[227] It has been held that s.30(1)(f) requires only that the person identified as landlord by s.44 should have the necessary intention to redevelop and that the capacity in which the intention is held is irrelevant. Thus, where a local authority was both freeholder and underlessee, its intention to grant qua freeholder a new building lease, with a surrender of both the existing headlease and its underlease, was

---

219 [1957] E.G.D. 128; (1957) 107 L.J. 556.

220 Repealed by the 2003 Order. See now s.30(1A) and (1B).

221 [2002] 1 E.G.L.R. 49.

222 [1955] 2 Q.B. 636 CA.

223 [1963] 1 W.L.R. 1008; [1963] 3 All E.R. 28 CA.

224 [1957] 1 W.L.R. 156; [1957] 1 All E.R. 151 CA. It was said by Denning L.J. that even if the intention of the executors was material, as the title of the executor derives from the will and speaks from the will (*Meyappa Chetty v Supramanian Chetty* [1916] 1 A.C. 603) the court was able to hear from the executor as to the intention of the executors, although probate was not taken out until sometime afterwards. The judge, it was said was right to adjourn the case before any formal order was made until probate had been obtained, because until probate had been obtained the court could not enter judgment.

225 [1957] 1 W.L.R. 156; [1957] 1 All E.R. 151 CA.

226 Subject in the case of ground (g) (own occupation) to the special provisions relating to controlling interests, group member companies and beneficiaries under a trust. See paras 7–254, 7–257 and 7–258.

227 See *Re Crowhurst Park* [1974] 1 W.L.R. 583, a case under para.(g) (see para.7–248). There are no provisions, as are contained in ss.41(2) and 42(3)(b) for the purposes of ground (g) of s.30(1), treating the intention of the beneficiaries under a trust or a member company of a group of companies respectively, as the intention of the landlord for the purposes of ground (f). Thus, for the purpose of ground (f) the relevant intention is that of the landlord trustees or of the landlord company and not the beneficiaries or of the member of the group. There is no reason why, however, the landlord cannot intend to do work falling within ground (f) to enable the beneficiaries or a member of the group to occupy the premises for business purposes.

sufficient for the purposes of the Act to oppose the renewal of the various tenancies held by various sub-underlessees from the local authority. It was unnecessary for the local authority to hold the intention to redevelop in its capacity as underlessee.[228]

7–137 ***XL Fisheries v Leeds Corp***[229] The tenants made a request for a new tenancy at a time when their landlord was an individual. The landlord sold her reversion to the Leeds Corporation, which applied for a certificate pursuant to s.57(1) of the 1954 Act that the land was required for local government purposes. The Court of Appeal held that it was sufficient that the landlord's interest was vested in the corporation at the dates when it made application for a certificate and when it notified the tenants of that application, notwithstanding that the landlord had been an individual when the request was made. Accordingly, s.57(1) took effect and the tenant's application was dismissed.

7–138 ***Morris Marks v British Waterways Board***[230] M held a sub-tenancy from mesne landlords who in turn held from predecessors in title of the British Waterways Board. M served a s.26 request on the mesne landlords who had by then agreed to surrender what remained of their leasehold interest to the Board. At the Board's request, the mesne landlords served a counter-notice opposing the grant of a new tenancy to M on ground (f). The mesne landlords subsequently surrendered their interest to the Board, who were thus M's direct landlord when his application came to court. The Board proved that it intended to carry out works coming within ground (f) and the Court of Appeal held that the Board was entitled to rely on the counter-notice served by the mesne landlords.

7–139 For the circumstances in which a superior landlord who becomes a competent landlord may withdraw a s.25 notice, see Sch.6 para.6 (discussed in para.7–08).

Building leases

7–140 The landlord must show that he intends to carry out the work,[231] although it is obviously sufficient for him to prove that he intends to have it done by his servants or agents, such as building contractors. As the landlord may employ building contractors so it has been held that the landlord may implement the work by granting a building lease. The only real distinction between an ordinary building contract and a building lease is that the building contractor is remunerated by money, while the building lessee is remunerated by the grant of a lease: *Gilmour Caterers Ltd v St Bartholomew's Hospital Governors*[232] (digested in para.7–145). The all important criterion is one of control. Although a building contractor is not a servant or agent but an independent contractor, nevertheless it

[228] *Sheil v St Helens BC* [1997] C.L.Y. 3266.
[229] [1955] 2 Q.B. 636 CA.
[230] [1963] 1 W.L.R. 1008; [1963] 3 All E.R. 28 CA.
[231] See *Edwards v Thompson* [1990] 2 E.G.L.R. 71 CA (digested in para.7–147) for an illustration of where the landlord failed to establish a sufficiently firm and settled intention to implement a planning permission for the construction of five houses, no developer having been selected or estimates obtained at the date of the hearing.
[232] [1956] 1 Q.B. 387; [1956] 2 W.L.R. 419; [1956] 1 All E.R. 314 CA.

is the landlord that specifies what is to be done to ensure that the work is undertaken in accordance with the building contract. Similarly, in the context of a building lease, it is important to ensure that everything which is to be done is done with the approval of the landlord and under his inspection. In *Gilmour Caterers Ltd v St Bartholomew's Hospital Governors*, Denning L.J. said:

> "This agreement for a building lease is in the usual terms. The lessee is to hold as a tenant at will until the new building is completed, and, when he has completed the new building, he is to be granted a lease 48 years as from the beginning. The landlord, St. Bartholomew's Hospital, under the terms of the agreement have full control over that work that has to be done. Everything has to be done to their approval and is under their inspection, and if anything unto-ward happens they can immediately re-enter.[233]"

Although the landlord must maintain control there is no reason why the development proposal should not emanate from the building lessee. As a matter of common sense it is invariably the case that it is the developer who will put forward the proposals for development which are then accepted by the landlord and the element of control is the obligation contained within the covenant to build provided for by the terms of the building lease. In *Gilmour Caterers Ltd v St Bartholomew's Hospital Governors*[234] (digested in para.7–145) the building to be erected was in accordance with plans previously agreed by the landlord, being proposals which were forthcoming from the developer. Parker L.J. indicated that the landlords had "complete control of the nature and design of the reconstruction". The building lease specifically provided that the lessee was to build in conformity "in every respect with plans elevations and sections and specifications already approved of and signed by the surveyor for the time being of the lessors". In *Aberdeen Steak Houses Group Plc v Crown Estate Commissioners*[235] the landlord's proposal involved the grant of a building lease. The landlord had shortlisted five bids. All involved schemes prepared by the developers. No suggestion was made that the landlord did not thereby intend to carry out the necessary work for the purposes of the statutory provisions. **7–141**

Is it necessary for the landlord to seek and obtain the planning permission? It is unclear from *Gilmour Caterers Ltd v St Bartholomew's Hospital Governors*[236] (digested in para.7–145) as to who obtained the planning permission, if such was required in that case. In both *PF Ahern & Sons v Hunt*[237] (digested in para.7–179) and *Spook Erection Ltd v British Railways Board*[238] (digested in para.7–146) the planning permission had been obtained by the landlord. However, it is not considered that it is necessary for the landlord itself to obtain the planning permission. As long as a planning permission has been obtained or there is at the date of the hearing a reasonable prospect of obtaining permission and the landlord ensures by way of an obligation contained in the building lease that the work in accordance with the planning permission has to be undertaken, the landlord will establish the appropriate intention for the purposes of para.(f) of **7–142**

233 At 391.
234 [1956] 1 Q.B. 387; [1956] 2 W.L.R. 419; [1956] 1 All E.R. 314 CA.
235 [1997] 2 E.G.L.R. 107.
236 [1956] 1 Q.B. 387; [1956] 2 W.L.R. 419; [1956] 1 All E.R. 314 CA.
237 [1988] 2 E.G.L.R. 74 CA.
238 [1988] 1 E.G.L.R. 76 CA.

s.30(1) of the 1954 Act. It is, of course, important to establish that there is, or there is a reasonable prospect of obtaining, a planning permission.[239]

7–143 It will usually be necessary for the developer to establish that he has sufficient funds available to enable the development to be implemented: *Peter Goddard & Sons v Hounslow LBC*[240] (digested in para.7–181). The developer will ordinarily give evidence about the proposed development. Where the landlord proposed to grant a building lease but no one from the development company was called, no architects' drawings had been made, no relevant statutory consents had been obtained, and no contract with the development company had yet been signed, the landlord failed in it opposition to the tenant's renewal: *Reohorn v Barry Corp*[241] (digested in para.7–155). Each case depends on its own facts but it is unnecessary to for the building lessee to show that he has entered into a building contract as at the date of the hearing: *AJA Smith Transport v British Railways Board*[242] (digested in para.7–148).

7–144 The length of the term of the building lease would seem to be irrelevant unless it is so short as to throw doubt upon the genuineness of the landlord's intention. In *PF Ahern & Sons v Hunt*[243] (digested in para.7–179), the term was 125 years, as was also the case in *Aberdeen Steak Houses Group Plc v Crown Estate Commissioners*[244]; in *Spook Erection Ltd v British Railways Board*[245] (digested in para.7–146) the term was 99 years; in *Gilmour Caterers Ltd v St Bartholomew's Hospital Governors*[246] (digested in para.7–145) it was 48 years and in *Turner v Wandsworth LBC*[247] (digested in para.7–163), it was only four years. It would be otherwise where the landlord had obtained planning permission for redevelopment but intended, once he had obtained possession, to sell the site to a developer. Since the developer would then be free either to redevelop or not as he chose—a decision which was outside the control of the landlord—it could not be said that the landlord intended to do anything except to sell the site: see Mann L.J. in *PF Ahern & Sons v Hunt* (digested in para.7–179). It is important that the building lease is not executed before the hearing, as in those circumstances[248] the "landlord"[249] would appear to be the building lessee and not the landlord under the building lease, in which case the relevant intention is that of the building lessee. There is no objection to the landlord entering into an agreement for a building lease prior to the hearing, which agreement is conditional upon the landlord succeeding in his opposition to the renewal. It is unnecessary, however,

---

239 See para.7–153.
240 [1992] 1 E.G.L.R. 281 CA.
241 [1956] 1 W.L.R. 845; [1956] 2 All E.R. 742 CA.
242 [1981] 1 E.G.L.R. 54 CA.
243 [1988] 2 E.G.L.R. 74.
244 [1997] 2 E.G.L.R. 107.
245 [1988] 21 E.G. 73 CA.
246 [1956] 1 Q.B. 387; [1956] 2 W.L.R. 419; [1956] 1 All E.R. 314 CA.
247 [1994] 1 E.G.L.R. 134 CA.
248 Assuming it to be one in excess of 14 months, see para.3–87 as to the meaning of "landlord". See also *Capocci v Goble* [1987] 2 E.G.L.R. 102 CA (digested in para.7–178) and *PF Ahern & Sons v Hunt* [1988] 2 E.G.L.R. 74 CA (digested in para.7–179).
249 That is to say the competent "landlord" within s.44.

for the landlord to have signed an agreement with the selected developer by the date of the hearing: *AJA Smith Transport v British Railways Board*[250] (digested in para.7–148).

Gilmour Caterers v St Bartholomew's Hospital Governors[251] The landlords intended to carry out a redevelopment of war-damaged premises through a 48-year building lease equated with the value of the freehold. The county court judge dismissed the tenant's application. The tenant argued that the building lease was in effect an outright disposal and that accordingly the landlord did not intend to carry out the redevelopment itself. It was held that in the absence of any allegation that the building lease was a sham, the motive for entering into the building lease was irrelevant. The building lease was what it purported to be and, accordingly, the appeal was dismissed. **7–145**

Spook Erection v British Railways Board[252] The landlord opposed the tenant's renewal under ground (f) of s.30(1). The landlord had obtained planning permission for redevelopment of the demised premises as a supermarket. The landlord had in mind a disposal of the freehold to a well-known supermarket chain. However, upon it becoming clear that the tenant would not vacate, the landlord entered into a building lease with the supermarket under the terms of which the landlords would retain full control of the work to be done. The building lease was for a term of 99 years on completion of the building and payment of a premium was provided for, although pending completion the licence fee was payable. The Court of Appeal upheld the judge's decision that an intention under ground (f) had been proved. **7–146**

Edwards v Thompson[253] The subject premises consisted of a smithy and were part of a larger area of land belonging to the landlord, including a barn. The landlord obtained planning permission for conversion of the barn and the tenant's premises into a single dwelling house and for the construction of five new houses with an access way on the landlord's remaining land. The permission was subject to a condition that "the development to which this permission relates shall not be occupied until it has been completed in accordance with the approved plans". There was also a condition restricting occupation of any part of the development until the access way had been constructed. The landlord proved that she had engaged a builder to carry out the conversion of the barn and the tenant's premises and had prepared a detailed specification and had arranged to borrow the funds necessary to finance the work. As to the rest of the land which was subject to the planning permission, the evidence was that it was intended that the remainder of the development should be carried out by an independent developer at the same time as the works of conversion. The Court of Appeal assumed that this was to be assumed to be by way of a building lease to enable full control over the development. However, no specific developer had been selected, and no **7–147**

---

[250] [1981] 1 E.G.L.R. 54 CA.

[251] [1956] 1 Q.B. 387; [1956] 2 W.L.R. 419; [1956] 1 All E.R. 314 CA.

[252] [1988] 1 E.G.L.R. 76 CA.

[253] [1990] 2 E.G.L.R. 71 CA.

estimates had been made as to the cost of constructing the five houses and access road. Nor had advice been received as to what the developer might be prepared to pay for the land. The Court of Appeal held that the requisite intention had not been proved. There was a very real possibility that an acceptable price could not be agreed with an independent developer within a period which would allow the whole development to go ahead at the termination of the tenancy. It might well have been necessary to wait for a matter of months, or even longer. Thus the landlord had not shown a firm and settled intention, not likely to be changed, to carry out the conversion of the barn and tenant's premises at the necessary time. The planning permission made no provision for a phased development.

7–148 ***AJA Smith Transport v British Railways Board***[254] The landlord intended to carry out its proposed redevelopment by granting a building lease to E Ltd, but the agreement had not been signed by the date of the hearing. E Ltd had agreed terms with a building contractor for the work to be carried out, but had not signed any building contract. E Ltd, however, had a builder in mind who they had no doubt would be willing to undertake the work and had retained an architect for the purposes of providing plans. The Court of Appeal held that there was overwhelming evidence to support the landlord's intention under ground (f).

Factors affecting firmness of intention

7–149 Lord Denning M.R. has said "that when the landlord has in the past fluctuated in his mind as to what to do with the premises", the court is not bound to accept the landlord's assertion that he has a firm and settled intention: *Reohorn v Barry Corp*[255] (digested in para.7–155). However, it has been held that a landlord's settled intention to redevelop was not vitiated by evidence that they had accepted a previous offer from a third party to purchase the whole of the property and that they were continuing to consider such offers: *Edwards v Thompson*[256] (digested in para.7–147). A failure to progress the development of other land which is to be developed in conjunction with the tenant's demise may adversely affect the ability of the landlord to establish the requisite intention. Thus, in *Edwards v Thompson*, although the landlord would have satisfied the statutory criteria if the development had consisted of the tenant's premises in isolation, the development of the tenant's premises was dependent on implementing a planning permission for the construction of five houses on adjoining land which the landlord had intended should be undertaken by an independent developer. At the date of hearing the evidence was that no developer had been selected, no estimates obtained nor advice received as to what a developer would pay for the adjoining land[257] (the receipt of which was necessary to enable the landlord to fund the development of the tenant's premises). Accordingly, the landlord had failed to make out the necessary intention; there was a very real possibility that an

254 [1981] 1 E.G.L.R. 54 CA.
255 [1956] 1 W.L.R. 845 CA at 849–850.
256 [1990] 2 E.G.L.R. 72 CA.
257 [1990] 2 E.G.L.R. 72 CA.

acceptable price would not be achieved for the adjoining land in time to enable the landlord to fund the intended development of the tenant's premises.

Meaning of "intends": the second aspect

Objective Test

The second aspect of "intention" involves an objective assessment of the realistic prospects of implementing the intention held: *Zarvos v Pradhan*[258] (digested in para.7–160). It is not principally concerned with the genuineness of the landlord's decision, but with whether it is practicable to carry it out. In *Betty's Cafes*,[259] the House of Lords adopted for the purposes of ground (f) the definition of intention given by Asquith L.J. in *Cunliffe v Goodman*,[260] a decision under s.18 of the Landlord and Tenant Act 1927. In that case, Asquith L.J. said: **7–150**

> "An 'intention' to my mind connotes a state of affairs which the party intending ... does more than merely contemplate: it connotes a state of affairs which, on the contrary, he decides, so far as in him lies, to bring about, and which, in point of possibility, he has a reasonable prospect of being able to bring about, by his own act of volition."

In a later passage, Asquith L.J. stated that the "intention" was not proved "if the person professing it has too many hurdles to overcome, or too little control of events". The existence of those "hurdles" and the reasonable likelihood of the landlord overcoming them are to be viewed objectively. In order to establish an intention within ground (f), the landlord has to satisfy the court that a reasonable landlord would believe that he had a reasonable prospect of overcoming any existing hurdle, such as obtaining the finance[261] or the planning permission necessary for his proposed development or occupation: *Gregson v Cyril Lord Ltd*[262] (digested in para.7–154) and *Cadogan v McCarthy & Stone Developments Ltd*.[263] Thus, where the landlord proposed to enter into a building lease for the construction of a hotel and commercial complex, the absence of any coach lay-by facility, apparently contrary to the then requirements of the local highways department in connection with hotel sites, did not prevent the landlord from succeeding in establishing the relevant intention, where expert evidence was given on behalf of the landlord that the requirement was not a problem and that the restriction would probably be relaxed by the highway authority. Although if it were not relaxed it would be critical to the success or failure of the development

[258] [2003] EWCA Civ 208; [2003] 2 E.G.L.R. 37. See also para.7–135 above.

[259] *Betty's Cafes Ltd v Phillips Furnishing Stores Ltd* [1959] A.C. 20; [1958] 2 W.L.R. 513; [1958] 1 All E.R. 607 HL.

[260] [1950] 1 All E.R. 720 CA.

[261] See, e.g. *DAF Motoring Centre (Gosport) v Hatfield and Wheeler* [1982] 2 E.G.L.R. 59 CA, where it was said that it was not incumbent on the landlords to place before the court a fully particularised scheme, such as might have been necessary to place before a finance house in order to obtain a loan, as this would involve saying that it was incumbent upon the landlords to show, not only that they intended to carry out the scheme, but that they were ready and in all respects able to carry it out.

[262] [1963] 1 W.L.R. 41; [1962] 3 All E.R. 907 CA.

[263] [2000] L. & T.R. 249 CA.

scheme the court was satisfied that, on the evidence before it, it was very probable that this potential stumbling block would be overcome: *Aberdeen Steak Houses Group Plc v Crown Estate Commissioners*.[264]

Test applied on assumption landlord has possession

7–151 The test propounded in *Gregson v Cyril Lord*[265] was approved by the House of Lords in *Westminster City Council v British Waterways Board*[266] (digested in para.7–186). It was emphasised that the test is to be applied upon the assumption that the landlord has obtained possession. Thus any impediment which arises by reason of the tenant's occupation will be ignored.[267]

Scheme need not be financially viable

7–152 If the landlord is genuine in his intention and has the ability and financial means to bring it about, the fact that the proposed scheme is not financially viable is irrelevant. The landlord does not have to establish that he has a reasonable prospect of making an economic success of his proposals, e.g. to run a proprietary golf club: *Dolgellau Golf Club v Hett*[268] (digested in para.7–183). The court is not concerned with whether the landlord's decision is a prudent business decision provided the landlord has a reasonable prospect of fulfilling it: *Humber Oil Terminals Trustee Ltd v Associated British Ports*.[269]

Uncertainty over need for planning permission

7–153 In a situation where there is any uncertainty as to whether the landlord's plans require planning permission in order to be carried out, the court need not and normally should not try to resolve that question. What is necessary is to apply an objective test, that is:

> "... An enquiry whether the landlords on the evidence have established a reasonable prospect either that planning permission is not required or, if it is, that they would obtain it. That does not necessitate the determination by the court of any of the questions which may one day be submitted to the planning authority or to the Minister; it is the practical appraisal upon the evidence before the Court as to whether the landlords upon whom ... the onus lies, have established a reasonable prospect of success"[270]

In the later decision of *Cadogan v McCarthy and Stone (Developments) Ltd*,[271] Saville L.J. said:

---

[264] [1997] 2 E.G.L.R. 107 CA.
[265] [1963] 1 W.L.R. 41 CA. See fn.35.
[266] [1985] A.C. 676; [1984] 3 W.L.R. 1047; [1984] 3 All E.R. 737 HL.
[267] One assumes that the tenant is not in occupation and that the use carried on by the tenant has ceased: see paras 7–186 and 7–217.
[268] [1988] 2 E.G.L.R. 75 CA.
[269] [2011] EWHC 2043 (Ch) at [129].
[270] Upjohn L.J. in *Gregson v Cyril Lord* [1963] 1 W.L.R. 41 at 48.
[271] [2000] L. & T.R. 249 CA at 254.

> "A reasonable prospect in this context accordingly means a real chance, a prospect that is strong enough to be acted on by a reasonable landlord minded to go ahead with plans which require permission, as opposed to a prospect that should be treated as merely fanciful or as one that should sensibly be ignored by a reasonable landlord. A reasonable prospect does not entail that it is more likely than not that permission will be obtained."

Thus it is wrong for the court to consider whether on a balance of probabilities permission will be obtained; the court's task is to consider whether on a balance of probabilities there is a reasonable prospect of obtaining permission. It is sufficient for the landlord to show that he has a real as opposed to a fanciful prospect of success; it is sufficient for him to show no more than an even chance: *Gatwick Parking Services Ltd v Sargent*[272] (digested in para.7–156). A recent example of the application of this test is the decision of *Dogan v Semali Investments Ltd*.[273] The Court of Appeal referred with approval to what Laws L.J. had said in *Gatwick Parking Services Ltd v Sargent*[274]:

> "I emphasise that the hurdle to be surmounted by the appellant under section 30(1) (g), in the light of the authorities on the subject, is by no means a high one. He does not have to demonstrate a balance of probability that permission will be granted. He has to show that there is a real, not merely a fanciful, chance."

Gregson v Cyril Lord[275] The landlord proved an intention, which was accepted as bona fide, of occupying the premises as offices. There was a difference of opinion between the expert witnesses at the hearing whether planning permission was needed for the landlords' proposals and, if it was, whether it would be obtained. The evidence was that the landlords did not, in any event, intend to apply for permission. They gave evidence that they had occupied other suites as offices in the same building over the years, had never applied for planning permission, and had never been subject to enforcement proceedings. The judge declined to go into the question of whether planning permission was necessary or could be obtained, but held that it was sufficient that the landlord had shown a bona fide intention to occupy. The Court of Appeal ordered a new trial because the county court judge had not applied the correct test. **7–154**

---

[272] [2000] 2 E.G.L.R. 45 CA.

[273] [2005] EWCA Civ 1036. In that case the landlord opposed renewal relying on ground (f). The judge held that the landlord did not have a firm and settled intention and did not have a reasonable prospect of obtaining planning permission albeit the only evidence before him was that of the landlord's expert. The Court of Appeal said that even if the judge were correct in his view that the state of the landlord's intention before the trial was "wishy washy" this mattered not as long as there was a settled and firm intention established at the trial. Further there was no evidence before the judge to enable him to reject the landlord's evidence. Since the trial at first instance the council had in fact granted planning permission to the landlord for its stated plans. The court was entitled to take this into account, following *Gatwick Parking Services Ltd v Sargent* [2000] 2 E.G.L.R. 45 CA. It was confirmatory of the view that the judge had reached the wrong conclusion below.

[274] [2000] 2 E.G.L.R. 45 CA at 49J (having referred to the judgment of Upjohn L.J. in *Gregson v Cyril Lord* [1963] 1 W.L.R. 41 at 47 and the passage from the judgment of Savile L.J. in *Cadogan v McCarthy & Stone Developments Ltd* [2000] L. & T.R. 249).

[275] [1963] 1 W.L.R. 41; [1962] 3 All E.R. 907 CA.

7–155 ***Reohorn v Barry Corp***[276] The landlord, the local corporation, proposed to develop the premises, which consisted of about six-and-a-half acres used as a car park, by erecting shops, hotels, boarding houses and a garage and building a new road. This was to be done by granting a building lease to a development company which would carry out the work. At the hearing no one from the development company was called and it emerged that no architects' drawings had been made, no relevant statutory consents had been obtained, and no contract with the development company had yet been signed. The county court judge nonetheless held that the corporation had sufficiently proved its intention. This decision was reversed by the Court of Appeal which held that, although the premises were ripe for development and the proposed work was obviously desirable, the evidence showed that plans for the development had hardly started, the corporation's ability to do the work or have it done was very much in doubt, and difficulties might arise which would cause the scheme to be abandoned.

7–156 ***Gatwick Parking Services Ltd v Sargent***[277] L opposed T's application for renewal in respect of T's off-airport car parking service near Gatwick Airport on the grounds that the landlord intended to carry on such a car parking service from the tenant's holding. The planning permission for the user was subject to a condition that the use would only be carried on by the tenant company. The landlord however subsequently obtained permission to use the site for car parking purposes but prior to trial that permission was quashed pursuant to a largely unopposed application by the tenant for judicial review of the local authority's decision. Upon reconsideration of the matter the council refused L's application notwithstanding their own planning officer's advice that Government policy towards conditions confining use to a particular limited company had changed and that Government policy was firmly set against such conditions. At trial T contended that the planning difficulties meant that the landlord was unable to establish the requisite intention. The county court judge agreed and refused leave to appeal. After judgment and before permission had been obtained from the Court of Appeal to appeal, the council, considering a fresh application, and receiving similar advice to that given on the previous occasion granted planning permission to L and removed the previous condition confining the use to the tenant company. Prior to the hearing of the appeal T obtained leave to apply for a judicial review of the council's decision. The Court of Appeal allowed L's appeal holding that it was sufficient for the landlord to show a real as opposed to a fanciful prospect of obtaining the necessary planning consent; L was not required to show more than an even chance. The reports of the council's planning officers clearly supported L's prospects as was evident from the fresh evidence furnished by L's successful application since the date of the decision appealed against. The possibility that the pending judicial review proceedings might go against the council did not prevent L from establishing that he had an even chance of achieving his purpose, as the council would have to reconsider the application in light of all the guidance available, which guidance was in favour of removing the condition that the use could only be carried on by the tenant company.

---

[276] [1956] 1 W.L.R. 845; [1956] 2 All E.R. 742 CA.

[277] [2000] 2 E.G.L.R. 45 CA.

Meaning of "intends": are there really two aspects?

Although for purposes of analysis it has been convenient to discuss the two aspects of intention separately, the decided cases recognise a connection between the two aspects. In *Cunliffe v Goodman*[278] Asquith L.J. made the connection in the following terms: **7–157**

> "Not merely is the term 'intention' unsatisfied if the person professing it has too many hurdles to overcome, or too little control of events: it is equally inappropriate if at the material date that person is in effect not deciding to proceed but feeling his way and reserving his decision until he shall be in possession of financial data sufficient to enable him to determine whether the project will be commercially worthwhile."

He said of the plaintiff in that case and her alternative proposals to demolish the premises:

> "In the case of neither scheme did she form a settled intention to proceed. Neither project moved out of the zone of contemplation–out of the sphere of the tentative, the provisional and the exploratory–into the valley of decision."

In *Fisher v Taylors Furnishing Stores*,[279] Denning L.J. connected the various elements of ground (f) thus:

> "The court must be satisfied that the intention to reconstruct is genuine and not colourable [*bona fides*]; that it is a firm and settled intention, not likely to be changed [*firmness*]; that the reconstruction is of a substantial part of the premises [*nature of works*], indeed so substantial that it cannot be thought to be a device to get a possession [*bona fides*]; that the work is so extensive that it is necessary to get possession of the holding in order to do it [*reasonableness*]; and that it is intended to do the work at once and not after a time [*date and practicability of implementation*]." (Our additions in parentheses and italics.)

As these quotations show, the more hurdles that there are in the way of the landlord in implementing his intention, the more difficult it is for him to show that he really has reached a "firm and settled intention, not likely to be changed" and that he has "moved out of the zone of contemplation . . . into the valley of decision".

There is no requirement to deal with the two limbs in sequential order: *Zarvos v Pradhan*[280] (digested in para.7–160) Ward L.J. said: **7–158**

> "If a judge found that there was no genuine intention to run the business and that the expression of that intent was a colourable device to obtain possession and then do something different with the premises, then that is the end of the matter. The landlord falls at the first fence. One need not investigate the reality or the fantasy of his business plan. That inquiry is undertaken if it appears to be a case where, with the best will in the world, the landlord has no real prospect of succeeding in his aim of starting a business. There may, therefore, be cases where his subjective intent can be taken as read and where the case will, therefore, stand or fall on this second limb."

The true position, to be gathered from the authorities, is perhaps this: **7–159**

---

278 [1950] 2 K.B. 237; [1950] 1 All E.R. 720 CA.
279 [1956] 2 Q.B. 78; [1956] 2 W.L.R. 985; [1956] 2 All E.R. 78 CA.
280 [2003] EWCA Civ 208; [2003] 2 E.G.L.R. 37.

(1) A landlord may be perfectly genuine in his intention to redevelop, but matters may be at such a provisional and tentative stage that his genuine intention is not a sufficiently fixed intention for the purposes of grounds (f) or (g).
(2) Even where the landlord has a fixed and settled intention which he is not likely to change, it may nonetheless be the case that, viewed objectively, there are so many difficulties still unresolved that there is little reasonable likelihood of him being able to implement that intention.

In either of the above cases the landlord would not prove a sufficient intention under grounds (f) or (g).

7–160 ***Zarvos v Pradhan***[281] L opposed renewal of T's tenancy of an Indian restaurant situated on the ground and basement of a building the freehold of which was owned by L. L stated that he intended to carry on a restaurant/wine bar business from the premises. L had previously carried on a Greek restaurant business from T's demise prior to his letting out the property and now lived on the first floor above the Indian restaurant. L did not intend to resurrect the old restaurant that he had carried on. The evidence of L was that L would require to borrow some £40,000 to set up the new business. Evidence was given that he had £100 in his bank account. There was some other evidence (although it was not clear to what extent it was vouched for by the documents) suggesting that L had between £37,000 to £47,000 in joint or sole accounts of L and his wife. L would, on obtaining possession, have to pay compensation of £13,750. Three charges securing some £80,000 were registered against the building. There was no formal valuation of the building, although L valued it at £750,000. L produced from his accountant cash flow forecasts and projections of a profit and loss account. There was no evidence that the accountant was an expert in the restaurant business. The evidence of income used by the accountant derived principally from L's daughter, who had come up with some specimen menus and prices. L's bank had indicated that they would be interested in financing the refurbishment of the restaurant but there was no evidence as to the sum L had asked his bank for, nor what information had been put before the bank. Two weeks after the hearing L's bank wrote to him offering a fixed term loan of £60,000 to fund the refurbishment to be secured on the building.

The county court judge held that L had not satisfied the court that he would be able to raise sufficient funds to be able to run the restaurant and decided against L. L appealed on the basis that the judge had not made it clear whether he had found that L had no genuine intention or whether he had found that he was unable to carry out a genuine intention which he in fact held, and that the judge failed to take into account L's substantial equity in the building.

The Court of Appeal held:

(1) There is nothing in principle or in practice which demands a sequential treatment of the genuineness of the landlord's plans and the practicality of the implementation of his stated intention.

[281] [2003] EWCA Civ 208; [2003] 2 E.G.L.R. 37.

(2) The judge was considering whether there was a reasonable prospect of implementing the landlord's stated intention.
(3) Albeit on L's valuation there was an equity in the building of well over £600,000, it could not be said on the evidence that the judge was not entitled to find as he did. His decision was not so outside the ambit within which reasonable views may have been taken about the prospects of raising capital that it could be said that he was wrong and that his findings were against the weight of the evidence.
(4) The application to admit the fresh evidence of the proposed loan was refused. The evidence was evidence which could have been obtained prior to the trial: *Ladd v Marshall*[282]; *Hertfordshire Investments Ltd v Bubb*.[283]

Motive

The motive of the landlord in wishing to carry out the ground (f) works is irrelevant provided there is a genuine intention to do the relevant works: *Fisher v Taylor's Furnishing Stores*[284]; *Housleys Ltd v Bloomer-Holt Ltd*[285] (digested in para.7–109); *Turner v Wandsworth LBC*[286] (digested in para.7–163); *Betty's Cafes Ltd v Phillips Furnishing Stores Ltd*[287]; *Zarvos v Pradhan*[288] (digested in para.7–155) (a case under paragraph (g)). **7–161**

Thus Parker L.J. in *Fisher v Taylor's Furnishing Stores*[289] said:

> "... if ground (f) is proved to the satisfaction of the Court, it matters not to what use the landlord ultimately intends to put the building–he may intend to let it when the work is done to a third party. He may intend ultimately to occupy it himself for his own business; or he may not have made up his mind at all ...".

The landlord's reason for carrying out the work, therefore, may be of assistance only insofar as it undermines the genuineness of the landlord's intention. Thus, as Denning L.J. said in a passage already quoted from *Fisher v Taylors Furnishing Stores Ltd*[290]:

> "... the Court must be satisfied that the intention to reconstruct is genuine and not colourable."

Thus the landlord who wishes to do the work because he intends to occupy the premises for his own business purposes will, nevertheless, still be entitled to rely on ground (f): *Fisher v Taylor's Furnishing Stores Ltd*approved in *Betty's Cafes Ltd v Phillips Furnishing Stores Ltd.* Similarly, where the landlord desires to **7–162**

282 [1954] 1 W.L.R. 1489 CA.
283 [2000] 1 W.L.R. 2318 CA.
284 [1956] 2 Q.B. 78; [1956] 2 W.L.R. 985.
285 [1966] 1 W.L.R. 1244; [1966] 2 All E.R. 966 CA.
286 [1994] 1 E.G.L.R. 134 CA.
287 [1959] A.C. 20; [1958] 2 W.L.R. 513; [1958] 1 All E.R. 607 HL.
288 [2003] EWCA Civ 208.
289 [1956] 2 Q.B. 78 at 91 CA.
290 [1956] 2 Q.B. 78 at 84.

demolish the premises in order to let them out for agricultural purposes (*Craddock v Hampshire CC*)[291] or in order to sell them.

7–163 ***Turner v Wandsworth LBC***[292] The tenant's premises were used as an inner-city farm visited by children, deriving enjoyment and education in seeing what the animals on the farm got up to. The landlords opposed renewal on the grounds of s.30(1)(f). The landlords had entered into a building agreement with a company which ran a private school. The terms of the agreement were that the company would, once the tenant's tenancy had been terminated, demolish the buildings and dig up the hard-standing on the site, create a car parking area and landscape the remainder. On doing that, the company would be entitled to a lease of four years. The judge at first instance held that as the landlord eventually wanted to sell the freehold, the landlord's intention was colourable, not genuine, a ploy and not long term. The Court of Appeal held that the landlord's motive was irrelevant; the landlord had a genuine intention within the meaning of the section.

Evidence of intention

7–164 Where the landlord is an individual, he will often seek to prove his intention by giving oral evidence. It is not, however, essential, in order for the landlord to discharge the burden of proof, for the landlord to give evidence himself and submit himself to cross-examination, if there is evidence available to the court to find the requisite intention: *Grinnell v Deeley*.[293] Thus, evidence given by the person responsible for the management of the property, e.g. the landlord's son, may be sufficient (*Grinnell v Deeley*).There is no requirement that if only the landlord gives evidence in support of the ground of opposition the court must have corroborative evidence in order of the burden upon him to be discharged.[294]

The intention can be proved by evidence that the landlord acted upon advice of its surveyor, and that the substance of that advice was to implement a scheme under ground (f): *PF Ahern & Sons v Hunt* (digested in para.7–179). L may establish a sufficient intention by his evidence in cross-examination in answer to a previously uncontemplated scenario: *Yoga for Health Foundation v Guest*[295] (digested in para.7–165). One of two joint landlords, who is tendered as a witness

[291] [1958] 1 W.L.R. 202; [1958] 1 All E.R. 449 CA.
[292] [1994] 1 E.G.L.R. 134 CA.
[293] (2000) 80 P. & C.R. D15 CA.
[294] *Mirza v Nicola* [1990] 2 E.G.L.R. 73 CA. Russell L.J. said:

"What is said on behalf of the appellant tenants is that in a case such as this the judge should look for corroboration of the landlord's assertion that he desires to occupy the premises for the purposes of a business. That may very well be a desirable state of affairs . . . I am quite unable to accept the submission made . . . on behalf of the tenants that there is in some way an obligation on the judge not to accept resistance to an application for a new lease on the grounds disclosed in section 30(1)(g) unless there is in existence some corroborative material of the landlord's assertions.

In my judgment, provided that the judge asks himself the right question—which is whether it is established that there is in fact at the date of the hearing a fixed and firm intention on the part of the landlord to occupy the premises for business purposes—he is entitled, on the sworn testimony of the landlord alone, to come to the conclusion that the burden of proof has been discharged."

[295] [2002] EWCA 2658 (Ch); [2003] 1 P. & C.R. DG15.

for the landlords jointly is able to speak for them all subject to any suggestion made otherwise in cross-examination: *Yoga for Health Foundation v Guest.*

Yoga for Health Foundation v Guest[296] T was lessee of a mansion house with outbuildings situated in a courtyard area. T used the entirety for business purposes. The relevant policy in the local plan provided that buildings in the countryside could be reused for residential purposes only where a commercial use was inappropriate because of access or amenity considerations. L had planning permission to split the mansion house into two dwellings. That scheme envisaged that the outbuildings in the courtyard would be used as auxiliary to the residential accommodation in the two new houses. However, this overlooked the fact that to use the outbuildings for residential purposes would involve a change of user from commercial to residential, for which L did not have permission and any such permission would require overcoming the policy objection. L's evidence did not contemplate a variation of the scheme for the use of the outbuildings. L would either have to sell off the houses without the courtyard (scheme 1) or each house would be sold with half the courtyard and the purchasers would either use it for commercial purposes or leave it empty. T had indicated that it was prepared to take a new tenancy of the courtyard area only and that there would be no access or amenity problems in so doing. **7–165**

In cross-examination G, being one of the joint landlords, accepted that he had not considered what he would do if the court granted T a new tenancy of the outbuildings alone and had not actively given any consideration to the development of the mansion house on its own. During cross-examination G said that "if I am forced to make a statement on that issue here, then I would say that we would sub-divide the main house as per the existing plans, but without the outbuildings". There was no evidence of the financial effects of L being forced to implement scheme 1. The county court judge held that L had established a firm and settled intention to carry out scheme 1. On appeal T contended that G's evidence represented "a move at supersonic speed from the zone of doubt into the valley of decision", and submitted that it could not be taken as evidence that the landlords had formed the necessary intention in the sense of having definitely decided to carry out scheme 1. The appeal was dismissed. The court held that G had by his oral evidence established L's clear intention to effect scheme 1:

(1) G had in his evidence stated that his business was development. It was not necessary for L to alight upon a precise scheme where L's stated intention was to exploit whatever development potential the property had in the most economic way that was feasible given the planning constraints;
(2) the inherent economics also made it clear that L was intending to carry out a development. L had paid £560,000 for the site, which with T in occupation was worth only £427,000. Thus in that context L's only conceivable route out of financial disaster would be by exploiting whatever development potential the property had;
(3) there was nothing implausible about the speed with which G was able to respond to the previously uncontemplated scenario put to him in

[296] [2002] EWCA 2658 (Ch); [2003] 1 P. & C.R. DG15.

cross-examination. Indeed the speed with which G reacted to the hypothesis put to him emphasised rather than detracted from the settled nature of the basic intention;

(4) albeit G was a joint landlord no objection could be taken that his evidence alone was insufficient: G had been tendered as a witness for the landlords jointly and T had not in cross-examination suggested otherwise.

7–166 Where a company or local authority is the landlord, difficulties may arise as to how it is to prove that it has formed an intention. The best evidence of intention is a formal resolution of the company, such as was before the court in the *Betty's Cafes* case, or a formal resolution of the local authority[297] or a duly authorised sub-committee. However, this is not necessary in every case. A formal resolution may be unnecessary if the directors of the landlord company who are giving evidence represent its directing mind and will and control what it does: *HL Bolton Engineering Co Ltd v TJ Graham & Sons Ltd*[298] (digested on this point in para.7–169). As Denning L.J. said in that case[299]:

> "A company may in many ways be likened to a human body. It has a brain and nerve centre which controls what it does. It also has hands which hold the tools and act in accordance with directions from the centre. Some of the people in the company are mere servants and agents who are nothing more than hands to do the work and cannot be said to represent the mind or will. Others are directors and managers who represent the directing mind and will of the company, and control what it does. The state of mind of these managers is the state of mind of the company and is treated by the law as such ... So here, the intention of the company can be derived from the intention of its officers and agents. Whether their intention is the company's intention depends on the nature of the matter under consideration, the relative position of the officer or agent and the other relevant facts and circumstances of the case."

7–167 In the case of a company the absence of any board resolution to carry out the intended scheme will not prevent the landlord from establishing the appropriate intention if there is other evidence which shows that the landlord has a settled intention, unlikely to be changed, to carry out the development. Thus, where the landlord had entered into an agreement to pre-let the accommodation to be developed and was under a contractual obligation with the prospective lessees to

[297] See *Poppett's (Caterers) Ltd v Maidenhead Corp* [1971] 1 W.L.R. 69 CA (digested in para.7–172). It may be that a local authority's decision to carry out the works is susceptible to judicial review: *R. v Watford BC Ex p. Incorporated West Herts Golf Club* [1990] 1 E.G.L.R. 263 (judicial review granted of decision not to renew club's lease of golf course); *R. v Bexley LBC Ex p. Barnehurst Golf Club*[1992] E.G.C.S. 39 (judicial review refused of resolution to oppose grant of new tenancy).

[298] [1957] 1 Q.B. 159; [1956] 3 W.L.R. 804; [1956] 3 All E.R. 624 CA. See also *Manchester Garages v Petrofina (UK)* [1995] 1 E.G.L.R. 62 (digested in para.7–171); *Europark (Midlands) v Town Centre Securities* [1985] 1 E.G.L.R. 88 (digested in para.7–176).

[299] [1957] 1 Q.B. 159 at 172. As to the general position whether, at law, the act of an individual is to be attributed to or count as the act of the company, see: *Meridian Global Funds Management Asia Ltd v Securities Commission* [1995] A.C. 500 PC; *KR v Royal Sun Alliance Plc* [2006] EWCA Civ 1454; [2007] B.C.C. 522.

use its reasonable endeavours to bring about the termination or surrender of the tenant's lease, that was said to be "powerful evidence that the landlord does intend to do the development."[300]

The landlord may, in support of his case, provide to the court an undertaking to carry out the proposed work. As to the weight to be attached by the court to such an undertaking, see paras 7–184 and 7–221 et seq. **7–168**

HL Bolton Engineering Co Ltd v TJ Graham & Sons Ltd[301] The evidence at trial of the intention of the landlords (a company) showed that there had been no meeting of the board of directors but that each of the three directors of the landlords had individually played some part in the proposed development of the premises for occupation by the landlords. The directors had discussed the plans with the architect and had authorised the giving of the s.25 notice and other work preparatory to the occupation of the premises by the landlords. The Court of Appeal held that there had been sufficient proof of an intention under ground (g) because the directors were more than mere servants or agents of the company, but represented its mind and will and controlled what it did. Thus, the intention of the landlords could be derived from the intention of its directors. **7–169**

A&W Birch v PB (Sloane) and Cadogan Settled Estates Co[302] It was held that evidence of the landlord company's intention under ground (f) of s.30(1) of the Act could not be given by the company's secretary and individual directors. The judge adjourned the hearing in order to enable the landlord company to convene the necessary meetings of the board of directors and pass the necessary resolutions and, if it were beyond their powers to do so, to have them passed by the company in general meeting. **7–170**

Manchester Garages v Petrofina (UK)[303] On the hearing of the tenant's application for a new tenancy the landlord, a petrol company, opposed on ground (g). It appeared that no resolution had been passed by the board of the landlord about its proposed occupation, no evidence was given by any director and no evidence by anyone on what the intentions of the board, as a board, were. The only evidence was given by the north-west regional director of the landlord's business, who was totally responsible for the landlord's affairs in the region where the premises were situated. He stated that he had full authority to take the decision. The Court of Appeal upheld the county court judge's decision that the intention had been sufficiently proved. It was sufficient if the intention was formed by an agent of the company within whose authority it lay to make the decision without reference to any superior authority, unless his decision was shown to be inconsistent with some concurrent intention of some superior authority. **7–171**

---

[300] *Crossco No.4 Unlimited v Jolan Ltd* [2011] EWHC 803 (Ch) at [383] per Morgan J., unaffected on this point on appeal [2011] EWCA Civ 1619. The landlord had also obtained planning permission and assembled a professional team to advise and assist with the development.

[301] [1957] 1 Q.B. 159; [1956] 3 W.L.R. 804; [1956] 3 All E.R. 624 CA. See also para.7–279, where the case is digested on the question of the five-year bar under ground (g).

[302] 167 E.G. 283; [1956] E.G.D. 184; (1957) 106 L.J. 204.

[303] [1975] 1 E.G.L.R. 62 CA.

7–172 ***Poppett's (Caterers) Ltd v Maidenhead Corp***[304] The landlord, a local authority, served a notice specifying ground (f). Long before the service of the notice, various committees of the landlord had looked into the potential development of the premises and the minutes of those committees were subsequently confirmed by the local authority. However, neither the local authority nor any committee thereof had passed any resolution formally expressing an intention to demolish any part of the premises. The Court of Appeal upheld the county court judge's decision that the intention had been sufficiently proved.

Examples of sufficiency/insufficiency of evidence as to intention

7–173 There have been a number of cases where the tenant has alleged that the evidence before the court was not such as to justify the court concluding that the landlord had a firm and settled intention or was insufficient to show that it was probable that the landlord would be able to implement his stated intention. What is evident from a consideration of these cases is that it is a question of fact and degree for the trial judge as to whether the landlord has established the relevant intention. The cases are useful, however, in illustrating the state of preparation which a landlord is required to reach in order to persuade the court that he has a sufficient intention for the purposes of the ground of opposition.[305]

7–174 ***Joss v Bennett***[306] The landlord desired to redevelop the tenant's premises. At trial the landlord's application for outline planning consent had been refused although the reason for refusal was something which was likely to be overcome. No detailed plans of the proposed redevelopment had been prepared and the financial and economic aspects of the proposed redevelopment had only been investigated in a general way. It was held that the landlord had not established a sufficient intention under para.(f) but that it was likely that he would have a genuine intention to demolish in the future such that the grant of a long tenancy was inappropriate and, accordingly, a lease for three years was to be granted to the applicant.

7–175 ***Pelosi v Bourne***[307] The landlord opposed the tenant's application for renewal on the ground that he wished to occupy the tenant's premises as an extension of the landlord's own drapery business. The landlord's drapery business was situated next door to the tenant's premises. Evidence was given that the landlord's business was prosperous and expanding and that it was financially strong enough to justify the occupation of the tenant's adjoining premises. The landlord's present accommodation was inadequate. It was held that the landlord had established a sufficient intention for the purposes of ground (g) albeit "there

---

304 [1971] 1 W.L.R. 69; [1970] 3 All E.R. 289 CA.

305 In addition to those digested here, see also *Edwards v Thompson* [1990] 2 E.G.L.R. 71 CA (digested at para.7–147) and *Reohorn v Barry Corp* [1956] 1 W.L.R. 845; [1956] 2 All E.R. 742 CA (digested at para.7–155).

306 [1956] E.G.D. 228; (1956) 167 E.G. 207.

307 (1957) 169 E.G. 656; [1957] E.G.D. 144.

might be some fluctuation in [the] intention about the size of the shop counters or the colour of the paint to be used, or other matters which had to be decided when one expanded one's business".

Europark (Midlands) v Town Centre Securities[308] The landlord of a car park near to a shopping centre served a s.25 notice relying on ground (g) (own occupation). At the trial of a preliminary point on the tenant's application, the landlord's property director gave evidence that the landlord intended to run the car park itself, hoping to increase the occupancy and thus to enhance the trading position in the shopping centre, which the landlord also owned. The landlord had passed a resolution to this effect and also relied on an earlier resolution which showed that it was looking into the viability of the proposition. Some quotations had been obtained for the supply of various items of equipment necessary to run the car park, but no architect's plans were produced, nor had the landlord started to recruit staff. It was held that the evidence was sufficient to show that the landlord intended to occupy the premises for its own business. **7–176**

A Levy & Son v Martin Brent Developments[309] The landlord intended to redevelop the tenant's premises which formed part of a parade of shops by demolishing the parade and erecting thereon new retail units. Planning permission had been obtained. One of the units forming the development site was subject to a lease which did not expire until approximately four years after the date of the hearing. The tenant of that unit was not willing to co-operate. However, at trial evidence was called to show that an associated company of the landlord had contracted to purchase that unit. Finance was to be forthcoming from the landlord's parent company. Evidence was given that the parent had carried out a development through a number of subsidiaries including the landlord company, which itself had been responsible for 30 developments during the six years preceding the trial. The parent was a public limited company with a property portfolio, via one of its property developing companies, of a value of £150 million, with an annual development programme in excess of £40 million. There was no contract for demolition, no contract for building and no materials for the redevelopment had been purchased at the date of trial. The judge held that the landlord had established a sufficient intention under para.(f). It was pedantic in the circumstances to expect the court to go into questions of the precise origin of any funds that were to be used, which bank account was to provide them or anything of that nature. The landlord was clearly a very large operation dealing with properties on a grand scale and over the years was able to provide funds for developments much larger than the one which was before the court. The evidence, furthermore, showed that the intention was capable of implementation. **7–177**

Capocci v Goble[310] The landlord intended to develop the tenant's premises, which consisted of a site for a cold store and garage for vehicles used in connection with the tenant's ice-cream business, into 10 residential flats. The **7–178**

[308] [1985] 1 E.G.L.R. 88.
[309] [1987] 2 E.G.L.R. 93.
[310] [1987] 2 E.G.L.R. 102 CA.

evidence at trial was that outline planning permission would be obtained without difficulty in due course. The landlord had intended to carry out the development by entering into a commercial arrangement with a developer, which developer had undertaken a similar successful development in the area. The director and shareholder of the development company gave evidence to the effect that he was interested in carrying out the development and that the company's bank had agreed in principle to assist in lending the necessary money. No development agreement had been entered into and no evidence was given as to the viability of the project. The Court of Appeal upheld the judge's decision to the effect that the landlord had established a sufficient intention for the purposes of ground (f). It was said that it was not necessary either for there to be a concluded agreement nor for the basic terms of any agreement between the landlord and the developer to be established. It was probable on the evidence that an agreement would be reached between them; that was sufficient.

7–179 ***PF Ahern & Sons v Hunt***[311] The tenant had a tenancy of premises which it used for its business as industrial rubbish disposal contractors. The interest of the landlord was vested in trustees who had obtained planning permission for a residential development in connection with the demised premises and surrounding land. Several developers had already shown an interest. The trustees were throughout advised by a surveyor and had on his advice made a decision to sell the freehold interest outright. That decision was taken by the trustees before they were advised about the existence of business tenancies. The trustees served a s.25 notice opposing the grant of a new tenancy under ground (f) of s.30(1) of the Act. At trial the trustees called evidence that they wished to realise the development value of the site. The surveyor had considered three proposals:

(1) outright sale;
(2) joint venture with developer; and
(3) building lease at a premium.

The second scheme for various reasons could not be pursued. The surveyors evidence at the hearing was that the freehold of the site would not be sold but that a 125-year building lease would be granted. It was held on appeal that there was ample evidence on which the judge could find that the trustees had established a sufficient intention.

7–180 ***Skeet v Powell-Sheddon***[312] The tenant carried on the business of a private hotel or lodging house from two properties demised by the landlords. The landlord opposed renewal under s.30(1)(g). The evidence before the judge was that the landlord intended to carry on the hotel business from the premises by entering into partnership with her husband, who would be responsible for the day-to-day management of the hotel. The landlord's daughter was studying hotel management and would become manageress after obtaining her qualification but, while a student, would give limited assistance in the running of the hotel. No

[311] [1988] 2 E.G.L.R. 74 CA.
[312] [1988] 2 E.G.L.R. 112 CA.

partnership agreement had been entered into and no application for a licence to sell alcohol from the premises had been made by the landlord. The county court judge held that the landlord had shown a genuine intention to occupy the premises for the purposes of carrying on a business and the Court of Appeal refused to interfere with that finding.

Peter Goddard & Sons v Hounslow LBC[313] The landlord local authority opposed the tenant's application for renewal on the grounds that it wished to redevelop the premises, not by themselves, but through a development company under a building lease. Outline planning permission had been obtained for the development. The various sub-tenants occupied parts of the site. It was suggested by the tenant that there would be difficulties in proceeding with the outline planning permission because the site was a riverside one with various underground works holding up the river bank and that there could be problems in bringing forward detailed specifications and drawings without having possession of the site in order that surveys might be undertaken. Furthermore, the development company was largely dependent upon bank finance in order to implement the development and at the date of the hearing the bank's agreement to advance money to it on overdraft was about to be reviewed. It was said that there was no firm evidence that it would be renewed. The development company had in fact spent an initial £70,000 on the project. The Court of Appeal dismissed the tenant's appeal from the judge's decision that the landlord had proved a sufficient intention under para.(f). The expenditure of £70,000 indicated that it was a case of "intention" rather than "hope" and the judge's view that there would be no problem in getting rid of the occupiers and that finance would be forthcoming was essentially a finding upon a question of fact and degree for the judge. There were no grounds for interfering with his conclusions. **7–181**

Palisade Investments v Collin Estate[314] The landlord intended to redevelop the tenant's premises which were within a conservation area. The planning consent imposed a condition that the demolition of the premises was not to be undertaken before a contract for the carrying out of the works of redevelopment of the site had been made. The evidence at trial as to the landlord's proposed programme indicated that the contract for the development was not going out to tender until after the demolition work had begun. Thus there was proposed a technical breach of the planning conditions. The Court of Appeal rejected the tenant's appeal and upheld the judge's decision that the landlord had made out a sufficient intention under ground (f). There were several ways in which the breach could be dealt with; either by a renegotiation of the condition or by altering the programme for the redevelopment itself. The judge was entitled to infer that that was a possible course. There was, in any event, no absolute rule that any prospective illegality would prevent a landlord from establishing the requisite intention to demolish and reconstruct or, as the case may be, under **7–182**

313 [1992] 1 E.G.L.R. 281 CA.
314 [1992] 2 E.G.L.R. 94 CA.

ground (g) occupy the premises for its own purposes. Possible illegality was relevant only so far as it went to show that the landlord had no reasonable prospect of carrying out his intention.

7–183 ***Dolgellau Golf Club v Hett***[315] The tenant was a members club operating a 9-hole golf course. The landlord opposed renewal under ground (g). The landlord was an individual. He gave evidence that he intended to operate a proprietary golf club, making use of the existing 9-hole golf course. He said that if the club decided to remove its temporary club buildings, for which the terms of the lease provided, he would replace them with temporary constructions of his own; otherwise he hoped to negotiate with the club for the purchase of its buildings. One way or another his intention was to rely on temporary buildings at the outset with a view, later, to building a new permanent club house. He produced no schemes in the form of sketch drawings or outline specifications of what he had in mind, and gave no indication of the likely cost of his proposal.

The landlord suggested a figure of about £8,000 to provide and equip temporary buildings to replace those of the club. He said that he intended to boost the club's income from membership subscription and green fees by the sale of alcohol and the provision of a gaming machine in the club house. He also spoke of supplementing the club's income from winter grazing of sheep and haymaking. However, he had not made any application for, or seemingly investigated the possibility of obtaining, planning permission for any new building. Nor had he investigated what was involved or the possible difficulties for a proprietary club in obtaining a new liquor licence for temporary buildings of the sort he had in mind or in obtaining a licence for a gaming machine. He hoped to increase the income from green fees by attracting more visitors than it currently attracted. The landlord gave evidence as to his financial assets but there was no confirmation, documentary or otherwise, of much of his evidence about the value of those assets. The expert accountancy evidence suggested that the landlord would make either a very small profit or an operating loss.

The judge was of the view that the cost of providing the club with new equipment to maintain the course was likely to be much more expensive than the landlord had estimated. Furthermore, it was the judge's view that in the first or early years, the landlord's venture was likely to lose members and would operate at best at an annual loss of about £12,000. However, notwithstanding this, the judge accepted that albeit the landlord's proposal was unprepared and risky, he had a genuine intention to carry out the scheme and had the ability and financial means to bring it about and accordingly upheld the landlord's opposition. The Court of Appeal dismissed the tenant's appeal.

[315] [1998] 2 E.G.L.R. 75 CA.

Undertaking to the court

In the *Betty's Cafes* case,[316] the court accepted an undertaking from the landlord to carry out the proposed works. In *Espresso v Guardian* (digested in para.7–225) the court accepted an undertaking to carry out certain works and to occupy for business purposes under ground (g). It was stated that where a responsible landlord offers such an undertaking to the court it will be powerful evidence of fixity of intention, although not conclusive. There is some doubt as to the appropriateness of the court accepting an undertaking in a case falling under ground (g), although the same objections would not appear to extend to an undertaking given under ground (f). (See the discussion of this point in para.7–221 et seq.) **7–184**

Date upon which landlord is to implement intention

Termination of the current tenancy

The landlord's intention must be one which he intends to implement "on the termination of the current tenancy". Clearly, the reference to "the termination of the current tenancy" includes the continuation thereof pursuant to ss.24 and 64, since the landlord cannot possibly implement his intention until the current tenancy has come to an end and he is entitled to vacant possession. In *Westminster City Council v British Waterways Board*[317] (digested in para.7–186) the House of Lords held that the question whether the landlord's intention was capable of being implemented must be judged upon the assumption that the current tenancy would come to an end and the landlord would be entitled to vacant possession. Accordingly, any argument that planning permission would not be obtained, because the planning authority would desire to protect the use of the premises by the existing occupier, would cease to apply once the current tenancy, and thus the occupation of the tenant, had come to an end.[318] **7–185**

Westminster City Council v British Waterways Board[319] The British Waterways Board was the landlord of premises adjacent to the Paddington Basin of the Grand Union Canal, which had for many years been occupied by the tenants, Westminster City Council, and used by them as a street cleansing depot. The landlord opposed the tenants' application for a new tenancy under ground (g) of s.30(1) (own occupation). The landlord proved at trial an intention, which the judge held to be bona fide, to go into occupation of the premises at the end of the tenancy and thereafter to use them for marina and leisure purposes in connection **7–186**

---

[316] *Betty's Cafes Ltd v Phillips Furnishing Stores Ltd* [1959] A.C. 20; [1958] 2 W.L.R. 513; [1958] 1 All E.R. 607 HL.

[317] [1985] A.C. 676; [1984] 3 W.L.R. 1047; [1984] 3 All E.R. 737 HL.

[318] However, if the planning policy in question requires a consideration of the fact that a proposed development would preclude the possibility of a resumption of the existing use, i.e. the potential for such use would be lost, the court is entitled to have regard to it in considering whether or not the landlord has a reasonable prospect of obtaining planning permission: *Cadogan v McCarthy & Stone (Developments) Ltd* [2000] L. & T.R. 249 CA.

[319] [1985] A.C. 676; [1984] 3 W.L.R. 1047; [1984] 3 All E.R. 737 HL.

with the canal. However, the judge held that the board's proposed use would involve a change of use from the existing planning use, namely as a depot. He went on to hold that planning permission to change the use would be refused by the city council, which also happened to be the local planning authority, on the ground that it would disturb the present use of the premises as a street cleansing depot. Accordingly, the board had not sufficiently proved its intention and a new tenancy should be granted. The board appealed to the Court of Appeal which allowed the appeal. The tenants appealed to the House of Lords. It was held:

(1) The correct test to be applied was the objective test set out by the Court of Appeal in *Gregson v Cyril Lord*[320] (digested in para.7–154) namely whether the landlord had established a reasonable prospect either that planning permission was not required or, if it was, that he would obtain it.
(2) The prospect of success in obtaining planning permission should be assessed on the footing that the landlord was entitled to possession.
(3) On that footing, the preservation of the existing use would not be a reason for refusing planning permission, for refusal on that ground alone is only justified if the refusal may reasonably be expected to lead to a resumption of the existing use.
(4) In any event, the existing use of the premises was not as a street cleansing depot but as a depot simpliciter. The council's stated reason for refusing consent was not, therefore, directed to preservation of the existing planning use, but to preserve its own occupation, which was not a legitimate planning ground.

7–187 Although the reference is to the "termination of the current tenancy", it is thought that if the landlord could prove an intention to start the works within a short period after obtaining possession that would be sufficient: the landlord might, e.g. wish to carry out a survey of the premises and finalise his detailed plans for their redevelopment only after he had obtained possession. In *Livestock Underwriting Agency Ltd v Corbett and Newson Ltd*[321] the judge said:

> "... I accept [counsel's] submissions that in these matters one cannot say that this is a question of demolishing the moment other people walk out. You have to take a reasonable view of the matter and ... if they start work within the quarter after the termination of the tenancy ... they are within the meaning of 'demolishing' at the termination of the current tenancy."

Taking into account new evidence on appeal

7–188 As the relevant date for determining the intention is the date of the termination of the current tenancy, that date may move if there is an appeal, for until disposal of the appeal the tenancy is continuing pursuant to ss.24 and 64. Thus, it often arises that on appeal a party, usually the landlord, seeks to adduce fresh evidence in support of his intention. There is a difference between taking account of matters which arise after trial, and which could not with reasonable diligence have been made available at the trial, and taking account of matters which arise after trial,

320 [1963] 1 W.L.R. 41; [1962] 3 All E.R. 907 CA.
321 (1955) 165 E.G. 469.

but which could with reasonable diligence have been made available at the trial. The former will ordinarily be permitted; the latter will not be. Thus, upon an appeal the court will be entitled to have regard to developments, e.g. in relation to the obtaining of planning permission since the date of trial: *Accountancy Personnel v Worshipful Company of Salters*[322] (digested in para.7–295); *Gatwick Parking Services Ltd v Sargent*[323] (digested in para.7–156). However, where the landlord failed under para.(g) on the ground that the court was not satisfied that he would be able to raise the funds necessary to commence the business intended, the court on appeal refused to admit evidence of a letter from the landlord's bank, written two weeks after the trial, which offered appropriate financing facilities, as such evidence could reasonably have been made available at trial. *Ladd v Marshall*[324] is still an "appropriate starting point for the consideration of the admission of fresh evidence": *Hertfordshire Investments Ltd v Bubb*[325]; *Zarvos v Pradhan*[326] (digested in para.7–160). The consideration by the court on appeal of fresh evidence is not dependent upon establishing that the judge can be shown to have been wrong. Once it has been decided that fresh evidence should be admitted, the court should consider it notwithstanding that the appeal is a review of the judge's decision rather than a re-hearing: *Davy's of London (Wine Merchants) Ltd v City of London Corp.*[327]

Interrelation with redevelopment break clauses

Often the landlord is able to break the term of the lease prior to its expiry by effluxion of time by serving upon the tenant a redevelopment break notice in accordance with the terms of the lease. The question which arises where, as is frequently the case, the wording of the break clause reflects the terms of para.(f) of s.30(1), is whether the intention to redevelop must be shown at the earlier date of the service of the notice rather than the date of the hearing.[328] Much depends on the exact wording of the break clause[329] but it is considered that if the break clause were to mirror the statutory ground of opposition the court is likely to **7–189**

322 (1972) 116 E.G. 240.

323 [2000] 2 E.G.L.R. 45CA.

324 [1954] 1 W.L.R. 1489 CA. Where the question which has to be considered is whether the evidence could not have been obtained with reasonable diligence for use at the trial.

325 [2000] 1 W.L.R. 2318 CA.

326 [2003] EWCA Civ 208; [2003] 2 E.G.L.R. 37.

327 [2004] EWHC 2224 (Ch) Lewison J.

328 The date of the hearing being the relevant date for the purposes of para.(f): see para.7–136.

329 There are numerous cases. For example in *Gough v The Worcester and Birmingham Canal Company* (1801) 6 Ves. Jr. 354, the break clause provided:

"that if the [landlord] . . . shall be minded to set out any part of the ground hereby demised . . . for a street or streets, or to set or sell any part or parts thereof to build upon, and shall at any time during the said term give to the said lessee…two months notice in writing of such intention, then it shall be lawful for the lessor. . . . to enter upon such ground of the said demised premises as shall be set out for a street . . . [etc]".

In *Johnson v The Edgware Railway Company* (1866) 35 Beav. 480. The break clause in this case provided:

"Provided always and it is hereby agreed that in case any portion or portions of the said demised lands shall be required for the purposes of building, planting accommodation or otherwise, or for the purpose of working clay, sand or gravel in, under or upon the same, by [the landlord] . . . it shall be

require, in order for the break notice to be valid, that for the relevant intention to be established at the date of the service of the break notice as well as in respect of the s.25 notice at the date of the hearing. It is accordingly advisable at the drafting stage to avoid incorporating the statutory wording.

7–190 A case in which the difference between the wording of the break clause and that of the statute proved to be of importance is *Aberdeen Steak Houses Group Plc v Crown Estate Commissioners*[330] the tenant's lease contained the following redevelopment break clause:

> "If the [commissioners] shall desire to demolish or reconstruct the Building or a substantial part thereof or to carry out substantial work of construction on part thereof on or after the 10th day of October in the years 1995 or 2000 or 2005 and of such desire shall give to [Aberdeen] at least six months' previous notice in writing to expire on the relevant of the aforementioned dates then on the expiration of the said notice the term hereby granted shall cease . . ."

The argument of the tenant that "desire" was akin to "intention" was rejected. The learned judge said:

> "On behalf of [the tenant it was] submitted that 'desire' was stronger than 'wish', it was akin to 'intention' and connoted 'a firm and a settled desire' . . . [that] the effect of the operation of a break clause was analogous to the operation of a forfeiture clause it should be strictly construed against the landlord and in favour of the tenant. Accordingly, [it was] submitted that there must in addition have been a reasonable expectation, as at April 5 1995 [the date of the service of the break notice], that the desire could be implemented. [It was] submitted that it would not be sufficient for the commissioners to show a desire to carry out some form of refurbishment or even a form of refurbishment that might have involved works falling within the scope of the break clause. What must be established is that there was a desire to carry out works which would have fallen within the scope of the break clause.
>
> On behalf of the commissioners it was submitted that in order to prove the existence of the requisite desire it was not necessary to satisfy the test of intention under para.(f). It was submitted that the commissioners only have to prove the existence of their wish to carry out a demolition or reconstruction of the building or a substantial part thereof on or after October 10, 1995. In particular, it was submitted that the commissioners do not have to prove that on or before April 5, 1995 they had a reasonable prospect of bringing about the relevant demolition or reconstruction: it was sufficient if the commissioners wished to carry out such work notwithstanding the fact that as at April 5, 1995 there were hurdles which had to be overcome before the work could be done.
>
> On this point I prefer the submissions made on behalf of the commissioners. 'Desire' is an ordinary English word meaning simply to wish for something. As a matter of plain language it is, I think, quite different from the word 'intention' . . . the commissioners . . . do not have to prove a desire as at April 5, 1995 to carry out a specific scheme of demolition or reconstruction of the building or a substantial part thereof. It is sufficient if the commissioners contemplated, in general terms, demolition or reconstruction of the building or a substantial part of it. The desired works must fall within the general rubric of demolition or reconstruction, but there is no necessity for the commissioners to be able to point to a 'finished' scheme of demolition or reconstruction as at April 5, 1995."

---

lawful for the [landlord] . . . to resume and take any portion or portions accordingly, on giving to [the tenant] three calendar months' previous notice of his intention so to do . . .".

In these two decisions it is to be noted that the clause pursuant to which the right to break was conferred provided by its terms that the landlord had, effectively, to "intend" to do something. The court held that the landlord had to have a bona fide intention to do the thing in question which permitted the lease to be broken.

[330] [1997] 2 E.G.L.R. 107 CA.

The landlord may operate the break notice by service of a notice pursuant to s.25: see para.3–182. The covering letter to service of the s.25 notice may be referred to to give effect to the notice as one pursuant to the terms of the contract as well as the statutory provisions: *Aberdeen Steak Houses Group Plc v Crown Estate Commissioners*.[331] **7–191**

Tenant willing to grant access for works

By s.31A(1)(a), it is provided that the court shall not hold that the landlord could not reasonably carry out the intended works "without obtaining possession of the holding" if: **7–192**

> "... the tenant agrees to the inclusion in the terms of the new tenancy of terms giving the landlord access and other facilities for carrying out the work intended and, given that access and those facilities, the landlord could reasonably carry out the work without obtaining possession of the holding and without interfering to a substantial extent or for a substantial time with the use of the holding for the purposes of the business carried on by the tenant."

It has been held by the Court of Appeal in *Romulus Trading Co Ltd v Trustees of Henry Smith's Charity (No.2)*[332] that there is no particular stage in the proceedings by which the tenant is required to elect to rely upon s.31A, although it is desirable that he should indicate from the earliest possible moment that an issue arises under the section.[333]

The tenant will only need to rely upon this provision if his current tenancy does not contain a reservation of sufficient width to enable the landlord to carry out the intended work (see para.7–95). A landlord is arguably in a better position if the tenant seeks to rely on s.31A than he is if there is reservation within the terms of the current lease, for the protection conferred upon the tenant by s.31A is cut down by the second condition to s.31A(1)(a). This is illustrated by *Price v Esso*[334] (digested in para.7–104), where the tenant lost on the application of s.31A but won because the landlord could carry out the intended work under a term of the existing lease. **7–193**

If the tenant wishes to rely upon s.31A(1)(a), a number of matters will need to be considered, namely: **7–194**

(1) The identification of what are the relevant works intended by the landlord. Section 31A does not come into play until the landlord has proved his intention to do works sufficient to satisfy ground (f).[335]

---

331 [1997] 2 E.G.L.R. 107. See also para.3–182.

332 [1991] 1 E.G.L.R. 95. See also para.14–76.

333 Although in light of the new procedure under CPR Pt 56 and in particular the requirement for the tenant to produce the evidence upon which he relies at quite an early stage in the litigation, the tenant's election is equally likely to be made at a fairly early stage in the proceedings. A tenant is now required to state in response to a landlord's Part 7 termination application as to whether he relies on s.31A and, if so, the basis on which he does so: see paras 14–74 and 14–76.

334 [1980] 2 E.G.L.R. 58 CA.

335 See further para.7–195.

(2) The tenant must agree to the inclusion in the terms of the new tenancy of rights of access and other facilities for carrying out the works.
(3) The right of access and the facilities to which the tenant has agreed must be such as will enable the landlord "reasonably" to carry out the works.[336]
(4) The right of access and the facilities to which the tenant has agreed must be such as will enable the landlord to reasonably carry out the works "without obtaining possession of the holding"[337] (the first condition).
(5) The effect of the granting of the rights of access and the facilities may well result in some interference with the use of the holding by the tenant for the purposes of his business. Section 31A(1)(a) will not apply if that interference will be substantial in extent "or" in time[338] (the second condition).

The ground (f) works

7–195 It is not open to a tenant who seeks to rely upon s.31A to contend that the landlord ought reasonably to do different works from those which he has proved he intends to do—*Decca Navigator Co v Greater London Council*[339] (digested in para.7–196). It is the works which the landlord actually intends to do which are relevant for the purpose, not other work which might be said to achieve the same object. However, in considering the application of s.31A(1)(a) the court should consider whether the terms of the lease as proposed by the tenant make provision for (1) some of the works carried out by the landlord to be undone and (2) additional work to be carried out by the tenant so as to enable the tenant to occupy and trade from the holding. Such additional work may be taken into account in considering both whether the landlord's works could reasonably be carried out without obtaining possession (the first condition) and whether the interference with the use of the tenant's holding would be for a substantial extent and time (the second condition): *Pumperninks of Piccadilly Ltd v Land Securities Plc*[340] (digested on this point in para.7–197). Each aspect of the tenant's works should be considered against the background that s.31A is directed to the works that the landlord intends to do. Thus, in the context of its application to the first condition, this would mean that the court would be entitled to have regard to the fact that the tenant was ultimately seeking, by the incorporation of the new terms of the lease as to access and facilities, something which was wholly incompatible with the effect of the landlord's works. In the context of the second condition, the extent and time of the interference should include consideration of the nature, extent and period of the tenant works pursuant to the terms of the new lease to enable the tenant to occupy the holding.

7–196 ***Decca Navigator Co v Greater London Council***[341] A tenancy of half an acre of land used as a car park contained a provision that it could be determined if the

[336] See further para.7–198.
[337] See further para.7–200 et seq.
[338] See further para.7–202 et seq. The word "or" is to be read conjunctively: see para.7–204.
[339] [1974] 1 W.L.R. 748; [1974] 1 All E.R. 1178 CA.
[340] [2002] EWCA Civ 621; [2002] 3 All E.R. 609.
[341] [1974] 1 W.L.R. 748; [1974] 1 All E.R. 1178 CA.

landlord required the land for a fire station. The landlords decided to build a fire station and gave notice terminating the tenancy. The tenant applied for a new tenancy and relied upon s.31A(1)(b) to support its contention that the landlords could achieve their purpose satisfactorily by building the fire station not where they said they wished to put it, but upon another part of the holding. The judge found that the landlords' intended work required all the land and, holding that the words "intended work" in the section meant the work which the landlords in fact intended to carry out, found the landlords required possession of the whole of the holding. It was held that the question was not whether the landlords were reasonable in intending to do the work, but whether they were, having that intention, reasonable in dispossessing the tenant completely in order to carry it out. If it should appear that part of the work was such as no reasonable person would execute, this might be a ground for doubting the bona fides of the landlords' intentions. There was no such doubt here and the appeal was accordingly dismissed.

Pumperninks of Piccadilly Ltd v Land Securities Plc[342] T's demise was what was known as an "egg-shell" demise, i.e. one which demised only the internal skin of the part of the building occupied. L proposed to do work to T's shop. The overall effect of the work involved the removal of every physical built thing in the demise; effectively the egg-shell and thus the material enclosing the "demised premises" would be removed and what was T's shop would become part of an open space, which would include adjacent units, to be fitted out by any new occupier or occupiers, providing a floor, a ceiling, plastering or other wall covering and such internal partitions as may be appropriate. **7–197**

T argued, inter alia,[343] that it was prepared to provide means of access to enable L to carry out the work (it being agreed that the work could not be undertaken pursuant to the terms of the existing lease). T also sought, as terms of the new tenancy, provisions the effect of which would be intended to secure that, if the works were carried out under the terms of any new tenancy, the tenant could reinstate the premises in such a manner as would enable it to carry out its existing business.

The landlord's work would take some 17 to 23 days if carried out in a single operation, during which T could not occupy the premises for the purposes of his business. This the judge said was not a substantial interference. However, T proposed terms for a new tenancy which would enable him to undo most of that which was undertaken by the landlord. The judge held that where the necessity of permitting the tenant to undo what the landlord intends would leave little purpose in the landlord's doing what he intends, the landlord could not reasonably do that which he otherwise intends without possession. As a matter of fact and degree that point was reached in the case before him and T was not entitled to rely on s.31A as precluding a finding that L could not reasonably carry out the works within s.30(1)(f) without obtaining possession.

---

342 [2002] Ch. 332; [2002] 3 All E.R. 609. This decision is also important on the question of works falling within ground (f) where the demise consists of an internal skin only: see para.7–94.

343 T also argued that the work did not fall within ground (f). On this aspect of the decision see para.7–94.

On appeal, T argued the judge was wrong under s.31A(1) to look beyond the programme of works that L intended to carry out and that the court was to look only at the effect on the tenant's holding whilst the works intended by L were carried out.

It was held:

(1) Per Charles J. with whom Simon Brown L.J. agreed: T's argument that when considering s.31A the court should only have regard to the period of the programme and period of works of demolition, etc. intended by the landlord in considering the application of the first condition to s.31A(1)(a) was wrong; the court should in considering the application of s.31A have regard to the terms of the new lease where those terms made provision for (a) some of the works carried out by the landlord to be undone and (b) additional work to be carried out by T so as to enable T to occupy and trade from the holding. If, after the intended works are carried out, the premises would not exist precisely as they had before, this would be a relevant factor in deciding whether those works could be carried out without obtaining possession.

(2) Per Charles J. with whom Simon Brown L.J. agreed: when a tenant agrees to the inclusion in the terms of the new tenancy of terms giving access and other facilities for carrying out the work intended, and that work will have the result that the holding will no longer exist, they cannot be terms that enable the landlord to carry out the works without obtaining possession of the holding: dicta of Parker L.J. in *Blackburn v Hussain*[344] followed.

(3) Per Charles J. with whom Simon Brown L.J. agreed: in some circumstances when a landlord intends to do work that the tenant wants to undo, and further or alternatively when the tenant will need to do work after the landlord has finished his work to enable him to use the holding, the tenant should be able to take advantage of s.31A.

(4) Per Charles J. with whom Simon Brown L.J. agreed: in the context of the second condition of s.31A(1)(a) (time and extent of interference) the extent and time of the interference should include consideration of the nature, extent and period of the works that would have to be done pursuant to terms of the new lease to enable the tenant to occupy and use the holding. The decisions in *Cerex Jewels v Peachey Property Corp*[345] (digested in para.7–205); *Redfern v Reeves*[346] (digested in para.7–203) and *Price v Esso*[347] (digested in para.7–104) were not binding authority preventing consideration of the physical effect of the landlord's works where, when completed, further work has to be done to enable the tenant to occupy and use the holding.

(5) Per Chadwick L.J. with whom Simon Brown L.J. agreed: s.31A(1)(a) of the 1954 Act does not apply in a case (such as the instant case) where it would

344 [1988] 1 E.G.L.R. 77 at 78.
345 [1986] 2 E.G.L.R. 65.
346 [1978] 2 E.G.L.R. 52 CA.
347 [1980] 2 E.G.L.R. 58 CA.

be a necessary consequence of carrying out the landlord's work that the holding would become unusable, indefinitely, for the purpose of the tenant's business.

Access and facilities must enable landlord "reasonably" to carry out the work

The word "reasonably" indicates that the landlord may have to adjust his method or sequence of work in order to carry out his intended works: *Pumperninks of Piccadilly Ltd v Land Securities Plc*[348] (digested in para.7–197). However, given the access and the facilities proposed by the tenant the works must not be made unreasonably more lengthy or expensive for the landlord. Thus, where the tenant suggested that the landlord could carry out work over the weekend so as to reduce the contract period, the evidence that this gave rise to an unreasonable additional cost meant that it would be an uneconomical way of proceeding and thus not "reasonable": *Graysim Holdings Ltd v P&O Property Holdings Ltd.*[349] The tenant is entitled to say that the landlord should have the work done by a contractor—rather than doing it himself—so that the work could be done more speedily, unless it is uneconomic to do so: *Jones v Thomas*[350] (digested in para.7–199). The court is not precluded from considering offers made by the tenant outside the terms of the new tenancy, e.g. by way of an offer of an indemnity in respect of extra costs in considering the test of reasonableness: *Pumperninks of Piccadilly Ltd v Land Securities Ltd.*[351] **7–198**

Jones v Thomas[352] The landlord owned a group of buildings, consisting of a dwelling/house, which she occupied with her husband, and premises let to the tenant comprising a workshop forge and covered shed. The demised premises were dilapidated to the extent that they had become dangerous and liable to fall down. Neither landlord nor tenant had any repairing obligation to the other. The landlord served a s.25 notice specifying ground (f) (demolition and reconstruction) as one of her grounds of opposition under s.30(1). At the hearing of the tenant's application for a new tenancy, the landlord stated an intention to rebuild the bulging main walls of the workshop from the footings up, to replace the whole of the existing steel sheet roofing and to demolish the forge and the covered yard. The landlord's husband gave evidence that he intended to do the **7–199**

[348] [2002] Ch. 332; [2002] 3 All E.R. 609 at [61] approving of comments of the judge at first instance.

[349] [1993] 1 E.G.L.R. 96 at 101E (first instance).

[350] (1963) 186 E.G. 1053; [1963] E.G.D. 314.

[351] [2002] Ch. 332; [2002] 3 All E.R. 609 at [61], per Charles J.

[352] (1963) 186 E.G. 1053; [1963] E.G.D. 314. Note: the case was decided on the basis, since disapproved by the House of Lords in *Heath v Drown* (digested in para.7–103), that "if the work could be done whilst the tenant was there putting up with the inconvenience of having workmen about the place" the landlord had not shown that he was not reasonably able to carry out the works without obtaining possession. The matter is now to be judged not as one of the practicability of the tenant putting up with the inconvenience of works, but with the landlord's legal ability to carry them out while there is a subsisting tenancy. Nevertheless, the main point in this case, that economic necessity may make it reasonable for the landlord to "do it himself", remains highly relevant under s.31A.

work himself in his spare time in stages. The landlord and her surveyor gave evidence that it would be uneconomic to pay a contractor to do the work. The county court judge found:

> "If the [landlord's husband] were to do this work himself in his spare time then it would take a long time and would be difficult without obtaining possession; but the [landlord] is not entitled to say, 'Because I am going to do it myself I want him out'. The work which the building requires could be done quite expeditiously while the [tenant] is still in occupation. As the [tenant] and his sons are not there the whole time the work could be done in his absence."

The county court judge granted a seven-year tenancy. It was held on appeal, allowing the appeal:

(1) The premises were so dilapidated and dangerous and the work proposed so extensive that the work proposed to the workshop was properly described as "reconstruction".
(2) In view of the evidence that it was not economic to employ contractors to do the work, the only practical way for the landlord to do the work was to get her husband to do it himself. On the basis, she could not reasonably do so without obtaining possession.
(3) The s.25 notice made it clear that the landlord was intending to rely on ground (f) and it was not necessary to go into detail in the notice as to the exact work contemplated. In any event, "reconstruction", as applied to the whole holding was sufficient to embrace some degree of demolition.

Access and facilities must enable landlord reasonably to carry out the work "without obtaining possession of the holding"

7–200 The subsection, as construed by the courts, produces some curious anomalies. If the long-term effect of the landlord's proposals upon the tenant's business is irrelevant, it might appear to follow that, where a tenant is able to grant facilities which would not result in a substantial interference with his business, it is irrelevant that the effect of the works once they are completed is to make the premises totally inappropriate for that business.

7–201 **Example** If a garage with upper part were used by the tenant merely for storage purposes, he might well be able to show under s.31A(1)(a) that his business would not be substantially interfered with if the landlord were to implement an intention to convert the premises to a shop and offices. The physical work would not seriously disrupt the tenant's storage use, but when the works had been completed he would be using for storage purposes premises quite inappropriate to that use.

However, in *Blackburn v Hussain*[353] (digested in para.7–206) Parker L.J.,[354] without finally deciding the point, said that there was great force in the contention

---

353 [1988] 1 E.G.L.R. 77 CA.

354 At [1988] 1 E.G.L.R. 77 at 78 where he said:

"That is sufficient to dispose of the issue arising on this appeal, but it was also submitted on behalf of the appellant that section 31A did not really arise at all, because it cannot have contemplated an agreement which involved the destruction of the subject matter of the original holding. Were it

that it was not possible for the tenants to avoid the plain meaning of s.31A(1)(a) in that way. In *Pumperninks of Piccadilly Ltd v Land Securities Plc*[355] (digested in para.7–197) Chadwick L.J., with whom Simon Brown L.J. agreed,[356] held that s.31A(1)(a) could not be utilised by a tenant where the consequence of the landlord's works were that the holding would become unusable, indefinitely, for the purpose of the tenant's business. It was said by the Learned Lord Justice that this was either because if s.31A(1)(a) applied the landlord could not, adopting the reasoning of Parker L.J., reasonably carry out the landlord's works without obtaining legal possession of the holding, or because (Chadwick L.J.'s preferred approach) s.31A(1)(a) simply could not have been intended to apply to such a case. Charles J., in the same case, was of the view that when a tenant agrees to the inclusion in the terms of the new tenancy of terms giving access and other facilities for carrying out the work intended and that work will have the result that the holding will no longer exist they cannot be terms that enable the landlord to carry out the works without obtaining possession of the holding.[357] However, in some circumstances when a landlord intends to do work that the tenant wants to undo, and further or alternatively, when the tenant will need to do work after the landlord has finished his work to enable him to use the holding, the tenant should be able to take advantage of s.31A and that in those circumstances issues of fact and degree are likely to arise.[358] An example could be one in which a landlord intends to produce a shell for letting and fitting out by a tenant.

See also *Leathwoods Ltd v Total Oil Great Britain Ltd*[359] (digested in para.7–106).

Interference for a substantial time or extent

The court is not concerned with the long-term effect of the carrying out of the works upon the tenant's business; it is concerned with the question of whether, during the course of the works, the tenant's use of the holding will be substantially interfered with: *Redfern v Reeves*[360] (digested in para.7–203). Thus, the court is concerned with the physical impact of the work upon the tenant's holding. The court will have regard in considering the extent and time of the interference not only with the works proposed by the landlord but also additional work to be carried out by the tenant undoing the landlord's works and work to **7–202**

otherwise it would involve a tenant's being able to say: 'I agree to the destruction of the subject matter of the original holding, but I demand that, it having been destroyed, I am granted a new tenancy, not of my holding, but of some entirely different entity.' Without finally deciding the matter, I should say that I accept that there is great force in that contention and that for my part I do not, as presently advised, accept that it is possible for a tenant by any such agreement to avoid the plain meaning of section 30(1)(f)."

355 [2002] Ch. 332; [2002] 3 All E.R. 609.

356 Simon Brown L.J. agreed with both Charles J. and Chadwick L.J., see at [97], and although the reasoning of Charles J. and Chadwick L.J. was slightly different.

357 Citing with approval the dicta of Parker L.J. in *Blackburn v Hussain* [1988] 1 E.G.L.R. 77 CA.

358 Charles J. at [48].

359 [1985] E.G.L.R. 237.

360 [1978] 2 E.G.L.R. 52 CA.

enable the tenant to occupy and trade from the holding after completion of the landlord's works: *Pumperninks of Piccadilly Ltd v Land Securities Plc*[361] (digested in para.7–197).

7–203 ***Redfern v Reeves***[362] The landlord intended substantially to alter premises in order that he might move his jeweller's business there and opposed the tenant's application for a new tenancy on ground (f). The tenant stated in her application that, in accordance with s.31A(1)(a), if she were granted a new tenancy she would give the landlord access for the purpose of carrying out the intended works. The county court judge found that the proposed works could not be done without the tenant leaving the premises but that during the works, which were estimated to take between two and four months, the tenant could transfer to nearby premises while preserving the goodwill of her business. He held that there would be no substantial interference with the tenant's use of the premises and therefore that she was entitled to rely on s.31A(1)(a). The Court of Appeal held that under the subsection the court must look to the physical effects of the work and not to the consequences of it from a business point of view (e.g. the effect on the goodwill of the business). Since it was manifest that the totality of the work would undoubtedly interfere to a substantial extent and for a substantial time with the tenant's use of the demised premises the judge's decision would be reversed.

"Or"

7–204 The use of the word "or" might appear to indicate that the section will be inapplicable if the interference is substantial in time (but not extent) or substantial in extent (but not in time). It has been held by the Court of Appeal that this is not the correct interpretation. The relevant words are to be read conjunctively so that the questions of the extent of the interference and its duration must be considered together as a matter of fact and degree: *Cerex Jewels v Peachey Property Corp*[363] (digested in para.7–205).

7–205 ***Cerex Jewels v Peachey Property Corp***[364] The ground-floor shop and basement at 40 Carnaby Street, London W1, were let to the applicant to be used as a jewellers' shop. The respondent landlords served notice under s.25 stating that they would oppose any application for a new tenancy on ground (f) (demolition and reconstruction). Before the county court judge, the respondents gave evidence as to works which they proposed to carry out to the building as a whole so as to demonstrate an intention to carry out works within ground (f). The applicants sought to show: (1) that many of the works could be carried out by the respondents as necessary repairs in respect of which they had power of entry under the current tenancy; (2) that the remainder of the intended work was such that "the landlord could reasonably carry out the work without interfering to a substantial extent or for a substantial time with the use of the holding for the

[361] [2002] Ch. 332; [2002] 3 All E.R. 609.
[362] [1978] 2 E.G.L.R. 52 CA.
[363] [1986] 2 E.G.L.R. 65 CA.
[364] [1986] 2 E.G.L.R. 65 CA.

purposes of the business carried on by the tenant" within s.31A(1)(a). The judge carefully considered the detail of the work intended by the respondents and the question of how much of it could be done within the terms of the existing tenancy. He also considered how far the carrying out of the works which could not be done within the terms of the existing agreement would interfere with the tenant's business and for how long.

He found as a fact that works of replacement of the floor of the shop would make it impossible for the applicants to carry on their business for a period of six weeks, and that this was a "substantial" period. He dismissed the tenant's application.

On appeal it was held:

(a) The word "or" was to be construed as "and" so that the question of the extent of the interference and its duration should be considered together. It was a question of fact and degree, and the probable duration of the interference should not be disregarded in considering whether it would be "to a substantial extent", nor should its extent be disregarded in deciding whether it would continue "for a substantial time".

(b) The judge had been correct in his approach in identifying the intended work which could not be done under the terms of the current tenancy and in considering whether the physical carrying out of that work would interfere to a substantial extent and for a substantial time with the tenant's business. However, he had misunderstood the evidence on this point and should have concluded that the period during which the applicants would be unable to carry on business would be only two weeks. To hold that such a short period in the context of the present case would deprive a tenant of the protection of s.31A(a) would involve an emasculation of the subsection such as to render it almost nugatory. The applicant's appeal was therefore allowed.

Blackburn v Hussain[365] The tenant carried on the business of a cafe. The landlord owned a shop adjoining the demised premises and another shop, access to which was obtained by a passageway at the rear of the building of which all three shops formed part. The landlord opposed renewal under s.30(1)(f) of the Act. The three shops were separate self-contained units. There were no toilets in the demised premises but the tenant had the use of lavatories laying behind a neighbouring shop. The landlord's proposals involved the demolition of the walls between the shops and converting them into one large open area. The work required the removal and replacement of all existing shop fronts, the removal of the lavatories and the provision of a staircase which was to be situated within the demised premises. The landlord also intended to carry out a complete refurbishment of the premises once converted. 7–206

It was accepted by the tenant that the landlord would, apart from the provisions of s.31A, succeed in establishing the appropriate intention under

[365] [1988] 1 E.G.L.R. 77 CA.

s.30(1)(f). The tenant at trial indicated that he would be prepared to afford the landlord all facilities and access which he required for carrying out the work which he intended to do.

It was common ground that for a minimum period of 12 weeks it would be impossible to run the cafe and that for part of that period the landlord would require the use of the whole of the demised premises although it was possible for cafe equipment to be shifted from one place to another without actually moving it from the demised premises.

The county court judge held that the tenant could rely on s.31A as the landlord did not intend to interfere with the carrying on of the tenant's business for a substantial time or extent. The tenant appealed to the Court of Appeal, where the main issue was whether the judge had been correct in coming to the decision as a matter of fact and degree that the interference was not substantial.

The Court of Appeal held that, on the evidence, the nature of the interference for a period of 12 weeks was interference to a substantial extent and for a substantial time with the use of the cafe for the purpose of the business carried on by the tenant.

Examples of "substantial interference"

7–207 Although the question of "substantial interference" must be decided in each case upon its particular facts and as a matter of fact and degree, it may be helpful to practitioners to summarise here the decisions of the courts on the question in the various decided cases:

(1) In *Cerex Jewels v Peachey*[366] (digested in para.7–205), the qualifying works would have totally excluded the tenant from the holding for a period of two weeks. This was held not to be "substantial interference".

(2) In *Redfern v Reeves*[367] (digested in para.7–203), the qualifying work would have prevented the tenant from carrying on her business for a period of between two and four months (although the evidence was not entirely clear on the point). This was held to be "substantial interference".

(3) In *Blackburn v Hussain*[368] (digested in para.7–206), there would have been more or less total interference with the tenant's cafe business for a period of 12 weeks. This was held to be "substantial interference".

(4) In *Graysim Holdings v P&O Property Holdings*,[369] total exclusion of the tenant from the holding for the period of eight weeks was held to be "substantial interference". (This was the decision of the deputy judge at first instance; it was technically *obiter* and was not the subject of further appeal.)

(5) In *Price v Esso*[370] (digested in para.7–104), the exclusion by the tenant for a period of 16 weeks was held to be "substantial interference".

---

366 [1986] 2 E.G.L.R. 65 CA.
367 [1978] 2 E.G.L.R. 52.
368 [1988] 1 E.G.L.R. 77 CA.
369 [1993] 1 E.G.L.R. 96.
370 [1980] 2 E.G.L.R. 58 CA.

(6) In *Pumperninks of Piccadilly Ltd v Land Securities Plc*[371] (digested in para.7–197), at first instance, a period of 17 to 23 days was held not to be substantial.

Economically separable part

Under s.31A(1)(b), the court shall not hold that the landlord cannot reasonably carry out the intended works without obtaining possession of the holding if: **7–208**

> "... the tenant is willing to accept a tenancy of an economically separable part of the holding and either paragraph (a) of this section is satisfied with respect to that part or possession of the remainder of the holding would be reasonably sufficient to enable the landlord to carry out the intended work."

The following matters need to be considered under this head:

(1) Once again, "the intended works" are the works which the landlord has proved he intends to carry out: see *Decca Navigator Co v Greater London Council*[372] (digested in para.7–196), above.

(2) The tenant must be willing to accept a tenancy of "an economically separable part of the holding". The tenant is not to be deemed to have elected to take only a new tenancy of the "economically separate part" merely because he relies upon s.31A(1)(b) as an alternative to s.31A(1)(a): see *Romulus Trading Co Ltd v Trustees of Henry Smith's Charity (No.2)*.[373] By subs.(2) a part of the holding is to be deemed to be an economically separable part

> "if, and only if, the aggregate of the rents which, after the completion of the intended work, would be reasonably obtainable on separate lettings of that part and the remainder of the premises affected by or resulting from the work would not be substantially less than the rent which would then be reasonably obtainable on a letting of those premises as a whole."

In order to apply this test, it is necessary to assume that the intended works have been carried out and that there are then separate lettings of (a) the part of the holding which is alleged to be economically separable and (b) the remainder of the premises (not the remainder of the "holding") insofar as those premises are affected by or result from the work. Those rents are then aggregated and the test is satisfied if the aggregate of those rents is not substantially less than could be obtained upon a letting of the premises (a) and (b) as a whole. Accordingly, whether or not the separation of the part is "economic" is judged from the point of view of the landlord's rental income, not from the point of view of the tenant's requirements for the carrying on of his business.

(3) Once it has been determined that the part of the holding is "economically separable", the remaining condition in s.31A(1)(b) can be satisfied in one of two ways. Under the first limb the tenant may show that, so far as the economically separable part is concerned, he is willing to grant access and

[371] [2002] Ch. 332; [2002] 3 All E.R. 609.
[372] [1974] 1 W.L.R. 748; [1974] 1 All E.R. 1178 CA.
[373] [1991] 1 E.G.L.R. 95 CA.

facilities under s.31A(1)(a) in respect of that part and that the intended work can be carried out without substantially interfering with his business. This gives the tenant greater flexibility than under s.31A(1)(a) itself, because the excluded part of the holding may be the part where the landlord requires to carry on works which would substantially interfere with the tenant's business. In the alternative, the tenant may show that, without being granted facilities or access over the economically separable part, the landlord is nonetheless able reasonably to carry out his intended works on the excluded part of the holding.

7–209 The effect of the tenant succeeding under s.31A(1)(b) is not to defeat the landlord's ground (f) altogether—see *Romulus Trading Co Ltd v Trustees of Henry Smith's Charity (No.2)*[374]—but to give him a "fallback position". In such a case the order for a new tenancy will not be of the whole holding, but only of the economically separable part: s.32(1A).

The practical operation of the two limbs of section 31A(1)(b)

7–210 Where the only work which the landlord intends to carry out is outside the economically separable part, the tenant can rely upon the second limb. Where the work is mainly concentrated outside the economically separable part, but the landlord either requires to carry out some work on the economically separable part, or requires some facilities over it, such as access, then the tenant must rely, in addition, upon the first limb. Although the word "or" is used, it is thought that the tenant can rely in part upon the second limb and in part upon the first. This can be illustrated by an example.

7–211 **Example** Suppose a tenancy of a shop with a large yard, each having a separate access. The tenant uses the whole of the yard for storing goods. The landlord's proposal under ground (f) is to build an office building taking up four-fifths of the area of the yard and using the yard's access. On these facts, the tenant could probably not rely upon s.31A(1)(a), because his business would be substantially interfered with by the landlord requiring possession of four-fifths of his storage space for the period of the works. However, the tenant might well be able to establish that, once the new office building was erected the rent which could be obtained for it, when aggregated with the rent which could be obtained for the shop with its small remaining part of the yard, would be greater than could be obtained on a letting of the shop and office building together. Such mixed premises might not have much appeal in the open market. Given that the shop and part of the yard are an "economically separable part", the tenant could then establish under s.31A(1)(b) that the landlord would be able to carry out his intended works without obtaining possession of the shop part, because he only needed possession of the four-fifths of the yard plus the access. The tenant might need to rely in addition upon the first limb of s.31A(1)(b), if the works intended

[374] [1991] 1 E.G.L.R. 95 CA.

by the landlord required for some practical reason limited rights of access over the shop part or over the retained part of yard.

The landlord's prospects of success under ground (f)

The practical difficulties which a landlord may encounter under each of the categories of work falling within ground (f) may be broadly described as follows: **7–212**

(1) Where the landlord intends a total demolition, he is unlikely to encounter any difficulty in showing that his works come within ground (f) and that he reasonably requires possession of the holding in order to carry them out (unless he has a reservation of exceptional width as in *Price v Esso*[375] (digested in para.7–104)). In such a case the tenant will not be able to succeed under s.31A(1)(a) or (b): *Mularczyk v Azralnove Investments*[376] (digested in para.7–213).

(2) Where the landlord intends to demolish a substantial part, he may become involved in arguments as to the substantiality of the part which he intends to demolish. It may also be that he has a reservation in sufficiently wide terms to entitle him to carry out partial demolition and the tenant may well have a good argument under s.31A(1)(a) or (b).

(3) Where the landlord intends to reconstruct the whole of the premises, the same considerations apply as in (1) above.

(4) Where the landlord intends to reconstruct a substantial part of the premises, the same considerations apply as in (2) above.

(5) Where the landlord intends to carry out work of construction on the holding (meaning for present purposes work of construction upon the whole or substantially on the whole, of the holding) he will once again be involved in an argument as to substantiality. The landlord is unlikely, once he has established the substantiality of his work of construction, to encounter any greater difficulties than would a landlord under categories (1) or (2) above.

Where the landlord intends to carry out work of construction on part of the holding, he will be involved in an argument about substantiality. Since part of the holding will be unaffected by his works, the tenant may establish a sufficient reservation in the landlord's favour in order to enable him to carry out the works, or may be able to show that the carrying out of the works will not substantially interfere with his business, or that the unaffected part is an "economically separable part" within s.31A.

Mularczyk v Azralnove Investments[377] The tenant carried on the business of clipping poodles at a single-storey building, with two reception rooms and another room, which was in so bad a state of repair that the only economic thing to do was to demolish it, and rebuild. The landlord served a s.25 notice, specifying ground (f) (demolition and reconstruction) and the judge found as a **7–213**

375 [1980] 2 E.G.L.R. 58 CA.
376 [1985] 2 E.G.L.R. 141 CA.
377 [1985] 2 E.G.L.R. 141 CA.

fact that the landlord did intend to demolish and rebuild the buildings and to clear the whole site. The tenant, however, relied on s.31A(1)(a). The tenant was prepared to provide access and other facilities to enable the work to be carried out.[378] The judge dismissed her application for a new tenancy. It was held that on the basis that the whole site was going to be cleared and all the buildings demolished, there would be interference to a substantial extent, or for a substantial time, with the business. Even if the work was phased, it would be impractical to carry on a business involving the care of animals while substantial building works were being carried on nearby.

9. GROUND (G)—OWN OCCUPATION

The statutory wording

7–214 Under para.(g), a landlord is entitled to oppose an application for a new tenancy on the following ground[379]:

> "That on the termination of the current tenancy the landlord intends to occupy the holding for the purposes or partly for the purposes of a business to be carried on by him therein or as his residence."

This is subject to the provisions of subs.(2), dealing with the five-year bar, which are discussed in detail below (see para.7–264 et seq.).

Meaning of "intends"

7–215 The word "intends" is to be given the same meaning as under ground (f) (see paras 7–134 to 7–160).

Second limb: Assumption that landlord is in possession

7–216 The landlord's intention to occupy for his own business may require a number of hurdles to be overcome. If these are outside the landlord's control the court may find that there is no reasonable prospect of the landlord being able to implement its decision to occupy. In determining whether the landlord has satisfied the second (objective) element of the relevant test,[380] the court is to assume that the tenant's tenancy has determined and the landlord is in possession: *Humber Oil Terminals Trustee Ltd v Associated British Ports*,[381] following the approach of the House of Lords in *Westminster City Council v British Waterways Board*[382]

---

[378] Although it is unclear from the terms of the report what were the actual terms for access which were proposed by the tenant, it would seem that the tenant's proposals envisaged some kind of staggered development.

[379] For a consideration of the evidence to be relied upon by the parties in support of, or in opposition to, this ground, see para.11–58 et seq.

[380] See para.7–150.

[381] [2011] EWHC 2043 (Ch); affirmed on appeal [2012] EWCA Civ 596. The case is digested at para.7–220.

[382] [1985] A.C. 676 HL (a case under para.(f) of s.30(1)).

(digested in para.7–186). Thus, where the landlord sought to take over the tenant's business and the tenant alleged it's cooperation was needed to enable the landlord to carry on the intended business the court was to assess whether the landlord would be likely to implement its stated intention on the hypothesis that the tenant's tenancy had ended and the landlord was in possession.[383]

Taking over tenant's business

There is nothing in the Act which prevents the landlord from taking over the tenant's business.[384] Even if one were to describe this pejoratively as "expropriation" the policy of the Act is that the tenant is to be protected in the carrying on of his business unless, inter alia, the landlord establishes an intention to occupy the holding for the purposes of his business.[385] Where the tenant has expressed the view that it will not co-operate with the landlord to enable the landlord to carry on the business on termination of the current tenancy, the court is nonetheless entitled to consider and make findings as to what the tenant would do once the tenant's lease has terminated.[386] Thus, where the landlord wished to take over the tenant's jetty which was used for the supply of oil to third party refineries, the court was entitled to find, on the assumption that the tenant's lease **7–217**

---

[383] Rimer L.J. giving the judgment of the court said:

"25. In my judgment, exactly the same approach [as in *Westminster City Council v British Waterways Board*] fell to be applied in the present case. The judge had to assess the objective element of ABP's stated intention by making the required statutory assumption that it is ABP and not HOTT that is in possession of the premises; and, therefore, necessarily on the assumption that HOTT's tenancies had determined. That is what he did and he made his findings of fact referred to above as to the probabilities of what would then happen. Those findings were, in my judgment, made on the correct statutory assumption and were findings that showed that the objective element of the required intention was met.

26. [It was] submitted that the judge's approach involved a misapplication of what was decided in the *Westminster City Council* case. [It was argued that] the correct statutory hypothesis upon which the landlord's intention must be tested is that the tenant's tenancy has come to an end and that the landlord has resumed possession. Whilst the assessment of the landlord's claimed intention on that hypothesis can legitimately take into account its notional dealings in such circumstances with a third party (in that case, the Secretary of State), it cannot take into account its dealings with the former tenant. For myself, I do not accept that such a limitation on the application of the statutory hypothesis is supported by the *Westminster City Council* case itself or is otherwise justified as a matter of principle ..."

See also para.7–151.

[384] *Humber Oil Terminals Trustee Ltd v Associated British Ports* [2011] EWHC 2043 (Ch) at [143]. As Vos J. said:

"There is no objection to a supermarket chain buying up freehold interests in other supermarkets' shop premises (provided they do so more than five years before the termination of the lease – see s 30(2)), just because they wish to oppose the grant of a new tenancy so they can take over their competitor's site. I am sure that worldly-wise supermarkets are alive to this possibility, but if it were to happen, I cannot see how the target supermarket could cry foul, when the predator took over its building and operation and simply changed the name above the door." at [143].

[385] *Humber Oil Terminals Trustee Ltd v Associated British Ports* [2011] EWHC 352 (Ch); upheld at [2012] EWCA Civ 36.

[386] *Humber Oil Terminals Trustee Ltd v Associated British Ports* [2011] EWHC 352 (Ch); upheld at [2012] EWCA Civ 36 at [116] and [132]–[133].

had terminated,[387] that the tenant would most likely enter into a commercial arrangement with the landlord to enable oil to continue to be supplied to the refineries rather than seek to remove its equipment and seek to find alternative jetty facilities.

7–218 Reliance on para.(g) of s.30(1) of the 1954 Act is not an abuse of a dominant position by the landlord contrary to s.18 of the Competition Act 1998.[388] A proposal of a rent which is excessive cannot without more constitute the imposition of an unfair rent for the purposes of s.18 of the 1998 Act. Any element of compulsion which might arise from the dominant position of the landlord is negatived, in the context of the 1954 Act by the jurisdiction of the court, absent agreement between the parties, to assess the rent on the basis of a statutory formula, which by reason of its direction to assess a market rent, excludes any ransom element.[389] A landlord is not precluded from relying on s.30(1)(g) by reason of s.18 of the 1998 simply because it originally negotiated for new leases at excessive rents and only decided to rely upon s.30(1)(g) having failed to secure agreement to those rents.[390]

Potential sale

7–219 The settled intention of the landlord was held not to be vitiated by evidence that they had accepted a previous offer from a third party to purchase the whole of the property and that they were continuing to consider such offers: *Edwards v Thompson*[391] (digested in para.7–147) (a case under para.(f)). The position may be different if there was actual evidence that an offer would be made and that such an offer was likely to be accepted.[392] The fact that unexpected offers and events may in the future occur, which the landlord would have to consider (as not

---

387 *Westminster CC v British Waterways Board* [1985] 1 A.C. 676 HL (digested in para.7–186) and see para.7–151.

388 See *Humber Oil Terminal Trustee Ltd v Associated British Ports* [2011] EWHC 352 (Ch) (The Chancellor of the High Court); upheld at [2012] EWCA Civ 36. Section 18 of the Competition Act 1998 provides, in so far as is material:

"(1) Subject to section 19, any conduct on the part of one or more undertakings which amounts to the abuse of a dominant position in a market is prohibited if it may affect trade within the United Kingdom.

(2) Conduct may, in particular, constitute such an abuse if it consists in—

(a) directly or indirectly imposing unfair purchase or selling prices or other unfair trading conditions;

(b) limiting production, markets or technical development to the prejudice of consumers;

(c) applying dissimilar conditions to equivalent transactions with other trading parties, thereby placing them at a competitive disadvantage;

(d) making the conclusion of contracts subject to acceptance by the other parties of supplementary obligations which, by their nature or according to commercial usage, have no connection with the subject of the contracts.

(3) In this section—'dominant position' means a dominant position within the United Kingdom; and'the United Kingdom' means the United Kingdom or any part of it."

389 *Humber Oil Terminals Trustee Ltd v Associated British Ports* [2011] EWHC 352 (Ch) at [34]; [2012] EWCA Civ 36 at [38] per Etherton L.J.

390 *Humber Oil Terminal Trustee Ltd v Associated British Ports* [2012] EWCA Civ 36 at [37] per Etherton L.J.

391 [1990] 2 E.G.L.R. 72 CA.

392 *Humber Oil Terminals Trustee Ltd v Associated British Ports* [2011] EWHC 2043 (Ch) at [130].

to do so would be a breach of fiduciary duty by the director's of the landlord company) does not render the landlord's decision uncertain or conditional.[393]

Humber Oil Terminals Trustee Ltd v Associated British Ports[394] T was lessee of the Immingham Oil Terminal ("the IOT") under four leases covering a jetty, onshore oil depot, substantial pipe and storage works and other land. The tenant was a joint venture company between Total and Conoco. The IOT was operated by another joint venture company of Total and Conco, APT. The jetty protruded about 1km into the Humber Estuary. The jetty was used to supply oil and related products to two oil refineries owned by Total and Conoco which were some 5km away from the IOT. The IOT was owned by ABP who opposed T's renewal of its leases on the basis that it intended to occupy and manage the IOT and the jetty itself with a view both to the maintenance of supply to the refineries and to open the jetty to third party users. T pointed to the fact that, when its lease terminated, it was entitled to remove its pipelines, equipment and infrastructure from the jetty. That would cost some £10 million. The cost of replacing what could be removed would be £60 million and take two years. The tenant had refused to engage with the landlord in any negotiations. The tenant argued that: **7–220**

(i) ABP did not have a firm and settled intention as it was more interested in achieving a higher rental on renewal than seeking to occupy for the purposes of its own business.
(ii) ABP's case relied on showing a seamless transition without interrupting supplies to the refineries. The landlord could not pray in aid the fact that if it obtained possession the tenant would co-operate with the landlord. Allowing the landlord to rely on what the tenant would or might do was circular as it allowed the landlord to rely on what would happen if the landlord was successful to decide whether the landlord would be successful.
(iii) There were too many hurdles for ABP to overcome. There was no detailed plan and no terms were agreed with APT or any other operator to operate the IOT.
(iv) If a deal was not struck with the tenant, in all probability APT not ABP would be in occupation.
(v) That ABP was not occupying the IOT for its own business but was expropriating the business of the tenant.
(vi) It could not be said that ABP intended to occupy the IOT at the termination of the current tenancy but only at a much later stage.

The court held:

(i) that although early board minutes and memoranda suggested ABP's primary motivation was to seek to obtain the most money for the IOT the true position on the evidence was that ABP did intend to run the IOT itself. It was not necessary for the court to determine whether that was a prudent

[393] *Humber Oil Terminals Trustee Ltd v Associated British Ports* [2011] EWHC 2043 (Ch) at [130].
[394] [2011] EWHC 2043 (Ch); affirmed on appeal [2012] EWCA Civ 596.

business decision. The fact that offers for a new lease, if made, would have to be considered did not render the landlord's intention uncertain or conditional.

(ii) The court was required in considering s.30(1)(g) to look at the position at the termination of the current tenancy: *Westminster CC v British Waterways Board*[395] (digested in para.7–186). The court was not precluded from making findings as to what the tenant was likely to do at the termination of the tenancy. The most likely option at the termination of the lease was that the tenant would seek to negotiate a commercial arrangement with ABP rather than to move its equipment from the jetty and interfere with the refinery business; the economics made it most likely that a deal would be struck to enable the IOT to be used by the tenant (other than by way of a lease) to continue to service the refineries.

(iii) Given that the court had found that the tenant would most likely negotiate a commercial arrangement with ABP, ABP would, in practice, be able to achieve their stated intention. The evidence given by the tenant was that if it decided to enter into a commercial arrangement with ABP it would make it work. Even if the tenant did walk away from negotiations ABP still had a reasonable prospect of operating the jetty with new third party customers. ABP would offer port service to third parties even though at the beginning this was likely to be small scale.

(iv) The court was satisfied that ABP would occupy whether or not it used the service of APT. ABP would, absent the tenant, have necessarily to enter into a management or commercial agreement of some kind with APT for APT to operate the IOT on its behalf.

(v) There was nothing in the suggestion that ABP was expropriating the business of the tenant rather than carrying on its own business. The landlord was entitled under the Act to carry on the same business as that carried on by the tenant.

(vi) Although it may take time for the commercial arrangement with the tenant and the landlord to be reached, that did not mean that ABP's intention could not be implemented. It was likely that some interim arrangement would be made with the finer details worked out later so as to ensure continuity of supplies to the refineries.

Undertaking to the court

7–221 It is common for a landlord to give an undertaking to the court under ground (f), but there may be some doubt as to the propriety of the court accepting an equivalent undertaking under ground (g). In *Espresso v Guardian*[396] (digested in para.7–225), such an undertaking was accepted under both grounds (f) and (g). In *London Hilton Jewellers v Hilton International Hotels*,[397] the Court of Appeal held that the giving of an undertaking to implement ground (g) "compelled fixity

395 [1985] 1 A.C. 676 HL.
396 [1959] 1 W.L.R. 250 CA.
397 [1990] 1 E.G.L.R. 112 CA.

of intention" and "was decisive". In *Lennox v Bell*[398] (digested in para.7–226), an undertaking was offered under ground (g) but the court declined to regard the offering of that undertaking as being conclusive either of the bona fides of the landlord's intention or of its firmness. In *Lightcliffe v Walton*, the Court of Appeal held that the giving of an undertaking under ground (g) did not create a legal presumption that the landlord's stated intention was genuine and, if the judge had ground for doubting the landlord's veracity, he was entitled to disregard the undertaking altogether.

A rather different point was taken in *Chez Gerard v Greene*. There it was argued that the court should not, as a matter of principle, accept an undertaking under ground (g), because an undertaking to carry on a business is not enforceable by the court. The Court of Appeal did not expressly accept or reject this argument, which is based upon a line of authority establishing that the court will not grant specific performance of an obligation to carry on a business, nor grant a mandatory injunction which would have the same effect. In *Cooperative Insurance Society Ltd v Argyll Stores (Holdings) Ltd*[399] the Court of Appeal ordered the tenants of a Safeway supermarket in the Hillsborough Shopping Centre to re-open a store which they had covenanted to keep open. The House of Lords[400] reversed the Court of Appeal and held that the previous practice of not ordering specific performance of a covenant to run a business was soundly based in that: **7–222**

(1) such orders would require constant supervision in the sense of an indefinite series of rulings to ensure execution of the order;
(2) the sanctions for contempt are disproportionate and inappropriate;
(3) orders to carry on an activity are inherently different from orders to achieve a result (e.g. build or repair a building);
(4) such an order would be too imprecise;
(5) an order for specific performance would enable the claimant to hold the defendant to ransom if performance were more expensive than the claimant's loss;
(6) it was not in the public interest to require a person to carry on business at a loss if the other party can be compensated, because it wastes resources and prolongs litigation.

Where the landlord has provided an undertaking to the court, and there is a subsequent change of mind, the landlord will have to apply to the court to be released from the undertaking. Where the landlord's proposals have changed so that he no longer intends to comply with the undertaking, e.g. to carry a scheme of development, an acceptance by the tenant of a new lease from the landlord has the effect of relieving the landlord from compliance with the undertaking: *Bentley & Skinner (Bond Street Jewellers) Ltd v Searchmap Ltd*[401] (digested in para.7–229).

398 (1957) 169 E.G. 753 CA.
399 [1996] 3 W.L.R. 27; [1996] 3 All E.R. 934; [1996] 1 E.G.L.R. 71 CA.
400 [1998] A.C. 1; [1997] 2 W.L.R. 898; [1997] 3 All E.R. 297 HL.
401 [2003] EWHC 1621 (Ch); [2003] P.L.S.C.S. 169 Lightman J.

7–223 It is often suggested that the decision in *Cooperative Insurance Society v Argyll Stores*[402] limits the value of an undertaking given by a landlord to the court. However, it is considered that any potential difficulty caused by this case may be substantially overcome by the landlord agreeing to undertake in a form which is negative both in form and substance, namely, to undertake "not to use the premises for [an agreed period] for any purposes other than a business carried on by the landlord"; or "not to use the premises for any purpose other than [the specified business]." Although by this form of wording the landlord is not obliged to carry on the intended business he may be prevented from using the property for anything other than a business or the specified business, respectively.[403] The negative form of undertaking was accepted by the county court judge in *Sundowner Ltd v Lawrence*[404] as an answer to the potential problems, both in terms of weight to be attached to and of the enforceability of the landlord proffering a positive undertaking to carry on a business, raised by the decision in *Cooperative Insurance Society v Argyll Stores*.[405]

7–224 However, in *Patel v Keles*[406] an undertaking in the negative form suggested in para.7–223 was said to throw doubt upon the landlord's intention. In that case the landlord gave an undertaking that he would not to use the premises for two years for any purpose other than as a newsagents' business. The judge was not impressed by that undertaking and held that it called into question the landlord's intention, which ought to have been a substantial and genuine intention of running the business for the foreseeable future. The judge noted that the undertaking, being one in a negative form, could enable the premises to remain empty. The judge concluded that he was far from satisfied that there was a real intention such as the 1954 Act required. The judge at first instance said:

> "I have to say that I am very disturbed about what I can only say is the temporary nature of the undertaking for a two year period. It does indicate to me that the intention is a temporary one, to run for two years and no more. It reflects in turn on the real nature of the intention for effectively there is an end date. It is not the foreseeable future, it has an end date to it; an end date which is clearly in contemplation. It does not stem from a positive need for the premises, or a positive requirement, which one might ordinarily expect there to be in the case, for example, of a landlord who was out of work but who owned premises which he could use for his own livelihood, perhaps his only premises. It is the limited nature of that undertaking which I find really very unsatisfactory."[407]

The appeal was dismissed.

7–225 ***Espresso Coffee Machine Co Ltd v Guardian Assurance Co***[408] The landlords served a counter-notice to the tenants' request for a new tenancy, on the ground that they intended to occupy the premises for the purposes of their own business under s.30(1)(g). The tenants accepted the landlords' evidence that the landlords

[402] [1996] 3 W.L.R. 27; [1996] 3 All E.R. 934; [1996] 1 E.G.L.R. 71 CA.

[403] If the tenant has adjoining property the covenant may be enforced against successors in title to the landlord as a restrictive covenant.

[404] Unreported Norwich CC 2000.

[405] [1998] A.C. 1; [1997] 2 W.L.R. 898; [1997] 3 All E.R. 297 HL.

[406] [2009] EWCA Civ 1187; [2010] Ch. 332.

[407] See the judgment of Arden L.J at [11].

[408] [1959] 1 W.L.R. 250; [1959] 1 All E.R. 458 CA.

had bought the freehold of the premises in 1951 with a view to the possible occupation of it in 1960 when the lease of the premises they presently occupied expired, but contended that in January 1958 the landlords had become interested in other possibly more suitable premises, which were undergoing extensive reconstruction. In the High Court, however, the landlords gave evidence that a resolution to occupy the subject premises for business if possession were obtained had been passed by their board in February 1958 and gave an undertaking by their counsel in the terms of the board resolution, whereupon Harman J. held that the landlords had established a sufficiently fixed present intention to occupy within s.30(1)(g) and refused to grant a new tenancy. It was held that the landlords had satisfied the requirements of s.30(1)(g); the board resolution was an adequate indication of a fixed, settled and real intention and counsel's undertaking on behalf of such a responsible body acted to "compel fixity of intention".

Lennox v Bell[409] The landlord carried on the business of a greengrocer for several years. Due to the illness of her husband she let the premises to the tenant who carried on the same business. After the landlord's husband died, she has various jobs, including work which involved heavy lifting, until on her doctor's advice she gave it up. The tenant's lease was coming to an end and there was a quarrel between the parties over who was to pay the rates on the tenanted property that led to a good deal of unpleasantness. Seeing that the lease was about to come to an end, the landlord put the business into the hands of business agents to sell it for her when the lease fell in. The landlord served on the tenant a notice under s.25, opposing the grant of a new tenancy under ground (g) of s.30(1) (own occupation). **7–226**

At the hearing of the tenant's application for a new tenancy, the landlord gave an undertaking to the court that she would commence business "as soon as practicable" if she obtained possession of the shop. The county court judge held that having regard to the landlord's health it was unlikely that she could carry on the greengrocery business, albeit she would receive assistance from close family; it was a "dream", not a real intention and what was at the back of the whole matter was the quarrel with the tenant and the desire to get rid of the tenant in order to sell the property with vacant possession. Although the undertaking was not made in bad faith, it was in those circumstances of little worth. He granted a new tenancy. On appeal by the landlord: the question of the genuineness of the landlord's intention was said to be one of fact and since the judge had taken into account all the relevant considerations, the Court of Appeal could not interfere with his decision.

Lightcliffe and District Cricket and Lawn Tennis Club v Walton[410] The landlord owned some 20 acres of land and let to the tenant some three and-a-half acres forming an "island" in the middle of the whole of the land. The tenant used the land occupied by it for the purpose of a cricket and tennis club. The remainder of the land occupied by the landlord was used by him for the purposes of grazing **7–227**

[409] (1957) 169 E.G. 753 CA.
[410] [1978] 1 E.G.L.R. 35 CA.

cattle. When the tenant's lease expired, the landlord opposed the grant of a new tenancy under ground (g) of s.30(1) (own occupation). At the hearing in the county court on the tenant's application for a new tenancy, the evidence was that the landlord, according to his own estimate, was using the land already available to him to only 50 per cent of its capacity. There was evidence that the tenant's land was land of poor quality and that, as it had been occupied by the tenant for a long time, it would require considerable treatment before it could become suitable for grazing. That would have involved a substantial expenditure by the landlord. The landlord offered an undertaking that if the tenant's application for a new tenancy was refused the land would be used for and only for the purposes of the landlord's business as a farmer. The judge held that the intention of the landlord was not genuine or bona fide and ignored the undertaking in reaching his decision on the bona fides of the landlord's intention. On appeal by the landlords it was held:

(1) The giving of an undertaking, whoever gives it and in whatever circumstances, does not create a legal presumption in favour of a landlord in establishing the genuineness of his intention under ground (g) of s.30(1). The fact that an undertaking is given is not conclusive that the intention which is behind it is a genuine one.
(2) An undertaking which is given by a substantial company of good reputation is likely to be more dependable than an undertaking given by an individual who may for personal reasons find it necessary or expedient to change his mind.

The appeal was therefore dismissed.

7–228 ***Chez Gerard v Greene***[411] The premises, in Charlotte Street, London W1, had for some years been successfully operated by the tenant as a restaurant. At the end of the term, the landlord, which was a Liberian shipping company, with no record of operating restaurants, opposed the tenant's application for a new tenancy on the ground that it intended to occupy the premises for the purposes of a restaurant business. The evidence was that a board resolution to this effect had been passed, a provisional contract with an experienced restaurateur to act as manager had been entered into, preliminary costings had been worked out, finance was available and no planning permission was required. In addition the landlords, through their representative who gave evidence, gave an undertaking to the court to enter into occupation of the premises and run the business. The judge held that the intention had been proved and concluded: "In order to ensure justice I will find in favour of the landlord only if the appropriate undertaking is given . . . It is essential for the protection of the tenant that this should be only on the undertaking that has been proffered."

The tenant appealed. The Court of Appeal held that the only interpretation of the judgment which "might carry the judgment down" was that the judge had relied upon the undertaking as being itself sufficient to establish the landlord's intentions. But, on a true interpretation, the judge was only saying that the

[411] [1983] 2 E.G.L.R. 79 CA.

undertaking was one of the factors which he had taken into account for its evidential value, and that approach could not be criticised.

Bentley & Skinner (Bond Street Jewellers) Ltd v Searchmap Ltd[412] In proceedings by T for the grant of a new tenancy, L opposed on the ground that L intended to redevelop the demised premises, involving connecting the demised premises with L's own adjoining retail premises and demolishing the first floor to create a salon of two storeys in height. T argued unsuccessfully that L had not a firm and settled intention to carry out the work. The landlord showed to the satisfaction of the county court judge that he had the necessary intention to develop and that he had a realistic and not fanciful chance of obtaining the necessary planning consent. In support of the stated intention the landlord offered an undertaking to the court that the works described in the evidence before the court would be carried out as soon as practicable in event of obtaining possession. The judge accepted that undertaking as decisive of the fixity of intention. The judge stated that if L could not honour his undertaking "I would be unlikely to release him unless he consented to a new lease on acceptable terms." **7–229**

Subsequent to the hearing L told T that it had withdrawn its plans for redevelopment and had acquired property elsewhere, and so T took a new lease of the demised premises outside the 1954 Act. Subsequently T became aware of the fact that L had in fact acquired the alternative property on the first day of the hearing of his opposition to renewal. T sought to appeal the original order and have the original proceedings restored on the basis that credible new evidence relevant to L's intention had become available which could not with reasonable diligence have been obtained for use at the trial.

In any event T argued that L did not have a fixed and settled intention at the date of the hearing as (1) it offered a new lease to T; (2) L had not pursued negotiations with the planning authority and (3) at about the time of the offer L had stopped all further preparatory work for the development.

On appeal to Lightman J. the appeal was dismissed as:

(a) the "alternative" property acquired by L was office not retail premises and thus was never an alternative to the retail development proposed by L affecting the demised premises; the acquisition of the "alternative" property was therefore wholly irrelevant;
(b) the new lease taken by T operated as a surrender by operation of law of T's original lease and all and any rights to a new lease under the Act;
(c) that the matters raised by T, even if they were allowed to be raised, were not cogent evidence of the absence of fixity of intention. L had abandoned the scheme as it was no longer financially attractive. The undertaking was an obstacle to the landlord's change of heart. However, when T was offered a new lease it had a choice, either to accept or to require L to seek a release from the undertaking. As T had accepted the offer L was "off the hook" in respect of the undertaking.

[412] [2003] EWHC 1621 (Ch); [2003] P.L.S.C.S. 169 Lightman J.

Meaning of "occupy"

7–230 Under ground (g), the landlord has to show that he intends to "occupy" the holding. Occupy has the same meaning as in s.23.[413]

Occupation of the holding

Occupation of new buildings

7–231 The intention must be to occupy "the holding". This is defined by s.23(3) as meaning "the property comprised in the tenancy, there being excluded any part thereof which is occupied neither by the tenant nor by a person employed by the tenant and so employed for the purposes of a business ...".[414] In *Nursey v Currie*[415] (digested in para.7–234) the court held that the landlord had failed to establish ground (g) where what he intended to do was to demolish the building comprised in the existing holding, build new premises and then occupy those new premises. The Court of Appeal took the view that what the landlord was intending to occupy was not "the holding", but new premises substituted for "the holding". Wynn-Parry J. in his judgment said:

> "It seems to me that the language circumscribes the use of the phrase 'the holding' in that paragraph and makes it necessary to concentrate the whole of one's attention on the particular piece of land, whether it has buildings on it or not, which is the subject-matter of the tenancy in question. So viewed, it appears to me that the contention for the landlords in the present case is too wide, and that when one is looking at the material time at 'the holding' under paragraph (g), it is not permissible to take into account the wider scheme which the landlords had in mind, and merely to treat the land comprised in the holding as land which, in one way or another, will be used for the purpose of the wider undertaking."

There are two possible interpretations to this. The first (narrower) ratio: (1) the landlord can rely upon s.30(1)(g) only where he intends to occupy the subject matter of the tenancy; or the second (wider) ratio: (2) the landlord cannot rely upon s.30(1)(g) if he intends to occupy the holding in an unaltered state, together with adjoining land as part of a larger complex and not as a separate holding on its own. The Court of Appeal in *Cam Gears Ltd v Cunningham*[416] (digested in para.7–235) restricted the ratio of *Nursey v Currie*[417] to the narrower ratio. In *Cam Gears Ltd v Cunningham*, premises consisted of a vacant site with a concrete surface, used as a car park. The landlord proved that he intended to erect a commercial building on part of the car park and to occupy that building, together with the rest of the land comprised in the holding, for the purposes of his business. The Court of Appeal held that *Nursey v Currie*[418] was distinguishable, apparently upon the ground that the landlord was going to occupy all of the premises comprised in the holding, that is to say the land, and it was irrelevant

[413] See para.1–42 et seq.
[414] See para.8–06 et seq.
[415] [1959] 1 W.L.R. 273; [1959] 1 All E.R. 497 CA.
[416] [1981] 1 W.L.R. 1011; [1981] 2 All E.R. 560 CA.
[417] [1959] 1 W.L.R. 273; [1959] 1 All E.R. 497 CA.
[418] [1959] 1 W.L.R. 273; [1959] 1 All E.R. 497 CA.

that the landlord was, in addition, going to occupy premises which had not yet been erected upon the holding. *Nursey v Currie* was, similarly, given a narrow interpretation in *Leathwoods v Total Oil*[419] (digested in para.7–106) where it was said to apply only where "the holding" consists entirely of buildings. In *Method Development v Jones*[420] (digested in para.7–238), Salmon L.J. expressed reservations whether *Nursey v Currie* was correctly decided. In *JW Thornton Ltd v Blacks*[421] (digested in para.7–236) the Court of Appeal had the task of attempting to reconcile these decisions and dicta. It was said in that case to be unreasonable to apply the ratio of *Nursey v Currie*to a case where the only work of alteration which the landlord intended was the removal of two non-load-bearing partition walls.

The current position appears to be that a landlord of bare land who intends to build thereon and occupy the new building will succeed under ground (g), whereas a landlord of land which is built upon who intends to demolish and reconstruct and occupy the new building will fail. There would appear to be little merit in this distinction and it may be that *Nursey v Currie*[422] was decided per incuriam, since the Privy Council decision in *McKenna v Porter Motors*[423] was not cited to the Court of Appeal. In that case, the Privy Council approved the statement made in the Court of Appeal of New Zealand that: **7–232**

> "a landlord may, in our opinion, enter into occupation of premises intending as part of his enjoyment thereof to demolish the buildings and substitute others therefore which he in turn will occupy; he is occupying the premises if he occupies the land and such buildings as from time to time are situate thereon".

This point was not apparently argued in *Thornton v Blacks* (digested in para.7–236) and may have to be considered if the Court of Appeal is confronted with a case which reproduces the facts of *Nursey v Currie*.[424]

Date of determination of holding

An important matter to consider in this context is the date at which one must determine the "holding". If the demised premises at the date of grant consisted of bare land but by the date of the court hearing included buildings constructed by the tenant, does the landlord, in order to ensure that he does not fall foul of *Nursey v Currie*, need to establish an intention only to occupy the land (in which case the landlord can succeed albeit he proposes to build upon it[425]) or does he have to establish an intention to occupy the buildings (in which case he is unable to show an appropriate intention by demolishing and re-building)? In determining the extent of the property to be comprised in any new tenancy, s.32(1) makes it clear that in the absence of agreement between the landlord and the tenant that **7–233**

419 [1985] 2 E.G.L.R. 237 CA.
420 [1971] 1 W.L.R. 168; [1971] 1 All E.R. 1027 CA.
421 [1986] 2 E.G.L.R. 61 CA.
422 [1959] 1 W.L.R. 273; [1959] 1 All E.R. 497 CA.
423 [1956] A.C. 688; [1956] 3 W.L.R. 658; [1956] 3 All E.R. 262 PC.
424 [1959] 1 W.L.R. 273; [1959] 1 All E.R. 497 CA.
425 *Cam Gears Ltd v Cunningham* [1981] 1 W.L.R. 1011; [1981] 2 All E.R. 560 CA.

any new tenancy is to consist of the property which constitutes the holding as at the date of the order of the court. However, it is possible to read *Nursey v Currie*as supporting the view that for the purposes of ground (g) what constitutes the "property comprised in the tenancy" within s.32(1) is that which was demised at the date of grant.[426]

However, it is to be noted that in *Nursey v Currie* there the "holding" equated to the demised premises at the date of grant. It is considered that the better view is that for the purposes of para.(g) "the holding" is to be determined at the date of the hearing of the ground of opposition under para.(g).

7–234 ***Nursey v P Currie (Dartford) Ltd***[427] The tenant's premises consisted of several small buildings standing in a yard. The landlord relied upon ground (g) of s.30 (own occupation). The landlord intended to demolish the buildings on the premises and develop the property as a petrol filling station to be occupied by him. The county court judge dismissed the tenant's application. It was held on appeal, allowing the appeal, that the "holding" intended to be occupied for the purposes of s.30(1)(g) must be the subject matter of the tenancy, including existing buildings, in the state it exists at the hearing. The landlord by intending to demolish the existing buildings could not, therefore, be said to be intending to occupy the holding.

7–235 ***Cam Gears Ltd v Cunningham***[428] The tenant's premises consisted of a vacant site constituting a car park which he used in connection with a business carried on nearby. The landlord opposed the grant of a new tenancy relying upon ground (g) of s.30(1) (own occupation). The landlord, if he obtained possession of the premises, intended to erect buildings on it, which would cover about one-third of the total area of the site, and to occupy the buildings and land for the purposes of his business. It was held that, even assuming that *Nursey v Currie*[429] was rightly decided, "the holding" consisted of the vacant site, being the subject matter of the tenancy, and this the landlord intended to occupy, albeit he intended also to erect new buildings thereon.

---

426 Willmer L.J. in *Nursey v Currie* said:

"It appears to me, therefore, that in applying section 30(1)(g), one must look at the particular holding comprised in the particular tenancy which is before the court in the particular case. Here the building is described in the tenancy agreement as:

'the buildings forming part of premises known as No. 248, Broadway, Bexley Heath in the County of Kent, and comprising the drivers' room, can store, pump and the spirit store, together with the right of ingress and egress thereto . . .'

In relation to this case, therefore, para (g) must be construed as though, instead of the word 'holding', those words which I have read from the tenancy agreement were set out in the paragraph. The question to be determined then is whether the landlords proved that on the termination of the current tenancy they intended to occupy:

'the buildings forming part of the premises known as No. 248, Broadway, Bexley Heath in the County of Kent and comprising the drivers' room, can store, pump and the spirit store.'"

427 [1959] 1 W.L.R. 273; [1959] 1 All E.R. 497 CA.

428 [1981] 1 W.L.R. 1011; [1981] 2 All E.R. 560 CA.

429 [1959] 1 W.L.R. 273; [1959] 1 All E.R. 497 CA.

JW Thornton Ltd v Blacks Leisure Group Plc[430] The respondents occupied most of the ground floor of a building known as Bradburn House in Northumberland Street, Newcastle-upon-Tyne, for the purposes of their leisurewear business. A small portion of the ground floor was let by the respondents to the applicants, who sold confectionery. The respondents served a s.25 notice on the applicants, stating that they would oppose any application for a new tenancy on ground (g) (own occupation). The county court tried, as a preliminary issue, the question of whether this ground was made out. As first presented to the court, the respondents' case was that their intention was to carry out physical works of alteration so that about half of the applicant's holding would be used for a new staircase, and the other half as retail space. At a late stage in the hearing the respondents modified their proposals so that they involved the removal of two non-load-bearing partitions separating the applicant's shop from the rest of the ground floor. The intention was then that the whole of this space should be occupied for retailing purposes by the respondents. Evidence was presented to the court showing that the finances were available for the necessary work; that planning permission was likely to be obtained; and that the respondents' board had approved the revised proposals. An undertaking was given to the court that the board would be recommended to carry out the revised proposals without any further alterations. **7–236**

The judge accepted that the respondents had established an intention within ground (g) and dismissed the application.

On appeal it was held that the decision in *Nursey v Currie*[431] (digested in para.7–234), upon which the applicant relied, should be regarded only as establishing that, if a landlord intends to demolish buildings which form part of the holding before going into occupation, he does not intend to occupy "the holding" (which is defined in s.23 as "the property comprised in the tenancy"). It was quite unrealistic to suggest that the respondents did not intend to occupy the holding for the purposes of their business merely because the partition walls would no longer be present when they resumed possession of the property and had carried out the intended works.

Occupation of part

Although it would appear from the wording of ground (g) that an intention to occupy part only of "the holding" would be insufficient, the Court of Appeal held in *Method Development v Jones*[432] (digested in para.7–238) that it was sufficient for the purposes of ground (g) for the landlord to show that within a reasonable time after the termination of the current tenancy he intended to enter into occupation of all or substantially all of the holding and use a part of it for the purposes of his business. **7–237**

[430] [1986] 2 E.G.L.R. 61 CA.
[431] [1959] 1 W.L.R. 273; [1959] 1 All E.R. 497 CA.
[432] [1971] 1 W.L.R. 168; [1971] 1 All E.R. 1027 CA.

7–238 ***Method Development v Jones***[433] The landlord was leasehold owner of an office floor, part of which it occupied and part of which was sub-let to the tenant. The landlord served a notice pursuant to s.25 specifying ground (g) of s.30(1). At the hearing of the tenant's application for a new tenancy, the landlord gave evidence of its intention with regard to its future occupation of the tenant's holding which was over 1,800 square feet of office space, three-quarters of which was one large room and a quarter of which was another room. The landlord intended to provide itself immediately with a store and despatch room, a room for an administrative assistant and a typist, and a waiting-room, which would initially occupy 700 square feet. Within 12 months the landlord's need for space would expand to the extent that only 400 square feet of the holding would remain unoccupied by them. It had not really made up its mind about what would happen to the 400 square feet. The Court of Appeal held that this was sufficient for the purposes of ground (g).

Date of intended entry into occupation

7–239 The intention under ground (g) is to be fulfilled "on the termination of the current tenancy". In *Method Developments Ltd v Jones*[434] (digested in para.7–238), Salmon L.J. glossed this by talking of "a situation such as the present where the landlords intend at the termination of the lease—which must mean within a reasonable time from the date of its termination". This remark was applied by the Court of Appeal in *London Hilton Jewellers v Hilton International Hotels*,[435] where Lloyd L.J. said:

> "That gives a sensible and business-like construction of section 30(1)(f) and (g). It is cited, as authoritative, in Woodfall on Landlord and Tenant... What is a reasonable time after termination of the tenancy is, of course, a question of fact in each case; I do not accept... that the 'month or so' referred to by the [judge in the instant case] was unreasonably long."

Intended length of occupation

7–240 No period of time is specified by the Act which the landlord must show as his intended length of occupation in order to succeed under ground (g). As Lord Denning M.R. said in *Willis v Association of Universities*[436]:

> "Section 30(1) (g) of the Landlord and Tenant Act, 1954, does not say for how long the landlord must intend to occupy himself, and the courts must fill the gap. It seems to me that in some cases, even a short time may suffice. Take the case where the landlord intends to occupy the premises and to carry on business himself there for six months, and then transfer the business to his son as a family arrangement. I should have thought that the father would have sufficient intention to satisfy section .30(1) (g). But suppose the intention was after six months to transfer to a purchaser for cash, I should not expect that intention to suffice."

---

433 [1971] 1 W.L.R. 168; [1971] 1 All E.R. 1027 CA.

434 [1971] 1 W.L.R. 168 CA.

435 [1990] 1 E.G.L.R. 112 CA.

436 [1965] 1 Q.B. 140; [1964] 2 W.L.R. 946; [1964] 2 All E.R. 39 CA; *Patel v Keles* [2010] EWCA Civ 1187; [2010] Ch. 115 at [36] per Arden L.J.

Although section 30(1)(g) does not require that the landlord should intend to occupy the premises for any particular length of time, his intended occupation must not be fleeting or illusory. It has been said that this is a minimum requirement which might be an appropriate test to apply where the business is to be continued through successors in title.[437] In other circumstances, there must be some substance in the intended occupation for the purpose of carrying on the landlord's business and the occupation must be more than short-term. What is short-term must depend on the facts of the particular case. The landlord is not required to show positively that he has no intention of selling for a five year period by way of analogy to s.30(2): *Patel v Keles*.[438] If the landlord has a sufficient intention (as that is understood within the 1954 Act) to sell the premises within five years, he will be treated as not having the requisite intention to occupy.[439] **7–241**

Occupation for business purposes

In most cases, the landlord relying upon ground (g) will seek to establish an intention to occupy for the purposes of a business. The meaning of "business" and the question whether the occupation is "for the purposes of a business" have been considered above.[440] It is sufficient if the landlord intends to occupy the holding "partly" for the purposes of a business to be carried on by him therein. Provided there is some business occupation, occupation for mixed purposes is sufficient. For the purposes of ground (g) the business need not be independent: e.g. the storage or holding of equipment manufactured elsewhere, or the provision of parking or canteen facilities for employees working nearby, would be occupation for the purposes of a business carried on the holding (and elsewhere). In *Hunt v Decca Navigator Co*[441] (digested in para.7–243) it was held **7–242**

[437] *Patel v Keles* [2010] EWCA Civ 1187; [2010] Ch. 115 at [36]. The court here was contemplating a scenario of a transfer not by way of sale but to a successor in title to the business.
[438] [2010] EWCA Civ 1187; [2010] Ch. 115.
[439] [2010] EWCA Civ 1187; [2010] Ch. 115 at [36] per Arden L.J. This proposition Arden L.J. derived from dicta of Denning M.R. in *Willis v Association of Universities of the British Commonwealth* [1965] 1 Q.B. 140; [1964] 2 All E.R. 39; [1964] 2 W.L.R. 946 where he said:

"Section 30(1)(g) of the Act of 1954 does not say for how long the landlord must intend to occupy himself, and the courts must fill the gap. It seems to me that in some cases even a short time may suffice. Take the case where the landlord intends to occupy the premises and to carry on business himself there for six months, and then transfer the business to his son as a family arrangement. I should have thought that the father would have sufficient intention to satisfy section 30(1)(g). But suppose the intention was after six months to transfer to a purchaser for cash, I should not expect that intention to suffice. Just as a purchaser within the previous five years cannot defeat the tenant (see section 30(2)), so also a purchaser shortly afterwards should not be able to defeat him. The matters that influence me are these. It is open to the landlord to complete the transfer before the day of hearing, in which case it is the successor's intention which counts – see section 30(1)(g) – save only that if that successor falls foul of section 30(2) his intention does not count. Hence I would say that if the landlord intends to occupy the premises and carry on business himself there for a time, and then to transfer to a successor, his intention is sufficient to satisfy section 30(1)(g), unless the intended transfer is one which, if it had been made before the hearing, would have fallen within section 30(2) so as to render section 30(1)(g) unavailable." at 150.
[440] See paras 1–111 et seq., and 1–107 et seq., respectively.
[441] (1972) 222 E.G. 625.

that an intention to occupy the holding as a car park for the use of visitors and staff at the landlords' adjoining premises was sufficient. It is sufficient that the landlord intends to occupy part of the holding for business purposes. However, the landlord, in those circumstances, must still go on to show that he intends to occupy the remainder of "the holding".

7–243 ***Hunt v Decca Navigator Co***[442] The landlords opposed the grant of a new tenancy on ground (g) (own occupation). The intention proved was to use the holding as a car park, to be used by the landlords' employees and visitors to their business premises which were adjacent. The tenants argued that the business was not intended to be carried on "therein" (i.e. in or on the holding), because the landlords' business was not to be carried on on the holding, but in the adjacent premises. It was held that the landlord had made out a sufficient intention.

7–244 In *Jones v Jenkins*[443] (digested in para.7–245) the question arose whether the landlord's intention to re-let the premises as two residential flats came within the ground (g). The Court of Appeal applied the same test of "occupation" as under s.23(1) (see para.1–42 et seq.) and held that the ground of opposition failed. This result is confirmed by the decision of the House of Lords in *Graysim Property Holdings Ltd v P&O Property Holdings Ltd.*[444]

7–245 ***Jones v Jenkins***[445] The tenant had a business tenancy of premises used as a "nature cure centre", and was also granted a tenancy (by the same landlord) of two residential flats in an adjoining house. For the purpose of the tenant's application for a new tenancy of the two residential flats, it was assumed by the parties and the court that the 1954 Act applied and that the two flats together constituted "the holding" within the meaning of s.23. The landlord opposed on, inter alia, ground (c) (other breaches) and ground (g) (own occupation).

On ground (c), the judge held that it had been agreed that the flats should be used as a residential annex to the nature cure business, but one had been converted to use as a laundry and the other was used as a massage parlour.

On ground (g), the judge accepted that the landlord intended to re-let the flats as residential accommodation, and held that this was business occupation within the meaning of ground (g).

The judge dismissed the application and the tenant appealed. On appeal it was held:

(1) On ground (c) there was no evidence that one of the flats was being used as a laundry, but there was evidence that the other flat was being used as a massage parlour. Since the judge had correctly found one-half of the breach proved, but had not been entitled on the evidence to find the other half, it was impossible to say how he ought properly to have exercised his discretion. A retrial would have to be ordered.

---

442 (1972) 222 E.G. 625.
443 [1986] 1 E.G.L.R. 113 CA.
444 [1996] A.C. 329; [1995] 3 W.L.R. 854 HL.
445 [1986] 1 E.G.L.R. 113 CA.

(2) On ground (g) the landlord's intention to relet the flats as residential accommodation did not amount to an intention to occupy them for business purposes.

Business may have to be carried on in the holding

Unlike s.23(1), there is a further requirement in ground (g) that the business must be intended to be carried on "therein", by which is meant it must be carried on in the holding. Thus it may be that occupation for the purposes of a business which is carried on elsewhere will be insufficient: see *Hillil Property & Investment Co Ltd v Naraine Pharmacy Ltd*[446] (digested in para.1–119). "Therein" includes "thereon": *Hunt v Decca Navigator Co*[447] (digested in para.7–196), where it was held that using a car park for staff visiting an adjoining building was not the carrying on of a business elsewhere, but was the use of a car park for a business carried on on the site and elsewhere as well. It appears from *Method Development v Jones*[448] (digested in para.7–238) that the carrying on of a business in a substantial part of the holding will be sufficient. **7–246**

Business must be carried on by landlord

Generally

Just as under s.23(1) the business must be carried on by the tenant, so under ground (g) the business must be intended to be carried on by the landlord. The special provisions governing the situation where the landlord has a controlling interest in a company,[449] or where the landlord is a company and a person has a controlling interest in the company,[450] or where the landlord's interest is held on trust,[451] are set out below. The position where a tenant claims to occupy and carry on business at premises through an agent, rather than in person, has been considered previously.[452] What is said in those paragraphs and the cases which are there discussed are equally applicable to the case where the landlord intends, under ground (g), to occupy and carry on a business through an agent or manager: see in particular *Cafeteria (Keighley) Ltd v Harrison*[453] (digested in para.1–85). One, perhaps unexpected, effect of this is illustrated by the case of *Chez Gerard v Greene*[454] (digested in para.7–228), where a Liberian shipping company with no experience of running restaurants was able to establish an intention to run a restaurant under ground (g) through a management agreement with an experienced restaurateur. **7–247**

---

446 [1979] 2 E.G.L.R. 65 CA.
447 (1972) 222 E.G. 625.
448 [1971] 1 W.L.R. 168; [1971] 1 All E.R. 1027 CA.
449 s.30(1A). See para.7–254 et seq.
450 s.30(1B). See para.7–254 et seq.
451 s.41(2). See para.7–258.
452 See paras 1–76 and 1–82 et seq.
453 (1956) 168 E.G. 668 CA.
454 (1983) 268 E.G. 575 CA.

Occupation in partnership

7–248 In *Re Crowhurst Park*[455] the landlord proved that he intended to occupy the holding for the purposes of a business to be carried on by himself and his wife in partnership. It was held that where two persons carry on business in common as partners, each of them occupies the firm's premises and each of them carries on business there, so that the landlord had established the necessary intention. In *Skeet v Powell-Sheddon*[456] (digested in para.7–180) the landlord intended to carry on business in partnership with her husband. It was held that there was no need to demonstrate that she intended on carrying on the business exclusively. See also *Clift v Taylor*,[457] a case under the Landlord and Tenant Act 1927, where the equivalent words were "that the premises are required for occupation by himself" and it was held that occupation by a firm of which the landlord was a partner was occupation by the landlord himself within the meaning of the enactment.

7–249 In *Re Crowhurst Park*[458] and *Skeet v Powell-Sheddon*[459] the landlord intended to occupy in partnership with others. The partnership in those cases was an intended partnership; it was not pre-existing. There is no specific statutory provision (as there is for instance in the case of the service of notices upon or service of notices by tenant partners as contained in s.41A[460]) dealing with the intended occupation of a landlord where the landlord's interest is held by partners on trust for a partnership. In most cases the landlord partners will rely on the provisions of s.41(2), i.e. to say the intention is that of beneficiaries under a trust (i.e. the trust of the partnership property which will include the reversionary interest). These provisions are discussed in para.7–258. However, it is appropriate to consider here the difficulties which may arise where the landlord's interest is held in partnership. There are several potential difficulties:

(i) What happens if some or all of the legal owners have ceased to members of the partnership?
(ii) Is it possible for the legal owners to be said to "intend" to occupy where the beneficiaries under the partnership include persons other than the legal owners?
(iii) What is the date of the "creation" of the partnership?

7–250 **(i) Where "the landlord" comprises some or all of the retired partners** The legal owners of the landlord's interest will be holding the reversionary interest on trust. The retired partners will not, qua landlord, be intending to occupy the holding for business purposes. It will be necessary, therefore, in order for "the landlord" to be able to oppose the renewal, for there to be either a transfer of the legal estate to the current partners or for the current holders of the legal estate to rely on the provisions of s.41(2), namely upon the intended occupation of the

[455] [1974] 1 W.L.R. 583; [1974] 1 All E.R. 991.
[456] [1988] 2 E.G.L.R. 112 CA.
[457] [1948] 2 K.B. 394; [1948] 2 All E.R. 113 CA.
[458] [1974] 1 W.L.R. 583; [1974] 1 All E.R. 991.
[459] [1988] 2 E.G.L.R. 112 CA.
[460] As to which see at para.3–101.

beneficiaries (or some of them) under the partnership. The transfer to the current partners should not give rise to problems under the five year bar contained within s.30(2): see para.7–264 et seq. If there is a simple transfer from the current registered proprietors (who consist of all or some retired partners) to the current partners without any form of purchase, there should be no difficulty: see *Morar v Chauhan*[461] (considered in para.7–251).

(ii) Is it possible to say that the legal owners "intend" to occupy? The position being postulated here is that some only of the current partners hold the landlord's interest. The concern here is not so much that the legal owners cannot form a firm and settled intention to occupy—they clearly can—but whether they are able to implement the intention which is held. The legal owners (being partners of a partnership) will hold that legal estate on trust for the partners (including themselves). Thus, can it be said that, where the intention is for the trustee partners qua legal owners to enter and carry on a business, they cannot do so, because they have no right qua trustees of the legal estate, vis-à-vis the other beneficiaries under the partnership, effectively to oust those beneficiaries from occupation? Thus, it will be said that they cannot, from a practical point of view, show that they can implement the intention to occupy. There are a number of ways of overcoming this potential problem. **7–251**

First, there seems to be no reason why the beneficiaries under the partnership cannot simply agree that occupation by the legal owners qua trustees is in the best interests of the partnership. In *Morar v Chauhan*[462] (which was not a partnership case) the landlord declared a trust of the freehold for his children. He opposed the tenant's renewal on the ground that he intended to carry on a dry-cleaning laundry business. The court saw no difficulty in that. There was no discussion, however, in that case of the terms of the trust or of the trustees' right qua legal owner to occupy and run a business notwithstanding the existence of the trust and the beneficiaries rights under it.[463] It would seem, however, arguable that occupation by the partner landlords as part of the partnership is nevertheless occupation by "the landlord". In *Clift v Taylor*,[464] which was a case under the provisions of the Landlord and Tenant Act 1927 (now repealed), the landlord could oppose renewal

---

[461] [1985] 1 W.L.R. 1263; [1985] 3 All E.R. 493 CA.

[462] [1985] 1 W.L.R. 1263; [1985] 3 All E.R. 493 CA.

[463] In *I&H Caplan v Caplan (No.2)* [1963] 1 W.L.R. 1247 (digested in para.1–46), the tenant carried on business as outfitters. The judgment of Cross J. deals with the question as to whether or not the tenant had ceased to occupy the premises for business purposes. However, from the judge's recitation of the procedural history it would seem that the landlord's interest was held on trust for their infant children. The landlord opposed renewal under para.(g) of s.30(1) on the basis that they intended to carry on from the premises the business of a retail outfitters. The tenant company contended that the landlords had not and could not have such an intention as the Act required, because as they held the freehold not beneficially but as trustees they could not lawfully carry on business themselves on the premises without an order of the court enabling them to do it, which order they might in the circumstances very well not obtain. This issue was decided at first instance in favour of the landlord but was reversed in the Court of Appeal on the ground that the uncertainty as to whether or not the court would allow the landlords to carry on business on the premises as trustees for their children made it impossible to say that the landlords had an "intention" to do so within the meaning of s.30(1)(g) of the Act. Neither the judgment at first instance nor that of the Court of Appeal on the issue of ground (g) is reported.

[464] [1948] 2 K.B. 394.

if he showed "that the premises are required for occupation by himself." The landlord was one of five partners and had a staff of 41 people. It was said that the intended occupation by the firm satisfied the statutory provisions. Scott L.J. said:

> "The existing arrangement with his partners as to the firm's occupation of the building (excluding the tea-shop) was that the firm as a whole had a tenancy from him as landlord and he assumed that a similar arrangement would be made in regard to the premises previously let for a tea-shop. On this [counsel] for the tenant contended that such a lease would not constitute 'occupation by the landlord'... [Counsel for the landlord's] answer was that it was open to the landlord to give a mere licence to the firm to use the new premises; which would dispose of that objection. We agree; but we go further. On the reasonable interpretation of the Act it would be ridiculous to suppose that Parliament had intended to complicate the simple business concept of occupation by the landlord by pursuing the irrelevant further inquiry whether he had a partner or partners, or whether he let the premises in question to the firm or gave them a licence. But even if so artificial and technical a construction of the Act... was proper, [counsel for the landlord] pointed out that on the basis of the position now obtaining both in equity and at law, as explained with authorities on pp. 550 and 554 of the fifth edition of Cheshire's 'Modern Real Property,' land or any interest in land owned by a partnership and in its possession is occupied by all the partners and by each of them, because they are tenants in common. That, in our view, disposes of [the tenant's] contention of real property law." (at 402/403)

Secondly, the trustee legal owners, as landlord, may rely on s.41(2), that is to say that they do not intend to occupy qua legal owners but rely on the intention of the beneficiaries under the trust (of which they constitute some but not all) to carry on the partnership business from the tenant's premises. This should not cause a difficulty subject to any potential problem over the date of creation of the relevant trust.

7–252 **(iii)** If, as will be the case in most cases where the landlord's interest is subject to a partnership, the trustee landlords oppose renewal in reliance upon s.41(2), an issue may arise as to when the relevant trust is created for the purposes of the five year bar in s.30(2). This is discussed in para.7–283.

Occupation by one only of several persons who constitute the landlord

7–253 A different question arises where there are joint landlords, and the intention is that only some of them will occupy. In *Weatherall & Co v Stone*[465] occupation by two out of three landlords did not satisfy the statutory wording of the Landlord and Tenant Act 1927, where s.5(3)(b) used the wording "that the premises are required for occupation by himself...". Landlords faced with this problem may, however, rely on the trust provisions of s.41(2).[466]

Controlling interests

7–254 Prior to the amendments introduced by the 2003 Order it was provided by s.30(3), that where the landlord had a controlling interest in a company, any business to be carried on by the company should be treated for the purposes of ground (g) as a business to be carried on by the landlord. "Controlling interest"

---

[465] [1950] 2 All E.R. 1209 CA.

[466] See para.7–258.

was defined. This provision was introduced by amendment in 1969 and was intended to overrule *Tunstall v Steigmann*,[467] where it was held that a landlord could not succeed under ground (g) if the business was to be carried on by a company controlled by the landlord, rather than by the landlord herself. However, the provision appeared only partially to achieve its intended purpose; although the business was deemed to be that of the landlord, there remained a difficulty since it was the company, and not the landlord, which intended to "occupy". Section 30(3) did not expressly deem the occupation in such circumstances to be that of the landlord, although it could probably have been said that he would be intending to occupy through the agency of the company.

For the purposes of s.30(3) a person had a controlling interest in a company if and only if either: **7–255**

(1) he is a member of it and able, without the consent of any other person, to appoint or remove the holders of at least a majority of the directorships; or
(2) he holds more than one-half of its equity share capital, there being disregarded any shares held by him in a fiduciary capacity or as a nominee for another person: s.30(3).

Two new sub-sections have been added to s.30(1) by art.14(1). They provide: **7–256**

> "30(1A) where the landlord has a controlling interest in a company, the reference in sub-section (1)(g) above to the landlord shall be construed as a reference to the landlord or that company.
>
> 30(1B) subject to sub-section (2A)2 below, where the landlord is a company and the person has a controlling interest in the company, the reference in sub-section (1)(g) above to the landlord shall be construed as a reference to the landlord or that person."

These two subsections reflect the amendments contained within s.23(1A) and (1B).[468] Thus a landlord may oppose renewal under para.(g):

(1) where the landlord, being a controlling shareholder in a company, intends to occupy via the company with the company carrying on the business;
(2) where the landlord is a company and the business is intended to be undertaken by the controlling shareholder.

A person has a controlling interest in a company if, had that person been a company, the other company would have been a subsidiary within the meaning of s.459 of the Companies Act 2006[469]: s.46(2) as inserted by art.17 of the 2003 Order.

Company: occupation by member of a group

Where the landlord's interest is held by a member of a group the landlord is able to succeed in opposing renewal if any member of the group intends to occupy the **7–257**

[467] [1962] 2 W.L.R. 1045; [1962] 2 All E.R. 417 CA.

[468] As to which, see para.1–86 et seq.

[469] An identical definition of "subsidiary" was to be found in the Companies Act 1985 s.736.

holding for the purposes of a business to be carried on by that member: s.42(3). Two bodies corporate shall be taken to be members of a group if and only if one is a subsidiary of the other or both are subsidiaries of a third body corporate: s.42(1). "Subsidiary" has the meaning given to it by s.1159 of the Companies Act 2006.[470] A company is a "subsidiary" of another, it's "holding company", if that other company:

(1) holds a majority of the voting rights in it, or
(2) is a member of it and has the right to appoint or remove a majority of its board of directors, or
(3) is a member of it and controls alone, pursuant to an agreement with other shareholders or members, a majority of the voting rights in it, or is a subsidiary of a company which is itself a subsidiary of that other company.

Beneficiaries

7–258 Where the landlord's interest is held on trust, it is provided by s.41(2) that references in s.30(1)(g) to the landlord are to be construed as including references to the beneficiaries under the trust or any of them. Thus the intention of the beneficiaries is equated with the intention of the landlords. It has been held in the county court that the intention of an infant beneficiary can be taken into account: *Gundry v Stewart.*[471] As has been seen from the decisions discussed in para.1–92 et seq., "beneficiaries under the trust" has a restricted meaning. Difficulties may be encountered where there are two or more beneficiaries, only some of whom intend to occupy the premises, for something may then have to be done as to the remaining beneficiary's entitlement to otherwise occupy. Dealing with that beneficiary's entitlement may prevent reliance on ground (g) by reason of the five-year bar: see *Meyer v Riddick*[472] (digested in para.1–103).

Occupation as residence

7–259 As an alternative to intended occupation for business purposes, a landlord can rely upon ground (g) where he intends to occupy the premises "as his residence". In order to establish this limb of ground (g), it would appear that the landlord must occupy only for residential purposes and not for mixed purposes, although if the intention is to occupy for mixed residential and business purposes he would succeed under the first limb of ground (g) (see paras 7–237 and 7–242).

7–260 "Residence" is not defined. An interesting question which arises is whether the holding must be used as a residence in the sense that all the activities which are usually associated with the use of premises as a residence, such as cooking and sleeping, must be undertaken on the holding. Is it possible, for instance, for the landlord to succeed albeit he has a second home? In the context of the Rent Acts the question of whether or not the tenant is occupying premises as a residence

[470] See para.A1.073.
[471] [1959] C.L.Y. 1818.
[472] [1990] 1 E.G.L.R. 107 CA. See also para.7–283.

arises particularly when considering whether the tenant is a statutory tenant. By s.2(1) of the Rent Act 1977 it is provided that:

> "Subject to this Part of this Act—(*a*) after the termination of a protected tenancy of a dwelling-house the person who, immediately before that termination, was the protected tenant of the dwelling-house shall, if and so long as he occupies the dwelling-house as his residence, be the statutory tenant of it . . ."

Thus where the tenant has two homes or where the tenant's living activities are divided between two properties the question arises whether the tenant is occupying the relevant premises as a residence. In *Hampstead Way Investments Ltd v Lewis-Weare*[473] (digested in para.7–263), the House of Lords did not, in the context of the Rent Acts, discount the possibility that someone's could have more than one home. Lord Brandon said:

> "(1) A person may have two dwelling houses, each of which he occupies as his home, so that, if either of them is let to him, his tenancy of it is protected by the Rent Act 1977 (see *Langford Property Co Ltd v. Athanassoglou*[474]) . . . (3) Where a person owns one dwelling house which he occupies as his home for most of his time and is at the same time the tenant of another dwelling house which he only occupies rarely or for limited purposes it is a question of fact and degree whether he occupies the latter dwelling house as his second home (see *Langford Property Co Ltd v Athanassoglou*,[475] *Beck v. Scholz*[476]). That principle has been followed and applied in cases since 1968: see *Roland House Gardens Ltd v Cravitz*[477] and *Regalian Securities Ltd v Scheuer*."[478]

It has been held in the context of s.30(1)(g) that the landlord may intend to occupy the holding as a residence albeit the holding is not inter-connected, e.g. where the holding consisted of two flats separated by two front doors and a staircase: *Shearum Ltd v Savill*[479] (digested in para.7–262).

Occupation as a residence does not require personal use of each and every part of the holding. Thus allocation of accommodation for use by guests is still occupation by the landlord of the holding as his residence: *Shearum Ltd v Savill*[480] (digested in para.7–262). In the judgment of Nourse L.J. in *Shearum Ltd v Savill*, it was said that it was necessary for the landlord to show that he intended to occupy "the whole of the premises, not just part, for use as a permanent residence". However, it is clear having regard to the facts of that decision, that the court was not suggesting that the landlord has to personally occupy each and every part of the holding. In *Method Development v Jones*[481] (digested in para.7–238), the landlord had no stated intention in relation to 400 square feet of a building of 1,866 square feet. Nevertheless, the landlord succeeded. Fenton Atkinson L.J. said in that case: **7–261**

---

[473] [1985] 1 W.L.R. 164; [1985] 1 All E.R. 564 HL.
[474] *Langford Property Co v Tureman* [1949] 1 K.B. 29; [1948] 2 All E.R. 722 CA.
[475] *Langford Property Co v Tureman* [1949] 1 K.B. 29; [1948] 2 All E.R. 722 CA.
[476] [1953] 1 Q.B. 570; [1953] 2 W.L.R. 651; [1953] 1 All E.R. 814 CA.
[477] (1975) 29 P. & C.R. 432 CA.
[478] (1982) 1322 N.L.J. 20 CA.
[479] Unreported April 1, 1996 CA.
[480] Unreported April 1, 1996 CA.
[481] [1971] 1 W.L.R. 168; [1971] 1 All E.R. 1027 CA.

> "... It seems to me plain that one can occupy a holding for the purposes of one's business under s.30(1) (g) even though one may not intend at present to make actual or physical use of the whole of the holding. There is a settled intention here to use a very substantial part, something like four-fifths; and just as one can plainly occupy a dwelling-house as one's residence even though one leaves a couple of rooms empty, I think here that the landlord's proven intention to occupy the whole of this holding for the purposes of their business."

Although this was not a case of intended residential use, there seems to be no reason why an analogous principle should not apply.

7–262 ***Shearum Ltd v Savill***[482] The tenant's holding consisted of two separate flats on the ground and first floors, each having its own front door. Access to the first floor flat was by a staircase. The landlord, who was elderly, stated that he intended to occupy the two floors as his residence. There were two rooms on the first floor. The landlord's stated intention was to live mainly on the ground floor (due to his age) and would use the first floor for three purposes—as a guest room, as a study/workroom and his surplus furniture and other belongings would be spread between the rooms. He stated that he wished to install a lift but had not yet prepared any plans or estimates or obtained any necessary consents. The Court of Appeal dismissed the tenant's appeal from the county court judge's decision in favour of the landlord holding that use as a guest room, although not used by the landlord personally, was clearly used as part of his residence as was the spreading of surplus furniture and other belongings between the rooms. Notwithstanding the fact that the landlord did not have a sufficient intention with regard to the lift, there was no finding that the landlord could not get up and down the stairs between the two flats if there was no lift.

7–263 ***Hampstead Way Investments Ltd v Lewis-Weare***[483] The premises demised to the tenant comprised two living rooms, two bedrooms and a small box-room. The tenancy was for three years. Living with him in the flat were his wife, stepson, stepdaughter and, after her birth, his daughter. Several years later (after the contractual term had expired) the tenant and his wife bought a three-bedroom house half a mile from the flat and, except for the stepdaughter (who went abroad), the family moved there and occupied it as their home. The tenant was employed by a night club and worked five nights a week. The tenant often returned from work early in the morning. In order not to disturb his wife the tenant retained a room in the flat to which he returned after work to sleep. This arrangement continued five days a week. The tenant would sleep until the afternoon, after which he went to the house and had a light meal prepared by his wife. When he was off work he was at the house. The remainder of the flat was occupied for all usual living activities by the stepson. The flat was used by the tenant as his mail address and he kept his working clothes there. No meals were eaten at the flat nor did the tenant entertain his friends there; all entertaining was done at the house. All the outgoings of the flat except for the gas bill, which was paid by his stepson, were paid by the tenant. The landlords sought possession of the flat on the ground that the tenant had ceased to occupy it as his residence after

---

482 Unreported April 1, 1996 CA.

483 [1985] 1 W.L.R. 164; [1985] 1 All E.R. 564; [1985] 1 E.G.L.R. 120 HL.

the move to the house and, by virtue of s.2(1)(a) of the Rent Act 1977 as construed with s.3(2) of the Rent Act 1968, was no longer a protected tenant. The county court judge dismissed the landlords' claim for possession on the ground that the house and flat constituted one unit of living accommodation. The Court of Appeal allowed their appeal. The tenant and the stepson appealed to the House of Lords.

It was held that where a person had two places of residence, one of which was occupied as a home for most of the time and another which was occupied for limited purposes, the question whether the occupation of the second dwelling house was as a second home was a question of fact and degree. The court should, in determining that question, consider not only whether the second home was occupied separately as a complete home in itself but also whether the tenant occupied both homes as a combined unit. The house and flat being half a mile from each other could not possibly be regarded as constituting together a single unit of living accommodation. The very limited use of the flat by the tenant for his occupation was insufficient to make the flat as his second home. Accordingly, the tenant was not occupying the flat as his residence, and the tenancy was therefore not a protected tenancy for the purposes of the 1977 Act. The possession order had, therefore, been rightly made and the appeal would be dismissed.

The "five-year bar"

By virtue of s.30(2), the landlord cannot rely upon ground (g): **7–264**

> "... if the interest of the landlord, or an interest which has merged in that interest and but for the merger would be the interest of the landlord, was purchased or created after the beginning of the period of five years which ends with the termination of the current tenancy, and at all times since the purchase or creation thereof the holding has been comprised in a tenancy or successive tenancies within the Act."

Whether the five-year bar applies can be tested as follows: **7–265**

(1) It is necessary to identify "the interest of the landlord"; that is to say the interest of the "landlord" as defined in ss.44 (see para.3–87). In addition it is necessary to consider whether an interest has merged in the landlord's interest which would be "the interest of the landlord" if it had not merged.[484]

(2) It is necessary to look at the s.25 notice or s.26 request to ascertain the date therein specified, for the termination of the current tenancy referred to in s.30(2) is the date specified in the s.25 notice or s.26 request, as the case may be, and not the date upon which the tenancy will come to an end pursuant to s.24 and 64: see *Frederick Lawrence Ltd v Freeman Hardy & Willis Ltd*[485] (digested in para.7–280).

---

[484] As to the date for determining whether the interest which has merged would have been the interest of the landlord, see para.7–269 et seq.

[485] [1959] 3 W.L.R. 275; [1959] 3 All E.R. 77 CA.

(3) Taking that date, it is necessary to count back five years to find the date from which the statutory bar commences (hereinafter referred to as "the relevant commencement date"). If the interest of the landlord has been purchased or created after the relevant commencement date and if the holding has at all times thereafter been comprised in a tenancy or successive tenancies within the Act, the landlord may not rely on ground (g).

7–266 The application of s.30(2) can be illustrated by two examples.

7–267 **Example 1** The tenant under the current tenancy, S, is a sub-tenant holding from T. T has surrendered his tenancy to the freeholder, F, for valuable consideration. By virtue of the surrender and merger of T's interest, F becomes S's "landlord". F serves a s.25 notice on S. The tenancy surrendered by T to F would, let us say, have had 20 years unexpired at the date specified in the s.25 notice. If it had not been surrendered, it would have been T who would have been S's landlord. Accordingly T's interest is an "interest which has merged in" F's interest and "but for the merger would be the interest of the landlord". If the surrender and merger took place after the relevant commencement date it follows that F has "purchased" that interest and is thus barred by s.30(2).

7–268 **Example 2** The facts are the same as above, but the duration of T's tenancy was such that he would, at the date of expiry of the s.25 notice, have had less than 14 months unexpired if he had not surrendered his interest. That being so, he would not have been S's "landlord". Therefore it is irrelevant that F has purchased T's interest for the purposes of applying the five-year rule. F will not be barred by the rule provided that he purchased his freehold interest after the relevant commencement date: see *Diploma Laundry v Surrey Timber*[486] (digested in para.7–270).

The date for determining whether the relevant interest would have been the "interest of the landlord"

7–269 The date for determining whether the relevant interest would have been the "interest of the landlord" is the date of service of the s.25 notice (or possibly the date of the counter-notice to the tenant' s.26 request) and not the date of the merger: *Diploma Laundry Ltd v Surrey Timber Ltd*[487] (digested in para.7–270). Accordingly, if the superior landlord accepts a surrender from his tenant and the tenant's interest is not, at the date of the service of the s.25 notice, of such length as to constitute the interest of the landlord for the purposes of s.44, although it would have been at the date of the surrender, the superior landlord will not be caught by the five-year bar in opposing renewal of the sub-tenant's lease, to which the superior landlord is, by virtue of the surrender, the immediate reversioner.

---

486 [1955] 2 Q.B. 604; [1955] 3 W.L.R. 404; [1955] 2 All E.R. 922 CA.

487 [1955] 2 Q.B. 604; [1955] 3 W.L.R. 404; [1955] 2 All E.R. 922 CA.

Diploma Laundry Ltd v Surrey Timber Ltd[488] F Ltd were the tenants of business premises under a lease expiring on March 25, 1955. F Ltd granted a sub-tenancy of the whole of the demised premises to D Ltd for the remainder of their term, less one day. ST Ltd purchased the freehold reversion in 1949. On March 25, 1953, F Ltd surrendered its lease to ST Ltd for consideration and D Ltd thereby became the immediate tenants of ST Ltd. On September 23, 1954, D Ltd served on ST Ltd a request for a new tenancy from March 24, 1955. On October 19, 1954, ST Ltd served a counter-notice specifying ground (g) as the ground of opposition to the grant of a new tenancy. D Ltd contended that ST Ltd could not rely on ground (g) by reason of s.30(2) of the Act. **7–270**

It was held:

(1) The date for considering whether F Ltd's interest would have been the interest of the landlord within the meaning of s.44 was either the date of the tenant's request or the date of the landlord's counter-notice, although for present purposes it was unnecessary to decide which was correct.
(2) F Ltd's interest at the date of the tenant's request (being September 23, 1954) or at the date of the landlord's counter-notice in response thereto (being October 19, 1954) was not the interest of the landlord within the meaning of s.44, because at either of those dates it had less than 14 months unexpired and did not, therefore, satisfy s.44(1)(b). Accordingly, F Ltd's interest was irrelevant for the purposes of s.30(2).
(3) ST Ltd's freehold interest was, therefore, the relevant interest to consider. As they had purchased that interest in 1949 it was not purchased or created within five years of the date D Ltd's current tenancy terminated (being March 24, 1955).
(4) As F Ltd's interest was irrelevant, it was unnecessary to consider whether it had been purchased or created within five years of the date on which D Ltd's current tenancy determined.

Creation of landlord's interest

The word "created" in s.30(2) is referable to the creation of the landlord's interest and not to the creation of the landlord's title: *Frederick Lawrence Ltd v Freeman Hardy & Willis Ltd*[489] (digested in para.7–280). Where the party opposing is the freehold owner (whether as sole beneficial owner or as trustee) the only limitation is one of "purchase". One cannot "create" a freehold interest. Thus, where the landlord executed a trust within the five year period for his children but opposed qua trustee, there was held to be no creation of the landlord's interest for the purposes of s.30(2): *Morar v Chauhan.*[490] The Court of Appeal held that the trustee landlord was not barred from relying on ground (g) qua trustee by the five-year bar by the creation of the trust within that period. If the creation or **7–271**

[488] [1955] 2 Q.B. 604; [1955] 3 W.L.R. 404; [1955] 2 All E.R. 922 CA.

[489] [1959] 3 W.L.R. 275; [1959] 3 All E.R. 77 CA.

[490] [1985] 1 W.L.R. 1263; [1985] 3 All E.R. 493; [1985] 2 E.G.L.R. 137 CA. It should be noted that in this case it was the trustee—not the beneficiaries—who intended to occupy. If the beneficiaries had intended to occupy, relying on s.41(2), the five-year period would have run from the date of creation of the trust.

purchase of the landlord's interest pre-dates the grant of the current tenancy (or any previous business tenancy which was vested in the tenant who is the tenant under the current tenancy), s.30(2) will not apply, because there has been a time (if only a scintilla of time) since the creation or purchase of the landlord's interest when "the holding" has not been "comprised in a tenancy or successive tenancies" within the Act: see *Northcote Laundry v Donnelly*[491] (digested in para.7–275). For the same reason, it would appear that the landlord will not be barred if, at any time since the creation or purchase of his interest, the tenancy has for any reason ceased to be one to which the Act applies, e.g. as a result of non-occupation. In *Northcote Laundry v Donnelly*,[492] Russell L.J. suggested that if the landlord's interest had been created on the same day as the landlord granted the lease, the landlord would have been caught by s.30(2). This interpretation seems to be contrary to the policy of the Act, as identified in *Artemiou v Procopiou*[493] (digested in para.7–276), namely to prevent the exploitation of sitting tenants by speculators. In the circumstances suggested by Russell L.J. the tenant would not have been a "sitting tenant", nor could the landlord be said to be a speculator.[494] It is, therefore, suggested that the decision in *Northcote Laundry v Donnelly*[495] is to be supported on the further, and primary, ground that s.30(2) simply has no application where the landlord has himself granted the tenancy in question.

7–272 Where the interest of the landlord is a leasehold one, the interest is created upon execution and not at the date on which the leaseholders' interest in the land commenced according to that lease: *Northcote Laundry v Donnelly*.[496] If the grant is registrable at HM Land Registry, it has been held at County Court level that the landlord's interest is also the date of grant notwithstanding the requirement of registration of the lease: *Denny Thorn & Co v George Harker & Co*.[497] This conclusion seems questionable in light of the view expressed in *Pearson v Alyo*[498] that "the subsection [here referring to s.44(1)] is concerned only with legal owners." Under the Land Registration Act 2002 the legal estate of a lease granted out of a registered estate will not pass until registration of the lease at the Land Registry.[499] The position is otherwise where the court is concerned with whether there has been a purchase of "the landlord's interest". It has been held that the interest is purchased within s.30(2) of the Act when the

---

491 [1968] 1 W.L.R. 562; [1968] 2 All E.R. 50 CA.

492 [1968] 1 W.L.R. 562; [1968] 2 All E.R. 50 CA.

493 [1966] 1 Q.B. 878; [1965] 3 W.L.R. 1011; [1965] 3 All E.R. 539 CA.

494 See also in *VCS Car Park Management Ltd v Regional Railways North East Ltd* [2000] 3 W.L.R. 370 CA (digested in para.7–285), which supports this view.

495 [1968] 1 W.L.R. 562; [1968] 2 All E.R. 50 CA.

496 [1968] 1 W.L.R. 562; [1968] 2 All E.R. 50 CA.

497 (1957) 108 L.J. 348 CC. This was a case of a sale and lease back. The sale occurred on December 16, 1952 with the date of termination being December 25, 1957. Registration of the lease was not effected until December 30, 1957. Held, that the interest was created on grant not registration. In light of *VCS Car Park Management Ltd v Regional Railways North East Ltd* [2001] Ch. 121 CA (digested in para.7–285) it would seem that it would not have mattered, if the case were being decided today, if the court were to have found that the date of registration was the relevant date of creation.

498 [1990] 1 E.G.L.R. 114 CA per Nourse L.J.

499 ss.27(1) (2)(b) and Sch.2 para 3 of the 2002 Act. In general the grant of a lease of not less than seven years is registrable in order to be effective at law: see s.27(2).

agreement to acquire the landlord's interest is entered into albeit the purchaser does not acquire the status of "landlord" within s.44 until registration: *Frederick Lawrence Ltd v Freeman Hardy & Willis Ltd*[500] (digested at para.7–280).

In *Artemiou v Procopiou*[501] (above) the Court of Appeal held that an interest of a landlord which consists of a series of successive leases, is created at the moment of the first lease in the series. In that case it was held that a landlord who had purchased a leasehold interest in 1960 and who had renewed that interest by taking a new lease in 1961 was, for the purpose of ground (g), to be taken to have acquired his interest not in 1961, but in 1960. However, in order for a landlord to take advantage of successive leases, the landlord must have been the "landlord" within s.44 of the 1954 Act at all times under the successive leases. Thus, if there is a period of time when, before the grant of the further lease, the landlord, albeit the immediate landlord of the tenant, has ceased to be the competent landlord, the landlord will, upon the grant of the further lease, be caught by the five-year bar: *Frozen Value Ltd v Heron Foods Ltd*[502] (digested in para.7–277). Thus, if L is T's immediate landlord and competent landlord for the purposes of the 1954 Act, any grant to L of a new leasehold interest at any time within 14 months of the expiry of L's leasehold interest (assuming L is not in occupation for business purposes of any part of the premises demised to L) will trigger s.30(2) of the Act, for L will have ceased (under L's old lease) to be competent landlord of T once there was less than 14 months unexpired of his term. What is unclear from the decision of the Court of Appeal in *Frozen Value Ltd v Heron Foods Ltd*[503] is whether any period of time, no matter how short, will prevent L from relying on a succession of leases. Thus, one may envisage a situation where L, prior to the 14 month period of expiry of his leasehold interest, seeks the grant of a new lease from his landlord to ensure his continuity as competent landlord. If he does obtain a new lease from his landlord, may it be said that there was a moment in time when, upon the surrender of L's existing lease (by operation of law or otherwise), he ceased to be competent landlord and thus only became competent landlord upon the grant of the new lease?[504] One can see that the court would be resistant to an argument based on a fraction of a time, but what if the new grant is delayed after the surrender by, e.g. a few hours or a day? Further, the grant of a new lease of not less than seven years will only confer the status of landlord within the meaning of s.44 when registered at the Land Registry.[505] Thus, if the new lease takes some time to be registered the registration may only occur at a time when the landlord has less than 14 months remaining of his current lease. **7–273**

[500] [1959] Ch. 731 CA at 738 per Romer L.J. delivering the judgment of the court.

[501] [1966] 1 Q.B. 878; [1965] 3 W.L.R. 1011; [1965] 3 All E.R. 539 CA.

[502] [2012] EWCA Civ 473; [2012] 3 W.L.R. 437.

[503] [2012] EWCA Civ 473; [2012] 3 W.L.R. 437.

[504] Lloyd L.J. in giving judgment for the tenant said that, had L take a new tenancy before May 17, 2009 (being the date 14 months prior to the expiry of L's lease), there could have been no doubt that L would have been competent landlord and the creation of its successor interest would seamlessly have extended its interest as such for the foreseeable future: at [79].

[505] See para.7–272.

7–274 A conditional agreement for lease does not give rise to the creation of any interest in land.[506] Thus where the mesne landlord, whose tenancy (which was created more than five years prior to the termination date in the s.25 notice served on the sub-tenant) was continuing pursuant to s.24, had entered into an agreement for lease with the superior landlord, which agreement was conditional upon the completion of certain building work, the landlord's interest remained the continuation tenancy and his opposition to the renewal of the sub-tenant's lease was not caught by s.30(2): *Cornish v Brook Green Laundry.*[507] If the landlord's leasehold interest was created by way of a lease back from the sale by him of his freehold interest, the landlord's interest is to be treated as commencing with the commencement of the landlord's period as freehold owner, the successive periods as freeholder and then leaseholder being taken together: *VCS Car Park Management Ltd v Regional Railways North East Ltd*[508] (digested in para.7–285).

7–275 ***Northcote Laundry v Donnelly (Frederick)***[509] N Ltd were the freehold owners of business premises. By a lease dated September 23, 1964, they demised those premises to FD Ltd for a term of 21 years from September 29, 1964. FD Ltd entered into occupation on September 29, 1964. N Ltd retained a part of the premises under a yearly periodic tenancy commencing on September 29, 1964. FD Ltd served upon N Ltd a s.25 notice dated November 2, 1966, specifying September 29, 1967, as the date of termination and specifying ground (g) (own occupation) in opposition to the grant of a new tenancy. N Ltd argued that FD Ltd could not rely on ground (g) by reason of s.30(2) of the Act. It was held:

(1) The landlord's interest was created on the date of execution of the lease (being September 23, 1964) and not the date the landlord entered into possession.
(2) As the landlord's interest was created on September 23, 1964, it could not be said that at all times since that date there had been a business tenancy of the holding, namely that part occupied by N Ltd, because N Ltd's business tenancy did not commence until September 29, 1964.
(3) Accordingly, s.30(2) of the Act did not apply.

7–276 ***Artemiou v Procopiou***[510] In March 1960, the landlord took an assignment of the leasehold interest in cafe premises. In March 1961, he renewed his lease for a term of seven years. In November 1963 he sub-let the premises to the tenant. The landlord gave notice under s.25 terminating the tenancy in October 1965 and specifying ground (g) of s.30(1). It was held that the interest of the landlord was

[506] It is not an equitable lease as specific performance cannot be ordered until satisfaction of the condition: *Walsh v Lonsdale* (1882) L.R. 21 Ch. D. 9 CA; *Cornish v Brook Green Laundry* [1959] 2 W.L.R. 295.

[507] [1959] 2 W.L.R. 215; [1959] 1 All E.R. 373 CA. Even if the court had found that there had been an unconditional agreement for lease, it would seem that, in light of the later decision in *Artemiou v Procopiou* [1966] 1 Q.B. 878; [1965] 3 W.L.R. 1011; [1965] 3 All E.R. 539 CA, the mesne landlord would still have not been caught by the five-year bar, as his interest would be treated as being created when it originally arose under the first of the succession of leases.

[508] [2000] 3 W.L.R. 370; [2000] 1 All E.R. 403; [2000] 1 E.G.L.R. 57 CA.

[509] [1968] 1 W.L.R. 562; [1968] 2 All E.R. 50 CA.

[510] [1966] 1 Q.B. 878; [1965] 3 W.L.R. 1011; [1965] 3 All E.R. 539 CA.

purchased or created in March 1960. The mischief at which s.30(2) was aimed was the exploitation of sitting tenants for speculators. As the tenant's tenancy did not commence until November 1963 he was not a sitting tenant. Further (Danckwerts and Salmon L.JJ.) "the interest of the landlord" means the interest of the landlord in the holding when it first arose by purchase or creation. The landlord's interest was comprised in two successive leases and taken together the landlord's interest commenced on a date which was before the five year period began. The two leases together constituted an "the interest of the landlord" which satisfied the requirements of s.30(2).

Frozen Value Ltd v Heron Foods Ltd[511] L was leasehold owner of a ground floor supermarket with first floor residential accommodation under a lease dated May 8, 1981. The lease was for a term of 35 years expiring on July 17, 2010. L granted an underlease on October 1, 2011 expiring on July 14, 2010. L did not occupy any part of the premises demised to T for business purposes. On January 27, 2010 (that is at a time when L's leasehold interest had less than 14 months unexpired) T served a s.26 request on the freehold owner for the grant of a new tenancy seeking the grant of a new lease with effect from July 29, 2010. On February 24, 2010 the freehold owner granted L a new lease of the premises for a term of 15 years commencing on July 18, 2010. L opposed renewal under para.(g) of s.30(1). The Court of Appeal,[512] reversing the trial judge, held that L was caught by the five-year bar by reason of the grant of the new lease. The Court of Appeal held: **7–277**

(1) That L was not the (competent) landlord at all for the purposes of s.30(2) of the 1954 Act between May 17, 2009 (being the date 14 months prior to the expiry of L's lease which had been granted in 1981) and February 24, 2010 (the date of the grant of the new lease to L);
(2) The decisions in *Artemiou v Procopiou*[513] (digested in para.7–276) and *VCS Car Park Management Ltd v Regional Railways North East Ltd*[514] (digested in para.7–285) were distinguishable as in neither of those cases did the landlord's interest suffer an interruption during the relevant five period.

Meaning of "purchase"

The word "purchase" is used in the sense of "buying for money": *Bolton v Graham*[515] (digested in para.7–279). "Money" in this context is not confined to cash in its strict sense, but excludes the acquisition of property in consideration of giving a covenant: *Frederick Lawrence v Freeman Hardy & Willis*[516] (digested in para.7–280). Thus, a surrender by operation of law which is not for valuable **7–278**

[511] [2012] EWCA Civ 473; [2012] 3 W.L.R. 437.
[512] By a majority, Rimer L.J. dissenting.
[513] [1966] 1 Q.B. 878; [1965] 3 W.L.R. 1011; [1965] 3 All E.R. 539 CA.
[514] [2001] Ch. 121; [2000] 3 W.L.R. 370; [2000] 1 All E.R. 403 CA.
[515] [1957] 1 Q.B. 159; [1956] 3 W.L.R. 804; [1956] 3 All E.R. 624 CA. This case is also digested on the issue of establishing "introduction" within s.30(1)(g) in para.7–169.
[516] [1959] 3 W.L.R. 275; [1959] 3 All E.R. 77 CA.

consideration does not constitute the "purchase" of an interest: *Bolton v Graham.*[517] In *Frederick Lawrence v Freeman Hardy & Willis*,[518] it was held that there was a purchase albeit the acquisition was not expressed to be for valuable consideration and it would be difficult to say how much, in light of the absence of any apportionment of the consideration, the landlord had "paid" for the relevant interest, when, on a true consideration of the transaction embodied in the parties' agreement it was intended by the contracting parties to be one of sale and purchase. The "purchase" takes place at the date of exchange of contracts: *Frederick Lawrence v Freeman Hardy & Willis.*[519] The purchase of the shares of a company which owns the landlord's interest is unlikely to be held a purchase of the interest within the meaning of s.30(2). This certainly seems to have been assumed in *Wates Estate Agency Services Ltd v Bartleys Ltd.*[520]

7–279 ***HL Bolton Engineering Co Ltd v TJ Graham & Sons Ltd***[521] In 1941 the landlords (a company) granted a lease of business premises to Tubes Ltd, who sub-let part thereof to the tenants. In 1955 Tubes Ltd vacated the part they occupied and their leasehold interest was surrendered by operation of law. No consideration was paid to Tubes Ltd by the landlords for the surrender. In 1955 the landlords served a notice under s.25 on the tenants, specifying ground (g) of s.30(1). The question for the court was whether, by accepting the surrender of the intermediate lease from Tubes Ltd, the landlords had "purchased" the interest of the landlord or an interest which had merged in that interest and, but for the merger, would be the interest of the landlord within the five-year period laid down in s.30(2). It was held that "purchase" in s.30(2) has its popular meaning of buying for money and does not include a surrender for no consideration. The five-year bar did not therefore apply.

7–280 ***Frederick Lawrence Ltd v Freeman Hardy & Willis Ltd***[522] By an underlease dated December 30, 1933, Sears Ltd demised business premises to F.J. Cartwright Ltd for a term expiring on March 22, 1959. That term was, by an assignment dated November 29, 1934, vested in the applicants, Frederick Lawrence Ltd, the tenants. By a reversionary lease dated March 10, 1952, the premises were demised to Sears Ltd for a term of 99 years, subject to the tenancies affecting the premises. By the third recital of an agreement dated June 30, 1954, Sears Ltd agreed to "sell" and Freeman, Hardy and Willis to "purchase" the business of Sears Ltd and certain freehold and leasehold premises which included the underlease. In conformity with this recital, cl.1 of the agreement provided that "Sears sell and Freeman purchase as at January 1, 1954 (hereinafter called 'the sale date')" the said freehold and leasehold interests. Clause 2 of the agreement provided that the consideration for the sale and purchase was to be apportioned between the freehold and leasehold properties. However, in respect

[517] [1956] 3 W.L.R. 804; [1956] 3 All E.R. 624 CA.
[518] [1959] 3 W.L.R. 275; [1959] 3 All E.R. 77 CA.
[519] [1959] 3 W.L.R. 275; [1959] 3 All E.R. 77 CA.
[520] [1989] 2 E.G.L.R. 87 CA.
[521] [1957] 1 Q.B. 159 CA. A further issue in this case was whether the landlord has established a sufficient intention for the purposes of para.(g). This aspect of the case is digested at para.7–169.
[522] [1959] Ch. 731 CA.

of the leasehold interests comprising the underlease, no amount was attributed at all; the consideration for the leasehold interests was expressed to be the covenant by the landlords to pay the rents reserved and to observe and perform the covenants and conditions contained in the leases under which the properties were held and to indemnify Sears Ltd in respect of any breach thereof. Apart from this covenant and indemnity, no cash consideration, even a nominal one, was attributed to the leasehold interests including the underlease.

Pursuant to the agreement by a transfer dated November 1, 1954, the reversionary lease was assigned to Freeman, Hardy and Willis Ltd, the landlords. No monetary consideration was expressed in the transfer. The only consideration moving from the landlords to Sears Ltd were the covenants implied under s.77(1)(c) of the Law of Property Act 1925 (being covenants to pay rent and observe the covenant of the lease and to indemnify the assignor), which were expressly incorporated in the transfer. Upon the registration at the Land Registry of the transfer on November 13, 1954, the landlords became entitled to the leasehold reversion expectant upon the determination of the tenant's tenancy.

On March 28, 1958, the landlords served on the tenants a notice under s.25, terminating the tenancy on March 22, 1959, and opposed the grant of a new tenancy on ground (g) in s.30(1) (own occupation).

It was held that:

(1) The landlord's interest had not been "created" after the beginning of five years ending with the termination of the tenant's current tenancy, for the word "created" in s.30(2) is referable to the creation of the landlord's interest and not to the creation of the landlord's title. Accordingly, the interest of the landlords had been "created" by the reversionary lease dated March 10, 1952, albeit the landlords did not acquire this interest until 1954.

(2) The word "purchased" in s.30(2) means "bought for money". "Money" in this context is not confined to cash in its strict sense, but would exclude the acquisition of property in consideration for giving a covenant. If the agreement and the transfer were looked at independently, neither could be regarded as a "purchase" of the leasehold interests comprising the underlease. However, it was wrong to split up what was one single and indivisible agreement. As such it was clear from the third recital, cl.1 and cl.2 of the agreement, that the transaction embodied in the agreement was intended by the contracting parties to be one of sale and purchase. Although it would be difficult to say how much the landlords "paid" for the relevant interests, if the amount had to be assessed in terms of money, the ordinary commercial view of the transaction would be that the landlords bought Sears Ltd's leaseholds, along with its business and other assets.

(3) The "interest of the landlord" within s.30(2) is the interest by virtue of which the landlord opposes a tenant's application for a new lease. That interest in this case was the legal interest in reversion expectant on the termination of the tenancy and the landlords "purchased" that interest on the date when the agreement with Sears Ltd was signed, namely June 30, 1954.

(4) Although the landlords did not acquire the position or status of landlord until November 13, 1954, when the purchase was completed and registered, the relevant date of purchase for the purposes of s.30(2) was when the landlords entered into the agreement for sale.

(5) The date of "the termination of the current tenancy" for the purposes of s.30(2) is the date specified in the landlord's notice served under s.25; it is not to be construed as incorporating an extension of time granted under s.64.

Accordingly, the landlords were held to have purchased the premises within the five-year period and s.30(2) therefore applied.

Group companies and the five-year bar

7–281 Where the landlord's interest is held by a member of a group[523] the purchase or creation that is required to be considered is that of the purchase from or creation by a person other than a member of the group.[524] Accordingly, inter group transfers or arrangements are not caught by the five-year bar. If, therefore, a group company were to grant an intermediate leasehold interest to a member of the same group so as to render that member the immediate reversioner to the tenant's lease, the grant is not the relevant interest to be considered for the purposes of s.30(2).

Controlling interests

7–282 By reason of the provisions of s.30(1B), where a landlord is a company and a person has a controlling interest in it, the landlord company can oppose renewal under s.30(1)(g) either in reliance on the company's own occupation or that of the person with the controlling interest it. However, the prohibition upon relying on s.30(1)(g) where the reversion has been acquired in the last five years ending with the termination of the current tenancy is extended to catch changes in the controlling interest. The person with the controlling interest is prohibited from opposing renewal where there has been a change in the controlling interest in the company in the period of five years ending with the termination of the current tenancy: s.30(2A) to the 1954 Act. The "termination of the current tenancy" is the date specified in the s.25 notice or the s.26 request, as the case may be, for termination of the current tenancy/the commencement of the new tenancy. Section 30(2A) provides:

> "Sub-section (1B) above shall not apply if the controlling interest was acquired after the beginning of the period of 5 years which ends with the termination of the current tenancy, and at all times since the acquisition of the controlling interest the holding has been comprised in a tenancy or successive tenancies of a description specified in section 23(1) of this Act."

It would seem that the effect of this provision it limited:

---

523 As to which, see para.7–257.

524 s.42(3)(b).

(1) The prohibition does not apply to the company landlord only the person who has the controlling interest.[525] Thus, albeit there may have been a change in the controlling interest of the company landlord in the relevant period, that will simply prevent the person with the controlling interest from occupying; it will not prevent the company landlord from opposing.

(2) This extension of the five-year bar does not apply where the landlord is an individual and intends to occupy through a company, the controlling interest in which has only recently been acquired by the landlord.[526] The reason for this is that the purpose of the bar is to prevent those who have recently acquired the reversion from opposing renewal under ground (g); there is no objection to a landlord individual opposing renewal under the amended provisions of the Act simply because that individual intends to run the business through a newly acquired company. However, a landlord, who has formed a company incorporated specifically for the purpose of running the business intended to be carried on from the premises, cannot transfer the reversion to the company and oppose renewal through the company, even though the individual may possess a controlling interest in the company. For example, suppose an individual landlord who has held the reversion to a lease for 20 years, and intends to occupy the premises for the purposes of a business to be carried on by him. On advice, shortly before the hearing, he transfers the reversion to a newly incorporated company which intends to hold the reversion solely as a property-holding concern. The company is non-trading and is wholly owned by the individual. The individual controlling shareholder intends to carry on the business. None of the new sections would appear to assist here. The new company is the landlord and the normal provisions of s.30(2) would apply to its acquisition of the reversion. Even if the company can be said not to have "purchased" the interest of the landlord, the individual would still need to rely on s.30(1B) to which s.30(2A) applies. As the controlling interest was only acquired when the company was incorporated it would seem that the attempt by the individual to occupy in reliance on s.30(1B) would be thwarted by s.30(2A). Care must therefore be taken to ensure that the individual retains the landlord's interest until the procedures of the Act have been completed.

Beneficiaries under trust

By virtue of s.41(2), where the landlord's interest is held on trust, the references in para.(g) to the landlord shall be construed as including references to the beneficiaries under the trust or any of them–see *Sevenarts v Busvine*.[527] The apparently wide meaning of this provision has been cut down by judicial decisions (noted in para.1–89 et seq.). Where a landlord seeks to rely upon the trust provisions (i.e. by relying on the intention of the beneficiaries or any of **7–283**

[525] The terms of s.30(2A) apply only to s.30(1B) not s.30(1A).

[526] As to the meaning of "controlling interest", see para.7–254. There is no provision corresponding to s.30(2A) applicable to a situation where s.30(1A) applies.

[527] [1968] 1 W.L.R. 1929; [1969] 1 All E.R. 392 CA.

them[528]), the "five-year bar" will apply, if the trust was created within the five-year period: *Morar v Chauhan.*[529] In the case of a trust arising under a will or intestacy the interest of the landlord will be treated as having been purchased or created when it was purchased or created by or in favour of the deceased testator or intestate: *Gundry v Stewart.*[530] Difficulties may be encountered where there are two or more beneficiaries, only some of whom intend to occupy the premises, for something may then have to be done as to the remaining beneficiary's entitlement to otherwise occupy. Dealing with that beneficiary's entitlement may prevent reliance on ground (g) by reason of the five-year bar: see *Carshalton Beeches Bowling Club v Cameron*[531] (digested in para.1–101) and *Meyer v Riddick*[532] (digested in para.1–103).

Purchase by tenant of the reversion

7–284 What happens if an intermediate tenant, who himself would have had no difficulty under s.30(2), buys his landlord's interest after the relevant commencement date? If merger occurs, his interest will, prima facie, fall foul of s.30(2). The interest which he had before merger would not have done so but the wording of s.30(2) does not seem apt to enable him to rely upon his former interest. In other words, s.30(2) seems to be placing alternative hurdles in the landlord's way, rather than providing the landlord with alternative ways in which he can surmount the hurdle. If this is a correct analysis of s.30(2), the result seems harsh in cases such as the example given, since the transaction could easily have been arranged in such a way that merger did not occur and no relevant policy objective of the Act seems to be achieved in imposing the s.30(2) bar in one case if not in the other. In *Akin v Ward*[533] the mesne landlord, who had been granted a 10-year term, acquired the immediate freehold reversion to his lease. At the date of the tenant's application for renewal the mesne landlord's prior leasehold interest would, but for the merger upon his acquisition of the freehold reversion, have had less than 14 months to run. The mesne landlord was said to be caught by the five-year bar as his only qualifying interest under s.44 was as owner of the freehold and that interest had been purchased less than five years ago. However, it is considered that in light of *VCS Car Park Management Ltd v Regional Railways North East Ltd*[534] (digested in para.7–285), an intermediate tenant[535] who acquires the immediate reversion to his own leasehold interest will not be caught by the five-year bar so as to prevent him from relying on ground (g). In that case the landlord's interest was transferred pursuant to a statutory scheme with the landlord taking a lease back so as to remain the tenant's "landlord" for the purposes of the Act. It was held that the object of the subsection was not

[528] As opposed to his own interest as trustee.

[529] [1985] 1 W.L.R. 1263; [1985] 3 All E.R. 493; [1985] 2 E.G.L.R. 137 CA.

[530] [1959] C.L.Y. 1818 CA.

[531] [1979] 1 E.G.L.R. 80 CA.

[532] [1990] 1 E.G.L.R. 80 CA.

[533] [1981] C.L.Y. 1510 CC.

[534] [2001] Ch. 121; [2000] 3 W.L.R. 370; [2000] 1 All E.R. 403 CA.

[535] Being someone who qualified as competent landlord for the purposes of s.44, i.e. someone who had an interest in reversion in excess of 14 months.

undermined by allowing the landlord to object to the renewal of the tenant's lease. It was said that the object to the Act was to prevent exploitation of sitting tenants by landlords who acquired the reversion. This mischief has been held not to be present in the case of a landlord who obtains successive tenancies going back over a period exceeding the requisite five years.[536] It was said that this reasoning applied equally where the person claiming the interest starts as a freeholder and then becomes a lease-holder.

VCS Car Park Management Ltd v Regional Railways North East Ltd[537] VCS was granted a six-year tenancy on December 18, 1992 for a term commencing from August 21, 1991 to August 23, 1997. The premises consisted of a car park at Whitby Station in North Yorkshire and the landlord was British Railways Board ("the Board"). By October 2, 1996 the landlord under the lease had become Regional Railways North East Limited ("Regional Railways"). On October 2, 1996 Regional Railways served notice on VCS under s.25 terminating the tenancy with effect from August 23, 1997 and opposing renewal under para.(g). **7–285**

Regional Railways became landlord under the lease in a convoluted fashion. On March 30, 1994 the Secretary of State, in exercising its power under the Railways Act 1993, directed the Board to transfer to a new company, Railtrack, the undertaking of the Board. Railtrack was a company incorporated by statute. On the same day the transfer scheme was signed by the Board and by Railtrack. The transfer scheme effected, as from a date to be fixed by the Secretary of State, the transfer of the Board's undertaking to Railtrack. The demised premises were included in the transfer.

The transfer scheme was to take effect from April 1, 1994. Pursuant to the scheme there was also to be a lease back to the Board of all the property comprised in the transfer, including the demised premises, for a term of five years from April 1, 1994 to April 1, 1999. The effect of the transfer followed by the leaseback was, vis-à-vis the car park, that the Board had gone from being a freeholder to being a leaseholder under a five-year lease. The Board, lessee under the lease, became, as it had been as freeholder, the landlord of VCS under its lease.

On September 14, 1995 the Secretary of State made another direction under the Railways Act 1993 directing the Board to transfer to Railtrack the property comprised in the lease. This involved a surrender of the Board's existing reversionary lease with a new lease back to the Board of the car park. This lease ran for a term from September 17, 1995 to April 1, 1999.

On December 8, 1995 the Board surrendered to Railtrack the premises comprised in the second reversionary lease. However on the same day Railtrack granted yet another lease to the Board of the car park which ran from December 8, 1995 to March 21, 2001. On the same day, pursuant to another transfer scheme which had been directed by the Secretary of State, the Board's interest under this new, third reversionary lease, was transferred to Regional Railways. This came

[536] *Artemiou v Procopiou* [1965] 3 W.L.R. 1011; [1965] 3 All E.R. 539 CA (digested in para.7–276).
[537] [2001] Ch. 121; [2000] 3 W.L.R. 370; [2000] 1 All E.R. 403 CA.

into effect on December 10, 1995 so with effect from that date Regional Railways became landlord of VCS under the third reversionary lease which was to continue until March 31, 2001.

Finally, on March 2, 1997, yet another lease of the car park was granted by Railtrack to Regional Railway, the fourth reversionary lease, running from March 2, 1997 to December 1, 2004.

There was no appeal from the county court judge's determination that Regional Railways intended to occupy the premises for the purposes of a business to be carried on by them. It was contended, however, by the tenant that Regional Railways' interest was caught by s.30(2) in that its interest was created only in 1995.

It was held:

(1) as the Board was the holding company of Regional Railways, they were members of the same group for the purposes of s.42(3)(b) and thus the interest that had to be considered was that of the Board not Regional Railways;
(2) the mischief at which the Act is aimed is not offended by allowing a person in the position of the Board to object to the grant of a new tenancy under ground (g).

Where only part of the landlord's interest is caught by the five-year bar

7–286 A question arises as to whether the "interest" of the landlord includes circumstances where only part of the landlord's interest is caught by the five-year bar rule. It may happen, for instance, that the landlord acquires premises which are the subject matter of the tenancy in parts, for instance, the demised premises consist of, say, five warehouses demised under one lease. The landlord acquires three under one transaction and the remaining two under another. The first transaction is completed several years before the second is entered into and completed. In relation to the two warehouses viewed in isolation the landlord's interest is caught by the five-year bar. However, the landlord's interest in relation to the entirety is not caught by the five-year bar. It is unclear whether in these circumstances it can be said the "landlord's interest" has been purchased so as to fall foul of the five-year bar.

10. DISPOSAL OF APPLICATION

Dismissal where ground of opposition established

Tenant's application for renewal

7–287 Section 31(1) provides that where the landlord in opposition to the tenant's application for renewal has established any of the grounds of opposition under s.30(1) to the satisfaction of the court, the court shall dismiss the tenant's application for a new tenancy. Upon the dismissal of the tenant's application the current tenancy will continue for a period of three months beginning with the date on which the application is finally disposed of: s.64(1)(c), unless the landlord's s.25 notice or the tenant's s.26 request specifies a date of termination later than the said period of three months (which in practice is unlikely to be the case).

Landlord's termination application

By s.29(4), it is provided that where the landlord establishes to the satisfaction of the court any of the grounds of opposition under s.30(1): "the court shall make an order for termination of the current tenancy in accordance with s.64 of this Act without the grant of a new tenancy."[538] If the landlord does not establish any of the grounds of opposition the court shall make an order for the grant of a new tenancy and accordingly for the termination of the current tenancy immediately before the commencement of the new tenancy: s.29(4)(b). **7–288**

"Finally disposed of"

The reference to the date on which the "application is finally disposed of" is construed as a reference to the earliest date by which the proceedings on the application (including any proceedings on or in consequence of an appeal) have been determined and any time for appealing or further appealing has expired: s.64(2).[539] **7–289**

Dismissal under section 31(2)

Even where the landlord has not established a ground of opposition under s.30(1), the tenant will not be granted a new tenancy in certain circumstances, by virtue of s.31(2).[540] The provisions of this subsection apply where: **7–290**

(1) the landlord has specified ground (d) (suitable alternative accommodation), ground (e) (sub-letting of part) and/or ground (f) (demolition and reconstruction) in his s.25 notice or counter-notice[541];
(2) the landlord has failed to establish any of these grounds to the satisfaction of the court;
(3) the court would, however, have been satisfied of one of those grounds if the date specified in the s.25 notice or s.26 request had been a date later than was in fact specified (but not more than a year later).

If these conditions are satisfied, then:

(a) the court shall make a declaration to the effect that the ground or grounds would have been satisfied, if a different date had been specified in the s.25 notice or s.26 request, and the court shall specify that "different date";
(b) the court shall not make an order for a new tenancy.

---

538 s.29(4)(a).
539 See further para.3–227 et seq.
540 As amended by the 2003 Order.
541 As to the payment of compensation, see para.12–14.

This disposes of the tenant's application for a new tenancy or of the landlord's termination application so that, if he does nothing, his current tenancy will come to an end in the ordinary way pursuant to s.64 (see para.3–229). However, where the court has made such a declaration and has specified the "different date", the tenant may, within 14 days, apply to the court for an order substituting the "different date" for the date which was actually specified in the s.25 notice or s.26 request.[542] The effect of this is that the current tenancy continues until the "different date", rather than coming to an end on the date specified in the original s.25 notice or s.26 request, or the date upon which the current tenancy would have come to an end by virtue of s.64. The 14-day limit within which the tenant may apply for an order is a statutory time limit and therefore, presumably, cannot be extended by the court. However, since it is only procedural, it can presumably be dispensed with by agreement of the parties or waived by the landlord in accordance with the principle of *Kammins Ballrooms Co Ltd v Zenith Investments (Torquay) Ltd*[543] (digested in para.3–245). For a general discussion of "Waiver and estoppel", see para.3–232 et seq.

7–291 The effect of these provisions can be illustrated by an example[544] under each of grounds (d), (e) and (f).

7–292 **Example 1: Suitable alternative accommodation** The landlord has specified ground (d) (suitable alternative accommodation) in a s.25 notice which specifies as the date of termination March 25, 2008. At the trial on February 1, 2008, he proves all the necessary elements of ground (d) except for one–the premises which are intended to be offered as suitable alternative accommodation are subject to a unprotected tenancy the contractual term of which will not expire until December 25, 2008. He is thus unable to show that the date of availability is suitable for the tenant's requirements, because the current tenancy will determine on June 1, 2008, and the alternative premises will not, by that date, be available. However, if he had specified in his s.25 notice not March 25, 2008, but December 25, 2008, the current tenancy would have continued up to December 25, 2008. Since the landlord has proved that the alternative premises will be available by December 25, 2008, he would have satisfied ground (d), if he had specified that later date. Since December 25, 2008, is not more than one year later than March 25, 2008, the court would make a declaration substituting December 25, 2008, for the date specified in the s.25 notice. If the tenant took no action, his tenancy would come to an end on June 1, 2008. If he applied for December 25, 2008, to be substituted in the s.25 notice, then his tenancy would continue until that date.

It is to be noted that the provisions of s.31(2) assist the landlord only in respect of the date of availability of the suitable accommodation; they do not enable him to postpone the date at which he must satisfy the other elements of ground (d), such as the fact that he has made an offer of suitable alternative accommodation, or that he is "willing" at the date of the hearing to provide alternative accommodation at a further date.

542 As to the procedure for making such an application; see para.14–115 et seq.

543 [1970] 3 W.L.R. 287; [1970] 2 All E.R. 871 HL.

544 See also *Accountancy Personnel v Worshipful Company of Salters* (1972) 222 E.G. 1589 (digested in para.7–295).

Example 2: Current tenancy created by sub-letting of part The position under ground (e) (current tenancy created by sub-letting of part) can be illustrated by the following supposed facts. F is the freeholder, T is the tenant of the whole and S is the sub-tenant of part. F has served a s.25 notice on T, who has not applied for a new tenancy. F, as the "landlord" of S within the definition in s.44, has served a s.25 notice on him, relying on ground (e) and specifying March 25, 2008, as the date of termination. The trial takes place on February 1, 2008. F proves all the necessary elements of ground (e), save that he is unable to show that he "requires possession of the holding for the purpose of letting or otherwise disposing of" the property as a whole, because, due to an oversight, the date which he specified in the s.25 notice served upon T was December 25, 2008. On the termination of S's current tenancy on June 1, 2008, F will not "require" possession of the holding, because he will not be able to let it or otherwise dispose of it together with the rest of the property until T's tenancy has come to an end on December 25, 2008. However, if the date specified in the s.25 notice served upon S had been December 25, 2008, not March 25, 2002, S's current tenancy would not have come to an end until December 25, 2008, and F would have satisfied the court that he required possession on that date. Accordingly, the court would make a declaration to that effect and, if S made an application, would substitute December 25, 2008, for the date of March 25, 2008. **7–293**

Example 3: Demolition and reconstruction The landlord relies on ground (f) (demolition and reconstruction) and specifies March 25, 2008, as the date of termination. The trial takes place on February 1, 2008. The landlord proves all the necessary elements of ground (f), save that his application for planning permission has been refused by the local planning authority. The landlord's planning witness gives evidence, however, which the court accepts, that it is highly likely that permission will be given on appeal to the Secretary of State, but that the result of such an appeal will not be known before December 25, 2008. On these facts, the land-lord has failed to prove that "on the termination of the current tenancy", namely June 1, 2008, he will be in a position to implement his intention. However, if he had specified December 25, 2008, in his s.25 notice, the current tenancy would have continued until that date. Accordingly, the landlord could have satisfied the court that, if the tenancy had come to an end on that later date, he would have been in a position to implement his intention. Accordingly, the court would make a declaration to that effect and, if the tenant applied for December 25, 2008, to be substituted in the s.25 notice, his tenancy would continue until that date. It should be noted that s.31(2) does not relieve the landlord of proving, at the date of the hearing, that he has a genuine, firm and settled intention to carry out the relevant works. **7–294**

Accountancy Personnel Ltd v Worshipful Company of Salters[545] At the hearing in July 1971 of the tenant's application for a new tenancy the landlord opposed under ground (f). The evidence indicated that the premises were in a conservation area and that the redevelopment site included a number of listed buildings. The judge thought, on a consideration of the evidence, that permission **7–295**

545 (1972) 222 E.G. 1589; (1972) 116 S.J. 240.

would be obtained by (at the latest) June 1972. He accordingly held that the ground of opposition existed and was established, not at the termination of the tenancy (December 1971) but as at June 1972, and made a declaration in accordance with s.31(2). The tenant appealed and when the appeal came on in March 1972, it appeared that matters had not progressed as anticipated at the hearing and that permission was not likely to be obtained until sometime later. The Court of Appeal dismissed the appeal but substituted the date of September 29, 1972. Denning L.J. commented that, in this sort of case, it was proper for the Court of Appeal to take into account events which had happened since the date of the hearing.

Other circumstances in which an application will be dismissed or struck out

7–296 These include the following:

(1) Where the tenancy ceases to be one to which the Act applies after an application has been made for a new tenancy (see para.2–55 et seq.).
(2) Where the application is dismissed for want of prosecution, or failure to comply with the rules of the court as to service, or with a direction of the court.

Grant of new tenancy

7–297 Unless the landlord establishes a ground of opposition under s.30(1), or the court makes a declaration under s.31(2), or the tenant's renewal application is dismissed or struck out for some other reason, the court "shall make an order for the grant of a new tenancy and accordingly for the termination of the current tenancy immediately before the commencement of the new tenancy": s.29(1) and 29(4)(b). The new tenancy shall comprise such property, at such rent and on such other terms" as are provided by ss.32 to 35 inclusive. The terms of the new tenancy are determined according to the principles which we discuss in Ch.8. Where the landlord would have succeeded on ground (f) but for the tenant's willingness to accept a tenancy of an economically separable part, the court will order a new tenancy confined to that part: s.32(1A).

Compromise

7–298 The parties may agree that the application should, by consent, be dismissed, struck out or granted. As to the factors which need to be considered in determining whether an enforceable agreement has been reached and in submitting a consent order to the court see Ch.15.

11. MISREPRESENTATION

The statutory provision: old regime: pre June 1, 2004

Section 55 of the Act provided: **7–299**

> "Where under ... Part I of this Act the Court refuses an order for the grant of a new tenancy, and it is subsequently made to appear to the Court that the order was obtained, or the Court induced to refuse the grant, by misrepresentation or the concealment of material facts, the Court may order the landlord to pay to the tenant such sum as appears sufficient as compensation for damage or loss sustained by the tenant as the result of the order or refusal."

The landlord referred to in the Act was the landlord opposing the application for the new tenancy. The tenant was the person in respect of whom the grant of the new tenancy was refused: s.55(2). **7–300**

The most usual occasions upon which this section was considered was where the landlord had opposed the grant of a new tenancy under ground (f) or (g) of s.30(1). Sometimes the tenant was willing, without taking any steps to apply for a new tenancy, to accept the landlord's assertion that he intended to demolish or rebuild the premises or to occupy them for his own business purposes and agreed to go out of possession either when the current tenancy came to an end by effluxion of time, or earlier, by agreeing to surrender so as to accelerate the date upon which the landlord could resume possession. In those circumstances, if the tenant was induced by an innocent misrepresentation or concealment of material facts, the tenant would not be able to claim compensation under s.55. Section 55 applied only where *the court was induced*, by misrepresentation or concealment of material facts, to refuse an order for a new tenancy. In these circumstances the tenant could, of course, be able to establish a misrepresentation actionable at common law: see *Deeley v Maison AEL*.[546] **7–301**

New regime: post May 30, 2004

Section 55 has been repealed: s.28(2) and Sch.6 of the 2003 Order. New provisions have been inserted. A new s.37A has been inserted by art.20 of the 2003 Order. It provides: **7–302**

> "37A(1) Where the court–
> (a) makes an order for the termination of the current tenancy but does not make an order for the grant of a new tenancy, or
> (b) refuses an order for the grant of a new tenancy
> and it is subsequently made to appear to the court that the order was obtained, or the court was induced to refuse the grant, by misrepresentation or the concealment of material facts, the court may order the landlord to pay the tenant such sum as appears to be sufficient as compensation for damage or loss sustained by the tenant as a result of the order or refusal.
> (2) Where–
> (a) the tenant has quit the holding–
> (i) after making but withdrawing an application under s.24(1) of this Act; or

[546] Unreported July 28, 1989 CA.

(ii) without making such an application; and
(b) it is made to appear to the court that he did so by reason of misrepresentation or the concealment of material facts,

the court may order the landlord to pay to the tenant such sum as appears sufficient as compensation for damage or loss sustained by the tenant as the result of quitting the holding."

7–303 These provisions are much wider than s.55 of the 1954 Act. Section 55 did not apply to a tenant, who had accepted, in response to a landlord's s.25 notice opposing renewal, that the landlord would succeed in his renewal and, therefore, had declined to make an application. Nor did the section apply where the tenant, having instituted an application, subsequently withdrew it on the strength of the landlord's evidence. In both cases the tenant was unable to obtain compensation under s.55 albeit there was a material misrepresentation or concealment of material facts, although there might have been circumstances where the tenant could make a claim at common law. The new provisions enable compensation to be obtained where the misrepresentation or concealment of material facts has led to any of the following situations occurring:

(1) When the court has made an order terminating the current tenancy but not ordering the grant of a new tenancy. This will occur where the tenant, having made his application, then agrees for it to be dismissed. This reflects the wording of the new s.29(4)(a).
(2) Where the tenant has made an application under s.24(1) but the court has refused an order for the grant of a new tenancy.
(3) Where the tenant has made an application for renewal under s.24(1) and the tenant has subsequently withdrawn the application and quit the holding. This is likely to occur where the tenant has seen the evidence in support of the landlord's opposition and takes the view, based on that evidence, that the landlord will succeed and, therefore, rather than incurring the cost of going to court, simply quits. However, there must be a withdrawal of the application. If the tenant accepts a new but very short term by way of a compromise of the landlord's opposition to the renewal of his current tenancy there has been no withdrawal of the application: *McAleese v Menary*.[547]
(4) Where the tenant has simply quit the holding without making any application under s.24(1) of the Act. It is to be noted that there is nothing in s.37A(2)(ii) and (2)(b) to suggest that the tenant must have quit the holding in response to a ground of opposition contained in a landlord's s.25 notice or counter-notice to the tenant's s.26 request. There is nothing, therefore, preventing a tenant from making an application for damages for misrepresentation/concealment of material facts where the landlord has made various representations in correspondence leading up to the termination of the tenancy.

---

[547] [2010] Westlaw 4483760, Lands Tribunal for Northern Ireland, where the court refused to read "withdraw" as meaning "the disposal of the proceedings" under the virtually identical provisions contained in art.27(2)(a)(i) of the Business Tenancies (Northern Ireland) Order 1996.

Misrepresentation or concealment

There must, as with any claim for misrepresentation, be a representation of fact which is false. A statement of intent can be a relevant representation. However, the mere service of a s.25 notice relying on ground (f) cannot be taken as a representation, as the date that it is served, that the landlord has an intention to carry out the relevant work: *Inclusive Technology v Williamson*.[548] There must be more. If the landlord serves a covering letter in which he makes it clear that he has an intention at that time[549] or expresses orally to the tenant that he intends to do the work, such representations may amount to representations of fact, namely as to the state of mind of the landlord at that time. Any such representation by the landlord as to his intention is a continuing representation as to his state of mind.[550] If that changes over the course of time a failure to notify the tenant will give rise to a misrepresentation or concealment. However, the falsity of the continuing representation does not arise simply because the landlord is exploring other commercial options. As Hughes L.J. said: **7–304**

> "It is, I think, important to say in a case of this kind that a continuing representation of the kind given here, of an intention to renovate or refurbish, would not be rendered false simply because the landlord explored other commercial options; that is almost inevitably going to happen in a large number of cases. Accordingly, there is no question that there arises a duty upon the landlord to make periodic, or indeed continuous, fresh, informative statements to the tenant as to the progress of such other options as he may be exploring, the progress of any planning application, negotiations for finance, or for anything of that kind."[551]

Quitting before June 1, 2004

If the tenant has quit the holding before the 2003 Order came into force, any claim for misrepresentation will be governed by s.55, not s.37A: art.29(5) of the 2003 Order. **7–305**

Changes of mind

The Act does not seem to provide any safeguard to the tenant against a change of mind on the landlord's part between the time of the court hearing and the time that the landlord's interest vests in possession. As Denning L.J. said in *Fisher v Taylors Furnishing Stores*[552]: **7–306**

---

[548] [2009] EWCA Civ 718; [2010] 1 P. & C.R. 2.

[549] In *Inclusive Technology v Williamson* [2009] EWCA Civ 718; [2010] 1 P. & C.R. 2, the landlord had written to the tenant enclosing the s.25 and in the covering letter had stated that it was "... necessary to obtain vacant possession to carry out the intended work." The Court of Appeal held that the judge's finding that the landlord had formed the necessary intention at the time of the letter was "unassailable" (Carnwath L.J. at [5]). The letter it was said had to be read in the context of the fact that it had been preceded by a friendly warning of the possibility of refurbishment such as to require vacant possession and conversations with the landlord's agent and that the refurbishment was going ahead and would require vacant possession.

[550] *Inclusive Technology v Williamson* [2009] EWCA Civ 718; [2010] 1 P. & C.R. 2 following the contractual position as reflected in the well known decision of *With v O'Flanagan* [1936] Ch. 575 CA.

[551] [2009] EWCA Civ 718; [2010] 1 P. & C.R. 2 at [34].

[552] [1956] 2 Q.B. 78 at 84; [1956] 2 W.L.R. 985; [1956] 2 All E.R. 78 CA.

> "it must be remembered that if the landlord, having got possession, [under ground (f)], honestly changes his mind and does not do any work of reconstruction, the tenant has no remedy. Hence the necessity for a firm and settled intention".

One way to overcome this particular problem of a change of mind is for the tenant to enter into an agreement to surrender containing provision that the landlord will, in the event that he fails to carry out his stated intention, pay to the tenant such sum as will compensate the tenant for damage or loss sustained by him as a result of the surrender. It is not necessary there should be any reference specifically to misrepresentation and concealment, since the required effect will be achieved by the provision that compensation becomes payable (1) if at any time after the date of the agreement it appears that the landlord has no intention to demolish or rebuild, etc. or has abandoned any such intention, or (2) if the demolition, rebuilding, etc. is not begun/completed by the landlord within a specified time. The tenant will, of course, have received the statutory compensation (assuming the only specified grounds are (e), (f) and/or (g)). The agreement will have to comply with s.38A(2).

CHAPTER 8

THE TERMS OF THE NEW TENANCY

1. PROPERTY, DURATION, RENT AND OTHER TERMS OF NEW TENANCY TO BE AGREED BETWEEN THE PARTIES OR DETERMINED BY THE COURT

The Act deals, in four separate sections, with the four fundamental constituents of the new tenancy to be granted by the court. What property is to be comprised in the new tenancy is governed by s.32, which is discussed in detail below (para.8–06 et seq.). What is to be the duration of the new tenancy is governed by s.33, which will also be discussed in detail (para.8–21 et seq.). What is to be the rent payable under the new tenancy is governed by s.34 (para.8–90). The "other terms" of the tenancy are governed by s.35 (para.8–45 et seq.). No amendments were made by the 2003 Order to ss.32, 34 or 35 (other than consequential amendments and amendments to s.34 to reflect the controlling interest provisions contained within s.23(1A)). Section 33 has been amended so as to extend the court's jurisdiction to grant a term of 15 years.[1] **8–01**

Agreement on all or some of the terms

In relation to property, duration, rent and other terms each of the relevant sections provides, first, for agreement between the parties and, in default of agreement, for the matter to be determined by the court. The wording of s.32 differs slightly from that of the other sections since it speaks of "absence of agreement" rather than "default of agreement" and the court is to "designate" rather than "determine" the matter in dispute. However, it is not considered that there is any significance in the difference in wording between the sections. **8–02**

By virtue of s.69(2) "agreement" means "agreement in writing". Clearly, there may be agreement under one of the sections binding upon landlord and tenant without there necessarily being agreement upon matters arising under one or more of the other sections. In other words agreement need not be total, it may be piecemeal. In *Derby v ITC*[2] (digested in para.8–04), the court had to consider the position where the parties had reached agreement "subject to contract" for the grant of a new contractual tenancy. The "subject to contract" agreement embraced all the matters mentioned in ss.32 to 35. The court held that this agreement did not bind the parties for the purpose of the application, because (1) it was **8–03**

[1] See para.8–26.
[2] [1977] 2 All E.R. 890.

expressed to be "subject to contract" and was not therefore intended to be binding and (2) it was not intended to be an agreement for the purposes of ss.32 to 35.

8–04 ***Derby & Co Ltd v ITC Pension Trust Ltd***[3] The landlords served a s.25 notice stating that they would not oppose the grant of a new tenancy and the tenants duly gave counter-notice and applied to the court. The summons was adjourned generally by consent, pending negotiations between surveyors. The tenants' surveyor wrote to the landlords' surveyor a letter marked "subject to contract", in which they confirmed that terms as to rent, duration and certain other terms had been "agreed on behalf of the tenants without prejudice to their rights under the Landlord and Tenant Act procedures". The parties' solicitor agreed the form of draft lease, which was duly engrossed, but not executed or exchanged. Then the tenants wrote to the landlords' surveyors, stating that in view of changes in the market they wished to renegotiate the agreed terms. The adjourned summons was brought on for hearing.

The issue before the court was whether there had been an agreement between landlords and tenants on the duration, rent and other terms for the purposes of ss.33, 34 and 35, so that the court was required to order a new tenancy in those terms, or whether there had been no such agreement so that the court, in default, retained jurisdiction to determine those matters itself.

The landlord argued that there was an agreement between the parties for the purposes of the Act or, alternatively, that the tenants were estopped from resiling from their agreement because the landlords had thereby been induced to refrain from applying for an interim rent pursuant to s.24A.

(1) It was held that the agreement on terms was not an "agreement" within the meaning of ss.33, 34 and 35, because that was a reference to an agreement made for the purposes of an application to the court. The agreement in the present case was not such an agreement, because it was made in an attempt to avoid the necessity of an application to the court and was made without prejudice to the tenants' rights under the 1954 Act and "subject to contract".
(2) No estoppel arose because there was no evidence that the tenants had requested the landlords not to make any application for an interim rent and there was always the risk, when parties negotiated "subject to contract", that one of the parties would back out of the negotiations before leases were exchanged.

8–05 It follows that negotiations between the parties may result in one of the four following situations:

(1) The parties may reach agreement, as a matter of contract, for the grant of a future tenancy within the meaning of s.28. The effect of this is considered later (para.15–21 et seq.). For such an agreement to be binding, however, it will have to comply with all the normal requirements, in particular those of the Law of Property (Miscellaneous Provisions) Act 1989. An "agreement

[3] [1977] 2 All E.R. 890.

by correspondence" would not be sufficient: see *Commission for the New Towns v Cooper (Great Britain) Ltd*.[4]

(2) The parties may reach agreement, for the purposes of the application, upon all four matters dealt with in ss.32 to 35. The effect of this, as recognised in *Derby v ITC*[5] (digested in para.8–04), is that the court is bound to make a formal order embodying the terms which have been agreed.[6] It is thought that such an agreement, being one made for the purposes of, and in accordance with, the 1954 Act, does not have to comply with the Law of Property (Miscellaneous Provisions) Act 1989, but the point remains undecided.

(3) The parties may reach an agreement for the purposes of the application on some only of the matters governed by ss.32 to 35. They will not then be able to resile from that agreement and the court will be bound by the agreed terms in making its order for a new tenancy.[7] The matters which have not been agreed remain to be determined by the court.

(4) There may be no agreement for the purposes of the application on any of the matters governed by ss.32 to 35, in which case they must all be determined by the court. The remaining paragraphs of this Part assume that this is the position which has been reached.

2. THE PROPERTY (SECTION 32)

Usually confined to the "holding"

Subject to special considerations which are discussed below,[8] the property to be comprised in the new tenancy is to consist of "the holding". In determining what is the holding, one starts with the property comprised in the current tenancy and then subtracts any part thereof which is not occupied by the tenant or by a person employed by the tenant for the purposes of the business which brings the tenancy within the Act: s.23(3). The test is one of occupation (see paras 1–42 et seq. and 1–80 et seq.). It is not necessary that the tenant should occupy the whole of the premises for business purposes; if he occupies part for business purposes and the rest for some other purpose, the holding comprises both parts which he occupies. However, when the occupation relied upon is that of employees of the tenant, their employment must be in the same business as that which attracts the protection of the Act. For example, if the tenant runs a restaurant and accommodates his waiters in residential accommodation above, both the restaurant and the residential accommodation will comprise "the holding". If, however, the residential accommodation was occupied by persons employed by the tenant in connection with another business which he carried on elsewhere, the residential accommodation would be excluded from the holding. **8–06**

---

[4] [1995] 2 E.G.L.R. 113 CA.

[5] [1977] 2 All E.R. 890.

[6] See also *Behar, Ellis & Parnell v Territorial Investments Ltd* [1973] CAT 237 CA considered in para.15–23.

[7] See *Boots v Pinkland* [1992] 2 E.G.L.R. 58.

[8] Paras 8–19 and 8–20.

Date of designation of the "holding"

8–07 Section 32(1) provides that the court shall "designate [the property which constitutes the holding] by reference to the circumstances existing at the date of the order". The "date of the order" is the date when an order is made for a new tenancy, not the hearing at first instance or on appeal of a preliminary point: see *I&H Caplan Ltd v Caplan (No.1)*[9] (digested on this point in para.8–09).

8–08 In *Narcissi v Wolfe*[10] (digested in para.8–10), it was held that the premises genuinely occupied by the tenant at the date of the order constituted the "holding" irrespective of his motive for occupying them. Roxburgh J. in that case indicated in somewhat tentative terms that at least for the purposes of s.23(3) and s.32 occupation in breach of covenant has to be ignored. This goes further than s.23(4) which provides that the Act will apply where the business is being carried on in breach of covenant prohibiting business use of a particular kind, but not prohibiting business use generally: see para.1–129 et seq.

8–09 ***I&H Caplan Ltd v Caplan***[11] On December 23, 1958, the landlords gave notice terminating the tenants' tenancy and opposed the grant of a new tenancy under ground (g) of s.30. On April 14, 1959, the tenants applied to the High Court by originating summons for the grant of a new tenancy. The question of the landlords' intention to occupy was treated as a separate issue and was decided by the judge in favour of the landlords. The parties then agreed that the originating summons should be treated as being before the judge and the judge thereupon made an order dismissing it with costs. The tenants appealed to have the judge's decision set aside and sought an order that they be entitled to a new tenancy. The landlords then sought an order that the tenants' appeal be struck out on the ground that the tenants had ceased to carry on business in the premises and had no intention of remaining there and, therefore, there was no "holding" at the date of the appeal in respect of which there could be granted a new tenancy. The Court of Appeal decided in favour of the landlords. The position when the Court of Appeal made their order was that there had been no inquiry into the facts except on the question of the landlords' intention to occupy under s.30(1)(g). The Court of Appeal, therefore, referred the matter back to the Chancery Division to determine whether, at the date of the order by the Court of Appeal, the tenants were entitled to the grant of a new tenancy of the premises. The tenants appealed against the order of the Court of Appeal. The House of Lords held that "the holding" for the purposes of s.32 should be determined by an investigation into the factual position not at the date of the order made by the Court of Appeal but at the later date of the order for the grant of a new tenancy. The tenants' appeal, therefore, succeeded.

---

[9] [1962] 1 W.L.R. 55; [1961] 3 All E.R. 1174 HL.

[10] [1960] Ch. 10; [1959] 3 W.L.R. 431; [1959] 3 All E.R. 71.

[11] [1962] 1 W.L.R. 55; [1961] 3 All E.R. 1174 HL. On the issue of whether or not the tenant was in "occupation", see the case digest at para.1–46.

Narcissi v Wolfe[12] The tenant was granted a lease of premises consisting of a ground floor, basement and three upper floors. The tenant used the basement and ground floor in connection with his business of a restaurateur and the three upper floors were sub-let. The sub-tenant of the first floor left and the tenant then began using that floor as temporary storage space for food and furniture and occasional office use. The tenant made an application for a new tenancy. 8–10

(1) It was held that the holding for the purposes of the new tenancy was to consist of the ground floor, basement and first floor only.
(2) In determining whether the tenant was in occupation of the first floor the evidence of office use was to be excluded, for it was negligible and in breach of covenant; occupation cannot be based upon acts which are in breach of covenant. The tenant was, however, in occupation of the first floor as the tenant was using that for storage in connection with his business as restaurateur.

It follows from these two decisions that the tenant has considerable scope for improving his position by enlarging the "holding" before the date of the order. For example, part of the premises might be sub-let at the date when the landlord serves s.25 notices on the tenant and sub-tenant. If the sub-tenant does not apply for a new tenancy, but vacates the sub-let part before the hearing of the tenant's application for a new tenancy, the tenant can, if he wishes, move into occupation of the sub-let part before the date of the hearing, in which case he will be entitled to a new tenancy of the whole of the property. 8–11

We have discussed[13] the test of economic separability of part of the holding under s.31A(2). The tenant who fears that he will have difficulty in showing that the part which he wishes to retain satisfies this test can, it is suggested, rearrange his affairs before the hearing in such a way as to circumvent the statutory test of economic separability. Since the works to be considered under ground (f) are those which are to be carried out on "the holding" and since the question of what is "the holding" depends upon what parts of the premises comprised in the current tenancy are occupied by the tenant at the date of the hearing, the tenant can simply move out of those parts other than that which he wishes to be treated as "economically separable", in which case the size of the holding will be reduced to that smaller part which he still occupies and the application of ground (f) and of s.31 must be considered in relation to that smaller holding.

Includes certain rights

The tenancy ordered by the court may also include "rights enjoyed by the tenant in connection with the holding" under the current tenancy: s.32(3). The word "rights" is clearly apt to include easements such as rights of way, rights of light, etc. (See *Nevill Long v Firmenich*[14] (digested in para.1–35) and para.1–30 et seq.) It was held under s.5 of the Landlord and Tenant Act 1927 that fishing rights 8–12

[12] [1960] Ch. 10; [1959] 3 W.L.R. 431; [1959] 3 All E.R. 71.
[13] In para.7–208 et seq.
[14] [1983] 2 E.G.L.R. 76 CA.

might be included as part of the premises demised by a lease: *Whitley v Stumbles*.[15] However it has been held in *Re No.1 Albemarle Street*[16] (digested in para.8–16) that a mere licence, such as a right to maintain an advertising hoarding on the face of a building, was not a "right" within s.32(3) (although such a right may be included as a term of the new lease under s.35). The court cannot treat the tenancy as including under s.32(3) or confer in relation to a tenancy under s.35(1), rights which are not conferred by a lease. Thus, in *Orlik v Hastings and Thanet*[17] (digested in para.8–18), it was held that a licence to park cars on land not comprised in the holding was not to be included in the new tenancy as a "right" under s.32(3). Similarly in *J Murphy & Sons Ltd v Railtrack Plc*[18] (digested in para.8–142) it was held that no right of access to premises, where none existed under the terms of the existing lease, could be implied under s.32(3). In *Kirkwood v Johnson* (digested in para.8–17), the current tenancy contained an option to purchase the freehold reversion. The option had not been exercised within the time limit laid down in the current tenancy and the Court of Appeal, without deciding whether the option was a "right" within the meaning of s.32(3), held that because the option had lapsed it could not be said to be a right "enjoyed by the tenant" at the date the matter came before the court.

8–13 The only rights which can be included are those which "attach to the holding". It follows that if the tenant of a shop and upper part had sub-let the upper part so that it was excluded from the holding, he would not be entitled to have included in his new tenancy rights of access exclusively enjoyed by the upper part. Although it is clear from the foregoing that the tenant cannot acquire greater rights in respect of his new tenancy than subsist under the current tenancy at the date the matter comes before the court, he is not necessarily entitled to all rights which do subsist. It is provided by s.32(3) that the parties may agree, or the court may determine in default of agreement, that some rights previously enjoyed should not be included in the new tenancy.[19] This is to be contrasted with the court's role in determining "the holding" which involves no discretion to cut down the holding, as defined. Where a right contained in the current tenancy is inappropriate because of the passage of time, or where, e.g. the landlord offers in substitution for an existing right of way one which is equally beneficial to the tenant but which is more convenient to the landlord, the old right need not be included in the new tenancy.

8–14 A right enjoyed by the tenant during his tenancy but which falls outside s.32(3) may, nevertheless, be imposed as a term of the new lease pursuant to s.35(1): *Picture Warehouse Ltd v Cornhill Investments Ltd*.[20] Whether or not such an order is to be made will depend on the facts.

---

[15] [1930] A.C. 544 HL.

[16] [1959] 2 W.L.R. 171; [1959] 1 All E.R. 250.

[17] (1975) 29 P. & C.R. 126; [1975] E.G.D. 104 CA.

[18] [2002] EWCA Civ 679; [2012] 1 E.G.L.R. 48.

[19] See as an interesting example the comments by Chadwick L.J. with respect to the tenant's rights to retain chattels and tenant's fixtures on the land where the tenant was under an obligation to deliver up the site clear of all buildings: see *Wessex Reserve Forces and Cadets Association v White* [2005] EWHC 983 (QB); [2005] 3 E.G.L.R. 127; upheld on appeal [2005] EWCA 1744; [2006] 2 P. & C.R. 45.

[20] [2008] EWHC 45 (QB); [2008] E.G.L.R. 29.

Picture Warehouse Ltd v Cornhill Investments Ltd[21] T was, and had been for some years, the tenant of premises on the second floor in a building used principally as a multi-storey car park. T had three parking spaces on the first floor. At the end of that lease T agreed to surrender the second floor premises and to take a new lease of the ground floor and to surrender two of its three spaces in return for two spaces the forecourt at the front of the building. T's rent was to be reduced by £500 per annum. L was not the freehold owner of the land. A dispute arose between L and the freehold owner of the forecourt. T became concerned about its ability to use the forecourt. L wrote in October 2000 to T informing it that parking on the forecourt would be allowed for a maximum of 30 mins at a time. No designated spaces were in fact provided. Several years later, in 2003, a new three-year lease was entered into. It made no reference to T's use of the forecourt. On the expiry of the three-year lease T sought a renewal and argued that it was entitled as a term of the renewed lease to a right to park two vehicles on the forecourt for no more than 30 mins at a time. It was held: **8–15**

(1) That whatever rights T had over the front land were outside the terms of the lease and thus could not fall within s.32(3).
(2) That the court could grant a right equivalent to that conferred by the letter pursuant to s.35 but that it was inappropriate to do so on the facts of the case as:
    (a) The licence although contractual and not simply gratuitous, was revocable.
    (b) T had accepted that as the position in 2000 and 2003.
    (c) The right conferred by the letter was not one to the certainty of two spaces but was a right to share with others.
(3) T had not established a case for the right to be one for two spaces which was irrevocable; the rights under the letter were still available to T.

Re No.1 Albemarle Street[22] The current tenancy contained the following clause: "The lessors hereby permit and authorise the lessees to maintain during the continuance of this lease the advertising signs . . . in their present position . . . outside the building of which the demised premises form part." When the tenant applied for a new tenancy under the 1954 Act the landlord resisted the inclusion of this clause. It was held that the court did not have jurisdiction to insert such a clause under s.32 as a "right enjoyed by the tenant in connection with the holding" so as to be included in the new tenancy as part of "the holding". However, it was a "term" of the new tenancy within the meaning of s.35. On the facts, the discretion was exercised by including the clause in the new tenancy. **8–16**

Kirkwood v Johnson[23] Premises were demised for a term of a little over five years by a lease which contained an option for the tenant to acquire the freehold of the premises for a stated price, exercisable by notice given not less than three **8–17**

21 [2008] EWHC 45 (QB); [2008] E.G.L.R. 29. T could have avoided the problem which he encountered by ensuring that the rights were set out in a document expressed to be supplemental to the lease.
22 [1959] Ch. 531; [1959] 2 W.L.R. 171; [1959] 1 All E.R. 250.
23 [1979] E.G.L.R. 82 CA.

months before expiration of the term. The tenant did not exercise the option. The landlord served a s.25 notice and the tenant applied for a new tenancy. The deputy judge granted a new tenancy of five years and included as a term thereof an option to purchase the freehold, at an increased price. It was held on appeal that the court had no jurisdiction under s.35 to include a new option, because to do so would be to create a new saleable asset in the hands of the tenant, enlarge "the holding" as defined by s.32(3) and interfere with the landlord's property rights in a way that would require express statutory authority.

8–18 ***G Orlik Meat Products Ltd v Hastings and Thanet Building Society***[24] The tenants had a seven-year lease of a rectangular piece of yard ("the demised premises") adjoining the tenant's main premises (which were held under a different title). Part of the yard ("the landlord's part"), at the far side of the tenant's main premises was excluded from the demise and remained in the possession of the landlord. The tenant had an express right to use the landlord's part for the purposes of access to and egress from the demised premises. There was a covenant in the lease prohibiting obstruction of the landlord's part by permitting or suffering vehicles or merchandise to stand thereon. When the tenant came to apply for a new tenancy, it claimed that there should have been included in the lease the right to park two vehicles, partly on the landlord's part. The Court of Appeal reversed the county court judge's finding that the right to park the two vehicles was included in the current tenancy, and rejected an alternative argument based on proprietary estoppel, stating: "We conclude that neither by the effect of a grant contained in the lease, nor by the effect of an irrevocable licence or any equity have the tenants as against the landlords any such right of parking as is claimed." Accordingly, s.32(3) (which defines the premises to be included in the new tenancy as being "the holding") could not assist the tenant. The Court of Appeal then considered whether, by virtue of s.35, the court had jurisdiction to include the rights of parking in the new tenancy. It was held that the court had no jurisdiction to enlarge "the holding" by ordering the grant of an easement over the landlord's part, or conferring rights over the landlord's part not hitherto enjoyed.

Where the tenancy comprises property other than "the holding"

8–19 Although the tenant is only entitled to apply for a new tenancy of "the holding", the landlord can insist under s.32(2) that, in addition to the holding, the tenancy should comprise the rest of the property comprised in the current tenancy. This enables a landlord, who is reluctant to see his property sub-divided, to require the tenant to take an overriding lease of the whole, and with it, all problems connected with the management of the sub-tenants, e.g. see *Atkey v Collman*.[25] Section 32(2) does not expressly impose any time limit upon the landlord for exercising this right. The landlord is required to make his election in his acknowledgement of service: CPR PD 56 para.3.6(5).

---

[24] (1975) 29 P. & C.R. 126; [1975] E.G.D. 104 CA.
[25] (1955) 105 L.J. 396 CC.

Economically separable part of the holding

Where s.31A(1)(b) applies, the court will order the grant of a new tenancy of the economically separable part of the holding.[26] **8–20**

3. DURATION OF NEW TENANCY (SECTION 33)

Date upon which new tenancy is to commence

The date upon which the new tenancy will commence is not within the discretion of the court. It is provided by s.33 that it "shall begin on the coming to an end of the current tenancy". The date on which the current tenancy comes to an end is governed by ss.24, 25, 26 and 64 (see para.3–228 et seq. and *Re 88 High Road, Kilburn*[27] (digested in para.8–22). **8–21**

Re 88 High Road, Kilburn: Meakers v DAW Consolidated Properties[28] The tenant held business premises under a lease for a term of 36-and-three-quarter years from September 29, 1921. The landlord served a notice under s.25 terminating the tenancy on June 24, 1958, and stating that it would not oppose an application to the court for a new tenancy. The tenant made an application to the court for a new tenancy. The landlord accepted that a new tenancy should be granted, but was in dispute with the tenant over the date from which the new lease was to begin. **8–22**

It was held that the effect of the provision in s.25(1) is to apply s.64 and the provisions relating to interim continuation contained therein and, if the conditions stated in paras (a), (b) and (c) of s.64(1) are fulfilled, then the notice given by the landlord under s.25(1) ceases to be of any effect so far as terminating the tenancy at the date specified in the notice and the tenancy will be continued and will only be terminated under the provisions of s.64. Accordingly, the new tenancy was to begin, at the earliest, three months from the decision of the court.

Length of tenancy

Form of court order

Although the commencement date of the current tenancy is, as has been stated, defined as a matter of law, the courts in the past adopted the somewhat confusing practice of ordering the grant of a term of years from a particular date, even though the court cannot know at that time when the current tenancy will come to an end and, accordingly, when the new tenancy will begin. This practice has been disapproved by the Court of Appeal in *Michael Chipperfield v Shell (UK) Ltd*[29] (digested in para.8–32), where it was suggested that the court should instead make an order for a tenancy from the termination of the current tenancy (without **8–23**

---

[26] See para.7–209.
[27] [1959] 1 W.L.R. 279; [1959] 1 All E.R. 527.
[28] [1959] 1 W.L.R. 279; [1959] 1 All E.R. 527.
[29] [1980] 1 E.G.L.R. 51 CA.

naming a date) with a specified date of termination. This practice was followed in *Turone v Howard de Walden Estates*[30] (digested in para.8–24). Ironically, this can lead to the result that, if the date of termination is not very far ahead, it may have passed before the termination of the current tenancy. See, by way of example, *O'May v City of London Real Property Co Ltd*[31] (digested in para.8–47).

8–24 ***Turone v Howard de Walden Estates***[32] The county court judge, when granting the tenant a new tenancy, ordered that it was to be for a term of seven years without expressing a commencement date. The landlords appealed to the Court of Appeal against the judge's order relating to the rent to be paid on the new tenancy. After that appeal, the parties applied to the judge for clarification of his order. The judge, having rejected a submission that he had no jurisdiction to correct the order, ordered that the new tenancy was to commence on January 15, 1981. However, by reason of s.64, the current tenancy did not expire until May 11, 1982. On appeal by the tenant it was held that when the judge grants a new tenancy, its commencement date will in most cases be uncertain because of the possibility of appeals and the effect of s.64. However, the expiry date of the new tenancy can be specified and the judge should order that when the new lease comes to be executed—that is, when the matter is finally disposed of—the term of the lease to be executed shall be for a term ending on a date specified.

8–25 The date of commencement of the new tenancy is of some importance, because so long as the current tenancy subsists the tenant is required only to pay the old rent (or an interim rent) and to abide by the terms of the current tenancy. Once the new tenancy has begun, the tenant is obliged to pay the new rent and abide by the terms of the new tenancy.

Maximum duration to be ordered by court

8–26 Although the parties are permitted by s.33 to agree that the tenancy will be for as long a term of years as they wish, the jurisdiction of the court in default of agreement is circumscribed. The court may either grant a periodic tenancy or a tenancy for a term of years not exceeding 15 years.[33] The court can, by consent, order a longer term: see *Janes v Harlow*[34] (digested in para.8–148) (20-year term granted).

---

30 [1983] 2 E.G.L.R. 65 CA.

31 [1983] A.C. 726; [1982] 2 W.L.R. 407; [1982] 1 All E.R. 660 HL.

32 [1983] 2 E.G.L.R. 65 CA.

33 The maximum period which, prior to June 1, 2004, could be granted by the court, in the absence of agreement between the parties, was 14 years.

34 [1980] 1 E.G.L.R. 52.

Court's discretion as to length

Circumstances affecting exercise of discretion

Subject to the limit upon the maximum term which can be granted, it is for the court to determine what is "reasonable in all the circumstances".[35] These circumstances may include: **8–27**

(1) The difficulty which the landlord may have if he has to re-let the premises after a very short term. The court has a discretion, if it thinks fit, to grant the tenant a term longer than the tenant wants: *Re Sunlight House*[36] (digested in para.8–29).

(2) The length of the current tenancy; this was the reason given by the Court of Appeal in *Betty's Cafes*[37] for cutting down from 14 to 5 years the length of term granted to the tenants by the trial judge. The House of Lords did not have to consider this point, since it reversed the Court of Appeal's ruling on the question of whether there should be a new tenancy at all.

(3) The fact that the tenant has been in occupation, under a series of tenancies, for a number of years.

(4) The length of time the current tenancy has been continued under s.24: see *London and Provincial Millinery Stores v Barclays Bank Ltd*[38] and *Frederick Lawrence Ltd v Freeman Hardy & Willis Ltd*[39] (digested in para.7–280) (compare *Becker v Hill Street Properties*[40] (digested in para.8–85)).

(5) The nature of the tenant's business; it may be such that a long period of security of tenure is essential in order to preserve the tenant's good-will and to enable him to make sufficient capital investment in his business. Conversely, in *CBS UK Ltd v London Scottish Properties*[41] the court granted the tenant the short term it desired, although the landlord wished it to take a 14-year term. The court attached little weight to evidence of what term would have been granted in the market, but instead considered all the circumstances, including the tenant's desire to relocate its business in the near future. This is to be contrasted with *Charles Follett Ltd v Cabtell Investments Ltd*[42] where the court required the tenant to take the 10-year term contended for by the landlord, but gave the tenant the right to break on six months' notice exercisable "once and for all" at the commencement of the new tenancy.

---

35 s.35.

36 (1959) 173 E.G. 311.

37 *Betty's Cafes Ltd v Phillips Furnishings Stores Ltd* [1957] Ch. 67; [1956] 3 W.L.R. 1134; [1957] 1 All E.R. 1 CA.

38 [1962] 1 W.L.R. 510; [1962] 2 All E.R. 163 CA.

39 [1959] Ch. 731; [1959] 3 W.L.R. 275; [1959] 3 All E.R. 77 CA.

40 [1990] 2 E.G.L.R. 78 CA. Where the tenant paid a higher rent during the continuation tenancy than that reserved by the lease, this made the length of holding over irrelevant. It would appear that the rent so paid was not pursuant to a determination as to an interim rent, but arose out of negotiations between the parties.

41 [1986] 2 E.G.L.R. 125.

42 [1986] 2 E.G.L.R. 76 (first instance).

(6) The tenant's impending retirement: *Becker v Hill Street Properties*[43] (digested in para.8–85).

(7) The fact that the landlord, although barred by the five-year rule, wishes to occupy the premises for its own business: *Upsons v Robins*[44]; *Michael Chipperfield v Shell (UK) Ltd*[45]; (digested in para.8–32); *Wig Creations v Colour Film Services Ltd.*[46] However, the fact that the landlord has purchased the reversionary interest with the intention of occupying the relevant premises for the purposes of his own business does not enable the landlord to contend that the five-year period from the date of purchase represents a ceiling beyond which the Court ought not, in its discretion, extend the term of the new tenancy: *Wig Creations v Colour Film Services Ltd.*[47]

(8) The hardship to the landlord if a long term were to be granted: *Upsons v Robins*[48] (above).

(9) The hardship to the tenant if a short term were granted: *Amika Motors v Colebrook Holdings*[49] (digested in para.8–84). The relative status of the parties: *Upsons v Robins*[50] (above).

(10) The fact that the tenant's tenancy will be one to which the 1954 Act applies: *Adams v Green*[51] (digested in para.8–82); *National Car Parks Ltd v Paternoster Consortium Ltd*[52] (digested in para.8–86).

(11) The fact that the tenant wishes to limit original tenant liability: *Rumbelows v Tameside Metropolitan BC*[53] (digested in para.8–31).

(12) The fact that the relationship between the parties is such that it should not be unnecessarily prolonged: *Orenstein v Duan.*[54]

(13) The fact that the application is being pursued for the benefit of a purchaser from the tenant: *Lyons v Central Commercial Properties Ltd.*[55]

Short term

8–28 In most of the reported cases from which some of the above points are gleaned, the tenant was seeking a long term and the landlord was trying to cut it down. However, during the recent recession tenants have started to seek short terms. A number of arguments have been advanced on behalf of tenants: (1) the rental market is such that the premises will be over-rentalised. A long lease with upward

---

43 [1990] 2 E.G.L.R. 78 CA.
44 [1955] 3 W.L.R. 584; [1955] 3 All E.R. 348 CA.
45 [1980] 1 E.G.L.R. 51 CA.
46 [1969] 20 P. & C.R. 870 CA.
47 [1969] 20 P. & C.R. 870 CA, where the court ordered a term for a period one year in excess of the five-year period of ownership which the landlord required to oppose under s.30(1)(g).
48 [1955] 3 W.L.R. 584; [1955] 3 All E.R. 348 CA. See also *Joss v Bennett* [1956] E.G.D. 228 (digested in para.7–167).
49 (1981) 259 E.G. 243 CA.
50 [1955] 3 W.L.R. 584 CA.
51 [1978] 2 E.G.L.R. 46 CA.
52 [1990] 1 E.G.L.R. 99.
53 Unreported 1994 but noted at [1994] 13 E.G. 102.
54 Unreported May 5, 1983 CA.
55 [1958] 1 W.L.R. 869 CA at 1881, per Harman J. (digested in para.7–21).

only reviews will have the effect that the tenant is paying more than the market rent; (2) the fact that in such circumstances the tenant will find it difficult to assign the lease; and (3) the tenant wishes to avoid some of the disadvantages of the original tenant's ability. The landlord's arguments against a short term have included: (a) that the value of the landlord's reversionary interest will be diminished; (b) that the value of the landlord's surrounding property will be diminished; (c) the fact that a short term would not be granted in the market place; and (d) that it is inconvenient to deal with a short term in that renewal under the 1954 Act occurs more frequently. The decisions have invariably favoured tenants.

Factors which have been given little weight by the court are:

(i) The fact that the tenant has a rigid policy of wanting a particular (short) term: *Rumbelows v Tameside Metropolitan BC*.[56]
(ii) What would be granted to the tenant in the market; *CBS UK Ltd v London Scottish Properties*[57] (digested in para.8–30).
(iii) The diminution to the landlord's reversion where there is no evidence of the landlord intending to sell; *CBS UK Ltd v London Scottish Properties*.[58]

Re Sunlight House, Quay Street, Manchester[59] The tenant of an office building, having been granted a 10-year term in September 1948, requested a renewal of the tenancy for a term commencing from February 4, 1959 to August 4, 1959. The landlord wanted a three-year term to be granted. The application for a new tenancy was heard on February 3, 1959. The likely termination of the tenant's current tenancy was, in light of the operation of the provisions of s.64 of the Act and of the possibility of appeal, June 20, 1959, which would, if the tenant's request were granted, leave the landlord only six weeks before the term expired. The landlord was entitled to a reasonable period to enable him to re-let the premises. Accordingly, a term expiring on December 25, 1959, was reasonable in all the circumstances. **8–29**

CBS UK Ltd v London Scottish Properties[60] The tenant was granted a lease of factory premises for a term of 10 years from March 25, 1974. The landlord was itself the tenant under a head lease for a term of 150 years. The tenant's application came before the court on June 27, 1985. The tenant at trial asked for a term expiring on August 31, 1986, whereas the landlord asked for a 14-year term. **8–30**

The reason why the tenant wanted a short term was that it was in the process of moving from the premises to other premises and that all it needed was sufficient time to make an orderly departure. The landlord resisted the grant of such a short term as it argued that the capital value of its interest would be substantially diminished unless the longer term was granted. The evidence was that, if pure market forces were to prevail, a landlord would seek to grant a term

[56] Unreported 1994 but noted at [1994] 13 E.G. 102.
[57] [1985] 2 E.G.L.R. 125.
[58] [1985] 2 E.G.L.R. 125.
[59] (1959) 174 E.G. 311.
[60] [1985] 2 E.G.L.R. 125.

of 15–20 years with five-yearly rent reviews and no landlord would let the premises for a period of a year save in exceptional circumstances.

The premises were readily marketable. The parties had in fact agreed a rental of £260,000 whatever the outcome, which was £10,000 more than the landlord's agent had originally advised was the appropriate rent. On the evidence the judge accepted that the market would regard the landlord's interest subject to the lease to August 31, 1986, which was not contracted out of the 1954 Act, as significantly less valuable than the same property subject to a 14-year lease: there was a potential uncertainty as to whether the tenant would in fact leave at the expiration of the contractual term; there were re-letting costs to be considered; and there would be a negative cash flow of some £75,000 per annum so long as the premises remained vacant after the tenant's departure. The tenant had in fact offered to pay the landlord £50,000 if the tenant did not vacate by August 31, 1986.

In deciding what was reasonable in all the circumstances, little weight was to be attached to the landlord's argument that in the market place a term of a year would not be granted. In the absence of evidence that the landlord was intending to sell its interest, so that there was no realistic possibility of a realisable loss on sale, it was, in all the circumstances, reasonable to grant the tenant what it wanted; the landlord had in effect 11 months to find a new tenant to avoid a negative cash flow and there was little likelihood of that in light of the demand for the premises. Although a 14-year lease was also readily marketable and it was proper for the landlord to seek to maximise the marketability of his asset, the purpose of the Act is to protect the tenant and he was being given the protection he needed and no more by the grant of the shorter term. In the circumstances the landlord was properly protected and it would be reasonable to grant the term the tenant asked for.

8–31 ***Rumbelows v Tameside Metropolitan BC***[61] The tenant, having been granted a lease of 20 years, wanted a lease of five years. The landlord wanted to grant a tenancy of 14 years and, in any event, not less than 10 years. A tenancy of five years was granted.

8–32 ***Michael Chipperfield v Shell (UK) Ltd; Warwick & Warwick (Philately) Ltd v Shell (UK) Ltd***[62] C and W were both tenants, each occupying a stall in a stamp-dealing emporium ("The Bourse") containing 17 such stalls in a larger complex owned by the landlords. In 1977 the landlords decided to determine all the tenancies of the stalls in order to obtain more space for their staff and accordingly, in June 1977, served s.25 notices on C, W and S, another stallholder, determining their tenancies on March 25, 1978. When the tenants requested new tenancies, the landlords opposed the requests under, inter alia, ground (g) of s.30(1) (occupation for own business). The matter was referred to the county court, where the landlords conceded that the notices which had been served on S were invalid and, since the consequence of S's s.26 notice was that the earliest the landlords could possibly gain possession of "The Bourse" would have been in

[61] Unreported but noted at [1994] 13 E.G. 10.

[62] [1980] 1 E.G.L.R. 51 CA.

May 1980, they were also forced to concede that they could not substantiate their opposition under ground (g) to the grants of new tenancies to C and W. The parties were unable to agree the durations of the new tenancies, which were eventually decided under s.33 by the judge in February 1980 to be three years "to commence with reference to the provisions of section 64". In considering the exercise of the discretion under s.33, the judge directed herself in the following terms:

> "Dealing with the issue of duration and other terms, where there is no agreement, section 33 of the Act of 1954 comes into operation. It provides discretion to grant terms reasonable in all the circumstances and entitles me to take into consideration all factors. It includes the grounds of opposition of the landlords under s.30(1)(g), their intentions and plans and the hardships and needs of each party. I must give proper protection to the tenants but not be unfair to the landlords, nor allow the grant of a new tenancy to defeat development or reduce the value of the building; and must weigh up and reasonably protect the interests of both parties."

The landlords appealed, contending that a proper exercise of the judge's discretion required her to grant new tenancies no longer than 12 months, which would have enabled them to obtain possession of "The Bourse" by serving fresh notices on C and W to coincide more or less with S's case. The landlord argued that the judge had failed properly to exercise her discretion under s.33 by not giving consideration to factors including the effect of the length of term granted to C and W on the landlords' plans to obtain possession from other tenants and by giving too much weight to C, W and S's offer to move to one end of "The Bourse" to allow the landlords as much room as possible therein.

It was held that:

(1) Although the judge made no express reference to the possible effect on S's case, she was well aware of it and, in any case, if and when S's case came before the court the result of C's and Ws case might be taken into consideration.
(2) The judge had rightly taken into account the tenants' offer to move their stalls.

The Court of Appeal made observations as to the proper form of order in such a case:

It was in the interests of both landlord and tenant that the termination date of the new tenancy should be established when the order for a new tenancy was made, even though it was not possible because of the effect of s.64 to determine when the tenancy would start. The shorter the duration the more important this was. The end of the new tenancy should always be expressed in this way. Accordingly, the order would be varied by substituting for "3 years to commence with reference to the provisions of Section 64" the words "a term expiring on July 31, 1983".

It remains common in 2012 as it was at the date of the last edition (2007) for tenants to seek short terms of around five years. In the absence of a desire to redevelop at the end of the term, such a term tends to be contrary to the landlord's **8–33** interest, for the institutional market looks for a longer term. What is the court's approach likely to be? In considering the various authorities a number of general principles can be extracted, namely:

(1) each application for renewal of a tenancy turns on its own facts;
(2) the court will seek to confer upon the tenant a term sufficient to protect the tenant in the carrying on of his business; the primary purpose of the legislation is to protect the tenant;
(3) it is perfectly valid for a landlord to seek to maximise the value and marketability of its reversion but any paper diminution will be ignored;
(4) what is likely to be granted in the market is of only limited value in assisting the court in determining, in the exercise of its discretion, what is reasonable;
(5) any rigid policy of either party as to the length of term to be taken or granted is irrelevant to the exercise of the court's discretion;
(6) the determination of the duration of the term is an exercise of discretion with the court seeking to strike a balance between the degree of protection to which the tenant is entitled in the exercise of his business interests and the need to ensure that the decision is neither unfair on or oppressive to the landlord.

8–34 A consideration of the facts of all of the relevant decisions shows that on each case there was a specific reason being put forward by the tenant as to why it wanted a particularly short term. In *CBS UK Ltd v London and Scottish*[63] (digested in para.8–30) the tenant simply wanted time to effect an orderly departure, the tenant having made the decision to move his business out of the holding to other premises which it owned. In the *Charles Follett v Cabtell*[64] decision the tenant wanted the short term because it could not afford the rent. In *Ganton House Investments v Crossman Investments*[65] the tenant was looking for somewhere else to go, wishing to find somewhere more desirable in which to locate their business. In *Rumbelows v Tameside Metropolitan BC*[66] the tenant had a rigid policy of seeking a term of only five years being particularly concerned with the difficulties of assignment of an over-rentalised property and of continuing original tenant liability.

8–35 The court's attitude towards the tenant's proposal will depend very much upon the reasons that are being put forward by the tenant. For instance it is quite apparent that today if *Rumbelows v Tameside Metropolitan BC*[67] were to be decided again the Landlord and Tenant (Covenants) Act 1995 might have a material impact. The 1995 Act would have alleviated the problems associated with original tenant liability. Furthermore, the court will have regard to the landlord's proposals to seek to accommodate the tenant's concerns, e.g. as in the

[63] [1985] 2 E.G.L.R 125.
[64] [1986] 2 E.G.L.R. 76 (first instance).
[65] [1995] 1 E.G.L.R. 239 CC.
[66] Unreported but noted at [1994] 13 E.G. 10.
[67] Unreported but noted at [1994] 13 E.G. 10.

Charles Follett v Cabtell[68] decision where the landlord proposed a break clause. In both *Charles Follett v Cabtell*[69] and *Ganton House Investments v Crossman Investments*[70] the court effectively gave the tenant an opportunity of finding alternative premises and if it could not it was stuck with the length of term sought by the landlord.

Since the cases considered above were decided there have come to the fore new arguments which are the product of statutory and market changes which affect the argument as to (short) lease duration[71]: **8–36**

(1) the Landlord and Tenant (Covenants) Act 1995 has affected original tenant liability;
(2) the market is not in a recession as it was, for instance, when *Ganton House Investments v Crossman Investments*[72] was decided; it is, therefore, arguable, in favour of the tenant, that the landlord will find it easier to let and therefore the prospect of a void is minimal;
(3) on the other hand a buoyant market arguably favours the landlord's requirement for a longer lease, and ought to allay the tenant's concerns about difficulties with assignment, in that insofar as it could be shown that market rents increase in excess of the rent reserved the tenant should have little difficulty in effecting an assignment and may even obtain a premium.

Undoubtedly the giving of concessions aids the landlord's argument in seeking to oppose a shorter term. The decisions in *Charles Follett v Cabtell*[73] and *Ganton House Investments v Crossman Investments*[74] reflect this. Undoubtedly the offer of a break clause or a concession concerning continuing liability, i.e. an automatic release, or the nature of the rent review clause will have an impact upon the court's approach in relation to the length of term to be granted. **8–37**

The special considerations which are applicable where the premises are ripe for redevelopment, or where the landlord will shortly be able to rely upon ground (g) (own occupation), are considered in the next paragraph. **8–38**

---

68 [1986] 2 E.G.L.R. 76 (first instance).
69 [1986] 2 E.G.L.R. 76 (first instance).
70 [1995] 1 E.G.L.R. 239 CC.
71 In the 2002 edition of this Work reference was also made to the proposed changes to accountancy practice, in terms of how leasehold liabilities were to dealt with in the profit and loss account and balance sheet. The proposed changes were to treat a lease transaction as an asset financing and thus result in the capitalisation of the rental liability over the whole of the lease term. The then accountancy practice showed rental liability as an expense on a year-by-year basis. There was a view current at that time that this change might give rise to an argument that long-term lease liabilities impact on key accounting ratios (used to assess the financial position and performance of companies) and would alter the financial ranking of companies. This perceived argument in fact found no expression in practice.
72 [1995] 1 E.G.L.R. 239 CC.
73 [1986] 2 E.G.L.R. 76 (first instance).
74 [1995] 1 E.G.L.R. 239 CC.

Special considerations where premises ripe for development, etc.

8–39 In a number of cases, the courts have had to consider the question of duration in a context where the premises to be comprised in the new tenancy were "ripe for redevelopment", so that the landlord could be expected shortly to be able to formulate the necessary intention under ground (f) (demolition and reconstruction), or where the circumstances were such that the landlord, although unable to rely upon ground (g) (own occupation) because he had purchased the landlord's interests within the five-year period, would nonetheless shortly be able to establish that ground. The approach of the courts in these circumstances is very similar to their approach to the analogous question of whether a break clause should be inserted as a term of the new tenancy.

8–40 In *Reohorn v Barry*[75] (digested in para.7–155), the Court of Appeal held that the landlord's plans for redevelopment were insufficiently far advanced to enable it to rely upon ground (f) (demolition and reconstruction). However, so that it should not impede the redevelopment of the premises if the landlord formed the necessary intention, the court granted the tenant a short fixed term terminable thereafter on six months' notice given by either party. Similarly, in *London and Provincial v Barclays Bank*,[76] the Court of Appeal held that the judge had erred in failing to take into account, in determining the question of duration, the fact that the premises were "ripe for redevelopment" and that by granting a long term he would impede that redevelopment.

8–41 Similar considerations arise when the landlord is unable to rely upon ground (g) (own occupation) because he is barred by the five-year rule. In *Wig Creations v Colour Film Services*,[77] the judge found that the landlords wished to occupy the premises for the purposes of their own business, but were barred by the five-year rule. Balancing the interests of landlord and tenant, he granted a tenancy to expire one year after the landlords would have qualified under the five-year rule; the Court of Appeal declined to interfere with the exercise of his discretion. Lord Denning M.R. said:

> "Section 33 is in very wide terms. It empowers the court to do what is 'reasonable in all the circumstances'. Suppose a landlord bought five years ago, plus one day. He could resist a new tenancy altogether on the ground that he wanted the place for his own business. Suppose he buys it five years ago less one day. Should he be kept out of the place for several years simply by the terms of the two-day difference? I think not. The policy of the Act is to give a landlord (who has purchased more than five years ago) an absolute right to get possession for his own business: leaving it to the court to do what is reasonable, the five-year period is a factor which it is permissible for the judge to take into account. The weight of it is for him.[78]"

---

[75] [1956] 1 W.L.R. 845; [1956] 2 All E.R. 742 CA.

[76] [1962] 1 W.L.R. 510; [1962] 2 All E.R. 163 CA.

[77] (1969) 20 P. & C.R. 870; (1969) 113 S.J. 688 CA.

[78] (1969) 20 P. & C.R. 870; (1969) 113 S.J. 688 CA at 874.

Own occupation

An alternative to ordering a new short term is to enable the landlord to break upon notice if the landlord desires to occupy for his own business: *Peter Millett v Salisbury Handbags*[79] (digested in para.8–43). **8–42**

Peter Millett v Salisbury Handbags[80] The landlord opposed the tenant's request for a term of 14 years, arguing that only a six-month term should be granted as the premises were required by a subsidiary. Although this suggestion emerged late in the day and the evidence in connection with it was "sketchy", the judge held that the landlord was to be given an opportunity to establish a genuine and workable intention to trade in the premises through the subsidiary. Accordingly the judge ordered a three-year term subject to a landlord's break clause, exercisable by six-months' notice, expiring at any time, but only if a company in the same group as the landlord, as defined in the Act, intended to occupy the premises for the purposes of a business to be carried on by that company. **8–43**

Duration can exceed length of immediate landlord's tenancy

Where there is a chain of interests and the duration of the term granted by the court is longer than the length of the immediate landlord's tenancy, the court has power to grant such reversionary tenancies as may be required to secure the combined effect of a grant of such a term—see para.2 of Sch.6.[81] **8–44**

4. TERMS OTHER THAN AS TO PROPERTY, DURATION AND RENT (SECTION 35)

The "other terms" governed by s.35(1) are those terms of the tenancy other than as to the property, the duration and the rent. For the reasons given (in para.8–90) it is necessary for the parties to agree, or the court to determine, any question as to the property, the duration and other terms, before it embarks upon a consideration of the proper rent to be paid under the new tenancy. It is for this reason that the "other terms" are discussed at this stage. **8–45**

Exercise of discretion as to the other terms: *O'May*

In determining what should be the "other terms", the court is required by s.35(1) to "have regard to the terms of the current tenancy and to all relevant circumstances". The Landlord and Tenant (Covenants) Act 1995 inserted by amendment a new subs.(2) as follows: **8–46**

> "In subsection (1) of this section the reference to all relevant circumstances includes (without prejudice to the generality of that reference) a reference to the operation of the provisions of the Landlord and Tenant (Covenants) Act 1995."

---

[79] [1987] 2 E.G.L.R. 104.

[80] [1987] 2 E.G.L.R. 104.

[81] Discussed in para.10–42 et seq.

In *O'May v City of London Real Property Ltd*[82] (para.8–47), the House of Lords gave guidance on how the court was to exercise its discretion under s.35(1). In considering the effect of the Landlord and Tenant (Covenants) Act 1995 when determining the terms of the new lease, it has been said that the 1995 Act has changed the law substantially. In particular, it prevents a landlord from enjoying the sort of rights that he had under the old law, once the tenant assigns the lease. In these circumstances, the terms of s.35 of the 1954 Act, as interpreted in *O'May v City of London Real Property Ltd*,[83] do not entitle the landlord to say that, on a renewal under the 1954 Act, he should be given as generous terms as the 1995 Act provides. The 1995 Act represented a sea change in the law relating to a tenant's liability after he assigns the lease, and it also altered the law relating to the landlord's power to impose terms on assigning the lease. It did not merely represent a sea change in what had been common practice, but in what a landlord can lawfully require, both in terms of what is to be included in the lease initially and what he can demand upon an assignment: *Wallis Fashion Group Ltd v CGU Life Assurance Ltd*[84] (digested in para.8–68).

8–47 ***O'May v City of London Real Property Co Ltd***[85] A firm of solicitors applied for a new tenancy of premises consisting primarily of one floor in an office block. The landlords did not object to the grant of a new tenancy, but a dispute arose over the terms thereof and the matter was referred to court. The tenants contended that the new tenancy should be on the same terms as the current tenancy with, in particular, a provision that the tenants should pay a proportion of the heating and lighting expenses of the common parts of the building. The landlords proposed instead a "clear lease" whereby the fluctuating costs of the landlords' responsibilities for service, maintenance, repair and redecoration of the structural, exterior and common parts of the building were to be reimbursed by the tenants. The landlords produced evidence to the effect that the capital value of the landlord's interests, subject to the clear lease was far greater than that if it were subject to a lease incorporating the current terms. The parties' valuers also agreed that a reduction in the proposed rental level of 50p per square foot would be appropriate if the "clear lease" was granted. The landlords further gave evidence that "clear leases" of this nature were gaining acceptability in the property market. Goulding J. accepted the landlords' contentions and granted a renewal of the tenancy on the terms suggested by the landlords. The tenants' appeal was allowed by the Court of Appeal, whereupon the landlords appealed to the House of Lords.

The issue before the court was whether the court should exercise its discretion so as to impose, in place of the tenants' existing liability to pay a proportion of the heating and lighting expenses of the common parts, against the tenants' will, a provision that they should pay a fluctuating charge, being a proportion of all the costs of the landlords' responsibilities for service and repair, in return for a flat diminution in the rent of the new tenancy.

---

[82] [1983] A.C. 726; [1982] 2 W.L.R. 407; [1982] 1 All E.R. 660 HL.

[83] [1983] A.C. 726; [1982] 2 W.L.R. 407; [1982] 1 All E.R. 660 HL.

[84] [2000] 2 E.G.L.R. 49.

[85] [1983] A.C. 726; [1982] 2 W.L.R. 407; [1982] 1 All E.R. 660 HL.

The House of Lords held:

(1) In "having regard to the terms of the current tenancy and to all relevant circumstances" under s.35(1) the court must begin by considering the terms of the current tenancy and the burden of persuading the court to impose a charge in those terms against the will of either party must rest on the party proposing the change, and that change proposed must, in the circumstances of the case, be fair and reasonable, and should take into account, amongst other things, the comparatively weak negotiating position of a sitting tenant requiring renewal, particularly in conditions of scarcity, and the general purpose of the Act which is to protect the business interests of the tenant so far as they are affected by the approaching termination of the current lease in particular as regards his security of tenure;

(2) The landlords' proposed change would be a real and serious detriment to the tenants, involving as it did a fluctuating charge compensated for on the face of it by a flat reduction in the rent. The landlords had not discharged the burden of showing that it was reasonable for the tenants to bear that risk and, accordingly, the appeal would be dismissed.

(3) The nature of the parties' interests in the land was such as to call for the assumption of long-term risks by the landlords. A transfer of those risks to the tenants created a risk disproportionate to their interest.

General principles as to other terms

The following points of general principle emerge: **8–48**

(1) The requirement that the court is to "have regard to the terms of the current tenancy" indicates that there is an onus on the party seeking any change from those terms to justify that change: see, e.g. *Cardshops v Davies*.[86] It has been said that the words "have regard to" are elastic: they compel something between an obligation to reproduce existing terms and an unfettered right to substitute others.[87]

(2) It is insufficient justification for the change that one party will thereby benefit greatly.

(3) The court would be unlikely to allow any change which prejudiced the security of tenure of the tenant in his business, because it is the policy of the Act to protect the tenant in his business: see *Gold v Brighton Corp*[88] (digested in para.8–61). Thus, the court should not narrow the user clause contained in the current tenancy so as to restrict the business actually carried on, although there may be good reason why a wide user clause should be narrowed so as to restrict the use of the premises to the business actually being carried on: *Gold v Brighton Corp*.[89]

---

[86] [1971] 1 W.L.R. 591 at 596 per Widgery L.J.; [1971] 2 All E.R. 721 CA; *O'May* v *City of London Real Property Co Ltd* [1983] 2 A.C. 726 at 740 per Lord Hailsham and at 747 per Lord Wilberforce.

[87] *O'May v City of London Real Property Co Ltd* [1983] 2 A.C. 726 at 747 per Lord Wilberforce.

[88] [1956] 1 W.L.R. 1291; [1956] 3 All E.R. 442 CA.

[89] [1956] 1 W.L.R. 1291; [1956] 3 All E.R. 442 CA.

(4) The court is unlikely to allow any change in the terms of the tenancy which is sought to be introduced for the sole purpose of increasing the rent payable, by making the lease more favourable to the tenant, if the tenant does not wish that change: see *Charles Clements (London) v Rank City Wall*[90] (digested in para.8–58).

(5) The court will recognise that the terms of the current tenancy are either the result of a free bargain between the parties or their predecessors, or the result of some previous decision of the court under the Act.

(6) It is the court and not market forces which determines the terms of the tenancy.[91] The fact that other tenants in the market may be prepared to accept the term sought is not irrelevant but is simply one factor to which the court will have regard: *Wallis Fashion Group Ltd v CGU Life Assurance Ltd*[92] (digested in para.8–68).

(7) This does not, however, mean that the court will seek to "petrify" the terms of the lease.[93] If the terms of the current tenancy are obsolete or deficient, the court may consider this an adequate reason for change.

(8) In particular, the incidence of inflation in recent years will justify the court in introducing a rent review clause, even if the current tenancy was a lengthy term of years at a fixed rent.

(9) The court will bear in mind all relevant circumstances, in particular the fact that the tenant may be in a weak negotiating position.[94]

(10) Special considerations may apply to a proposal by the landlord to introduce a redevelopment break clause, because that is a term which is concerned

---

[90] [1978] 1 E.G.L.R. 47.

[91] *O'May v City of London Real Property Co Ltd* [1983] 2 A.C. 726 Lord Hailsham said at 740:

"(1) It is clear from section 34 [dealing with the rent under the new tenancy] that, in contrast to the enactments relating to residential property, Parliament did not intend, apart from certain limitations to protect the tenant from the operation of market forces in the determination of rent. (2) In contrast to the determination of rent, it is the court and not the market forces which, with one vital qualification, has an almost complete discretion as to the other terms of the tenancy … And (3) in deciding the terms of the new tenancy, as to which its discretion is otherwise not expressly fettered, the court must start by 'having regard to' the terms of the current tenancy, which ex hypothesi must either have been originally the subject of agreement between the parties, or themselves the result of a previous determination by the court in earlier proceedings for renewal …"

Lord Wilberforce placed rather more weight on market forces. He said at 747C:

"I accept therefore the landlord's contention that, in principle, tenants are not to be protected from market forces; as regards rent, indeed, this is expressly laid down in section 34 … The same underlying principle ought to be applied to the determination of other terms in the new lease, subject, however, to the guidelines laid down in section 35—as to which see below."

However, Lord Wilberforce's reference to market forces is tempered by the words immediately following those quoted where he speaks of the court being required to have "regard to the terms of the current tenancy" and the onus being on the party seeking change to justify it.

[92] [2000] 2 E.G.L.R. 49. In this particular case the landlord sought the incorporation of a requirement in the new lease for the tenant, upon assignment, to enter into an Authorised Guarantee Agreement under the terms of the Landlord and Tenant (Covenants) Act 1995 whether or not it was reasonable for the landlord to so require, pointing to the fact that all but one of the 15 other tenants in the centre had agreed to the term. Neuberger J. recognised that it was a factor which favoured the landlord but nevertheless held that the term should be incorporated subject to a qualification that the landlord could only insist on the tenant entering into an AGA upon assignment if it was reasonable to do so. See further paras 8–66 and 8–67.

[93] Lord Wilberforce at p.747.

[94] *O'May v City of London Real Property Co Ltd* [1983] 2 A.C. 726 at 740 per Lord Hailsham.

not merely with the rights and obligations of the parties under the current tenancy, but also requires a recognition of the policy considerations which govern the exercise of the discretion of the court under s.35(3) in relation to the duration of tenancies (see paras 8–39 and 8–77 et seq.).

(11) The fact that, at least on paper, the landlord or tenant can be said to be compensated for the proposed change by an increase or reduction in the rent payable under the new tenancy does not of itself justify the change. In particular, if a tenant is being asked to shoulder a risk which is more appropriately borne by the freeholder in return for a reduction in rent, he is being made an involuntary insurer of that risk. (Compare the approach of Goulding J. in *O'May*[95] at first instance on this point with that of the Court of Appeal[96] and House of Lords.)

(12) All the preceding considerations are subject to the overriding question: whether the proposed change can be justified on grounds of "essential fairness" between landlord and tenant.

Service charges

The court will not normally incorporate as a term of a new lease a service charge provision which requires the tenant to contribute to the total costs of repairing the main structure of the building of which the demised premises form part where the current tenancy contains no equivalent provision. To do so would require the tenant to accept risks which could not be quantified and were not capable of being compensated for by a reduction in the proposed level of rent: *O'May v City of London Real Property Co Ltd*[97] (digested in para.8–47). This is not to say, however, that a service charge clause cannot be updated or the services added to or incorporated where none existed before. The reason for rejecting the landlord's argument in *O'May v City of London Real Property Co Ltd* was that in considering the parties' interests in the premises, the landlord having a freehold interest and the tenant taking a term of five years, it was more appropriate that the burden of the depreciation of the landlord's capital asset be borne by the landlord. As Lord Wilberforce said: **8–49**

> "The character of the two parties' interests in the land—the landlord's indefinite one by freehold, the tenant's a limited one over a comparatively short period, even though capable of renewal if the tenant so wishes, is such as to call for the assumption of long term risks by the former . . ."

These sentiments were reflected also in the judgments in the Court of Appeal of Shaw and Brightman L.JJ. Thus, as Brightman L.J. said: "A short-term tenant was not adequately compensated by a small reduction in rent for the assumption of the financial risks implicit in the maintenance . . ."[98] It is thus clear that the length of the term will have an effect on the court's approach to the risks which

---

[95] [1979] 1 E.G.L.R. 74.

[96] [1981] Ch. 216; [1980] 3 W.L.R. 881; [1980] 3 All E.R. 466 CA.

[97] [1983] 2 A.C. 726; [1982] 2 W.L.R. 407; [1982] 1 All E.R. 660 HL; affirming [1981] Ch. 216; [1980] 3 W.L.R. 881; [1980] 3 All E.R. 466 CA.

[98] [1981] Ch. 216 at 227.

the landlord is seeking to transfer to the tenant. It may be, therefore, that where the lessee's interest is not a short-term but a long-term one, the landlord may persuade the court that the risk of a fluctuating service charge relating to the structure should be borne by the tenant if that risk is not disproportionate to their interests. There is no indication either in the House of Lords or the Court of Appeal as to what would be viewed as a long-term interest, other than the fact that the landlord had a freehold interest which was viewed as a long-term one and the tenant had a five-year term which was viewed as a short-term interest.

8–50 It is to be noted that the landlord in *O'May v City of London Real Property Co Ltd*[99] (digested in para.8–47) wanted a "clear lease". It did not seek an intermediate position on the service charge provisions. The most onerous risk which the landlord was seeking to transfer to the tenant was that of the repair and maintenance of the structure and exterior of the building of which the demised premises formed part. A service charge which does not seek to make the tenant liable for maintenance, repair and redecoration of the premises is more likely to be upheld by the court: *Leslie & Godwin Investments v Prudential Assurance Co.*[100] It would appear that in *Boots v Pinkland*,[101] the county court judge upheld the landlord's contention for the incorporation of service charge to cover management fees. The report is unclear on this issue.

8–51 Where the current tenancy contains a fixed service charge in respect of the provision of services by the landlord, the Court of Appeal has held that it is appropriate, especially in conditions of anticipated inflation, to substitute a variable service charge in the new tenancy granted pursuant to the Act: *Hyams v Titan Properties.*[102] The correctness of this decision, at least on one particular point, must be uncertain in the light of *O'May v City of London Real Property Co Ltd*[103] (digested in para.8–47). The service charge provisions in *Hyams v Titan Properties*[104] included the cost of repairing the main structure of the building and, by converting a fixed payment into an obligation to pay a proportion of the actual cost, the Court of Appeal was, in effect, making the tenant a insurer for the future structural well-being of the building in the way deprecated in *O'May v City of London Real Property Co Ltd*[105] where the tenants of units within the landlord's market had, under earlier lease arrangements, paid a rent and a variable service charge, but had moved, under their current leases, to an all inclusive rent to accommodate a refurbishment by the landlord of the market, which move was intended to be temporary, little weight was to be attached to the terms of the current leases in determining whether the tenants should remain on an all inclusive rent: *Edwards & Walkden (Norfolk) Ltd v City of London.*[106]

---

[99] [1983] 2 A.C. 726; [1982] 2 W.L.R. 407; [1982] 1 All E.R. 660 HL; affirming [1981] Ch. 216; [1980] 3 W.L.R. 881; [1980] 3 All E.R. 466 CA.

[100] [1983] 2 A.C. 726; [1982] 2 W.L.R. 407; [1982] 1 All E.R. 660 HL; affirming [1981] Ch. 216; [1980] 3 W.L.R. 881; [1980] 3 All E.R. 466 CA.

[101] [1992] 2 E.G.L.R. 98.

[102] (1972) 24 P. & C.R. 359 CA.

[103] [1983] 2 A.C. 726; [1982] 2 W.L.R. 407; [1982] 1 All E.R. 660 HL.

[104] (1972) 24 P. & C.R. 359 CA.

[105] [1983] 2 A.C. 726; [1982] 2 W.L.R. 407; [1982] 1 All E.R. 660 HL.

[106] [2012] EWHC 2527 (Ch). As the parties agreed that the principle governing the new tenancies to be granted was that the landlord should be able to recover in full from the tenants the ongoing

In *Amarjee v Barrowfen Properties*[107] (digested in para.8–151), the tenant had occupied business premises as a furniture warehouse on an oral yearly periodic tenancy. On renewal the parties agreed a 14-year term. The tenant's premises formed part of a parade of shops owned by the landlord which had been built between the wars. The landlord proposed a service charge which included the maintenance of the exterior and common parts of the parade and of a sprinkler system serving the whole parade. All the leases in the parade contained such a service charge provision. The tenant argued that the service charge be limited to his premises and an adjoining unit but accepted a liability to pay a fair proportion of maintaining the common sprinkler system serving the whole parade, the car park and the maintenance of fire escape routes. The judge included the service charge provision as argued by the landlord. The judge indicated that the position would have been different if he had been dealing with a written tenancy agreement which had not included such a service charge provision. However, it is difficult to see why this should make any distinction as to the application of the principles set out in *O'May v City of London Real Property Co Ltd*[108] (digested in para.8–47). **8–52**

If the landlord adduces no evidence to justify the proposed change but relies instead on inferences to be drawn from the lease provisions, he is unlikely to discharge the burden upon him to show that a change from the terms of the existing tenancy should be determined: *Davy's of London (Wine Merchants) Ltd v City of London Corp*[109] (digested in para.8–54). **8–53**

It has been said that current market practice supports the inference that adoption of a variable service charge to cover the provision of services by a landlord to a tenant in multi occupied commercial premises is generally regarded as fair by both landlords and tenants.[110] A fair balance between the interests of commercial landlords and commercial tenants is, it is said, reflected in the RICS guidance, Service Charges in Commercial Property, 2nd edn (2011).[111] It is, however, unclear to what extent weight should be attached to market forces in determining the terms of the new lease and in particular the service charge provisions.[112] **8–53A**

---

operational and maintenance costs in running the market, that principle was most fairly and accurately reflected in the landlord's proposal for a variable service charge.

107 [1993] 2 E.G.L.R. 133.

108 [1983] 2 A.C. 726 HL.

109 Unreported November 27, 2003, Mayor's and City of London Court.

110 *Edwards & Walkden (Norfolk) Ltd v City of London* [2012] EWHC 2527 (Ch) at [90].

111 [2012] EWHC 2527 (Ch) at [90].

112 See the remarks of Lord Hailsham and Lord Wilberforce at fn.91 above. In other contexts market forces have been given little weight, see, e.g. *CBS UK Ltd v London Scottish Properties* [1985] 2 E.G.L.R. 125 (digested at para.8–30), where the length of term which would be granted in the market was essentially ignored in determining the length of the term to be granted to the tenant (see para.8–27(5)) and *Wallis Fashion Group Ltd v CGU Life Assurance Ltd* [2000] 2 E.G.L.R. 49 Ch (digested in para.8–68), where the fact that the landlord had obtained an AGA from most of its tenants in terms similar to that which it sought in the new lease proposed, was only a limited factor to which the court had regard in determining the form of the relevant clause to be incorporated into the tenant's new lease.

8–54 ***Davy's of London (Wine Merchants) Ltd v City of London Corp***[113] T was tenant of basement restaurant/wine bar premises. At the time of the grant of the lease a considerable amount of fit out was undertaken. No further refurbishment had been undertaken since that date. Under the terms of the original lease T was required to pay a service charge of 8.5 per cent of the costs of running the building, of the repair of the demised premises and of the repair, maintenance and renewal of all pipes, wires, conduits, sewers, drains and vents supplying or carrying services serving the building. It was also to pay 75 per cent of the maintenance, running repair and replacement of the goods lift. The figure of 8.5 per cent represented mathematically the proportion that the demised premises bore to the whole of the building. L was unable to recover the remaining 91.5 per cent of the costs of repair to the demised premises from the remainder of the tenants in the building. L sought a variation to the effect that T should bear 100 per cent of the cost of the repair to the demised premises, including the foundations of the building. L argued that the terms of the lease placed an unfair burden on L, as T was effectively only bearing a small proportion of the cost of repair to the demised premises. No evidence was given before the court (1) as to what led to the agreement over the original terms (2) what were the terms in the other leases within the building or (3) to justify the change. As the onus was on L and as it must be assumed in the absence of evidence to the contrary that the original terms were the result of a commercial negotiation between the original parties, L had not even begun to discharge the onus which it had to discharge in order to justify the change.

User

8–55 A change in the terms of the user provision may arise for a variety of reasons, e.g. because the landlord seeks to widen the user (to increase the rent) or the tenant may want to narrow the user to obtain a rental advantage or the tenant wishes to widen the market of potential assignees or the landlord wishes to narrow the user to the activity actually undertaken by the tenant. A restriction on use in the new lease which is not contained in the comparables may be an appropriate reason for reducing the rent payable under the new tenancy: *UDS Tailoring v BL Holdings*.[114] There is not, however, likely to be any reduction merely because of a restriction on use where the user can be altered with the consent of the landlord which consent cannot be unreasonably withheld: *Aldwych Club v Copthall Property Co*[115] (digested in para.8–62) and *Owen v Nightingale Page and Bennett*.[116]

8–56 If the landlord seeks to widen the user clause to obtain a rental advantage the landlord's proposal is unlikely to meet with success notwithstanding the fact that the relaxation of the user covenant would enable the tenant to carry on a business

[113] Unreported November 27, 2003, Mayor's and City of London Court.

[114] [1982] 1 E.G.L.R. 61.

[115] (1962) 185 E.G. 219.

[116] (1955) 165 E.G. 761.

other than his present one and make the property more readily assignable: *Charles Clements v Rank City Wall*[117] (digested in para.8–58). See also *Gorleston Golf Club v Links Estate (Gorleston)*.[118]

8–57 If the existing lease contains a user covenant not to use the premises save for a specified purpose without first obtaining the landlord's consent, the landlord cannot unilaterally widen the user clause for the purposes of seeking a rental advantage on renewal: *C&A Pensions Trustees v British Vita Investments*[119] (a rent review case, commented on in *Tea Trade Properties v CIN Properties Ltd*[120]). Of course, if the covenant is subject to the qualification that it cannot be unreasonably withheld, a valuer can seek to value the premises on the basis of the most profitable use of the premises for which consent could not be unreasonably withheld: see *Aldwych Club v Copthall Property Co*[121] (digested in para.8–62).

8–58 ***Charles Clements (London) v Rank City Wall***[122] The landlord agreed to grant the tenant a new tenancy. The tenant's business was that of a cutler and the terms of the current tenancy restricted the user to that of a cutler. The parties agreed that the terms of the new lease should be those of the current tenancy, save that the landlord desired to relax the restraint on user by including a proviso that the landlord's consent was not to be unreasonably withheld to a change of use. It was agreed between the parties that if this proviso was included in the new lease the rent would be higher. The tenant objected to its inclusion.

It was held that the court should not include as a term of the new tenancy a user covenant in less restrictive terms than those of the current tenancy. The scheme of the Act is to protect the tenant in his character of an occupying business tenant carrying on his business in the premises. The proposed modification did not benefit the tenant in that respect for, although the relaxation of the user covenant would enable the tenant to carry on a business other than his present one and made the property more readily assignable, these were collateral advantages which arose only if the tenant wished to discontinue his present business. On the other hand the correlative burden on the tenant of paying a higher rent to the landlord in consequence of the proposed modification was something that affected the tenant in the carrying on of his business because further out goings had to be met before any profit could be arrived at. Accordingly, as the landlord's proposal was burdensome rather than beneficial to the tenant and, since the tenant objected to it, it would not receive the court's sanction.

8–59 It is considered that the tenant will have difficulty in persuading the court to widen a user clause if the only reason is to enable him to assign more readily. It has been said that the object of the Act was to protect the tenant in the carrying on of his business, "not to put a saleable asset into [the tenant's] hands": per

[117] [1978] 1 E.G.L.R. 47.
[118] (1959) 109 L.J. 140 CC.
[119] [1984] 2 E.G.L.R. 75.
[120] [1990] 1 E.G.L.R. 155.
[121] (1962) 185 E.G. 219.
[122] [1978] 1 E.G.L.R. 47.

Denning L.J. in *Gold v Brighton Corp*[123] (digested in para.8–61). Where the tenant's existing user is in breach of covenant, he is unlikely to obtain a new lease with that user but will be left with the terms of the existing lease and be required to apply to the landlord for a change of use: *Davis v Brighton Corp.*[124]

8–60 A landlord will ordinarily find it difficult to narrow the permitted user. In *Gold v Brighton Corp*[125] (digested in para.8–61), Parker L.J. said:

> "Undoubtedly under section 35[(1)] of the Act the County Court Judge is given a very wide discretion, but in the ordinary case, at any rate, it is difficult to think of any consideration which would justify changing the restrictions on user in such a way as to alter or limit the nature of the business which the tenant has lawfully carried out on those premises and which it is clearly the object of the Act to preserve.[126]"

However, there may be good reasons why a wide user clause should be narrowed so as to restrict the use of the premises to the business actually carried on. If, for instance, the tenancy contains an open-user covenant, by reason of the fact that the tenancy was made orally, the court may well limit the user clause to the use carried on by the tenant: *Amarjee v Barrowfen Properties*[127] (digested in para.8–151). Furthermore, there may be circumstances justifying a narrowing of the user clause if it relates to a part (at least, perhaps, if it is not an important part) of the tenant's business. In *Gold v Brighton Corp*,[128] the landlord sought to prevent the tenant from selling second-hand clothes. However, the landlord failed to provide any evidence as to why it wanted the change. Denning L.J. said:

> "In as much as the tenant is to be protected in respect of his business, the terms of the new tenancy should be such as to enable him to carry on his business as it is. They should not prevent him from carrying on an important part of it. At any rate, if he is to be prevented from using the premises in the future in the way in which has used it in the past, it is for the landlord to justify the restriction: and there ought to be strong and cogent evidence for the purpose. I find no such evidence here. The mere suggestion or hint that the tone of the street would be lowered is not enough.[129]"

If the current tenancy contains a user clause which prevents the landlord from unreasonably withholding consent to a change of use, the court will not at the request of the tenant impose a more restrictive clause in the new tenancy so as to reduce the amount of rent payable under s.34.

8–61 ***Gold v Brighton Corp***[130] The tenant carried on a business, Adrienne, Furs and Fashions, as a dealer in mainly second-hand furs and ladies' wear. The tenant sought a new tenancy on terms similar to the existing agreement. In particular, the user clause thereof was very widely drafted, entitling the tenant to use the premises as, inter alia, "shops [and] offices". The landlord did not oppose the

[123] [1956] 1 W.L.R. 1291 CA.
[124] (1956) 106 L.J. 556 CC.
[125] [1956] 1 W.L.R. 1291 CA.
[126] [1956] 1 W.L.R. 1291 CA at 1296.
[127] [1993] 2 E.G.L.R. 133.
[128] [1956] 1 W.L.R. 1291 CA.
[129] [1956] 1 W.L.R. 1291 CA at 1293.
[130] [1956] 1 W.L.R. 1291; [1956] 3 All E.R. 442 CA.

grant of a new tenancy, but objected to the user clause, proposing instead that the tenant be restricted to the business of furriers and the sale of ladies' wear and be specifically prohibited from dealing in second-hand goods (except with the landlord's consent). At the hearing, the landlord's valuer stated that he "would expect a prudent landlord to restrict the user of the premises so as not to lower the tone of the district". The judge granted a new tenancy but, holding that it was reasonable to restrict the user of the premises, ordered that the tenancy should contain a term prohibiting the sale of second-hand goods without consent. The tenant was ordered to pay half the landlord's costs of the hearing. Subsequently, but before the hearing of the appeal, the same landlord granted a new tenancy to a tenant of adjacent premises, on terms allowing the sale of second-hand clothes. It was held:

(1) The Act was plainly intended to protect the tenant in his business and the terms of a new tenancy should consequently enable the tenant to carry on the business as it is and should not prevent him from carrying on an important part of it, except on the basis of strong and cogent evidence.
(2) However, it would not be right to insert in the new tenancy the former widely drafted user clause; the object of the Act was to protect the tenant in his business and not to "put a new saleable asset in his hands". If a change of user were reasonable in the future, no doubt the landlord would consent to it. Accordingly, the new terms should provide that the tenant might carry on the existing business of a dealer in new and second-hand furs and ladies' (and children's) wear.

Aldwych Club v Copthall Property Co[131] The tenant, a members' club which had occupied the premises since their erection in 1911, applied to the court for a new tenancy. The existing lease contained a covenant by the tenant to use the premises only as a club, unless the landlord consented to any other use, such consent not to be unreasonably withheld. Before the hearing, the landlord had obtained planning permission for the use of the premises as offices. It was common ground between the parties that the tenant was entitled to a new tenancy; that the landlord could not reasonably refuse and, if asked, would have given consent to the change of user to offices; and that the rent for the premises restricted to club use would be £2,500, but £5,200 if restricted to both club and office use. It was held that: **8–62**

(1) The court had a very wide discretion under s.35, when ascertaining the terms of the new tenancy, but it could not properly introduce a restriction on user at the instance of the tenant "with the consequence and indeed, the sole purpose, of bringing about a diminution of the rent to be determined under section 34", when the premises were suitable for use as offices, planning permission had been obtained, and the landlord was willing to consent to the user as offices.
(2) Even if the tenant was willing to accept an absolute prohibition on user as anything but a club, the court would not "sterilise the use of the premises to

[131] (1963) 185 E.G. 219.

their present use with the consequences that there would be excluded from the hypothetical open market the class of would-be tenants most likely to pay the best rent, namely, those wishing to use the premises as offices".

8–63 In *Amarjee v Barrowfen Properties*[132] (digested in para.8–151) the previous tenancy contained no written terms. The parties had agreed a 14-year term. The user was, therefore, effectively open. The tenant wanted to restrict the user covenant to his business. The judge indicated that "had there been a previous lease with an open user clause, I would not have considered a change to a restricted user clause being justified". The judge accordingly restricted the user to the tenant's business which was furniture and carpet sales. However, the judge's distinction is questionable. There being no written terms the user was, effectively, an open one. There is no reason why this should not be viewed as a previous lease with an open-user clause within the terms of the judge's own language.

8–64 A positive user covenant may be of value to a landlord and other tenants, e.g. in a shopping centre. If multiple retailers close their outlets in a shopping centre this may be a severe disadvantage to other shopkeepers within the centre, as a closed unit not only detracts from the attractiveness of the appearance of the centre but is likely to result in fewer shoppers being attracted to the centre. However, the landlord is limited to damages for breach of such a covenant. He is not entitled to an injunction requiring the tenant to reopen: see *Cooperative Insurance Society Ltd v Argyll Stores (Holdings) Ltd*.[133] An attempt by a tenant to delete an existing positive covenant failed in the county court in *Boots v Pinkland*[134] (digested in para.8–152).

---

[132] [1993] 2 E.G.L.R. 133.

[133] [1998] A.C. 1 HL Lord Hoffmann said:

"The principles of equity have always had a strong ethical content and nothing which I say is intended to *diminish* the influence of moral values in their application. I can envisage cases of gross breach of personal faith, or attempts to use the threat of non-performance as blackmail, in which the needs of justice will override all the considerations which support the settled practice. But although any breach of covenant is regrettable, the exercise of the discretion as to whether or not to grant specific performance starts from the fact that the covenant has been broken. Both landlord and tenant in this case are large sophisticated commercial organisations and I have no doubt that both were perfectly aware that the remedy for breach of the covenant was likely to be limited to an award of damages. The interests of both were purely financial: there was no element of personal breach of faith, as in Victorian cases of railway companies which refused to honour obligations to build stations for landowners whose property they had taken: compare *Greene v West Cheshire Railway Co* (1871) L.R. 13 Eq. 44. No doubt there was an effect on the businesses of other traders in the Centre, but Argyll had made no promises to them and it is not suggested that C.I.S. warranted to other tenants that Argyll would remain. Their departure, with or without the consent of C.I.S., was a commercial risk which the tenants were able to deploy in negotiations for the next rent review. On the scale of broken promises, I can think of worse cases . . .".

Compare the position in Scotland: *Highland Universal Properties Ltd v Safeway Properties Ltd* [2000] 3 E.G.L.R. 110.

[134] [1992] 2 E.G.L.R. 98.

Alienation

If the landlord seeks to limit an existing alienation clause he will have to show very powerful reasons for doing so: *Cardshops v Davies*.[135] Thus, where the existing lease contained the usual qualified provision that the tenant could not assign without first obtaining the consent of the landlord, such consent not to be unreasonably withheld, the landlord could not seek to impose a requirement that the tenant first offer to surrender the tenancy to the landlord: *Cardshops Ltd v Davies*. See also *Fitzpatrick Bros v Bradford Corp*[136] (where the county court rejected an attempt to limit the tenant's right to assign). In *Turone v Howard de Walden Estates*[137] it was said that it was proper to exclude from the terms of the new tenancy a clause (contained in the current tenancy) prohibiting absolutely assigning or sub-letting part of the premises where the premises could not, having regard to the physical layout of the premises, be the subject matter of an assignment or sub-letting of part. **8–65**

Many tenants were, prior to the coming into force of the Landlord and Tenant (Covenants) Act 1995, particularly concerned over the continuing liability of a tenant by reason of the doctrine of privity of contract. This had led some tenants to seek to limit the length of the term taken on renewal. Others sought to provide for a term in the new lease that the tenant be relieved from liability under the terms of the lease after the tenant has assigned the lease on. In the county court an attempt to impose a term limiting the liability of the tenant under the lease for the duration that the lease was vested in the tenant failed: *Amarjee v Barrowfen Properties Ltd*[138] (digested in para.8–151). The judge rejected the tenant's argument, notwithstanding evidence that this is what tenants were seeking in the market on new lettings. The judge was of the view that (1) such a provision was "almost unheard of" and (2) it would have a potentially adverse affect on the value of the landlord's investment in the property. **8–66**

However, since the passing of the Landlord and Tenant (Covenants) Act 1995[139] any renewal will be a new tenancy within the meaning of that Act. The 1995 Act limits the tenant's liability to the time that the lease is vested in the tenant. On assignment the tenant may be required to enter into an authorised guarantee agreement ("AGA") (s.16 of the 1995 Act) requiring the tenant to guarantee the performance and observance of the covenants by the assignee but only for so long as the lease is vested in the assignee. By s.35(2) of the 1954 Act (inserted by para.4 of Sch.1 to the 1995 Act) it is provided that:

> "(2) in subsection (1) of this section the reference to all relevant circumstances includes (without prejudice to the generality of that reference) a reference to the operation of the provisions of the Landlord and Tenant (Covenants) Act 1995."

135 [1971] 1 W.L.R. 591; [1971] 2 All E.R. 721 CA.
136 (1960) 110 L.J. 208 CC.
137 [1982] 1 E.G.L.R. 92 CA.
138 [1993] 2 E.G.L.R. 133.
139 Which came into force on January 1, 1996: see Landlord and Tenant (Covenants) Act 1995 (Commencement) Order (SI 1995/2963).

Accordingly, on any renewal the tenant's liability cannot enure for a period longer than the time that the lease is vested in the tenant or, if an AGA is entered into upon assignment by the tenant, for so long as the tenancy is vested in the assignee. Section 16 of the 1995 Act does not permit the landlord to request an AGA upon assignment as of right. The requirement for an AGA must be reasonable. By virtue of s.16(3)(b) of the 1995 Act, a landlord's requirement for an AGA is valid and enforceable only if it is a requirement that is "lawfully imposed". Where an assignment requires the landlord's consent, and the alienation covenant is silent on the specific issue of whether or not he can demand an AGA, then the landlord can only refuse consent if it is reasonable to do so: see s.19(1) of the Landlord and Tenant Act 1927. In those circumstances, the landlord can only impose a condition upon the grant of his consent if that condition is reasonable. If it was reasonable to demand an AGA as a condition of his consent, then the demand is lawfully imposed. If it is unreasonable to make such a demand, then it was not lawfully imposed: *Wallis Fashion Group Ltd v CGU Life Assurance Ltd*[140] (digested in para.8–68).

8–67 As a result of the provisions of the 1995 Act the landlord will be entitled to seek as a term of the new lease a condition that the tenant, upon assignment, enter into an AGA. However, it is unlikely that the court will provide for this right to be automatic rather than permitting the landlord to insist upon an AGA only where such a requirement is reasonable. The court in *Wallis Fashion Group Ltd v CGU Life Assurance Ltd*[141] (digested in para.8–68) when faced with this argument decided on the facts of that case that the landlord could only insist upon an AGA if reasonable to do so. It was said that although a qualification of reasonableness as to the requirement of the outgoing tenant to enter into an AGA could lead to disputes and to litigation, a dispute as to the reasonableness of the landlord's requirement for an AGA would not normally be likely to raise a reasonableness debate, unless there was a wider reasonableness debate already on foot, in relation to the proposed assignment. In practice, at least normally, either the parties will agree all the terms upon which an assignment will take place or they will agree none of them. Furthermore, the standard of unreasonableness was not ungenerous to the landlord. In order to show that the landlord's requirement for an AGA was unreasonable, the tenant would have to show that no reasonable landlord could, in the circumstances, require it. This struck a fair balance between the interests of the parties. The suggestion by the landlord in that case that all, bar one (due to an oversight), of the tenants in the landlord's shopping centre had accepted the provision for an automatic AGA, although a factor for the court to consider, was not conclusive in the landlord's favour. It was said that one had to bear in mind that each of the other tenants who agreed the clause may not have regarded the point as one worth holding out for if all other issues were agreed. In the context of another type of dispute, namely as to the value of freeholds under the Leasehold Reform Act 1967, the Lands Tribunal has developed the concept of the "*Delaforce* effect", which is occasionally invoked to answer reliance by landlords upon what other tenants have agreed. Many tenants may be prepared to concede a particular point in negotiations because it is not a point of great

[140] [2000] 2 E.G.L.R. 49 Ch D.
[141] [2000] 2 E.G.L.R. 49 Ch D.

importance in relation to a particular case, but the landlord is prepared to insist on it, as he has far wider interests. So far as estate management factors were concerned, the court was prepared to accept that it is more convenient for a landlord to have all leases in a given development on as similar terms as possible. However, particularly in the age of computers, it was unrealistic to suggest that the landlord's records would have any difficulty in coping with the fact that the tenant's tenancy would contain a slightly different provision so far as a landlord's right to demand an AGA on an assignment was concerned.

Wallis Fashion Group Ltd v CGU Life Assurance Ltd[142] Wallis Fashion Group Ltd (Wallis), had been granted a lease of business premises for 25 years from June 24, 1974. The premises formed part of a shopping centre which comprised some 18 units. The lease included covenants by the tenant: (1) not to assign part only of the premises comprised in the lease (the premises); (2) not to assign the whole of the premises without obtaining the consent of the landlord; and (3) not to assign the whole of the premises unless the assignee enters into a covenant with the landlord to observe all the covenants in the lease for its duration. Under its current lease (the lease), Wallis was liable throughout the whole contractual term on the tenant's covenants, whether it had assigned or not. Further, because of cl.(3), an assignee of the lease from Wallis could have been made similarly liable if the landlord had required it. Apart from this, the lease could only be assigned with the landlord's consent, which was not to be unreasonably withheld. If Wallis had assigned the lease, it would not be liable under the tenant's covenants beyond June 24, 1999 (the contractual expiry date of the lease). As the present lease was granted in 1974, the 1995 Act has no relevant application to it. However, the new tenancy (the tenancy) to be granted to Wallis, being granted after January 1, 1996, would be subject to the Landlord and Tenant (Covenants) Act 1995 (the 1995 Act). **8–68**

The alienation covenant in the proposed new lease provided that the landlord's consent could be subject to various conditions as is permitted by s.19(1)(a) of the Landlord and Tenant Act 1927 as amended by the 1995 Act. Wallis proposed that one of the conditions should be in these terms:

> "For the purpose of s.19(1)(a) of the 1927 Act it is further agreed that any consent of the landlord to an assignment of the whole of the demised premises may be subject to a condition that (where reasonable) the tenant shall prior to the proposed assignment being completed execute and deliver to the landlord a deed which shall be prepared by the landlord's solicitors containing covenants on the part of the tenant in the form of those contained in the seventh schedule therein defined as the present tenant."

The provisions of the Seventh Schedule provided for an AGA to be entered into by the outgoing tenant in accordance with s.16 of the 1995 Act. The dispute between the parties was whether the words, "where reasonable", should be included, as Wallis contended, or should not be included, as the landlord contended. On Wallis's construction, on an assignment by the tenant for the time being, the landlord could require an AGA in the form agreed in the Seventh

142 [2000] 2 E.G.L.R. 49 Ch D.

Schedule, but only if it is reasonable to do so. On the landlord's construction, an AGA could be required in such circumstances as an automatic matter of right.

The landlord contended he was as a matter of the interpretation of the 1995 Act entitled to require an AGA as of right without needing to show that such a requirement was reasonable. If that were wrong the landlord in support of the omission of the words "where reasonable" relied on three factors. First, even as proposed by the landlord, the alienation provisions in the tenancy would be more generous to the tenant, and less beneficial to the landlord, than under the lease, and the court should lean in favour of following the terms of the current lease: see s.35(1) and *O'May*.[143] Secondly, a reasonableness requirement can, even with the best will in the world on both sides, lead to uncertainty, and to costly and time-consuming disputes. Thirdly, all but one (due to an oversight) of the 15 other tenants who had agreed new tenancies in the landlord's shopping centre, 14 had consented to the inclusion of the alienation provision in the form contended for by the landlord. The judge accepted Wallis' proposal.

(1) First, a landlord, whose consent cannot be unreasonably withheld to an assignment, is not, where the alienation covenant is silent as to the landlord's right to an AGA, automatically entitled to require an AGA when his consent to an assignment is sought.

(2) So far as the landlord's first reason was concerned, the terms of s.35 of the 1954 Act, as interpreted in *O'May*,[144] did not entitle the landlord to say that, on a renewal under the 1954 Act, he should be given as generous terms as the 1995 Act provides.

(3) So far as the landlord's second point was concerned, albeit the court saw the force of the argument, in a covenant of the sort proposed by Wallis, the standard of unreasonableness was not ungenerous to the landlord. In order to show that the landlord's requirement for an AGA was unreasonable, the tenant would have to show that no reasonable landlord could, in the circumstances, require it.

(4) So far as the third factor was concerned, the fact that, with one exception (due to an oversight), the other 15 tenants had agreed the clause in the form for which the landlord contended indicated that market forces tend to produce a form of covenant as contended for by the landlord and was a factor that assisted the landlord (particularly following what Lord Wilberforce, rather than Lord Hailsham, said in *O'May*.[145]) However, one had to bear in mind that each of the other tenants who agreed the clause may not have regarded the point as one worth holding out for if all other issues were agreed.

[143] [1983] 2 A.C. 726; [1982] 2 W.L.R. 407; [1982] 1 All E.R. 660 HL.

[144] [1983] 2 A.C. 726; [1982] 2 W.L.R. 407; [1982] 1 All E.R. 660 HL.

[145] [1983] 2 A.C. 726; [1982] 2 W.L.R. 407; [1982] 1 All E.R. 660 HL.

Guarantors

Section 41A(6) expressly provides that, in the special circumstances where only one of two or more joint tenants formerly in partnership obtains a new tenancy, the court has power to order the grant to be made subject to the satisfaction, within a time specified by the order, of conditions as to guarantors, sureties or otherwise as appear to the court equitable, having regard to the omission of the other joint tenants from the persons who will be the joint tenant under the new tenancy. **8–69**

Where s.41A does not apply, the power of the court in relation to guarantors is somewhat different. It would appear that the court is not entitled to refuse the grant of a new tenancy upon the ground that the tenant is not willing to provide a guarantor, even when there was a guarantor party to the current tenancy, because that is not one of the grounds for dismissal specified in s.30(1). However, the Court of Appeal has held in *Cairnplace v CBL*[146] (digested in para.8–71) that the court has a discretion, under s.35, to insert a term in the new tenancy obliging the tenant, within a specified period, to secure that a satisfactory guarantor shall join in the lease. Presumably the way in which this is to be enforced is that, if a satisfactory guarantor has not been provided within the said time, the landlord can serve a notice pursuant to s.146 of the Law of Property Act 1925, complaining of that breach of the terms of the tenancy, and then forfeit the lease. The tenant would be entitled to apply for relief, but this would be unlikely to be granted without the provision of a satisfactory guarantor. **8–70**

Cairnplace v CBL (Property Investment) Co[147] The landlord granted to X a lease which contained, inter alia, a covenant in the usual form restricting alienation by the tenant with a proviso that upon assignment to a limited company, if so required by the landlord, two directors of the company should join the sureties to guarantee the observance by the tenant of the tenant's covenants. The lease also contained a covenant requiring the tenant to pay the landlord's costs of preparing the lease. X assigned the lease to a limited company. One year of the term then remained and it was obvious at that time that an eventual application for a new tenancy by the company was contemplated. Two of the company's four directors acted as guarantors of the company's obligations under the lease. The tenant company applied for a new tenancy, which the landlords did not oppose. The terms of the new tenancy were agreed, save that the landlord wished to retain the guarantors of the old lease as guarantors of the new lease and wanted the tenant company to pay the costs of the preparation of the new lease. **8–71**

At the hearing before the county court judge it was found that the tenant company, having been recently incorporated, was unable to produce accounts. Evidence was given of its turnover by one of its directors which showed that its profit margin was low. The tenant company had a bank overdraft of about £30,000, security for which was provided by two houses belonging to two directors of the company. The tenant company's outgoings, by way of rent, in respect of the new tenancy would be increased. The judge held, inter alia, that the

[146] [1984] 1 W.L.R. 696; [1984] 1 All E.R. 315 CA.

[147] [1984] 1 W.L.R. 696; [1984] 1 All E.R. 315 CA.

new lease of the premises was to include: (1) a term requiring the tenant company to provide two guarantors, who were to be directors of the tenant company, within six months of the execution of the lease, to guarantee observance of its obligations under the lease throughout the new tenancy; (2) a term providing that the costs of preparing the new lease were to be borne by the tenant. The tenant appealed against the order. It was held that:

(a) The court had a discretion under s.35 to include a term in the new lease requiring the tenant to provide guarantors of his obligations thereunder.
(b) The judge was wrong in requiring the tenant company to pay the landlord's costs of preparing the new lease, for the tenant, by virtue of s.1 of the Costs of Leases Act 1958, was under an obligation to pay the landlord's costs of preparation of the new lease only where the parties had expressly so agreed. The court should not, in determining the term of the new lease, exercise its discretion under s.35 so as to deprive the tenant of protection conferred on him by the 1958 Act. Thus, although the parties had provided for costs of preparation to be borne by the tenant in the old lease, no such provision was to be incorporated as a term of the new lease.

8–72 The requirement to obtain guarantors is likely to be imposed where the tenant company has recently been incorporated, the tenant having taken an assignment shortly prior to the expiration of the term: as in *Cairnplace v CBL*[148] (digested in para.8–71). There would appear to be no limit to the number of guarantors the court can require the tenant to provide. Thus in *Cairnplace v CBL*[149] a term was imposed requiring the tenant company to provide two guarantors. It would also appear that the court may in the exercise of its discretion under s.35(1) identify the status of the guarantors, e.g. as directors of the tenant: *Cairnplace v CBL*.[150] The Court of Appeal gave detailed reasons for requiring that guarantors be procured. Some of the more important points to emerge are the following:

(1) There were many terms in leases which depended for their efficacy on the co-operation of third parties; e.g. an obligation to insure. Admittedly there would be a ready market of insurers enabling the tenant to comply with that obligation without difficulty; however, that did not mean that the court had no jurisdiction to include a term where the market was more restricted or of a small class (e.g. director guarantors), thus rendering it more difficult for the tenant to comply with the obligation. The fact that the tenant would find it more difficult to comply with the obligation was, however, relevant in considering whether the court should exercise its discretion to include such a term.
(2) Section 41A(6) of the Act did not preclude the court from imposing a term requiring the tenant to supply guarantors: that subsection contemplates a termination of the obligation of one or more partners who are party to the

[148] [1984] 1 W.L.R. 696; [1984] 1 All E.R. 315 CA.
[149] [1984] 1 W.L.R. 696; [1984] 1 All E.R. 315 CA.
[150] [1984] 1 W.L.R. 696; [1984] 1 All E.R. 315 CA.

old lease which, therefore, necessarily gave a different security to the landlord than that under the new lease.

(3) The application for a new lease by the tenant company was clearly contemplated on the assignment; the risks of the tenant defaulting over a 10-year period, which was the duration of the new lease, were greater than that of one year, the tail-end of the old lease; the whole adventure was promoted by two directors who by their voting rights controlled the tenant company. In those circumstances it could not be said that the judge had erred in exercising her discretion to include a term in the new lease requiring two directors of the tenant company to act as guarantors.

(4) The jurisdiction of the court to impose such a term was not confined to the special facts of the instant case and there were circumstances differing widely from those in the instant case in which such a term could properly be incorporated.

Costs of leases

The court should not, in exercising its discretion under s.35(1), include a term in the new lease requiring the tenant to pay the costs of the new lease, even where the current tenancy contains a term to that effect: *Cairnplace v CBL*[151] (digested in para.8–71). The reason is that by virtue of s.1 of the Costs of Leases Act 1958 the tenant is under an obligation to pay the landlord's costs of preparation of the new lease only where the parties have expressly so agreed. It was said that the court should not in determining the terms of the new lease deprive the tenant of the protection conferred on him by the 1958 Act. **8–73**

Repairs and alterations

Where the landlord is under a pre-existing obligation to repair the structure and exterior he will probably not be able to relieve himself of that liability by passing the risk on to the tenant via a service charge provision: *O'May v City of London Real Property Co Ltd*[152] (digested in para.8–47). However, one can envisage circumstances where the landlord may, for instance, wish to incorporate an entry provision to enable him to carry out work in default of the tenant and recover the costs as a debt, if the existing lease fails to contain such a provision. Where the parties are agreed as to the terms of repair, care should be taken to ensure that any order accurately reflects the new terms: *Bullen v Goodland*.[153] It was suggested by Harman L.J. in that case that "in a short tenancy of seven years, responsibility for [the] structure could be and was normally left out" of the terms of a lease and "that was [a] sensible course". It is not clear from the report what were the terms of the earlier lease between the parties. **8–74**

[151] [1984] 1 W.L.R. 696; [1984] 1 All E.R. 315 CA.

[152] [1983] 2 A.C. 726; [1982] 2 W.L.R. 407 HL.

[153] (1961) 105 S.J. 231 CA.

8–75 If the property is out of repair the landlord may seek to oppose renewal under para.(a) of s.30(1) of the Act.[154] However, if the landlord does not wish to oppose renewal nor forfeit the current lease, how can the landlord bring about a state of affairs under the terms of the new lease to be granted which requires the tenant to bring the property up to the state and condition required by the lease covenants? One solution is for the landlord to seek as a term of the new lease a provision requiring the tenant to effect repairs within a specified time[155] of grant. Such a clause of the new lease will be a departure from the terms of the old lease. As with any such departure the burden of proof will be on the landlord to justify its inclusion: *O'May v City of London Real Property Company Limited*.[156] There are several arguments justifying the imposition of a clause requiring work to be done within a specified period of time upon the grant of a new lease:

(1) that (and this will be dependent upon evidence) the existence of the dilapidations gives rise to a diminution to the landlord's reversion[157];
(2) the landlord should not have to wait until the expiration of the new lease (or at least until the last three years of the new lease[158]) in order to be able to ensure that the tenant complies with his obligations;
(3) that as a matter of essential fairness as between landlord and tenant there is no reason why the tenant should not be required to comply with his obligations and the imposition of this clause is the best means available to the court to ensure that he does so.

The arguments for opposing the introduction of this term include the following:

(a) that if there is any diminution to the landlord's reversion there is no reason why the landlord should be entitled to circumvent the Leasehold Property (Repairs) Act 1938 Act. A diminution to the landlord's reversion is a ground for the court granting consent under the 1938 Act in any event. Thus, the tenant's position will be to say that the court should let the landlord take his chance under the 1938 Act during the term of the new lease;
(b) that most modern commercial leases contain a *Jervis v Harris*[159] clause entitling the landlord to enter upon default of the tenant and recover any monies expended by way of a debt. This, as is well known, enables the landlord to circumvent the restrictions imposed by the 1938 Act. However, it does first require the landlord to expend money in effecting the repairs. The tenant will, in those circumstances, be able to say that if the landlord is

---

[154] See para.7–10 et seq.

[155] The relevant period of time being that recommended by the landlord's surveyor as being the appropriate period needed in order to remedy the disrepair.

[156] [1983] 2 A.C. 726; [1982] 2 W.L.R. 407; [1982] 1 All E.R. 660 HL.

[157] It is considered that this will have little impact on the court's approach unless the landlord is either seeking, or within the not too distant future will be seeking, to dispose of the reversion.

[158] To avoid the application of the Leasehold Property (Repairs) Act 1938, which requires the landlord to obtain leave from the court to bring a claim for damages or forfeiture in respect of dilapidations in case of leases of seven years or more with more than three years remaining unexpired.

[159] [1996] 1 E.G.L.R. 78 CA.

so concerned and the tenant defaults upon receipt of any notice, the landlord has his remedy under the *Jervis v Harris* clause.

In a case where the lease contained no restriction on alterations, for there were no written terms, the landlord nevertheless succeeded in limiting the tenant's ability to carry out alterations to non-structural alterations: *Amarjee v Barrowfen Properties*[160] (digested in para.8–151). In that case the tenant sought a term which permitted him to carry out any alterations to the premises subject to the landlord's consent, such consent not to be unreasonably withheld and subject to a provision for reinstatement at the end of the term. As there was no other lease containing such a covenant within the parade of shops owned by the landlord of which the demised premises formed part, the judge saw difficulties in permitting one tenant to do something denied to the others, including his immediate neighbour, whose premises formed part of the same structure. There were, furthermore, no immediate plans produced by the tenant as to the structural alterations it wished to effect. **8–76**

Redevelopment break clauses

In *Reohorn v Barry*[161] (digested in para.7–155) it was pointed out that "the Act should clearly not be used as an instrument to defeat development". This appears from the fact that ground (f) is a mandatory ground, in the sense that, once the landlord has proved it, the court has no discretion to grant a new tenancy. Thus, if it so happens that the landlord's plans for redevelopment have come to fruition by the term date of the current tenancy, he has an indefeasible right to deprive the tenant of security of tenure by opposing his application for a new tenancy. The Act would not have allowed a landlord to oppose on this ground as of right had it not been part of the overriding policy of the Act that the security of tenure of the tenant in his business was not absolute, but must be subject to the national interest that worn out or obsolete commercial buildings should, from time to time, be rebuilt or reconstructed. This factor may incline the court to grant only a short term of years, as has been noted above (para.8–39 et seq.). **8–77**

Alternatively, the court may grant a long term of years, but include a redevelopment break clause. The jurisdiction to do this is established by *McCombie v Grand Junction*.[162] In *Adams v Green*[163] (digested in para.8–82), this policy was expressed in strong terms by the Court of Appeal. It was there held that it is sufficient that there is a "possibility" of redevelopment of the premises within the period of the new tenancy to justify the insertion of a redevelopment break clause. It was pointed out that the tenant has certain safeguards, since the landlord will have to prove his intention under ground (f) (demolition and reconstruction) when the time comes to exercise the break, and the tenant will be entitled to his statutory compensation. **8–78**

160 [1993] 2 E.G.L.R. 133.

161 [1956] 1 W.L.R. 845; [1956] 2 All E.R. 742 CA; [1982] 2 W.L.R. 407; [1982] 1 All E.R. 660 HL.

162 [1962] 1 W.L.R. 581; [1962] 2 All E.R. 65n CA.

163 [1978] 2 E.G.L.R. 46 CA.

8–79 It is considered that the authorities support the following propositions:

(1) The court, in considering what term should be granted to the tenant, must strike a reasonable balance between two conflicting considerations: (a) that so far as reasonable the lease should not prevent the landlord from using the premises for redevelopment; (b) a reasonable degree of security of tenure should be provided to the tenants: *JH Edwards & Sons v Central London Commercial Estates*[164] (digested in para.8–83); *Becker v Hill Street Properties*[165] (digested in para.8–85). Fox L.J. said in *JH Edwards & Sons v Central London Commercial Estates*:

> "In considering what would be proper leases in the circumstances of this case, I think that the predominant considerations are two. First, that so far as reasonable the lease should not prevent the superior landlord from using premises for the purposes of development. Secondly, that a reasonable degree of security of tenure should be provided for the tenants. Those considerations are to some degree in conflict. The function of the court is to strike a reasonable balance between them in all the circumstances of the case."

(2) The legal test for determining whether or not a redevelopment break clause should be incorporated in the new lease has been formulated as whether redevelopment is "on the cards" or there is a "real possibility" of redevelopment occurring: *Adams v Green*[166] (digested in para.8–82); *National Car Parks Ltd v Paternoster Consortium Ltd*[167] (digested in para.8–86). However, as noted above, there is no indication in the formulation of the legal test for incorporating a break clause that the landlord's desire to redevelop necessarily trumps the tenant's desire for security of tenure.[168] A good example of this is the unreported decision in *Horserace Betting Levy Board v Grosvenor Properties*.[169] The tenant wanted a two-year term but the landlord wanted a one-year term as it intended to develop (the landlord having been granted planning permission for such development). The tenant was a statutory body which was about to be abolished at the end of the two-year period and needed, it said, to stay where it was to enable it to undertake an orderly closure of its work. The evidence was that it would be extremely difficult to find a two-year term in the market, that it would be disruptive to move when seeking to wind up

---

[164] [1984] 1 E.G.L.R. 103 CA.

[165] [1990] 2 E.G.L.R. 78 CA.

[166] [1978] 2 E.G.L.R. 46 CA.

[167] [1990] 1 E.G.L.R. 99.

[168] *Davy's of London (Wine Merchants) Ltd v The Mayor and Commonalty and Citizens of the City of London* [2004] 3 E.G.L.R. 39 (digested in para.8–87) per Lewison J. at [29]. In his judgment Lewison J. said:

"[22] In deciding whether a new tenancy should or should not include a break clause, the usual starting point is the statement of Stamp LJ in *Adams v Green* [1978] 2 E.G.L.R. 46, at p.47G, that:

It was no part of the policy . . . of the 1954 Act to give security of tenure to a business tenant at the expense of preventing redevelopment.

[23] *I emphasise the word 'preventing', which is not the same as 'delaying'*. In that case, the landlord had no plans for redevelopment but wished to have the flexibility to sell to a developer. The Court of Appeal, reversing the decision of the trial judge, ordered the inclusion in the new tenancy of a break clause operable on two years' notice. In other words, the tenant had guaranteed security of tenure of two years." (Emphasis supplied)

[169] Unreported 2001, Central London County Court, H.H. Judge Cooke QC.

and that it was likely to lose key staff if it had to move. The landlord had organised its affairs within the building to enable it to undertake a development after one year. However, the evidence was that it would not lose a substantial sum by way of income during the additional year if the tenant were to be granted a two-year term and certain works to the building could be effected around the tenant. The tenant won.

(3) The function of the court to strike a fair balance between the two competing aspirations necessarily presupposes that the landlord may have to wait for some time (though not so long as to prevent redevelopment) before being able to regain possession: *Davy's of London (Wine Merchants) Ltd v City of London Corp*[170] (digested in para.8–87). Thus albeit the landlord may satisfy the court that the break should be incorporated in the new lease the court may defer the date from which the break is to operate as part of the balancing exercise.

(4) The landlord may establish that there is a real possibility, albeit he calls no evidence of financial viability or of specific plans for redevelopment: *Adams v Green*.[171]

(5) The landlord does not have to show that the premises are "ripe for redevelopment": *Adams v Green*.[172]

(6) The landlord need not himself wish to carry out the redevelopment; it is sufficient that the landlord does not want to be saddled with a lease which would prevent redevelopment: *Adams v Green*[173]; nor does the landlord have to show that he will benefit in some way from its incorporation. Thus, it matters not that the landlord may have already agreed to sell the reversion for a price unaffected by the existence of a break: *Davy's of London (Wine Merchants) Ltd v City of London Corp*.[174]

(7) It is not necessary for the landlord to show that he has possession of the redevelopment site. Where the landlord will have difficulties in obtaining vacant possession of the site which is the subject of the proposed redevelopment he can give evidence that he will seek to buy out the relevant interests: *National Car Parks v Paternoster*[175] (digested in para.8–86).

(8) The landlord does not need to show he has planning permission for redevelopment: *Adams v Green*[176]; *Becker v Hill Street Properties*.[177]

(9) It is not for the court to determine whether, objectively, the scheme proposed by the landlord is desirable: *Becker v Hill Street Properties*.[178]

---

170 See fn.168 above.
171 [1978] 2 E.G.L.R. 46 CA.
172 [1978] 2 E.G.L.R. 46 CA.
173 [1978] 2 E.G.L.R. 46 CA.
174 See fn.168 above.
175 [1990] 1 E.G.L.R. 99.
176 [1978] 2 E.G.L.R. 46 CA.
177 [1990] 1 E.G.L.R. 78 CA.
178 [1990] 2 E.G.L.R. 78 CA.

(10) It is not the policy of the Act to confer upon the tenant a saleable asset: *Gold v Brighton Corp*[179] (digested in para.8–61), approved in *Adams v Green*[180] and *JH Edwards v Central London Commercial Estates.*[181]

(11) The fact that the compensation payable to the tenant would be inadequate (upon the landlord exercising the break and opposing renewal under s.30(1)(f)) is an irrelevant consideration; the question of the adequacy of the statutory compensation is a matter for Parliament: *JH Edwards v Central London Commercial Estates.*[182]

(12) The court may insert a redevelopment break clause albeit this would cause financial hardship to the tenant, if it were to be exercised, because of the substantial investment which the tenant has made to the premises: *Amika Motors v Colebrook Holdings*[183] (digested in para.8–84).

Tenant's break clauses

8–80 Tenants often seek the incorporation of a break clause. There is no reported English authority in respect of the incorporation of a break clause by a tenant, although the test for incorporation of a landlord's redevelopment break clause[184] may apply by analogy, i.e. is there a realistic prospect of the event happening (usually affecting the tenant's relocation of its business), for which the break is sought during the duration of the term to be granted. In *First Secretary of State v Greatestates Ltd*[185] both parties were content with a 10-year term of office premises in Hackney but the tenant wanted a break after the fifth year of the term, as it was said that its property requirements generally, and in particular whether or not it needed the subject property, were uncertain. It was said by the tenant, a government department, that there was a realistic possibility of relocation by the end of the fifth year of the term. Interestingly, in this case the judge accepted, by analogy, that the test for determining whether the tenant should be entitled to his break, was the same test as that for determining whether a landlord should be able to obtain a redevelopment break clause, i.e. was there a realistic possibility (as opposed to a probability) that the tenant would need to vacate at the end of the five-year period. However, even on this beneficial test the tenant did not succeed. The evidence of the tenant was that there was no need for flexibility at the demised premises specifically. The tenant as a statutory body had a general policy over the whole of its estate to have short but commercially realistic terms for office premises. The tenant had no evidence, oral or documentary, that the subject property was earmarked for a possible, let alone probable, move. On the contrary the evidence that the tenant did have was that it had in fact vacated other premises in Hackney and had relocated staff to the subject property. The inference, in the absence of evidence to the contrary, was that there was therefore no realistic possibility of a move in five years time. The fact that the government department

179 [1956] 1 W.L.R. 1291 at 1294.
180 [1978] 2 E.G.L.R. 46 CA.
181 [1984] 2 E.G.L.R. 103 CA.
182 [1984] 2 E.G.L.R. 103 CA.
183 [1981] 2 E.G.L.R. 62 CA.
184 As to which test, see para.8–79(2).
185 Unreported 2005, Central London County Court, H.H. Judge Dean QC.

had a policy to retain employment opportunities in deprived areas (of which Hackney was one) was a fact in support of that conclusion.

As is apparent from the facts of *First Secretary of State v Greatestates Ltd*[186] the tenant will be required to justify the incorporation of the break by reference to factors affecting the premises demised and not by reference to general policy considerations, e.g. to retain flexibility. Thus, for instance a concern about competition adversely affecting the business will not of itself justify the incorporation of a break clause if the competition about which concern is expressed affects tenants generally rather than the tenant in particular with respect to his occupation of the demised premises. Thus, in *Eason and Son (NI) Ltd v Central Craigavon Ltd*,[187] a tenant within a shopping centre sought to incorporate a break clause at Years 6 and 11 in an agreed term of 15 years. Of the 16 tenants within the shopping centre only two had been granted breaks, and the landlord gave evidence as to why it was that in those particular cases break clauses were incorporated for the benefit of those two tenants. The tenant's reason for seeking a break was essentially driven by a concern about its ability to assign the premises because the premises were unusually large and his business was, he considered, likely to be adversely affected by increased competition. The Court declined to incorporate a break clause. It said: **8–81**

> "The user permits the sale of items such as newspapers, periodicals, magazines, books, stationery and greeting cards etc. There is a qualified permission for change of use within Use Class 1 of the Planning (Use Classes) (NI) Order 1989 [equivalent to the 1987 Use Classes Order]. The unit is unusually large and the market for such a unit may be limited. There is increased competition within the tenant's trade particularly as a result of the abolition of the Net Book Agreement, a wider availability of newspapers in supermarkets etc, the arrival of specialist greeting card retailers and the prospect of strong competition from a national multiple. Mr Tinsley [a director of the tenant company who gave evidence] illustrated the effects of the competition from supermarkets in particular was having on its trade. *The Tribunal is not persuaded that there is any significantly greater danger to the tenant from the prospects of increased competition nearby than that which might affect other classes of retailers.* It also accepts Mr Cassidy's [the valuer on behalf of the landlord] suggestion that the agreed new user clause with its qualified permission for change of use permits trade flexibility through the capacity for Class 1 retailing and that provides a degree of comfort in the context of both continuing occupation and alienation." (emphasis supplied) (at [16])

Adams v Green[188] The tenant carried on business from shop premises which formed part of a row of 12 shops owned by the landlord. The entire row was approximately 100 years of age. The landlords had, in granting tenancies to seven of the 12 tenants, insisted on a redevelopment break clause. The tenant's current tenancy did not contain a redevelopment break clause. At the hearing of the tenant's application for a new tenancy, the landlords contended, inter alia, for a tenancy of 14 years subject to a right for the landlords to determine the tenancy at any time by giving not less than two years' prior notice in writing if the landlord wished to demolish or reconstruct the premises. The landlords were themselves **8–82**

[186] Unreported 2005, Central London County Court, H.H. Judge Dean QC.

[187] June 19, 2003 (Westlaw Case No.21729343) (Lands Tribunal of Northern Ireland, where the Tribunal is concerned with the Business (Northern Ireland) Order 1996, which is, in this context, identical to that of the 1954 Act).

[188] [1978] 2 E.G.L.R. 46 CA.

unlikely to implement any redevelopment of the premises as they were probably unable to obtain the necessary finance. However, the landlords were soon to retire and wanted the redevelopment clause so as not to be saddled with a lease of premises which would be unattractive to a prospective developer/purchaser. The landlords did not, however, produce any study on the financial viability of redevelopment of the premises. The county court judge held that although the premises were not ripe for redevelopment, redevelopment was sufficiently likely to make it unjust to impose upon the landlords a 14-year lease with no break and accordingly granted the tenant a term of seven years without a break clause.

The Court of Appeal ordered that a new lease should be for 14 years with a break clause as contended for by the landlords, which was a break clause operable at any time on two years' notice.

8–83 ***JH Edwards & Sons v Central London Commercial Estates; Eastern Bazaar v Central London Commercial Estates***[189] Two tenant companies occupied shops which flanked the north of the main entrance to a large hotel which the landlords also owned. One of the tenants had traded there since 1958 under three consecutive leases, while the other was of more recent origin. Both the expired tenancies, which had been for five years each, contained break clauses providing for development at the landlord's option. The evidence revealed that the reason the break clauses had been inserted was with a view to the comprehensive redevelopment of the whole site (including the hotel and the shops). By the hearing of the tenants' applications for new tenancies the landlords had abandoned this scheme and had instead entered into an agreement to grant a long lease of the whole site to a hotel company which intended to carry out substantial work thereto.[190] This might in due course involve making the shops into part of an enlarged hotel entrance hall. The landlords satisfied the county court judge that there was a "possibility of a bona fide decision to operate a break clause" if one were granted, in respect of each renewal. The judge ordered, however, that the new tenancies should be of 12 and 10 years' duration and should not contain break clauses, since the tenants would suffer greater hardship if breaks were inserted than the landlords would if they were not. It was held:

(1) Where it was likely that the landlords might wish to develop property then, since it is not the policy of the Act to inhibit development, they "should not be saddled with a lease which may prevent such development".
(2) It was, in such circumstances, wrong to order the grant of new tenancies for such substantial periods as 12 and 10 years without development break clauses.

---

[189] [1984] 2 E.G.L.R. 103 CA.

[190] The landlord had abandoned its scheme involving a comprehensive development of hotel premises, with shops on the ground floor, and had let the hotel under a long lease to the hotel company. The hotel company was soon to become landlord of the shops and the issue was whether the landlord was entitled to break clauses, effectively for the benefit of the hotel, in respect of the new shop leases. The hotel wished to reserve to itself the right to carry out work to the shops. The evidence in that case was not terribly satisfactory so far as the landlord was concerned.

(3) In substitution therefore the tenants should each be granted new tenancies for seven years with rent reviews to take effect from the end of the fifth year and with redevelopment break clauses not to take effect until the end of the fifth year.

Amika Motors v Colebrook Holdings[191] The tenant carried on the business of motor dealers at premises consisting of showrooms fronted by an open forecourt area. The tenant had obtained a franchise for Toyota motorcars and required as a consequence the use of service facilities. The tenant duly bought premises next door to the business premises and converted them at considerable capital expense as a workshop for cars. A few days after the completion of the works, the landlord served a notice under s.25 in respect of the business premises stating that it did not oppose the grant of a new tenancy. The landlord at the hearing before the county court judge contended that although it could not oppose the grant of a new tenancy under ground (f) of s.30 (demolition and reconstruction) it did, in fact, have the intention and ability to carry out a scheme which would fall within ground (f) and therefore any new tenancy granted to the tenant should contain a redevelopment break clause. **8–84**

The judge found that the landlord intended to carry out a scheme of redevelopment which included the tenant's holding, but that if the tenant did not obtain a new long-term lease it would be in grave difficulties as it could lead to the loss of its franchise rights and of its capital invested in the development of the workshop. The judge held, however, that the landlord could not reasonably carry out the development without access to the whole of the tenant's holding and accordingly he granted a five-year term with an option to the landlord to terminate the lease for the purpose of reconstruction by giving not less than six-months' notice, such notice not to expire before three years from the date of the commencement of the lease—effectively being a break two years after the hearing. The tenant appealed. It was held on appeal that where the landlord has a bona fide intention of developing his land, even if that intention is not capable of immediate realisation, the terms of the new tenancy should not impede the realisation of that intention. Although the tenant would suffer hardship if it was not given a new long-term lease, redevelopment of land should not be prevented. Accordingly the judge's decision, having taken into account all the considerations, was in conformity with the scheme of the Act. The appeal was, therefore, dismissed.

Becker v Hill Street Properties[192] Mr Salter, the long leasehold owner of 6 Upper Wimpole Street, London W1, occupied the second and third floors as a residential maisonette and let the other parts to three medical practitioners. One of these was Mr Becker who in January 1980 took an underlease of two rooms on the first floor for a term expiring on December 25, 1984. There he carried on practice as a dentist. On June 21, 1984, Mr Salter served a notice on Mr Becker under s.25 stating that he would not oppose the grant of a new tenancy. Mr Becker applied to the court and there followed prolonged negotiations which led **8–85**

[191] [1981] 2 E.G.L.R. 62 CA.
[192] [1990] 2 E.G.L.R. 78 CA.

to nothing. In 1987 Mr Salter died and his executrices indicated to Mr Becker that they intended to redevelop the premises. In the event, they sold their long leasehold interest to Hill Street Properties Ltd, who bought with full notice of Mr Becker's rights and those of the other two medical tenants, one of whom had a lease which did not expire until December 24, 1993. When Mr Becker's application came before the county court the only issue was the duration of the new tenancy and the possibility of including a redevelopment break clause. The judge granted a term expiring on December 24, 1993, with no break clause. The principal reasons for his decision were that in his view the premises were not "ripe for redevelopment". He said:

> "I do not know if there is any urgency to refurbish in reality . . . In my judgment this building is not ripe for redevelopment. I think it has got many years of use ahead of it and can be used for its present purposes . . . It is not evidence that conversion into luxury flats [as the new landlords proposed] is desirable."

The landlords appealed to the Court of Appeal. It was held:

(1) That it was irrelevant whether a particular development proposed by the landlord was objectively desirable. The question was what the landlord bona fide wants to do with the premises, not whether, considered objectively, the premises were so worn out, so old and so tired that they were in need of complete redevelopment.

(2) It was important to have in mind that the term awarded by the judge was not a very long term; that there should be a reasonable degree of security of tenure for tenants; that Mr Becker had been practising in the Harley Street area since 1962 and from the premises since 1979; that he was 66 and due to retire in December 1993; that it would be difficult to find alternative premises for a short period; and that it would take the landlords at least 12 months, probably longer, to get on site. Weighing all the factors it was appropriate that the term should be one expiring on December 24, 1993 without any break. The appeal was dismissed.

8–86 ***National Car Parks Ltd v Paternoster Consortium Ltd***[193] The tenants, NCP, were holding over under the terms of a lease of a large purpose-built car park under Paternoster Square, part of a large 1960s development adjacent to St Paul's Cathedral. A long leasehold interest in the Paternoster site, including the car park, six large office buildings and numerous retail units, was acquired by the Paternoster Consortium. The consortium began to implement plans aimed at a comprehensive redevelopment of the site, including the car park. NCP applied to the court for a new tenancy of the car park for a term of 10 years. The consortium asked for a redevelopment break clause to be inserted, operable on six months' notice. The court ordered that the question of the break clause should be tried as a preliminary issue.

At trial the consortium led detailed evidence as to its efforts to obtain planning permission and to obtain vacant possession from the office and retail tenants, and as to how the scheme was to be financed. It hoped to make a start on demolition

193 [1990] 1 E.G.L.R. 99.

work to the car park site in June 1990.[194] NCP pointed to the uncertainties inherent in the position, since planning permission had not yet been applied for, a number of interests remained to be bought out, and the future ownership of the site itself seemed in doubt. NCP asked for 10 years without break; alternatively, for a break operable not earlier than December 1993, when most of the shop leases fell in; alternatively, for a break exercisable only when planning permission and full vacant possession had actually been obtained.

It was held that the test for determining whether a redevelopment break clause should be incorporated was whether there was a real possibility, as opposed to a probability, that redevelopment would be practicable within the term of the lease. This had been demonstrated to be the case, and since the disturbance to NCP's business was very small compared to other businesses, a break clause should be included. Furthermore, there was no logic in limiting operation of the clause to 1993, since the retail leases might well be bought out before that date. Nor would it be right to make the exercise of the break subject to the precondition that planning permission and vacant possession should actually have been obtained. Because the new tenancy would be protected by the Act, the security of tenure afforded by the Act would in effect allow NCP to delay redevelopment for up to a year, at great cost to the developers if such a precondition were inserted. Accordingly, the break clause was to be operable on six months' notice.

Davy's of London (Wine Merchants) Ltd v The Mayor and Commonalty and Citizens of the City of London[195] L sought the introduction of a rolling break clause operable on six-months' notice (being a change at trial from the original 11 months' notice proposed in L's acknowledgement of service) but not to be operated before September 2005, being approximately 18 months after the commencement of the new term. The building of which the demised premises formed part was some 25 years old. The corporation wished to demolish the building and carry out a major redevelopment. The corporation did not intend to carry out the work themselves, but had negotiated a sale of the building to a development company. However, the development of the building formed part of a large site intended to be the subject of development. The assembly of the development site was complicated and it was considered that it would take some two to three years to complete the site assembly. No planning application had been made, it being considered better to wait until the site had been assembled before doing so. T objected to the incorporation of the break clause on four grounds: 8–87

(1) that in order for a redevelopment break clause to be incorporated L had to show that the redevelopment was to be carried out by or at least for the benefit of the landlord seeking the incorporation of the break clause. T pointed out that the purchase price had been agreed and thus the break was of no benefit to L. L argued that this was wrong and that the question was

[194] As things turned out the comprehensive redevelopment of the Paternoster Square site was delayed by the recession and only commenced in 2002. It has now been completed and occupied.

[195] Unreported November 27, 2003 Mayor and City of London Court. On appeal: *Davy's of London (Wine Merchants) Ltd v City of London Corp* [2004] 3 E.G.L.R. 39.

not whether the landlord ultimately intends to develop or benefit from the development but simply whether the development was a real possibility by whomsoever it be accomplished;

(2) that because of the difficulties in the site assembly, the prospect of the development was so speculative that it should be disregarded;

(3) that there was an over supply of office space and the economic climate meant that any development was not economically viable;

(4) that T wished to incur substantial expenditure in modernising the demised premises. Although the premises were reasonably successful T wanted to spend some £70,000 to £80,000 on refurbishment and such an investment required a reasonable degree of security of tenure and accordingly if a break clause were to be incorporated T needed a term of between seven and 10 years without a break in order properly to invest in the business and obtain a return on the expenditure to be incurred.

The learned judge held:

(a) as to the first argument L was correct. In *JH Edwards v Central London Commercial Estates*[196] Fox L.J. had emphasised that, in considering the incorporation of a break clause it was not "satisfactory to look at the matter simply from the point of view of the present landlord." Similarly in *National Car Parks v Paternoster Consortium Ltd*[197] the landlord's interest was, at the date of the hearing, the subject of negotiation, and it was the proposed purchaser of the landlord's interest, who had not yet completed the transaction, who was intending to develop the site;

(b) that, on the evidence, L had underestimated the time that it would take to assemble the redevelopment site. However, the economics of the project were such that, at some stage during the currency of the new lease, the development would be economically viable;

(c) T's expressed intention to invest in his business was to be disregarded. For nearly 20 years T had incurred costs only on repair and replacement and the business was profitable. T did not voice any concerns over the impact of a break clause on investment until the need arose to make the application for renewal. Further, any investment would in any event result in a return on capital (having regard to the agreed rents between the parties);

(d) in the circumstances, L was to have a break operable after the fifth year of the term, but subject to 11 and not six-months' notice.

On appeal, having regard to new evidence admitted on the appeal, Lewison J. varied the break clause enabling the landlord to terminate the tenancy on or after June 1, 2008 by service of not less than 11 months' notice.

8–88 A form of compromise might be the insertion not of a redevelopment break clause, but of a reservation similar to that in *Heath v Drown*[198] (digested in para.7–103), which would enable the landlord to carry out certain works of

196 [1984] 1 E.G.L.R. 103 CA.

197 [1990] 1 E.G.L.R. 99.

198 [1973] A.C. 498; [1972] 2 W.L.R. 1306; [1972] 2 All E.R. 561 HL.

reconstruction and improvement to the premises during the new tenancy. In *Fernandez v Walding*,[199] it was tacitly assumed that the court had no power to do so–an assumption which Lord Kilbrandon apparently accepted in *Heath v Drown*. Nonetheless, such a compromise would enable the landlord to improve his asset, while preserving for the tenant his security of tenure and the goodwill of his business. The fact that the premises had been improved by the landlord at his own expense and would accordingly be of greater value to the tenant could be reflected by a suitable provision for rent review to take effect upon completion of the works. This would, of course, only be an acceptable solution to the problem if the works were of a comparatively limited nature and if the premises as reconstructed or improved were still suitable for the purposes of the tenant's business.

Special provisions

Section 60(2) contains special provisions for premises provided under the Local Employment Acts, enabling the appropriate minister to certify that certain terms should be included in a new tenancy. It is not appropriate to summarise the detailed provisions of this subsection here and any interested readers are referred to the statutory provision for its terms. The same can be said to any readers interested in s.60A or 60B (special provisions relating to Wales). **8–89**

5. RENT (SECTION 34)

Last matter to be determined

In *Cardshops v Davies*[200] the Court of Appeal pointed out that it is inappropriate for the court to consider the question of rent until the parties have agreed, or the court has determined, what should be the property comprised in the tenancy, what should be the length of tenancy and what should be its other terms, since each of these matters is, in principle, capable of affecting the amount of rent payable. In practice it is not unusual for the amount of rent to be agreed, even when there are other matters in dispute or for rent to be agreed on alternative bases, depending upon what the court should decide about the matters in dispute: see, e.g. *O'May v City of London Real Property*[201] (digested in para.8–47). Rent for the purposes of s.34 should be considered to exclude other payments by the tenant to the landlord such as service charges or insurance payments, even if they are reserved as further or additional rent. **8–90**

199 [1968] 2 Q.B. 606; [1968] 2 W.L.R. 583; [1968] 1 All E.R. 994 CA. See para.7–92 fn.109.
200 [1971] 1 W.L.R. 591; [1971] 2 All E.R. 721 CA.
201 [1983] 2 A.C. 726; [1982] 2 W.L.R. 407; [1982] 1 All E.R. 660 HL.

Rent determined by process of valuation

8–91 As is pointed out in *O'May v City of London Real Property Ltd*[202] (digested in para.8–47), a sharp distinction is to be drawn between the process which the court carries out under s.34 and that which it carries out under s.35, or for that matter s.33. The power under s.34 is not a matter of discretion but a matter of valuation. Evidence about the appropriate market rent for a property is admissible only if it is an objective valuation by an expert valuer. Thus, although a trader can give evidence on the trading conditions in his area, he cannot, for the purpose of being used as a comparable, give evidence about the appropriate market for his own property: *Rogers v Rosedimond Investments*[203] (digested in para.11–34).

Turnover rent

8–92 A question of principle arises as to whether the court has power under s.34 to determine that the rent is to be payable by reference to a formula, such as one which relates it to the tenant's turnover, rather than simply carrying out a valuation by reference to open market rack rents payable for comparable properties. Turnover rent provisions are commonly found in leases of licensed premises and are becoming more common (as a component part of an aggregate rental) in leases of retail premises in shopping centres. In practical terms the question is most likely to be raised where the rent under the current tenancy is assessed, in whole or in part, by reference to some agreed formula although, strictly speaking, the provisions of the current tenancy as to rent have no direct part to play in the assessment under s.34(1) which is concerned with the new tenancy, not the current tenancy.

8–93 The argument that the court has jurisdiction to assess a "turnover rent" (or some other rent linked to a formula) in an appropriate case is based upon the words "might reasonably be expected to be let in the open market". It may be argued that one is being directed by these words to ask how the rent for the demised premises would be assessed in the open market if the premises were being let on the relevant valuation date. If the court finds, on the evidence presented at the hearing, that rents in the open market for premises like the demised premises would be assessed by reference to a turnover rent, such a rent would be the "market rent" for such premises, not a rent of a fixed amount assessed by reference to rack rent transactions. This argument may be supported by reference to *Naylor v Uttoxeter Urban DC*[204] where Brightman J. determined the rent under the new tenancy of a cattle market as being 20 per cent of the gross commission earned by the tenant, a firm of auctioneers. What is not clear from that case is how the judge's determination was reflected in the terms of the new tenancy, since the matter was adjourned for the precise terms of the lease to be agreed, having regard to the judgment given. Another decision, *Stride & Son v Chichester Corp*,[205] is often cited as an example of the court awarding a rent by reference to

[202] [1983] 2 A.C. 726; [1982] 2 W.L.R. 407; [1982] 1 All E.R. 660 HL.
[203] [1978] 2 E.G.L.R. 48 CA.
[204] (1974) 231 E.G. 619.
[205] [1960] E.G.D. 117.

the tenant's turnover. However, in that case the parties' surveyors had agreed that that was how the rent was to be assessed and the rent was fixed for the duration of the lease; it was not expressed as a varying sum referable to the percentage of the turnover from time to time. In *Inntrepreneur Pub Co Ltd v Palmer*[206]it was held that the court did have jurisdiction to fix an interim rent by reference to a percentage of turnover in an appropriate case. This was not a cattle market case but was of shop premises.

There are, however, powerful countervailing arguments to the effect that the court has no jurisdiction either to fix an initial rent by reference to the tenant's turnover (as was done by agreement in the *Stride* case) or as a variable turnover figure. It can be argued that such an approach conflicts with the express disregards of the effect upon rent of the tenant's occupation of the holding and of the goodwill of the tenant's business (as to which see para.8–138 et seq. below). Any fixing of an initial rent by reference to what the tenant has, in the period leading up to the grant of the new tenancy, been able to earn by way of turnover or commission, would seem to include an element attributable both to the tenant's occupation and to his goodwill. It is not easy to see how the rent could be adjusted so as to give effect to those disregards.[207] Similarly, where the court orders that the rent will vary from time to time during the new tenancy by reference to the tenant's actual turnover, it is even more difficult to say that that rent will, at all material times, give full effect to the disregards. It remains to be seen how a court would decide between these conflicting arguments. **8–94**

---

206 Unreported April 16, 1998, Brighton CC, H.H. Judge Viner.

207 This is a concern expressed in *Woodfall, Law of Landlord and Tenant* (London: Sweet & Maxwell) Vol.2, para.22.149.6 where it is stated:

"(g) Turnover In appropriate circumstances, the court may fix the rent by reference to a percentage of the tenant's turnover or commission. To date this has only been done in the case of livestock markets, but it may be that the court would have such power in relation to retail units where there are no comparables (e.g. motorway shop) or where the current tenancy provides for rent to be assessed on that basis. It is not entirely clear how the problem of disregarding the tenant's goodwill can be overcome in these circumstances."

It is common practice in undertaking a profits method of valuation to make use of past trading accounts as a guide to the future. The actual trading accounts are those of the actual operator of the demised premises. Assuming these are available (and there is an argument that they are not available, as they would not be documents in the public domain: *Cornwall Coast Country Club v Cardgrange* [1987] 1 E.G.L.R. 146; *Lynall v IRC* [1972] A.C. 680 HL and see para.11–70 et seq.) the valuer will be faced with the task of having to eliminate the effect on his valuation of the fact that he is using accounts of an up and running business of a tenant who is in occupation. A willing lessee of premises such as a hotel would be likely to be faced with substantial initial expenditure. Similarly, an existing hotel operation would have built up considerable goodwill. This has to be assumed not to be in existence so that, again, it will take the willing lessee some years before he can build up a trading reputation and a body of customers likely to return. The result of these two factors is that the hypothetical willing lessee would expect the initial years as one of reduced profits before he built up a full and sustainable level of profitability. Albeit the usual practice is to base the calculations on the anticipated full level of profitability, the existence of the early less profitable years, is reflected in a lower proportion of the full anticipated profit being paid as rent. It is arguable, therefore, that as a matter of valuation practice one is able to disregard the effect of the tenant's occupation/goodwill and that, therefore, the impact of those disregards is not a factor preventing the court from awarding a turnover rent.

8–95 If the court has jurisdiction in what circumstances will the court award such a rental? In the *Inntrepreneur Pub Co Ltd v Palmer*[208] decision the learned judge considered that a turnover rent was inappropriate in that case as:

(1) it was unfair to both parties as such a rent relied on the personality and performance of the actual tenant;
(2) the turnover percentage was not liable to change and the risk of inaccuracy fell solely on the landlord;
(3) turnover leases were out of fashion since at least 1986/1987;
(4) there was no evidence of turnover leases being granted in the market;
(5) there was no evidence to guide the court as to what the appropriate percentage would be.

Thus if the court were to have jurisdiction, the decision as to whether in fact, with regard to any actual renewal, a turnover provision should be incorporated will be determined, principally, by reference to what was happening in the market. This is consistent with the wording of s.34, namely, that the rent is that for which the holding might reasonably be expected to be let in the open market.

Profits valuation

8–96 The jurisdiction to order a rent determined by reference to a fixed or variable percentage of the tenant's turnover should not be confused with a profits approach to valuation, which is an accepted methodology for calculating the rent to be paid in respect of certain types of premises, such as licensed premises, cinemas and petrol filling stations. The profits method involves the hypothetical parties attempting to forecast the probable profit and ultimately to derive a sum to be paid by way of rent. To do this the following calculations need to be undertaken:

(1) Calculate the anticipated turnover (e.g. in the case of licensed premises from sales of beer and cider, wines, spirits and minerals, food and retained income from gambling machines).
(2) Calculate the anticipated gross profit on turnover.
(3) Deduct the likely expenses so as to produce the divisible balance (or notional profit).
(4) Ascertain the hypothetical tenant's bid by way of a particular proportion of that divisible balance as rent.

There may of course be a number of disputes at each of these stages: see, by way of example, *Brooker v Unique Pub Properties Ltd*.[209]

A profits valuation often gives rise to the issue as to whether or not the actual tenant's trading accounts are admissible. See para.11–70 et seq. on this matter.

[208] Unreported April 16, 1998, Brighton CC, H.H. Judge Viner.
[209] [2009] EWHC 2599 (Ch).

Evidence as to rent

In the majority of cases the open market rent will be determined by evidence of lettings of comparable properties.[210] The remark of Judge Hamilton in the county court decision of *Barrett (W) & Co v Harrison*,[211] that "the ideal comparable property hardly ever exists", rings very true in practice. Particular regard in considering the comparable transactions must be had to the terms of the tenancy of the comparable and the terms to which the new tenancy is to be subject. Thus, for instance, a restriction on user, being one more onerous than the restrictions found in the comparable transactions, may result in a reduction in the rent payable: see *UDS Tailoring v BL Holdings*[212]; *Amarjee v Barrowfen Properties*[213] (digested in para.8–151). However, it may be that no reduction is required in the rent where the new lease contains a qualified-user covenant, i.e. one which permits change of user with the landlord's consent which cannot be unreasonably withheld: see *Aldwych Club v Copthall Property Co*[214] (digested in para.8–62); *Owen v Nightingale, Page and Bennett*[215] (user covenant restricting premises to the sale of toys and prams only subject to obtaining the landlord's consent such consent not to be unreasonably withheld). As Forbes J. said in *GREA Real Property Investments v Williams*[216]: **8–97**

> "It is a fundamental aspect of valuation that it proceeds by analogy. The valuer isolates those characteristics of the object to be valued which in his view affects the value and then seeks another object of known or ascertainable value possessing some or all of those characteristics with which he may compare the object he is valuing. Where no directly comparable object exists the valuer must make allowances of one kind or another, interpolating or extrapolating from his given data. The less closely analogous the object chosen for comparison the greater the allowances which have to be made and the greater the opportunity for error."

An actual offer for the premises may be a very useful piece of evidence for the landlord to adduce. Thus, in *Re Osnaburgh Street*,[217] the landlord was able to establish that he had a firm offer at a particular figure for the rent. He adduced in evidence the written contract entered between him and a third party whereby the third party agreed, conditionally, to take a new 21-year lease upon vacant possession being given by a specified date. Harman L.J. held that the evidence of the contract was preferable to the valuation evidence of the experts which both sides had called. However, it will be very rare that a landlord will be able to produce evidence of an offer made in respect of the premises which is both bona fide and sufficiently firm to be of any relevance. **8–98**

The mere fact that the landlord owns the property in a particular location does not prevent the comparable transaction from being an open market one: *Baptiste v* **8–99**

---

[210] As to the comparable method of valuation and the use of expert valuation evidence, see para.11–66 et seq. As to the use of the tenant's trading accounts, see para.11–70 et seq.
[211] [1956] E.G.D. 178.
[212] [1982] 1 E.G.L.R. 61.
[213] [1993] 2 E.G.L.R. 133 CC.
[214] (1962) 185 E.G. 219.
[215] (1955) 165 E.G. 761.
[216] [1979] 1 E.G.L.R. 121.
[217] (1957) 169 E.G. 656 at 691.

Gray's Inn.[218] Comparable transactions which are achieved by tender are often regarded with suspicion, although the court can bear them in mind: *Simonite v Sheffield City Council*.[219] If there are no reliable comparables, the court can have regard to the general increase in rent levels in the locality: *National Car Parks v Colebrook Estates*.[220] For examples of the way in which the court deals with comparables, see *Turone v Howard de Walden Estates*[221]; *Newey & Eyre v J Curtis & Son*[222] (wholesale warehouse of electrical goods); *Oriani v Dorita Properties*[223]; and *French v Commercial Union Assurance Co*[224] (shops in a shopping centre). The rents under the current lease and of comparable adjoining properties are relevant valuation evidence of the market rent of the subject property without the need for the court to require the party relying on those rents to produce positive evidence of the circumstances in which they were determined. Rather it is for the party who challenges the relevance of the passing rent and/or the rent of the adjoining property to adduce evidence of circumstances relied on to show that the rents are not relevant factors in the valuation exercise of determining the open market rent: *Trans-World Investments Ltd v Dadarwalla*.[225]

8–100 The parties' experts often rely on arbitrator's awards or previous expert determinations in respect of rent reviews of comparable properties. Awards of an arbitrator are likely to be inadmissible as opinion evidence: *Land Securities Plc v Westminster CC*.[226] Reliance on an earlier expert determination, without the benefit of the expert being present to be cross examined, is also likely to be held to be of little assistance.[227]

8–101 The values for rating shown in the valuation list are not a reliable guide as to market value. As Judge Barrington said in *Chambers Wolfe & Gold Stores v Denny*[228]; "the values put upon such property as this for rating purposes, whatever may be the theoretical position, in fact generally lag well behind the open market rental values and are therefore not of assistance in assessing rent under s.34 of the Act". See also *Jeffreys v Hutton Investment*[229]: "it would be unwise to follow rateable values slavishly . . ."; and *Davis v Brighton Corp*.[230] It may be, however, that as the rateable value is assessed on the basis of a tenancy from year to year, such evidence will be relevant where, unusually, a yearly periodic tenancy for a one-year fixed term is to be granted. Contrast *Robinson v*

---

218 [1993] 2 E.G.L.R. 136.

219 [1992] 1 E.G.L.R. 105.

220 [1983] 1 E.G.L.R. 78.

221 [1982] 1 E.G.L.R. 89 CA.

222 [1984] 2 E.G.L.R. 105.

223 [1987] 1 E.G.L.R. 88 CA.

224 [1993] 1 E.G.L.R. 113 CA.

225 [2007] EWCA Civ 480; [2008] 1 P. & C.R. 314 at [30]. See also *Earlrose Golf & Leisure Ltd v Fair Acre Investments Ltd* [2009] EWCA Civ 1295 at [41] (assessment of damages for trespass).

226 [1993] 1W.L.R. 286. The further basis for its inadmissibility, namely that it was hearsay, has been swept away by the Civil Evidence Act 1995.

227 *Glenfield Motor Spares Ltd v Smith*[2011] EWHC 3130 (Ch) (determination as to s.34 rent by judge in reliance on expert determination under earlier rent review as to the usable area of the demised premises set aside).

228 (1956) 168 E.G. 120.

229 (1956) 168 E.G. 203.

230 (1956) 106 L.J. 556 CC.

Shaw,[231] where the judge thought that evidence of rateable values was inadmissible. The authors have rarely encountered the court attaching any weight to the rateable value on the question of the rent to be payable under s.34. Nonetheless, it would appear that such evidence is in principle admissible although the weight to be attached to it depends on all the circumstances.

The valuation will, for practical purposes, be based on rents prevailing at the date of the hearing (see para.8–108). However, as under the Act the new tenancy will not commence until three months after final disposal, regard should be had to matters which could reasonably be expected to happen between the date of the hearing and the date of the commencement of the new term: *Lovely and Orchard Services v Daejan Investments Ltd*[232] (digested in para.6–48). **8–102**

Formula for valuation under section 34(1)

As is the case in the analogous areas of rating valuation and rent review, the amount of rent to be determined by the court is based not upon matters as they are, but upon matters as they are deemed to be by virtue of the valuation formula set out in s.34(1). The most significant parts of that formula are discussed in detail in succeeding paragraphs. **8–103**

Letting in "open market" by "willing lessor"

The rent to be determined by the court is to be "that at which . . . the holding might reasonably be expected to be let in the open market by a willing lessor . . .". The reference to "open market" makes it clear that what is envisaged is that the holding is notionally available to let. Mention is made of "a willing lessor," although a "willing lessee" is not expressly referred to. However, a willing lessee must be assumed to exist because that is inherent in the concept of the premises being let "in the open market" (see *Dennis & Robinson Ltd v Kiossos Establishment*[233]—a rent review case).[234] In *Stride & Son v Chichester Corp*,[235] Dankwerts J. said: **8–104**

> "It has been pointed out . . . that there is no reference to a willing lessee. I do not know quite what the effect of that is, whether he is to be taken as more hard-headed and less willing than the landlord to enter into the transaction, but I think at any rate I must take it that I have to ascertain what rent would be paid in the open market by a lessee who was prepared to take the premises".

In *Naylor v Uttoxeter Urban DC*,[236] Brightman J. said:

---

[231] (1956) 167 E.G. 192.

[232] [1978] 1 E.G.L.R. 44.

[233] [1987] 1 E.G.L.R. 133 CA.

[234] In *Humber Oil Terminals Trustee Ltd v Associated British Ports* [2012] EWHC 1336 (Ch), it was common ground that although s.34 did not refer to a willing lessee such was to be assumed as it was implied from the concept of a letting "in the open market": at [39].

[235] [1960] E.G.D. 117.

[236] [1974] E.G.D. 357.

> "No doubt the court must assume that there would exist some or more firms of auctioneers who would be willing lessees, and that such firm or firms would be ordinarily competent and be prepared to tender at a proper price . . .".

8–105 The meaning of "willing lessor" and "willing lessee" in the context of rent review has been considered by Donaldson J. in *FR Evans (Leeds) Ltd v English Electric Co Ltd*.[237] It was there emphasised that the "willing lessor" was an abstraction, not the actual landlord, but a hypothetical person with a right to grant a lease of the premises and who wished to let the premises at an appropriate rent. Similarly, the "willing lessee" was an abstraction, a hypothetical person actively seeking premises to fulfil his needs. The fact that both lessor and lessee are "willing" does not mean that they are "anxious" to reach agreement and the negotiations must be assumed to be fair and friendly, but must be conducted in the light of all the advantages and disadvantages which on the relevant date would affect the property and any lessee of the property. The personal circumstances of the tenant are not relevant. There is nothing in the Act which enables the rent to be fixed at a lower rate because the tenant cannot afford a rent which s.34 would produce: *Giannoukakis v Saltfleet Ltd*.[238]

8–106 A letting is an open market letting even if there may be only one interested bidder. Thus, where the tenant's only means of access was over his own adjoining land, there being no right of access provided for by the terms of his lease, the statute was not to be subject to any implied disregard of the fact that the demised premises were landlocked: *J Murphy & Sons Ltd v Railtrack Plc*[239] (digested in para.8–142). In *Northern Electric Plc v Addison*,[240] the original lease had contained a prohibition on use of the demised premises other than as an electricity substation, and the landlord unsuccessfully sought to contend that the limited restriction on use gave rise to a ransom value, as no landlord would be willing to let premises on that basis without some form of premium element. It was held by the Court of Appeal that the rent was to be assessed upon the basis of the rent at which the premises might reasonably be expected to be let on the open market by a willing lessor. That rent was to be determined having regard to the terms of the tenancy other than those relating to rent. Therefore the valuation exercise required one to assume a willing lessor of premises limited to use as an electricity substation. That combination of considerations necessarily precluded a notional lessor *unwilling* to let the premises for such restricted use, unless a premium was paid to take into account other potential uses. It follows that a ransom value is excluded where the hypothetical negotiation is between willing lessor and lessee.

8–107 There is no reason why one should exclude from the market, in calculating the open market value of the premises the presence (and thus potential bid by) an adjoining occupier (who may be a "special bidder" in the sense that he has a special interest in bidding for the premises by reason of his needs/proximity):

---

237 (1978) 36 P. & C.R. 185 QBD.

238 [1988] 1 E.G.L.R. 73 CA. See also *Brooker v Unique Pub Properties Ltd* [2009] EWHC 2599 (Ch).

239 [2002] EWCA Civ 679; [2002] 2 E.G.L.R. 48.

240 [1997] 2 E.G.L.R 111 CA.

IRC v Clay[241] where the court held that a valuation of a property should take into account the likely bid of the owners of any adjoining property in order to obtain the subject property for their purposes. As has been stated "the principle is that, unless the rent review clause excludes any potential bid from a special purchaser, that bid should be taken into account in assessing the open market rent".[242]

Valuation date

It may be of importance to know at what date the premises are notionally being let in the market, since the state of the market may change from time to time while the application for a new tenancy is pending. It has been held, in *English Exporters (London) v Eldonwall Ltd*[243] and *Lovely and Orchard Services v Daejan Investments Ltd*[244] (digested in para.6–48), that the valuation date is technically the date of commencement of the new tenancy, but that in practice the court must do its best with the evidence available at the date of hearing to assess the rent appropriate to the new tenancy which will, by virtue of s.64, not begin until some months after the hearing. Thus the judge has to assess the rent on the basis of the evidence presented at the hearing, including evidence of any changes in the market likely to occur between the date of the hearing and the date on which the tenancy will commence. For this purpose, the court must assume that there will be no appeal such as to delay the commencement of the new tenancy beyond the three months contemplated by s.64. **8–108**

---

241 [1914] 3 K.B. 466 CA. See also *Raja v Revenue Divisional Officer* [1939] A.C. 302; *Lynall v IRC* [1972] A.C. 680; and rent review cases such as *First Leisure Trading Ltd v Dorita Properties Ltd* [1991] 1 E.G.L.R. 133 and *British Airways Plc v Heathrow Airport* [1992] 1 E.G.L.R. 141.

242 *Hill & Redman's Law of Landlord and Tenant* (London: LexisNexis) para.A3702. The true position on a proper consideration of *IRC v Clay* is that the existence of the special purchaser is to be taken into account but any overbid by him is not. The effect of this distinction is, at first sight to a non-valuer, obscure but it is elucidated by the commentary in the *Red Book* (At PS 4.2.18(f)) as follows:

"The definition of Open Market Value does not require the Valuer to ignore the existence of a special purchaser, but to take no account of that special purchaser's additional bid, i.e. the amount by which his offer might exceed offers made by non-special purchasers. In practice, the existence of a special purchaser may affect (usually to a limited degree) the level of offers made by non-special purchasers and, to that extent, may be taken into account in arriving at Open Market Value."

The concept is, therefore, that the presence or potential presence in the market of the special purchaser may push up the open-market value but not necessarily to the level to which the special purchaser would himself be prepared to go. In *IRC v Clay*, the special purchaser's overbid was not in fact determined as the open-market value and dicta in that case are wholly consistent with the commentary in the Red Book. In the case it was found that the value of a house as a private residence was not more than £750; in fact the house was purchased by the trustees of the next door nursing home for £1,000; the trustees would have been prepared to go to £1,100; knowing of the interest of the trustees, the vendor had not been willing to sell for less than £1,000. A determination of the open market value at £1,000 was upheld by the Court of Appeal. Therefore, the determination of the court shows that regard is to be had to the effect on the market of the presence in it of a special purchaser but not his "overbid". "Overbid" here meaning the amount which the special purchaser would have been prepared to but did not have to pay.

243 [1973] 2 W.L.R. 435; [1973] 1 All E.R. 726.

244 (1977) 246 E.G. 651; (1977) 121 S.J. 711.

Effect on valuation of length of term

8–109 The length of term granted by the court may have an effect on the amount of rent. Whether this is so in any particular case, and what the effect is, is a matter of valuation dependent upon market conditions prevailing at the time. It was once thought that a tenant would always be prepared to pay a higher rent for a long term of, say, 14 years than he would for a shorter term of, say, five years. The opposite is now quite often the case and, especially in times of economic recession, tenants may well prefer a relatively short lease rather than the long-term commitment to the property required by a lease of 14 years. The view which once prevailed that a tenant would pay less for a tenancy from year to year than he would for a term of five years certain also needs to be reconsidered, especially when one is dealing with small premises in a secondary position in times of economic recession.

Effect on valuation of terms of tenancy

8–110 The rent is to be that at which the holding might reasonably be expected to fetch in the open market "having regard to the terms of the tenancy (other than those relating to rent)": s.34(1). It is expressly provided by s.34(4) (as added by the Landlord and Tenant (Covenants) Act 1995) that:

> "It is hereby declared that the matters which are to be taken into account by the court in determining the rent include any effect on rent of the operation of the provisions of the Landlord and Tenant (Covenants) Act 1995."

8–111 The words "other than those relating to rent" in s.34(1) have been explained in *Regis v Lewis & Peat*[245] and *English Exporters v Eldonwall*,[246] on the footing that the whole process would otherwise be nonsensical, because one cannot have regard to rent when the whole object of the exercise is to find out what the rent is to be. Although the words "other than those relating to rent" might, on one interpretation, appear to preclude the court from having regard to the fact that there are rent review provisions in the new tenancy, such an interpretation is contrary to common sense, because the question of whether there are or are not reviews will almost always have a material effect on what the tenant is willing to pay. Indeed, if such a wide interpretation were to be pushed to its logical conclusion, the court would be forced to disregard not merely the existence of rent review clauses in the new tenancy, but also provisions such as the covenant to pay rent, a covenant to pay service charges or insurance as rent, a covenant to pay interest on late rent, the proviso for re-entry in the case of non-payment of rent and, perhaps, whether the rent is payable in advance or in arrear. This question has been much discussed by the courts in the special context of rent review: see, in particular, *British Gas Corp v Universities Superannuation*

---

[245] [1970] 3 W.L.R. 361; [1970] 3 All E.R. 227.

[246] [1973] Ch. 415; [1973] 2 W.L.R. 435; [1973] 1 All E.R. 726.

Scheme Ltd[247] and *Equity & Law Life Assurance Society Plc v Bodfield Ltd*.[248] The position as stated in this paragraph is consistent with these decisions.

Clearly, the reference to "the terms of the tenancy" is a reference to the terms of the new tenancy, not to those of the current tenancy, although, as explained above (para.8–44), the terms of the new tenancy are often substantially similar to those of the current tenancy. The terms of the current tenancy which may have an effect on rent include provisions which require the tenant to pay a service charge (as in *O'May v City of London Real Property Co Ltd*[249] (digested in para.8–47)), repairing obligations, insuring obligations, provisions restricting alienation and provisions restricting user.

In determining the rent the court will value the premises having regard to the use permitted by the terms of the proposed new lease. In *Gorleston Golf Club v Links Estate*,[250] a county court decision, the premises were valued on the basis of the only use permitted by the user clause, rather than (as the landlord contended) on the basis of the most profitable use to which they could be put in the absence of such a user clause. If the lease contains a qualified user covenant the premises may be valued by reference to the most profitable use for which consent may be obtained. In *Aldwych Club v Copthall*[251] (digested in para.8–62), the user clause restricted use of the premises to that of a gentleman's club, subject to change of use with the landlord's consent (such consent not to be unreasonably withheld). By the date of the hearing the landlord had obtained planning permission for office use of the premises and satisfied the court that, if consent were to be sought for change of use under the terms of the tenancy to offices, it could not be refused. The court accordingly determined a rent on the basis that the premises could be used as offices. **8–112**

If the user covenant is absolute the court must assume that the hypothetical landlord will enforce the covenant. Thus no hope value can be attributed to the possibility of the landlord relaxing the covenant. In *Plinth Property Investments Ltd v Mott, Hay & Anderson*,[252] a rent review case, the lease contained a clause restricting use of the premises to that of offices of consulting engineers. The landlords argued that, in assessing the rent, the arbitrator should take into account the possibility that the landlord might agree to a variation of that user clause so as to mitigate the depressing effect on rent of such a narrow restriction. The Court of Appeal held that this was not permissible, and that the premises had to be valued upon the assumption that the landlords would strictly enforce their rights under the lease. In *Forte & Co v General Accident Life Assurance Ltd*,[253] the judge distinguished *Plinth* on the grounds that the covenant governing user expressly contemplated that the landlord might consent to a change of use. **8–113**

247 [1986] 1 W.L.R. 398; [1986] 1 All E.R. 978.
248 [1987] 1 E.G.L.R. 124 CA.
249 [1983] 2 A.C. 726; [1982] 2 W.L.R. 407; [1982] 1 All E.R. 660 HL.
250 (1959) 173 E.G. 298; (1959) 109 L.J. 140 CC.
251 (1962) 185 E.G. 219.
252 [1979] 1 E.G.L.R. 17 CA.
253 [1986] 2 E.G.L.R. 115.

8–114 The user clause if restrictive may reduce the value of the premises. In another rent review case, *Law Land Co Ltd v Consumers Association*[254] the user clause in the lease restricted use to that of the Consumers' Association and its associated organisations. The tenants argued that this meant that there was only one tenant in the market for the premises, namely themselves, so the user clause would have a most dramatically depressing effect on rent. It was, however, held by the Court of Appeal that such an argument was contrary to the concept of a letting in the open market and that the premises must be valued on the basis that they could be used as offices by the willing lessee (whoever that might be) and not merely by the Consumers' Association. However, the tenants scored a partial success, because the effect of such a user clause, limiting use to that of the willing lessee, would itself depress the rent, because the willing lessee would know that the lease was not easily assignable.

8–115 The court will not relax the user covenant in the proposed new lease if the tenant's business is sufficiently protected by the existing user covenant.[255] In *Charles Clements v Rank City Wall*[256] (digested in para.8–58), the current tenancy contained a clause restricting the user of the premises to that of a cutler, which was the business carried on by the tenant. The landlord sought to have inserted as a term of the new tenancy a proviso that consent to a change of use would not be unreasonably withheld. It was common ground between the parties that the effect of inserting that proviso would be to increase the rent payable under s.34. The court refused to make this change on the ground that the tenant's business, which it was the policy of the Act to protect, was sufficiently safeguarded by the terms of the existing user clause and that the alleged benefit to the tenant deriving from the proposed proviso, namely that the tenancy would become more easily assignable, was purely collateral and should not be imposed upon the tenant against its will.

8–116 Similar considerations as apply to user covenants apply to statutory restrictions on use, which will arise principally under the Town and Country Planning Act 1990. Clearly, since the court will not grant a new tenancy for a use which is in breach of planning control (see *Turner & Bell v Searles (Stanford-le-Hope)* (digested in para.7–48)), the valuation under s.34 must be conducted on the basis that the premises cannot be used in breach of such control. However, the fact that planning permission does not exist for a particular use at the date of the hearing is not, it is thought, conclusive; it would be open to the landlord to prove by expert evidence that the willing lessee would be able to obtain planning permission for a more valuable use and would accordingly pay a greater rent on account of this "hope value". See *Rushmoor BC v Goacher*[257] and *Sixth Centre Ltd v Guildville*[258] (both rent review cases).

---

[254] [1980] 2 E.G.L.R. 109 CA.

[255] As to the courts' approach to alterations to the user covenant contained in the new lease, see para.8–53 et seq.

[256] [1978] 1 E.G.L.R. 47.

[257] [1985] 2 E.G.L.R. 140.

[258] [1989] 1 E.G.L.R. 260.

The property to be valued

Section 34(1) directs the court to determine the rent which "the holding" might reasonably be expected to be let in the open market. The words "the holding" in s.34(1) refer to the property of the landlord which is being let but excludes the property of the tenant and therefore excludes property installed by the tenant which he has a right to detach and remove: *Humber Oil Terminals Trustee Ltd v Associated British Ports.*[259] The right to detach and remove may arise by contract, common law or by statute. Thus in determining "the holding" to be valued there is to be excluded: **8–117**

(i) That which the tenant has a contractual right to remove. This may be more extensive that a simple right to remove tenant's fixtures. Thus, the contractual right may extend to "all or . . . some of the Lessee's works" at the election of the lessee.[260] The effect of a contractual right to remove is that even those matters which would otherwise be treated as part of the realty as being "landlord's fixtures" are to be excluded from the property to be valued. "It is the right of removal by the tenant which shows that the property is to be regarded as his [the tenant's] own for the purposes of working out the open market rent to be paid in respect of the demised premises, not whether the fixtures happen to be regarded as 'tenant's fixtures' as such."[261]

(ii) Those parts of the holding which constitute tenant's fixtures: Although removable tenant's fixtures are not "improvements" within the disregard of s.34(1),[262] they do not form part of the premises which are to be valued.[263]

(iii) Improvements falling within the statutory disregard contained within s.34(1)(c).[264]

The method to be adopted so as to give effect to the exclusion from the valuation is considered at para.8–118.[265]

---

[259] [2012] EWHC 1336 (Ch) at [175]. Although the case was one dealing with interim rent under s.24D of the Act the judge dealt with s.34 and the meaning of "the holding".

[260] See the terms of the contractual provision for removal in *Humber Oil Terminals Trustee Ltd v Associated British Ports* [2012] EWHC 1336 (Ch) at [22].

[261] *Humber Oil Terminals Trustee Ltd v Associated British Ports* [2012] EWHC 1336 (Ch) at [177]. The effect of a contractual right of removal may mean that on analysis there is no relevant property to which s.34(1)(c) applies. This was the case in *Humber Oil* due to the width of the contractual provision for removal.

[262] See para.8–125.

[263] As noted by Sales J. in *Humber Oil Terminals Trustee Ltd v Associated British Ports* [2012] EWHC 1336 (Ch), it would be bizarre if rent had to be paid for all tenant's fixtures while an exemption was provided in relation to most landlord's fixtures: at [175].

[264] See para.8–125. Sales J. said that s.34(1)(c) provides for an additional disregard for the protection of a tenant in relation to improvements made to the demised property which the tenant has no right to detach and remove and which have thus become property of the landlord: [2012] EWHC 1336 (Ch) at [170].

[265] Consider also the position on interim rent at para.9–34 et seq.

How is effect to be given to the exclusion of property from the valuation?

8–118 If property which the tenant has the right to detach and remove is excluded from the valuation of the rent under s.34(1), how is that to be reflected in the valuation process? Is the property in question to be assumed not to be there or is there some other method which should be adopted to give effect to the exclusion? In the context of the claim for interim rent under s.24D(1),[266] where the direction is for the rent to be that "which it is reasonable for the tenant to pay," it has been held that any disregard of the tenant's property, on whatever basis,[267] is given proper effect not by making an assumption that the matters covered by the disregard are not present at all, but by reducing the overall value of the property being valued by an amount in proportion to the cost of installing the property in question and by reducing the rent to be paid by an appropriate amount accordingly: *Humber Oil Terminals Trustee Ltd v Associated British Ports*.[268] In adopting this approach the valuer can undertake the task in a number of ways:

(i) First, by ascertaining the rental value of the entire property and then deducting the rentalised value of the tenant's property.
(ii) Secondly, by ascertaining the capital cost of replacing the property let without the benefit of the tenant's property, and then de-capitalising the resultant sum by at an appropriate rate to obtain an annual rent (which was in fact the approach adopted in *Humber Oil Terminals Trustee Ltd v Associated British Ports*[269]).[270]

8–119 The practical difference between these two approaches and that of disregarding the existence of the tenant's property is that the former, unlike the latter, does not require any assumption to be made about the cost which would be incurred to

[266] Which governs the determination of an interim rent where the landlord is opposing renewal or where there is a renewal of less than the whole of the property comprised in the relevant tenancy: see the terms of s.24C and 24D(1).

[267] As to the basis for disregarding the tenant's property, see para.9–34 et seq.

[268] [2012] EWHC 1336 (Ch).

[269] A depreciation allowance was made of 40% to the capital cost of the jetty to take account of the age of the jetty.

[270] The approach is the Depreciated Replacement Cost. Sales J. described this method as follows:

"[82] As explained in the RICS Guidance, the DRC method is used where there is no active market for the asset being valued, so that there is no useful or relevant evidence of recent sales transactions due to the specialised nature of the asset (para 3.1). It is a method for ascribing a capital value to the asset in question. The method is based on the economic theory of substitution, whereby it is assumed that the potential willing buyer of the asset would not pay more to acquire the asset being valued than the cost of acquiring an equivalent new one: 'The technique involves assessing all the costs of providing a modern equivalent asset using pricing at the date of valuation' (para 2.3). Both the expert valuers used the DRC method to assess the present capital value of the Oil Jetty, by relying on evidence from other experts regarding the current costs of providing a replacement (there being argument as to what, if any, equipment installed on the jetty should be treated as being included in the calculation and in relation to differences between those other experts) and then applying a depreciation allowance of 40% – a figure which they agree on – to take account of the age of the Oil Jetty in order to arrive at a figure representing its current capital value. Having gone through this process, they agreed that a further step was required (which was not the subject of the RICS Guidance), to apply some suitable decapitalisation rate to that notional capital value to arrive at an appropriate annual rental figure. They disagreed about the decapitalisation rate."

make reinstall the tenant's property or the time it would take to do so. This is illustrated by *Humber Oil Terminals Trustee Ltd v Associated British Ports* where the tenant unsuccessfully sought to argue (on the calculation of interim rent under s.24D)[271] that by disregarding the tenant's property the rent was to be ascertained on the basis of a bare jetty without any of the equipment which had been provided by the tenant, such that the valuer had to factor into the rental valuation the cost of re-equipping the jetty and the time it would take to make it operational. Some support for the landlord's approach may be said to be derived from *GREA Real Property Investments v Williams*[272] and *Estates Projects v Greenwich LBC*,[273] where Forbes J. gave some guidance, in the analogous context of rent review, on the relevant principles to be applied to the disregard of improvements.[274]

Is vacant possession to be assumed?

Section 34 does not expressly require the court to assume that the premises are being let in the open market with vacant possession, although it must be assumed that the tenant himself is not in occupation and any effect on rent of the fact that he has been in occupation is expressly required to be disregarded (see para.8–138). Consequently, in the normal case the valuation will be on a full vacant possession basis but where the tenant has sub-let part of the premises, it appears that the valuation under s.34 is to be on the basis that the premises are being let in the open market subject to and with the benefit of that sub-tenancy. In *Oscroft v Benabo*,[275] the Court of Appeal held that the court should take into account the fact that the upper parts of the premises were subject to a residential sub-tenancy at a rent which was controlled by the Rent Act 1957. Presumably, the position would be the same if the sub-tenancy were one which was protected by the 1954 Act. Some support for an assumption of full vacant possession may, however, be derived from Lord Evershed's approval in *Harewood Hotels v Harris*[276] of the statement in *Woodfall* that the disregard contained in paragraph (a) means that "the premises have to be envisaged as empty premises in the market".[277] **8–120**

In *Forte v General Accident Fire & Life Assurance Plc*,[278] a rent review case, the judge stated that vacant possession of the premises was generally to be assumed **8–121**

271 See para.9–33 et seq.

272 [1979] 1 E.G.L.R. 121 at 124C.

273 [1979] 2 E.G.L.R. 85 at 87E–F.

274 See para.8–137. It may be thought that an approach which values the landlord's property on the basis that the tenant's property does not have to be re-installed, albeit no rental value is being given to the tenant's property, still takes into account an effect on value. The tenant in *Humber Oil Terminals Trustee Ltd v Associated British Ports* relied on the New Zealand decision of *S&M Property Holdings v Waterloo Investments* [1999] 3 N.Z.L.R. 189, where the lease was granted of a bare site and the tenant had built a hotel on the site. The rent review clause provided that on review the rent was to be "the full ground rental" of the land but "no account shall be taken of the value of any buildings".

275 [1967] 1 W.L.R. 1087; [1967] 2 All E.R. 548 CA.

276 [1958] 1 W.L.R. 108; [1958] 1 All E.R. 104 CA.

277 In determining an interim rent under the new provisions of s.24D (as to which, see para.9–33), it is expressly provided that regard is to be had "to the rent payable under any sub-tenancy of part of the property comprised in the relevant tenancy": 24D(2)(b).

278 [1986] 2 E.G.L.R. 115.

even where the rent review provisions contain no express assumption as to vacant possession. However, on the facts of that case an existing sub-tenancy of part of the premises was to be taken into account on valuation and not disregarded because (1) the lease was granted subject to the existing sub-tenancy and (2) it was contemplated at the date of grant of the lease that the sub-tenancy would continue up to and beyond the rent review date. *Oscroft v Benabo*[279] was cited, but distinguished on the basis that it was concerned specifically with the position under the 1954 Act.

Various consequences may flow, as a matter of valuation, from a failure to assume vacant possession. First, the fact that there is a sub-tenant obviously prevents the willing lessee from occupying the whole of the premises and it may be that they are less attractive for that reason. Secondly, where the rent under the sub-tenancy is restricted by, e.g. the Rent Acts, the value of the sub-let part may be depressed and the willing lessee will not be prepared to pay in respect of that part a rent reflecting its value if let, e.g. on an assured tenancy. A third effect is that if the tenant takes subject to a sub-tenancy he may well find that he has obligations, express or implied, owed to the sub-tenant, such as obligations to repair, which are greater than the obligations he owes to the landlord under the terms of the new tenancy. Fourthly, the tenant may seek to deduct a percentage from the rent which he receives from the sub-tenant to reflect the trouble and expense of management.

8–122 It is thought that the court can, in principle, take into account the likelihood of the sub-tenancy coming to an end during the term of the new tenancy, as might be anticipated if the Rent Act tenant was elderly and in poor health and had no members of his family living with him. In many cases, however, such factors will be too intangible to be valued.

Assumption as to state of repair

8–123 The court is not expressly required to make an assumption about the physical state of the holding. Prima facie, the holding is to be valued as it stands. Where the landlord has a full repairing obligation, no injustice is caused by a valuation of the holding in its actual physical state, since, if it is in disrepair, that is the landlord's fault and the tenant will benefit by having to pay a lower rent.

8–124 The same is not, however, true where the tenant has a full repairing obligation but the premises are dilapidated due to his default at the date of the hearing. The landlord has other remedies, such as forfeiture, opposition to the grant of a new tenancy under ground (a), or insisting that the new tenancy should contain an obligation on the tenant forthwith to carry out an appropriate schedule of works. In addition, there are statements in the decided cases which, although technically obiter dicta, strongly suggest that if the disrepair results from the tenant's default that disrepair must be disregarded in assessing the rent under s.34, because the tenant would otherwise be benefiting from his own wrong. In *Family Management v Gray*,[280] Shaw L.J. said:

[279] [1967] 1 W.L.R. 1087; [1967] 2 All E.R. 548 CA.
[280] [1980] 1 E.G.L.R. 46 CA.

> "When the negotiation of the terms of those new leases [under the 1954 Act] came to be dealt with between the reversioners and the prospective lessees they could not, in diminution of what was the proper rent to be paid, urge their own default in having failed to comply with the repairing covenants under the lease as a justification or reason for a lower rent, whether arrived at by negotiation or determined by the court."

Similar statements were made in, *Hibernian Property Co v Liverpool Corp*[281] (a compulsory purchase case) and in *Harmsworth Pension Funds Trustees v Charringtons Industrial Holdings*[282] and *Little Hayes Nursing Home v Marshall*[283] (rent review cases).

Disregard of improvements

The court, in determining a rent, is expressly required by s.34(1) to disregard four matters. The disregard of improvements, pursuant to para.(c), is discussed first because of its pre-eminent importance. Significant amendments to para.(c) were introduced by the Law of Property Act 1969, and the paragraph is considered in its amended form. The court is required to disregard "any effect on rent of any improvement to which this paragraph applies". Subsection (2) then specifies the circumstances in which the paragraph is to apply. The effect of this is set out in the following paragraphs.[284] **8–125**

(1) The disregard applies only to "improvements"

"Improvements" is a term which is not defined. In the context of s.19(2) of the Landlord and Tenant Act 1927, the word "improvements" has been held to be any work of physical alteration which, from the tenant's point of view, improves the holding; it is irrelevant that, from the landlord's point of view, it may not be an improvement: *Lambert v Woolworth*.[285] In the context of Pt 1 of the Landlord and Tenant Act 1927, which is discussed in detail in Ch.13 of this book,[286] it has been held that the complete demolition of the premises comprised in the holding and the erection of buildings of an entirely different nature is an "improvement": see *National Electric Theatres Ltd v Hudgell*.[287] In *Price v Esso*[288] (digested in para.7–104) the phrase "improvements, alterations or additions" was held to include the total demolition of the existing buildings comprised in the holding and the erection of buildings of a different layout and design. **8–126**

By virtue of the rule that fixtures which are attached to the freehold become part of the freehold, it would appear that, if they are installed by the tenant and

---

281 [1973] 1 W.L.R. 751; (1973) 2 All E.R. 1117.

282 [1985] 1 E.G.L.R. 97.

283 (1993) 66 P. & C.R. 90.

284 (1993) 66 P. & C.R. 90.

285 [1938] Ch. 883 CA.

286 See para.13–19 et seq.

287 [1939] Ch. 553. The cases under s.19(2) were not considered by the judge to be of assistance in determining the meaning of improvement under Pt 1 of the 1927 Act. See para.13–19.

288 [1980] 2 E.G.L.R. 58 CA.

are not removable by him, they are "improvements".[289] They will thus fall to be disregarded provided they come within the further conditions for the application of para.(c) discussed below. Even if they do not fulfil those conditions they will not fall to be valued if they are, at the date of the hearing, "tenant's fixtures" in the sense that they can be removed by the tenant: see *New Zealand Government Property Corp v HM&S*[290] (digested in para.8–127), a rent review case. Although removable tenant's fixtures are not "improvements" within the disregard, they do not form part of the premises which are to be valued.[291]

8–127 ***New Zealand Government Property Corp v HM&S Ltd***[292] By an indenture made in 1896, the landlords' predecessors granted to the tenants' predecessors a long lease of a theatre. During the course of that lease, the premises were fully fitted out with the tenants' fixtures. The indenture contained a covenant to yield up the premises and all fixtures excluding tenants' fixtures. In 1973, the lease was renewed; in the demise, however, no mention was made of fixtures, although the lease contained a similar covenant to yield up the premises (tenants' fixtures excepted). The new lease also contained provision for rent review, whereby on review the premises were to be valued assuming, inter alia, vacant possession and disregarding the matters set out in s.34(1)(a), (b) and (c). On the first review the tenants contended: (1) that the assumption of "vacant possession" required the valuer to value on the basis that the tenants had left taking all their fixtures with them; (2) that these fixtures comprised all trade fixtures installed in the premises since 1896.

The landlords contended that no such assumption was required and that in any event any trade fixtures in the premises in 1973 were, by virtue of the grant of the new lease, transformed from tenants' into landlords' fixtures.

The tenants contended in the alternative that if the landlords were right then, by leaving their trade fixtures in the premises in 1973, they had at that date effected a tenants' improvement to the premises which should accordingly be disregarded. The parties appointed as arbitrator Judge Hawser QC, official referee, who by an interim award held for the tenants on contention (1) but against them on contention (2) and on their alternative contention. On the tenants' appeal by way of case stated the landlords did not challenge the arbitrator's holding on contention (1). As to the other contentions, Woolf J. held that the authorities who show that a tenant loses his right to remove trade fixtures on an express surrender by deed were not applicable to a surrender by operation of law on the making of a new lease between the same parties. The question whether the tenants had lost the right to remove the fixtures was to be decided by looking at the intention of the parties and here the inference was clear that the tenants had

---

[289] In *New Zealand Government Property Corporation Ltd v HM&S* [1982] Q.B. 1145 CA (para.8–119). Lord Denning said that the disregard of improvements in s.34 applied only "to improvements made by the tenant which are landlord's fixtures" which the tenant is unable to remove. It does not apply to tenant's fixtures: ibid p.1160B-C. Dunn and Fox L.JJ. specifically agreed with this analysis: p.1161G and 1165H, respectively.

[290] [1982] Q.B. 1145; [1982] 2 W.L.R. 837; [1982] 1 All E.R. 624 CA.

[291] *Humber Oil Terminals Trustee Ltd v Associated British Ports* [2012] EWHC 1336 (Ch) at [175] and [176].

[292] [1982] Q.B. 1145; [1982] 2 W.L.R. 837; [1982] 1 All E.R. 624 CA.

not, by taking a new lease, intended to give up that right. Alternatively, even if the fixtures were to be regarded as landlords' fixtures but as tenants' improvements, they were to be assessed as improvements which had been carried out at the date they were installed and not when they became landlords' fixtures. The landlords appealed.

It was held by the Court of Appeal:

(a) When an existing lease expires or is surrendered by operation of law and is followed immediately by another to the same tenant remaining in possession, the tenant does not lose the right to remove the tenants' fixtures.
(b) Where an express surrender takes place, but the tenant remains in possession under a new lease, it is a question of construction of the instrument of surrender whether or not he has also given up his right to remove his fixtures: per Fox and Dunn L.JJ.
(c) "Improvements" under s.34 does not include improvements made by the tenant which are tenants' fixtures.
(d) The rent should be assessed on the basis that the tenants' fixtures had been removed by the tenants and were therefore not part of the demised premises.

(2) The improvement must have been "carried out by a person who at the time it was carried out was the tenant"

As noted,[293] the term "tenant" is not expressly defined. It presumably bears its ordinary meaning of the person or persons in whom the tenancy is vested. It would seem to follow that, if the improvement is carried out during a period prior to the grant of the tenancy while the prospective tenant is a licensee only, the improvement will not be disregarded: see *Euston Centre Properties v H&J Wilson*,[294] a rent review case. As Scott J. commented in another rent review case, *Hambros Bank Executor & Trustee Co v Superdrug Stores*,[295] "the statutory provision is clear and unambiguous. It requires the person to be the tenant at the time the improvement is carried out". Similarly, it is probable that improvements carried out by a sub-tenant will not be disregarded so far as the tenant is concerned; consider, however, *Pelosi v Newcastle Arms Brewery*[296] (digested in para.13–68), a case decided under the Landlord and Tenant Act 1927. **8–128**

It is to be noted that s.41, which deals with the position where the tenancy is held upon trust does not, for the purposes of s.34, deem improvements carried out by the beneficiaries under the trust who are in occupation of the holding to be improvements carried out by "the tenant". Nor does s.42, which deals with tenancies held by members of a group of companies, treat improvements carried out by a member of the group which is not the tenant as if they were carried out by the tenant. Compare s.41(1)(b) which provides that the reference in para.(d) of s.34(1) (dealing with the case where the holding comprises licensed premises) to **8–129**

293 See para.3–101, et seq.
294 [1982] 1 E.G.L.R. 57.
295 [1985] 1 E.G.L.R. 99.
296 [1989] 1 E.G.L.R. 99 CA.

"the tenant" includes the beneficiary or beneficiaries under a trust. The express reference to para.(d) of s.34(1) in s.41 underlines the fact that it does not apply to para.(c). See also s.42(2)(b) (dealing with group companies) which has the same effect.

(3) The improvement must have been "carried out" by the tenant

8–130 The tenant need not physically have done the works himself. The tenant will at least normally satisfy the statutory requirement if he can establish that he either physically effected the works himself, or got a third party to do so. The tenant will usually satisfy the statutory test if he can show that he had entered into an arrangement with a third party which arrangement will typically, be but need not necessarily be, a contract, under which that party agreed with the tenant to do the specific works involved in effecting the improvements: *Durley House Ltd v Cadogan*.[297]

8–131 ***Durley House Ltd v Cadogan***[298] D was tenant under a lease dated October 9, 1979 being for a term of 65 years from March 25, 1979 at a yearly rent of £5,000 per annum subject to review every seven years. The property demised by the lease was to be used as 11 serviced residential apartments. The rent review provisions provided that the rent was to be reviewed to five per cent of the freehold value of the property as at the relevant review date on certain assumptions and "disregarding those matters set out in paragraphs (a), (b) and (c) of s.34 of the Landlord and Tenant Act 1954 as amended by the Law of Property Act 1969".

The issue was whether certain improvements were to be taken into account on review. On January 20, 1989 D had entered into an agreement with F, whereby F agreed to manage the property. F was under an obligation under the terms of the agreement to fit out the apartments to a luxury standard, subject to D approving conceptual plans and estimates to be submitted by F for the upgrading and refurbishment of the apartments. The detailed plans for the work had to be submitted to D and its landlord for approval and the approval of D was not to be unreasonably withheld. The work had to be completed within two years. D could determine the agreement if the apartments were not maintained to a luxury standard. D did not pay for the improvements effected by F. It was held that nevertheless the improvements were within the terms of s.34(2) of the 1954 Act "carried out" by the tenant.

> "Once it is accepted, as it is and plainly must be, that an arrangement under which the tenant gets a building contractor to do the works would not take the tenant out of the ambit of s.34(2) in a particular case, I do not find it easy, at any rate at first sight, to see at what point or on what logical basis it could be said that any arrangement with a third party under which the tenant gets that third party to effect the works would take the tenant out of the section."

---

[297] [2000] 1 W.L.R. 246; [2000] 1 E.G.L.R. 60 Ch D. Neuberger J. said:

[298] [2000] 1 W.L.R. 246; [2000] 1 E.G.L.R. 60 Ch D.

If it was insufficient to show that D had merely arranged for a third party to carry out the work and that D had to be more involved in the relevant works than merely requiring them to be done, D was more involved in that the present case because:

(1) D had to approve the conceptual terms and estimates for the relevant works;
(2) the carrying out of the relevant improvements was part of the initial condition for the grant of the agreement;
(3) detailed plans for the relevant works required the approval of D and they had to be completed within a specific time;
(4) the nature and standard of the relevant improvements had at least, to some extent, been laid down by D;
(5) the provisions for termination of the agreement enabled D to put an end to the agreement if F failed to comply with their obligations in connection with the relevant works;
(6) D had a right to inspect the relevant works;
(7) the relevant works enured for the benefit of D when the agreement expired, the improvements were obviously intended to increase the profitability of the business, the beneficial effects of which would be enjoyed by D during the currency of the agreement with F.

(4) The improvement must not have been carried out "in pursuance of an obligation to [the] immediate landlord"

The wide terms of this exclusion should be noted. Clearly, where there is a term in the tenancy agreement itself requiring the tenant to carry out the works of improvement, they will not be disregarded, whether that obligation is a specific obligation to carry out a schedule of works, or whether the works are done pursuant to some general obligation, such as an obligation to repair or to comply with the requirements of statute. Thus, in *Forte v General Accident Life Assurance Ltd*,[299] a rent review case, works of improvement carried out by the tenant pursuant to the Fire Precautions Act 1971 were to be taken into account where the tenant had covenanted to comply with all statutory requirements. Further, it would appear that improvements carried out pursuant to a collateral agreement, such as a building contract between the immediate landlord and tenant, would not be disregarded, nor would work carried out pursuant to a covenant in a licence which placed an obligation upon the tenant to carry out the works. Contrast *Godbold v Martin the Newsagent*,[300] a rent review case, where it was held that the licence, upon its true construction, imposed no obligation upon the tenant to carry out the improvements but merely permitted him to do so. A recital in a lease to the effect that the tenants had, at their expense, with the approval of the lessors, constructed a new soakaway pump to the demised premises and in consideration thereof the landlord had agreed to reduce the rent, did not mean that the soakaway pump was constructed "in pursuance of an 8–132

[299] [1986] 2 E.G.L.R. 115.
[300] [1983] 2 E.G.L.R. 128.

obligation" to the landlord. The words were not words of obligation but merely words of narrative: *Rombus Materials Ltd v WT Lamb Properties*.[301]

The correctness of the county court case of *Appleton v Abrahamson*[302] (where it was decided that an improvement was not to be disregarded if it had been carried out pursuant to a moral, but not a legal, obligation to the immediate landlord), may be doubted.

8–133 The obligation must be owed "to the immediate landlord", so that an agreement between, e.g. the tenant and his sub-tenant, that the tenant would carry out works of improvement would not require the improvement to be rentalised as between the landlord and tenant. Contrast *Owen Owen Estate Ltd v Livett*[303] (digested in para.13–74) under the differently worded provisions of the 1927 Act.

(5) Further conditions must be complied with if the improvement was not carried out during the current tenancy

8–134 If the improvement was carried out during the current tenancy and fulfils the foregoing conditions, it is to be disregarded. If it was not carried out during the current tenancy, it will only be disregarded if it fulfils all of the following further conditions:

(1) that it was completed not more than 21 years before the application to the court[304] was made. This is self-explanatory, although it should be noted that it is the date of completion of the improvement which is relevant and the date of application which defines the 21-year period; and
(2) that the holding or any part of it affected by the improvement has at all times since the completion of the improvement been comprised in tenancies of the description specified in s.23(1) of the Act (see Ch.1).

8–135 It is difficult to interpret this provision. Let us suppose that a tenancy was granted in 1970 and that an improvement was carried out during the term of that tenancy in 1986. In 1990, because of adverse business conditions, the tenant ceased trading from the premises which remained vacant for two years. During that two-year period the tenancy would arguably not have been one "of the description specified in section 23(1)" because there would have been no business occupation. If the lease was then assigned to a successor in title who commenced trading in 1992, the tenancy would once again come within the description in s.23(1). Supposing the tenancy to be renewed in 1994 for a term of 14 years, the question would arise upon an application for a new tenancy in 2008 whether the improvement carried out in 1986 should or should not be disregarded. Although each of the tenancies, including the current tenancy, was during most of its existence a tenancy within the description specified in s.23(1),

---

301 Unreported February 18, 1999 CA.

302 (1956) 167 E.G. 633.

303 [1956] Ch. 1; [1955] 3 W.L.R. 1; [1955] 2 All E.R. 513.

304 The words "for the new tenancy" were substituted by the words "the court" by the 2003 Order to reflect the fact that an application may now consist of an application for renewal or termination.

can it really be said that "at all times" since the improvement was carried out the holding was comprised in a tenancy of that description? This point remains to be resolved.

It should also be noted that a tenancy which fulfils the description in s.23(1) does not lose that quality merely because the security of tenure provisions of ss.24 to 28 are excluded by agreement of the parties with the leave of the court. Thus, if one of the previous tenancies had been subject to such an exclusion, condition (b) would nonetheless be fulfilled, assuming, of course, that by agreement between landlord and tenant upon the expiry of the unprotected tenancy the tenant had in fact been granted a new tenancy within s.23(1), and condition (c) that at the termination of each of these tenancies the tenant did not quit. The point of this is that, if vacant possession of the holding has been delivered back to the landlord by the tenant, the benefit of the improvements passes from the tenant to the landlord and cannot be taken advantage of by any successive tenant. The position is, of course, otherwise where the tenant has assigned his tenancy; in that case the benefit of the improvements will also be taken to have been assigned and the tenant will not have quit "at the termination" of the tenancy. **8–136**

How disregard of improvements affects valuation

The Act gives no guidance on the valuation method by which improvements are to be disregarded. In *GREA Real Property Investments v Williams*[305] and *Estates Projects v Greenwich LBC*,[306] Forbes J. gave guidance, in the analogous context of rent review, on the relevant principles to be applied.[307] From those judgments the following propositions can, it is suggested, be distilled: **8–137**

(1) The question of how improvements are to be disregarded is primarily one of fact, that is to say of valuation method, and not of law. It follows that, although a court may be able to declare that a particular method is invalid, because no reasonable valuer properly applying the relevant principles could adopt it, there may be a variety of different methods from which it is open to the valuer to choose as it appears to him to be best in the light of his knowledge and experience.
(2) If it is practicable to value the subject premises by reference to comparables which are themselves unimproved, then that is a permissible method. Whether it is practicable will depend partly upon the nature of the comparables and partly upon the nature of the improvements. In a case where one is valuing offices which were originally let as a shell, there may be little difficulty in finding suitable shell comparables, if it is market practice for offices to be let in shell condition.
(3) If the comparable method is not practicable, it is for the valuer to devise some suitable method for isolating, from the full value of the premises as

[305] [1979] 1 E.G.L.R. 121.
[306] [1979] 2 E.G.L.R. 85.
[307] See also the discussion at paras 8–117 and 8–118 of *Humber Oil Terminals Trustee Ltd v Associated British Port* [2012] EWHC 1336 (Ch), in the context of disregarding the tenant's property when assessing the rent.

they are, that element which represents the effect on rent of the improvements carried out by the tenant. The cost of carrying out the improvements at the date of valuation may be relevant if and so far as the willing lessee, if offered unimproved premises, would reduce his bid by reference to the cost to him of carrying out the improvements.

(4) A criticism of both the comparable method and the method which requires an adjustment to be made on the assumption that the willing lessee is going to have to carry out the improvements himself is that this flies in the face of reality. The improvements will have been carried out some years prior to the date of the application, but if the willing lessee did them again he would have to pay a full price and he would obtain new (and not old) improvements. Further, the willing lessee would bear in mind the fact that the carrying out of the improvements would either prevent him from going into occupation of the premises for some time, or would make his occupation of the premises during the course of the works less convenient. In reality, there is no reason why the tenant should obtain an allowance for this notional disruption when he is not in fact going to be disrupted at all.

(5) It is suggested that the answer to the conundrum is to be found in the knowledge and experience of the valuer. He must have in mind the value of the premises including the question of how old they are and how far they conform to modern standards. He should have in mind the cost of these improvements in terms of both labour and materials as a capital sum in relation to the amount of the full rental value of the premises. Considering all those factors, he should reach a judgment, based upon his own skill and experience, of what is an appropriate deduction to be made from the full rental value for the effect of the improvements carried out by the tenant.

Other "disregards"

8–138 The other matters required to be disregarded by s.34(1) can be dealt with more shortly. Under para.(a) it is provided that the court must disregard "any effect on rent of the fact that the tenant has or his predecessors in title have been in occupation of the holding". This is closely connected with the disregard in para.(b) which requires there to be disregarded "any good-will attached to the holding by reason of the carrying on thereat of the business of the tenant (whether by him or a predecessor of his in that business)". In *Harewood v Harris*,[308] Romer L.J. said:

> "It seems to me that paragraphs (a) and (b) are really directed to saying that, for example, the fact that the sitting tenant has been in occupation for some time past and has built up a goodwill is to be disregarded in assessing the rent which he is to pay under his new lease. Normally, of course, a man who is in the position of a sitting tenant and has built up a business and been there for some years and established himself would be prepared to pay a higher rent than anybody else then coming in for the first time. It is that kind of thing, in my view, to which paragraphs (a) and (b) are directed."

[308] [1958] 1 W.L.R. 108; [1958] 1 All E.R. 104 CA.

In the same case, Lord Evershed M.R. stated that he was entirely willing to accept the following passage from *Woodfall on Landlord and Tenant*:

> "This seems to dispose equally of any accretion to the rent attributable to such occupation (the premises have to be envisaged as empty premises in the market) and of the 'sitting tenant' concession which was sometimes allowed for in assessing a 'reasonable' rent under the Act of 1951."

This approach to para.(a) was adopted recently by Sales J. in *Humber Oil Terminals Trustee v Associated British Ports*.[309] He said that the provision was "directed at removing the effect of what is sometimes called 'the sitting tenant overbid', the idea that a sitting tenant might be prepared to pay a premium to avoid the disturbance of having to move out."

It has been held in the county court that the disregard under para.(a) of s.34(1) did not enable a tenant to argue for a discount on the rent to reflect the absence of a rent-free period for fitting out as part of the hypothetical letting when such rent-frees were being granted in the comparable transactions. *Max Mara Ltd v Pearl Assurance Plc*.[310] It was said: **8–139**

> "What is central to the bargaining for a genuine rent free period at the outset of a new lease is not the tenant's occupation or previous lack of occupation but the need and intention of the tenant at that particular time to fit the premises out. The heavy costs involved affect the bargaining process and those include the rent of the period in which the work is being done and the premises cannot be used commercially. The rent free period is assessed, as the comparables . . . show, to meet the particular circumstances in each case to compensate for the genuine factual situation. The rental effect stems from that factual situation and where it does not exist, as on renewal, should be kept out of the equation. Section 34(a) read simply prevents any accretion to rent attributable to the occupation by the tenant entitled to a lease renewal and on the other side any sitting tenant concession. It does not require the court to import a fiction with all the uncertainties and distortions that would inevitably follow."

The difference between paras (a) and (b) is that under (a) one is required to disregard not merely the "sitting tenant's overbid", but also the fact that the tenant has been in occupation of the premises and has carried on business there. This is not necessarily identical with the "goodwill" of the business referred to under (b), because in certain kinds of business it may be the personality of the tenant as much as the name and reputation of the business which attract customers. For example, a restaurant might be thriving while under the management and control of a famous chef. That chef might sell the business and its goodwill to a person who did not enjoy the same renown and the business might suffer. This shows that the two elements, although often closely related, are not identical. The relevant goodwill is that which attaches to the business which is carried out by the tenant, whether or not that goodwill was built up by him or by a predecessor in title and whether built up during the current tenancy or during a previous tenancy. The goodwill of any previous different business carried on by the tenant or a predecessor in title at the premises would be unlikely, in any event, to have any effect on rental value, because by ceasing the business and starting up a new business the tenant or his predecessor in title will already have destroyed that **8–140**

---

309 [2012] EWHC 1336 (Ch) at [179].

310 Unreported May 16, 1996, Central London County Court, H.H. Judge White.

goodwill. It appears from the decision in *Cramas Properties v Connaught Fur Trimmings*,[311] that the reference to "business" is to the particular business carried on, not to the kind of business carried on by the tenant or his predecessor. In *Prudential Assurance Co Ltd v Grand Metropolitan Estates*,[312] a rent review case, the judge considered the effect on the rental value of a public house of these disregards.

8–141 In *Jefferies v O'Neill*,[313] a rent review case, the only means of access to the demised premises was over adjoining freehold property owned by the tenant himself. Nourse J. held that, for the purposes of the rent review, this limitation on access should be ignored and the valuer should assume that access could be obtained to the demised premises. A similar result was reached in *British Airways Plc v Heathrow Airport*,[314] also a decision on a contractual rent review clause. In *J Murphy & Sons Ltd v Railtrack Plc*[315] (digested in para.8–142) it was sought to apply this principle to the operation of s.34 by implying a disregard as to the lack of access. The Court of Appeal declined to accept that any such term could be implied into the statute. The rent review cases, being cases concerning the construction of contracts, depended on the intention of the parties to those contracts; this could not be an approach adopted in relation to a statutory provision which was not lease specific but which was to apply irrespective of the parties' intentions.

8–142 ***J Murphy & Sons Ltd v Railtrack Plc***[316] L let premises to T, the only means of access to which was over T's adjoining land. On renewal L argued that, in determining the rent under s.34 of the Act, the lack of access was to be disregarded. It was said that the rent under s.34 should be determined in the same way as a standard rent review clause relying on *Jefferies v O'Neill*.[317]

The court held:

(1) that the lack of access was not to be disregarded. The rent review cases were not applicable. In a rent review one is looking at the intention of the parties to the lease having regard to the language they have used and the surrounding circumstances. In the case of a statutory renewal of a lease the statutory provisions apply in the same way to all leases. The intention of the parties to a particular lease cannot be written into the statutory language[318] (digested in para.8–16);

---

311 [1965] 1 W.L.R. 892; [1965] 2 All E.R. 382 HL. See paras 12–38 and 12–39.
312 [1993] 2 E.G.L.R. 153.
313 [1984] 1 E.G.L.R. 106.
314 [1992] 1 E.G.L.R. 141.
315 [2002] EWCA Civ 679; [2002] 2 E.G.L.R. 48.
316 [2002] EWCA Civ 679; [2002] 2 E.G.L.R. 48.
317 [1984] 1 E.G.L.R. 106.
318 Peter Gibson L.J. said:

"34(1), as it seems to me, contains within itself all the essential guidance needed for the determination of the rent on the hypothesis of a letting of the holding in the open market by a willing lessor with the specific statutory disregards referred to in the subsection, and only those disregards. I of course accept that the counterpart of a willing lessor in the open market is a willing lessee. The phrase 'the holding' means the premises demised under the tenancy: see s.23(3). The holding cannot, in my view, be enlarged to include an easement, or indeed any other right, not previously enjoyed.

(2) no right of access could be implied under s.32(3) or s.35(1). The court cannot treat the tenancy as including under s.32(3), or confer in relation to a tenancy under s.35(1), rights which are not conferred by the lease: *Orlik v Hasting and Thanet*[319] (digested in para.8–16);

(3) the judge at first instance was right to reject the suggestion that the absence of access prevented the valuation from being one in an open market. Even if there was only one person with a special interest in acquiring the property, nevertheless the valuation was one in the open market. An open market is one from which no one is excluded and, if there is a purchaser interested, there can be a sale in the open market: *Gajapaitiraju v Revenue Divisional Officer Vizagaptam*[320] followed.

It is provided by s.34(1)(d) that there is to be disregarded in the case of a holding comprising licensed premises, any addition to its value attributable to the licence, if it appears to the court that having regard to the terms of the current tenancy and any other relevant circumstances the benefit of the licence belongs to the tenant. It is provided that if the Act applies by virtue of s.23(1A) the benefit of the licence is equally disregarded where the licence belongs to a company in which the tenant has a controlling interest or where the licence belongs to a person who has a controlling interest in the tenant company. A person has a controlling interest in a company if, had he been a company, the other company would have been its subsidiary: s.46(2). "Subsidiary" has the same meaning as given by s.1159 of the Companies Act 2006. **8–143**

Provision for review of rent in new tenancy

It was not entirely clear whether the court had power, prior to 1969, to include provision for rent review as one of the terms of the new tenancy. In *Re 88 High Road, Kilburn*[321] (digested in para.8–149), it was held that the court had jurisdiction to insert such a clause and such a provision was inserted operable, apparently, by the landlord alone. The judge seems to have considered that the way in which the review would operate would be that the landlord would apply to the court to fix the reviewed rent, but the parties subsequently agreed that the review should be conducted by a surveyor. However, it is not clear from that decision from which provisions of the Act the court derived jurisdiction to assess **8–144**

When Parliament has specified what should be taken into account and what should be disregarded, it is a bold submission that it is permissible, nevertheless, for the court to imply a further disregard. That is particularly so where the suggested further disregard of the lack of access, requires the holding to be treated as having some right of access, such as an easement, over neighbouring land which is not conferred by the tenancy and which the landlord is not able to grant . . . Unless there is some principle that the rental value of any premises is to be maximized for the benefit of the landlord—and I cannot see how there can be any such principle—it seems to me impossible for the court to depart from the reality of the situation as a matter of statutory interpretation in order to imply into the tenancy some right which it does not confer. It would be very surprising if Parliament intended that a tenant should be required to pay rent for a right which he already has by reason of his ownership of land adjoining the demised premises."

[319] (1975) 29 P. & C.R. 126.

[320] [1939] A.C. 302 PC.

[321] [1959] 1 W.L.R. 279; [1959] 1 All E.R. 527.

a rent subject to review rather than the single rent which appears to be contemplated by s.34. The jurisdiction under s.34 is not discretionary, so it may be that the rent review provisions were inserted by the court pursuant to its powers under s.35, which enable it to deal with the "other terms" of the tenancy. An objection to this approach might be that a rent review clause is not an "other term", because it is a term which relates to rent. The Law Commission certainly considered the matter to be sufficiently doubtful to recommend in its report in 1969 that an express power to insert rent review provisions should be included by way of amendment in the Act. Accordingly, what is now s.34(2) was inserted as follows:

> "Where the rent is determined by the Court the Court may, if it thinks fit, determine that the terms of the tenancy shall include such provision for varying the rent as may be specified in the determination."

8–145 The power to incorporate as a term of the new lease provision for review of the rent is now almost invariably exercised where the court grants a term of longer than five years. As was the case at the time of writing the previous editions of this work in 1996 and 2002, the courts appear to have settled upon a five-year pattern of rent review as doing justice between landlord and tenant, although landlords sometimes argue for a shorter period and tenants for a longer one. In a period of acute inflation and rapidly rising property values such as prevailed in the late 1980s, landlords may argue that five years is too long a period during which their rent is to be fixed. On the other hand, tenants will wish to know with some certainty what are their future outgoings in terms of rent and will also wish to avoid the trouble and expense of over frequent rent reviews. As well as giving weight to these arguments on both sides, the court is usually influenced by market practice. Evidence is often given that a particular pattern of rent review is acceptable in particular areas, in respect of particular kinds of properties, or by particular classes of tenant and landlord. Provided that all relevant factors are taken into account, the decision on what is the appropriate period between reviews is a matter for the discretion of the court. See *WH Smith v Bath*[322] (digested in para.8–137), below and *Graham v Hodgson*,[323] for examples of cases where the county court judge ordered a four-year and three-year review pattern respectively. In *Northern Electric Plc v Addison*,[324] the Court of Appeal upheld the judge's refusal to incorporate provision for review in a lease of 14 years of an electricity sub-station. The rent was only £40 per annum and the cost of the implementation of the review process was likely to exceed the increase in any rent achieved on review. It was said that the judge was entitled to reach the conclusion that it would be wrong to provide for a rent review clause on the basis that something might turn up in the future or that some unforeseen circumstance might arise about which he had heard no evidence, whereby an increase would be justified sufficient to recover the costly matter of renegotiation.

When a rent review clause is negotiated between parties in the open market it is almost invariably the case that it is "upwards only". The reason for this is that

---

322 Unreported November 6, 1984, County Court.

323 Unreported, but noted at [1994] 13 E.G. 102.

324 [1997] 2 E.G.L.R. 111 CA. See also para.8–106 for a summary of this case.

institutional landlords such as pension funds or insurance companies, which now constitute the majority of owners of commercial freeholds, will insist upon a minimum guaranteed return from their investments in order to be able to satisfy their commitment to their beneficiaries. However, from the earliest days of the Act, the court has treated the question as being one of striking a fair balance between the landlord and the tenant, stating that there was no reason in principle why if at the review date it turned out that rental values had fallen, the rent should not be decreased. This inclination against upwards only reviews, and in favour of upwards-and-downwards clauses, has been adopted in all save one of the reported cases where the issue has been joined between landlord and tenant.[325]

WH Smith & Son Ltd v Bath City Council[326] WH Smith sought a new tenancy of a shop in a prime shopping street in Bath. The city council, who were the leaseholders of many of the city centre properties, were willing to grant a new tenancy and the parties were able to agree all the terms of the new tenancy but one: the frequency of reviews in the rent review clause. The city council sought four-yearly reviews and WH Smith reviews at five-yearly intervals. The city council's arguments can be summarised as follows: **8–146**

(1) It had since 1974 with very few exceptions been its policy to grant new tenancies with four-year reviews; this arose from its soundly motivated management needs in a city where rental growth had out-stripped inflation to the extent of nearly doubling, in some instances in three years.
(2) It would not be fair or desirable to concede a five-year review pattern when nearly all the other tenants on its estate in the past 10 years had been compelled to take four-year patterns.
(3) There was no shortage of demand by tenants for premises in the subject street, despite the city council's insistence on four-yearly reviews.

WH Smith contended in turn that:

(a) They had 300 retail outlets across the country, the vast majority of which were on five-yearly reviews; a four-yearly review would be a dangerous precedent in that it would encourage other freeholders to apply pressure to bring the periods down across the board to four years.
(b) An increase in the frequency of rent reviews would result in an extra work load necessitating the engagement of more staff with attendant experience.
(c) Rent reviews were occasions where the harmony essential to good landlord and tenant relationships might be disturbed and thus the fewer opportunities for reviews the better.
(d) An increase in the frequency of reviews would lead to greater uncertainty and difficulty in forward business planning.

---

[325] See the cases in paras 8–137 to 8–144.
[326] Unreported November 6, 1984, County Court.

(e) Even though the parties had agreed that the adjustment in the annual agreed rent on the basis of four- or five-yearly reviews should be £300, such compensation would not be an adequate remedy to the tenant for the disadvantages it would suffer.

It was held that:

(i) The court's function was not to interfere with the negotiating positions of the parties, but to ensure that the tenant derived a benefit which was just and that the landlord could not seek to impose a term which was unfair and unreasonable.
(ii) The landlords had shown generally and in this particular case that their policy of insisting on four-yearly rent reviews in the special circumstances of Bath was prudent and right; the proposed four-year periodicity was fair and reasonable and the new tenancy would be ordered on the terms agreed with a four-yearly rent review.

8–147 ***Stylo Shoes v Manchester Royal Exchange***[327] The landlord was willing to grant a new tenancy of 14 years, contending that the rent should be £8,000 per annum with provision for upwards only reviews. The tenant agreed the rent should be £4,000 per annum but said that it should be entitled itself to exercise a right to review the rent if there appeared to be a downward trend in market rents. Cross J. fixed the rent at £5,000 and inserted a right for the tenant (as well as the landlords) to exercise the review in the rent review clause. After all, he saw "no reason why sauce for the goose should not be sauce for the gander". The judge awarded the tenant one-half of its costs against the landlord.

8–148 ***Janes (Gowns) v Harlow Development Corp***[328] At the hearing of the tenant's application for a new tenancy there was evidence that, due to recent developments in the locality, it was quite possible that rents might go up or down in the future. On this basis the judge held that an upwards-or-downwards clause should be included as a term of the new tenancy. Since there was no evidence that the insertion of upwards only rent review clauses in leases of comparable properties had affected the rents payable, it was not appropriate to make any consequential adjustment upwards in assessing the rent to be paid pursuant to the current tenancy to reflect the insertion of the upwards-and-downwards rent review clause.

8–149 ***Re 88 High Road, Kilburn***[329] The tenant asked for a new lease for a term of 14 years, while the landlords contended for a term of seven years only. The reason given by the landlords was:

> "that if the tenants are to have security of tenure in the shape of the longer term, then a guard against inflation should be provided for them, and that a provision should therefore be included in the lease that, at the end of the first half, a right should be given to the landlords by

---

[327] [1967] E.G.D. 743.
[328] [1980] 1 E.G.L.R. 52.
[329] [1959] 1 W.L.R. 279; [1959] 1 All E.R. 527.

> the lease, to have the rent reviewed, provided that any review shall not have the effect of lowering the rent but only of increasing it, if on review it is considered that, in the circumstances then obtaining, the rental value of the property has increased."

The judge held that the tenants should be granted the 14-year term which they sought, but directed that there should be included in the lease a provision for the review of rent at the end of the first half of the term for which the landlords had asked.

Blythewood Plant Hire v Spiers[330] The tenants had been holding over as yearly tenants of land since the expiry of the original five-year term in 1946. The tenants applied for a new tenancy and the judge awarded a 10-year term with a redevelopment break clause operable at the expiry of the seventh or any subsequent year. (The landlords had contended that the lease should be for five years only.) On the question of whether the rent review provisions operable at the end of the fifth year of the term should be upwards-and-downwards the judge commented that: **8–150**

> "neither of the two valuers who gave evidence had any practical experience of a two-way clause and until recently such clauses were virtually unknown in the real world. A clause in this form would have the result that the landlord's interest would become more difficult to market. It would therefore have an immediate impact on the value of the landlord's interest. On the other hand, the evidence suggested that a tenant would not pay substantially more rent for an upward/downward clause as such a clause is likely to be of little immediate benefit to the tenant."

The judge ordered that the clause should be upwards only.

Amarjee v Barrowfen Properties Ltd[331] The tenant had occupied the premises for some years without any written lease or tenancy agreement, as a tenant from year to year. Upon the hearing of his application for a new tenancy under the Act, it was agreed that he should be granted a new term of 14 years with a five-year rent review provision. The judge accepted the tenant's proposal for an upwards-and-downwards rent review clause. He noted that all the other leases which were in evidence had upwards only clauses but commented that they were granted at a time when, on the expert evidence, property and rental values were rising. He said: **8–151**

> "Now that the unthinkable has started to occur, and property prices are falling, I see no reason why upwards/downwards clauses should not be incorporated in leases. They have the obvious merit offairness and the only disadvantage I can see is that they may give rise to disputes, in some instances, at the end of review periods, which would not have occurred with an upwards only clause. That potential disadvantage does not, in my judgment, outweigh the advantage of fairness . . ."

Boots the Chemists Ltd v Pinkland[332] One of the applications before the court was for a term which it had been agreed should be 14 years with rent reviews at **8–152**

---

[330] [1992] 2 E.G.L.R. 103 CC.
[331] [1993] 2 E.G.L.R. 133 CC.
[332] [1992] 2 E.G.L.R. 98 CC.

the end of the fifth and tenth years. The judge referred to the *Jane's (Gowns)*[333] case (digested in para.8–148) and *Stylo Shoes*[334] (digested in para.8–147). He said that he had no means of knowing whether the decline in rental values over the previous two years was merely a "bear phase" in the continuing "bull market" or whether it was the beginning a new "bear market", indicating that the long running "bull market" had now come to an end. Accordingly, it would be appropriate to include an upwards and downwards review clause because:

> "if it be the case that we are now in the incipient stages of a prolonged 'bear market' then present-day rents will seem exorbitant later in this decade and in the beginning of the next century. As a consequence, fixed rents, or rents which can only be revised upwards, will wreak the same sort of injustice upon tenants as that which has been suffered by landlords in previous decades when leases contained no provision for rent review at all. On the other hand, if the present period of decline in rental values is merely an aberration in a continuing 'bull market', the landlords will in no way be prejudiced by the inclusion of a provision for rents to be reviewed downwards as well as upwards."

8–153 ***Forboys Plc v Newport Borough Council***[335] The tenant agreed a nine-year lease of a shop unit in a shopping centre. The tenant's old lease was for a term of 21 years without provision for review of the rent. The parties agreed that the new lease was to contain provision for review every three years. Evidence was given by the landlord that other units within the centre had upwards only rent review provisions. The judge was persuaded, however, that this lease had been agreed at the time when the full effects of the recession had not been felt. He was of the view on the evidence that, at the date of trial, "the recession is still bumping along the bottom". It was held that the review provisions were to be upwards-and-downwards as this was fair to both parties.

8–154 It is interesting to note that in none of the decided cases concerning upwards/downwards rent review clauses was there any provision whatsoever for rent review in the current tenancy. The court did not, accordingly, have to decide what weight (if any) to give to the upwards only, or upwards-and-downwards, nature of such a provision in deciding whether the rent review provisions of the new tenancy should be of the same or of a different nature. Nor is there any specific consideration in any of the decided cases of the question whether the court is precluded from inserting an upwards only rent review provision on the basis that such a clause does not conform with the requirement to assess a market rent to prevail throughout the entire period of the lease. Such an argument is not, of course, consistent with the actual decision of the court in *Re 88 High Road, Kilburn*[336] (digested in para.8–149) or *Blythewood Plant Hire v Spiers*[337] (digested in para.8–150), but the point does not seem to have been specifically argued. It has been held by the Court of Appeal in *Fawke v Chelsea*[338] (digested in para.9–41), below, that the court has jurisdiction under s.34 to assess a "differential" rent, namely a rent which increased by fixed amounts, or which

---

[333] [1980] 1 E.G.L.R. 52.
[334] [1967] E.G.D. 743.
[335] [1994] 1 E.G.L.R. 138 CC.
[336] [1959] 1 W.L.R. 279; [1959] 1 All E.R. 527.
[337] [1992] 2 E.G.L.R. 103 CC.
[338] [1980] Ch. 441; [1979] 3 W.L.R. 508; [1979] 3 All E.R. 568 CA.

increased when repairs which the landlords were required to carry out were completed, if the evidence indicated that, in the market, the parties would have agreed a rent on that basis.

8–155 In practice, the detailed terms of the rent review clause are often agreed between landlord and tenant once the court has decided in principle that a clause is to be inserted, for what period and whether "upwards only" or "upwards-and-downwards". If landlord and tenant were to be in disagreement on the detailed terms of the rent review provisions, it is thought that the court would be strongly influenced by the terms of s.34, which has been considered by parliament to be a fair basis upon which the rent is to be assessed when the matter comes before the court. Many rent review clauses in fact incorporate, with suitable modifications, the terms of s.34 and the court would be likely to do so also.

8–156 One part of the rent review clause which might cause controversy between landlord and tenant is the extent to which the tenant's improvements should be disregarded. The tenant might argue that the clause should be drafted so as to ensure that the landlord was not entitled, at any time during the new tenancy, to obtain the benefit of any improvements carried out by the tenant, even if they were carried out longer ago than 21 years before the rent review date. The answer to this argument would appear to be that Parliament, on the advice of the Law Commission, has made a decision in principle, by virtue of its amendments to s.34 in the Law of Property Act 1969, that if tenants' improvements are older than 21 years they should not be disregarded. The justification for this is either that improvements of such an age would be unlikely to have any real effect on rental value, or that a disregard which applied for a longer period would lead to practical difficulties for landlords and tenants in proving what works had in fact been done by whom. Since the effect of the court granting a tenancy for a term of five years only, without review, would be that upon any renewal of the tenancy any tenant's improvements older than 21 years would not be disregarded, there seems to be no reason in principle why a rent review clause inserted by the court to take effect in five years' time should not have precisely the same effect.[339]

[339] See para.8–125 et seq. for a detailed discussion of the statutory disregard of improvements.

CHAPTER 9

INTERIM RENT

The 1954 Act as originally enacted conferred no power on the court to vary the rent payable pursuant to the current tenancy during such time as it was being continued by virtue of ss.24 and 64. Since that rent was in most cases considerably lower than that which would have been obtainable in the market during the period of continuation and since the period of continuation could, for various reasons beyond the control of the landlord, be extremely lengthy, the position was generally considered to be unfair to landlords. It was in order to mitigate this injustice to landlords that s.24A was introduced by the Law of Property Act 1969. For the relatively simple provisions contained in s.24A of the 1954 Act under the old regime, the 2003 Order substitutes no less than four sections containing 17 sub-sections. The position is not straightforward. The changes brought about by the 2003 Order are essentially twofold: **9–01**

(1) an entitlement is given to the tenant to seek an interim rent[1];
(2) a new methodology, as an alternative to that provided for by the old provisions, has been introduced for calculating the interim rent.

Which methodology is to be adopted depends upon whether the application for renewal is unopposed and the tenant ends up with a new tenancy or the landlord is opposing (whether by way of opposition to the tenant's claim for a new tenancy or by way of the landlord's own claim for termination). In summary:

(a) Where there is no opposition to renewal, the prima facie position is that the rent payable under the new tenancy at the commencement of the new tenancy will also be the interim rent. This prima facie position is subject to two exceptions which are likely to be utilised often in practice;
(b) in any other case, i.e. where there is opposition to the tenant having a renewal, the calculation of the interim rent is very similar to that under the old regime.

[1] This of course applies, as with any claims made by the landlord, only in respect of claims made pursuant to a s.25 notice or s.26 request served after May 31, 2004.

1. RIGHT TO APPLY FOR INTERIM RENT

9–02 Section 24A(1) confers a right to apply for an interim rent "while the tenancy continues by virtue of section 24". It follows that there is no right to apply where the tenancy is being continued by ss.28[2] and 36(2),[3] which continue tenancies independently of the provisions of s.24. Furthermore, either the landlord must have given notice under s.25 of the Act or the tenant must have made a request for a new lease under s.26. No interim rent is payable if the tenancy is simply allowed to continue under s.24 without either party serving a s.25 notice or s.26 request and the tenancy comes to an end, e.g. by surrender or forfeiture.

9–03 Prior to June 1, 2004 the right to apply for an interim rent could be exercised only by the landlord; no such right was given to the tenant. The reason for this was that, as explained above, the purpose of s.24A was to amend a perceived injustice to landlords. The possibility that (as in fact happened in the early 1990s) business rents might fall considerably below the level reserved by the lease, thus causing a corresponding injustice to tenants, was not foreseen or, at any rate, not provided for. The 2003 Order has now made provision with effect from June 1, 2004 for the tenant, in addition to the landlord, to apply for an interim rent.

9–04 The landlord who may apply for an interim rent is presumably "the landlord" as defined in s.44 (see para.3–87). This produces the odd result, where the current tenancy is a sub-tenancy and the mesne tenancy is itself being continued by s.24, that the person to whom the rent under the current tenancy is payable during the period of the continuation, namely the immediate landlord, is not himself entitled to apply for an interim rent. This can be illustrated by an example.

9–05 **Example** If F is the freeholder, T is the tenant of the whole occupying part for the purposes of his business and S is the sub-tenant occupying the rest for the purposes of his business, F will satisfy the definition of "landlord", assuming the appropriate notices to have been served. If T and S both apply for new tenancies of the parts which they respectively occupy, both T's tenancy and S's sub-tenancy will be continued by virtue of ss.24 and 64. However, since F is "the landlord," only he may apply for an interim rent to be assessed in respect of the tenancy and the sub-tenancy. If he applies in respect only of the tenancy, T is faced with the prospect of receiving a low rent from S while having to pay a higher interim rent to F. It is suggested that T, in these circumstances, should ask F to apply for an interim rent in S's proceedings and, if F refuses to do so, should ask the court to exercise its discretion against F when he claims an interim rent from T. An alternative argument, which does not depend upon the court's discretion, is that the interim rent payable by T should in any event be diminished because his tenancy is subject to S's sub-tenancy at a low rent.

9–06 Where an application for an interim rent has been made by a person who has ceased to be "the landlord" before the application is heard, the person who has become the landlord must be joined in order that the application to be properly constituted. (It is unclear whether it is sufficient that he be substituted for the

[2] See para.15–14 et seq.

[3] See para.10–10 et seq.

landlord who made the application.) In *Bloomfield v Ashwright*[4] (digested in para.9–45) the reversion had been assigned after an application for an interim rent had been made, but before the application was heard. The Court of Appeal held that the jurisdiction to award an interim rent was a jurisdiction in respect of the premises, not a jurisdiction to order payment to a particular person. Since both the assignor and the assignee remained parties to the interim rent application, it was validly constituted and it was for them and not the court to decide who was to take the benefit of the award. If, however, the application has been heard and an interim rent has been determined, a subsequent change in the identity of "the landlord" would have no effect.

If either of the landlord or the tenant has already made an application, the other may not himself do so unless the application made by the other is withdrawn.[5] Thus, for instance, if the landlord were to make an application for an interim rent but then withdraw it, there would appear to be nothing preventing the tenant from making his own application or, come to that, to prevent the landlord from subsequently making a second application. **9–07**

2. TIME FOR MAKING APPLICATION

Other than the requirement that a s.25 notice or s.26 request shall have first been served, there is no time limit as to the earliest date at which the application for interim rent may be made.[6] The application may be made, it would appear, at any time after service of a s.25 notice or s.26 request. However, there is a time limit as to the latest date by which an application for an interim rent may be made. Section 24A(3) provides that the application must not be "made more than six months after the termination of the relevant tenancy". It is considered that "termination of the relevant tenancy" is here referring to the termination of the relevant tenancy in accordance with the 1954 Act, not the date on which the term would, but for the Act, have expired by effluxion of time[7] or the date of termination or commencement specified in the landlord's s.25 notice or the tenant's s.26 request respectively.[8] Thus, there is no reason why, where a tenant **9–08**

4 [1983] 1 E.G.L.R. 82 CA.

5 s.24A(2).

6 As to the procedure for making an application for interim rent, see para.14–110 et seq.

7 It clearly is not this date, as this date may pass before any notice or request has in fact been served before initiating the 1954 Act procedure. If it were this date, its effect would be that a landlord, if he wanted to claim interim rent, would have to ensure that he served a s.25 notice within six months of the contractual term date. If he did not, he would be unable to claim an interim rent, albeit he subsequently served a s.25 and irrespective of the duration of the continuation tenancy.

8 Neither of these dates seems appropriate although the dates correspond to the "statutory period," this being the last date by which the application for renewal or termination must be made: s.29B(1) and (2) (As to the meaning of "statutory period" see para.6–17 et seq.) If the draftsman had intended to correlate the last date for making an application for interim rent with that for making an application for renewal/termination he could have done so by referring to the definition of "statutory period", rather than referring to the termination of the relevant tenancy. It is also to be noted that in s.30(1) the various references to "termination of the current tenancy" mean the date of termination in accordance with the Act. If the dates specified in the s.25 notice or s.26 request were to be viewed as the relevant date of termination, it would encourage applications for interim rent to be made before it is known whether or not the tenant has made an application for renewal. Take the following example: T serves

has been granted a new tenancy whether by agreement with the landlord or by order of the court, the landlord cannot within six months thereafter seek an interim rent.[9]

9–09 Although the application can be made at any time after the service of a s.25 notice or the making of a s.26 request, it is unusual in practice for the application to be made before the tenant has applied for a new tenancy, because, unless the tenant does so, the period of continuation during which an interim rent is payable will usually be short. In special circumstances, such as where it is anticipated that there will be a change in the identity of "the landlord" in the near future, there might be tactical reasons for the making of an application as soon as a s.25 notice has been served or a s.26 request made. In practice a landlord will not bother to apply for an interim rent, unless there may be a significant period of continuation after the tenant makes his application or unless rents have increased so dramatically that the "cash-flow" benefits of obtaining the earliest possible determination are significant.

3. JURISDICTION DISCRETIONARY

9–10 Section 24A provides that if the landlord applies for an interim rent the court may determine a rent accordingly. The word "may" confers a discretion on the court which, in most cases, will be exercised in favour of the landlord: *English Exporters v Eldonwall*.[10] In *Bloomfield v Ashwright Ltd*[11] (digested in para.9–45) Lawton L.J. accepted as being "well founded" a submission that the judge had a discretion to order an interim rent and that there might be circumstances when it would be unjust to make a tenant pay an interim rent. He went on to say: "I find it myself difficult to imagine such circumstances but no doubt others with a more fertile imagination than I have can do so." The views of Megarry J. in *English Exporters v Eldonwall*[12] and Lawton L.J. in *Bloomfield v Ashwright*[13] were

---

a s.26 request giving six months notice. The landlord does not oppose renewal. The tenant has to wait two months in order to issue a renewal claim unless the landlord serves a counter-notice opposing renewal. The tenant is not, however, obliged to serve the application before the expiry of the "statutory period", for after issue he then has four months in which to serve the claim form (see para.14–56 et seq.). However, CPR PD 56 para.3.17 requires the interim rent application, "where proceedings have already been commenced for the grant of a new tenancy" to be made in those proceedings. The landlord will not, however, know of the existence of the proceedings until service by which time it may be too late to make the application. The landlord could only avoid this consequence by making an application for interim rent without knowing whether the tenant will be making an application for renewal.

The view that the "termination of the tenancy" is termination of the old tenancy, i.e. in accordance with s.64, in fact accords with the view of the Government and the Regulatory Reform Committee: see the Explanatory Statement by the Office of the Deputy Prime Minister, September 2003, Appendix F, para.5 when the draft Order was laid before Parliament and the 14th Report of the Regulatory Reform Committee, dated October 21, 2003, para.19. Both of those documents refer to the time limit being one requiring the application to be made not later than "six months after the termination *of the old tenancy*." The old tenancy does not end, where an application for renewal is made or a termination application is made, other than in accordance with s.64.

[9] See also para.9–14.

[10] [1973] Ch. 415; [1973] 2 W.L.R. 435; [1973] 1 All E.R. 726.

[11] [1983] 1 E.G.L.R. 82 CA.

[12] [1973] Ch. 415; [1973] 2 W.L.R. 435.

approved by Nourse L.J. in *Charles Follett Ltd v Cabtell Investments Ltd*[14] (digested in para.9–23), where the Court of Appeal held that there is no discretion in the court to order (or to extract by way of undertaking) that the tenant pay something other than an interim rent: it is "all or nothing".[15]

If a claim for an interim rent is made the claimant must make sure that appropriate evidence is before the court to enable the court to deal with it: *Arora v Bose*,[16] where the interim rent application having been made, was adjourned for what appeared to be a four-year period, without the landlord during that period seeking any directions in relation to evidence. The Court of Appeal refused to interfere with the learned judge's decision to decline to entertain the application for interim rent during the course of the substantive hearing concerning the terms, in particular, the terms as to rent, of a new lease for the premises. **9–11**

4. DATE FROM WHICH INTERIM RENT PAYABLE

Under the old provisions the date from which the interim rent was payable was the later of the following possible dates: (1) the date specified in the s.25 notice or s.26 request; or (2) "the date on which the proceedings were commenced".[17] **9–12**

Under the new regime, the position is different. The interim rent commences from the "appropriate date".[18] The "appropriate date" is: **9–13**

(1) if an application under s.24A(1) is made in a case where the landlord has given a notice under s.25, the earliest date of termination that could have been specified in the landlord's s.25 notice: s.24B(2);
(2) if an application under s.24A(1) is made in a case where the tenant has made a request for a new tenancy under s.26, the earliest date that could have been specified in the tenant's s.26 request as the date from which the new tenancy is to be begin: s.24B(3).

The obligation to pay the interim rent commences as from the "appropriate date" notwithstanding that the actual application may be made later than the "appropriate date". Thus, it will be important, e.g. in any agreement for renewal at the door of the court, to deal with the landlord's entitlement to make an application, whether by way of the landlord waiving his entitlement to interim rent or by the parties agreeing an interim rent in lieu of the landlord's entitlement **9–14**

---

13 [1983] 1 E.G.L.R. 82 CA.
14 [1986] 2 E.G.L.R. 76 CA.
15 This remains the position notwithstanding the amendments made by the 2003 Order.
16 (1998) 76 P. & C.R. D1 CA.
17 This being the wording in the now repealed s.24(2). In *Stream Properties v Davis*, Pennycuick V.C. held that the "proceedings" in question were the landlord's application for an interim rent and not the tenant's application for a new tenancy. Despite an obiter dictum of Lord Denning M.R. in *Secretary of State v Rossetti Lodge Investment Co*, suggesting that *Stream Properties v Davis* may have been wrongly decided, it was followed in the Chancery Division in *Victor Blake v Westminster* [1979] 1 E.G.L.R. 714, and approved by the Court of Appeal in *Lloyds Bank v City of London* [1982] 3 W.L.R. 1138; [1983] 1 All E.R. 92 CA.
18 s.24B.

otherwise to make a claim. This problem would not have arisen under the old regime. The reason for this was, as noted above, that the interim rent ran only from the latest of the date of the making of the application or the date of termination or commencement contained in the relevant s.25 notice or s.26 request respectively. Thus, if by the date of agreement at court on the tenant's claim for renewal, the landlord had not made an application for an interim rent, the landlord had for all practical purposes waived his entitlement to an interim rent, for if he made an application for an interim rent the very next day he would, at best, obtain an interim rent for three months and three weeks (s.64 providing that the current tenancy would continue for three months together with the time for appeal after final disposal). However, under the new regime, the "appropriate date" from which the interim rent is payable is not related to the date of the making of the application for interim rent. It is a date which is historic and may be many months, in some cases, years prior to the date of the agreement for renewal.

9–15 In the exceptional circumstances in which s.31(2) operates,[19] the court will make an order substituting a later date for the date originally specified in the landlord's s.25 notice or s.26 request. Under the old regime it was unclear whether in such circumstances the interim rent would be payable from the date originally specified. If not, the practical effect would be that no interim rent could be awarded. However, under the new provisions as the date from which the interim rent is payable is the earliest date which could have been specified in the relevant notice or request the mere alteration of the date by the court under s.31(2) has no impact on the date from which the interim rent is payable.

5. VALUATION DATES

9–16 Under the old provisions it was held that the valuation of the interim rent was by reference to market values at the commencement of the interim rent period: *Fawke v Viscount Chelsea*[20] (digested in para.9–41); *English Exporters v Eldonwall*[21]; *Charles Follett Ltd v Cabtell Investments Ltd*[22] (digested in para.9–23). The matter post June 1, 2004 is now complicated. There are valuation dates for determining the assessment of the interim rent as well as for determining the application of various exceptions to the basis of assessment. After June 1, 2004 the position is as follows:

(1) where the interim rent is one determined in accordance with s.24C(2)[23] the interim rent will be the s.34 rent and thus the interim rent is not separately assessed to the s.34 rent determined for the new tenancy;
(2) where a party seeks to rely on the exception provided for by s.24C(3)(a)[24] to the application of s.24C(2), "the appropriate date is the valuation date"

[19] See para.7–290 et seq.
[20] [1979] 3 W.L.R. 508; [1979] 3 All E.R. 568 CA.
[21] [1973] Ch. 415 at 431 C–431D.
[22] [1986] 2 E.G.L.R. 76 CA.
[23] As to which see para.9–25.
[24] As to which see para.9–27.

for the alternative s.34 rent assessment for the purposes of establishing the application of the exception[25]: s.24C(4). If the exception applies the s.34 assessment as at the "appropriate date" will become the interim rent: s.24C(5);

(3) where a party seeks to rely on the exception provided for by s.24C(3)(b)[26] to the application of s.24C(2), the valuation date for the alternative s.34 rent assessment for the purposes of establishing the exception is the s.34 valuation date, i.e. for practical purposes the date of the hearing subject to any appropriate adjustment to take account of the delay prior to the grant of the new lease (the date in accordance with s.64 which is three months and three weeks (being the period for appeal[27]) after final disposal). If the exception provided for by s.24C(3)(b) applies the interim rent will be that provided for by s.24C(7). The valuation date for the assessment under s.24C(7) is considered in (4) below;

(4) the valuation dates applicable to the exceptions to the application of s.24C(2) are as mentioned above. If the exception within s.24C(3)(b) alone is, or that exception together with that contained within s.24C(3)(a) are, established, it is provided that the interim rent will be the "rent which it is reasonable for the tenant to pay while the relevant tenancy continues by virtue of section 24 of this Act": s.24C(6). The rent which it is reasonable for the tenant to pay is that provided for by s.24C(7), i.e. the interim rent is on the basis provided for by s.24C(7).[28] As will be seen, the basis of assessment under s.24C(7) is essentially the application of s.34 assessed on the terms of the relevant tenancy (i.e. the current tenancy). It is unclear whether the valuation date is the s.34 valuation date or the "appropriate date". The wording of subss.(6) and (7) are not dissimilar to that under the old s.24A(3) and under that wording the case law decided that the valuation date was the date of the commencement of the interim rent period, which under the new rules is the "appropriate date".

(5) where the interim rent is determined in accordance with s.24D no express reference is made as to what is the valuation date. However, the wording contained within s.24D(2) is very similar to that of the old s.24A(3) and under that wording the case law decided that the valuation date was the date of the commencement of the interim rent period, which under the new rules is the "appropriate date".[29]

[25] As to the meaning of which see para.9–13.

[26] As to which see para.9–27.

[27] See para.14–137 et seq.

[28] s.24C(7) is considered in para.9–31.

[29] As to the meaning of which see para.9–13. The "appropriate date" was the valuation date which was adopted in *Humber Oil Terminals Trustee Ltd v Associated British Ports* [2012] EWHC 1336 (Ch).

6. VALUATION METHODOLOGIES

Pre June 1, 2004

General

9–17 Under the old regime there was only one valuation methodology, namely that provided for by the terms of s.24(A)(3)(now repealed). This provided that in determining the rent under s.24A the court was to have regard:

> "to the rent payable under the terms of the tenancy, but otherwise subsections (1) and (2) of section 34 shall apply to the determination as they would apply to the determination of a rent under that section if a new tenancy from year to year of the whole of the property comprised in the tenancy were granted to the tenant."

In *English Exporters v Eldonwall*,[30] Megarry J. explained the principles applicable to the determination of an interim rent. They may be summarised as follows:

(1) The hypothetical tenancy is a tenancy from year to year.
(2) The commencement date of that tenancy is the beginning of the interim rent period.
(3) The other terms of the hypothetical yearly tenancy are the same as those of the current tenancy which is being continued so far as consistent with a tenancy from year to year.
(4) The rent payable in respect of the hypothetical yearly tenancy is to be determined by the court on the same valuation principles as are appropriate under s.34 to the determination of a rent under the new tenancy, but upon the basis of a hypothetical yearly tenancy.
(5) The court is required to "have regard to the rent payable under the current tenancy"; this confers upon the court a discretion to "cushion" or "temper" the market rent which it would have assessed in accordance with the foregoing principles.

9–18 In *Regis Property v Lewis & Peat*,[31] Stamp J. adopted a somewhat different approach, but in *Fawke v Viscount Chelsea*[32] (digested in para.9–41) the Court of Appeal stated that that of Megarry J. was to be preferred. In *Charles Follett v Cabtell*[33] (digested in para.9–23), the Court of Appeal largely affirmed Megarry

---

[30] [1973] Ch. 415.

[31] [1970] 3 W.L.R. 361; [1970] 3 All E.R. 227.

[32] [1979] 3 W.L.R. 508 CA.

[33] In *English Exporters (London) Ltd v Eldonwall Ltd* [1973] Ch. 415 at 433–34, Megarry J. said:

"I doubt if the two elements of market rent and the existing rent are intended to be given equal weight. Section 24A(3) provides that section 34 'shall apply' to the determination in the manner stated, and merely requires the court to 'have regard' to the existing rent. I think the process envisaged is not that of striking a balance between two factors of equal weight, but is that of applying one factor, namely, the market rent, and, where appropriate, suitably tempering it by reference to the existing rent."

This was, however, to some extent qualified by Nourse L.J. in the *Charles Follett* case at 90 as follows:

J.'s approach, but disapproved of that part of his judgment where he suggested that more weight was necessarily to be given to the "new rent" than to the "old rent". On the somewhat unusual facts of that case, the Court of Appeal refused to disturb the judge's decision that a "cushion" of 50 per cent was to be applied.

Cushion

The intention behind the statutory declaration to have regard to the old rent was expressed by Nourse L.J. in *Charles Follett v Cabtell*[34] in the following terms: **9–19**

> "What was the intention of Parliament in requiring regard to be had to the old rent? While sympathising with the pleas for clarification which have been made by Megarry J. and others, I think the circumstances in which section 24A came into existence provide a reliable answer to this question. By 1969 it had been demonstrated that a tenant, in times of inflation, could readily spin out the steps prescribed by the 1954 Act and the rules of the court, so as unfairly to prolong the continuation of the old rent under section 24. The defeat of such practices was the primary legislative purpose of section 24A. At the same time it was recognised that while inflation benefits the tenant during the currency of a lease at an inflated rent, it exposes him to an inordinate shock if its consequences are visited on him in full directly the lease has determined. The legislative purpose of the requirement that regard should be had to the old rent was, where appropriate, to cushion the tenant against that shock."

A number of propositions can be put forward, based upon the decided cases under the old provisions of s.24A, as to the principles upon which the quantum (if any) of the cushion is to be assessed. The application of the cushion remains relevant under the new regime[35] and thus a consideration of the decided cases is appropriate. The table (at the end of this Chapter) shows how various judges have adjusted the rent determined in respect of the new tenancy in order to arrive at an interim rent. This table although based on decisions under the old regime is still of some assistance in considering the cushion to be applied, if any, under s.24C(7) or 24D(2). It is considered that the authorities support the following propositions: **9–20**

(1) A cushion does not have to be provided in every case. It is only necessary to temper the market rent by reference to the existing rent where appropriate: *Halberstam v Tandalco Corp NV*[36] (digested in para.9–22); *Dept of the Environment v Allied Freehold Property Trust*.[37]

"... I cannot see that there was intended to be an invariable rule that the interim market rent should be given greater weight than the old rent or that regard to the latter should only be capable in resulting in some marginal or not very significant reduction.If, as I think, the purpose of the requirement is, where appropriate, to cushion the tenant against the shock that I have described it is not impossible to conceive of circumstances in which it might well be thought that that object could be achieved only by applying a reduction which was far from marginal, and certainly significant. If Megarry J did indeed intend to propound an invariable rule to the contrary, then I must express my respectful disagreement with his view."

[34] [1987] 2 E.G.L.R. 88 CA at 90F–H.

[35] Under s.24C(7) and 24D(2) as to which see paras 9–31 and 9–34, respectively.

[36] [1985] 1 E.G.L.R. 90 CA.

[37] [1992] 45 E.G. 156.

(2) The court ought not to award an interim rent so close to the market rent determined for the new tenancy that the tenant effectively ends up paying in excess of the market rent at the commencement of the interim rent period: see *Conway v Arthur*.[38]
(3) The court ought not to pay mere lip service to the direction to have regard to the old rent: *Charles Follett v Cabtell* (digested in para.9–23).[39]
(4) The length of the s.24 continuation period may be relevant in considering the "cushion" to be given. The longer the continuation the less the cushion discount is likely to be: *French v Commercial Union Assurance Co*.[40]

9–21 In the recent decision of *Humber Oil Terminals Trustee Ltd v Associated British Ports*[41] Sales J. stated that the provision of a cushion was one purpose (but he did not consider that it was the exclusive purpose) of the direction (within s.24D(2)(a)[42]) to "have regard to the rent payable under the terms of the relevant tenancy."

9–22 ***Halberstam v Tandalco Corp NV***[43] The tenant of business premises held the premises under a lease for a term of seven years and one month, expiring on September 30, 1976, at a rent of £650 per annum. A s.25 notice was served specifying September 30, 1976, as the date of termination. The tenant duly served a counter-notice and made an originating application to the court for the grant of a new tenancy. The landlord and the tenant entered into negotiations for the grant of a new lease. In 1979 the reversionary interest was assigned to Tandalco. The negotiations for a new lease ceased and on December 9, 1980, Tandalco made an application for determination of an interim rent. On November 25, 1983, the tenant's originating application was determined and a new lease of five years with no rent review was awarded (this having been agreed between the parties) at a rent of £6,500 per annum with an interim rent of £5,200 from December 9, 1980 (the agreed date of the interim rent commencement period).

In coming to his determination on interim rent the learned county court judge refused to take into account the rent of £650 payable under the current tenancy because of the delay which had ensued between the date of the expiry of the contractual term and the date of the hearing.

On appeal it was held that an interim rent could be tempered where appropriate, by reference to the rent under the current tenancy. However, it was not always necessary to provide a "cushion" between the old rent and the new rent.

The tenant in this case had the benefit of the rent under the old tenancy for a considerable period of time from the expiration of the contractual term to the commencement of the interim period. Further, there had been long delay in the proceedings (even though that delay had not been any fault of the tenant). Accordingly, the rent under the current tenancy could not in any way be

[38] [1988] 2 E.G.L.R. 113 CA.
[39] [1987] 2 E.G.L.R. 88 CA.
[40] [1993] 1 E.G.L.R. 113 CA.
[41] [2012] EWHC 1336 (Ch).
[42] Effective post June 1, 2004.
[43] [1985] 1 E.G.L.R. 90 CA.

considered relevant, either as a guide to the market rent of December 9, 1980 (the commencement of the interim rent period), nor was it a case where reference to the old rent was necessary for the purposes of providing a cushion between that rent and the impact of the market rent payable.

Charles Follett Ltd v Cabtell Investments Ltd[44] Upon the expiry of the tenant's tenancy of basement garage premises, the tenant applied for a new tenancy in the usual way. The tenant in its originating summons requested a new tenancy of 14 years at a rent of £14,500 with seven yearly rent reviews on the same terms and conditions as the current tenancy. The landlord in its affidavit and reply to the originating summons requested a 10-year term with five-year reviews at a rent of £25,000 per annum. When the matter came on for trial, the tenant altered its position and requested a new tenancy of one year only at a rent of £57,500. This was because it could not afford the new rent and required a period of one year to look for alternative accommodation. The landlord also changed its position and claimed a rent for a new tenancy of £125,000 per annum. The landlord suggested that the tenant could be accommodated by granting a 10-year term with a right to break at the beginning of the new term on six months' written notice. **9–23**

The current tenancy contained a rent review clause which made time of the essence of the service of relevant notices and was upwards only. The tenant requested that any new tenancy granted with a rent review provision should be both upwards and downwards.

The landlord had also made an application for interim rent, the commencing date of which was July 7, 1983, and a dispute existed between the parties as to the various discounts which ought to be made from the market rent determined in assessing an interim rent.

The subject of the appeal was that part of the deputy's judge's order dealing with the interim rent in which, having first held that there was to be a discount in the interim rent of 25 per cent to reflect the difference between a fixed-term tenancy and a tenancy from year to year, he went on to hold that:

(1) there was to be a further discount of 50 per cent so as to "cushion" the increase to market rent, but
(2) there was to be no interim rent in the exercise of the court's discretion unless the landlord agreed to accept £25,000 per annum only during the period when that had been its own claimed figure.

On appeal it was held:

(a) The requirement in s.24A that the court should have regard to the rent under the current tenancy is to cushion the effect of the new rent on the tenant. Here the deputy judge had, in view of the exceptional increase in rents, exercised his discretion in a way which could not be said to be wrong in principle. The 50 per cent reduction would be upheld.

---

[44] [1987] 2 E.G.L.R. 88 CA.

(b) However, the judge could only have ordered an interim rent determined in accordance with the statutory requirements, or refused to order one at all. It was not open to him, by requiring an undertaking, in effect to order an interim rent.

Post June 1, 2004

9–24 There are essentially two valuation methodologies. Either:

(1) the interim rent is the new rent under the new tenancy; or
(2) the interim rent is a "rent which it is reasonable for the tenant to pay" but otherwise determined in accordance with s.34 on the assumptions made under the old regime, namely, that the tenancy is on the terms of the current tenancy[45] and is one from year to year.

These two methodologies are discussed in detail in the paragraphs below.

Methodology (1)

9–25 **Section 24C(2): Interim rent equating to rent under new tenancy** The circumstances in which an interim rent may be awarded by reference to the rate of the annual rent reserved by the new tenancy are strictly defined, although it is considered that these circumstances will not often be encountered in practice. Furthermore, even where those circumstances apply, there are two exceptions to the general rule that the rent under the new tenancy is the interim rent.

An interim rent calculated by reference to the rent under the new tenancy applies where:

(1) the landlord has given the tenant a s.25 notice or the tenant has served a s.26 request for a new tenancy; and
(2) at the date of service of the s.25 notice or the s.26 request the tenant was in occupation of *the whole* of the property comprised in the relevant tenancy for the purposes or partly for the purposes of a business carried on by him[46]; and
(3) the landlord has not opposed the grant of a new tenancy either by specifying grounds of opposition in the s.25 notice or in the counter-notice to the s.26 request[47]; and

---

[45] The tenancy which the tenant holds under is referred to as "the current tenancy" in the unamended provisions: s.26(1) and s.46(1). However, s.26(1) has been amended but the definition of current tenancy remains the same: see art.28 para.6 amending s.46. Section 24A(1) of the new provisions refers to the tenancy which is continuing under s.24 as "the relevant tenancy". Why the draftsman considered the reference to "the current tenancy" to be inappropriate is unclear.

[46] Accordingly, if the tenant has sub-let part or is simply not in occupation of part, the provisions of s.24C will not apply.

[47] Thus, if the landlord has opposed renewal the interim rent will not be determined in accordance with s.24C. Presumably because of the inherent delay in dealing with a claim which is opposed, the point in time before which the rent under the new tenancy would be determined would be such that if s.24C had applied the parties would have invariably invoked s.24C(3)(a) (see para.9–27 sub-para.(1)

(4) the landlord grants a new tenancy of the whole of the property comprised in the relevant tenancy to the tenant (whether as a result of an order for the grant of a new tenancy or otherwise) (e.g. by agreement).

If all the above-mentioned conditions are satisfied, then the rent payable under and at the commencement of the new tenancy shall also be the interim rent.[48]

Thus, it can be seen that s.24C(2) will not apply where the tenant is not occupying part (no matter how small[49]) for purposes falling within s.23(1); if any part is sub-let; if the whole was occupied for purposes falling within s.23(1) as at the date of the s.25 notice or s.26 request but as at the date of the hearing the holding consists of part only of the premises (because of a subsequent sub-letting by the tenant) and the landlord does not require the tenant pursuant to s.32(2) to take a new lease of the entirety; if the landlord opposes renewal (albeit the landlord may subsequently withdraw his opposition or loses at court in opposing the tenant's renewal) or if the tenant takes a new lease by agreement consisting of premises different to those previously demised (e.g. by the tenant agreeing to surrender back to the landlord accommodation which the tenant considers is surplus to its requirements). 9–26

Exceptions to section 24C(2) The rent payable under and at the commencement of the new tenancy will not be the interim rent in circumstances where either of the following exceptions applies: 9–27

(1) Where either the landlord or the tenant shows to the satisfaction of the court that the interim rent differs substantially from the rent that would have been payable under s.34 if the tenancy had commenced on the "appropriate date": s.24C(3)(a) and (4).[50] This is obviously to cater for situations where there would have been a substantial difference between the rent payable under the new tenancy and the rent that would have been determined as the new rent for a new lease at the commencement of the date from which the interim rent is payable. This is most likely to arise in circumstances where a substantial period of time has elapsed between the "appropriate date" for the purposes of s.24B and the determination of the rent under s.34 for the purposes of the new lease. No guidance is given in Act in seeking to ascertain what is substantial.
(2) Where either the landlord or the tenant shows to the satisfaction of the court that the terms of the new tenancy are substantially different to those of the current tenancy (referred to as "the relevant tenancy") and the effect is such that the interim rent under s.24(2) (i.e. the s.34 rent for the new tenancy)

---

and para.9–29 below). Thus, it was probably considered more appropriate to make separate provision for the valuation of the interim rent in these circumstances.

[48] There is, therefore, no "cushion" as was provided under the old regime. As to the "cushion" under the old regime, see para.9–19 et seq.

[49] Subject presumably to the application of the de minimis rule.

[50] The valuation date is considered at para.9–16(2).

will be substantially different to the new rent which would have been determined in accordance with s.34 in respect of a tenancy on the terms of the relevant tenancy: s.24C(3)(b).[51]

9–28 There is no indication in the new provisions as to what constitutes a substantial difference in rent for the purposes of s.24C(3)(a) and (b). It is thought that this word will be likely to be given the same meaning as it was in a different context in *Palser v Grinling*[52]; that is to say, "great, weighty, big or solid." Accordingly, it will be insufficient simply to show that the difference is other than de minimis. A submission that anything more than 10 per cent was to be treated as substantial was rejected in *Brooker v Unique Pub Properties Ltd.*[53]

9–29 **What is the effect if the two exceptions apply? The first exception** If either of the parties is able to show that the interim rent would be substantially different from that determined under s.34, if the s.34 determination had been made as at the "appropriate date", then the interim rent is the rent so determined, i.e. the rent which has been determined under s.34 under as if the new tenancy had commenced on the appropriate date.

9–30 **The second exception** If either of the parties shows that the s.34 rent on the terms of the old lease would have been substantially different from the rent under the new tenancy as determined,[54] there is then a further valuation formula which operates. In these circumstances the interim rent is "the rent which it is reasonable for the tenant to pay while the relevant tenancy [i.e. the current tenancy] continues by virtue of section 24": s.24C(6).

9–31 What is a "rent which it is reasonable for the tenant to pay"? Section 24C(7) provides that the reasonable rent is such rent as would be determined in accordance with s.34(1) and (2) on the same terms of the new tenancy and for the same duration of the new tenancy as that which was actually granted to the tenant having regard:

(1) to the rent payable under the terms of the relevant tenancy[55]; and
(2) to the rent payable under any sub-tenancy of part of the property comprised in the relevant tenancy.[56]

9–32 The valuation date for s.24C((7) would appear to be the "appropriate date": see para.9–16, sub-para.(4).

---

[51] The valuation date is considered at para.9–16(3).
[52] [1948] A.C. 291 HL.
[53] [2009] EWHC 2599 (Ch).
[54] It is sufficient that this is shown either in isolation or together with s.24C(3)(a) for s.24C(6) and (7) to apply.
[55] This would appear to reintroduce in the new regime the cushioning effect under the old regime: see para.9–19 et seq.
[56] This is a rather odd direction with regard to the valuation, as s.24C applies only where at the date of s.25 notice or s.26 request the tenant was in occupation of the whole of the property comprised in the relevant tenancy. Thus, this direction it would seem is intended to deal only with sub-lettings which the tenant has effected after receipt of s.25 notice or service of a s.26 request.

Methodology (2)

Amount of interim rent in any other case Where s.24C does not apply[57] the interim rent is the rent "which it is reasonable for the tenant to pay while the relevant tenancy continues by virtue of section 24": s.24D(1). It has been held in *Humber Oil Terminals Trustee Ltd v Associated British Ports*[58] that the direction contained within s.24D(1) is the governing obligation on the court and that the requirements of s.24D(2) fall to be read and applied in light of that obligation. **9–33**

A reasonable rent for the tenant to pay is determined[59]:

(1) By assessing it in a fair and practical way, having regard to the actual circumstances which it is contemplated at the start of the interim rent period it is contemplated will apply during the period for which the rent is to be paid.[60]
(2) By assuming a notional tenancy on the terms of the relevant tenancy (i.e. the current tenancy).
(3) On the assumption that the notional tenancy is one from year to year.
(4) By reference to the provisions of s.34(1) and (2) as applicable to that notional tenancy.
(5) Having regard to:
    (a) the rent payable under the terms of the relevant tenancy (i.e. current tenancy)[61]; and
    (b) to the rent payable under any sub-tenancy of part of the property comprised in the relevant tenancy (i.e. current tenancy).[62]

The current passing rent is not a limit on the amount which may be determined as an interim rent: *Humber Oil Terminals Trustee Ltd v Associated British Ports*.[63]

"of the whole property" The interim rent under s.24D is determined on the basis of a notional yearly tenancy "of the whole property comprised in the relevant tenancy": s.24D(2). The notional tenancy provided for by s.24D(2) is not to be treated as a demise which includes property which the tenant has installed and has a right to detach and remove. The reference to "the whole property" **9–34**

---

[57] That is to say that the conditions set out in para.9–25 are not satisfied.
[58] [2012] EWHC 1336 (Ch) at [154].
[59] s.24(7).
[60] *Humber Oil Terminals Trustee Ltd v Associated British Ports* [2012] EWHC 1336 (Ch) at [154] and [181].
[61] This would appear to reintroduce in the new regime the cushioning effect under the old regime: see para.9–19 et seq.
[62] This direction follows approach of the Court of Appeal in *Oscroft v Benabo* [1967] 1 W.L.R. 1087 which considered that it was appropriate to take into account the existence of a residential sub-tenant. See para.8–121.
[63] [2012] EWHC 1336 (Ch) at [154] and [181].

means the whole of the property owned by the landlord which the tenant has no right to detach and remove: *Humber Oil Terminals Trustee Ltd v Associated British Ports*.[64]

9–35 However, where the tenant has a right to remove and detach property which would otherwise form part of the relevant tenancy, it does not follow that that property is presumed to have been removed and does not exist. Such an assumption is not required by the statute. Thus, where the tenant had use of a fully fitted jetty, which fittings had been undertaken by the tenant and in respect of which the tenant had a contractual right to remove, the interim rent could fairly disregard the value of the tenant's property by ascertaining the cost of a replacement jetty ignoring the cost of installing replacements for the tenant's property: *Humber Oil Terminals Trustee Ltd v Associated British Ports*.[65]

9–36 ***Humber Oil Terminals Trustee Ltd v Associated British Ports***[66] The landlord sought an interim rent in respect of a jetty. The jetty protruded into the Humber Estuary for about 1km and was constructed as a bare jetty by the landlord. It was leased to the tenant, H, which was a joint venture company operated by two oil companies which used the jetty for crude oil and other products to be loaded on or off-loaded from ships mooring up at the jetty. The tenant carried out various works ("the tenant's works") to the jetty which included, inter alia, booms for the berths for ships, a pipeline system between the berths and the shore for the loading and unloading of the oil and other products, and the installation of fire equipment which health and safety legislation required to enable the jetty to operate. Part of the tenant's works consisted of fixtures which at law would constitute landlord's fixtures, and had become part of the realty. The lease to the tenant provided that at the end of the lease the tenant could remove all of the tenant's works. It also exempted ("the exemption") the tenant from paying charges which the landlord, as harbour authority, could charge in respect of ships using the jetty. The tenant's current rent as at the term date of the lease was £4,045,244 per annum. The landlord successfully opposed the tenant's claim for renewal under para.(g) of s.30(1) of the 1954 Act.[67] It sought an interim rent under s.24D of just under £25 million. The tenant sought an interim rent of £2.3 million.

The tenant argued that in assessing the interim rent:

(1) The tenant's works were to be assumed not to exist either because of the contractual provision providing for their removal, or because they were tenant's fixtures or by reason of the disregard under s.34(1)(c) and (2) of the Act.

---

[64] [2012] EWHC 1336 (Ch) at [168]. See also the discussion at para.8–117 et seq. on the question of the property to be valued for the purposes of s.34(1).

[65] [2012] EWHC 1336 (Ch). See also the discussion at paras 8–117 and 8–118.

[66] [2012] EWHC 1336 (Ch).

[67] Digested in para.7–220 on this point.

(2) That accordingly the terms of s.24D required a valuation to be undertaken on the basis of a yearly tenancy of a bare jetty and that a notional incoming tenant would have to incur the costs of providing the tenant's works in order to get the jetty up and running.
(3) That the exemption was of no value to the hypothetical tenant, as it would take the notional incoming tenant longer than the interim rent period to install the relevant equipment to the jetty to make it operational and thus there would be no ships utilising the jetty which would enable the tenant to benefit from the exemption.

The Judge held, agreeing with the landlord's contentions, that:

(1) In determining an interim rent under s.24D the governing obligation of the court was to assess an interim rent "which it is reasonable for the tenant to pay". The requirements of s.24D(2) fell to be read and applied in light of that overriding obligation.
(2) The rent which it is reasonable for the tenant to pay should be assessed in a practical and fair way, having regard to the actual circumstances which it is contemplated at the start of the interim rent period will apply during the period for which the rent is to be paid. Since it was always contemplated that the tenant would be operating the jetty in the usual way in the interim period, it was obvious that it was reasonable for it to pay rent which reflected such actual usage, which was foreseeable when the interim period commenced. The court should not assume that, contrary to the facts, there was only a bare jetty structure in place.
(3) The tenant was only required to pay an interim rent for "the whole of the property comprised in the relevant tenancy." Although "the whole of the property" excluded the tenant's works by reason of the contractual right for the tenant to remove the same, it was not necessary in order to give proper effect to the statutory direction in s.24D(1) to assume that the tenant's works were not present at all. Rather it was appropriate to reduce the overall value of the jetty (as furnished with pipelines and equipment) by an amount in proportion to the cost of installing them and reducing the rent to be paid by an appropriate amount accordingly.
(4) The current passing rent did not provide helpful guidance on the rent it would be reasonable for the tenant to pay as it was rooted in circumstances from long ago. Furthermore, it was possible for the court to "have regard" to the current passing rent in its particular contractual setting and to infer from it and from a change in circumstances that "the rent which it is reasonable for the tenant to pay" for the interim period should be increased above the current passing rent. The current passing rent was not a limit on the amount which could be set as an interim rent.
(5) As the jetty was not assumed to be bare, the exemption was of value to the notional incoming tenant.
(6) As the notional tenancy to be assumed was a yearly tenancy, the rental figure was to be reduced by 10 per cent.

(7) This was not a case in which it was appropriate to allow for a distinct cushioning effect to take account of the increase in market rents above the current passing rent due to inflation or the impact of unexpected events, which might lead to the conclusion that it is reasonable to protect a tenant against "an inordinate shock" of suddenly being required to pay a much higher rent.

(8) The interim rent was assessed at £14,800,306 per annum.

9–37 **Valuation date** The valuation date for assessing the interim rent in accordance with s.24D would appear to be the "appropriate date": see para.9–16, sub-para.(5).

9–38 **Discretion** A judge under s.24D has a broad discretion: *Neale v Witney Electric Theatre*.[68] Where the interim rent is not determined at a figure higher than the passing rent, it is not necessarily the case that the s.34 rent (as assessed on the basis of a tenancy from year to year) should be given greater weight.[69] Thus, where the interim rent determined on a tenancy from year to year was 25 per cent less than the passing rent (which passing rent was more or less around the market rent at the valuation date) the judge was not required to award the reduced rent in circumstances where the tenant was not going to be entitled to a new tenancy and was receiving an undiscounted rent from a sub-tenant of part of the demised premises.[70]

9–39 **Interim rent upon revocation of the order for the grant of a new tenancy or upon the parties agreeing not to act on the order** Where an interim rent has been awarded under s.24C, i.e. the interim rent has been awarded where the requirements set out in para.9–24 above have been satisfied, and either there is a revocation of the order pursuant to s.36(2) (upon application made by the tenant)[71] or the landlord and tenant agree not to act on the order, either party may then apply for a new interim rent to be determined under s.24D, i.e. a reasonable rent for the tenant to pay. In these circumstances the court will determine a new interim rent in accordance with s.24D without a requirement for a further application under s.24A(1).

7. DIFFERENTIAL INTERIM RENT

9–40 The Court of Appeal has held in *Fawke v Viscount Chelsea*[72] (digested in para.9–41) in respect of s.24A in its unamended form that the interim rent need not be a constant figure throughout the entirety of the period of the continuation. In that case, the premises were in a state of disrepair, although remedial works were planned. It was held that, during such time as the premises remained in disrepair, the interim rent would be a lower figure than that which should become

68 [2011] EWCA Civ 1032.

69 See also para.9–18 and fn.33 above.

70 *Neale v Witney Electric Theatre* [2011] EWCA Civ 1032.

71 As to which, see para.10–10.

72 [1980] Q.B. 441; [1979] 3 W.L.R. 508; [1979] 3 All E.R. 568 CA.

payable once the repairs were effected. The cases in which the court could fix a differential interim rent are extremely rare (as was indeed emphasised in *Fawke v Viscount Chelsea*). There is no reason why, notwithstanding the more sophisticated treatment of interim rent as a consequence of the amendments made by the 2003 Order, the decision of *Fawke v Viscount Chelsea* could not equally apply, depending on the circumstances, to interim rents awarded under the new provisions.

Fawke v Viscount Chelsea[73] On the hearing of the tenant's application for a new tenancy, it was proved that the premises had been extensively affected by dry rot, due to seepage of water from a defective drain. The interior decorations were also affected by water penetration. Extensive works of repair were required in order to eradicate the dry rot, but these were likely to be completed before the commencement of the new tenancy. For the purposes of the determination of the interim rent under s.24A and of the rent payable pursuant to the new tenancy under s.34, it was conceded that the landlord was under a full exterior repairing obligation. The county court judge held that he should not take into account the state of repair of the premises in fixing an interim rent under s.24A, but in fixing the rent to be paid under the new tenancy he ordered a review after seven years in order to reflect the fact that works of redecoration and repair were needed before the tenant could settle down to quiet enjoyment of his holding. **9–41**

On appeal, the Court of Appeal had to consider the following issues:

(1) Whether it was proper to take into account the state of the repair of the premises in fixing the interim rent.
(2) At what valuation date the interim rent should be assessed.
(3) Whether evidence on the state of the repair of the premises as they in fact were at the valuation date (but were only known to have been subsequently) could be taken into account.
(4) Whether the court had power under s.24A to fix a "differential" interim rent, i.e. a rent which would increase once the necessary repairs were completed.
(5) Whether it was proper under s.34 to take into account the state of repair of the premises in fixing the rent payable under the new tenancy.
(6) Whether the court had power under s.34 to fix a "differential" rent as the rent payable under the new tenancy.

The Court of Appeal held that:

(a) The state of repair of the premises, whatever the cause, should be taken into account under s.24A. Whether and how the market rent would thereby have been affected was a matter for evidence in each particular case.
(b) The proper valuation date for the interim rent was the commencement of the interim rent period.
(c) The court should take into account all the evidence before it on the state of repair of the premises on the material date.

---

73 [1980] Q.B. 441; [1979] 3 W.L.R. 508.

(d) If the evidence indicated that a "differential rent" would have been agreed in the market as the rent to be paid during the interim rent period, the court should fix a differential interim rent accordingly.

(e) Similarly, under s.34, the state of repair of the premises, whatever its cause, should be taken into account. Whether and how the market rent under the new tenancy would thereby have been affected was a matter for evidence in each particular case.

(f) If the evidence indicated that, in the market, parties would have agreed a rent which increased by fixed amounts, or which increased when repairs were completed, the court should fix the rent under the new tenancy on that basis.

9–42 There is a different context in which the concept of a "differential interim rent" may be relevant. Since the question of the amount of the interim rent is normally considered at the hearing, there will often, in practice, have elapsed a considerable period of time since the interim rent began to run.[74] Unless rents have remained more or less constant during the period in question it may be argued by one party or the other that, as a matter of valuation, or as a matter of discretion, that an interim rent determined in accordance with s.24D[75] ought not to remain constant for the whole of the relevant period. One approach is to consider whether the hypothetical tenancy assumed for the purposes of s.24D permits the possibility of the continuation tenancy itself having provision for rent review. It is thought that such an approach is unhelpful, since it would be highly unusual for a tenancy from year to year (as opposed to a tenancy for a term of years certain) to contain any rent review provisions whatsoever. The suggestion is particularly artificial since it is difficult to see how the contractual provisions for rent review, which are designed to be operated by the parties themselves, are to be adapted to what is essentially an exercise by the court of its discretion, without the direct intervention of the parties. An alternative way of supporting the same argument is to point to the fact that it is one of the features inherent in a tenancy from year to year that it is open to the parties to seek to agree a different rent as from the end of the first year and, in the absence of agreement, to terminate the tenancy. Such an approach, however, appears to conflict with the principle that the valuation date for the s.24D interim rent is the date of commencement of the interim rent period; the effect of the argument is that the valuation date is not this one date, but, in addition, each anniversary of that date. Further, there seems to be an inconsistency between the suggestion that the court may, in effect, assess the interim rent retrospectively by reference to market conditions throughout the period, and the undoubted right of the parties to ask the court to assess the interim rent payable at the start of the interim rent period or, at any rate, before it has come to an end. It is, therefore, tentatively suggested that the correct position is

---

[74] This is particularly so now that the commencement date for the payment of the interim rent is a date which, in many cases, does not accord with the reality. The "appropriate date", being the earliest date which could have been specified in the s.25 notice or s.26 request, will in most cases be different from the actual date specified albeit even if only by a few days, as it is rare to find either a landlord or tenant serving a notice or request specifying the earliest date possible, if not only to take account of and avoid any problems caused by the vagaries of the postal system.

[75] As to which, see para.9–33 et seq.

as follows. As a matter of valuation, the rate at which the interim rent determined in accordance with s.24D is payable is that which would have been agreed between a hypothetical landlord and a hypothetical tenant negotiating a tenancy from year to year beginning at the start of the interim rent period, without there being any possibility of the rent being renegotiated so long as the tenancy continues. Depending upon market conditions, either landlord or tenant might argue that the rate to be agreed should be enhanced or discounted to take account of the fact that the possibility of renegotiation normally inherent in a tenancy from year to year was not open to either party. There would seem to be no reason why the court, having fixed the rate of interim rent in this way, should not take into account the way the market had moved over the entire period in deciding what, if any, "cushion" should be applied to the figure finally assessed.

8. EFFECT OF DISCONTINUANCE

Under the old regime, prior to the introduction of the Civil Procedure Rules, it was held that an application for interim rent was not "parasitic" on the application for a new tenancy and accordingly survived discontinuance thereof, whether made by separate claim, counter-claim, or in the answer[76]: see *Michael Kramer v Airways Pension Fund*[77] and *Artoc v Prudential*.[78] It is considered that the same conclusion should be adopted under the new CPR, Pt 56 procedure and in respect of the new ss.24A to 24D provisions. **9–43**

9. EFFECT OF TRANSFER OF THE REVERSION

Under the old regime, it was held that where a landlord had made an application for an interim rent, the subsequent assignment of the reversion did not deprive the court of jurisdiction to determine an interim rent under s.24A: *Bloomfield v Ashwright*[79] (digested in para.9–45). It is considered that this remains the position under the new regime.[80] **9–44**

Bloomfield v Ashwright[81] The landlord served a s.25 notice on the tenant of business premises, specifying ground (g) of s.30(1) (own occupation), expressed to expire on September 14, 1978. The landlord applied for an interim rent pursuant to s.24A and, in August 1981, assigned its reversion to Shelgate Property Co Ltd. There was no evidence before the court as to the detailed terms **9–45**

[76] Under the previous practice, a landlord could include in his Answer a claim for interim rent under s.24A: *Thomas v Hammond-Lawrence* [1986] 1 W.L.R. 456; [1986] 2 All E.R. 214; [1986] 1 E.G.L.R. 141 CA. The practice form N400 was retained upon the introduction of CPR and the form continued to include provision for the making of a claim for interim rent in the Answer. CPR 8.7 provides that no counter-claim is permitted to a Pt 8 claim without the court's permission. However, the Practice Direction to Pt 56 of the CPR PD56 para.3.4, enables a landlord to include in his acknowledgement of service to a Pt 8 claim, a claim for interim rent: see para.14–110 et seq.

[77] [1978] 1 E.G.L.R. 49 CA.

[78] [1984] 1 W.L.R. 1181; [1984] 3 All E.R. 538.

[79] [1983] 1 E.G.L.R. 82 CA.

[80] See further para.9–06.

[81] [1984] 1 W.L.R. 710 CA.

of that assignment. The landlord notified the tenant of the assignment and Shelgate was added to the proceedings as an additional respondent. The proceedings were protracted and it was not finally determined that the tenant should have a new tenancy, and what should be the terms and rent thereof, until February 19, 1982. The judge made an order determining that the interim rent should be payable at the rate of £2,340 per annum. It was held that the assignment of the reversion to Shelgate, before the court had determined the interim rent pursuant to s.24A, did not deprive the court of jurisdiction to make a determination. Under s.24A the court was concerned with the rent payable during the interim continuation of the tenancy and the landlord (assignor) was duty bound to the new reversioner, Shelgate, to safeguard its interests in the interim rent application, even if there had been no specific assignment of the benefit thereof. Both the landlord and Shelgate were therefore before the court and the court did not have to decide which of them was entitled to the interim rent, but what interim rent was payable.

10. DATE WHEN INTERIM RENT IS TO BE PAID

9–46 The 1954 Act does not specify the date upon which any "arrears" which have built up since the start of the interim rent period fall to be paid by the tenant to the landlord. It would see that the difference, if any, between the interim rent and the rent payable under the current tenancy for the interim rent period becomes payable immediately following the determination of the court, or, by way of analogy to rent review, upon the quarter day under the lease immediately following determination: *South Tottenham v R&A Millett*.[82] The difficulty with the latter date is that one can have a determination of an interim rent in circumstances where the tenant has discontinued his claim for a new lease and the current tenancy has come to an end before the determination of the interim rent.

11. TACTICS

9–47 The new provisions have altered some of the tactics which were adopted pre June 1, 2004.

It was often the case that where the premises were over-rentalised a landlord would refrain from seeking an interim rent. Now that the tenant has the entitlement to make an interim rent application the landlord's opportunity to hold onto the old (high) rent until the grant of the new lease has evaporated.

The ability of tenants to postpone the interim rent by serving a 12-months' s.26 request has gone. The date from which the interim rent is payable is now not governed by the actual date specified in the s.25 notice or s.26 request but by the earliest date which could have been specified.

As mentioned above, neither party is able to make an application for interim rent where there exists an extant application made by the other: s.24A(2). An application must be made not more than six months after the termination of the tenancy. It is considered that there is very little room for tactical manoeuvring.

[82] [1983] 1 E.G.L.R. 82 CA.

Circumstances may arise, however, where a party needs to be alert as to a possible attempt to negate the entitlement to an interim rent.

Example The tenant has made an unopposed application for renewal and has made an application for interim rent. The parties reach agreement on the terms of the new lease and the new lease is executed (so as to bring about a surrender of the current tenancy). Prima facie the landlord will be entitled to an interim rent equating to the rent for the new lease: s.24C. If six months elapse from the execution of the new lease there would appear nothing to stop the tenant from withdrawing the interim rent application so as to avoid the payment of interim rent. The landlord will then be unable to make such an application as the application will be made "more than six months after the termination of the relevant tenancy" within s.24A(3) of the Act. **9–48**

Where the tenant's lease is subject to a sub-tenancy or sub-tenancies of part, an anomaly arises in that the "landlord" (assuming the landlord for the purposes of s.44 is the superior landlord, i.e. superior landlord is the competent landlord of both the tenant and the sub-tenant) will (probably) as against the sub-tenant be able to obtain a rent equal to the s.34 rent (i.e. a rent under s.24(2)) but as against the tenant will only be able to obtain an interim rent on the less favourable basis under s.24D (because the existence of a sub-tenancy of part precludes the application of s.24C(2)). **9–49**

CHAPTER 10

CARRYING OUT THE ORDER

1. ORDER REFUSING/GRANTING NEW TENANCY

Refusal of new tenancy

There are several provisions which deal with what the court is to do if it finds that the landlord's opposition to the tenant's renewal of his lease is successfully opposed. It is provided by s.31(1) that if the landlord opposes an application under subs.(1) of s.24 on one of the grounds under s.30(1) and establishes any of those grounds to the satisfaction of the court, the court shall not make an order for the grant of a new tenancy. The court will in these circumstances simply order the tenant's application for renewal to be dismissed. Section 31(1) by its terms (1) is limited to an application for renewal by a tenant under s.24(1) (for a landlord who makes an application under s.24(1) is necessarily not opposing renewal) and (2) does not provide for what is to happen to the current tenancy which is not renewed. The latter is dealt with by s.64. The tenant's tenancy[1] will expire three months and 21 days[2] after the disposal of the tenant's application for renewal. **10–01**

Section 29(4)(a) provides that where a landlord makes an application for termination under s.29(2) and establishes to the satisfaction of the court any of the grounds of opposition under s.30(1) the court shall make an order for the termination of the current tenancy in accordance with s.64 without the grant of a new tenancy. The provision for ordering termination of the current tenancy is the final disposal of the landlord's termination application triggering the terms of s.64.

[1] s.64 does not refer to the tenant's "current tenancy." Sections 29(1) and (4)(a) and (b) make reference to the tenant's "current tenancy". Section 26(1) of the Act (prior to its amendment by the 2003 Order) defined the tenant's "current tenancy" as " the tenancy under which he holds for the time being". However, s.26(1) has been amended by the 2003 Order and the definition within it was deleted. But the definition of "current tenancy" is now to be found in s.46(1) and remains the same as that previously within s.26: art.26 para.6 of the 2003 Order amending s.46(1) of the 1954 Act. Section 24A(1) of the new provisions refers to the tenancy which is continuing under s.24 as "the relevant tenancy". Why the draftsman considered that the reference to current tenancy in s.26 in its unamended form needed to be amended is unclear.

[2] See s.64(2). The 21-day period is the period for appeal: para.14–137 et seq.

Grant of new tenancy

10–02 A new tenancy may be ordered either pursuant to an application (either by the tenant or the landlord) under s.24(1) or upon the landlord's failure to successfully obtain a termination order under the landlord's termination application under s.29(2). It is provided by s.29(1) that on an application under s.24(1), the court shall make an order for the grant of a new tenancy and accordingly for termination of the current tenancy immediately before the commencement of the new tenancy.

By s.29(4)(b) it is provided that where a landlord has made a termination application pursuant to s.29(2) and the landlord does not establish to the satisfaction of the court a ground of opposition upon which he relies, the court "shall make an order for the grant of a new tenancy and accordingly for the termination of the current tenancy immediately before the commencement of the new tenancy."[3]

2. THE EFFECT OF THE ORDER FOR THE GRANT OF A NEW TENANCY

Landlord and tenant bound by order

10–03 Section 36(1) sets out the consequences of the making of an order for a new tenancy by the court, unless that order is revoked, or the landlord and the tenant agree not to act upon it.[4] Subject to those exceptions, the effect of the making of an order is that (s.36(1)):

> "the landlord shall be bound to execute or make in favour of the tenant, and the tenant shall be bound to accept, a lease or agreement for a tenancy of the holding embodying the terms agreed between the landlord and tenant or determined by the court . . . and where the landlord executes or makes such a lease or agreement the tenant shall be bound, if so required by the landlord, to execute a counterpart or duplicate thereof."

10–04 The subsection does not expressly state at what date the landlord and the tenant are respectively bound to execute and accept a lease embodying the terms comprised in the order, but it must be borne in mind that the new tenancy will not come into effect until the termination of the current tenancy in accordance with the provisions of ss.24 and 64. Where the new tenancy is to be granted by order of the court, as opposed to an agreement between the parties, this date will necessarily be at least three months later than the date of the order. In view of this, and in particular in view of the tenant's right to apply for revocation,[5] it may be that the landlord and tenant are not bound to comply with the order until the date specified for the commencement of the new tenancy.

10–05 By virtue of s.36(4), in a case where the interest of the lessor is subject to a mortgage, a lease executed or agreement made under s.36(1) is deemed to be authorised by s.99 of the Law of Property Act 1925, notwithstanding any

[3] See also paras 6–15 and 6–16 as to withdrawal of the landlord's termination application.

[4] See paras 10–09 and 10–10.

[5] See para.10–10.

provision purporting to restrict or exclude the right to do so. There is no equivalent provision exempting the lessor from obtaining other necessary consents, such as that of a superior landlord and such consent should always be sought whether the new (sub) tenancy is granted by agreement or order of the court. Problems could arise when the superior landlord has an absolute right to refuse consent.

Enforcement of order

Section 36(1) gives no clear guidance as to how the tenant can force the landlord to grant him a new tenancy, or how the landlord can force the tenant to execute a counterpart. Where one of the parties is in default three possible means of enforcement suggest themselves: **10–06**

(1) First, it could be argued that a party who is "bound" by an order of the court to do a positive act is in contempt of court if he fails to comply with that order. In *Mills (IS) (Yardley) v Curdworth Investments*[6] Lawton L.J. said that once an order had been made the landlord was under a "statutory duty" under s.36 to execute in favour of the tenant a lease embodying the terms settled by the court. If that analysis is correct, the ordinary penalties for contempt of court, such as a fine or committal, might be sought as a means of enforcing compliance. We consider this view of the effect of s.36(1) to be unlikely to be correct, especially as the order would not normally provide any specific date by which the lease (or counterpart) was to be executed. Enforcement by committal requires a judgment or order to do an act within a specified time: RSC Ord.45 r.5(1)(a) Sch.1 CPR. However, where a judgment or order requiring a person to do an act does not specify a time within which the act is to be done, the court has power to make an order requiring the act to be done within such time after service of that order, or such other time, as may be specified therein: RSC Ord.45 r.6 Sch.1. In *Greaves Organisation v Stanhope Gate Property Co*[7] the tenant obtained an order of the court on July 31, 1968 for the grant of a new tenancy. No new tenancy was granted by the landlord and accordingly the tenant returned to court and on November 25, 1970 obtained an order against the landlord that the landlord execute and deliver a new lease to the tenant within four days.

(2) Secondly, it may be that the effect of the word "bound" is to create a sort of statutory contract enforceable in the same way as if the parties had entered into an agreement respectively to grant and accept a tenancy. On this view, the way that landlord or tenant would enforce the statutory contract would be by proceedings for specific performance. In *Pulleng v Curran.*[8] Sir George Baker said:

---

[6] [1975] 2 E.G.L.R. 54 CA.
[7] [1973] E.G.D. 991.
[8] (1980) 44 P. & C.R. 58 CA.

> "No lease was entered into by the parties pursuant to the order of the court, and so the situation that has since prevailed is, as a matter of analysis, to be regarded as an agreement for lease on the same terms as the original lease, pursuant to the order of the court under section 29."

(3) The third possibility, which we consider to be the most likely, is that the effect of the order is analogous to the position where an order of the court has been obtained for specific performance of an agreement for lease. If that is so, the landlord or tenant could, in the case of default by the other party, apply to the appropriate officer of the court itself to execute the lease or counterpart in the name of the defaulting party.

10–07 Whichever of the above views is correct, the doctrine of *Walsh v Lonsdale*[9] presumably applies as from the date when the parties are bound to comply with the order. The effect of this is that an equitable tenancy arises between the parties, even though no formal documents have been executed. In *Greaves Organisation v Stanhope Gate Property Co*[10] Foster J. said:

> "[The tenants] were in many ways in a stronger position than they would be in according to the doctrine in *Walsh v Lonsdale*, where the parties were treated very nearly as if the lease has been granted, for that doctrine applied only if specific performance would be ordered: here there was a court order that had to be enforced. [The tenants] had a right to obtain a lease from the landlord and in equity were in the same position as if a lease had been granted. [The tenants] thus had an equitable interest . . ."

As the tenant has a lease in equity the tenant is, after the order of the court but before grant, able to carve an underlease out of his equitable interest: *Greaves Organisation v Stanhope Gate Property Co.*[11]

Termination of current tenancy three months after final disposal

10–08 The grant of a new tenancy pursuant to the tenant's application amounts to the "final disposal" of the application within the terms of s.64. The effect of this is that the tenant's current tenancy will end three months (together with the time for any appeal) after the order of the court granting the new tenancy: see para.3–218 et seq.

3. ORDER CEASING TO HAVE EFFECT

By agreement of parties

10–09 When an order has been made by the court, the landlord and the tenant may "agree not to act upon the order", in which case the order will not have the effect described above. The agreement must be in writing: s.69(2). Presumably the agreement must also be one which would be binding according to the ordinary principles of the law of contract. If it is the case that, as suggested in para.10–07, a lease exists in equity from the date of the order of the court an agreement not to

[9] (1882) L.R. 21 Ch. D. 9 CA.
[10] [1973] E.G.D. 991.
[11] [1973] E.G.D. 991.

act on the order must be viewed as a surrender of the tenant's equitable interest. As such the agreement would need to comply with the provisions of s.2 of the Law of Property (Miscellaneous Provisions) Act 1989.

On application of tenant

By virtue of s.36(2), the tenant is entitled to apply to the court for the revocation of the order within 14 days after it has been made.[12] If the court has ordered the grant of one or more new tenancies, whether claimed in one claim form or in separate claim forms, the tenant is entitled to seek revocation of the order for the grant of one of the tenancies, while relying on the order for the grant of the others: *Broadmead v Corben Brown.*[13] The purpose of this provision is to enable a tenant who is dissatisfied with the terms of the new tenancy granted by the court to reconsider, within the 14-day period, his willingness to take on the burden of a new tenancy. If the tenant applies for revocation, the court has no discretion to refuse it. When an order for revocation has been made, the current tenancy will continue until at least the date upon which it would, in any event, have been continued by virtue of ss.24 and 64. The parties may, however, agree that it should continue for a longer period and, in default of agreement, the tenancy will continue for such period as may be determined by the court as being necessary to afford the landlord a reasonable opportunity for reletting or otherwise disposing of the premises which would have been comprised in the new tenancy. It will be for the court to decide, upon the evidence available, what period is necessary. The premises to be considered for the purposes of reletting are not confined to "the holding", but extend to all the premises which would have been comprised in the new tenancy. Accordingly, where the landlord has elected to require the tenant to take a new tenancy of the whole of the premises (part being sub-let or unoccupied)[14], the landlord is presumably entitled to have the current tenancy continue for such period as is necessary in order reasonably to enable him to relet on a reversionary lease, subject to and with the benefit of the sub-tenancies (if any). **10–10**

Where premises are difficult or even impossible to relet and the tenant perceives a real possibility of a new tenancy being ordered on terms unacceptable to him, he should consider carefully whether he would not be better to withdraw his application entirely, rather than run the risk of being required to remain as a tenant for such period as the court might order pursuant to s.36(2). On the other hand, it is clear that under s.36(2) it is the current tenancy which is being prolonged, so that the tenant will not be required to pay rent at the level fixed as appropriate for the new tenancy: it is even arguable that during such period as the tenancy is continued by virtue of s.36(2) (as opposed to ss.24 and 64) the landlord is not entitled to claim an interim rent, because s.24A provides that such rent is payable "while the tenancy continues by virtue of section 24". **10–11**

---

[12] As to the costs implications of an application for revocation, see para.10–25. For the procedure for making such an application, see paras 14–119 and 14–120.

[13] [1966] E.G.D. 756.

[14] See para.8–19.

10–12 A problem which may be encountered in practice is where the tenant wishes to appeal against some part of the court's determination of the terms of the new tenancy and would be unwilling to take the new tenancy unless the appeal is successful (in whole or in part). In such a case the tenant will not be able to wait until the result of the appeal is known before applying for revocation: the 14-day period dates from the making of the original order, not the order on appeal. Rather, he should apply within the 14 days for revocation but seek an adjournment of the application until the result of the appeal is known.

4. COSTS

Judicial discretion as to costs

General

10–13 The questions of who should pay the costs of the tenant's application to the court for a new tenancy and the amount of such costs are decided according to ordinary principles. An agreement contained within the tenant's lease imposing upon the tenant, if he makes an application for a new tenancy, an obligation to pay the landlords costs in respect of that application will be void under s.38(1) as being the imposition of a "*penalty*" within the meaning of that section: *Stevenson and Rush (Holdings) v Langdon.*[15]

10–14 The practice had arisen prior to 1974 of the court making no order as to costs in both opposed and unopposed renewal proceedings. However, it was held in *Decca Navigator Co v GLC*[16] that the former practice should not be followed and that costs should be in the discretion of the judge.[17] The discretion must be exercised judicially, that is to say according to settled principles: *Decca Navigator v GLC*[18] (digested in para.7–196). It is usual in contentious matters for the costs to "follow the event", that is to say costs should be awarded in favour of the winning party: CPR r.44.3(2)(a).

---

[15] [1979] 1 E.G.L.R. 72 CA.

[16] [1974] 1 W.L.R. 748.

[17] Denning M.R. said at 752:

"There is only one further matter which Mr. French raised before us. It is as to the question of costs. The judge dismissed the application with costs on Scale 4. Mr. French does not challenge that order. But he draws attention to a note in the County Court Practice 1973, at pp.885–86, where it says:

'The administration of [the Landlord and Tenant Act 1954] by the courts often gives rise to special problems as to costs, but it seems that frequently each side is left to bear its own costs of an application to the court for the grant of a new lease. Thus, where both parties negotiated, but were unable to agree the terms on which a new lease should be granted, and an application was made to the court under the provisions of the Act, an order was made for the grant of a new lease but no order was made as to costs, leaving each side to bear its own costs.'

That was the usual practice which was noted in *Willis v. Association of Universities of the British Commonwealth (No. 2)* [1965] 1 W.L.R. 836. But since that case, there have been amendments made by the Law of Property Act 1969. So much so that the former practice should no longer be followed. The costs should be in the discretion of the county court judge to do as he thinks just."

[18] [1974] 1 W.L.R. 748; [1974] 1 All E.R. 1178 CA.

Issue based orders

In the case of an application under the Act, it may sometimes be difficult to know who has "won". If there is an issue of principle between the parties, such as whether the landlord is entitled to oppose the grant of a new tenancy upon one of the grounds set out in s.30(1), it will often be obvious who has "won". In other cases, where the parties are in disagreement on a number of the terms of the new tenancy, the landlord may win on some points, the tenant may win on others and the court may decide between them on yet others. Similarly, where the amount of rent to be paid is the sole or principal issue, the court may find that the true figure is not sufficiently close to that put forward by either landlord or tenant to enable the court to say who has "won". **10–15**

The position pre-CPR was that if a claimant succeeded in any part of a disputed claim he was entitled to his costs, the reasoning being that it had been necessary for him to come to court in order to recover anything. This approach is exemplified in *Re Elgindata Ltd (No.2)*.[19] The CPR brought about a change of approach. It is an approach which emphasises the need for the court to consider the issues and whether or not to make orders reflecting the outcome of those issues. That the court should be more ready to make an issues based cost order was made clear by Lord Woolf in *AEI Redeffusion Music Ltd v Phonographic Performance Ltd*.[20] **10–16**

Thus the emphasis of the new court rules is to require the courts to be more ready to make separate orders which reflect the outcome of different issues.[21] A judge **10–17**

[19] [1992] 1 W.L.R. 1207. Nourse L.J. said:

"The principles are these. (i) Costs are in the discretion of the court. (ii) They should follow the event, except when it appears to the court that in the circumstances of the case some other order should be made. (iii) The general rule does not cease to apply simply because the successful party raises issues or makes allegations on which he fails, but where that has caused a significant increase in the length or cost of the proceedings he may be deprived of the whole or a part of his costs. (iv) Where the successful party raises issues or makes allegations improperly or unreasonably, the court may not only deprive him of his costs but may order him to pay the whole or a part of the unsuccessful party's costs. Of these principles the first, second and fourth are expressly recognised or provided for by [RSC O.62] rules 2(4), 3(3) and 10 respectively. The third depends on well established practice. Moreover, the fourth implies that a successful party who neither improperly nor unreasonably raises issues or makes allegations on which he fails ought not to be ordered to pay any part of the unsuccessful party's costs."

[20] [1999] 1 W.L.R. 1507 CA. He said:

"I draw attention to the new Rules because, while they make clear that the general rule remains, that the successful party will normally be entitled to costs, they at the same time indicate the wide range of considerations which will result in the court making different orders as to costs. From 26 April 1999 the 'follow the event principle' will still play a significant role, but it will be a starting point from which a court can readily depart. This is also the position prior to the new Rules coming into force. The most significant change of emphasis of the new Rules is to require courts to be more ready to make separate orders which reflect the outcome of different issues. In doing this the new Rules are reflecting a change of practice which has already started. It is now clear that too robust an application of the 'follow the event principle' encourages litigants to increase the costs of litigation, since it discourages litigants from being selective as to the points they take. If you recover all your costs as long as you win, you are encouraged to leave no stone unturned in your effort to do so." (at 1522/1523)

[21] *AIE Rediffusion Music Ltd v Photographic Performance Ltd* [1999] 1 W.L.R. 1507 CA; *Summit Property Ltd v Pitmans* [2001] EWCA 2020.

may make different orders for costs in relation to discrete issues. He should consider doing so where a party has been successful on one issue but unsuccessful on another issue.[22] A judge may deprive a party of costs on an issue on which he has been successful. It is not necessary in order for a judge to make such an order for him to be satisfied that the issue was raised improperly or unreasonably.[23]

Relevant factors to consider in making order as to costs

10–18 In deciding what order (if any) to make about costs, the court must have regard to all the circumstances, including the conduct of the parties; whether a party has succeeded on part of his case, even if he has not been wholly successful; and any payment into court or admissible offer to settle made by a party which is drawn to the court's attention (whether or not made in accordance with CPR Pt 36[24]): CPR r.44.3(4). The conduct of the parties includes: (1) conduct before, as well as during, the proceedings, and in particular the extent to which the parties followed any relevant pre-action protocol; (2) whether it was reasonable for a party to raise, pursue or contest a particular allegation or issue; (3) the manner in which a party has pursued or defended his case or a particular allegation or issue; (4) whether a claimant who has succeeded in his claim, in whole or part, exaggerated his claim: CPR r.44.3(5). The orders which the court may make include an order that a party must pay a proportion of another's party's costs; a stated amount in respect of another party's costs; costs from or until a certain date only; costs incurred before proceedings have begun; costs in relation to particular steps taken in the proceedings; costs relating only to a distinct part of the proceedings; and interest on costs from or until a certain date, including a date before judgment: CPR r.44.3(6).

Unopposed renewal-lease terms

10–19 An unopposed renewal application need not and often does not involve more than one or two issues in dispute. Often the parties are agreed as to the terms of the new lease save as to rent.[25] Alternatively, where, for instance, the landlord has redevelopment proposals in mind it is often the case that the terms of the new lease can be agreed save for the incorporation of the landlord's proposed redevelopment break clause and the impact that will have on the rent to be paid. The break clause issue identifies a fairly clear cut event which may be said to have been "won" or "lost" by a party. If for instance a tenant opposed the incorporation of such a clause, the landlord would clearly be at risk as to paying the tenant's costs of the unopposed renewal if the landlord were to withdraw his insistence upon the incorporation of a redevelopment break clause or lost the issue at trial. In those circumstances one would expect the court to adhere to the

---

22 *Johnsey Estates (1990) Ltd v Secretary of State for the Environment* [2001] EWCA Civ 535.
23 *Summit Property Ltd v Pitmans* [2001] EWCA Civ 2020.
24 See para.10–26.
25 As to costs where the issue is one of rent, see para.10–21.

principle reflected in CPR r.44(2) that costs follow the event.[26] Some examples may be found in the reported cases of costs orders in unopposed lease renewals[27]:

(1) In *O'May v City of London Real Property Co Ltd*[28] (digested in para.8–47) (pre-CPR) the landlord sought a "clean lease", requiring the new lease to contain provision for the payment of a service charge relating to inter alia the state and condition of the exterior. At first instance the landlord won and the tenant was required to pay one-half of the costs of the adjournment of the tenant's originating summons into court. The landlord lost on appeal and in the Court of Appeal.[29] The court ordered that the tenant was to have the whole of the costs below[30];
(2) In *Cairnplace v CBL*[31] (digested in para.8–71) (pre-CPR) there were two issues. First, whether the new lease should contain provision for a surety and secondly whether the new lease should contain provision requiring the tenant to pay for the costs incurred by the landlord in the preparation of the new lease. The tenant lost the first but won the second issue. The court made an order that the tenant pay 85 per cent of the landlord's costs and the landlord pay 15 per cent of the tenant's costs.
(3) In *Wallis Fashion Group Ltd v CGU Life Assurance Ltd*[32] (digested in para.8–68) the parties were in dispute as to whether as a term of the new lease the landlord should, on assignment, be entitled as of right to an authorised guarantee agreement from the outgoing tenant (as contended for by the landlord) or only insofar as such a requirement was reasonable (as contended for by the tenant). Neuberger J., as he then was, is recorded as saying that:

> "The question of costs has been touched upon, and the parties agreed before they knew the result, to my mind rightly and sensibly, that the successful party should have the costs of the application only in so far as they relate to the issue that I have just decided..."

---

[26] Of course each case must be considered on its own facts. In *Samuel Smith (Southern) Ltd v Howard de Walden Estates Ltd* Unreported June 21/22, 2006, Central London CC, H.H. Judge Dean QC, the landlord sought the incorporation of a redevelopment break clause operable at any time after the commencement of the new term upon service of six months notice. This was the principal issue between the parties. The tenant opposed the incorporation of the break but on the day of the trial conceded that the break was to be inserted but contended that the date from which it was to operate was to be not earlier than the expiry of the fifth year of the term. The judge held that the break was not to operate until after the expiry of the third year of the term. He made an order that there was to be no order as to costs, accepting that the costs which the landlord had incurred in preparing its evidence as to why a break should be inserted would have been necessary in any event to deal with the date from which the break was to operate. Thus, the tenant's last minute change of heart over the principle as to whether or not a break clause should go in had not given rise to any wasted costs. The landlord had, he said, maintained an unreasonable position as to the date from which the break was to operate, having regard to the lack of evidence from the landlord as to the imminence of any redevelopment. In all the circumstances the judge thought the appropriate order was for each party to bear its own costs.

[27] See also *Charles Clements (London) v Rank City Wall*[1978] 1 E.G.L.R. 47 Ch D.

[28] [1983] 2 A.C. 726; [1982] 2 W.L.R. 407 HL.

[29] [1981] 1 Ch. 216 CA.

[30] The landlord went to the House of Lords but the appeal was dismissed with costs.

[31] [1984] 1 W.L.R. 696 CA.

[32] [2000] 2 E.G.L.R. 49.

10–20 Where an unopposed renewal involves a number of lease terms the court will, in determining costs in such cases, have regard to a number of factors in the exercise of its discretion but these will include in our experience:

(1) the importance of each issue relative to the other issues in dispute with regard to the lease renewal[33];
(2) the impact if any of any issue on the rent;
(3) the time taken at trial to deal with the issue;
(4) the parties respective positions before trial on the issue;
(5) any offers made in respect of the issue.

Cost where issue is one of rent only

10–21 Where the issue is one only as to the rent to be paid under the new lease, difficulty may arise in identifying the "event" which it is said a party has won. With rent it is unusual for the trial judge to award the rent contended for by one party. There are undoubtedly cases where one party succeeds to a greater extent than the other. However, there are equally a large number of cases where the rent awarded is nearer to the mid point than to either of the rival contentions. In uncomplicated cases where the rent is fixed at the mid point the judge would be entitled to (and probably should) direct each party to bear its own costs. This approach was adopted by the Court of Appeal in *Le Witt v Brookes.*[34] The principal dispute in that case was as to rent. The tenant contended for £200 and the landlord for £350.The court awarded a rent of £300. This was on the landlord's side of the mid-way point. The judge at first instance sought to apply the analogy of a payment into court to the landlord's contentions and awarded the tenant one-half of its costs. The Court of Appeal said that this was wrong and that each side should bear its own costs. Although the rent of £300 awarded was nearer to the landlord's figure than that of the tenant's, the court plainly felt that neither party had done sufficiently better than the other to justify an award of costs in that party's favour.[35]

---

[33] In *Boots the Chemist Ltd v Pinkland*; *Thorn EMI v Pinkland* [1992] 2 E.G.L.R. 95, in addition to the determination of the rents the parties were at issue as to (1) positive trading covenant (Boots only); (2) upwards/downwards or upwards-only rent reviews (Boots only); (3) hypothetical term at rent review (Boots only): (4) management fees and (5) length of term (Thorn only). Although not reported on this issue the landlord won the rental dispute between the parties. The court ordered the tenants to pay 80% of the landlord's costs as the rent was the major issue between the parties in the case. Another example is the *Cairnplace v CBL* decision mentioned in para.10–19 above. Here the issue of whether or not the tenant should pay the landlord's costs of the preparation of the new lease was a minor one (being governed by a statutory provision) when compared with the issue as to whether the tenant was required to provide guarantors.

[34] [1956] 1 W.L.R. 1438 CA. Contrast this with *Harewood Hotels v Harris* [1958] 1 W.L.R. 108 CA. In that case the court awarded a rent very close to the rent contended for by the tenant but the tenant lost on another point (the judge having ordered a term shorter than that contended for by the tenant). The judge ordered the landlord to pay one-half of the tenant's costs. The Court of Appeal refused to intervene.

[35] Denning L.J. said that the court in the exercise of its discretion should consider the reasonableness or unreasonableness of offers on each side amongst other things: at 1439. Hodson L.J. said that "This is not to say that any hard and fast rule is to be laid down, that in all cases where the court fixes an

Cases relating to rent are, however, not always straightforward. Arguments in cases where the issue is one of rent may include legal issues (e.g. the construction of the lease terms), valuation issues and other technical issues (e.g. as to appropriate methodology for valuing the premises) and issues of fact (e.g. as to the extent to which improvements are to be disregarded). In some cases, the issues are argued in the alternative to one another so that it is possible for one party to lose on one issue and win on another. Thus, it may be possible for the rent to be nearer the figure contended for by that party even though he may have put forward a case on an issue which failed. In those circumstances one would expect that it would be right to award that party part of his costs but to deprive him of some part of his costs to reflect the time and expense involved in the disputed issue which he lost. This approach is reflected in the CPR Pt. 44. **10–22**

While it must be emphasised that there are usually a number of factors influencing the court in the exercise of its discretion in each case, some help may be derived from the following table which analyses the court's decisions on costs in various reported cases where the only dispute was over the amount of rent.[36] **10–23**

COSTS WHERE ISSUE ONE OF RENT ONLY

Case	Landlord's figure	Tenant's figure	Rent determined by court	Order as to cost
English Exporters (London) Ltd v Eldonwall Ltd[37]	£16,000	£10,206	£16,000	Tenant to pay half of landlord's costs
Le Witt v Brookes[38]	£350	200	300	No order as to costs
National Car Parks v Colebrook Estates[39]	£50,000	£26,500	£29,000	Tenants entitled to two-thirds of their costs
Thoms v O&C Estates Ltd[40]	£31,632	£17,224	£24,000	No order as to costs

intermediate figure between counter offers there should be no order as to costs, but it is an indication as to (as I think) a natural practice to follow in a situation like this, which must often arise." (at 1441).

[36] It must also be remembered that these decisions pre date the introduction of the Civil Procedure Rules.

[37] [1973] Ch. 415; [1973] 2 W.L.R. 435; [1973] 1 All E.R. 726.

[38] [1956] 1 W.L.R. 1438; [1956] 3 All E.R. 676 CA.

[39] [1983] 1 E.G.L.R. 78.

[40] Unreported May 19, 1983.

Orders by consent

10–24 Where an order under the Act is made by consent, the parties should provide for costs by the terms of the agreed order. This is discussed in para.15–31.

Revocation of order for grant of new lease

10–25 It is expressly provided by s.36(3) that, where an order has been revoked on the application of the tenant pursuant to s.36(2), the court may, if it thinks fit, revoke or vary any provision in the order as to costs and may award costs even if no order for costs was included in the original order. In *Re 88 High Road, Kilburn*[41] (digested in para.8–149), the court ordered the tenant to pay the whole of the landlord's costs of the application including the application to revoke. In *Commercial Veneer Co Ltd v Printing House Properties Ltd*[42] and *Rom Tyre & Accessories Ltd v Crawford Street Properties Ltd*[43] the tenant was ordered to pay the landlord's costs on a party-and-party basis[44] upon the tenant's application to revoke. Whether it is right to do so in any particular case will depend to some degree upon whether the tenant was reasonable in pressing his application so far as to obtain an order for a new tenancy and then to seek to have the order revoked. If, upon an application to revoke under s.36(2), the court does not specifically direct otherwise, the order as to costs made in the original order will stand.

Calderbank offers

10–26 A party wishing to protect its position on costs can make an offer on a "without prejudice save as to costs" basis offering to settle the proceedings (or specified issues) on particular terms. This form of offer, known as a Calderbank offer[45] has been largely obviated by the provisions of Pt 36 of the Civil Procedure Rules. Part 36 sets out the costs consequences of an offer to settle a claim. However, those consequences apply only if the offer complies with the requirements of Pt 36. The concept of a Calderbank letter which does not in its terms comply with the provisions of Pt 36 and other non-complying offers have been preserved (r.36(2)). However, the costs consequences specified in Pt 36 do not follow unless the court otherwise orders (r.36.1(2)).

10–27 It is our experience that the parties will be reluctant to make a CPR Pt 36 offer, because of the costs consequences if accepted: CPR 36.13. It is for that reason that a party who wishes to propose settlement on the basis that there is no order as to costs, or some other order as to costs, will make a Calderbank Offer.

---

41 [1959] 1 W.L.R. 279; [1959] 1 All E.R. 527.

42 [1957] E.G.D. 119.

43 (1966) 197 E.G. 565.

44 Now the standard basis.

45 *Calderbank v Calderbank* [1976] Fam. 73; [1975] 3 W.L.R. 586; [1975] 3 All E.R. 333 CA. See also para.15–55 et seq.

Costs of lease

The costs of executing the lease and counterpart are to be distinguished from the costs of the proceedings. It is open to the parties to agree expressly that the new tenancy should contain a term providing for the payment of such costs by one party or the other. In the absence of express agreement, however, the court should not insert such a term, even where the current tenancy contains a provision which required the tenant to bear the costs of preparing and executing the lease creating the current tenancy: *Cairnplace v CBL*[46] (digested in para.8–71). The reason for this is that the Costs of Leases Act 1958 provides that: **10–28**

> "notwithstanding any custom to the contrary, a party to a lease shall, unless the parties thereto agree otherwise in writing, be under no obligation to pay the whole or any part of any other party's solicitor's costs of the lease".

In the *Cairnplace v CBL* case, the Court of Appeal held that it would not be a correct exercise of judicial discretion to use the wide power conferred on the court by the general words of s.35 to deprive the tenant of the protection conferred on him by a later Act dealing specifically with that very obligation.

5. PROVISIONS AS TO REVERSIONS

The complex provisions of s.65 can only be understood in the context of the evolution of the law of landlord and tenant as it applies to the situation where a head landlord (L) has granted to a tenant (T) a lease of land out of which T has, in turn, granted to a sub-tenant (S) a sub-lease. At common law, problems arose in two situations. First, difficulties arose where the lease granted to T disappeared in circumstances which gave rise to no rights and obligations, whether by privity of contract or privity of estate, enjoyed by or binding on L and S respectively. Secondly, a similar set of problems arose where the creation of T's interest occurred after the grant by L to S of a direct lease, so that T was S's landlord not by virtue of any contract between T and S, nor of any estate created by T in favour of S, but by the direct grant by L to T of an interest expectant in reversion upon S's interest. The common law did provide a solution to the second problem by treating the grant of a lease of the reversion as being equivalent to an assignment pro tanto of the freehold. The common law was, however, unable to provide a solution to the first of these problems, because the doctrines of privity of contract and privity of estate were insufficiently flexible. Accordingly, it was by virtue of legislation in the mid-nineteenth century that a statutory solution of this first problem was provided. To the draftsman of the 1954 Act it must have been readily apparent that potentially the scheme of the Act might recreate the problems inherent in the common law, as it stood before the intervention of statute, since the Act created a new way in which S's sub-tenancy might continue beyond T's tenancy, and a new way in which a reversionary tenancy in favour of T might be granted in circumstances which the common law would have regarded as being inconsistent with the continuation or renewal of S's sub-tenancy. In the **10–29**

[46] [1984] 1 W.L.R. 696; [1984] 1 All E.R. 315 CA.

following paragraphs we seek to explain the anomalous situation prevailing at common law, the way in which those problems were resolved by statute, and, finally, the way in which the draftsman of the Act ensured that such anomalies would not recur in the new situation which the Act created.

Continuation of tenancy beyond term of superior tenancy

10–30 Section 65(1) provides:

> "Where by virtue of a provision of this Act a tenancy (in this subsection referred to as 'the inferior tenancy') is continued for a period such as to extend to or beyond the end of the term of a superior tenancy, the superior tenancy shall, for the purposes of this Act and of any other enactment and of any rule of law, be deemed so long as it subsists to be an interest in reversion expectant upon the termination of the inferior tenancy and, if there is no intermediate tenancy, to be the interest in reversion immediately expectant upon the termination thereof."

10–31 Thus, where, by virtue of the Act, a tenancy is continued up to or beyond the contractual term of a superior tenancy, the superior tenancy is to be deemed to be an interest in reversion expectant upon the determination of the inferior tenancy so long as the superior tenancy subsists and, if there is no intermediate tenancy, it is further deemed to be the interest in reversion immediately expectant upon the determination of the inferior tenancy. This is best illustrated by an example.

10–32 **Example** F grants to L a tenancy expiring on December 25, 2012. L grants to T a tenancy of part of the premises expiring on December 20, 2012. T grants to S a sub-tenancy of part of his premises for a term expiring on December 15, 2012. For the purposes of this example we assume that L, T, and S are all occupying at least part of the premises demised to them respectively for the purposes of a business, so that each has a tenancy protected by the Act. On December 15, 2012, S's sub-tenancy would, at common law, have come to an end by effluxion of time, but it does not because it is continued by the Act. Similarly, T's tenancy would have come to an end on December 20, 20012 but it does not because it is continued by the Act. Likewise, L's tenancy would have come to an end on December 25, 2012, but does not because it is continued by the Act. In this situation the effect of s.65(1) is as follows. L's tenancy is deemed to be an interest in reversion expectant upon the determination of T's tenancy and S's sub-tenancy, because they are both "inferior tenancies" within the meaning of the subsection. So far as T's tenancy is concerned, L's tenancy is also deemed to be the interest in reversion immediately expectant upon the determination of T's tenancy, because there is no interest intermediate between them. So far as T is concerned, his interest is an interest in reversion expectant upon the termination of S's sub-tenancy and it is also the interest in reversion immediately expectant upon the termination of S's sub-tenancy, because there is no interest intermediate between them. The effect is that, so long as L's tenancy and T's tenancy subsist, L remains bound by his obligations to T and has his rights against T, such as the right to receive rent, the right to enforce the covenants of T's tenancy, the right to distrain against T for arrears of rent and the right to forfeit T's tenancy for failure to pay rent or breach of covenant. Similarly, T is able to enforce against L all of

L's obligations so long as L's tenancy subsists. Similarly, between T and S, so long as T's tenancy subsists they have the rights, and are bound by the obligations, of S's sub-tenancy.

Intermediate tenancy coming to end but sub-tenancy continuing

Section 65(2) provides: **10–33**

> "In the case of a tenancy continuing by virtue of any provision of this Act after the coming to an end of the interest in reversion immediately expectant upon the termination thereof, subsection (1) of section one hundred and thirty-nine of the Law of Property Act 1925 (which relates to the effect of the extinguishment of a reversion) shall apply as if references in the said subsection (1) to the surrender or merger of the reversion included references to the coming to an end of the reversion for any reason other than surrender or merger."

Section 65(2) deals with the position where L has granted a tenancy to T, who has in turn sub-let all or part of the premises to S, and S's sub-tenancy is continued by the Act after the coming to an end of T's tenancy. It is necessary to consider the common law situation, as altered by statute, to understand the way in which the Act deals with this situation. At common law, the basic rule was that where T's tenancy came to an end by effluxion of time, notice to quit or forfeiture, any derivative interest, such as S's sub-tenancy, would fall in with it: *Pennell v Payne*.[47] This would either occur at the same time as the termination of T's tenancy (in the case of notice to quit or forfeiture), or at an earlier date (since the sub-tenancy would necessarily determine by effluxion of time at a date earlier than the date on which the tenancy would determine by effluxion of time). The common law recognised, however, that a sub-tenancy would not come to an end when the termination of the tenancy was effected by surrender or merger. Thus, it was only in the case of surrender and merger that the common law had to confront the problem of T's tenancy disappearing while S's sub-tenancy subsisted. This situation created difficulties, because the common law of landlord and tenant recognised only rights and obligations which arose either out of privity of contract or privity of estate. Where T's tenancy had disappeared by surrender or merger, there was no contract between L and S, nor was there any privity of estate. Thus the paradoxical situation arose that, although S had an interest in land derived from his sub-tenancy, he had no obligations towards L and likewise had no rights against him. L for similar reasons had no obligations to S and no rights against him. Accordingly, the Real Property Act 1845 s.9, which is re-enacted in s.139 of the Law of Property Act 1925, provided that, where a reversion expectant on a lease of land is surrendered or merged, the estate or interest which as against the lessee for the time being confers the next best right to the land shall be deemed to be the reversion for the purpose of preserving the same incidents and obligations as would have affected the original reversion had there been no surrender or merger thereof. The effect of this is that, when T's tenancy comes to an end, L steps into T's shoes for all purposes, so that he becomes bound by the covenants which T gave to S and can enforce against S the covenants which S gave to T. **10–34**

---

[47] [1995] Q.B. 192; [1995] 2 W.L.R. 261; [1995] 2 All E.R. 592 CA.

10–35 The effect of the Act of 1954 was to create a new situation in which T's tenancy might come to an end, yet S's sub-tenancy would survive. Accordingly, it is provided by s.65(2) that the position created by s.139 of the Law of Property Act 1925 will apply also where T's interest comes to an end for any reason whatsoever, while S's sub-tenancy is continued by the Act. Thus the practical effect is that, where T's tenancy is not protected by the Act so that it comes to an end by effluxion of time, or where it is duly terminated in accordance with the Act yet S's sub-tenancy thereafter continues, L steps into T's shoes in the same way as he would have if T's tenancy had come to an end by surrender or merger. In the context of an old lease[48] it has been suggested, although the court did not decide the point, that upon the termination of T's tenancy the right to sue for arrears accrued due, or for breaches of covenant committed under, S's sub-tenancy prior to the termination of T's tenancy passes to the head lessor: *Electricity Supply Nominees Ltd v Thorn EMI Ltd.*[49]

10–36 One result of the provisions of s.65(2) which is not sufficiently recognised is that it makes it important for landlords whose consent is requested to a sub-letting of premises to which the Act applies (or may apply) to look carefully at the covenants and conditions of the proposed sub-lease. Except in the case of surrender or merger, the landlord would not be at all concerned at common law with what covenants and conditions were entered into between T and S. The reason for this is that, if the tenancy came to an end by effluxion of time or notice to quit, both T and S would be bound to vacate so there was no possibility of L being liable to S for covenants entered into by T. Even in the case of surrender or merger, although the consequence would be (by virtue of s.139 of the Law of Property Act 1925) that L would step into the shoes of T, L would at least have the choice whether or not to proceed with the surrender or merger in the light of his knowledge of the covenants and conditions which would become binding upon him. As a result of s.65(2) of the 1954 Act, L has no choice over whether he is prepared to step into T's shoes in circumstances where T's tenancy determines, but S's sub-tenancy is continued. Thus, if he has been so foolish as to permit T to grant a sub-tenancy to S upon terms and conditions which are disadvantageous to T, L will find himself bound by those disadvantageous terms and conditions if T's tenancy comes to an end yet S's sub-tenancy continues.

Continuation of tenancy beyond commencement of reversionary tenancy

10–37 Section 65(3) of the Act provides:

---

[48] That is one which is not governed by the provisions of the Landlord and Tenant (Covenants) Act 1995, which came into force on January 1, 1996.

[49] [1991] 2 E.G.L.R. 46 CA. The argument for transfer of the right to sue centres upon the wording of s.141(3) of the Law of Property Act 1925, which refers to a person becoming entitled "by conveyance or otherwise" to a covenant to take advantage of, and enforce, it. The wording suggests that s.141 is not confined to assignments only. Under a new lease governed by the Landlord and Tenant (Covenants) Act 1995 the provisions of s.141 of the Law of Property Act have been repealed and are inapplicable.

> "Where by virtue of any provision of this Act a tenancy (in this subsection referred to as 'the continuing tenancy') is continued beyond the beginning of a reversionary tenancy which was granted (whether before or after the commencement of this Act) so as to begin on or after the date on which apart from this Act the continuing tenancy would have come to an end, the reversionary tenancy shall have effect as if it had been granted subject to the continuing tenancy."

Section 65(3) deals with the position where a tenancy continues by virtue of the Act beyond the date on which a reversionary tenancy is to commence. Once again, it is necessary to illustrate, by example, the position at common law.

Example Suppose that L grants a tenancy to T. Clearly, the relationship of landlord and tenant exists between them as a matter of both contract and estate. Suppose that L grants to R a reversionary tenancy (also called a concurrent lease or lease of the reversion). The common law regarded this as being, in effect, an assignment by L of his reversion, so that R became T's landlord subject to the benefit and burden of the covenants and conditions contained in T's tenancy from the date of commencement of R's reversionary tenancy until the expiry thereof, whereupon L would once again become T's landlord subject to the benefit and burdens of T's tenancy. Accordingly, by what may be regarded as the legal fiction of treating the reversionary tenancy as being an assignment, the common law avoided the difficulties which would otherwise have arisen from the lack of any privity of estate (as well as of any privity of contract) between R and T. Section 65(3) similarly provides that where a tenancy continues by virtue of the Act up to or after the date upon which a reversionary tenancy comes into effect, the reversionary tenant is bound by the covenants and conditions of the continuing tenancy as if the reversionary tenancy had been made expressly subject thereto. **10–38**

The grant of a reversionary lease may constitute an agreement for the grant of a future tenancy within s.28.[50] Where the grant of the reversionary lease falls within s.28, the grant has the effect of determining the tenant's protection under the Act in respect of any existing tenancy. The grant of the reversionary tenancy in order to be an agreement within s.28 must be made with the person who constitutes the tenant's "landlord" within s.44: *Bowes-Lyon v Green*[51] (digested in para.15–17). It remains to be decided whether the "landlord" must also be the tenant's immediate landlord. **10–39**

New tenancy granted to commence after reversionary tenancy

Section 65(4) provides: **10–40**

> "Where by virtue of any provision of this Act a tenancy (in this subsection referred to as 'the new tenancy') is granted for a period beginning on the same date as a reversionary tenancy or for a period such as to extend beyond the beginning of the term of a reversionary tenancy, whether the reversionary tenancy in question was granted before or after the commencement of this Act, the reversionary tenancy shall have effect as if it had been granted subject to the new tenancy."

---

[50] As to s.28 generally, see para.15–14 et seq.

[51] [1961] 3 W.L.R. 1044; [1961] 3 All E.R. 843 HL.

10–41 Section 65(4) deals with the situation where a new tenancy is granted pursuant to the Act to take effect from a date which is the same as or later than the date upon which a reversionary tenancy is to take effect. At common law the position would have been that, because the new tenancy granted to T took effect after the commencement of the tenancy granted to R, R would be entitled to possession and T would merely have a reversionary tenancy expectant upon the termination of R's tenancy. Section 65(4), in effect, reverses the common law position. R's tenancy takes effect subject to T's new tenancy granted pursuant to the Act, so that T is entitled to possession and R has a tenancy which is reversionary to T's new tenancy.

New tenancy granted for term longer than immediate landlord's interest

10–42 The position where a new tenancy is granted for a term longer than the immediate landlord's term is governed by the provisions of para.2 of Sch.6. This paragraph provides:

> "Where the period for which in accordance with the provisions of Part II of this Act it is agreed or determined by the court that a new tenancy should be granted thereunder will extend beyond the date on which the interest of the immediate landlord will come to an end, the power of the court under Part II of this Act to order such a grant shall include power to order the grant of a new tenancy until the expiration of that interest and also to order the grant of such a reversionary tenancy or reversionary tenancies as may be required to secure that the combined effects of those grants will be equivalent to the grant of a tenancy for that period; and the provisions of Part II of this Act shall, subject to the necessary modifications, apply in relation to the grant of a tenancy together with one or more reversionary tenancies as they apply in relation to the grant of one new tenancy."

The basic scheme of this paragraph is that the tenant whose immediate landlord has an insufficiently long interest to grant him the full term intended to be ordered by the court will receive not one tenancy but two or more, each to be granted by that landlord whose interest enables him to grant it, which will take effect in succession to each other in the same way as if one grant had been possible. The way in which this operates in practice can be illustrated by the following examples.

10–43 **Example 1** Suppose the following chain of interests: L is the superior landlord and is the owner of the freehold. C is the competent landlord for the purposes of Sch.6 and is "the landlord" as defined by s.44.[52] C's term is expressed to expire on December 31, 2018.

M is the mesne landlord as defined by Sch.6 and his term is due to expire on December 31, 2014.

T has a continuation tenancy and is applying for a new tenancy pursuant to the Act. Neither C nor M is in occupation of any part of the premises and neither of their tenancies is one to which the Act applies.

If the court decides that T should be granted a new tenancy expiring on December 31, 2020, that will be a tenancy extending beyond the expiry dates of

[52] As to the meaning of which, see para.3–87 et seq.

M's tenancy and C's tenancy. Accordingly, in order that T should have a tenancy of that duration, it is necessary that he should be granted new tenancies by M, C and L, respectively.

In this example the court would accordingly make the following order:

> "That M grants to T a tenancy commencing on the date of termination of T's current tenancy and determining on December 31, 2014.
> That C grants to T a tenancy commencing on January 1, 2015, and terminating on December 31, 2018.
> That L grants to T a tenancy commencing on January 1, 2019, and determining on December 31, 2020."

The provisions of this paragraph accordingly appear to create a statutory exception to the rule that a tenant who grants a sub-tenancy for the whole of the length of his unexpired term effects an assignment of that tenancy. The paragraph expressly provides that T's succession of tenancies should be treated as if they were, in effect, the grant of one tenancy and the continuation provisions of the Act are modified accordingly, so that the first tenancy is not continued by virtue of the Act beyond the date when the succeeding tenancy has been ordered to commence.

Example 2 An additional complication arises if one supposes that M's tenancy is protected by the Act, as would be the case where he has sub-let only part of the premises to T and occupies the remainder for business purposes. Making this modification to the above example and further supposing that C has served a s.25 notice upon M and that M has applied for a new tenancy, considerable difficulties can arise if T's application for a new tenancy is considered by the court before it has decided the terms of M's new tenancy. The court may refuse to grant M a new tenancy at all, in which case the position will be that the new tenancy to be granted by M to T will be one which will determine on the date on which M's current tenancy will determine pursuant to the provisions of s.64. M may be granted a new tenancy of five years' duration, in which case the new tenancy to T would be granted by M for the first five years and by C and L respectively for the balance. If, however, M were granted a term of 14 years, the paragraph would not apply at all, because M would be able to grant to T the full term ordered by the court. Very great difficulties will arise as to the correct form of order in any case where M is granted a new tenancy for a lesser term than that granted to T, because M's new tenancy will necessarily be one protected by the Act. Accordingly, at the date of the order granting the new tenancy to T, it will be impossible to predict whether M's tenancy will in fact come to an end on the contractual expiry date, or whether it will continue and perhaps be renewed beyond that date pursuant to the provisions of the Act. Thus it will not be known whether C will, in fact, be the appropriate person to grant a tenancy to T. Although a literal reading of s.65(3) might suggest that T's second tenancy which has been ordered to be granted by C would be a "reversionary tenancy" which would take effect in reversion to M's continuing tenancy, this would produce absurd results, because T would become M's landlord although the purpose of para.2 is to put T in the same position as if he had been granted not three tenancies but one. The paragraph also applies where the new tenancy to T is granted not by order of the court but by agreement. 10–44

Such an agreement must be made not with the immediate landlord of T, but with the "competent landlord", which in this example will be C.[53]

Power of competent landlord to bind mesne landlords

10–45 Paragraphs 3 and 4 of Sch.6 provide:

> `3(1) Any notice given by the competent landlord under Part I of this Act to terminate the relevant tenancy, and any agreement made between that landlord and the tenant as to the granting, duration, or terms of a future tenancy, being an agreement made for the purposes of the said Part I, shall bind the interest of any mesne landlord notwithstanding that he has not consented to the giving of the notice or was not a party to the agreement.
>
> (2) The competent landlord shall have power for the purposes of Part I of this Act to give effect to any agreement with the tenant for the grant of a new tenancy beginning with the coming to an end of the relevant tenancy, notwithstanding that the competent landlord will not be the immediate landlord at the commencement of the new tenancy, and any instrument made in the exercise of the power conferred by this sub-paragraph shall have effect as if the mesne landlord had been a party thereto.
>
> (3) Nothing in the foregoing provisions of this paragraph shall prejudice the provisions of the next following paragraph.
>
> 4(1) If the competent landlord, not being the immediate landlord, gives any such notice or makes any such agreement as is mentioned in sub-paragraph (1) of the last foregoing paragraph without the consent of every mesne landlord, any mesne landlord whose consent has not been given thereto shall be entitled to compensation from the competent landlord for any loss arising in consequence of the giving of the notice or the making of the agreement.
>
> (2) If the competent landlord applies to any mesne landlord for his consent to such a notice or agreement, that consent shall not be unreasonably withheld, but may be given subject to any conditions which may be reasonable (including conditions as to the modification of the proposed notice or agreement or as to the payment of compensation by the competent landlord).
>
> (3) Any question arising under this paragraph whether consent has been unreasonably withheld or whether any conditions imposed on the giving of consent are unreasonable shall be determined by the court.`

10–46 Paragraphs 3 and 4 of Sch.6 provide for the situation where the person who fulfils the definition of "landlord" within s.44 (who is referred to as "the competent landlord") is not the immediate landlord of the tenant under the relevant tenancy, there being one or more intervening mesne landlords. It is "the competent landlord" and he alone who is entitled to give a s.25 notice to the tenant under the relevant tenancy and it is he alone who is entitled to agree with the tenant for the grant of a new tenancy and to agree its duration, the rent payable thereunder and its other terms. Paragraph 3 provides that any such notice and any such agreement is binding upon each of the mesne landlords without their consent: *Lewis v MTC Cars Ltd*[54] (digested in para.10–49).

10–47 Effectively, therefore, para.3 of Sch.6 gives the competent landlord the power to control the terms of the relationship of landlord and tenant between the tenant and his immediate landlord. This may have far-reaching consequences for the immediate landlord. It may be that he is in occupation of part only of the

---

[53] As to the power of the "competent landlord" to bind other reversioners, see para.10–45.

[54] [1975] 1 W.L.R. 457.

premises, but is required by the competent landlord to take a new tenancy of the whole of the premises, so that he will be the tenant's immediate landlord for a long term of years. Yet it is for the competent landlord and not the immediate landlord to agree with the tenant what rent the tenant shall pay and what are the terms upon which the tenant shall hold of his immediate landlord. The rent may be too low, the terms may be disadvantageous to the immediate landlord; indeed, the immediate landlord may be deprived of the opportunity of ridding himself of the tenant because the competent landlord does not choose to oppose the grant of a new tenancy upon grounds which would have been available to the immediate landlord. It may even be that the power of the competent landlord goes so far as to agree that the tenant will have a new tenancy of premises greater than those to which he is entitled under the terms of the Act; perhaps the premises may even by agreement be increased so as to encroach upon the premises which are occupied by the immediate landlord.

The remedy which is provided by para.4 for this possible injustice to the immediate landlord is to give him a right of compensation against the competent landlord in all cases where the immediate landlord's consent has not been obtained. Thus, in the example quoted above, the immediate landlord might obtain compensation from the competent landlord for the fact that the tenant is paying too low a rent, or for the fact that an onerous liability has been put upon the immediate landlord or because the immediate landlord has been deprived of the opportunity of getting rid of the tenant. Such claims might be difficult to prove and, perhaps for this reason, are rare in practice. The "competent landlord" from whom compensation can be obtained is presumably the "competent landlord" who has made the agreement binding the mesne landlord and causing him loss. It would be contrary to principle to make compensation payable by whoever fulfilled the definition of "competent landlord" at the date that the damage was actually suffered or that a claim for compensation was made. Nonetheless, it is the counsel of prudence in every case where a landlord, who is the competent landlord, but not the immediate landlord, intends to serve a s.25 notice, or to agree to the grant of a new tenancy which will be binding upon a mesne landlord, first to seek that mesne landlord's consent, except in a case where it is obvious that no loss or damage could be caused. If consent is sought from a mesne landlord, he may not with-hold it unreasonably, but may attach conditions to his consent, provided those conditions are themselves reasonable. In a case of dispute between the competent landlord and a mesne landlord over reasonableness, it is for the court to decide. Clearly, this process can be somewhat cumbersome and could result in considerable delay with consequent loss of tactical advantage between the competent landlord, the mesne landlord and the tenant. It is perhaps, for this reason also, that consent is so seldom sought in practice. **10–48**

Lewis v MTC Cars Ltd[55] A was the freeholder of the business premises in question. B had a term of years expiring on December 23, 1968; and C, who was the defendant, had a sub-term expiring on December 20, 1968, and was in **10–49**

[55] [1975] 1 W.L.R. 457; [1975] 1 All E.R. 874 CA.

occupation of the premises for its business purposes. B's tenancy was unprotected since B was not in occupation. After the expiry of their contractual terms, B and C continued to pay their respective rents to A and B. In those circumstances, B became tenant of A as a yearly tenant, or tenant from year to year. C, however, remained in occupation and paying rent to B, not as a yearly sub-tenant of B, but, by virtue of the 1954 Act, on a statutory continuation of that sub-tenancy. A, on November 13, 1972, gave to B due notice to quit, determining B's yearly contractual tenancy on December 23, 1973. On November 21, 1972 A gave to C a s.25 notice to determine C's sub-tenancy on May 31, 1973, which was a date prior to the termination of B's mesne tenancy. The defendant, C, contended that that notice was ineffective. It was not disputed that A was the competent landlord to serve a s.25 statutory notice on C when he did so, notwithstanding the existence at the time of the mesne tenancy of B. It was, however, asserted in that there was no power to serve a notice under s.25 with a termination date earlier than the expiry of the contractual mesne tenancy of B. It was held that the notice was valid. Russell L.J. said:

> "Now it may—and at first sight would—appear strange that by a section 25 notice (in the present case given by A to C) the sub-tenancy of C from B can in effect be terminated by A's action without reference to C's mesne landlord B; that is to say, before the end of B's contractual head tenancy. Is B to be, for example, deprived of his profit rental while remaining liable for rent to A under the headlease? It appears to me that this situation is covered, and indeed exactly envisaged, elsewhere in the Act. In this case, A was only in a position to give a section 25 notice to C because of the relatively short interest of B in reversion to C's tenancy once the notice to quite had been given to B. This is under section 44 of the 1954 Act. Section 44 applies the provisions of Schedule 6 to a case such as the present, where the immediate landlord B is not the freeholder... under paragraph 3 of that schedule the acts of A as the competent landlord (able to give, therefore, a section 25 notice) are made binding on the intermediate land-lord B; and by paragraph 4, if the mesne landlord B has not consented to the acts of A, he will be entitled to compensation from A for any loss that may be caused to him. It seems to me that those provisions deprive what appears to me to be the plain result of the language of section 25 of the strangeness or oddity that without them might have occurred to the ordinary common law or indeed equity mind. Accordingly in my judgment, the judge was quite correct in concluding that the date specified in the section 25 notice could not in law be criticised."

Superior landlords

10–50 Paragraphs 5, 6 and 7 of Sch.6 provide:

> "5. An agreement between the competent landlord and the tenant made for the purposes of Part I of this Act in a case where—
> (a) the competent landlord is himself a tenant, and
> (b) the agreement would apart from this paragraph operate as respects any period after the coming to an end of the interest of the competent landlord,
>
> shall not have effect unless every superior landlord who will be the immediate landlord of the tenant during any part of that period is a party to the agreement.
>
> 6. Where the competent landlord has given a notice under section 25 of this Act to terminate the relevant tenancy and, within two months after the giving of the notice, a superior landlord—
> (a) becomes the competent landlord; and
> (b) gives to the tenant notice in the prescribed form that he withdraws the notice previously given;

the notice under section 25 of this Act shall cease to have effect, but without prejudice to the giving of a further notice under that section by the competent landlord.

7. If the competent landlord's interest in the property comprised in the relevant tenancy is a tenancy which will come or can be brought to an end within sixteen months (or any further time by which it may be continued under section 36(2) or section 64 of this Act and he gives to the tenant under the relevant tenancy a notice under section 25 of this Act to terminate the tenancy or is given by him a notice under section 26(3) of this Act:—

(a) the competent landlord shall forthwith send a copy of the notice to his immediate landlord; and

(b) any superior landlord whose interest in the property is a tenancy shall forthwith send to his immediate landlord any copy which has been sent to him in pursuance of the preceding sub-paragraph or this sub-paragraph."

The provisions of paras 5, 6 and 7, which deal with the position of landlords whose interests are superior to those of the competent landlord, operate in a quite different way from those relating to mesne landlords contained in paras 3 and 4. The competent landlord is entitled to serve a s.25 notice without the consent of any superior landlord. However, if the competent landlord is himself a person whose interest may come to an end within 16 months (or any further time by which it may be continued under s.36(2) or s.64 of the Act), he is obliged by para.7 forthwith to send a copy of the notice to his immediate landlord, and every superior landlord who is himself a tenant must forthwith send a copy to his immediate landlord. These provisions apply equally to the case where such a competent landlord receives a tenant's request pursuant to s.26. **10–51**

Paragraph 6 provides for the situation where a notice pursuant to s.25 has been given by the competent landlord, but that person subsequently ceases to be the competent landlord.[56] Where there has been a change in the identity of the competent landlord within three months of the giving of the s.25 notice, the new competent landlord may give notice to the tenant withdrawing the s.25 notice. Such a notice must be in the form[57] prescribed by the Landlord and Tenant Act 1954 Pt 2 (Notices) Regulations 2004.[58] If the new competent landlord exercises his power to withdraw the notice he is then free, if he so chooses, to serve a fresh notice. This may differ from the notice served by the previous competent landlord in that it may specify a different date for termination of the current tenancy and/or may seek to oppose the grant of a new tenancy, whereas the previous notice stated that the landlord would not oppose, or vice versa. The new competent landlord would also have the opportunity of specifying additional or different grounds of opposition. Curiously, although the provisions of para.7 cater equally for the case of a s.25 notice and a s.26 request, para.6 provides no corresponding right for the new competent landlord to withdraw a counter-notice given pursuant to s.26(6). A possible reason for this omission is that the furnishing of a copy of the s.26 request pursuant to para.7 may enable the superior landlord to bring himself within the definition of "competent landlord" before the competent landlord has had the opportunity to serve a counter-notice. Once the superior landlord has become the new competent landlord he can, of course, himself then serve a **10–52**

---

[56] For a discussion of the meaning of "landlord" and "competent landlord", see para.3–87. Paragraph 3–67 et seq. explains how the identity of "the landlord" may change from time to time.

[57] Form 6. See para.A2–039.

[58] The 1983 Regulations were revoked by the 2004 Regulations (SI 2004/1005) with effect from June 1, 2004.

counter-notice relying upon such grounds of opposition as he chooses. Nonetheless, this does not cater for the case where the competent landlord receives a s.26 request, forthwith sends a copy to his immediate landlord as required by para.7, but also forthwith serves a counter-notice pursuant to s.26(6). It would seem that in such circumstances the superior landlord would be bound by the contents of that counter-notice, would not be entitled to withdraw it and would not be entitled to claim compensation against the previous competent landlord.

10–53 There is considerable scope for tactical manoeuvring, which may be important where the tenant and the sub-tenant are connected companies or persons, or otherwise have a common commercial interest adverse to the superior landlord. Since it will necessarily be the case that the contractual expiry date of the sub-tenancy is an earlier date than the contractual expiry date of the tenancy, it follows that the earliest date upon which the sub-tenant may make a request pursuant to s.26 will always be earlier than the earliest date upon which the superior landlord can give a notice pursuant to s.25 to determine the tenancy (although it will be the same date as the earliest date upon which the superior landlord could give notice terminating the sub-tenancy). It follows that there will always be a period of at least a day (but usually longer) when: (1) the tenant is "the competent landlord"; (2) the sub-tenant is entitled to serve his request upon him; (3) the superior landlord is in no position to make himself the competent landlord; and (4) the tenant can comply with his statutory duty to forward a copy of the s.26 request, while shortly thereafter serving a counter-notice stating that he does not intend to oppose the sub-tenant's application for a new tenancy. Such a tactical manoeuvre may be particularly effective where the ground of opposition is one such as arrears of rent under the sub-tenancy or some past breach by the sub-tenant. It will be less effective in the case of ground (f) (demolition and reconstruction) because the landlord will probably be able to argue successfully in such circumstances for the grant to the sub-tenant of a very short tenancy or of a tenancy with a redevelopment break clause.[59]

10–54 Although no express sanction is provided for failure by the competent landlord to serve copies upon his immediate landlord pursuant to para.7, it is thought that in a suitable case an action would lie for breach of statutory duty for any damage suffered as a result of such failure.

10–55 Unlike the provisions governing the position of mesne landlords under paras 3 and 4, para.5 expressly provides that superior landlords are not bound, without their consent, by agreements made by the competent landlord purporting to affect their interests. Where the agreement would, apart from that paragraph, operate as respects any period after the coming to an end of the interest of the competent landlord, it shall not have effect unless every superior landlord who would be the immediate landlord of the tenant during any part of that period is a party to the agreement. The operation of this paragraph could give rise to considerable difficulties where there is a chain of superior interests, all or some of which are, as well as the current tenancy, protected by the Act. In any particular case, it may be impossible to predict with certainty whether the grant of a term of years to the

---

[59] See paras 8–39 et seq. and 8–77 et seq.

tenant under the current tenancy will require a grant to him only by his immediate landlord, or by his landlord and the next superior landlord, and so on. This position has already been illustrated.[60] Since para.5 provides that such an agreement "shall not have effect unless" all relevant superior landlords have consented, it is essential in every case that the consent of every landlord who might come within the paragraph is obtained, otherwise the agreement will, presumably, be void, even respecting those landlords who did consent. This could cause considerable practical difficulties where a complex chain of title is involved.

[60] See para.10–44.

CHAPTER 11

PREPARING FOR THE HEARING

1. GENERAL

Considerations to which parties should have regard

The scheme of the Act gives considerable scope to both landlord and tenant for tactical manoeuvring. In Ch.4 the tactical considerations for landlord and tenant in relation to the service of notices have been discussed. Similar considerations can apply after service of the notice in relation to the progress of the claim for a new tenancy (whether by the landlord or the tenant) or in respect of the landlord's termination application.[1] The landlord and the tenant will often be concerned with the time which it will take for the court to deal with the issues arising in the claim for renewal/termination and, depending upon the circumstances, may wish the court's decision to be delayed or advanced. Both the landlord and the tenant will also wish to be sure that, by the date of the hearing, circumstances are such as enable them to prove their case and that they have had sufficient time in order to accumulate the necessary evidence. In practice, because of the high rate of settlement of claims under the Act without the intervention of the court, the parties to a claim tend to consider these matters only when a hearing is in prospect. The prudent landlord and tenant will consider at an early stage what are the matters likely to be in issue between them; what is the likely timetable for the claim; how that timetable can strengthen or weaken their respective cases; how that timetable can work to their economic advantage or disadvantage; and what steps need to be taken in order to gather the necessary evidence. These considerations are reinforced by the new CPR Pt 56, the effect of which is to require the parties at an early stage of the litigation to identify the differences between them. **11–01**

[1] As to procedure, see Ch.14. The claim is required to be served within four months of its issue whether the claim be for renewal (either by the tenant or the landlord) or a landlord's termination application: CPR r.56.3(3)(b) and (4)(b) respectively. See further paras 14–56 to 14–65.

Time tabling[2]

Renewal (whether by tenant or landlord)

11–02 The lapse of time between issuing the Pt 8 claim for a new tenancy and its final disposal will depend upon many factors, the operation of which will often be difficult to predict. However, it is often important for the landlord and tenant to attempt, at an early stage, some forecast of the probable future timetable of the application. The following examples in relation to applications raising a variety of issues are based upon our general experience, but it must be stressed that the periods of time mentioned in them are illustrative only and that in any particular case quite different periods of time may apply. In these examples we make reference to the distinction between applications consequent upon the serving of a s.25 notice and those consequent upon the making of a s.26 request, since the timetable may not be the same in each case. In each example we assume that the relevant notice or request has been given on January 2, 2013.

11–03 **Example 1: Where there is no ground of opposition and the only issue is as to the amount of rent to be paid pursuant to the new tenancy** Either party may make an application for renewal immediately after service of a landlord's s.25 notice. The application must be served within two months of issue, whoever has made the application.[3] Assuming that the landlord makes the application as soon as possible[4] (because for instance the landlord wishes to take advantage of the substantial increase in rents since the last review). The tenant will be required to serve an acknowledgment of service within 14 days of the service upon him of the landlord's claim form.[5] The landlord's evidence need not be filed with the claim form nor within a specified time following receipt of the acknowledgement of service.[6] As the claim for renewal by a landlord must necessarily be one which is unopposed it is provided that no evidence need by filed unless and until the court directs.[7] The court will then issue directions for the further management of the case as part of its management functions.[8] The date of the case management conference will depend upon the state of the court lists and its holiday arrangements. We assume that this takes place on by the latest March 1, 2013. If it is apparent at the directions stage that the only issue is rent, the district judge

---

2 The examples in this section deal with the CPR having regard to the amendments made by the Civil Procedure (Amendment) Rules 2004 (SI 1306/2004), which were enacted to deal with the changes made to the 1954 Act by the 2003 Order.

3 As the claim is a Pt 8 claim the provisions contained within CPR r.8.3 for filing an acknowledgement of service apply: see para.14–67 et seq.

4 And the landlord is in the driving seat in this regard: see paras 6–53 to 6–56.

5 See paras 14–67 and 14–71.

6 The previous practice of requiring service of evidence within 14 days of receipt of the acknowledge of service has not been continued with respect to the new regime in light of the 2003 Order amendments. (The position was previously that in the case of a claim for renewal by a tenant—which was the only form of claim prior to June 1, 2004—the evidence had to be filed within 14 days of receipt of the acknowledgment of service (CPR r.56.3(10) (now repealed)) with the landlord's evidence being served 14 days thereafter (CPR r.56.3(11) (now repealed)).

7 PD 56 para.3.14. See further paras 14–81 to 14–83.

8 See paras 14–84 and 14–85.

will give directions for exchange of experts' reports or possibly for the appointment of a single joint expert. A reasonable time for this would appear to be four/six weeks, but, bearing in mind the holiday period, we will assume that they are ordered to be exchanged by April 14, 2013. After exchange of reports there is normally a further lapse of time, during which the parties consider each other's reports to see whether they can reach agreement on any matters arising out of them.[9] A reasonable period of time for this would be about two weeks and thus the application might come on for hearing (depending on the state of the court's lists) in May/June 2007. Assuming a hearing date of, say June 1, 2013 then, by virtue of s.64 the new tenancy would come into effect on September 22, 2013,[10] assuming no appeals.

Example 1A: If we take the same type of case—rent only—but this time preceded by a tenant's s.26 request, we can see that there will be a slightly longer period before the new tenancy comes in effect. If a s.26 request is served the landlord must if he wishes to oppose renewal serve a counter-notice to a s.26 request.[11] It is provided that the court shall not entertain an application under s.24(1)(for renewal) if it is made before the end of the period of two months beginning with the date of the making of the request, unless the application is made after the landlord has given a notice under s.26(6). Section 26(6) does not contemplate a positive counter-notice by the landlord.[12] Thus, it would seem that the landlord has to wait two months, albeit he does not intend to oppose, before he can make an application for renewal. Thus, in the above example, assuming a s.26 request is served in January 2013 the application could not be made before March 2, 2013. As essentially everything is put back two months one would expect expert evidence to be dealt with before the summer vacation. However, bearing in mind the holiday period it is perfectly conceivable that the trial window will not be until September/October. Assuming a trial date of October 1, 2013 the new tenancy will take effect from January 22, 2008. 11–04

Example 2: Where there is no ground of opposition and there is agreement between the parties on what the rent should be on alternative bases, but issues arise about the terms of the new tenancy We assume again that the landlord has made the application. Assuming a directions hearing on March 1, 2013, the district judge would not direct the exchange of experts' reports, unless (as sometimes happens) the question of what terms should be included in the new tenancy required to be decided upon expert evidence. The district judge would no doubt require the parties to formulate the issue or issues between them, with witness statements of fact and the preparation of a draft lease identifying the landlord's proposals upon which the tenant's counter-proposals would be shown in red. Since the preparation of such a document should not in principle take any great length of time, the parties could immediately seek the earliest open date in the court lists. We assume that a date could be found in say not later than three 11–05

---

9 See para.11–32.

10 This date being the period of three months provided for by s.64 together with the period of 21 days to take account of the period for appeal: see para.14–137 et seq. as to the time for appealing.

11 s.26(6). See para.5–03 et seq.

12 As to the implications of this, see para.5–08.

months, taking account of the time for serving witness statements of fact and the travelling lease. The hearing would take place some time in June 2013. Assuming a hearing date of June 15, 2013 the new tenancy would come into effect on October 6, 2013,[13] assuming no appeals.

11–06 **Example 3: Where the landlord opposes the grant of a new tenancy on ground (f) (demolition and reconstruction) and where there is no agreement on the terms of any new tenancy to be granted nor on the rent** In this example it probably matters not whether the matter starts off by way of a claim for renewal or by way of a landlord's termination application. The reason is that as the landlord is opposing he can serve a counter-notice and immediately make an application for termination. Assuming a landlord's termination application, the landlord is not required to serve with the application evidence in support of it. The tenant will be required to serve a defence as a termination application is dealt with under the Pt 7 procedure of the CPR.[14] The tenant will be required to serve the defence in 14 days of service of the claim form or if he first serves an acknowledgement of service to the claim, within 28 days after service of the particulars of claim.[15] Thus, we shall assume, as before, a directions hearing on March 1, 2013. It is provided that grounds of opposition are to be tried as preliminary issues.[16] The tenant would also require disclosure of the documents relevant to the landlord's intention. Such disclosure might be quite voluminous and we assume that an order would be made for discovery to take place. We would expect standard disclosure by lists within say 21 days with inspection seven days thereafter. Expert evidence might well be appropriate and we assume that reports would be ordered. We would expect these to be exchanged within say four weeks after disclosure. Since disputes often arise about whether full disclosure has been given in the first instance by the landlord, the court would probably be unwilling to fix a date, but would instead require the parties to furnish a certificate of readiness upon the completion of disclosure. Assuming adequate disclosure to have been given the preliminary issue might come on for hearing on October 1, 2013. If that issue was decided in favour of the landlord, the court shall make an order for the termination of the current tenancy in accordance with s.64 of the Act without the grant of a new tenancy.[17] The tenancy would come to an end on January 21/22, 2014, assuming no appeals. If the landlord failed in his ground of opposition, it is provided that "the court shall make an order for the grant of a new tenancy and accordingly for the termination of the current tenancy immediately before the commencement of the new tenancy."[18]

---

[13] See fn.10 above.

[14] See paras 14–72 to 14–76.

[15] CPR r.15.4. A defendant thus obtains an extra 14 days within which to serve a defence by serving an acknowledgment of service in accordance with CPR Pt 10.

[16] See paras 14–88 to 14–91.

[17] s.29(4)(a).

[18] s.29(4)(b). See para.10–02.

Defining the issues

Pre-October 15, 2001

It was previously the case[19] that in the High Court the parties' respective contentions were contained not in the originating summons or any other pleading, but in affidavits sworn by the parties. In practice, such affidavits were often insufficiently detailed to define with any precision what were the real issues between the parties. In the county court, the position was even more unsatisfactory. It had become customary for the tenant in his application to suggest terms for a new tenancy which were quite unrealistic and far from what he really expected to obtain from the court. It was not unknown for a tenant to suggest that the new tenancy should be at the same rent as was payable under the current tenancy. In the county court although the landlord's answer to the tenant's application would itself usually contain an element of "shadow-boxing", it was likely to represent more accurately what the landlord was seeking from the court, if only because it would have been formulated in response to the tenant's proposals and under less immediate pressure of time. This slap-dash approach to pleadings which had grown up in practice was no doubt encouraged by the decision of the Court of Appeal in *Morgan v Jones*[20] (digested in para.14–79) to the effect that, even if the landlord did not state his objection to the terms proposed by the tenant, the court must nonetheless consider, in all the circumstances, what terms are reasonable. **11–07**

Part 56[21]

As a result of CPR Pt 56 and the Practice Direction thereto the parties' respective contentions ought to be identified at a fairly early stage of the litigation. This is particularly so after June 1, 2004.[22] In particular it is to be noted that: **11–08**

(1) A tenant is required either in his claim form[23] (where he is the claimant), or in his acknowledgement of service[24] to a landlord's claim for renewal, to particularise, inter alia:
    (a) whether he relies on ss.23(1A),[25] 41[26] or 42[27];
    (b) the nature of the business carried on and whether any part of it is occupied by someone other than the tenant;
    (c) the terms of the tenancy he proposes.

---

[19] That is prior to the coming into effect on October 15, 2001 of CPR Pt.56 and the Practice Direction thereto.

[20] [1960] 1 W.L.R. 1220; [1960] 3 All E.R. 583 CA.

[21] This rule and the Practice Direction to it, is dealt with in detail in Ch.13.

[22] CPR Pt.56 and the Practice Direction thereto were amended with effect from June 1, 2004 to take account of the amendments to the Act by the 2003 Order.

[23] PD 56 para.3.5.

[24] PD 56 para.3.11.

[25] Controlling interest in company occupier: see para.1–86 et seq.

[26] Occupation pursuant to a trust: see para.1–92 et seq.

[27] Occupation as a member of a group company: see para.1–104.

(2) A landlord is required, where he makes a claim for renewal, to particularise inter alia:
   (a) the terms of the new tenancy he requires;
   (b) whether he requires the tenant pursuant to s.32(2) to take a new tenancy of the whole where the tenant is occupying part only of the holding.[28]
(3) A landlord is required, where he makes a termination application or he opposes the tenants renewal application, to particularise inter alia:
   (a) the grounds of opposition;
   (b) full details of those grounds;
   (c) the terms of the tenancy proposed if he fails on those grounds.[29]
(4) A tenant is required, in his acknowledgement of service to a landlord's termination application, to state, inter alia:
   (a) whether he relies on ss.23(1A), 41 or 42[30] and if he does so the basis on which he does so;
   (b) whether he relies on s.31A[31] and if so the basis on which he does so.[32]

These requirements ought to enable the court, upon the directions hearing to gear the directions towards the real issues between the parties. It is hoped that CPR Pt 56 will now require both parties to consider exactly what it is they are intending to present to the court at a much earlier stage than otherwise would be the case.[33]

Evidence: witness statements and oral evidence

11–09 The claimant's evidence in support of the claim as well as that of the defendant in opposition (whether this be a renewal claim or an opposed renewal/termination application) will be in the form of a witness statement, which is governed by CPR Pt 32.[34] It is to be noted that the witness statement will ordinarily stand as the witness's evidence in chief: CPR r.32.5(2). Amplification of the witness statement may be permitted with permission of the court as well as being able to give evidence in relation to new matters which have arisen since the witness statement was served: CPR r.32.5(3). The court will give permission only y if it considers that there is good reason not to confine the evidence of the witness to the contents of his witness statement: CPR r.32.5(4). Once a witness statement

---

[28] PD 56 para.3.7.

[29] PD 56 paras 3.9 and 3.12.

[30] As to these sections, see fnn.25, 26 and 27 above.

[31] That is to say whether the tenant is prepared to grant to the landlord, in response to the landlord's opposition under para.(f) of s.30(1), terms as to access to enable the landlord to carry out the work (s.31A(a)) or is prepared to accept an economically separable part (s.31A(b)): see para.7–192 et seq.

[32] PD 56 para.3.13.

[33] As to the evidence to be served in support of the tenant's claim and on behalf of the landlord in response, see paras 14–81 to 14–83.

[34] Nothing in the rules prevents a witness giving evidence by affidavit, at a hearing other than the trial, if he chooses to do so but the party putting forward the affidavit may not recover the additional cost of making it from any other party unless the court orders otherwise: CPR r.32.15. The *Chancery Guide*, Appendix 9, contains guidelines on witness statements for Chancery actions.

has been served it is to be noted that a failure to call the witness to give evidence at trial does not prevent any other party from relying upon it. The other party may put it in as hearsay evidence: CPR r.32.5(5).[35]

Evidence: documents

The amount of documentary evidence will vary according to the nature of the issues arising in the application (whether one for renewal or termination).[36] Where only rent is in issue it will be comparatively small, since the bulk of the evidence to be considered by the court will be contained in the proofs of the expert witnesses. Where on the other hand the landlord is proving an intention under para.(f) (demolition and reconstruction), the amount of documentary evidence necessary to establish his intention can be very extensive. It is clearly desirable in the interests of economy for the documents put in evidence to be confined to those which really are necessary. Often, especially in a case under ground (f), documents which have been disclosed to the other side and which were relevant at the time that they were disclosed, have ceased to be relevant by the date of the hearing. For example, if planning permission had not been obtained by the date of disclosure it would be necessary to disclose to the other side all communications with the planning authority which were relevant to the question of whether planning permission was likely to be granted. If, however, planning permission had been obtained by the date of the hearing, all those documents would probably have ceased to be relevant. Clearly, on those facts, the only documents which should be put before the court would be the application for planning permission and the permission itself, together with any supporting drawings or other relevant supporting documents. The bulk of documents can also be reduced in many cases by the parties establishing, either informally or by the service of notices to admit facts, which matters are truly in issue and which are conceded on the basis of the documents which have been disclosed. **11–10**

Once it has been determined which documents are relevant, the parties should seek to agree a bundle.[37] The effect of this agreement is merely that both parties agree that the documents appearing in the bundle are authentic and not forgeries and can be considered by the court without strict proof. The agreement does not prevent either party from criticising the documents, commenting thereon, or suggesting that they do not represent the truth of the matter asserted.[38] Experience has shown that much time can be wasted and much irritation caused **11–11**

---

[35] As to hearsay evidence and evidence as to comparable transactions for the purposes of valuation, see para.11–65 et seq.

[36] Disclosure is dealt with by CPR Pt 31.

[37] See the *Chancery Guide*, para.7.12.

[38] However, note para.7.13 of the *Chancery Guide* which provides:

".13 When agreeing bundles for trial, the parties should establish through their legal representatives, and record in correspondence, whether the agreement of bundles:

(1) extends no further than agreement of the composition and preparation of the bundles; or

(2) includes agreement that the documents in the bundles are authentic (see rule 32.19); or

(3) includes agreement that the documents may be treated as evidence of the facts stated in them.

The court will normally expect parties to agree that the documents, or at any rate the great majority of them, may be treated as evidence of the facts stated in them. A party not willing to agree should,

by the inefficient preparation of bundles of documents. The following suggestions are based upon practical experience[39]:

(1) although it is sometimes convenient to separate various categories of documents into separate bundles, it is usually better to arrange them in strict chronological order[40];
(2) the bundle should be arranged in such a way that the document which is earliest in time appears at the front of the bundle; the practice of arranging them from the back of the bundle causes great inconvenience in relation to any document of more than one page;
(3) the documents should be photocopied on one side of the paper only;
(4) the bundle should be numbered from the front, and it is important that each sheet of paper should have a number; the practice of giving a number to each document causes difficulty where a document has more than one page;
(5) pagination must be agreed between the parties, and experience indicates that the most practical way of achieving uniformity of pagination is for one party to accept the responsibility of preparing all the paginated bundles;
(6) care should be taken to ensure that all photocopies are clearly legible;
(7) normally, six copies of the bundle are required: two for each party; one for the witness; and one for the judge;
(8) where plans or drawings will be put in evidence, the most convenient format in which they are to be prepared for the court will depend upon their size and number. It is often best to prepare a "brochure" of plans and drawings, each of them being open flat rather than folded and bound together either at the top left-hand corner or along the whole of the left-hand side. The plans and drawings themselves will probably have numbers, but it may be convenient for a new numbering system to be devised for easy reference; those numbers should be prominently written on the relevant plan or drawing;
(9) a similar treatment is usually appropriate for photographs. If possible they should be numbered on the front. An index of photographs and a location plan showing where each was taken and in what direction the camera was facing will often be invaluable.

11–12 The practice, which so far as the authors' experience is concerned still appears to be prevalent, of the Claimants' solicitors simply sending to the other parties an index of the bundles, rather than the bundles themselves, is contrary to PD 39. It is provided by PD 39 that "the party filing the trial bundle should supply identical bundles to all the parties to the proceedings and for the use of the witnesses."[41]

---

when the trial bundles are lodged, write a letter to the court (with a copy to all other parties) stating that it is not willing to agree, and explaining why."

[39] Detailed guidelines on the preparation of bundles for trial are to be found in the *Chancery Guide*, paras 7.9 to 7.17 and Appendix 6 thereto, in addition to those contained in PD Pt 39A, miscellaneous provisions relating to hearings, para.3.

[40] This comment is apposite in particular to correspondence bundles. It is usual to have separate bundles for the pleadings, witnesses, expert reports and correspondence depending on the size of the documentation.

[41] PD 39 para.3.10.

Evidence: expert evidence

General

In many cases the parties will seek to rely upon expert evidence either to deal with issues of valuation, e.g. as to the rent for the new tenancy or in seeking to substantiate or resist the landlord's grounds of opposition, e.g. valuation evidence will be required to establish ground (e) and expert evidence may be necessary to deal with the question of the landlord's intention for the purposes of ground (f), e.g. as to the landlord's prospects of obtaining planning permission (where it has not yet been granted), the impact that the proposed works will have on the tenant's business and the duration of the works, etc. **11–13**

Admissibility

Expert evidence is dealt with by CPR Pt 35. The admission of expert evidence is within the complete control of the court in the exercise of its management powers. The CPR makes it clear that: **11–14**

(1) expert evidence is not admissible without permission of the Court (CPR r.35.4(1));
(2) expert evidence may be limited to that which is reasonably required to resolve the proceedings (CPR r.35.1);
(3) the overriding duty of the expert is to the Court (CPR r.35.3).

The underlying objective of the court's control over the admission of expert evidence is to reduce the inappropriate use and the cost of expert evidence. The court in furthering the overriding objective to "actively manage cases" (CPR r.1.4(1)) is required to have regard to "whether the likely benefits of taking a particular step justifies the cost of taking it" (CPR r.1.4(2)(h)). In particular, especially in cases involving the rental value of the premises, the Court will consider whether it is appropriate for a single joint expert to be appointed under CPR r.35.7.[42] The court must examine whether the evidence sought to adduced is admissible expert evidence. It has been said that the party seeking to call the evidence must satisfy the court of the existence of a body of expertise governed by recognised standards of rules of conduct capable of influencing the court's decision on any of the issues which it has to decide and that the witness to be called has a sufficient familiarity with and knowledge of the expertise in question to render his opinion potentially of value in resolving any of those issues.[43] Where the question is one of law, expert evidence will be excluded because that is within the expertise of the court and the expert evidence does not assist.[44]

---

[42] See paras 11–25 to 11–26 for the court's power to direct a single joint expert.

[43] *Barings Plc (In Liquidation) v Coopers & Lybrand*, *Times*, March 7, 2001 Ch. D; *Liverpool Roman Catholic Archdiocesan Trustees Inc v Goldberg* [2001] 4 All E.R. 950, Evans-Lombe J.

[44] *Liverpool Roman Catholic Archdiocesan Trustees Inc v Goldberg* [2001] 4 All E.R. 950 citing *Midland Bank Trust Co Ltd v Hett Stubbs & Kemp* [1979] 1 Ch. 384.

Who is an expert?

11–15 It is said:

> "An expert is a person with a high degree of skill and knowledge in a particular subject, who has relevant and up to date expertise with regard to issues in the case, and sufficient education and communication skills to produce a clear written report, and if necessary, to provide helpful oral evidence to the Court."[45]

An expert may be someone who is employed by one of the parties so long as he is fully familiar with the need for objectivity and aware of the difficult nature of the role of an expert: *Field v Leeds City Council*.[46] Where it is demonstrated that there exists a relationship between the proposed expert and the party calling him which a reasonable observer might think was capable of affecting the views of the expert so as to make them unduly favourable to that party, his evidence should not be admitted however unbiased the conclusions of the expert might probably be.[47]

Court's permission required

11–16 No party may call an expert or put in evidence in an expert's report without the court's permission[48]: CPR r.35.1. In applying for permission the field of expertise

[45] *White Book* (London: Sweet & Maxwell) Vol.1, 2012, notes to CPR 35.2.1. This definition reflects the same definition as appeared in *Civil Procedure*, Autumn 2007, Vol.1, p.950 as was referred to in the previous edition of this work. The definition has remained unchanged since 2001.

[46] [2000] 1 E.G.L.R. 54 CA, a case of housing disrepair. Use of an in-house surveyor may give rise to problems as to the provision of information under CPRr.35.9. It was suggested in that case that, in the circumstances, it may be better to use a third party expert. *Field v Leeds CC* was followed in *Admiral Management Services Ltd v Para Protect Europe Ltd* [2002] EWHC 233 (Ch), a dispute concerning the alleged poaching of employees and intellectual property. The claimant, the first employer, was allowed in principle, to recover the costs of "expert" staff time in searching for, and analysing, material found on the defendant's, the second employer's, computers.

[47] *Liverpool Roman Catholic Archdiocesan Trustees Inc v Goldberg* [2001] 4 All E.R. 950 (expert was barrister in same chambers as defendant). The approach taken by the Judge in that case as to admissibility of the expert evidence was adversely commented upon in *Factortame Ltd v Secretary of State (No.2)* [2002] EWCA Civ 932; [2003] Q.B. 381 at [70]. In *Franks v Towse* [2001] EWCA Civ 9, the Court of Appeal decided that one person could not appear as an advocate and give expert opinion evidence before the Lands Tribunal. Cresswell J. said:

"An expert witness in the High Court should never when giving evidence assume the role of an advocate... Where exceptionally the tribunal grants permission for a chartered surveyor, valuer or estate agent to act both as advocate and as expert witness, when giving evidence as an expert the surveyor, valuer or agent still owes a duty to help the tribunal on matters within his or her expertise, and this duty overrides any obligation to the person from whom he or she receives instructions."

In *Toth v Jarman* [2006] EWCA Civ 1028, the Court of Appeal said that experts' potential conflicts of interest should be disclosed at an early stage in proceedings, and experts might add to the declaration at the end of their report that they had no such conflict.

[48] Pt 56 has been substantially amended to take into account the amendments made by the 2003 Order. It was formerly the case that that claimant was required to file the evidence upon which he intends to rely within 14 days of receipt of the acknowledgment of service, and for the defendant to file his evidence within 14 days of service on him of the claimant's evidence: CPR r.56.3(10) and (11) respectively (now repealed). It was considered that the requirement to obtain the court's permission for expert evidence was not overridden by the requirement for the claimant to file his evidence with his acknowledgement. The position is now made clear. Where the claim is unopposed, no evidence

must be identified and where practicable the name of the expert in that field intended to be relied on: CPR r.35.4(2). The permission will only relate to a named expert in the identified field: CPR r.35.4(3). The practical difficulty for both parties is that invariably they will have retained an expert from whom advice has been sought from very early on in the dispute, possibly pre-institution of proceedings, without knowing whether the court will allow expert evidence to be admitted, or, if it does, whether it will allow more than one expert in any particular field. There is no reason why, however, such an expert should not act as an expert witness for the party who has instructed him. A court may limit the amount of the expert's fees and expenses that the party who wishes to rely on the expert may recover from any other party: CPR r.35.4(4).

The form of expert evidence

Expert evidence is to be given in a written report unless the court directs otherwise: CPR r.35.5. The report must comply with the requirements set out in the Practice Direction and contain the following (CPR r.35.10 and PD 35 paras 2.1 and 2.2): **11–17**

(1) be addressed to the court and not the party from whom the expert has received his instructions;
(2) give details of his qualifications;
(3) give details of any literature or other material which the expert has relied on in making the report;
(4) say who carried out any test or experiment which the expert has used for the report and whether or not the test or experiment has been carried out under the expert's supervision and to give the qualifications of the person who carried out any such test or experiment;
(5) where there is a range of opinion on matters dealt with in the report, to summarise the range of opinion and to give reasons for his own opinion;
(6) contain a summary of the conclusions reached;
(7) contain a statement that the expert understands his duty to the court and has complied with that duty (CPR r.35.10(2) and PD35 para.3(9)); and
(8) contain a statement setting out the substance of all material instructions (whether written or oral). The statement should summarise the facts and instructions given to the expert which are material to the opinions expressed in the report or upon which those opinions are based (CPR r.35.10(3)).

The expert's report must be verified by a statement of truth (PD 35 para.3.3) in the following form, namely:

---

need be filed unless and until the court directs it to be filed: PD 56 para.3.14. Where the claim is opposed it is provided that the evidence (including expert evidence) must be filed by the parties as the court directs and the landlord shall be required to file his evidence first: PD56 para.3.15. Where the claim is a landlord's termination application, the evidence will be directed in accordance with the usual directions given at the management conference held on a Pt 7 claim.

> "I confirm that I have made clear which facts and matters referred to in this report are within my own knowledge and which are not. Those that are within my own knowledge I confirm to be true. The opinions I have expressed represent my true and complete professional opinions on the matters to which they refer."

It is to be noted that the instruction referred to in item (8) above will not be protected by privilege: CPR r.35.10(4). However, cross-examination of the expert on the contents of his instructions will not be allowed unless the court permits (or unless the party who gave the instructions consents to it). Before it gives permission the court must be satisfied that there are reasonable grounds to consider that the statement in the report of the substance of the instructions is inaccurate or incomplete. If the court is so satisfied it will allow the cross-examination of where it appears to be in the interests of justice to do so: CPR r.35.10(4); PD 35 para.5.

Exchange of expert evidence

11–18 The court will usually direct there to be a simultaneous exchange of expert evidence.[49] If the report is not exchanged on the date directed by the court it is not necessary for the other party to enquire whether a report is being served or seek a debarring order: *Baron v Lovell*.[50] It is for the party who seeks to rely on the expert evidence to seek permission and such permission should be sought promptly.[51] Serving expert evidence late may not be fatal to its admission. In *Meredith v Colleys Valuation Services Ltd*[52] the Court of Appeal reversed the first instance decision, preventing a defendant from relying upon an expert report served two weeks late, because the delay was short, there was no unless order, the claimant had the report and costs penalties were a preferable alternative sanction. In *RC Residuals Ltd v Linton Fuel Oils Ltd*[53] both parties were late serving their expert evidence, and the trial was adjourned. The claimant served expert reports respectively 10 and 20 minutes beyond the time specified in an "unless" order.

---

[49] In an appropriate case the court may order sequential exchange: see the *Chancery Guide,* Ch.4, para.4.15. It is said that "Sequential reports may, for example, be appropriate if the service of the first expert's report would help to define and limit the issues on which such evidence may be relevant."

[50] [1999] C.P.L.R. 630 CA.

[51] [1999] C.P.L.R. 630 CA.

[52] [2001] EWCA Civ 1456. A party who fails to serve an expert report in time will need leave of the court for an extension of time. By CPR r.35.13 it is provided that:

"A party who fails to disclose an expert's report may not use the report at the trial or call the expert to give evidence orally unless the court gives permission."

In *Meredith v Colleys Valuation Services Ltd*[2001] EWCA Civ 1456, the Court of Appeal followed the earlier decision of *Bansal v Cheema* [2001] C.P. Rep. 6 CA, to the effect that it was essential for courts, in exercising their discretion to extend time for service, to consider each matter listed under CPR r.3.9(1) (which lists a number of matters which the court must consider in dealing with an application for an extension of time for compliance). See also *Keith v CPM Field Marketing Ltd* [2001] C.P. Rep. 35. More recently the Court of Appeal has stated that the court must conduct an appropriate review and balancing exercise but need not mention expressly all of the circumstances in the list: *Khatib v Ramco International* [2011] EWCA Civ 605.

[53] [2002] EWCA Civ 911; [2002] 1 W.L.R. 2782.

The judge struck out the evidence, but the Court of Appeal allowed the appeal as the defendant had refused service of the reports by email,[54] and the new trial date would not be affected.

The expert's duty to the court

The duty of the expert is to the court: CPR r.35.3.[55] In this regard it is to be noted: **11–19**

(1) that the report shall be addressed to the court and not the party from whom the expert has received his instructions (PD 35 para.3.1); and
(2) at the end of his report there must be a statement that (a) the expert understands his duty to the court and (b) he has complied with that duty (CPR r.35.10(2); PD 35 para.3.2(9)).

The duties and responsibilities of experts, in relation to the court was considered by Cresswell J. in *National Justice Compania Naviera SA v Prudential Assurance Co Ltd*, commonly known as "the *Ikarian Reefer*".[56] It was said: **11–20**

> "1. Expert evidence presented to the Court should be, and should be seen to be, the independent product of the expert uninfluenced as to the form or content by the exigencies of litigation (*Whitehouse v Jordan* [1981] 1 W.L.R. 246, House of Lords at 256 per Lord Wilberforce).
> 2. An expert witness should provide independent assistance to the Court by way of objective unbiased opinion in relation to matters within his expertise (see *Polivitte Ltd v Commercial Union Assurance Co Plc* [1987] 1 Lloyd's Rep. 379 at 386 per Garland J; and *Re Jay* [1990] F.C.R 193 per Cazalet J. An expert witness in the High Court should never assume the role of an advocate.
> 3. An expert witness should state the facts or assumption on which his opinion is based. He should not omit to consider material facts which could detract from his concluded opinion (*Re Jay*, above).
> 4. An expert witness should make it clear when a particular question or issue falls outside his expertise.
> 5. If an expert's opinion is not properly researched because he considers that insufficient data are available then this must be stated with an indication that the opinion is no more than a provisional one (*Re Jay*, above). In cases where an expert witness who has prepared a report could not assert that the report contained the truth, the whole truth and nothing but the truth without some qualification that qualification should be stated in the report (*Darby & Co Ltd v Welldon (No.9)*, *The Times*, November 9, 1990, CA, per Staughton L.J.).
> 6. If, after exchange of reports, an expert witness changes his view on the material having read the other side's expert report or for any other reason, such change of view should be communicated (through legal representatives), to the other side without delay and when appropriate to the Court.

---

[54] It was said that a solicitor who adopted a rigid policy of not accepting service by e-mail could not expect the court, in an age where electronic communication is now becoming more and more common, to take an unsympathetic stance to an application by the other side for an extension of time when the matter, being one of urgency, could have been dealt with in the time limit if electronic means had been used.

[55] As the expert's first duty is to the court, he has direct access to it in that he may, without giving notice to any party, file a written request with the court for directions to assist him in carrying out his functions as an expert: CPR r.35.14.

[56] [1993] 2 E.G.L.R. 183. The approach of Cresswell J. was approved by Otton L.J. in *Stanton v Callaghan* [1992] Q.B. 936 CA.

7. Where expert evidence refers to photographs, plans, calculations, analyses, measurements survey reports or other similar documents, these must be provided to the opposite party at the same time as the exchange of reports."

11–21 The expert's duties as set out in the *Ikarian Reefer* are reflected in the CPR—CPR r.35.3, CRP 35.10 and the accompanying Practice Direction. The general requirements reflected in PD 35 paras 2 and 3 are expanded upon in the Protocol (the Protocol for the Instruction of Experts to give Evidence in Civil Claims) annexed to the Practice Direction: PD35 Protocol para.4. A failure by the expert to understand that his duty is the court may entitle the court to debar the expert from acting as a witness in the proceedings: *Stevens v Gullis*.[57]

11–22 In *Anglo Group Plc v Winther Brown & Co Ltd*,[58] Judge Toulmin QC said that Cresswell J.'s analysis needed to be extended to accommodate the CPR. He said:

"1. An expert witness should at all stages in the procedure, on the basis of the evidence as he understands it, provide independent assistance to the Court and the parties by way of objective unbiased opinion in relation to matters within his expertise. This applies as much to the initial meetings of experts as to evidence at trial. An expert witness should never assume the role of an advocate.

2. The expert's evidence should normally be confined to technical matters on which the Court will be assisted by receiving an explanation, or to evidence of common professional practice or to evidence of common professional practice. The expert witness should not give evidence or opinions as to what the expert himself would have done in similar circumstances or otherwise seek to usurp the role of the Judge.

3. He should co-operate with the expert or the other party or parties in attempting to narrow the technical issues in dispute at the earliest possible stage of the procedure and to eliminate or place in context any peripheral issues. He should co-operate with the other expert(s) in attending without prejudice meetings as necessary and in seeking to find areas of agreement and to define precisely areas of disagreement to be set out in the joint statement of experts ordered by the Court.

4. The evidence presented to the Court should be, and be seen to be, the independent product of the expert uninfluenced as to form or content by the exigencies of the litigation.

5. An expert witness should state the facts or assumptions upon which his opinion is based. He should not omit to consider material facts which could detract from his concluded opinion.

6. An expert witness should make it clear when a particular question or issue falls outside his expertise.

7. Where an expert is of the opinion that his conclusions are based on inadequate factual information he should say so explicitly.

8. An expert should be ready to reconsider his opinion, and if appropriate, to change his mind when he has received new information or has considered the opinion of the other expert. He should do so at the earliest opportunity".

11–23 The RICS issued a practice statement in 1997. The third edition of its practice statement was published in 2009 and is combined with guidance notes for surveyors acting as expert witnesses. The practice statement and guidance notes emphasise the need for independence. The importance of complying with the

---

[57] [2000] 1 All E.R. 527; [1999] 3 E.G.L.R. 71 CA, where the expert had demonstrated that he had no conception of the requirements of the court with regard to experts.

[58] [2000] All E.R. (D) 294. The role of the expert witness as expounded in the *Ikarian Reefer* was said to be in need of extension in accordance with the CPR.

RICS guidance is reflected in the observations of A.J. Trott FRICS in *Re Pottier*[59] where he said (in the context of a case concerning restrictive covenants):

> "… Neither expert has, in my opinion, complied with the requirements of the RICS Practice Statement "Surveyors Acting as Expert Witnesses" Third Edition (effective 3 January 2009) despite having declared their compliance with it. It is not sufficient for expert Chartered Surveyor witnesses to pay lip service to this practice statement while ignoring its substantive requirements. Such failure to comply will inevitably mean that the expert's evidence will carry little or no weight, as is the case here."

Although the RICS Code is not the subject of a Practice Direction, the Code, as with other professional codes, may be taken into consideration by the court in dealing with expert evidence.

A code of guidance for expert evidence has been prepared: the *Protocol for the Instruction of Experts to give Evidence in Civil Claims* is annexed to CPR PD35. **11–24**

Single joint expert

Where two or more parties wish to submit expert evidence on a particular issue, the court may direct that the evidence on that issue is to be given by one expert only: CPR r.35.7.[60] It is said: **11–25**

> "It may be anticipated that the Court is likely to direct that the evidence on a particular issue is to be given by a single joint expert where it appears to the Court, on the information then available, that the issue falls within a substantially established area of knowledge and where it is not necessary for the Court to sample a range of opinion."[61]

The objective of appointing a single joint expert is to reduce costs and to reduce delay. One perennial problem is, however, that the parties will ordinarily have received expert advice at an early stage from an expert (and in many cases often prior to the institution of proceedings). When the court considers the question of expert evidence at directions, it may be disproportionate to order a single joint expert, which will involve new instructions and further expense. Furthermore, even if a single joint expert is appointed, it is likely that the parties will wish to retain their own appointed expert to advise on the report of the single joint expert. The court may, instead of ordering a single joint expert, seek to reduce costs by framing the directions in an attempt to narrow issues between the experts, e.g. by requiring service of written questions and of without prejudice discussions (as to which see further below).

A single joint expert is either a person agreed upon by the parties or such other person (where the parties are unable to agree) who is selected in such manner as the court may direct, e.g. by the appointment of a valuer by the RICS (CPR r.35.7(2)). Each instructing party may give instructions to the expert: CPR **11–26**

---

[59] [2010] UKUT 206 (LC).

[60] The parties may, of course, agree to instructing a single joint expert but this is rare.

[61] *Civil Procedure*, Vol.1, 2012, notes to para.35.7.1. See also the *Chancery Guide*, Ch.4, paras 4.11 to 4.14.

r.35.8(1).[62] It is preferable that the form of the instructions should be agreed if possible: *Daniels v Walker*.[63] If the expert receives conflicting instructions he may apply to the court for directions: CPR r.35.14. The parties are jointly and severally liable, unless the court otherwise orders, for the costs of the single joint expert: CPR r.35.8(5). In appointing a single joint expert, the court may give directions about the payment of his fees and expenses and any inspections examination or experiments which he may wish to carry out: CPR r.35.8(3) The court may, before an expert is instructed, limit the amount that can be paid by way of fees and expenses to the expert and direct that the instructing parties pay that amount into court: CPR r.3 5.8(4).

Challenging report

11–27 What if either party is unhappy with the single joint expert's report? What can be done? Permission may be granted to enable the dissatisfied party to appoint another expert to challenge the report of the single joint expert: *Daniels v Walker*.[64] In that case Lord Woolf M.R. said:

> "In a substantial case such as this, the correct approach is to regard the instruction of an expert jointly by the parties as the first step in obtaining expert evidence on a particular issue. It is to be hoped that in the majority of cases it will not only be the first step but the last step. If, having obtained a joint expert's report, a party, for reasons which are not fanciful, wishes to obtain further information before making a decision as to whether or not there is a particular part (or indeed the whole) of the expert's report which he or she may wish to challenge, then they should, subject to the discretion of the court, be permitted to obtain that evidence.
>
> In the majority of cases, the sensible approach will not be to ask the court straight away to allow the dissatisfied party to call a second expert. In many cases it would be wrong to make a decision until one is in a position to consider the position in the round. You cannot make generalisations, but in a case where there is a modest sum involved a court may take a more rigorous approach. It may be said in a case where there is a modest amount involved that it would be disproportionate to obtain a second report in any circumstances. At most what should be allowed is merely to put a question to the expert who has already prepared a report . . .
>
> In a case where there is a substantial sum involved, one starts, as I have indicated, from the position that, wherever possible, a joint report is obtained. If there is disagreement on that report, then there would be an issue as to whether to ask questions or whether to get your own expert's report. If questions do not resolve the matter and a party, or both parties, obtain their own expert's reports, then that will result in a decision having to be reached as to what evidence should be called. That decision should not be taken until there has been a meeting between the experts involved. It may be that agreement could then be reached; it may be that agreement is reached as a result of asking the appropriate questions. It is only as a last resort that you accept that it is necessary for oral evidence to be given by the experts before the court. The expense of cross examination of expert witnesses at the hearing, even in a substantial case, can be very expensive."

---

[62] It is impermissible for one party to attend a conference with the joint single expert in the absence of a representative of the other: *Peet v Mid-Kent Area Healthcare National Health Service Trust*, November 5, 2001 CA.

[63] [2000] 1 W.L.R. 1382 CA.

[64] [2000] 1 W.L.R. 1382 CA. In *Peet v Mid-Kent Area Healthcare NHS Trust* [2001] EWCA Civ 1703 the Court of Appeal expressed the view that a good reason was required for the appointment of a further expert witness following the appointment of a joint single expert, particularly in the case of non-medical expert evidence.

In *Cosgrove v Pattison*[65] a party was given leave to call evidence from a second expert when that party alleged that the single joint expert might be biased and the appointment of and the giving of evidence by that party's own expert would not give rise to any further delay or additional costs, as he was already involved in the case as a witness of fact. Neuberger J. said:

> "In my judgment although it would be wrong to pretend that this is an exhaustive list, the factors to be taken into account when considering an application to permit a further expert to be called are these. First, the nature of the issue or issues; secondly, the number of issues between the parties; thirdly, the reason the new expert is wanted; fourthly, the amount at stake and, if it is not purely money, the nature of the issues at stake and their importance; fifthly, the effect of permitting one party to call further expert evidence on the conduct of the trial; sixthly, the delay, if any, in making the application, seventhly, any delay that the instructing and calling of the new expert will cause; eighthly, any other special features of the case; and, finally, and in a sense all embracing, the overall justice to the parties in the context of the litigation."

Later he said:

> "As [counsel], who appears on behalf of the respondents argues, it cannot be enough for a person who wants to call a new expert, simply to say: 'I have a report from another expert and it is inconsistent with the agreed expert's conclusion'. Otherwise, anyone who had the money and the inclination to instruct another expert would always have the right to call him. Having said that, it does seem to me that if a new expert can be found who has a contrary view to the joint expert that is a reason for perm itting that new expert to be called. It is certainly not a sufficient reason in every case, but if there are grounds for thinking that the joint expert may be wrong, because another expert takes a different view, that is certainly a factor which is to be borne in mind."

Cross-examination of single joint expert

In the ordinary course of events it is inappropriate where a single joint expert gives oral evidence for him to be cross-examined.[66] **11–28**

---

[65] [2001] C.P. Rep. 68; [2001] C.P.L.R. 177 Ch D, case involving a boundary dispute.

[66] *Peet v Mid-Kent Area Healthcare NHS Trust* [2001] EWCA Civ 1703; [2002] 1 W.L.R. 210. The contrary view is expressed in *Civil Procedure*, Vol.1 2012, notes to CPR r.35.7.1 ("If a single joint expert is called to give oral evidence at trial, it is submitted, although the rule and the practice direction do not make this clear, that both parties will have the opportunity to cross-examine him/her, but with a degree of restraint, given that the expert has been instructed by the parties"), and this seems to have been assumed in *Daniels v Walker* [2000] 1 W.L.R. 1382 CA, where Lord Woolf said that each party has "an opportunity to question the expert". However, Lord Woolf was the presiding judge in *Peet v Mid-Kent Area Healthcare NHS Trust*. In *Peet v Mid-Kent Area Healthcare NHS Trust* Lord Woolf C.J. said:

"28 That paragraph [i.e. that text in the notes to the White Book] may be applicable in some cases, but it certainly should not be regarded as being of general application. I summarise my reasons for so saying. The starting point is: unless there is reason for not having a single expert, there should be only a single expert. If there is no reason which justifies more evidence than that from a single expert on any particular topic, then again in the normal way the report prepared by the single expert should be the evidence in the case on the issues covered by that expert's report. In the normal way, therefore, there should be no need for that report to be amplified or tested by cross-examination. If it needs amplification, or if it should be subject to cross-examination, the court has a discretion to allow that to happen. The court may permit that to happen either prior to the hearing or at the hearing. But the assumption should be that the single joint expert's report is the evidence. Any amplification or any cross-examination should be restricted as far as possible. Equally, where parties agree that there should be a single joint expert, and a single joint expert produces a report, it is possible for the court

Written questions to experts

11–29 After receipt of an expert report, either an expert instructed by another party, or of a report of a single joint expert, the recipient has an opportunity (once only without the court's permission) to put questions to the expert. Such questions must be in writing and put within 28 days of the service of the report: CPR r.35.6.[67] The questions are limited to questions for the purposes of clarification unless the court or the other party otherwise agrees.[68] The answer to the questions form part of the evidence of the expert: r.35.6(3). They should be verified by a statement of truth: PD 35 para.3.3.[69] If the expert does not answer questions asked of him the court may order that the party who instructed the expert cannot rely on the evidence of that expert or recover the fees of that expert from any other party: CPR r.35.6(4). No time period is specified for answering the questions unless this has already been the subject of a court direction.

Use of expert report

11–30 Once an expert report has been prepared and disclosed, any party may use it as evidence at the trial: CPR r.35.11. If a party fails to disclose an expert report contrary to an order of the court, that party may not use it at trial or call the expert to give oral evidence without the permission of the court: CPR r.35.13. It is now no longer acceptable for expert evidence to be served late: *Baron v Lovell*.[70] The court has wide powers as to the sequence of exchange of expert reports. The court may order simultaneous or sequential exchange.[71]

Power of court to direct a party to provide information

11–31 Where a party has access to information which is not reasonably available to the other party, the court may direct the party who has access to it to prepare and file a document recording the information and serve a copy of that document on the other party: CPR r.35.9. Thus one can envisage circumstances where the issue is one of rent and the landlord has a portfolio of properties and, therefore, an available source of comparables unavailable to the tenant.

---

still to permit a party to instruct his or her own expert and for that expert to be called at the hearing. However, there must be good reason for that course to be adopted. Normally, where the issue is of the sort that is covered by non-medical evidence, as in this case, the court should be slow to allow a second expert to be instructed."

[67] A copy of the questions should be sent to the solicitors for the party instructing the expert: PD 35 para.6.1. The fees for answering the questions are to be paid by the party instructing the expert: PD 35 para.6.2.This does not affect any decision of the court as to the party who is ultimately to bear the experts costs: para.6.2.

[68] See the *Chancery Guide*, Ch.4, para.4.19.

[69] The PD does not say so expressly but as the material is treated as part of the expert's evidence it is considered that PD35 para.3.3 would apply.

[70] [1999] C.P.L.R. 630 CA. See also para.11–18.

[71] See fn.52, para.11–18.

Without prejudice discussions

The court will, as part of the directions relating to the admissibility of expert evidence, order that there be a discussion between the experts before and/or after the exchange of expert reports in order to narrow the issues between the parties: CPR r.35.12.[72] The rule refers to a discussion and although usually the nature of the discussion is by way of a meeting, it need not be, e.g. it may be by telephone. The purpose of such discussions is (1) to identify the issues of the proceedings and (2) where possible, to reach agreement on an issue. The content of the discussion between the experts is not referred to at trial unless the parties agree. Ordinarily the court directs that the experts produce a statement of what is and what is not agreed and a summary of their reasons for disagreeing. However, CPR r.35.12(5) provides that where experts reach agreement on an issue during the discussions the agreement shall not bind the parties unless the parties expressly agree to be bound by the agreement: CPR r.35.12(5). **11–32**

Inadmissible material contained in report

If, upon perusal of the other side's expert report it appears to contain material which is or may be inadmissible, it is prudent to raise any objection before the report is put in evidence. By that time, the damage may have been done (*Rogers v Rosedimond*[73] (digested in para.11–34)) or the point as to inadmissibility may be taken to have been waived (*Town Centre Securities v Wm Morrison*[74] (digested in para.11–35)). Although these decisions concern the admissibility of hearsay evidence, and must now be read subject to the Civil Evidence Act 1995 which renders hearsay evidence admissible in any event, they illustrate the need for early objection to the contents of an expert report if objection is to be taken, e.g. it may be that the report strays into matters which are outside the relevant field of expertise or refers to without prejudice negotiations. **11–33**

Rogers v Rosedimond Investments (Blakes Market)[75] The only issue on the hearing of the tenant's application for a new tenancy was how much the rent should be for the ensuing term. The tenant under his old tenancy of a shop unit in an arcade of similar units was paying £1,500. He was willing to increase this to £2,000 subject to rent reviews, but the landlord wanted a rent of £2,500. The tenant called as witnesses two traders of neighbouring shop units similar to that of the tenant's. Those two traders were already paying the rent asked for by the landlord from the tenant under the new tenancy. They gave evidence that the trading conditions of the arcade were not as good as they had expected when they took on their tenancies and that, in their opinion, the rent they were paying was too high and that a reasonable rent for their properties was £1,800–£2,000. The tenant also called an expert witness who gave evidence of comparables. That witness had not, however, seen the leases which provided for the rents that he **11–34**

[72] See also, the *Chancery Guide*, Ch.4, para.4.16 et seq.

[73] [1978] 2 E.G.L.R. 48 CA.

[74] [1982] 2 E.G.L.R. 114.

[75] [1978] 2 E.G.L.R. 48 CA.

said were being paid for the comparables. The judge reached the conclusion, on the evidence, that the proper rent was £1,750, though he increased this to £2,000 because the tenant was willing to pay £2,000. The judge, however, in reaching that decision, said that he relied heavily on the evidence of the two traders. It was held that although the traders could give admissible evidence on the trading conditions of the arcade, that evidence had to be carefully and critically considered as it was tainted by the personal trading experience of the witness, such as his individual trading capacity and opportunities. In accepting their entire evidence without considered reflection, the judge accepted totally their rental valuations for their own particular shop units. This was inadmissible and a retrial had to be ordered. As the first point had been decided in favour of the landlord, it was unnecessary to express any view on the inadmissibility of the evidence of the expert witness. However, Roskill L.J. was of the view that if the only objection to the judge's decision was hearsay evidence having been admitted, he would have hesitated before ordering a retrial. The issue of hearsay had not been raised before final speeches before the trial judge, the judge may have ordered an adjournment, albeit at the landlord's risk and the landlord may, under pressure of costs, have felt it reasonable to allow the evidence, albeit hearsay, to be admitted.

11–35 ***Town Centre Securities Ltd v Wm Morrison Supermarkets Ltd***[76] An expert giving oral evidence at a rent review arbitration relied upon comparables of which he did not have a first-hand knowledge. No objection was taken to the admission of that evidence at the hearing. On appeal from the arbitrator on the ground that the expert's evidence ought not to have been admitted, it was held that although evidence of comparables on which an expert relies in support of his opinion ought to be direct not hearsay evidence, the failure to object to inadmissible evidence at the hearing resulted in an implied agreement or waiver of the right to insist upon strict compliance with the rules of evidence.

2. EVIDENCING GROUND (A) (DILAPIDATIONS)[77]

The landlord's case

11–36 In practical terms, the landlord is unlikely to have specified ground (a) unless he has satisfied himself at the date he serves the notice that there are substantial breaches of the repairing covenants contained in the current tenancy. Normally his surveyor will have inspected and carried out an interim schedule of dilapidations. This may or may not have been served upon the tenant under cover of a s.146 notice. In order to substantiate his case at trial the landlord will have to rely upon that schedule, and his surveyor will have to give expert evidence as to his estimate of the cost of complying with the works and the time necessary for doing so. It will also be relevant for the court to be informed of the length of time during which the dilapidations have existed, whether this has been brought to the tenant's attention by the landlord and whether any earlier schedules have been served. The court will also be concerned to know whether the dilapidations have,

[76] [1982] 2 E.G.L.R. 114.

[77] As to this ground of opposition, see para.7–10 et seq.

in reality, caused any damage to the landlord's reversion or whether they are items of a trivial nature which a reasonably minded tenant in occupation might be content to put up with. All these matters affect the manner in which the court will exercise its discretion.

"Scott" schedules

Normally, the tenant will himself appoint a surveyor to advise on the landlord's schedule of dilapidations. In giving that advice, the surveyor will probably agree with some of the items and pricings contained in the landlord's schedule, while disagreeing with others. Where there are many items on the schedule and there is a substantial difference of opinion between the surveyors, it is usually convenient for their respective contentions to be set out in a schedule prepared in official referee's form (a "Scott schedule"). This will be arranged in several columns. The headings of those columns will vary according to the facts of each particular case but the following is the most common format: **11–37**

(1) The items of alleged disrepair are set out, numbered separately.
(2) The landlord states his contention as to the price of each item.
(3) The landlord sets out any particular comment which he wishes to make upon any item.
(4) The tenant states whether he accepts that the particular disrepair covered by the item exists.
(5) The tenant states the price of remedying the disrepair in respect to each item which he admits and, sometimes, in the alternative to his contention that there is no disrepair, in relation to some of the disputed items.
(6) The tenant makes such comments as he wishes in respect of each item.
(7) A column is left for the use of the judge, who will indicate there his finding in relation to each item. In respect of items upon which the parties are in agreement, an appropriate figure is sometimes put as an agreed figure in the judge's column.

It should, however, be emphasised that a Scott schedule will not be appropriate in all cases because exact quantification of the disrepairs is not always required, as it would be in a claim for damages. Since the court is required to decide whether the landlord has established his ground of opposition under para.(a) as at the date of the hearing, both surveyors should inspect shortly before the trial and inform the court of the up-to-date position in their oral evidence.

The tenant's case

Since the tenant's proposals for the future are relevant to the exercise by the court of its discretion, he may decide to offer an undertaking to carry out all or some of the works contained in the landlord's schedule within a specified time. The court will take such a proposal more seriously if the tenant is able to state in detail which items are accepted and which are not and what is a realistic timetable in **11–38** which those works can be completed. The court may also require to be satisfied that the tenant has sufficient funds to carry out the proposed programme of works.

3. EVIDENCING GROUND (B) (PERSISTENT ARREARS)[78]

The landlord's case: evidence of arrears

11–39 The most convenient way in which a landlord can demonstrate to the court that there has been persistent delay in paying rent which has become due is to prepare a schedule of arrears. This should set out the following matters in chronological order:

(1) When rent has become due pursuant to the terms of the lease and in what amount.
(2) When payments have been made by the tenant (including, in each case, how many days late).
(3) A running total showing how much rent has been due and unpaid from time to time.
(4) What reminders have been sent and in what form, e.g. rent demands, reminders from managing agents or solicitors' letters.
(5) What enforcement action has had to be taken, such as the issue of proceedings, the obtaining of judgment, or the issuing of writs of possession.

If possible, this schedule, which is of a purely factual nature, should be agreed with the tenant. If the tenant is not prepared to agree the schedule, the landlord will need to prove the case set out in the schedule, by producing the originals of the relevant documents and by the oral evidence of those instructed to receive rent on the landlord's behalf, the solicitors who wrote the letters, etc. A tenant who is unwilling or reluctant to agree a schedule may be induced to change his mind by service of a notice to admit facts: CPR r.32.18.[79]

Evidence of prejudice to landlord

11–40 Since the ground under (b) is discretionary, the landlord in seeking to persuade the court not to grant a new tenancy will wish to emphasise the trouble and expense caused by the tenant's past failure to pay rent. If the landlord is an individual, he may give evidence of the time and trouble which he has had to take in order to chase the arrears, or if he has had to pay a managing agent, the extra expense which has been involved because of the tenant's default. If the landlord is a company, it may be able to show how many hours of administrative time have been taken up in dealing with the tenant's arrears. Where proceedings have been brought, the landlord may wish to show how much legal expense has been

[78] As to this ground of opposition, see para.7–27 et seq.

[79] The failure to admit facts without good reason would undoubtedly be a factor to which the court will have regard in considering costs: CPR r.44.3 and 44.4.

involved, and especially the amount by which solicitor-and-own-client costs have exceeded any costs which may have been awarded to the landlord by the court.

The tenant's case

11–41 The tenant will wish to tip the balance of the court's discretion in his favour. He may have some excuse or explanation for the failure to pay rent which he should put before the court, supported by suitable documentary and oral evidence. Equally importantly, he will wish to satisfy the court that, whatever may have been his past record, it will not be repeated under any new tenancy. The court should be informed in detail of the tenant's financial resources and how he expects to meet his obligation to pay the new rent. As an earnest of good faith, it is often wise for a tenant to offer to give some form of security to the landlord, such as the payment of rent in advance for, say, a year, the depositing of a sum by way of security, or the provision of satisfactory guarantors.

4. EVIDENCING GROUND (C) (OTHER BREACHES)[80]

The landlord's case

11–42 The ambit of ground (c) is extremely wide.[81] Where the landlord is relying upon breaches of the terms of the tenancy, he should prove those breaches to the satisfaction of the court in the ordinary way, as he would in an action for forfeiture or damages. Where "other reasons" are relied upon, the landlord may have to show that the tenant's use or management of the holding is illegal or immoral or contrary to public policy. This may involve the landlord in proof of the exact planning status of the premises, or other matters of a general nature.

Evidence of prejudice to landlord

11–43 Since the ground specified in para.(c) is discretionary, the landlord may have to satisfy the court that the breaches of covenant or other matters relied upon are not merely technical breaches, but have caused loss and inconvenience to the landlord or to the public at large. In particular, it will be relevant whether the landlord has complained about the breaches during the current tenancy and, if so, what action the tenant has taken to remedy them.

The tenant's case

11–44 As in all the discretionary grounds, an explanation by the tenant for his past conduct and his proposals as to the future will be relevant. Where some sort of explanation or excuse is offered for past breaches and an undertaking not to repeat them is considered by the court to be sincere, it may exercise its discretion in favour of the tenant. Whether the court would be entitled to accept an

[80] As to this ground of opposition, see para.7–42 et seq.
[81] See para.7–47.

undertaking by the tenant to do something positive in the future (as opposed to a negative undertaking not to do something in the future) has been covered earlier.[82]

5. EVIDENCING GROUND (D) (SUITABLE ALTERNATIVE ACCOMMODATION)[83]

The offer

11–45 Normally a landlord will prove that he has offered accommodation by putting in evidence the letter in which the offer was made. A discussion of what sort of offer is required to have been made has been considered in Ch.7.[84]

Intention

11–46 Where a landlord is an individual, he should show his willingness at the date of the hearing to provide, or secure the provision of, alternative accommodation by oral testimony. Where the landlord is a company, the willingness can be proved in the same way as a landlord proves his intention under ground (f) or (g) (see paras 11–54 and 11–55). Clearly, in giving that evidence, the landlord must explain precisely what is the accommodation that he is offering and how it is that he is able to provide it or secure its provision. Where the landlord proves that he himself is the owner of the accommodation, he will also have to show that he is able to let it to the tenant with vacant possession. Where the landlord does not own the alternative accommodation, he will have to prove that the owner is willing to let it to the tenant; usually it will be necessary for the owner of the property to give evidence of this fact. If the landlord does not own the alternative premises, but intends to purchase them or to take them on lease before letting them to the tenant, he will have to provide evidence of his financial ability to do so.

Terms of offer

11–47 The landlord must establish the detailed terms upon which the alternative accommodation is offered, since the court must consider whether they are reasonable having regard to the terms of the current tenancy.

Nature of premises offered

11–48 When the court is deciding the question of suitability, the first element to be considered is the nature of the offered premises. The court will have to be informed of the location of the premises, which is best done by a location plan showing the offered and the existing premises, supplemented by oral evidence (probably of an expert) on how those locations compare. The physical dimensions

[82] See para.7–222.
[83] As to this ground of opposition, see para.7–56 et seq.
[84] See paras 7–57 to 7–62.

and layout of the offered premises can best be demonstrated by a suitable floor plan, which can once again be supplemented by oral evidence, probably of an expert. For purposes of comparison, equivalent information should be supplied in respect of the existing premises. The court may require to be satisfied that the offered premises are in good condition by the evidence of a surveyor. Where it is apparent that the tenant is likely to make detailed criticism of the offered premises, it may be helpful for the court to view both the existing and the offered premises.

Nature of tenant's business

The second element to be considered in relation to reasonableness concerns the nature and requirements of the tenant's business, including the requirement to preserve goodwill. In some cases the nature of the tenant's business, its requirements, and the way in which its goodwill would or would not be affected by a change in location, will be readily apparent. In others, it may be necessary for both parties to call expert evidence about the nature and requirements of a particular kind of business and as to how the goodwill of such a kind of business would be affected by a move. The tenant may wish to adduce evidence in relation to the special requirements of his particular business. Where these matters are fiercely in controversy, the landlord will probably seek extensive disclosure from the tenant of documents showing the nature of the business, the extent to which it is dependent on passing trade or attracts a clientele from a particular location, and of the accounts. **11–49**

6. EVIDENCING GROUND (E) (SUB-LETTING OF PART)[85]

The conveyancing background

In order to prove that the current tenancy was created by the sub-letting of part only of the property comprised in a superior tenancy and that the landlord is the owner of an interest in reversion expectant on the termination of that superior tenancy, it will be necessary to produce documentary evidence of the landlord's title, the creation of the superior tenancy and the creation of the sub-tenancy. Insofar as the original positions of landlord, superior tenant and sub-tenant have been affected by deeds of variation, deeds of assignment, deeds of surrender and notices, these too must be put in evidence before the court. **11–50**

Valuation evidence

Expert evidence from a valuer is necessary in order to prove: (1) what rent could be obtained on a separate letting of the holding; (2) what rent could be obtained on a separate letting of the rest of the property comprised in the superior tenancy; **11–51**

[85] As to this ground of opposition, see para.7–76 et seq.

and (3) what rent could be obtained on a letting of the whole. In the absence of such valuation evidence, the landlord will be unable to prove his case under ground (e).[86]

The landlord's requirement

11–52 In order to prove that, on the termination of the current tenancy, the landlord requires possession of the holding for the purpose of letting or otherwise disposing of the property as a whole, the landlord will have to provide evidence of his intention for the future of the premises and his ability to implement that intention. The evidence necessary to establish both elements of his intention are similar to those arising under ground (f).[87]

7. EVIDENCING GROUND (F) (DEMOLITION AND RECONSTRUCTION)[88]

The works

11–53 Central to the landlord's case under ground (f) is the extent of the works which he claims to intend to carry out. Normally the landlord will produce plans drawn up by an architect or surveyor showing the holding in its existing state. Either by means of suitable notation upon those plans or by another set of plans, he will show what works are intended. Often the landlord will have gone out to tender by the date of the hearing and the bills of specification and tender can be usefully put before the court in order to provide a verbal description of what is intended. The landlord should be in a position to cost the works, at least in approximate terms, since this will both inform the court of their substantiality and will relate to the issue of whether the landlord has the capacity to carry out his plans. A programme of works, perhaps supported by a bar chart, indicating at what stage particular phases or items are to be completed, will show the substantiality of the works in terms of time and may be relevant under s.31A.[89] Although to a certain extent these documents may be self explanatory, it is usually desirable that oral evidence should be called from an architect, surveyor, engineer, or project manager for the purposes of explaining them to the court and answering any questions arising out of them. In preparing such evidence for trial it is important to bear in mind the general guidance given above.[90]

---

[86] As to expert evidence generally, see para.11–13 et seq.

[87] See paras 11–54 to 11–55.

[88] As to this ground of opposition, see para.7–87.

[89] See para.11–56.

[90] See paras 11–09 (oral evidence), 11–10, 11–11 (documentary evidence) and paras 11–13 to 11–35 (expert evidence).

Intention

In order to satisfy the court that he has a firm, settled and bona fide intention to carry out the works, a landlord who is an individual should give oral evidence of his intention. Where the landlord is a body corporate, the best way of evidencing such an intention is the production of a formal board resolution to that effect. Where, for some reason, it is not practicable or desirable to obtain such a resolution, a witness should be called to prove that he has sufficient authority to reach such decisions on behalf of the company and to state that he has in fact formed such a decision on the company's behalf. Reference should be made[91] to cases considering the sufficiency of evidence of intention. If it is desired to give an undertaking to the court, an individual landlord may do so in person in the witness box, or counsel may be authorised by resolution of a body corporate or a responsible officer of a body corporate so to do. **11–54**

Other matters relevant to intention

The practical considerations which arise out of the landlord's proposal to carry out works are relevant both to the question of whether he has a firm, settled and bona fide intention and to the interrelated question whether he has a reasonable prospect, in practical terms, of carrying out his proposals. It will therefore usually be necessary for the landlord to adduce evidence on a number of matters relating to the history of the project and to the practical possibilities of carrying it into effect. The landlord should be prepared to deal with the following matters: **11–55**

(1) The way in which the project has evolved. It will be of some importance for the court to understand how it is that the landlord has come to the decision to carry out the works which he proposes. In particular, it will be relevant if the existing buildings are in a poor state of repair, are obsolete, or are uneconomic in their size, layout or permitted user. The holding may be only one element in a larger projected redevelopment. It will be a matter of judgment in each case how much evidence of such background matters will be of assistance to the court.

(2) The viability of the project. Although the landlord does not have to prove under ground (f) that what he is doing is reasonable, the court is less likely to believe that he has a firm and settled intention if the proposed redevelopment does not make economic sense. Accordingly, the landlord should be prepared to defend the viability of the project which will normally be evidenced by calculations as to the cost, on the one hand, of carrying out the proposed works and the return, on the other hand, from the premises after the works have been carried out, as opposed to the return from the premises without the carrying out of such works.

(3) Planning permission. The court may have to decide whether planning permission is required for the proposed works; normally this would be done by calling the evidence of a planning witness although the decision, in the

[91] See paras 7–164 to 7–183.

end, is one of law for the court. If planning permission is required and has been obtained, the permission should be before the court together with the application and supporting plans. If planning permission has not been obtained, evidence must be led such as to satisfy the court that the landlord has a reasonable prospect of obtaining it. The history of any previous planning permission and the expressed grounds for refusal will be relevant. The planning witness will give much the same evidence as he would to an inspector on a planning enquiry, dealing with any relevant statutory development plans and any relevant statements by the local planning authority of its policy, as well as his own views as to the merits of the proposals. It may be possible for one side or the other to call a witness from the local planning authority, although he is unlikely to be able to do more than indicate what advice he might give to the relevant committee. Similar considerations apply to other statutory permissions, such as a listed building consent where the premises are listed, or are in a conservation area.

(4) Other consents. The landlord should also give careful consideration to what consents, if any, he may require from third parties in order to carry out his proposals. He may require to take access over adjoining land not in his ownership; in such a case he would wish to prove to the court that he has, at least in principle, reached agreement with the adjoining owner. His building may to some degree infringe rights of light or air to adjoining properties; he will have to satisfy the court that he is likely to be able to reach a satisfactory accommodation with those adjoining owners. The landlord may himself be a leaseholder, in which case he will have to satisfy the court that, if any consents are necessary under the terms of his lease in order to carry out the works, that it has been, or can be, obtained from the superior lessors. Likewise where the land is burdened with restrictive covenants.

(5) Financial resources. The landlord must prove his financial ability to carry out the proposed works. A substantial development company may prove this through its annual report or some other evidence of its assets. An individual may prove that he has sufficient moneys in the bank, or sufficient moneys promised to him. Normally, the production of bank statements and/or a letter from a reputable bank or financial institution will be accepted by the tenant as evidence, but in cases where the landlord's financial ability is seriously in issue it may be necessary to call a witness from the bank or financial institution.

(6) Development agreements, building leases, etc. Where the landlord intends that the development be carried out pursuant to a development agreement or building lease, he must prove either that a binding (albeit conditional) agreement exists, or that there is a sufficiently firm understanding in principle with the proposed developer or building lessee to show that the landlord can procure the carrying out of the development. Where no formal agreement has been reached, it will usually be necessary to call a representative of the other party to give evidence of the firmness of the understanding in principle.

(7) Other matters. The landlord should also put before the court evidence of any other matters showing how far his plans have progressed. For example, although it is not essential that the landlord should have gone out to tender, still less have entered into the binding building contract by the date of the hearing, it would be relevant if he had in fact done so.

Evidence under section 31A

As a result of the decision of the House of Lords in *Heath v Drown*[92] (digested in para.7–103), the only evidence now necessary in order to demonstrate to the court that the landlord requires possession in order to carry out his work is the evidence showing the nature of those works[93] and the terms of the current tenancy, which will show whether that work can or cannot be lawfully done by the landlord without obtaining possession. **11–56**

However, the questions which arose under the law as it was formerly understood to be now arise, in modified form, under s.31A.[94] Under limb (a) of s.31A, expert evidence should be adduced on whether the access and facilities offered by the tenant would render the work proposed by the landlord more difficult to carry out, more expensive, or more lengthy. Furthermore, the court will have to be satisfied by the tenant of the extent of the holding, the use thereof by the tenant for the purposes of the tenant's business and what interference would be caused to that use if the landlords were to carry out the proposed works with the benefit of the offered facilities. The landlord may himself rely upon expert evidence about the nature of the works and of the tenant's business in order to demonstrate that such interference would be substantial. In order to rely upon limb (b), the tenant must adduce valuation evidence on: (1) the rent reasonably obtainable on a separate letting of the part of the holding which he alleges to be "economically separable"; (2) the rent reasonably obtainable in respect of the rest of the holding affected by the works; and (3) the rent reasonably obtainable on a letting as a whole of those parts of the premises affected by the works, taken together with the part of the holding which is alleged to be economically separable. In each case the valuation must be carried out upon the assumption that the works have been done. In the absence of expert valuation evidence on these three matters, the court has no material upon which to decide whether the part of the holding is or is not "economically separable". **11–57**

[92] [1973] A.C. 498; [1972] 2 W.L.R. 1306 HL.

[93] See para.11–53.

[94] See para.7–192 et seq.

8. EVIDENCING GROUND (G) (OWN OCCUPATION)[95]

Intention

11–58 A landlord has to prove his intention within ground (g) in much the same way as under ground (f) (demolition and reconstruction). The meaning of "intends" has been discussed in Chapter 7.[96] The evidence necessary to prove such an intention has also been considered.[97] Undertakings to enter into and carry on a business are sometimes offered to the court under ground (g) as under ground (f). The propriety of the court accepting such an undertaking has already been considered.[98]

Other matters relevant to intention

11–59 As under ground (f), the landlord must prove that he has the practical possibility of carrying out his intention. He should show that he has given serious thought to the manner in which the business will be carried out and to its potential profitability. Advice may have been taken on how the business is to be run, what turnover can be expected and what net profit can be expected on that turnover. If the landlord has business experience in the proposed, or any other, business this should be put in evidence, if necessary by showing balance sheets or other evidence of the way in which those businesses have been carried on. If the landlord is intending to operate the premises through a manager, or to employ staff, he should put in evidence any arrangements which he has made to employ them. Other matters preparatory to the starting up of a business may also be relevant and should be proved, such as proposals for the acquisition of stock, or the obtaining of estimates for shopfittings. If the proposal involves a change of business from that carried on by the tenant under the current tenancy, the landlord will have to show either that no planning permission is required, or, if it is, that he is reasonable in considering that it could be obtained. Planning witnesses may be required.

11–60 If the tenant wishes to raise a point of law, such as an argument that the landlord does not fulfil the requirements s.30(1A) or (1B)[99], it is incumbent upon the tenant to raise it at an early stage. Thus where the point that the landlord did not satisfy the provisions of s.30(3)[100] was raised by the tenant for the first time only in his closing submissions, the court was entitled to adjourn the hearing to permit the landlord to admit further evidence to meet the objection.[101]

---

95 As to this ground of opposition, see para.7–214 et seq.

96 See paras 7–134 et seq. and 7–215.

97 See paras 11–54 and 11–55.

98 See para.7–221 et seq.

99 See para.7–254 et seq.

100 Now repealed and replaced by s.30(1A) and (1B).

101 *Ambrose v Kaye* [2002] EWCA Civ 91; [2002] 1 E.G.L.R. 49 at [43]. As to the five-year bar, see para.7–264 et seq.

The five-year bar

It is for the landlord to show that he is not barred by the five-year rule; this he can prove by adducing in evidence the necessary documents, such as deeds of title, leases, assignments, trust deeds, etc. 11–61

9. EVIDENCE WHERE "THE OTHER TERMS" OF THE NEW TENANCY ARE IN DISPUTE[102]

Defining the issues

It is important for the parties to formulate precisely what has, and what has not, been agreed between them. Where there is substantial disagreement over the terms of the new tenancy, a draft lease should be put before the court showing what is proposed by the landlord and what is proposed by the tenant. If the tenant is insisting upon the terms of the current tenancy being continued into the new tenancy and the landlord is seeking only a few changes, it would be convenient to put before the court a photocopy of the lease creating the current tenancy with the landlord's proposed amendments written on it in red. Where the landlord is proposing to go to his standard form lease, which is entirely different from the terms of the current tenancy, and the tenant is objecting only to particular clauses, it is convenient to put before the court the landlord's standard draft with the tenant's proposed amendments in red. A court will, of course, also have to have before it a copy of the current lease, so that it can be compared with what the landlord now proposes. Where there is little common ground between landlord and tenant, it may be necessary for the court to be presented with two documents showing their respective contentions. Normally the parties will be able to agree upon what is the most convenient way in which matters should be presented to the court; if not, a direction should be sought, preferably well before the hearing. 11–62

Justifying changes of term

In relation to each proposed change from the current tenancy, the party proposing the change should adduce evidence of why the change is wanted and of its financial impact on landlord and tenant. In some cases, it may be relevant to justify the proposed change by reference to market practice or to changes in conveyancing practice. Sometimes the reason for wanting the change may be connected with what has happened under the current tenancy; e.g. the landlord may seek a provision for interest upon late rent, partly on the grounds that the tenant under the current tenancy has been frequently in arrears. In such a case, the matters relied upon as justifying the change should be proved in the ordinary way. A tenant may wish to resist a change proposed by the landlord on the ground that it would materially affect him in his enjoyment of the holding for the purposes of his business; this requires evidence of the way in which the tenant carries on his business and of why the proposed change will adversely affect it. 11–63

[102] As to the other terms, see para.8–45 et seq.

Break clauses

11–64 As explained[103] special considerations arise in relation to a proposal by the landlord for a redevelopment break clause. In practice, the evidence which the landlord will seek to adduce in support of the insertion of such a clause will be very similar to the evidence upon which he would rely if proving ground (f) (demolition and reconstruction). The nature of such evidence is considered above.[104] In particular, the court will often be persuaded to insert such a break clause if it can be shown that the premises are "ripe for redevelopment", which often requires expert evidence. In resisting the insertion of a redevelopment break clause, the tenant will probably have to rely upon evidence showing that the insertion of such a clause would be greatly damaging to the goodwill of his business. Evidence of this will usually come from the tenant himself, but may be supplemented by the evidence of an expert in that business, or of a valuer.

10. EVIDENCE OF RENTAL VALUE

Valuer's reports

11–65 Where the amount of rent to be paid under the new tenancy is in issue it is usual for both parties to rely upon expert valuation evidence of a surveyor.[105] The contents of the valuer's report will depend upon the circumstances of each case. Once the valuer has produced a draft report he will need to discuss it with solicitor or counsel before it is exchanged in its final form. When reports have been exchanged each valuer should prepare, for the benefit of his client's solicitor or counsel, a critique of the other side's report. This can then be used in cross-examination at the hearing. He may also wish, with the leave of the court, to put in a supplementary report rebutting what has been said by his opposite number. If it is intended to rely upon a supplementary report this should, where time permits, be served on the opposing party.

Valuation methods and supporting evidence

11–66 It is for the valuer to advise what evidence appears to him to be appropriate in order to substantiate his opinion on rent. Normally he will adopt the "comparable" method. Where, as is usual, each valuer is intending to rely upon allegedly comparable transactions in order to support the rent contended for, particular care must be taken over the proof of the comparable transactions relied upon. This is still the case notwithstanding the admissibility of hearsay evidence in civil proceedings. In *English Exporters v Eldonwall*[106] Megarry J. stated the principles governing the proof of comparable transactions in valuation cases, as follows:

---

[103] In paras 8–39 et seq. and 8–77 et seq.
[104] See paras 11–54 to 11–55.
[105] As to expert evidence generally, see para.11–13 et seq.
[106] [1973] 2 W.L.R. 435; [1973] 1 All E.R. 726.

> "Putting matters shortly, and leaving on one side the matters that I have mentioned, such as the Civil Evidence Act 1968 and anything made admissible by questions in cross-examination, in my judgment a valuer giving expert evidence in chief (or in re-examination): (a) may express the opinions that he has formed as to values even though substantial contributions to the formation of those opinions have been made by matters of which he has no first-hand knowledge; (b) may give evidence as to the details of any transactions within his personal knowledge, in order to establish them as matters of fact; and (c) may express his opinion as to the significance of any transactions which are or will be proved by admissible evidence (whether or not given by him) in relation to the valuation with which he is concerned; but (d) may not give hearsay evidence stating the details of any transactions not within his personal knowledge in order to establish them as matters of fact. To those propositions I would add that for counsel to put in a list of comparables ought to amount to a warranty by him of his intention to tender admissible evidence of all that is shown on the list."

It can be seen from this quotation that, prior to the enactment of the Civil Evidence Act 1995, it was important for both parties, at an early stage, to consider how to prove the comparables from which they relied. No problem arose if all the comparables were first hand, that is to say, within the personal knowledge of the expert witness. If some comparables were not "first hand", attempts were often made to agree the relevant facts with the other party. It was often the case that parties wished to rely upon comparable transactions which neither could strictly prove. In the absence of agreement the facts relating to the comparables had to be proved strictly. This may have involved calling, as witnesses of fact, people who were directly involved in the transaction in question. **11–67**

The rule against hearsay evidence however is now much diminished. The Civil Evidence Act 1995 abrogates the rule against hearsay evidence. Although there are certain procedural requirements for reliance upon hearsay evidence contained within the 1995 Act (as well as CPR r.33.2) a failure to comply with the requirements of the 1995 Act does not effect admissibility of the hearsay evidence. It is simply a matter which goes to weight.[107] It may also be taken into account by the court in considering the exercise of its powers with respect to the course of proceedings and costs.[108] No problem arises if all the comparables are first hand, that is to say within the personal knowledge of the expert witness. If some comparables are not "first hand", an attempt should be made with the other party to agree the relevant facts. This may be acceptable where the other party has his own knowledge of the transaction in question, or where he can be satisfied of the salient facts, as by being given a letter from one of the surveyors who took part in the transaction. It often happens, of course, that both parties wish to rely upon comparable transactions which they cannot strictly prove, which provides an inducement to each party to agree the other's comparables. Where agreement cannot be reached, an attempt should be made to prove the comparables strictly. This may involve the calling, as witnesses of fact, of people who were directly involved in the transaction in question. Alternatively, the procedure under the Civil Evidence Act 1995 may be adopted. It may be that a comparable transaction can be strictly proved simply by putting in evidence the document, such as a lease, by which it was effected. **11–68**

[107] Civil Evidence Act 1995 s.2(4).
[108] Civil Evidence Act 1995 s.2(4).

11–69 The expert will throughout his career have read large quantities of professional literature. The expert will be entitled to rely on these documentary sources. Thus, Megarry J. in *English Exporters v Eldonwall*[109] said he saw no objection to the valuer employing:

> "... textbooks, journals, reports of auctions and other dealings, and information obtained from his professional brethren and others, some related to particular transactions and some more general and indefinite ... doubtless much, or most, of this will be accurate, though some will not; and even what is accurate so far as it goes may be incomplete, in that nothing may have been said of some special element which affects value. Nevertheless, the opinion that the expert expresses is none the worse because it is in part derived from the matters or which he could give no direct evidence. Even if some of the extraneous information which he acquires in this way is inaccurate or incomplete, the errors and omissions will often tend to cancel each other out; and the valuer, after all, is an expert in this field, so that the less reliable the knowledge that he has about the details of some reported transaction, the more his experience will tell him that he should be ready to make some discount from the weight that he gives it in contributing to his overall sense of value. Some aberrant transactions may stand so far out of line that he will give little or no weight. No question of giving hearsay evidence arises in such case; the witness states his opinion from his general experience."

However, one must be careful of the expert who seeks to rely on a specific article or report or statistical table prepared by others for purposes other than the proceedings in question and seeks to cite it as specific authority or support for the opinion he expresses. On this topic see *R. v Abadom*.[110]

Relevance of trading accounts

11–70 In an early decision under the 1954 Act, *Re St Martin's Theatre*,[111] it was said that the tenant's financial position was relevant to his ability to pay the rent and perform his covenants under the lease and that the landlord may, therefore, in a proper case, be entitled to disclosure of the tenant's financial documents for the period of the current tenancy, particularly if the tenant was a limited company. One can certainly see the relevance of such documentation if the landlord is opposing the grant of a new tenancy under, for instance, ground (b). The judge made a somewhat general statement that wherever a tenant is asking for a lease of property his financial situation is always of the greatest materiality and should, of course, be read in context. The landlord was, in *Re St Martin's Theatre*, opposing on, inter alia, grounds (a) and (c) which put in issue the behaviour of the tenant in the past and its probable behaviour in the future. It must not be thought that a tenant's accounts will be discloseable whenever he applies for a tenancy under the Act. This is particularly so on the issue of the rent under s.34.

11–71 In *Harewood Hotels v Harris*[112] evidence of the earnings of the tenant's business was held to be admissible as to the question of what rent could be obtained in the open market for hotel premises. It was said, however, that such evidence was not admissible for the purpose of showing what the particular tenant could afford to pay. However, the Court of Appeal subsequently held in *WJ Barton Ltd v*

109 [1973] Ch. 415; [1973] 2 W.L.R. 435; [1973] 1 All E.R. 726.
110 [1983] 1 W.L.R. 126.
111 [1959] 1 W.L.R. 872.
112 [1958] 1 W.L.R. 108.

Longacre Securities Ltd[113] that the tenant's trading accounts are normally irrelevant in determining the market rent, except in the rare case where a valuation by the "comparable method" was impossible. The categories of premises in which trading accounts may be relevant was not defined or limited but it was suggested that it might include a hotel (as in *Harewood Hotels v Harris*[114]), a petrol filling station, a theatre or a racecourse. To this may be added a casino: *Electricity Supply Nominees v London Clubs*[115]; *Cornwall Coast Country Club v Cardgrange*[116] (rent review cases).

The accounts which will be admissible will, however, be limited to those accounts which are available to the hypothetical bidder in the open market rather than the tenant's confidential accounts. In *Cornwall Coast Country Club v Cardgrange*,[117] Scott J. reviewed all the authorities and, in reliance upon *Lynall v IRC*[118] held that "confidential information was not to be admitted into evidence unless it represented information which would be available in the hypothetical market". Thus the only accounts which will be discoverable are published accounts or those required by statute to be filed at Companies House. Scott J.'s decision was followed in *Electricity Supply Nominees Ltd v London Clubs Ltd.*[119] In *Humber Oil Terminals Trustee Ltd v Associated British Ports*[120] the tenant, in the context of a claim for an interim rent under s.24D(1)[121] of the Act of a jetty operated by the tenant, sought disclosure of the cost incurred by the landlord of operating, maintaining or investing in the port. The tenant alleged this was relevant to the determination of the interim rent of the jetty as its lease of the jetty exempted the tenant from paying harbour dues. One of the reasons given by the judge for refusing disclosure[122] was that there was no real basis for supposing that the hypothetical tenant negotiating the amount of rent payable for an annual tenancy (the hypothesis under s.24D(1)—see s.24D(2)) of the jetty would be aware of the information as to the costs incurred or to be incurred by the landlord. **11–72**

The various decisions have, however, been criticised by the learned authors of *Handbook of Rent Review*, where at para.7.7.4 the authors suggest that, as a result of these decisions, the rule as to the admissibility of trading accounts is precisely the opposite of what it should be. **11–73**

> "... Accounts which would have been available to the hypothetical lessee should not be admitted because to do so would fail to give effect to the usual requirement to disregard the effect on rent of ... the occupation of the tenant [see s.34(1)(a)].
>
> If the tenant had not been in occupation, there would have been no published accounts

---

[113] [1982] 1 W.L.R. 398 CA.
[114] [1958] 1 W.L.R. 108 CA.
[115] [1988] 2 E.G.L.R. 152.
[116] [1987] 1 E.G.L.R. 146.
[117] [1987] 1 E.G.L.R. 146.
[118] [1971] 3 W.L.R. 759.
[119] [1988] 2 E.G.L.R. 152.
[120] [2011] EWHC 1184 (Morgan J.). As to the facts of this case which involved a claim by the landlord opposing renewal under para.(g) of s.30(1), see para.7–220.
[121] As to which see para.9–33 et seq.
[122] The other was one of relevance. The landlord had simply failed to establish any connection between the harbour costs and the hypothetical negotiations between the hypothetical parties with respect to a rent assessed in accordance with s.24D.

> available to the hypothetical lessee and the disregard requires that any effect which such accounts would have had on the mind of the hypothetical tenant, and thus on the market, must be ignored. Yet the same criticism cannot be made of accounts which were not public and thus could not directly have affected the market. Such accounts should be admitted because, without infringing the disregard, they bear direct relevance to the central question in a notional profit valuation, namely what is the profit-earning potential of the premises.
> The proposition can be illustrated by an example: in the rent review of a casino, both landlord and tenant might adopt the notional profits method. The landlord might allege that a casino of the quality and in the location of the subject premises might be expected to achieve a turnover of £40 million per annum. The tenant might assert that a properly-run casino of that size in that location could only be expected to achieve a turnover of £10 million. In deciding who was right, surely the arbitrator ought to be entitled to receive evidence as to the actual turnover achieved by the tenant over the previous five years. If he had in fact been turning over some £40 million then, in the absence of some explanation, the arbitrator would be justified in treating the tenant's case with some scepticism."

The learned authors of the *Handbook* recognise, however, that their view has received no support from the English authorities but is said to be consistent with the approach of the Court of Appeal in New Zealand in *Modick RC v H Mahoney*.[123]

Plans, surveys, views and schedules

11–74 It is usually convenient to put before the court a location plan of the premises and floor plans showing their extent and layout. If any point is being taken on the state of repair of the premises, both sides will probably call building surveyors who should exchange their reports in the ordinary way. Where the tenant is claiming that improvements should be disregarded, a schedule of alleged improvements should be put before the court, together with the date that such improvements were alleged to be carried out. The facts of this schedule should be agreed it possible. In some, though by no means all, cases where rent is in issue the court may well be assisted by a view of the premises. Normally this is a question which is raised with the judge at an early stage of the hearing so that he can indicate at what stage of the proceedings (if any) he would find a view most helpful. In a case where the premises are in disrepair at the date of the hearing due to the landlord's default, but the landlord undertakes to carry out works of repair, the court will have to be informed how long those works will take and what disruption they will cause to the tenant's business so that it can consider whether to order a variable rent and, if so, of what amount.

[123] [1992] 1 N.Z.L.R. 150 CA (NZ).

CHAPTER 12

COMPENSATION FOR DISTURBANCE

1. CIRCUMSTANCES IN WHICH RIGHT TO COMPENSATION ARISES

Section 37(1), as amended by the Law of Property Act 1969, specified the circumstances in which the tenant was entitled to compensation on quitting the holding. The provisions of the Act with regard to compensation have been substantially amended by the 2003 Order.[1] The policy of the earlier legislation remains, namely to give financial compensation to a tenant where the ground relied upon by the landlord for opposing his application for a new tenancy, or in support of the landlord's termination application, is one of the mandatory grounds which does not depend upon the fault of the tenant, namely grounds (e) (sub-letting of part), (demolition and reconstruction) and/or (g) (own occupation by landlord). The 2003 Order, as with the 1969 amendments, provides for the right to compensation to arise in three distinct sets of circumstances. These are similar but not identical to those provided for by the 1969 amendments. **12–01**

The three compensation cases

The provisions of s.37(1) have been repealed and there is substituted in its place the following: **12–02**

> "(1) Subject to the provisions of this Act, in a case specified in sub-section (1A), (1B) or (1C) below ('a compensation case') the tenant shall be entitled on quitting the holding to recover from the landlord by way of compensation an amount determined in accordance with this section.
>
> (1A) The first compensation case is where on the making of an application by the tenant under section 24(1) of this Act the court is precluded (whether by sub-section (1) or sub-section (2) of section 31 of this Act) from making an order for the grant of a new tenancy by reason of any of the grounds specified in paragraphs (e), (f) and (g) of section 30(1) of this Act ('the compensation grounds') and not of any grounds specified in any other paragraph of section 30(1).
>
> (1B) The second compensation case is where on the making of an application under section 29(2) of this Act the court is precluded (whether by section 29(4)(a) or section 31(2) of this Act) from making an order for the grant of a new tenancy by reason of any of the compensation grounds and not of any other grounds specified in section 30(1) of this Act.
>
> (1C) The third compensation case is where—

[1] In particular the provisions as to payment of "double compensation" have been altered so as to apply only in circumstances where the whole of the holding has been occupied for business purposes for 14 years. This is to be contrasted with the previous position where double compensation could be awarded so long as at least part of the premises comprised in the holding had been occupied for business purposes for 14 years. See para.12–35 et seq.

(a) the landlord's notice under section 25 of this Act or, as the case may be, under section 26(6) of this Act, states his opposition to the grant of a new tenancy on any of the compensation grounds and not on any other grounds specified in compensation 30(1) of this Act; and

(b) either—

(i) no application is made by the tenant under section 24(1) of this Act or by the landlord under section 29(2) of this Act; or

(ii) such an application is made but is subsequently withdrawn."

The first compensation case

12–03 There is little difficulty, it is considered, with respect to the provisions for the first compensation case. If the tenant makes an application for renewal and the landlord opposes it (the landlord himself not having made any termination application) and the landlord makes out his compensation grounds, the tenant obtains his compensation. The first compensation case is thus really no different to the position under the old regime.

The second compensation case

12–04 This applies where the landlord himself makes an application for termination. If he makes good that application on compensation grounds and not on any other ground, he must pay compensation.

The third compensation case

12–05 This is where the landlord has specified compensation grounds and no other grounds in his s.25 notice or counter-notice to the tenant's s.26 request, and either (1) the tenant makes no application for renewal or the landlord makes no application for termination or (2) if any such application is made it is subsequently withdrawn. Thus, the third compensation case provides for three circumstances in which compensation becomes payable (the landlord having specified in all cases the compensation grounds in his s.25 notice or counter-notice to the tenant's s.26 request and no other ground of opposition):

(a) no application is made by the tenant for renewal or by the landlord for termination and thus the current tenancy is simply allowed to terminate on the date specified in the landlord's s.25 notice or in the tenant's s.26 request;

(b) an application for renewal is made by the tenant but is subsequently withdrawn by the tenant[2];

(c) an application for termination is made by the landlord and is subsequently withdrawn.[3]

---

[2] The tenant does not need the consent of the landlord to withdraw the application: CPR Pt 38, see para.14–95.

[3] The landlord cannot withdraw the application without the consent of the tenant: s.29(6). As to the tactical possibilities available to a landlord by reason of the right to apply for termination, see para.12–19.

Withdrawal of grounds of opposition

12–06 It follows from the wording of s.37(1C) that if a compensation ground is specified (and no other) in the relevant notice the landlord becomes liable to pay compensation. This is so even if, as happens not infrequently, the landlord subsequently notifies the tenant that he is no longer seeking to oppose renewal. The subsequent "withdrawal" of the opposition to renewal will not relieve the landlord of liability to pay compensation. The only circumstance where the landlord can avoid such a liability arises where there is a change in the person who is the competent landlord within the meaning of the Act following which there is a withdrawal of the notice. The special circumstances in which a s.25 notice can be withdrawn by a superior landlord who subsequently becomes "the landlord" have been discussed above (see para.7–08 et seq.).

Withdrawal of application for renewal pre-CPR

12–07 Prior to 1982, where an application had been made to the High Court, it could not be discontinued without the leave of the court, which might have ordered it to be discontinued "on such terms as to costs, the bringing of a subsequent action, or otherwise as it thinks just". In *Covell Matthews v French Wools*[4] and *Young, Austen & Young v BMA*,[5] the court held that it had jurisdiction to impose a term, as a condition of giving leave to discontinue, that the tenant would not claim compensation under s.37. In both those cases, such a term was in fact imposed on the ground that the tenants who had made the application had subsequently decided that they did not want new tenancies for reasons unconnected with the landlord's opposition to their applications. In *Lloyds Bank v City of London*,[6] the Court of Appeal confirmed that the court had jurisdiction to impose such a term, but disapproved of the manner in which that jurisdiction had been exercised in the two cases previously mentioned. The Court of Appeal held that a tenant should be allowed unconditionally to withdraw his application, even if the landlord had abandoned his ground of opposition, unless the landlord had been prejudiced by delay in seeking leave to discontinue, or by events which had occurred between the date when the landlord notified the tenant that he withdrew his ground of opposition and the date when the tenant informed the landlord that he did not propose to proceed with his application. The fact that the tenant had decided for its own reasons not to seek a new tenancy was not sufficient ground for depriving it of the compensation to which it would have been entitled if it had not made any application at all. The Court of Appeal noted the anomalous difference between procedure in the county court and procedure in the High Court, which was less favourable to a tenant who sought to withdraw his application, but stated that the anomaly had no relevance to the way in which the High Court's jurisdiction should be exercised. See also *Fribourg & Treyer v Northdale Investments Ltd*[7] and *Ove Arup Inc v Howland Property Investment*

4 [1978] 1 W.L.R. 1477; [1978] 2 All E.R. 800; [1978] 1 E.G.L.R. 42 CA.

5 [1977] 1 W.L.R. 881; [1977] 2 All E.R. 884; [1977] 2 E.G.L.R. 57.

6 [1983] Ch. 192; [1982] 3 W.L.R. 1138; [1983] 1 All E.R. 92 CA.

7 [1982] 2 E.G.L.R. 52.

Co,[8] where the tenant was also allowed to discontinue without giving up its right to compensation. By an amendment to the Rules of the Supreme Court in 1982, it was provided (by RSC Ord.21 r.2(3A)) that no leave was required to discontinue proceedings commenced by originating summons up to 14 days after service of the defendant's affidavit. This applied to summonses claiming new tenancies pursuant to the Act: *Artoc v Prudential*.[9] After expiry of the 14-day period, leave was still required.

Under the CPR

12–08 Under the CPR no leave is required to discontinue all or part of a claim: CPR r.38.2(1). A landlord cannot, however, withdraw an application for termination without the consent of the tenant: s.29(6).[10]

Subsequent termination of lease following withdrawal

12–09 If the tenant's claim is withdrawn then the subsequent forfeiture of the lease by the landlord does not deprive the tenant of his entitlement to compensation: *Webb v Sandown Sports Club Ltd*[11] (digested in para.12–60). It is essential, however, in these circumstances that the tenant has quit the holding by the date of the forfeiture.[12]

Where the tenant's renewal application is not withdrawn

12–10 Section 37(1C) provides that compensation is payable where, inter alia, the tenant's application for renewal is withdrawn. It is considered that the withdrawal of the application is a condition precedent to the entitlement to the payment of compensation. For example, if the tenant having received an appropriate form of s.25 notice makes an application for renewal but quits the holding upon agreeing a surrender prior to any withdrawal of the application, the tenant is, arguably, not entitled to compensation. It is true to say that the tenant has quit the holding but he has not withdrawn the application. Any subsequent withdrawal will be at a time when the tenancy has ceased to exist. It seems difficult to suggest that the subsequent withdrawal at a time when the tenancy which was the subject matter of the application has ceased to exist satisfies the statutory requirements. Although not stated expressly, it appears the intention of Parliament to have been that the tenant was to receive compensation where the tenant's interest came to an end in consequence of the grounds of opposition relied on by the landlord, by the tenant accepting the ground(s) of opposition stated in the landlord's notice; by subsequently accepting the landlord's grounds of opposition by withdrawing any application made; or, upon the court determining that the tenant lost his right to renewal by reason only of the relevant grounds giving rise to the payment of

8 [1982] 1 E.G.L.R. 63.

9 [1984] 1 W.L.R. 1181; [1984] 3 All E.R. 538.

10 As to the potential problems of a tenant requiring to give his consent, see para.6–16. See also para.14–98.

11 [2000] E.G. 13 (C.S.).

12 See further para.12–56 et seq.

compensation. A surrender of the lease does not fit any one of those circumstances. On the other hand depriving the tenant of compensation in these circumstances (i.e. where a surrender has occurred) would appear to make the payment of compensation dependent upon the, possibly fortuitous, sequence of events. If before any surrender the tenant had withdrawn his application (albeit only one day before) the tenant on the above analysis would still be entitled to compensation.

Specifying additional grounds

Where the landlord has specified ground (e), ground (f) and/or ground (g) (whether any other ground has or has not also been specified), the tenant will be entitled to compensation if the landlord successfully opposes the application upon grounds (e), ground (f) and/or ground (g) and on no other ground: s.37(1A). It follows that a tenant who receives a s.25 notice or counter-notice under s.26(6), which contains a ground of opposition other than that under ground (e), ground (f) and/or ground (g), can only obtain compensation if he makes an application and pursues it to judgment. It was a common tactic for a landlord, who wished to rely upon ground (e), ground (f) and/or ground (g), but who suspected that the tenant did not want a new tenancy for reasons of his own, to include in addition some other ground of opposition (provided that there is a bona fide intention to rely on that other ground). If that was done, the tenant would not be entitled to compensation without making an application and pursuing it, which he might not be willing to do. **12–11**

Ground of opposition contained within section 25 notice or counter-notice must be specified bona fide

A landlord's grounds of opposition must be specified bona fide. If the grounds of opposition are not stated honestly and truthfully the notice is likely to be invalid. See the discussion in para.3–158 et seq. **12–12**

Section 26 proposals—must they be bona fide?

The insistence by the court that the landlord's intention as to the grounds of opposition upon which he relies must not be misrepresented was sought to be extended to the tenant's proposals for a new tenancy contained in the tenant's s.26 request. However, in *Sun Life Assurance Plc v Thales Tracs Ltd*[13] (digested in para.3–220) the Court of Appeal held that a s.26 request contains no requirement for the tenant to state his intention or belief and thus the genuineness of any intention on the part of the tenant to seek a renewal is irrelevant to the validity of the request. As the court pointed out, if it were right that the tenant's entitlement to compensation, where a s.26 request was served, depended on the investigation as to his state of mind, the entitlement to compensation would depend on who **12–13**

[13] [2000] 1 E.G.L.R. 138 QBD.

initiated the procedure, for if the procedure is initiated by the landlord,[14] the tenant is entitled to compensation irrespective of his intention as to whether or not he wishes to renew.[15] Thus where the tenant's only reason for serving a s.26 request was to obtain compensation, the tenant had been aware of the landlords' intention to redevelop prior to service of the s.26 request and thus anticipated a hostile counter-notice, but without any intention of seeking a renewal, and the tenant had, prior to the s.26 request, arranged alternative accommodation into which the tenant was to move, it was held that the tenant's request was valid.[16]

Where application is dismissed

Dismissal under section 31(1) and (2)

12–14 Compensation is payable where the tenant's application for renewal is defeated under s.31(2)[17] as well as where it is defeated under s.31(1). By virtue of s.37(4), a tenant whose application for renewal has been defeated can apply to the court for a certificate to the effect that the landlord has succeeded only on grounds (e), (f) and/or ground (g) and on no other ground, so that he will be entitled to compensation.[18] It is to be noted that the effect of s.37(4) is simply to entitle the tenant to obtain a certificate as to the ground upon which the court has been precluded from granting a new tenancy. It does not entitle the tenant to seek declaratory relief as to what would have happened if the tenant had made and pursued its application. These tactical considerations have been discussed in more detail (see para.7–269 et seq.).

No compensation where dismissal on other grounds

12–15 We have already noted the decision of the Court of Appeal in *Zenith v Kammins*[19] (digested in para.6–22) to the effect that an invalid application is nonetheless an "application" for the purposes of the Act which prolongs the current tenancy. Presumably it also follows that a tenant who has made an application for a new tenancy which is invalid (perhaps because it was premature[20]) will be unable to obtain compensation under s.37(1), even if the landlord has specified ground (e), ground (f) and/or ground (g), unless the invalid application is withdrawn. If the landlord succeeds in striking out the application on grounds of prematurity (as happened in *Kammins v Zenith*[21] (digested in para.3–245)), no compensation would be payable because dismissal of an application on such grounds does not come within any of the sets of circumstances envisaged by s.37(1). In cases where a tenant has agreed to accept a new tenancy of an "economically separable

[14] By serving a s.25 notice specifying the appropriate ground giving rise to compensation.
[15] See para.12–06.
[16] *Sun Life Assurance Plc v Thales Tracs Ltd* [2001] 1 W.L.R. 1562; [2001] 2 E.G.L.R. 57 CA.
[17] See para.7–290 et seq. with respect to the application of s.31(2).
[18] As to the making of an application for such a certificate, see para.14–115.
[19] [1971] 1 W.L.R. 1751 CA.
[20] Although the circumstances in which an application can be premature are now limited: see para.6–20.
[21] [1971] A.C. 850; [1970] 3 W.L.R. 287 HL.

part" of the holding within the meaning of s.31A there would appear to be no provision for him to receive compensation appropriate to that part of the holding not included in his new tenancy.

Tactical use of right by landlord to make termination application

This wording of s.37(1C) is similar to the wording under the old regime but there is an important difference. Under the old regime procedure a landlord could not make an application for termination. Under the new legislation he can make an application for termination. It seems to the authors that there are two tactical uses of the landlord's new rights to make an application. **12–16**

Forcing tenant to go to court

By making an application for termination and not withdrawing it the landlord forces the tenant to go to court to obtain his compensation. Under the old wording the tenant was entitled to receive his compensation where the landlord had opposed renewal on compensation grounds and the tenant accepted that the landlord would succeed. The tenant could walk away and obtain his compensation. Now, however, the landlord has the opportunity of forcing the tenant to go to court in order to obtain his compensation. As the landlord has the opportunity of getting his termination application in first,[22] the landlord may, tactically, force the tenant to have to face the prospect of having to force the tenant to face the prospect of litigation in order to secure his compensation. **12–17**

However, the court, albeit only at Master level of the High Court, has indicated that it is not prepared to tolerate the tactical abuse of the landlord's new rights. In *Felber Jucker & Co Ltd Sabreleague Ltd*,[23] the landlord had specified ground (f) in his s.25 notice. The landlord changed his mind about redeveloping the premises and in order to avoid paying compensation to the tenant made a termination application, the intention being that the landlord would fail in his application such that the court would have to award a new tenancy. The court struck out the landlord's application as an abuse of process. This decision was of course one where the landlord's termination application was not made bona fide, the landlord having abandoned his plans for redevelopment. **12–18**

Eleventh-hour termination application

Another potential problem arises where a tenant proposes to vacate in response to the landlord's statement of opposition only to find himself faced at the eleventh hour with a termination application. If the tenant is faced with a termination application in these circumstances there is of course nothing stopping a tenant who wishes to obtain his compensation without incurring unnecessary court cost admitting the landlord's claim. **12–19**

[22] See para.6–53 et seq.
[23] [2005] P.L.S.C.S. 162, Master Moncaster.

12–20 The time limit for making an application for termination is "the statutory period".[24] Thus the tenant may be lulled into a false sense of security, thinking that he will receive his compensation. The tenant having received a s.25 notice opposing renewal is, let us assume, prepared to accept that the landlord would succeed without the landlord having to establish the relevant ground of opposition. However, the tenant will not know until the expiry of the statutory period, i.e. the date of termination specified in the s.25 notice, whether or not the landlord will suddenly make an application at the last moment forcing the tenant to go to court to obtain his compensation. The issue of the application for termination by the landlord will, of course, continue the current tenancy under s.24 beyond the date of termination.

12–21 **Example** L serves s.25 notice specifying compensation grounds. T does not respond as he knows that L will succeed, e.g. he is known to be intending to demolish the whole of the premises. Say a day before the expiry of the statutory period (the time period for making an application under s.29(2): s.29A(2)) L issues an application under s.29(2). The new legislation does not reverse *Esselte AB v Pearl Assurance Plc*[25] (digested in para.2–53) nor *Surrey CC v Single Horse Properties Ltd*[26] (digested in para.2–54). Thus, if T vacates, his tenancy will come to an end. But how does he get compensation? The circumstances do not fit any of the compensation cases. Let us assume, however, that albeit T's tenancy has come to an end he continues to fight L's claim in the hope of getting compensation. L naturally wins as he is demolishing the whole. However, the application has not been "withdrawn" for L has succeeded and thus it is not a third compensation case. Nor can it be said that the matter comes within the second compensation case, as the court is not "precluded" from granting a new tenancy by reason of the grounds of opposition but by reason of the fact that the tenant no longer has a tenancy!

Severed reversions

12–22 Where a tenant makes a claim for compensation pursuant to s.37 of the Act, s.37(3B) makes it clear that the compensation for each part separately held is to be determined separately and recoverable only from the person who is the "landlord" for the purposes of s.44 with respect to that part. It would seem that in the absence of agreement the apportionment of the compensation payable as between the persons who constitute the "landlord" is to be made by the court.

2. AMOUNT OF COMPENSATION

12–23 By virtue of s.37(2), the amount of compensation to which a tenant will be entitled under s.37(1) is either:

[24] As to the meaning of which, see para.6–17.
[25] [1997] 1 E.G.L.R. 73 CA.
[26] [2002] 1 W.L.R. 2016; [2002] 2 E.G.L.R. 43 CA.

(1) the rateable value of the holding (or such part[27] as satisfies the relevant conditions[28]) × the "appropriate multiplier" × 2; or
(2) the rateable value of the holding × the "appropriate multiplier" × 1.

We examine in turn how each of these elements in the calculation is to be ascertained, and the circumstances in which the more generous compensation under limb (a) will be appropriate.

Ascertaining the rateable value

Section 37(5) contains detailed provisions for ascertaining the rateable value of the holding. (For the meaning of "the holding", see para.8–06 et seq.) The rateable value is ascertained by reference to the valuation list in force at the date of service of the s.25 notice or s.26 request, as the case may be.[29] If the holding is separately rated in the valuation list, that valuation is taken. The Lands Tribunal on appeal from a valuation officer has held that where the valuation list is subject to a proposal for alteration and the list is subsequently altered, the rateable value is, nevertheless, the value found on inspection of the list on the valuation date; a later rateable value cannot be applied retrospectively: *Plessey Co v Eagle Pension Funds*[30] (digested in para.12–25). **12–24**

Plessey Co v Eagle Pension Funds[31] The building of which the demised premises formed part had their rateable value reduced (from £74,472 to £60) because they had been damaged by fire. The tenant reoccupied the premises after they had been restored. A proposal was made as to assessment of the rateable value of the restored premises. The landlord served a s.25 notice before the rateable value of the building shown in the list (£60) was altered. It was held the rateable value was an apportioned part of £60, not the rateable value of the holding as subsequently altered (namely £21,097). **12–25**

If the holding is part only of a hereditament for which a rateable value is shown, that value has to be apportioned. If parts of the holding are separately rated, the separate values for those parts are aggregated. It may be necessary both to apportion and to aggregate, as where one part of the holding is separately rated and another part of the holding forms only a part of a rateable hereditament. **12–26**

Example Imagine two buildings, each of two storeys, the ground floor in each case being a shop and the first floor in each case being offices. If the holding comprises both sets of offices but only one of the shops and if each building is separately rated, the rateable value of the holding is to be ascertained by adding to the rateable value of the shop and office comprised in the building which is included in the holding the rateable value (determined by apportionment) of the additional offices. **12–27**

---

27 s.37(3A).

28 Being those referred to in s.37(3).

29 s.37(5).

30 [1990] 2 E.G.L.R. 209.

31 [1990] 2 E.G.L.R. 209.

12–28 After April 1, 1990, in determining the rateable value of the holding under s.37(5) such part of the holding as constitutes "domestic property" is disregarded: para.2(3)(a) of Sch.7 to the Local Government and Housing Act 1989 ("the 1989 Act"). "Domestic property" is defined in accordance with s.66 of the Local Government Finance Act 1988.[32] Thus, in the common case of a shop with residential accommodation above, the residential accommodation is excluded in determining the rateable value of the holding. This is not to say, however, that the tenant will not receive compensation for the domestic property: see para.12–48.

12–29 Where it is not possible to ascertain the rateable value of the holding by either of the foregoing methods, the subsection provides for a determination of what the rateable value would have been if it had appeared in the valuation list (presumably at the date of the s.25 notice or s.26 request). Disputes arising in relation to any of these matters are to be determined by reference to the Commissioners of the Inland Revenue for decision by a valuation officer, with a right of appeal to the Lands Tribunal.[33]

"Appropriate multiplier"

12–30 The "appropriate multiplier" means such multiplier as the Secretary of State may prescribe by statutory instrument: s.37(8). The Secretary of State may prescribe different multipliers for different cases: s.37(8). The figure of two-and-a-quarter was prescribed as the appropriate multiplier with effect from March 25, 1981.[34] This was increased to three with effect from April 1, 1985.[35] It was unclear whether the multiplier prescribed by those regulations applied to tenancies terminated by notices served before those regulations came into force. The Court of Appeal held, in *International Military Services Ltd v Capital & Counties Plc*[36] and *Cardshops Ltd v John Lewis Properties Ltd*,[37] that a tenant is entitled to compensation at the rate prescribed by those rules which are in force at the date of his quitting the holding, even though a different rate prevailed at the date of service of the s.25 notice or s.26 request, as the case may be. This principle does not hold good in relation to the most recent variation. The appropriate multiplier with effect from April 1, 1990 is one.[38] However this applies only where the s.25 notice is given after April 1, 1990.[39]

---

[32] See Appendix, para.A.1.085.

[33] The Commissioners have, by statutory instrument, made the Landlord and Tenant (Determination of Rateable Value Procedure) Rules 1954 governing the procedure to be adopted.

[34] Landlord and Tenant Act 1954 (Appropriate Multiplier) Regulations (SI 1981/69).

[35] Landlord and Tenant Act (Appropriate Multiplier) Order (SI 1984/1932).

[36] [1982] 1 W.L.R. 575; [1982] 2 All E.R. 20; [1982] 1 E.G.L.R. 71 CA.

[37] [1983] Q.B. 161; [1982] 3 W.L.R. 803; [1982] 3 All E.R. 746; [1982] 2 E.G.L.R. 53 CA.

[38] Landlord and Tenant Act 1954 (Appropriate Multiplier) Order 1990 (SI 1990/363).

[39] art.4. Where the s.25 notice was given after April 1, 1990, a tenant was for a period which expired in April 2000 able to take advantage of provisions enabling him to elect to be paid compensation by reference to the rateable value of the holding on March 31, 1990 (see para.12–55), in which case the multiplier was eight (Landlord and Tenant Act 1954 (Appropriate Multiplier) Order 1990, art.4).

Single or double compensation?

General

A tenant will be entitled to compensation calculated by the method described under the second limb referred to above[40] unless he can bring himself within the conditions for double compensation, which are set out in s.37(2) and (3). The tenant in order to be entitled to double compensation must show: **12–31**

(1) that business occupation has endured for a period of 14 years "immediately preceding the termination of the current tenancy"[41];
(2) that premises "being or comprised in the holding" have been occupied for the purposes of a business or for those and other purposes[42];
(3) that the business has been carried on by "the occupier"[43];
(4) that if during the period of 14 years there was a change in the occupier of the premises, the person who was the occupier immediately after the change was the successor to the business carried on by the person who was the occupier immediately before the change[44];
(5) that the above conditions are satisfied in relation to the whole of the holding.[45] If the conditions can be satisfied with respect to part only of the holding, double compensation is payable in respect of that part only.[46]

14 years "immediately preceding the termination of the current tenancy"

The first step is to ascertain the date of "the termination of the current tenancy", which is defined by s.37(7) to mean the date of termination specified in the relevant s.25 notice or s.26 request. The second step is to calculate the commencement of a period of 14 years ending on that date. It is then necessary to ask the question: have "premises being or comprised in the holding" been occupied for the purposes of a business carried on by the occupier or for those or other purposes during the whole of that 14-year period? Section 37(3)(a) refers to "the whole of the 14 years immediately preceding the termination of the current tenancy . . .". The requirement that the tenant should have occupied for the period of 14 years immediately preceding the date of termination specified in the landlord's s.25 notice or date of commencement specified in the tenant's s.26 request gives rise to difficulties for a tenant who wishes to vacate before that date: *Sight & Sound Education Ltd v Books Etc Ltd*[47] (digested in para.12–33). **12–32**

[40] As described in para.12–23.
[41] Discussed in para.12–32 et seq.
[42] Discussed in para.12–35 et seq.
[43] Discussed in para.12–37.
[44] Discussed in para.12–38, et seq.
[45] This is a new requirement introduced by the 2003 Order: s.37(2).
[46] s.37(3A). This matter is discussed in para.12–35.
[47] [1999] 3 E.G.L.R. 45 Ch D.

12–33 ***Sight & Sound Education Ltd v Books Etc Ltd***[48] The tenant held a tenancy of business premises for a term expiring on September 28, 1997. The landlord gave notice determining the tenancy on February 25, 1998; the notice stated that the landlord would oppose the grant of a new tenancy on grounds (f) and (g) of s.30(1) of the Act. The tenant gave up possession of the premises shortly before the contractual term date. The tenant claimed double compensation based on 14 years' actual occupation. The landlord contended that the eligible period of occupation must be 14 years expiring on the date of termination specified in the landlord's s.25 notice, and that because the tenant gave up possession by September 28, 1997, it could not satisfy the requirement of 14 years' occupation ending on February 25, 1998. It was held that the tenant was not entitled to double compensation. As the tenant gave up possession by the contractual term date, the tenant ceased to enjoy the protection of the 1954 Act thereafter. The effect of s.37(3) and (7) was that the 14-year period of occupation had to be satisfied up to the date of termination of the tenancy specified in the landlord's s.25 notice. The tenant was not in occupation after September 28, 1997, and did not occupy up to Feburary 25, 1998.

12–34 In considering the question as to whether or not the tenant has been in occupation for the relevant 14-year period, the tenant may still be able to establish the relevant 14-year period albeit there have been periods of non-business activity, e.g. at the commencement of the lease where the tenant has entered to fit out for the purposes of undertaking his business[49] or at the termination where the tenant has vacated in order to ensure an orderly delivery up of possession to the landlord. In *Department of the Environment v Royal Insurance Plc*,[50] the tenant had been in occupation for 14 years, less one day at the commencement of the tenancy utilised for fitting out. It was held that only single compensation was payable, since there was no room for the application of the de minimis principle and the tenant had not been in occupation for the required 14-year period. This decision was overruled by the Court of Appeal in *Bacchiocchi v Academic Agency Ltd*[51] (discussed also in paras 1–59 and 1–60). In that case the tenant had been in occupation for 14 years "immediately preceding the termination of the current tenancy" being the date of termination specified in the landlord's s.25 notice. However, the tenant discontinued his application for a new lease such that the date of termination in accordance with s.64 of the Act was post the date of termination specified in the s.25 notice. The tenant vacated the premises 12 days prior to the date upon which the tenancy would come to an end in accordance with s.64 of the Act. The tenancy excluded the right to compensation under s.37 but by s.38(2) that clause would be void if the tenant had occupied the premises for "the whole of the five years immediately preceding the date on which the tenant [was] to quit the holding". It was held that the vacation by the tenant was incidental to the ordinary course or conduct of business activity which involved

48 [1999] 3 E.G.L.R. 45 Ch D.

49 See *Pointon York Group Plc v Poulton* [2007] 1 P. & C.R. 6, considered at para.1–30 et seq., and para.1–43.

50 [1987] 1 E.G.L.R. 83.

51 [1998] 1 W.L.R. 1313; [1998] 2 All E.R. 241 CA. See also *Pointon York Group Plc v Poulton* at para.1–43.

running down a business in order to vacate the premises and to quit on the proper date. It was not necessary for there to be a precise coincidence of time between cessation of all activity and the moment when the obligation to quit arises. Whether the cessation of activity prior to the term date will be such as to break the thread of continuity is a matter of fact and degree. If, of course, premises are left vacant for a matter of months, the court would be readier to conclude that the thread of continuity has been broken: *Bacchiocchi v Academic Agency Ltd.*[52] In *Sight & Sound v Books Etc*[53] (digested in para.12–33) it was stated, obiter, that a period on non-occupation of five months was too long.

Premises being or comprised in the holding

Prior to the amendments introduced by the 2003 Order, a tenant who satisfied the relevant conditions for the payment of double compensation with respect to part only of the holding was entitled to double compensation calculated by reference to the whole of the holding. The Court of Appeal, in *Edicron Ltd v William Whiteley Ltd*[54] decided, with respect to the pre-2003 Order wording, that the premises to be considered are premises "being or comprised in the holding", so that it was sufficient that part of the holding had been occupied for the purposes of a business for a continuous period of 14 years immediately preceding the end of the current tenancy; it was not necessary that the whole of the premises comprised in the holding should have been so occupied.[55] **12–35**

The position after June 1, 2004 has been altered by the 2003 Order. If the relevant conditions[56] for the payment of double compensation are satisfied in relation to part of the holding but not in relation to any other part, the amount of compensation shall be the aggregate of sums calculated separately as compensation in respect of each part.[57] This is a change from the position under the old regime. Each part of the holding is now to be looked at for the purposes of considering whether double compensation is payable and in order for double compensation to be obtained in relation to the entirety, the entirety will need to have satisfied s.37(3)(a). As only part may be subject to a claim for double compensation and another part subject to a claim for single compensation, the total compensation payable will be an aggregate of the compensation sums payable in respect of each part. **12–36**

[52] [1998] 2 All E.R. 241 at 250, per Simon Brown L.J.
[53] [1999] 3 E.G.L.R. 45 Ch D.
[54] [1984] 1 W.L.R. 59; [1984] 1 All E.R. 219 CA.
[55] The meaning of "holding" and the date at which its extent is to be judged are discussed below: para.12–46 et seq.
[56] Being those in s.37(3).
[57] Accordingly, it is provided that for the purpose of calculating compensation in respect of a part any reference in s.37 to the holding shall be construed as a reference to that part: s.37(3A).

Occupier

12–37 It is to be noted that the business is to be carried on by "the occupier". "The occupier" need not necessarily be the tenant or a predecessor-in-title of his in the tenancy. This is made clear in the debates in *Hansard*, June 17, 1954, para.2394, where it was said:

> "... it will [not] ... be necessary for the business to have been carried on by the tenant during the 14 years. It will be enough if the business has been carried on by the occupier of the premises for the time being, whether he was the tenant or whether the business was carried on by the freeholder and passed from the freeholder to the tenant."

Thus, one could have a situation where the owner of premises has been in occupation for say 10 years. He then enters into a sale and lease-back. The previous owner, now tenant, will be entitled to double compensation after a further four years business occupancy. Contrast the position under the (now repealed) provisions of the Landlord and Tenant Act 1927, exemplified by *Corsini v Montague Burton*.[58] See also *Department of the Environment v Royal Insurance Plc*,[59] where the legislative intent was not brought to the attention of the court, and the fact that the tenant had occupied the premises as a licensee prior to grant, which if taken together with the period of occupation qua tenant would have satisfied the 14-year period, was ignored.

Change in occupier/successor to business

12–38 If there has been no change in the occupier of the premises the tenant will be entitled to double compensation.[60] If there has been a change of occupier during the 14-year period it is necessary to pose the further question: was the person who became the occupier immediately after that change the successor to the business carried on by the person who was the occupier immediately before the change? If so, the tenant is entitled to double compensation. If not, he is entitled only to single compensation. The meaning of "the successor to the business" is uncertain: it is probably insufficient for the successor to carry on the same kind of business, if he has not bought the goodwill of the tenant's business and has none of the same clientele: *Cramas Properties v Connaught Fur Trimmings*[61] (digested in para.12–39) a case decided under the transitional provisions of the 1954 Act. Lord Reid said:

> "If one simply makes a comparison of the crucial words in para.5[62] with similar words in other parts of the Act of 1954 it is quite possible to arrive at the result reached by the Court of

---

[58] [1953] 2 W.L.R. 1092; [1953] 1 All E.R. 8 CA, where it was held that a person is a "predecessor in title" within s.25 of the Landlord and Tenant Act 1927 only if he had title to the premises to which the tenant has succeeded. Mere occupation of the premises pursuant to a licence or other friendly arrangement was insufficient: see para.13–76.

[59] [1987] 1 E.G.L.R. 83. See the discussion of this case at para.12–34.

[60] An inter-group company assignment will not give rise to a change in the occupier (s.42(2)(c)) nor, where the tenancy is held on trust, will an assignment upon the appointment of a new trustee (s.41(1)(c)).

[61] [1965] 1 W.L.R. 892; [1965] 2 All E.R. 382 HL.

[62] Of Sch.9 to the Act.

> Appeal [that 'the tenant's business' meant the tenant's type of business rather than the tenant's actual business]. The Act of 1954 deals in various connexions with change of ownership of a business during a particular period. For example in s 34(b)[63] there is reference to '... the carrying on thereat of the business of the tenant (whether by him or by a predecessor of his in that business)': in s 37(3) (b) and s 38(2) (b) there is reference to '... the successor to the business carried on by...' the former occupier: in s 43(3) (b) there is reference to '... any predecessor in the carrying on of the business carried on by the tenant...' and in para.4(c) of Sch 9 there is reference to '... a successor to his business...' So there is a marked change of language in para.5 of Sch 9 and we must look to see what can have been the reason for this ... The words in para.5 'the carrying on of the tenant's business (whether by him or by any other person)' are quite different from those in the sections to which I have referred: they make no reference to a predecessor or successor in the business. So it must be presumed that they have a different meaning. They can have a different meaning because 'the tenant's business' can mean the tenant's type of business and then the next words 'whether by him or by any other person' are appropriate. So this different meaning must be held to be their true meaning.
> I think, however, that that is much too narrow an approach... There does not appear to be any other provision in the Act of 1954 where 'the tenant's business' could be held to mean the tenant's type of business, or any reference anywhere to a type of business...".

Cramas Properties v Connaught Fur Trimmings[64] Premises were sub-let to G for 14 years from June 24, 1949 expiring on June 21, 1963. G occupied the premises for their business of manufacturing furriers until 1961. They then moved their business to other premises and on March 1, 1961, assigned the underlease of the demised premises to Connaught, who occupied them for their own business of manufacturing furriers which was unconnected with G's business. On December 20, 1962, the reversion to the underlease was surrendered to the superior landlord who became the immediate landlords of Connaught. The parties negotiated and agreed that in consideration of the respondents refraining from applying to the court for a new tenancy the appellants would pay them on quitting the premises the compensation, if any, that they would have been entitled to receive (under s.37) if they had applied to the court for a new tenancy and the court were precluded from granting it. Under the transitional provisions of para.5(1) of Sch.9 to the Act of 1954 regarding tenancies current at the commencement of the Act, Connaught would not have been entitled to compensation under s.37 unless at the date on which they were to quit, the holding had "continuously been occupied for the purposes of the carrying on of the tenant's business (whether by him or by any other person) for at least five years". Connaught had carried on their own business on the premises for less than three years prior to June 25, 1963 (being the date of termination specified in the s.25 notice) though the business of manufacturing furriers had been carried on on the premises by G and then by Connaught for more than five years prior to that date. It was held that Connaught were not entitled to compensation because the words "the tenant's business" in para.5(1) of Sch.9 meant the business carried on by the particular tenant and not his type of business, and the premises had not been continuously occupied for the purpose of the respondents' business for at least five years prior to June 25, 1963. 12–39

The natural and only meaning of the words "the tenant's business" was the actual business belonging to the tenant as:

---

63 See now s.34(1)(b).

64 [1965] 1 W.L.R. 892; [1965] 2 All E.R. 382 HL.

(1) nowhere in the Act did "the tenant's business" mean the tenant's type of business;
(2) it would be irrational to make the tenant's right to compensation depend precisely how the premises were used by a former occupier;
(3) the Act gave no guidance on the criteria by which types of business could be ascertained and, if the argument that "the tenant's business" meant type of business were accepted, it would be necessary to invent them; but when it was appreciated, from s.23, that the Act applied to all businesses, trade, professions, employments and activities, it was evident that the task of indentifying a business by type or class would present insuperable difficulties to the courts.

Part only of the holding satisfying the conditions

12–40 As mentioned above,[65] the amendments brought about by the 2003 Order have made in clear that in order to obtain double compensation the conditions must be satisfied with respect to the whole of the holding and not simply part of it.

Illustrations of the operation of the provisions

12–41 The effect of these provisions can be illustrated by the following:

12–42 **Example 1** The tenant has a tenancy on three floors of an office building which comprises "the holding" at the material date. He has occupied the first floor for a continuous period of 14 years ending with the date of termination of the current tenancy, but not the second and third floors, which were sub-let during part of that period. Prior to June 1, 2004 the tenant would have been entitled to double compensation because he had been in occupation of part of the holding (that is to say the first floor) for the full 14-year period even though he had not been in occupation of the whole of the holding during that period. Post June 1, 2004 the tenant is entitled to double compensation in respect of the first floor only and single compensation in respect of the other floors.

12–43 **Example 2** Suppose that T is a solicitor occupying a suite of offices. After seven years he is struck off the roll of solicitors for professional misconduct and carries on business from the offices as a management consultant. If his occupation as a solicitor and management consultant lasts for more than 14 years up to the date of termination of his current tenancy, he will be entitled to double compensation because there has been no change in the occupier of the holding, even though there has been a change in the business carried on.

12–44 **Example 3** Suppose the same facts as in Example 2, save that after T has been struck off he assigns the tenancy to A, who carries on the business of a management consultant. A will not be entitled to double compensation because there has been a change in the occupier and A is not the successor to T's business as a solicitor.

---

[65] See para.12–35.

Since the computation of the 14-year period is by reference to the date specified in the relevant s.25 notice or s.26 request, there is scope for tactical manoeuvring by landlord or tenant in order to ensure that there is single or double compensation (see para.4–24 et seq.). **12–45**

Extent of "the holding"

Compensation is payable by reference to the rateable value of "the holding".[66] In *Edicron v William Whiteley*[67] it was held at first instance that the extent of "the holding" is to be judged by reference to circumstances as they are at the date of service of the landlord's s.25 notice. This is to be contrasted with the position where a new tenancy is granted, in which case it is expressly provided by s.32(1) that the property which constitutes the holding is to be designated by reference to the circumstances existing at the date of the order.[68] The judge gave two reasons for his decision on this point: **12–46**

(1) That the express provision contained in s.37(5)(a) that the rateable value should be determined by reference to the valuation list in force on the date of service of the s.25 notice suggested that it was intended that the extent of "the holding" in respect of which that rateable value was shown should be ascertained at the same date.
(2) That this interpretation enabled the landlord to know, at the date that he served his s.25 notice specifying a ground of opposition, what was the extent of the compensation which he had to pay and enabled the tenant to know, upon receipt of the s.25 notice, the extent of the compensation to which he was entitled.

The second reason given in *Edicron v William Whiteley*[69] must be qualified by the decision of the Court of Appeal in *Cardshops Ltd v John Lewis Properties Ltd*,[70] where it was held that a change in the multiplier provisions subsequent to the service of a s.25 notice could increase the amount of compensation payable. Furthermore, the second reason does not apply to the case where the tenant makes a s.26 request, since the landlord's liability to pay compensation and the tenant's right to receive it will not crystallise unless and until the landlord serves a counter-notice within s.26(6), which will be a date later than the making of the tenant's s.26 request. However, the first reason applies with equal force to the case where the tenant has made a s.26 request, since s.37(5)(a) provides for the rateable value to be ascertained by reference to the valuation list in force on the date when the tenant makes a s.26 request. This part of the judge's decision in *Edicron v William Whiteley* was not challenged on appeal. The tactical considerations arising from this decision are illustrated by the facts of *Edicron v William Whiteley*. If the tenant has sub-let part of the premises comprised in the **12–47**

[66] s.37(2). As to the meaning of "the holding", see para.8–06 et seq.
[67] [1984] 1 W.L.R. 59; [1984] 1 All E.R. 219; [1983] 1 E.G.L.R. 79 CA.
[68] See para.8–07.
[69] [1984] 1 W.L.R. 59; [1984] 1 All E.R. 219; [1983] 1 E.G.L.R. 79 CA.
[70] [1983] Q.B. 161; [1982] 3 W.L.R. 803; [1982] 3 All E.R. 746; [1982] 2 E.G.L.R. 53 CA.

tenancy and has reason to believe that the landlord intends to serve a notice specifying ground (e), (f) and/or ground (g), he can increase the size of "the holding" and thus increase his entitlement to compensation, if he is able to obtain vacant possession of the sub-let parts and go into occupation of them himself before the date of service of a s.25 notice or the making of a s.26 request.

Domestic property

12–48 The Local Government and Housing Act 1989 has amended the provisions for quantifying the compensation payable in that one must now consider whether any part of the holding constitutes "domestic property" as defined in s.66 of the Local Government Finance Act 1988.[71] The amendments were brought into effect to provide for the abolition of domestic rates. The question of whether any part of the holding constitutes "domestic property" is relevant only where the valuation date is on or after April 1, 1990. A number of categories need to be considered:

Where the holding does not include domestic property

12–49 Where the tenant's holding does not include domestic property the amount of the compensation is calculated in accordance with the conditions set out in para.12–23, that is to say, it will be the product of: (1) the rateable value or twice the rateable value of the holding multiplied by (2) the appropriate multiplier.

Where the holding includes domestic property

12–50 If part of the holding includes domestic property, the amount of the compensation is calculated by reference to: (1) the rateable value or twice the rateable value of the holding excluding such part as constitutes domestic property, multiplied by (2) the appropriate multiplier together with (3) an addition of a sum equal to the tenant's reasonable expenses in removing from the domestic property (s.37(5A)(b)). Any question as to the amount of the sum in (3) shall be determined by agreement between the landlord and the tenant or, in default of agreement, by the court: s.37(5B).

Where the whole of the holding constitutes domestic property

12–51 Where the whole of the holding constitutes domestic property as defined in s.66 of the Local Government Finance Act 1988, the rateable value of the holding is to be taken to be an amount equal to the rent at which it is estimated the holding might reasonably be expected to let from year to year if the tenant undertook to pay all usual tenant's rates and taxes[72] and to bear out the cost of repairs (defined in s.69(1) of the Act) and insurance and the other expenses (if any) necessary to maintain the holding in a state to command that rent: s.37(5C).

[71] See Appendix 1, para.A.1.085.
[72] As to which see *Halsbury's Laws of England* (London: LexisNexis), Vol.27(1) (Reissue 4th edn), para.424 et seq.

The relevant date for determining the rateable value of the holding in accordance with the s.37(5C) formula is at the date of the s.25 notice or of the landlord's counter-notice under s.26(6) as the case may be: s.37(5D)(a). **12–52**

If there is a dispute as to the value of the holding to which the s.35(5C) formula gives rise, the dispute, whether arising in proceedings before the court or otherwise, is to be referred to the Commissioners of the Inland Revenue for a decision by a valuation officer (defined in s.37(7)): s.37(5D)(b). An appeal from the valuation officer lies to the Lands Tribunal: s.37(5D)(c). Accordingly, the amount of the compensation will be the product of: (1) the rateable value or twice the rateable value of the holding as calculated in accordance with s.37(5C) multiplied by (2) the appropriate multiplier. **12–53**

It may be considered that there will be very few circumstances in which the whole of the holding constitutes domestic property, because the 1954 Act is concerned with business not residential use. By s.66 of the Local Government Finance Act 1988 it is provided that property is domestic if "... it is used wholly for the purposes of living accommodation" (s.66(1)(a) of the Local Government Finance Act 1988).[73] It will be remembered that the provision of residential accommodation may constitute a business (see para.1–120). **12–54**

Transitional provisions

In certain cases a tenant was, until April 1, 2000, given an opportunity to elect for a special basis of compensation, which was effectively compensation calculated by reference to the pre-April 1, 1990 rateable value multiplied by a higher multiplier than applied post-April 1, 1990.[74] These provisions are discussed in detail in the first edition of this work and the reader is referred to it.[75] **12–55**

3. PAYMENT OF COMPENSATION

Quitting the holding

The date at which the tenant is entitled to compensation

Under the previous wording of s.37(1) the tenant was "entitled on quitting the holding to recover from the landlord by way of compensation" the amount determined in accordance with the remaining provisions of s.37. This wording is repeated in s.37(1) of the new wording. **12–56**

Where s.37(1) applies, the tenant is entitled "on quitting the holding" to recover from the landlord by way of compensation an amount determined in accordance with the foregoing principles. Clearly, the reference to "quitting" means that the tenant is not entitled to receive compensation until he has physically yielded up vacant possession of the holding to his landlord. Where the tenant vacates before **12–57**

---

73 See Appendix, para.A1.086.

74 See generally, para.4 of Sch.7 to the Local Government and Housing Act 1989.

75 See para.12–55 (1st edn, 1997).

the termination of his tenancy, but after his right to compensation has crystallised, two questions arise. First, does the tenant destroy his right to compensation by vacating before the termination of the tenancy. Secondly, if vacating does not destroy the tenant's entitlement, is he entitled to be paid compensation upon vacating.

Vacating after the right to compensation has crystallised

12–58 It is considered that once the tenant's right to compensation has crystallised the fact that the tenant thereafter vacates the premises ought not to affect his entitlement to be paid compensation, notwithstanding the fact that by vacating the premises the tenancy will cease to be one to which the Act applies. The provisions of s.37(1) refer to the tenant being entitled to compensation (assuming the other criteria for entitlement to be satisfied) upon quitting the holding. There is nothing in the Act requiring the quitting of the holding to coincide with the termination of the tenancy. Support for this view derives from two decisions. First, on the facts of the Court of Appeal decision of *Bacchiocchi v Academic Agency Ltd*[76] (discussed in paras 1–59, 1–60 and 12–34) it was accepted that the tenant was entitled to double compensation but for the existence of the agreement contained within the tenant's lease which sought to exclude the tenant's right to compensation. In order to strike down that exclusion agreement, the tenant was required to show for the purposes of s.38(2) that he was in occupation for business purposes until the date of termination of the tenancy in accordance with s.64 (the tenant in that case having made an application for renewal which was subsequently withdrawn). However, the case proceeded on the assumption that but for the exclusion agreement the tenant would have been entitled to double compensation notwithstanding the fact that the tenant had vacated 12 days before the termination of the tenancy as provided for by s.64. It was only to overcome the exclusion agreement that it was necessary to consider whether, as the court found, the tenancy was one to which the Act applied during the 12-day period. Secondly, in *Webb v Sandown Sports Club Ltd*[77] (digested in para.12–60) the tenant was entitled to double compensation where, having vacated the premises prior to withdrawing the application for renewal, the landlord subsequently (after the tenant's withdrawal of his application) forfeited the lease by peaceable re-entry. In this case the tenant vacated the premises three months prior to the date of the termination of the tenancy provided for by the terms of s.64. However, the tenant had in fact quit the holding and had been in occupation for 14 years immediately prior to the termination of the current tenancy (i.e. 14 years prior to the date of termination specified in the landlord's s.25 notice). The fact that the tenancy was not one to which the Act applied at the date of the forfeiture was irrelevant to the tenant's entitlement to compensation.

12–59 Vacating the premises prior to the termination of the tenancy may, however, involve a risk for the tenant if there happens to be, as is often the case in modern commercial leases, a provision excluding the right to compensation. The difficulties that may be encountered by an early cessation of occupation are well

76 [1998] 1 W.L.R. 1313; [1998] 2 All E.R. 241 CA.

77 [2000] E.G. 13 (C.S.).

illustrated by the *Bacchiocchi v Academic Agency Ltd*[78] decision (see paras 1–59, 1–60 and 12–34, above). Non-occupation will validate the exclusion agreement as the tenancy is no longer one to which the Act applies and accordingly will not be struck down by s.38(2). If there is an exclusion agreement contained in the tenant's lease, the tenant is, if he wishes to defeat it, required to remain in occupation until "the date on which the tenant under a tenancy to which this Part of this Act applies is to quit the holding" within the terms of s.38(2).[79]

Webb v Sandown Sports Club Ltd[80] L served upon T a notice pursuant to s.25 specifying June 19, 1997, as the date of termination and opposing renewal under ground (g) of s.30(1) of the Act. The tenant applied for a new tenancy. In July 1998 the tenant advertised his intention to relocate the business. On October 4, 1998, having found alternative premises, the tenant ceased trading and removed most of the stock from the premises. The tenant did, however, return to the premises to collect the remaining stock and papers on October 19, 1998. The tenant served a notice discontinuing his application for a new tenancy on October 22, 1998. L purported to forfeit the lease by effecting a peaceable re-entry in November 1998, L having earlier served a notice under s.146 alleging breach of covenant. T did not pursue a claim for relief. T claimed that as he had withdrawn his application and quit the holding he was entitled to compensation under s.37 of the Act. L contended that T had not quit the holding at any material time. It was held that T had quit and that accordingly T was entitled to his compensation. **12–60**

Is the tenant entitled to compensation on vacating?

If the tenant vacates the premises after the entitlement has crystallised, is the tenant entitled to immediate payment upon quitting the holding? We think not, because such a construction would lead to the absurd result that a tenant, who had quit "the holding" as ascertained at the date of service of the relevant s.25 or s.26 request, could thereupon claim compensation, even though he had subsequently resumed possession of sub-let parts (which would then constitute "the holding" for the purposes of his application for a new tenancy). At that date it could not, of course, be known whether the landlord would be able to defeat the tenant's application by establishing the relevant ground and it would accordingly not be known whether the tenant would be entitled to compensation at all. A result consistent with our conclusion, based on rather different wording, was reached under s.4 (now repealed) of the Landlord and Tenant Act 1927: *Smith v Metropolitan Properties Co Ltd*.[81] **12–61**

To whom is payment effected

Payment is to be made to the person or persons constituting the tenant at the date of quitting the holding. Where the tenant is a partnership the Act provides that the **12–62**

[78] [1998] 1 W.L.R. 1313; [1998] 2 All E.R. 241 CA
[79] See further paras 12–63, et seq.
[80] [2000] E.G. 13 (C.S.).
[81] [1932] 1 K.B. 314.

compensation is recoverable by those of them who constitute the "business tenants": s.41A(7). Accordingly, the landlord should be able to discharge his obligation under the Act by making payment to the business tenants albeit those persons may consist of some only of the persons constituting the tenant under the tenancy.

4. CONTRACTING OUT OF COMPENSATION FOR DISTURBANCE: SECTION 38(2)

Contracting out prohibited, subject to exceptions

12–63 Section 38(2) renders void any "agreement (whether contained in the instrument creating the tenancy or not and whether made before or after the termination of that tenancy) which purports to exclude or reduce compensation" under s.37, subject to two important exceptions.

First exception

12–64 The first exception is where the parties have entered into "any agreement as to the amount of any such compensation which is made after the right to compensation has accrued". The question arises as to what is the date upon which such a right accrues. There are, in principle, three possibilities. First, it could be said that the right to compensation accrues when the landlord serves a s.25 notice or counter-notice under s.26(6) specifying only ground (e), ground (f) and/or ground (g). Secondly, it could be said that the right does not accrue until such a notice or counter-notice has been served and the tenant has either not made an application within the relevant time limit,[82] or has withdrawn an application, or that application has been successfully opposed on one of the relevant grounds. At that date one can be certain that the tenant will obtain compensation. Thirdly, it can be said that the right does not accrue until the tenant has quit the holding, because it is not until that date that he can demand to be paid the compensation. Since the subsection contemplates an agreement being rendered void even if made after the termination of the tenancy, it appears that the third possibility must be the correct interpretation, if the reference to "termination of the tenancy" is a reference to termination of the current tenancy as continued by the Act. Inevitably, any agreement after that date must be one made at a time when the right to compensation has accrued according to the first two possible interpretations. It may be, however, that the reference to termination of the tenancy is a reference to the contractual expiry date, in which case there are arguments in favour of any of the three possibilities.

---

[82] After post June 1, 2004, there is the further condition, namely, that the landlord has also not made a termination application within the relevant time limit or if he has done so, the same has been withdrawn.

Second exception

The second exception to the prohibition of agreements excluding or modifying the tenant's right to compensation for disturbance arises because s.38(2) is expressed to apply only: 12–65

> "where (a) during the whole of the five years immediately preceding the date on which the tenant under a tenancy to which this Part of this Act applies is to quit the holding, premises being or comprised in the holding have been occupied for the purposes of a business carried on by the occupier or for those and other purposes, and (b) if during those five years there was a change in the occupier of the premises, the person who was the occupier immediately after the change was the successor to the business carried on by the person who was the occupier immediately before the change."

The wording of this exception is clearly modelled upon that of s.37(3), which lays down the conditions to be fulfilled in order for the tenant to be entitled to double compensation. The meaning of those provisions has been discussed.[83] Three differences should, however, be noted. First, the use of the word "*and*" in s.38(2), which is not used in s.37(3), reinforces the decision of the Court of Appeal in *Edicron v William Whiteley*[84] on the meaning of "*premises*" under limb (a). Secondly, the relevant period is five years, not 14 years. Thirdly, the date by reference to which the period is computed is not "*the termination of the current tenancy*" as defined in s.37(7), but "*the date on which the tenant under a tenancy to which this Part of this Act applies is to quit the holding*". The meaning of this is obscure. It may mean the contractual expiry date of the tenancy, so that any tenancy granted for a term of less than five years certain can validly contain a provision excluding or modifying the right to compensation.[85] It may, however, mean the date of termination specified in the relevant s.25 notice or s.26 request. This is thought to be an unlikely interpretation, both because the date so specified

---

[83] See para.12–31 et seq. and in particular para.12–32.

[84] [1984] 1 W.L.R. 59; [1984] 1 All E.R. 219 CA.

[85] There are a number of reasons why it is considered that this date is not the appropriate date:

(i) First, it would mean that any tenancy of less than five years could never, in any circumstances, carry with it an entitlement to compensation. Thus one could have a scenario of, say, a tenancy of four years with the tenant continuing to hold over after the contractual expiry date, such that the holding over period had the effect that the tenant had been in occupation in excess of five years. There is no clear justification, having regard to the purpose of the compensation provisions, which compensate for the disturbance *of business occupancy* (*Cramas Properties v Connaught Fur Trimmings* [1965] 1 W.L.R. 892, 898, per Lord Reid), for limiting the entitlement to compensation by reference to the contractual period of occupation rather than occupation under the Act.

(ii) Secondly, the concept of a contractual term date is inappropriate in the context of a periodic tenancy. In the case of a periodic tenancy there is in one sense no contractual termination date. There is no fixed period which one can point to as the expiry of the contractual term.

(iii) Thirdly, one cannot properly refer to the tenant as being required to "quit the holding" at the contractual termination date where the tenant is in occupation for business purposes, for the 1954 Act actually continues the contract of tenancy between the parties. Unlike the position in the Rent Acts, where the contractual term expires and a new, statutory form of tenancy, is substituted, the tenancy continued by s.24 of the 1954 Act is a continuation of the estate in land and is capable therefore of being assigned or forfeited in the usual way: *HL Bolton Engineering Co Ltd v TJ Graham & Sons Ltd* [1957] 1 Q.B. 159 CA—"the common law tenancy subsisted with a statutory variation as to the mode of determination" at 168 per Denning L.J. Thus, the contract of tenancy actually does not end but continues.

will not, in most circumstances, be the date upon which either landlord or tenant expects that the tenant will quit the holding, and because the draftsman could easily have incorporated the express definition in s.37(7) to give the phrase that meaning.[86] The third possibility is that the reference to the date upon which the tenant "*is to quit*" the holding means the date upon which he is legally obliged to give up vacant possession, which, by virtue of the continuation provisions of ss.24 and 64 of the Act, may be later than both the contractual expiry date and the date specified in any relevant notice or request. The reference to "*the holding*", which is a concept relevant at the termination rather than the commencement of a tenancy, suggests that it is the third possibility which is correct.

12–66 In *Bacchiocchi v Academic Agency Ltd*[87] (discussed in paras 1–59, 1–60 and 12–34) the Court of Appeal proceeded (there being no argument to the contrary) on the assumption that the reference to the date on which the tenant was to "*quit the holding*" was the date on which the tenant was legally obliged to give up vacant possession, i.e. the third possibility considered above. In that case the landlord served a s.25 notice terminating the tenant's tenancy on April 8, 1994. The tenant duly served a counter-notice and made an originating application but subsequently discontinued it such that by the operation of s.64 of the Act, the tenancy was continued until August 11, 1994 and terminated on that date. The tenant was mistakenly advised by solicitors that the lease terminated on July 29, 1994 and duly made arrangements to vacate by that date. The premises were vacant for the period of 12 days from July 29, 1994 to August 11, 1994. The Court of Appeal held that the exclusion of the right to compensation contained within the tenant's lease was, nevertheless, caught by s.38(2) as the premises had been occupied for business purposes during the whole of the five years immediately preceding August 11, 1994.

12–67 The view of Simon Brown L.J.[88] is also consistent with the approach that the Court of Appeal has taken as to the meaning of the words "on quitting the holding" in s.37(1) of the 1954 Act. This section provides that "on quitting the holding" the tenant is entitled "to recover from the landlord by way of compensation an amount determined in accordance with this section." In *Cardshops Ltd v John Lewis Properties Ltd*,[89] the court had to consider whether, in determining the quantum of compensation to be received, the relevant multiplier was that in force at the date of the landlord's s.25 notice or the later

[86] It is considered that there is force in this point. The draftsman has not sought to define the quitting of the holding in some particular way, so that it seems to require an application of the relevant law. The service of a s.25 notice or s.26 request is only one means of bringing about a termination of the tenancy. It is not necessarily a sufficient means in itself, e.g. if an application for renewal were to be made this would result in an continuation of the tenancy and thus the entitlement of the tenant to carry on occupying the holding such that he is not obliged to quit.

[87] [1998] 1 W.L.R. 1313 at 1315; [1998] 2 All E.R. 241 at 243 CA.

[88] In *Bacchiocchi v Academic Agency Ltd*[1998] 1 W.L.R. 1313 at 1315; [1998] 2 All E.R. 241 at 243 CA.

[89] [1983] Q.B. 161 CA. The Divisional Court in *Smith v Metropolitan Properties Co* [1932] 1 K.B. 314, in an analogous context under earlier business legislation dealing with the payment of compensation, held that the words "on quitting the holding" under s.4 of the Landlord and Tenant Act 1927 (since repealed) (providing for the tenants' entitlement to compensation for loss of goodwill), meant the termination of the tenancy, i.e. when the tenant was required to quit the holding at law.

date when the tenant "quit the holding." The Court of Appeal followed the reasoning of Slade J. in *International Military Services Ltd v Capital & Counties Plc*[90] that as the entitlement arose on the quitting of the holding and not before it was "quite plain that the amount of the entitlement must be assessed in accordance with the law as it stands at the date of quitting …". Ackner L.J. in *Cardshops Ltd v John Lewis Properties Ltd*[91] expressed the view that he had no doubt that "Slade J. was treating the date of the quitting as being the date upon which the tenancy continued by section 64 expired…."

What is the date upon which "*the tenant is to quit the holding*" where no application for a new tenancy is made by the tenant? If that date is, according to the *Bacchiocchi v Academic Agency Ltd*[92] decision, the date on which the tenant is legally required to deliver up vacant possession to the landlord, it would appear that where no application for a new tenancy has been made, logically the date upon which the tenant is to quit the holding should be the date of termination specified in the landlord's s.25 notice or the date of commencement specified in the tenant's s.26 request. In *Cramas Properties v Connaught Fur Trimmings*[93] (digested in para.12–39) the court was concerned with the transitional provisions of the Act. If the tenancy was in existence when the Act of 1954 was passed, the tenant only received compensation if he satisfied the requirements of para.5(1) of Sch.9. That paragraph is in these terms: **12–68**

> "(1) A tenant under a tenancy which was current at the commencement of this Act shall not in any case be entitled to compensation under s. 37 or s. 59 of this Act unless at the date on which he is to quit the holding the holding or part thereof has continuously been occupied for the purposes of the carrying on of the tenant's business (whether by him or by any other person) for at least five years."

The court proceeded on the basis that the date on which the tenant was "*to quit the holding*" was (the tenant having made no application for the grant of a new tenancy) the date of termination specified in the landlord's s.25 notice.[94]

If the tenant remains in occupation after the expiry of the tenancy and quits later, the period of holding over is ignored in determining whether: **12–69**

> "during the whole of the five years immediately preceding the date on which the tenant under a tenancy to which this Part of this Act applies is to quit the holding, premises being or comprised in the holding have been occupied for the purposes of a business carried on by the occupier or for those and other purposes".

Albeit "the holding" has been quitted after a period of five years immediately preceding which the holding has been occupied for business purposes, only the

---

[90] [1982] 1 W.L.R. 575.

[91] [1983] Q.B. 161 CA at 178. It is also clear from a consideration of the facts of that case that the date of "quitting the holding" was the date when the tenant's tenancy terminated in accordance with s.64, i.e. when his right lawfully to remain in occupation had come to an end.

[92] [1998] 1 W.L.R. 1313.

[93] [1965] 1 W.L.R. 892; [1965] 2 All E.R. 382 HL.

[94] It is considered that this view remains valid notwithstanding the opportunity which now exists for a landlord to make an application for renewal or for a termination application. If neither the tenant nor the landlord has made an application for renewal or renewal/termination respectively, the tenant's tenancy will end on the date specified in the s.25 notice or s.26 request.

period of occupation referable to the holding having been comprised in a tenancy to which the Act applied is to be taken into account: *London Baggage Co (Charing Cross) Ltd v Railtrack Plc (No.2)*.[95] Thus, where the tenant's lease was one of only four years and contained a clause excluding the right to compensation, that clause was not struck down by s.38(2) where the tenant had remained in occupation of the holding after the expiry of his lease as tenant-at-will and did not quit until he had been in occupation for business purposes for a period in excess of five years: *London Baggage Co (Charing Cross) Ltd v Railtrack Plc (No.2)*.[96]

Change in occupier

12–70 The provisions of s.38(2)(b) make it clear that the agreement excluding or reducing the amount of the compensation payable shall not be struck down where there has been a change in the occupier of the premises, unless the new occupier is a successor to the business carried on by the occupier immediately before the change. The words make it clear that the succession must be to the actual business carried on by the previous occupier and not simply the same kind of business. However, the Act makes it clear that no change in occupier will be treated as having occurred where the change has occurred as a result of:

(1) an inter-group company assignment: s.42(2)(c);
(2) changes in occupation by members of the same group where such occupation continues to satisfy the requirements of s.42;
(3) changes in occupation by companies in whom the tenant has a controlling interest where such occupation satisfies s.23(1A)(a);
(4) an assignment upon the appointment of a new trustee, where the tenancy is held on trust: s.41(1)(c).

Modification of right to compensation: section 38(3)

12–71 Where s.38(2) does not apply, it is expressly provided by s.38(3) that the landlord and tenant may agree to "*exclude*" or "*modify*" the right to compensation. Clearly, an agreement to "*exclude*" is an agreement that no compensation shall be payable. An agreement to "*modify*" the rights would be one which purported to limit them to a particular figure or provided for them to be computed in a particular way differing from that laid down by s.37. Section 38(3) of the 1954 Act refers to an exclusion or modification of "*the right*" to compensation. In the House of Lords decision of *Jones v Wrotham Park Settles Estates*[97] an agreement to modify the amount of the price payable for the freehold interest was held not to be a modification of the right to acquire the freehold. In that case two companies entered into a scheme (the grant of a concurrent lease) which was described as having been devised with "care and ingenuity", the effect of which was substantially to enhance the price payable by the resident tenant on acquiring the

---

[95] [2003] 1 E.G.L.R. 141.
[96] [2003] 1 E.G.L.R. 141.
[97] [1980] A.C. 74; [1979] 2 W.L.R. 132; [1979] 1 All E.R. 286 HL.

freehold pursuant to his rights under the Leasehold Reform Act 1967. The House of Lords held that s.23 of that Act (which renders void any agreement insofar as it purports to exclude or modify the right to acquire the freehold or an extended lease) had no application as the provision under attack "may modify the terms upon which the tenant may acquire the freehold, but does not modify the right itself": see Lord Russell at 113C–113D. A genuine modification of the situation to which the statutory system of calculation of the price applied was not a modification of the right of enfranchisement, which remained untouched save as to the cost of enforcement of the right.

It would appear that even if the special circumstances mentioned (in para.12–63 et seq.) are not satisfied, the landlord could be held to an agreement which increased the amount of compensation payable to the tenant for disturbance, since that would not be an exclusion or reduction within s.38(2) (but a modification) of the tenant's rights under the Act. **12–72**

Leases in existence as at October 1, 1954

If one encounters (as would happen, the authors imagine, vary rarely) a long business lease which was current at the commencement of the 1954 Act (October 1, 1954) the tenant is not entitled to any compensation, not even single compensation, unless at the date on which the tenant is to quit the holding, the holding or part thereof has continuously been occupied for the purposes of the carrying on of the tenant's business (whether by him or by any other person) for at least five years: para.5 of Sch.9 to the 1954 Act. As to the meaning of "*is to quit*" within s.38(2)(a), see para.12–65 et seq. **12–73**

If the lease current as at October 1, 1954 contains a contractual provision for compensation on the termination of the tenancy, the tenant must elect whether to pursue his contractual claim or his claim under s.37. He cannot have both: para.6 of Sch.9 to the Act. **12–74**

Compulsory purchase

A tenant who is displaced by an authority possessing compulsory purchase powers and, who is entitled to compensation under s.37 of the 1954 Act, is not precluded from claiming, in addition, a disturbance payment under s.37(1)(a) of the Land Compensation Act 1973: *Evis v Commission for the New Towns*.[98] **12–75**

[98] [2002] 2 E.G.L.R. 167 Lands Tribunal.

CHAPTER 13

IMPROVEMENTS[1]

1. INTRODUCTION

Those provisions of the Landlord and Tenant Act 1927 ("the 1927 Act") which entitled business tenants to compensation for loss of goodwill if their landlords declined to renew their leases have been abolished and replaced by the provisions of the 1954 Act relating to security of tenure and compensation for disturbance. However, the provisions of Pt 1 of the 1927 Act which relate to improvements remain in force. These enable tenants of holdings to which the 1927 Act applies to carry out improvements on their holdings, subject to certain conditions and formalities, and further entitle them to compensation for those improvements, subject to certain further conditions and formalities.[2] **13–01**

The right to contract out of the 1927 Act is restricted. By virtue of s.9 the Act applies notwithstanding any contract to the contrary if that contract was made after February 8, 1927. By a proviso to that section, contracting-out for adequate consideration is permitted, but by s.49 of the 1954 Act that proviso ceased to have effect in relation to contracts made after December 10, 1953. **13–02**

2. DOES THE 1927 ACT APPLY?

Applies to holdings

The Act is expressed to apply to certain kinds of "holding". The definition is very different from that of "holding" under the 1954 Act, since the 1927 Act definition includes the entirety of the premises held under the lease in question, not just that part of those premises which are occupied by the tenant for the purposes of a **13–03**

---

[1] All references to sections in this Chapter are to sections of the Landlord and Tenant Act 1927 unless otherwise stated. It should be noted that no amendments are made by the 2003 Order to the 1927 Act as to the entitlement to carry out and claim compensation for improvements.

[2] The 1927 Act s.19(2), implies into covenants against the making of improvements without the licence or consent of the landlord a qualification that the covenant shall be deemed, notwithstanding any express provision to the contrary, to be subject to a proviso that licence or consent is not to be unreasonably withheld. This extends to all leases other than agricultural holdings, farm business leases and mining leases: s.19(4). It is not intended in this work to deal with the provisions of s.19. This Chapter is confined to the provisions of Pt 1 of the 1927 Act, which enables improvements to be carried out albeit there is an absolute prohibition against the making of alterations (s.3) and provides for a limited right to the payment of compensation (s.1). A tenant who has a qualified right to carry out improvements, whether expressly or by reason of s.19(2), may still seek to obtain compensation at the end of the lease by following the Pt 1 procedure.

business.[3] Agricultural holdings as defined by the Agricultural Holdings Act 1986 are expressly excluded, as are holdings held under farm-business tenancies within the meaning of the Agricultural Tenancies Act 1995.[4]

13–04 Part 1 of the Act does not apply to any holding let to a tenant as the holder of any office, appointment or employment, from the landlord, and continuing so long as the tenant holds such office, appointment or employment.[5] This is considered further in para.13–10.

Must be held under a lease

Meaning of "lease"

13–05 In order to come within the 1927 Act, the holding must consist of premises "held under a lease". "Lease" is defined in s.25(1) to mean a lease, underlease or other tenancy, an assignment operating as a lease or underlease, or an agreement for such a lease, underlease, tenancy or assignment. It follows that premises held under a licence are not holdings to which the 1927 Act applies. The question whether a tenancy at will comes within this definition must be open to doubt.[6]

13–06 There is no limitation under the 1927 Act as to the duration of the lease in order for Pt 1 to apply. Under the 1954 Act short leases are excluded from protection.[7] However, there is no corresponding exclusion of such a lease from the application of Pt 1 of the 1927 Act. Thus the 1927 Act applies to fixed-term tenancies, however short the term, and to periodic tenancies. Similarly, a tenancy may be excluded by agreement from the protection of the 1954 Act.[8] However, Pt 1 of the 1927 Act will apply to such an excluded business tenancy. By analogy with the position under the 1954 Act it is considered that the 1927 Act would apply to an unlawful sub-lease.[9]

Mining leases

13–07 The 1927 Act does not apply to premises held under a "mining lease", which is defined by s.25(1) to mean a lease "for any mining purposes or purposes connected therewith". Presumably the purpose of the lease is to be ascertained by an examination of the user clause and other internal evidence, although extrinsic evidence about the purpose of both parties to the lease is, perhaps, admissible. It is to be noted that it is irrelevant that the tenant is not, in fact, using the premises for mining: *O'Callaghan v Elliott*.[10]

---

[3] s.17(1). Compare the 1954 Act definition (discussed in para.8–06 et seq.). As to the difference between occupation and use see further below, para.13–12 et seq.

[4] s.17(1).

[5] s.17(2).

[6] Compare the position under the 1954 Act (discussed in para.1–17 et seq.).

[7] See para.1–148 et seq.

[8] See para.2–02 et seq.

[9] *D'Silva v Lister House Developments Ltd* [1970] 2 W.L.R. 563; [1970] 1 All E.R. 858, see para.1–28.

[10] [1966] 1 Q.B. 60; [1965] 3 W.L.R. 746; [1965] 3 All E.R. 111 CA.

"Mining purposes" are defined[11] in wide terms so as to include: **13–08**

> "the seeking and searching for, winning, working, getting, making merchant-able, smelting or otherwise converting or working for the purposes of any manufacture, carrying away and disposing of mines and minerals in or under land, and the erection of buildings, and the execution of engineering and other works suit able for those purposes."[12]

In *O'Callaghan v Elliott*[13] it was held that "mines and minerals" for the purpose of the definition include all substances capable of being worked for a profit below the top surface of the land, such as sand, gravel and clay, but not peat. In *Earl of Lonsdale v Attorney-General*[14] this phrase in the context of a nineteenth-century conveyance was held to include only solid substances capable of being dug out of a mine and therefore not oil or natural gas. On a literal reading the definition in the 1927 Act would apparently include the lease of a factory where sand is graded and put into sacks (because that is the "making merchantable" of a mineral) and also the lease of an iron-smelting plant. Whether the courts would give the definition such a wide interpretation, so as to exclude such leases from the 1927 Act (and the 1954 Act), remains to be seen. **13–09**

Holder of office, etc.

By virtue of s.17(2), the Act does not apply to any holding let to a tenant as the holder of any office, appointment or employment from the landlord and continuing so long as the tenant holds such office, appointment or employment. In the case of tenancies created after the commencement of the Act (which must, in the nature of things, almost certainly now be all tenancies), the contract must be in writing and express the purpose for which the tenancy is created. "The contract" referred to can presumably be either a tenancy agreement or a contract of employment which includes a term granting a tenancy to the employee. In order to be excepted from the Act the landlord and the employer must be the same person and the tenancy must be expressed to come to an end when the tenant ceases to hold the office, appointment or employment. **13–10**

Date of lease

The 1927 Act applies to leases made before or after the commencement of the Act. **13–11**

Must be used for trade or business

The 1927 Act applies only where such premises are "used wholly or partly for carrying on thereat any trade or business". The differences between this provision and that of the 1954 Act should be noted. The test under the 1927 Act is whether **13–12**

[11] s.25.

[12] The definition is contained within the definition of "mining lease": s.25(1).

[13] [1966] 1 Q.B. 60; [1965] 3 W.L.R. 746; [1965] 3 All E.R. 111 CA.

[14] [1982] 1 W.L.R. 887; [1982] 3 All E.R. 579.

the premises are "used", not whether they are "occupied".[15] Under the 1927 Act there is no requirement that the premises should be used by the tenant.[16] Nor is there any requirement that the business should be that of the tenant.[17] However, unlike the 1954 Act definition, the 1927 Act requires that the business should be carried on "thereat", that is to say at the holding.

13–13 The 1927 Act provides no general definition of "trade or business" and it should be noted in particular that the wide definition of "business" for the purposes of the 1954 Act[18] does not apply (see para.1–111 et seq.). The absence of any reference to "business" including an activity of a body of persons whether corporate or unincorporate would appear to exclude the application of Pt 1 to activities carried on by a members club.[19]

13–14 The words "trade or business" have been considered by the courts in other contexts, especially in revenue cases. It appears that the word "business" necessarily connotes the motive of making profits. In *Smith v Anderson*[20] Jessel M.R. said that "business" was "anything which occupies the time and attention and labour of a man for the purpose of profit". "Trade" does not necessarily mean something by which a profit is made. In *Re Incorporated Council of Law Reporting for England and Wales*[21] Coleridge C.J. said:

> "... it is not essential to the carrying on of a trade that the persons engaged in it should make or desire to make, a profit by it. Though it may be true in the great majority of cases the carrying-on of a trade does, in fact, include the idea of profit, yet the definition of the mere word 'trade' does not necessarily mean something by which a profit is made."

In *Brighton College v Marriott*,[22] a company limited by guarantee had as its principal object to provide a general education in conformity with the doctrines of the Church of England—an object admittedly charitable. It was held that the company in providing education for money was carrying on a trade, notwithstanding that the whole purpose and object of the charity was the carrying

---

[15] Compare para.1–42 et seq.

[16] Compare para.1–80 et seq.

[17] Compare para.1–122 et seq.

[18] s.23(2) of the 1954 Act.

[19] See, e.g. under the 1954 Act, *Addiscombe Garden Estates v Crabbe* [1957] 3 W.L.R. 980; [1957] 3 All E.R. 563 CA (digested in para.1–111) and para.1–115. Contrast *Carlisle and Silloth Golf Club v Smith* [1913] 3 K.B. 75 CA, where in addition to the members of the club, who were entitled on payment of an annual subscription to play on the links and to other privileges for the current year, a considerable number of visitors were permitted to use the club premises and to play on the links in accordance with a provision contained in the lease which required the club to allow such visitors to play on payment of certain green fees. Buckley L.J. said: "If it were necessary (which it is not) to decide whether the club were carrying on 'an adventure or concern in the nature of trade,' I am of opinion that they were. To determine this question it is not the character of the person who carries on but the character of the concern which is carried on that has to be regarded. If a landowner laid down upon his land a golf course and charged fees for admission and user—if, that is to say, the links were a proprietary golf links carried on with a view to profit—there can be no question but that the proprietor would be assessable. The adventure of maintaining golf links and charging for the use of them is an 'adventure or concern in the nature of trade.'"

[20] (1880) L.R. 15 Ch. D. 247 CA.

[21] (1888) L.R. 22 Q.B.D. 279.

[22] [1926] A.C. 192.

on of the school. The business of sub-letting residential flats is expressly excluded from the 1927 Act by s.17(3)(b).

By virtue of the proviso to s.17(3), "premises regularly used for carrying on a profession" shall be deemed to be premises used for carrying on a trade or business "so far as this Part of this Act relates to improvements". Since those parts of the 1927 Act which did not relate to improvements have now been abolished, the effect is that all such premises are now deemed to be used for carrying on a trade or business. Accordingly, the case of *Stuchbery v General Accident*,[23] where it was held that a solicitor did not carry on a "trade or business" within the meaning of s.17 for the purposes of obtaining compensation for loss of goodwill, has ceased to be relevant. Reference to regular use is presumably intended to exclude from protection a lease granted to a professional man of premises where the use is mainly residential, but only intermittently for professional purposes.[24] There is no definition within the Act of the term "profession". Scrutton L.J. has said that: **13–15**

> "A profession in the present use of language involves the idea of an occupation requiring either purely intellectual skill or manual skill controlled, as in painting, sculpture, or surgery, by the intellectual skill of the operator, as distinguished from an occupation which is substantially the production or sale of commodities. The line of demarcation may vary from time to time. The word 'profession' used to be confined to the three learned professions, the Church, Medicine and Law. It has now, I think, a wider meaning."[25]

It is provided that where premises are used partly for the purposes of a trade or business and partly for other purposes, the provisions of Pt 1 apply only to improvements which are improvements to the trade or business.[26] Subsection (4) of s.17 does not mean that the alterations must still result in the same business being carried on throughout. The subsection is contrasting the improvements in relation to the trade or business for which the premises are partly used and improvements in relation to the other purposes for which the premises are used, and is applying the Act only to the former: *National Electric v Hudgell.*[27] Thus, it is clear that Pt 1 applies to mixed-use premises, e.g. shop with residential upper part. Work to the residential part would not prima facie appear to be work capable of certification under the Act nor eligible for compensation, unless it can be said that the work is, within the wording of s.17(4) "*in relation* to the trade and business". **13–16**

In the remainder of this Part, the expressions "holding", "lease", "land- lord" and "tenant" refer to holdings, leases, landlords, and tenants, to which the 1927 Act applies. **13–17**

---

[23] [1949] 1 All E.R. 1026 CA.

[24] Compare the substantial purpose of occupation test under the 1954 Act: *Cheryl Investments Ltd v Saldanha* [1978] 1 W.L.R. 1329; [1979] 1 All E.R. 5 CA (digested at para.1–39).

[25] *Inland Revenue Commrs v Maxse* [1919] 1 K.B. 647 CA.

[26] s.17(4).

[27] [1939] Ch. 553 at 565; [1939] 1 All E.R. 567.

3. THE RIGHT TO MAKE IMPROVEMENTS

Proper improvement

13–18 The provisions of the 1927 Act are sometimes considered solely in terms of the right which they confer upon a tenant in certain circumstances to claim compensation for improvements. For example, in *Owen Owen v Livett*[28] (digested in para.13–74) the tenant applied for a certificate that proposed improvements were proper improvements and the entire case appears to have been argued upon the footing that no certificate should be granted unless its effect would be to entitle the tenant to claim compensation at the termination of his tenancy. But this is open to question. Why should the landlord be able to object, in his notice of objection, to an improvement being carried out merely because the tenant would not be able to claim compensation? The right to carry out an improvement is distinct from the tenant's right to compensation for the improvement. It would appear that an improvement is a proper improvement, within the meaning of s.3(1) of the 1927 Act, if it complies with s.3(1)(a), (b) and (c). In other words, the landlord is entitled to object to the granting of a certificate by the tribunal only upon the merits of the proposed works. Furthermore, to limit proper improvements to those in respect of which the tenant will be entitled to compensation overlooks, it is suggested, two further important rights granted by the Act. First, the tenant of a holding to which the Act applies has the right, in certain circumstances, to carry out an improvement to the holding which he would otherwise not be permitted to carry out under the terms of his tenancy. Secondly, the situation can arise in which the landlord is entitled to carry out improvements at his own expense in return for a reasonable increase in the rent.

"Improvement"

13–19 The meaning of the word "improvement" must first be considered. The word is not defined anywhere in the 1927 Act although the right to obtain compensation conferred by s.1(1) is said to relate to any improvement "(including the erection of any building)". Although a tenant is not entitled to compensation for "a trade or other fixture which the tenant is by law entitled to remove",[29] this express exception contained in s.1(1) suggests that for all purposes other than the claiming of compensation at the end of the term the installation of tenant's fixtures might constitute an improvement.

13–20 The words "an improvement on his holding"[30] do not impose any condition that some part of the original bricks and mortar of the buildings upon the holding must be retained. In *National Electric v Hudgell*[31] it was held that demolition of

[28] [1956] Ch. 1; [1955] 3 W.L.R. 1; [1955] 2 All E.R. 513.
[29] See para.13–71.
[30] ss.1(1) and 3(1).
[31] [1939] Ch. 553; [1939] 1 All E.R. 567.

all the existing buildings on the site and the erection of new buildings of a different size and design and intended to be used for different purposes was an "improvement" within the Act.[32]

Morton J. said:

> "Thus the plaintiffs' holding under the two leases is a piece of land having a front-age of 120 ft for each piece, with a frontage of 60 ft to the Great North Road and a depth of 125 ft, with a cinematograph theatre upon it which cannot now be used for any form of public entertainment. If the proposed works are carried out, the holding will consist of the same piece of land, having upon it a row of new shops, with residential flats over them. It is admitted that the works to be carried out would enable the holding to be used profitably, and would forthwith greatly increase the value of the holding for letting purposes and otherwise, and that they are works which are calculated to add to the letting value of the holding at the termination of the term. All these allegations are admitted. So far, the change, to use for the moment a neutral word, is clearly for the benefit of the tenant, and it seems equally clear that the landlord's rent would be more amply secured throughout the term. It seems to me that these works would be an improvement of the holding in any ordinary use of the word 'improvement.' Supposing, for example, the plaintiffs were to say: 'We have pulled down the cinematograph theatre, which is no longer any use for this purpose. We have substituted for that a row of shops with residential flats over them. The result is greatly to increase the letting value of the holding, and to increase also the letting value of the holding at the end of the term.' It would surely be a natural use of the words if the plaintiffs said: 'We have carried out an improvement on our holding.' To take a still stronger example, supposing that the holding consisted of a piece of land with a row of extremely badly built and possibly insanitary shops, and that the lessees of that holding pulled down those shops and erected a row of modern well-built shops, with every sanitary convenience, that would surely, in the ordinary use of the word 'improvement,' be an improvement of the holding."

It was also said in *National Electric v Hudgell* that it was unnecessary for the holding to be improved in its character as premises for the trade or business for which it was already being used. This may mean that works will be held to constitute an improvement even if their effect is to make the 1927 Act cease to apply to the holding. The work may equally be an improvement albeit it may impose an onerous burden upon the landlord to pay compensation at the end to the term. For instance, an investor might invest a small sum in a comparatively modest property, which was subject to a lease, and the lessee might pull down the property and erect an expensive block of shops with flats over it and thereby impose upon the landlord against his will an obligation to pay a very substantial sum by way of compensation at the end of the lease. It has been said that might be the result of the Act in certain cases. However, it was considered that there was a potential safeguard inserted in s.3 itself, because the improvement cannot be carried out under the section unless the tribunal is satisfied that it is reasonable and suitable to the character of the holding: *National Electric v Hudgell.*[33] **13–21**

For the purposes of s.19(2) of the Act, which attaches to covenants against the making of the improvements without consent a proviso that such consent will not be unreasonably withheld, the Court of Appeal has held that anything which, from the tenant's point of view, renders his occupation of the premises more **13–22**

[32] It has been said that Morton J.'s interpretation of "improvement" as covering demolition and re-erection was a very natural interpretation of the words: Parker C.J. in *Sainty v Minister of Housing and Local Government* (1964) 15 P. & C.R. 432 DC (not a case under the 1927 Act).

[33] [1939] Ch. 553; [1939] 1 All E.R. 567.

beneficial is an improvement: *Woolworth v Lambert*[34] and *Lambert v Woolworth*.[35] However, in *National Electric v Hudgell*[36] this was not considered to be a helpful analogy for the purpose of Pt 1 of the 1927 Act In *Price v Esso*[37] (digested in para.7–104), it was held that a contractual stipulation which entitled the landlord to enter the premises during the tenancy for the purpose of effecting "alterations additions or improvements" allowed the landlord to enter and demolish the entirety of the buildings comprised in the tenancy and to rebuild them according to a new design of his own choosing.[38]

13–23 In summary, it appears that all physical works which the tenant wishes to do to his premises whether they be works of demolition, alteration or building, are likely to come within the meaning of the word "improvement", although this by no means necessarily means that the tenant intending to carry out such works will be able to satisfy the other conditions imposed by the Act which must also be fulfilled before he can do so and before he can claim compensation.

Tenant must give notice of intention to effect improvement

13–24 The Act gives the initiative for proposing an improvement to the tenant; there is no equivalent provision entitling a landlord to initiate the process, as he might well wish to do if the enhanced rent which he could obtain would be sufficient return upon the capital which he would need to expend in making the improvement. Section 3(1) provides that where a tenant proposes to make an improvement "he shall serve on his landlord notice of his intention to make such improvement". The mandatory terms of this provision might appear to suggest that in every case a tenant who intends to carry out an improvement must give notice to his landlord, even if the improvement is one which he is entitled to carry out under the terms of his tenancy and even if he has no intention to claim compensation at the end of term. It is most doubtful whether the courts would in fact adopt such an interpretation, so as to render a tenant liable for damages for breach of statutory duty where he carried out works of improvement which were not prohibited by any covenant, but which he had not notified to his landlord. The point must remain open but it provides a useful argument for a landlord who wishes to prevent alterations to the premises which are not caught by the terms of any express covenant in the lease. Where the tenant is under a statutory obligation to carry out the improvement he must still serve on his landlord a notice of intention: s.48(1) of the 1954 Act.

13–25 The subsection further provides that the notice of intention must be accompanied by a specification and plan showing the proposed improvement and the part of the existing premises affected thereby. In *Deerfield v Leathersellers*[39] (case

[34] [1937] Ch. 37.
[35] [1938] Ch. 883; [1938] 2 All E.R. 664.
[36] [1939] Ch. 553; [1939] 1 All E.R. 567.
[37] [1980] 2 E.G.L.R. 58 CA.
[38] *National Electric v Hudgell* was cited by Megaw L.J. in support of that conclusion.
[39] (1983) 46 P. & C.R. 132 CA.

13–26) the court made the following observations (some based on con-cessions made by counsel and accepted by the court) on the requirements of a notice of intention:

(1) There is no prescribed form.
(2) The notice must be in writing.
(3) The notice need not expressly refer to the 1927 Act.[40]
(4) The notice may include a statement by the tenant that he intends to carry out additional works which are not, in fact, improvements. It need not distinguish between the two categories of work.
(5) There is no need for the notice, plan and specification to be separate documents. One, or two, pieces of paper, suitably annotated, may suffice.
(6) Nor need the notice, plan and specification all be served at the same time. There is sufficient "togetherness" if documents served at different times are connected by their wording, or by circumstances.
(7) The "specification" must give to the landlord substantially all the information which he would want in order to deal with his various options during the three-month period following service of the notice.
(8) Whether a document or documents can be treated as a notice is to be judged objectively, as an ordinary matter of construction.
(9) The notice must be served on the landlord or his agent authorised to receive such a notice, but it is sufficient if an authorised agent in fact subsequently passes on the notice to the landlord.
(10) If separate documents are served, the three-month period commences when the last of them is served.

Deerfield Travel Services v Wardens and Society of the Mistery or Art of the Leather Sellers of the City of London[41] Before sub-letting, the tenants planned to execute substantial works of refurbishment to the premises, some of which it was thought would qualify as "improvements" within the Landlord and Tenant Act 1927. On June 23, 1978, the tenants' solicitor wrote to the landlords' solicitor and referred to "various modernisations and improvements" which the tenants proposed to carry out, involving "a considerable sum of money", and enclosed "a set of plans prepared by the architects to the lessees". Finally he requested confirmation that "consent to the alterations being made is, in principle, available" and an indication as to "the proportion of the monies spent the Leathersellers will be prepared to reimburse on termination of the tenancy". The letter was passed to the landlords and thence to their surveyors, who on August 11, 1978, wrote to the tenants' solicitors to suggest that the tenants discuss the proposed alterations with them, the landlords' surveyors. Thereafter, the **13–26**

[40] However, the notice must at least impliedly refer to the Act. Although Lawton and Templeman L.JJ. declined in *Deerfield Travel Services v Wardens and Society of the Mistery or Art of the Leather Sellers of the City of London*, to decide whether a notice which did not expressly or impliedly refer to the Act would be valid, it would appear that Gray QC sitting as a deputy judge to the High Court has so held: see *Oldschool v Caplin* Unreported August 8, 1994, cited in Haley, *The Statutory Regulation of Business Tenancies*, 1st edn (Oxford: OUP, 2000).

[41] (1981) 43 P. & C.R. 143; (1982) 263 E.G. 254 (first instance); (1983) 46 P. & C.R. 132; [1982] 2 E.G.L.R. 39 CA.

surveyors communicated on the landlords' behalf from time to time with the tenants' architect. On August 29, 1978, the tenants' architect sent the landlords' surveyors the detailed plans which had been requested. Subsequently, the landlords' surveyors indicated to the tenants' architect that there were no objections to the work going ahead and advised the landlords that some of the work amounted to improvements, but that no compensation should be paid. The tenants, however, had given instructions and the work had been commenced, when it transpired that the landlords were not willing to make any contribution. The tenants applied by originating summons to the Chancery Division for declarations on, inter alia, the following preliminary issues:

(1) Whether the letter dated June 23, 1978, constituted a notice of intention to make improvements under s.3(1) of the Landlord and Tenant Act 1927.
(2) If so, whether the landlords had served a notice of objection within three months of such notice.
(3) Whether the court had jurisdiction under the 1927 Act to certify that the works executed by the tenants (a) were proper improvements; or (b) had been duly executed.

Peter Gibson J. found that as from August 11, 1978, the landlords were to be taken as holding out their surveyors to act as their agents to negotiate the proposed alterations, thereby impliedly authorising them to deal with any matters that arose. He also found that it would have been obvious to the surveyors that the outline plan supplied with the letter of June 23, 1978, was likely to be supplemented by a detailed drawing at a later date, and that the plans which were eventually supplied together with the matters in correspondence contained all the information on which the surveyors needed to be in a position to advise the landlords for the purposes of s.3(1) of the 1927 Act. Accordingly, the landlords were to be taken as having been informed of what was to be done by way of improvements and alterations and the judge granted the declarations sought in the affirmative, restricting the declaration on jurisdiction, however, to certifying that the works had been duly executed.

The landlords appealed and the issue before the Court of Appeal was whether the judge had erred in law: (a) in holding that the tenants' letter of June 23, 1978, was a valid notice of intention to make improvements pursuant to s.3(1) of the Landlord and Tenant Act 1927; (b) in holding that the accompanying plan was a "specification" within the meaning of the Act.

The Court of Appeal held that:

(i) On a true construction of the letter dated June 23, 1978, the tenants had by implication made known to the landlords that they were making a claim which "complied broadly" with the provision of s.1 of the 1927 Act. The letter would have alerted a "reasonably sensible businessman" at least to the extent of prompting him to seek advice and since in this case the letter had been sent to the landlords' solicitors, advice should have been available.

(ii) The outline plan which accompanied the letter dated June 23, 1978, was not in itself a sufficient plan or "specification". It was not necessary, however, for the purposes of s.3 of the 1927 Act that the sending of plans and specifications should be contemporaneous with the notice of intention because "as a matter of common sense" very often in these cases the tenant is able to give notice of intention to make improvements but he may have to wait some time for detailed plans and specifications to be drawn up. It was sufficient that there was some "linkage" between the notice and the detailed plans and that was provided here by the "inevitable expectation" that the outline plan would be followed by detailed plans.

(iii) Accordingly, since notice of intention, plans and a specification satisfying the provision of the 1927 Act had been served, the land-lords' appeal was dismissed.

Time for service of notice of intention

Section 3(1) does not lay down any time limits within which the tenant is to make his proposal. Presumably, he can give notice as soon as the tenancy is granted to him and can do so at any time during the term. However, it is likely to be implied that a notice of intention to carry out works given less than three months before the expiry of the term would be invalid, since to hold otherwise would be to deprive the landlord of the full three-months' period during which he has the right to serve notice of objection.[42] The provisions of s.23 as to service of the notice are discussed above (para.3–49 et seq.). **13–27**

The tenant is required to serve on his landlord notice of his intention to make the improvement together with a specification and plan, and must supply copies to any superior landlord, albeit the tenant is obliged by statute to carry out the improvements.[43] However, the landlord has no right to object to such improvements.[44] A certificate that the improvement is a proper one need not be obtained, but the tenant may apply to the court for a certificate that the improvement has been duly executed.[45] **13–28**

Service of notice on superior landlords

The duty of the tenant under s.3(1) is to serve a notice on his immediate landlord. Where the immediate landlord is himself a tenant, he should serve on his immediate landlord copies of all documents relating to proposed improvements and claims which have been sent to him by his tenant. Service of these copies must be made "within the time and in the manner prescribed": s.8(1). "Prescribed" means prescribed by rules of court or by a practice direction.[46] Prior **13–29**

---

42 As to the landlord's right to object, see para.13–30 et seq.

43 s.48(1) 1954 Act.

44 s.48(1) 1954 Act.

45 s.48(1) 1954 Act.

46 See s.25(1) of the Landlord and Tenant Act 1927, as amended by the Civil Procedure (Modification of Enactments) Order 2001 (SI 2001/2717), which came into force on October 15, 2001.

to CPR Pt 56, it was provided by CPR Sch.1, RSC Ord.97 r.4(2) (High Court), and CPR Sch.2, CCR Ord.43 r.3(2), (county court) that such copies must be served "forthwith" and the copy must be accompanied by a notice in writing stating the date when the document was received by the immediate landlord. It is unclear, now that the whole of CPR Sch. 1, RSC Ord.97 and CPR Sch.2, CCR Ord.43 have been revoked what, if any, requirement exists for service upon superior landlords of the notice of proposed improvements. The Practice Direction to Pt 56 makes provision only for the service up the chain of interests of the claim form and documents served with it: PD 56 para.5.5. Unlike the provisions of para.6 of Sch.6 to the 1954 Act, s.8(1) of the 1927 Act does not impose any statutory duty to serve copies on superior landlords. The sanction imposed is that a landlord who fails to serve such copies will be unable himself to claim from his landlord such compensation for the improvement as he may become liable to pay to the tenant.

Landlord may serve notice of objection

13–30 The landlord who has received notice of the tenant's intention to do works of improvement may give notice of objection: s.3(1). Any superior landlord who has been served with a copy of the tenant's notice of intention is also entitled to object by giving notice to the tenant proposing to carry out the improvement.[47] A superior landlord who has not been served with such a copy has no right to object on his own behalf. Notice of objection, whether by the immediate or any other landlord, must be served within three months of service of the tenant's notice of intention. The landlord cannot serve a notice of objection where the tenant is required to carry out an improvement pursuant to a statutory obligation: s.48(1) of the 1954 Act.

Notice of objection

13–31 No definition of "notice of objection" is contained in the Act and no form of notice is prescribed. However, in *Deerfield v Leather Sellers*[48] (digested in para.13–26) the court held that "the objection in question must be an objection to the tenant making the proposed improvements". There the fact that the landlord had maintained that the works were works of repair (not improvement) did not mean that the landlord had objected to their being carried out by the tenant. It is not, however, entirely clear whether the notice must indicate that the landlord objects to the improvement as such, or whether it is sufficient that he objects to it being carried out by the tenant (rather than by the landlord). It may be that an offer by the landlord himself to carry out the improvement, if made within the three-month period, would be construed as a notice of objection.

13–32 If no notice of objection is received within the three-month period, the tenant is able to carry out the work according to the tenant's notice of intention as detailed

---

47 s.8(1).

48 [1982] 2 E.G.L.R. 89 CA.

in the specification and plan.[49] There is no time limit on when, in these circumstances, the tenant is to carry out the work. It may be, therefore, that the tenant has the right to carry out the work at any time during the remainder of the term.

The landlord is not entitled to object to an improvement made in pursuance of a statutory obligation.[50] **13–33**

Landlord's offer to carry out improvements

Form of offer

Instead of serving a notice of objection, the landlord may himself offer to execute the improvement in consideration of a reasonable increase of rent, or of such increase of rent as the tribunal may determine. This appears to give the landlord a choice of offer which he can make. He can say, "I will do the work in return for an increase of £1,000 per annum", in which case the tribunal will refuse a certificate if, but only if, £1,000 is a reasonable figure. Or he can say, "I will do the work in return for such increase as the tribunal may determine". In that case it would seem that the tribunal should determine the proper increase and refuse a certificate accordingly. Presumably the landlord could combine an offer of the first type with an alternative offer to accept what the tribunal determined if it decided against him on reasonableness. **13–34**

It would appear that the offer must relate to the whole of those works in respect of which (but for the offer) the tribunal would have granted a certificate; the landlord cannot offer to do some only of those works, still less propose an alternative scheme of works which he prefers. Although it is not so stated in s.3(1), the landlord's offer must presumably contain some time limit within which he undertakes to carry out the improvement. This would seem to follow from the provision that the effect of an offer is to prevent the tribunal from furnishing a certificate "unless it is subsequently shown to the satisfaction of the tribunal that the landlord has failed to carry out his undertaking". No time limit is imposed for the making of this offer; it does not have to be made within the three-month period available for notice of objection. In practical terms, the landlord should serve a notice of objection within the three-month period, even if he intends to make an offer, otherwise the tenant can simply ignore the offer and carry out the improvement himself; if no notice of objection has been served, the matter never comes before the tribunal. **13–35**

It has been held in *Norfolk Capital Group Ltd v Cadogan Estates Ltd*[51] that a landlord who has had served upon him a notice pursuant to s.3(1) does not, upon serving notice upon the tenant that he would carry out the improvements in consideration of a reasonable increase in rent, acquire a right to carry out the improvements where the tenant does not accept the landlord's offer. **13–36**

[49] As to the ability to override absolute covenants in the lease or contained in a headlease, see para.13–50.

[50] s.48(1) of the 1954 Act. See also paras 13–28 and 13–30.

[51] [2004] EWHC 384 (Ch).

Reasonable increase in rent

13–37 The 1927 Act does not contain any definition of, and nor is there any decided authority on, the meaning of the expression "reasonable increase of rent". There would appear to be three possibilities: first, that the reasonable increase in rent is to reflect a proportion of the increase in the capital value of the improved property; secondly, that it is to reflect a percentage of the increase in the current letting value of the improved property; and thirdly, that it is to represent a fair return on the capital that the landlord has to expend in carrying out the improvements pursuant to his offer; in other words, a fair return on capital invested.

13–38 The first possibility, it is considered, can be disregarded, for there is no basis for suggesting that this section is looking at determining an increase in rent by reference to the increased capital value of the improved property. There is, however, some support within the terms of the 1927 Act for the view that the appropriate basis for determining the reasonable increase in rent is by reference to the increase in letting value. The tenant, in order to obtain a certificate that the improvement is a proper one, is required to satisfy the relevant tribunal that, inter alia, the improvement "is of such a nature to be calculated to add to the letting value of the holding at the termination of the tenancy" (s.3(1)(a) of the 1927 Act). It is, therefore, arguable that as the tribunal has to consider in determining whether a certificate is to be granted the increase in letting value of the holding, albeit at the termination of the tenancy, the letting value of the holding is the relevant criterion in determining the reasonable increase of rent, particularly since the purpose of making an offer is to prevent a certificate being granted. Further, the landlord could seek to argue that the (unimproved) property would have been let at a greater rental if the proposed works of improvement had existed at the date of grant. Why should not the landlord now seek to recoup by way of a reasonable increase of rent a percentage of the increase in the letting value of the improved premises? That is surely the whole basis of the limitation imposed by s.3(1)(a) upon what is an "improvement", namely the requirement that it should add to the letting value of the holding at the termination of the tenancy; the landlord is not to be left with premises which during the course of the term the tenant has by force of statute altered to the detriment of the landlord.

13–39 So far as the third possibility is concerned, some support for this view is to be found in the level of compensation to which the tenant would be entitled if he had carried out the work at his own cost. The tenant's compensation is not to exceed the net addition to the value of the holding as a whole which may be determined to be the direct result of the improvement (s.1(1)(a)) or the reasonable cost of carrying out the improvement at the termination of the tenancy, subject to a deduction of an amount equal to the cost (if any) of putting the works constituting the improvement into a reasonable state of repair, except so far as such cost is covered by the liability of the tenant under any covenant or agreement as to the repair of the premises (s.1(1)(b)). The tenant may therefore recoup under limb (b) the capital which he has invested. If the landlord offers to carry out the work at his own cost it is appropriate, therefore, that the landlord should only obtain a fair return on the capital which he has invested for the remainder of the term.

The Act does not state when the increase of rent becomes payable nor whether the offer is to make any suggestion as to the date of payment. It is considered that the most likely date from which payment is to commence is the date of completion of the works of improvement by the landlord. **13–40**

Right of entry

Although s.10 appears to confer upon any landlord who has "undertaken" to execute improvements a right of entry to carry out such works, the better view would appear to be that the landlord who has made such an offer is not entitled forthwith to enter and carry out the works unless and until the tenant has accepted his offer (see para.13–36). If the tenant would prefer that the improvement be not carried out instead of his paying an increased rent, he is not bound to accept the landlord's offer, but will be unable to carry out the improvements himself. **13–41**

Application to tribunal for certificate

If the tenant has received a notice of objection within the three-month period he may "in the prescribed manner" apply to the tribunal for a certificate that the improvement is a proper improvement: s.3(1). "Prescribed" means prescribed by rules of court or by a practice direction.[52] The manner was until October 2001 prescribed by Sch.1, RSC Ord.97 r.5 (High Court) and Sch.2, CCR Ord.43 r.4 (county court). The procedure is now governed by CPR Pt 56, and the Practice Direction thereto, para.5.[53] The tribunal is defined by s.21 as being the court which has jurisdiction pursuant to s.63 of the Landlord and Tenant Act 1954, which will be either the High Court or the county court (now that there is no longer any rateable value limit on the county court jurisdiction). The tenant need not apply to the tribunal for a certificate where the improvement has been carried out in pursuance of a statutory obligation: s.48(1) of the 1954 Act. The tenant may, however, apply for a certificate that the improvement has been duly executed (see para.13–54). **13–42**

Upon the hearing of an application pursuant to s.3(1), the tribunal is required to ascertain that notice of intention has been served upon "any superior landlords interested". The effect of this provision is unclear, since, as has been noted,[54] the immediate landlord may have decided not to serve copies upon superior landlords or may have omitted by error to do so, in which case the only consequence appears to be that he is unable to claim compensation from them and they are not entitled to serve notice of objection. Nonetheless, such superior landlords may, for reasons other than compensation, be "interested" in the question whether the tenant should be entitled to carry out the improvement. For example, the superior landlord may himself be bound by a covenant which would be broken if the improvement is carried out. If the tribunal ascertains that no notice has been served upon such superior landlords, what is the effect? It can hardly be that the **13–43**

[52] See s.25(1) of the Landlord and Tenant Act 1927, as amended by the Civil Procedure (Modification of Enactments) Order 2001 (SI 2001/2717), which came into force on October 15, 2001.

[53] As to the procedure, see para.14–121 et seq.

[54] See para.13–54.

application is invalid, because the tenant was under no duty to do more than serve his notice of intention upon his immediate landlord. Nor, as has been pointed out, was the immediate landlord under any duty to serve copies on his immediate landlord, although he should do so if he wishes to claim compensation. Nor can the effect be that the tribunal orders the service of fresh notice upon those superior landlords, giving them the right to object within three months of that further notice. Since the immediate landlord has necessarily objected himself, otherwise the matter would not be before the tribunal, such a direction would be pointless. Because the tribunal is required to give the superior landlords an opportunity of being heard, the only practical effect of this would therefore appear to be that, where no notice of objection has been served on a superior landlord, the application should be adjourned for a sufficient time to allow the superior landlord to be represented before the tribunal.

Criteria for grant of certificate

13–44 The tenant must then satisfy the tribunal of three things concerning the improvement.

That it is of such a nature as to be calculated to add to the letting value of the holding at the termination of the tenancy

13–45 This requirement considerably cuts down the wide definition of "improvement".[55] Once the matter has come before the tribunal the question of whether the landlord's reversion will be enhanced at the termination of the tenancy becomes relevant. The following difficult question may arise where a substantial term of years remains unexpired. If the tenant proposes to erect an office building and 80 years of his lease remain unexpired, it is quite likely that the building will have been pulled down and another one erected in its place before the lease falls in. Unless the tribunal is satisfied to the contrary, it would appear that in such a case the tenant would not succeed under limb (a) of s.3(1).

That it is reasonable and suitable to the character of the holding

13–46 Section 3(2) provides that in considering whether the improvement is reasonable and suitable to the character of the holding, the tribunal shall have regard to any evidence brought before it by the landlord or any superior landlord (but not any other person) that the improvement is calculated to injure the amenity or convenience of the neighbourhood. This prevents the tenant's application being turned into a sort of "planning enquiry" by local amenity groups and other objectors who are not themselves the immediate or superior landlord of the tenant.

---

[55] As to which, see para.13–19 et seq.

That it will not diminish the value of any other property belonging to the same landlord, or to any superior landlord from whom the immediate landlord of the tenant directly or indirectly holds

Proof of *any*diminution in the value of such property is apparently sufficient to defeat the tenant's application; it is not necessary to prove that such diminution would be substantial. Nor does it appear, from the structure of s.3(1), that it is open to the tribunal, if it is satisfied that there will be diminution to the value of such property, to allow the application upon condition that the tenant makes suitable financial recompense to the landlord for the diminution. **13–47**

It seems to us that once the tribunal is satisfied on the above three matters, it should grant a certificate, even if it has no reason to believe that the effect of such a grant will be to enable the tenant to claim compensation at the termination of his tenancy. Insofar as the language used in *Owen Owen v Livett*[56] (digested in para.13–74) may, on one reading, suggest the contrary, we consider that it is misleading. If the tribunal is so satisfied it is provided by s.3(1) that, after making such modifications (if any) in the specification or plan as it thinks fit and imposing such other conditions as it thinks reasonable, the tribunal may certify "in the prescribed manner"[57] that the improvement is a proper improvement. The court has no jurisdiction to grant a certificate in respect of works which have been executed or even started; in such a case all it can do is to certify that the improvement has been "duly executed": *Deerfield v Leather Sellers*[58] (digested in para.13–26) and *Hogarth Health Club v Westbourne Investments Ltd*[59] (digested in para.13–49). The manner of certification was prescribed by CPR Sch.1, RSC Ord.97 r.5 (High Court) and CPR Sch.2, CCR Ord.43 r.4 (county court), which provided that any such certificate shall be embodied in an order. The procedure for Pt 1 is, in respect of claims issued after October 15, 2001, governed by CPR Pt 56 and the Practice Direction thereto, PD 56 para.5. It is provided that if the court intends to certify under s.3 of the 1927 Act that an improvement is a proper improvement or has been duly executed, it shall do so by way of an order: PD 56 para.5.7.[60] **13–48**

Hogarth Health Club v Westbourne Investments Ltd[61] A sports club and sports ground in Chiswick, London, was demised for a term of 28 years from September 1960. In June 1979 the tenants gave notice to their landlords of the intention to make certain improvements. In November 1979 the landlords gave notice of objection. In December 1979 the tenants applied to the county court for a certificate that the proposed works were proper improvements within the meaning of s.3 of the Landlord and Tenant Act 1927. The works were in fact commenced in 1979 (probably before the issue of the application) and were completed in October 1981. Meanwhile the proceedings followed a desultory **13–49**

[56] [1956] Ch. 1; [1955] 3 W.L.R. 1; [1955] 2 All E.R. 513.
[57] As to the meaning of "prescribed", see fn.52 above.
[58] (1983) 43 P. & C.R. 143.
[59] [1990] 1 E.G.L.R. 89 CA.
[60] As to procedure, see para.14–121 et seq.
[61] [1990] 1 E.G.L.R. 89 CA.

course. The landlords applied to strike out the tenants' proceedings on the ground of inordinate and inexcusable delay. This application was dismissed. On appeal it was held that an application for a certificate could not be heard and determined by the court after the improvements had been completed. There were numerous indications in the Act that when the application comes before the court it must relate to improvements yet to be made in the future. The intent and purpose of s.3 was to provide the tenant with the means of knowing in advance whether improvements that he proposed to carry out would be lawful and would be proper for the purpose of calculating compensation at the end of his tenancy. The whole tenor of the section was consistent only with a certificate being granted before the works are completed.

Entitlement to carry out proposed improvement

13–50 Section 3(4) provides that, where no notice of objection has been served within the three-month time limit, or where the tribunal has given a certificate that the improvement is a proper one:

> "it shall be lawful for the tenant as against the immediate and any superior landlord to execute the improvement according to the plan and specification served on the landlord, or according to such plan and specification as modified by the Tribunal or by agreement between the tenant and the landlord or landlords affected, anything in any lease of the premises to the contrary notwithstanding."[62]

The far-reaching effects of this provision are often overlooked. The lease may contain an absolute prohibition on the making of the proposed improvement and such a prohibition may be contained in one or more of the superior leases. Nonetheless, if there has been no notice of objection or if the tenant has obtained his certificate, he is able to override the provisions of those leases and it is lawful for him to carry out the works. This is particularly startling in its effect upon superior landlords, since, as has been noted,[63] there is no statutory duty upon the tenant or the landlord to serve notice of intention upon any superior landlord, and no right in any superior landlord who has not been served with a copy of the notice of intention to object on his own behalf. The courts have not yet been required to consider the full implications of this section.

4. CARRYING OUT THE IMPROVEMENT

By landlord pursuant to undertaking

13–51 The improvement may be carried out by the landlord where he has offered to do so and the tenant has accepted that offer (see paras 13–34 to 13–41). In such a case, the tribunal will have refused to certify that the improvement is a proper

---

[62] This subsection does not permit a tenant to carry out an improvement in contravention of any restriction created or imposed for naval, military or air-force purposes or for civil aviation purposes under the powers of the Civil Aviation Act 1982, or for securing any rights of the public over the foreshore or seabed: s.3(4).

[63] See para.13–29.

improvement, but it may reconsider the matter if it is subsequently shown that the landlord has failed to carry out his undertaking: s.3(1). The landlord is presumably also contractually bound to the tenant by such undertaking, so that if he fails to comply with it the tenant will have the remedy against him of damages and specific performance.[64] Where the landlord has given such an undertaking which has been accepted and the landlord wishes to carry it out, it is provided by s.10 that he has a right of entry at all reasonable times for the purposes of executing the improvement and of making any inspection of the premises which may reasonably be required.

By tenant pursuant to certificate

A tenant who has obtained a certificate from the tribunal is entitled, but not bound, to carry out the works certified. If he wishes subsequently to claim compensation, he must carry out the works certified, comply with any conditions imposed by the tribunal and complete the improvement within such time as has been agreed between landlord and tenant or fixed by the tribunal: see s.3(5). It may be that even if a tenant does not comply with such conditions, or does not complete the improvement within the time agreed or fixed, the improvement will nonetheless be taken to have been lawfully made, albeit the right to claim compensation will have been lost. On the other hand it may be objected that circumstances may have changed between the hearing before the tribunal and the date (after expiry of the time limit) when the tenant decided to carry out the improvement. In such a case it might be unjust to the landlord to allow the tenant to carry out the improvement without once again going through the procedure of the 1927 Act. **13–52**

By tenant where no notice of objection has been served

Likewise a tenant who has served notice of intention, but has received no notice of objection within the three-month period is entitled, but not bound, to carry out the works specified in his notice. In such a case there would appear to be no limitation upon the time within which he is entitled to carry them out. **13–53**

Certificate of execution

Once the tenant has duly carried out the improvement, he may require the landlord to furnish him with a certificate that the improvement has been duly executed: s.3(6). This is so even if the tenant has commenced the works within three months of his notice of intention, provided the landlord has not served a notice of objection within that period: *Deerfield v Leather Sellers*[65] (digested in para.13–26). If the landlord refuses or fails within one month to do so, the tenant **13–54**

[64] The contract would not have to comply with the provisions of the Law of Property (Miscellaneous Provisions) Act 1989, s.2 as the contract is not one for the sale or other disposition of an interest in land.
[65] (1983) 46 P. & C.R. 132 CA.

may instead apply to the tribunal which shall, if satisfied that the improvement has been duly executed, give a certificate to that effect. The tenant is liable to pay the landlord's reasonable costs of furnishing a certificate. The purpose of such a certificate is that it evidences due compliance with the provisions of the Act in relation to the improvement. This may be of some importance if the improvement is carried out many years before the termination of the tenancy, since otherwise due compliance might be difficult to prove.

Increase in rates or fire insurance to be borne by tenant

13–55 The effect of an improvement to the holding may be to increase the rateable value thereof or to increase the amount of insurance premiums. Section 16 provides that, where the landlord is liable to pay any rates or fire insurance premiums, which are increased in consequence of an improvement, the rent payable by the tenant to the landlord shall be increased accordingly.

5. THE RIGHT TO COMPENSATION FOR IMPROVEMENTS

Conditions for compensation

13–56 The Act of 1927 confers upon tenants the right to compensation for improvements, subject to a number of conditions. One would think that such a right would be of considerable value, yet claims under the Act for compensation are made with surprising infrequency.[66] This may be because tenants believe that the amount of such compensation is unlikely to be worth the bother of going through the procedures of the Act, because the existence of the right to compensation is not sufficiently well appreciated by tenants and their advisers, because the provisions of the Act are so technical that tenants and their advisers simply fail to operate the procedures properly, or a combination of these and other factors. Needless to say, we would recommend as good practice to tenants and advisers that they should at least contemplate, in every case where the tenant intends to carry out works of alteration to the premises within the 1927 Act, whether any steps should be taken in order to safeguard the tenant's right to compensation.

Checklist of preconditions

13–57 The following checklist is provided for easy reference in order to determine whether compensation is payable. Each point in the checklist is considered in detail in the following paragraphs. In order for compensation to be payable it is necessary to answer each of the following questions in the affirmative:

(1) Is there a tenancy of a holding to which the 1927 Act applies?

---

[66] Neuberger J., noted in *Daejan Properties v Holmes* [1996] E.G.C.S. 185, that the tenant's rights under Pt 1 of the 1927 Act are infrequently invoked because the procedure is often unfamiliar, and lengthy and the outcome uncertain.

(2) Has the tenant under that tenancy (or a predecessor in title of his) observed the necessary formalities under s.3?
(3) Has the tenant made a claim for compensation within the time limit specified in s.47 of the 1954 Act?
(4) Has the tenant quit the holding?
(5) Has the tenancy come to an end?
(6) Has work of improvement, not being a trade or other fixture which the tenant is by law entitled to remove, been carried out on the holding?
(7) Was that work of improvement carried out otherwise than in pursuance of a contract entered into for valuable consideration?
(8) Was the work of improvement carried out by the tenant or his predecessor in title?
(9) Does the work of improvement add to the letting value of the holding at the termination of the tenancy?

Holding must be one to which the Act applies

Only a tenant of a holding to which the 1927 Act applies is entitled to claim compensation. The conditions which must be fulfilled in order for the 1927 Act to apply have already been discussed.[67] Since those conditions may be fulfilled, or cease to be fulfilled from time to time, it follows that tenancies can go in and out of the 1927 Act. It is therefore of importance to consider at what time it is necessary for the tenancy to be one to which the 1927 Act applies if the tenant is to be entitled to compensation. Although the 1927 Act gives no express guidance it appears from the way in which its machinery is intended to operate that the 1927 Act must apply both at the date when the tenant serves his notice of claim pursuant to s.47 and on his quitting at the termination of the tenancy. Thus, an intervening period when Pt 1 does not apply to the holding would appear to be irrelevant. This is in accordance with the construction placed upon s.4 of the 1927 Act (now repealed) in *Smith v Metropolitan Properties Co Ltd.*[68] **13–58**

Necessary formalities must have been observed

Section 3(5) provides that a tenant shall not be entitled to claim compensation under the 1927 Act unless he has, or his predecessors in title have, gone through the formal procedures under s.3. These have already been fully considered.[69] **13–59**

Must have given notice of claim in due time

Section 47 of the 1954 Act lays down strict time limits within which the tenant must make a notice of claim if he is subsequently to be entitled to compensation for improvements. In practice, a tenant will often fail to make his claim within due time, because he first comes to consider the question of compensation for **13–60**

---

[67] See paras 13–03 to 13–17.
[68] [1932] 1 K.B. 314.
[69] See para.13–18 et seq.

improvements when his current tenancy has come to an end and he is on the point of quitting. Indeed, the operation of the time limits is such that the tenant may have to serve a notice of claim even in circumstances where he does not yet know whether he will or will not obtain a new tenancy from the court under the 1954 Act. In such circumstances, of course, it is good practice for notice of claim to be served, in any event, to guard against the eventuality of a new tenancy being refused.

The relevant time limits

13–61 (1) Where the tenancy is terminated by notice to quit (whether given by the landlord and whether given under the 1954 Act or at common law). The claim must be made not more than three months after the giving of the relevant notice, except where the tenant has made a request for a new tenancy under s.26, in which case the claim must be made within three months of the landlord's counter-notice stating whether he will oppose the grant of a new tenancy, or (if he has not served a counter-notice) within three months of the latest date upon which he could have done so. Where a landlord, himself a tenant, served a notice to quit on his sub-tenant, but before the expiration of the notice the head lease came to an end, it was held for the purposes of s.5(5) of the 1927 Act (repealed) (which required a claim for a new tenancy to be made "not less than nine months before the termination of the tenancy or where the tenancy is terminated by notice within eighteen months after service of the notice . . .") that the sub-lease was terminated not by the notice to quit but by the termination of the head lease: *Allied Ironfounders Ltd v John Smedley Ltd.*[70]

(2) Where the tenancy comes to an end by effluxion of time. The claim must be made not earlier than six nor later than three months before the coming to an end of the tenancy.

(3) Where the tenancy is terminated by forfeiture or re-entry. The claim must be made within three months of the "effective date" of the order of the court for the recovery of possession or (in the case of peaceable re-entry) within three months of re-entry. The "effective date" of the order is defined by s.47(4) of the 1954 Act to mean the date on which the order is to take effect according to the terms thereof or the date on which it ceases to be subject to appeal, whichever is the later.

No extension of time possible

13–62 In *Donegal Tweed v Stephenson*[71] it was held that the court had no jurisdiction to extend the statutory time limits for applying for a new tenancy under s.5 of the 1927 Act (now repealed). Presumably the same principle applies to the time limits imposed by s.47 of the 1954 Act.

[70] [1952] 1 All E.R. 1344.

[71] [1929] E.G.D. 210.

Procedure for making claim

In order to be valid, a claim must be made "in the prescribed manner".[72] The manner was prescribed by CPR Sch.1, RSC Ord.97 r.4 (High Court) and CPR Sch.2, CCR 1981 Ord.43 r.3 (county court). These rules provided that any claim for compensation must be in writing and be signed by the claimant, his solicitor or agent and should contain: **13–63**

(1) A statement of the name and address of the claimant and of the landlord against whom the claim is made.
(2) A description of the holding in respect of which the claim arises and of the trade or business carried on there.
(3) A concise statement of the nature of the claim.
(4) Particulars of the improvement including the date when it was completed and the cost thereof.
(5) A statement of the amount claimed.

These rules have been revoked with effect from October 15, 2001. The procedure for instituting proceedings under Pt 1 of the 1927 Act is governed by CPR Pt 56 and the Practice Direction thereto in respect of claims made after October 15, 2001. The new rules, PD 56, para.5.8, make virtually identical provision as to the contents of the notice of claim *which precedes* the institution of the proceedings under Pt 1.[73] The service of the notice of claim is regulated by s.23.[74]

It was held in *British Colonial v William McIlroy*[75] that a notice of claim for compensation for disturbance under s.4 of the 1927 Act (now repealed) was invalid if it failed to state any of the prescribed particulars and that the courts had no jurisdiction to give leave to amend. The notice of claim could not be read together with the proceedings, which did refer to the amount of the compensation, in order to validate it as the proceedings were issued one month after the expiration of the time for making the notice of claim. Presumably, the reasoning behind this decision applies also to notices of claim for compensation for improvements made pursuant to s.1 of the 1927 Act. **13–64**

By the provisions of s.8(1) a mesne landlord shall not be entitled to make a claim for compensation unless "in the time and manner prescribed" he had served on his immediate superior landlord copies of all documents relating to claims for compensation sent to him in pursuance to Pt 1 of the 1927 Act. The time and manner were prescribed by CPR Sch.1, RSC Ord.97 r.4(2) and CPR Sch.2, CCR Ord.43(3), which provided for mesne landlords to serve copies of notices of claim received by them upon their superior landlord. These provisions were revoked with effect from October 15, 2001 as a result of the introduction of CPR Pt 56 and the Practice Direction thereto. There is, however, corresponding **13–65**

---

72 As to the meaning of "prescribed", see s.25(1) of the 1927 Act, fn.52 above.
73 As to court procedure, see para.14–121 et seq.
74 See para.3–49 et seq.
75 [1952] 1 K.B. 107.

provision in the new rules for notification of superior landlords by mesne landlords of claims for compensation: see PD 56 para.5.9.

The tenant must have quit the holding

13–66 It is a precondition of entitlement to compensation that the tenant has quit the holding. Thus, if a tenant holds over after the termination of his current tenancy, his claim to compensation will not crystallise until he has actually moved out. It is considered that a tenant who renews his tenancy cannot carry forward his claim for compensation. There are several reasons for this.[76] First, the offer by the landlord of the grant of a new tenancy was originally a ground for refusing compensation.[77] The grant of the new lease was in substitution of the right to compensation. By the grant of the new lease the tenant continues to enjoy the benefit of the improvement. Secondly, the Jenkins' Committee, considered that a claim to compensation did not survive the renewal of the tenancy.[78] Thirdly, if the right to compensation survives the renewal "it is difficult to see what effect could be given to the inclusion of 'predecessors in title' if the title under which the improvements were carried out was not the same title as that in respect of which the claim for compensation is made".[79]

13–67 In *Pelosi v Newcastle*[80] (digested in para.13–68), the Court of Appeal distinguished between the entitlement to be paid compensation, which arises only when the tenant has quit the holding upon termination of his tenancy, and his right to claim compensation which can be said to arise earlier. The court pointed out that in order to serve his notice of claim the tenant must be entitled to do so and by reason of the time limits laid down by s.47 of the 1954 Act this right must necessarily arise before termination of the tenancy[81] and will probably arise before the tenant has quit the holding. Further, the court observed that the "claim" referred to in s.1(1) of the 1927 Act is a notice of claim in accordance with the then RSC Ord.97 or CCR Ord.43 (now PD 56 para.5.8), and not a formal application by originating summons to the court. The court dismissed arguments, such as impressed the Divisional Court in *Smith v Metropolitan Properties Co Ltd*[82] to the effect that it was premature to determine the tenant's entitlement to compensation before the termination of his tenancy. Indeed, the court observed that it might in many cases be possible to determine the amount of compensation before that date. In any event, the Court of Appeal thought that the ratio decidendi of the *Smith v Metropolitan Properties*decision, which was in any event not binding on the Court of Appeal, no longer had any application because of the procedural changes since the decision was made. The County Court Rules in force when *Smith v Metropolitan Properties* was decided required the tenant to proceed "by action commenced by Plaint and ordinary summons". The ratio of

---

76 See *Woodfall, Law of Landlord and Tenant* (London: Sweet & Maxwell), Vol.2, para.22.200.
77 s.2(1)(d). This section can no longer be implemented: s.48(2) of the 1954 Act.
78 The *Jenkins Report, Final Report of the Leasehold Committee* (1950) Cmnd. 7982, para.295.
79 See *Woodfall, Law of Landlord and Tenant* (London: Sweet & Maxwell), Vol.2, para.22.200.
80 [1981] 2 E.G.L.R. 36 CA.
81 Save in the case of forfeiture of the lease.
82 [1932] 1 K.B. 314.

the judgment of the Divisional Court was that "no sum of money can be recovered by action unless the action be begun after the money is due". That reasoning was, said that court in *Pelosi*, inapplicable where the procedure for determination was by originating application.[83] However, as Ormrod L.J. noted, the County Court Rules (then in force) did refer to proceedings for the "determination of a right to compensation" and not for the recovery of the compensation due. In any event, it is now clear in light of the Court of Appeal's decision in *Pelosi* that the right to compensation may be determined prior to the quitting of the holding by the tenant, whatever one may make of *Smith v Metropolitan Properties Company Ltd.*

Pelosi v Newcastle Arms Brewery (Nottingham) Ltd[84] The landlord granted a lease to the tenant. The tenant granted a sub-lease. The sub-lessees carried out works of improvement with the landlord's consent to the premises. The sub-lessees assigned their sub-lease to X who subsequently obtained an assignment of the reversionary interest of the tenant, thereby merging the sub-lease with the lease. X, prior to the expiration of the term created by the lease, sought compensation for the works of improvement. It was accepted that he would only obtain compensation if he could establish that, pursuant to s.1(1) of the 1927 Act, the improvements were made by his "predecessor in title" as defined in s.25(1) of the Act. It was held: **13–68**

(1) That a tenant can institute proceedings for determination of the right to compensation and the amount thereof before the lease is terminated and he has quitted the holding; the right to payment, however, does not arise until termination of the lease and the quitting of the holding by the tenant.
(2) "Predecessor in title" within s.25(1) of the Act was not to be interpreted according to its strict conveyancing meaning. The tenant under the Act was the person entitled in possession to the "holding". Accordingly, the "tenant's predecessor in title" was the person from whom the tenant derived the right to possession. X could only establish his right to possession of the holding by reference to the sub-lease.

The tenancy must have terminated

It is also a precondition of the entitlement to compensation that the tenancy has terminated: see *Smith v Metropolitan Properties Co Ltd*[85] a case decided under s.4 of the 1927 Act (now repealed), where the construction of s.1 was also considered. For a discussion of the position under s.37 of the 1954 Act, which is different in its wording, see para.12–56 et seq. **13–69**

---

83 This applies equally to the institution of proceedings by way of a Pt 8 claim under the CPR.
84 [1981] 2 E.G.L.R. 36 CA.
85 [1932] 1 K.B. 314.

Must be a qualifying improvement

13–70 Certain works which would otherwise be in the nature of an improvement are specifically accepted from the compensation provisions of the 1927 Act.

13–71 Section 1(1) excepts any "trade or other fixture which the tenant is by law entitled to remove". Presumably the question of whether the tenant is or is not entitled to remove his fixtures is to be considered at the date of termination of the tenancy, since otherwise a tenant who wrongfully held over and failed to remove his fixtures within a reasonable period of termination of his tenancy would, ironically, obtain the right to be compensated for them.[86] On the question of the duration of the tenant's right to remove fixtures, see *New Zealand Government Property Corporation v HM&S Ltd*[87] (digested in para.8–127).

13–72 Section 2(1)(a) excludes compensation for any improvement carried out pursuant to a statutory obligation unless the improvement was carried out after October 1, 1954.[88] Improvements undertaken pursuant to a statutory obligation are unlikely to give rise to an entitlement to compensation, as it is common for modern commercial leases to require the tenant to comply with statutory requirements. A tenant's covenant to this effect is likely to render the improvement as one undertaken by the tenant "in pursuance of a contract" within s.2(1)(b) (see para.13–70) thereby defeating the claim for compensation.

13–73 Section 2(1)(b) excepts:

> "any improvement which the tenant or his predecessors in title were under an obligation to make in pursuance of a contract entered into, whether before or after the passing of the 1927 Act, for valuable consideration, including a building lease".

This exception has been given a wide construction; e.g. in *Owen Owen v Livett*[89] (digested in para.13–74) Upjohn J. held that works carried out pursuant to a contract made between the tenant and his sub-tenant, not between the tenant and his landlord, did not qualify for compensation. In s.9 of the 1927 Act, "contract" refers only to a contract made between landlord and tenant. However, Upjohn J. thought that "contract" in one section of the 1927 Act could have a different meaning in another section. Upjohn J.'s reason for the construction that he placed on s.2(1)(b) was that if "contract" was to be restricted to contracts made between landlord and tenant, then, if the tenant made an improvement pursuant to a contract with another party, such as a sub-tenant, he could get his quid pro quo twice over; once from the sub-tenant and again from the landlord under the terms of the Act. It will also be necessary in most cases to examine the terms of any licence entered into between the landlord and tenant relating to the improvements in order to see whether, upon its true construction, the tenant therein covenanted that it would carry out the improvements, see, e.g. *Godbold v Martin the*

---

[86] The Act does not provide for what is to happen if the improvement is a tenant's fixture but the lease requires the tenant to deliver it up at the end of the term.

[87] [1982] 2 W.L.R. 837; [1982] 1 All E.R. 624 CA.

[88] s.48(1) of the 1954 Act.

[89] [1956] Ch. 1.

Newsagents Ltd,[90] a rent review case. Section 2(3) provides a sort of "half-way house" for a case where there has been no contract pursuant to which the improvements were undertaken, but the tenant or his predecessors in title have nonetheless received from the landlord or his predecessors in title some benefit in consideration of the improvement. In that event, the tenant is entitled to compensation, but the tribunal may reduce its amount accordingly. No guidance is given on how the amount of this reduction is to be assessed.

Owen Owen Estate Ltd v Livett[91] The tenant served on the landlord a notice of intention to carry out certain works of improvement. The landlord within the time prescribed by s.3(1) of the 1927 Act served on the tenant notice of objection. The landlord's objection was that the tenant had sub-let the premises and was required to carry out the improvements pursuant to a covenant contained in the sub-lease and that accordingly, as the tenant was under an obligation to make the improvement pursuant to a contract entered into for valuable consideration within s.2(1)(b) of the 1927 Act, the improvement was not a proper improvement as the tenant would not be able to claim compensation at the expiry of the term. The tenant applied to the High Court as the tribunal under s.63 of the Landlord and Tenant Act 1954, for a certificate under s.3(1) of the 1927 Act that the improvements were proper. It was held that the sub-lease plainly put the tenant under an obligation to make an improvement and therefore it was an improvement which the tenant was under an obligation to make in pursuance of a contract entered into for valuable consideration; the expression "contract" within s.2(1)(b) of the 1927 Act could not be limited to a contract made between the landlord and the tenant. **13–74**

It must have been carried out by tenant or predecessor in title

Section 1(1) entitles "a tenant of a holding to which this Part of this Act applies" to be paid compensation "in respect of any improvement . . . made by him or his predecessors in title". **13–75**

The way in which the words "tenant" and "predecessor in title" have been interpreted in the decided cases may be thought, perhaps, to reveal a difference of judicial opinion. In *Pasmore v Whitbread*,[92] it was held that for a person to be a "predecessor in title" within the meaning of s.25 of the 1927 Act he must have had title to the tenancy in which the tenant has succeeded. If there has been a new grant to the tenant and the tenant has succeeded to the business carried on by another person in those premises, that person is not his "predecessor in title" within the meaning of the section. In *Williams v Portman*,[93] it was held that a sub-tenant who surrendered his interest to the tenant was not a predecessor in title of the tenant; accordingly, the tenant could not claim compensation pursuant to s.4 of the 1927 Act (now repealed) by relying upon the occupation of the **13–76**

[90] [1983] 2 E.G.L.R. 128.
[91] [1956] Ch. 1; [1955] 3 W.L.R. 1; [1955] 2 All E.R. 513.
[92] [1953] 2 W.L.R. 359; [1953] 1 All E.R. 361 CA.
[93] [1951] 2 K.B. 948; [1951] 2 All E.R. 539 CA.

sub-tenant. In *Corsini v Montague Burton*[94] it was held that a person is not a "predecessor in title" of the tenant if he occupied the premises not as tenant but pursuant to a licence or other friendly arrangement. However, in *Pelosi v Newcastle*[95] (digested in para.13–68) the Court of Appeal was prepared to give a rather wider and more purposive interpretation to s.25, which defines the tenant as "any person entitled in possession to the holding under any contract of tenancy" and "predecessor in title" as "in relation to a tenant or landlord . . . any person through whom the tenant or landlord has derived title, whether by assignment, by will, by intestacy, or by operation of law". The facts there were as follows. Certain improvements had been carried out by sub-tenants. At the time proper notices pursuant to s.3 had been served by the sub-tenants upon the tenant and by the tenant upon the landlord. Subsequently, the sub-tenancy was assigned and later the successors to the sub-tenants bought the tenant's interest. It was common ground that, as a result of this transaction, the sub-tenancy became merged in the tenancy. At the end of the tenancy the tenants claimed compensation for the improvements carried out by the sub-tenants. The Court of Appeal held that the tenant's entitlement to compensation involved them in showing a right to possession of the holding and that, in order to do so, it was necessary for them to prove title derived both from the sub-tenants and from the tenant. Accordingly, the Court of Appeal held, the tenants did indeed derive title from the sub-tenants, and were accordingly successors in title to the sub-tenants for the purposes of claiming compensation for their improvements. This may have the surprising result that a tenant who has carried out improvements, but has subsequently sub-let the premises, would be unable, upon the termination of his tenancy to claim compensation for those improvements, because he would be unable to prove that he was entitled to possession of the holding. This would be the case, even though the sub-tenant eventually quit the holding so that the landlord had the benefit of the premises together with valuable improvements. For the position in relation to sub-tenants' improvements under the 1954 Act, see para.8–120.

Must add to letting value of holding

Date at which ascertained

13–77 Section 1(1) entitles a tenant to be paid compensation only in respect of an improvement "which at the termination of the tenancy adds to the letting value of the holding". The policy behind this would appear to be, on the one hand, to compensate tenants for the cost of improvements to the holding, but, on the other hand, to avoid the landlord having to pay for such improvements if he in fact derives no benefit from them. This is particularly important because, as has been noted, whether something is an "improvement" is judged solely from the tenant's point of view. Whether it adds to the letting value of the holding, however, is to be judged at the date of termination of the tenancy on the basis of a valuation between the landlord and a hypothetical tenant thereof. If it is proved that the

[94] [1953] 2 W.L.R. 1092; [1953] 1 All E.R. 8 CA.
[95] [1981] 2 E.G.L.R. 36 CA.

improvement does not add to the letting value of the holding at the termination of the tenancy, then no compensation is payable.

Obligation to reinstate

Is it possible to avoid the payment of compensation by ensuring that the lease contains a provision requiring reinstatement at the end of the lease of any work undertaken pursuant to a certificate under the 1927 Act? If the tenant has to reinstate how can it be said that the improvement will add to the letting value of the holding? In order to obtain the certificate that the improvement is a proper improvement, the tenant need only show that the work *is calculated to add* to the letting value of the holding at the termination of the tenancy: s.3(1). However, for the purposes of compensation he must, under s.1(1), show that it adds to the letting value at the termination of the tenancy. The authors are not aware of any practice of incorporating reinstatement clauses of this nature which seek to negate the entitlement to compensation under the Act in this way. It may be said that such a clause in any event is an attempt to contract out of the Act contrary to the provisions of s.9.[96] **13–78**

6. AMOUNT OF COMPENSATION

May be agreed

Section 1(3) provides that "in the absence of agreement between the parties" all questions as to the right of compensation under s.1, or as to the amount thereof, shall be determined by the tribunal. For the procedure before the tribunal, see para.14–115 et seq. Clearly, under this provision it is possible for the parties to agree that compensation is payable, and/or to agree in respect of which works it is payable, even if they cannot agree how much should be paid in respect of those works. It is then only those matters which have not been agreed which need be referred to the tribunal. **13–79**

Quantification of amount of compensation

By virtue of the proviso to s.1(1), the sum to be paid as compensation for any improvement is limited to the lesser of the following amounts: (1) the net addition to the value of the holding as a whole which results directly from the improvement; or (2) the reasonable cost of carrying out the improvement at the termination of the tenancy, making allowance for any necessary repairs. Since each of these bases operates independently to fix a "ceiling" on the amount of compensation, it is necessary in every case to consider each basis separately. **13–80**

[96] On contracting out, see para.13–86 et seq.

The net addition to the value of the holding

13–81 Section 1(2) provides that in determining the amount of such net addition, regard shall be had to the purposes for which it is intended that the premises shall be used after the termination of the tenancy. Accordingly, the matter appears to be looked at from the landlord's point of view in the light of the purpose for which he, or some prospective tenant of his, will use the holding in future. This means that if the tenant has carried out improvements of a specialist nature which benefited the tenant in his business, but would be of little value to an incomer, he may receive no, or very little, compensation. In particular, in terms somewhat similar to those of s.18 of the 1927 Act (which limits the amount of damages recoverable in an action for dilapidations), s.1(2) further specifies that if it is intended to demolish or to make structural alterations in the premises or any part thereof or to use the premises for a different purpose, regard shall be had to the effect of such demolition, alteration or change of user on the additional value attributable to the improvement. Regard is also to be had to the length of time likely to elapse between the termination of the tenancy and the demolition, alteration or change of user. This means in effect that if the landlord intends to use the premises as improved for a year but then to demolish them, the tenant should be entitled to one year's purchase of the value of the improvements rather than to their value in perpetuity. It is unclear whether the landlord's intention must be assessed on the basis of the facts as they are found to be on the termination of the tenancy, as is the case under s.18 of the 1927 Act. An alternative view would be that the situation has to be assessed as it appears at the date of hearing of the tenant's application for compensation. Under this head, it is the "net" addition to the holding which is to be assessed; this indicates that it may be that an improvement may in some ways enhance the value of the holding, while in other ways diminish it. It is the net result of this benefit and detriment which is represented by the net addition to the value. It is thought that the value referred to is the capital value of the holding, not its value by the year.

13–82 **Example** Suppose that an office block was let in 1980 without air conditioning. Suppose that the tenant, at its own expense, and in compliance with s.3 of the 1927 Act, installed a full air-conditioning system in 1995. If the tenant claimed compensation upon expiry of its lease in 2005, the valuation under head (a) of s.1(1) would proceed as follows. First, one would have to value the premises upon the assumption that they had no air conditioning. Assume that in this condition they would have obtained a rental value of £400,000 per annum, and that a suitable year's purchase is five. On that basis, the capital value of the premises, unimproved, would be £2 million. In order to determine the net addition to the value of the block which is the direct result of the air conditioning, it is necessary to determine the value of the premises as improved. Assume that with its air-conditioning system the annual value of the premises is £500,000. Taking the same rate of return the capital value thereof would be £2,500,000 and the "net addition" would accordingly be £500,000.

The reasonable cost of carrying out the improvement, subject to a deduction in respect of repairs

The second basis of limitation of compensation for improvements is that it is not to exceed the reasonable cost of carrying out the improvement at the termination of the tenancy. In most cases this presumably is to be assessed by a building surveyor estimating that it would require at current costs to carry out the improvement. This is then subjected to a deduction of: **13–83**

> "an amount equal to the cost (if any) of putting the works constituting the improvement into a reasonable state of repair, except so far as such cost is covered by the liability of the tenant under any covenant or agreement as to the repair of the premises."[97]

The reason why this deduction is made is that if the improvement is not in a reasonable state of repair, compensation should not be computed by reference to the cost of carrying it out at the termination of the tenancy when presumably, as newly done work, it would be in good repair. However, if the disrepair is already covered by the tenant's obligations contained in the lease, as will often be the case, the disrepair is ignored, since the landlord will have his remedy in the form of an action for damages for dilapidations.

Example Taking the same facts as have been assumed in the example above under limb (a) it is possible to illustrate the operation of limb (b), assuming the tenant to have no liability for repair of the air-conditioning system. Suppose that the air conditioning system in 2005 would cost £400,000 to install, but that the existing system requires £100,000 to be spent on repairing it if it is to be brought into a reasonable state of repair. In that case compensation under (b) would be £300,000. **13–84**

Reduction on account of benefits

By virtue of s.2(3) as noted above, the tribunal is to take into account any benefits which the tenant or his predecessors in title may have received from the landlord or his predecessors in title in consideration expressly or impliedly of the improvement, such as a rent-free period attributable to the time when the carrying out of the improvement deprives the tenant of beneficial occupation. No express direction is given how the tribunal is to evaluate the appropriate reduction in this amount, but since compensation is being calculated by reference to current prices it is thought probable that the value of the benefit should also be taken at current prices. **13–85**

7. CONTRACTING OUT

Section 9

Section 9 of the 1927 Act provides as follows: **13–86**

[97] s.1(1)(b).

> "This Part of this Act shall apply notwithstanding any contract to the contrary, being a contract made at any time after the 8th day of February, nineteen hundred and twenty seven:
> Provided that, if on the hearing of the claim or application under this Part of the Act it appears to the tribunal that a contract made after such date as aforesaid, so far as it deprives any person of any right under this Part of this Act, was made for adequate consideration, the tribunal shall in determining the matter give effect thereto."

The proviso was repealed with respect to agreements made post 1953: s.49 of the 1954 Act.

Agreement of nominal sum

13–87 Does an agreement of a nominal sum in advance of the compensation being claimed fall foul of s.9?

13–88 It is to be noted that the proviso to s.9 required the tribunal to give effect to any agreement albeit it deprived "any person of any right under this Part of this Act", where the agreement was made "for adequate consideration". What was adequate consideration? In *Holt v Lord Cadogan*[98] the Divisional Court had to consider the proviso in connection with the provisions (since repealed) of s.4 to the 1927 Act, which conferred upon the tenant upon quitting the holding to compensation for disturbance (which was then calculated by reference to the value of the goodwill of the business). The tenant had a lease of six years from 1924. In 1927 the landlord granted consent to improvements carried out by the tenant. It was agreed between the parties that if the landlord did not enforce the repairing obligation at the end of the term the tenant in consideration agreed not to make a claim for compensation for disturbance. The tenant claimed compensation of £220 and in response to the landlord relying on the tenant's undertaking argued that the undertaking was void as it was caught by s.9 of the 1927 Act. The county court judge held that the consideration for the undertaking was not adequate. The premises were going to be demolished by the landlord at the end of the term and thus by reason of s.18 the damages to which the landlord would be entitled would be nil and thus the landlord's promise not to enforce the repairing covenant was of no value. His decision was reversed by the Court of Appeal. Lord Hanworth M.R. said:

> "The view of the County Court Judge was that . . . there was no adequate consideration, but it appeared to the Court that in considering the advantages which accrued to the tenant under the licence [to carry out the work], the . . . Judge had overlooked two things; first, that the tenant was relieved of the liability imposed on him to paint the inside and outside of the premises in . . . 1927, which must have involved an outlay of at least £40 or £50; and, secondly, that the tenant was given the advantage of being allowed to alter the premises, an alteration not necessarily for the benefit of the landlord . . . They . . . [were] solid and valuable benefits and it seemed impossible to cast them aside and to hold that the tenant did not get adequate consideration for giving up his claim for compensation."

Accordingly, the tenant's claim for compensation for disturbance was held to be barred.

---

[98] [1930] 46 T.L.R. 271 DC.

The proviso to s.9 dealt with *depriving* someone of a right under the Act. One could do so if one provided adequate consideration. However, after the repeal of the proviso one cannot deprive anyone of any right he has under the 1927 Act even for consideration. One must, however, distinguish between contracting out (which is a deprivation of rights) and agreeing the amount of the compensation (which is not a deprivation).[99] *Holt v Lord Cadogan* was a case where the tenant was agreeing not to exercise any right to claim compensation under the 1927 Act. Section 9 does not stop the parties from agreeing the amount of the compensation. It is considered that it remains possible to agree the amount of compensation so long as this does not amount to a contracting out. **13–89**

When does an agreement as to the amount of compensation constitute contracting out? The concern expressed in the *Jenkins Report* which led to the repeal of the proviso, was that the tribunal could find it difficult to determine, often many years after the grant, whether the consideration given at the date of grant was adequate. Now may it be argued that notwithstanding the repeal of the proviso the court should, in determining whether the tenant has agreed the amount of compensation or has alternatively contracted out of his rights, still have regard to what the tenant has received in return for the agreement? If the tenant has entered into a bona fide agreement and it is clear that notwithstanding the passing of time the tenant had received adequate consideration for agreeing a nominal sum by way of compensation, why should the court construe that as a contracting out? The *Jenkins Report* proposed that contracting out should be with the consent of the court and in considering whether or not to give consent the adequacy of the consideration would be taken into account. That proposal was not adopted. **13–90**

It has been said that: **13–91**

> "It is not possible to state categorically where the dividing line is to be drawn between agreeing the amount of compensation (e.g. at a nominal amount) and purporting to contract out of the Act. It is possible that the parties cannot agree in advance that any improvements carried out by the tenant will attract nominal compensation, but that such an agreement may be made in relation to a formulated scheme. On the other hand, since compensation is payable by reference to values and costs prevailing at the end of the tenancy, it may be that any agreement in advance is ineffective."[100]

The potential problem envisaged by this passage of agreeing a nominal amount may be sought to be overcome by having bands of compensation (descending in quantum with every passing year of the term) which is agreed to be payable over

---

[99] See, for instance, by analogy the decision in the House of Lords in *Wentworth Securities Ltd v Jones* [1980] A.C. 74 HL, considered in para.12–71, where an agreement to modify the price payable for the freehold interest was held not to be a modification of the right to acquire the freehold and therefore not struck down by s.23 of the Leasehold Reform Act 1967 which renders void any agreement insofar as it purports to exclude or modify the right to acquire the freehold or an extended lease.

[100] *Woodfall, Law of Landlord and Tenant* (London: Sweet & Maxwell) Vol.2, para.22.215. In passing it is also to be noted that notwithstanding the reservations in *Woodfall* about agreeing the amount of the compensation in advance, the 1927 Act does not contain words such as are to be found in s.38 of the 1954 Act, dealing with compensation for disturbance, which provide that there may be an agreement as to the amount of compensation but only after "the right to compensation has accrued": s.38(2) of the 1954 Act.

the term and which ultimately leads to payment at the end of the term of a "nominal" sum by reference to the anticipated value/cost of the improvements. Compensation under the 1927 Act is calculated on two bases. The tenant receives the lesser of first the net addition by the improvements to the value of the holding as a whole, or secondly, the reasonable cost of carrying out the improvement at the termination of the tenancy, making allowance for any necessary repairs.[101] As these are matters which are determined at the end of the lease one can see the force of the comments that an agreement in advance is ineffective. However, as one of the bases of quantifying the compensation is by reference to the addition to the letting value the parties may agree to write off the value over time such that by the end of the lease it is agreed that the net addition is limited so as to be nominal only.[102] Under this arrangement the agreement between the parties confers on the tenant an entitlement to compensation which reduces each year of the passing of the term. Thus if the tenancy is brought to an end prematurely, e.g. by surrender or forfeiture, the tenant receives more compensation than if it is brought to an end at a later date. If the term runs its course there is only nominal consideration payable being (and it being so recited as) a genuine pre-estimate of the net addition to the letting value at the end of the term.

13–92 It seems to the authors therefore that:

(1) for a tenant to agree not to claim compensation is a contracting out even if the agreement not to claim compensation is for consideration;
(2) for a tenant to agree no or only nominal compensation simpliciter is to be equated to a contracting out;
(3) that an arrangement which seeks to be a genuine pre-estimate of the compensation at the end of the term albeit agreed in advance at the beginning of the term may be upheld.

Obligation to reinstate

13–93 As to whether an agreement contained within the tenancy for reinstatement at the expiry of the term of the improvements effected is an effective means of preventing compensation being payable, see para.13–78.

8. PAYMENT OF COMPENSATION

Time of payment

13–94 As is confirmed by the decision of the Court of Appeal in *Pelosi v Newcastle*[103] (digested in para.13–68) the tenant is not entitled to be paid his compensation until his tenancy has come to an end and he has quit the holding. Sometimes, of

[101] See para.13–80 et seq.
[102] In very long leases the tenant would have considerable difficulties in obtaining a certificate for carrying out the improvement, due to the fact that a "proper improvement" must be one which is likely to add to the letting value at the termination of the current tenancy. It would be hard to show this at the start of, for example, a tenancy with a term of 125 years.
[103] [1981] 2 E.G.L.R. 36 CA.

course, there will at this date still be a dispute over the tenant's entitlement to compensation and/or as to the amount thereof. In such circumstances the landlord would not, it is thought, be held to be in breach of statutory duty in failing to pay an amount which was still in dispute, but would be liable to pay it forthwith upon the tribunal ruling on the matter. There would appear to be no provision for interest to be payable on the moneys, so interest would not run unless and until the tenant commenced proceedings claiming payment.

Payment "by his landlord"

By virtue of s.1(1) the compensation is to be paid to the tenant "by his landlord". **13–95** "Landlord" is defined in s.25(1) to mean any person who under a lease is, as between himself and the tenant or other lessee, for the time being entitled to the rents and profits of the demised premises payable under the lease; that is to say it means the immediate landlord.

The question of what person fulfils this definition, and is thus required to pay **13–96** compensation, is to be judged at the date of termination of the tenancy—this was certainly assumed on all sides in *GC&E Nuthall (1917) Ltd v Entertainments & General Investment Corp Ltd.*[104] By virtue of s.23(2), unless or until a tenant of a holding shall have received notice that the person entitled to the rents and profits has ceased to be so entitled and been told the name and address of the person who has become entitled, the tenant is entitled to look to the original landlord for his compensation.

Rights of mesne landlords

Section 8 governs the position where there is a chain of interests in reversion to **13–97** the tenancy in respect of which compensation for improvements is successfully claimed. In essence, as was said by Ormrod L.J. in *Pelosi v Newcastle*[105] (digested at para.13–48) "the scheme of the Act is to pass this liability back eventually to the person who benefits financially from the improvement". Thus, by virtue of s.8, any mesne landlord who has paid or is liable to pay compensation is entitled, at the end of his term, to compensation from his immediate landlord in like manner and on the same conditions as if he had himself made the improvements in question. The reference to "in like manner" incorporates the provisions of s.1 of the 1927 Act and s.47 of the 1954 Act.

The reference in s.8 to "on the same conditions" incorporates the provisions of **13–98** s.3 on the giving of notice of a proposal to make improvements and the obtaining, where necessary, of a certificate. It may be, of course, that a sub-tenant successfully claims compensation from the tenant, who is unable to pass on the liability to his landlord, because the tenant has not gone through the necessary statutory procedure. Section 8(1) further expressly provides that a mesne landlord is not entitled to claim compensation unless he has furnished his immediate

104 [1947] 2 All E.R. 384.
105 [1981] 2 E.G.L.R. 36 CA.

landlord with copies of all documents relevant to the making of the improvement and where he has done so the superior landlord, as well as the mesne landlord, has all the powers conferred by the 1927 Act as if he were the immediate landlord of the tenant. Thus, he may appear before the tribunal and is bound by the proceedings. A claim for compensation by a mesne landlord must be made at least two months before the expiration of his term.[106]

Right to make deductions

13–99 Section 11 gives to the landlord and the tenant a mutual right of set-off in respect of sums payable by way of compensation and sums due under or in respect of the tenancy.

Right of landlord to charge the holding

13–100 Schedule 1 contains provisions enabling a landlord who has paid compensation, or himself carried out an improvement, to obtain an order charging the holding. Such a charge acts as a security for the eventual repayment from his superior landlord of sums laid out by him.

9. CROWN LAND

13–101 The 1927 Act applies to land belonging to Her Majesty in right of the Crown or the Duchy of Lancaster and to land belonging to the Duchy of Cornwall, and to the land belonging to any Government Department.[107]

---

[106] s.8(1).

[107] s.24(1) and Sch.2.

CHAPTER 14

PROCEDURE

In this Chapter the following abbreviations are used: **14–01**

CCA—County Courts Act 1984
CCR—County Court Rules 1981
RSC—Rules of the Supreme Court
CPR—Civil Procedure Rules
PD—Practice Direction of the CPR
CG—Chancery Guide

1. PROCEDURE UNDER THE LANDLORD AND TENANT ACT 1954

Changes brought about by the 2003 Order

Prior to June 1, 2004 only a tenant could make an application and the claim was required to be made in accordance with the Pt 8 procedure of the CPR subject to amendment with regard to the filing of evidence as provided for by CPR Pt 56. The position was changed quite radically with effect from June 1, 2004. In summary the changes which were made were: **14–02**

(1) to make provision for renewal and termination claims by landlords[1];
(2) to provide for opposed claims to be dealt with by way of the Pt 7 procedure rather than by way of the Pt 8 procedure[2];
(3) the removal of any requirement for evidence to be filed with the claim form or with the defendant's acknowledgement of service[3];
(4) the removal of the entitlement to seek a stay.[4]

Jurisdiction

The application for a new tenancy under s.24(1) (whether by a tenant or a landlord) or a landlord's termination application under s.29(2) must be made in the court of competent jurisdiction, which may be either the High Court or the county court. The claim must be started in the county court save in exceptional circumstances: CPR r.56.2. The claim may be started in the High Court but the **14–03**

---

[1] As to which see paras 14–20 et seq. and 14–31 et seq.
[2] As to which see para.14–31.
[3] As to which see paras 14–81 et seq.
[4] Previously to be found in CPR r.56.3(4)(a) and (5). This does not prevent the court from ordering a stay pursuant to the general provisions of the CPR. See further paras 14–29 and 14–30.

claimant must file with the claim a certificate stating the reasons for bringing the claim in the High Court: CPR r.56.2(2). The circumstances[5] which may justify bringing the claim in the High Court are if there are complicated disputes of fact or there are points of law of general importance: PD 56 para.2(4). The value of the property and the amount of any financial claim may be relevant as to whether or not a claim should be started in the High Court but they are not conclusive and these factors alone will not normally justify starting the claim in the High Court: PD 56 para.2(5).

Jurisdiction of the county court

14–04 The jurisdiction of the county court was formerly limited to premises where the rateable value of the holding did not exceed £5,000: s.63 of the 1954 Act as amended by s.6(1) of and Sch.2 to the Administration of Justice Act 1973. Since July 1, 1991 the jurisdiction of the county court has been unlimited: s.63(2) of the 1954 Act as amended by the High Court and County Courts Jurisdiction Order 1991.[6]

Jurisdiction of High Court unlimited

14–05 The Chancery Division of the High Court has jurisdiction whatever the rateable value of the holding[7] (s.63(2) of the Act as amended). The claim[8] must be brought in the Chancery Division: PD 56 para.2(6); CG Ch.18.1(15). A master or a district judge may not, without the consent of the Vice-Chancellor, make a final order for the grant of a new tenancy except by consent: PD 2B para.5.1(j).[9]

The court of issue

14–06 The majority of claims will be issued in the county court. Prior to October 15, 2001[10] the claimant could only start his claim in the county court for the district in which (1) the defendant or one of the Defendants lived or carried on business or (2) the property, the subject of the claim for renewal, was situated. In respect of all claims issued after October 15, 2001 the claim must be issued in the county court for the district in which the land is situated: CPR r.56.2(1).

---

[5] The circumstances referred to in the Practice Direction are neither exhaustive nor conclusive. Both CPR r.56.2(3) and PD 56, para.2.4 refer to the circumstances which "may" justify starting in the High Court.

[6] SI 1991/724, art.2(1)(d).

[7] For the meaning of "holding" see para.8–06 et seq.

[8] Which will be by way of a Pt 8 claim in the case of an unopposed renewal or by way of a Pt 7 claim in the case of an opposed renewal or a landlord's termination application: see further below.

[9] They can make orders for interim rent: see further para.14–104 et seq. as to the procedure for making an application for interim rent.

[10] The coming into effect of Pt 56 and PD 56.

2. TRANSFER

Wrong county court

Now that the county court has jurisdiction whatever the rateable value of the holding, the only potential problem faced by the tenant's advisers is the possibility of issuing in the wrong court. Where the tenant has for some reason commenced proceedings in the wrong county court a judge[11] of the county court may order the proceedings: **14–07**

(1) to be transferred to the county court in which they ought to have been started;
(2) continue in the county court in which they have been started; or
(3) be struck out (CPR r.30.2).

This rule reflects the fact that although a county court is held for a particular district the jurisdiction of the county court is a general one: *Sharma v Knight*.[12] Thus, in that case an originating application made to a county court in the wrong district in time but forwarded (by that court) to the county court in the correct district so as to arrive out of time was held to have been made in time.

Transfer to the High Court

By the High Court

By s.41 of the CCA (preserved by s.63(9) of the 1954 Act) the High Court may, at any stage in proceedings commenced in the county court or transferred to the county court, order the proceedings or part of them to be transferred to the High Court if it thinks that the proceedings or any part of them should be heard and determined in the High Court. The jurisdiction of the court to exercise the powers conferred on the High Court by the County Courts Act 1984 is dealt with in CPR r.30.3. **14–08**

The matters to which the court must have regard include:

(1) the financial value of the claim and the amount in dispute, if different;
(2) whether it would be more convenient or fair for hearings (including the trial) to be held in some other court;
(3) the availability of a judge specialising in the type of claim in question;
(4) whether the facts, legal issues, remedies or procedures involved are simple or complex;

---

[11] Although CPR r.30.2(2) refers to the order being made by a "judge" this means, unless the context otherwise requires, a judge, master or district judge or a person authorised to act as such: CPR r.2.3(1).

[12] [1986] 1 W.L.R. 757 CA. See also *Gwynedd CC v Grunshaw* [2000] 1 W.L.R. 494 CA, where it was held that an appeal notice, which should have been issued in Caernarfon CC as the court in which the order, decision or award appealed was made but which was attempted to be made in the appellant's local county court in Skegness in Lincolnshire, was made within time, albeit the Skegness court had refused to file the appeal.

(5) the importance of the outcome of the claim to the public in general;
(6) the facilities available at the court where the claim is being dealt with and whether they may be inadequate because of any disabilities of the party or potential witness.

14–09 Upon an order for transfer, the transferring court will immediately send notice of the transfer to the receiving court. That notice will contain (1) the name of the case, and (2) the number of the case and at the same time as the transferring court notifies the receiving court it will also notify the parties of the transfer: CPR r.30.4.1; PD 30 paras 4.1 and 4.2. Any order made before the transfer of the proceedings is not affected by the order to transfer: CPR r.30.4(2). There is a right of appeal against the order for transfer. The procedure for appeal is dealt with in PD 30 para.5. An application can be made to set aside the order which should be made to the court which made the order (PD 30 para.6.1) and such an application should be made in accordance with CPR Pt 23 and the Practice Direction which supplements it: PD 30 para.6.2. The application to set aside the order for transfer may be made, for instance, where one of the parties was not present (e.g. under CPR r.23.10) or where neither party is present and the court made the order of its own initiative (CPR r.3.3(4) and (5)).

14–10 The High Court may on the application of any person interested order that the 1954 Act proceedings be transferred to the county court, if it appears to the court that the 1954 Act proceedings in the High Court and any proceedings before the county court should be heard together by the county court: 1954 Act s.63(4)(b).

By the county court

14–11 The county court by s.42 of CCA may at any stage in the county court proceedings, whether commenced in or transferred to the county Court, either of its own motion or upon the application of any party order the transfer of the whole or any part of the proceedings to the High Court. In the case of an application (whether by the tenant or the landlord) under the 1954 Act this power will most commonly be exercised where the court considers that some important question of law or fact is likely to arise: see PD 56 para.2(4). The governing criterion is that set out in CPR r.30.3(2) (set out above). PD 30 sets out the procedure on transfer, procedure for an appeal and application to set aside.

Transfer to the county court

By the High Court

14–12 The High Court may on its own motion or on the application of any party to the proceedings order the transfer of the High Court proceedings to the county court: CCA s.40. The question of transfer is most likely to be considered by the master on the hearing for directions. The criteria to which the court should have regard in making an order for transfer are those set out in CPR r.30.3(2) referred to above. If proceedings are commenced in the High Court when they should have been commenced in the county court, the High Court will normally strike out the claim or transfer it to the county court on its own initiative: PD 56 para.2(3). The costs of starting the claim in the High Court and of any transfer will normally be disallowed: PD 56 para.2(3). If the person bringing the proceedings knew, or ought to have known, that they should have been brought in the county court, there is a discretion to strike out. However, in view of the overriding objective (CPR r. 1.1(1) and (2)(b)) it is considered that the power to strike out is likely to be exercised only in extreme cases.

A claim with an estimated value of less than £50,000 would generally be transferred to a county court (PD 29 para.2.2). The court may still transfer to a county court a claim with an estimated value that exceeds £50,000: PD 29 para.2.3; PD 56 para.2.5. The decision to transfer may be made at any stage in the proceedings. The case if transferred, being of a Chancery nature, will ordinarily be transferred to the Central London county court (Chancery List) where the case will be heard by specialist Chancery circuit judges or recorders and a continuous Chancery List is maintained, and if the parties prefer a transfer to a local county court which coincides with a Chancery District Registry: CG, Ch.13 para.13.6. **14–13**

The High Court may on the application of any person interested order that the 1954 Act proceedings be transferred to the county court, if it appears to the court that the 1954 Act proceedings in the High Court and any other proceedings before the county court should be heard by the county court: 1954 Act s.63(4)(b). One can envisage circumstances where tenancies of a number of shops owned by the same landlord and let to various tenants have come up for renewal and most of the actions have been made in the county court whilst a few have been commenced in the High Court. If, e.g. the landlord invoked s.30(1) (demolition and reconstruction) in respect of all of the properties, it will be desirable for the proceedings to be decided by the same court. **14–14**

Costs of transferred matters

As has been seen, an application for a new tenancy or a termination application, whether commenced in the county court or the High Court, may be transferred pursuant to a number of provisions, namely ss.41 and 42 of the CCA and s.63(4) of the 1954 Act. The effect on costs of a transfer is dealt with by s.45 of the CCA. Where a matter has been transferred to the county court from the High Court, s.45 of the CCA gives the county court judge the same discretion as to costs as he would have had if the matter had been commenced in the county court, subject to any order made by the transferring court. **14–15**

The costs incurred, however, of any proceedings in the High Court prior to transfer may either be disallowed or awarded on the county court scale if the trial judge thinks the action should have been commenced in the county court. It is provided by PD 56 that if a claimant starts a claim in the High Court and the court decides that it should have started in the county court, the court will normally disallow the costs of starting the claim in the High Court and of any transfer: PD 56 para.2.3. **14–16**

14–17 Section 45 of the CCA deals also with the costs of actions transferred from the county court to the High Court. The position is identical to that in the county court in the sense that the High Court judge has the same discretion as to costs as if the application had been commenced in the High Court, subject to any order as to costs made by the transferring court.

Effect of transfer

To the High Court

14–18 Where the High Court makes an order for transfer pursuant to s.41 of the CCA or the county court makes an order pursuant to s.42 of the CCA it was previously the case that RSC Ord.78 provided that the proceedings were to be treated as if begun in the High Court by originating summons. However, there is now a common procedure and even more so since the introduction of CPR Pt 56 and PD 56. Where an order for transfer has been made the transferring court will immediately send notice of the transfer to the receiving court. The notice will contain the name of the case and the number of the case and at the same time as the transferring court notifies the receiving court it will also notify the parties of the transfer under CPR r.30.4(1): PD 30 para.4(2). The order for transfer takes effect from the date it is made by the court: PD 30 para.3.

To the county court

14–19 Where the claim form is transferred to the county court pursuant to s.63(4) of the 1954 Act it was previously provided, i.e. prior to the coming into force of the CPR, that the matter was to be treated as a county court action for all purposes: CCR Ord.16 r.6 providing for general provisions on transfer from the High Court. There appears to be no express provision in relation to proceedings transferred to a county court equivalent to CCR Ord.16 r.6 nor RSC Ord.97 r.11. The provisions contained within PD 30 for notification by the transferring court of the transfer (as noted in para.14–18) apply.

3. THE CLAIM FOR A NEW TENANCY

Claim form

14–20 The procedure for making an application for a new tenancy was, prior to the introduction of CPR, by way of an originating summons (RSC Ord.97 r.2) in the High Court and by way of an originating application (CCR Ord.43 r.2(1)) in the county court. In the county court albeit there was a practice form (Form N397) it was not prescribed. There was, until PD 8B (in its then form), some doubt as to the procedure for 1954 Act applications under the CPR, its form and the information which was required to be contained within it. However, PD 8B was itself difficult to follow and continued to distinguish between High Court and county court renewal proceedings. Since October 15, 2001 the claim form for both High Court and county court applications for renewal is to be in the claim form for Pt 8.[13]

By CPR r.56.3(3) and PD 56 para.2.1 it is provided that a claimant in a landlord and tenant claim[14] must use the Pt 8 procedure as modified by Pt 56 and the practice direction thereto.[15] Thus, an application for an unopposed new lease claim, whether made[16] by the landlord or the tenant, will be by way of a Pt 8 claim. The Pt 8 claim form is Form N208: CPR Pt 4, PD 4. Notwithstanding the introduction of CPR Pt 56, the Lord Chancellors Department has stated that it is not proposing to produce additional forms in respect of it. Thus, Form N208 continues to bear a resemblance to the forms previously used in the High Court and county court for pre-October 15, 2001 claims. Where a tenant's claims is opposed, the tenant must use the Pt 7 procedure (see para.14–31 et seq.). **14–21**

Prescribed information

Information to be provided in all claims (whether by landlord or tenant)

The claim form must contain information required by both Pt 8 and PD 56. By CPR r.8.2 it must state: **14–22**

(1) that Pt 8 applies to the claim;
(2) (a) the question which the claimant wants the court to decide; or (b) the remedy which the claimant is seeking and the legal basis for the claim to that remedy;
(3) if the claim is being made under an enactment, what that enactment is;
(4) if the claimant is claiming in a representative capacity, what that capacity is; and
(5) if the defendant is sued in a representative capacity, what that capacity is.

By PD 56 para.3.4 the claim form must also state: **14–23**

(1) the property to which the claim relates;
(2) particulars of the current tenancy (including date, parties and duration), the current rent (if not the original rent) and the date and method of termination;
(3) particulars of every notice or request given or made in respect of that tenancy under ss.25 or 26 of the 1954 Act; and
(4) the expiry date of—
    (a) the statutory period under s.29A(2);

---

[13] October 15, 2001 is the date when Pt 56 came into effect pursuant to Update 23 to the CPR.
[14] This is defined by CPR r.56.1(1) as meaning a claim under, inter alia, the Landlord and Tenant Act 1954.
[15] As to the conditions to be met in order for a claim for renewal to be made, see para.6–03 et seq. (claim by tenants) and para.6–07 (claim by landlords). As to the time by which the claim must be made, see para.6–17 et seq.
[16] As to when an application is "made", see paras 6–42 to 6–45.

(b) an agreed extended period made under s.29B.

Information to be provided where the claimant is the tenant

14–24 Where the claimant is the tenant, the claim form must in addition to the information referred to above, include[17]:

(1) the nature of the business carried on at the property;
(2) whether the claimant relies on ss.23(1A), 41 or 42 of the 1954 Act and, if so, the basis on which he does so;
(3) whether the claimant relies on s.31A of the 1954 Act and, if so, the basis on which he does so;
(4) whether any, and if so what part, of the property comprised in the tenancy is occupied neither by the claimant nor by a person employed by the claimant for the purpose of the claimant's business;
(5) the claimant's proposed terms of the new tenancy; and
(6) the name and address of—
    (a) anyone known to the claimant who has an interest in the reversion in the property (whether immediate or in not more than 15 years) on the termination of the claimant's current tenancy and who is likely to be affected by the grant of a new tenancy; or
    (b) if the claimant does not know of anyone specified by sub-para.(6)(a), anyone who has a freehold interest in the property.

Information to be provided where the landlord is the claimant

14–25 Where the claimant is the landlord making a claim for a new tenancy under s.24, the landlord, must, in addition to the details specified in para.3.4 of PD 56,[18] ensure that the claim form contains details of[19]:

(1) the claimant's proposed terms of the new tenancy;
(2) whether the claimant is aware that the defendant's tenancy is one to which s.32(2) applies and, if so, whether the claimant requires that any new tenancy shall be a tenancy of the whole of the property comprised in the defendant's current tenancy or just of the holding as defined by s.23(3); and
(3) the name and address of—
    (a) anyone known to the claimant who has an interest in the reversion in the property (whether immediate or in not more than 15 years) on the termination of the claimant's current tenancy[20] and who is likely to be affected by the grant of a new tenancy; or
    (b) if the claimant does not know of anyone specified by sub-para.(3)(a), anyone who has a freehold interest in the property.

---

[17] CPR PD 56 para.3.5.

[18] See para.14–23 above.

[19] PD 56 para.3.7.

[20] The words "on the termination of the claimant's current tenancy" should presumably be read as meaning "on the termination of the defendant's current tenancy", for the claimant within PD 56 para.3.7 is the landlord.

Failure to provide information in accordance with CPR

It has been held, under the pre-CPR provisions, that a failure by the tenant to state his proposals in his originating application did not invalidate it. In *Williams v Hillcroft Garage*[21] the tenant in purported compliance with what is now PD 56 para.3.5, stated that "the following are my proposals as to the period rent and other terms which I am applying—renewal of the tenancy for a period of five or seven years at a rent to be agreed upon or decided by the Court". No further information or particulars were given. The Court of Appeal held that the application ought not to have been struck out because, although it was defective in failing to give the information required by the CCR, it was not a nullity. It was said that the landlord should have asked the tenant to supply the necessary information and, if it failed to do so, then the landlord should have asked the court to direct that if the information was not supplied the application should be struck out. This case was decided under CCR 1936 Ord.40 r.8 which did not specifically require that such details "shall" and "must" be stated, unlike CCR 1981 Ord.43 r.6, RSC Ord.97 r.6[22] and now PD 56. However, notwithstanding these mandatory words, it is considered that a failure to supply the information required by PD 56 does not render the application a nullity. CPR r.3.10 makes it clear that an error of procedure, such as a failure to comply with a rule or a practice direction, does not invalidate any step taken in the proceedings unless the court so orders.[23] The court may make an order to remedy the error. It is clear that if the court requires the tenant to provide particulars and he fails to do so the court will have the power to strike out the claim: CPR r.3.4(2)(c). **14–26**

Statement of truth

The claim form must be verified by a statement of truth: CPR r.22.1. It is to be noted that as r.8.5 does not apply to renewal applications (see CPR r.56.3(3)(a)) the claimant is unable to rely on CPR r.8.5(7), so that notwithstanding the verification of the claim form by a statement of truth the claimant is unable, it would seem, to rely on the matters set out in the claim form as evidence. **14–27**

Assignment of claim

In the High Court the claim will be assigned to the Chancery Division: CG Ch.18, para.18.1(15). It will be allocated to the multi-track: CPR r.8.9(c). In the High Court, the claim form is issued out of Chancery Chambers, or, if outside London, may be issued in the district registry. CG Ch.12 contains detailed provisions in **14–28**

---

21 [1971] 22 P. & C.R. 402; (1971) 115 S.J. 127 CA. This was applied in *G Orlik Meat Products Ltd v Hastings and Thanet Building Society* (1975) 29 P. & C.R. 126 CA, where it was held that the amendment to the tenant's originating application could be made notwithstanding the then time limit contained within s.29(3) for the tenant to make an application to the court for renewal. See on this question of amendment, para.14–53.

22 Both in their pre-CPR format. Those rules were retained under the CPR until October 15, 2001 in Sch.1 to the CPR.

23 This also appears consistent with the overriding objective: CPR rr.1.1(1) and (2)(b) and 3.10.

relation to hearings by district registries. Claims issued in the Central London County Court may be issued in the Chancery List of that court.[24]

Stay of proceedings for negotiation

14–29 The previous practice in respect of originating summonses issued in the High Court was that the court office would not seal the summons unless the particulars of the hearing which was to be before the master had been inserted. In other words a date for hearing before the master must have been inserted in the originating summons upon issue. However, if the parties were in negotiation and neither side wanted to press on with the proceedings, it was permissible for the summons to be stated to be for "a day to be fixed", in which case either party could at any time thereafter issue a notice of appointment to hear the summons. This did not relieve the tenant from serving the originating summons within the time limits prescribed by the rules.

14–30 Prior to October 15, 2001 the CPR made no provision for requesting a stay whilst parties tried to settle,[25] as the provisions permitting a request for a stay to allow for settlement contained within CPR r.26.4 were inapplicable to a Pt 8 claim (CPR r.8.9(c)). CPR r.56, prior to the amendments brought about to CPR r.56 by the enactment of the 2003 Order, made provision for a stay, although only at the request of the landlord: CPR r.56.3(4)–(9) (since repealed). By those rules provision was made for the landlord, whether the claim was in the High Court or the county court, to request a three-month stay in order to facilitate negotiation of a new tenancy. However, CPR r.56.3(4)–(9) have been repealed by the amendments made by the Civil Procedure (Amendment) Rules 2004 (SI 2004/1306) to reflect the amendments made to the 1954 Act by the 2003 Order. The provisions for a three-month stay have gone. It is said[26] that the provision for a stay is no longer necessary because of the existence of the power conferred upon the parties to extend the time for applying to court.[27]

4. TERMINATION APPLICATION AND OPPOSITION TO TENANT'S RENEWAL CLAIM

The form of claim

14–31 Where a new tenancy is opposed by a landlord the claimant must use the Pt 7 procedure: CPR r.56.3(4) and PD 56 para.2.1A.[28] An opposed claim means[29] a claim for:

(a) a new tenancy under s.24 of the 1954 Act in circumstances where the grant of a new tenancy is opposed; or

[24] See CG, Appendix 15, "the Chancery Business at Central London Civil Justice Centre", para.1.4.
[25] Provision was made by the Chancery Guide for a stay in the High Court.
[26] *White Book*, Vol.1, p.1935 (2012 edition).
[27] That is to say, extending the "statutory period". As to which see para.6–17 et seq.
[28] As to the conditions to be met in order for a landlord to make a termination application, see paras 6–13 to 6–14. As to the time by which the application must be made, see para.6–17 et seq.
[29] CPR r.56.3(2)(c).

(b) the termination of a tenancy under s.29(2) of the 1954 Act.

Thus Pt 7 will need to be used:

(1) by a tenant who makes an application under s.24 where the renewal is opposed;
(2) by a landlord who makes a termination application pursuant to s.29(2).

Part 7 claims: opposition on grounds other than the grounds of opposition contained in section 30(1) of the Act

Termination applications under section 29(2)

A claim by a landlord that the tenant has no security of tenure is not a termination application within s.29(2) and would not appear to be an "opposed claim" for the purposes of the CPR albeit the Practice Direction contemplates such a situation.[30] By PD 56 para.3.9 it is provided that: **14–32**

> "where the claimant is the landlord making an application for the termination of a tenancy under section 29(2) of the 1954 Act, in addition to the details specified in paragraph 3.4, the claim form must contain (1) the claimant's grounds of opposition . . ."

The expression "grounds of opposition" is defined in PD 56 para.3.1(3) so as to include not only the grounds of opposition under s.30(1) but in addition "any other basis on which the landlord asserts that a new tenancy ought not to be granted." This would include opposition on the ground that the tenant was not in occupation for business purposes. Such a ground of opposition is not, however, one which is required to be stated in a landlord's s.25 notice[31] or in his counter-notice to the tenant's s.26 request and cannot form the basis of a claim for termination under s.29(2). The definition of "an opposed claim"[32] does not on the face of it include the extended definition of "grounds of opposition", at least where the landlord is making a termination application.

Thus, although the procedural provisions of the CPR contemplate that a termination application includes a situation where the landlord opposes renewal on some basis other than the grounds of opposition contained in s.30(1) this is not to be found in s.29(2) itself. Section 29(2) provides that: **14–33**

> "a landlord may apply to the court for an order for the termination of a tenancy to which this Part of this Act applies without the grant of a new tenancy – (a) if he has given notice under s.25 of this Act that he is opposed to the grant of a new tenancy to the tenant; or (b) if the tenant has made a request for a new tenancy in accordance with s.26 of this Act and the landlord has given notice under subs.(6) of that section."

---

[30] The reason being that s.29(2) refers to an application for termination where the landlord has opposed renewal in his s.25 notice or in his counter-notice to the tenant's s.26 request. Such notices contemplate opposition only on grounds within s.30(1). See para.14–32 for the terms of s.29(2).

[31] Which the landlord is unlikely to serve anyway. As the tenancy is not one to which the Act applies, any s.25 notice has nothing to bite on.

[32] See para.14–31.

Thus opposition to the grant of a new tenancy on the basis that the tenant is not in occupation is not a "a claim for the termination of a tenancy under s.29(2) of the 1954 Act" within para.2.1A(2) of PD 56. Thus the landlord is not in these circumstances required to make his claim under Pt 7. If a landlord wanted to seek a declaration as to the tenant's status prior to any application being issued by the tenant (to which the landlord may respond by his acknowledgment of service) there seems to the authors no reason why the landlord cannot simply issue a Pt 8 claim form for declaratory relief. Such a claim would not be governed by Pt 56. Alternatively, the landlord could simply issue a claim for possession (assuming for instance that the contractual term date has come to an end) under Pt 7 on the basis that the tenant has no protection under the Act. This equally is not a claim governed by CPR Pt 56 as it is not a claim under "the Landlord and Tenant Act 1954": CPR r.56.1(1). However, if the landlord opposes the tenant's renewal claim on the basis of the tenant's alleged non-occupation this would seem to be caught by CPR Pt 56 (see para.14–34 below).

Where the tenant's renewal claim is opposed on grounds other than those contained in section 30(1)

14–34 This is probably an "opposed claim" and is certainly assumed to be one by the PD 56. If a tenant is faced with a claim that is opposed only on the basis that the tenant is not within the Act at all, it would seems that the claim is, nevertheless, an "opposed claim" within the rules albeit that definition does not, as noted above, refer to the extended meaning of "grounds of opposition". However, opposition to renewal on the basis that the tenant is not protected at all would seem to fall within the words CPR r.56.3(2)(c) and para.3.1 (2) PD 56 as the claim is for "a new tenancy under s.24 of the 1954 Act in circumstances where the grant of a new tenancy is opposed". The draftsman has certainly assumed that in these circumstances the tenant will issue his claim under Pt 7 rather than by way of Pt 8. That this appears to have been the intention of the rule changes is apparent from a consideration of the provisions for the landlord's acknowledgment of service. Where the tenant is the claimant the landlord's acknowledgment must state with particulars "in his defence (a) the defendant's grounds of opposition". As we have seen in para.14–31 above, "grounds of opposition" include non-s.30(1) grounds. Thus, the draftsman was anticipating that where the tenant's claim for renewal was being opposed on non-s.30(1) grounds, the claim would have to be commenced by a Pt 7 claim. The difficulty for the tenant, however, is that he may not know at the time he issues his claim that it will be opposed on the basis that he has no security of tenure.

Where the tenant's renewal claim is opposed on the grounds contained in section 30(1)

14–35 This is clearly an "opposed claim". However, the requirement for the tenant to use Pt 7 is slightly odd in the case of a tenant seeking renewal, in that albeit the landlord may have indicated, in his s.25 notice or counter-notice to the tenant's s.26 request, that he intends to oppose, the landlord is not, of course, obliged to continue with his opposition to the renewal. However, a tenant faced with opposition in the landlord's s.25 notice must commence his claim under Pt 7. Presumably, if the landlord has indicated prior to the claim being made, that notwithstanding what is said in the s.25 notice he is not intending to oppose, there is no reason why the tenant cannot make a claim under Pt 8. Where a claim is made by the tenant which is unopposed the acknowledgement of service has to be in form N210. If the claim is opposed the landlord's acknowledgement of service has to be in form N9. It is unclear what a landlord should do where he has indicated that he does oppose in his s.25 notice, but decides not to oppose in response to the tenant's Pt 7 claim. Not only are the forms of acknowledgements of service different but the particulars to be included in them also differ. It is probably the case that in form N9 the landlord should simply state that he is no longer opposing. The court will probably order, at the directions hearing, that the claim is to continue as if it were a Pt 8 claim.

Part 7 claims: opposition on the grounds of opposition contained in section 30(1) of the Act

It is suggested that a landlord cannot rely on a ground of opposition not pleaded in his claim form,[33] for the onus is upon him to establish it: *Desbroderie v Segalov*.[34] It has been held in cases dealing with pre-CPR and 2003 Order provisions, that a landlord could not in his answer to a tenant's claim for renewal rely on any ground of opposition to the grant of a new tenancy which has not been stated in his s.25 notice or counter-notice to the s.26 request: *Nursey v P Currie (Dartford) Ltd*[35] (digested in para.7–224); *Hutchinson v Lambeth*[36] (digested in para.3–169). It follows that the Pt 7 claim should not include any ground of opposition which has not been so stated and the landlord would not be given leave to amend his acknowledgement of service to include such a ground. If the s.25 notice contains a ground of opposition, but the claim form states that the landlord does not oppose the grant of a new tenancy on that ground, or does not state the relevant ground, the landlord can subsequently rely on the ground of opposition. In *Olley v Hemsby Estates*[37] it was held, with respect to pre-CPR procedure in the county court, that the landlord was entitled to amend his answer so as to include the ground or grounds of opposition contained in the s.25 notice that had not been included in the answer. Under the CPR the provisions as to amendment apply only to a statement of case: CPR Pt 17. The definition of "statement of case" in CPR r.2.3(1) does not include an acknowledgement of service. It does, however, include a particulars of claim or defence. 14–36

---

[33] Or defence where the landlord is serving a defence to the tenant's Pt 7 claim.

[34] [1956] E.G.D. 211; [1956] J.P.L. 892; [1956] 106 L.J. 764 CC (where the landlord had failed to file an answer to the tenant's originating application as required by the then rules of court the judge held that the landlord could not oppose but could defend as to the rent payable under the proposed new lease). See also para.14–78 et seq.

[35] [1959] 1 W.L.R. 273; [1959] 1 All E.R. 497 CA.

[36] [1984] 1 E.G.L.R. 75.

[37] [1965] C.L.Y. 2205; [1965] E.G.D. 340 CA, applied in *Nurit Bar v Pathwood Investments Ltd* (1987) 54 P. & C.R. 178 CA (digested in para.14–55).

The contents of the Part 7 claim

14–37 By PD 56 para.3.4 the claim form must state:

(1) the property to which the claim relates;
(2) particulars of the current tenancy (including date, parties and duration), the current rent (if not the original rent) and the date and method of termination;
(3) particulars of every notice or request given or made in respect of that tenancy under ss.25 or 26 of the 1954 Act; and
(4) the expiry date of—
    (a) the statutory period under s.29A(2);
    (b) an agreed extended period made under s.29B.

14–38 Where the claimant is the landlord making an application for the termination of a tenancy under s.29(2) of the 1954 Act, in addition to the details specified in para.3.4 of PD 56, the claim form must contain[38]:

(1) the claimant's grounds of opposition;
(2) full details of those grounds of opposition; and
(3) the terms of a new tenancy that the claimant proposes in the event that his claim fails.

Priority of claims

14–39 Where more than one application to the court under s.24(1) or s.29(2) of the 1954 Act is made, para.3.2 of PD 56 makes provision as to which of the applications take precedence. This is considered in detail in para.6–07 fn.20 and para.6–14.

5. PARTIES TO THE CLAIM

The claimant

14–40 Where the tenant makes an application for renewal, the person who fulfils the definition of the tenant at the date of the issue of the claim should be made the claimant.[39] In the rare case of the tenant assigning his tenancy to another after the claim has been issued and served, it is essential that the assignee apply to the court to substitute himself as the proper applicant: CPR r.19.2 and 19.4. Such an application will be made pursuant to CPR Pt 23. When the court makes an order for the substitution of a party, it may give consequential directions and may direct a copy of the order be served on every party to the proceedings and any other person affected by the order as well as filing an amended claim form within 14 days: CPR r.19.4(5) and (6); PD 19 paras 2.1 to 2.3.

---

[38] PD 56 para.3.9.

[39] This matter is considered in paras 3–101 and 6–24 et seq. generally.

The claimant in respect of landlord's claim for renewal or a termination application will be the landlord as defined by s.44.[40] 14–41

The defendant

In respect of a tenant's application for renewal, the person who, in relation to the tenant's current tenancy, is the landlord as defined by s.44 of the Act must be made defendant to the claim.[41] The question of who falls within s.44 is to be considered as at the date of issue. However, it is clear from the wording of s.44 that the person who falls within the definition of "landlord" may change during the course of the proceedings. At every stage of the proceedings down to final judgment the person joined as the "defendant" should in fact be the person answering the description of the "landlord" in s.44. It is insufficient merely to serve notice of proceedings on that party: *Piper v Muggleton*.[42] If the proceedings are improperly constituted, the court has no jurisdiction to grant a new tenancy: *Meah v Mouskos*.[43] Where a person who has become the "landlord" as defined by s.44 after proceedings have been issued has not been made a party to the proceedings by the time the matter comes on for trial, the judge should normally allow the new landlord to apply to be joined and should adjourn the matter for that purpose: *Meah v Mouskos*. The application to substitute the defendant by the new landlord may be made either by the applicant or by the new landlord: CPR r.19.4. An application for substitution may be made without notice: CPR r.19.3(3)(a). The application must be supported by evidence showing the stage the proceedings have reached and what changes occurred to cause the transfer of interest: PD 19 para.5.2. Upon the court making an order substituting a defendant the court may direct[44]: 14–42

(1) the claimant to file with the court within 14 days (or as ordered) an amended claim form;
(2) a copy of the order to be served on all parties to the proceedings and any other person affected by it;
(3) the pleadings, together with any other document referred to in the statement of case, to be served on the new defendant;
(4) unless the court otherwise orders, the amended claim form to be served on any other defendants.

A new defendant does not become a party to proceedings until the amended claim form has been served on him: PD 19 para.3.3.

A defendant to the claim who is not the competent landlord may nevertheless be estopped from denying that he is the competent landlord. If the defendant has served a s.25 notice, the notice contains a representation that the server is the 14–43

40 As to who constitutes "the landlord" see paras 3–87 and 6–36 generally.
41 As to who constitutes "the landlord" see paras 3–87 and 6–36 generally.
42 [1956] 2 W.L.R. 1093; (1956) 2 All E.R. 249 CA.
43 [1964] 2 W.L.R. 27; (1963) 3 All E.R. 908 CA.
44 PD 19 para.3.2.

competent landlord: *Shelley v United Artists Corp Ltd*[45] (digested in para.14–45). In those circumstances the claim, albeit issued in the name of the person who is not the competent landlord, will nevertheless be valid.

14–44 The defendant to a landlord's renewal application under s.24 or a termination application under s.29(2) should be the tenant.[46]

14–45 ***Shelley v United Artists Corp Ltd***[47] The claimants were business tenants of premises under a lease expiring on June 20, 1988. United Artists Corporation Limited ("UA") was the landlord. UA was head lessee of the building of which the demised premises formed part. The head lease expired on June 24, 1988. The reversion to the head lease was vested in a company called Benesco Limited ("B"). By the terms of the head lease UA had an option to take a new head lease for a term of 14 years commencing on the expiration of the head lease.

UA on July 28, 1987 gave the plaintiffs a s.25 notice terminating the plaintiffs' tenancy with effect from June 20, 1988. UA was at the date of the service of that notice competent landlord as no notice had been served by B upon UA. On July 30, 1987 UA gave B two notices, one exercising the option and the other a request under s.26, requesting a new lease with effect from June 24, 1988. The plaintiffs gave UA a counter-notice on August 6, 1987 and UA passed this on to B within the statutory time limit. On October 22, 1987 the plaintiffs applied for a new lease making UA the sole defendant not knowing of the notices served by UA. B did not hear about the originating summons until 1988. On October 7, 1988 B granted MGM, a member of the same group of companies as UA, a new head lease for a term of 25 years from June 24, 1988. The plaintiffs sought to have MGM substituted as defendant to the originating summons. UA argued that the originating summons was invalid in that at the date of the making of the application B, not UA, was the competent landlord.

The Court of Appeal held:

(1) that UA was competent landlord, for as a result of the exercise of the option and the doctrine in *Walsh v Lonsdale*,[48] the "interest" of UA at the date of the originating summons consisted of the combination of the fag-end of the original term plus the equitable term of 14 years from that date. Although UA had the right under the option to cancel its exercise this was not a condition precedent preventing the application of the *Walsh v Lonsdale* doctrine. Furthermore, even though the rent under the new 14-year lease had not been ascertained, complete machinery for its ascertainment had been agreed within the terms of the option.
(2) If the view in (1) were incorrect, UA and MGM were estopped from denying that they were competent landlords. UA by serving a s.25 notice represented that it was a competent landlord and when it had ceased to be

[45] [1990] 1 E.G.L.R. 103 CA. See also *Lay v Ackerman* [2004] EWCA Civ 184; [2005] 1 E.G.L.R. 139, where a similar point was taken in the context of the Leasehold Reform, Housing and Urban Development Act 1993. See also para.3–93 and fn.168 thereto.
[46] See para.6–37.
[47] [1990] 1 E.G.L.R. 103 CA.
[48] (1882) L.R. 21 Ch. D. 9 CA.

such by serving a s.26 request on B, their earlier representation was false and it was accordingly under a duty to correct it (*With v O'Flanagan*[49]). UA had realised that the plaintiffs were labouring under a mistake and in the circumstances UA was estopped from denying it was competent landlord at the date of the making of the originating summons. MGM were in no better position than UA, since MGM were granted the head lease at the request of UA and MGM were fellow subsidiaries in the same group and were represented by the same solicitors who at all stages knew the facts.

Amendment of claim form where misdescription of landlord

Pre CPR

Where a tenant[50] has, in his claim form for a new tenancy, incorrectly named the defendant, the court has power to amend the application albeit the time for making the application in the name of the correct defendant may have passed. Prior to the CPR the powers in this respect of the High Court and county court were identical. RSC Ord.20, r.5 applied to the county court by CCR Ord.15 r.1. RSC Ord.20 r.5 provided by sub-rule 3 that: **14–46**

> "An amendment to correct the name of a party may be allowed under paragraph (2) [after the relevant period of limitation has expired] notwithstanding that it is alleged that the effect of the amendment will be to substitute a new party if the Court is satisfied that the mistake sought to be corrected was a genuine mistake and was not misleading or such as to cause any reasonable doubt as to the identity of the party intending to sue or, as the case may be, intended to be sued."

The practice of the court was to permit a substitution, albeit of a different name, if the original mistake was one as to nomendature rather than identity[51] and was not such as to mislead or cause reasonable doubt as to whom was really intended to be sued. If the applicant was aware of the facts or could have discovered them if he had enquired, the amendment would not have been permitted. The power to **14–47**

---

[49] [1936] Ch. 575.

[50] Of course what is said here applies equally where a landlord as claimant names the defendant incorrectly. However, it will usually be of most concern to the claimant tenant by reason of the fact that he may be faced with a claim by the landlord that he has no protection by reason of the invalidity of the claim.

[51] The distinction is often not easy to draw and may be difficult to apply in any given case. In what has become known as *The Sardinia Sulcis* test (*The Al Tawwab* [1991] 1 Lloyds Rep. 201), Lloyd L.J. said:

"In one sense a Plaintiff always intends to sue the person who is liable for the wrong which he has suffered. But the test cannot be as wide as that. Otherwise there could never be any doubt as to the person intended to be sued, and leave to amend would always be given. So there must be some narrower test. In *Mitchell v Harris Engineering* the identity of the person intended to be sued was the Plaintiff's employers. In *Evans v Charrington* it was the current landlord. In *Thistle Hotels v McAlpine* the identity of the person intending to sue was the proprietor of the hotel . . . In all these cases it was possible to identify the intending Plaintiff or intended Defendant by reference to a description which was more or less specific to the particular case. Thus if, in the case of an intended Defendant, the Plaintiff gets the right description but the wrong name, there is unlikely to be any doubt as to the identity of the person intended to be sued. But if he gets the wrong description, it will be otherwise."

grant leave to amend extended to cover the case where an entirely wrong name had been used; that is, where B was sought to be sued, but was mistakenly named as A. Leave was not given where the mistake was one of responsibility, that is to say, where A (rather than B) was sued under the mistaken belief that A (rather than B) was responsible for the matters complained of. Thus amendments were permitted in the following cases:

(1) where the competent landlord was named as the plaintiff and the tenant as defendant to the originating summons: *Teltscher Bros Ltd v London & India Dock Investments Ltd*[52];
(2) where the tenant had made his application in the name of the landlord's managing agents, which managing agents formed part of the same group of companies of the landlord and had formerly been the tenant's landlord and had served the s.25 notice as agents for the landlord: *Evans Construction Co Ltd v Charrington & Co Ltd*[53];
(3) where the landlord had assigned the reversion after service by the tenant of a s.26 request and had not informed the tenant of the change in ownership such that the tenant issued proceedings against the former landlord: *Eburne (SW) Ltd v Toome Investments*.[54] The amendment was allowed notwithstanding the fact that the statutory time limit for making the originating application had expired. This would, on its face, appear to be a mistake not as to identity but as to responsibility: the tenant intended to name the former landlord for it was considered that it was he who was the competent landlord.

An amendment was not allowed, however, where the original landlords were Birch Bros Ltd but had subsequently become Birch Bros (Properties) Ltd, which was not a subsidiary or related to the original landlord: *Beardmore Motors v Birch Bros (Properties) Ltd; Re Holmes Road, Kentish Town*.[55]

Post CPR

14–48 The correction of the name of a party is now dealt with in two rules of the CPR, namely CPR r.17.4(3) and r.19.5(2), (3). By r.17.4(3) it is provided:

> "The Court may allow an amendment to correct a mistake as to the name of the party, but only where the mistake was genuine and not one which would cause reasonable doubt as to the identity of the party in question."

By CPR r.19.5(2) and (3) it is provided:

> "(2) The Court may add or substitute a party only if—
> (a) the relevant limitation period was current when the proceedings were started; and
> (b) the addition or substitution is necessary.

---

52 [1989] 1 W.L.R. 770; [1989] 2 E.G.L.R. 261.
53 [1983] 1 Q.B. 810; [1983] 2 W.L.R. 117; (1983) 1 All E.R. 310 CA.
54 [1977] C.L.Y. 445.
55 [1958] 2 W.L.R. 975; [1958] 2 All E.R. 311.

(3) The addition or substitution of a party is necessary only if the Court is satisfied that—
   (a) the new party is to be substituted for a party who is named in the claim form in mistake for the new party;
   (b) the claim cannot properly be carried on by or against the original party unless the new party is added or substituted as claimant or defendant; or
   (c) the original party has died or had a bankruptcy order made against him and his interest or liability has passed to the new party."

Gregson v Channel 4 Television Corp

In *Gregson v Channel 4 Television Corp*[56] the Court of Appeal considered the interrelation between CPR rr.17.4(3) and 19.5(2). The claimant issued a claim for damages for libel in respect of a television broadcast published by Channel 4 Television Corporation. By mistake he named as defendant "Channel 4 Television Company Limited", which was a wholly-owned dormant subsidiary of Channel 4 Television Corporation. The claimant served his claim form on the last day for service. It was accepted by the defendant that the mistake was genuine and not one that could cause reasonable doubt as to the identity of the party in question. It was held that in those circumstances CPR r.17.4(3) applied. The Court of Appeal made it clear that CPR r.19.5 deals with cases where the claimant mistakenly names the wrong party as defendant, whereas CPR r.17.4 deals with cases where the claimant misnames the defendant. It was argued that where the claimant misnames the defendant and the misnomer is an existing person, natural or corporate, the application has to be made under CPR r.19.5. This was rejected by the court. It was said that it was impossible to know whether there was any other existing person, natural or corporate, of their mistaken names somewhere and if the argument were correct the court would always have to go to CPR r.19.5 where the mistake was as to a name. It was said that this was inconsistent with the scheme of the rules and the distinction between CPR r.17.4(3) and CPR r.19.5.. It is to be noted that in *Gregson v Channel 4 Television Corp* both May L.J. and Peter Gibson L.J. stated that they did not find assistance from a comparison between the CPR and the old rules and the cases decided thereunder.[57] **14–49**

Adelson v Associated Newspapers Ltd

The Court of Appeal in *Adelson v Associated Newspapers Ltd*[58] has now made it clear, differing from the view of May L.J. and Gibson L.J. in *Gregson v Channel 4 Television Corp*,[59] that CPR 17.4(3) and CPR 19.5 were intended to replicate the provisions of RSC Ord.20 r.5 discussed above. The mistake must thus be one as to the name of a party rather than one of identity. Accordingly, in order to rely **14–50**

---

[56] [2000] C.P. Rep. 60 CA.

[57] May L.J. said:

"There were provisions in the former Rules of the Supreme Court providing for cases where an application was made to correct a mistake in the name of a party or to substitute a new party for one had been joined by a mistake. The Civil Procedure Rules are a new procedural code and there is, in my view, no basis for supposing that these new rules were intended to replicate, or for that matter not to replicate, the former provisions. It is not generally appropriate to refer to authorities decided under the former rules to determine what the new rules mean or how they should be applied."

[58] [2007] EWCA 701.

[59] [2000] C.P. Rep. 60 CA.

on CPR 19.5 it has to be shown that the person who issued the claim form would have named the new party in the statement of case had the mistake not been made. The court provided some general guidance:

> "(1) Most of the problems in this area arise out of the difference, sometimes elusive, between an error of identification and an error of nomenclature [29]. In order to come within the rule the mistake must be as to the name of a party not as to identity [43].
>
> (2) An error of identification will occur where a claimant identifies an individual as the person who has caused him an injury, intends to sue that person, describes him in the pleadings by the correct name, but then discovers that he has identified the wrong person as the person who has injured him. An error of nomenclature occurs where the claimant identifies the correct person as having caused him the injury, but describes him in the pleadings by the wrong name [29].
>
> (3) A problem arises in distinguishing between the two types of error where the claimant knows the attributes of the person that he wishes to sue, for example their landlord, or the manufacturer of an object, but has no personal knowledge of the identity of that person. If on inquiry he is incorrectly informed that a named third party has those attributes and he commences an action naming that third party as defendant but describing in the pleading the attributes of the person intended to be sued, the case is more likely to be one of misnomer of the person intended to be sued rather than an error of identification [30] and [56]. Where the pleading give a description of the party but give the party the wrong name a "mistake as to name" is given a generous interpretation [43]. That generous test of this type of mistake is laid down in *The Sardinia Sulcis*.[60][56]
>
> (4) CPR 19.5 presupposes that there is a person intending to sue. The mistake envisaged in relation to the name of the claimant is one under which the name used for the claimant is not the name of the person wishing to sue. Such a mistake is likely to be made by an agent of the person intending to sue. Where the claimant is a company the mistake will always be that of an agent, but identifying the person intending to sue may create difficulties [31].
>
> (5) The rule also envisages that there will be a person intended to be sued. The mistake envisaged in relation to the defendant will be one under which the name used for the defendant is not the appropriate name to describe the person that the claimant intends to sue. Thus the rule envisages a defendant identified by the claimant but described by a name which is not correct [32].
>
> (6) In either case the mistake that the rule envisages is one of nomenclature, not of identification [33].
>
> (7) Where the correct defendant is unaware of the claim until after the limitation period had expired the court will be unlikely to grant permission to make the amendment [57]."

If time has expired

14–51 Can an application to amend the name of a party be made after the expiration of the period provided for making the relevant claim, whether that be a claim for renewal or for making a termination application? As has been seen, any application for renewal or termination must be made before the end of the "statutory period".[61] If a party is misdescribed in proceedings which were issued in time, i.e. before the statutory period, but the application for amendment is made only after the expiration of the statutory period, will the amendment be permitted? CPR r.19.5(1) provides that CPR 19.5 "applies to a change of parties after the end of a period of limitation under . . . (c) any other enactment which allows such a change or under which such a change is allowed." The wording of

---

[60] As to which see fn.51.

[61] See para.6–17.

CPR r.19.5 originally provided (in an earlier incarnation in CPR r.19.4) that it applied "to a change of parties after the end of a period of limitation under . . . (d) any other statutory provision." CPR r.19.4 became r.19.5 with effect from CPR update 14, effective from April 18, 2000. CPR r.19.5(1) was amended to its present wording (as set out above) by CPR update 22 effective from March 12, 2001. In the context of the 1954 Act, a change of a party after the expiration of the period for making a claim for renewal could well have been described (under the original wording) as a change after "the end of a period of limitation under . . . (d) any other statutory provision". However, it might have seemed less clear that such a change comes within the amended wording since it could have been argued that the 1954 Act is not an "enactment which allows such a change, or under which such a change is allowed" other than in the sense that no provision is made by the terms of the Act prohibiting such a change. The Court of Appeal in *Parsons v George*[62] held that CPR r.19.5 was to be so read. It was held that CPR r.19.5 confers jurisdiction on the court to enable a claim made under the 1954 Act to be amended notwithstanding that the application for amendment is made after the expiry of the time which the tenant has to make the application (being then, with respect to the pre-2003 Order position, within four months of the receipt or service of a s.25 notice or s.26 request, respectively). It was said that the 1954 Act was an enactment under which "such a change is allowed" in the sense that it was not prohibited by the Act.

Service

The change in the name of the defendant may be such that the court concludes that there was ineffective service of the claim form upon the new substituted party. Under the rules which applied prior to the CPR it was held that where an amendment is permitted and is such as to change completely the name of the defendant, so that there has been ineffective service, the court should also, generally, grant an extension of time for service on the substituted party under the then CCR 1981 Ord.13 r.5 or RSC Ord.6 r.8 and Ord.7 r.6. There are corresponding provisions in CPR r.3.10 and 3.1(2)(a) respectively. However, in light of CPR r.7.6(3) and the decision in *Vinos v Marks & Spencer Plc*[63] it would appear that a similar approach cannot be taken pursuant to CPR r.3.1(2)(a). The court in *Gregson v Channel 4 Television Corp*[64] went on to consider the circumstances in which an extension for time for service may have to be granted. The court took into account what Donaldson L.J. said in *Evans Construction Co v Charrington*,[65] a decision under the former rules. It was said in that case that the incorrect naming of a defendant would not necessarily affect service, but might well do so. It was said that the likelihood of the wrong person being served was greater in respect of companies. If there was service by post addressed to the wrong member of a group of companies at the registered office of each of the companies in the group, that would inevitably lead to service on the wrong **14–52**

[62] [2004] EWCA Civ 912.

[63] [2001] 3 All E.R. 784. See further paras 14–59 to 14–63.

[64] [2000] C.P. Rep. 60 CA.

[65] [1983] 1 Q.B. 810 at 823C.

company rather than the intended company. The Court of Appeal in *Gregson* stated that under the CPR the court had to give effect to the overriding objective to enable the court to deal with cases justly. It was said that if the court decides to allow a new party to be added or substituted it was not necessarily the case that a consequential order for the service of the claim form on the new party has to be rigidly confined by CPR r.7.6(3). May L.J. said that there were three reasons for this:

> "Firstly, until the Court has permitted a new party to be added or substituted, there is no question of that party being served simply because, until then, they were not a party. It is not, therefore a question of extending time for serving the claim form, but of giving directions as to its service. Secondly, the sense of my first reason is recognised in paragraph 3.2 of the Part 19 Practice Direction, by which the Court may direct the amended claim form to be served on the new Defendant. Thirdly, if consideration such as those referred to in rule 7.6(3) are relevant to a particular application, they will come into play when the Court decides whether or not to allow the new party to be added or substituted. If, having taken those considerations into account, the Court decides to allow the addition or substitution, it would make no sense if the order were ineffective because the amended claim form could not be served."

It was contended in the *Gregson v Channel 4 Television Corp* decision above that an extension for time for service was required pursuant to CPR r.7.6(3) on the basis that there had not been any effective service of the original claim on the appropriate party and the application for an extension had accordingly been made after the time for service of the claim form had expired. The court, also, rejected this argument. The claim form had been served upon a senior business advisor of Channel 4 Television Corp who was authorised to accept service of documents on behalf of the company secretary. Albeit he was employed by the corporation it was said that this was personal service on "a company or other corporation" under CPR r.6.4(4). It was said that the fact that the individual in question might also be regarded as authorised to accept service on behalf of the dormant subsidiary was at best a "technical quibble unrelated to substantial justice".

Amendment where amendment other than name of defendant

14–53 Under the previous procedure it has been held that a claim which had been validly made could be amended, subject to the court's discretion, even though the statutory time limit for making the originating application expired. Thus a tenant has been allowed to amend his application:

(1) to alter the particulars of the nature of the tenant's business and as to the parts of the premises occupied by the tenant: *De Costa v Chartered Society of Queen Square*[66] (digested in para.14–54);
(2) where there was a misdescription of the holding, referring only to part of the demised premises which constituted the holding: *Bar v Pathwood*[67] (digested in para.14–55);

---

[66] (1961) 177 E.G. 447 CA.
[67] [1987] 1 E.G.L.R. 90 CA.

(3) to seek to include as part of the terms of the new tenancy to be granted by the court a right to park on the landlord's adjacent land: *G Orlik Meat Products Ltd v Hastings and Thanet Building Society* (digested in para.8–18).

There seems no reason why this approach should not be equally applicable under CPR.

De Costa v Chartered Society of Queen Square[68] The tenant of a hotel or boarding house had covenanted not to carry on any business "except the business (to be carried on only by the tenant) of sub-letting one or more rooms to respectable persons for residential purposes". The landlord, apparently taking the view that the tenancy was protected by the 1954 Act, served a s.25 notice stating that it would not oppose the grant of a new tenancy. The tenant applied to the county court for a new tenancy in the appropriate form. The tenant's business was there stated to be "sub-letting rooms for residential purposes (hotel)". By way of answers to a request for further and better particulars, the tenant stated that two rooms were sub-let, but that the other rooms were used for the boarding-house business. The landlord put in an answer denying that that 1954 Act applied to the tenant. After expiry of the four-month period allowed for the making of an application for a new tenancy, the tenant sought leave to amend the application, so as to state that the business was of "granting licenses" (not sub-letting), and the further particulars, so as to state that no part of the premises were sub-let. Leave to amend was granted. It was held that the amendment had been properly allowed because the court must ascertain the true facts and decide on them whether the 1954 Act applied to the tenancy. **14–54**

Bar v Pathwood[69] The tenant in her originating application misdescribed the "holding", referring to only part of the demised premises which constituted the "holding". It was conceded that the originating application was valid when made. The tenant's application to amend the proceedings, made after the four-month time limit for the making of an originating application had expired, was opposed by the landlord. The Court of Appeal held that the county court judge was wrong to hold that the court had no jurisdiction to amend the proceedings after the expiry of the four-month time limit. On the question of whether the court should exercise its discretion to grant leave to amend, the landlord argued that, the tenant having chosen to limit her application to only part of the "holding", the landlord had, in light of the fact that the time limit of four months for the making of an originating application had passed acquired a vested right to resist the renewal of a new tenancy of the whole of the "holding". The court rejected this argument, for what constitutes the "holding" was a matter for the court to consider at the hearing. The amendment merely made clear the description of the "holding" to which the originating application necessarily related. The amendment was allowed. **14–55**

---

68 (1961) 177 E.G. 447 CA.

69 [1987] 1 E.G.L.R. 90 CA.

6. SERVICE OF CLAIM FORM

Application for renewal

Time for service

14–56 The general rule is that a claim form must be served within four months after the date of issue (CPR r.7.5(2) applied to Pt 8 claims by PD 8 para.2.1).[70]

Upon whom should service be effected

14–57 Where the claim is made by the tenant the claim form is required to be served upon the persons named in the claim form in compliance with PD 56 para.3.5(6): PD 56 para.3.6.[71]

14–58 Where the claim is made by the landlord the claim form is required to be served upon the persons named in the claim form in compliance with PD 56 para.3.7(3): PD para.3.8.[72]

Extension of time for service

14–59 The court may extend the validity of the claim form: CPR r.7.6(1). The general rule is that the application for an extension should be made to the court before the expiry of the four-month period: CPR r.7.6(2)(a). Under the RSC it was held that the court had jurisdiction to extend time if the application was made after the expiry of the four month period: *Chappell v Cooper*[73]; *Singh v Duport Harper Foundries Ltd*.[74] By CPR r.7.6(3) the court's discretion to extend time for service of the claim form where the application is made after the expiry of the period specified for service is limited. A court may make such an order only if:

(1) the court has been unable to serve the claim form; or

---

[70] The general rule did not until October 1, 2008 apply to 1954 Act proceedings. Prior to that date the claim form was required to be served within two months after the date of issue.

[71] This provides that the claim form should specify:

"(6) the name and address of—

(a) anyone known to the claimant who has an interest in the reversion in the property (whether immediate or in not more than 15 years) on the termination of the claimant's current tenancy and who is likely to be affected by the grant of a new tenancy; or

(b) if the claimant does not know of anyone specified by sub-paragraph (6)(a), anyone who has a freehold interest in the property."

[72] This provides that the claim form should specify:

"(3) the name and address of—

(a) anyone known to the claimant who has an interest in the reversion in the property (whether immediate or in not more than 15 years) on the termination of the claimant's current tenancy and who is likely to be affected by the grant of a new tenancy; or

(b) if the claimant does not know of anyone specified by sub-paragraph (3)(a), anyone who has a freehold interest in the property."

[73] [1980] 1 W.L.R. 958 CA.

[74] [1994] 1 W.L.R. 769; [1994] 2 All E.R. 889 CA.

(2) the claimant has taken all reasonable steps to serve the claim form but has been unable to do so; and
(3) in either case, the claimant has acted promptly in making the application.

Thus, where the failure to serve in the four-month period is as a result of the failure of the tenant's solicitors to appreciate that the time for service is a four-month period specified by CPR r.7.5(1), the failure is likely to be fatal to the tenant's claim: *Chabba v Turbogame Ltd.*[75]

In *Singh v Duport Harper Foundries Ltd*[76] the Court of Appeal held that, following *Leal v Dunlop Bio-Processes International*[77] (see also *Ward-Lee v Linehan*[78]) that the court had power to grant an extension for the validity of the originating summons albeit the application for it was made after the expiry of the period of extension which the court could grant, relying upon RSC Ord.2 r.1 whereby a failure to comply with the rules of the court may be treated as an irregularity and RSC Ord.3 r.5 which empowered the court to extend the period within which a person was required to do any act in proceedings. There are corresponding provisions in CPR r.3.10 and r.3.1(2)(a) respectively. However, CPR r.3.1(2)(a) is unavailable where the application is caught by CPR r.7.6(3): *Vinos v Marks & Spencer Plc.*[79] In that case May L.J. said: 14–60

> "The meaning of rule 7.6(3) is plain. The court has power to extend the time for serving the claim form after the period for its service has run out 'only if' the stipulated conditions are fulfilled. That means that the court does not have power to do so otherwise. The discretionary power in the rules to extend time periods—rule 3.1(2) (a)—does not apply because of the introductory words. The general words of Rule 3.10 cannot extend to enable the court to do what rule 7.6(3) specifically forbids, nor to extend time when the specific provision of the rules which enables extensions of time specifically does not extend to making this extension of time."

This decision was followed in *Kaur v CPT Coil Ltd.*[80]

The words "has been unable to serve" in CPR r.7.6(3)(a) include all cases where the court has failed to serve, including mere oversight on its part: *Cranfield v Bridgegrove Ltd.*[81] Most cases have turned on the interpretation of "reasonable steps" by the claimant to effect service in CPR r.7.6(3)(b). In determining 14–61

---

[75] [2001] EWCA Civ 1073. In this case the court was concerned with the rules in their form pre-October 15, 2001 and when the period for service was two months. The tenant's solicitors thought as a result of the "Notes for Guidance", (which were in fact misleading so far as 1954 Act applications were concerned), that the time for service was four months. The application for the extension was made after the expiry of two months but before the expiry of the four-month period. The court held, on the then CPR, that albeit the time for service was two months, the time within which an application could be made to extend the time for service without the guillotine of CPR r.7.6(3) descending was four months. As the application for the extension was made within the four month period CPR r.7.6(3) did not apply and the court had a general discretion to extend time, which it did on the facts of that case.

[76] [1994] 1 W.L.R. 769; [1994] 2 All E.R. 889 CA.

[77] [1984] 1 W.L.R. 874; [1984] 2 All E.R. 207 CA.

[78] [1993] 1 W.L.R. 754 CA.

[79] [2001] 3 All E.R. 784 CA.

[80] [2001] C.P. Rep. 34 CA.

[81] [2003] EWCA Civ 656; [2003] 3 All E.R. 129; [2003] P.L.S.C.S. 113.

whether a claimant has taken such steps the court is limited to considering the steps that the claimant did take in the four month period for service.[82]

14–62 ***Cranfield v Bridgegrove Ltd***[83] On February 12, 2001, T's solicitors sent the claim form to the county court asking the court to issue and serve the proceedings. The proceedings were issued on February 15, 2001. The date for expiry for service of the claim was April 15, 2001. However, due to an oversight the court had failed to serve the proceedings. L, who had served a s.25 notice stating that he would not oppose renewal, contended that accordingly T's lease came to an end on September 28, 2001, being the date of termination specified in the notice. On contacting the court on August 23, the court informed T's solicitors that the claim form had been put on the court file by mistake. T served a copy of the claim form on that day on L and the court served L the following day. On September 18, 2001 T made an application for an extension of time for service of the claim form pursuant to CPR r.7.6. In *Vinos v Marks & Spencer Plc*,[84] it was decided that, after the expiry of the time limit for service of a claim form, the court had no power to extend time for service if the circumstances fell outside CPR r.7.6(3). The court upheld the county court judge in granting an extension of time holding that the words "has been unable to serve" in r.7.6(3)(a) includes all cases where the court has failed to serve, including mere oversight on its part.

14–63 An extension of the time for service cannot be obtained by invoking CPR r.6.9.[85] In *Godwin v Swindon BC*,[86] which was principally concerned with the interpretation of CPR r.6.7(1), the court also said (at [50] per May L.J.) that r.6.9(1) cannot be invoked to dispense with service "when what would be done is in substance that which rule 7.6(3) forbids."[87]

Requiring claimant to serve

14–64 Often the tenant issues but does not serve immediately in an attempt to remain in occupation for as long as possible, particularly where it is obvious that the landlord was going to succeed in his ground of opposition, e.g. where the landlord proposes to demolish the premises. Although service must be effected within four months, a delay of that period can be very inconvenient to a landlord who wishes to get on to the premises to implement his development as soon as possible. Where a claim form has been issued against a defendant, but has not yet been served on him, the defendant may serve a notice on the claimant requiring him to serve the claim form or discontinue within a period specified in the notice, which period must be at least 14 days after service of the notice: CPR r.7.7(1) and

[82] *Carnegie v Drury* [2007] EWCA Civ 497.

[83] [2003] EWCA Civ 656; [2003] 3 All E.R. 129; [2003] P.L.S.C.S. 113..

[84] [2001] 3 All E.R. 784 CA.

[85] This provides "(1) The court may dispense with service of a document. (2) An application for an order to dispense with service may be made without notice."

[86] [2001] EWCA Civ 1478; [2001] 4 All E.R. 641; [2002] 1 W.L.R. 997.

[87] See further *Anderton v Clwyd CC* [2002] EWCA Civ 933; [2002] 3 All E.R. 813; [2002] 1 W.L.R. 3174 and *Wilkey v BBC* [2002] EWCA Civ 1561; [2002] 4 All E.R. 1177; [2003] 1 W.L.R. 1 per Simon Brown L.J. at para.18 as to the ambit of CPR r.6.9. The authorities are reviewed in *Kuenyehia v International Hospitals Group Ltd* [2006] EWCA Civ 21.

(2).[88] If the claimant fails to comply with the notice, the court may, on the application of the defendant, dismiss the claim or make any other order it thinks just: r.7.7(3).

Landlord's termination application

Time for service

The Pt 7 claim form must be served within four months of issue and CPR r.7.5: applied by CPR r.56.3(4). **14–65**

How service is to be effected: renewal or termination

The provisions as to how a claim form may be served are set out in Pt 6 to the CPR. It is to be noted that service can be effected by fax or other means of electronic communication: CPR r.6.3(1). PD 6A paras 3.1 and 4.1 make provision in relation to service by electronic means. **14–66**

7. ACKNOWLEDGEMENT OF SERVICE

Time and occasion for service

The CPR provide for a defendant to a claim, of whatever description, to indicate, by serving an acknowledgement of service, whether he proposes to defend the claim. The form of the acknowledgement as well as its contents differs depending on whether the claim is one for renewal under Pt 8 or is in response to a claim under Pt 7.[89] Whatever form the acknowledgement is required to take it will ordinarily be required to be served within 14 days after service of the claim form: CPR r.10.3.[90] An acknowledgement of service to a Pt 8 (but not to a Pt 7 claim) is required to have a statement of truth appended to it: CPR r.22.1(1)(d).[91] **14–67**

In considering the claim for an extension of time for service of the acknowledgement it is considered the court should have regard to: **14–68**

(1) the overriding objective contained in CPR Pt 1;
(2) the list of matters in CPR r.3.9[92];

---

[88] There seems to be no reason why these rules cannot be invoked in connection with a tenant's claim under Pt 8. Part 8 specifically refers to CPR r.7.5 in connection with service: see CPR r.8.2.

[89] It must not be forgotten that a Pt 7 claim may consist not only of a termination application made by a landlord but also a claim for renewal by a tenant where he knows that it will be opposed: see paras 14–31 and 14–35.

[90] As will be seen below a party to a Pt 7 claim may obtain an extra 14 days for serving a defence by serving an acknowledgement of service.

[91] A defendant to a Pt 7 claim is not required to serve an acknowledgement of service. See para.14–72.

[92] *Sayers v Clarke Walker* [2002] EWCA Civ 645; [2002] 3 All E.R. 490. The decision in *Sayers* was distinguished in *Robert v Momentum Services Ltd* [2003] EWCA Civ 299; [2003] 1 W.L.R. 1577. It was held that where an application for an extension of time is made before the expiry of the time limit

(3) the fact that post-CPR litigation is not to be viewed as a game of skill and chance[93];

(4) the fact that but for the failure to acknowledge service the Claimant would have been in no position to obtain judgment in default or summary judgment for the terms it seeks in its claim form.

Landlord's acknowledgement to tenant's Part 8 claim for renewal

14–69 The Pt 8 procedure disapplies the provisions as to Pt 15, which deal with service of a defence.[94] A defendant to a Pt 8 claim must, however, file an acknowledgement of service in the relevant practice form not more than 14 days after service of the claim form and serve the acknowledgement of service on the claimant: CPR r.8.3(1).[95] CPR r.8.3(2) provides that the acknowledgement of service must state (1) whether the defendant contests the claim; and (2) if the defendant seeks a different remedy from that set out in the claim form, what that remedy is. This rule is not disapplied by CPR Pt 56 or the Practice Direction. However, "contesting the claim" must here refer to the terms of the new tenancy as opposed to contesting the right of renewal. If the landlord had indicated prior to any claim being instituted that he was opposing renewal the tenant should have commenced his claim by the Pt 7 procedure.[96]

14–70 Where the claim is an unopposed claim and the claimant is the tenant, the acknowledgment of service is to be in form N210 and must state with particulars[97]:

(1) whether, if a new tenancy is granted, the defendant objects to any of the terms proposed by the claimant and if so—
   (a) the terms to which he objects; and
   (b) the terms that he proposes insofar as they differ from those proposed by the claimant;

(2) whether the defendant is a tenant under a lease having less than 15 years unexpired at the date of the termination of the claimant's current tenancy and, if so, the name and address of any person who, to the knowledge of the defendant, has an interest in the reversion in the property expectant (whether immediate or in not more than 15 years from that date) on the termination of the defendant's tenancy;

---

sought to be extended it was not necessary to go through the checklist contained in r.3.9. In such cases the discretion should be exercised having regard to the overriding objective of enabling the court to deal with cases justly, including, so far as practicable, the matters set out in r.1.1(2).

[93] *Ambrose v Kaye* [2002] EWCA Civ 91; [2002] 1 E.G.L.R. 49, per Chadwick L.J.

[94] CPR r.8.9(a)(ii).

[95] In the county court the landlord was, prior to CPR, obliged to file an answer in reply to the tenant's originating application: CCR Ord.43 r.2(1). This rule was retained in the Schedule rules to the CPR, prior to the CPR amendments made in October 2001, and, accordingly, a respondent landlord to a claim for the grant of a new tenancy was after the coming into force of the CPR still required to file an answer to the application. This was so notwithstanding the fact that the CPR made no other reference to an "answer" and such a document was not within the definition of "statement of case" in r.2.3(1).

[96] See paras 14–31, 14–34 and 14–35 above.

[97] CPR PD 56 para.3.10.

(3) the name and address of any person having an interest in the property who is likely to be affected by the grant of a new tenancy; and
(4) if the claimant's current tenancy is one to which s.32(2) of the 1954 Act applies, whether the defendant requires that any new tenancy shall be a tenancy of the whole of the property comprised in the claimant's current tenancy.

Tenant's acknowledgement to landlord's Part 8 claim for renewal

Where the claim is an unopposed claim and the claimant is the landlord, the acknowledgment of service is to be in form N210 and must state with particulars[98]: **14–71**

(1) the nature of the business carried on at the property;
(2) if the defendant relies on ss.23(1A), 41 or 42 of the 1954 Act, the basis on which he does so;
(3) whether any, and if so what part, of the property comprised in the tenancy is occupied neither by the defendant nor by a person employed by the defendant for the purpose of the defendant's business;
(4) the name and address of:
  (a) anyone known to the defendant who has an interest in the reversion in the property (whether immediate or in not more than 15 years) on the termination of the defendant's current tenancy and who is likely to be affected by the grant of a new tenancy; or
  (b) if the defendant does not know of anyone specified by sub-para.(4)(a), anyone who has a freehold interest in the property; and
(5) whether, if a new tenancy is granted, the defendant objects to any of the terms proposed by the claimant and, if so:
  (a) the terms to which he objects; and
  (b) the terms that he proposes insofar as they differ from those proposed by the claimant.

Tenant's response to landlord's Part 7 termination application

Where the landlord opposes renewal the tenant is not in fact required to serve an acknowledgement of service. The tenant has the option, as with any Pt 7 claim, of missing out an acknowledgment and serving a defence immediately. It is provided by CPR r.9.2 that where particulars of claim are served on a defendant,[99] the defendant may: **14–72**

(1) file or serve an admission in accordance with CPR Pt 14;
(2) file a defence in accordance with CPR Pt 15 (or do both, if he admits part of the claim); or

---

[98] CPR PD 56 para.3.11.

[99] The particulars of claim are to be contained in or served with the claim form or served within 14 days of service of the claim form: CPR r.7.4.

(3) file an acknowledgement of service in accordance with CPR Pt 10.

14–73 The benefit to a defendant to a Pt 7 claim of serving an acknowledgement of service is that it provides the defendant with more time for serving a defence. CPR r.10.1(3) provides that a defendant may file an acknowledgment of service if he is unable to file a defence within the period specified by CPR r.15.4 or if he wishes to dispute the court's jurisdiction. By CPR r.15.4 a defence is required to be served within 14 days of service of the particulars of claim. However, if an acknowledgment of service is filed the defence does not need to be served until 28 days after service of the particulars of claim.

14–74 Where the claim is an opposed claim and the claimant is the landlord:

(1) the acknowledgment of service is to be in form N9; and
(2) in his defence the defendant must state with particulars:
  (a) whether the defendant relies on ss.23(1A), 41 or 42 of the 1954 Act and, if so, the basis on which he does so;
  (b) whether the defendant relies on s.31A of the 1954 Act and, if so, the basis on which he does so; and
  (c) the terms of the new tenancy that the defendant would propose in the event that the claimant's claim to terminate the current tenancy fails.[100]

14–75 Section 23(1A) refers to the position where the tenant claims protection of the Act by reason of the occupation or the carrying on of a business by a company in which the tenant has a controlling interest, or where the tenant is a company, by a person with a controlling interest in the company. In either case the occupation or the carrying on of the business shall be treated for the purposes of the Act as equivalent to occupation or, as the case may be, the carrying on of a business by the tenant.[101]

14–76 The requirement for the tenant to state whether or not he intends to rely on s.31A is welcomed. Previously there was no time limit imposed on the tenant as to when he was required to express an intention to rely on these provisions.[102] However, what the tenant can actually say at this stage of the procedure may be rather limited. In an opposed claim the evidence is to be filed as the court directs.[103] The landlord's evidence is to be filed first.[104] However, until the tenant has seen the detailed evidence of the landlord's proposals he may not be in a position to state, other than in very general terms, the terms in the new tenancy which he proposes to provide by way of access nor identify that part of the holding which he alleges is an economically separable part.

---

[100] PD 56 para.3.13.
[101] See para.1–86 et seq.
[102] *Romulus Trading Co Ltd v Trustees of Henry Smith's Charity (No.2)* [1991] 1 E.G.L.R. 95 CA, where it was held that there was no particular stage in the proceedings by which the tenant was required to elect to rely on s.31A. See also para.7–192.
[103] PD 56 para.3.15.
[104] PD 56 para.3.15.

Landlord's response to tenant's Part 7 claim for renewal

Where the claim is an opposed claim and the claimant is the tenant the landlord it is provided that: **14–77**

(1) the acknowledgment of service is to be in form N9[105]; and
(2) in his defence the defendant must state with particulars:
  (a) the defendant's grounds of opposition;
  (b) full details of those grounds of opposition;
  (c) whether, if a new tenancy is granted, the defendant objects to any of the terms proposed by the claimant and if so:
    (i) the terms to which he objects; and
    (ii) the terms that he proposes insofar as they differ from those proposed by the claimant;
  (d) whether the defendant is a tenant under a lease having less than 15 years unexpired at the date of the termination of the claimant's current tenancy and, if so, the name and address of any person who, to the knowledge of the defendant, has an interest in the reversion in the property expectant (whether immediately or in not more than 15 years from that date) on the termination of the defendant's tenancy;
  (e) the name and address of any person having an interest in the property who is likely to be affected by the grant of a new tenancy; and
  (f) if the claimant's current tenancy is one to which s.32(2) of the 1954 Act applies, whether the defendant requires that any new tenancy shall be a tenancy of the whole of the property comprised in the claimant's current tenancy.[106]

Failure to serve acknowledgement of service

Party entitled to attend hearing

Under the former rules it was held that, where the landlord failed to serve an answer in the county court, this prevented him from opposing the grant of a new tenancy. He was, nevertheless, entitled to be heard as to the rent and other terms on which the court must decide on the basis of the evidence put before it: *Morgan v Jones*[107] (digested in para.14–79). It is provided by the CPR that if the **14–78**

---

[105] A landlord need not serve an acknowledgment: see para.14–72, where the position of the tenant is concerned. What is said there applies equally to the position of a landlord in response to a tenant's Pt 7 claim form.

[106] PD 56 para.3.12. The tenant is not obliged in his defence to state the nature of the business carried on at the property nor whether any part of it is occupied neither by the tenant or by any person employed by him for the purposes of the tenant's business. Contrast the position with respect to the contents of the tenant's acknowledgement of service in response to a landlord's Pt 8 claim for renewal: see para.14–71.

[107] [1960] 1 W.L.R. 1220; [1960] 3 All E.R. 583 CA. See also *Desbroderie v Segalov* [1956] J.P.L. 892; [1956] 106 L.J. 764; [1956] E.G.D. 211 CC (where the landlord had failed to file an answer to the tenant's originating application as required by the then rules of court. The judge held that the landlord could not oppose but could defend as to the rent payable under the proposed new lease).

defendant has failed to file an acknowledgement of service and the time period for doing so has expired the defendant may attend the hearing of the claim but may not take part in the hearing unless the court gives permission: CPR r.8.4. The claimant is unable to obtain judgment in default under Pt 12: CPR r. 12.2(b).[108]

14–79 ***Morgan v Jones***[109] The tenants, having been served with a s.25 notice, applied to the county court for a new tenancy, the application being on form 335 of the county court forms, pursuant to the County Court Rules 1936 (as amended) Ord. 40 r.8(1) and containing the tenants' proposals for the terms (including the rent payable) of the new tenancy. The landlord in his answer stated that he opposed the grant of a new tenancy on the ground stated in his s.25 notice, namely ground (b) of s.30(1). The county court judge decided in favour of the tenants and held that a new tenancy should be granted. The learned judge held that, as on the "pleadings" the landlords had not specifically opposed the terms of the new tenancy proposed by the tenants, the landlords could not be allowed to call evidence of whether those terms were reasonable. The landlords appealed. It was held that in the absence of a written agreement between the parties, the judge in determining the terms of a new tenancy under ss.33 and 34 must hear evidence on the reasonableness of those terms. Mere proposals put forward by the tenants for a new tenancy are insufficient to enable a judge, on those proposals alone, to come to any conclusion on the matter at all. There must be evidence before him to support the reasonableness of those proposals. It could not be inferred from the landlords' failure to object in their answer to the tenants' proposed terms that the landlords thereby agree with those terms. Accordingly, the judgment could not be supported on the question of the reasonableness of the proposed terms and the case was ordered to be remitted to the judge to determine whether those terms were reasonable and whether the rent was one which could be reasonably expected to be obtained by a willing lessor.

14–80 **Amending acknowledgement of service** The landlord may wish to amend where, for instance, he has stated that he requires any new tenancy to be one comprising the whole of the property demised under the current tenancy but has subsequently changed his mind, or where he wishes to alter the terms proposed for the new tenancy. Under the CPR the provisions as to amendment apply only to a statement of case: CPR Pt 17. The definition of "statement of case" in CPR r.2.3(1) does not include an acknowledgement of service. If the landlord is unable to formally amend the acknowledgement of service, he may be able to amend his case indirectly by referring to, for instance, the terms of the new lease which he is now proposing, in his evidence in response to that of the tenant.

---

[108] Although he may seek summary judgment: see para.14–100 et seq.

[109] [1960] 1 W.L.R 1220 CA.

8. Evidence[110]

In support of a Part 8 claim

Part 8, without modification, provides that the claimant must serve any written evidence on which he intends to rely when he files his claim form: CPR r.8.5(1). This would in the context of the 1954 Act in most cases cause unnecessary expenditure and it may be impossible. CPR r.8.5(1) is disapplied to claims for renewal or termination: CPR r.56.3(3)(a). Prior to the amendments to CPR Pt 56 brought about by the 2003 Order, CPR r.56.3(10) (since repealed) provided that the claimant must file and serve any written evidence on which he intended to rely within 14 days of the service upon him of the landlord's acknowledgement of service. Evidence was also required to be served with the acknowledgement. The evidence required to be served under CPR r.56.3(10) was that supporting the parties positions so that the court could identify the issues and give appropriate further directions. **14–81**

The position now is fairly simple. Where the claim is unopposed, no evidence need be filed in support of the claim or with the defendant's acknowledgement of service unless and until the court directs it to be filed: PD 56 para.3.14. Thus, the rules relating to the filing of evidence contained within CPR rr.8.5 and 8.6 do not apply. It should be noted, however, that the claim form may not be relied on as evidence.[111] **14–82**

In support of a Part 7 claim

The provisions of PD 56 again make the position clear. Where the claim is an opposed claim,[112] evidence, including expert evidence, must be filed by the parties as the court directs and the landlord shall be required to file his evidence first.[113] **14–83**

---

[110] As to evidence generally, see Ch.11.

[111] See para.14–27.

[112] And this includes a landlord's termination application as well as a claim for renewal by the tenant in circumstances where the claim is opposed: PD 56 para.3.1(2).

[113] PD 56 para 3.15. It would be contrary to the overriding objective to require the parties to incur the costs of providing evidence on the terms of the new lease and on the rent where the landlord is opposing renewal at the same time as the evidence relevant to the ground of opposition. The reasons are that: (1) those issues may never arise if the landlord is successful in his ground of opposition; (2) the parties are, in light of the landlord's opposition, unlikely to have brought their minds to bear on the terms of any draft lease which is to form the subject of any renewal; (3) the valuation date for the rent may be many months ahead and the preparation of valuation evidence is simply premature.

9. DIRECTIONS

Time for giving directions

Part 8 claims

14–84 It is provided by PD 8A para.6.1 that the court may give directions immediately a Pt 8 claim form is issued either on application of a party or on its own initiative, and that such directions may include the fixing of a hearing date.[114] The court will give directions about the future management of the claim in accordance with CPR 29.

Part 7 claims

14–85 Where a defendant files a defence the court will serve an allocation questionnaire on each party. Each party must file the allocation questionnaire, which shall be at least 14 days after the date on which it is deemed to be served on the party in question.[115] The purpose of the allocation questionnaire is to determine the track to which the case is to be allocated. There are three tracks[116]: the small claims track; the fast track and the multi-track. Allocation will be by the court.[117] The court may order an allocation hearing.[118] Landlord and tenant claims will ordinarily be allocated to the multi-track (as they are automatically under Pt 8 claims).[119] It is not unknown, however, for cases to be allocated to the fast track. If allocation is to the multi-track the court will, upon allocation, give directions or fix a case management conference: CPR r.29.2.

Track allocation

Part 8 claims

14–86 A claim form under Pt 8 is automatically allocated to the multi-track: CPR r.8.9(c).[120] Part 29 contains detailed provisions as to case management concerning cases which have been allocated to the multi-track. The master (High Court) or the district judge (county court) will consider what directions to make as to the further conduct of the proceedings in respect of, for instance, disclosure, provision for the determination of preliminary issues, the joinder or substitution of parties and any other direction which is considered desirable. It has been known, for instance, for the court to reallocate the case away from the multi-track and onto the fast track (where the case is expected to last not more than a day and

---

114 See also CPR r.29.2 which provides that "the Court will fix the trial date or the period in which the trial is to take place as soon as practicable" upon allocation to a multi-track. A Pt 8 claim is automatically allocated to the multi-track: CPR r.8.9(c).

115 CPR r.26.3 generally.

116 CPR r.26.1(2).

117 CPR r.26.5.

118 CPR r.26.5(4).

119 As to which, see para.14–86.

120 Which provides that accordingly CPR Pt 26 does not apply.

where the expert evidence is limited[121]: CPR r.26.6(5)). If allocated to the fast track the court when giving directions will fix the trial date or fix a period, not exceeding three weeks, within which the trial is to take place: CPR r.28.2(2). The trial date or trial period will be not more than 30 weeks from the giving of directions: CPR r.28.2(4).

Part 7 claims

This has been considered in para.14–85 above. **14–87**

Preliminary issue

Part 8 claims

The parties are required to assist the court in furthering the overriding objective contained in CPR r.1.1, to deal with cases justly by raising the issues they wish to take at an early stage.[122] The Pt 8 claim form should include any preliminary points which are sought to be contested, for instance whether the s.25 notice is valid (see *British Railways Board v AJA Smith Transport Ltd*[123] (digested in para.3–243). If the preliminary point arises after service of the claim form, the claim form or the landlord's acknowledgement of service should be amended *(Bolton v Oppenheim*[124] and see also *I&H Caplan v Caplan (No.2)*[125] (digested in para.7–44). Under the rules in force prior to the CPR, if the landlord wished to raise a preliminary issue, he would do so either by taking out a summons in the action or by raising it in his affidavit in reply to the summons. Under the Pt 8 procedure the landlord is entitled to raise the issue by making a Pt 20 claim, although he cannot do so without obtaining the court's permission: CPR r.8.7. An application for consent would have to be made in accordance with Pt 23 or, alternatively, at the hearing for directions. **14–88**

Part 7 claims

The consideration of whether or not to direct the hearing of a preliminary issue is particularly appropriate where the court has to decide whether the landlord's ground of opposition has been made out. It is now specifically provided by PD 56 **14–89**

---

[121] In such a case the court is likely to order the appointment of a single joint expert. As to the appointment of a single joint expert, see para.11–25 et seq.

[122] *Ambrose v Kaye* [2002] EWCA Civ 91; [2002] P.L.S.C.S. 5. The court may adjourn the hearing to allow further evidence to be admitted to a point raised for the first time by the tenant in his closing submissions. Thus where on a preliminary issue as to whether the landlord could prove ground (g) the tenant raised in his closing submissions the argument that the landlord could not satisfy s.30(3) as he did not have a controlling interest in the company intending to occupy, it would be unjust to deprive the landlord of the opportunity of meeting the objection simply because it was raised late, where he would have been able to deal with it if the issue had been raised at an earlier stage. Accordingly it was a proper exercise of discretion to adjourn the hearing to permit the landlord to effect a transfer of shares so as to satisfy the statutory permissions and for evidence of that to be admitted.

[123] [1981] 2 E.G.L.R. 66.

[124] [1959] 1 W.L.R. 913; [1959] 3 All E.R. 90 CA.

[125] [1963] 1 W.L.R. 1247; [1963] 2 All E.R. 930.

para.3.16 that unless in the circumstances of the case it is unreasonable to do so, any grounds of opposition shall be tried as a preliminary issue: PD 56 para.3.16. This reflects the view of Megarry J. in *Dutch Oven Ltd v Egham Estate & Investment Co.*[126] The convenience and economy of this course is plain. The cost and expenditure of labour involved in preparing to adduce evidence is often considerable. If the landlord succeeds on the ground of opposition, none of that evidence will be required and the waste on each side will be substantial. If, on the other hand, the landlord fails under his ground of opposition, then during an adjournment each can prepare for the conflict as regards the terms of the new tenancy. In some cases, of course, there will be an overlapping of issues which will make it inappropriate to attempt to try a separate preliminary point. For example, where a landlord opposes on ground (a)—disrepair—the tenant may offer a covenant in the new lease to carry out certain specified works and there may be a dispute as to what (if any) damage to the reversion has resulted from the disrepair and this might itself require expert evidence on the rental value of the holding. To attempt to state a preliminary issue in such a case might increase, rather than decrease, expense and delay. It may also be inconvenient to have a hearing in two stages, e.g. where the differences between the two parties on the terms of the new tenancy (if the landlord were to fail in his opposition) are small.

14–90 Where there is a preliminary issue the parties should, before any hearing for directions before the master, agree between themselves as to the formulation of that preliminary issue and have a draft of that formulation ready to hand to the master for his consideration. If no agreement can be reached between the parties as to what is the proper formulation of the preliminary issue, its formulation will be determined by the master having regard to the oral representations of the parties.

14–91 A preliminary issue should not form the subject matter of separate proceedings if it can be raised as part of the claim: see *Royal Bank of Scotland Ltd v Citrusdal Investments Ltd*[127] (which concerned a tenant's originating application to the county court but the principle seems equally applicable to the Pt 8 claim).

Failure to comply with the directions

14–92 When making an order the court may specify the consequence of failure to comply with the order: CPR 3.1(3)(b). The court may strike out the claim if there has been a failure to comply with a court order: CPR r.3.4(2)(c). If the order does contain a sanction for failure to comply that sanction has effect unless the party in default applies for and obtains relief from the sanction: CPR r.3.8(1). Where the court order requires something to be done within a specified time, and specifies the consequence of failure to comply, the time for doing the act may not be extended by agreement between the parties: CPR r.3.8(3).The circumstances to which the court may have regard in considering whether to grant relief from any sanction imposed for a failure to comply with the court order is set out in CPR r.3.9. The court has power under CPR r.3.9(2) to grant relief even where the order

[126] [1968] 1 W.L.R. 1483; [1968] 3 All E.R. 100.

[127] [1971] 1 W.L.R. 1469; [1971] 3 All E.R. 558.

was made by consent.[128] The application must be supported by evidence: CPR r.3.9(2). Where no sanction is specified an application to impose a sanction for non-compliance will need to be made pursuant to Pt 23.

10. JOINDER OF INTERESTED PARTIES

Generally

By CPR Sch.1, RSC Ord.97 r.8(1)[129] it was provided that any person affected by the proceedings for a new tenancy may apply to be made a party to the proceedings and the court may give such directions on the application as appear necessary. Where the tenant or landlord make a Pt 8 claim they are as claimant required[130] to include in the claim form the name and address of anyone known to the claimant who: **14–93**

(1) has an interest in the reversion in the property (whether immediate or in not more than 14 years) on the termination of the tenant's current tenancy;
(2) who is likely to be affected by the grant of a new tenancy (other than a person whose only interest is a freeholder); and
(3) if no person falling within (2) is known, of anyone who has a freehold interest in the property.

If such a person served with the claim form wishes to be made a party the application should be made on notice. It is provided that, generally, notice must be served at least three days before the court is to deal with the application: CPR r.23.7. Whether or not such an application is made, the master or district judge on any hearing for directions will wish to know whether there is any superior landlord or other interested party affected by the claim. It will be clear from the landlord's acknowledgement of service whether or not he is himself a tenant[131] and whether the notification or joining of the superior landlord is necessary. Such a case might arise where the landlord has only four years of his term remaining and the tenant is seeking the grant of a term of 10 years, which may require the court to grant a reversionary lease from the superior landlord. In such a case the court will, whether or not an application has been made to it, order that notice of the proceedings be given to the superior landlord and that he be made a party to the proceedings. The matter is, however, in the court's discretion and if it considers that a person is not sufficiently affected, the court will refuse to order a notice to be given or the party to be joined. Where there is an adjournment to enable a person to be added or served with notice of proceedings, it is likely that a date will be fixed for a further hearing of the claim so as to enable that person to

---

[128] *Pannone LLP v Aardvark Digital Ltd* [2011] EWCA Civ 803.

[129] The pre-CPR corresponding provision in the county court, contained in CCR Ord.43 r.14, was not retained by the CPR Sch.2 rules when the CPR were enacted.

[130] By PD 56 para.3.5(6) (in the case of a Pt 8 claim made by the tenant) and PD 56 para.3.7(3) (in the case of a Pt 8 claim by a landlord).

[131] Because of the information which is required to be served pursuant to PD 56 para.3.10(2). The same is equally true where the landlord is the claimant: see PD 56 para.3.11(4) as to the information required to be provided by the tenant in his acknowledgment of service.

consider the matter and appropriate directions then to be given, such as for the filing of evidence by the added party or by the other parties.

Mortgagees

14–94 It was held in *Meah v Mouskos*[132] that there was no need for the landlord's mortgagee to be made a party to the proceedings if the mortgagee has neither gone into possession nor appointed a receiver. The reason is that by s.36(4) it is provided that a lease granted pursuant to the 1954 Act is deemed to be one authorised by s.99 of the Law of Property Act 1925 (dealing with the power of the mortgagor to grant leases), notwithstanding an exclusion of s.99 by the mortgage. It was said in that case that it is proper to give the mortgagee notice of the proceedings and that it is then for him to decide whether he wishes to apply to be made a party to the proceedings. If, however, the mortgagee is in possession or has appointed a receiver, it was provided by CPR Sch.1, RSC Ord.97 r.1(2) (High Court) and CPR Sch.2, CCR Ord.43 r.1(2) (county court)[133] that the mortgagee was to be treated as a "landlord" for the purposes of the 1954 Act and, therefore, should be made the defendant to the claim. There is no corresponding provision contained within CPR Pt 56 or PD 56. However, it seems to matter not as by virtue of the 1954 Act the mortgagee is treated in those circumstances as the "competent landlord" for the purpose of the 1954 Act: s.67. It is provided by PD 56 para.3.3 that it is the person who is the landlord as defined by s.44 of the 1954 Act who must be made the defendant to the tenant's Pt 8 claim. It is probably prudent to make both the landlord and the mortgagee as defendants to the claim if there is doubt as to whether or not the mortgagee is in possession.

11. DISCONTINUING PROCEEDINGS

Discontinuance of Part 8 claim by tenant as of right

14–95 The provisions of the CPR effectively give the claimant tenant a right to discontinue his Pt 8 claim without first having to seek the permission of the court: CPR Pt 38. Permission is required only in the special situations provided for by CPR r.38.2(2)(a) and (b) which are highly unlikely to arise in the context of a claim for a new tenancy. Where there is more than one claimant all must consent or the court's permission must be obtained to the discontinuance: CPR 38.2(2)(c). The discontinuance takes effect on the date when notice of discontinuance is served on the defendant: CPR r.38.5(1). Unless the court orders otherwise, a claimant who discontinues is liable for the costs which a defendant against whom he discontinues incurred on or before the date on which notice of discontinuance was served on him: CPR r.38.6(1). A notice of discontinuance served in error may be set aside by the court pursuant to CPR 3.10: *Toplain Ltd v Orange Retail*.[134]

[132] [1964] 2 W.L.R. 27; [1963] 3 All E.R. 908 CA.

[133] The RSC and CC Rules were retained in Schs 1 and 2 to the CPR upon the initial introduction of the CPR. These provisions were repealed on October 15, 2001 (see Civil Procedure (Amendment) Rules (SI 2001/256) with the introduction of CPR Pt 56.

[134] Unreported July 26, 2012, Roth J.

Withdrawal/ discontinuance of Part 8 claim made by landlord

The position is different in the case of a Pt 8 claim by a landlord. The landlord cannot withdraw the application once made unless the tenant consents to its withdrawal: s.24(2C). The tenant can, however, invite the court to dismiss the claim, where he informs the court that he does not want a new tenancy: s.29(5). The filing a notice of discontinuance on the court by a tenant under s.29(5) imposes a positive mandatory obligation on the court to dismiss the landlord's application and the application is to be treated as automatically dismissed upon receipt by the court of the tenant's notification: *Windsor Life Assurance Co Ltd v Lloyds TSB Bank Plc*.[135] **14–96**

Discontinuance of Part 7 claim by tenant

There seems to be no reason why the general provisions for discontinuance in CPR Pt 38 referred to above[136] should not apply to a tenant's Pt 7 claim. **14–97**

Discontinuance of landlord's Part 7 claim

Oddly, at least to the authors, the landlord is required to obtain the tenant's consent in order to withdraw his termination application: s.29(6). This requirement may have something to do with the wording of s.29(4)(b). This provides that if the landlord makes a termination application but does not establish to the satisfaction of the court any of the grounds on which he is entitled to make the application in accordance with s.30, the court shall make an order for the grant of a new tenancy and accordingly for the termination of the current tenancy immediately before the commencement of the new tenancy. It may have been thought that if the landlord could simply withdraw his termination application without consent there would be no mechanism for ensuring that the tenant obtained a new tenancy and thus required the withdrawal to be subject to the tenant's veto. The tenant will only grant consent subject to the landlord agreeing to the grant of a new tenancy or for the landlord to withdraw subject to directions to be given by the court for consideration of a renewal by the tenant. **14–98**

Costs of discontinuance

The normal order on discontinuance is that the claimant bears the defendant's costs up to the date on which notice of discontinuance is served. The court may order otherwise but the burden is on the party who seeks to persuade the court that some other consequence should follow: *Ian Walker v John Graham Walker*.[137] Where the landlord makes a claim for a new tenancy, service by the defendant tenant of a notice under s.29(5) is equivalent to a notice of **14–99**

---

135 [2009] 3 E.G.L.R. 53 CC.

136 See para.14–95.

137 [2005] EWCA Civ 247.

discontinuance[138]. Accordingly, the burden of proof is on the tenant defendant to justify the departure of the court from the normal order: *Lay v Drexler*.[139]

12. SUMMARY JUDGMENT

Entitlement to claim

14–100 It is now possible under the CPR to seek summary judgment either in relation to the claim for the new tenancy or in relation to the landlord's grounds of opposition. A claim for summary judgment under RSC Ord.14[140] could not be brought in relation to proceedings concerning the 1954 Act, insofar as it related to the tenant's claim for a new tenancy or the landlord's grounds of opposition, for summary judgment could be sought only in an action "begun by writ": RSC Ord.14 r.1(2).

14–101 The CPR make it clear that summary judgment may be given against a claimant "in any type of proceedings": CPR r.24.3(1). Summary judgment may also be given against a defendant "in any type of proceedings" save for three exceptions which do not impact upon proceedings under the 1954 Act: CPR r.24.3(2). "Any type of proceedings" encompasses claims made under Pt 7 or Pt 8. The claim cannot be made by the claimant until the service of an acknowledgement of service unless the court otherwise gives permission: CPR r.24.4(1). The application for summary judgment will be made pursuant to Pt 23: CPR r.24.4(3). An application made pursuant to Pt 23 requires the evidence to be filed at the same time as the filing of the application: CPR r.23.7(2). If the respondent to an application for summary judgment wishes to rely on written evidence at the hearing he must file and serve it at least seven days before the hearing: CPR r.24.5(1). Evidence in reply must be served at least three days before the hearing: CPR r.24.5(2). At least 14 days' notice must be given of the date for the hearing and the issues which it is proposed the court would decide at the hearing: CPR r.24.4(3). The application for summary judgment will normally be listed before a master: CG: Ch.6, para.6–27.

Test for summary judgment

14–102 The court may grant summary judgment against a claimant or defendant on the whole claim or on a particular issue if (CPR r.24.2):

(1) It considers that:

---

[138] It has been held at County Court level that the notification by the tenant takes effect as an automatic dismissal: *Windsor Life Assurance Co Ltd v Lloyds TSB Bank Plc* [2009] 3 E.G.L.R. 53 CC, H.H. Judge Peter Cowell.

[139] [2007] EWCA Civ 464; [2007] 2 E.G.L.R. 46.

[140] Summary judgment in the county court could be obtained only where "the defendant has delivered a defence," and this, therefore, excluded applications under the Act for which there was service not of a defence but an answer. It was also available only to the plaintiff, whether by way of original action or by way of counterclaim.

(a) the claimant has no real prospect of succeeding on the claim or issue; or

(b) the defendant has no real prospect of successfully defending the claim or issue; and

(2) there is no other compelling reason why the case or issue should be disposed of at a trial.

The respondent to a claim for summary judgment need only show a real prospect of succeeding (where the claimant to the claim is respondent to the summary judgment application) or of successfully defending the claim or issue (where the defendant to the claim is respondent to the summary judgment application). The court will disregard prospects which are false, fanciful or imaginary. In *Swain v Hillman*[141] Lord Woolf M.R. said:

> "The words 'no real prospect of being successful or succeeding' do not need any amplification, they speak for themselves. The word 'real' distinguishes fanciful prospects of success or, as [counsel for the defendant] submits, they direct the court to the need to see whether there is a 'realistic' as opposed to a 'fanciful' prospect of success."

And[142]:

> "Useful though the power is under Pt 24, it is important that it is kept to its proper role. It is not meant to dispense with the need for a trial where there are issues which should be investigated at the trial. As [counsel for the defendant] put it in his submissions, the proper disposal of an issue under Pt 24 does not involve the judge conducting a mini-trial, that is not the object of the provisions; it is to enable cases, where there is no real prospect of success either way, to be disposed of summarily."

Judge L.J. said:

> "This ['no real prospect of success'] is simple language, not susceptible to much elaboration, even forensically. If there is a real prospect of success, the discretion to give summary judgment does not arise merely because the court concludes that success is improbable. If that were the court's conclusion, then it is provided with a different discretion, which is that the case should proceed but subject to appropriate conditions imposed by the court."

---

[141] [2001] 1 All E.R. 91 at 92; [2001] C.P.L.R. 779; [2000] P.I.Q.R. P51 CA. See also *Three Rivers DC v Bank of England* (*No.3*) [2001] UKHL 16; [2001] 2 All E.R. 513, Lord Hope said at [95]:

"I would approach that further question in this way. The method by which issues of fact are tried in our courts is well settled. After the normal processes of discovery and interrogatories have been completed, the parties are allowed to lead their evidence so that the trial judge can determine where the truth lies in the light of that evidence. To that rule there are some well-recognised exceptions. For example, it may be clear as a matter of law at the outset that even if a party were to succeed in proving all the facts that he offers to prove he will not be entitled to the remedy that he seeks. In that event a trial of the facts would be a waste of time and money, and it is proper that the action should be taken out of court as soon as possible. In other cases it may be possible to say with confidence before trial that the factual basis for the claim is fanciful because it is entirely without substance. It may be clear beyond question that the statement of facts is contradicted by all the documents or other material on which it is based. The simpler the case the easier it is likely to be take that view and resort to what is properly called summary judgment. But more complex cases are unlikely to be capable of being resolved in that way without conducting a mini-trial on the documents without discovery and without oral evidence. As Lord Woolf MR said in *Swain v Hillman* [2001] 1 All ER 91 at 95, that is not the object of the rule. It is designed to deal with cases that are not fit for trial at all."

[142] At 95.

Application to 1954 Act proceedings

14–103 It is considered that CPR Pt 24 is unlikely to be utilised in 1954 Act applications save in exceptional circumstances. Thus, for instance, it will be difficult to envisage circumstances where it could be used where there is a dispute over the terms of the new lease, with arguments as to the variation as to the terms thereof capable of being put on both sides, or where the dispute is as to rent. It is considered that the most likely ambit of Pt 24 in the context of the 1954 Act proceedings is in connection with the landlord's grounds of opposition. One of the authors at least has encountered Pt 24 being utilised successfully by a landlord in relation to opposing the tenant's renewal under paras (f) and (g) of s.30(1) (own occupation). Ground (g) is a ground of opposition which, in practice, is ordinarily fairly easy to establish. No evidence of opinion will usually be required (unless the business to be carried on by the landlord requires planning permission and he has only made an application for it by the date of the hearing) and as long as the landlord can satisfy the court that he has a fixed and settled intention to occupy for the statutory purposes, i.e. his own business or residence and the tenant has no real prospect of seeking to persuade the court that the tenant has no such genuine intention, there is no good reason why the matter should go to trial. The position may be different, however, when one considers para.(f) (demolition and redevelopment). One can well see that where what the landlord proposes to do is demolish the entirety of the tenant's premises, the claim may justify an application for summary judgment. However, it is difficult to see how Pt 24 could be utilised where there is a dispute as to the extent to which the works are qualifying works within the statutory wording or the extent to which the landlord could be said to reasonably require possession unless the latter argument was based solely on the true construction of the terms of a reservation in the existing lease.

14–104 However, if a tenant considers that the landlord is insufficiently prepared he cannot, in most cases, attempt to obtain a tactical advantage by seeking summary judgment to dismiss the landlord's claim opposing renewal. The reason for this is that relevant question is not whether as at the date of the summary judgment hearing, the landlord has the requisite intention but whether at that date he can show that he has reasonable prospects of showing such an intention as at the trial date (whenever that may be): *Somerfield Stores Ltd v Spring (Sutton Coldfield) Ltd (In Administration)*.[143]In that case Spring, the landlord, having received notices under s.26 of the 1954 Act served by Somerfield in relation to a supermarket site held under three leases, opposed renewal under para.(f) of s.30(1) of the 1954 Act. Spring went into administration. Somerfield, seeking to take advantage of the hiatus that had arisen due to Spring's administration, applied for summary judgment[144] to dismiss the grounds of opposition which would have left the way clear for them to be granted a new tenancy. As matters stood at the date of the summary judgment hearing it was unlikely that Spring

[143] [2010] EWHC 2084 (Ch); [2010] 3 E.G.L.R. 37; [2011] L. & T.R. 8.

[144] The tenant having applied earlier for and obtained the court's permission to continue the proceedings pursuant to para.43(6) of Sch. B1 to the Insolvency Act 1986: see [2009] EWHC 2084 (Ch) ; [2011] L. & T.R. 8.

was able to carry out its redevelopment plans. H.H. Judge Cooke held that the landlord did not have to establish the requisite intention as at the date of the summary judgment hearing. The issue was not whether the landlord had, as at the date of the summary judgment hearing, formulated a sufficient intention for the purposes of para.(f) but whether the landlord had, at that date, a real prospect of forming, and proving that he has formed, the requisite intention at the anticipated trial date.[145]

14–105 The decision in *Somerfield Stores Ltd v Spring (Sutton Coldfield) Ltd (In Administration)*[146] does not mean that the summary judgment procedure can never been invoked in 1954 Act termination proceedings. All that it means is that a *tenant* cannot, save in exceptional circumstances, seek to utilise summary judgment as a tactic for seeking to accelerate the date by which the landlord has to establish the appropriate intention. This is not to say, however, that *a landlord* whose case is sufficiently strong should not contemplate seeking summary judgment *as against the tenant*. There is a clear distinction between a claim by a tenant for summary judgment against a landlord under para.(f) and a summary judgment claim by a landlord against a tenant under para.(f). The nature of a claim under para.(f) usually involves evidence from the landlord and the landlord alone. Unless a tenant is relying upon s.31A of the 1954 Act or is seeking to assert that there is no realistic prospect of obtaining planning permission, or that the works proposed are insufficient for para.(f), it is rare for tenants to put forward a positive case in relation to a ground (f) opposition. If the landlord's evidence is so strong that it is unlikely that anything could arise between the date of the summary judgment hearing and the date of trial which would undermine the strength of the landlord's case, there seems to be no reason why a landlord should not seek summary judgment in reliance upon the ground of opposition. The test on a landlord's claim for summary judgment is whether or not *the tenant* has a reasonable prospect of resisting the ground of opposition. The tenant is, in those circumstances, in a fundamentally different position to that of a tenant seeking summary judgment. Logically, if the landlord's evidence is overwhelming then, subject to exceptional circumstances (e.g. if it has planning permission but there is a judicial review pending as at the date of the summary judgment hearing and one could not predict the outcome of the review), there is no reason why it should not be equally overwhelming at trial. Thus, there should be no need to wait until trial to determine the opposition to the tenant's claim for renewal. By contrast, where the landlord is seeking to resist summary judgment by the tenant he will often be able to point to a number of matters which could occur between the date of the summary judgment hearing and the date of trial to enhance his opposition to the renewal. There is good reason why, therefore, the landlord merely has to show that he has reasonable prospects of proving the appropriate intention at the trial date.

14–106 What if the landlord needs to rely on expert opinion evidence in support of his claim for summary judgment? There is nothing in the Civil Procedure Rules

[145] As the learned Judge said, "if it were open to a tenant to bring forward the date at which the intention must be formed by the simple expedient of putting in a summary judgment application, it would result in an application for summary judgment being made in virtually every case."
[146] [2010] EWHC 2084 (Ch); [2010] 3 E.G.L.R. 37.

permitting expert opinion evidence to be put before the court under Pt 24 without leave of the court. The general position provided for by CPR 35.4(1) is that "no party may call an expert or put in evidence an expert's report without the court's permission." This rule seems geared towards evidence at trial. On a Pt 24 claim an expert will not be called, for there is no oral evidence, and it may be that there is no report as such to which the expert will refer in providing his statement. In practice expert opinion evidence is often relied on in support of Pt 24 claims under the 1954 Act.[147] If objection is taken the permission of the court can be sought at the hearing. If permission for such evidence is not obtained in advance, the landlord runs the risk that permission will be refused or there will be an adjournment to enable the tenant to put in its own expert evidence. A Pt 24 hearing which has before it conflicting expert evidence presented by the parties is not one which is unlikely to be amenable to the summary judgment process.

14–107 The court may on an application for summary judgment make an order for judgment on the claim, strike out or dismiss the claim, dismiss the application or make a conditional order: PD 24 para.5.1. A conditional order may involve the payment of a sum of money into court or provide for the taking of a specified step in relation to the claim as the case may be, with the claim or statement of case being dismissed in the event of non-compliance: PD 24 para.5.2(2). It is important to note that the court will not follow its former practice of granting leave to a defendant to defend a claim, whether conditionally or unconditionally: PD 24 para.5.2(2).

13. ASSESSORS

Appointment and use of

14–108 By s.70(1) of the Senior Courts Act 1981 the High Court may, if it thinks expedient to do so, call in the aid of one or more assessors specially qualified and hear and dispose of the cause or matter wholly or partially with their assistance. The CCA s.63(1) is to similar effect. The court may exercise the power of its own motion: s.63(5) of the 1954 Act and CPR r35.15. Not less than 21 days before making the appointment of an assessor, the court will notify each party in writing of the name of the proposed assessor, the matter in respect of which the assistance of the assessor will be sought and of the qualifications of the assessor to give assistance: PD 35 para.10.1. Where any person has been proposed for appointment as an assessor, objection to him, either personally or in respect of his qualification, may be taken by any party: PD 35 para.10.2. It is provided by CPR r.35.15(2) that the assessor assists the court in dealing with the matter in which he has skill and experience and may take such part in the proceedings as the court may direct. He may:

(1) prepare a report for the court (CPR r.35.15(3)(a));

[147] In *Roche Products Ltd v Kent Pharmaceuticals Ltd* [2006] EWCA Civ 1775, Neuberger L.J. said that "If *prima facie* convincing expert evidence is available which supports [the Defendant's] case, then no reason has been put forward as to why such expert evidence has not been provided in the form of a witness statement for the purposes of this CPR Pt 24 application." At [48].

(2) inspect the land to which the proceedings relate without the judge and report to the judge in writing thereon (s.63(6)(a) of the 1954 Act);
(3) attend the whole or any part of the trial to advise the court on any matter at issue in the proceedings (CPR r.35.15(3)(b)).

It is to be noted, however, that albeit the assessor may be directed to prepare a report and albeit that will be sent to each of the parties and may be used by the parties at trial (CPR r.35.15(4)), the assessor will not give oral evidence or be open to cross-examination or questioning: PD 35 para.10.4. The remuneration of the assessor is to form part of the costs of the proceedings unless the assessor was appointed upon the motion of the judge, whereupon the costs are defrayed by Parliament: CPR r.35.15(5), (7); s.63(6)(c) of the 1954 Act.

The use of assessors in practice prior to the implementation of the CPR was extremely rare. Albeit little used, their use could have been extremely valuable where, for instance, the main issue to be decided was one of rent. However, it is considered that assessors will continue to be a rarity in light of the court's power to direct that there be a single joint expert: CPR r.35.7; see paras 11–22 and 11–23. **14–109**

14. CLAIM FOR INTERIM RENT

Making of claim

Under the previous practice a landlord could, in the county court, include in his answer a claim for interim rent under s.24A: *Thomas v Hammond-Lawrence*.[148] Alternatively, if no application for a new tenancy had yet been made the landlord could claim an interim rent by way of an originating application: CCR Ord.3 r.4. It is provided by CPR r.8.7 that no counterclaim is permitted to a Pt 8 claim without the court's permission. Prior to the amendments to CPR Pt 56 to take on aboard the amendments to the Act made by the 2003 Order, PD 56 para.3.7 provided that the acknowledgement of service to the tenant's Pt 8 claim could include or be accompanied by an application by the defendant for an order for an interim rent. The 2003 Order substantially revised the provisions as to interim rent. The procedural provisions are now contained within PD 56 paras 3.17 to 3.19. **14–110**

No existing proceedings

If there are no proceedings (whether for renewal or termination) up and running, or where such proceedings have been disposed of, an application for interim rent under s.24A shall be made under the procedure in Pt 8: PD 56 para.3.19. In these circumstances the Pt 8 claim form shall include details of[149]: **14–111**

[148] [1986] 1 W.L.R. 456; [1986] 2 All E.R. 214; [1986] 1 E.G.L.R. 141 CA. As to the previous provisions in the High Court, see the second edition of this Work at para.13.13.1.2.
[149] PD 56 para.3.19.

(1) the property to which the claim relates;
(2) the particulars of the relevant tenancy (including date, parties and duration) and the current rent (if not the original rent);
(3) every notice or request given or made under ss.25 or 26;
(4) if the relevant tenancy has terminated, the date and mode of termination; and
(5) if the relevant tenancy has been terminated and the landlord has granted a new tenancy of the property to the tenant:
    (a) particulars of the new tenancy (including date, parties and duration) and the rent; and
    (b) in a case where s.24C(2) of the 1954 Act applies[150] but the claimant seeks a different rent under s.24C(3)[151] of that Act, particulars and matters on which the claimant relies as satisfying s.24C(3).

Where the landlord issues his own claim for an interim rent it would appear that the claim must be served within four months of issue as provided for by CPR r.7.5(2).

Proceedings in existence

14–112 Where proceedings have already been commenced for the grant of a new tenancy or the termination of an existing tenancy, the claim for interim rent under s.24A shall be made in those proceedings by[152]:

(1) the claim form;
(2) the acknowledgment of service or defence; or
(3) an application on notice under Pt 23.

Thus, in a Pt 7 claim, the landlord can make his application in the Pt 7 claim. Alternatively, if the tenant makes a Pt 7 claim, the landlord can make the application in the defence. Where the tenant has made a Pt 8 claim the landlord can make the application in the acknowledgement of service.

Revocation of order for the grant of a new tenancy

14–113 Any application under s.24D(3)[153] shall be made by an application on notice under Pt 23 in the original proceedings.

---

[150] See para.9–24 et seq., i.e. where one of the parties is arguing that the usual provisions as to the calculation of interim rent should not apply because of one of the qualifications set out in the section is applicable.

[151] See para.9–27.

[152] PD56 para.3.17.

[153] This provides:"(3) If the court:

(a) has made an order for the grant of a new tenancy and has ordered payment of interim rent in accordance with section 24C of this Act, but

(b) either—

(i) it subsequently revokes under section 36(2) of this Act the order for the grant of a new tenancy; or

(ii) the landlord and tenant agree not to act on the order,

Nature of claim for interim rent

Under the old RSC and county court procedure, pre-CPR, it was held that an application by the landlord for an interim rent whether made by originating summons or by a summons in the proceedings survived the discontinuance of the tenant's application for a new tenancy: *Michael Kramer & Co v Airways Pension Fund Trustees Ltd*[154]; *Artoc Bank & Trust Ltd v Prudential Assurance Co Plc*[155] and *Coates Brothers v General Accident Life Assurance*.[156] The claim by a landlord under the present provisions of the CPR, however effected, i.e. whether under Pt 8 or by way of what is effectively a Pt 20 claim to the tenant's own Pt 7 claim, is equally not a claim which can be said to be parasitic on the tenant's claim but is to be treated as a wholly distinct claim for independent relief and ought, therefore, to survive the discontinuance of the tenant's claim. **14–114**

15. DECLARATION PURSUANT TO SECTION 31(2) OF THE ACT

The application

Where the court makes a declaration pursuant to s.31(2) of the Act that one of the grounds of opposition in (d), (e) and (f) of s.30(1) of the Act would have been satisfied if a date later than that specified in the s.25 notice or the s.26 request (being a date not more than one year after the date so specified) had been specified, the effect is that no tenancy is ordered, but the tenant has 14 days after the making of the declaration to require the court to substitute the later date for the date specified. The tenant may wish to consider his position. It was previously provided under the RSC and CCR as retained by Schs 1 and 2 to the CPR until October 15, 2001 (the coming into force of CPR Pt 56), that the application to substitute the later date could be made by an application in chambers without notice within 14 days after the date of the declaration: RSC Ord.97 r.10; CCR Ord.43 r.9. No affidavit with supporting evidence was required. **14–115**

No specific provision was substituted under CPR Pt 56 so as to deal with the matters with which those previous rules were concerned, notwithstanding the repeal of those rules by CPR Pt 56 and PD 56. This remains the position under the present CPR as at the time of writing. It is considered that the application should be dealt with by way of an application pursuant to CPR Pt 23 as before without the need to give notice. CPR Pt 23 contemplates that applications may be served without notice: CPR r.23.4(2) and PD 23A para.3. **14–116**

The statutory time limit of 14 days cannot be extended. **14–117**

---

the court on the application of the landlord or the tenant shall determine a new interim rent in accordance with subsections (1) and (2) above without a further application under section 24A(1) of this Act."

[154] [1978] 1 E.G.L.R. 49 CA.

[155] [1984] 1 W.L.R. 1181; [1984] 3 All E.R. 538.

[156] [1991] 1 W.L.R. 712.

16. CERTIFICATE UNDER SECTION 37(4) OF THE ACT

The application

14–118 Where the court decided that it was precluded from granting a tenancy on one of the grounds specified in s.30(1) of the Act, the court was required to state all the grounds on which the court is so precluded (CPR Sch.1 RSC Ord.97 r.9 and Sch.2, CCR Ord.43 r.8) (now repealed). There is no corresponding provision in CPR Pt 56 or PD 56. The ground on which the landlord successfully opposes the grant of a new tenancy may be important from the tenant's point of view, for it is only if the court was precluded from granting a new tenancy by reason of grounds (e), (f) and (g) of s.30(1) of the Act that the tenant will be entitled to compensation under s.37 of the Act. Where the court is so precluded, it may, upon application by the tenant, certify that fact: s.37(4) of the Act. Prior to October 15, 2001 it was provided that the application for certification was made either at the hearing or by way of an application without notice: CPR Sch.1, RSC Ord.97 r.10(1); Sch.2, CCR Ord.43 r.9. Again neither CPR Pt 56 nor PD 56 make any provision as to the manner in which such an application should be made. It is considered that the application should be dealt with by way of an application pursuant to CPR Pt 23 or orally at the hearing. This rule contemplates that applications may be served without notice: CPR r.23.4(2) and PD 23A para.3.

17. REVOCATION OF ORDER GRANTING NEW TENANCY

The application

14–119 Where a new tenancy has been granted, the tenant has 14 days within which to determine whether he wishes to accept the grant of the new tenancy. If he decides not to, he should apply to the court for an order revoking the order for the grant of a new tenancy. The 14-day period is a statutory time limit and cannot be extended: s.36(2) of the Act. If the tenant makes such an application, the court must revoke the order: s.36(2) of the Act. The award as to costs made at the hearing is not affected by the revocation unless the court hearing the application for revocation otherwise orders: s.36(3) of the Act. See *Nihad v Chain*,[157] where the court revoked the order as to costs made on the hearing of the originating application that the tenant pay one-third of the landlord's costs (there having been a dispute as to the rent payable and the landlord was closer) and ordered that the tenant pay the costs of the action.

14–120 There is no express provision contained in CPR Pt 56 or PD 56 dealing with the procedure by which an application for revocation is to be made. It would seem that the application should be in accordance with CPR Pt 23. The application for revocation should be made pursuant to CPR Pt 23 upon notice.

---

[157] [1956] E.G.D. 234 CC.

18. PROCEDURE UNDER THE LANDLORD AND TENANT ACT 1927

The procedure discussed in the following paragraphs applies whether the claim is one for a certificate that works are works of improvement or for claims for compensation. **14–121**

The appropriate court

An application for a certificate that works of improvement are "proper improvements" pursuant to s.3 of the 1927 Act may be made either in the High Court or the county court: s.21 of the 1927 Act and s.63(2) of the 1954 Act. The claim should normally be brought in the county court, in the district in which the land is situated: CPR r.56.2(1) and PD 56 para.2.2.[158] **14–122**

The claim form

The application for a certificate is made by a claim form in accordance with Pt 8; CPR r.56.1, PD 56 para.2.1. As the claim form is in accordance with Pt 8 it must include the matters referred to in para.14–22 above. In addition it is provided by PD 56 para.5.2 that it must also include details of: **14–123**

(1) the nature of the claim or the matter to be determined;
(2) the property to which the claim relates;
(3) the nature of the business carried on at the property;
(4) particulars of the lease or agreement for the tenancy including:
    (a) the names and addresses of the parties to the lease or agreement;
    (b) its duration;
    (c) the rent payable;
    (d) details of any assignment or other devolution of the lease or agreement;
(5) the date and mode of termination of the tenancy;
(6) if the claimant has left the property, the date on which he did so;
(7) particulars of the improvement or proposed improvement to which the claim relates; and
(8) if the claim is for payment of compensation, the amount claimed.

The particulars required in a claim for compensation are not dissimilar: CPR PD 56 para.5.8.

The parties

The claimant will be the person who is seeking to carry out the improvement or claim the compensation. The claimant's immediate landlord must be a defendant to the claim: PD 56 para.5.4. Immediately upon receipt of the claim a defendant must serve a copy of the claim form and any document served with it and of his **14–124**

[158] See also para.14–06.

acknowledgement of service upon his immediate landlord. If the person so served is not the freeholder, he must serve a copy of these documents on his landlord and so on from landlord to landlord: PD 56 para.5.5.

Service

14–125 The general rule is that a claim form must be served within four months after the date of issue (CPR r.7.5(2) applying to Pt 8 claims by PD 8 para.2.1).

Acknowledgement of service

14–126 The defendant must file an acknowledgement of service not more than 14 days after service of the claim form: CPR r.8.3(1). It must state whether the defendant contests the claim and if the defendant seeks a different remedy to that set out in the claim form what it is: CPR r.8.3(2). The acknowledgement of service may be made informally by way of a letter: PD 8 para.3.2. If no acknowledgement of service is filed in time the defendant may attend the hearing but may not unless the court gives permission take part in the hearing.

Evidence

14–127 Part 8 provides that the claimant must serve any written evidence on which he intends to rely when he files his claim form: CPR r.8.5(1). The defendant is required to serve his evidence with his acknowledgement of service: CPR r.8.5(3).[159] However, by PD 56 para.5.6 it is provided that for the purposes of claims under Pt 1 to the Landlord and Tenant Act 1927 the evidence need not be filed either with the claim form or acknowledgement of service. The filing of evidence will accordingly be a matter which will be dealt with on the hearing for directions, for the court's permission is required for the admission of evidence in the absence of evidence being filed with the claim/acknowledgement: CPR r.8.6(1).

Directions

14–128 The claim is automatically allocated to the multi-track: CPR r.8.9(c). The court will fix a date for a hearing when it issues the claim form: PD 56 para.5.3. In light of the absence of any obligation to file evidence with the claim or with the acknowledgement of service,[160] the first hearing will invariably be a hearing for directions only. The claim will proceed in the normal way as a Pt 8 claim and consequently, the master/district judge may, upon hearing the application, order evidence, including expert evidence, to be submitted by the parties to the claim.

---

[159] CPR r.8.5 is disapplied to claims for renewal under the 1954 Act: CPR r.56.3(2)(b).

[160] See para.14–81 et seq.

As in the case of claims for renewal, the court may also upon the first hearing make orders relating to persons affected by the application for a certificate, e.g. a superior landlord.

Order on certification

Where the court certifies an improvement as a proper improvement or has been duly executed, it shall do so by way of order: PD 56 para.5.7. **14–129**

Compensation—the need to claim

The requirements of s.47 of the 1954 Act as to the making of a written claim to the landlord must be complied with in order for a valid claim for compensation to be made. These time limits are discussed in para.13–60. **14–130**

19. APPEALS

Restructure

By s.56 of the Access to Justice Act 1999, the Lord Chancellor was empowered to prescribe an alternative destination for appeals which would otherwise lie to a county court, the High Court or the Court of Appeal. By the Access to Justice Act 1999 (Destination of Appeals) Order 2000,[161] which came into force on May 20, 2000, the Lord Chancellor re-organised the structure of appeals. The 2000 Order provides a uniform procedure for appeals. **14–131**

Route of appeal: Pt 8 claims

In respect of Pt 8 claims[162] the structure is[163]: **14–132**

---

161 SI 2000/1071, referred to in the remainder of this text as the "2000 Order".

162 It should be noted that the routes of appeal for case management decisions and decisions, such as striking out or relating to summary judgment under Pt 24 are identical. Such proceedings are not final (as defined in art.1(1)(c)) for the purposes of 2000 Order art.4. Orders striking out the proceedings or a statement of case, and orders giving summary judgment under CPR Pt 24 are not final decisions because they are not decisions that would finally determine the entire proceedings whichever way the court decided the issues before it: Brooke L.J. in *Tanfern v Cameron-MacDonald* [2000] 1 W.L.R. 1311; [2000] 2 All E.R. 801 CA.

163 If the normal route of a first appeal would be to a circuit judge or to a High Court judge, either the lower court or the appeal court may order the appeal to be transferred to the Court of Appeal if they consider that it would raise an important point of principle or practice or there is some other compelling reason for the Court of Appeal to hear it (CPR r.52.14(1)). This rule refers to first appeals, because what is in question is whether the appeal in question should be heard in the county court or the High Court on the one hand or in the Court of Appeal on the other. By the 2000 Order art.5, all second appeals lie to the Court of Appeal and nowhere else, so that this question could not arise in that context. The Master of the Rolls also has the power to direct that an appeal which would normally be heard by a circuit judge or a High Court judge should be heard instead by the Court of Appeal (the

(1) An appeal of the decision of the county court district judge (e.g. in relation to a claim to strike out) is to the circuit judge of the county court as a first appeal.[164]

(2) An appeal from a decision of the county court circuit judge not sitting in an appellate capacity is to the High Court.[165] This will cover most 1954 Act hearings relating to renewal. Although art.4(a) of the 2000 Order provides that an appeal shall lie to the Court of Appeal where the decision to be appealed is a final decision and a claim allocated by a court to the multi-track, this applies only where the claim is a Pt 7 claim and allocation to the multi-track is pursuant to CPR rr.12.7, 14.8 or 26.5. Thus art.4(a) does not apply to Pt 8 claim and in any event, as Pt 8 claims are automatically treated as allocated to the multi-track pursuant to CPR r.8.9(c), art.4(a) of the 2000 Order would not apply to them.

(3) An appeal from the county court circuit judge, which is itself a determination of an appeal from a district judge, i.e. the circuit judge was acting in an appellate capacity, is to the Court of Appeal as a second appeal.[166]

(4) An appeal from a decision of a master or a district judge of the High Court is to a judge of the High Court.[167]

(5) An appeal from the decision of the High Court not sitting in an appellate capacity is by way of first appeal to the Court of Appeal.

(6) An appeal against a decision of a judge of the High Court, where the determination is itself consideration of an appeal from a circuit judge by way of first appeal, is to the Court of Appeal as a second appeal.[168]

Route of appeal: Part 7 claims

14–133 The structure is the same for Pt 7 claims as it is for Pt 8 claims, save for one important difference. Ordinarily, an appeal from a Pt 8 claim under the 1954 Act will be to a High Court judge. However, an appeal of a final decision under a Pt 7 claim where the Pt 7 claim has been allocated to the multi-track will be to the Court of Appeal.[169]

Permission to appeal

14–134 (1) *District Judge to Circuit Judge of County Court.* Permission for such an appeal is required: CPR r.52.3(1)(a). If the district judge refuses permission, a further application for permission may be made to the Appeal

1999 Act s.57(1)). In such cases the Master of the Rolls and the Court of Appeal also have the power to remit an appeal to the court in which the original appeal was or would have been brought (CPR r.52.14(2)).

164 2000 Order art.3(2).

165 2000 Order art.3(1).

166 2000 Order art.5.

167 2000 Order art.2.

168 2000 Order art.5.

169 2000 Order art.4(a). Under Pt 7 there is no automatic allocation of track as there is under Pt 8. See paras 14–86 and 14–87.

Court, i.e. the county court judge: CPR r.52.3(3). If the county court judge, as an appeal court, refuses permission to appeal, then no further right of appeal exists.[170]

(2) *County Court to High Court.* Permission for such an appeal is required: CPR r.52.3(1)(a). If the county court judge refuses permission, a further application for permission may be made to the Appeal Court, i.e. the High Court: CPR r.52.3(3). If the judge, as an appeal court, refuses permission to appeal, no further right of appeal exists.[171]

(3) *Appeal from Circuit Judge to Court of Appeal as second appeal.* Where the county court circuit judge dismisses an appeal from a district judge the Court of Appeal is the appropriate appeal court but such an appeal is a second appeal.[172] An appeal from the county court judge, being a second appeal to the Court of Appeal, needs the permission of the Court of Appeal: CPR r.52.13(1).

(4) *Master or District Judge to High Court.* Permission to appeal is required: CPR r.52.3. An application for permission to appeal may be made either to the master/district judge at the hearing of which the decision to appeal was made or to the Appeal Court in an appeal notice: CPR r.52.3(2). Where the lower court refuses an application for permission to appeal, a further application for permission to appeal may be made to the Appeal Court: CPR r.52.3(3). If the Appeal Court, without a hearing, refuses permission to appeal, the person seeking permission may request the decision to be reconsidered at a hearing: CPR r.52.3(4). No further right to appeal exists if the Appeal Court refuses permission.[173]

(5) *High Court to Court of Appeal.* Permission to appeal is required: CPR r.52.3. An application for permission to appeal may be made either to the High Court judge at the hearing of which the decision to appeal was made or to the Appeal Court in an appeal notice: CPR r.52.3(2). Where the lower court refuses an application for permission to appeal, a further application for permission to appeal may be made to the Appeal Court: CPR r.52.3(3). If the Appeal court, without a hearing, refuses permission to appeal, the person seeking permission may request the decision to be reconsidered at a hearing: CPR r.52.3(4). Where the Court of Appeal refuses permission to appeal without a hearing, it may, if it considers that the application is totally without merit, make an order that the person seeking permission may not request the decision to be reconsidered at a hearing.[174] No further right to appeal exists if the Appeal Court refuses permission.[175]

---

170 Access to Justice Act 1999 s.54(4). Where the Appeal Court refuses permission without considering the matter at a hearing, the person seeking permission may, within seven days after service of the notice that permission has been refused, request that the decision be reconsidered at a hearing: CPR r.52.3(4) and (5).

171 Access to Justice Act 1999 s.54(4).

172 2000 Order art.5.

173 Access to Justice Act 1999 s.54(4).

174 CPR r.52.3(4A).

175 Access to Justice Act 1999 s.54(4).

(6) *Appeal from High Court to Court of Appeal as second appeal*. The position here is identical to that considered in (3) above of an appeal from the county court judge where the county court judge was acting in an appellate capacity.

Thus, in summary all appeals need permission to appeal. Second appeals will be to the Court of Appeal and consent of that court is required. Where after hearing an application for permission to appeal the Appeal Court refuses permission, there is no right to appeal that decision.[176]

Tests for permission to appeal

First appeal

14–135 On a first appeal, permission to appeal will only be given where:

(1) the court considers that the appeal would have a real prospect of success; or
(2) there is some other compelling reason why the appeal should be heard (CPR r.52.3(6)).

The meaning of "real prospect of success" has been considered in relation to summary judgment claims for[177] and in particular in the judgment of Lord Woolf M.R. in *Swain v Hillman*.[178] In *Tanfern Ltd v Cameron-MacDonald*[179] Brooke L.J. cited *Swain v Hillman* and stated that the same approach should be adopted in relation to CPR r.52.3(6)(a).

Second appeal

14–136 Permission will not be granted unless the Court of Appeal[180] considers that:

[176] The principle which underlies the rule in s.54(4) of the 1999 Act (insofar as it refers to the refusal of leave to appeal) is that if both a lower court and an appeal court at a lower level of the judicial hierarchy have decided that a proposed appeal has no real prospect of success, and that there is no other compelling reason why the appeal should be heard (see CPR r.52.3(6)), that must be the end of the matter, and the issue cannot be relitigated higher up the judicial chain. This principle does not, however, apply to an order not to extend time for an appeal where the prospects of the appeal have not been considered on its merits. The logic of this decision is that if a circuit judge or a High Court judge sitting in an appeal court has the choice of disposing of a belated and unmeritorious appeal either by refusing to extend time for appealing or by refusing permission to appeal, he/she, it has been said, should bear in mind that taking the latter course will bring the appellate proceedings to an end. The adoption of the former course, on the other hand, may entail further expense and delay while a challenge is launched at a higher appeal court against the decision not to extend time for appealing: Brooke L.J. in *Foenander v Bond Lewis & Co* [2001] EWCA Civ 759; [2001] 2 All E.R. 1019.

[177] Discussed in para.14–102.

[178] [2001] 1 All E.R. 91 CA.

[179] [2000] 1 W.L.R. 1311 CA.

[180] Permission can only be obtained from the Court of Appeal itself; CPR r.52.13. Thus, if a judge in the lower court, whether the county court or the High Court, purports to grant permission for a second appeal, that grant of permission is a nullity: *Clark (Inspector of Taxes) v Perks* [2001] 1 W.L.R. 17; [2000] 4 All E.R. 1 CA.

(1) the appeal would raise an important point of principle or practice, or
(2) there is some other compelling reason for the Court of Appeal to hear it (CPR r.52.13(2); Access to Justice Act 1999 s.55(1)).

Time for appealing

The time for appealing is an important consideration in connection with the 1954 Act, as s.64 continues the tenancy until it is finally disposed of. "Final disposal" includes any proceedings on or in consequence of an appeal and "any time for appealing or further appealing has expired", except that if the application is withdrawn or an appeal is abandoned then the "final disposal" is construed as a reference to the date of withdrawal or abandonment: s.64(2) of the 1954 Act.[181] **14–137**

The time limit for an appellant's notice is 21 days after the date of the decision appealed against, unless a longer period is directed by the lower court: CPR r.52.4(2). Where the lower court directs a different period under CPR r.52.4(2)(a), that period should not normally exceed 35 days: CPR PD 52 para.5.19. The appellant's notice is a prescribed form, N161: CPR Pt 4 and PD 52 para.5.1. **14–138**

Where it is not possible to file the appellant's notice in time, the appellant must seek an extension of time in his appellant's notice and provide evidence in support of that application, stating the reason for the delay and the steps taken prior to the application being made: CPR PD 52 para.5.2. Where the tenant makes an application for leave to appeal out of time and leave is refused, the "final disposal" for the purposes of s.64 is calculated from the date upon which the time for appealing expired, and not the date when the application to extend time was dismissed: *Shotley Point Marina (1986) Ltd v Spalding*.[182] **14–139**

The nature of the appeal

Review only of decision

The appeal is in the nature of a review[183] of the decision of the lower court unless: **14–140**

(1) a practice direction makes different provision for a particular category of appeal; or
(2) the court considers that in the circumstances of an individual appeal it would be in the interests of justice to hold a re-hearing.[184]

---

[181] See para.3–227 et seq.

[182] [1997] 1 E.G.L.R. 223 CA.

[183] For the difference between a review and rehearing see *ST Du Pont v EI Du Pont Nemours & Co* [2003] EWCA Civ 1368; [2006] 1 W.L.R. 2793.

[184] CPR r.52.11(1). See *Asiansky Television Plc v Bayer Rosin (A Firm)* [2001] EWCA Civ 1792; approving of the decision of Steel J. to conduct an appeal by way of a review. See also *Audergon v La Baguette Ltd* [2002] EWCA Civ 10; *Assicurazioni Generali SpA v Arab Insurance Group* [2002] EWCA Civ 1642; [2003] 1 W.L.R. 577; and *ST Du Pont v EI Du Pont Nemours & Co*[2003] EWCA Civ 1368; [2006] 1 W.L.R. 2793.

The court will allow the appeal if the court concludes on such review that the decision was wrong: CPR r.52.11(3)(a). The general powers of the appeal court are set out in CPR r.52.10. The fact that the appeal is by way of a review does not preclude the court from admitting and considering fresh evidence: *Davy's of London (Wine Merchants) Ltd v City of London Corp.*[185]

Procedural irregularity

14–141 The appeal court will allow an appeal where the decision in the lower court was wrong[186] or unjust because of a serious procedural irregularity[187] in the proceedings in the lower court: CPR r.52.11(3).

---

[185] [2004] EWHC 2224 (Ch), Lewison J. See also para.7–188.

[186] By PD 52 para.13.1 it is provided that "the Appeal Court will not normally make an order allowing an appeal unless satisfied that the decision of the lower court was wrong". The court will not, accordingly, make an order allowing an appeal albeit both parties to the appeal consent, unless the court is satisfied that it is wrong: *Cinnamon Ltd v Morgan* [2001] EWCA Civ 1616.

[187] As to procedural irregularity see *Tanfern v Cameron-MacDonald* [2000] 1 W.L.R. 1311; [2000] 2 All E.R. 801 CA; Brooke L.J. said:

"This [the rule] marks a significant change in practice, in relation to what used to be called 'interlocutory appeals' from district judges or masters. Under the old practice, the appeal to a judge was a rehearing in the fullest sense of the word, and the judge exercised his/her discretion afresh, while giving appropriate weight to the way the lower court had exercised its discretion in the matter. Under the new practice, the decision of the lower court will attract much greater significance. The appeal court's duty is now limited to a review of that decision, and it may only interfere in the quite limited circumstances set out in r.52.11(3).

The first ground for interference speaks for itself. The epithet 'wrong' is to be applied to the substance of the decision made by the lower court. If the appeal is against the exercise of a discretion by the lower court, the decision of the House of Lords in *G v G* [1985] 2 All E.R. 225, [1985] 1 W.L.R. 647 warrants attention. In that case Lord Fraser of Tullybelton said:

'Certainly it would not be useful to inquire whether different shades of meaning are intended to be conveyed by words such as "blatant error" used by Sir John Arnold P. in the present case, and words such as "clearly wrong", "plainly wrong" or simply "wrong" used by other judges in other cases. All these various expressions were used in order to emphasise the point that the appellate court should only interfere when it considers that the judge of first instance has not merely preferred an imperfect solution which is different from an alternative imperfect solution which the Court of Appeal might or would have adopted, but has exceeded the generous ambit within which a reasonable disagreement is possible.' (See [1985] 2 All E.R. 225 at 229, [1985] 1 W.L.R. 647 at 652.).

So far as the second ground for interference is concerned, it must be noted that the appeal court only has power to interfere if the procedural or other irregularity which it has detected in the proceedings in the lower court was a serious one, and that this irregularity caused the decision of the lower court to be an unjust decision".

An alternative formulation of the threshold test for interference with the exercise of discretion by the appeal court is that stated by Lord Woolf M.R. in *Phonographic Performance Ltd v AEI Rediffusion Music Ltd* [1999] 1 W.L.R. 1507 at 1523:

"Before the court can interfere it must be shown that the judge has either erred in principle in his approach or has left out of account or has taken into account some feature that he should, or should not, have considered, or that his decision was wholly wrong because the court is forced to the conclusion that he has not balanced the various factors fairly in the scale."

This passage was cited and applied by the Court of Appeal in *Price v Price (t/a Poppyland Headware)* [2003] EWCA Civ 888; [2003] 3 All E.R. 911 at [26]–[27].

See also *Audergon v La Baguette Ltd* [2002] EWCA Civ 10.

A court is slow to interfere on an appeal against the exercise by a first instance judge of discretion: *Tanfern Ltd v Cameron-MacDonald*.[188] An appeal, not against a determination which requires an evaluation of the facts, the conclusion upon which is often a matter of degree upon which different judges may legitimately differ, is closely analogous to the exercise of a discretion and it has been said that appellate courts should approach appeals with respect to such findings in a similar way to an appeal against the exercise of a discretion: *Assicurazioni Generali SpA v Arab Insurance Group (BSC)*[189]; *Marazzi v Global Grange Ltd*[190] (digested in para.7–119). In the *Marazzi* case the questions for determination were whether, if the landlord carried out the proposed works said to fall within s.30(1)(f) of the Act, it would be demolishing or reconstructing a substantial part of the premises or be carrying out substantial work of construction on the holding or part of it. Those questions were questions in the nature of an evaluation and thus the appellate court could interfere only if the first instance judge: **14–142**

(1) had misstated the law;
(2) had misunderstood, in a material way, some point of fact about what the proposed works were; or
(3) while correctly stating the law and correctly understanding the facts, had nevertheless come to a conclusion that could not be right.

[188] [2000] 1 W.L.R. 1311 CA.
[189] [2002] EWCA Civ 1642; [2003] 1 W.L.R. 577, Clarke L.J. at [16]. Approved in *Datec Electronic Holdings Ltd v United Parcels Service Ltd* [2007] UKHL 23.
[190] [2002] EWCA 3010 (Ch), Lawrence Collins J., citing Clarke L.J. (above).

CHAPTER 15

COMPROMISE

1. CIRCUMSTANCES IN WHICH COMPROMISE ARISES

A compromise of an application for renewal or a landlord's termination application may occur at any time during the pendency of the claim. The settlement between the parties may involve either an agreement for renewal, or an agreement for possession with or without the payment of compensation[1]. A number of matters need to be kept in mind when dealing with the settlement of 1954 Act disputes to ensure that the same are legally binding. We propose to deal with, first a settlement giving rise to the grant of a new lease and secondly, a settlement involving the termination of the tenant's current tenancy, which invariably involves the giving up of possession and the payment of compensation.[2] As to agreements for the grant of a new lease, such agreements may be (1) an agreement which is intended to be documented other than by way of an order of the court for the grant of a new lease[3] or (2) an agreement for the purposes of the proceedings, including an order of the court for the grant of a new tenancy in accordance with the Act.[4] **15–01**

2. AGREEMENT FOR NEW LEASE OTHER THAN BY WAY OF A GRANT PURSUANT TO A COURT ORDER

Is there a binding agreement?

In order for the parties to be bound there must be a contractually binding agreement. There is usually little difficulty where the parties have entered into a written agreement[5] which is signed by the parties or their duly authorised agents.[6] **15–02**

---

[1] It should be noted in passing that there are no special rules for interpreting compromise agreements: *BCCI v Ali* [2001] UKHL 8; [2002] 1 A.C. 251 at [8] and [26]. See also *Barrett v Universal-Island Records* [2006] EWHC 1009 (Ch), Lewison J. at [152].

[2] See para.15–36 et seq. as to agreements settling the landlord's termination application and para.15–39 as to the position concerning an agreement to deliver up possession.

[3] See para.15–02 et seq.

[4] See para.15–21 et seq.

[5] Whether an application by a tenant for renewal is in the nature of an offer is a matter which is considered in para.6–47. However, in light of the terms of the Law of Property (Miscellaneous Provisions) Act 1989 (see para.15–12) even if an offer any "acceptance" by the landlord of the terms expressed by the tenant in his application form is unlikely to give rise to a binding contract. But the "acceptance" may be sufficient for the purposes of ss.32–35 (see para.15–21 et seq.).

[6] Note the formal requirements for the execution of documents by companies: ss.43 and 44 of the Companies Act 2006. Notwithstanding the dicta of Lewison J. at [12] in *Redcard Ltd v Williams*

However, any such written agreement will need to comply with the terms of s.2 of the Law of Property (Miscellaneous) Provisions Act 1989.[7] The 1989 Act does not apply to contracts to grant a lease taking effect in possession for a term not exceeding three years at the best rent reasonably obtainable without taking a fine.[8] Difficulties often arise where one party seeks to assert that a binding agreement has arisen out of the parties' written negotiations. Two questions arise: First, has any contractual intent been excluded by use of the qualification "subject to contract?" Secondly, is the correspondence admissible in any event, i.e. is the correspondence protected by "without prejudice" privilege?

(1) Subject to contract

15–03 Normally, the existence of the rubric "subject to contract" in correspondence will negate contractual intention. Where there are negotiations relating to the disposal of an interest in land and those negotiations are expressed to be "subject to contract", the negotiations cannot mature into a concluded agreement unless and until there is an exchange of contracts in accordance with ordinary conveyancing practice.[9] Before that, either party can withdraw and costs incurred will be irrecoverable.[10] In some cases, however, the words may be ignored as meaningless. Thus, the qualification was held to be inapplicable where the words were found at the end of an acceptance letter of tender documents which contained full particulars and special conditions of sale, incorporating the *National Conditions of Sale* 18th edn, with amendments, such that the Court was able to hold that the tender documents set out all the terms of the contract, so that nothing remained to be negotiated and thus there was no need for a further formal contract: *Michael Richards Properties Ltd v St Saviour's Wardens*.[11] See also, to similar effect, *Alpenstow Ltd v Regalian Properties Ltd*[12] where the terms of the agreement between the parties were contained within a detailed and "conscientiously drawn" document which supported a "strong and exceptional contention that the words 'subject to contract' were not to be given their prima facie meaning".

[2010] EWHC 1078 (Ch) at [10]–[12], Lewison J., (on appeal) [2011] EWCA Civ 466, (which on one reading suggests that a contract for the disposition of an interest in land must comply with s.44 of the Companies Act 2006), there would seem to be no reason why a contract cannot be signed *on behalf of* a company, e.g. by a single director in accordance with s.43(1)(b) of the 2006 Act. The Law of Property (Miscellaneous Provisions) Act 1989 does not provide that a contract must be signed by a company in order to be effective; it may be signed on behalf of the contracting party: s.2(3). The position is otherwise where the statute requires the relevant document to be signed by the company: see *Hilmi & Associates Ltd v 20 Pembridge Villas Freehold Ltd* [2010] EWCA Civ 314; [2010] 1 W.L.R. 2750 (notice under the Leasehold Reform, Housing and Urban Development Act 1993 required to be signed by tenant).

[7] As to which see para.15–12.

[8] Law of Property (Miscellaneous Provisions) Act 1989 s.2(5).

[9] "As everybody . . . knows, that expression, when used in relation to the sale of land, means that, although the parties have reached an agreement, no legally binding contract comes into existence until the exchange of formal written contracts takes place:" *Christos v Secretary of State for Transport* [2004] 1 E.G.L.R. 5 at 7 per Mummery L.J. CA.

[10] *Regalian Properties Plc v London Docklands Development Corp* [1995] 1 W.L.R. 212.

[11] [1975] 3 All E.R. 416.

[12] [1985] 1 W.L.R. 721.

One still finds, in practice, a liberal use of the "subject to contract"qualification. Although it is now extremely difficult, if not impossible, to bring about an agreement relating to the disposition of an interest in land by way of an exchange of correspondence,[13] one advantage of still continuing to endorse correspondence with the "subject to contract" qualification is that it may prevent any argument based on estoppel being run against the party that is seeking to withdraw from the negotiations. As Lord Templeman said in *AG of Hong Kong v Humphreys Estate*[14]: **15–04**

> "It is possible but unlikely that in circumstances at present unforeseeable a party to negotiations set out in a document expressed to be "subject to contract" will be able to satisfy the court that the parties have subsequently agreed to convert the document into a contract or that some form of estoppel had arisen to prevent both parties from refusing to proceed with the transactions envisaged by the document."[15]

More recently Lord Scott said in *Yeoman's Row Management Ltd v Cobbe*[16] (where the negotiations were oral):

> "The reason why, in a 'subject to contract' case, a proprietary estoppel cannot ordinarily arise is that the would-be purchaser's expectation of acquiring an interest in the property in question is subject to a contingency that is entirely under the control of the other party to the negotiations . . . The expectation is therefore speculative."

The subject to contract nature of correspondence or discussions may be express or implied. It should be noted that where parties are proceeding directly towards the exchange of lease and counterpart, *without formal contract*, there is a presumption (or ordinary expectation) that the parties are proceeding "subject to lease" and are not contractually bound until formal exchange of lease and counterpart: *Leveson v Parfum Marcel Rochas (England) Ltd*[17]; *Longman v Viscount Chelsea*.[18] The presumption may be rebutted: *Stratton (RJ) Ltd v Wallis Tomlin & Co*[19] (digested at para.15–20). This presumption does not apply where the parties are negotiating for a new lease to be granted within the context of **15–05**

---

[13] Because of the decision in *New Towns v Cooper (Great Britain) Ltd* [1995] Ch. 259; [1995] 2 W.L.R. 677 CA.

[14] [1987] A.C. 114.

[15] There are other more recent authorities taking a similar approach, e.g. *Edwin Shirley Production Ltd v Works Space Management Ltd* [2001] 2 E.G.L.R. 16 (no proprietary estoppel was held to exist where occupation of a prospective lessee occurred during "subject to contract" negotiations notwithstanding the fact that the lessee had incurred expenditure on improvements); *Loubatieres v Mornington Estates (UK)* [2004] EWHC 825 (Ch) (subject to contract negotiations did not give rise an estoppel notwithstanding the fact that the prospective purchaser had incurred expenditure in seeking planning permission). The real difficulty is showing detrimental reliance, for a party cannot usually be said to have acted to his detriment in reliance on a "subject to contract" representation which he knows enables either party to withdraw from the arrangement. See also the recent decision of *Haq v Island Homes Housing Association* [2011] 2 P. & C.R. 17 CA where the tenant failed in his claim to a 60 year term as the negotiations were at all times subject to contract and the local authority had done nothing to waive the subject to contract qualification (digested in para.3–261).

[16] [2008] 1 W.L.R. 1752 HL.

[17] [1966] 200 E.G. 407.

[18] (1989) 58 P. & C.R. 189 CA.

[19] [1986] 1 E.G.L.R. 104 CA.

existing 1954 Act proceedings and reach an agreement over the terms to be granted: *Behar, Ellis and Parnell v Territorial Investments Ltd.*[20]

15–06 Once used, the expression "subject to contract" qualifies all subsequent correspondence and negotiations between the parties, notwithstanding the omission of that phrase in subsequent correspondence, unless and until the qualification is expressly or impliedly expunged: *Sherbrook v Dipple.*[21]

15–07 Where the parties are negotiating for the grant of a new lease "subject to contract" the tenant must ensure that he continues to protect his 1954 Act rights: *Akiens v Salomon*[22] (digested in para.15–07A).

15–07A ***Akiens v Salomon***[23] In that case the tenant's lease of business premises expired on September 29, 1986. On December 21, 1990, the landlord served a s.25 notice specifying July 1, 1991, as the date of termination. The tenant's time for making an originating application expired on April 21, 1990. Correspondence ensued between the parties' respective solicitors over the terms of a new lease. The correspondence was headed either "subject to contract" or "subject to lease". On April 15, 1991, the landlord accepted the tenant's proposals. The letter of acceptance was headed "subject to lease". On May 15, 1991, the landlord's solicitors enclosed the counterpart lease for signature. This was returned on June 24, 1991. The landlord refused to complete, and claimed possession on the ground that as the tenant had failed to protect its position by making an originating application for the grant of a new tenancy. The Court of Appeal upheld the landlord's entitlement to possession as the case was an ordinary one of negotiation subject to lease. Moreover, no estoppel arose as nothing had been said or done which could reasonably have encouraged the tenant to conclude that the landlord was content to treat the time limit under s.25 as in suspense.

(2) Without prejudice correspondence

15–08 Correspondence which is marked "without prejudice" will ordinarily be inadmissible before the court. The most comprehensive summary of the exceptions to the privilege is set out in the judgment of Walker L.J. in *Unilever Plc v Proctor and Gamble.*[24] The "without prejudice" privilege can apply to "opening shots": *Norwich Union Life Assurance Society v Waller*[25]; *South Shropshire DC v Amos*[26]; *Buckingham CC v Moran*[27]; *Standrin v Yenton Minster Homes Ltd.*[28] In *Standrin v Yenton* Lloyd L.J. said:

---

[20] [1973] CAT, 237 CA. See further para.15–23.

[21] (1980) 41 P. & C.R. 173 CA. See also *Cohen v Nessdale* [1982] 2 All E.R. 97.

[22] (1993) P. & C.R. 364 CA. Contrast *JT Developments v Quinn* (1991) 62 P. & C.R. 33 CA (digested in para.3–260).

[23] (1993) P. & C.R. 364 CA.

[24] [2000] 1 W.L.R. 2436 at 2444–2445.

[25] [1984] 1 E.G.L.R. 126 (rent review notice trigger notice not covered by "without prejudice").

[26] [1986] 1 W.L.R. 1271 CA (20 page document setting out clam for statutory compensation).

[27] [1989] 2 All E.R. 225 (assertion of rights not an attempt to negotiate).

[28] *Times*, July 22, 1991 CA.

> "The opening shot in negotiations may well be subject to privilege where, for example, a person puts forward a claim and in the same breath offers to take something less in settlement, or . . . . . .where a person offers to accept a sum in settlement of an as yet unquantified claim. But where the opening shot is an assertion of a person's claim and nothing more than that, then prima facie it is not protected."

For the purposes of settlements in the context of 1954 Act proceedings, it is unnecessary to consider all of the exceptions to the "without prejudice" privilege set out in *Unilever Plc v Proctor and Gamble*.[29] Two, should, however, be noted. **15–09**

First, when a dispute arises as to whether without prejudice communications have resulted in a concluded compromise agreement, then those communications are admissible in order to determine whether or upon what terms the agreement has been reached: *Tomlin v Standard Telephone and Cables Ltd.*[30] Further, the settlement negotiations are admissible as an aid to construction of the compromise agreement to which they give rise: *Admiral Management Services Ltd v Para-Protect Europe Ltd*[31]; *Oceanbulk Shipping and Trading SA v TMT Asia Ltd.*[32] **15–10**

Secondly, without prejudice correspondence may be admissible on the issue of costs, e.g. *Calderbank* offers.[33] **15–11**

(3) The Law of Property (Miscellaneous Provisions) Act 1989[34]

Section 2 of the 1989 Act provides that a contract for the sale or other disposition of an interest in land made on or after September 27, 1989 can only be made in writing and only by incorporating all the terms which the parties have expressly agreed in one document or, where contracts are exchanged, in each. The document incorporating the terms or, where contracts are exchanged, one of the documents incorporating them (but not necessarily the same one) must be signed by or on behalf of each party to the contract.[35] It would seem that an agreement complying with s.2 of the 1989 Act cannot arise out of an exchange of **15–12**

---

[29] [2000] 1 W.L.R. 2436 at 2444–2445.

[30] [1969] 1 W.L.R. 1378.

[31] [2002] 1 W.L.R. 2722 (where without prejudice correspondence which was impliedly referred to in the consent order was admitted in order to assist its construction).

[32] [2011] 1 A.C. 662; [2010] UKSC 44. This is not an exception to the rule, reaffirmed by the House of Lords in *Chartbrook Ltd v Persimmon Homes Ltd* [2009] 1 A.C. 1101 HL, that subjective statements of intent are inadmissible as an aid to interpretation. Objective facts communicated by one party to the other in the course of the negotiations (albeit those negotiations may have been without prejudice) are admissible as an aid to interpretation and constitute material which forms part of the factual matrix. The distinction between objective facts and other statements made in the course of negotiations was clearly stated by Lord Hoffmann in *Chartbrook*: "Whereas the surrounding circumstances are, by definition, objective facts, which will usually be uncontroversial, statements in the course of pre-contractual negotiations will be drenched in subjectivity and may, if oral, be very much in dispute" at [38].

[33] As to such offers, see paras 10–26 et seq. and 15–55 et seq.

[34] It is not possible in this work to undertake a detailed analysis of the provisions of the 1989 Act. Readers are referred to *Hill and Redman's Law of Landlord and Tenant*, A502 to A549 for a more detailed treatment.

[35] s.2(3) of the 1989 Act.

correspondence: *New Towns v Cooper (Great Britain) Ltd*[36]; *Valentine v Allen.*[37] If a settlement occurs outside the door of the court the single written document signed by both parties will often, in practice, be found in the Tomlin order,[38] signed by or on behalf of both parties and submitted to the court and which reflects the terms agreed. When reaching an agreement at the door of the court an issue of authority may arise.[39]

(4) Certainty of terms

15–13 A common problem which arises in practice is that the parties reach agreement on the principal terms, such as the property to be demised, the length of term and the rent to be paid but leave the remaining terms to be incorporated into a lease to be agreed subsequently between the parties' solicitors. Such an agreement is unlikely to satisfy the requirements of the 1989 Act since it will be difficult to say that all of the terms are agreed and contained in a single document signed by both parties.[40] An agreement to agree will be too uncertain to enforce.[41] Any potential invalidity due to uncertainty may be overcome, however, if the parties' obligations can be given an objective content. Thus, an agreement between parties for a lease which provided that the lease was to contain "such other covenants and conditions as shall reasonably be required *by the lessor*" was held to be sufficiently certain: *Sweet & Maxwell Ltd v Universal News Services Ltd.*[42] In *Stratton (RJ) Ltd v Wallis Tomlin Co Ltd*[43] (digested in para.15–20) the parties' agreement provided that "it is also understood that a covenant will be incorporated to prevent the premises being used for an offensive trade, such as the preparation and sale of fish & chips, fried chicken, Chinese food, etc." The court held that those words did not render the agreement too uncertain. It was

---

[36] [1995] Ch. 259; [1995] 2 W.L.R. 677 CA. Thus, it is not essential for the correspondence to be qualified "subject to contract".

[37] [2003] EWCA Civ 915 at [25].

[38] As to which see para.15–60.

[39] See para.15–25.

[40] Although the court will lean in favour of upholding the agreement: *Brown v Gould* [1972] Ch. 53 at 56–57 Megarry J. In *Trustees of National Deposit Friendly Society v Beatties of London Ltd* [1985] 2 E.G.L.R. 59.

[41] *Foley v Classique Coaches Ltd* [1934] 2 K.B. 1 CA at 13; *May & Butcher Ltd v The King* [1934] 1 K.B. 17 HL. In *Walford v Miles* [1992] A.C. 128 HL. Lord Ackner said at [138]:'"The reason why an agreement to negotiate, like an agreement to agree, is unenforceable, is simply because it lacks the necessary certainty … This uncertainty is demonstrated in the instant case by the provision which it is said has to be implied in the agreement for the determination of the negotiations. How can a court be expected to decide whether, subjectively, a proper reason existed for the termination of negotiations?"'

[42] [1964] 2 Q.B. 699 CA. Pearson L.J. said: "The second condition enables the Court to decide on the reasonableness of a requirement if the parties are unable to agree. A formula such as that used in [the clause] is a convenient and effective means of dealing with the position where the parties have agreed on the main points but have not yet settled the details, and wish to make a binding agreement immediately. By using a formula such as this, introducing the objective test of reasonableness, the parties avoid making a mere agreement to agree, which would be unenforceable." at 733.

[43] [1986] 1 E.G.L.R. 104 CA.

said that the type of foods expressly referred to were merely examples of the general prohibition which was intended.[44]

Alternatively, the parties' agreement may make provision for a third party dispute resolution procedure (such as arbitration or determination by an independent expert) in the absence of agreement over the terms.

Section 28

Generally

Section 28 of the Act provides that the Act shall not apply to a tenancy once an agreement for a future tenancy complying with the terms of that section has been entered into. The effect of such a s.28 agreement is that the current tenancy continues until the date specified for commencement of the future tenancy, but is not a tenancy to which the Act applies, so that neither party may thereafter serve any notices and the tenant may not apply to the court for a new tenancy. Once the date for the grant of the future tenancy has arrived, the current tenancy will cease, but the tenant will, of course, be entitled to enforce the agreement and thus obtain a new tenancy from the landlord. Section 28 provides: **15–14**

> "Where the landlord and tenant agree for the grant to the tenant of a future tenancy of the holding, or of the holding with other land, on terms and from a date specified in the agreement, the current tenancy shall continue until that date but no longer, and shall not be a tenancy to which this Part of this Act applies."

Requirements for an agreement to be a section 28 agreement

There are a number of limitations to this section which are probably fairly obvious: **15–15**

The agreement must at be in writing: s.69(2).[45]

The agreement for the new lease must be between "the landlord" and "the tenant". The "landlord" is the person who qualifies as "landlord" within s.44(1), i.e. the competent landlord: *Bowes-Lyon v Green*[46] (digested in para.15–17). It is unclear from that decision whether the "landlord" must also be the tenant's immediate landlord.

---

[44] May L.J. relied on Lord Wright's dictum in *Hillas & Co Ltd v Arcos Ltd* (1932) 147 L.T. 503, 514, to the following effect:"Businessmen often record the most important agreements in crude and summary fashion; modes of expression sufficient and clear to them in the course of their business may appear to those unfamiliar with the business far from complete or precise. It is accordingly the duty of the court to construe such documents fairly and broadly, without being too astute or subtle in finding defects, but on the contrary the court should seek to apply the old maxim of English law *verba ita sunt intelligenda ut res magis valeat quam pereat*. That maxim, however, does not mean that the court is to make a contract for the parties or to go outside the words they have used, except in so far as there are appropriate implications of law."

[45] Which provides that references in the Act to an agreement between the landlord and the tenant (except in s.38(1) and (2)) are to be construed as references to an agreement in writing between them.

[46] [1963] A.C. 420 HL. As to the meaning of "landlord" within s.44, see para.3–87.

An agreement between the tenant and a third party may be caught by s.38(1)[47] but will not be one as between landlord and tenant for the purposes of s.28. Thus, an agreement between a superior landlord and a business sub-tenant to grant the sub-tenant a lease at a future date would not be within s.28.[48] Such an agreement is presumably unenforceable since it is an agreement to surrender the current tenancy at a future date that does not comply either with the provisions of s.28 or of s.38A. (see para.3–19 et seq.);

The tenancy must be of "the holding" (as defined in s.23(3))[49] or of the holding with other land. Thus an agreement of part only of the holding is probably not within s.28 but an agreement for more than the holding (as may arise in the case where part of the premises is sub-let) is within s.28. The question of what is "the holding" is, it would seem, to be determined at the date of the agreement in question. However, there may still be room for argument as to what constituted "the holding" at the date that the agreement was entered into. If there is a dispute over what constituted the "holding" at the date on which the agreement falling within s.28 is said to have arisen, it will be necessary to have factual evidence of what was in fact being occupied by the tenant unless one can draw appropriate inferences from the admitted facts.

The agreement must be for a "future tenancy" from a specified date. This is to be distinguished from an agreement between landlord and tenant for the immediate grant of a new tenancy which would have the effect of determining the current tenancy by surrender by operation of law.

It has been said that the agreement envisaged by the section is one which is "a binding contractual arrangement enforceable by the parties at law".[50] In *Stratton (RJ) Ltd v Wallis Tomlin Co Ltd*[51] (digested in para.15–20) an agreement between surveyors in correspondence was held to constitute an enforceable agreement for these purposes. Since the coming into force of the Law of Property (Miscellaneous Provisions) Act 1989[52] such an agreement must, it is considered, now comply with the more stringent requirements of that Act.[53]

The dictum of May L.J. in *Stratton (RJ) Ltd v Wallis Tomlin Co Ltd*[54] (digested in para.15–20) would suggest that a conditional but binding agreement for lease (e.g. conditional on planning permission being obtained, with the date fixed for commencement of the new lease to be a specified number of days upon planning having been granted) would be within the terms of s.28. Section 28 requires the

---

47 See para.3–13 et seq.

48 This could arise in a number of ways, e.g. the superior landlord may approach the sub-tenant at a time when there is less than 14 months left of the tenant tenant's lease (which may also be 1954 Act protected) (and so that the superior landlord will be the "competent landlord" within s.44) and agree to grant the sub-tenant a new lease directly upon the coming to an end of the tenant's lease of the sub-let premises.

49 See para.8–06 as to the meaning of "holding".

50 Per May L.J., *Stratton (RJ) Ltd v Wallis Tomlin Co Ltd* [1986] 1 E.G.L.R. 104 CA (digested in para.15–20).

51 [1986] 1 E.G.L.R. 104 CA.

52 On the provisions for the 1989 Act, see generally *Hill & Redman's Law of Landlord and Tenant*, paras 1002–1089.

53 The provisions of the 1989 Act do not apply to contracts for the grant of leases of less than three years at the best rent without fine or premium: s.2(5) of the Law of Property (Miscellaneous Provisions) Act 1989. See further para.15–18.

54 [1986] 1 E.G.L.R. 104 CA.

term of the new tenancy to be from "a date [to be] specified in the agreement". A conditional agreement providing for a date of commencement once the condition has been satisfied would appear to be fulfill this requirement.

In those cases where s.28 does not apply the current tenancy will, notwithstanding the agreement for the grant of a new tenancy, continue to be one to which the Act applies. It seems that in those circumstances the agreement is, arguably, void under s.38 unless s.38A has been complied with. Of course if the parties actually execute the new lease, the fact that the agreement pursuant to which that lease has been executed is void matters not: *Gibbs Mew v Gemmell*.[55] 15–16

Bowes-Lyon v Green[56] A building was subject to a complicated chain of leasehold interests. Rye was the long leasehold owner of the whole building at all material times. Rye had granted Wells a tenancy of the whole building expiring on May 4, 1959. Wells sub-let the ground floor and basement premises to Bowes-Lyon for a term expiring on April 1, 1959. Bowes-Lyon granted a sub-underlease to Green of the ground floor only to expire on March 31, 1959. Wells was not in occupation of any part of the building. Bowes-Lyon occupied the basement premises for business purposes. Green occupied the ground floor shop for business purposes. On March 19, 1958, Rye granted to Green a reversionary lease of the ground floor shop for a term a seven years commencing on April 5, 1959. Bowes-Lyon sued Green for the rent for the quarter alleged to be due on June 24, 1959. Bowes-Lyon argued that both her sub-lease and Green's sub-underlease were continuing pursuant to s.24 and thus the reversionary lease to Green took subject to the sub-lease and the sub-underlease. Green argued that the reversionary lease granted by Rye had the effect of bringing Greens sub-underlease to an end as the reversionary lease fell within s.28. It was held that the reversionary lease was not an agreement within s.28, because Rye was not "the landlord", as defined by s.44, at the material time in respect of Green's continuation sub-underlease. Green's "landlord" was Bowes-Lyon, because her sub-lease was continuing by virtue of s.24 and was thus "a tenancy which would not come to an end within 14 months or less by effluxion of time" within s.44(1)(b). Accordingly Green remained liable as the tenant of Bowes-Lyon of the ground floor and was liable for the June quarter's rent. 15–17

Law of Property (Miscellaneous Provisions) Act 1989

It is a matter of doubt whether an agreement for the purposes of s.28 of the 1954 Act is one which is required to comply with the provisions of the Law of Property (Miscellaneous Provisions) Act 1989 s.2. In *Lambert v Keymood*[57] Laws, J. suggested, obiter, that the court would not in the context of s.28 insist on strict legal formalities. He said: 15–18

---

[55] [1999] 1 E.G.L.R. 43 CA.

[56] [1963] A.C. 420 HL.

[57] [1997] 2 E.G.L.R. 70; [1997] 43 E.G. 131 QBD. The learned judge was not referred to any authority on s.28 and his comments seem difficult to reconcile with the requirement that the agreement be one which is contractually binding arrangement enforceable by the parties at law: May L.J., *Stratton (RJ) Ltd v Wallis Tomlin Co Ltd.*

> "The purpose of s.69(2) is no doubt to ensure a degree of certainty, and thus the avoidance of dispute, when in the context of s.28 it is asserted that a 1954 Act tenancy has been superseded by a later agreement. It is not to insist on legal formalities. It certainly does not require the formal execution of a lease. I do not think it necessarily requires the execution of a document exhaustively containing all the terms agreed, such that no parol evidence could be introduced to explain the full intentions of the parties. The writing must, in my judgment, demonstrate that the parties have come to terms upon a new contract for the tenancy of the property in question. One would expect it to be signed by both parties, but if it is only signed by the party against whom it is raised in later proceedings (as here), that will be sufficient. Otherwise the statute could be deployed to defeat what on any remotely sensible view of the evidence was in fact the parties' contractual intention"

The language used by the learned judge is reminiscent of the application of the provisions of s.40 of the Law of Property Act 1925.[58]

However, the authors consider it arguable that the dictum of Laws J. was wrong. It is to be noted that the Judge was not referred to any authority on s.28. The case has not been referred to in any subsequent authority and his comments seem difficult to reconcile with the requirement that the agreement be one which is contractually binding arrangement enforceable by the parties at law: May L.J., *Stratton (RJ) Ltd v Wallis Tomlin Co Ltd*.[59] If that statement is applied in the context of the 1989 Act it is difficult to see how an agreement which does not comply comes within that description.

Protection of section 28 agreement

15–19 If a s.28 agreement is entered into with the "landlord", it is imperative that the tenant protect his position in case the reversionary interest is sold. As the effect of a s.28 agreement is that the current tenancy is not a tenancy to which the Act applies, unless the tenant has protected the s.28 agreement against third parties, the new landlord may acquire the land free of the s.28 agreement and thus effectively be able to obtain vacant possession: see *Stratton (RJ) Ltd v Wallis Tomlin & Co Ltd* (digested in para.15–20). In the case of unregistered land the s.28 agreement ought to be protected as an estate contract, registered as a Class C(iv) land charge.[60] In the case of registered land the s.28 agreement may be protected by way of entry of a notice or, in most cases, will be protected as an overriding interest within Land Registration Act 2002.[61]

[58] Repealed with effect from September 27, 1989, in respect of contracts for the creation or disposition of an interest in land made on or after that date. In the case of agreements for lease made prior to the coming into force of the Law of Property (Miscellaneous Provisions) Act 1989, no action could be brought to enforce an agreement for a lease unless either: (1) there was an agreement in writing of the agreement signed by the person against whom the action is brought; or (2) there had been part performance of the agreement: Law of Property Act 1925 s.40. Although there was no memorandum of an agreement for a lease such as to satisfy the statute, yet, if the agreement had been partly performed, parol evidence of it could be given in an action for specific performance. Parol evidence was not admissible to contradict or vary a written document; but it was admissible in order to show the external circumstances which enabled its effect to be ascertained, such as the condition of the property at the time when the lease was granted.

[59] [1986] 1 E.G.L.R. 104 CA.

[60] See s.2(4), Class C(iv) of the Land Charges Act 1972. See also para.15–54.

[61] Being the rights of every person in actual occupation of the land: see para.2 of Sch.1 to the Land Registration Act 2002 (first registrations) and para.2 of Sch.3 (registered dispositions). See also para.15–54.

Stratton (RJ) Ltd v Wallis Tomlin & Co Ltd[62] The tenants applied for a new tenancy and entered into negotiations with their then landlord's surveyors as to the terms thereof. This resulted in an agreement for a new tenancy, evidenced by the correspondence between surveyors. Subsequently a receiver was appointed in respect of the landlord's undertaking, and the landlord's interest was sold to a new landlord. The new landlord (apparently) claimed not to be bound by the agreement for a new tenancy, because it was not registered as an estate contract (presumably under the Land Charges Act 1972). The new landlord also contended that the effect of s.28 of the Act was that, once the agreement to a future tenancy had become binding, the tenant ceased to be entitled to apply for a new tenancy under the Act, by virtue of s.28 which states that after such an agreement "the current tenancy . . . shall not be a tenancy to which this Part of this Act applies". The judge upheld this contention and dismissed the tenant's application. On appeal it was held that the surveyors were duly authorised to conclude an agreement on behalf of their respective clients; an agreement in writing had been reached on all material terms and the correspondence was not expressly or impliedly "subject to contract"[63]; there was an agreement within the meaning of s.28 and the application had been properly dismissed. (It is to be noted that this case pre-dated the coming into force of the Law of Property (Miscellaneous Provisions) Act 1989, but there is no reason to doubt that the same result would now occur, if it is assumed that the s.28 agreement was itself enforceable). **15–20**

3. AGREEMENT FOR NEW LEASE TO BE GRANTED BY COURT IN THE 1954 ACT PROCEEDINGS

Is there a binding agreement?

The terms of ss.32, 33, 34 and 35 of the Act refer to there being a determination by the court in "the absence of agreement" or in "default of agreement". By s.69(2) "agreement" means "agreement in writing". What if there is an agreement upon some of the matters to be incorporated within the terms of the new lease but not others? Is it possible for there to be an agreement on a piecemeal basis? **15–21**

The Act certainly supports the view that there may be agreement on one or other matters for the purposes of any renewal.[64] The agreement must, however, be one made for the purposes of an application to the court. Thus, for instance, if the **15–22**

---

[62] [1986] 1 E.G.L.R. 104 CA.

[63] As noted in para.15–05 it is ordinarily to be presumed that where the parties are proceeding directly towards the exchange of lease and counterpart without entering into a formal agreement for lease, they are negotiating "subject to lease": *Leveson v Parfum Marcel Rochas (England) Ltd* (1996) 200 E.G. 407 at 408; *Longman v Viscount Chelsea* [1989] 2 E.G.L.R. 242 CA. The presumption was rebutted in *Stratton (RJ) Ltd v Wallis Tomlin & Co Ltd*.

Since the coming into force of the Law of Property (Miscellaneous Provisions) Act 1989, no binding contract can arise by an exchange of offer and acceptance in correspondence save in respect of an agreement to grant a lease for less than three years: *Commission for the New Towns v Cooper (Great Britain) Ltd* [1995] 2 W.L.R. 677, and s.2(5) of the 1989 Act.

[64] See *Boots v Pinkland Ltd* [1992] 2 E.G.L.R. 98 CC, where the judge held that, unless the landlord agreed, the tenant was not permitted to resile from a statement made in opening by its counsel that the parties had agreed a 10-year term.

parties are seeking to negotiate the grant of a new lease outside the court procedures, the agreement is not an agreement for the purposes of the 1954 Act: *Derby & Co Ltd v ITC Pension Trust Ltd*[65] (digested in para.8–04). Thus, in that case, where the parties had reached agreement "subject to contract" it was said that the agreement on the various terms of the new lease did not bind the parties for the purposes of the 1954 Act application because not only did the "subject to contract" qualification prevent there from being a binding arrangement but, in any event, it was not a agreement which was intended to be one for the purposes of ss.32 to 35. The agreement was one which was an attempt to avoid the necessity of an application to the court and was made without prejudice to the tenant's rights under the 1954 Act.[66]

15–23 As noted above, where the parties are negotiating for the grant of a new lease other than by way of the compromise of court proceedings, it is presumed that the parties are not contractually bound until formal exchange of lease and counterpart: see *Leveson v Parfum Marcel Rochas (England) Ltd*[67]; *Longman v Viscount Chelsea*.[68] However, the presumption will not apply in the case of an attempt to compromise litigation which is pending: *Behar v Territorial Investments Ltd*.[69] In *Behar* James L.J. said:

> "In the Landlord and Tenant Act 1954, in sections 33, 34 and 35, are terms which encourage the parties of such litigation to agree on the terms of a new tenancy, and it is when the parties cannot agree that the court makes a determination. By their solicitors, the parties have followed the course contemplated by the legislation, designed to dispose of the pending litigation. They reached agreement on every point, and at the moment of time when agreement was so reached, the subject matter of the litigation was compromised and the inevitable new tenancy had to be granted on the terms agreed."

Stamp L.J. said:

> "The relations between the parties were not the ordinary relations of a proposed lessor and proposed lessee free to enter into a lease or not; for the landlord, if the tenant pursued his application, was bound to grant a lease. The situation was not such that, on a failure if negotiations, there would be a lease, but one in which, on those negotiations breaking down, the landlord could be bound to grant a lease on terms, which, so far as not agreed, would be determined by the court. This being the situation, I can see no room for concluding that because the parties intended the result of their negotiations to be embodied in an executed lease, they were negotiating on the footing that they would not be bound to enter into such a lease and there would be no contract until the lease was actually executed. On the contrary, they were negotiating the terms of a lease which each would be bound to execute . . . if necessary. I would imply a contract to that effect from the outset."

The Law of Property (Miscellaneous Provisions) Act 1989

15–24 If there is an agreement for the purposes of one of the four matters dealt with in ss.32 to 35 the effect of this is that the court is bound to make a formal order embodying the terms which have been agreed. It is considered that such an

---

[65] [1977] 2 All E.R. 890 Ch D.

[66] See also paras 8–02 to 8–05.

[67] [1966] 200 E.G. 407.

[68] (1989) 58 P. & C.R. 189 CA.

[69] [1973] CAT 229 CA.

agreement, being one made for the purposes of, and in accordance with, the 1954 Act, does not have to comply with the Law of Property (Miscellaneous Provisions) Act 1989. Once an agreement has been reached on some or all of the matters governed by ss.32 to 35, the parties will not be able to resile from that agreement.[70]

Authority

Who is to sign the settlement? A barrister or solicitor may be given express authority by a client in connection with a compromise. In the absence of an express authority there may be an implied or ostensible authority. The matter has been considered in *Waugh v HB Clifford & Sons Ltd*[71] where Brightman L.J. said: **15–25**

> "The law thus became well established that the solicitor or counsel retained in an action has an *implied* authority as between himself and his client to compromise the suit without reference to the client, provided that the compromise does not involve matters 'collateral to the action'; and *ostensible* authority, as between himself and the opposing litigant, to compromise the suit without actual proof of authority, subject to the same limitation; and that a compromise does not involve 'collateral matters' merely because it contains terms which the court could not have ordered by way of judgment in the action; for example, the return of the piano in the *Prestwich* case, 18 C.B.N.S. 806; the withdrawal of the imputations in the *Matthews* case, 20 Q.B.D. 141
>
> . . . . ..
>
> It follows, in my view, that a solicitor (or counsel) may in a particular case have ostensible authority vis-à-vis the opposing litigant where he has no implied authority vis-à-vis his client. I see no objection to that. All that the opposing litigant need ask himself when testing the ostensible authority of the solicitor or counsel, is the question whether the compromise contains matter 'collateral to the suit.' The magnitude of the compromise, or the burden which its terms impose on the other party, is irrelevant. But much more than that question may need to be asked by a solicitor when deciding whether he can safely compromise without reference to his client."

General matters for consideration

In settling a claim for renewal (by whomsoever made) by way of an order for the grant of a new tenancy the parties need to consider: **15–26**

(i) The form of order.
(ii) The date when the new tenancy is to commence and thus when the current tenancy is to end.
(iii) Interim rent.
(iv) Costs.

Form of order

There is no prescribed form of order. It will be usual to annex in a schedule the agreed form of lease to be granted pursuant to the order. The substantive part of the order will ordinarily: **15–27**

---

[70] See fn.64 above.
[71] [1982] Ch. 374.

(i) Recite that it is "By Consent".
(ii) Order, e.g. "that a new tenancy of the premises known as [. . ..] and more particularly described in the schedule hereto be granted to the applicant for the period, at the rent and on the terms and conditions as set out in the form of lease contained in the said schedule."
(iii) Make provision for interim rent, whether or not applied for.
(iv) Deal with costs.

Date of commencement of new tenancy

15–28 The new tenancy will, subject to agreement to the contrary, commence three months after final disposal in accordance with s.64[72] (usually a further 21 days, being the time for appealing must be added to the three months, but this does not apply to a consent order). Parties to a settlement of a lease renewal often agree to "backdate" the commencement of the term to the expiration of the contractual term of the old tenancy. The lease does not become vested in the tenant until execution, for a term is only vested from the date of grant notwithstanding that the date of commencement predates the date of grant: *Bradshaw v Pawley*[73] (digested in para.15–29). However, by backdating the date of commencement the parties agree the date which will be used for ascertaining the date on which the term will expire, and this backdating may also, depending on the true construction of the agreement, give rise to an obligation to make payments in respect of past periods. There is nothing preventing the parties from imposing obligations in respect of any period prior to the execution of the lease; whether in fact any such obligation has been created depends on the true construction of the lease: *Bradshaw v Pawley*.

15–29 ***Bradshaw v Pawley***[74] The tenancy of business premises terminated on March 24, 1974. The tenant applied for a new lease for a term of 10 years from March 25, 1974 at a rent of £1,750 per annum. The parties reached an agreement and entered into a consent order dated January 11, 1977. The parties had in fact agreed that the new tenancy was to be outside the provisions of the 1954 Act. An order of the court was made on May 16, 1977 excluding any new tenancy from the security of tenure provisions of the 1954 Act. The new lease was not executed until March 10, 1978. By the habendum, the premises were demised to the lessee to hold the same unto the lessee "from March 25, 1974, for the term of 10 years but determinable as hereinafter provided yielding and paying therefor during the said term yearly and proportionately for any fraction of a year the rents hereinafter set out". The yearly rent was specified at £1,750 per annum. The reddendum required the rent to be paid "during the said term". It was held that the tenant was liable to pay rent at the sum of £750 per annum from March 25, 1974.

---

[72] See para.14–137.

[73] [1980] 1 W.L.R. 10. The parties may agree a term longer than that provided for by s.33: see para.8–26.

[74] [1980] 1 W.L.R. 10.

Interim rent

Any settlement of a 1954 Act renewal claim ought to deal with the question of interim rent, even if an interim rent application has yet to be made. The reason for this is that s.24A(3) provides that the application for interim rent must not be "made more than six months after the termination of the relevant tenancy". It is considered that "termination of the relevant tenancy" is here referring to the termination of the relevant tenancy in accordance with the 1954 Act, not the date on which the term would, but for the Act, have expired by effluxion of time, or the date of termination or commencement specified in the landlord's s.25 notice of the tenant's s.26 request respectively.[75] Thus, there is no reason why, where a new tenancy is entered into pursuant to a settlement, either party cannot seek to make an application for an interim rent (subject, it is considered, to any contrary agreement contained within the settlement). **15–30**

Costs

Where an order under the Act is made by consent, the parties should provide for costs by the terms of the agreed order. If they do not, the court may decline to make any order as to costs, leaving the parties to bear their own costs. Where the parties have compromised their dispute and agreed an order, e.g. in the form of a *Tomlin* order,[76] settling all their disputes save that of costs, it has been said that the court should not, save in a reasonably obvious case, embark on making an order for costs because the court will have no proper basis of agreed or determined facts upon which to base its decision. In these circumstances the court should put the parties to their election either to proceed with the trial or accept no order as to costs: *BTC Software Ltd v Brewer & Sons Ltd*.[77] The court may exercise the jurisdiction to decide the issue of costs by reference to what is apparent from the terms of the *Tomlin* order supplemented by what is common ground: *Carlisle and Cumbria United Independence Supporters Society Ltd v CUFC Holdings Ltd*.[78] A notice by a tenant pursuant to s.29(5) (being a notice served by the tenant in a claim by a landlord under Pt 8 for renewal, inviting the court to dismiss the claim) is not to be equated with a compromise of litigation but is analogous to a notice of discontinuance, where the ordinary rule is that the party discontinuing should pay the costs: *Lay v Drexler*.[79] **15–31**

---

[75] See para.9–08 et seq.

[76] See para.15–60 et seq.

[77] [2003] EWCA Civ 939; [2004] F.S.R. 9. In *Gossage v Biston* [2012] EWCA Civ 717.

Jackson L.J. said: "15 … Parties to litigation should be encouraged to settle as many issues as they can and if they can settle all issues except costs it would be wrong to discourage them from doing so. I would prefer to say that where parties reach an agreement which involves all issues save as to costs being agreed then … first they should be encouraged to try and settle the issue of costs but, secondly, if they cannot do so then they should appreciate that there is a real risk that the court will make no order for costs."

[78] [2010] EWCA Civ 463. Thus, where the terms on which a Part 8 claim were settled were compared to the declarations sought and it was clear that the claimants were successful, the defendant was ordered to pay the costs: *Re Shree Swaminarayan Satsang* [2012] EWHC 1645 (Ch).

[79] [2007] EWCA Civ 464. See para.14–99 et seq.

4. SECTION 38 AND 38A OF THE 1954 ACT

15–32 An agreement which has the effect of precluding the tenant from making an application or request or providing for the termination or surrender of the tenant's current tenancy, in the event of his making an application or request is void: s.38(1).[80] An agreement for the surrender of a tenancy on such date or in such circumstances as may be specified in the agreement, and which agreement is made between the parties *who are* the landlord and the tenant in relation to that tenancy is void unless the requirements of s.38A are complied with: s.38A(2) and (4).

Grant of new lease

15–33 One matter that is rarely considered in relation to settlement negotiations (whether those negotiations are for the grant of a lease outside the context of the existing proceedings or within the proceedings) is whether or not there is any requirement to ensure that there is compliance with s.38A (i.e. sanctioning an agreement to surrender) in order to be able to grant the new lease pursuant to the compromise that has been or is about to be concluded. In *Gibbs Mews Plc v Gemmell*[81] the tenant entered into a tenancy at will which had the effect of surrendering his existing protected business tenancy. The tenant subsequently argued that the tenancy at will was void as it was an agreement relating to the prior tenancy, which agreement had the effect of precluding the tenant from making an application under the 1954 Act in respect of that business tenancy. The Court of Appeal held that the tenant was in fact estopped from denying that there had been a surrender of the earlier tenancy and therefore felt that s.38 had no application. However it was said that, even if it did apply, s.38 did not prevent an actual surrender by operation of law. In *Gibbs Mews Plc v Gemmell*[82] the new lease had been duly executed, but often all that one has in the case of a settlement at the door of the court, is an agreement signed by both parties. Will this agreement be void if s.38A has not been complied with? There are two arguments to overcome any suggested invalidity: (i) that the matter is incorporated into a court order and does not therefore simply rest in contract (indeed as noted above, there may not in fact be a contract satisfying the contractual requirements of s.2 of the Law of Property (Miscellaneous Provisions) Act 1989[83]); alternatively, (ii) s.28 applies to the agreement, the effect of which will be to exclude the 1954 Act in relation to the tenant's current tenancy. It is considered that, in most cases, such an agreement will be caught by s.28 of the 1954 Act.

Agreement to surrender as term of new lease

15–34 The parties may reach an agreement that the tenant's new lease should contain provision for its surrender on specified terms. It is unclear in practice how this

---

[80] See para.3–07 et seq.

[81] [1999] 1 E.G.L.R. 43 CA. See also para.3–11.

[82] [1999] 1 E.G.L.R. 43 CA.

[83] See para.15–24 above.

can be achieved. The terms of s.38(2) render any agreement to surrender void in relation to a tenancy to which the Act applies. An agreement for a tenancy to be granted pursuant to an order of the court is not caught by s.38(2), for the agreement is contained in a tenancy which has yet to be granted. However, immediately upon its grant, the effect of that agreement to surrender will be to preclude the tenant from making an application in relation to that tenancy. The agreement will thus be void by reason of s.38(1) and 38A(2) unless the notice requirements of s.38A(4) are complied with. However, it is difficult to see how the notice requirements of s.38A(4) of the Act and Sch.4 to the 2003 Order can be complied with respect to a tenancy which has yet to be granted, for the parties cannot be described as the persons who "are the landlord and tenant" in relation to it; it is a tenancy which does not exist at the date of the court's order.

New lease to be outside the 1954 Act

What should be done if the new lease which is agreed between the parties is one in respect of which the security of tenure provisions of the 1954 Act are intended to be excluded? Of course if there is time to serve the relevant notice and declaration provided for by s.38A(3) no difficulty arises.[84] Problems may, however, be encountered where agreement is reached at court and the relevant court order needs to be agreed and submitted. For example, the parties may agree that the landlord's termination application is to succeed but with a short term tenancy to be granted to the tenant (whether immediately[85] or upon the coming to an end of the tenant's current tenancy) which short term tenancy is to be outside the Act. One cannot, it would seem, make the court order conditional on the requirements of s.38A(3) having been complied with, for it is probably the case that the very submission of the signed *Tomlin* order will have the effect that the tenant will be "contractually bound" before the s.38A(3) matters have been completed[86]. If the court order has been signed before the s.38A(3) requirements have been fulfilled any potential security of tenure may be overcome upon re-execution of any agreement for lease: *Evenlex v Essexcrest*.[87] But this requires the tenant's co-operation. **15–35**

5. SETTLING TERMINATION APPLICATION

General matters for consideration

In compromising a termination application (in favour of the claimant landlord) the parties need to consider: **15–36**

(i) The form of order.

---

[84] As to which see para.2–13 et seq.

[85] If the agreement is for a new tenancy to take effect immediately, this will give rise to a surrender of the tenant's current tenancy and one may also have to comply with the requirements of s.38A(4): see para.3–11.

[86] As to the meaning of this expression see para.3–26. As to *Tomlin* orders, see para.15–60 et seq.

[87] [1988] 1 E.G.L.R. 69 CA.

(ii) The date when the tenant's current tenancy is to end.
(iii) The delivery up of possession.
(iv) The payment of compensation, both as to the amount and the date when payment is to be effected.
(v) Interim rent.
(vi) Costs.

The form of order

15–37 If the parties agree simply for the landlord to succeed in his termination application without any ancillary relief, the parties can enter into a consent order providing for the termination of the tenant's current tenancy. There is no need to specify the date of termination as this will be in accordance with the terms of s.64.[88] However, the agreement will usually involve more than the simple agreement that the landlord succeed in his termination application. Compensation will ordinarily be agreed to be paid (and often the landlord will have agreed to pay a larger sum than the statutory compensation to which the tenant is entitled in order to obtain an early termination of the tenant's tenancy). In these circumstances the order should take the form of a *Tomlin* order.[89]

Date of termination

15–38 The tenant's current tenancy will ordinarily terminate three months from the date of final disposal.[90] However, the parties may seek to provide for a longer period or a shorter period. The agreed date of termination will be the date upon which the landlord wishes not only that the tenancy should end but upon which the tenant is to deliver up vacant possession. It would seem from the decision of *Johns v Chatalos*[91] (digested in para.15–47) that the court has jurisdiction to make an order for possession in the 1954 Act proceedings. As noted below, it is unclear whether the court may order possession to be given on a date earlier than that provided for by s.64. There is nothing stopping the parties agreeing, however, an earlier date for termination, with an agreed term to that effect contained in the Schedule to the *Tomlin* order. Such a term would not be inconsistent with the substantive order of the court, which will provide simply for the termination of the tenant's current tenancy without the grant of any new tenancy. The agreement of the parties as to the earlier date of termination is effectively an agreement for the surrender of the tenant's current tenancy (which is being continued by s.64) on a date earlier than the tenancy would otherwise come to an end in accordance with that section. Accordingly, it may also be necessary for the parties to have complied with the terms of s.38A(2) and (4) of the 1954 Act, and Sch.4 to the 2003 Order, in order for the agreement providing

---

88 See para.3–227 et seq.
89 As to which see para.15–60 et seq.
90 See para.3–227 et seq.
91 [1973] 1 W.L.R. 1437; [1973] 3 All E.R. 410. This case is discussed further in paras 15–40 and 15–46.

for the earlier termination to be valid and enforceable.[92] Compliance with these provisions should be recited in the Schedule to the Tomlin order.

Delivery up of possession

15–39 The court has jurisdiction to make an order for possession as part of the parties' compromise of the application: see paras 15–45 and 15–46. If the parties have agreed a date of termination (and consequential delivery up of possession) on a date earlier than the provided for by s.64, it is considered that the landlord will need to ensure that there has been due compliance with s.38A (agreements to surrender) in order for the agreement to be binding and enforceable.[93]

15–40 There would appear to be no legal difficulty in providing for a later date of termination as in *Johns v Chatalos*[94] (digested in para.15–47) itself. An important consideration for the landlord in these circumstances is to make satisfactory provision as to the tenant's status after the date fixed by s.64 for termination of the current tenancy.[95] Payment by the tenant during the period of continuation pursuant to s.64 would not, of course, give rise to any new tenancy as the payment of rent and occupation is referable to the tenant's current tenancy.[96] If the date of termination is later than that provided for by s.64, however, the tenant is clearly not a tenant post the s.64 termination date. His status could be said to be akin to that of the "tolerated trespasser", a status which was said to exist in relation to secure tenants of residential premises.[97] It would be sensible to

---

[92] See further para.3–23 as to the requirements of s.38A(2) and (4) and para.15–46 where the issue is discussed further.

[93] See paras 15–45 and 15–46.

[94] [1973] 1 W.L.R. 1437; [1973] 3 All E.R. 410. This case is discussed further on the issue of the date of the delivering up of possession in paras 15–45 and 15–46.

[95] This was not a problem which the landlord in *Johns v Chatalos* [1973] 1 W.L.R. 1437; [1973] 3 All E.R. 410 had to contend with, as it was agreed between the parties that the tenant was to occupy rent free from the date of the making of the consent order.

[96] See para.1–17.

[97] Where a landlord has obtained an order for possession he may (in the context of a residential possession claim) agree not to execute an outright order, which will usually be on terms, e.g. to pay an amount off arrears. In *Burrows v Brent LBC* [1996] 1 W.L.R. 1448; (1997) 29 H.L.R. 167, the House of Lords held that where the landlord under a secure tenancy of residential premises decides not to enforce an order but agrees to allow the former tenant to remain in occupation on terms, no new tenancy (or licence) is created (in the absence of special circumstances). The position was held to be the same if a postponed order had been made and the secure tenancy ended because the conditions had not been complied with, but the landlord nonetheless allowed the former tenant to remain on terms: *Greenwich LBC v Regan* (1996) 28 H.L.R. 469 CA, approved in *Burrows*. During the period when the former secure tenant was allowed to remain without the creation of a new tenancy, he was categorised as a "tolerated trespasser." In *Burrows* Lord Browne-Wilkinson said, at 1455B–D: "… In my judgment little guidance is to be obtained from the cases where a tenant holds over after the termination of an ordinary tenancy where there is no possibility that the expired tenancy can revive. The position in relation to secure tenancies is *sui generis*. In my judgment, the agreement [by a landlord to allow the secure tenant to remain in occupation albeit he had no complied with the conditions for staying the order for possession] can and should take effect in the way the parties intend, i.e. it is an agreement by the landlords that, upon the tenant complying with the agreed conditions, the landlords will forbear from executing the order, i.e. from taking the step which would finally put an end to the tenant's right to apply to the court for an order reviving the tenancy. There is no need to impute to the parties an intention to create a new tenancy or licence: the retention of

provide in the *Tomlin* order,[98] that as from the termination of the current tenancy in accordance with s.64, all further payments made by the tenant should be made by way of mesne profits until the delivery up of possession. Payment of mesne profits pending the execution of an order (or agreed date for possession) will not give rise the grant of a new tenancy as the occupation is referable to the order rather than an intention to grant a new tenancy.[99] However, an increase in the mesne profits to be paid by the occupier above the rate laid down in the order may give rise to the grant of a new tenancy: *Stirling v Leadenhall Residential Ltd*.[100]

The payment of compensation

15–41 The parties will usually agree that the order should provide for payment of any statutory compensation to which the tenant would ordinarily be entitled under s.37 of the Act. Sometimes indeed, the landlord will agree to pay the tenant a sum in excess of the statutory compensation as an incentive to agree to the order for termination. Since a termination application does not itself involve a claim for compensation under s.37, any agreement as to the quantum of compensation should be put into the Schedule to the *Tomlin* order,[101] rather than as part of the substantive order of the court. The parties may agree that no compensation is payable. This may arise where, for instance, the landlord would have a claim for dilapidations and the quantum of the claim is used to offset the sum that would otherwise be paid as damages for breach of covenant.[102] Where the compensation to be paid is less than that to which the tenant would otherwise be entitled in accordance with the statutory provisions, the landlord needs to ensure that any such agreement does not fall foul of the anti avoidance provisions of s.38(2). Any agreement to exclude or reduce the compensation payable under s.37 may be made without being rendered void under s.38(2), if it is made "after the right to compensation has accrued."[103] The meaning of this expression is unclear.[104]

15–42 The landlord will usually wish to ensure that payment of compensation is made to coincide with the delivery up of possession. This is a matter of drafting.

---

possession and the payment of rent relate to occupation under the old tenancy which is in limbo but which may be revived. In these circumstances I think it is fair to characterise the former tenant as a trespasser whom the landlord has agreed not to evict — a "tolerated trespasser" — pending either the revival of the old tenancy or the breach of the agreed conditions." The concept of a tolerated trespasser was brought to an end by Sch.11 to the Housing and Regeneration Act 2008 amending the Housing Act 1985. In *Austin v Southwark* [2010] UKSC 28 the Supreme Court held that the whole concept of the "tolerated trespasser" was based on an erroneous construction of the (unamended) Housing Act 1985.

[98] As to which see para.15–60.

[99] See, by way of example, *Essex Plan v Broadminster* (1988) 56 P. & C.R. 353 Ch D (where the exclusive possession was referable to occupation pending sale).

[100] [2001] 3 All E.R. 645 CA.

[101] As to *Tomlin* orders see para.15–60.

[102] Such a claim will not usually arise where the landlord opposes under para.(f) (redevelopment) of s.30(1) of the Act, for often an intended redevelopment of the tenant's holding will negate any claim. However, a claim for dilapidations may arise where the landlord opposes under para.(g) (own occupation).

[103] The proviso to s.38(2).

[104] See paras 12–63 and 12–64.

Interim rent

An interim rent is payable by the tenant "while the tenancy... continues by virtue of section 24 of this Act" (s.24A(1)). A tenancy which is terminated pursuant to a termination application is, nevertheless, one continuing under s.24 (in combination with s.64) until termination. An application for interim rent must be made not later "than six months after the termination of the relevant [i.e. the tenant's current] tenancy" (s.24(3)).[105] Accordingly, both parties should be alive to the possibility that either may make an interim rent application notwithstanding the fact that the termination application has been disposed of by consent. If an application for interim rent has already been made the parties can agree what that interim rent figure should be. Often a landlord who is about to obtain possession will agree, where the interim rent period is relatively short, to the interim rent being no greater than the passing rent. If no application has been made by either party for an interim rent as at the date of the entry into the *Tomlin* order disposing of the landlord's termination application a recital should be included in the Schedule to the *Tomlin* order that the agreement is in full and final settlement of all claims each has against the other under (inter alia) the 1954 Act, including any claim for interim rent under s.24A to 24D. **15–43**

Costs

The parties' agreement should deal with costs. If the parties agree everything other than costs the court may decline only to decide the issue of costs: see para.15–31. **15–44**

Agreement to give up possession

Possession after section 64 date

In *Johns v Chatalos*[106] (digested in para.15–47) it was held that the court may also, by consent, make an order for possession of the premises by way of compromise of an application for a new tenancy. In that case the tenant's claim for renewal was withdrawn by consent together with an order for the delivery up of possession and payment of compensation upon the date that possession was given.[107] **15–45**

Possession prior to section 64 date

It is not clear whether the court may order possession prior to the date on which the tenancy would otherwise come to an end in accordance with the Act. This problem did not arise for consideration in *Johns v Chatalos* as the order for possession was to take effect on a date later than the date on which the tenancy **15–46**

---

105 As to when the six-month period starts see para.9–08.

106 [1973] 1 W.L.R. 1437; [1973] 3 All E.R. 410.

107 It would seem from the report that the matter was dealt with by way of a consent order rather than a *Tomlin* order. Thus, the order for possession was a substantive order of the court.

would otherwise come to an end. It would accordingly be prudent in a case where the termination date is accelerated to a date earlier than that provided for by s.64 for the parties to enter into an agreement to surrender the tenancy in accordance with s.38A(2).[108] An agreement to bring the tenancy to an end on an earlier date than that provided for by s.64 may be caught by s.38A(2). Prior to the amendments brought about by the 2003 Order any such agreement (ordinarily reached at the door of the court) did not cause any practical difficulty. Counsel for the parties would simply present the signed consent order to the court and invite the court to make a formal order under what was s.38(4)(since repealed) and the court's authorisation would be recited in the court order. However, under the new procedure brought in by s.38A(4) and Sch.4 to the 2003 Order, the relevant notice and statutory declaration must be served before the agreement to surrender under s.38(2) is entered into or the tenant becomes contractually bound to enter into the agreement for surrender.[109] If the parties sign a consent order before any form of notice and declaration required by Sch.4 is served it would seem that the agreement to determine the tenancy on a date earlier than that provided for by s.64 is void and unenforceable.

15–47 ***Johns v Chatalos***[110] The tenant of business premises applied for a new tenancy by summons in the county court. By way of compromise of those proceedings, the county court made an order by consent for possession of the premises in six months' time, the tenant to remain in occupation rent free during that period, to be released from liability for dilapidations and to be given £250 on quitting. The tenant came to regret the bargain, did not give possession of the premises on the agreed date and applied to the county court to vary the consent order. The county court dismissed the application and gave the landlord leave to execute the order for possession. The tenant issued proceedings in the High Court claiming a declaration, inter alia, that the consent order was null and void. It was held that the county court had jurisdiction to make an order by consent for possession in proceedings under the 1954 Act. The order was by way of compromise of the tenant's claim for a new tenancy. It was accordingly unnecessary for the order of the court to be confined to the ambit of the original dispute between the parties or to be kept within the limits of the relief competent to be granted had the application proceeded to a conclusion instead of being compromised.

Practical importance of decision

15–48 The decision that a court has jurisdiction, by consent, to make an order for possession in compromise of a tenant's application for a new tenancy under the Act is of considerable practical importance. Especially where the landlord is opposing the grant of a new tenancy, such applications are often compromised at the door of the court on terms that the application is withdrawn or dismissed, a

[108] See para.3–21 et seq. generally on the procedural requirements for there to be a valid agreement to surrender.

[109] See paras 3–24 and 3–26.

[110] [1973] 1 W.L.R. 1437; [1973] 3 All E.R. 410.

date for possession is agreed, and financial arrangements (including compensation, payment for dilapidations, etc.) are settled. It would be inconvenient if the landlords had to wait for a further three months for the current tenancy to expire and then seek an order for possession in fresh proceedings. There is no reason why the jurisdiction to make an order for possession should not apply equally where the agreement to give possession is reached in a termination application under s.29(2) of the Act.

6. PROTECTION BY REGISTRATION

Protection of agreement for lease

Unregistered land

An agreement for lease is registrable as an estate contract within the meaning of the Land Charges Act 1972, s.2(1), Class C(iv). The registration at the Land Charges Registry is against the name of the estate owner or the person entitled at the date of the agreement to have a legal estate conveyed to him.[111] An error in the name registered does not invalidate the registration if the name given may fairly be called a version of the name; but a person who searches in the correct name is protected even if it fails to reveal an entry.[112] **15–49**

If an agreement which is required to be registered has not been, it is void against a purchaser for money or money's worth of a legal estate in the land charged with it.[113] There is no requirement that the purchaser must take in good faith or that the money paid on purchase must be more than nominal.[114] **15–50**

As noted above, any agreement which is not registered is void against a purchaser of a legal estate for money or money's worth.[115] As the purchaser is not required to act in good faith the contract has been held not to be binding on a purchaser where he did not diligently investigate title[116]; had knowledge of the contract[117]; deliberately intended to defeat it[118] and or where the land was expressly conveyed subject to the contract.[119] The party who under the agreement is to be granted a **15–51**

---

[111] Land Charges Act 1972, s.2(1), Class C(iv).

[112] *Oak Co-Operative Building Society v Blackburn* [1968] Ch. 730.

[113] Land Charges Act 1972, s.4(6). A purchaser is defined as as any person (including a mortgagee or lessee) which, for valuable consideration, takes any interest in land or is a charge on land (s.17(1) of the 1972 Act) and see *Sharp v Coates* [1949] 1 K.B. 285; [1948] 2 All E.R. 871; *Coventry Permanent Economic Building Society v Jones* [1951] 1 All E.R. 901.

[114] *Midland Bank Trust Co Ltd v Green* [1981] A.C. 513; [1981] 1 All E.R. 153 HL.

[115] Land Charges Act 1972, s.4(6).

[116] *Sharpe v Coates* [1949] 1 K.B. 285; [1948] 2 All E.R. 871 (owner of interest in possession and therefore purchaser had constructive notice of it).

[117] *Coventry Permanent Economic Building Society v Jones* [1951] 1 All E.R. 901; *Hollington Bros Ltd v Rhodes* [1951] 2 T.L.R. 691 at 696.

[118] *Midland Bank Trust Co Ltd v Green* [1981] A.G. 513.

[119] *Hollington Bros Ltd v Rhodes* [1951] 2 All E.R. 578n. It may be possible in these circumstances to impose a constructive trust upon the purchaser: *Lyus v Prowsa Developments Ltd* [1982] 2 All E.R. 963; [1982] 1 W.L.R. 1044. The *Lyus* case fell within the principle enunciated in *Rochefoucauld v Bowstead* [1897] 1 Ch. 196 where Lindley L.J. at 206 said:

lease has a claim in damages against the other party thereto where the agreement is not binding on the purchaser of the reversion notwithstanding the fact that this may be due to prospective tenant's the failure to protect the contract by registration.[120]

Registered land

15–52 Where the agreement for lease relates to registered land, the agreement may be protected by entry of a unilateral notice.[121] The rights of persons in actual occupation are overriding interests and the agreement will be binding on any purchaser of the land albeit not protected by the entry of a unilateral notice.[122] The agreement will not, however, constitute an overidding interest if (i) it belongs to a person whose occupation would not have been obvious on a reasonably careful inspection of the land at the time of the disposition, and (ii) of which the person to whom the disposition is made does not have actual knowledge at that time.[123]

15–53 It is unclear what a tenant should do in response to a landlord's application for renewal. This too constitutes a pending land action and ought to be protected. It is submitted that the tenant is, albeit by reason of the actions of the landlord, seeking a renewal of his tenancy.

Protection of renewal claim

15–54 It is rare for a tenant who is negotiating the grant of a new lease whilst proceedings for a new tenancy are afoot to seek to protect the application for renewal. Whether the tenant should protect the claim and the consequences of not doing so are discussed at para.6–64 et seq.

Protection of section 28 agreement

15–54A Where the land is registered any contract should, notwithstanding the absence of any entry in the register of the landlord's title protecting the agreement, be protected as an overriding interest (assuming the tenant to be in actual occupation). If one is dealing with unregistered land the contract must be protected as a land charge. This is illustrated by *Stratton (RJ) Ltd v Wallis Tomlin*

"… it is a fraud on the part of a person to whom land is conveyed as a trustee and who knows it was so conveyed to deny the trust and to claim the land himself. Consequently, notwithstanding the statute, it is competent for a person claiming land conveyed to another to prove by parol evidence that it was so conveyed upon trust for the claimant, and that the grantee, knowing the facts, it denying the trust in relying upon the form of conveyance and the statute, in order to keep the land himself."

See also *Initial Development Concept Group Limited v Clark* [1992] 1 E.G.L.R. 187 and *Chattey v Farndale Holdings* [1997] 1 E.G.L.R. 153. It may also be possible for the purchaser to be estopped from asserting that the unregistered charge is ineffective: *Taylor Fashions Ltd v Liverpool Victoria Trustees Co Ltd* [1982] Q.B. 133.

[120] *Wright v Dean* [1948] Ch. 686; *Hollington Bros Ltd v Rhodes* [1951] 2 All E.R. 578n.

[121] Land Registration Act 2002, ss.34(2)(b) and 35.

[122] Land Registration Act 2002, Sch.3, para.2.

[123] Land Registration Act 2002, Sch.3, para.2(c).

& Co Ltd[124] (digested in para.15–20) where the tenants failed to protect the agreement that they had entered into with the landlord, who sold his interest to a third party. The s.28 agreement was not enforceable against the third party but had the effect of depriving the tenant's current tenancy of any statutory protection.

7. PART 36 AND *CALDERBANK* OFFERS

Part 36 generally

An offer to settle may be made in the form provided for by Pt 36. The criteria for such an offer are set out in CPR r.36.2. There are substantial advantages to a claimant making a Pt 36 offer. CPR r.36.14(3) allows a court to reflect the fact that a claimant obtains a judgment at trial at least as advantageous as his Pt 36 offer by ordering (unless it considers it unjust to do so) (i) interest on any money element of the claim up to 10 per cent above the base rate; (ii) costs on an indemnity basis and (iii) interest on those costs up to 10 per cent above the base rate. Where a claimant fails to obtain a judgment more advantageous than a defendant's Pt 36 offer CRP r.36.14(2) provides that the court will, unless it considers it unjust to do so, order that the defendant is entitled to (i) his costs from the date on which the period for accepting the offer expired, and (ii) interest on those costs up to 10 per cent above the base rate. In considering whether it would be unjust to make the orders referred to above, the court will take into account all the circumstances of the case including (a) the terms of any Pt 36 offer; (b) the stage in the proceedings when any Pt 36 offer was made, including in particular how long before the trial started the offer was made; (c) the information available to the parties at the time when the Pt 36 offer was made; and (d) the conduct of the parties with regard to the giving or refusing to give information for the purposes of enabling the offer to be made or evaluated (CPR r.36.14(4)). **15–55**

1954 Act proceedings

It is not appropriate to make an offer under Pt 36 (as opposed to a *Calderbank* offer)[125] in the context of 1954 Act disputes. To start with the most obvious reason, those parts of Pt 36 dealing with money claims cannot be used against a defendant in the context of 1954 Act litigation, whether as landlord or tenant, because they cannot appropriately be adapted to a renewal context, which often involves considering a whole host of terms (e.g. where terms of the proposed lease are in dispute) in respect of which it is often very difficult to predict the outcome. **15–56**

A further disadvantage of using Pt 36, particularly in unopposed renewals, is that the rules provide that upon any acceptance of a Pt 36 offer, the claimant's costs up to the date when the offer is accepted are to be paid by the defendant, provided that the acceptance did not require the court's permission: CPR r.36.10.

---

[124] [1986] 1 E.G.L.R. 104 CA.

[125] As to which see para.15–58.

This is particularly problematic in the case of unopposed lease renewals, where the usual understanding (especially at an early stage of the litigation) is that on settlement each party pays its own costs. However, Pt 36 provides that whether the landlord or tenant is claimant to a renewal claim, an acceptance of an offer provides the claimant with its costs. Thus, a defendant to an unopposed lease renewal is unlikely to accept any Pt 36 offer which is made by the claimant. Nor is the defendant likely to make a Pt 36 offer when acceptance will result in a costs liability. Moreover, there is no flexibility in the Pt 36 offer with respect to costs, as a claimant in a Pt 36 offer cannot, as part of that offer, offer a "drop hands" position.[126]

15–57 However, is there a way for a defendant to use Pt 36 to exert pressure (i.e. because of the penalties expressly provided for in CPR r.36.14) but without worrying about acceptance? It occurs to the Authors that there may be such a way where the claim includes a claim for interim rent. Suppose that the defendant to the claim makes a Pt 36 offer which is an offer which does not include the claim for interim rent. The offer is then one dealing with the substantive claim for renewal but is still an offer which "relates to only part of the claim" for the purpose of CPR r.36.11(3). This means that the court is to determine costs if the offer is accepted (CPR r.36.11(3) and 36.10(2)). The defendant can then argue that costs should not be awarded to the claimant, as the usual costs order in 1954 Act settlements is that each party pays its own costs . He will seek to settle the interim rent once the offer is accepted. Of course the difficulty with this course of action is that the defendant faces *the risk* that costs may be awarded against him. The burden is on him to persuade the court: CPR r.36.10(2). On balance it is probably not worth taking the risk for the potential benefits, and therefore the *Calderbank* route is recommended (see para.15–58).

Calderbank offers

15–58 Nothing in Pt 36 prevents a party making an offer to settle in whatever way he chooses, but if the offer is not made in accordance with CPR r.36.2, it will not have the consequences specified by Pt 36: CPR r.31(2). It is, of course, possible for parties to make *Calderbank* offers (i.e. offers without prejudice save as to costs), but such offers are not Pt 36 offers. The court retains in those circumstances its general discretion in respect of costs under CPR r.44.3. Under that rule it can take account of any settlement offers made. The court may award indemnity costs together with interest on those costs. However, the list of potential costs orders contained in r.44.3(6) makes no express provision for the high rate of interest (of up to 10 per cent above base rate) referred to in Pt 36, but it seems that the court's discretion in such cases remains a wide one albeit that the list of Pt 36 penalties is only expressly made available for Pt 36 offers. As a result, the recipient of a non-Pt 36 offer may feel under less pressure to accept it because it may feel that it is less likely to face the clear and severe penalties

[126] This is a product of CPR r.36.2(2) which provides that the Pt 36 offer (in order to be such) must "(c) specify a period of not less than 21 days within which the defendant will be liable for the claimant's costs in accordance with rule 36.10 if the offer is accepted." This rule thus applies whether the offer is made by the claimant or defendant.

available under Pt 36 for a party that fails to improve on an offer at trial. It remains to be seen, however, whether the court will take the view that it is not right to make such a distinction between its approach to costs in a case where Pt 36 applies and one where the *Calderbank* route is the only practical possibility.

Contract for disposition of an interest in land?

15–59 In Foskett, *The Law and Practice of Compromise* (7th edn para.15–16 fn.31), it is said that "It is thought that in most cases where no further involvement of the court is contemplated other than enforcement of the terms of the agreement it is right to say that ordinarily a contract of compromise has been concluded." However, in special cases, of which a compromise involving a disposition of land is one, an acceptance of a Pt 36 offer gives rise not to an enforceable contract, but to an obligation which is enforceable by other means: *Orton v Collins*,[127] *Warren v Radmon House Group Ltd*.[128] An acceptance of a Pt 36 offer which involves the disposition of an interest in land would not ordinarily give rise to a contract which complies with s.2 of the Law of Property (Miscellaneous Provisions) Act 1989, comprising a single document incorporating all the express terms of the contract, signed by both sides. In *Orton v Collins* it was held that the acceptance of a Pt 36 offer need not create a contract at all; rather, it can be characterised as creating an obligation sui generis that the court could enforce by requiring the parties to do what was necessary to implement the settlement. If necessary it could enforce that obligation by ordering the parties to enter into a contract that did comply with the formalities of s.2 of the Act. The Judge said:

> "The mischief that section 2 of the 1989 Act must have been intended to redress can have no relevance whatever to the settlement of existing court proceedings under the machinery now provided by CPR Part 36. There is no question of lack of mutuality, nor of the uncertainties said to arise out of the doctrine of part performance. If a Part 36 offer is made and accepted according to the rules there can be no doubt that the acceptance should be read together with the offer and the problems illustrated by *Timmins v. Moreland Street Property Co Ltd* do not arise. Furthermore the parties know that they are entering into a solemn and binding legal transaction. They have the opportunity to seek legal advice: a Part 36 offer, if not withdrawn, remains open for 21 days (unless the trial is imminent, in which case the permission of the court is required). Indeed in the ordinary way the parties will be advised by lawyers throughout, much more so than when most vendors and purchasers are in the initial stages of negotiating a land contract."

8. THE *TOMLIN* ORDER

15–60 An order made "in *Tomlin* form" more commonly known simply as "a *Tomlin* order" is one which is aimed at dealing with arrangements which have been agreed between the parties not all of which could appropriately have been made the subject of a direct order or judgment of the court. The general form of wording of a *Tomlin* order is:

---

[127] [2007] 1 W.L.R. 2953.

[128] [2009] 2 All E.R. 245 CA at [21] per Sir Anthony Clarke M.R.

> "*AND UPON the parties having agreed the terms of settlement*
> *BY CONSENT*
> *IT IS ORDERED that all further proceedings in this case be stayed upon the terms set out in the Schedule to this order except for the purposes of enforcing those terms.*
> *AND IT IS FURTHER ORDERED that either party may be permitted to apply to the court to enforce the terms upon which this case has been stayed without the need to bring a new claim.*"

The order then appends a Schedule in which all the detailed terms of settlement are set out.

15–61 The *Tomlin* order ought also to deal with costs. They should be dealt with in the body of the order. It is to be noted that in *Marchant v Marchant*,[129] Dankwerts L.J. expressed the view that the words "liberty to apply" without more were ineffective to keep alive the proceedings for the purposes of enforcement. The full expression "liberty to apply for the purpose of enforcing the said terms" must be used.

15–62 The benefit of the *Tomlin* procedure is that it enables the enforcement of the terms of settlement within the existing action. No new action is needed to be instituted in order to enforce the terms. The compromise reached gives rise to a new legal relationship, often in the case of property a contract for the grant of interest in land. If there is default in adhering to the terms the innocent party will have a cause of action either for damages or specific performance or an injunction, etc. Ordinarily a new action would need to be instituted. However, the *Tomlin* order enables the parties to obtain enforcement without the need to issue fresh proceedings for the purposes of enforcement.

[129] [1967] CAT 26.

CHAPTER 16

THE ELECTRONIC COMMUNICATIONS CODE ("THE CODE") AND THE 1954 ACT[1]

1. THE CODE

Electronic communications infrastructure and equipment are commonplace features on the rooftops of buildings. The Code enables operators of communications networks to acquire rights to install and maintain equipment on other people's land. The installation may be the subject of an express agreement or one conferred by the court pursuant to the electronic communications code.[2] The agreement may constitute a licence or a tenancy; if it is a tenancy it may or may not be one contracted out of Pt II of the Landlord and Tenant Act 1954 ("the 1954 Act"). The interrelationship between the provisions of the Code and the 1954 Act remains to be resolved by judicial determination.[3] The Code deals with the exercise of rights by operators and the removal of electronic apparatus. **16–01**

In referring to "the occupier" or "the owner" this Chapter refers to the person upon whose land the electronic communications apparatus[4] ("the apparatus") is situated, or the person over whose land Code rights are sought to be exercised, or the person who seeks to effect an alteration to that land affecting the apparatus or to remove the apparatus. The person who exercises rights under the Code pursuant to an express agreement, or who seeks the court's dispensation of the **16–02**

---

[1] This Chapter calls heavily upon the lecture given by Wayne Clark as part of the Blundell Lecture Series, entitled "*Property Problems Under the Electronic Communications Code*" delivered on June 29, 2011 as part of the 36th Annual Series Blundell Lectures ("*Clark*").

[2] s.10 of the Telecommunications Act 1984 introduced a Code known as the Telecommunications Code granting extensive powers over land to telecommunications operators. The operative section has now been replaced by the Communications Act 2003 and the Code itself referred to in the 2003 Act as "the Electronic Communications Code", with the modifications introduced by s.106 and Sch.3 to that Act. Although s.106 of the 2003 Act says that the Code set out in Sch.2 to the 1984 Act is referred to as "the electronic communications code" in "this Chapter", the amendments made by the 2003 Act did not include changing the title to Sch.2, so that in Sch.2 itself it is still called "The Telecommunications Code". In this Chapter reference to "the Code" is to the Telecommunications Code as modified.

[3] It has been said that the Code "… must rank as one of the least coherent and thought-through pieces of legislation on the statute book" per Lewison J. in *The Bridgewater Canal Co Ltd v Geo Networks Ltd* [2010] 1 W.L.R. 2576 at [7]. The judge's actual decision was reversed on appeal: [2011] 1 W.L.R. 1487 CA.

The Law Commission has recently issued a consultation paper upon the Code: Consultation Paper No.205. One of its recommendations is that "where a Code Operator has vested in it a lease of land for the installation and/or use of apparatus the removal of which is subject to the security provisions of a revised code, Part 2 of the Landlord and Tenant Act 1954 shall not apply to a lease", para.8.22.

[4] "Electronic communications apparatus" has a very wide definition which is to be found in para.1.

owner's consent in order to exercise such rights, will be referred to as "the operator".[5] References in this Chapter to paragraph numbers are to the paragraphs of the Code unless otherwise stated.

General regime

16–03 The Code provides for a number of rights exercisable by or against occupiers/owners and operators. The Code draws a distinction between general and special regimes.[6] The general regime of the Code is contained in paras 2 to 7. In the ordinary case, an operator of an electronic communications network requires the agreement of an occupier of land in order to exercise rights under the Code. These rights include the right to execute works connected with the installation, maintenance, adjustment, repair or alteration of apparatus; the keeping of apparatus on under or over the land; or the entry on to the land to inspect apparatus: para.2(1). The occupier's consent is needed before any of these rights can be exercised. The Code provides, in general, for:

(1) The extent to which any consent granted by the occupier of land for the exercise of Code rights binds third parties.
(2) The right of an operator to obtain an entitlement to exercise Code rights notwithstanding the absence of the express consent of the occupier/owner.
(3) The right of a person with an interest in the relevant land to seek the alteration or removal of the apparatus.

This Chapter will touch briefly upon the matters in (1) and (2) but consider (3) in more detail, as it is that element of the Code which gives rise to a consideration of the inter action, if any, with the 1954 Act.

Special regimes

16–04 The special regimes run alongside the general regime. There are a number of them. They are dealt with by paras 9 to 12, which are expressly excluded from the general regime: para.2(9). Thus, for example, an operator has the right to install apparatus over, under, along or across a publicly maintainable highway without going through the process of seeking agreement or going to court: para.9; an operator may fly lines over land if the lines connect apparatus on adjacent or neighbouring land: para.10; an operator also has the right to install apparatus on or under tidal waters or land: para.11 and paras 12 to 14 deal with linear

[5] As will be seen the operator, in order to have Code protection with respect to the removal of apparatus, need not own the apparatus.

[6] As so described by Lewison J. in *The Bridgewater Canal Co Ltd v Geo Networks Ltd* [2010] 1 W.L.R. 2576. This dichotomy was adopted by the Court of Appeal.

obstacles.[7] The special regimes are not considered in this Chapter, which is confined to a consideration of the general regime.

General regime

Agreement

Rights under the Code need to be exercised with the consent of the occupier unless consent is dispensed with by the court. It is sufficient in order to confer Code rights upon the operator for *the occupier for the time being of the land* to have entered into an agreement with the operator "for the statutory purposes." The Code[8] deals with the extent to which an agreement by the occupier of the land binds persons having superior or inferior interests to that of the occupier. The provisions are complex but draw a distinction between: **16–05**

(a) A situation where the agreement is being entered into by the occupier of any land for purposes connected with the provision *to the occupier* from time to time of that land of any electronic communications services.
(b) A situation where the agreement is being entered into by the occupier other than for the provision to the occupier from time to time of the land of any electronic communications services.

The first class of case is confined to an agreement for provision of electronic communications services to the occupier from time to time of the land to which the agreement relates. The terms of para.2(3) enable agreements entered into to be binding on anyone having an interest in the land so long as someone who is bound by the agreement (whether because they conferred the right or agreed to be bound by it or because they derive an interest from the person who conferred the right) is in occupation of the land. One point to note about these provisions is that it enables a lessee of a year or more to enter into an agreement which will be binding on a superior interest.[9] This particular type of arrangement does not give rise to the problems that commonly arise in practice and accordingly is not considered further. **16–06**

The position with respect to the second category of case is a follows: **16–07**

(i) An agreement[10] by the freeholder, whether or not an occupier at the time, is binding on any derivative interest (so long as that derivative interest was

---

[7] Special provisions also apply to undertakers' works. An undertaker is a person authorised by Act of Parliament to carry on any railway, tramway, road transport, water transport, canal, inland navigation, dock, harbour, pier or lighthouse undertaking: para.23(10). Again, these provisions are not considered in this Chapter.

[8] Para.2.

[9] A detailed consideration of the terms of para.2(3) are contained in *Clark*.

[10] This also applies where the freeholder is not the grantor but has agreed in writing to be bound. As to whether an agreement is required, if in excess of seven years, to be registered at HM Land Registry, see *Clark*.

created after the right is conferred) or occupier (whose contractual interest derives from someone who is bound) (para.2(4)).

(ii) An agreement[11] by a lessee (of any length), whether or not an occupier at the time, is binding on any derivative interest (so long as that derivative interest was created after the right is conferred) or occupier (whose contractual interest derives from someone who is bound) (para.2(4)).Thus, if one has a lease followed by an overriding lease, and the overriding lessee enters into an agreement with the operator, that agreement is arguably not binding on the lessee (now sub-lessee), as the interest of the lessee does not derive from that of the overriding lessee.

16–08 **Statutory purposes** It is an important qualification to the exercise of rights under the Code that the agreement conferring the right is one conferring rights "for the statutory purposes". The "statutory purposes" are defined as meaning "the purposes of the provision of the operator's network" (para.1).

16–09 **Lease/licence** For the purposes of this Chapter we shall assume that any agreement will constitute a lease falling within security of tenure of the 1954 Act. This Chapter does not consider the question as to whether or not an agreement relating to the provision of facilities for the installation or use of electronic communications apparatus is more likely to be held to be a lease or licence. This important issue will have to be addressed by reference to the relevant facts of each case, applying the principles set out in para.1–03 et seq.

Consent of occupier dispensed with by court: Paragraph 5

16–10 If an operator requires an occupier to agree that any of the Code rights should be conferred on an operator, he may give notice to that effect (para.5(1)). Such a notice may also be given if the operator wants consent given by an occupier to bind holders of other interests in the land. If no agreement has been given after 28 days of service of the notice, the operator can apply to the court for an order conferring the proposed right (para.5(2)). On such an application the court must make an order in the operator's favour; but only if one of two conditions is satisfied. The first is that any prejudice caused by the order is capable of being compensated by money. The second is that any such prejudice is outweighed by the benefit accruing from the order (para.5(3)). In determining the extent of the prejudice and the weight of that benefit "the court shall have regard to all the circumstances and to the principle that no person should unreasonably be denied access to an electronic communications network or to electronic communications services": para.5(3).

16–11 It would seem from the decision of *Leger-Davey v First Secretary of State*[12] that the circumstances to which the court has regard are site specific. In other words

[11] This also applies where the lessee is not the grantor but has agreed in writing to be bound.

[12] [2004] EWCA Civ 1612; [2005] 2 P. & C.R. 86. The consideration of para.5 arose in the context of an appeal against a decision of an inspector, following an inquiry, to grant planning permission to an operator for the erection of a telecommunications mast and equipment cabin. The inspector, in considering the question for planning purposes whether the proposed site was the best location, had

the court cannot refuse to make an order under para.5 because of the existence of a better and more feasible location. Accordingly, the fact that the occupier/owner may be able to point to an alternative site which is more suitable and confers upon users of the network a potentially greater benefit than the proposed site is irrelevant to the Court's determination under para.5(3).

The terms of an order must include terms and conditions to ensure that the least possible loss and damage is caused by the exercise of the right (para.5(5)). In addition the order must include financial terms. The financial terms that the order must include are: **16–12**

(i) Terms for the payment of such consideration as appear to the court would have been fair and reasonable if the agreement had been given willingly; and
(ii) Terms ensuring that persons bound by the right are adequately compensated for loss and damage (para.7(1)).

The payments may be periodical and the court may require their amount to be determined by arbitration (para.7(4)). The court may also determine the persons to whom payments must be made.[13]

Alteration or removal

The Code

The rights The Code contains two rights which entitle the occupier/owner to seek alteration or removal of the apparatus. They are contained in paras 20 and 21. An important point of difference between these two provisions is that the latter applies only where the right to keep the apparatus on the land has come to an end. It is often used in conjunction with reliance upon a s.25 notice under the 1954 Act. **16–13**

considered para.5 of the Code with respect to alternative sites which had been suggested at the inquiry. The inspector had concluded in relation to these alternative sites that because of the objections by the land owners to the use of their land for the installation of the mast, there was no achievable alternative site available. Thus, he had concluded that a county court would have refused an order under para.5 on the ground that the appeal site was more suitable. The appellants argued that this was to misunderstand the nature of the para.5 right. Although the appeal did not succeed for reasons which are not material for present purposes, the Court nevertheless endorsed the criticism which was levelled at the inspector's approach to para.5. It was said that: "the limitations on the power are narrowly confined and do not permit the court to make an environmental appraisal as between sites. The "circumstances" to which the court, under the closing part of the para, shall have regard, are the circumstances relevant to determining the extent of the prejudice and the weight of the benefit of the site to users, as specified in the sub-para. It does not permit the court to conduct that overall assessment of the benefits and disbenefits of land use which is appropriate to the decision of a planning authority."

[13] Where an operator exercises a right under the Code he may be liable to pay compensation for injurious affection to neighbouring land. This is assessed in the same way as compensation for injurious affection under s.10 of the Compulsory Purchase Act 1965 (para.16).

Paragraph 20

16–14 The heading to para.20 is "Power to require alteration of apparatus". That statutory heading is both accurate and misleading. It is accurate in that, unlike para.21, it is not a restriction but an enabling provision. As one commentator has noted, it amplifies rather than restricts the rights of the owner. It is misleading in that "alteration" is not confined to what one would ordinarily consider is an alteration[14]; it includes removal or replacement.[15]

16–15 In summary, para.20 enables any person with an interest in the land on, under or over which the apparatus is installed to serve notice on the operator that the owner requires alteration of the electronic communications apparatus on the ground that it is necessary to enable the owner to carry out a proposed improvement of the land. The operator must serve a counter notice within 28 days from the giving of the para.20 notice in order to secure his rights. If a counter notice is served the alteration can be required only if the court so orders. If no counter notice is served the operator must comply with the notice requiring the alteration to be effected. A number of features of para.20 can be highlighted at this stage before consideration is given to the 1954 Act. In particular:

(i) The power is not exhaustive.
(ii) The power is exercisable notwithstanding the terms of the agreement.
(iii) It may be invoked by "any person with an interest in land or any adjacent land."
(iv) It applies to an alteration of "electronic communications apparatus."
(v) The alteration must be necessary to carry out a proposed improvement of the land.
(vi) The court will only make an order if the statutory criteria are satisfied.
(vii) Costs of removal are payable by the owner not the operator.

Some, but not all, of these matters will be considered in further detail below.

16–16 **Not exhaustive** As para.20 is conferring an additional power to the occupier/owner, it is not intended to be exhaustive of the circumstances in which an alteration to the electronic communications apparatus may be required. It is clear from the terms of para.27(2) that the provisions of the Code, except paras 8(5) and 21, are without prejudice to any rights arising under the agreement. Thus, the power need not be invoked if there exists a contractual entitlement enabling the owner to require the operator to effect an alteration which is an alteration falling short of full removal. If there is a contractual provision providing for a unilateral right requiring the operator to remove the electronic communications apparatus this will not be enforceable because of the restriction contained in para.21 and para.21 is not capable of being excluded by the express terms of the agreement: para.27(2). Removal other than in reliance on para.21 can be required only by relying on para.20 and satisfying the various criteria under it.

---

[14] See, e.g. some form of reconfiguration.
[15] Para.1(2).

Notwithstanding the terms of the agreement Paragraph 20 may be invoked irrespective of what is said in the terms of the agreement. Obviously it may be invoked notwithstanding the absence of a contractual entitlement to require alterations. It would also seem that para.20 would override a contractual prohibition restricting the owner from carrying out alterations. Paragraph 27(3) provides that no compensation is payable to the operator for exercising a Code right other than that provided for by the Code. Thus, if and in so far as the exercise of the Code right is contrary to the terms of the agreement, there would appear to be no contractual entitlement to damages for breach of contract. 16–17

There is no limitation within the terms of para.20 as to when the notice may be served. Is it possible to enforce the order prior to the expiry of a fixed term agreement?[16] Ordinarily the alteration which the occupier/owner wishes to effect is one of removal.[17] Although it is not explicitly so stated in the Code, it may be thought obvious that the person giving the notice cannot enter upon the land demised to the operator until the lease has been terminated. Having said this there seems no reason why the court could not make an order prior to the expiry of the fixed term, and make a further order pursuant to para.20(7) enabling the person giving the notice to enter upon the land himself to remove the apparatus in default of the operator effecting the alteration. Of course in many cases the person giving the notice will want to undertake a whole host of other work (e.g. redevelopment of the demised premises) which it cannot do until termination of the fixed term agreement. Thus an order for removal of the apparatus in isolation would be of little assistance. Furthermore, there is the overriding requirement that the alteration is "necessary" to enable the carrying out of a "proposed improvement of the land" in which the giver of the notice has an interest. Removal would have to be shown to be necessary as at the date of the making of the order and in a case where the fixed term agreement will not expire for several years, it is difficult to see how this requirement could be satisfied. It is for this reason that where the tenancy is one protected by the provisions of Pt II of the 1954 Act the earliest time at which one normally encounters para.20 notices is in the 12 months preceding the contractual expiry date of the lease. 16–18

"Person with an interest in that land or adjacent land" The paragraph may be invoked by a "person with an interest in that land or adjacent land." The reference to an "interest in land" would ordinarily exclude a person who has a mere contractual interest. An "interest in land" would clearly include a freehold or leasehold interest. A specifically enforceable agreement for lease giving rise to a lease in equity would probably also, in the view of the Authors, come within the definition. 16–19

Alteration of apparatus As previously noted, "alteration" includes removal. Electronic communications apparatus is given a wide definition and clearly includes a mast from which apparatus is carried or suspended. Note the paragraph applies only "where any electronic communications apparatus is kept installed 16–20

[16] There is academic debate as to whether a notice served during the currency of a fixed term tenancy is a repudiation of the agreement.

[17] And it will be recalled that "alteration" is defined so as to include "removal". See para.16–14.

on, under or over any land *for the purposes of the operator's network*". Thus, a mast erected under a tenancy agreement, but which is utilised for apparatus serving networks of third party operators but not any network of the tenant, is not, vis-à-vis the tenant, one falling within para.20.

16–21 **Necessary for proposed improvement** A notice may be served only if the removal of the apparatus is "necessary" to enable the person serving the notice to carry out "a proposed improvement of the land in which he has an interest." "Improvement" is defined in para.20(9) as including "development and change of use". A number of matters arise here:

(i) First, the removal of the apparatus per se cannot be said to be a "development" of the land. The alteration is one which is required to be "necessary" to effect the development of the land. In other words it is the existence of the apparatus which would otherwise prevent a development of the land from being undertaken. The apparatus does not by its presence prevent a development of the land if all that is proposed is work to the apparatus itself.
(ii) Secondly, there is no indication within the Code as to how imminent that proposed improvement is required to be in order for a notice to be served and/or an order made. Like many such matters it is probably a question of degree. If there is an immediate requirement to undertake the work this will obviously satisfy the statutory wording. If an improvement is proposed but will not be undertaken for, say, two years the person serving the notice may have greater difficulty.
(iii) Thirdly, it is unclear whether planning permission is needed or its prospects of being obtained are required to be shown. Under the terms of para.(f) of s.30(1) of the 1954 Act it is sufficient that one can show that there is a reasonable prospect of obtaining planning permission.[18] Similarly, if one does not have planning permission nevertheless it may be said, in the context of the Code, that the improvement is "proposed" in the sense that it reflects the desire of the owner. However, it must be implicit that the proposal be a realistic one. If there is no prospect of planning permission then it is difficult to see how a court could find that the improvement is one which is proposed to be carried out.[19]

16–22 **Court conditions** The Code circumscribes the court's power to make an order. It must be shown that:

(i) The alteration is necessary to carry out the improvement to the land.
(ii) The alteration will not substantially interfere with any service which is or is likely to be provided using the operator's network.

[18] See para.7–153.

[19] It may be that "proposed" signifies an intention. The OED defines "propose" as meaning, inter alia, intend, resolve (on), propose (to do). The word "intends" is, of course, used in both grounds (f) and (g) in s.30(1) of the 1954 Act.

(iii) The operator has sufficient rights for making the alteration or would have such rights if an application were made under para.5 and the court were to dispense with the need for the occupier's/owner's agreement.

These criteria have to be considered against the backdrop of two overriding considerations, namely: that the court will have regard to all the circumstances, and the principle that no person should unreasonably be denied access to an electronic communications network or to electronic communications services. As Lewison J. put it in *Geo Networks Ltd v Bridgwater Canal Co Ltd*[20] at first instance:

> "The formulation of the principle ... is not that no person should be denied access to a network. It is that no person shall *unreasonably* be denied access. Necessarily, as it seems to me, formulating the principle in this way entails the conclusion that there may be circumstances in which it is reasonable to deny such access."

An order of the court may, subject to the consent of the applicant, provide for the alteration to be effected with such modifications and on such terms and subject to such conditions as the court thinks fit. If the applicant refuses to agree to any such modification, term or condition the court may refuse to make the order: para.20(7). There is no provision equivalent to that contained in para.21(7)[21] enabling the person serving the notice to seek the court's authorisation for the person serving the notice to remove the apparatus himself. However, in light of para.20(7) it would seem that there is no reason why the court should not be able to provide for a conditional order requiring the work to be undertaken by the operator and, in default, for the work to be undertaken by the owner. **16–23**

Costs of removal One of the principal deterrents to serving a para.20 notice is the requirement in para.20(8) that the person who serves the notice should reimburse the operator "in respect of any expenses which the operator incurs in or in connection with the execution of any works in compliance with the order". Those expenses are to be paid "unless the court otherwise thinks fit". The obligation is to pay "any expenses," and this is ordinarily interpreted as meaning a full indemnity of all of the costs which the operator will incur. There is no express qualification to the effect that such costs must be reasonable. Moreover what is referred to is expenditure incurred "in or in connection with the execution of any works". It seems, therefore, that the common case of requiring removal will only cover the costs of the removal of the apparatus not its installation elsewhere. It would be sensible for any order to provide that upon default not only may the server of the notice effect the work, but, furthermore, recover the costs of so doing. There appears to be no reason why para.20(7) of the Code could not cover this. **16–24**

[20] [2010] 1 W.L.R. 2576.

[21] As to which see para.16–27.

Paragraph 21

16–25 **Person must be entitled to require removal** Paragraph 21 imposes a restriction on the right to require removal of apparatus where any person "is for the time being entitled to require the removal of any of the operator's electronic communications apparatus from any land." The restriction applies whether the right of removal arises under "any enactment or because that apparatus is kept on, under or over that land otherwise than in pursuance of a right binding that person or for any other reason". An entitlement to serve a para.20 notice is not to be treated as an entitlement to enforce the removal of apparatus within the terms of para.21.[22] Thus the restriction on removal provided for by para.21 would arise where:

(i) The contractual term of the agreement (whether a tenancy or a licence) has come to an end.
(ii) The agreement constitutes a sub-lease and the intermediate lease is forfeited or terminated, e.g. by a break clause.[23]
(iii) The agreement constitutes a licence and the interest out of which the licence was created is assigned. As a licence does not create a proprietary interest in land it is not binding on successors of the licensor.[24]
(iv) Removal is sought by a person with title paramount, e.g. where a lessee has conferred the right on the operator but the freehold owner has not agreed to be bound pursuant to para.2(2)(b).
(v) Removal is required by a statutory body, e.g. the apparatus has been installed in breach of planning control and the planning authority is entitled to take enforcement action for its removal.[25]

In order for the occupier/owner to serve the para.21 notice, the entitlement of the operator to keep his apparatus on the land must have come to an end.[26] Some interesting questions arise in this regard where the operator's right to use the land constitutes a tenancy and that tenancy is one protected by the 1954. If the operator's tenancy is continuing by s.24 of the 1954 Act it cannot be said, in the context of para.21, that the owner "is for the time being entitled to require removal of" the operator's apparatus. No entitlement to require removal can be said to exist unless and until the tenant's interest pursuant to which the apparatus

---

22 Para.21(12).

23 The break clause served by the superior landlord upon the intermediate lessee will bring to an end all derivative interests: *Pennell v Payne* [1995] Q.B. 192 CA.

24 *Ashburn Anstalt v Arnold* [1989] Ch. 1 CA.

25 See the terms of the Electronic Communications Code (Conditions and Restrictions) Regulations 2003 (SI 2003/2553) as amended by the Electronic Communications Code (Conditions and Restrictions) Amendment Regulations 2009 (SI 2009/548), reg.5 relating to the requirement to serve notice on the planning authority of an intended installation of electronic communications apparatus.

26 It is to be noted that, notwithstanding the owner's entitlement to seek removal of the apparatus, it would appear that no claim for damages for trespass can be made. So long as the para.21 restriction applies the apparatus is deemed to have been lawfully kept on the land: para.21(9). Thus, for instance, in the case of a fixed term agreement which is not protected by the 1954 Act, service of a counter notice may arguably defer any entitlement to damages to the date of the court order providing for removal.

is situated on, under or over the relevant land has come to, or has been brought to, an end. On the face of it this would appear to be the date of termination provided for by s.64. However, this could cause difficulty in reliance on para.21: see further para.16–37.

The apparatus to be removed The restriction applies to prevent removal of "any of the operator's electronic apparatus" (para.21(1)). However the apparatus which is protected does not have to be vested in the user. It is sufficient that the operator is using electronic communications apparatus, albeit that apparatus may belong to others, so long as it is being used for the purposes of the operator's network: para.21(11). The all important criterion is whether the apparatus is being used for the purposes of the operator's network. Thus, if one has a mast vested in one operator who provides facilities to others and both are using the mast for apparatus in connection with their own networks each will have protection. If the mast owner is simply providing a structure for the carrying or suspension of the apparatus of others and is not utilising the mast in connection with his own network, the mast agreement is not caught by the restriction.[27] **16–26**

Notice procedure As with para.20, para.21 provides for a notice procedure. Any person who is entitled for the time being to require removal of the apparatus may give notice requiring its removal: para.21(2). The operator, in order to protect its rights under the Code, is required to give a counter notice within 28 days of service of the para.21 notice. Failure to serve a counter notice results in the person serving it becoming "entitled to enforce the removal of the apparatus": para.21(3). The owner may, upon default of the service of a counter notice, obtain court authority to remove it himself (para.21(7)) and recover the costs of so doing (para.21(8)). **16–27**

The counter notice served in response to a para.21 notice may: **16–28**

(a) state that the person giving the notice is not entitled to require the removal of the apparatus; and/or
(b) specify the steps which the operator proposes to take for the purpose of securing a right as against the person giving the notice to keep the apparatus on the land. The steps which the operator proposes can include steps for retention pursuant to a right to be acquired pursuant to para.5 (para.21(4)).

If a counter notice is served, removal can be effected only pursuant to an order of the court (para.21(6)). If the counter notice specifies steps that the operator proposes to take to keep the apparatus on the land the court shall not make an order unless it is satisfied either:

(a) that the operator is not intending to take those steps or is being unreasonably dilatory in the taking of those steps; or

[27] Although of course those operators using the mast in connection with their own networks will have the benefit of the restriction.

(b) that the taking of those steps will not secure for the operator as against the giver of the notice, any right to keep the apparatus installed on, under or over the land or as the case may be, to reinstall it if it is removed (para.21(6)).

16–29 **Contractual provision to the contrary** It is provided that the provisions of the Code are without prejudice "to any rights or liabilities arising under any agreement to which the operator is a party": para.27(2). However, this exception does not apply to para.21: para.27(2). Thus, any contractual entitlement to enforce removal which would have the effect of circumventing para.21 is simply ineffective. This is to be contrasted with para.20 where, as noted,[28] there is no prohibition within the Code on a contractual provision for the operator to effect an alteration which does not amount to removal.

16–30 **Costs of removal** As previously noted, under para.20 there is no entitlement for the server of the notice to recover the costs of the alteration. On the contrary, the giver of the notice will be required to pay the costs of the operator in effecting the alteration. In contrast, para.21 does entitle the giver of the notice to recover costs. Expenses incurred by the giver of the notice "in or in connection with the removal of the apparatus shall be recoverable by him from the operator" (para.21(8)). However, it is to be noted that this entitlement to recover costs arises where the apparatus "is removed by any person under any authority given by the court under sub-para.(7) above". The effect of this provision is that expenditure incurred by the giver of the notice is recoverable only where:

(i) there is a default in serving a counter notice, and the giver of the notice seeks and obtains the court's consent for authority to go in and do the work or
(ii) a counter notice is served and an order of the court is made and the order of the court confers authority to go in and remove the apparatus.

Use of paragraph 5 as defence to a paragraph 20 or 21 notice

16–31 There is no reason why an operator cannot seek to invoke paras 2 and 5 in response to either a para.20 or para.21 notice. Often one sees by way of response to such a notice a claim by the operator for an agreement for installation elsewhere on the land of the person serving the notice. Paragraph 5, as noted above,[29] itself requires service of a notice claiming the rights required and an application to the court for the dispensation of the occupier's consent. If the alteration is necessary for the purposes of carrying out the development, it might be difficult to satisfy the court that any prejudice caused by the order would be compensated by money, in which case one would not expect para.5 rights to override the para.20 rights which the occupier/owner is invoking.

16–32 As previously noted, para.21 provides for service of a counter notice and the counter notice can include steps which the operator proposes to take for the

---

[28] See para.16–16.

[29] See para.16–10.

purposes of securing a right to keep the apparatus on, under or over the land. This will reflect the para.5 rights that the operator will seek to acquire. Paragraph 21 specifically provides that that claim to such rights in the counter notice will not prevent a para.21 order being made, if the para.5 rights will "not secure for the operator against the landowner any right to keep the apparatus installed on, under or over the land or, as the case may be, to reinstall it if it is removed". The para.5 claim will not secure such a right if the prejudice cannot be compensated for in money or the benefit to the network or the service does not otherwise override the prejudice.

The 1954 Act

Interrelation with Code

It is difficult, to say the least, to fit the practices and procedures laid down by the Code with the parallel practices and procedures laid down by the 1954 Act. Yet, where both the Code and the 1954 Act apply, both must be accommodated. How can this be done? Are two sets of parallel proceedings necessary[30]? The potential difficulties can be stated (and this is not intended to be an exhaustive list): **16–33**

(i) Protection under the 1954 Act requires occupation for business purposes. Protection with respect to para.20 and 21 notices is dependent not on occupation for business purposes but use of apparatus installed on, under or over land for the purposes of the operator's network. Under the 1954 Act one can have only one occupier of land for business purposes. Under the Code sub-tenants and sub-licensees may all have Code protection in relation to a single piece of apparatus (whether or not owned by them) so long as it is used for their network purposes.

(ii) Notices under the 1954 Act, whether or not opposing renewal, cannot be served earlier than 12 months nor less than six months before the date specified in the notice and cannot be served so as to terminate earlier than the contractual term date. A para.20 notice can theoretically be served at any time. A para.21 notice can be served only after the contractual term date has come to an end.

(iii) Tenants under the 1954 Act do not have to a serve a counter notice in response to a s.25 notice to continue statutory protection. Tenants under the Code must serve a counter notice in a prescribed form in response to paras 20 and 21 notices in order to continue to enjoy rights under the Code.

(iv) Applications for renewal or termination under the 1954 Act must be made before the expiry of the "statutory period."[31] Once a tenant has served an appropriate counter notice to the para.20 or 21 notice there is, subject to

[30] Some commentators have suggested that two sets of proceedings are wholly impractical and could not have been intended. Two different regimes providing for different timing and criteria running in tandem seems very odd to say the least.

[31] s.29A of the 1954 Act. See para.6–17 et seq.

para.24A,[32] no time limit in the Code for the making of an application by the owner for an order under para.20 or 21.

(v) Opposition to renewal under the 1954 Act may be based only upon the statutory grounds, which include both tenant default or non-default grounds. Under the Code, the landowner can seek removal on only one of two grounds: development of the land on which the apparatus is situated necessitating the alteration of the apparatus, or the coming to an end of the lease pursuant to which the apparatus is situated on, under or over the land.[33]

(vi) Rent on renewal under the 1954 Act is determined by reference to a letting in the open market disregarding improvements (s.34 of the 1954 Act). A determination of the sum to be paid pursuant to an order of the court made under para.5 is such sum as is "fair and reasonable" assuming the parties had entered into the agreement willing (para.7(1)). This expression does not necessarily equate to a market rent.

(vii) Where the landlord successfully opposes renewal under the 1954 Act on one of the relevant grounds giving rise to the payment of compensation, the compensation is payable only by the landlord and is calculated by reference to the rateable value of "the holding". Under the Code, where the landowner successfully obtains an order requiring the removal of apparatus, compensation may be payable by either the landlord or the tenant and is calculated by reference to the cost of removal of the apparatus.

Interrelation with paragraph 20

16–34 Paragraph 20 of the Code is concerned with carrying out development. So is s.30(1)(f). That section entitles the landlord to oppose renewal if on the termination of the current tenancy he intends to carry out work of demolition reconstruction or construction. Although the statutory criteria are different, there seems little difficulty in combining a para.20 notice with a notice under s.25 of the 1954 Act.[34] A s.25 notice opposing renewal under s.30(1)(f) is often regarded in practice as a para.20 notice and invariably one sees counter notices under the Code being served in response.

16–35 There is no reason why a para.20 notice cannot be served in advance of the date upon which the current tenancy would otherwise come to an end in accordance with the provisions of the 1954 Act. Ordinarily, one would seek to combine service of a para.20 notice with the service of the s.25 notice. There are, as is well known, restrictions on the of s.25 notices, namely, that they are to be served not less than six months and not more than 12 months prior to the date of termination specified in the notice.[35] There is nothing within para.20 restricting the date at which a para.20 notice may be served other than, of course, the practical fact that

[32] As to para.24A, see para.16–41.

[33] These grounds would also appear to be mutually exclusive for para.20 assumes the continuing existence of an entitlement for the apparatus to be on, under or over the land.

[34] Or of course a counter notice in response to a s.26 request. What is said in the text applies equally to a counter notice to a s.26 request.

[35] See para.3–176 et seq.

the server may be unable to enforce the alteration (by reason of the inability to bring to an end the termination of the operator's interest in the land).[36] However, if it so happens that the para.20 proceedings are heard prior to the 1954 Act proceedings, there is no reason why the court cannot seek to provide, as a term of any order under the Code, that the alteration is to be effected upon, and subject to the determination of, the operator's tenancy under the provisions of the 1954 Act.

Ground (f) of section 30(1)

The interrelation of para.20 and s.30(1)(f) of the 1954 Act remains to be considered by the courts. A number of points of interest may be noted: **16–36**

(i) Under para.20 the relevant alteration must be "necessary" to enable the development to be undertaken. Under para.(f) of s.30(1) the landlord has to establish a firm and settled intention to carry out work which falls within one of the relevant grounds within para.(f). One might expect the court to direct that proceedings under para.20 and s.30(1)(f) (e.g. a termination application) be heard at the same time. But the tests are materially different. "Development" under the Code includes a change of use. A change of use may not involve any work which would otherwise fall within para.(f) but would be work which is necessary in order to enable the development to be effected, e.g. where the planning permission permitting the change of use imposed a condition for the removal of the apparatus. A court hearing both applications together would have to distinguish carefully between these two tests.

(ii) Under the 1954 Act it is "the landlord" within s.44 who must intend to do the work.[37] The landlord can intend, for instance, to do that work via a third party, e.g. by intending to grant a building lease. However, under the Code the alteration must be one to enable the person having an interest in the land to which the improvement is proposed to carry out the improvement. In *Durley House Ltd v Cadogan*[38] Neuberger J. held that, in order for the tenant to show that he had "carried out" works of improvement under the disregard of improvements contained in s.34(2) of the 1954 Act, it was probably necessary to show more than that he merely arranged for them to be done. He said that a tenant may well not satisfy s.34(2) in a case where he has arranged a third party to do the works unless he can establish some involvement in identifying supervising and/or financing the works resulting in the specific improvements concerned.[39]

---

[36] It may also give rise to a difficulty in establishing that the alteration "is necessary" in order to carry out the proposed development.

[37] As to the meaning of "landlord" within s.44 see para.3–87.

[38] [2000] 1 W.L.R. 246 Ch D.

[39] He said:

"Given that it is common ground that the tenant need not physically have done the works himself, and given the statutory language, it appears to me that, in the absence of good reason being shown to the contrary, the tenant will, at least normally, satisfy the statutory requirement if he can establish that he either physically did the specific works himself, or got a third party to do so. The tenant will usually satisfy that test if he could show that he had entered into an arrangement with a third party (which arrangement will typically be, but need not necessarily be, a contract) under which that party

(iii) Under the 1954 Act the landlord has to show that he requires possession to effect the intended work.[40] There is no requirement under the Code for the occupier/owner to show that he needs possession to do the work. It is sufficient that he shows that the alteration is necessary to enable an improvement to the land to be carried out. Thus it is conceivable that a case falling within the terms of para.20 of the Code may fail under the 1954 Act by reason of the terms of s.31A of the 1954 Act.[41]

(iv) Does para.21 need to be complied with where the court has made an order under para.20 and the landlord has also obtained an order terminating the tenant's rights (in reliance on s.30(1)(f)) under the 1954 Act? The landlord under the 1954 Act in opposing renewal is essentially seeking possession. The restriction on the right to require the removal of apparatus is dealt with by para.21. This would, on its face, suggest that the landlord would have to await the termination of the operator's leasehold interest under the 1954 Act and then serve a para.21 notice upon the coming to an end of the tenant's lease. That seems extremely cumbersome and there does not appear to any reason why the court cannot make an order under para.20 prior to any 1954 Act proceedings or at the same time as any 1954 Act proceedings without the landlord then having to invoke the provisions of para.21. If the court is minded to make a para.20 order requiring removal the landlord need not go on, additionally, to serve a para.21 notice upon the coming to an end of the tenant's interest under the 1954 Act. It is to be noted that para.21(1) provides that subject to the terms of para.21 the occupier/owner "shall not be entitled to force the removal of the apparatus except, subject to sub-para.(12) below, in accordance with" the provisions of para.21. Paragraph 21(12) provides that the provisions of para.21 are "without prejudice ... to the power to enforce an order of the court under the said para ... 20". It is true that the owner cannot *serve* a para.21 notice simply because he is in a position to serve *a para.20 notice* (para.21(12)). However, if he has obtained his para.20 *order* he is entitled to enforce that irrespective of the terms of para.21: para.21(2).

Interrelation with paragraph 21

16–37 There is much debate by commentators upon the interrelationship between the Code and the 1954 Act about the difficulty that landlord faces in seeking to oppose renewal under s.30(1)(f) (or (g)) because of the stipulation in para.21 that no notice for removal can be served until the person giving the notice is "*entitled*"

---

agreed with the tenant to do the specific works involved in effecting the improvements. Once it is accepted, as it plainly must be, that an arrangement under which the tenant gets a building contractor to do the works would not take the tenant out of the ambit of section 34(2) in a particular case, I do not find it easy to see at what point, or on what logical basis, it could be said that any arrangement with a third party under which the tenant gets that third party to do the works would take the tenant out of the section ... However, it seems to me that it would be right to add this. A tenant may well not satisfy section 34(2) in a case where he has got a third party to do the works unless he can establish some involvement in identifying supervising and/or financing the works resulting in the specific improvements concerned." at 250–252.

[40] See para.7–102.

[41] As to which see para.7–192 et seq.

to do so. He will not be entitled to do so until the operator's legal rights have come to an end. However, if the tenant makes an application to the court for renewal, there remains a legally binding right imposed upon the owner which prevents him from serving a para.21 notice, namely the continuation tenancy under the 1954 Act. Thus, the landlord is caught either way. He cannot serve a para.21 notice because the tenant remains entitled to keep the apparatus on the land by reason of the continuation of the tenancy under the 1954 Act. Equally, he cannot bring the tenancy to an end because he cannot serve a para.21 notice so is unable to show, for the purposes of the 1954 Act, an intention capable of being implemented within a reasonable time of termination of the current tenancy.

It has been suggested that one possible way of overcoming this absurdity would be to provide for a broad construction of the reference to "entitled" in para.21; according to this suggestion, the owner is "entitled" to require removal if he is entitled to serve a s.25 notice under the 1954 Act which will have the effect, eventually, of requiring the operator to remove the apparatus. However, as those commentators note, the s.25 notice is not per se a right to require removal, but a right to have the question of whether the tenant's 1954 Act continuation rights should be brought to an end determined. However one seeks to accommodate para.21 with the 1954 Act one will be required to strain the language of the Code to achieve a "fit". It seems to the authors that the difficulty, at least in relation to s.30(1)(f) of the 1954 Act, can be overcome by concentrating not on para.21 but upon para.20. As noted, once one has obtained an order under para.20, it may be enforced irrespective of the terms of para.21.[42] **16–38**

Ground (g) of section 30(1)

How does the Code interact with para.(g) of s.30(1) 1954, i.e. where the owner seeks possession on the basis of own occupation? The Code does not expressly provide for this, but the landlord may combine his proposal for own occupation with a proposal for development and may seek to take advantage of para.20. However, "development" requires more than simply a proposal to remove the electronic communications apparatus[43] and it is considered that a landlord will have certain difficulties in relying on s.30(1)(g) (quite apart from the difficulty over serving a para.21 notice until the entitlement for the apparatus to be on the land has come to an end[44]). The following appear to the authors to be potential difficulties: **16–39**

(i) First, one must consider what it is the owner is seeking to occupy. If, for example, he proposes himself to utilise the apparatus consisting of a mast situated on top his building for his own network he may not in fact be able to establish an intention to occupy "the holding". The "holding" is confined

[42] See para.16–36(iv). Para.20 is, of course, not as advantageous as para.21 so far as the question of costs is concerned. The costs of removal are to be borne by the landowner: para.20(8). This is subject to a court order to the contrary ("unless the court otherwise thinks fit"). The landowner will, therefore, end up having to pay (i) statutory compensation under s.37 of the 1954 Act and (ii) costs of removal.

[43] See para.16–21 above.

[44] As to which see para.16–37.

to property comprised in the tenancy. Electronic communications apparatus may, and probably would in the case of a mast affixed to a structure, constitute fixtures.[45] The general rule is that which constitutes a fixture becomes part of the realty: *Melluish v BMI (No.3) Ltd*.[46] However, para.27(4) provides that "the ownership of any property shall not be affected by the fact that it is installed on or under, or affixed to, any land by any person in exercise of a right conferred by it or in accordance with this Code". Thus if and insofar as the right for the apparatus to be on the land has arisen pursuant to a Code power, the effect of this provision may be that for all purposes (and not merely for the purposes of the Code) the normal rule relating to fixtures is displaced. This may mean that the apparatus is not part of the "holding" for 1954 Act purposes.[47]

(ii) The same result may be supported by a rather different argument. In so far as the owner proposes to use the operator's apparatus affixed to the land, the apparatus is likely to constitute a tenant's fixture and thus by analogy to *Wessex Reserve Forces and Cadets Association v White*[48] the equipment may be assumed to have been removed at the end of the term and thus not constitute part of "the holding" capable of being occupied.

(iii) But what if the demised premises consist of say the roof on top of which the operator had installed his apparatus? Even if the landlord cannot show an intention with respect to the apparatus itself surely he can show an intention to occupy a site by, e.g. by installing his own apparatus for his own network? However, even here the position is not clear cut. Unlike s.23(1) of the 1954 Act, a further requirement of ground (g) is that the business must be carried on "therein", by which is meant that it must be carried on in the holding.[49] The owner's network business is, arguably, not itself being carried on from the roof top.

Occupation

16–40 The apparatus (and the land on, under or over which it is installed) may be shared. Only one person can be in occupation of the same holding for business purposes so as to give rise to 1954 Act protection: *Graysim Holdings Ltd v P&O Property Ltd*.[50] Thus, where there is a sharing of networks who is in occupation of the relevant site? The question of occupation was considered in *Arqiva Ltd v*

[45] What constitutes a fixture depends on a number of factors. The two most important factors seem to be the manner in which the article in question has been annexed and the purpose of annexation.

[46] [1996] A.C. 454 HL.

[47] See para.7–92.

[48] [2006] 1 E.G.L.R. 56 CA. Where it was held that in considering the extent to which the landlord could succeed under ground (f), the court was to assume that the tenant would remove its chattels and fixtures upon termination of the tenancy, and thus any work which was to be undertaken to those elements was to be ignored in determining what work was being undertaken to "the holding" and thus to be ignored in assessing the landlord's prospects of success under ground (f). The landlord in that case could not establish it was going to demolish the buildings in question, for the buildings had to be assumed not to be there at the end of the term. See also para.7–111.

[49] See para.7–246.

[50] [1996] A.C. 329 HL. See para.1–66.

Everything Everywhere Ltd[51] but not in the context of the 1954 Act but rather in the context of whether or not new contractual rights had arisen upon the expiry of a fixed term agreement. The judge considered that roaming[52] did not give rise to a change in occupier of the site.[53] If this is right only the tenant (not the sharer) will have 1954 Act protection.

Paragraph 24A of the Code

The Electronic Communications and Wireless Telegraphy Regulations 2011 (SI 2011/1210), which came into force on May 26, 2011, make provision for a limitation on time in dealing with applications to install facilities. This would appear to apply to all applications, including a request to confer rights under para.2.[54] Regulation 2 and para.1 of Sch.1 to the regulations insert into the Code an entirely new provision, namely para.24A. This provides that: **16–41**

---

[51] [2011] EWHC 1411 TCC. The matter before the court arose out of the joint venture arrangement between T-Mobile (now Everything Everywhere) and Orange. Arqiva provided sites for use by Orange and T-Mobile. Those companies wished to roam over each other's networks which involved the sending, receipt and automatic changeover of signals by Everything Everywhere and Orange on each other's frequencies and equipment throughout the duration of a call and for internet access. There was no sharing of frequencies; each network operator still operated its own frequencies within the radio spectrum. In all cases it was the customer's handset that changed automatically the radio frequencies when switching between the networks. This arrangement was held to give rise to breaches of a whole host of covenants which had been entered into with Arqiva under various agreements.

[52] Roaming does not involve any physical access to a site or structure, e.g. a mast being operated by the tenant. It essentially involves a reconfiguration of network software and equipment. Seamless roaming allows a call to be uninterrupted as a customer moves between cells of two networks of two different network operators. Roaming occurs in very familiar everyday situations, e.g. by using a mobile phone abroad, where the network operator will have entered into an agreement with the operator of another network to permit that to happen, and the making of emergency calls in areas where customers to do not have access to their own operator's network. Thus, roaming involves the process of a customer of one network operator accessing the network and frequency of another operator of which it is not a customer.

[53] It is not clear how the judge reached this conclusion having already held that the roaming gave rise to a breach of a clause, cl.2.1.1(d), which permitted "the Client to share use of such part or parts of the Station(s) and such of the BBC's accommodation and equipment therein in common with others including the BBC, as the BBC may from time to time approve (such approval not to be unreasonably withheld or delayed);" The judge said:

"Clause 2.1.1(d) sets out the use which OPCS is permitted to make of Arqiva's Station, accommodation and equipment. It permits OPCS 'to share use . . . in common with others including the BBC, as the BBC may from time to time approve (such approval not to be unreasonably withheld or delayed).' By allowing roaming OPCS are allowing the voice and data traffic of EE's T-Mobile brand customers to use the OPCS equipment which is located at the Station. There is therefore shared use of the 'Client's Equipment' which is installed at the Station and is, in turn, making use of part of the Station, accommodation and equipment. This shared use of the 'Client's Equipment' is also shared use of the Station, accommodation and equipment." at [143].

It would seem that the distinction is that Orange remained in occupation and their occupation had not ceased but for the purposes of cl.2.1.1(d) they were to be treated as sharing such occupation without first obtaining consent.

[54] The Department for Culture Media and Sport, in their document entitled "*Implementing the Revised EU Electronic Communications Framework*", April 2011, (HMG response to consultation) indicate that the time limit runs from the point at which the decision-maker has received the information it requires to make a decision based on that information: para.45. That reg.3 is an aspiration for dealing with applications is apparent from its application to the time within which it is expected that County Courts will provide determinations under para.5. In the Department for Business

"Regulation 3 of the Electronic Communications and Wireless Telegraphy Regulation 2011 makes provision about the time within which certain applications under this code for the granting of rights to install facilities must be determined."

Regulation 3 of the 2011 regulations provides:

"6 month period for deciding application to install facilities
(1) This regulation applies where—
(a) a person authorised to provide public electronic communications networks applies to a competent authority for the granting of rights to install facilities on, over or under public or private property for the purposes of such a network,
(b) a person authorised to provide electronic communications networks other than to the public applies to a competent authority for the granting of rights to install facilities on, over or under public property for the purposes of such a network, or
(c) a person applies to OFCOM for a direction applying the electronic communications code in the person's case.
(2) Except in cases of expropriation, the competent authority must make its decision within 6 months of receiving the completed application.
(3) In this regulation 'public electronic communications network', 'electronic communications network' and 'OFCOM' have the same meanings as in Chapter 1 of Part 2 of the Communications Act 2003."

There is no definition within the regulations as to "competent authority" but there is no reason to suppose that it will not cover the Crown.

16–42 If and in so far as this six-month limit applies it is unclear what are the consequences, if any, of a failure to deal with the application within the prescribed time. It may be that a claim for damages for breach of statutory duty arises. Alternatively, the operator would have to seek an injunction requiring the competent authority to comply with the statutory obligation.

Innovation and Skills document of September 2011 it was said that such a timescale within the context of applicants seeking appropriate court orders was "challenging . . . but one which we will work with the Ministry of Justice and the courts to meet": see para.77.

The relevant part of the Framework Directive 2002/21/EC (common regulatory framework for electronic communications networks and services) (as amended by Directive 2009/140/EC) provides:

"Article 11

Rights of Way

1. Member States shall ensure that when a competent authority considers an application for the granting of rights to install facilities on, over or under public or private property to an undertaking authorised to provide public communications networks or an application for the granting of rights to install facilities on, over or under public property to an undertaking authorised to provide electronic communications networks other than to the public, the competent authority acts on the basis of simple, efficient, transparent and publicly available procedures, applied without discrimination and without delay and in any event makes its decision within six months of the application, except in cases of expropriation."

APPENDICES

Appendix 1
Statutes

Appendix 2
Statutory Regulations

APPENDIX I

STATUTES

Landlord and Tenant Act, 1927 A1.001

(17 & 18 GEO. 5. C. 36)[1]

An act to provide for the payment of compensation for improvements and goodwill to tenants of premises used for business purposes, or the grant of a new lease in lieu thereof, and to amend the law of landlord and tenant.

[22ND DECEMBER, 1927]

PART I

COMPENSATION FOR IMPROVEMENTS AND GOODWILL ON THE TERMINATION OF TENANCIES OF BUSINESS PREMISES

Tenant's right to compensation for improvements A1.002

1.—(1) Subject to the provisions of this Part of this Act, a tenant of a holding to which this Part of this Act applies shall, if a claim for the purpose is made in the prescribed manner and within the time limited by section 47 of the Landlord and Tenant Act, 1954, be entitled, at the termination of the tenancy, on quitting his holding, to be paid by his landlord compensation in respect of any improvement (including the erection of any building) on his holding made by him or his predecessors in title, not being a trade or other fixture which the tenant is by law entitled to remove, which at the termination of the tenancy adds to the letting value of the holding:

Provided that the sum to be paid as compensation for any improvements shall not exceed—

(a) the net addition to the value of the holding as a whole which may be determined to be the direct result of the improvement; or

[1] Printed as amended by the Landlord and Tenant Act, 1954, the Crown Estates Act 1961, the Statute Law Revision Act 1950, the Charities Act 1960, the Endowments and Glebe Measure 1976 (No. 4), the Rent Act 1977, Housing Act 1980, Agricultural Holdings Act 1986, Gas Act 1986, Water Act 1989, Electricity Act 1989.

For adaptations of this Act in respect of servicemen, see the Reserve and Auxiliary Forces (Protection of Civil interests) Act, 1951 (14 & 15 Geo. 6. c. 65). s.33.

(b) the reasonable cost of carrying out the improvement at the termination of the tenancy, subject to a deduction of an amount equal to the cost (if any) of putting the works constituting the improvement into a reasonable state of repair, except so far as such cost is covered by the liability of the tenant under any covenant or agreement as to the repair of the premises.

(2) In determining the amount of such net addition as aforesaid, regard shall be had to the purposes for which it is intended that the premises shall be used after the termination of the tenancy, and if it is shown that it is intended to demolish or to make structural alterations in the premises or any part thereof or to use the premises for a different purpose, regard shall be had to the effect of such demolition, alteration or change of user in the additional value attributable to the improvement, and to the length of time likely to elapse between the termination of the tenancy and the demolition, alteration or change of user.

(3) In the absence of agreement between the parties, all questions as to the right to compensation under this section, or as to the amount thereof, shall be determined by the tribunal hereinafter mentioned, and if the tribunal determines that, on account of the intention to demolish or alter or to change the user of the premises, no compensation or a reduced amount of compensation shall be paid, the tribunal may authorise a further application for compensation to be made by the tenant if effect is not given to the intention within such time as may be fixed by the tribunal.

A1.003 **Limitation on tenant's right to compensation in certain cases**

2.—(1) A tenant shall not be entitled to compensation under this Part of this Act—

(a) in respect of any improvement made before the commencement of this Act; or

(b) in respect of any improvement made in pursuance of a statutory obligation, or of any improvement which the tenant or his predecessors in title were under an obligation to make in pursuance of a contract entered into, whether before or after the passing of this Act, for valuable consideration, including a building lease[2]; or

(c) in respect of any improvement made less than three years before the termination of the tenancy[2]; or

(d) if within two months after making of the claim under section one, subsection (1), of this Act the landlord serves on the tenant notice that he is willing and able to grant to the tenant, or obtain the grant to him of, a renewal of the tenancy at such rent and for such term as, failing agreement, the tribunal may consider reasonable; and, where such a notice is so served and the tenant does not within one month from the service of the notice send to the landlord an acceptance in writing of the offer, the tenant shall be deemed to have declined the offer.[2]

(2) Where an offer of the renewal of a tenancy by the landlord under this section is accepted by the tenant, the rent fixed by the tribunal shall be the rent which in the opinion of the tribunal a willing lessee or other than the tenant would agree to give and a willing lessor would agree to accept for the premises,

[2] See the Landlord and Tenant Act, 1954, s.48, *post*.

having regard to the terms of the lease, but irrespective of the value attributable to the improvement in respect of which compensation would have been payable.

(3) The tribunal in determining the compensation for an improvement shall in reduction of the tenant's claim take into consideration any benefits which the tenant or his predecessors in title may have received from the landlord or his predecessors in title in consideration expressly or impliedly of the improvement.

Landlord's right to object **A1.004**

3.—(1) Where a tenant of a holding to which this Part of this Act applies proposes to make an improvement on his holding, he shall serve on his landlord notice of his intention to make such improvement, together with a specification and plan showing the proposed improvement and the part of the existing premises affected thereby, and if the landlord within three months after the service of the notice, serves on the tenant notice of objection, the tenant may, in the prescribed manner, apply to the tribunal, and the tribunal may, after ascertaining that notice of such intention has been served upon any superior landlords interested and after giving such persons an opportunity of being heard, if satisfied that the improvement—

(a) is of such a nature as to be calculated to add to the letting value of the holding at the termination of that tenancy; and

(b) is reasonable and suitable to the character thereof; and

(c) will not diminish the value of any other property belonging to the same landlord, or to any superior landlord whom the immediate landlord of the tenant directly or indirectly holds;

and after making such modifications (if any) in the specification or plan as the tribunal thinks fit, or imposing such other conditions as the tribunal may think reasonable, certify in the prescribed manner that the improvement is a proper improvement:

Provided that, if the landlord proves that he has offered to execute the improvement himself in consideration of a reasonable increase in rent, or of such increase of rent as the tribunal may determine, the tribunal shall not give a certificate under this section unless it is subsequently shown to the satisfaction of the tribunal that the landlord has failed to carry out his undertaking.

(2) In considering whether the improvement is reasonable and suitable to the character of the holding, the tribunal shall have regard to any evidence brought before it by the landlord or any superior landlord (but not any other person) that the improvement is calculated to injure the amenity or convenience of the neighbourhood.

(3) The tenant shall, at the request of any superior landlord or at the request of the tribunal, supply such copies of the plans and specifications of the proposed improvement as may be required.

(4) Where no such notice of objection as aforesaid to a proposed improvement has been served within the time allowed by this section, or where the tribunal has certified an improvement to be a proper improvement, it shall be lawful for the tenant as against the immediate and any superior landlord to execute the improvement according to the plan and specification served on the landlord, or according to such plan and specification as modified by the tribunal or by agreement between the tenant and the landlord or landlords affected, anything in any lease of the premises to the contrary notwithstanding:

Provided that nothing in this subsection shall authorise a tenant to execute an improvement in contravention of any restriction created or imposed—

(a) for naval, military or air force purposes;

(b) for civil aviation purposes under the powers of the Air Navigation Act, 1920;

(c) for securing any rights of the public over the foreshore or bed of the sea.

(5) A tenant shall not be entitled to claim compensation under this Part of this Act in respect of any improvement unless he has, or his predecessors in title have, served notice of the proposal to make the improvement under this section, and (in case the landlord has served notice of objection thereto) the improvement has been certified by the tribunal to be a proper improvement and the tenant has complied with the conditions, if any, imposed by the tribunal, nor unless the improvement is completed within such time after the service on the landlord of the notice of the proposed improvement as may be agreed between the tenant and the landlord or may be fixed by the tribunal, and where proceedings have been taken before the tribunal, the tribunal may defer making any order as to costs until the expiration of the time so fixed for the completion of the improvement.

(6) Where a tenant has executed an improvement of which he has served notice in accordance with this section and with respect to which either no notice of objection has been served by the landlord or a certificate that it is a proper improvement has been obtained from the tribunal, the tenant may require the landlord to furnish to him a certificate that the improvement has been duly executed; and if the landlord refuses or fails within one month after the service of the requisition to do so, the tenant may apply to the tribunal who, if satisfied that the improvement has been duly executed, shall give a certificate to that effect.

Where the landlord furnishes such a certificate, the tenant shall be liable to pay any reasonable expenses incurred for the purpose by the landlord, and if any question arises as to the reasonableness of such expenses, it shall be determined by the tribunal.

4–7. [*Repealed by the Landlord & Tenant Act 1954, s.45, Sched. 7.*]

A1.005 **Rights of mesne landlords**

8.—Where, in the case of any holding, there are several persons standing in the relation to each other of lessor and lessee, the following provisions shall apply:

Any mesne landlord who has paid or is liable to pay compensation under this Part of this Act shall, at the end of his term, be entitled to compensation from his immediate landlord in like manner and on the same conditions as if he had himself made the improvement [. . .][3] in question, except that it shall be sufficient if the claim for compensation is made at least two months before the expiration of his term:

A mesne landlord shall not be entitled to make a claim under this section unless he has, within the time and in the manner prescribed, served on his immediate superior landlord copies of all documents relating to proposed improvements and claims which have been sent to him in pursuance of this Part of this Act:

[3] The words omitted were repealed by the Landlord and Tenant Act 1954, ss.45 and 68(1) and Sched. 7.

Where such copies are so served, the said superior landlord shall have, in addition to the mesne landlord, the powers conferred by or in pursuance of this Part of this Act in like manner as if he were the immediate landlord of the occupying tenant, and shall, in the manner and to the extent prescribed, be at liberty to appear before the tribunal and shall be bound by the proceedings.

(2) In this section, references to a landlord shall include references to his predecessors in title.

Restriction on contracting out A1.006

9. This Part of this Act shall apply notwithstanding any contract to the contrary, being a contract made at any time after the eighth day of February, nineteen hundred and twenty-seven:

Provided that, if on the hearing of a claim or application under this Part of the Act it appears to the tribunal that a contract made after such date as aforesaid, so far as it deprives any person of any right under this Part of this Act, was made for adequate consideration, the tribunal shall in determining the matter give effect thereto.[4]

Right of entry A1.007

10. The landlord of a holding to which this Part of this Act applies, or any person authorised by him, may at all reasonable times enter on the holding or any part of it, for the purpose of executing any improvement he has undertaken to execute and of making any inspection of the premises which may reasonably be required for the purposes of this Part of this Act.

Right to make deductions A1.008

11.—(1) Out of any money payable to a tenant by way of compensation under this Part of this Act, the landlord shall be entitled to deduct any sum due to him from the tenant under or in respect of the tenancy.

(2) Out of any money due to the landlord from the tenant under or in respect of the tenancy, the tenants shall be entitled to deduct any sum payable to him by the landlord by way of compensation under this Part of this Act.

Application of 13 & 14 Geo. 5, c. 9, s. 20 A1.009

12. Section twenty of the Agricultural Holdings Act, 1923 (which relates to charges in respect of money paid for compensation), as set out and modified in the First Schedule to this Act, shall apply to the case of money paid for compensation under this Part of this Act, including any proper costs, charges, or expenses incurred by a landlord in opposing any proposal by a tenant to execute an improvement, or in contesting a claim for compensation, and to money expended by a landlord in executing an improvement the notice of a proposal to execute which has been served on him by a tenant under this Part of this Act.

[4] See the Landlord & Tenant Act 1954, s.49.

A1.010 Power to apply and raise capital money

13.—(1) Capital money arising under the Settled Land Act, 1925 [. . .][5] or under the University and College Estates Act, 1925, may be applied—

(a) in payment as for an improvement authorised by the Act of any money expended and costs incurred by a landlord under or in pursuance of this Part of this Act in or about the execution of any improvement;

(b) in payment of any sum due to a tenant under this Part of this Act in respect of compensation for an improvement, and any costs, charges, and expenses incidental thereto;

(c) in payment of the costs, charges, and expenses of opposing any proposal by a tenant to execute an improvement.

(2) The satisfaction of a claim for such compensation as aforesaid shall be included amongst the purposes for which a tenant for life, statutory owner, [. . .][6] may raise money under section seventy-one of the Settled Land Act, 1925.

(3) Where the landlord liable to pay compensation for an improvement [. . .][7] is a tenant for life or in a fiduciary position, he may require the sum payable as compensation and any costs, charges, and expenses incidental thereto, to be paid out of any capital money held on the same trusts as the settled land.

In this subsection "capital money" includes any personal estate held on the same trusts as the land [. . .][8]

A1.011 Power to sell or grant leases notwithstanding restrictions

14. Where the powers of a landlord to sell or grant leases are subject to any statutory or other restrictions, he shall, notwithstanding any such restrictions or any rule of law to the contrary, be entitled to offer to sell or grant any such reversion or lease as would under this Part of this Act relieve him from liability to pay compensation thereunder, and to convey and grant the same, and to execute any lease which he may be ordered to grant under this Part of this Act.

A1.012 Provisions as to reversionary leases

15.—(1) Where the amount which a landlord is liable to pay as compensation for an improvement under this Part of this Act has been determined by agreement or by an award of the tribunal, and the landlord had before the passing of this Act granted or agreed to grant a reversionary lease commencing on or after the termination of the then existing tenancy, the rent payable under the reversionary lease shall, if the tribunal so directs, be increased by such amount as, failing agreement, may be determined by the tribunal having regard to the addition to the letting value of the holding attributable to the improvement:

Provided that no such increase shall be permissible unless the landlord has served or caused to be served on the reversionary lessee copies of all

[5] The words omitted were repealed by the Trusts of Land and Appointment of Trustees Act 1996, Sched. 4.

[6] *ibid.*

[7] The words omitted were repealed by the Landlord and Tenant Act 1954, s.45 and Sched. 7, Pt I.

[8] The words omitted were repealed by the Trusts of Land and Appointment of Trustees Act 1996, Sched. 4.

documents relating to the improvement when proposed which were sent to the landlord in pursuance of this Part of this Act.

(2) The reversionary lessee shall have the same right of objection to the proposed improvement and of appearing and being heard at any proceedings before the tribunal relative to the proposed improvement as if he were a superior landlord, and if the amount of compensation for the improvement is determined by the tribunal, any question as to the increase of rent under the reversionary lease shall, where practicable, be settled in the course of the same proceedings.

[*Subs. (3) repealed: Landlord & Tenant Act 1954, s.45, Sched.7.*]

Landlord's right to reimbursement of increased taxes, rates or insurance premiums A1.013

16. Where the landlord is liable to pay any [. . .][9] rates (including water rate) in respect of any premises comprised in a holding or has undertaken to pay the premiums on any fire insurance policy on any such premises, and in consequence of any improvements executed by the tenant on the premises under this Act the assessment of the premises or the rate of premium on the policy is increased, the tenant shall be liable to pay to the landlord sums equal to the amount by which—

(a) the [. . .][10] rates payable by the landlord are increased by reason of the increase of such assessment;

(b) the fire premium payable by the landlord is increased by reason of the increase in the rate of premium;

and the sums so payable by the tenant shall be deemed to be in the nature of rent and shall be recovered as such from the tenant [. . .][11]

Holdings to which Part I applies A1.014

17.—(1) The holdings to which this Part of this Act applies are any premises held under a lease, other than a mining lease, made whether before or after the commencement of this Act, and used wholly or partly for carrying on thereat any trade or business [not being—

(a) agricultural holdings within the meaning of the Agricultural Holdings Act 1986 held under leases in relation to which that Act applies, or

(b) holdings held under farm business tenancies within the meaning of the Agricultural Tenancies Act 1995].[12]

(2) This Part of this Act shall not apply to any holding let to a tenant as the holder of any office, appointment or employment, from the landlord, and continuing so long as the tenant holds such office, appointment or employment, but in the case of a tenancy created after the commencement of this Act, only if the contract is in writing and expresses the purpose for which the tenancy is created.

(3) For the purposes of this section, premises shall not be deemed to be premises used for carrying on thereat a trade or business—

(a) by reason of their being used for the purpose of carrying on thereat any profession;

[9] The words omitted were repealed by the Finance Act 1963, s.73(7) and Sched. 13, Pt IV.

[10] *ibid.*

[11] The words omitted were repealed by the Housing Act 1980, s.152 and Sched. 26.

[12] Substituted by Agricultural Tenancies Act 1995 (c. 8), Sched.

(b) by reason that the tenant thereof carries on the business of subletting the premises as residential flats, whether or not the provision of meals or any other service for the occupants of the flats is undertaken by the tenant:

Provided that, so far as this Part of this Act relates to improvements, premises regularly used for carrying on a profession shall be deemed to be premises used for carrying on a trade or business.

(4) In the case of premises used partly for purposes of a trade or business and partly for other purposes, this Part of this Act shall apply to improvements only if and so far as they are improvements in relation to the trade or business.

PART III

GENERAL

A1.015 The tribunal

21.—The tribunal for the purposes of Part I of this Act shall be the court exercising jurisdiction in accordance with the provisions of section sixty-three of the Landlord and Tenant Act, 1954.[13]

22. [*Repealed by the Landlord & Tenant Act 1954, s.68, Sched. 7.*]

A1.016 Service of notices

23.—(1) Any notice, request, demand or other instrument under this Act shall be in writing and may be served on the person on whom it is to be served either personally, or by leaving it for him at his last known place of abode in England or Wales, or by sending it through the post in a registered letter addressed to him there, or, in the case of a local or public authority or a statutory or a public utility company, to the secretary or other proper officer at the principal office of such authority or company, and in the case of a notice to a landlord, the person on whom it is to be served shall include any agent of the landlord duly authorised in that behalf.

(2) Unless or until a tenant of a holding shall have received notice that the person theretofore entitled to the rents and profits of the holding (hereinafter referred to as "the original landlord") has ceased to be so entitled, and also notice of the name and address of the person who has become entitled to such rents and profits, any claim, notice, request, demand, or other instrument which the tenant shall serve upon or deliver to the original landlord shall be deemed to have been served upon or delivered to the landlord of such holding.

A1.017 Application to Crown, Duchy, ecclesiastical and charity lands

24.—(1) This Act shall apply to land belonging to His Majesty in right of the Crown or the Duchy of Lancaster and to land belonging to the Duchy of

[13] As amended by Landlord and Tenant Act, 1954. s.63(10).

Cornwall, and to land belonging to any Government department, and for that purpose the provisions of the Agricultural Holdings Act, 1923, relating to Crown and Duchy lands, as set out and adapted in Part I of the Second Schedule to this Act, shall have effect.

(2) The provisions of the Agricultural Holdings Act, 1923, with respect to the application of that Act to ecclesiastical and charity lands, as set out and adapted in Part II of the Second Schedule to this Act, shall apply for the purposes of this Act.

(3) [*Repealed by Endowments and Glebe Measure* 1976 (No. 4), *s.*47(4) *and Sched.* 8.]

(4) Where any land is vested in the official custodian for charities in trust for any charity, the trustees of the charity and not the custodian shall be deemed to be the landlord for the purposes of this Act.[14]

Interpretation **A1.018**

25.—(1) For the purposes of this Act, unless the context otherwise requires—

The expression "tenant" means any person entitled in possession to the holding under any contract of tenancy, whether the interest of such tenant was acquired by original contract, assignment, operation of law or otherwise;

The expression "landlord" means any person who under a lease is, as between himself and the tenant or other lessee, for the time being entitled to the rents and profits of the demised premises payable under the lease;

The expression "predecessor in title" in relation to a tenant or landlord means any person through whom the tenant or landlord has derived title, whether by assignment, by will, by intestacy, or by operation of law;

The expression "lease" means a lease, under-lease or other tenancy, assignment operating as a lease or under-lease, or an agreement for such lease, under-lease tenancy, or assignment;

The expression "mining lease" means a lease for any mining purpose or purposes connected therewith, and "mining purposes" include the sinking and searching for, winning, working, getting, making merchantable, smelting or otherwise converting or working for the purposes of any manufacture, carrying away, and disposing of mines and minerals, in or under land, and the erection of buildings, and the execution of engineering and other works suitable for those purposes;

The expression "term of years absolute" has the same meaning as in the Law of Property Act, 1925:

The expression "statutory company" means any company constituted by or under an Act of Parliament to construct, work or carry on any [. . .],[15] [. . .],[16] [. . .],[17] tramway, hydraulic power, dock, canal or railway undertaking; and the expression "public utility company" means any company within the meaning of the Companies (Consolidation) Act, 1908, or a society registered under the Industrial and Provident Societies Acts, 1893 to 1913, carrying on any such undertaking;

[14] As amended by Charities Act, 1960, s.48(1), Sched. 6.
[15] Omitted by the Gas Act 1986, Sched. 9.
[16] Omitted by the Water Act 1989, Sched. 27.
[17] Omitted by the Electricity Act 1989, Sched. 18.

The expression "prescribed" means [prescribed by rules of court or by a practice direction][18]
(2) The designation of landlord and tenant shall continue to apply to the parties until the conclusion of any proceedings taken under or in pursuance of this Act in respect of compensation.[19]

A1.019 **Short title, commencement and extent**

26.—(1) This Act may be cited as the Landlord and Tenant Act, 1927.
(2) [*Repealed by Statute Law Revision Act* 1950.]
(3) This Act shall extend to England and Wales only.

SCHEDULES

Section 12

A1.020

FIRST SCHEDULE

Provisions as to Charges

(1) As landlord, on paying to the tenant the amount due to him under Part I of this Act, in respect of compensation for an improvement [. . .][20] under that Part, or on expending after notice given in accordance with that Part such amount as may be necessary to execute an improvement, shall be entitled to obtain from the Minister of Agriculture and Fisheries (hereinafter referred to as the Minister) an order in favour of himself and the persons deriving title under him charging the holding, or any part thereof, with repayment of the amount paid or expended, including any proper costs, charges or expenses incurred by a landlord in opposing any proposal by a tenant to execute an improvement or in contesting a claim for compensation, and of all costs properly incurred by him in obtaining the charge, with such interest, and by such instalments, and with such directions for giving effect to the charge, as the Minister thinks fit.

(2) Where the landlord obtaining the charge is not an absolute owner of the holding for his own benefit, no instalment or interest shall be made payable after the time when the improvement [. . .][21] in respect whereof compensation is paid will, in the opinion of the Minister, have become exhausted.

(3) Where the estate or interest of a landlord is determinable or liable to forfeiture by reason of his creating or suffering any charge thereon, that estate or interest shall not be determined or forfeited by reason of his obtaining such a charge, anything in any deed, will or other instrument to the contrary thereof notwithstanding.

[18] Substituted by Civil Procedure (Modification of Enactments) Order (SI 2001/2717) art. 3
[19] Now Land Charges Act, 1972, s.2, Class A: see Act of 1972, s.18(6).
[20] The words omitted were repealed by the Landlord and Tenant Act 1954, s.45 and Sched. 7, Pt I.
[21] *ibid.*

(4) The sum charged shall be a charge on the holding, or the part thereof charged, for the landlord's interest therein and for interests in the reversion immediately expectant on the termination of the lease, but so that, in any case where the landlord's interest is an interest in a leasehold, the charge shall not extend beyond that leasehold interest.

(5) Any company now or hereafter incorporated by Parliament, and having power to advance money for the improvement of land, may take an assignment of any charge made under this Schedule, upon such terms and conditions as may be agreed upon between the company and the person entitled to the charge, and may assign any charge so acquired by them.

(6) Where a charge may be made under this Schedule for compensation due under an award, the tribunal making the award shall, at the request and cost of the person entitled to obtain the charge, certify the amount to be charged and the term for which the charge may properly be made, having regard to the time at which each improvement [. . .][22] in respect of which compensation is awarded is to be deemed to be exhausted.

(7) A charge under this Schedule may be registered under section ten of the Land Charges Act, 1925, as a land charge of Class A.

Section 24

SECOND SCHEDULE **A1.021**

PART I

APPLICATION TO CROWN AND DUCHY LAND

1.—(a) With respect to any land belonging to His Majesty in right of the Crown, or to a Government department, for the purposes of this Act, the Commissioners of Crown Lands, or other the proper officer or body having charge of the land for the time being, or, in case there is no such offer or body, then such person as His Majesty may appoint in writing under the Royal Sign Manual, shall represent His Majesty, and shall be deemed to be the landlord.

(b) [*Repealed by Crown Estates Act*, 1961, *Sched.* 3, *Pt.* II.]

2.—(a) With respect to land belonging to His Majesty in right of the Duchy of Lancaster, for the purposes of this Act, the Chancellor of the Duchy shall represent His Majesty, and shall be deemed to be the landlord.

(b) The amount of any compensation under Part I of this Act payable by the Chancellor of the Duchy shall be raised and paid as an expense incurred in improvement of land belonging to His Majesty in right of the Duchy within section twenty-five of the Act of the fifty-seventh year year of King George the Third, chapter ninety-seven.

3.—(a) With respect to land belonging to the Duchy of Cornwall, for the purposes of this Act, such person as the Duke of Cornwall, or the possessor for the time being of the Duchy of Cornwall appoints, shall represent the

[22] *ibid.*

Duke of Cornwall or other the possessor aforesaid, and be deemed to be the landlord, and may do any act or thing under this Act which a landlord is authorised or required to do thereunder.

(b) Any compensation under Part I of this Act payable by the Duke of Cornwall, or other the possessor aforesaid, shall be paid, and advances therefore made, in the manner and subject to the provisions of section eight of the Duchy of Cornwall Management Act, 1863, with respect to improvements of land mentioned in that section.

PART II

APPLICATION TO ECCLESIASTICAL AND CHARITY LAND

1.—(a) Where lands are assigned or secured as the endowment of a see, the powers by this Act conferred on a landlord in respect of charging land shall not be exercised by the bishop in respect of those lands, except with the previous approval in writing of the Estates Committee of the Ecclesiastical Commissioners.

(b) [. . .][23]

(c) The Ecclesiastical Commissioners may, if they think fit, on behalf of an ecclesiastical corporation, out of any money in their hands, pay to the tenant the amount of compensation due to him under Part I of this Act, and thereupon they may, instead of the corporation obtain from the minister a charge on the holding in respect thereof in favour of themselves, and every such charge shall where the landlord is the incumbent of a benefice be effectual notwithstanding any change of the incumbent.

2. The powers by this Act conferred on a landlord in respect of charging land shall not be exercised by trustees for ecclesiastical or charitable purposes, except with the approval in writing of the [Charity Commission][24] or the Board of Education, as the case may require.

[23] Repealed by the Endowments and Glebe Measure 1976, s.47(4) and Sched. 8.

[24] The words in square brackets in para.2 were substituted by the Charities Act 2006 (c.50) Sch.8 para.20

Landlord and Tenant Act, 1954[1] A1.022

(2 & 3 ELIZ. 2, C. 56)

An Act to provide security of tenure for occupying tenants under certain leases of residential property at low rents and for occupying sub-tenants of tenants under such leases; to enable tenants occupying property for business, professional or certain other purposes to obtain new tenancies in certain cases; to amend and extend the Landlord and Tenant Act, 1927, The Leasehold Property (Repairs) Act, 1938, and section eighty-four of the Law of Property Act, 1925; to confer jurisdiction on the County Court in certain disputes between landlords and tenants; to make provision for the termination of tenancies of derelict land; and for purposes connected with the matters of aforesaid.

[30TH JULY, 1954]

PART II

TENANCIES TO WHICH PART II APPLIES[2]

Tenancies to which Part II applies

23.—(1) Subject to the provisions of this Act, this Part of this Act applies to any tenancy where the property comprised in the tenancy is or includes premises which are occupied by the tenant and are so occupied for the purposes of a business carried on by him or for those and other purposes. **A1.023**

(1A) Occupation or the carrying on of a business—

- **(a) by a company in which the tenant has a controlling interest; or**
- **(b) where the tenant is a company, by a person with a controlling interest in the company, shall be treated for the purposes of this section as equivalent to occupation or, as the case may be, the carrying on of a business by the tenant.**

(1B) Accordingly references (however expressed) in this Part of this Act to the business of, or to use, occupation or enjoyment by, the tenant shall be construed as including references to the business of, or to use, occupation or enjoyment by, a company falling within subsection (1A)(a) above or a person falling within subsection (1A)(b) above.[3]

(2) In this Part of this Act the expression "business" includes a trade, profession or employment and includes any activity carried on by a body of persons, whether corporate or unincorporate.

[1] Printed as amended.
[2] See also Leasehold Reform Act, 1967, s.16(1).
[3] Added by Regulatory Reform (Business Tenancies) (England and Wales) Order (SI 2003/3096) art.13.

(3) In the following provisions of this Part of this Act the expression "the holding", in relation to a tenancy to which this Part of this Act applies, means the property comprised in the tenancy, there being excluded any party thereof which is occupied neither by the tenant nor by a person employed by the tenant and so employed for the purposes of a business by reason of which the tenancy is one to which this Part of this Act applies.

(4) Where the tenant is carrying on a business, in all or any part of the property comprised in a tenancy, in breach of a prohibition (however expressed) of use for business purposes which subsists under the terms of the tenancy and extends to the whole of that property, this Part of this Act shall not apply to the tenancy unless the immediate landlord or his predecessor in title has consented to the breach or the immediate landlord has acquiesced therein.

In this subsection the reference to a prohibition of use for business purposes does not include a prohibition of use for the purposes of a specified business, or of use for purposes of any but a specified business, but save as aforesaid includes a prohibition of use for the purposes of some one or more only of the classes of business specified in the definition of that expression in subsection (2) of this section.

Continuation and renewal of tenancies

A1.024 **Continuation of tenancies to which Part II applies and grant of new tenancies**

24.—(1) A tenancy to which this Part of this Act applies shall not come to an end unless terminated in accordance with the provisions of this Part of this Act; and, subject to the ~~provisions of section twenty nine of this Act, the tenant under such a tenancy may apply to the court for~~ **following provisions of this Act either the tenant or the landlord under such a tenancy may apply to the court for an order for the grant of**[4] a new tenancy—

(a) if the landlord has given notice under [section 25 of this Act][5] to terminate the tenancy,

(b) if the tenant has made a request for a new tenancy in accordance with section twenty-six of this Act.

(2) The last foregoing subsection shall not prevent the coming to an end of a tenancy by notice to quit given by the tenant, by surrender or forfeiture, or by the forfeiture of a superior tenancy, [unless—

(a) in the case of a notice to quit, the notice was given before the tenant had been in occupation in right of the tenancy for one month; or

~~(b) in the case of an instrument of surrender, the instrument was executed before, or was executed in pursuance of an agreement made before, the tenant had been in occupation in right of the tenancy for one month.~~[6]

(2A) Neither the tenant nor the landlord may make an application under subsection (1) above if the other has made such an application and the application has been served.

[4] Substituted by Regulatory Reform (Business Tenancies) (England and Wales) Order (SI 2003/3096) art.3.

[5] Substituted by the Law of Property Act 1969, s.3(2).

[6] Repealed by Regulatory Reform (Business Tenancies) (England and Wales) Order (SI 2003/3096) Sch.6, para.1.

(2B) Neither the tenant nor the landlord may make such an application if the landlord has made an application under section 29(2) of this Act and the application has been served.

(2C) The landlord may not withdraw an application under subsection (1) above unless the tenant consents to its withdrawal.[7]

(3) Notwithstanding anything in subsection (1) of this section—

(a) where a tenancy to which this Part of this Act applies ceases to be such a tenancy, it shall not come to an end by reason only of the cesser, but if it was granted for a term of years certain and has been continued by subsection (1) of this section then (without prejudice to the termination thereof in accordance with any terms of the tenancy) it may be terminated by not less than three nor more than six months' notice in writing given by the landlord to the tenant;

(b) where, at a time when a tenancy is not one to which this Part of this Act applies, the landlord gives notice to quit, the operation of the notice shall not be affected by reason that the tenancy becomes one to which this Part of this Act applies after the giving of the notice.

~~[**24A.** (1) The landlord of a tenancy to which this Part of this Act applies may,—~~

~~(a) if he has given notice under section 25 of this Act to terminate the tenancy; or~~

~~(b) if the tenant has made a request for a new tenancy in accordance with section 26 of this Act;~~

~~apply to the court to determine a rent which it would be reasonable for the tenant to pay while the tenancy continues by virtue of section 24 of this Act, and the court may determine a rent accordingly.~~

~~(2) A rent determined in proceedings under this section shall be deemed to be the rent payable under the tenancy from the date on which the proceedings were commenced or the date specified in the landlord's notice or the tenant's request, whichever is the later.~~

~~(3) In determining a rent under this section the court shall have regard to the rent payable under the terms of the tenancy, but otherwise subsections (1) and (2) of sections 34 of this Act shall apply to the determination as they would apply to the determination of a rent under that section if a new tenancy from year to year of the whole of the property comprised in the tenancy were granted to the tenant by order of the court.~~

Applications for determination of interim rent while tenancy continues **A1.025**

24A.—(1) Subject to subsection (2) below, if—

(a) the landlord of a tenancy to which this Part of this Act applies has given notice under section 25 of this Act to terminate the tenancy; or

(b) the tenant of such a tenancy has made a request for a new tenancy in accordance with section 26 of this Act,

either of them may make an application to the court to determine a rent (an "interim rent") which the tenant is to pay while the tenancy ("the relevant tenancy") continues by virtue of section 24 of this Act and the court may order payment of an interim rent in accordance with section 24C or 24D of this Act.

[7] Added by Regulatory Reform (Business Tenancies) (England and Wales) Order (SI 2003/3096) art.3.

(2) Neither the tenant nor the landlord may make an application under subsection (1) above if the other has made such an application and has not withdrawn it.

(3) No application shall be entertained under subsection (1) above if it is made more than six months after the termination of the relevant tenancy.][8]

A1.026 **Date from which interim rent is payable**

24B.—(1) The interim rent determined on an application under section 24A(1) of this Act shall be payable from the appropriate date.

(2) If an application under section 24A(1) of this Act is made in a case where the landlord has given a notice under section 25 of this Act, the appropriate date is the earliest date of termination that could have been specified in the landlord's notice.

(3) If an application under section 24A(1) of this Act is made in a case where the tenant has made a request for a new tenancy under section 26 of this Act, the appropriate date is the earliest date that could have been specified in the tenant's request as the date from which the new tenancy is to begin.[9]

A1.027 **Amount of interim rent where new tenancy of whole premises granted and landlord not opposed**

24C.—(1) This section applies where—

(a) the landlord gave a notice under section 25 of this Act at a time when the tenant was in occupation of the whole of the property comprised in the relevant tenancy for purposes such as are mentioned in section 23(1) of this Act and stated in the notice that he was not opposed to the grant of a new tenancy; or

(b) the tenant made a request for a new tenancy under section 26 of this Act at a time when he was in occupation of the whole of that property for such purposes and the landlord did not give notice under subsection (6) of that section,

and the landlord grants a new tenancy of the whole of the property comprised in the relevant tenancy to the tenant (whether as a result of an order for the grant of a new tenancy or otherwise).

(2) Subject to the following provisions of this section, the rent payable under and at the commencement of the new tenancy shall also be the interim rent.

(3) Subsection (2) above does not apply where—

(a) the landlord or the tenant shows to the satisfaction of the court that the interim rent under that subsection differs substantially from the relevant rent; or

(b) the landlord or the tenant shows to the satisfaction of the court that the terms of the new tenancy differ from the terms of the relevant tenancy to such an extent that the interim rent under that subsection is substantially different from the rent which (in default of such agreement) the court would have determined under section 34 of this Act to be payable under a tenancy which commenced on the same day as the

[8] Substituted by Regulatory Reform (Business Tenancies) (England and Wales) Order (SI 2003/3096) art.18.

[9] Added by Regulatory Reform (Business Tenancies) (England and Wales) Order (SI 2003/3096) art.18.

new tenancy and whose other terms were the same as the relevant tenancy.

(4) In this section "the relevant rent" means the rent which (in default of agreement between the landlord and the tenant) the court would have determined under section 34 of this Act to be payable under the new tenancy if the new tenancy had commenced on the appropriate date (within the meaning of section 24B of this Act).

(5) The interim rent in a case where subsection (2) above does not apply by virtue only of subsection (3)(a) above is the relevant rent.

(6) The interim rent in a case where subsection (2) above does not apply by virtue only of subsection (3)(b) above, or by virtue of subsection (3)(a) and (b) above, is the rent which it is reasonable for the tenant to pay while the relevant tenancy continues by virtue of section 24 of this Act.

(7) In determining the interim rent under subsection (6) above the court shall have regard—

(a) to the rent payable under the terms of the relevant tenancy; and
(b) to the rent payable under any sub-tenancy of part of the property comprised in the relevant tenancy,

but otherwise subsections (1) and (2) of section 34 of this Act shall apply to the determination as they would apply to the determination of a rent under that section if a new tenancy of the whole of the property comprised in the relevant tenancy were granted to the tenant by order of the court and the duration of that new tenancy were the same as the duration of the new tenancy which is actually granted to the tenant.

(8) In this section and section 24D of this Act "the relevant tenancy" has the same meaning as in section 24A of this Act.[9]

Amount of interim rent in any other case A1.028

24D.— (1) The interim rent in a case where section 24C of this Act does not apply is the rent which it is reasonable for the tenant to pay while the relevant tenancy continues by virtue of section 24 of this Act.

(2) In determining the interim rent under subsection (1) above the court shall have regard—

(a) to the rent payable under the terms of the relevant tenancy; and
(b) to the rent payable under any sub-tenancy of part of the property comprised in the relevant tenancy,

but otherwise subsections (1) and (2) of section 34 of this Act shall apply to the determination as they would apply to the determination of a rent under that section if a new tenancy from year to year of the whole of the property comprised in the relevant tenancy were granted to the tenant by order of the court.

(3) If the court—

(a) has made an order for the grant of a new tenancy and has ordered payment of interim rent in accordance with section 24C of this Act, but
(b) either—
    (i) it subsequently revokes under section 36(2) of this Act the order for the grant of a new tenancy; or
    (ii) the landlord and tenant agree not to act on the order,

the court on the application of the landlord or the tenant shall determine a new interim rent in accordance with subsections (1) and (2) above without a further application under section 24A(1) of this Act.[9]

Termination of tenancy by the landlord[10]

A1.029 **25.**—(1) The landlord may terminate a tenancy to which this Part of this Act applies by a notice given to the tenant in the prescribed form specifying the date at which the tenancy is to come to an end (hereinafter referred to as "the date of termination"):

Provided that this subsection has effect subject to [the provisions of section 29B(4) of this Act and][11] the provisions of Part IV of this Act as to the interim continuation of tenancies pending the disposal of applications to the court.

(2) Subject to the provisions of the next following subsection, a notice under this section shall not have effect unless it is given not more than twelve nor less than six months before the date of termination specified therein.

(3) In the case of a tenancy which apart from this Act could have been brought to an end by notice to quit given by the landlord—

(a) the date of termination specified in a notice under this section shall not be earlier than the earliest date on which apart from this Part of this Act the tenancy could have been brought to an end by notice to quit given by the landlord on the date of the giving of the notice under this section; and

(b) where apart from this Part of this Act more than six months' notice to quit would have been required to bring the tenancy to an end, the last foregoing subsection shall have effect with the substitution for twelve months of a period six months longer than the length of notice to quit which would have been required as aforesaid.

(4) In the case of any other tenancy, a notice under this section shall not specify a date of termination earlier than the date on which apart from this Part of this Act the tenancy would have come to an end by effluxion of time.

~~(5) A notice under this section shall not have effect unless it requires the tenant, within two months after the giving of the notice, to notify the landlord in writing whether or not, at the date of termination, the tenant will be willing to give up possession of the property comprised in the tenancy.~~

~~(6) A notice under this section shall not have effect unless it states whether the landlord would oppose an application to the court under this Part of this Act for the grant of a new tenancy and, if so, also states on which of the grounds mentioned in section thirty of this Act he would do so.~~[12]

(6) A notice under this section shall not have effect unless it states whether the landlord is opposed to the grant of a new tenancy to the tenant.

(7) A notice under this section which states that the landlord is opposed to the grant of a new tenancy to the tenant shall not have effect unless it also specifies one or more of the grounds specified in section 30(1) of this Act as the ground or grounds for his opposition.

(8) A notice under this section which states that the landlord is not opposed to the grant of a new tenancy to the tenant shall not have effect unless it sets out the landlord's proposals as to—

(a) the property to be comprised in the new tenancy (being either the whole or part of the property comprised in the current tenancy);

10 See also Leasehold Reform Act 1967, s.34(5), Sch.3.

11 Added by Regulatory Reform (Business Tenancies) (England and Wales) Order (SI 2003/3096) art.11.

12 Repealed by Regulatory Reform (Business Tenancies) (England and Wales) Order (SI 2003/3096) Sch.6, para.1.

(b) the rent to be payable under the new tenancy; and
(c) the other terms of the new tenancy.[13]

Tenant's request for a new tenancy[14] **A1.030**

26.—(1) A tenant's request for a new tenancy may be made where the ~~tenancy under which he holds for the time being (hereinafter referred to as "the current tenancy")~~ **current tenancy**[15] is a tenancy granted for a term of years certain exceeding one year, whether or not continued by section 24 of this Act, or granted for a term of years certain and thereafter from year to year.

(2) A tenant's request for a new tenancy shall be for a tenancy beginning with such date, not more than twelve nor less than six months after the making of the request, as may be specified therein:

Provided that the said date shall not be earlier than the date on which apart from this Act the current tenancy would come to an end by effluxion of time or could be brought to an end by notice to quit given by the tenant.

(3) A tenant's request for a new tenancy shall not have effect unless it is made by notice in the prescribed form given to the landlord and sets out the tenant's proposals as to the property to be comprised in the new tenancy (being either the whole or part of the property comprised in the current tenancy), as to the rent to be payable under the new tenancy and as to the other terms of the new tenancy.

(4) A tenant's request for a new tenancy shall not be made if the landlord has already given notice under the last foregoing section to terminate the current tenancy, or if the tenant has already given notice to quit or notice under the next following section; and no such notice shall be given by the landlord or the tenant after the making by the tenant of a request for a new tenancy.

(5) Where the tenant makes a request for a new tenancy in accordance with the foregoing provisions of this section, the current tenancy shall, subject to the provisions of ~~subsection (2) of section 36~~ **sections 29B(4) and 36(2)**[16] of this Act and the provisions of Part IV of this Act as to the interim continuation of tenancies, terminate immediately before the date specified in the request for the beginning of the new tenancy.

(6) Within two months of the making of a tenant's request for a new tenancy the landlord may give notice to the tenant that he will oppose an application to the court for the grant of a new tenancy, and any such notice shall state on which of the grounds mentioned in section thirty of this Act the landlord will oppose the application.

Termination by tenant of tenancy for fixed term **A1.031**

27.—(1) Where the tenant under a tenancy to which this Part of this Act applies, being a tenancy granted for a term of years certain, gives to the immediate landlord, not later than three months before the date on which apart from this Act the tenancy would come to an end by effluxion of time, a notice in

[13] Substituted by Regulatory Reform (Business Tenancies) (England and Wales) Order (SI 2003/3096) art.4.
[14] See also Leasehold Reform Act 1967, s.34(3), (5), Sch.2 para.6 and Sch.3
[15] Substituted by Regulatory Reform (Business Tenancies) (England and Wales) Order (SI 2003/3096) Sch.5, para.3.
[16] Substituted by Regulatory Reform (Business Tenancies) (England and Wales) Order (SI 2003/3096) art.12.

writing that the tenant not desire the tenancy to be continued, section 24 of this Act shall not have effect in relation to the tenancy, **unless the notice is given before the tenant has been in occupation in right of the tenancy for one month**.[17]

(1A) Section 24 of this Act shall not have effect in relation to a tenancy for a term of years certain where the tenant is not in occupation of the property comprised in the tenancy at the time when, apart from this Act, the tenancy would come to an end by effluxion of time.[18]

(2) A tenancy granted for a term of years certain which is continuing by virtue of section 24 of this Act **shall not come to an end by reason only of the tenant ceasing to occupy the property comprised in the tenancy but**[19] may be brought to an end on any ~~quarter~~[20] day by not less than three months' notice in writing given by the tenant to the immediate landlord, whether the notice is given [. . .][21] after the date on which apart from this Act the tenancy would have come to an end [or before that date, but not before the tenant has been in occupation in right of the tenancy for one month].[22]

(3) Where a tenancy is terminated under subsection (2) above, any rent payable in respect of a period which begins before, and ends after, the tenancy is terminated shall be apportioned, and any rent paid by the tenant in excess of the amount apportioned to the period before termination shall be recoverable by him.[23]

A1.032 **Renewal of tenancies by agreement**[24]

28.—Where the landlord and tenant agree for the grant to the tenant of a future tenancy of the holding, or of the holding with other land, on terms and from a date specified in the agreement, the current tenancy shall continue until that date but no longer, and shall not be a tenancy to which this Part of this Act applies.

Application to court for new tenancies

~~**Order by court for grant of a new tenancy**~~

~~**29.**—(1) Subject to the provisions of this Act, on an application under subsection (1) of section 24 of this Act for a new tenancy the court shall make an order for the grant of a tenancy comprising such property, at such rent and on such other terms, as are hereinafter provided.~~

~~(2) Where such an application is made in consequence of a notice given by the landlord under section 25 of this Act, it shall not be entertained unless the tenant has duly notified the landlord that he will not be willing at the date of termination to give up possession of the property comprised in the tenancy.~~

17 Inserted by Law of Property Act, 1969, s.4(2).
18 Added by Regulatory Reform (Business Tenancies) (England and Wales) Order (SI 2003/3096) art.25.
19 Added by Regulatory Reform (Business Tenancies) (England and Wales) Order (SI 2003/3096) art.25.
20 Repealed by Regulatory Reform (Business Tenancies) (England and Wales) Order (SI 2003/3096) art.25.
21 Repealed by Law of Property Act 1969, s.4(2).
22 Inserted by the Law of Property Act 1969, s.4(2).
23 Added by Regulatory Reform (Business Tenancies) (England and Wales) Order (SI 2003/3096) art.25.
24 See also Leasehold Reform Act, 1967, ss.34, 35, Sched. 3.

~~(3) No application under subsection (1) of section 24 of this Act shall be entertained unless it is made not less than two nor more than four months after the giving of the landlord's notice under section 25 of this Act or, as the case may be, after the making of the tenant's request for a new tenancy.~~

Applications to court **A1.033**

29.—Order by court for grant of new tenancy or termination of current tenancy
(1) Subject to the provisions of this Act, on an application under section 24(1) of this Act, the court shall make an order for the grant of a new tenancy and accordingly for the termination of the current tenancy immediately before the commencement of the new tenancy.

(2) Subject to the following provisions of this Act, a landlord may apply to the court for an order for the termination of a tenancy to which this Part of this Act applies without the grant of a new tenancy—

- **(a) if he has given notice under section 25 of this Act that he is opposed to the grant of a new tenancy to the tenant; or**
- **(b) if the tenant has made a request for a new tenancy in accordance with section 26 of this Act and the landlord has given notice under subsection (6) of that section.**

(3) The landlord may not make an application under subsection (2) above if either the tenant or the landlord has made an application under section 24(1) of this Act.

(4) Subject to the provisions of this Act, where the landlord makes an application under subsection (2) above—

- **(a) if he establishes, to the satisfaction of the court, any of the grounds on which he is entitled to make the application in accordance with section 30 of this Act, the court shall make an order for the termination of the current tenancy in accordance with section 64 of this Act without the grant of a new tenancy; and**
- **(b) if not, it shall make an order for the grant of a new tenancy and accordingly for the termination of the current tenancy immediately before the commencement of the new tenancy.**

(5) The court shall dismiss an application by the landlord under section 24(1) of this Act if the tenant informs the court that he does not want a new tenancy.

(6) The landlord may not withdraw an application under subsection (2) above unless the tenant consents to its withdrawal.[25]

Time limits for applications to court **A1.034**

29A.—(1) Subject to section 29B of this Act, the court shall not entertain an application—

- **(a) by the tenant or the landlord under section 24(1) of this Act; or**
- **(b) by the landlord under section 29(2) of this Act,**

if it is made after the end of the statutory period.

(2) In this section and section 29B of this Act "the statutory period" means a period ending—

- **(a) where the landlord gave a notice under section 25 of this Act, on the date specified in his notice; and**

[25] Substituted by Regulatory Reform (Business Tenancies) (England and Wales) Order (SI 2003/3096) art.5.

(b) where the tenant made a request for a new tenancy under section 26 of this Act, immediately before the date specified in his request.

(3) Where the tenant has made a request for a new tenancy under section 26 of this Act, the court shall not entertain an application under section 24(1) of this Act which is made before the end of the period of two months beginning with the date of the making of the request, unless the application is made after the landlord has given a notice under section 26(6) of this Act.

A1.035 **Agreements extending time limits**

29B.—(1) After the landlord has given a notice under section 25 of this Act, or the tenant has made a request under section 26 of this Act, but before the end of the statutory period, the landlord and tenant may agree that an application such as is mentioned in section 29A(1) of this Act, may be made before the end of a period specified in the agreement which will expire after the end of the statutory period.

(2) The landlord and tenant may from time to time by agreement further extend the period for making such an application, but any such agreement must be made before the end of the period specified in the current agreement.

(3) Where an agreement is made under this section, the court may entertain an application such as is mentioned in section 29A(1) of this Act if it is made before the end of the period specified in the agreement.

(4) Where an agreement is made under this section, or two or more agreements are made under this section, the landlord's notice under section 25 of this Act or tenant's request under section 26 of this Act shall be treated as terminating the tenancy at the end of the period specified in the agreement or, as the case may be, at the end of the period specified in the last of those agreements.[26]

A1.036 **Opposition by landlord to application for new tenancy**

30.—(1) The grounds on which a landlord may oppose an application under ~~subsection (1) of section 24 of this Act~~ **section 24(1) of this Act, or make an application under section 29(2) of this Act,**[27] are such of the following grounds as may be stated in the landlord's notice under section 25 of this Act or, as the case may be, under subsection (6) of section 26 thereof, that is to say:—

(a) where under the current tenancy the tenant has any obligations as respects the repair and maintenance of the holding, that the tenant ought not to be granted a new tenancy in view of the state of repair of the holding, being a state resulting from the tenant's failure to comply with the said obligations;

(b) that the tenant ought not to be granted a new tenancy in view of his persistent delay in paying rent which has become due;

(c) that the tenant ought not to be granted a new tenancy in view of other substantial breaches by him of his obligations under the current tenancy, or for any other reason connected with the tenant's use or management of the holding;

(d) that the landlord has offered and is willing to provide or secure the provision of alternative accommodation for the tenant, that the terms on which the alternative accommodation is available are

[26] Added by Regulatory Reform (Business Tenancies) (England and Wales) Order (SI 2003/3096) art.10.

[27] Substituted by Regulatory Reform (Business Tenancies) (England and Wales) Order (SI 2003/3096) art.6.

reasonable having regard to the terms of the current tenancy and to all other relevant circumstances, and that the accommodation and the time at which it will be available are suitable for the tenant's requirements (including the requirement to preserve goodwill) having regard to the nature and class of his business and to the situation and extent of, and facilities afforded by, the holding;

(e) where the current tenancy was created by the subletting of part only of the property comprised in a superior tenancy and the landlord is the owner of an interest in reversion expectant on the termination of that superior tenancy, that the aggregate of the rents reasonably obtainable on separate lettings of the holding and the remainder of that property would be substantially less than the rent reasonably obtainable on a letting of that property as a whole, that on the termination of the current tenancy the landlord requires possession of the holding for the purpose of letting or otherwise disposing of the said property as a whole, and that in view thereof of the tenant ought to be granted a new tenancy;

(f) that on the termination of the current tenancy the landlord intends to demolish or reconstruct the premises comprised in the holding or a substantial part of those premises or to carry out substantial work of construction on the holding or part thereof and that he could not reasonably do so without obtaining possession of the holding;

(g) subject as hereinafter provided, that on the termination of the current tenancy the landlord intends to occupy the holding for the purposes, or partly for the purposes, of a business to be carried on by him therein, or as his residence.

(1A) Where the landlord has a controlling interest in a company, the reference in subsection (1)(g) above to the landlord shall be construed as a reference to the landlord or that company.

(1B) Subject to subsection (2A) below, where the landlord is a company and a person has a controlling interest in the company, the reference in subsection (1)(g) above to the landlord shall be construed as a reference to the landlord or that person.[28]

(2) The landlord shall not be entitled to oppose an application **under section 24(1) of this Act, or make an application under section 29(2) of this Act,**[29] on the ground specified in paragraph (g) of the last foregoing subsection if the interest of the landlord, or an interest which has merged in that interest and but for the merger would be the interest of the landlord, was purchased or created after the beginning of the period of five years which ends with the termination of the current tenancy, and at all times since the purchase or creation thereof the holding has been comprised in a tenancy or successive tenancies of the description specified in subsection (1) of section 23 of this Act.

(2A) Subsection (1B) above shall not apply if the controlling interest was acquired after the beginning of the period of five years which ends with the termination of the current tenancy, and at all times since the acquisition of the controlling interest the holding has been comprised in a tenancy or successive tenancies of the description specified in section 23(1) of this Act.[28]

[28] Added by Regulatory Reform (Business Tenancies) (England and Wales) Order (SI 2003/3096) art.14.

[29] Added by Regulatory Reform (Business Tenancies) (England and Wales) Order (SI 2003/3096) art.6.

~~(3) Where the landlord has a controlling interest in a company any business to be carried on by the company shall be treated for the purposes of subsection (1)(g) of this section as a business to be carried on by him.~~

~~For the purposes of this subsection, a person has a controlling interest in a company if and only if either—~~

- ~~(a) he is a member of it and able, without the consent of any other person, to appoint or remove the holders of at least a majority of the directorships; or~~
- ~~(b) he holds more than one half of its equity share capital, there being disregarded any shares held by him in a fiduciary capacity or as nominee for another person;~~

~~and in this section "company" and "share" have the meanings assigned to them by section 455(1) of the Companies Act 1948 and "equity share capital" the meaning assigned to it by section 154(5) of that Act.~~[30]

A1.037 **Dismissal of application for new tenancy where landlord successfully opposes**[13]

31.—(1) If the landlord opposes an application under subsection (1) of section 24 of this Act on grounds on which he is entitled to oppose it in accordance with the last foregoing section and establishes any of those grounds to the satisfaction of the court, the court shall not make an order for the grant of a new tenancy.

(2) ~~Where in a case not falling within the last foregoing subsection the landlord opposes an application under the said subsection (1) on one or more of the grounds specified in paragraphs (d), (e) and (f) of subsection (1) of the last foregoing section but establishes none of those grounds to the satisfaction of the court, then if the court would have been satisfied of any of those grounds~~ **Where the landlord opposes an application under section 24(1) of this Act, or makes an application under section 29(2) of this Act, on one or more of the grounds specified in section 30(1)(d) to (f) of this Act but establishes none of those grounds, and none of the other grounds specified in section 30(1) of this Act, to the satisfaction of the court, then if the court would have been satisfied on any of the grounds specified in section 30(1)(d) to (f) of this Act**[31] if the date of termination specified in the landlord's notice or, as the case may be, the date specified in the tenant's request for a new tenancy as the date from which the new tenancy is to begin, had been such later date as the court may determine, being a date not more than one year later than the date so specified,—

- (a) the court shall make a declaration to that effect, stating of which of the said grounds the court would have been satisfied as aforesaid and specifying the date determined by the court as aforesaid, but shall not make an order for the grant of a new tenancy;
- (b) if, within fourteen days after the making of the declaration, the tenant so requires the court shall make an order substituting the said date for the date specified in the said landlord's notice or tenant's request, and thereupon that notice or request shall have effect accordingly.

[30] Repealed by Regulatory Reform (Business Tenancies) (England and Wales) Order (SI 2003/3096) Sch.6, para.1.

[31] Substituted by Regulatory Reform (Business Tenancies) (England and Wales) Order (SI 2003/3096) art. 7.

Grant of a new tenancy in some cases where section 30(1)(f) applies **A1.038**

[**31A.**—(1) Where the landlord opposes an application under section 24(1) of this Act on the ground specified in paragraph (f) of section 30(1) of this Act **or makes an application under section 29(2) of this Act on that ground,**[32] the court shall not hold that the landlord could not reasonably carry out the demolition, reconstruction or work of construction intended without obtaining possession of the holding if—

(a) the tenant agrees to the inclusion in the terms of the new tenancy of terms giving the landlord access and other facilities for carrying out the work intended and, given and other facilities for carrying out the work intended and, given that access and those facilities, the landlord could reasonably carry out the work without obtaining possession of the holding and without interfering to a substantial extent or for a substantial time with the use of the holding for the purposes of the business carried on by the tenant; or

(b) the tenant is willing to accept a tenancy of an economically separate part of the holding and either paragraph (a) of this section is satisfied with respect to that part or possession of the remainder of the holding would be reasonably sufficient to enable the landlord to carry out the intended work.

(2) for the purposes of subsection (1)(b) of this section a part of a holding shall be deemed to be an economically separate part if, and only if, the aggregate of the rents which, after the completion of the intended work, would be reasonably obtainable on separate lettings of that part and the remainder of the premises affected by or resulting from the work would not be substantially less than the rent which would then be reasonably obtainable on a letting of those premises as a whole.][33]

Property to be comprised in new tenancy **A1.039**

32.—(1) [Subject to the following provisions of this section,][34] an order under section 29 of this Act for the grant of a new tenancy shall be an order for the grant of a new tenancy of the holding; and in the absence of agreement between the landlord and the tenant as to the property which constitutes the holding the court shall in the order designate that property by reference to the circumstances existing at the date of the order.

[(1A) Where the court, by virtue of paragraph (b) of section 31A(1) of this Act, makes an order under section 29 of this Act for the grant of a new tenancy in a case where the tenant is willing to accept a tenancy of part of the holding, the order shall be an order for the grant of a new tenancy of that part only.][35]

(2) The foregoing provisions of this section shall not apply in a case where the property comprised in the current tenancy includes other property besides the holding and the landlord requires any new tenancy ordered to be granted under section 29 of this Act to be a tenancy of the whole of the property comprised in the current tenancy; but in any such case—

[32] Added by Regulatory Reform (Business Tenancies) (England and Wales) Order (SI 2003/3096) art.8.
[33] Inserted by Law of Property Act 1969, s.7(1).
[34] Substituted by Law of Property Act 1969, s.7(2).
[35] Inserted by Law of Property Act 1969.

(a) any order under the said section 29 for the grant of a new tenancy shall be an order for the grant of a new tenancy of the whole of the property comprised in the current tenancy, and

(b) references in the following provisions of this Part of this Act to the holding shall be construed as references to the whole of that property.

(3) Where the current tenancy includes rights enjoyed by the tenant in connection with the holding, those rights shall be included in a tenancy ordered to be granted under section 29 of this Act [except as otherwise agreed between the landlord and the tenant or, in default of such agreement, determined by the court].[36]

A1.040 Duration of new tenancy

33.—Where on an application under this Part of this Act the court makes an order for the grant of a new tenancy, the new tenancy shall be such tenancy as may be agreed between the landlord and the tenant, or, in default of such an agreement, shall be such a tenancy as may be determined by the court to be reasonable in all the circumstances, being, if it is a tenancy for a term of years certain, a tenancy for a term not exceeding ~~fourteen~~ fifteen[37] years, and shall begin on the coming to an end of the current tenancy.

A1.041 Rent under new tenancy

34.—[(1)][38] The rent payable under a tenancy granted by order of the court under this Part of this Act shall be such as may be agreed between the landlord and the tenant or as, in default of such agreement, may be determined by the court to be that at which, having regard to the terms of the tenancy (other than those relating to rent), the holding might reasonably be expected to be let in the open market by a willing lessor, there being disregarded—

(a) any effect on rent of the fact that the tenant has or his predecessors in title have been in occupation of the holding,

(b) any goodwill attached to the holding by reason of the carrying on thereat of the business of the tenant (whether by him or by a predecessor of his in that business),

[(c) any effect on rent of an improvement to which this paragraph applies,][39]

(d) in the case of a holding comprising licensed premises, any addition to its value attributable to the licence, if it appears to the court that having regard to the terms of the current tenancy and any other relevant circumstances the benefit of the licence belongs to the tenant.

[(2) Paragraph (c) of the foregoing subsection applies to any improvement carried out by a person who at the time it was carried out was the tenant, but only if it was carried out otherwise than in pursuance of an obligation to his immediate landlord and either it was carried out during the current tenancy or the following conditions are satisfied, that is to say,—

[36] Inserted by Law of Property Act 1969.

[37] Substituted by Regulatory Reform (Business Tenancies) (England and Wales) Order (SI 2003/3096) art. 26.

[38] Substituted by Law of Property Act 1969.

[39] Inserted by Law of Property Act 1969.

(a) that it was completed not more than twenty-one years before the application? ~~the new tenancy~~ **to the court**[40] was made; and
(b) that the holding or any part of it affected by the improvement has at all times since the completion of the improvement been comprised in tenancies of the description specified in section 23(1) of this Act; and
(c) that at the termination of each of those tenancies the tenant did not quit.

(2A) If this Part of this Act applies by virtue of section 23(1A) of this Act, the reference in subsection (1)(d) above to the tenant shall be construed as including—
(a) a company in which the tenant has a controlling interest, or
(b) where the tenant is a company, a person with a controlling interest in the company.[41]

(3) Where the rent is determined by the court the court may, if it thinks fit, further determine that the terms of the tenancy shall include such provision for varying the rent as may be specified in the determination.][42]

(4) It is hereby declared that the matters which are to be taken into account by the court in determining the rent include any effect on rent of the operation of the provisions of the Landlord and Tenant (Covenants) Act 1995.[43]

Other terms of new tenancy A1.042

35.—[(1)][44] The terms of a tenancy granted by order of the court under this Part of this Act (other than terms as to the duration thereof and as to the rent payable thereunder), **including, where different persons own interests which fulfil the conditions specified in section 44(1) of this Act in different parts of it, terms as to the apportionment of the rent**[45] shall be such as may be agreed between the landlord and the tenant or as, in default of such agreement, may be determined by the court; and in determining those terms the court shall have regard to the terms of the current tenancy and to all relevant circumstances.

[(2) In subsection (1) of this section the reference to all relevant circumstances includes (without prejudice to the generality of that reference) a reference to the operation of the provisions of the Landlord and Tenant (Covenants) Act 1995.][46]

Carrying out of order for new tenancy A1.043

36.—(1) Where under this Part of this Act the court makes an order for the grant of a new tenancy, then, unless the order is revoked under the next following subsection or the landlord and the tenant agree not to act upon the order, the landlord shall be bound to execute or make in favour of the tenant, and the tenant shall be bound to accept, a lease or agreement for a tenancy of the holding embodying the terms agreed between the landlord and the tenant

40 Substituted by Regulatory Reform (Business Tenancies) (England and Wales) Order (SI 2003/3096) art.9.
41 Added by Regulatory Reform (Business Tenancies) (England and Wales) Order (SI 2003/3096) art. 15
42 Inserted by Law of Property Act 1969.
43 Inserted by Landlord and Tenant (Covenants) Act 1995 (c. 30), Sched. 1.
44 Amended to Landlord and Tenant Act (Covenants) 1995, *ibid.*
45 Added by Regulatory Reform (Business Tenancies) (England and Wales) Order (SI 2003/3096) art. 27.
46 Inserted by Landlord and Tenant Act 1995, *ibid.*

or determined by the court in accordance with the foregoing provisions of this Part of this Act; and where the landlord executes or makes such a lease or agreement the tenant shall be bound, if so required by the landlord, to execute a counterpart or duplicate thereof.

(2) If the tenant, within fourteen days after the making of an order under this Part of this Act for the grant of a new tenancy, applies to the court for the revocation of the order the court shall revoke the order; and where the order is so revoked, then, if it is so agreed between the landlord and the tenant or determined by the court, the current tenancy shall continue, beyond the date at which it would have come to an end apart from this subsection, for such period as may be so agreed or determined to be necessary to afford to the landlord a reasonable opportunity for reletting or otherwise disposing of the premises which would have been comprised in the new tenancy; and while the current tenancy continues by virtue of this subsection it shall not be a tenancy to which this Part of this Act applies.

(3) Where an order is revoked under the last foregoing subsection any provision thereof as to payment of costs shall not cease to have effect by reason only of the revocation; but the court may, if it thinks fit, revoke or vary any such provision or, where no costs have been awarded in the proceedings for the revoked order, award such costs.

(4) A lease executed or agreement made under this section, in a case where the interest of the lessor is subject to a mortgage, shall be deemed to be one authorised by section ninety-nine of the Law of Property Act, 1925 (which confers certain powers of leasing on mortgagors in possession), and subsection (13) of that section (which allows those powers to be restricted or excluded by agreement) shall not have effect in relation to such a lease or agreement.

A1.044 **Compensation where order for new tenancy precluded on certain grounds**[47]

~~37.—(1) Where on the making of an application under section 24 of this Act the court is precluded (whether by subsection (1) or subsection (2) of section 31 of this Act) from making an order for the grant of a new tenancy by reason of any of the grounds specified in paragraphs (e), (f) and (g) of subsection (1) of section 30 of this Act and not of any grounds specified in any other paragraph of that subsection, [or where no other ground is specified in the landlord's notice under section 25 of this Act or, as the case may be, under section 26(6) thereof, than these specified in the said paragraphs (e), (f) and (g) and either no application under the said section 24 is made or such an application is withdrawn,] then, subject to the provisions of this Act, the tenant shall be entitled on quitting the holding to recover from the landlord by way of compensation an amount determined in accordance with the following provisions of this section.~~

37.—(1) Subject to the provisions of this Act, in a case specified in subsection (1A), (1B) or (1C) below (a "compensation case") the tenant shall be entitled on quitting the holding to recover from the landlord by way of compensation an amount determined in accordance with this section.[48]

[47] See Leasehold Reform Act 1967, s.35(6). In so far as this section applies to assured tenancies it should be applied in its substituted form as set out in the Housing Act 1980, Sched. 5, as amended by the Housing and Planning Act 1986, s.13(4) and (7).

[48] Substituted by Regulatory Reform (Business Tenancies) (England and Wales) Order (SI 2003/3096) art. 19.

(1A) The first compensation case is where on the making of an application by the tenant under section 24(1) of this Act the court is precluded (whether by subsection (1) or subsection (2) of section 31 of this Act) from making an order for the grant of a new tenancy by reason of any of the grounds specified in paragraphs (e), (f) and (g) of section 30(1) of this Act (the "compensation grounds") and not of any grounds specified in any other paragraph of section 30(1).

(1B) The second compensation case is where on the making of an application under section 29(2) of this Act the court is precluded (whether by section 29(4)(a) or section 31(2) of this Act) from making an order for the grant of a new tenancy by reason of any of the compensation grounds and not of any other grounds specified in section 30(1) of this Act.

(1C) The third compensation case is where—

- **(a) the landlord's notice under section 25 of this Act or, as the case may be, under section 26(6) of this Act, states his opposition to the grant of a new tenancy on any of the compensation grounds and not on any other grounds specified in section 30(1) of this Act; and**
- **(b) either—**
  - **(i) no application is made by the tenant under section 24(1) of this Act or by the landlord under section 29(2) of this Act; or**
  - **(ii) such an application is made but is subsequently withdrawn.**[49]

(2) [Subject to ~~subsections (5A) to (5D) of this section]~~ ~~the said amount~~ **the following provisions of this section, compensation under this section**[48] shall be as follows, that is to say,—

- (a) where the conditions specified in the next following subsection are satisfied **in relation to the whole of the holding**[49] it shall be [the product of the appropriate multiplier and][50] twice the rateable value of the holding.
- (b) in any other case it shall be [the product of the appropriate multiplier and][50] the rateable value of the holding].

(3) The said conditions are—

- (a) that, during the whole of the 14 years immediately preceding the termination of the current tenancy, premises being or comprised in the holding have been occupied for the purposes of a business carried on by the occupier or for those and other purposes;
- (b) that, if during those 14 years there was a change in the occupier of the premises, the person who was the occupier immediately after the change was the successor to the business carried on by the person who was the occupier immediately before the change.

(3A) If the conditions specified in subsection (3) above are satisfied in relation to part of the holding but not in relation to the other part, the amount of compensation shall be the aggregate of sums calculated separately as compensation in respect of each part, and accordingly, for the purpose of calculating compensation in respect of a part any reference in this section to the holding shall be construed as a reference to that part.

(3B) Where section 44(1A) of this Act applies, the compensation shall be determined separately for each part and compensation determined for any part

[49] Added by Regulatory Reform (Business Tenancies) (England and Wales) Order (SI 2003/3096) art. 19.

[50] Added by Local Government, Planning and Land Act 1980, Sched. 33, para.4(1).

shall be recoverable only from the person who is the owner of an interest in that part which fulfils the conditions specified in section 44(1) of this Act.[51]

(4) Where the court is precluded from making an order for the grant of a new tenancy under this Part of this Act in ~~the circumstances mentioned in subsection (1) of this section~~ **a compensation case**[52] the court shall on the application of the tenant certify that fact.

(5) For the purposes of subsection (2) of this section the rateable value of the holding shall be determined as follows.

(a) where in the valuation list in force at the date on which the landlord's notice under section 25 or, as the case may be, subsection (6) of section 26 of this Act is given a value is then shown as the annual value (as hereinafter defined) of the holding, the rateable value of the holding shall be taken to be that value;

(b) where no such value is so shown with respect to the holding but such a value or such values is or are so shown with respect to premises comprised in or comprising the holding or part of it, the rateable value of the holding shall be taken to be such value as is found by a proper apportionment or aggregation of the value or values so shown;

(c) where the rateable value of the holding cannot be ascertained in accordance with the foregoing paragraphs of this subsection, it shall be taken to be the value which, apart from any exemption from assessment to rates, would on a proper assessment be the value to be entered in the said valuation list as the annual value of the holding;

and any dispute arising, whether in proceedings before the court or otherwise, as to the determination for those purposes of the rateable value of the holding shall be referred to the Commissioners of Inland Revenue for decision by a valuation officer.

An appeal shall lie to the Lands Tribunal from any decision of a valuation officer under this subsection, but subject thereto any such decision shall be final.

[(5A) If part of the holding is domestic property, as defined in section 66 of the Local Government Finance Act 1988,—

(a) the domestic property shall be disregarded in determining the rateable value of the holding under subsection (5) of this section; and

(b) if, on the date specified in subsection (5)(a) of this section, the tenant occupied the whole or any part of the domestic property, the amount of compensation to which he is entitled under subsection (1) of this section shall be increased by the addition of a sum equal to his reasonable expenses in removing from the domestic property.

(5B) Any question as to the amount of the sum referred to in paragraph (b) of subsection (5A) of this section shall be determined by agreement between the landlord and the tenant or, in default of agreement, by the court.

(5C) If the whole of the holding is domestic property, as defined in section 66 of the Local Government Finance Act 1988, for the purposes of subsection (2) of this section the rateable value of the holding shall be taken to be an amount equal to the rent at which it is estimated the holding might reasonably be expected to let from year to year if the tenant undertook to pay all usual

[51] Added by Regulatory Reform (Business Tenancies) (England and Wales) Order (SI 2003/3096) art. 19.

[52] Substituted by Regulatory Reform (Business Tenancies) (England and Wales) Order (SI 2003/3096) art. 19.

tenant's rates and taxes and to bear the cost of the repairs and insurance and the other expenses (if any) necessary to maintain the holding in a state to command that rent.

(5D) The following provisions shall have effect as regards a determination of an amount mentioned in subsection (5C) of this section—

(a) the date by reference to which such a determination is to be made is the date on which the landlord's notice under section 25 or, as the case may be, subsection (6) of section 26 of this Act is given;

(b) any dispute arising, whether in proceedings before the court or otherwise, as to such a determination shall be referred to the Commissioners of Inland Revenue for decision by a valuation officer;

(c) an appeal shall lie to the Lands Tribunal from such a decision, but subject to that, such a decision shall be final.][53]

(5E) Any deduction made under paragraph 2A of schedule 6 of the Local Government Finance Act 1988 (deduction from valuation of hereditaments used for breeding horses etc.) shall be disregarded, to the extent that it relates to the holding, in determining the rateable value of the holding under subsection (5) of this section.][54]

(6) The commissioners of Inland Revenue may by statutory instrument make rules prescribing the procedure in connection with references under this section.

(7) In this section—

the reference to the termination of the current tenancy is a reference to the date of termination specified in the landlord's notice under section 25 of this Act or, as the case may be, the date specified in the tenant's request for a new tenancy as the date from which the new tenancy is to begin;

the expression "annual value" means rateable value except that where the rateable value differs from the net annual value the said expression means net annual value;

the expression "valuation officer" means any officer of the Commission of Inland Revenue for the time being authorised by a certificate of the Commissioners to act in relation to a valuation list.

[(8) in subsection (2) of this section "the appropriate multiplier" means such multiplier as the Secretary of State may by order made by statutory instrument prescribe [and different multipliers may be so prescribed in relation to different cases].[55]

(9) A statutory instrument containing an order under subsection (8) of this section shall be subject to annulment in pursuance of a resolution of either House of Parliament.][56]

Compensation for possession obtained by misrepresentation **A1.045**

37A.—(1) Where the court—

(a) makes an order for the termination of the current tenancy but does not make an order for the grant of a new tenancy, or

(b) refuses an order for the grant of a new tenancy,

[53] Added by Local Government and Housing Act 1989, Sched. 7.

[54] Inserted by the Local Government Finance (Miscellaneous Amendments and Repeal Order 1990 (S.I. 1990 No. 1285)).

[55] Added by the Local Government and Housing Act, Sched. 7.

[56] Added by Local Government, Planning and Land Act 1980, Sched. 33, para. 4(2).

and it subsequently made to appear to the court that the order was obtained, or the court was induced to refuse the grant, by misrepresentation or the concealment of material facts, the court may order the landlord to pay to the tenant such sum as appears sufficient as compensation for damage or loss sustained by the tenant as the result of the order or refusal.

(2) Where—

(a) the tenant has quit the holding—

(i) after making but withdrawing an application under section 24(1) of this Act; or

(ii) without making such an application; and

(b) it is made to appear to the court that he did so by reason of misrepresentation or the concealment of material facts,

the court may order the landlord to pay to the tenant such sum as appears sufficient as compensation for damage or loss sustained by the tenant as the result of quitting the holding.[57]

A1.046 **Restriction on agreements excluding provisions of Part II**

38.—(1) Any agreement relating to a tenancy to which this Part of this Act applies (whether contained in the instrument creating the tenancy or not) shall be void [(except as provided by ~~subsection (4) of this section~~) **section 38A of this Act**[58]] in so far as it purports to preclude the tenant from making an application or request under this Part of this Act or provides for the termination or the surrender of the tenancy in the event of his making such an application or request or for the imposition of any penalty or disability on the tenant in that event.

(2) Where—

(a) during the whole of the five years immediately preceding the date on which the tenant under a tenancy to which this Part of this Act applies is to quit the holding, premises being or comprised in the holding have been occupied for the purposes of a business carried on by the occupier or for those and other purposes, and

(b) if during those five years there was a change in the occupier of the premises, the person who was the occupier immediately after the change was the successor to the business carried on by the person who was the occupier immediately before the change,

any agreement (whether contained in the instrument creating the tenancy or not and whether made before or after the termination of that tenancy) which purports to exclude or reduce compensation under [section 37 of this Act][59] shall to that extent be void, so however that this subsection shall not affect any agreement as to the amount of any such compensation which is made after the right to compensation has accrued.

(3) In a case not falling within the last foregoing subsection the right to compensation conferred by [section 37 of this Act][60] may be excluded or modified by agreement.

[57] Added by Regulatory Reform (Business Tenancies) (England and Wales) Order (SI 2003/3096) art. 20.

[58] Substituted by Regulatory Reform (Business Tenancies) (England and Wales) Order (SI 2003/3096) art. 21.

[59] Substituted by Regulatory Reform (Business Tenancies) (England and Wales) Order (SI 2003/3096) Sch.5, para.4.

[60] Substituted by Regulatory Reform (Business Tenancies) (England and Wales) Order (SI 2003/3096) Sch.5, para.4.

~~(4) The court may—~~

~~(a) on the joint application of the persons who will be the landlord and the tenant in relation to a tenancy to be granted for a term of years certain which will be a tenancy to which this part of this Act applies, authorise an agreement excluding in relation to that tenancy the provisions of section 24 to 28 of this Act; and~~

~~(b) on the joint application of the persons who are the landlord and the tenant in relation to a tenancy to which this Part of this Act applies, authorise an agreement for the surrender of the tenancy on such date or in such circumstances as may be specified in the agreement and on such terms (if any) as may be so specified;~~

~~if the agreement is contained in or endorsed on the instrument creating the tenancy or such other instrument as the court may specify; and an agreement contained in or endorsed on an instrument in pursuance of an authorisation given under this subsection shall be valid notwithstanding anything in the preceding provisions of this section.~~[61]

Agreements to exclude provisions of Part 2

38A.—(1) The persons who will be the landlord and the tenant in relation to a tenancy to be granted for a term of years certain which will be a tenancy to which this Part of this Act applies may agree that the provisions of sections 24 to 28 of this Act shall be excluded in relation to that tenancy.

(2) The persons who are the landlord and the tenant in relation to a tenancy to which this Part of this Act applies may agree that the tenancy shall be surrendered on such date or in such circumstances as may be specified in the agreement and on such terms (if any) as may be so specified.

(3) An agreement under subsection (1) above shall be void unless—

(a) the landlord has served on the tenant a notice in the form, or substantially in the form, set out in Schedule 1 to the Regulatory Reform (Business Tenancies) (England and Wales) Order 2003 ("the 2003 Order"); and

(b) the requirements specified in Schedule 2 to that Order are met.

(4) An agreement under subsection (2) above shall be void unless—

(a) the landlord has served on the tenant a notice in the form, or substantially in the form, set out in Schedule 3 to the 2003 Order; and

(b) the requirements specified in Schedule 4 to that Order are met.[62]

General and supplementary provisions

Saving for compulsory acquisitions **A1.047**

39.—(1)[. . .][63]

(2) If the amount of the compensation which would have been payable under section 37 of this Act if the tenancy had come to an end in circumstances giving

[61] Repealed by Regulatory Reform (Business Tenancies) (England and Wales) Order (SI 2003/3096) art. 21. Sch.6, para.1.

[62] Added by Regulatory Reform (Business Tenancies) (England and Wales) Order (SI 2003/3096) art. 22.

[63] Repealed by the Land Compensation Act 1973, s.86 and Sched. 3.

rise to compensation under that section and the date at which the acquiring authority obtained possession had been the termination of the current tenancy exceeds the amount of [the compensation payable under section 121 of the Lands Clauses Consolidation Act 1845 or section 20 of the Compulsory Purchase Act 1965 in the case of a tenancy to which this Part of the Act applies,][64] that compensation shall be increased by the amount of the excess.

(3) Nothing in section 24 of this Act shall affect the operation of the said section 121.

A1.048 **Duties of tenants and landlords of business premises to give information to each other**

~~**40.** (1) Where any person having an interest in any business premises, being an interest in reversion expectant (whether immediately or not) on a tenancy of those premises, serves on the tenant a notice in the prescribed form requiring him to do so, it shall be the duty of the tenant to notify that person in writing within one month of the service of the notice—~~

- ~~(a) whether he occupies the premises or any part thereof wholly or partly for the purposes of a business carried on by him, and~~
- ~~(b) whether his tenancy has effect subject to any sub-tenancy on which his tenancy is immediately expectant and, if so, what premises are comprised in the sub-tenancy, for what term it has effect (or, if it is terminable by notice, by what notice it can be terminated), what is the rent payable thereunder, who is the sub-tenant, and (to the best of his knowledge and belief) whether the sub-tenant is in occupation of the premises or of part of the premises comprised in the sub-tenancy and, if not, what is the sub-tenant's address.~~

~~(2) Where the tenant of any business premises, being a tenant under such a tenancy as is mentioned in subsection (1) of section 26 of this Act, serves on any of the persons mentioned in the next following subsection a notice in the prescribed form requiring him to do so, it shall be the duty of that person to notify the tenant in writing within one month after the service of the notice—~~

- ~~(a) whether he is the owner of the fee simple in respect of those premises or any part thereof or the mortgage in possession of such an owner and, if not,~~
- ~~(b) (to the best of his knowledge and belief) the name and address of the person who is his or, as the case may be, his mortgagor's immediate landlord in respect of those premises or of the part in respect of which he or his mortgagor is not the owner in fee simple, for what term his or his mortgagor's tenancy thereof has effect and what is the earliest date (if any) at which that tenancy is terminable by notice to quit given by the landlord.~~

~~(3) The persons referred to in the last foregoing subsection are, in relation to the tenant of any business premises,—~~

- ~~(a) any person having an interest in the premises, being an interest in reversion expectant (whether immediately or not) on the tenant's, and~~
- ~~(b) any person being a mortgagee in possession in respect of such an interest in reversion as is mentioned in paragraph (a) of this subsection;~~

~~and the information which any such person as is mentioned in paragraph (a) of this subsection is required to give under the last foregoing subsection shall~~

[64] Substituted by the Land Compensation Act 1973, s.47(3).

~~include information whether there is a mortgagee in possession of his interest in the premises and, if so, what is the name and address of the mortgagee.~~

~~(4) The foregoing provisions of this section shall not apply to a notice served by or on the tenant more than two years before the date on which apart from this Act his tenancy would come to an end by effluxion of time or could be brought to an end by notice to quit given by the landlord.~~

~~(5) In this section—~~

~~the expression "business premises" means premises used wholly or partly for the purposes of a business;~~

~~the expression "mortgagee in possession" includes a receiver appointed by the mortgagee or by the court who is in receipt of the rents and profits, and the expression "his mortgagor" shall be construed accordingly;~~

~~the expression "sub-tenant" includes a person retaining possession of any premises by virtue of [the Rent Act 1977] after the coming to an end of a sub-tenancy, and the expression "sub-tenancy" includes a right so to retain possession.~~

40.—(1) Where a person who is an owner of an interest in reversion expectant (whether immediately or not) on a tenancy of any business premises has served on the tenant a notice in the prescribed form requiring him to do so, it shall be the duty of the tenant to give the appropriate person in writing the information specified in subsection (2) below.

(2) That information is—

(a) whether the tenant occupies the premises or any part of them wholly or partly for the purposes of a business carried on by him;

(b) whether his tenancy has effect subject to any sub-tenancy on which his tenancy is immediately expectant and, if so—

(i) what premises are comprised in the sub-tenancy;

(ii) for what term it has effect (or, if it is terminable by notice, by what notice it can be terminated);

(iii) what is the rent payable under it;

(iv) who is the sub-tenant;

(v) (to the best of his knowledge and belief) whether the sub-tenant is in occupation of the premises or of part of the premises comprised in the sub-tenancy and, if not, what is the sub-tenant's address;

(vi) whether an agreement is in force excluding in relation to the sub-tenancy the provisions of sections 24 to 28 of this Act; and

(vii) whether a notice has been given under section 25 or 26(6) of this Act, or a request has been made under section 26 of this Act, in relation to the sub-tenancy and, if so, details of the notice or request; and

(c) (to the best of his knowledge and belief) the name and address of any other person who owns an interest in reversion in any part of the premises.

(3) Where the tenant of any business premises who is a tenant under such a tenancy as is mentioned in section 26(1) of this Act has served on a reversioner or a reversioner's mortgagee in possession a notice in the prescribed form requiring him to do so, it shall be the duty of the person on whom the notice is served to give the appropriate person in writing the information specified in subsection (4) below.

(4) That information is—

(a) whether he is the owner of the fee simple in respect of the premises or any part of them or the mortgagee in possession of such an owner,

(b) if he is not, then (to the best of his knowledge and belief)—

(i) the name and address of the person who is his or, as the case may be, his mortgagor's immediate landlord in respect of those premises or of the part in respect of which he or his mortgagor is not the owner in fee simple;

(ii) for what term his or his mortgagor's tenancy has effect and what is the earliest date (if any) at which that tenancy is terminable by notice to quit given by the landlord; and

(iii) whether a notice has been given under section 25 or 26(6) of this Act, or a request has been made under section 26 of this Act, in relation to the tenancy and, if so, details of the notice or request;

(c) (to the best of his knowledge and belief) the name and address of any other person who owns an interest in reversion in any part of the premises; and

(d) if he is a reversioner, whether there is a mortgagee in possession of his interest in the premises and, if so, (to the best of his knowledge and belief) what is the name and address of the mortgagee.

(5) A duty imposed on a person by this section is a duty—

(a) to give the information concerned within the period of one month beginning with the date of service of the notice; and

(b) if within the period of six months beginning with the date of service of the notice that person becomes aware that any information which has been given in pursuance of the notice is not, or is no longer, correct, to give the appropriate person correct information within the period of one month beginning with the date on which he becomes aware.

(6) This section shall not apply to a notice served by or on the tenant more than two years before the date on which apart from this Act his tenancy would come to an end by effluxion of time or could be brought to an end by notice to quit given by the landlord.

(7) Except as provided by section 40A of this Act, the appropriate person for the purposes of this section and section 40A(1) of this Act is the person who served the notice under subsection (1) or (3) above.

(8) In this section—

"business premises" means premises used wholly or partly for the purposes of a business;

"mortgagee in possession" includes a receiver appointed by the mortgagee or by the court who is in receipt of the rents and profits, and "his mortgagor" shall be construed accordingly;

"reversioner" means any person having an interest in the premises, being an interest in reversion expectant (whether immediately or not) on the tenancy;

"reversioner's mortgagee in possession" means any person being a mortgagee in possession in respect of such an interest; and

"sub-tenant" includes a person retaining possession of any premises by virtue of the Rent (Agriculture) Act 1976 or the Rent Act 1977 after the coming to an end of a sub-tenancy, and "sub-tenancy" includes a right so to retain possession.[65]

[65] Substituted by Regulatory Reform (Business Tenancies) (England and Wales) Order (SI 2003/3096) art. 23.

Duties in transfer cases A1.049

40A.—(1) If a person on whom a notice under section 40(1) or (3) of this Act has been served has transferred his interest in the premises or any part of them to some other person and gives the appropriate person notice in writing—

(a) of the transfer of his interest; and

(b) of the name and address of the person to whom he transferred it,

on giving the notice he ceases in relation to the premises or (as the case may be) to that part to be under any duty imposed by section 40 of this Act.

(2) If—

(a) the person who served the notice under section 40(1) or (3) of this Act ("the transferor") has transferred his interest in the premises to some other person ("the transferee"); and

(b) the transferor or the transferee has given the person required to give the information notice in writing—

(i) of the transfer; and

(ii) of the transferee's name and address,

the appropriate person for the purposes of section 40 of this Act and subsection (1) above is the transferee.

(3) If—

(a) a transfer such as is mentioned in paragraph (a) of subsection (2) above has taken place; but

(b) neither the transferor nor the transferee has given a notice such as is mentioned in paragraph (b) of that subsection,

any duty imposed by section 40 of this Act may be performed by giving the information either to the transferor or to the transferee.[66]

Proceedings for breach of duties to give information A1.050

40B. A claim that a person has broken any duty imposed by section 40 of this Act may be made the subject of civil proceedings for breach of statutory duty; and in any such proceedings a court may order that person to comply with that duty and may make an award of damages.[67]

Trusts A1.051

41.—(1) Where a tenancy is held on trust, occupation by all or any of the beneficiaries under the trust, and the carrying on of a business by all or any of the beneficiaries, shall be treated for the purposes of section twenty-three of this Act as equivalent to occupation or the carrying on of a business by the tenant; and in relation to a tenancy to which this part of this Act applies by virtue of the foregoing provisions of this subsection—

(a) references (however expressed) in this Part of this Act and in the Ninth Schedule to this Act to the business of, or to carrying on of business, use, occupation or enjoyment by, the tenant shall be construed as including references to the business of, or to carrying on of business, use, occupation or enjoyment by, the beneficiaries or beneficiary;

[66] Added by Regulatory Reform (Business Tenancies) (England and Wales) Order (SI 2003/3096) art. 24.

[67] Added by Regulatory Reform (Business Tenancies) (England and Wales) Order (SI 2003/3096) art. 24.

(b) the reference in paragraph (d) of [subsection (1) of][68] section thirty-four of this Act to the tenant shall be construed as including the beneficiaries or beneficiary; and

(c) a change in the persons of the trustees shall not be treated as a change in the person of the tenant.

(2) Where the landlord's interests is held on trust the references in paragraph (g) of subsection (1) of section thirty of this Act to the landlord shall be construed as including references to the beneficiaries under the trust or any of them; but, except in the case of a trust arising under a will or on the intestacy of any person, the reference in subsection (2) of that section to the creation of the interest therein mentioned shall be construed as including the creation of the trust.

A1.052 **[Partnerships**

41A.—(1) The following provisions of this section shall apply where—

(a) a tenancy is held jointly by two or more persons (in this section referred to as the joint tenants); and

(b) the property comprised in the tenancy is or includes premises occupied for the purposes of a business; and

(c) the business (or some other business) was at some time during the existence of the tenancy carried on in partnership by all the persons who were then the joint tenants or by those and other persons and the joint tenants' interest in the premises was then partnership property; and

(d) the business is carried on (whether alone or in partnership with other persons) by one or some only of the joint tenants and no part of the property comprised in the tenancy is occupied, in the right of the tenancy, for the purposes of a business carried on (whether alone or in partnership with other persons) by the other or others.

(2) In the following provisions of this section those of the joint tenants who for the time being carry on the business are referred to as the business tenants and the others as the other joint tenants.

(3) Any notice given by the business tenants which, had it been given by all the joint tenants, would have been—

(a) a tenant's request for a new tenancy made in accordance with section 26 of this Act; or

(b) a notice under subsection (1) or subsection (2) of section 27 of this Act;

shall be treated as such if it states that it is given by virtue of this section and sets out the facts by virtue of which the persons giving it are the business tenants; and references in those sections and in section 24A of this Act to the tenant shall be construed accordingly.

(4) A notice given by the landlord to the business tenant which, had it been given to all the joint tenants, would have been a notice under section 25 of this Act shall be treated as such a notice, and references in that section to the tenant shall be construed accordingly.

(5) An application under section 24(1) of this Act for a new tenancy may, instead of being made by all the joint tenants, be made by the business tenants alone; and where it is so made—

[68] Inserted by Law of Property Act 1969, s.1(2).

(a) this Part of this Act shall have effect, in relation to it, as if the references therein to the tenant included references to the business tenants alone, and

(b) the business tenants shall be liable, to the exclusion of the other joint tenants, for the payment of rent and the discharge of any other obligation under the current tenancy for any rental period beginning after the date specified in the landlord's notice under section 25 of this Act or, as the case may be, beginning on or after the date specified in their request for a new tenancy.

(6) Where the court makes an order under ~~section 29(1) of this Act for the grant of a new tenancy on an application made by the business tenants, it may order the grant to be made to them or to them jointly~~ **section 29 of this Act for the grant of a new tenancy it may order the grant to be made to the business tenants or to them jointly**[69] with the persons carrying on the business in partnership with them, and may order the grant to be made subject to the satisfaction, within a time specified by the order, of such conditions as to guarantors, sureties or otherwise as appear to the court equitable, having regard to the omission of the other joint tenants from the persons who will be the tenant under the new tenancy.

(7) The business tenants shall be entitled to recover any amount payable by way of compensation under section 37 or section 59 of this Act.][70]

Groups of companies **A1.053**

42.—(1) For the purposes of this section two bodies corporate shall be taken to be members of a group if and only if one is a subsidiary of the other or both are subsidiaries of a third body corporate **or the same person has a controlling interest in both.**[71]

~~In this subsection "subsidiary" has [the meaning given by section 736 of the Companies Act 1985].~~[72]

(2) Where a tenancy is held by a member of a group, occupation by another member of the group, and the carrying on of a business by another member of the group, shall be treated for the purposes of section 23 of this Act as equivalent to occupation or the carrying on of a business by the member of the group holding the tenancy; and in relation to a tenancy to which this Part of this Act applies by virtue of the foregoing provisions of this subsection—

(a) references (however expressed) in this Part of this Act and in the Ninth Schedule to this Act to the business of or to use occupation or enjoyment by the tenant shall be construed as including references to the business of or to use occupation or enjoyment by the said other member;

(b) the reference in paragraph (d) of [subsection (1) of][73] section thirty-four of this Act to the tenant shall be construed as including the said other member; and

[69] Substituted by Regulatory Reform (Business Tenancies) (England and Wales) Order (SI 2003/3096) Sch.5, para.5.

[70] Inserted by the Law of Property Act 1969, s.9.

[71] Added by Regulatory Reform (Business Tenancies) (England and Wales) Order (SI 2003/3096) art. 16.

[72] Repealed by Regulatory Reform (Business Tenancies) (England and Wales) Order (SI 2003/3096) Sch.6, para.1.

[73] Inserted by Law of Property Act 1969, s.1(2).

(c) an assignment of the tenancy from one member of the group to another shall not be treated as a change in the person of the tenant.

[(3) Where the landlord's interest is held by a member of a group—

(a) the reference in paragraph (g) of subsection (1) of section 30 of this Act to intended occupation by the landlord for the purposes of a business to be carried on by him shall be construed as including intended occupation by any member of the group for the purposes of a business to be carried on by that member; and

(b) the reference in subsection (2) of that section to the purchase or creation of any interest shall be construed as a reference to a purchase from or creation by a person other than a member of the group.][74]

A1.054 Tenancies excluded from Part II

43.—(1) This Part of this Act does not apply—

(a) to a tenancy of an agricultural holding [which is a tenancy in relation to which the Agricultural Holdings Act 1986 applies on a tenancy which would be a tenancy of an agricultural holding in relation to which that Act applied if subsection (3) of section 2 of that Act][75] did not have effect or, in a case where approval was given under subsection (1) of that section][76] if that approval had not been given.[77]

[(aa) to a farm business tenancy].[78]

(b) to a tenancy created by a mining lease;

(c) [. . .][79]; or

(d) [. . .][80]

(2) This Part of this Act does not apply to a tenancy granted by reason that the tenant was the holder of an office, appointment or employment from the grantor thereof and continuing only so long as the tenant holds the office, appointment or employment, or terminable by the grantor on the tenant's ceasing to hold it, or coming to an end at a time fixed by reference to the time at which the tenant ceases to hold it:

Provided that this subsection shall not have effect in relation to a tenancy granted after the commencement of this Act unless the tenancy was granted by an instrument in writing which expressed the purpose for which the tenancy was granted.

(3) This Part of this Act does not apply to a tenancy granted for a term certain not exceeding [six months][81] unless—

(a) the tenancy contains provision for renewing the term or for extending it beyond [six months][82] from its beginning; or

(b) the tenant has been in occupation for a period which, together with any period during which any predecessor in the carrying on of the

[74] Substituted by Law of Property Act 1969, s.10.
[75] Inserted by Agricultural Tenancies Act 1995 (c.8). Sched.
[76] Substituted by Agricultural Holdings Act 1986, Sched. 14, para. 21.
[77] As amended by the Agriculture Act 1958.
[78] Inserted 1995, c. 8, Sched., *ibid.*
[79] Repealed by Housing Act 1980, s.152 and Sched. 26.
[80] Repealed by Landlord and Tenant (Licensed Premises) Act 1990, ss.1, 2.
[81] Substituted by the Law of Property Act 1969, s.12(1).
[82] Substituted by the Law of Property Act 1969, s.12(1).

business carried on by the tenant was in occupation, exceeds [twelve months].[83]

[Jurisdiction of county court to make declaration A1.055

43A.—Where the rateable value of the holding is such that the jurisdiction conferred on the court by any other provision of this Part of this Act is, by virtue of section 63 of this Act, exercisable by the county court, the county court shall have jurisdiction (but without prejudice to the jurisdiction of the High Court) to make any declaration as to any matter arising under this Part of this Act, whether or not any other relief is sought in the proceedings.][84]

Meaning of "the landlord" in Part II, and provisions as to mesne landlords, etc. A1.056

44.—(1) Subject to ~~the next following subsection~~ **subsections (1A) and (2) below,**[85] in this Part of this Act the expression "the landlord", in relation to a tenancy (in this section referred to as "the relevant tenancy"), means the person (whether or not he is the immediate landlord) who is the owner of that interest in the property comprised in the relevant tenancy which for the time being fulfils the following conditions, that is to say—

(a) that it is an interest in reversion expectant (whether immediately or not) on the termination of the relevant tenancy, and

[(b) that it is either the fee simple or a tenancy which will not come to an end within fourteen months by effluxion of time and, if it is such a tenancy, that no notice has been given by virtue of which it will come to an end within fourteen months or any further time by which it may be continued under section 36(2) or section 64 of this Act,][86]

and is not itself in reversion expectant (whether immediately or not) on an interest which fulfils those conditions.

(1A) The reference in subsection (1) above to a person who is the owner of an interest such as is mentioned in that subsection is to be construed, where different persons own such interests in different parts of the property, as a reference to all those persons collectively.

(2) References in this Part of this Act to a notice to quit given by the landlord are references to a notice to quit given by the immediate landlord.

(3) The provisions of the Sixth Schedule to this Act shall have effect for the application of this Part of this Act to cases where the immediate landlord of the tenant is not the owner of the fee simple in respect of the holding.

Interpretation of Part II A1.057

46.(1)—In this Part of this Act:—

"business" has the meaning assigned to it by subsection (2) of section 23 of this Act;

~~"current tenancy" has the meaning assigned to it by subsection (1) of section 26 of this Act;~~

[83] Substituted by the Law of Property Act 1969, s.12(1).

[84] Inserted by the Law of Property Act 1969, s.13.

[85] Substituted by Regulatory Reform (Business Tenancies) (England and Wales) Order (SI 2003/3096) art.27.

[86] Substituted by the Law of Property Act 1969, s.14(1).

"current tenancy" means the tenancy under which the tenant holds for the time being;[87]

"date of termination" has the meaning assigned to it by subsection (1) of section 25 of this Act;

subject to the provisions of section 32 of this Act, "the holding" has the meaning assigned to it by subsection (3) of section 23 of this Act;

"interim rent" has the meaning given by section 24A(1) of this Act;[88]

"mining lease" has the same meaning as in the Landlord and Tenant Act, 1927.

(2) For the purposes of this Part of this Act, a person has a controlling interest in a company, if, had he been a company, the other company would have been its subsidiary; and in this Part- "company" has the meaning given by section 735 of the Companies Act 1985; and

"subsidiary" has the meaning given by section 736 of that Act.[89]

Part III

Compensation for Improvements

A1.058 **Time for making claims for compensation for improvements**

47.—(1) Where a tenancy is terminated by notice to quit, whether given by the landlord or by the tenant, or by a notice given by any person under Part I or Part II of this Act, the time for making a claim for compensation at the termination of the tenancy shall be a time falling within the period of three months beginning on the date on which the notice is given:

Provided that where the tenancy is terminated by a tenant's request for a new tenancy under section 26 of this Act, the said time shall be a time falling within the period of three months beginning on the date on which the landlord gives notice, or (if he has not given such a notice), the latest date on which he could have given notice, under subsection (6) of the said section 26 or, as the case may be, paragraph (a) of subsection (4) of section 57 or paragraph (b) of subsection (1) of section 58 of this Act.

(2) Where a tenancy comes to an end by effluxion of time, the time for making such a claim shall be a time not earlier than six nor later than three months before the coming to an end of the tenancy.

(3) Where a tenancy is terminated by forfeiture or re-entry, the time for making such a claim shall be a time falling within the period of three months beginning with the effective date of the order of the court for the recovery of possession of the land comprised in the tenancy or, if the tenancy is terminated by re-entry without such an order, the period of three months beginning with the date of the re-entry.

87 Substituted by Regulatory Reform (Business Tenancies) (England and Wales) Order (SI 2003/3096) Sch 5, para.6.

88 Added by Regulatory Reform (Business Tenancies) (England and Wales) Order (SI 2003/3096) Sch 5, para.6.

89 Added by Regulatory Reform (Business Tenancies) (England and Wales) Order (SI 2003/3096) art.17.

(4) In the last foregoing subsection the reference to the effective date of an order is a reference to the date on which the order is to take effect according to the terms thereof or the date on which it ceases to be subject to appeal, whichever is the later.

(5) In subsection (1) of section one of the Act of 1927, for paragraphs (a) and (b) (which specify the time for making claims for compensation) there shall be substituted the words "and within the time limited by section forty-seven of the Landlord and Tenant Act, 1954".

Amendments as to limitations on tenant's right to compensation **A1.059**

48.—(1) So much of paragraph (b) of subsection (1) of section two of the Act of 1927 as provides that a tenant shall not be entitled to compensation in respect of any improvement made in pursuance of a statutory obligation shall not apply to any improvement begun after the commencement of this Act, but section three of the Act of 1927 (which enables a landlord to object to a proposed improvement) shall not have effect in relation to an improvement made in pursuance of a statutory obligation except so much thereof as—

(a) requires the tenant to serve on the landlord notice of his intention to make the improvement together with such a plan and specification as are mentioned in that section and to supply copies of the plan and specification at the request of any superior landlord; and

(b) enables the tenant to obtain at his expense a certificate from the landlord or the tribunal that the improvement has been duly executed.

(2) Paragraph (c) of the said subsection (1) (which provides that a tenant shall not be entitled to compensation in respect of any improvement made less than three years before the termination of the tenancy) shall not apply to any improvement begun after the commencement of this Act.

(3) No notice shall be served after the commencement of this Act under paragraph (d) of the said subsection (1) (which excludes rights to compensation where the landlord serves on the tenant notice offering a renewal of the tenancy on reasonable terms).

Restrictions on contracting out **A1.060**

49.—In section nine of the Act of 1927 (which provides that Part 1 of that Act shall apply notwithstanding any contract to the contrary made after the date specified in that section) the proviso (which requires effect to be given to such a contract where it appears to the tribunal that the contract was made for adequate consideration) shall cease to have effect except as respects a contract made before the tenth day of December, nineteen hundred and fifty-three.

Interpretation of Part III **A1.061**

50.—In this Part of this Act the expression "Act of 1927" means the Landlord and Tenant Act, 1927, the expression "compensation" means compensation under Part I of that Act in respect of an improvement, and other expressions used in this Part of this Act and in the Act of 1927 have the same meanings in this Part of this Act as in that Act.

PART IV

MISCELLANEOUS AND SUPPLEMENTARY

A1.062 Jurisdiction of county court where lessor refuses licence or consent

53.—(1) Where a landlord withholds his licence or consent—

(a) to an assignment of the tenancy or a subletting, charging or parting with the possession of the demised property or any part thereof, or

(b) to the making of an improvement on the demised property or any part thereof, or

(c) to a change in the use of the demised property or any part thereof, or to the making of a specified use of that property.

and the High Court has jurisdiction to make a declaration that the licence or consent was unreasonably withheld, then without prejudice to the jurisdiction of the High Court the country court shall have [the like jurisdiction whatever the net annual value for rating of the demised property is to be taken to be for the purposes of the County Courts Act 1984],[90] and notwithstanding that the tenant does not seek any relief other than the declaration.

(2) Where on the making of an application to the county court for such a declaration the court is satisfied that the licence or consent was unreasonably withheld, the court shall make a declaration accordingly.

(3) The foregoing provisions of this section shall have effect whether the tenancy in question was created before or after the commencement of this Act and whether the refusal of the licence or consent occurred before or after the commencement of this Act.

(4) Nothing in this section shall be construed as conferring jurisdiction on the county court to grant any relief other than such a declaration as aforesaid.

A1.063 Compensation for possession obtained by misrepresentation

55.—~~(1) Where under Part I of this Act an order is made for possession of the property comprised in a tenancy, or under Part II of this Act the court refuses an order for the grant of a new tenancy, and it is subsequently made to appear to the court that the order was obtained, or the court induced to refuse the grant, by misrepresentation or the concealment of material facts, the court may order the landlord to pay to the tenant such sum as appears sufficient as compensation for damage or loss sustained by the tenant as the result of the order or refusal.~~

~~(2) In this section the expression "the landlord" means the person applying for possession or opposing an application for the grant of a new tenancy, and the expression "the tenant" means the person against whom the order for possession was made or to whom the grant of a new tenancy was refused.~~[91]

[90] Substituted by the County Courts Act 1984, Sched. 2, para.23.

[91] Repealed by Regulatory Reform (Business Tenancies) (England and Wales) Order (SI 2003/3096) Sch 6, para.1.

Application to Crown[92] **A1.064**

56.—(1) Subject to the provisions of this and the four next following sections, Part II of this Act shall apply where there is an interest belonging to Her Majesty in right of the Crown or the Duchy of Lancaster or belonging to the Duchy of Cornwall, or belonging to a Government department or held on behalf of Her Majesty for the purposes of a Government department, in like manner as if that interest were an interest not so belonging or held.

(2) The provisions of the Eighth Schedule to this Act shall have effect as respects the application of Part II of this Act to cases where the interest of the landlord belongs to Her Majesty in right of the Crown or the Duchy of Lancaster or to the Duchy of Cornwall.

(3) Where a tenancy is held by or on behalf of a Government department and the property comprised therein is or includes premises occupied for any purposes of a Government department, the tenancy shall be one to which Part II of this Act applies; and for the purposes of any provision of the said Part II or the Ninth Schedule to this Act which is applicable only if either or both of the following conditions are satisfied, that is to say—

- (a) that any premises have during any period been occupied for the purposes of the tenant's business;
- (b) that on any change of occupier of any premises the new occupier succeeded to the business of the former occupier,

the said conditions shall be deemed to be satisfied respectively, in relation to such a tenancy, if during that period or, as the case may be, immediately before and immediately after the change, the premises were occupied for the purposes of a Government department.[93]

(4) The last foregoing subsection shall apply in relation to any premises provided by a Government department without any rent being payable to the department therefore as if the premises were occupied for the purposes of a Government department.

(5) The provisions of Parts III and IV of this Act amending any other enactment which binds the Crown or applies to land belonging to Her Majesty in right of the Crown or the Duchy of Lancaster, or land belonging to the Duchy of Cornwall, or to land belonging to any Government department, shall bind the Crown or apply to such land.

(6) Sections fifty-three and fifty-four of this Act shall apply where the interest of the landlord, or any other interest in the land in question, belongs to Her Majesty in right of the Crown or the Duchy of Lancaster or to the Duchy or Cornwall, or belongs to a Government department or is held on behalf of Her Majesty for the purposes of a Government department, in like manner as if that interest were an interest not so belonging or held.

[92] In s.56, any reference to a tenancy held by or on behalf of a Government department shall include a reference to a tenancy held by or on behalf of a visiting force or headquarters; and any reference to premises occupied for the purposes of a Government department shall include premises occupied for the purposes of a visiting force or headquarters; see the Visiting Forces and International Headquarters (Application of Law) Order 1999 (S.I. 1999 No. 1736), art. 12(2), Sched. 6.

[93] In this section and s.58 *post*, any reference to an interest in the property comprised in a tenancy held for the purposes of a Government department shall include a reference to such an interest where held for the purposes of a visiting force or headquarters; and the reference in s. 57(1) to "the first mentioned department" shall be construed accordingly; see the Visiting Forces and International Headquarters (Application of Law) Order 1999 (S.I. 1999 No. 1736), art. 12(2), Sched. 6.

[(7) Part I of this Act shall apply where—

(a) there is an interest belonging to Her Majesty in right of the Crown and that interest is under the management of the Crown Estate Commissioners; or

(b) there is an interest belonging to Her Majesty in right of the Duchy of Lancaster or belonging to the Duchy of Cornwall;

as if it were an interest not so belonging.][94]

A1.065 Modification on grounds of public interest of rights under Part II[95]

57.—(1) Where the interest of the landlord or any superior landlord in the property comprised in any tenancy belongs to or is held for the purposes of a Government department or is held by a local authority, statutory undertakers or a development corporation, the Minister or Board in charge of any Government department may certify that it is requisite for the purposes of the first-mentioned department, or, as the case may be, of the authority, undertakers or corporation, that the use or occupation of the property or a part thereof shall be changed by a specified date.

(2) A certificate under the last foregoing subsection shall not be given unless the owner of the interest belonging or held as mentioned in the last foregoing subsection has given to the tenant a notice stating—

(a) that the question of the giving of such a certificate is under consideration by the Minister or Board specified in the notice, and

(b) that if within twenty-one days of the giving of the notice the tenant makes to that Minister or Board representations in writing with respect to that question, they will be considered before the question is determined,

and if the tenant makes any such representations within the said twenty-one days the Minister or Board shall consider them before determining whether to give the certificate.

(3) Where a certificate has been given under subsection (1) of this section in relation to any tenancy, then,—

(a) if a notice given under subsection (1) of section 25 of this Act specifies as the date of termination a date not earlier than the date specified in the certificate and contains a copy of the certificate ~~subsections (5) and~~ **subsection**[96] (6) of that section shall not apply to the notice and no application for a new tenancy shall be made by the tenant under **subsection (1) of**[97] section 24 of this Act;

(b) if such a notice specifies an earlier date as the date of termination and contains a copy of the certificate, then if the court makes an order under Part II of this Act for the grant of a new tenancy the new tenancy shall be for a term expiring not later than the date specified in the certificate and shall not be a tenancy to which Part II of this Act applies.

(4) Where a tenant makes a request for a new tenancy under section 26 of this Act, and the interest of the landlord or any superior landlord in the

[94] Added by Housing Act 1980, s.73(4)(*a*).

[95] See also Leasehold Reform Act, 1967, ss.28(3), 38(2).

[96] Substituted by Regulatory Reform (Business Tenancies) (England and Wales) Order (SI 2003/3096) Sch. 5, para.7.

[97] Added by Regulatory Reform (Business Tenancies) (England and Wales) Order (SI 2003/3096) Sch. 5, para.7.

property comprised in the current tenancy belongs or is held as mentioned in subsection (1) of this section, the following provisions shall have effect:—

(a) if a certificate has been given under the said subsection (1) in relation to the current tenancy, and within two months after the making of the request the landlord gives notice to the tenant that the certificate has been given and the notice contains a copy of the certificate, then,—

(i) if the date specified in the certificate is not later than that specified in the tenant's request for a new tenancy, the tenant shall not make an application under section 24 of this Act for the grant of a new tenancy;

(ii) if, in any other case, the court makes an order under Part II of this Act for the grant of a new tenancy the new tenancy shall be for a term expiring not later than the date specified in the certificate and shall not be a tenancy to which Part II of this Act applies;

(b) if no such certificate has been given but notice under subsection (2) of this section has been given before the making of the request or within two months thereafter, the request shall not have effect, without prejudice however to the making of a new request when the Minister or Board has determined whether to give a certificate.

(5) Where application is made to the court under part II of this Act for the grant of a new tenancy and the landlord's interest in the property comprised in the tenancy belongs or is held as mentioned in subsection (1) of this section, the Minister or Board in charge of any Government department may certify that it is necessary in the public interest that if the landlord makes an application in that behalf the court shall determine as a term of the new tenancy that it shall be terminable by six months' notice to quit given by the landlord.

Subsection (2) of this section shall apply in relation to a certificate under this subsection, and if notice under the said subsection (2) has been given to the tenant—

(a) the court shall not determine the application for the grant of a new tenancy until the Minister or Board has determined whether to give a certificate,

(b) if a certificate is given, the court shall on the application of the landlord determine as a term of the new tenancy that it shall be terminable as aforesaid, and section 25 of this Act shall apply accordingly.

(6) The foregoing provisions of this section shall apply to an interest held by a [Health Authority or Special Health Authority][98] as they apply to an interest held by a local authority but with the substitution, for the references to the purposes of the authority, of a reference to the purposes of [~~National Health Service Act 1997~~] **the National Health Service Act 2006 or the National Health Service (Wales) Act 2006**.[99]

(7) Where the interest of the landlord or any superior landlord in the property comprised in any tenancy belongs to the National Trust the Minister of Works may certify that it is requisite, for the purpose of securing that the property will as from a specified date be used or occupied in a manner better suited

[98] Inserted by Health Authorities Act 1995 (c. 17), Sched. 1.

[99] Substituted by the National Health Service Act 1977, s.129 and Sched.15. Subsequently substituted by the National Health Service (Consequential Provisions) Act 2006 (c.43) Sch.1 para.15.

to the nature thereof, that the use or occupation of the property should be changed; and subsections (2) to (4) of this section shall apply in relation to certificates under this subsection, and to cases where the interest of the landlord or any superior landlord belongs to the National Trust, as those subsections apply in relation to certificates under subsection (1) of this section and to cases where the interest of the landlord or any superior landlord belongs or is held as mentioned in that subsection.

(8) In this and the next following section the expression "Government department" does not include the Commissioners of Crown Lands and the expression "landlord" has the same meaning as in Part II of this Act; and in the last foregoing subsection the expression "National Trust" means the National Trust for Places of Historic Interest or Natural Beauty.

A1.066 **Termination on special grounds of tenancies to which Part II applies**

58.—(1) Where the landlord's interest in the property comprised in any tenancy belongs to or is held for the purposes of a Government department, and the Minister or Board in charge of any Government department certifies that for reasons of national security it is necessary that the use or occupation of the property should be discontinued or changed, then—

- (a) if the landlord gives a notice under subsection (1) of section 25 of this Act containing a copy of the certificate, [subsection][100] (6) of that section shall not apply to the notice and no application for a new tenancy shall be made by the tenant under [subsection (1) of][101] section 24 of this Act;
- (b) if (whether before or after the giving of the certificate) the tenant makes a request for a new tenancy under section 26 of this Act, and within two months after the making of the request the landlord gives notice to the tenant that the certificate has been given and the notice contains a copy of the certificate,—
  - (i) the tenant shall not make an application under section 24 of this Act for the grant of a new tenancy, and
  - (ii) if the notice specifies as the date on which the tenancy is to terminate a date earlier than that specified in the tenant's request as the date on which the new tenancy is to begin but neither earlier than six months from the giving of the notice nor earlier than the earliest date at which apart from this Act the tenancy would come to an end or could be brought to an end, the tenancy shall terminate on the date specified in the notice instead of that specified in the request.

(2) Where the landlord's interest in the property comprised in any tenancy belongs to or is held for the purposes of a Government department, nothing in this Act shall invalidate an agreement to the effect—

- (a) that on the giving of such a certificate as is mentioned in the last foregoing subsection the tenancy may be terminated by notice to quit given by the landlord of such length as may be specified in the agreement, if the notice contains a copy of the certificate; and

[100] Substituted by Regulatory Reform (Business Tenancies) (England and Wales) Order (SI 2003/3096) Sch. 5, para.7.

[101] Added by Regulatory Reform (Business Tenancies) (England and Wales) Order (SI 2003/3096) Sch. 5, para.7.

(b) that after the giving of such a notice containing such a copy the tenancy shall not be one to which Part II of this Act applies.

(3) Where the landlord's interest in the property comprised in any tenancy is held by statutory undertakers, nothing in this Act shall invalidate an agreement to the effect—

(a) that where the Minister or Board in charge of a Government department certifies that possession of the property comprised in the tenancy or a part thereof is urgently required for carrying out repairs (whether on that property or elsewhere) which are needed for the proper operation of the landlord's undertaking, the tenancy may be terminated by notice to quit given by the landlord of such length as may be specified in the agreement, if the notice contains a copy of the certificate; and

(b) that after the giving of such a notice containing such a copy, the tenancy shall not be one to which Part II of this Act applies.

(4) Where the court makes an order under Part II of this Act for the grant of a new tenancy and the Minister or Board in charge of any Government department certifies that the public interest requires the tenancy to be subject to such a term as is mentioned in paragraph (a) or (b) of this subsection, as the case may be, then—

(a) if the landlord's interest in the property comprised in the tenancy belongs to or is held for the purposes of a Government department, the court shall on the application of the landlord determine as a term of the new tenancy that such an agreement as is mentioned in subsection (2) of this section and specifying such length of notice as is mentioned in the certificate shall be embodied in the new tenancy;

(b) if the landlord's interest in that property is held by statutory undertakers, the court shall on the application of the landlord determine as a term of the new tenancy that such an agreement as is mentioned in subsection (3) of this section and specifying such length of notice as is mentioned in the certificate shall be embodied in the new tenancy.

Compensation for exercise of powers under ss.57 and 58[102] A1.067

59.—(1) Where by virtue of any certificate given for the purposes of either of the two last foregoing sections [or, subject to subsection (1A) below, section 60A below.][103] the tenant is precluded from obtaining an order for the grant of a new tenancy, or of a new tenancy for a term expiring later than a specified date, the tenant shall be entitled on quitting the premises to recover from the owner of the interest by virtue of which the certificate was given an amount by way of compensation, and subsections (2), (3) **to (3B)**[104] and (5) to (7) of section 37 of this Act shall with the necessary modifications apply for the purposes of ascertaining the amount.

[(1A) No compensation shall be recoverable under subsection (1) above where the certificate was given under section 60A below and either—

(a) the premises vested in the Welsh Development Agency under section 7 (property of Welsh Industrial Estates Corporation) or 8 (land held under Local Employment Act 1972) of the Welsh Development

[102] See also Leasehold Reform Act 1967, S.28(3).

[103] Substituted by the Government of Wales Act 1998, s.129 and Sched. 15, para.1.

[104] Added by Regulatory Reform (Business Tenancies) (England and Wales) Order (SI 2003/3096) Sch. 5, para.8.

Agency Act 1975 **and were transferred to the National Assembly for Wales by virtue of the Welsh Development Agency (Transfer of Functions to the National Assembly for Wales and Abolition) Order 2005.**[105], or

~~(b) the tenant was not tenant of the premises when the said Agency acquired the interest by virtue of which the certificate was given.~~

(b) the tenant was not the tenant of the premises when the interest by virtue of which the certificate was given was acquired by the Welsh Development Agency or, if the interest was acquired on or after 1 April 2006, by the National Assembly for Wales in exercise of functions transferred to it by the Welsh Development Agency (Transfer of Functions to the National Assembly for Wales and Abolition) Order 2005[106]

(1B) [. . .][107]

(2) Subsections (2) and (3) of section 38 of this Act shall apply to compensation under this section as they apply to compensation under section 37 of this Act.

60.[108]—(1) Where the property comprised in a tenancy consists of premises of which the Minister of Technology or [the Urban Regeneration Agency][109] is the landlord, being premises situated in a locality which is either—

(a) a development area; or

(b) an intermediate area;

and the Minister of Technology certifies that it is necessary or expedient for achieving the purpose mentioned in section 2(1) of the said Act of 1972[110] that the use or occupation of the property should be changed, paragraphs (a) and (b) of subsection (1) of section 58 of this Act shall apply as they apply where such a certificate is given as is mentioned in that subsection.

(2) For the words "premises provided" there is to be substituted the words "any such premises" and for the words "the Board of Trade certify" there is to be substituted "the Minister of Technology certifies".

[(3) In this section "development area or, as the case may be, as an intermediate area by an order made, or having effect as if made, under section 1 of the Industrial Development Act 1982.][111]

A1.068 Welsh Development Agency premises

60A.—(1) Where the property comprised in a tenancy consists of premises of which the ~~Welsh Development Agency is the landlord, and the Secretary of State~~ **National Assembly for Wales is the landlord by virtue of the Welsh**

[105] Added subject to transitional provisions specified in SI 2005/3226 art.3 by Welsh Development Agency (Transfer of Functions to the National Assembly for Wales and Abolition) Order (SI 2005/3226) Sch.2, para.1.

[106] Substituted subject to transitional provisions specified in SI 2005/3226 art.3 by Welsh Development Agency (Transfer of Functions to the National Assembly for Wales and Abolition) Order (SI 2005/3226) Sch.2, para.1.

[107] Repealed by the Government of Wales Act 1998, s.152 and Sched. 18, Pt IV.

[108] As amended.

[109] Amended by the Leasehold Reform. Housing and Urban Development Act 1993, Sched. 21.

[110] S.2(1) of the Local Employment Act 1972 shall continue to have effect notwithstanding the repeal of the 1972 Act by the Industry Act 1972, Sched. 4.

[111] Substituted by Industrial Development Act 1982, Sched. 2.

Development Agency (Transfer of Functions to the National Assembly for Wales and Abolition) Order 2005 or by virtue of the Assembly exercising its functions under that Order, and the Assembly[112] certifies that it is necessary or expedient, for the purpose of providing employment appropriate to the needs of the area in which the premises are situated, that the use or occupation of the property should be changed, paragraphs (a) and (b) of section 58(1) above shall apply as they apply where such a certificate is given as is mentioned in that subsection.

(2) Where the court makes an order under Part II of this Act for the grant of a new tenancy of any such premises as aforesaid, and the [National Assembly for Wales][113] certifies that it is necessary or expedient as aforesaid that the tenancy should be subject to a term, specified in the certificate, prohibiting or restricting the tenant from assigning the tenancy or subletting, charging or parting with possession of the premises or any part of the premises or changing the use of the premises or any part of the premises, the court shall determine that the terms of the tenancy shall include the terms specified in the certificate.][114]

Development Board for Rural Wales premises **A1.069**

60B.—[. . .][115]

61. [. . .][116]

Exercise of powers of Board of Trade **A1.070**

62.—(1) [. . .][117]

(2) [. . .][118]

Jurisdiction of court for purposes of Parts I and II and of Part I of Landlord and Tenant Act, 1927 **A1.071**

63.—(1) Any jurisdiction conferred on the court by any provision of Part I of this Act shall be exercised by the county court.

(2) Any jurisdiction conferred on the court by any provision of Part II of this Act or conferred on the tribunal by Part I of the Landlord and Tenant Act, 1927, shall, subject to the provisions of this section, be exercised [by the High Court or a county court][119]

(3) [. . .][120]

112 Substituted subject to transitional provisions specified in SI 2005/3226 art.3 by Welsh Development Agency (Transfer of Functions to the National Assembly for Wales and Abolition) Order (SI 2005/3226) Sch.2, para.1.

113 Substituted subject to transitional provisions specified in SI 2005/3226 art.3 by Welsh Development Agency (Transfer of Functions to the National Assembly for Wales and Abolition) Order (SI 2005/3226) Sch.2, para.1.

114 Inserted by the Welsh Development Agency Act 1975, s.11(1).

115 Repealed by the Government of Wales Act 1998, s.152 and Sched. 18, Pt IV.

116 Repealed by the Endowments and Glebe Measure 1976 (No. 4) s.47(4) and Sched. 8.

117 Repealed by the Industrial Expansion Act 1968, s.18(2) and Sched. 4.

118 Repealed by the House of Commons Disqualification Act 1957, Sched. 4(1).

119 Substituted by the High Court and County Courts Jurisdiction Order 1991, Schedule (S.I. 1991 No. 724).

120 Repealed by the High Court and County Courts Jurisdiction Order 1991, Schedule (S.I. 1991 No. 724).

(4) The following provisions shall have effect as respects transfer of proceedings from or to the High Court or the county court, that is to say—

(a) where an application is made to the one but by virtue of subsection (2) of this section cannot be entertained except by the other, the application shall not be treated as improperly made but any proceedings thereon shall be transferred to the other court;

(b) any proceedings under the provisions of Part II of this Act or of Part I of the Landlord and Tenant Act, 1927, which are pending before one of those courts may by order of that court made on the application of any person interested be transferred to the other court, if it appears to the court making the order that it is desirable that the proceedings and any proceedings before the other court should both be entertained by the other court.

(5) In any proceedings where in accordance with the foregoing provisions of this section the county court exercises jurisdiction the powers of the judge of summoning one or more assessors under subsection (1) of section 88 of the County Courts Act, 1934, may be exercised notwithstanding that no application is made in that behalf by any party to the proceedings.

(6) Where in any such proceedings an assessor is summoned by a judge under the said subsection (1),—

(a) he may, if so directed by the judge, inspect the land to which the proceedings relate without the judge and report to the judge in writing thereon;

(b) the judge may on consideration of the report and any observations of the parties thereon give such judgment or make such order in the proceedings as may be just;

(c) the remuneration of the assessor shall be at such rate as may be determined by the Lord Chancellor with the approval of the Treasury and shall be defrayed out of moneys provided by Parliament.

(7) In this section the expression "the holding"—

(a) in relation to proceedings under Part II of this Act, has the meaning assigned to it by subsection (3) of section 23 of this Act,

(b) in relation to proceedings under Part I of the Landlord and Tenant Act, 1927, has the same meaning as in the said Part I.

(8) Subsections (5) to (7) of section of this Act shall apply for determining the rateable value of the holding for the purposes of this section as they apply for the purposes of subsection (2) of the said section 37 but with the substitution in paragraph (a) of the said subsection (5) of a reference to the time at which application is made to the court for the reference to the date mentioned in that subsection.

(9) Nothing in this section shall prejudice the operation of section 111 of the County Courts Act, 1934 (which relates to the removal into the High Court of proceedings commenced in a county court).

(10) In accordance with the foregoing provisions of this section, for section 21 of the Landlord and Tenant Act, 1927, there shall be substituted the following section—

"21. **The tribunal.**—The tribunal for the purposes of Part I of this Act shall be the court exercising jurisdiction in accordance with the provisions of section sixty-three of the Landlord and Tenant Act, 1954."

Interim continuation of tenancies pending determination by court **A1.072**

64.—(1) In any case where—

(a) a notice to terminate a tenancy has been given under Part I or Part II of this Act or a request for a new tenancy has been made under Part II thereof, and

(b) an application to the court has been made under the said Part I or ~~the said Part II~~ **under section 24(1) or 29(2) of this Act**[121], as the case may be, and

(c) apart from this section the effect of the notice or request would be to terminate the tenancy before the expiration of the period of three months beginning with the date on which the application is finally disposed of,

the effect of the notice or request shall be to terminate the tenancy at the expiration of the said period of three months and not at any other time.

(2) The reference in paragraph (c) of subsection (1) of this section to the date on which an application is finally disposed of shall be construed as a reference to the earliest date by which the proceedings on the application (including any proceedings on or in consequence of an appeal) have been determined and any time for appealing or further appealing has expired, except that if the application is withdrawn or any appeal is abandoned the reference shall be construed as a reference to the date of the withdrawal or abandonment.

Provisions as to reversions **A1.073**

65.—(1) Where by virtue of any provision of this Act a tenancy (in this subsection referred to as "the inferior tenancy") is continued for a period such as to extend to or beyond the end of the term of a superior tenancy, the superior tenancy shall, for the purposes of this Act and of any other enactment and of any rule of law, be deemed so long as it subsists to be an interest in reversion expectant upon the termination of the inferior tenancy and, if there is no immediate tenancy, to be the interest in reversion immediately expectant upon the termination thereof.

(2) In the case of a tenancy continuing by virtue of any provision of this Act after the coming to an end of the interest in reversion immediately expectant upon the termination thereof, subsection (1) of section 139 of the Law of Property Act, 1925 (which relates to the effect of the extinguishment of a reversion) shall apply as if references in the said subsection (1) to the surrender or merger of the reversion included references to the coming to an end of the reversion for any reason other than surrender or merger.

(3) Where by virtue of any provision of this Act a tenancy (in this subsection referred to as "the continuing tenancy") is continued beyond the beginning of a reversionary tenancy which was granted (whether before or after the commencement of this Act) so as to begin on or after the date on which apart from this Act the continuing tenancy would have come to an end, the reversionary tenancy shall have effect as if it had been granted subject to the continuing tenancy.

(4) Where by virtue of any provision of this Act a tenancy (in this subsection referred to as "the new tenancy") is granted for a period beginning on the

[121] Substituted by Regulatory Reform (Business Tenancies) (England and Wales) Order (SI 2003/3096) Sch.5, para.9.

same date as a reversionary tenancy or for a period such as to extend beyond the beginning of the term of a reversionary tenancy, whether the reversionary tenancy in question was granted before or after the commencement of this Act, the reversionary tenancy shall have effect as if it had been granted subject to the new tenancy.

A1.074 **Provisions as to notices**[122]

66.—(1) Any form of notice required by this Act to be prescribed shall be prescribed by regulations made by [the Secretary of State][123] by statutory instrument.

(2) Where the form of a notice to be served on persons of any description is to be prescribed for any of the purposes of this Act, the form to be prescribed shall include such an explanation of the relevant provisions of this Act as appears to [the Secretary of State][124] requisite for informing persons of that description of their rights and obligations under those provisions.

(3) Different forms of notice may be prescribed for the purposes of the operation of any provision of this Act in relation to different cases.

(4) Section 23 of the Landlord and Tenant Act, 1927 (which relates to the service of notices) shall apply for the purposes of this Act.

(5) Any statutory instrument under this section shall be subject to annulment in pursuance of a resolution of either House of Parliament.

A1.075 **Provisions as to mortgagees in possession**

67.—Anything authorised or required by the provisions of this Act, other than subsection ~~(2) or~~[125] (3) of section 40, to be done at any time by, to or with the landlord, or a landlord of a specified description, shall, if at that time the interest of the landlord in question is subject to a mortgage and the mortgagee is in possession or a receiver appointed by the mortgagee or by the court is in receipt of the rents and profits, be deemed to be authorised or required to be done by, to or with the mortgagee instead of that landlord.

A1.076 **Repeal of enactments and transitional provisions**

68.—(1) [. . .][126]

(2) The transitional provisions set out in the Ninth Schedule to this Act shall have effect.

A1.077 **Interpretation**

69.—(1) In this Act the following expressions have the meanings hereby assigned to them respectively, that is to say—

"agricultural holding" has the same meaning as in the [Agricultural Holdings Act 1986][127];

122 See also Leasehold Reform Act 1967, s.22(5).

123 The words in square brackets were substituted by the Transfer of Functions (Lord Chancellor and Secretary of State) Order 1974 (S.I. 1974 No. 1896), arts 2 and 3(2).

124 *ibid.*

125 Repealed by Regulatory Reform (Business Tenancies) (England and Wales) Order (SI 2003/3096) Sch.6, para.1.

126 Repealed by S.L.R. 1974.

127 Substituted by Agricultural Holdings Act 1986, Sched. 14, para. 22.

"development corporation" has the same meaning as in the New Towns Act, 1946;

["Farm business tenancy" has the same meaning as in the Agricultural Tenancies Act 1995][128];

"local authority" [means any local authority within the meaning of the Town and Country Planning Act 1990, any National Park Authority, the Broads Authority, **the London Fire and Emergency Planning Authority**[129] or].[130] [. . .][131] [joint authority established by Part IV of the Local Government Act 1985][132];

"mortgage" includes a charge or lien and "mortgagor" and "mortgagee" shall be construed accordingly;

"notice to quit" means a notice to terminate a tenancy (whether a periodical tenancy or a tenancy for a term of years certain) given in accordance with the provisions (whether express or implied) of that tenancy;

"repairs" includes any work of maintenance, decoration or restoration, and references to repairing, to keeping or yielding up in repair and to state of repair shall be construed accordingly;

"statutory undertakers" has the same meaning as in the Town and Country Planning Act, 1947, except that it includes the [British Coal Corporation][133];

"tenancy" means a tenancy created either immediately or derivitively out of the freehold, whether by lease or underlease, by an agreement for a lease or underlease or by a tenancy agreement or in pursuance of any enactment (including this Act), but does not include a mortgage term or any interest arising in favour of a mortgagor by his attorning tenant to his mortgagee, and references to the granting of a tenancy and to demised property shall be construed accordingly[134];

"terms", in relation to a tenancy, includes conditions.

(2) References in this Act to an agreement between the landlord and the tenant (except in section seventeen and subsections (1) and (2) of section 38 thereof) shall be construed as references to an agreement in writing between them.

(3) References in this Act to an action for any relief shall be construed as including references to a claim for that relief by way of counterclaim in any proceedings.

Short title and citation, commencement and exent A1.078

70.—(1) This Act may be cited as the Landlord and Tenant Act, 1954, and the Landlord and Tenant Act, 1927, and this Act may be cited together as the Landlord and Tenant Acts, 1927 and 1954.

(2) This Act shall come into operation on the first day of October, nineteen hundred and fifty-four.

(3) This Act shall not extend to Scotland or to Northern Ireland.

128 Added by the Agricultural Tenancies Act 1995, Sched., para. 12.
129 Added by Greater London Authority Act 1999, Sch.29, para.1.
130 Substituted by Environment Act 1995 (c. 25) Sched. 10.
131 Repealed by the Education Reform Act 1988, Sched. 13, Part I.
132 Inserted by Local Government Act 1985, Sched. 14, para. 36. S.I. 1985 No. 1884 reads that this enactment shall have effect as if references to a joint authority established by Part IV of the Local Government Act 1985 included references to an authority established by that order.
133 Substituted by the Coal Industry Act 1987, Sched. 1.
134 See 1957 Act, Sched. 4, paras.1(6) and 11.

SCHEDULES

Section 44

A1.079

SIXTH SCHEDULE

Provisions for purposes of Part II where Immediate Landlord is not the Freeholder

Definitions

1. In this Schedule the following expressions have the meanings hereby assigned to them in relation to a tenancy (in this Schedule referred to as "the relevant tenancy"), that is to say:—

"the competent landlord" means the person who in relation to the tenancy is for the time being the landlord (as defined by section forty-four of this Act) for the purposes of Part II of this Act;

"mesne landlord" means a tenant whose interest is intermediate between the relevant tenancy and the interest of the competent landlord; and

"superior landlord" means a person (whether the owner of the fee simple or a tenant) whose interest is superior to the interest of the competent landlord.

Power of court to order reversionary tenancies

2. Where the period for which in accordance with the provisions of Part II of this Act it is agreed or determined by the court that a new tenancy should be granted thereunder will extend beyond the date on which the interest of the immediate landlord will come to an end, the power of the court under Part II of this Act to order such a grant shall include power to order the grant of a new tenancy until the expiration of that interest and also to order the grant of such a reversionary tenancy or reversionary tenancies as may be required to secure that the combined effects of those grants will be equivalent to the grant of a tenancy for that period; and the provisions of Part II of this Act shall, subject to the necessary modifications, apply in relation to the grant of a tenancy together with one or more reversionary tenancies as they apply in relation to the grant of one new tenancy.

Acts of competent landlord binding on other landlords

3.—(1) Any notice given by the competent landlord under Part II of this Act to terminate the relevant tenancy, and any agreement made between that landlord and the tenant as to the granting, duration, or terms of a future tenancy, being an agreement made for the purposes of the said Part II, shall bind the interest of any mesne landlord notwithstanding that he has not consented to the giving of the notice or was not a party to the agreement.

(2) The competent landlord shall have power for the purposes of Part II of this Act to give effect to any agreement with the tenant for the grant of a new tenancy beginning with the coming to an end of the relevant tenancy, notwithstanding that the competent landlord will not be the immediate landlord at the commencement of the new tenancy, and any instrument made in the exercise of the power conferred by this sub-paragraph shall have effect as if the mesne landlord had been a party thereto.

(3) Nothing in the foregoing provisions of this paragraph shall prejudice the provisions of the next following paragraph.

Provisions as to consent of mesne landlord to acts of competent landlord

4.—(1) If the competent landlord, not being the immediate landlord, gives any such notice or makes any such agreement as is mentioned in sub-paragraph (1) of the last foregoing paragraph without the consent of every mesne landlord, any mesne landlord whose consent has not been given thereto shall be entitled to compensation from the competent landlord for any loss arising in consequence of the giving of the notice or the making of the agreement.

(2) If the competent landlord applies to any mesne landlord for his consent to such a notice or agreement, that consent shall not be unreasonably withheld, but may be given subject to any conditions which may be reasonable (including conditions as to the modification of the proposed notice or agreement or as to the payment of compensation by the competent landlord).

(3) Any question arising under this paragraph whether consent has been unreasonably withheld or whether any conditions imposed on the giving of consent are unreasonable shall be determined by the court.

Consent of superior landlord required for agreements affecting his interest

5. An agreement between the competent landlord and the tenant made for the purposes of Part II of this Act in a case where—

(a) the competent landlord is himself a tenant, and

(b) the agreement would apart from this paragraph operate as respects any period after the coming to an end of the interest of the competent landlord.

shall not have effect unless every superior landlord who will be the immediate landlord of the tenant during any part of that period is a party to the agreement.

[Withdrawal by competent landlord of notice given by mesne landlord

6. Where the competent landlord has given a notice under section 25 of this Act to terminate the relevant tenancy and, within two months after the giving of the notice, a superior landlord—

(a) becomes the competent landlord; and
(b) gives to the tenant notice in the prescribed form that he withdraws the notice previously given;

the notice under section 25 of this Act cease to have effect, but without prejudice to the giving of a further notice under that section by the competent landlord.

Duty to inform superior landlords

7. If the competent landlord's interest in the property comprised in the relevant tenancy is a tenancy which will come or can be brought to an end within sixteen months (or any further time by which it may be continued under section 36(2) or section 64 of this Act) and he gives to the tenant under the relevant tenancy a notice under section 25 of this Act to terminate the tenancy or is given by him a notice under section 26(3) of this Act:—
(a) the competent landlord shall forthwith send a copy of the notice to his immediate landlord; and
(b) any superior landlord whose interest in the property is a tenancy shall forthwith send to his immediate landlord any copy which has been sent to him in pursuance of the preceding sub-paragraph of this sub-paragraph.][135]

Section 56

A1.080

EIGHTH SCHEDULE

Application of Part II to land belonging to Crown and Duchies of Lancaster and Cornwall

1. Where an interest in any property comprised in a tenancy belongs to Her Majesty in right of the Duchy of Lancaster, then for the purposes of Part II of this Act the Chancellor of the Duchy shall represent Her Majesty and shall be deemed to be the owner of the interest.

2. Where an interest in any property comprised in a tenancy belongs to the Duchy of Cornwall, then for the purposes of Part II of this Act such person as the Duke of Cornwall, or other the possessor for the time being of the Duchy of Cornwall, appoints shall represent the Duke of Cornwall or other the possessor aforesaid, and shall be deemed to be the owner of the interest and may do any act or thing under the said Part II which the owner of that interest is authorised or required to do thereunder.

3. [. . .][136]

4. The amount of any compensation payable under section thirty-seven of this Act by the Chancellor of the Duchy of Lancaster shall be raised and paid as an expense incurred in improvement of land belonging to Her Majesty in

[135] Inserted by Law of Property Act 1969, s.14(2).
[136] Repealed by the Crown Estates Act 1961, s.9(4) and Sched. 3, Pt. II.

right of the Duchy within section twenty-five of the Act of the fifty-seventh year of King George the Third, Chapter ninety-seven.

5. Any compensation payable under section thirty-seven of this Act by the person representing the Duke of Cornwall or other the possessor for the time being of the Duchy of Cornwall shall be paid, and advances therefore made, in the manner and subject to the provisions of section eight of the Duchy of Cornwall Management Act, 1863, with respect to improvements of land mentioned in that section.

Sections 41, 42, 56, 68

NINTH SCHEDULE **A1.081**

TRANSITIONAL PROVISIONS

1. [. . .][137]

2. [. . .][138]

3. Where immediately before the commencement of this Act a person was protected by section seven of the Leasehold Property (Temporary Provisions) Act, 1951, against the making of an order or giving of a judgement for possession or ejectment, the Rent Acts shall apply in relation to the dwelling-house to which that person's protection extended immediately before the commencement of this Act if section fifteen of this Act had always had effect.

4. For the purposes of section twenty-six and subsection (2) of section forty of this Act a tenancy which is not such a tenancy as is mentioned in subsection (1) of the said section twenty-six but is a tenancy to which Part II of this Act applies and in respect of which the following conditions are satisfied, that is to say—

- (a) that it took effect before the commencement of this Act at the coming to an end by effluxion of time or notice to quit of a tenancy which is such a tenancy as is mentioned in subsection (1) of the said section twenty-six or is by virtue of this paragraph deemed to be such a tenancy; and
- (b) that if this Act had then been in force the tenancy at the coming to an end of which it took effect would have been one to which Part II of this Act applies; and
- (c) that the tenant is either the tenant under the tenancy at the coming to an end of which it took effect or a successor to his business,

shall be deemed to be such a tenancy as is mentioned in subsection (1) of the said section twenty-six.

5.—(1) A tenant under a tenancy which was current at the commencement of this Act shall not in any case be entitled to compensation under section thirty-seven or fifty-nine of this Act unless at the date on which he is to quit the holding the holding or part thereof has continuously been occupied for the

[137] Repealed by the S.L.R. 1976.
[138] Repealed by the S.L.R. 1976.

purposes of the carrying on of the tenant's business (whether by him or by any other person) for at least five years.

(2) Where a tenant under a tenancy which was current at the commencement of this Act would but for this sub-paragraph be entitled both to—

(a) compensation under section thirty-seven or section fifty-nine of this Act; and

(b) compensation payable, under the provisions creating the tenancy, on the termination of the tenancy,

he shall be entitled, at his option, to the one or the other, but not to both.

6.—(1) Where the landlord's interest in the property comprised in a tenancy which, immediately before the commencement of this Act, was terminable by less than six months' notice to quit given by the landlord belongs to or is held for the purposes of a Government Department or is held by statutory undertakers, the tenancy shall have effect as if that shorter length of notice were specified in such an agreement as is mentioned in subsection (2) or (3) of section fifty-eight of this Act, as the case may be, and the agreement were embodied in the tenancy.

(2) The last foregoing sub-paragraph shall apply in relation to a tenancy where the landlord's interest belongs or is held as aforesaid and which, immediately before the commencement of this Act, was terminable by the landlord without notice as if the tenancy had then been terminable by one month's notice to quit given by the landlord.

7. [. . .][139]

8. Where at the commencement of this Act any proceedings are pending on an application made before the commencement of this Act to the tribunal under section five of the Landlord and Tenant Act, 1927, no further step shall be taken in the proceedings except for the purposes of an order as to costs; and where the tribunal has made an interim order in the proceedings under subsection (13) of section five of that Act authorising the tenant to remain in possession of the property comprised in his tenancy for any period, the tenancy shall be deemed not to have come to an end before the expiration of that period, and section twenty-four of this Act shall have effect in relation to it accordingly.

9. [. . .][140]

10. [. . .][141]

11. Notwithstanding the repeal of Part II of the Leasehold Property (Temporary Provisions) Act, 1951, where immediately before the commencement of this Act a tenancy was being continued by subsection (3) of section eleven of that Act it shall not come to an end at the commencement of this Act, and section twenty-four of this Act shall have effect in relation to it accordingly.

[139] Repealed by the S.L.R. 1976.
[140] Repealed by the S.L.R. 1976.
[141] Repealed by the S.L.R. 1976.

(c. 46)

Meaning of "subsidiary" and related expressions

1159 Meaning of "subsidiary" etc A1.083

(1) A company is a "subsidiary" of another company, its "holding company", if that other company—

(a) holds a majority of the voting rights in it, or

(b) is a member of it and has the right to appoint or remove a majority of its board of directors, or

(c) is a member of it and controls alone, pursuant to an agreement with other members, a majority of the voting rights in it, or if it is a subsidiary of a company that is itself a subsidiary of that other company.

(2) A company is a "wholly-owned subsidiary" of another company if it has no members except that other and that other's wholly-owned subsidiaries or persons acting on behalf of that other or its wholly-owned subsidiaries.

(3) Schedule 6 contains provisions explaining expressions used in this section and otherwise supplementing this section.

(4) In this section and that Schedule "company" includes any body corporate.

1160 Meaning of "subsidiary" etc: power to amend A1.084

(1) The Secretary of State may by regulations amend the provisions of section 1159 (meaning of "subsidiary" etc) and Schedule 6 (meaning of "subsidiary" etc: supplementary provisions) so as to alter the meaning of the expressions "subsidiary", "holding company" or "wholly-owned subsidiary".

(2) Regulations under this section are subject to negative resolution procedure.

(3) Any amendment made by regulations under this section does not apply for the purposes of enactments outside the Companies Acts unless the regulations so provide.

(4) So much of section 23(3) of the Interpretation Act 1978 (c. 30) as applies section 17(2)(a) of that Act (effect of repeal and re-enactment) to deeds, instruments and documents other than enactments does not apply in relation to any repeal and re-enactment effected by regulations under this section.

(c. 41)

Domestic property A1.086

66.—(1) [Subject to subsections (2), (2B) and (2E) below][1] property is domestic if—

(a) it is used wholly for the purposes of living accommodation,
(b) it is a yard, garden, outhouse or other appurtenance belonging to or enjoyed with property falling within paragraph (a) above,
(c) it is a private garage [which either has a floor area of 25 square metres or less or is][2] used wholly or mainly for the accommodation of a private motor vehicle, or
(d) it is private storage premises used wholly or mainly for the storage of articles of domestic use.

[(2) Property is not domestic property if it is wholly or mainly used in the course of a business for the provision of short-stay accommodation, that is to say accommodation—

(a) which is provided for short periods to individuals whose sole or main residence is elsewhere, and
(b) which is not self-contained self-catering accommodation provided commercially.

[(2A) Subsection (2) above does not apply if—

(a) it is intended that within the year beginning with the end of the day in relation to which the question is being considered, short-stay accommodation will not be provided within the hereditament for more than six persons simultaneously; and
(b) the person intending to provide such accommodation intends to have his sole or main residence within that hereditament throughout any period when such accommodation is to be provided, and that any use of living accommodation within that hereditament which would, apart from this subsection, cause any part of it to be treated as non-domestic, will be subsidiary to the use of the hereditament for, or in connection with, his sole or main residence.][3]

(2B) A building or self-contained part of a building is not domestic property if—

(a) the relevant person intends that, in the year beginning with the end of the day in relation to which the question is being considered, the whole of the building or self-contained part will be available for

[1] Inserted by the Non-Domestic Rating (Definition of Domestic Property) Order 1993 (S.I. 1993 No. 542).

[2] Inserted by the Standard Community Charge and Non-Domestic Rating (Definition of Domestic Property) Order 1990 (S.I. 1990 No. 162).

[3] Substituted by the Standard Community Charge and Non-Domestic Rating (Definition of Domestic Property) (Amendment) Order 1991 (S.I. 1991 No. 474).

letting commercially, as self-catering accommodation, for short periods totalling 140 days or more, and

(b) on that day his interest in the building or part is such as to enable him to let it for such periods.

(2C) For the purposes of subsection (2B) the relevant person is—

(a) where the property in question is a building and is not subject as a whole to a relevant leasehold interest, the person having the freehold interest in the whole of the building; and

(b) in any other case, any person having a relevant leasehold interest in the building or self-contained part which is not subject (as a whole) to a single relevant leasehold interest inferior to his interest.

(2D) Subsection (2B) above does not apply where the building or self-contained part is used as the sole or main residence of any person other than a person who is treated as having such a residence there only by virtue of section 2(5A) above],[4] [and on the day in relation to which the question is being considered is not resident in the building or part.][5]

[(2D) Property is not domestic property if it is timeshare accommodation within the meaning of the Timeshare Act 1992.][6]

[(3) Subsection (1) above does not apply in the case of a pitch occupied by a caravan, but if in such a case the caravan is the sole or main residence of an individual, the pitch and the caravan, together with any garden, yard, outhouse or other appurtenance belonging to or enjoyed with them, are domestic property.][7]

[(4) Subsection (1) above does not apply in the case of a mooring occupied by a board, but if in such a case the boat is the sole or main residence of an individual, the mooring and the boat, together with any garden, yard, outhouse or other appurtenance belonging to or enjoyed with, are domestic property.

(4A) Subsection (3) or (4) above does not have effect in the case of a pitch occupied by a caravan, or a mooring occupied by a boat, which is an appurtenance enjoyed with other property to which subsection (1)(a) above applies.][8]

(5) Property not in use is domestic if it appears that when next in use it will be domestic.

(6) In applying subsection (5) above no assumption may be made that a site which is not a protected site will become one.

(7) Whether anything is a caravan shall be construed in accordance with Part I of the Caravan Sites and Control of Development Act 1960.

(8) Whether a site is a protected site shall be construed in accordance with Part I of the Caravan Sites Act 1968.

[(8A) In this section—

"business" includes—

(a) any activity carried on by a body of persons, whether corporate or unincorporate, and

[4] Substituted by the Standard Community Charge and Non-Domestic Rating (Definition of Domestic Property) Order 1990 (S.I. 1990 No. 162).

[5] Added by the Standard Community Charge and Non-Domestic Rating (Definition of Domestic Property) (Amendment) Order 1991 (S.I. 1991 No. 474).

[6] Added by the Non-Domestic Rating (Definition of Domestic Property) Order 1993 (S.I. 1993 No. 542).

[7] Substituted by the Rating (Caravans and Boats) Act 1996, s.1.

[8] *ibid.*

(b) any activity carried on by a charity;

"commercially" means on a commercial basis, and with a view to the realisation of profits; and

"relevant leasehold interest" means an interest under a lease or underlease which was granted for a term of 6 months or more and conferred the right to exclusive possession throughout the term.][9]

(9) The Secretary of State may by order amend, or substitute another definition for, any definition of domestic property for the time being effective for the purposes of this Part.

[9] Inserted by the Standard Community Change and Non-Domestic Rating (Definition of Domestic Property) Order 1990 (S.I. 1990 No. 162).

Local Government and Housing Act 1989 A1.087

(c. 42)

Section 149

SCHEDULE 7 A1.088

Compensation Provisions of Landlord and Tenant Act 1954, Part II

1. Any reference in this Schedule to a section which is not otherwise identified is a reference to that section of the Landlord and Tenant Act 1954, Part II of which relates to security of tenure for business, professional and other tenants.

2.—(1) Subject to the following provisions of this Schedule, section 37 (compensation where order for new tenancy precluded on certain grounds) shall have effect with the amendments set out below.

(2) At the beginning of subsection (2) there shall be inserted the words "Subject to subsections (5A) to (5D) of this section."

(3) After subsection (5) there shall be inserted the following subsections—

"(5A) If part of the holding is domestic property, as defined in section 66 of the Local Government Finance Act 1988,—

- (a) the domestic property shall be disregarded in determining the rateable value of the holding under subsection (5) of this section; and
- (b) if, on the date specified in subsection (5)(a) of this section, the tenant occupied the whole or any part of the domestic property, the amount of compensation to which he is entitled under subsection (1) of this section shall be increased by the addition of a sum equal to his reasonable expenses in removing from the domestic property.

(5B) Any question as to the amount of the sum referred to in paragraph (b) of subsection (5A) of this section shall be determined by agreement between the landlord and the tenant or, in default of agreement, by the court.

(5C) If the whole of the holding is domestic property, as defined in section 66 of the Local Government Finance Act 1988, for the purposes of subsection (2) of this section the rateable value of the holding shall be taken to be an amount equal to the rent at which it is estimated the holding might reasonably be expected to let from year to year if the tenant undertook to pay all usual tenant's rates and taxes and to bear the cost of the repairs and insurance and the other expenses (if any) necessary to maintain the holding in a state to command that rent.

(5D) The following provisions shall have effect as regards a determination of an amount mentioned in subsection (5C) of this section—

(a) the date by reference to which such a determination is to be made is the date on which the landlord's notice under section 25 or, as the case may be, subsection (6) of section 26 of this Act is given;

(b) any dispute arising, whether in proceedings before the court or otherwise, as to such a determination shall be referred to the Commissioners of Inland Revenue for decision by a valuation officer;

(c) an appeal shall lie to the Lands Tribunal from such a decision, but subject to that, such a decision shall be final."

(4) At the end of subsection (8) (definition of "the appropriate multiplier") there shall be added the words "and different multipliers may be so prescribed in relation to different cases."

3. The amendments made by paragraph 2 above do not have effect unless the date which, apart from paragraph 4 below, is relevant for determining the rateable value of the holding under subsection (5) of section 37 is on or after April 1, 1990.

4.—(1) Subject to paragraph 3 above and paragraph 5 below, in any case where—

(a) the tenancy concerned was entered into before April 1, 1990 or was entered into on or after that date in pursuance of a contract made before that date, and

(b) the landlord's notice under section 25 or, as the case may be, section 26(6) is given before April 1, 2000, and

(c) within the period referred to in section 29(3) for the making of an application under section 24(1), the tenant gives notice to the landlord that he wants the special basis of compensation provided for by this paragraph,

the amendments made by paragraph 2 above shall not have effect and section 37 shall, instead, have effect with the modification specified in sub-paragraph (2) below.

(2) The modification referred to in sub-paragraph (1) above is that the date which is relevant for the purposes of determining the rateable value of the holding under subsection (5) of section 37 shall be March 31, 1990 instead of the date on which the landlord's notice is given.

5. In any case where—

(a) paragraph 4(1)(a) above applies, and

(b) on March 31, 1990, the rateable value of the holding could be determined only in accordance with paragraph (c) of subsection (5) of section 37,

no notice may be given under paragraph 4(1)(b) above.

Landlord and Tenant (Licensed Premises) Act, 1990

(C. 39)

An Act to repeal section 43(1)(d) of the Landlord and Tenant Act 1954; and for connected purposes.

[November 1, 1990]

1.—(1) In the Landlord and Tenant Act 1954 (in this section referred to as "the 1954 Act"), in section 43 (tenancies excluded from Part II), paragraph (d) of subsection (1) (which excludes tenancies of premises licensed for the sale of intoxicating liquor for consumption on the premises) shall cease to have effect in relation to any tenancy entered into on or after July 11, 1989, otherwise than in pursuance of a contract made before that date.

(2) If a tenancy—

(a) is of a description mentioned in paragraph (d) of subsection (1) of section 43 of the 1954 Act, and

(b) is in existence on July 11, 1992, and

(c) does not fall within subsection (1) above,

that paragraph shall cease to have effect in relation to the tenancy on and after July 11, 1992; and section 24(3)(b) of the 1954 Act (which, in certain cases, preserves the effect of a notice to quit given in respect of a tenancy which becomes one to which Part II of the 1954 Act applies) shall not have effect in the case of a tenancy which becomes one to which that Part applies by virtue of this subsection.

(3) In relation to a tenancy falling within subsection (2) above, before July 11, 1992 the following notices may be given and any steps may be taken in consequence thereof as if section 43(1)(d) of the 1954 Act had already ceased to have effect—

(a) a notice under section 25 of the 1954 Act (termination of tenancy by landlord) specifying as the date of termination July 11, 1992 or any later date;

(b) a notice under section 26 of the 1954 Act (tenant's request for a new tenancy) requesting a new tenancy beginning not earlier than that date; and

(c) a notice under section 27(1) of the 1954 Act (termination by tenant of tenancy for fixed term) stating that the tenant does not desire his tenancy to be continued.

(4) In this section "tenancy" has the same meaning as in Part II of the 1954 Act.

2.—(1) This Act may be cited as the Landlord and Tenant (Licensed Premises) Act 1990.

(2) Subject to subsections (1) and (2) of section 1 of this Act,—

(a) section 43(1)(d) of the Landlord and Tenant Act 1954, and

(b) paragraph 5 of Schedule 2 to the Finance Act 1959 (which amended section 43 by substituting the present subsection (1)(d),

are hereby repealed.

(3) This Act shall come into force at the end of the period of two months beginning with the day on which it is passed.

(4) This Act does not extend to Scotland or Northern Ireland.

Appendix II

STATUTORY REGULATIONS

Civil Procedure Rules A2.001

Part 56

Landlord and Tenant Claims and Miscellaneous Provisions About Land A2.002

Note

These rules do not come into force until October 15, 2001.

I. Landlord and Tenant claims

Scope and interpretation A2.003

56.1—(1) In this section of this Part "landlord and tenant claim" means a claim under—

(a) the Landlord and Tenant Act 1927[1];
(b) the Leasehold Property (Repairs) Act 1938[2];
(c) the Landlord and Tenant Act 1954[3];
(d) the Landlord and Tenant Act 1985[4]; or
(e) the Landlord and Tenant Act 1987.[5]

(2) A practice direction may set out special provisions with regard to any particular category of landlord and tenant claim.

Starting the claim A2.004

56.2—(1) The claim must be started in the county court for the district in which the land is situated unless [paragraph (2) applies][6] or an enactment provides otherwise.

[1] 1927, c. 36.
[2] 1938, c. 34.
[3] 1954, c. 56.
[4] 1985, c. 70.
[5] 1987, c. 31.
[6] Substituted subject to transitional provisions specified in SI 2004/1306 r.20 by Civil Procedure (Amendment) Rules (SI 2004/1306) r.15

(2) The claim may be started in the High Court if the claimant files with his claim form a certificate stating the reasons for bringing the claim in that court verified by a statement of truth in accordance with rule 22.1(1).

(3) The practice direction referes to circumstances which may justify starting the claim in the High Court.

(4) [. . .][7]

[Claims for a new tenancy under section 24 and for the termination of a tenancy under section 29(2) of the Landlord and Tenant Act 1954?

A2.005 **56.3**—(1) This rule applies to a claim for a new tenancy under section 24 and to a claim for the termination of a tenancy under section 29(2) of the 1954 Act.

(2) In this rule—

- (a) "the 1954 Act" means the Landlord and Tenant Act 1954;
- (b) "an unopposed claim" means a claim for a new tenancy under section 24 of the 1954 Act in circumstances where the grant of a new tenancy is not opposed;?
- (c) "an opposed claim" means a claim for—
  - (i) a new tenancy under section 24 of the 1954 Act in circumstances where the grant of a new tenancy is opposed; or
  - (ii) the termination of a tenancy under section 29(2) of the 1954 Act.

(3) Where the claim is an unopposed claim—

- (a) the claimant must use the Part 8 procedure, but the following rules do not apply—
  - (i) rule 8.5; and?(ii) rule 8.6;
- (b) the claim form must be served within 2 months after the date of issue and rules 7.5 and 7.6 are modified accordingly; and
- (c) the court will give directions about the future management of the claim following receipt of the acknowledgment of service.

(4) Where the claim is an opposed claim—

- (a) the claimant must use the Part 7 procedure; but
- (b) the claim form must be served within 2 months after the date of issue, and rules 7.5 and 7.6 are modified accordingly.

(The practice direction to this Part contains provisions about evidence, including expert evidence in opposed).][8]

II. Miscellaneous provisions about land

A2.006 Scope

56.4 A practice direction may set out special provisions with regard to claims under the following enactments—

- (a) the Chancel Repairs Act 1932[9];

[7] Repealed subject to transitional provisions specified in SI 2004/1306 r.20 by Civil Procedure (Amendment) Rules (SI 2004/1306) r.15

[8] Substituted subject to transitional provisions specified in SI 2004/1306 r.20 by Civil Procedure (Amendment) Rules (SI 2004/1306) r.16

[9] 1932, c. 20.

(b) the leasehold Reform Act 1967[10];
(c) the Access to Neighbouring Land Act 1992[11]; [. . .][12]
(d) the Leasehold Reform, Housing and Urban Development Act 1993.[13]
[; and
(e) the Commonhold and Leasehold Reform Act 2002][14]

[10] 1967, c. 88.
[11] 1992, c. 23.
[12] Repealed by Civil Procedure (Amendment No. 2) Rules (SI 2003/3219) r.7
[13] 1993, c. 28.
[14] Added by Civil Procedure (Amendment No. 2) Rules (SI 2003/3219) r.7

Practice Direction—Landlord and Tenant Claims and Miscellaneous Provisions About Land A2.007

(PARAGARAPHS 1.1–5.7)

THIS PRACTICE DIRECTION SUPPLEMENTS PART 56

SECTION I—LANDLORD AND TENANT CLAIMS

1.1 In this section of this practice direction—
- (1) 'the 1927 Act' means the Landlord and Tenant Act 1927;
- (2) 'the 1954 Act' means the Landlord and Tenant Act 1954;
- (3) 'the 1985 Act' means the Landlord and Tenant Act 1985; and
- (4) 'the 1987 Act' means the Landlord and Tenant Act 1987.

56.2—Starting the claim A2.008

2.1 Subject to paragraph 2.1A, the claimant in a landlord and tenant claim must use the Part 8 procedure as modified by Part 56 and this practice direction.

2.1A Where the landlord and tenant claim is a claim for—
- (1) a new tenancy under section 24 of the 1954 Act in circumstances where the grant of a new tenancy is opposed; or
- (2) the termination of a tenancy under section 29(2) of the 1954 Act, the claimant must use the Part 7 procedure as modified by Part 56 and this practice direction.

2.2 Except where the county court does not have jurisdiction , landlord and tenant claims should normally be brought in the county court. Only exceptional circumstances justify starting a claim in the High Court.

2.3 If a claimant starts a claim in the High Court and the court decides that it should have been started in the county court, the court will normally either strike the claim out or transfer it to the county court on its own initiative. This is likely to result in delay and the court will normally disallow the costs of starting the claim in the High Court and of any transfer.

2.4 Circumstances which may, in an appropriate case, justify starting a claim in the High Court are if—
- (1) there are complicated disputes of fact; or
- (2) there are points of law of general importance.

2.5 The value of the property and the amount of any financial claim may be relevant circumstances, but these factors alone will not normally justify starting the claim in the High Court.

2.6 A landlord and tenant claim started in the High Court must be brought in the Chancery Division.

A2.009 Claims for a new tenancy under section 24 and termination of a tenancy under section 29(2) of the 1954 act

3.1 This paragraph applies to a claim for a new tenancy under section 24 and termination of a tenancy under section 29(2) of the 1954 Act where rule 56.3 applies and in this paragraph—

(1) 'an unopposed claim' means a claim for a new tenancy under section 24 of the 1954 Act in circumstances where the grant of a new tenancy is not opposed;

(2) 'an opposed claim' means a claim for—

(a) a new tenancy under section 24 of the 1954 Act in circumstances where the grant of a new tenancy is opposed; or

(b) the termination of a tenancy under section 29(2) of the 1954 Act; and

(3) 'grounds of opposition' means—

(a) the grounds specified in section 30(1) of the 1954 Act on which a landlord may oppose an application for a new tenancy under section 24(1) of the 1954 Act or make an application under section 29(2) of the 1954 Act; or

(b) any other basis on which the landlord asserts that a new tenancy ought not to be granted.

A2.010 Precedence of claim forms where there is more than one application to the court under section 24(1) or section 29(2) of the 1954 Act

3.2 Where more than one application to the court under section 24(1) or section 29(2) of the 1954 Act is made, the following provisions shall apply—

(1) once an application to the court under section 24(1) of the 1954 Act has been served on a defendant, no further application to the court in respect of the same tenancy whether under section 24(1) or section 29(2) of the 1954 Act may be served by that defendant without the permission of the court;

(2) if more than one application to the court under section 24(1) of the 1954 Act in respect of the same tenancy is served on the same day, any landlord's application shall stand stayed until further order of the court;

(3) if applications to the court under both section 24(1) and section 29(2) of the 1954 Act in respect of the same tenancy are served on the same day, any tenant's application shall stand stayed until further order of the court; and

(4) if a defendant is served with an application under section 29(2) of the 1954 Act ('the section 29(2) application') which was issued at a time when an application to the court had already been made by that defendant in respect of the same tenancy under section 24(1) of the 1954 Act ('the section 24(1) application'), the service of the section 29(2) application shall be deemed to be a notice under rule 7.7 requiring service or discontinuance of the section 24(1) application within a period of 14 days after the service of the section 29(2) application.

Defendant where the claimant is the tenant making a claim for a new tenancy under section 24 of the 1954 Act **A2.011**

3.3 Where a claim for a new tenancy under section 24 of the 1954 Act is made by a tenant, the person who, in relation to the claimant's current tenancy, is the landlord as defined in section 44 of the 1954 Act must be a defendant.

Contents of the claim form in all cases

3.4 The claim form must contain details of—
(1) the property to which the claim relates;
(2) the particulars of the current tenancy (including date, parties and duration), the current rent (if not the original rent) and the date and method of termination;
(3) every notice or request given or made under sections 25 or 26 of the 1954 Act; and
(4) the expiry date of—
(a) the statutory period under section 29A(2) of the 1954 Act; or
(b) any agreed extended period made under section 29B(1) or 29B(2) of the 1954 Act.

Claim form where the claimant is the tenant making a claim for a new tenancy under section 24 of the 1954 Act **A2.012**

3.5 Where the claimant is the tenant making a claim for a new tenancy under section 24 of the 1954 Act, in addition to the details specified in paragraph 3.4, the claim form must contain details of—
(1) the nature of the business carried on at the property;
(2) whether the claimant relies on section 23(1A), 41 or 42 of the 1954 Act and, if so, the basis on which he does so;
(3) whether the claimant relies on section 31A of the 1954 Act and, if so, the basis on which he does so;
(4) whether any, and if so what part, of the property comprised in the tenancy is occupied neither by the claimant nor by a person employed by the claimant for the purpose of the claimant's business;
(5) the claimant's proposed terms of the new tenancy; and
(6) the name and address of—
(a) anyone known to the claimant who has an interest in the reversion in the property (whether immediate or in not more than 15 years) on the termination of the claimant's current tenancy and who is likely to be affected by the grant of a new tenancy; or
(b) if the claimant does not know of anyone specified by sub-paragraph (6)(a), anyone who has a freehold interest in the property.

3.6 The claim form must be served on the persons referred to in paragraph 3.5(6)(a) or (b) as appropriate.

Claim form where the claimant is the landlord making a claim for a new tenancy under section 24 of the 1954 Act **A2.013**

3.7 Where the claimant is the landlord making a claim for a new tenancy under section 24 of the 1954 Act, in addition to the details specified in paragraph 3.4, the claim form must contain details of—

(1) the claimant's proposed terms of the new tenancy;
(2) whether the claimant is aware that the defendant's tenancy is one to which section 32(2) of the 1954 Act applies and, if so, whether the claimant requires that any new tenancy shall be a tenancy of the whole of the property comprised in the defendant's current tenancy or just of the holding as defined by section 23(3) of the 1954 Act; and
(3) the name and address of—
  (a) anyone known to the claimant who has an interest in the reversion in the property (whether immediate or in not more than 15 years) on the termination of the claimant's current tenancy and who is likely to be affected by the grant of a new tenancy; or
  (b) if the claimant does not know of anyone specified by subparagraph (3)(a), anyone who has a freehold interest in the property.

3.8 The claim form must be served on the persons referred to in paragraph 3.7(3)(a) or (b) as appropriate.

A2.014 **Claim form where the claimant is the landlord making an application for the termination of a tenancy under section 29(2) of the 1954 Act**

3.9 Where the claimant is the landlord making an application for the termination of a tenancy under section 29(2) of the 1954 Act, in addition to the details specified in paragraph 3.4, the claim form must contain—
(1) the claimant's grounds of opposition;
(2) full details of those grounds of opposition; and
(3) the terms of a new tenancy that the claimant proposes in the event that his claim fails.

A2.015 **Acknowledgment of service where the claim is an unopposed claim and where the claimant is the tenant**

3.10 Where the claim is an unopposed claim and the claimant is the tenant, the acknowledgment of service is to be in form N210 and must state with particulars—
(1) whether, if a new tenancy is granted, the defendant objects to any of the terms proposed by the claimant and if so—
  (a) the terms to which he objects; and
  (a) the terms that he proposes in so far as they differ from those proposed by the claimant;
(2) whether the defendant is a tenant under a lease having less than 15 years unexpired at the date of the termination of the claimant's current tenancy and, if so, the name and address of any person who, to the knowledge of the defendant, has an interest in the reversion in the property expectant (whether immediate or in not more than 15 years from that date) on the termination of the defendant's tenancy;
(3) the name and address of any person having an interest in the property who is likely to be affected by the grant of a new tenancy; and
(4) if the claimant's current tenancy is one to which section 32(2) of the 1954 Act applies, whether the defendant requires that any new tenancy shall be a tenancy of the whole of the property comprised in the claimant's current tenancy.

Acknowledgment of service where the claim is an unopposed claim and the claimant is the landlord A2.016

3.11 Where the claim is an unopposed claim and the claimant is the landlord, the acknowledgment of service is to be in form N210 and must state with particulars—

(1) the nature of the business carried on at the property;
(2) if the defendant relies on section 23(1A), 41 or 42 of the 1954 Act, the basis on which he does so;
(3) whether any, and if so what part, of the property comprised in the tenancy is occupied neither by the defendant nor by a person employed by the defendant for the purpose of the defendant's business;
(4) the name and address of—
  (a) anyone known to the defendant who has an interest in the reversion in the property (whether immediate or in not more than 15 years) on the termination of the defendant's current tenancy and who is likely to be affected by the grant of a new tenancy; or
  (b) if the defendant does not know of anyone specified by sub-paragraph (4)(a), anyone who has a freehold interest in the property; and
(5) whether, if a new tenancy is granted, the defendant objects to any of the terms proposed by the claimant and, if so—
  (a) the terms to which he objects; and
  (b) the terms that he proposes in so far as they differ from those proposed by the claimant.

Acknowledgment of service and defence where the claim is an opposed claim and where the claimant is the tenant A2.017

3.12 Where the claim is an opposed claim and the claimant is the tenant—

(1) the acknowledgment of service is to be in form N9; and
(2) in his defence the defendant must state with particulars—
  (a) the defendant's grounds of opposition;
  (b) full details of those grounds of opposition;
  (c) whether, if a new tenancy is granted, the defendant objects to any of the terms proposed by the claimant and if so—
    (i) the terms to which he objects; and
    (ii) the terms that he proposes in so far as they differ from those proposed by the claimant;
  (d) whether the defendant is a tenant under a lease having less than 15 years unexpired at the date of the termination of the claimant's current tenancy and, if so, the name and address of any person who, to the knowledge of the defendant, has an interest in the reversion in the property expectant (whether immediately or in not more than 15 years from that date) on the termination of the defendant's tenancy;
  (e) the name and address of any person having an interest in the property who is likely to be affected by the grant of a new tenancy; and
  (f) if the claimant's current tenancy is one to which section 32(2) of the 1954 Act applies, whether the defendant requires that any

new tenancy shall be a tenancy of the whole of the property comprised in the claimant's current tenancy.

A2.018 **Acknowledgment of service and defence where the claimant is the landlord making an application for the termination of a tenancy under section 29(2) of the 1954 Act**

3.13 Where the claim is an opposed claim and the claimant is the landlord—
(1) the acknowledgment of service is to be in form N9; and
(2) in his defence the defendant must state with particulars—
(a) whether the defendant relies on section 23(1A), 41 or 42 of the 1954 Act and, if so, the basis on which he does so;
(b) whether the defendant relies on section 31A of the 1954 Act and, if so, the basis on which he does so; and
(c) the terms of the new tenancy that the defendant would propose in the event that the claimant's claim to terminate the current tenancy fails.

A2.019 **Evidence in an unopposed claim**

3.14 Where the claim is an unopposed claim, no evidence need be filed unless and until the court directs it to be filed.

A2.020 **Evidence in an opposed claim**

3.15 Where the claim is an opposed claim, evidence (including expert evidence) must be filed by the parties as the court directs and the landlord shall be required to file his evidence first.

A2.021 **Grounds of opposition to be tried as a preliminary issue**

3.16 Unless in the circumstances of the case it is unreasonable to do so, any grounds of opposition shall be tried as a preliminary issue.

A2.022 **Applications for interim rent under section 24A to 24D of the 1954 Act**

3.17 Where proceedings have already been commenced for the grant of a new tenancy or the termination of an existing tenancy, the claim for interim rent under section 24A of the 1954 Act shall be made in those proceedings by—
(1) the claim form;
(2) the acknowledgment of service or defence; or
(3) an application on notice under Part 23.

3.18 Any application under section 24D(3) of the 1954 Act shall be made by an application on notice under Part 23 in the original proceedings.

3.19 Where no other proceedings have been commenced for the grant of a new tenancy or termination of an existing tenancy or where such proceedings have been disposed of, an application for interim rent under section 24A of the 1954 Act shall be made under the procedure in Part 8 and the claim form shall include details of—
(1) the property to which the claim relates;
(2) the particulars of the relevant tenancy (including date, parties and duration) and the current rent (if not the original rent);

(3) every notice or request given or made under sections 25 or 26 of the 1954 Act;
(4) if the relevant tenancy has terminated, the date and mode of termination; and
(5) if the relevant tenancy has been terminated and the landlord has granted a new tenancy of the property to the tenant—
  (a) particulars of the new tenancy (including date, parties and duration) and the rent; and
  (b) in a case where section 24C(2) of the 1954 Act applies but the claimant seeks a different rent under section 24C(3) of that Act, particulars and matters on which the claimant relies as satisfying section 24C(3).

Other claims under Part II of the 1954 act **A2.023**

4.1 The mesne landlord to whose consent a claim for the determination of any question arising under paragraph 4(3) of Schedule 6 to the 1954 Act shall be made a defendant to the claim.

4.2 If any dispute as to the rateable value of any holding has been referred under section 37(5) of the 1954 Act to the Commissioners for HM Revenue and Customs for decision by a valuation officer, any document purporting to be a statement of the valuation officer of his decision is admissible as evidence of the matters contained in it.

Claim for compensation for improvements under Part I of the 1927 act **A2.024**

5.1 This paragraph applies to a claim under Part I of the 1927 Act.

The claim form

5.2 The claim form must include details of:
(1) the nature of the claim or the matter to be determined;
(2) the property to which the claim relates;
(3) the nature of the business carried on at the property;
(4) particulars of the lease or agreement for the tenancy including:
  (a) the names and addresses of the parties to the lease or agreement;
  (b) its duration;
  (c) the rent payable;
  (d) details of any assignment or other devolution of the lease or agreement;
(5) the date and mode of termination of the tenancy;
(6) if the claimant has left the property, the date on which he did so;
(7) particulars of the improvement or proposed improvement to which the claim relates; and
(8) if the claim is for payment of compensation, the amount claimed.

5.3 The court will fix a date for a hearing when it issues the claim form.

Defendant

5.4 The claimant's immediate landlord must be a defendant to the claim.

5.5 The defendant must immediately serve a copy of the claim form and any document served with it and of his acknowledgment of service on his immediate landlord. If the person so served is not the freeholder, he must serve a copy of these documents on his landlord and so on from landlord to landlord.

Evidence

5.6 Evidence need not be filed – with the claim form or acknowledgment of service.

Certification under section 3 of the 1927 Act

5.7 If the court intends to certify under section 3 of the 1927 Act that an improvement is a proper improvement or has been duly executed, it shall do so by way of an order.

Compensation under section 1 or 8 of the 1927 Act

5.8 A claim under section 1(1) or 8(1) of the 1927 Act must be in writing, signed by the claimant, his solicitor or agent and include details of—

(1) the name and address of the claimant and of the landlord against whom the claim is made;
(2) the property to which the claim relates;
(3) the nature of the business carried on at the property;
(4) a concise statement of the nature of the claim;
(5) particulars of the improvement, including the date when it was completed and costs; and
(6) the amount claimed.

5.9 A mesne landlord must immediately serve a copy of the claim on his immediate superior landlord. If the person so served is not the freeholder, he must serve a copy of the document on his landlord and so on from landlord to landlord.

(Paragraphs 5.8 and 5.9 provide the procedure for making claims under section 1(1) and 8(1) of the 1927 Act—these 'claims' do not, at this stage, relate to proceedings before the court)

The Landlord and Tenant Act 1954, Part II (Notices) Regulations 2004

(S.I. 2004 No. 1005) **A2.025**

Made	*30th March 2004*
Laid before Parliament	*6th April 2004*
Coming into force	*1st June 2004*

The First Secretary of State, as respects England, and the National Assembly for Wales, as respects Wales, in exercise of the powers conferred by section 66 of the Landlord and Tenant Act 1954 (including that section as it has effect as mentioned in section 22(5) of the Leasehold Reform Act 1967), and of all other powers enabling them in that behalf, hereby make the following Regulations:

Citation and commencement **A2.026**

1. These Regulations may be cited as the Landlord and Tenant Act 1954, Part 2 (Notices) Regulations 2004 and shall come into force on 1st June 2004.

Interpretation **A2.027**

2.—(1) In these Regulations—

"the Act" means the Landlord and Tenant Act 1954;and
"the 1967 Act" means the Leasehold Reform Act 1967.

(2) Any reference in these Regulations to a numbered form (in whatever terms) is a reference to the form bearing that number in Schedule 2 to these Regulations or a form substantially to the same effect.

Prescribed forms, and purposes for which they are to be used. **A2.028**

3. The form with the number shown in column (1) of Schedule 1 to these Regulations is prescribed for use for the purpose shown in the corresponding entry in column (2) of that Schedule.

Revocation of Regulations **A2.029**

4. The Landlord and Tenant Act 1954, Part II (Notices) Regulations 1983 and the Landlord and Tenant Act 1954, Part II (Notices) (Amendment) Regulations 1989 are hereby revoked.

Signed by authority of the First Secretary of State

Keith Hill
Minister of State, Office of the Deputy Prime Minister

16th March 2004

Signed on behalf of the National Assembly for Wales

D. Elis- Thomas
Presiding Officer of the National Assembly

30th March 2004

A2.030 SCHEDULE 1

Regulations 2(2) and 3

PRESCRIBED FORMS, AND PURPOSES FOR WHICH THEY ARE TO BE USED[1]

(1)	*(2)*
Form number	*Purpose for which to be used*
1	Ending a tenancy to which Part 2 of the Act applies, where the landlord is not opposed to the grant of a new tenancy (notice under section 25 of the Act).
2	Ending a tenancy to which Part 2 of the Act applies, where— (a) the landlord is opposed to the grant of a new tenancy (notice under section 25 of the Act); and (b) the tenant is not entitled under the 1967 Act to buy the freehold or an extended lease.
3	Tenant's request for a new tenancy of premises where Part 2 of the Act applies (notice under section 26 of the Act).
4	Landlord's notice activating tenant's duty under section 40(1) of the Act to give information as to his or her occupation of the premises and as to any sub-tenancies.
5	Tenant's notice activating duty under section 40(3) of the Act of reversioner or reversioner's mortgagee in possession to give information about his or her interest in the premises.
6	Withdrawal of notice given under section 25 of the Act ending a tenancy to which Part 2 of the Act applies (notice under section 44 of, and paragraph 6 of Schedule 6 to, the Act).
7	Ending a tenancy to which Part 2 of the Act applies, where the landlord is opposed to the grant of a new tenancy but where the tenant may be entitled under the 1967 Act to buy the freehold or an extended lease (notice under section 25 of the Act and paragraph 10 of Schedule 3 to the 1967 Act).

[1] Only forms 1–7 or re-produced in these Appendicies.

(1)	*(2)*
Form number	*Purpose for which to be used*
8	Ending a tenancy to which Part 2 of the Act applies, where: (a) the notice under section 25 of the Act contains a copy of a certificate given under section 57 of the Act that the use or occupation of the property or part of it is to be changed by a specified date; (b) the date of termination of the tenancy specified in the notice is not earlier than the date specified in the certificate; and (c) the tenant is not entitled under the 1967 Act to buy the freehold or an extended lease.
9	Ending a tenancy to which Part 2 of the Act applies, where: (a) the notice under section 25 of the Act contains a copy of a certificate given under section 57 of the Act that the use or occupation of the property or part of it is to be changed at a future date; (b) the date of termination of the tenancy specified in the notice is earlier than the date specified in the certificate; (c) the landlord opposes the grant of a new tenancy; and (d) the tenant is not entitled under the 1967 Act to buy the freehold or an extended lease.
10	Ending a tenancy to which Part 2 of the Act applies, where: (a) the notice under section 25 of the Act contains a copy of a certificate given under section 57 of the Act that the use or occupation of the property or part of it is to be changed at a future date; (b) the date of termination of the tenancy specified in the notice is earlier than the date specified in the certificate; (c) the landlord does not oppose the grant of a new tenancy; and (d) the tenant is not entitled under the 1967 Act to buy the freehold or an extended lease.
11	Ending a tenancy to which Part 2 of the Act applies, where the notice under section 25 of the Act contains a copy of a certificate given under section 58 of the Act that for reasons of national security it is necessary that the use or occupation of the property should be discontinued or changed.
12	Ending a tenancy to which Part 2 of the Act applies, where—

(1)	(2)
Form number	*Purpose for which to be used*
	(a) the notice under section 25 of the Act contains a copy of a certificate given under section 58 of the Act (as applied by section 60 of the Act) that it is necessary or expedient for achieving the purpose mentioned in section 2(1) of the Local Employment Act 1972 that the use or occupation of the property should be changed; and (b) the tenant is not entitled under the 1967 Act to buy the freehold or an extended lease.
13	Ending a tenancy to which Part 2 of the Act applies, where: (a) the notice under section 25 of the Act contains a copy of a certificate given under section 57 of the Act that the use or occupation of the property or part of it is to be changed by a specified date; and (b) the date of termination of the tenancy specified in the notice is not earlier than the date specified in the certificate; and (c) the tenant may be entitled under the 1967 Act to buy the freehold or an extended lease.
14	Ending a tenancy to which Part 2 of the Act applies, where: (a) the notice under section 25 of the Act contains a copy of a certificate given under section 57 of the Act that the use or occupation of the property or part of it is to be changed at a future date; (b) the date of termination of the tenancy specified in the notice is earlier than the date specified in the certificate; and (c) the tenant may be entitled under the 1967 Act to buy the freehold or an extended lease the landlord opposes the grant of a new tenancy.
15	Ending a tenancy to which Part 2 of the Act applies, where: (a) he notice under section 25 of the Act contains a copy of a certificate given under section 58 of the Act (as applied by section 60 of the Act) that it is necessary or expedient for achieving the purpose mentioned in section 2(1) of the Local Employment Act 1972 that the use or occupation of the property should be changed; and (b) the tenant may be entitled under the 1967 Act to buy the freehold or an extended lease the landlord opposes the grant of a new tenancy.
16	Ending a tenancy of Welsh Development Agency Act 1975 premises where—

(1)	*(2)*
Form number	*Purpose for which to be used*
	(a) the notice under section 25 of the Act contains a copy of a certificate given under section 58 of the Act (as applied by section 60A of the Act) that it is necessary or expedient, for the purposes of providing employment appropriate to the needs of the area in which the premises are situated, that the use or occupation of the property should be changed; and (b) the tenant is not entitled under the 1967 Act to buy the freehold or an extended lease.
17	Ending a tenancy of Welsh Development Agency Act 1975 premises where: (a) the notice under section 25 of the Act contains a copy of a certificate given under section 58 of the Act (as applied by section 60A of the Act) that it is necessary or expedient, for the purposes of providing employment appropriate to the needs of the area in which the premises are situated, that the use or occupation of the property should be changed; and (b) the tenant may be entitled under the 1967 Act to buy the freehold or an extended lease.

SCHEDULE 2 A2.031

Regulation 2(2)

PRESCRIBED FORMS

FORM 1 A2.032

Landlord's Notice Ending a Business Tenancy with Proposals for a New One

SECTION 25 OF THE LANDLORD AND TENANT ACT 1954

IMPORTANT NOTE FOR THE LANDLORD: If you are willing to grant a new tenancy, complete this form and send it to the tenant. If you wish to oppose the grant of a new tenancy, use form 2 in Schedule 2 to the Landlord and Tenant Act 1954, Part 2 (Notices) Regulations 2004 or, where the tenant may be entitled to acquire the freehold or an extended lease, form 7 in that Schedule, instead of this form.

To: (*insert name and address of tenant*)
From: (*insert name and address of landlord*)

1. This notice applies to the following property: (*insert address or description of property*).

2. I am giving you notice under section 25 of the Landlord and Tenant Act 1954 to end your tenancy on (*insert date*).

3. I am not opposed to granting you a new tenancy. You will find my proposals for the new tenancy, which we can discuss, in the Schedule to this notice.

4. If we cannot agree on all the terms of a new tenancy, either you or I may ask the court to order the grant of a new tenancy and settle the terms on which we cannot agree.

5. If you wish to ask the court for a new tenancy you must do so by the date in paragraph 2, unless we agree in writing to a later date and do so before the date in paragraph 2.

6. Please send all correspondence about this notice to:

Name: . . . .

Address: . . . .

. . . .

. . . .

Signed: . . . . Date: . . . .

*(*delete if inapplicable*)

*[Landlord] *[On behalf of the landlord] *[Mortgagee] *[On behalf of the mortgagee]

A2.033

SCHEDULE

Landlord's Proposals for a New Tenancy

(*attach or insert proposed terms of the new tenancy*)

IMPORTANT NOTE FOR THE TENANT

This Notice is intended to bring your tenancy to an end. If you want to continue to occupy your property after the date specified in paragraph 2 you must act quickly. If you are in any doubt about the action that you should take, get advice immediately from a solicitor or a surveyor.

The landlord is prepared to offer you a new tenancy and has set out proposed terms in the Schedule to this notice. You are not bound to accept these terms. They are merely suggestions as a basis for negotiation. In the event of disagreement, ultimately the court would settle the terms of the new tenancy.

It would be wise to seek professional advice before agreeing to accept the landlord's terms or putting forward your own proposals.

Notes

The sections mentioned below are sections of the Landlord and Tenant Act 1954, as amended, (most recently by the Regulatory Reform (Business Tenancies) (England and Wales) Order 2003).

Ending of tenancy and grant of new tenancy

This notice is intended to bring your tenancy to an end on the date given in paragraph 2. Section 25 contains rules about the date that the landlord can put in that paragraph.

However, your landlord is prepared to offer you a new tenancy and has set out proposals for it in the Schedule to this notice (section 25(8)). You are not obliged to accept these proposals and may put forward your own.

If you and your landlord are unable to agree terms either one of you may apply to the court. You may not apply to the court if your landlord has already done so (section 24(2A)). If you wish to apply to the court you must do so by the date given in paragraph 2 of this notice, unless you and your landlord have agreed in writing to extend the deadline (sections 29A and 29B).

The court will settle the rent and other terms of the new tenancy or those on which you and your landlord cannot agree (sections 34 and 35). If you apply to the court your tenancy will continue after the date shown in paragraph 2 of this notice while your application is being considered (section 24).

If you are in any doubt about what action you should take, get advice immediately from a solicitor or a surveyor.

Negotiating a new tenancy

Most tenancies are renewed by negotiation. You and your landlord may agree in writing to extend the deadline for making an application to the court while negotiations continue. Either you or your landlord can ask the court to fix the rent that you will have to pay while the tenancy continues (sections 24A to 24D).

You may only stay in the property after the date in paragraph 2 (or if we have agreed in writing to a later date, that date), if by then you or the landlord has asked the court to order the grant of a new tenancy.

If you do try to agree a new tenancy with your landlord remember:

- that your present tenancy will not continue after the date in paragraph 2 of this notice without the agreement in writing mentioned above, unless you have applied to the court or your landlord has done so, and
- that you will lose your right to apply to the court once the deadline in paragraph 2 of this notice has passed, unless there is a written agreement extending the deadline.

Validity of this notice

The landlord who has given you this notice may not be the landlord to whom you pay your rent (sections 44 and 67). This does not necessarily mean that the notice is invalid.

If you have any doubts about whether this notice is valid, get advice immediately from a solicitor or a surveyor.

Further information

An explanation of the main points to consider when renewing or ending a business tenancy, "Renewing and Ending Business Leases: a Guide for Tenants and Landlords", can be found at www.odpm.gov.uk. Printed copies of the explanation, but not of this form, are available from 1st June 2004 from Free Literature, PO Box 236, Wetherby, West Yorkshire, LS23 7NB (0870 1226 236).

A2.034 FORM 2

Landlord's Notice Ending a Business Tenancy and Reasons for Refusing a New One

SECTION 25 OF THE LANDLORD AND TENANT ACT 1954

IMPORTANT NOTE FOR THE LANDLORD: If you wish to oppose the grant of a new tenancy on any of the grounds in section 30(1) of the Landlord and Tenant Act 1954, complete this form and send it to the tenant. If the tenant may be entitled to acquire the freehold or an extended lease, use form 7 in Schedule 2 to the Landlord and Tenant Act 1954, Part 2 (Notices) Regulations 2004 instead of this form.

To: (*insert name and address of tenant*)
From: (*insert name and address of landlord*)

1. This notice relates to the following property: (*insert address or description of property*)

2. I am giving you notice under section 25 of the Landlord and Tenant Act 1954 to end your tenancy on (*insert date*).

3. I am opposed to the grant of a new tenancy.

4. You may ask the court to order the grant of a new tenancy. If you do, I will oppose your application on the ground(s) mentioned in paragraph(s)* of section 30(1) of that Act. I draw your attention to the Table in the Notes below, which sets out all the grounds of opposition.

*(*insert letter(s) of the paragraph(s) relied on*)

5. If you wish to ask the court for a new tenancy you must do so before the date in paragraph 2 unless, before that date, we agree in writing to a later date.

6. I can ask the court to order the ending of your tenancy without granting you a new tenancy. I may have to pay you compensation if I have relied only on one or more of the grounds mentioned in paragraphs (e), (f) and (g) of section 30(1). If I ask the court to end your tenancy, you can challenge my application.

7. Please send all correspondence about this notice to:

Name: ....

Address: . . . .
. . . .
. . . .

Signed: . . . . Date: . . . .

*[Landlord] *[On behalf of the landlord] *[Mortgagee] *[On behalf of the mortgagee] *(*delete if inapplicable*)

IMPORTANT NOTE FOR THE TENANT

This notice is intended to bring your tenancy to an end on the date specified in paragraph 2.

Your landlord is not prepared to offer you a new tenancy. You will not get a new tenancy unless you successfully challenge in court the grounds on which your landlord opposes the grant of a new tenancy.

If you want to continue to occupy your property you must act quickly. The notes below should help you to decide what action you now need to take. If you want to challenge your landlord's refusal to renew your tenancy, get advice immediately from a solicitor or a surveyor.

NOTES

The sections mentioned below are sections of the Landlord and Tenant Act 1954, as amended, (most recently by the Regulatory Reform (Business Tenancies) (England and Wales) Order 2003)

Ending of your tenancy

This notice is intended to bring your tenancy to an end on the date given in paragraph 2. Section 25 contains rules about the date that the landlord can put in that paragraph.

Your landlord is not prepared to offer you a new tenancy. If you want a new tenancy you will need to apply to the court for a new tenancy and successfully challenge the landlord's grounds for opposition (see the section below headed "*Landlord's opposition to new tenancy*"). If you wish to apply to the court you must do so before the date given in paragraph 2 of this notice, unless you and your landlord have agreed in writing, before that date, to extend the deadline (sections 29A and 29B).

If you apply to the court your tenancy will continue after the date given in paragraph 2 of this notice while your application is being considered (section 24). You may not apply to the court if your landlord has already done so (section 24(2A) and (2B)).

You may only stay in the property after the date given in paragraph 2 (or such later date as you and the landlord may have agreed in writing) if before that date you have asked the court to order the grant of a new tenancy or the landlord has asked the court to order the ending of your tenancy without granting you a new one.

If you are in any doubt about what action you should take, get advice immediately from a solicitor or a surveyor.

Landlord's opposition to new tenancy

If you apply to the court for a new tenancy, the landlord can only oppose your application on one or more of the grounds set out in section 30(1). If you match the letter(s) specified in paragraph 4 of this notice with those in the first column in the Table below, you can see from the second column the ground(s) on which the landlord relies.

Paragraph of section 30(1)	*Grounds*
(a)	Where under the current tenancy the tenant has any obligations as respects the repair and maintenance of the holding, that the tenant ought not to be granted a new tenancy in view of the state of repair of the holding, being a state resulting from the tenant's failure to comply with the said obligations.
(b)	That the tenant ought not to be granted a new tenancy in view of his persistent delay in paying rent which has become due.
(c)	That the tenant ought not to be granted a new tenancy in view of other substantial breaches by him of his obligations under the current tenancy, or for any other reason connected with the tenant's use or management of the holding.
(d)	That the landlord has offered and is willing to provide or secure the provision of alternative accommodation for the tenant, that the terms on which the alternative accommodation is available are reasonable having regard to the terms of the current tenancy and to all other relevant circumstances, and that the accommodation and the time at which it will be available are suitable for the tenant's requirements (including the requirement to preserve goodwill) having regard to the nature and class of his business and to the situation and extent of, and facilities afforded by, the holding.
(e)	Where the current tenancy was created by the sub-letting of part only of the property comprised in a superior tenancy and the landlord is the owner of an interest in reversion expectant on the termination of that superior tenancy, that the aggregate of the rents reasonably obtainable on separate lettings of the holding and the remainder of that property would be substantially less than the rent reasonably obtainable on a letting of that property as a

Paragraph of section 30(1)	*Grounds*
	whole, that on the termination of the current tenancy the landlord requires possession of the holding for the purposes of letting or otherwise disposing of the said property as a whole, and that in view thereof the tenant ought not to be granted a new tenancy.
(f)	That on the termination of the current tenancy the landlord intends to demolish or reconstruct the premises comprised in the holding or a substantial part of those premises or to carry out substantial work of construction on the holding or part thereof and that he could not reasonably do so without obtaining possession of the holding.
(g)	On the termination of the current tenancy the landlord intends to occupy the holding for the purposes, or partly for the purposes, of a business to be carried on by him therein, or as his residence.

In this Table "the holding" means the property that is the subject of the tenancy.

In ground (e), "the landlord is the owner an interest in reversion expectant on the termination of that superior tenancy" means that the landlord has an interest in the property that will entitle him or her, when your immediate landlord's tenancy comes to an end, to exercise certain rights and obligations in relation to the property that are currently exercisable by your immediate landlord.

If the landlord relies on ground (f), the court can sometimes still grant a new tenancy if certain conditions set out in section 31A are met.

If the landlord relies on ground (g), please note that "the landlord" may have an extended meaning. Where a landlord has a controlling interest in a company then either the landlord or the company can rely on ground (g). Where the landlord is a company and a person has a controlling interest in that company then either of them can rely on ground (g) (section 30(1A) and (1B)). A person has a "controlling interest" in a company if, had he been a company, the other company would have been its subsidiary (section 46(2)).

The landlord must normally have been the landlord for at least five years before he or she can rely on ground (g).

Compensation

If you cannot get a new tenancy solely because one or more of grounds (e), (f) and (g) applies, you may be entitled to compensation under section 37. If your landlord has opposed your application on any of the other grounds as well as (e), (f) or (g) you can only get compensation if the court's refusal to grant a new tenancy is based solely on one or more of grounds (e), (f) and (g). In other words, you cannot get compensation under section 37 if the court has refused your tenancy on *other* grounds, even if one or more of grounds (e), (f) and (g) also applies.

If your landlord is an authority possessing compulsory purchase powers (such as a local authority) you may be entitled to a disturbance payment under Part 3 of the Land Compensation Act 1973.

Validity of this notice

The landlord who has given you this notice may not be the landlord to whom you pay your rent (sections 44 and 67). This does not necessarily mean that the notice is invalid.

If you have any doubts about whether this notice is valid, get advice immediately from a solicitor or a surveyor.

Further information

An explanation of the main points to consider when renewing or ending a business tenancy, "Renewing and Ending Business Leases: a Guide for Tenants and Landlords", can be found at www.odpm.gov.uk. Printed copies of the explanation, but not of this form, are available from 1st June 2004 from Free Literature, PO Box 236, Wetherby, West Yorkshire, LS23 7NB (0870 1226 236).

A2.035 FORM 3

Tenant's Request for a New Business Tenancy

SECTION 26 OF THE LANDLORD AND TENANT ACT 1954

To: (*insert name and address of landlord*)
From: (*insert name and address of tenant*)

1. This notice relates to the following property: (*insert address or description of property*).

2. I am giving you notice under section 26 of the Landlord and Tenant Act 1954 that I request a new tenancy beginning on (*insert date*).

3. You will find my proposals for the new tenancy, which we can discuss, in the Schedule to this notice.

4. If we cannot agree on all the terms of a new tenancy, either you or I may ask the court to order the grant of a new tenancy and settle the terms on which we cannot agree.

5. If you wish to ask the court to order the grant of a new tenancy you must do so by the date in paragraph 2, unless we agree in writing to a later date and do so before the date in paragraph 2.

6. You may oppose my request for a new tenancy only on one or more of the grounds set out in section 30(1) of the Landlord and Tenant Act 1954. You must tell me what your grounds are within two months of receiving this notice. If you miss this deadline you will not be able to oppose renewal of my tenancy and you will have to grant me a new tenancy.

7. Please send all correspondence about this notice to:

Name: ....
Address: ....
....
....

Signed: .... Date: ....

*[Tenant] *[On behalf of the tenant] (*delete whichever is inapplicable)

SCHEDULE **A2.036**

Tenant's Proposals for a New Tenancy

(*attach or insert proposed terms of the new tenancy*)

> **IMPORTANT NOTE FOR THE LANDLORD**
> **This notice requests a new tenancy of your property or part of it. If you want to oppose this request you must act quickly.**
> **Read the notice and all the Notes carefully. It would be wise to seek professional advice.**

NOTES

The sections mentioned below are sections of the Landlord and Tenant Act 1954, as amended, (most recently by the Regulatory Reform (Business Tenancies) (England and Wales) Order 2003)

Tenant's request for a new tenancy

This request by your tenant for a new tenancy brings his or her current tenancy to an end on the day before the date mentioned in paragraph 2 of this notice. Section 26 contains rules about the date that the tenant can put in paragraph 2 of this notice.

Your tenant can apply to the court under section 24 for a new tenancy. You may apply for a new tenancy yourself, under the same section, but not if your tenant has already served an application. Once an application has been made to the court, your tenant's cur-rent tenancy will continue after the date mentioned in paragraph 2 while the application is being considered by the court. Either you or your tenant can ask the court to fix the rent which your tenant will have to pay whilst the tenancy continues (sections 24A to 24D). The court will settle any terms of a new tenancy on which you and your tenant disagree (sections 34 and 35).

†Cross out words in square brackets if they do not apply

Time limit for opposing your tenant's request

If you do not want to grant a new tenancy, you have two months from the making of your tenant's request in which to notify him or her that you will oppose any appli-cation made to the court for a new tenancy. You do not need a special form to do this, but the notice must be in writing and it must state on which of the grounds set out in section 30(1) you will oppose the application. If you do not use the same wording of the ground (or grounds), as set out below, your notice may be ineffective.

If there has been any delay in your seeing this notice, you may need to act very quickly. If you are in any doubt about what action you should take, get advice immediately from a solicitor or a surveyor.

Grounds for opposing tenant's application

If you wish to oppose the renewal of the tenancy, you can do so by opposing your tenant's application to the court, or by making your own application to the court for termination without renewal. However, you can only oppose your tenant's application, or apply for termination without renewal, on one or more of the grounds set out in section 30(1). These grounds are set out below. You will only be able to rely on the ground(s) of opposition that you have mentioned in your written notice to your tenant.

In this Table "the holding" means the property that is the subject of the tenancy.

Paragraph of section 30(1)	*Grounds*
(a)	Where under the current tenancy the tenant has any obligations as respects the repair and maintenance of the holding, that the tenant ought not to be granted a new tenancy in view of the state of repair of the holding, being a state resulting from the tenant's failure to comply with the said obligations.
(b)	That the tenant ought not to be granted a new tenancy in view of his persistent delay in paying rent which has become due.
(c)	That the tenant ought not to be granted a new tenancy in view of other substantial breaches by him of his obligations under the current tenancy, or for any other reason connected with the tenant's use or management of the holding.
(d)	That the landlord has offered and is willing to provide or secure the provision of alternative accommodation for the tenant, that the terms on which the alternative accommodation is available are reasonable having regard to the terms of the current tenancy and to all other relevant circumstances, and that the accommodation and the time at which it will be available are suitable for the tenant's requirements (including the requirement to preserve goodwill) having regard to the nature and class of his business and to the situation and extent of, and facilities afforded by, the holding.

Paragraph of section 30(1)	*Grounds*
(e)	Where the current tenancy was created by the sub-letting of part only of the property comprised in a superior tenancy and the landlord is the owner of an interest in reversion expectant on the termination of that superior tenancy, that the aggregate of the rents reasonably obtainable on separate lettings of the holding and the remainder of that property would be substantially less than the rent reasonably obtainable on a letting of that property as a whole, that on the termination of the current tenancy the landlord requires possession of the holding for the purposes of letting or otherwise disposing of the said property as a whole, and that in view thereof the tenant ought not to be granted a new tenancy.
(f)	That on the termination of the current tenancy the landlord intends to demolish or reconstruct the premises comprised in the holding or a substantial part of those premises or to carry out substantial work of construction on the holding or part thereof and that he could not reasonably do so without obtaining possession of the holding.
(g)	On the termination of the current tenancy the landlord intends to occupy the holding for the purposes, or partly for the purposes, of a business to be carried on by him therein, or as his residence.

Compensation

If your tenant cannot get a new tenancy solely because one or more of grounds (e), (f) and (g) applies, he or she is entitled to compensation under section 37. If you have opposed your tenant's application on any of the other grounds mentioned in section 30(1), as well as on one or more of grounds (e), (f) and (g), your tenant can only get compensation if the court's refusal to grant a new tenancy is based solely on ground (e), (f) or (g). In other words, your tenant cannot get compensation under section 37 if the court has refused the tenancy on *other* grounds, even if one or more of grounds (e), (f) and (g) also applies.

If you are an authority possessing compulsory purchase powers (such as a local authority), your tenant may be entitled to a disturbance payment under Part 3 of the Land Compensation Act 1973.

Negotiating a new tenancy

Most tenancies are renewed by negotiation and your tenant has set out proposals for the new tenancy in paragraph 3 of this notice. You are not obliged to accept these proposals and may put forward your own. You and your tenant may agree in writing to extend the deadline for making an application to the court while negotiations continue. Your tenant may not apply to the court for a new tenancy until two months have passed from the date of the making of the request contained in this notice, unless you have already given notice opposing your tenant's request as mentioned in paragraph 6 of this notice (section 29A(3)).

If you try to agree a new tenancy with your tenant, remember:

- that one of you will need to apply to the court before the date in paragraph 2 of this notice, unless you both agree to extend the period for making an application.
- that any such agreement must be in writing and must be made before the date in paragraph 2 (sections 29A and 29B).

Validity of this notice

The tenant who has given you this notice may not be the person from whom you receive rent (sections 44 and 67). This does not necessarily mean that the notice is invalid.

If you have any doubts about whether this notice is valid, get advice immediately from a solicitor or a surveyor.

Further information

An explanation of the main points to consider when renewing or ending a business tenancy, "Renewing and Ending Business Leases: a Guide for Tenants and Landlords", can be found at www.odpm.gov.uk. Printed copies of the explanation, but not of this form, are available from 1st June 2004 from Free Literature, PO Box 236, Wetherby, West Yorkshire, LS23 7NB (0870 1226 236).

A2.037 FORM 4

Landlord's Request for Information about Occupation and Sub-tenancies

SECTION 40(1) OF THE LANDLORD AND TENANT ACT 1954

To: (*insert name and address of tenant*)
From: (*insert name and address of landlord*)

1. This notice relates to the following premises: (*insert address or description of premises*)

2. I give you notice under section 40(1) of the Landlord and Tenant Act 1954 that I require you to provide information—

(a) by answering questions (1) to (3) in the Table below;
(b) if you answer "yes" to question (2), by giving me the name and address of the person or persons concerned;
(c) if you answer "yes" to question (3), by also answering questions (4) to (10) in the Table below;
(d) if you answer "no" to question (8), by giving me the name and address of the sub-tenant; and
(e) if you answer "yes" to question (10), by giving me details of the notice or request.

TABLE

(1) Do you occupy the premises or any part of them wholly or partly for the purposes of a business that is carried on by you?
(2) To the best of your knowledge and belief, does any other person own an interest in reversion in any part of the premises?
(3) Does your tenancy have effect subject to any sub-tenancy on which your tenancy is immediately expectant?
(4) What premises are comprised in the sub-tenancy?
(5) For what term does it have effect or, if it is terminable by notice, by what notice can it be terminated?
(6) What is the rent payable under it?
(7) Who is the sub-tenant?
(8) To the best of your knowledge and belief, is the sub-tenant in occupation of the premises or of part of the premises comprised in the sub-tenancy?
(9) Is an agreement in force excluding, in relation to the sub-tenancy, the provisions of sections 24 to 28 of the Landlord and Tenant Act 1954?
(10) Has a notice been given under section 25 or 26(6) of that Act, or has a request been made under section 26 of that Act, in relation to the sub-tenancy?

3. You must give the information concerned in writing and within the period of one month beginning with the date of service of this notice.

4. Please send all correspondence about this notice to:

Name: . . . .

Address: . . . .

. . . .

. . . .

Signed: . . . . Date: . . . .

*[Landlord] *[on behalf of the landlord]

**delete whichever is inapplicable*

IMPORTANT NOTE FOR THE TENANT

This notice contains some words and phrases that you may not understand. The Notes below should help you, but it would be wise to seek professional advice, for example, from a solicitor or surveyor, before responding to this notice.

Once you have provided the information required by this notice, you must correct it if you realise that it is not, or is no longer, correct.

notice, but an exception is explained in the next paragraph. If you need to correct information already given, you must do so within one month of becoming aware that the information is incorrect.

The obligation will cease if, after transferring your tenancy, you notify the landlord of the transfer and of the name and address of the person to whom your tenancy has been transferred.

If you fail to comply with the requirements of this notice, or the obligation mentioned above, you may face civil proceedings for breach of the statutory duty that arises under section 40 of the Landlord and Tenant Act 1954. In any such proceedings a court may order you to comply with that duty and may make an award of damages.

NOTES

The sections mentioned below are sections of the Landlord and Tenant Act 1954, as amended, (most recently by the Regulatory Reform (Business Tenancies) (England and Wales) Order 2003)

Purpose of this notice

Your landlord (or, if he or she is a tenant, possibly your landlord's landlord) has sent you this notice in order to obtain information about your occupation and that of any sub-tenants. This information may be relevant to the taking of steps to end or renew your business tenancy.

Time limit for replying

You must provide the relevant information within one month of the date of service of this notice (section 40(1), (2) and (5)).

Information required

You do not have to give your answers on this form; you may use a separate sheet for this purpose. The notice requires you to provide, in writing, information in the form of answers to questions (1) to (3) in the Table above and, if you answer "yes" to question (3), also to provide information in the form of answers to questions (4) to (10) in that Table. Depending on your answer to question (2) and, if applicable in your case, questions (8) and (10), you must also provide the information referred to in paragraph 2(b), (d) and (e) of this notice. Question (2) refers to a person who owns an interest in reversion. You should answer "yes" to this question if you know or believe that there is a person who receives, or is entitled to receive, rent in respect of any part of the premises (other than the landlord who served this notice).

When you answer questions about sub-tenants, please bear in mind that, for these purposes, a sub-tenant includes a person retaining possession of premises by virtue of the Rent (Agriculture) Act 1976 or the Rent Act 1977 after the coming to an end of a sub-tenancy, and "sub-tenancy" includes a right so to retain possession (section 40(8)).

You should keep a copy of your answers and of any other information provided in response to questions (2), (8) or (10) above.

If, once you have given this information, you realise that it is not, or is no longer, correct, you must give the correct information within one month of becoming aware that the previous information is incorrect. Subject to the next paragraph, your duty to correct any information that you have already given continues for six months after you receive this notice (section 40(5)). You should give the correct information to the landlord who gave you this notice unless you receive notice of the transfer of his or her interest, and of the name and address of the person to whom that interest has been transferred. In that case, the correct information must be given to that person.

If you transfer your tenancy within the period of six months referred to above, your duty to correct information already given will cease if you notify the landlord of the transfer and of the name and address of the person to whom your tenancy has been transferred.

If you do not provide the information requested, or fail to correct information that you have provided earlier, after realising that it is not, or is no longer, correct, proceedings may be taken against you and you may have to pay damages (section 40B).

If you are in any doubt about the information that you should give, get immediate advice from a solicitor or a surveyor.

Validity of this notice

The landlord who has given you this notice may not be the landlord to whom you pay your rent (sections 44 and 67). This does not necessarily mean that the notice is invalid.

If you have any doubts about whether this notice is valid, get advice immediately from a solicitor or a surveyor.

Further information

An explanation of the main points to consider when renewing or ending a business tenancy, "Renewing and Ending Business Leases: a Guide for Tenants and Landlords", can be found at www.odpm.gov.uk. Printed copies of the explanation, but not of this form, are available from 1st June 2004 from Free Literature, PO Box 236, Wetherby, West Yorkshire, LS23 7NB (0870 1226 236).

FORM 5 **A2.038**

Tenant's Request for Information from Landlord or Landlord's Mortgagee about Landlord's Interest

SECTION 40(3) OF THE LANDLORD AND TENANT ACT 1954

To: (*insert name and address of reversioner or reversioner's mortgagee in possession [see the first note below]*)

From: (*insert name and address of tenant*)

1. This notice relates to the following premises: (*insert address or description of premises*)

2. In accordance with section 40(3) of the Landlord and Tenant Act 1954 I require you—

(a) to state in writing whether you are the owner of the fee simple in respect of the premises or any part of them or the mortgagee in possession of such an owner,

(b) if you answer "no" to (a), to state in writing, to the best of your knowledge and belief—

(i) the name and address of the person who is your or, as the case may be, your mortgagor's immediate landlord in respect of the premises or of the part in respect of which you are not, or your mortgagor is not, the owner in fee simple;

(ii) for what term your or your mortgagor's tenancy has effect and what is the earliest date (if any) at which that tenancy is terminable by notice to quit given by the landlord; and

(iii) whether a notice has been given under section 25 or 26(6) of the Landlord and Tenant Act 1954, or a request has been made under section 26 of that Act, in relation to the tenancy and, if so, details of the notice or request;

(c) to state in writing, to the best of your knowledge and belief, the name and address of any other person who owns an interest in reversion in any part of the premises;

(d) if you are a reversioner, to state in writing whether there is a mortgagee in possession of your interest in the premises; and

(e) if you answer "yes" to (d), to state in writing, to the best of your knowledge and belief, the name and address of the mortgagee in possession.

3. You must give the information concerned within the period of one month beginning with the date of service of this notice.

4. Please send all correspondence about this notice to:

Name: ....

Address: ....

....

....

Signed: .... Date: ....

(**delete whichever is inapplicable*) *[Tenant] *[on behalf of the tenant]

IMPORTANT NOTE FOR LANDLORD OR LANDLORD'S MORTGAGEE

This notice contains some words and phrases that you may not understand. The Notes below should help you, but it would be wise to seek professional advice, for example, from a solicitor or surveyor, before responding to this notice.

Once you have provided the information required by this notice, you must correct it if you realise that it is not, or is no longer, correct. This obligation lasts for six months from the date of service of this notice, but an exception is explained in the next paragraph. If you

need to correct information already given, you must do so within one month of becoming aware that the information is incorrect.

The obligation will cease if, after transferring your interest, you notify the tenant of the transfer and of the name and address of the person to whom your interest has been transferred.

If you fail to comply with the requirements of this notice, or the obligation mentioned above, you may face civil proceedings for breach of the statutory duty that arises under section 40 of the Landlord and Tenant Act 1954. In any such proceedings a court may order you to comply with that duty and may make an award of damages.

Notes

The sections mentioned below are sections of the Landlord and Tenant Act 1954, as amended, (most recently by the Regulatory Reform (Business Tenancies) (England and Wales) Order 2003)

Terms used in this notice

The following terms, which are used in paragraph 2 of this notice, are defined in section 40(8):

> "mortgagee in possession" includes a receiver appointed by the mortgagee or by the court who is in receipt of the rents and profits;
>
> "reversioner" means any person having an interest in the premises, being an interest in reversion expectant (whether immediately or not) on the tenancy; and
>
> "reversioner's mortgagee in possession" means any person being a mortgagee in possession in respect of such an interest.

Section 40(8) requires the reference in paragraph 2(b) of this notice to your mortgagor to be read in the light of the definition of "mortgagee in possession".

A mortgagee (mortgage lender) will be "in possession" if the mortgagor (the person who owes money to the mortgage lender) has failed to comply with the terms of the mortgage. The mortgagee may then be entitled to receive rent that would normally have been paid to the mortgagor.

The term "the owner of the fee simple" means the freehold owner.

The term "reversioner" includes the freehold owner and any intermediate landlord as well as the immediate landlord of the tenant who served this notice.

Purpose of this notice and information required

This notice requires you to provide, in writing, the information requested in paragraph 2(a) and (c) of the notice and, if applicable in your case, in paragraph 2(b), (d) and (e). You do not need to use a special form for this purpose.

If, once you have given this information, you realise that it is not, or is no longer, correct, you must give the correct information within one month of becoming aware that the previous information is incorrect. Subject to the last paragraph in this section of these Notes, your duty to correct any information that you have already given continues for six months after you receive this notice (section 40(5)).

You should give the correct information to the tenant who gave you this notice unless you receive notice of the transfer of his or her interest, and of the name and address of the person to whom that interest has been transferred. In that case, the correct information must be given to that person.

If you do not provide the information requested, or fail to correct information that you have provided earlier, after realising that it is not, or is no longer, correct, proceedings may be taken against you and you may have to pay damages (section 40B).

If you are in any doubt as to the information that you should give, get advice immediately from a solicitor or a surveyor.

If you transfer your interest within the period of six months referred to above, your duty to correct information already given will cease if you notify the tenant of that transfer and of the name and address of the person to whom your interest has been transferred.

Time limit for replying

You must provide the relevant information within one month of the date of service of this notice (section 40(3), (4) and (5)).

Validity of this notice

The tenant who has given you this notice may not be the person from whom you receive rent (sections 44 and 67). This does not necessarily mean that the notice is invalid.

If you have any doubts about the validity of the notice, get advice immediately from a solicitor or a surveyor.

Further information

An explanation of the main points to consider when renewing or ending a business tenancy, "Renewing and Ending Business Leases: a Guide for Tenants and Landlords", can be found at www.odpm.gov.uk. Printed copies of the explanation, but not of this form, are available from 1st June 2004 from Free Literature, PO Box 236, Wetherby, West Yorkshire, LS23 7NB (0870 1226 236).

FORM 6 **A2.039**

Landlord's Withdrawal of Notice Terminating Tenancy

SECTION 44 OF, AND PARAGRAPH 6 OF SCHEDULE 6 TO, THE LANDLORD AND TENANT ACT 1954

To: (*insert name and address of tenant*)
From: (*insert name and address of landlord*)

1. This notice is given under section 44 of, and paragraph 6 of Schedule 6 to, the Landlord and Tenant Act 1954 ("the 1954 Act").
2. It relates to the following property: (*insert address or description of property*)
3. 1 have become your landlord for the purposes of the 1954 Act.
4. I withdraw the notice given to you by (*insert name of former landlord*), terminating your tenancy on (*insert date*).
5. Please send any correspondence about this notice to:
Name: ....
Address: ....
....
....

Signed: .... Date: ....

*[Landlord] *[on behalf of the landlord] **delete whichever is inapplicable*

> **IMPORTANT NOTE FOR THE TENANT**
> **If you have any doubts about the validity of this notice, get advice immediately from a solicitor or a surveyor.**

NOTES

The sections and Schedule mentioned below are sections of, and a Schedule to, the Landlord and Tenant Act 1954, as amended, (most recently by the Regulatory Reform (Business Tenancies) (England and Wales) Order 2003).

Purpose of this notice

You were earlier given a notice bringing your tenancy to an end, but there has now been a change of landlord. This new notice is given to you by your new landlord and withdraws the earlier notice, which now has no effect. However, the new landlord can, if he or she wishes, give you a fresh notice with the intention of bringing your tenancy to an end (section 44 and paragraph 6 of Schedule 6).

Validity of this notice

The landlord who has given you this notice may not be the landlord to whom you pay your rent (sections 44 and 67). This does not necessarily mean that the notice is invalid.

If you have any doubts about whether this notice is valid, get advice immediately from a solicitor or a surveyor. If this notice is *not* valid, the original notice will have effect. Your tenancy will end on the date given in that notice (stated in paragraph 4 of this notice).

Further information

An explanation of the main points to consider when renewing or ending a business tenancy, "Renewing and Ending Business Leases: a Guide for Tenants and Landlords", can be found at **www.odpm.gov.uk** Printed copies of the explanation, but not of this form, are available from 1st June 2004 from Free Literature, PO Box 236, Wetherby, West Yorkshire, LS23 7NB (0870 1226 236).

A2.040 FORM 7

Landlord's Notice Ending a Business Tenancy (with Reasons for Refusing a New Tenancy) where the Leasehold Reform Act 1967 may apply

SECTION 25 OF THE LANDLORD AND TENANT ACT 1954 AND PARAGRAPH 10 OF SCHEDULE 3 TO THE LEASEHOLD REFORM ACT 1967

IMPORTANT NOTE FOR THE LANDLORD: Use this form where you wish to oppose the grant of a new tenancy, and the tenant may be entitled to acquire the freehold or an extended lease. Complete this form and send it to the tenant. If you are opposed to the grant of a new tenancy, and the tenant is not entitled to acquire the freehold or an extended lease, use form 2 in Schedule 2 to the Landlord and Tenant Act 1954, Part 2 (Notices) Regulations 2004 instead of this form.

To: (*insert name and address of tenant*)
From: (*insert name and address of landlord*)

1. This notice relates to the following property: (*insert address or description of property*)

2. I am giving you notice under section 25 of the Landlord and Tenant Act 1954 to end your tenancy on (*insert date*).

3. I am opposed to the grant of a new tenancy.

** insert letter(s) of the paragraph(s) relied on*

4. You may ask the court to order the grant of a new tenancy. If you do, I will oppose your application on the ground(s) mentioned in paragraph(s)* of section 30(1) of that Act. I draw your attention to the Table in the Notes below, which sets out all the grounds of opposition.

5. If you wish to ask the court for a new tenancy you must do so by the date in paragraph 2 unless, before that date, we agree in writing to a later date.

6. I can ask the court to order the ending of your tenancy without granting you a new tenancy. I may have to pay you compensation if I have relied only on one or more of the grounds mentioned in paragraph (e), (f) and (g) of section 30(1). If I ask the court to end your tenancy, you can challenge my application.

7. If you have a right under Part 1 of the Leasehold Reform Act 1967 to acquire the freehold or an extended lease of property comprised in the tenancy, notice of your desire to have the freehold or an extended lease cannot be given more than two months after the service of this notice. If you have that right, and give notice of your desire to have the freehold or an extended lease within those two months, this notice will not operate, and I may take no further proceedings under Part 2 of the Landlord and Tenant Act 1954.

***8.** If you give notice of your desire to have the freehold or an extended lease, I will be entitled to apply to the court under section 17/section 18** of the Leasehold Reform Act 1967, and propose to do so. If I am successful I may have to pay you compensation.

***delete the reference to section 17 or section 18, as the circumstances require*

OR

***8.** If you give notice of your desire to have the freehold or an extended lease, I will be entitled to apply to the court under section 17/section 18** of the Leasehold Reform Act 1967, but do not propose to do so.

***delete the reference to section 17 or section 18, as the circumstances require*

OR

***8.** If you give notice of your desire to have the freehold or an extended lease, I will not be entitled to apply to the court under section 17 or section 18 of the Leasehold Reform Act 1967.

** DELETE TWO versions of this paragraph, as the circumstances require*

***9.** I know or believe that the following persons have an interest superior to your tenancy or to be the agent concerned with the property on behalf of someone who has such an interest (*insert names and addresses*):

** delete if inapplicable*

10. Please send all correspondence about this notice to:

Name: ....

Address: ....

....

....

Signed: .... Date: ....

*[Landlord] *[On behalf of the landlord] *[Mortgagee] *[On behalf of the mortgagee]

** delete if inapplicable*

IMPORTANT NOTE FOR THE TENANT

This Notice is intended to bring your tenancy to an end on the date specified in paragraph 2.

Your landlord is not prepared to offer you a new tenancy. You will not get a new tenancy unless you successfully challenge in court the grounds on which your landlord opposes the grant of a new tenancy.

If you want to continue to occupy your property you must act quickly. The notes below should help you to decide what action you now need to take. If you want to challenge your landlord's refusal to renew your tenancy, get advice immediately from a solicitor or a surveyor.

NOTES

Unless otherwise stated, the sections mentioned below are sections of the Landlord and Tenant Act 1954, as amended, (most recently by the Regulatory Reform (Business Tenancies) (England and Wales) Order 2003)

Ending of your tenancy

This notice is intended to bring your tenancy to an end on the date given in paragraph 2. Section 25 contains rules about the date that the landlord can put in paragraph 2 of this notice.

Your landlord is not prepared to offer you a new tenancy. If you want a new tenancy you will need to apply to the court for a new tenancy and successfully challenge the landlord's opposition (see the section below headed "*Landlord's opposition to new tenancy*"). If you wish to apply to the court you must do so before the date given in paragraph 2 of this notice, unless you and your landlord have agreed in writing, before that date, to extend the deadline (sections 29A and 29B).

If you apply to the court your tenancy will continue after the date given in paragraph 2 of this notice while your application is being considered (section 24). You may not apply to the court if your landlord has already done so (section 24(2A) and (2B)).

You may only stay in the property after the date given in paragraph 2 (or such later date as you and the landlord may have agreed in writing) if before that date you have asked the court to order the grant of a new tenancy or the landlord has asked the court to order the ending of your tenancy without granting you a new one.

If you are in any doubt about what action you should take, get advice immediately from a solicitor or a surveyor.

Landlord's opposition to new tenancy

If you apply to the court for a new tenancy, the landlord can only oppose your application on one or more of the grounds set out in section 30(1). If you match the letter(s) specified in paragraph 4 of the notice with those in the first column in the Table below, you can see from the second column the ground(s) on which the landlord relies.

Paragraph of section 30(1)	*Grounds*
(a)	Where under the current tenancy the tenant has any obligations as respects the repair and maintenance of the holding, that the tenant ought not to be granted a new

Paragraph of section 30(1)	*Grounds*
	tenancy in view of the state of repair of the holding, being a state resulting from the tenant's failure to comply with the said obligations.
(b)	That the tenant ought not to be granted a new tenancy in view of his persistent delay in paying rent which has become due.
(c)	That the tenant ought not to be granted a new tenancy in view of other substantial breaches by him of his obligations under the current tenancy, or for any other reason connected with the tenant's use or management of the holding.
(d)	That the landlord has offered and is willing to provide or secure the provision of alternative accommodation for the tenant, that the terms on which the alternative accommodation is available are reasonable having regard to the terms of the current tenancy and to all other relevant circumstances, and that the accommodation and the time at which it will be available are suitable for the tenant's requirements (including the requirement to preserve goodwill) having regard to the nature and class of his business and to the situation and extent of, and facilities afforded by, the holding.
(e)	Where the current tenancy was created by the sub-letting of part only of the property comprised in a superior tenancy and the landlord is the owner of an interest in reversion expectant on the termination of that superior tenancy, that the aggregate of the rents reasonably obtainable on separate lettings of the holding and the remainder of that property would be substantially less than the rent reasonably obtainable on a letting of that property as a whole, that on the termination of the current tenancy the landlord requires possession of the holding for the purposes of letting or otherwise disposing of the said property as a whole, and that in view thereof the tenant ought not to be granted a new tenancy.
(f)	That on the termination of the current tenancy the landlord intends to demolish or reconstruct the premises comprised in the holding or a substantial part of those premises or to carry out substantial work of construction on the holding or part thereof and that he could not reasonably do so without obtaining possession of the holding.
(g)	On the termination of the current tenancy the landlord intends to occupy the holding for the purposes, or partly for the purposes, of a business to be carried on by him therein, or as his residence.

In this Table "the holding" means the property that is the subject of the tenancy.

In ground (e), "the landlord is the owner an interest in reversion expectant on the termination of that superior tenancy" means that the landlord has an interest in the property that will entitle him or her, when your immediate landlord's tenancy comes to an end, to exercise certain rights and obligations in relation to the property that are currently exercisable by your immediate landlord.

If the landlord relies on ground (f), the court can sometimes still grant a new tenancy if certain conditions set out in section 31A are met.

If the landlord relies on ground (g), please note that "the landlord" may have an extended meaning. Where a landlord has a controlling interest in a company then either the landlord or the company can rely on ground (g). Where the landlord is a company and a person has a controlling interest in that company then either of them can rely on ground (g) (section 30(1A) and (1B)). A person has a "controlling interest" in a company if, had he been a company, the other company would have been its subsidiary (section 46(2)).

The landlord must normally have been the landlord for at least five years before he or she can rely on ground (g).

Rights under the Leasehold Reform Act 1967

If the property comprised in your tenancy is a house, as defined in section 2 of the Leasehold Reform Act 1967 ("the 1967 Act"), you may have the right to buy the freehold of the property or an extended lease. If the house is for the time being let under two or more tenancies, you will not have that right if your tenancy is subject to a sub-tenancy and the sub-tenant is himself or herself entitled to that right.

You will have that right if all the following conditions are met:

(i) your lease was originally granted for a term of more than 35 years, or was preceded by such a lease which was granted or assigned to you; and

(ii) your lease is of the whole house; and

(iii) your lease is at a low rent. If your tenancy was entered into before 1 April 1990 (or later if you contracted before that date to enter into the tenancy) "low rent" means that your present annual rent is less than two-thirds of the rateable value of your house as assessed either on 23 March 1965, or on the first day of the term in the case of a lease granted to commence after 23 March 1965; and the property had a rateable value other than nil when the tenancy began or at any time before 1 April 1990. If your tenancy was granted on or after 1 April 1990, "low rent" means that the present annual rent is not more than £1,000 in London or £250 elsewhere; and

(iv) you have been occupying the house (or any part of it) as your only or main residence (whether or not it has been occupied for other purposes) either for the whole of the last two years, or for a total of two years in the last ten years; and

(v) the rateable value of your house was at one time within certain limits.

Claiming your rights under the 1967 Act

If you have a right to buy the freehold or an extended lease and wish to exercise it you must serve the appropriate notice on the landlord. A special form is prescribed for this purpose; it is Form 1 as set out in the Schedule to the Leasehold Reform (Notices) (Amendment) (England) Regulations 2002 (S.I. 2002/1715) or, if the property is in Wales, the Leasehold Reform (Notices) (Amendment) (Wales) Regulations 2002 (S.I. 2002/3187) (W.303). Subject to the two exceptions mentioned below, you must serve the notice claiming to buy the freehold or an extended lease within two months after the date of service of this notice. The first exception is where, within that two-month period, you apply to the court to order the grant of a new tenancy. In that case your claim to buy the freehold or an extended lease must be made when you make the application to the court. The second exception is where the landlord agrees in writing to your claim being made after the date on which it should have been made.

There are special rules about the service of notices. If there has been any delay in your seeing this notice, you may need to act very quickly.

If you are in any doubt about your rights under the 1967 Act or what action you should take, get advice immediately from a solicitor or a surveyor.

Landlord's opposition to claims under the 1967 Act

If your landlord acquired his or her interest in the house not later than 18 February 1966 he or she can object to your claim to buy the freehold or an extended lease on the grounds that he or she needs to occupy the house or that the house is needed for occupation by a member of his or her family. This objection will be under section 18 of the 1967 Act.

If you claim an extended lease, your landlord can object under section 17 of the 1967 Act on the grounds that he or she wishes to redevelop the property.

You will be able to tell from paragraph 8 of this notice whether your landlord intends to apply to the court and, if so, whether for the purposes of occupation or redevelopment of the house.

Compensation

If you cannot get a new tenancy solely because one or more of grounds (e), (f) and (g) in section 30(1) applies, you may be entitled to compensation under section 37. If your landlord has opposed your application on any of the other grounds as well as (e), (f) or (g) you can only get compensation if the court's refusal to grant a new tenancy is based solely on one or more of grounds (e), (f) and (g). In other words, you cannot get compensation under section 37 if the court has refused your tenancy on other grounds, even if one or more of grounds (e), (f) and (g) also applies.

If your landlord is an authority possessing compulsory purchase powers (such as a local authority) you may be entitled to a disturbance payment under Part 3 of the Land Compensation Act 1973.

If you have a right under the 1967 Act to buy the freehold or an extended lease but the landlord is able to obtain pos-session of the premises, compensation is payable under section 17(2) or section 18(4) of the 1967 Act. Your solicitor or surveyor will be able to advise you about this.

Negotiations with your landlord

If you try to buy the property by agreement or negotiate an extended lease with the landlord, remember:

- that your present tenancy will not be extended under the 1954 Act after the date in paragraph 2 of this notice unless you agree in writing to extend the deadline for applying to the court under the 1954 Act or you (or the landlord) has applied to the court before that date (sections 29, 29A and 29B), and
- that you may lose your right to serve a notice claiming to buy the freehold or an extended lease under the 1967 Act if you do not observe the two-month time limit referred to in the note headed *Claiming your rights under the 1967 Act*.

Validity of this notice

The landlord who has given you this notice may not be the landlord to whom you pay your rent (sections 44 and 67). This does not necessarily mean that the notice is invalid.

If you have any doubts about whether this notice is valid, get advice immediately from a solicitor or a surveyor.

Further information

An explanation of the main points to consider when renewing or ending a business tenancy, "Renewing and Ending Business Leases: a Guide for Tenants and Landlords", can be found at www.odpm.gov.uk. Printed copies of the explanation, but not of this form, are available from 1st June 2004 from Free Literature, PO Box 236, Wetherby, West Yorkshire, LS23 7NB (0870 1226 236).

Landlord and Tenant Act 1954 (Appropriate Multiplier) Order 1990

A2.041

(S.I. 1990 No. 363)

The Secretary of State for the Environment, as respects England, and the Secretary of State for Wales, as respects Wales, in exercise of the powers conferred by section 37(8) of the Landlord and Tenant Act 1954, and of all other powers enabling them in that behalf, hereby make the following order.

1. This Order may be cited as the Landlord and Tenant Act 1954 (Appropriate Multiplier) Order 1990 and shall come into force on April 1, 1990.
Appendices

2. In this Order references to section 37 are references to section 37 of the Landlord and Tenant Act 1954 and references to the 1989 Act are to the Local Government and Housing Act 1989.

3. Where the date which (apart from paragraph 4 of Schedule 7 to the 1989 Act) is relevant for determining the rateable value of the holding under section 37(5) is before April 1, 1990, the appropriate multiplier for the purposes of section 37(2) is 3.

4. Where the date which (apart from paragraph 4 of Schedule 7 to the 1989 Act) is relevant for determining the rateable value of the holding under section 37(5) is on or after April 1, 1990, the appropriate multiplier for the purposes of section 37(2) is—

(a) 1, except in a case specified in (b) below, and

(b) 8 in a case where section 37 has effect with the modification specified in paragraph 4(2) of Schedule 7 to the 1989 Act.

5. The Landlord and Tenant Act 1954 (Appropriate Multiplier) Order 1984 is hereby revoked.

A2.042 Local Government Finance (Repeals, Savings and Consequential Amendments) Order 1990

(S.I. 1990 No. 776)

The Secretary of State for the Environment, as respects England, and the Secretary of State for Wales, as respects Wales, in exercise of the powers conferred upon them by sections 140(4), 147(1) and (2) of the Local Government Finance Act 1988 section 194(2) of the Local Government and Housing Act 1989, and of all other powers enabling them in that behalf, hereby make the following Order:

A2.043 Citation, commencement and interpretation

1.—(1) his Order may be cited as the Local Government Finance (Repeals, Savings and Consequential Amendments) Order 1990 and shall come into force on April 1, 1990.

(2) In this Order "the 1967 Act" means the General Rate Act 1967.

A2.044 Application of the Order

2.—(1) The provisions of this Order apply only to so much of the provisions of enactments and instruments referred to herein as extend or apply to England or Wales.

(2) Nothing in this Order shall prejudice the effect of any regulations under section 117(8) of the Local Government Finance Act 1988 or order under section 147 of that Act or regulations under section 149 of the Local Government and Housing Act 1989 made before the making of this Order.

A2.045 Repeals, revocations and savings

3.—(1) Subject to paragraphs (2) and (3), the enactments and instruments mentioned in column (1) of Schedule 1 to this Order are hereby repealed and revoked to the extent mentioned in column (2).

(2) Without prejudice to section 16 of the Interpretation Act 1978, nothing in paragraph (1) shall have effect in relation to the operation on and after April 1, 1990 of the enactments mentioned in Schedule 1 for the purposes of, or for purposes connected with—

(a) any rate made, or precept issued, under the 1967 Act in respect of any period ending before April 1, 1990;

(b) any liability for rates in respect of any such period;

(c) the alteration of any valuation list in force immediately before April 1, 1990 pursuant to a proposal made before that date but to which effect had not been given immediately before that date.

(3) The repeal of section 133 of the Lands Clauses Consolidation Act 1845, section 2(7) of the Rating and Valuation Act 1925 and section 27 of the Compulsory Purchase Act 1965 shall not affect any liability (whenever

incurred) to make good a deficiency arising in respect of any period ending before April 1, 1990.

Amendments relating to the jurisdiction of county courts **A2.046**

4.—(1) In the following enactments, and in any other enactment relating to the jurisdiction of county courts, references to net annual value for rating or rateable value shall be construed as references to a sum equivalent to the last such value of the property concerned immediately before April 1, 1990:

(a) The Tithe Act 1891;
(b) sections 3(7), 30(2), 49(4), 66(4), 146 and 147(5) of, and Schedule 1 to, the Law of Property Act 1925;
(c) section 113 of the Settled Land Act 1925;
(d) sections 43A, 53 and 63 of the Landlord and Tenant Act 1954;
(e) section 1 of the Land Charges Act 1972;
(f) section 1 of the Matrimonial Homes Act 1983;
(g) sections 21, 22 and 139 of, and Schedule 1 to, the County Courts Act 1984; and
(h) paragraph 6(5) of Schedule 18 to the Housing Act 1985.

(2) In enactments to which paragraph (1) applies, references to the net annual value for rating or rateable value of a property which did not have such a value immediately before April 1, 1990 shall be construed as references to—

(a) the rateable value immediately before that date of a hereditament of which the property concerned forms or formed part; or
(b) where there is no such hereditament, or where it had no such value, the value by the year of the property concerned at the time when the relevant proceedings are commenced.

The Regulatory Reform (Business Tenancies) (England and Wales) Order 2003

S.I. 2003 No. 3096

Final provisions

Consequential amendments, repeals and subordinate provisions

28.—(1) Schedule 5 to this Order, which contains amendments consequential on the provisions of this Order, shall have effect. **A2.047**

(2) The enactments specified in Schedule 6 to this Order are repealed to the extent mentioned in the third column of that Schedule.

(3) Schedules 1 to 4 to this Order are designated as subordinate provisions for the purposes of section 4 of the Regulatory Reform Act 2001.

(4) A subordinate provisions order relating to the subordinate provisions designated by paragraph (3) above shall be subject to annulment in pursuance of a resolution of either House of Parliament.

(5) The power to make a subordinate provisions order relating to those provisions is to be exercisable in relation to Wales by the National Assembly for Wales concurrently with a Minister of the Crown.

(6) Paragraph (4) above does not apply to a subordinate provisions order made by the National Assembly for Wales.

(7) The notices and statutory declarations set out in Schedules 1 to 4 to this Order shall be treated for the purposes of section 26 of the Welsh Language Act 1993[1] (power to prescribe Welsh forms) as if they were specified by an Act of Parliament; and accordingly the power conferred by section 26(2) of that Act may be exercised in relation to those notices and declarations.

Transitional provisions

29.—(1) Where, before this Order came into force– **A2.048**

(a) the landlord gave the tenant notice under section 25 of the Act; or

(b) the tenant made a request for a new tenancy in accordance with section 26 of the Act,

nothing in this Order has effect in relation to the notice or request or anything done in consequence of it.

(2) Nothing in this Order has effect in relation–

(a) to an agreement–

(i) for the surrender of a tenancy which was made before this Order came into force and which fell within section 24(2)(b) of the Act; or

(ii) which was authorised by the court under section 38(4) of the Act before this Order came into force; or

(b) to a notice under section 27(2) of the Act which was given by the tenant to the immediate landlord before this Order came into force.

[1] 1993 c.38.

(3) Any provision in a tenancy which requires an order under section 38(4) of the Act to be obtained in respect of any subtenancy shall, so far as is necessary after the coming into force of this Order, be construed as if it required the procedure mentioned in section 38A of the Act to be followed, and any related requirement shall be construed accordingly.

(4) If a person has, before the coming into force of this Order, entered into an agreement to take a tenancy, any provision in that agreement which requires an order under section 38(4) of the Act to be obtained in respect of the tenancy shall continue to be effective, notwithstanding the repeal of that provision by Article 21(2) of this Order, and the court shall retain jurisdiction to make such an order.

(5) Article 20 above does not have effect where the tenant quit the holding before this Order came into force.

(6) Nothing in Articles 23 and 24 above applies to a notice under section 40 of the Act served before this Order came into force.

SCHEDULE 1

Article 22(2)

Form of notice that sections 24 to 28 of the Landlord and Tenant Act 1954 are not to apply to a business tenancy

To:

A2.049 ____

____

____

[*Name and address of tenant*]

From:

____

____

____

[*Name and address of landlord*][2]

IMPORTANT NOTICE

You are being offered a lease without security of tenure. Do not commit yourself to the lease unless you have read this message carefully and have discussed it with a professional adviser.

Business tenants normally have security of tenure – the right to stay in their business premises when the lease ends.

2 Amended by Correction Slip. On page 16, the following paragraph should be inserted before the paragraph starting "If you receive this notice...": "If you want to ensure that you can stay in the same business premises when the lease ends, you should consult your adviser about another form of lease that does not exclude the protection of the Landlord and Tenant Act 1954."

If you commit yourself to the lease you will be giving up these important legal rights.

- You will have no right to stay in the premises when the lease ends.
- Unless the landlord chooses to offer you another lease, you will need to leave the premises.
- You will be unable to claim compensation for the loss of your business premises, unless the lease specifically gives you this right.
- If the landlord offers you another lease, you will have no right to ask the court to fix the rent.

It is therefore important to get professional advice – from a qualified surveyor, lawyer or accountant – before agreeing to give up these rights.

If you want to ensure that you can stay in the same business premises when the lease ends, you should consult your adviser about another form of lease that does not exclude the protection of the Landlord and Tenant Act 1954,

If you receive this notice at least 14 days before committing yourself to the lease, you will need to sign a simple declaration that you have received this notice and have accepted its consequences, before signing the lease.

But if you do not receive at least 14 days notice, you will need to sign a "statutory" declaration. To do so, *you will need to visit an independent solicitor (for someone else empowered to administer oaths).*

Unless there is a special reason for committing yourself to the lease sooner, you may want to ask the landlord to let you have at least 14 days to consider whether you wish to give up your statutory rights. If you then decided to go ahead with the agreement to exclude the protection of the Landlord and Tenant Act 1954, you would only need to make a simple declaration, and so you would not need to make a separate visit to an independent solicitor.

SCHEDULE 2

Article 22(2)

Requirements for a valid agreement that sections 24 to 28 of the landlord and tenant act 1954 are not to apply to a business tenancy

1. The following are the requirements referred to in section 38A(3)(b) of the Act. **A2.050**

2. Subject to paragraph 4, the notice referred to in section 38A(3)(a) of the Act must be served on the tenant not less than 14 days before the tenant enters into the tenancy to which it applies, or (if earlier) becomes contractually bound to do so.

3. If the requirement in paragraph 2 is met, the tenant, or a person duly authorised by him to do so, must, before the tenant enters into the tenancy to which the notice applies, or (if earlier) becomes contractually bound to do so, make a declaration in the form, or substantially in the form, set out in paragraph 7.

4. If the requirement in paragraph 2 is not met, the notice referred to in section 38A(3)(a) of the Act must be served on the tenant before the tenant enters into the tenancy to which it applies, or (if earlier) becomes contactually bound to do so, and the tenant, or a person duly authorised by him to do so, must before that time make a statutory declaration in the form, or substantially in the form, set out in paragraph 8.

5. A reference to the notice and, where paragraph 3 applies, the declaration or, where paragraph 4 applies, the statutory declaration must be contained in or endorsed on the instrument creating the tenancy.

6. The agreement under section 38A(1) of the Act, or a reference to the agreement, must be contained in or endorsed upon the instrument creating the tenancy.

A2.051 **7.** The form of declaration referred to in paragraph 3 is as follows—

I

____

(*name of declarant*) of

____

(*address*) declare that–

1. I/

____

(*name of tenant*) propose(s) to enter into a tenancy of premises at

____

(*address of premises*) for a term commencing on

____

2. I/The tenant propose(s) to enter into an agreement with (*name of landlord*) that the provisions of sections 24 to 28 of the Landlord and Tenant Act 1954 (security of tenure) shall be excluded in relation to the tenancy.

3. The landlord has, not less than 14 days before I/the tenant enter(s) into the tenancy, or (if earlier) become(s) contractually bound to do so served on me/the tenant a notice in the form, or substantially in the form, set out in Schedule 1 to the Regulatory Reform (Business Tenancies) (England and Wales) Order 2003. The form of notice set out in that Schedule is reproduced below.

4. I have/The tenant has read the notice referred to in paragraph 3 above and accept(s) the consequences of entering into the agreement referred to in paragraph 2 above.

5. (*as appropriate*) I am duly authorised by the tenant to make this declaration.

DECLARED this

____

day of

____

To:

____

____

____

[*Name and address of tenant*]

From:

____

____

____

[*name and address of landlord*]

IMPORTANT NOTICE

You are being offered a lease without security of tenure. Do not commit yourself to the lease unless YOU have read this message carefully and have discussed it with a professional adviser.

Business tenants normally have security of tenure—the right to stay in their business premises when the lease ends.

If you commit yourself to the lease you will be giving up these important legal rights.

- You will have no right to stay in the premises when the lease ends.
- Unless the landlord chooses to offer you another lease, you will need to leave the premises.
- You will be unable to claim compensation for the loss of your business premises, unless the lease specifically gives you this right.
- If the landlord offers you another lease, you will have no right to ask the court to fix the rent.

It is therefore important to get professional advice – from a qualified surveyor, lawyer or accountant—before agreeing to give up these rights.

If you want to ensure that you can stay in the same business premises when the lease ends, you should consult your adviser about another form of lease that does not exclude the protection of the Landlord and Tenant Act 1954.

If you receive this notice at least 14 days before committing yourself to the lease, you will need to sign a simple declaration that you have received this notice and have accepted its consequences, before signing the lease.

But if you do not receive at least 14 days notice, you will need to sign a "statutory" declaration. To do so, you will need to visit an independent solicitor (or someone else empowered to administer oaths).

Unless there is a special reason for committing yourself to the lease sooner, you may want to ask the landlord to let you have at least 14 days to consider whether you wish to give up your statutory rights. If you then decided to go ahead with the agreement to exclude the protection of the Landlord and Tenant Act 1954, you would only need to make a simple declaration, and so you would not need to make a separate visit to an independent solicitor.

8. The form of statutory declaration referred to in paragraph 4 is as follows– **A2.052**

I

____

(*name of declarant*) of

____

(*address*) do solemnly and sincerely declare that—

1. I

____

(*name of tenant*) propose(s) to enter into a tenancy of premises at

____

(*address of premises*) for a term commencing on

____

2. I/The tenant propose(s) to enter into an agreement with (name of landlord) that the provisions of sections 24 to 28 of the Landlord and Tenant Act 1954 (security of tenure) shall be excluded in relation to the tenancy.

3. The landlord has served on me/the tenant a notice in the form, or substantially in the form, set out in Schedule 1 to the Regulatory Reform (Business Tenancies) (England and Wales) Order 2003. The form of notice set out in that Schedule is reproduced below.

4. I have/The tenant has read the notice referred to in paragraph 3 above and accept(s) the consequences of entering into the agreement referred to in paragraph 2 above.

5. (*as appropriate*) I am duly authorised by the tenant to make this declaration.

To:

____

____

____

[*Name and address of tenant*]

From:

____

____

____

[*name and address of landlord*]

IMPORTANT NOTICE

You are being offered a lease without security of tenure. Do not commit yourself to the lease unless you have read this message carefully and have discussed it with a professional adviser

Business tenants normally have security of tenure—the right to stay in their business premises when the lease ends.

If you commit yourself to the lease you will be giving up these important legal rights.

- You will have no right to stay in the premises when the lease ends.
- Unless the landlord chooses to offer you another lease, you will need to leave the premises.
- You will be unable to claim compensation for the loss of your business premises, unless the lease specifically gives you this right.
- If the landlord offers you another lease, you will have no right to ask the court to fix the rent.

It is therefore important to get professional advice—from a qualified surveyor, lawyer or accountant—before agreeing to give up these rights.

If you want to ensure that you can slay in the same business premises when the lease ends, you should consult your adviser about another form of lease that does not exclude the protection of the Landlord and Tenant Act 1954.

If you receive this notice at least 14 days before committing yourself to the lease, you will need to sign a simple declaration that you have received this notice and have accepted its consequences, before signing the lease.

But if you do not receive at least 14 days notice, you will need to sign a "statutory" declaration. To do so, you will need to visit an independent solicitor (for someone else empowered to administer oaths).

Unless there is a special reason for committing yourself to the lease sooner, you may want to ask the landlord to let you have at least 14 days to consider whether you wish to give up your statutory rights. If you then decided to go ahead with the agreement to exclude the protection of the Landlord and Tenant Act 1954, you would only need to make a simple declaration, and so you would not need to make a separate visit to a independent solicitor.

AND I make this solemn declaration conscientiously believing the same to be true and by virtue of the Statutory Declaration Act 1835.

DECLARED at

____

this

____

day of

____

Before me

(*signature of person before whom declaration is made*)

A commissioner for oaths or A solicitor empowered to administer oaths or (*as appropriate*)

SCHEDULE 3

Article 22(2)

Form of notice that an agreement to surrender a business tenancy is to be made

A2.053 **To:**

____

____

____

[*Name and address of tenant*]

From:

____

____

____

[*name and address of landlord*]

IMPORTANT NOTICE FOR TENANT

Do not commit yourself to any agreement to surrender your lease unless you have read this message carefully and discussed it with a professional adviser.

Normally, you have the right to renew your lease when it expires. By committing yourself to an agreement to surrender, *you will be giving up this important statutory right.*

- You will not be able to continue occupying the premises beyond the date provided for under the agreement for surrender, unless the landlord chooses to offer you a further term (in which case you would lose the right to ask the court to determine the new rent). You will need to leave the premises.
- You will be unable to claim compensation for the loss of your premises, unless the lease or agreement for surrender gives you this right.

A qualified surveyor, lawyer or accountant would be able to offer you professional advice on your options.

You do not have to commit yourself to the agreement to surrender your lease unless you want to.

If you receive this notice at least 14 days before committing yourself to the agreement to surrender, you will need to sign a simple declaration that you have received this notice and have accepted its consequences, before signing the agreement to surrender.

But if you do not receive at least 14 days notice, you will need to sign a "statutory" declaration. To do so, you will need to visit an independent solicitor (or someone else empowered to administer oaths).

Unless there is a special reason for committing yourself to the agreement to surrender sooner, you may want to ask the landlord to let you have at least 14 days to consider whether you wish to give up your statutory rights. If you then decided to go ahead with the agreement to end your lease, you would only need to make a simple declaration, and so you would not need to make a separate visit to an independent solicitor.

SCHEDULE 4

Article 22(2)

Requirements for a valid agreement to surrender a business tenancy

1. The following are the requirements referred to in section 38A(4)(b) of the Act. **A2.054**

2. Subject to paragraph 4, the notice referred to in section 38A(4)(a) of the Act must be served on the tenant not less than 14 days before the tenant enters into the agreement under section 38A(2) of the Act, or (if earlier) becomes contractually bound to do so.

3. If the requirement in paragraph 2 is met, the tenant or a person duly authorised by him to do so, must, before the tenant enters into the agreement under section 38A(2) of the Act, or (if earlier) becomes contractually bound to do so, make a declaration in the form, or substantially in the form, set out in paragraph 6.

4. If the requirement in paragraph 2 is not met, the notice referred to in section 38A(4)(a) of the Act must be served on the tenant before the tenant enters into the agreement under section 38A(2) of the Act, or (if earlier) becomes contractually bound to do so, and the tenant, or a person duly authorised by him to do so, must before that time make a statutory declaration in the form, or substantially in the form, set out in paragraph 7.

5. A reference to the notice and, where paragraph 3 applies, the declaration or, where paragraph 4 applies, the statutory declaration must be contained in or endorsed on the instrument creating the agreement under section 38A(2).

6. The form of declaration referred to in paragraph 3 is as follows— **A2.055**

I

____

(*name of declarant*) of

____

(*address*) declare that–

1. I have/

____

(*name of tenant*) has a tenancy of premises at

____

(*address of premises*) for a term commencing on

____

2. I/The tenant propose(s) to enter into an agreement with

____

(*name of landlord*) to surrender the tenancy on a date or in circumstances specified in the agreement.

3. The landlord has not less than 14 days before I/the tenant enter(s) into the agreement referred to in paragraph 2 above, or (if earlier) become(s) contractually bound to do so, served on me/the tenant a notice in the form, or substantially in the form, set out in Schedule 3 to Regulatory Reform (Business Tenancies) (England and Wales) Order 2003. The form of notice set out in that Schedule is reproduced below.

4. I have/The tenant has read the notice referred to in paragraph 3 above and accept(s) the consequences of entering into the agreement referred to in paragraph 2 above.

5. (*as appropriate*) I am duly authorised by the tenant to make this declaration.

DECLARED this

____

day of

____

To:

____

____

____

[*Name and address of tenant*]

From:

____

____

____

[*name and address of landlord*]

IMPORTANT NOTICE FOR TENANT

Do not commit yourself to any agreement to surrender your lease unless you have read this message carefully and discussed it with a professional adviser.

Normally, you have the right to renew your lease when it expires. By committing yourself to an agreement to surrender, *you will he giving up this important statutory right.*

- You will not be able to continue occupying the premises beyond the date provided for under the agreement for surrender, unless the landlord chooses to offer you a further term (in which case you would lose the right to ask the court to determine the new rent). You will need to leave the premises.
- You will be unable to claim compensation for the loss of your premises, unless the lease or agreement for surrender gives you this right.

A qualified surveyor, lawyer or accountant would be able to offer you professional advice on your options.

You do not have to commit yourself to the agreement to surrender your lease unless you want to.

If you receive this notice at least 14 days before committing yourself to the agreement to surrender, you will need to sign a simple declaration that you have received this notice and have accepted its consequences, before signing the agreement to surrender.

But if you do not receive at least 14 days notice, you will need to sign a "statutory" declaration. To do so, you will need to visit an independent solicitor (or someone else empowered to administer oaths).

Unless there is a special reason for committing yourself to the agreement to surrender sooner, you may want to ask the landlord to let you have at least 14 days to consider whether you wish to give up your statutory rights. If you then decided to go ahead with the agreement to end your lease, you would only need to make a simple declaration, and so you would not need to make a separate visit to an independent solicitor.

7. The form of statutory declaration referred to in paragraph 4 is as follows— **A2.056**

I

____

(*name of declarant*) of

____

(*address*) do solemnly and sincerely declare that–

1. I have/

____

(*name of tenant*) has a tenancy of premises at

____

(*address of premises*) for a term commencing on

____

2. I/The tenant propose(s) to enter into an agreement with

____

(*name of landlord*) to surrender the tenancy on a date or in circumstances specified in the agreement.

3. The landlord has served on me/the tenant a notice in the form, or substantially in the form, set out in Schedule 3 to the Regulatory Reform (Business Tenancies) (England and Wales) Order 2003. The form of notice set out in that Schedule is reproduced below.

4. I have/The tenant has read the notice referred to in paragraph 3 above and accept(s) the consequences of entering into the agreement referred to in paragraph 2 above.

5. (*as appropriate*) I am duly authorised by the tenant to make this declaration.

To:

____

____

____

[*Name and address of tenant*]

From:

____

____

____

[*name and address of landlord*]

IMPORTANT NOTICE FOR TENANT

Do not commit yourself to any agreement to surrender your lease unless you have read this message carefully and discussed it with a professional adviser.

Normally, you have the right to renew your lease when it expires. By committing yourself to an agreement to surrender, you will be giving up this important statutory right.

- You will not be able to continue occupying the premises beyond the date provided for under the agreement for surrender, unless the landlord chooses to offer you a further term (in which case you would lose the right to ask the court to determine the new rent). You will need to leave the premises.
- You will be unable to claim compensation for the loss of your premises, unless the lease or agreement for surrender gives you this right.

A qualified surveyor, lawyer or accountant would be able to offer you professional advice on your options.

You do not have to commit yourself to the agreement to surrender your lease unless you want to.

If you receive this notice at least 14 days before committing yourself to the agreement to surrender, you will need to sign a simple declaration that you have received this notice and have accepted its consequences, before signing the agreement to surrender.

But if you do not receive at least 14 days notice, you will need to sign a "statutory" declaration. To do so, you will need to visit an independent solicitor (or someone else empowered to administer oaths).

Unless there is a special reason for committing yourself to the agreement to surrender sooner, you may want to ask the landlord to let you have at least 14 days to consider whether you wish to give up your statutory rights. If you then decided to go ahead with the agreement to end your lease, you would only need to make a simple declaration, and so you would not need to make a separate visit to an independent solicitor.

AND I make this solemn declaration conscientiously believing the same to be true and by virtue of the Statutory Declarations Act 1835

DECLARED at

____

this

____

day of

Before me (*signature of person before whom declaration is made*)

A commissioner for oaths or a solicitor empowered to administer oaths *or* (*as appropriate*)

SCHEDULE 5

Article 28(1)

Consequential amendments

LANDLORD AND TENANT ACT 1954

1. The Act shall be amended as follows. **A2.057**

2. After section 14 insert–

"***Compensation for possession obtained by misrepresentation***

14A. Where an order is made for possession of the property comprised in a tenancy to which section 1 of this Act applies and it is subsequently made to appear to the court that the order was obtained by misrepresentation or the concealment of material facts, the court may order the landlord to pay to the tenant such a sum as appears sufficient as compensation for damage or loss sustained by the tenant as the result of the order."

3. In section 26(1), for the words "tenancy under which he holds for the time being (hereinafter referred to as "the current tenancy")" substitute "current tenancy".

4. In section 38(2) and (3) for the words "the last foregoing section" substitute the words "section 37 of this Act".

5. In section 41A(6) for the words from "section 29(1) " to "jointly" substitute "section 29 of this Act for the grant of a new tenancy it may order the grant to be made to the business tenants or to them jointly".

6. In section 46–

(a) for the definition of "current tenancy" substitute–

" "current tenancy" means the tenancy under which the tenant holds for the time being;"; and

(b) after the definition of "the holding" insert–

" "interim rent" has the meaning given by section 24A(1) of this Act;".

7. In sections 57(3)(a) and 58(1)(a)–

for the words "subsection (5) and" substitute the word "subsection"; and

after the word "under", in the second place where it occurs, insert the words "subsection (1) of".

8. In section 59(1), after "(3)" insert the words "to (3B)".

9. In section 64(1)(b), for the words "the said part II" substitute the words "under section 24(1) or 29(2) of this Act".

22. Agreements to exclude sections 24 to 28

(1) After section 38 insert—

"38A. Agreements to exclude provisions of Part 2

(1) The persons who will be the landlord and the tenant in relation to a tenancy to be granted for a term of years certain which will be a tenancy to which this Part of this Act applies may agree that the provisions of sections 24 to 28 of this Act shall be excluded in relation to that tenancy.

(2) The persons who are the landlord and the tenant in relation to a tenancy to which this Part of this Act applies may agree that the tenancy shall be surrendered on such date or in such circumstances as may be specified in the agreement and on such terms (if any) as may be so specified.

(3) An agreement under subsection (1) above shall be void unless—

(a) the landlord has served on the tenant a notice in the form, or substantially in the form, set out in Schedule 1 to the Regulatory Reform (Business Tenancies) (England and Wales) Order 2003 ("the 2003 Order"); and

(b) the requirements specified in Schedule 2 to that Order are met.

(4) An agreement under subsection (2) above shall be void unless—

(a) the landlord has served on the tenant a notice in the form, or substantially in the form, set out in Schedule 3 to the 2003 Order; and

(b) the requirements specified in Schedule 4 to that Order are met."

(2) Schedules 1 to 4 to this Order shall have effect.

INDEX

This index has been prepared using Sweet and Maxwell's Legal Taxonomy. Main index entries conform to keywords provided by the Legal Taxonomy except where references to specific documents or non-standard terms (denoted by quotation marks) have been included. These keywords provide a means of identifying similar concepts in other Sweet and Maxwell publications and online services to which keywords from the Legal Taxonomy have been applied. Readers may find some minor differences between terms used in the text and those which appear in the index. Suggestions to *sweetandmaxwell.taxonomy@thomson.com*.

All references are to paragraph number